W9-BSC-338

MORRIS AUTOMATED INFORMATION NETWORK

0 1021 0101053 0

ON LINE

Short Story Criticism

Guide to Gale Literary Criticism Series

For criticism on	Consult these Gale series
Authors now living or who died after December 31, 1959	*CONTEMPORARY LITERARY CRITICISM (CLC)*
Authors who died between 1900 and 1959	*TWENTIETH-CENTURY LITERARY CRITICISM (TCLC)*
Authors who died between 1800 and 1899	*NINETEENTH-CENTURY LITERATURE CRITICISM (NCLC)*
Authors who died between 1400 and 1799	*LITERATURE CRITICISM FROM 1400 TO 1800 (LC)* *SHAKESPEAREAN CRITICISM (SC)*
Authors who died before 1400	*CLASSICAL AND MEDIEVAL LITERATURE CRITICISM (CMLC)*
Authors of books for children and young adults	*CHILDREN'S LITERATURE REVIEW (CLR)*
Black writers of the past two hundred years	*BLACK LITERATURE CRITICISM (BLC)*
Short story writers	*SHORT STORY CRITICISM (SSC)*
Poets	*POETRY CRITICISM (PC)*
Dramatists	*DRAMA CRITICISM (DC)*
Major authors from the Renaissance to the present	*WORLD LITERATURE CRITICISM, 1500 TO THE PRESENT (WLC)*

For criticism on visual artists since 1850, see

MODERN ARTS CRITICISM (MAC)

ISSN 0895-9439

Volume 13

Short Story Criticism

Excerpts from Criticism of the Works of Short Fiction Writers

David Segal
Editor

Laurie DiMauro
Jennifer Gariepy
Drew Kalasky
Thomas Ligotti
Janet M. Witalec
Associate Editors

 **Gale Research Inc.** ·DETROIT · WASHINGTON, D.C. · LONDON

Library of Congress Catalog Card Number 88-641014
ISBN 0-8103-8469-8
ISSN 0895-9439

Printed in the United States of America
Published simultaneously in the United Kingdom
by Gale Research International Limited
(An affiliated company of Gale Research Inc.)
10 9 8 7 6 5 4 3 2 1

I(T)P™

The trademark **ITP** is used under license.

Contents

Preface   vii

Acknowledgments   xi

Preface

A Comprehensive Information Source on World Short Fiction

S hort Story Criticism (SSC) presents significant passages from criticism of the worlds's greatest short story writers and provides supplementary biographical and bibliographical materials to guide the interested reader to a greater understanding of the authors of short fiction. This series was developed in response to suggestions from librarians serving high school, college, and public library patrons, who had noted a considerable number of requests for critical material on short story writers. Although major short story writers are covered in such Gale series as *Contemporary Literary Criticism (CLC), Twentieth-Century Literary Criticism (TCLC), Nineteenth-Century Literature Criticism (NCLC)*, and *Literature Criticism from 1400 to 1800 (LC)*, librarians perceived the need for a series devoted solely to writers of the short story genre.

Coverage

SSC is designed to serve as an introduction to major short story writers of all eras and nationalities. Since these authors have inspired a great deal of relevant critical material, *SSC* is necessarily selective, and the editors have chosen the most important published criticism to aid readers and students in their research.

Approximately eight to ten authors are included in each volume, and each entry presents a historical survey of the critical response to that author's work. The length of an entry is intended to reflect the amount of critical attention the author has received from critics writing in English and from foreign critics in translation. Every attempt has been made to identify and include excerpts from the most significant essays on each author's work. In order to provide these important critical pieces, the editors will sometimes reprint essays that have appeared in previous volumes of Gale's Literary Criticism Series. Such duplication, however, never exceeds twenty percent of an *SSC* volume.

Organization

An *SSC* author entry consists of the following elements:

- The **Author Heading** cites the name under which the author most commonly wrote, followed by birth and death dates. If the author wrote consistently under a pseudonym, the pseudonym will be listed in the author heading and the author's actual name given in parentheses on the first line of the biographical and critical introduction.

- The **Biographical and Critical Introduction** contains background information designed to introduce a reader to the author and the critical debates surrounding his or her work. Parenthetical material following the introduction provides references to other biographical and critical series published by Gale, including *CLC, TCLC, NCLC, Contemporary Authors*, and *Dictionary of Literary Biography*.

- A **Portrait of the Author** is included when available. Many entries also contain illustrations of materials pertinent to an author's career, including holographs of manuscript pages, title pages, dust jackets, letters, or representations of important people, places and events in the author's life.

- The list of **Principal Works** is chronological by date of first publication and lists the most important works by the author. The first section comprises short story collections, novellas, and novella collections. The second section gives information on other major works by the author. For foreign authors, the editors have provided original foreign-language publication information and have selected what are considered the best and most complete English-language editions of their works.

- **Criticism** is arranged chronologically in each author entry to provide a useful perspective on changes in critical evaluation over the years. All short story, novella, and collection titles by the author featured in the entry are printed in boldface type to enable a reader to ascertain without difficulty the works discussed. Also for purposes of easier identification, the critic's name and the publication date of the essay are given at the beginning of each piece of criticism. Unsigned criticism is preceded by the title of the journal in which it appeared.

- Critical essays are prefaced with **Explanatory Notes** as an additional aid to students and readers using *SSC*. The explanatory notes provide several types of useful information, including: the reputation of a critic, the importance of a work of criticism, and the specific type of criticism (biographical, psychoanalytic, structuralist, etc.).

- A complete **Bibliographical Citation,** designed to help the interested reader locate the original essay or book, follows each piece of criticism.

- The **Further Reading List** appearing at the end of each author entry suggests additional materials on the author. In some cases it includes essays for which the editors could not obtain reprint rights.

Beginning with volume six, *SSC* contains two additional features designed to enhance the reader's understanding of short fiction writers and their works:

- Each *SSC* entry now includes, when available, **Comments by the Author** that illuminate his or her own works of the short story genre in general. These statements are set within boxes or bold rules to distinguish them from the criticism.

- A **Select Bibliography of General Sources on Short Fiction** is included as an appendix. Updated and amended with each new *SSC* volume, this listing of materials for further research provides readers with a selection of the best available general studies of the short story genre.

Other Features

A **Cumulative Author Index** lists all the authors who have appeared in *SSC, CLC, TCLC, NCLC, LC,* and *Classical and Medieval Literature Criticism (CMLC),* as well as cross-references to other Gale series. Users will welcome this cumulated index as a useful tool for locating an author within the Literary Criticism Series.

A **Cumulative Nationality Index** lists all authors featured in *SSC* by nationality, followed by the number of the *SSC* volume in which their entry appears.

A **Cumulative Title Index** lists in alphabetical order all short story, novella, and collection titles contained in the *SSC* series. Titles of short collections, separately published novellas, and novella collections are printed in italics, while titles of individual short stories are printed in roman type with quotation marks. Each title is followed by the author's name and the corresponding volume and page numbers where commentary on the work may be located. English-language translations of original foreign-language titles are cross-referenced to the foreign titles so that all references to discussion of a work are combined in one listing.

Citing *Short Story Criticism*

When writing papers, students who quote directly from any volume in the Literary Criticism Series may use the following general forms to footnote reprinted criticism. The first example pertains to material drawn from periodicals, the second to material reprinted from books:

[1]Henry James, Jr., "Honoré de Balzac," *The Galaxy 20* (December 1875), 814-36; excerpted and reprinted in *Short Story Criticism,* Vol. 5, ed. Thomas Votteler (Detroit: Gale Research, 1990), pp. 8-11.

[2]F. R. Leavis, *D. H. Lawrence: Novelist* (Alfred A. Knopf, 1956); excerpted and reprinted in *Short Story Criticism,* Vol. 4, ed. Thomas Votteler (Detroit: Gale Research, 1990), pp. 202-06.

Comments

Readers who wish to suggest authors to appear in future volumes, or who have other suggestions, are invited to contact the editors by writing to Gale Research Inc., Literary Criticism Division, 835 Penobscot Building, Detroit, MI 48226-4094.

Acknowledgments

The editors wish to thank the copyright holders of the excerpted criticism included in this volume, the permissions managers of many book and magazine publishing companies for assisting us in securing reprint rights, and Anthony Bogucki for assistance with copyright research. We are also grateful to the staffs of the Detroit Public Library, the Library of Congress, the University of Detroit Library, Wayne State University Purdy/Kresge Library Complex, and the University of Michigan Libraries for making their resources available to us. Following is a list of the copyright holders who have granted us permission to reprint material in this volume of *SSC*. Every effort has been made to trace copyright, but if omissions have been made, please let us know.

COPYRIGHTED EXCERPTS IN *SSC*, VOLUME 13, WERE REPRINTED FROM THE FOLLOWING PERIODICALS:

American Imago, v. 40, Fall, 1983; v. 42, Fall, 1985. Copyright 1983, 1985 by The Association for Applied Psychoanalysis, Inc. Both reprinted by permission of the publisher.—*American Literary Realism 1870-1910.* v. 8, Summer, 1975. Copyright © 1975 by the Department of English, The University of Texas at Arlington. Reprinted by permission of the publisher.—*Arizona Quarterly,* v. 47, Spring, 1991 for "Realism, Reform, and the Audience: Charlotte Perkins Gilman's Unreadable Wallpaper" by Conrad Shumaker. Copyright © 1991 by Arizona Board of Regents. Reprinted by permission of the publisher and the author./ v. 43, Autumn, 1987. Copyright © 1987 by Arizona Board of Regents. Reprinted by permission of the publisher.—*Book World,* May 10, 1987. © 1987, *The Washington Post*. Reprinted by permission of the publisher.—*Books and Bookmen,* v. 20, 1975 for "Gothic Pyrotechnics" by James Brockway. © copyright the author 1975. Reprinted by permission of the author.—*The Christian Science Monitor,* October 12, 1983 for "Seán O'Faoláin Collection: Evocative but Uneven" by Bruce Allen. © 1983 The Christian Science Publishing Society. All rights reserved. Reprinted by permission of the author.—*Criticism,* v. XXXI, Fall, 1989. Copyright, 1989, Wayne State University Press. Reprinted by permission of the publisher.—*Éire-Ireland,* v. VI, Fall, 1971 for "The Short Stories of Seán O'Faoláin: Theory and Practice" by Katherine Hanley. Copyright © 1971 Irish American Cultural Institute, 2115 Summit Ave., No. 5026, St. Paul, MN 55105. Reprinted by permission of the publisher and the author.—*Essays in French Literature,* n. 14, November, 1977. © Department of French Studies, The University of Western Australia. Reprinted by permission of the publisher.—*Feminist Studies,* v. 15, Fall, 1989. Copyright © 1989 by Feminist Studies, Inc. Reprinted by permission of the publisher, c/o Women's Studies Program, University of Maryland, College Park, MD 20742.—*Germanic Notes,* v. 21, 1990. All rights reserved. Reprinted by permission of the publisher.—*Irish University Review,* v. 6, Spring, 1976. © *Irish University Review*. Reprinted by permission of the publisher.—*Journal of the Midwest Modern Language Association,* v. 21, Spring, 1988 for "Out of the Maze: A Reading of Gide's 'Thésée' " by Winifred Woodhull. Copyright 1988 by The Midwest Modern Language Association. Reprinted by permission of the publisher and the author.—*Journal of the Short Story in English,* n. 10, Spring, 1988. © Universite d'Angers, 1988. Reprinted by permission of the publisher.—*LEGACY,* v. 5, Fall, 1988. Copyright © 1988 by The Pennsylvania State University. All rights reserved. Reproduced by permission of The Pennsylvania State University Press.—*The Literary Criterion,* v. XX, 1985. Reprinted by permission of the publisher.—*Literature and History,* v. 10, Spring, 1984 for "Re-Imagining the Fairy Tales: Angela Carter's Bloody Chambers" by Patricia Duncker. © 1984. Reprinted by permission of the publisher and the author.—*Literature and Psychology,* v. XXXVI, 1990. Copyright © *Literature and Psychology,* 1990. Reprinted by permission of the publisher.—*Midway,* v. 8, June, 1967. © 1967 by The University of Chicago. Reprinted by permission of The University of Chicago Press.—*The Nation,* New York, v. 243, October 4, 1986. Copyright 1986 *The Nation* magazine/The Nation Company, Inc. Reprinted by permission of the publisher.—*The New Republic,* v. 174, May 1, 1976; v. 195, December 22, 1986. © 1976, 1986 The New Republic, Inc. Both reprinted by permission of *The New Republic.*—*New Statesman,* v. 88, August 16, 1974, v. 97, May 25, 1979. © 1974, 1979 The Statesman & Nation Publishing Co. Ltd. Both reprinted by permission of the publisher.—*New York Herald Tribune Books,*

COPYRIGHTED EXCERPTS IN *SSC,* VOLUME 13, WERE REPRINTED FROM THE FOLLOWING BOOKS:

xiii

Angela Carter

1940-1992

(Full name Angela Olive Carter) English novelist, short
story writer, nonfiction writer, scriptwriter, and author of
children's books.

INTRODUCTION

Carter is best known for writings in which she undertakes
a feminist critique of Western history and culture. Combining components of Gothicism, surrealism, eroticism,
and myth, Carter explores such themes as violence, the
distribution of power in contemporary society, and female
sexuality. Like her novels, which incorporate elements
from several genres, including fantasy and science fiction,
Carter's short stories are often derived from fables, fairy
tales, and popular legends, all of which, she purports, reflect and perpetuate the dominant political, cultural, and
socioeconomic myths of patriarchal society. Alternately
praised and faulted for her extravagant Gothic approach,
Carter is esteemed as a writer of highly imaginative fiction.

In the oft-cited "Afterword" from *Fireworks: Nine Profane Pieces*, which many critics have identified as her literary manifesto, Carter argued that the tale, unlike the short
story, "interprets everyday experience through a system
of imagery derived from subterranean areas behind everyday experience." She also defined the literary tradition
that informs her work, stating that Gothicism "grandly ignores the value systems of our institutions; it deals entirely
with the profane. Its great themes are incest and cannibalism. Characters and events are exaggerated beyond reality, to become symbols, ideas, passions. Its style will tend
to be ornate, unnatural—and thus operate against the perennial human desire to believe the world of fact. Its only
humour is black humour. It retains a singular moral function—that of provoking unease." Critics find that Carter
typically employed violence and eroticism in her work and
that her images subsequently challenge popular myths and
attitudes regarding female sexuality. For example, the
image of blood, as a symbol of menstruation and defloration-
tion, is prominently featured in her short fiction. In a story
from *The Bloody Chamber, and Other Stories*, for instance,
Carter described a necklace as "a bloody bandage of rubies," concurrently emphasizing the violence of sexual intercourse and the loss of virginity through the image of a
slit throat as well as the economic value that society attaches to virginity. "The Courtship of Mr. Lyon," a retelling of the "Beauty and the Beast" tale, similarly discusses
the connection between money and gender in a patriarchal
society—women are regarded as passive, subservient objects to be bought, sold, and provided for by men. Carter
offered another version of "Beauty and the Beast" in "The
Tiger's Bride," in which the girl, as narrator, takes control

of her own story and destiny, describing a reciprocal relationship with the beast based on mutual trust, sacrifice,
and animalistic desire.

Carter's stories about historical figures expose and attack
the cultural conventions that influence judgments of the
past and determine what society deems proper, particularly the passive roles traditionally assigned to women. Suggesting alternative readings for historical events, Carter
questions the concept of an objective history unaffected by
legend. For example, in "The Fall River Axe Murders,"
Carter described from a woman's perspective the events
that motivated Lizzie Borden to murder her family. In
"Black Venus," the story of Jeanne Duval, the mistress of
French poet Charles Baudelaire, Carter similarly challenged the politics and assumptions associated with depictions of women as purveyors of evil, disease, and corruption.

While lauding Carter's critiques of fairy tales and attempts
at historical revisionism, some commentators lament the
absence of concrete alternatives for her heroines. Critics
argue that because Carter rewrote the tales within their
original structures, she robbed her protagonists of any real
sense of choice and actually perpetuated patriarchal views

regarding women, particularly the concepts which posit that female sexuality is merely a response to male arousal and that a mother and daughter will inevitably engage in the Electra complex. Nonetheless, commentators agree that Carter's tales succeed in provoking unease and uncovering the inequalities implicit in modern society and its cultural heritage. As Jill Matus observed: "A characteristic procedure of Carter's is to seize upon some image, icon or bit of mythology and draw out its implications, making gorgeous what is denigrated or scorned, blaspheming against what is held sacred, and exposing what is usually kept covert."

PRINCIPAL WORKS

SHORT FICTION

Fireworks: Nine Profane Pieces 1974; also published as *Fireworks: Nine Stories in Various Disguises*, 1981
The Bloody Chamber, and Other Stories 1979
Black Venus's Tale 1980
Black Venus 1985; also published as *Saints and Strangers*, 1986
Artificial Fire 1988

OTHER MAJOR WORKS

Shadow Dance (novel) 1966; also published as *Honey-buzzard*, 1967
Unicorn (poetry) 1966
The Magic Toyshop (novel) 1967
Several Perceptions (novel) 1968
Heroes and Villains (novel) 1969
The Donkey Prince (juvenilia) 1970
Miss Z, the Dark Young Landy (juvenilia) 1970
Love (novel) 1971; revised edition, 1987
The Infernal Desire Machines of Dr. Hoffman (novel) 1972; also published as *The War of Dreams*, 1974
The Passion of New Eve (novel) 1977
The Sadeian Woman and the Ideology of Pornography (nonfiction) 1979; also published as *The Sadeian Woman: An Exercise in Cultural History*, 1979
Nothing Sacred: Selected Writings (essays) 1982
Nights at the Circus (novel) 1984
Come Into These Yellow Sands (scripts) 1985
Wise Children (novel) 1991

CRITICISM

Victoria Glendinning (essay date 1974)

[*Glendinning is an English educator, biographer, novelist, and critic. In the following excerpt, she praises Carter's wordplay and imagery in* Fireworks, *but suggests that the themes are hackneyed.*]

[Angela Carter's] *Fireworks* are Gothic tales, not stories,

as she explains in an Afterword. Written 'in a room too small to write a novel in', they are the result of her preoccupation with the imagery of the unconscious. Some of these tales refer to a primitive past, or rework myths. The real world—principally, here, her experience of Japan—is reshaped subjectively so that real cities, real situations, blossom strangely. Her phrasing is superb, and her imagery sometimes unforgettable: 'stagnant eyes' for example. She stalks through many of her own tales, a wanderer 'sad by nature' and attracted to anguish.

The tales are full of puppets, mirrors, forests, sequined eyes, shells, flowers and diffuse lust, like the Dadd pictures at the Tate. It is exciting and provocative; but it is familiar. There have been so many literary variations on the themes of reality, identity, sexual duality. It is the world of Freudian dream and futuristic fiction and pornography; of Edgar Allan Poe, Pirandello, J. G. Ballard and Borges. Familiarity comes perhaps from the fact that the collective unconscious is everyone's stock-pot. But Angela Carter is too aware of its contents. The essence of the Gothic tale—as epitomised by Poe—is its apparent possible innocence. So there may be incest, bestiality, cannibalism; but it is never quite spelled out. Some of her best and most electric encounters are earthed by a pedantic need to explain. Sometimes this is done with a disarming self-irony. 'Do not think I do not realise what I am doing', as she writes at the end of **'The Smile of Winter'**, proceeding to analyse how it was done. But more often it seems a lack of literary tact. Take a small example from **'Reflections'**:

> 'Kiss yourself' commanded the androgyne in a swooning voice. 'Kiss yourself in the mirror, the symbolic matrix of this and that, hither and thither, outside and inside.'

The mirror-kiss and its weird consequences had their own force. Talk of symbolic matrices belongs to American Ph.D. theses. We are grounded. Or are we to learn from the author a depth of irony that can make suspect the very symbols that obsess her? Angela Carter is a genius as a word-spinner. She deserves a room big enough to write the new novel in.

Victoria Glendinning, "Real Cities," in New Statesman, *Vol. 88, No. 2265, August 16, 1974, p. 229.*

The Times Literary Supplement (essay date 1974)

[*In the following review of* Fireworks, *the critic praises the shock value of the stories, but faults Carter's prose style.*]

Like social workers, reviewers are supposed to be unshockable; incest, cannibalism, vampirism, perversion: they are all part of life's rich fabric. But these stories of Angela Carter's [*Fireworks*]—she prefers to call them tales, with thoughts of Poe and Hoffmann—are exotic, erotic, clever, and rather shocking. Perhaps this is a better tribute to her writing than imperturbability.

She *can* write. But one is never quite sure, as with fashionable modern naïf paintings, whether a competent talent is being boosted with gimmicks; or, to change the pictorial metaphor, whether we are dealing with a Dali or a Magritte. Are the histrionics genuine or, so to speak, histrionic? She calls her tales fireworks, but they are not at all like fireworks, which are noisy and pretty; the impression she works for, in prose strenuously bad and good, is one of tinniness, hollowness, deception, of a pervading sense of absence; of a small, bloodless wound smothered in tomato ketchup.

Three of the nine tales are set in Japan and related in semirealistic and autobiographical terms. The description of a beach in winter is the least forced; the other two evoke Tokyo—or a version of it, no doubt as individual as Durrell's Alexandria—as a setting for solipsistic love and loneliness. The rest of the stories are set in the fairytale (Grimm, not Andersen) jungles, cities and gardens. A life-sized puppet of unimaginable depravity vampirizes her puppet-master; incestuous orphaned twins find poisoned fruit in the forest; a hooded executioner rapes his daughter on the chopping-block where he decapitated her brother. Aged transvestites totter out in stilletoes and fox-fur scarves with little beady eyes. The executioner has his omelette made of fertilized eggs that taste of embryonic claw. The obsessions are mirrors, blood, androgynes, puppets, costumes, fetishes of every kind. As the props accumulate, so do the adjectives—"feverish", "remorseless", "hysterical", "strange", etc—and the language loses energy.

The artistic intention is to deny meaning to the word "real". Waves have the "artfully flawed incandescence of Art Nouveau glass", street lamps throw out the "yellow light that bleaches the blood out of road accidents so it doesn't look real". In art this has always been a recurrent intention; if it is not shocking, what is? The mirrors are there only to reflect reflections; the violence to consume itself repetitively; the disguises to reveal nothingness underneath.

> The world stretched out from my eye like spokes from a sensitized hub that galvanized all to life when I looked at it. . . . But all the time I was pulling the strings of my own puppet; it was this puppet who was moving about on the other side of the glass. And I eyed the most marvellous adventures with the bored eye of the agent with the cigar watching another audition. I tapped out the ash and asked of events: "What else can you do?"

> *"Only Reflect,"* in The Times Literary Supplement, *No. 3781, August 23, 1974, p. 897.*

James Brockway (essay date 1975)

[*In the following excerpt, Brockway provides a highly favorable assessment of* Fireworks.]

Shabby and Vulgar as our age sounds and appears to be—the achievement of our ubiquitous media men—it nevertheless has a few geniuses. In the world of the modern English novel one of these is Angela Carter. She is our Lady Edgar Allan Poe (and she knows it). So virile is her prose, we may also call her Our Bearded Lady. But she is more still. Like all genuine art, hers breaks through the bounda-

ries of one department of art and extends to others. So she is also a female Nijinsky, possessed by a devil, perhaps by Mephistopheles himself. She is Aubrey Beardsley, but wondrously transformed: divested of two of his essential features, his black-and-white and his consumption, and invested with all the wicked colour and glitter of Gustave Moreau, invested with life. She has also the decadence, the hysteria and the preciosity of Huysmans and Maeterlinck, the doll-like romance of Hoffmann (which she also knows). We can go to the film world, too, to definition: she is also a female Polanski, especially the delightful Polanski of *The Dance of the Vampires,* though, unlike him, never roguish, yet very much a rogue. And like all geniuses, she walks the tight-rope on one side of which yawns the chasm of madness, on the other the chasm of bathos. Again like all geniuses, she can topple over and down into both and the next minute be progressing, in full control again, along her tight-rope, on tiptoe. In short, she is the anti-thesis of the bourgeois.

This year, instead of a novel, Angela Carter has offered us a fireworks display: [in her collection, *Fireworks: Nine Profane Pieces*]. Tales, not short stories, which she explains in a lucid note on her work, and on this book in particular, in a brief 'Afterword'. As distinct from the short story, the tale, she tells us here, 'interprets everyday experience through a system of imagery derived from subterranean areas behind everyday experience . . .' She goes on to say of the Gothic tradition in which she writes that it:

> grandly ignores the value systems of our institutions; it deals entirely with the profane. Its great themes are incest and cannibalism. Characters and events are exaggerated beyond reality, to become symbols, ideas, passions. Its style will tend to be ornate, unnatural—and thus operate against the perennial human desire to believe the world of fact. Its only humour is black humour. It retains a singular moral function—that of provoking unease.

A long quote, which I hope both author and publisher will excuse, my excuse being that no one could have said it better than Angela Carter herself.

So there you have it. One touch of demurral: though the boards, inside and out, of this edition are right—they are in purple—the title and the harsh, unaesthetic colours of the jacket are not. It is true that fireworks have a brilliance we find in this writing. But theirs is a dead brilliance, while the brilliance of this book is alive. Fireworks, too, can turn out to be damp squibs, so it is a risky term too. Some of Angela Carter's fireworks here come close to turning into damp squibs, but not sufficiently so to justify so precarious a title. Greatest objection of all: fireworks are essentially artificial, and although all art is artifice, all art is not artificial. This writing aspires to be art and nearly everywhere succeeds. Fireworks do not. Fireworks die out. Art does not. The book deserved far subtler labelling. (p. 55)

It would be possible almost to give an account of the contents and nature of *Fireworks* by quoting from Angela Carter's own words in these tales. From the magnificent story **'The Loves of Lady Purple',** to my taste the finest in the book and one which harks back happily to the puppets in *The Magic Toyshop,* one could take 'freedom from actuality' and 'immune to the drab world of here and now' and 'bewildering entertainment' and 'Here the grotesque is the order of the day' and 'Everything in the play was entirely exotic' and, best of all, I think: 'a thick, lascivious murmur like fur soaked in honey which sent unwilling shudders of pleasure down the spines of the watchers', except that I also think Angela Carter will find plenty of readers who shudder most willingly.

One could also quote some of her idiosyncratic adjectives to say all: appalling, ghastly, violet, violent, perverse, torrid, desolate, vicious, viscous, cavernous, subaqueous, indecent, lewd, fernal, leprous, lycanthropic, stagnant, demented. But this would be to suggest a gothic orgy, whereas for all the highly deliberate, deliberately ornamental embroidery of this laden prose, it is the intelligence at work beneath it all which raises almost everything here to the level of art. For intelligence is another attribute of genuine art, and intelligence here is both active and unusual. The author tells us in her 'Afterword' that she began these tales during her stay in Japan and the first tale, **'A Souvenir of Japan'**, is an atmospheric scene painting of that country a la Carter. It is very much her atmosphere. Of the Samurai she comments: 'The magnificence of such objects hardly pertains to the human.' One could define her technique too by slightly paraphrasing another sentence from this beautiful piece, by substituting 'writing' for 'country' and 'embroidery' for 'hypocrisy' and arriving at: 'This writing has elevated embroidery to the level of the highest style.'

Like all geniuses, Carter walks the tight-rope on one side of which yawns the chasm of madness, on the other the chasm of bathos. Again like all geniuses, she can topple over and down into both and the next minute be progressing, in full control again, along her tight-rope, on tiptoe.

—James Brockway

The next piece, about 'shaggy', 'rough', 'filthy' and 'verminous' people living in a mountain community, displays a Carter fault: the splendid beginning tends to get bogged down in heavy verbal impasto. The next, **'The Loves of Lady Purple'**, does not and is magnificent all through. We are very close to Polanski here in this ultra-exotic glittering and pagan version of Pygmalion and Galatea, in which Lady Purple, the old professor's puppet, devours her maker. My only regret here was that Carter has mists floating about where there are also 'small winds' and where little clouds can be seen drifting across the face of the moon. But I'll let that pass, disliking as I do the schoolmaster approach, absurdly inappropriate here, anyway. Just imagine a schoolmaster caught up in Angela Carter's world! How soon he would lose what balls he had!

There are pieces here, **'The Smile of Winter'**, **'Flesh and the Mirror'**, a Woman-Friday piece, called **'Master'** (tribute to Daniel Defoe, 'father of the *bourgeois* novel'—for which, see the author's own farewell note) that don't seem quite to jell—or which didn't seem quite to jell in my mind. This cannot be said of the mirror-world, horror story, **'Reflections'**, which begins as science fiction with some splendidly written pages. Here my objection, and I'm sorry to have them, is that the horror becomes a bit bathetic. I wanted to laugh at the too realistic comparison of a spidery network which 'resembled nothing so much as open-work knitting', even if that is what it turns out to be. I wanted to laugh, too, where I shouldn't have, at the aged old androgyne's outsize 'phallic insignia of maleness', especially when, toppling momentarily from the tight-rope, Carter suddenly refers to it as a 'cock'. I admit that there is something in the likening of this old hag's voice to 'a very old lace handkerchief put away long ago in a drawer with pot-pourri and forgotten'. (After all, in *The Sacred and Profane Love Machine,* Iris Murdoch recently had strawberries giving off a 'thick dappled smell' which 'hung in the room like a gaudy cloud' . . . everything connects, everything connects, we merely divide life up and stick our labels on the fragments.) Nevertheless, such similes come just a little too close to the risible, imaginative though we all hope and aspire to be. 'The odour of her violence deafened me.' 'Your kisses along my arm were like tracer bullets.' 'X made love to me like the storming of the Bastille.' No. Here the tight-rope walker seems to have accomplished the amazing feat of having toppled down into both chasms, madness and bathos, simultaneously. The same applies to sand described as fudge: 'walking across a panful is a promenade in the Kingdom of Sweets', which is acceptable only as a parody of our age's (bad) taste for science fiction.

It is true, all the same, it was the sheer, assidious excellence of this prose that sent me searching for dissonances, waiting to see where the tight-rope walker toppled. True, too, that there are so many clever and happy turns of phrase to render the bad examples I have quoted of academic importance only. There is, for example: 'sea-boots freighted with sand'; 'the indecipherable clarity of dreams'—so much conveyed in only three key-words; the discernment of the remark about a dipsomaniac: 'Dismayed, he clung to the bottle as if it were a teat.' There is sudden, satirical humour in **'Master'**, where the savage girl's father 'made sandals from the rubber tyre to shoe his family's feet and they walked a little way into the twentieth century in them, but not far'. And the works of Graham Greene are both summed up and rolled up in the same story with the words: 'an ancient whisky priest sat all day in the ruins of a forsaken church brewing fire-water from wild bananas and keening the stations of the cross'. Yes, Carter can be wickedly satirical and funny too. Not all her humour is black.

The last piece, **'Elegy for a Freelance'**, is one of the most successful tales here. In it London is referred to as an 'old cow'—'so old she ought to be superannuated'. The girl narrator, remembering 'velvet nights spiked with menace' (quintessential Carter), says of herself: 'I was the innocent slave of *bourgeois* aesthetics, that always sees an elegiac charm in decay.' Here fireworks have turned into bombs, revolutionary explosions. However, the frowsty hippy-squatter scene ('A perpetual twilight dominated that house, with its characteristic odours of stale cooking, phantom bacon, lavatories and the cats who pissed in the hall') is only one side of this writing. To me, Carter seems at her best in the lush, exotic world of the stage, the puppet scene, the brothel, where the lighting is not twilight but darkness of the deepest black, wondrously illuminated by her own beautiful, garish, glittering, frightening dolls, in which 'sign and sense can fuse to an extent impossible to achieve among the multiplying ambiguities of an extended narrative . . . I am not so much exploring them as making abstractions from them'.

We are always moaning about our modern fiction. In a recent review of William Trevor's latest novel, I found myself quoting Doris Lessing's censure, admittedly of some years ago: 'We are not living in an exciting literary period.' But now we are. Just look around you. More than that: Look around you and *buy*. Only £2.50 for all this? **'The Loves of Lady Purple'** alone is worth £5. Given the devaluation of the pound, £10.

This review has become almost a compendium of felicities with one or two infelicities noted. And this is as it should be. I leave general assessments to the academics. I have no time for that. Besides, I need the time to read all these tales again. And again. (p. 56)

> *James Brockway, "Gothic Pyrotechnics," in* Books and Bookmen, *Vol. 20, No. 5, 1975, pp. 55-6.*

Patricia Craig (essay date 1979)

[*In the following excerpt, Craig praises Carter's imaginative use of symbolism and sexual allegory in* The Bloody Chamber.]

The content of traditional fairy and folk tales has been subjected to fairly rigorous scrutiny in the light of psychoanalysis; no one remains in any doubt that popular fables are informed to a remarkable extent by profound undercurrents, many of them erotic. When we stop taking these stories at their face value we have to recognise (without undue seriousness) that Tom Thumb can be a phallic projection, that 'Cinderella' can be about foot-fetishism and virginity, and that the forbidden can always have a sexual—often incestuous—connotation. Once we've learnt to interpret the symbols, in fact, they become almost ludicrously suggestive: 'for the life of her she could not imagine there was anything unpardonable in opening so small a chamber,' we read with glee in Sir Arthur Quiller-Couch's retelling of 'Bluebeard'. The sexual implications have become palpable, but sexual feeling is entirely absent from the original stories which are standard nursery fare.

To supply the missing erotic quality at the narrative level is one of Angela Carter's objectives in *The Bloody Chamber*; but she is by no means dealing in gross clinical exposition. Each of the ten stories in this collection has a starting-point in a fairy tale or legend, but from this point it expands into a new, more elaborate and fanciful sexual alle-

gory. 'Nothing,' as Angela Carter remarked in *The Sadeian Woman*, 'exercises such power over the imagination as the nature of sexual relationships.' The substance of the old tales can accommodate fresh varieties of meaning and reverberation, and although the imagery remains traditional its range of associations is easily extended. In Perrault, Andersen and Grimm the fundamental emotions of fear, relief, horror, triumph and so on are unambiguous, but the pattern of events is often more complex than it appears. The story of Little Red Riding Hood, for example, raises interesting questions about exactly what is embodied in whom, and Angela Carter (in **'The Werewolf'** and **'The Company of Wolves'**) with impressive economy draws out two alternative strands of meaning: only the sturdy figure of the child remains constant. Wise, and armed only with her father's hunting knife and her own integrity, she stands up to confront whatever is coming to her. In both cases she *is* the wolfsbane.

Angela Carter's themes are vampirism, lycanthropy, fear of corruption, the apprehension of malignity in natural forces; but in accordance with the somewhat ruthless optimism which underlines the therapeutic function of the prototypes, each ending signifies an action accomplished, a consummation effected, a fear dissolved. The snow child melts in the process of intercourse—an act preceded by a necessary pricking and bleeding, symbolically enacted by means of a rose with thorns. The overblown, androgynous rose, in fact, is the emblem most perfectly fashioned to express both sweetness and decadence: blood-red, blooming magically in the snow or nurtured on remnants of flesh discarded by a necrophagous queen. Blood-sucking and blood-letting have their metaphorical inverse in the innocuous blood of menstruation and defloration, and the psychological motif appertaining to each is superimposed endlessly upon the other: the slit throat, which represents the broken hymen, is itself represented by a necklace described as 'a bloody bandage of rubies' which brings us back to the 'jewel' of virginity. Hints, connections and associations proliferate, like the image of the bride in the bedroom filled with arum lilies, reflected to infinity in a wilderness of mirrors. Ms Carter's stories are too rich and heady for casual consumption; but they do provide, at a very high level, romantic nourishment for the imagination.

> *Patricia Craig, "Gory," in* New Statesman, *Vol. 97, No. 2514, May 25, 1979, p. 762.*

Ellen Cronan Rose (essay date 1983)

[*In the following excerpt, Rose discusses Carter's revisionist approach to female identity, sexuality, and traditional fairy tales in* The Bloody Chamber.]

What Adrienne Rich calls "the great unwritten story" of the "cathexis between mother and daughter" can be written many ways. As a lesbian, [Olga] Broumas understandably wants to explore the erotic ramifications of the mother/daughter bond [in her *Beginning with O*]. But a mother is not only her daughter's first love object. She is also her first and therefore most impressive image of adult womanhood. It is this aspect of the mother/daughter relationship that Angela Carter emphasizes in her retelling of "Blue-beard," the first and title story of *The Bloody Chamber.*

Here the strong bond between mother and daughter figures as a kind of "maternal telepathy" that sends not her brothers (as in the original) but her mother to the curious bride's rescue. As Bluebeard's sword ascends for the fatal blow, his young bride's mother bursts through the gate like a Valkyrie—or an Amazon—and fires "a single, irreproachable bullet" through his head.

It is significant that this fighting mother appears in the first story of *The Bloody Chamber.* "What do we mean by the nurture of daughters?" Adrienne Rich asks. Since "women growing into a world so hostile to us need a very profound kind of loving in order to learn to love ourselves," she concludes that "the most important thing one woman [a mother] can do for another [her daughter] is to illuminate and expand her sense of actual possibilities." A mother "who is a fighter" gives her daughter a sense of life's possibilities. Following her example, Bluebeard's widow and her "sisters" in the stories that follow are enabled to explore life's possibilities, to develop into adult women by learning to love themselves. (pp. 221-22)

The Bloody Chamber contains two versions of "Beauty and the Beast," the first a fairly straightforward retelling of the original version by Mme. Le Prince de Beaumont, the second a fanciful improvisation on it. Together they constitute a critique of the ideal of adult womanhood sanctioned by patriarchy and a suggested alternative to it.

[Bruno] Bettelheim concludes *The Uses of Enchantment* with a lengthy discussion of "Beauty and the Beast" because for him it represents the apex of the development to adult womanhood: the successful transfer of a girl's Oedipal attachment to her father to an appropriate partner of the opposite sex. But what seems to Bettelheim "all gentleness and loving devotion" in "Beauty and the Beast"—the attachment of Beauty to her father, the Beast's supplication of her love—is perceived differently by Angela Carter. In her first retelling of the tale, **"The Courtship of Mr. Lyon,"** Carter . . . keeps intact the plot of the original. But . . . she highlights and subtly modifies certain of its features. Beauty's father, for instance, thinks of his daughter as "his girl-child, his pet." Unlike the timid father in the original story, he is not frightened when he discovers an apparently empty mansion in the snow storm; he seems to recognize in its masculine provision for his needs (a decanter of whiskey and a rare roast beef sandwich) something of the comfort of a men's club. And when the beast materializes, he addresses him accordingly—"My good fellow."

Beauty remains with the Beast as long as she does "because her father wanted her to do so." "Do not think she had no will of her own," the narrator cautions. And yet one must wonder whether she does. Or if she does, whether the conditions of her life will allow it to have efficacy. She seems a mere pawn, tugged in one direction by her father's call to join him in his recovered prosperity and in another by the Beast's appeal to her pity. Self-sacrifice wins out over hedonism, proving that Beauty is a truly feminine woman. In effect, the Beast blackmails Beauty into marrying him by going on a hunger strike:

> "I'm dying, Beauty," he said in a cracked whisper of his former purr. "Since you left me, I have been sick. I could not go hunting. I had not the stomach to kill the gentle beasts. I could not eat. I am sick and I must die; but I shall die happy because you have come to say goodbye to me."
>
> She flung herself upon him, so that the iron bedstead groaned, and covered his poor paws with her kisses.
>
> "Don't die, Beast! If you'll have me, I'll never leave you."

You can almost hear his contented purr as the Beast-turned-Prince says, "Do you know, I think I might be able to manage a little breakfast today, Beauty, if you would eat something with me." In retelling "Beauty and the Beast," Carter has indicated that, in patriarchal cultural myths, women do not grow up. They simply change masters—from a beastly father to a fatherly beast. Having discovered this, she is free to invent a tale in which Beauty breaks free from paternal domination.

The patriarchal bonding implicit in **"The Courtship of Mr. Lyon"** is made explicit in **"The Tiger's Bride,"** where Beauty's "profligate" father gambles with the Beast, who beggars him. He is left with nothing. "Except the girl," the Beast reminds him and persuades the father to gamble further. "My father said he loved me yet he staked his daughter on a hand of cards." He loses. Beauty wins, because in **"The Tiger's Bride,"** the Beast is not an enchanted prince, a father-in-the-making. He is an animal, "a great, feline, tawny shape," who wears the mask and clothing of a man awkwardly and with discomfort. Moreover, he does not assume the prerogatives of patriarchy, does not ask Beauty to marry him. He asks only that Beauty strip off her clothes and stand before him naked.

What is naked is the metaphor. Earlier during her stay with the Beast, attended by a clockwork maid, Beauty had discovered her identity, as patriarchy has decreed it:

> I was a young girl, a virgin, and therefore men denied me rationality just as they denied it to all those who were not exactly like themselves. . . . I meditated on the nature of my own state, how I had been bought and sold, passed from hand to hand. That clockwork girl who powdered my cheeks for me; had I not been allotted only the same kind of imitative life amongst men that the doll-maker had given her?

So, although it is not easy for her to obey the Beast's command, Beauty has nothing to lose and everything to gain by stripping herself of her clothes and her socialized identity. Abandoned by men, she turns to the Beast and discovers herself. The tale ends with the Beast licking Beauty: "And each stroke of his tongue ripped off skin after successive skin, all the skins of a life in the world, and left behind a nascent patina of shining hairs."

According to Bettelheim, animals in fairy tales represent our animal nature—in general terms our "untamed id," more specifically our sexual impulses. The significance, for him, of "Beauty and the Beast" is that it suggests "that eventually there comes a time when we must learn what we have not known before—or, to put it psychoanalytically, to undo the repression of sex. What we had experienced as dangerous, loathsome, something to be shunned, must change its appearance so that it is experienced as truly beautiful." Carter's tale is just as much about "undoing the repression of sex" as is the original. But it is also about undoing the oppression of gender. Beauty discovers the animal in herself—her sexuality—only by stripping herself of the veneer of civilization which has socialized her as a woman.

Carter's retelling of "Beauty and the Beast" also questions the Freudian account of female development, in which a woman achieves sexual maturity by shifting her attachment from a father to a male lover. In her two versions of "Little Red Riding Hood" she offers a (nonlesbian) alternative, suggesting that a woman achieves (hetero)-sexual maturity by affirming her own sexuality through identifying with her (grand) mother. The process, as it unfolds in **"The Werewolf"** and **"The Company of Wolves,"** is complex. First, as the title should suggest, in **"The Werewolf"** Little Red Riding Hood discovers that her grandmother and the wolf are one and the same. In so doing, she is making a very important discovery: that to be a mature woman means to be sexual, animal. Understandably, this horrifies the young girl. So she calls out to the neighbors, who drive her werewolf grandmother out of the house and stone her to death. But although the little girl kills her grandmother, she does not then go home to mother and safety. Instead "the child lived in her grandmother's house; she prospered." Little Red Riding Hood may have been initially repulsed by the knowledge that becoming an adult woman will involve acknowledging the animal in herself. But the second step in her negotiation of that developmental process is signaled by her decision to remain in her grandmother's house. She is symbolically declaring her readiness to grow up.

That process of growth is completed in **"The Company of Wolves,"** where Little Red Riding Hood ends up "sweet and sound . . . in granny's bed, between the paws of the tender wolf." Inhabiting not only granny's house but her bed, Red Riding Hood has in a sense become her grandmother. Making love with the wolf, in a "savage marriage ceremony," she is also embracing her grandmother and thus acknowledging and affirming her adult female sexuality. Bettelheim says that it is love which transforms adult sexuality into something beautiful. Carter seems to be saying that love is not possible until one has come to accept and enjoy her sexuality, an accomplishment she associates in these stories with the mother/daughter relationship. (pp. 222-25)

"Wolf-Alice," the last story in *The Bloody Chamber,* is full of wolves and mirrors. Not a retelling of any fairy tale I know, it is nonetheless an appropriate text for concluding remarks about women writers' radical revision of traditional fairy tales.

Alice is a child raised by wolves, "not a wolf herself, although suckled by wolves. . . . Nothing about her is human except that she is *not* a wolf; it is as if the fur she thought she wore had melted into her skin and become part of it, although it does not exist." The hunters who kill her "foster mother" deliver her to some nuns, but they do not succeed in "civilizing" her. So they send her as a servant to the local Duke, who "lives in a gloomy mansion, all alone but for this child who has as little in common with the rest of us as he does." What he and Alice have in common is their dual nature; she is both wolf and human and so is he. He is a werewolf, who casts no image in the mirror. Some time after becoming the Duke's servant, Alice has her first menstrual period. As in [Ann Sexton's version of] "Snow White," the onset of her menses sends the woman in quest of her identity to a mirror. Prowling through the Duke's bedroom in search of some rags to stanch her bleeding, Alice bumps into his mirror. At first she thinks her reflection is another creature and tries to play with it. But "she bruised her muzzle on the cold glass and broke her claws trying to tussle with this stranger. . . . She felt a cool, solid, immovable surface between herself and she—some kind, possibly, of invisible cage?" Like the Queen's looking glass, this is "the rational glass, the master of the visible." As it denies the existence of the wolf-man, so it frustrates the wolf-woman's desire to know herself.

Earlier in the story, the narrator—one of the "rest of us"—says of Alice, "we secluded her in animal privacy out of fear of her imperfection because it showed us what we might have been." Her imperfection—she thinks of it as "her wound"—is her female sexuality, represented by her monthly bleeding. But unlike the rest of us—certainly unlike Adrienne Rich's Marie Curie, who died "denying / her wounds / denying / her wounds came from the same source as her power"—Wolf-Alice affirms her wound, her womanhood, as she had earlier refused to renounce her animal (foster) mother. She "learn[s] to expect these bleedings . . . so that you might say she discovered the very action of time by means of this returning cycle." With this acceptance comes a power the Queen in "Snow White" lacked, the power to look behind the mirror and discover there no patriarchal dictator, but "only dust, a spider stuck in his web, a heap of rags." Consequently, Wolf-Alice's "relation with the mirror was now far more intimate since she knew she saw herself within it."

The haunting conclusion of Carter's original fairy tale suggests that women would not be the only beneficiaries of liberation from the patriarchal dictates of the Queen's looking glass. The Duke, on one of his forays through the graveyard in search of food, is ambushed and shot. Wounded, he limps home where Alice later finds him, bleeding and in pain. Although puzzled, because "his wound . . . does not smell like her wound," Alice proceeds, "without hesitation, without disgust, with a quick, tender gravity," to lick the blood and dirt from his face. The story ends with these brief paragraphs:

> The lucidity of the moonlight lit the mirror propped against the red wall; the rational glass, the master of the visible, impartially recorded the crooning girl.
>
> As she continued her ministrations, this glass, with infinite slowness, yielded to the reflexive strength of its own material construction. Little by little, there appeared within it, like the image

Carter in 1974, the year she published Fireworks: Nine Profane Pieces, *her first short story collection.*

on photographic paper that emerges, first, a formless web of tracery, the prey caught in its own fishing net, then in firmer yet still shadowed outline until at last as vivid as real life itself, as if brought into being by her soft, moist, gentle tongue, finally, the face of the Duke.

What can fairy tales, retold by women, tell us about female development? That it has been distorted by patriarchy; that it is and must be grounded in the mother-daughter matrix; that it involves not only the discovery but the glad acceptance of our sexuality. That a woman who loves the woman who is herself has the power of loving another person. And perhaps someday even patriarchy will "yield" to that power. (pp. 226-27)

> Ellen Cronan Rose, "Through the Looking Glass: When Women Tell Fairy Tales," in The Voyage In: Fictions of Female Development, *Elizabeth Able, Marianne Hirsch, Elizabeth Langland, eds., University Press of New England, 1983, pp. 209-27.*

Patricia Duncker   (essay date 1984)

[*In the following excerpt, Duncker examines Carter's*

feminist treatment of traditional fairy-tale narratives in The Bloody Chamber *and argues that in these works Carter views herself as a "moral pornographer."*]

> I started to write short pieces when I was living in a room too small to write a novel in. So the size of my room modified what I did inside it and it was the same with the pieces themselves. The limited trajectory of the short narrative concentrates its meaning. Sign and sense can fuse to an extent impossible to achieve among the multiplying ambiguities of an extended narrative.
> Angela Carter—From the Afterword to
> *Fireworks: Nine Profane Pieces* (1974)

The Afterword to *Fireworks* (1974) and the Polemical Preface to *The Sadeian Woman* (1979) are both literary manifestos, maps for the territory and enterprise of Angela Carter's fiction. In her most recent work two strands sever and combine; firstly, her translations of the fairy tales of Charles Perrault (1977), ancient wisdom reborn as didactic little pieces of enlightened self-interest, the short tale in which sign and sense become utterly fused, with the moral, often a contradictory one, chugging along behind like the guardsman; and secondly, her critique of the mythology of sexuality in her novel, *The Passion of New Eve* (1977), a fantastic Gothic quest across an America riven by approaching apocalypse, an invading voyage into the forbidden places of sexual taboo. The psychology of pornography and the Gothic, submerged in the sexual translations of Eve, are subjected to speculative, non-fictional treatment in *The Sadeian Woman;* out of the last metamorphosis come the fairy tales of Charles Perrault, rewritten by the woman disguised, self-styled as the moral pornographer, the tales in *The Bloody Chamber.*

We must stand back to applaud her ambition, for the success of her enterprise, re-shaping and re-imagining the archetypes of imagination, re-casting the bricks of our inner worlds, would require extraordinary resourcefulness. The lure of her chosen form, tales rather than short stories, is easily explicable. For Carter the strength of the tale lies in the fact that it does not sink into the slough of dailiness, rather, it un-fetters the imagination. For the tale interprets rather than presents everyday experience, through 'a system of imagery derived from subterranean areas behind everyday experience, and therefore the tale cannot betray its readers into a false knowledge . . .' (Afterword to *Fireworks*). But here, I believe, she is wrong. The unconscious is not a treasure vault containing visionary revelations about ourselves. It is rather the cesspool of our fears and desires, filled with the common patterns that are also projections of the ways in which we have been taught to perceive the world. And the deep structure of those patterns will reflect the political, social and psychological realities within which we exist as best we can. The unconscious mirrors these changing realities. Nothing else. And the fairy tales, the received collective wisdom of the past, which, as Carter rightly perceives, reflect the myths of sexuality under patriarchy, have been and still are used as the text books through which those lessons are learned. Thus the tale, especially the fairy tale, is the vessel of false knowledge, or more bluntly, interested propaganda. Andrea Dworkin, in *Woman Hating* (1974), discusses the process by which women are taught fear, through the fairy tales, as a function of their femininity.

> The lessons are simple, and we learn them well.
>
> Men and women are different, absolute opposites.
>
> The heroic prince can never be confused with Cinderella, or
>
> Snow-white, or Sleeping Beauty. She could never do what he does
>
> at all, let alone better . . .
>
> Where he is erect, she is supine. Where he is awake, she is asleep.
>
> Where he is active, she is passive. Where she is erect, or awake, or
>
> active, she is evil and must be destroyed . . .

The fairy tales, with all the unfettered cruelty that is permissible in fantasy, spell out the punishment for rebellion or dissent. Dworkin again,

> There are two definitions of woman. There is the good woman. She is a victim. There is the bad woman. She must be destroyed. The good woman must be possessed. The bad woman must be killed, or punished. Both must be nullified.

Her analysis is perfectly correct. So far as she goes. She sees the fairy tales as parables handed out to children as working tools, ways of dealing with the world, the way to knuckle down into uncongenial shapes, rather than as weapons of understanding and change. The fairy tales are, in fact, about power, and about the struggle for possession, by fair or magical means, of kingdoms, goods, children, money, land, and—naturally, specifically,—the possession of women. And even the fairy (more properly folk) tale itself, as the narrative art of the people, communally owned, has been appropriated by the ruling class at a specific point in history, transformed, rewritten, possessed. For the fairy tales became children's literature at a particular moment in the history of their transmission. Originally, they were nothing of the kind. (pp. 3-4)

Charles Perrault and the Countess d'Aulnoy, both writing in the last years of the seventeenth century transcribed the tales from a living oral tradition, as did the Brothers Grimm, who rewrote and reshaped the Rhineland tales in their collection for a supposedly more sophisticated audience. But the tales, coming out of history, continue to mirror the times which produced them. There was nothing particularly remarkable about stepmothers in a period when lives were short, childbirth often fatal and a surviving husband would probably marry again; nor, in a medieval community, is there anything extraordinary about wells as the centre of village life or marriage at puberty. But, inexorably, the fairy tales became the property of childhood. And now, whether they are read or told, they have become narratives passed on from adults to children. The teller traditionally bears the face of age. They are the parables of wisdom and experience addressed to the apprehension of innocence, in which the pleasure of fiction is carefully fenced off and contained within the ritual parentheses, 'Once upon a time. . .', 'They lived happily ever after. . .' These are the limits of fantasy, and the fairy tale is necessarily fantastic, a world of extremes, excess, an inversion of dailiness. But the tales continue to expose the raw nerves of real conflicts between classes, families, men and women, mothers and daughters, fathers and sons. The transition from adolescence through puberty to adulthood is brutally taught through the tales in which inequalities are painted unambiguously in the characters of excess. The sexual symbolism of the fairy tales may now appear to us to be ludicrous, transparent, but to the child their meanings remain mysterious. Carter's rewriting of the tales is an exercise in making the mystery sexually explicit.

Apart from **'The Erl-King'**, which she presumably adapts from Goethe's ballad, Carter chooses a sequence of classic tales most of which are to be found in Perrault; the story of Bluebeard and his wives in **'The Bloody Chamber'**, two versions of 'Beauty and the Beast' in **'The Courtship of Mr Lyon'** and **'The Tiger's Bride'**, an operatic Puss-in-Boots which deliberately suggests the Baroque ornamentation of Rossini's music, Snow-White in **'The Snow Child'**, Sleeping Beauty as a Gothic vampire in **'The Lady of the House of Love'**, two versions of Red Riding Hood and a tale that combines motifs from several of these, **'Wolf-Alice'**. The animal aspects of human sexuality are her particular concern; thus the wolf and the lion roam through the tales seeking whom they may erotically devour. Carter's style is genuinely original; perhaps this is the most startling departure from the simplicity of form and directness characteristic of Perrault's narratives, as stark and uncompromising as ballads. Perrault's morals may be knowingly smug: his narratives are not. Carter's method is quite deliberate; the tales are rewritten as elaborate pieces of pure Gothic, in the manner of Poe.

> Character and events are exaggerated beyond reality, to become symbols, ideas, passions. Its (the Gothic tradition of Poe) style will tend to be ornate, unnatural. . . Its only humour is black humour.
>
> (Afterword to *Fireworks*)

But the infernal trap inherent in the fairy tale, which fits the form to its purpose, to be the carrier of ideology, proves too complex and pervasive to avoid. Carter is rewriting the tales within the strait-jacket of their original structures. The characters she re-creates must to some extent, continue to exist as abstractions. Identity continues to be defined by role, so that shifting the perspective from the impersonal voice to the inner confessional narrative as she does in several of the tales, merely explains, amplifies and re-produces rather than alters the original, deeply, rigidly sexist psychology of the erotic. The disarming of aggressive male sexuality by the virtuous bride is at the root of 'The Frog Prince' and 'Beauty and the Beast'. Carter transposes this moral into the narrative **'The Company of Wolves'**. So that the erotic confrontation and reversal at the end becomes a meeting of sexual aggression and the cliché of female erotic ingenuity. Red Riding Hood sees that rape is inevitable—'The Wolf is carnivore incarnate'—and decides to strip off, lie back and enjoy it. She wants it really. They all do. The message spelt out. **'The Tiger's Bride'** argues a variation on the original bargain;

the heroine is sold to the highest bidder in the marriage pact, but she too strips off all artifice, the lies inherent in borrowed garments, and reveals herself as she is, the mirror image of his feline predatory sexuality. Authorial comment surrounding this encounter is contradictory; on the one hand Beauty's body is 'the cold white meat of contract' but on the other, 'I, white, shaking, raw, approaching him as if offering, in myself, the key to a peaceable kingdom in which his appetite need not be my extinction.' I would suggest that all we are watching, beautifully packaged and unveiled, is the ritual disrobing of the willing victim of pornography.

Carter's tales are, supposedly, celebrations of erotic desire. But male sexuality has too long, too tenaciously been linked with power and possession, the capture, breaking and ownership of women. The explicitly erotic currents in her tales mirror these realities. Pornography, that is, the representation of overtly sexual material with the intention to arouse prurient, vicarious desire, uses the language of male sexuality. Even the women's equivalent of soft porn, romance novels and 'bodice-rippers', all conform to recognisably male fantasies of domination, submission and possession. Heterosexual feminists have not yet invented an alternative, anti-sexist language of the erotic. Carter envisages women's sensuality simply as a response to male arousal. She has no conception of women's sexuality as autonomous desire.

One of the deftest, most disturbing pieces in the book is her version of 'Snow-White', **'The Snow Child'**. Here Carter exposes the Oedipal conflict between Mother and Daughter: the snow maiden is the father's child, 'the child of his desire' who threatens to usurp the Mother's place. With one small touch Carter reveals the Mother as a sister to Sade's Juliette, the sexual terrorist, with a motif taken from the literature of pornography, 'she wore high, black shining boots with scarlet heels and spurs.' If the Mother ever fails the child in the fairy tales that child's life is always in jeopardy. In Carter's version the Mother offers up the child, as her sexuality blossoms in the rose, to the Father's lust, which destroys her. Carter removes the supposedly comforting denouement to the tale in which the mother is destroyed and the child successfully navigates the dangerous transition into sexual maturity. But she doesn't question the ideology implicit in the story, that the Mother and Daughter will—necessarily—become rivals for the Father's love and be prepared to countenance one another's destruction. The division between Mother and Daughter, and between Sisters, is one of the cornerstones of patriarchy. The fact that so many of the tales suggest and endorse those old enmities is both sinister and predictable. 'Cinderella', 'Snow-White', 'Beauty and the Beast' all argue the case for women, beware women. The logic of the fairy tales travels on into the structures of orthodox literature; *King Lear* is cast in the fairy tale mould of the old father dividing his kingdom between the three daughters, two are destructive and predatory, only the youngest daughter, carefully constructed out of masculine desire as the Snow Child had been, remains loyal to the father. Carter rings the sexual changes cheerfully enough.

Red Riding Hood sleeps between the paws of the Wolf, the Grandmother actually *is* the Wolf, Beauty becomes the Beast; but she still leaves the central taboos unspoken. Some things are unthinkable. She could never imagine Cinderella in bed with the Fairy Godmother.

Carter's extraordinary fascination with De Sade simmers at the root of what is both disturbing reactionary and sadly unoriginal in her work. She knows that 'the tale has relations with the subliterary forms of pornography, ballad and dream'. In *The Sadeian Woman* she suggests that the Devil is best slain with his own weapons and argues the case for the moral pornographer, who is, curiously, envisaged as male.

> The moral pornographer would be an artist who uses pornographic material as part of the acceptance of the logic of a world of absolute sexual licence for all the genders, and projects a model of the way such a world might work. A moral pornographer might use pornography as a critique of current relations between the sexes. His business would be the total demystification of the flesh and the subsequent revelation, through the infinite modulations of the sexual act, of the real relations between man and his kind. Such a pornographer would not be the enemy of women, perhaps because he might begin to penetrate to the heart of the contempt for women that distorts our culture even as he entered the realms of true obscenity as he describes it.

This is, I would suggest, utter nonsense. Pornography, indeed, the representation of all sexual relations between men and women, will necessarily 'render explicit the nature of social relations in the society in which they take place'. That is why most bourgeois fiction concentrates upon the choices surrounding courtship and marriage, for it is there that the values and realities upon which a society is based will be most sharply revealed. The realities of power perhaps, but not the imagined experience of desire. Pornography, heightened, stylised, remote, mirrors precisely these socially-constructed realities. The realities of male desire, aggression, force; the reality of women, compliant and submissive. Where then shall imagined desire, the expression of feminist eroticism, be found, apprehended, expressed? Andrea Dworkin argues that this can only emerge when the division of sexual polarity is destroyed, when male and female sexual identities are reborn.

> . . . we will have to abandon phallic worth and female masochism altogether as normative, sanctioned identities, as modes of erotic behaviour, as basic indicators of 'male' and 'female'.
>
> As we are destroying the structure of culture, we will have to build a new culture—nonhierarchical, nonsexist, noncoercive, nonexploitative—in other words, a culture which is not based on dominance and submission in any way.
>
> And as we are destroying the phallic identities of men and the masochistic identities of women, we will have to create, out of our own ashes, new erotic identities.

This passage, taken from her essay 'The Politics of Fear

and Courage' is very much to the point in that the fairy tales are used to teach precisely these things; phallic worth, female masochism, fear and courage. The fairy tales are bridges across the straits of adolescence. The child becomes a man or a woman; the rite of passage is marriage and sexual maturity, but within the architecture of the fairy tale this will have a different meaning for a boy and a girl. 'Tom Thumb', 'Puss-in-Boots' carry the classical Oedipal message of puberty; the Father, the ogre, must be slain by the adolescent who then possesses his inheritance, the ogre's castle, the princess. The Father is never killed by name in the fairy tales, but his threatening, confining destructiveness is emphasized. He is masked by superlatives, but with courage, ingenuity and strength he may be overcome. So the tales send the boys out into the world to seek their fortunes, create their wealth, possess their women. The boys must be taught courage. The girls must be taught fear. For girls the critical metamorphosis is sexual, menstruation, puberty, marriage. For Sleeping Beauty the symbolic curse that comes upon her is puberty, the first shedding of blood, the curse that can only be redeemed by marriage, her rightful place. This is the first of the tales in Perrault's collection *Histoires ou contes du temps passé* (1697). Perrault tells the tale up to the 'happy ending' of the Prince's kiss which redeems the time and awakens the Princess from her long stupor of adolescence. All the women have to do is wait. She must not initiate sexual activity, a potential she now possesses that is fraught with danger. She must wait and sleep out the years until she is possessed. Perrault, with all the unctuousness of a civil servant adds the moral.

> The Tale of Sleeping Beauty shows how long engagements make for happy marriages, but young girls these days want so much to be married I do not have the heart to press the moral.

> **Carter's tales are, supposedly, celebrations of erotic desire. But male sexuality has too long, too tenaciously been linked with power and possession, the capture, breaking and ownership of women. The explicitly erotic currents in her tales mirror these realities.**
>
> —*Patricia Duncker*

But Perrault only tells us a version of an older Neapolitan story to be found in Basile's *Pentamerone* (1636). In that version a king is out hunting, he passes the locked and deserted castle, his falcon flies in through the open window, he follows the bird and comes upon the sleeping princess, he is unable to rouse her or to control himself, rapes her, leaves and forgets her. The result of this little exploit is twins, Sun and Moon, who awaken their mother. The king eventually returns, but he is, unfortunately, already married to an ogress, a sister of Medea who tries to organise a meal in which his two children are served up in a pie and

the Sleeping Beauty is to be burnt. The link here between Sleeping Beauty and Snow White is clear, in both cases she is the Oedipal child who arouses the desire of the Father and the hatred of the Mother. Perrault's desire to curtail the narrative before it became too unpleasant need not be attributed to prudery; his stories were addressed to the Court where it was scarcely tactful to speak of cannibal queens and raping kings.

Carter's Gothic version of the tale is a peculiar nemesis for radical feminism. The lady of the House of Love is both the Sleeping Beauty and the Vampire Queen, the voracious witch of Hansel and Gretel.

> Everything about this beautiful and ghastly lady is as it should be, queen of night, queen of terror—except her horrible reluctance for the role.

In fact what the Countess longs for is the grande finale of all 'snuff' movies in which the woman is sexually used and ritually killed, the oldest cliché of them all, sex and death. She can abandon her predatory sexuality, the unnatural force, as her own blood flows, the symbolic breaking of the virgin hymen, the initiation into sexual maturity and then into death.

> In death, she looked far older, less beautiful and so, for the first time fully human.

> I will vanish in the morning light; I was only an invention of darkness.

> And I leave you as a souvenir the dark, fanged rose I plucked from between my thighs, like a flower laid on a grave. On a grave.

Only in death does she pass into womanhood, and the handsome British cyclist passes out of the innocent security of fairy tale into the terror of history and the trenches of the First World War.

The most successful narrative in Carter's collection is the most elaborate and expansive, the modern Bluebeard, **'The Bloody Chamber'**. This is a tour de force. The confessional voice of the tale is that of experience, the girl recalling her initiation into the adult world. Carter's story—and indeed all the earlier versions—are about women's masochistic complicity in male sexual aggression; and about husbands. Perrault was in no doubt about this either. He draws the moral from the story; an admonition to nosey women who seek to know the truth about the men they marry. 'Curiosity is the most fleeting of pleasures; the moment it is satisfied, it ceases to exist and it always proves, very, very expensive. It is easy to see that the events described in this story took place many years ago'. He then adds, embarrassed, 'no modern husband would dare to be half so terrible'. Carter's Bluebeard is simply a husband, he is given no other name. (pp. 5-10)

Carter's **'Bloody Chamber'** uses all the iconography of the Gothic; the remote castle, the virgin at the mercy of the tormented hero-villain, the enclosed spaces, hidden atrocities, women voraciously, masochistically eager for the corruption of sexuality. All the pervading themes of pornography are there too; domination, control, humiliation, mutilation, possession through murder. All perpetrated on willing, eager victims. The marriage bargain becomes explicit, the bride as the bought woman, acting out the 'ritual from the brothel.' Carter's tale carefully creates the classical pornographic model of sexuality, which has a definite meaning and endorses a particular kind of fantasy, that of male sexual tyranny within a marriage that is grossly unequal; the child bride responsive to her husband's desire, ready to be 'impaled' among the lilies of death, the face with its 'promise of debauchery', a rare talent for corruption. Here is the sexual model which endorses the 'normal and natural sadism of the male, happily complemented by the normal and natural masochism of the female.' The husband of **'The Bloody Chamber'** is a connoisseur, a collector of pornography. When the child bride peers at the titles in his bookcase she finds the texts for the knowledge she reads in blood, a guide to her fate, *The Initiation, The Key to Mysteries, The Secret of Pandora's Box,* imaged in the Sultan's murdered wives.

But there are two other figures that Carter has created in her re-writing of the tale whose actions and presence alter the terms of the unequal conflict between husband and wife. In Perrault's original version the bride's sister Anne, about whom we are told nothing but her name, looks out from the tower as Bluebeard sharpens his cutlass in the courtyard, to proclaim the galloping arrival of the bride's two brothers. In Carter's version this figure becomes the blinded piano tuner, Jean-Yves, who loves the child bride not for her ambiguous beauty, the veil across corruption, but for her single gift of music. Only with the blinded boy who humbly serves her music can Carter envisage a marriage of equality for Bluebeard's bride. Men as invalids are constant figures in women's fiction; most remarkably in the writing of Charlotte Brontë: her heroes suffer on the point of her pen, she blinds them, maims them, drowns them. This is easy to understand; if a man is damaged and hurt a woman is released from the habitual sexual constraint forced upon her, she can take action, initiate contact, speak out, the power imbalance inherent in all heterosexual relationships, is levelled off.

This attempt to break down the traditional erotic identities is also implied by the pervasive tranvestism in Brontë's novels: Rochester dressed as a gypsy woman, De Hamal as a nun, Shirley, behind the ambiguous sexuality of her name talks, acts, commands, swaggers like a man, Ginevra Fanshawe is wooed by Lucy Snowe, taking the part of a man in the school play. The man whose eyes are extinguished can no longer evaluate, dominate, control. He is reduced to dependence. Only when Rochester is blinded can Jane Eyre return. Blindness is the curse of Oedipus, a symbolic reckoning. But the blinded man has a further significance. This figure suggests that although men observe women constantly they do not see us; they do not perceive who we really are, we remain invisible. But while blindness, as symbolic castration, may signal the end of male sexual aggression, it is also mutilation. As such it cannot be offered as the answer, the new male erotic identity. In the case of Bluebeard's bride it is as well that her lover cannot see her, for she carries the mark of her complicity and corruption forever, the complicity of women who have been made in man's image, who have desired to be possessed, who walk after the diva of Isolde, the model

of Montmartre, the Romanian Countess, who meet the reward of that complicity in the bloody chamber.

It is not the brothers who arrive armed with muskets and rapiers to save Bluebeard's bride, but a figure who never appears in the fairy tales, the mother as travelling heroine.

> My eagle-featured, indomitable mother; what other student at the Conservatoire could boast that her mother had outfaced a junkful of Chinese pirates, nursed a village through a visitation of the plague, shot a man-eating tiger with her own hand and all before she was as old as I?

This is the mother who invests in her daughter's career rather than her price on the marriage market; and it is the mother's spirit, the courage incidentally of the Gothic heroines who pass unraped, unharmed down into the dungeons of the castle, which accompanies her daughter to learn the truth of the bloody chamber.

> My mother's spirit drove me on, into that dreadful place, in a cold ecstasy to know the very worst.

And the hand of vengeance against Bluebeard is the woman's hand, the mother's hand bearing the father's weapon. Only the women have suffered, only the women can be avenged.

> . . . without a moment's hesitation, she raised my father's gun, took aim and put a single, irreproachable bullet through my husband's head.

Here Carter is transforming the sexual politics of the fairy tales in significant ways. The mother of Bluebeard's bride never deserts her child. She has the wisdom to give her child the freedom demanded by sexual maturity, the freedom denied to Sleeping Beauty by her royal parents when they seek to protect her from the fairy's curse, that her hand shall be pierced by a spindle. But the mother arrives with melodramatic timeliness, giving the lie to Papa Freud's Oedipal realities.

> . . . I felt a pang of loss as if, when he put the gold band on my finger, I had, in some way, ceased to be her child in becoming his wife.

In fact, the bond between Mother and Daughter is never broken. Carter's tale, perhaps unwittingly, carries an uncompromisingly feminist message; for the women's revolution would seal up the door of the bloody chamber forever.

All Carter's books are either short novels or tales, fantastic narratives. *The Sadeian Woman* and her collected essays, *Nothing Sacred* (1982) are her only non-fictional work to date. Her style is as lavish and ornate as the detail on the architecture Puss-in-Boots finds easy to climb— 'Nothing to it once you know how, rococo's no problem.' This is her great strength. Her re-writing, re-imagining of the fairy tales could have been more intriguing than it is, had she studied the ambivalent sexual language that is there in the original tales. Perrault's Red Riding Hood is—in French—designated by a masculine name, Le petit Chaperon rouge. At the moment when the ritual words are uttered—'draw the bolt and the latch will open'—she is the one who enters; the wolf wears the grandmother's clothes. In later versions the woodcutters find both Red Riding Hood and the grandmother safe in the womb of the wolf. These ambiguities are partially acknowledged in **'The Company of Wolves'**, but follow the sexual symbolism of Cinderella thrusting her foot into the envoy's slipper, of Bluebeard's wife penetrating the secret space of the bloody chamber. These currents are there too in Carter's tales. She cannot avoid them. And she could go much further than she does.

Carter chooses to inhabit a tiny room of her own in the house of fiction. For women, that space has always been paralysingly, cripplingly small, I think we need the 'multiplying ambiguities of an extended narrative'. To imagine ourselves whole. We cannot fit neatly into patterns or models as Cinderellas, ugly sisters, wicked step-mothers, fairy God-mothers, and still acknowledge our several existences, experienced or imagined. We need the space to carve out our own erotic identities, as free women. And then to rewrite the fairy tales—with a bolder hand. (pp. 10-12)

> Patricia Duncker, "Re-Imagining the Fairy Tales: Angela Carter's Bloody Chambers," in Literature and History, *Vol. 10, No. 1, Spring, 1984, pp. 3-14.*

Ann Snitow   (essay date 1986)

[*In the following essay, Snitow examines the radicalism in Carter's works and offers praise for* Saints and Strangers.]

Angela Carter, famous and much read in England, has come to American readers only piecemeal, almost as if American publishers see her as a wine that won't travel well. Demon fiction writer though she is, her first real U.S. *succès d'estime* was for her feminist study of the Marquis de Sade, *The Sadeian Woman: And the Ideology of Pornography.* I remember the puzzling reviews of that book when it came out here in 1979. Most were grudgingly admiring but, taken together, they gave contradictory accounts of what the book said, agreeing only that Carter had somehow become besotted with de Sade and had misunderstood what a bad, bad man (or what a sad, sad man) he really was. One was totally unprepared, then, for the book itself:

> Sade's work concerns the nature of sexual freedom and is of particular significance to women because of his refusal to see female sexuality in relation to its reproductive function, a refusal as unusual in the late eighteenth century as it is now.

In that year, in the United States, it was startling to hear a feminist voice so unapologetic for engaging the archenemy. *The Sadeian Woman* was misread for good reasons: It is a threatening book. Carter speculated in a number of unpleasant directions (can women be as monstrous as men?); she was flexible enough to contain opposites (an appreciation and a contempt for de Sade); and peremptory enough to read or willfully misread de Sade for her own subversive, emancipatory purposes. The book suggested a shameless and aggressively probing stance for a woman

who would be the critic of male culture. It was phallic criticism consciously ironic about all phallic authority, and at its culminating moment it turned on its hero and excoriated him for making the mother figure in *Philosophy in the Boudoir* fall into a faint just before the moment of orgasm:

> He is as much afraid of freedom as the next man. So he makes her faint. He makes her faint because he can only conceive of freedom as existing in opposition, freedom as defined by tyranny.

Hardly besotted with de Sade, Carter is bitterly disappointed that freedom has no savor for him unless the prohibited woman is in chains, unconscious of her sexuality. Just when he seemed to Carter so close to being a revolutionary pornographer, one who can see that everyone, even the mother, is sexual, and that anyone can cross the boundaries of gender and taboo, he lapses into the myths common in most pornography, reinstating the old rigidity, reasserting the safe laws of transgression. How much does the concept of freedom depend on the pre-existence of prohibition? Carter tortures herself with this question in all her work. Meanwhile, to Carter's sorrow, the mother faints, the French Revolution fails, de Sade's freedom's just another word for naughty little boy.

No wonder the book caused consternation. It was an invention, a counterfiction to de Sade's, an intellectual interlude from a writer of extreme cunning who takes the imagination seriously as the place where we tell stories to ourselves and where we can best see—inside the form itself—the structure of our own rules.

Like most bad girls, Carter has a love/hate relationship to rules: she gives them their due, but defiantly demands a good time. Constantly at play, she writes fairy tales, Gothic horror stories, romances, phantasmagorical science fictions, allegories, fables—and her virtuosity at manipulating the laws of these conventional forms is dazzling. (She can skew them with irony or play them straight.) Reading a lot of Angela Carter at once is like being galloped on a child's hobbyhorse through the culture attic. You're choking on the fumes of greasepaint; you're startled as a bunch of waxwork Bluebeards, beasts and beauties blunder into you; you're tangled in string by some grand puppeteer who jerks you around, then cuts the connection, leaving you free to play with whatever toy you want. You wind one up. It's a gorgeous tableau of a terrible, deep forest, where the Wolf and Little Red Riding Hood couple in the glittering dark. The whole thing sparkles and revolves, then runs down.

For some readers, perhaps, once the mechanism winds to a halt, the whole illusion will evaporate like a midsummer night's dream. (In [***Saints and Strangers***], Carter has written an exquisitely silly spoof of that play, full of concupiscent fairies with bad head colds.) Certainly, Carter runs the risk of the true littérateur: How to resist the temptations of virtuosity? In an introduction to a marvelous essay, "Sixties Style," in her collection of occasional pieces, *Nothing Sacred*, she disarms criticism by simply apologizing: "I note that [this essay] is over-written and over-literary, but a person can only walk the one way and that is the way I still walk." Love me as I am, and don't hold it against me if what you love melts at a touch; infinite variety is the best of a lover's tricks.

Sometimes called a pornographic writer, she is one only in a very special sense. Pleasure—and the fear that is so often pleasure's sauce—are her subjects, but the most exciting moments in her fiction are literary: the splendid verbal coups, the sensuous unfolding of the story line. She can write narrative turns of such beauty you fall in love with the romance itself—forget the princes. Each book is a fresh experiment in form and tone, a trip down the possible paths inherent in yet another style. Carter tries everything and I'm sure is indifferent to the fact that, inevitably, the results of so much freedom are uneven.

In general, I think her talent for decoration, for magic textures of color and light, works better in her stories than in her novels. Some Carter fans will disagree, particularly those who like their metafictions long. I see the novels I've read as stories that got out of hand. In one very fine one, *The Magic Toyshop,* for example, she writes of a cruel, brilliant uncle who makes children's toys, "He was too big and wicked to be true." This is so, and why not? But the wicked uncle is one of her windup toys, an evil totem she must drag the whole length of this otherwise psychologically suggestive book. Wooden and unexplained, he eventually becomes a dead weight. In the stories, violent men who jump out at young girls make more sense. They serve their single function, to set the blood beating so that Carter can get a clear reading on the agitated human heart.

Why is Carter telling fairy tales while Rome indulges in what she calls, in one of her always witty essays, "bed and circuses"? How are her circuses better than the ones she finds pusillanimous, dead or sad? What saves the books from being kitsch? Well, not much, sometimes. If you've no taste for the turns and twists and tricks of narrative for their own sake, Carter will pale on you too fast; you'll leave before she tells you her secrets. But secrets she has— sometimes as rich as her prose. By telling fairy tales, she chooses a fictional world ruled by the brutal economy of roles: pattern determines that little girls will run away and big wolves give chase. But the unconscious always erupts in a Carter story: Beauty falls in love with the beast *as a beast*; she doesn't want a prince. Neither freedom nor pleasure is rational or safe, though, ironically, both have their own determining structures.

To me, even the more clanking of Angela Carter's artifices seem poignant, perhaps because through one persona or another she keeps signaling the *Angst* of entrapment inside pattern. The pain in her best stories is the pain of a real toad in an imaginary garden. A few of her more realistic pieces from an early volume, *Fireworks*, are moving precisely because the narrator wants so much to be authentic, to feel directly, and suffers the fate of the ironic and self-conscious, the fate of alienation from anything simple or sentimental. Carter's sophistication is curse and blessing. She can't go naked, no matter how many layers she strips off; a postlapsarian Eve, she is infernally knowing.

In *Saints and Strangers,* her new collection, Carter gives of her very best. The opening story, about Lizzie Borden ("**The Fall River Axe Murders**"), is particularly beautiful

in design and density. Carter assembles Lizzie's dreadful crime by picturing the Borden household at the moment before the family wakes on the fateful day in August 1892. In this atmosphere of unbearable immanence, Carter tours the sleeping house like an *hallucinée*. Her eyes like cameras, she witnesses each variable: the heat; Lizzie's menstrual blood; the experimental chemistry of unrefrigerated food; the circulation of boredom, madness and money; relevant snatches of the past represented by the sparse objects in this miserly house. She passes through the construction of locked doors to observe the architecture of the patriarchal family: father Borden and his captive womenfolk, wife, daughter, maid, each half swooning in sweat and unremembered dreams.

But whenever this authorial omniscience seems too complete Carter draws back and reminds us of how she is straining to imagine these people. Explanations are all very well, but the author loses confidence as she gazes at an old photograph of Lizzie which "secretes mystery." Is Lizzie Borden utterly other—"as taut as the strings of a wind-harp from which random currents of the air pluck out tunes that are not our tunes"—or is she continuous with us, perhaps even a reasonable assassin, exacting a just retribution for the suppressed violence of her terrible, woman-wasting world? By the end, Carter has let us see the ax, and the reasons Lizzie uses it, but the act itself need hardly be mentioned since, by now, the rival intensities of knowledge and mystery are so impacted that *everything* in the story cuts.

Freud broods over a psychological study like this, not only as a source of explanation but equally as a source of myth. In another fine story here, "**Peter and the Wolf**," Carter conflates a Freudian reading of a fairy tale with a rediscovery of the tale's original mystery. The story hangs in the balance between the power of the unconscious and the analysis of that power; Carter's art lies in her refusal to finally tip the scale to one side or the other:

> A girl from a village on the lower slopes [of the Alps] left her widowed mother to marry a man who lived up in the empty places. Soon she was pregnant. In October, there was a severe storm. The old woman knew her daughter was near her time and waited for a message but none arrived. After the storm passed, the old woman went up to see for herself, taking her grown son with her because she was afraid.

> From a long way off, they saw no smoke rising from the chimney. . . . There were traces of wolf-dung on the floor so they knew wolves had been in the house but left the corpse of the young mother alone although of her baby nothing was left except some mess that showed it had been born. Nor was there a trace of the son-in-law but a gnawed foot in a boot.

> They wrapped the dead in a quilt and took it home with them.

Time passes; the old woman has other grandchildren, among them Peter who at age 7 is taken above the timber line to tend the goats. A pack of wolves appears, "the thing he had been taught most to fear," among them a filthy, hairy little girl, obviously his lost cousin. The family captures this "marvel . . . on all fours" and brings her down to the village. But her wildness is more terrible and absolute than they can encompass. In a frenzy she ruins the house, delivers a death wound to the grandmother and howls until the wolves rescue her in a marauding pack. Peter watches it all, including

> the crevice of her girl-child's sex. . . . a view of a set of Chinese boxes of whorled flesh that seemed to open one upon another into herself, drawing him into an inner, secret place in which destination perpetually receded before him, his first, devastating, vertiginous intimation of infinity.

After that, he turns to piety and books as a fence against the unknown. He studies until he is a "stranger" to the peasants of his village and they let him leave to become a priest.

Down he comes from the mountains of his trauma and meets his cousin once again as she comes to drink at dawn from the river. He reacquaints himself with the power of her animal freedom, the oneness and grace that come from a perfect unconsciousness. This was what he had longed for all these years of pious self-abasement: sex without guilt, mortality without fear. His cry of "visionary ecstasy" startles the wolf-woman, who runs off, leaving him to continue his journey: "but what would he do at the seminary, now? For now he knew there was nothing to be afraid of. He experienced the vertigo of freedom." Under a "cool, rational sun," he gives one last look at the exotic mountain fastnesses now flattened like views on picture post cards. No longer circumscribed by old country tales, Peter is marked instead by the knowledge of one who has descended from the superstitious wilderness "into a different story."

Carter never patronizes "the primitive, vast, magnificent, barren, unkind simplicity of the mountain." She sees through it, but often returns to it because, she says, "The Gothic tradition . . . retains a singular moral function—that of provoking unease." A radical too rarely recognized by radicals, Carter insists that we count the power of the unconscious in our politics. If there are tyrants, she insists we examine our own hearts to find the unacknowledged place where we, too, love them. (pp. 315-17)

Ann Snitow, "The Post-Lapsarian Eve," in The Nation, *New York, Vol. 243, No. 10, October 4, 1986, pp. 315-17.*

Jennifer Krauss   (essay date 1986)

[*In the following essay, Krauss applauds Carter's revisionist approach to history in* Saints and Strangers.]

Angela Carter, throwing her voice back over the centuries, displays the talents of a skilled ventriloquist—with one important difference: Carter wants us to see her lips move. [In **Saints and Strangers,** her third collection of short stories], she takes apart the accepted morality tales that constitute the sacred cow called History, and exposes,

through her own manipulation of them, the cultural conventions that shape our view of the past.

She begins with **"The Fall River Axe Murders,"** a riveting psychological portrait of Lizzie Borden that draws on the textbook determinism of novels like Wharton's *Ethan Frome.* Descended from "the industrious, self-mortifying saints who imported the Protestant ethic wholesale into a land intended for the siesta," a land where "summer and salmonella came in together," Lizzie is doomed from the start. Born in post-Edenic Massachusetts (her town is called Fall River) and christened by her father with a "diminutive"— "a miser in everything, he even cropped off half her name before he gave it to her"—Lizzie slides passively toward the apocalyptic moment that will fix her place in history and its attendant iconography:

> On this burning morning when, after breakfast and the performance of a few household duties, Lizzie Borden will murder her parents, she will, on rising, don a simple cotton frock that, if worn by itself, might be right for the weather. But, underneath, has gone a long, starched cotton petticoat; another starched petticoat, a short one; long drawers; woolen stockings; a chemise; and a whalebone corset that takes her viscera in an unkind hand and squeezes them very tightly.
>
> There is also a heavy linen napkin strapped between her legs because she is menstruating.
>
> In all these clothes, out of sorts and nauseous as she is, in this dementing heat, her belly in a vice, she will heat up a flatiron on a stove and press handkerchiefs with the heated iron . . . .

But the social and physical actualities of Lizzie's time and place account for only a part of Carter's narrative. The Freudian fairy tale that consigns Lizzie to a "fictive, protracted childhood"—and to which any life, given the right storyteller, could logically be reduced—is offered as yet another explanation of the parricidal crime toward which Lizzie's history builds. When she is two her mother dies, making room for an archetypally wicked stepmother—a gluttonous parasite who grows ever more obese as she nibbles away at the family's emotional and financial resources, to the point of driving her husband to chop off the heads of Lizzie's prized pigeons because she "fancies" them for a pie.

Add to these sociopolitical, psychoanalytical reductions of the Borden tragedy Carter's own condensation of Lizzie's tale and you have the final gloss on a multilayered fiction. For Carter's tale is the product of a fictive "memory," and memory, by its very nature, is selective and imperfect.

Early on, Carter sets the stage for the narrative acrobatics to come, by turning the genre of "The House That Jack Built" on its head. Rather than adding descriptive information bit by bit to a skeletal outline, Carter strips her story down, in full view of the reader, to what she considers its bare emblematic bones, and then steps back to highlight her distortion of historical truth:

> In a mean house on Second Street . . . five living creatures are sleeping in the still, warm early morning.

> The other old man is some kind of kin of Borden's. He doesn't belong here; he is a chance bystander, he is irrelevant.
>
> Write him out of the script.
>
> . . .
>
> *One* old man and three of his women sleep in the house on Second Street.

Yet despite the fiction writer/historian's attempts to define Lizzie Borden for all time, to provide the Ur-reading of her life story, Lizzie remains "a stranger to herself," unable to distinguish in any of the "distorting mirrors" with which her tale is filled ("no mirror in this house does not take your face and twist it out of shape for you") the real Lizzie Borden. Although Carter mounts an extensive tour of the Borden house, she quite pointedly doesn't show us the interior of Lizzie's room. That "yet other door" is "kept securely locked," enabling Carter to clean the historical slate and bring us, in the final sentence of her story, to the pre-symbolic, prehistoric instant when "the Bordens's fatal day trembles on the brink of beginning."

These twice and thrice told tales (a genre in which Carter has dabbled for years) all begin with a literary fait accompli hermetically sealed by historical "fact." In other words, not only are they *about* the fallen world, but they call into question the very notion of an objective, retrievable history unclouded by legend. Carter supplies the missing prologues to these sanctified stories—some of which we learn by rote in grade school—and crafts a "brave new world" of strangers out of a long since colonized past. Returning to the peaceable kingdom of history where Brits befriend Indians and children in baptismal gowns romp unharmed amid wide-eyed and docile beasts—Edward Hicks's mid-19th-century primitive adorns the book's cover—Carter stirs up this settled and sainted fiction, and in the process pits life against art, brother against brother, self against self.

Having shown us, in **"The Fall River Axe Murders,"** the multiplicity of readings (and tellings) that fit any historical event, Carter hones in on the particular axes she wishes to grind. **"Our Lady of the Massacre,"** for instance, unmasks the ethnocentricity that's responsible for so much of the fiction of Early American history. It is the story of a "Lancashire milkmaid" become petty thief and whore who travels by way of Newgate prison to Virginia, there to live among the Indians, most of whom are soon massacred by the British. At the opening of the story, this nameless young woman's future is foretold by her Old World benefactress (the quintessential myopic historian) using a zodiacal chart and knowledge of the stars obtained through "a great telescope" left the old woman by her father: "Though her sight was too bad to make out much . . . what she did not see, she made up, for she said she had poor sight for the things of *this* world but clear sight into the one to come." The old woman prophesies that once in Virginia, whose "rivers flow directly from Eden," her precious charge will be "nowt less than Our Lady of the Red Men." She will bear a "blessed babe whose fathers' fathers never sailed in Noah's Ark" and will convert the natives to the "true religion." Her child will sit "smiling over everything with a gold crown on his head." In short, the American myth of manifest destiny.

But it isn't the way things happened. For "although the Minister would have it otherwise," the blasphemous intruders on this native ground were not, of course, the Indians, and no amount of Christian prophecy can smooth over the annihilation of a race. Carter's repentant harlot, who at the very end of the story takes the name of Mary (after her English guardian), repents not of her errant life among the "savages," but of the impulse toward thieving and prostitution with which her mother country has tainted her:

> For all the Minister swears they've come to build the *City of God* in the *New World*, I was the same skivvy as I'd been in Lancashire and no openings for a whore in the *Community of Saints*, either, if I could have found in my heart the least desire to take up my old trade again. But I could not; the Indians had damned me for a *good woman* once and for all.

"Our Lady of the Massacre" is more, however, than a sentimental treatise in reverse. Carter injects the moral seriousness of her authentic first-person narrative with a broad, ironic humor. Early on, having escaped from a sexually abusive overseer, Carter's heroine meets her first "red" woman ("not red but wondrous brown," weaponless and picking herbs), who asks her in sign language to surrender the knife she's stuck in her apron: " 'Now I'm for it!' I thinks but hands it over and she smiles, though not much, for these savages are not half so free with their feelings as we are. . . ." Behind this naive backhandedness lurks a harsh reality, for it is the colonists who transform "Our Lady of the Red Men" into "Our Lady of the Massacre"—leaving "a fair garden blasted of folk," a river "running blood," and a half-breed child who bears the mark of Cain surveying the ruins with a crown "of tears" rather than of gold. At the end of her narrative "Our Lady" weeps "by the waters of Babylon," but the Zion she remembers is the now conquered territory of a heathen tribe, not her "Christian" homeland in Merry Old England. The saints of history's parables, Carter exhorts, appear—by virtue of history's protective veil—to be strangers to the realities of imperialism and fratricide.

With **"The Cabinet of Edgar Allan Poe,"** Carter takes this war of fiction versus reality inside the psyche. She chronicles the decay of experience into theater, and of history (through the reflexive quality of her prose) into literary cliché. Imitating the structure and style of the classic German expressionist film *The Cabinet of Dr. Caligari* (1920), as well as the work of Edgar Allan Poe, Carter allies the filmic dissolve of truth into fiction with the chiaroscuro of democracy and tyranny, the revolving janus of freedom and repression. Poe, who has grown up "under the blackstars of the slave states," is transported to the "austere morning" of the Republic where "stern, democratic light scrubs apparitions off the streets" and "a man must make his own penumbra if he wants concealment." In this setting that "admits of no ambiguities," and in the simplistic categories of historical legend, "Either you are a saint or a stranger." But as the lights dim on Carter's Gothic tale and she begins to create her own fictional penumbras, it becomes more and more difficult to tell the strangers from the saints.

The Cabinet of Dr. Caligari, from which Carter borrows here, centers on the relationship between two characters whose uncertain identities are the crux of the film. Francis is either a criminal who has performed murders for a showman at a local fair or a delusive and unreliable narrator in the process of being cured; Caligari is either a manipulative tyrant committing murders-by-proxy or a benevolent healer. Carter's **"Cabinet"** ends with Poe, within whom both these figures are contained, staring into a "reflective glass" (after shaving off his moustache) at features that are "his own and yet not his own." Instead of what he believes to be his reverse image, Poe sees his wife, Virginia, "the loved and lost one" whom he may or may not have killed. The specter of this imagined offense haunts him, as does his native loyalty to the "slave state" whose name she shares. Unable to reconcile his nation's idea of health with the stranger within and to create a whole, democratic self, Poe surrealistically disintegrates as he stands at the mirror, engulfed by the shadow of past crimes—even as he calls melodramatically for "Lights!" The parody of Whitman's ebullient "Song of Myself" that helps to introduce this tale, then, goes to the heart of Carter's project: "So you say he overacts? Very well; he overacts. There is a past history of histrionics in his family."

It is the interaction between history and histrionics, between life and art, that most fascinates Carter. The literary models that stand behind her retellings of historical legends—*Ethan Frome* behind **"The Fall River Axe Murders,"** *Moll Flanders* behind **"Our Lady of the Massacre,"** *Caligari* behind **"The Cabinet of Edgar Allan Poe"**—heighten our sense that what Carter herself is doing, as she reopens the closed books of history, is fiction, indeed cannot help but be fiction. But then so is history.

Even in the somewhat less dazzling pieces in her collection—although these, too, are impressive—Carter retraces the steps of her precursors, and daringly breaks new ground. **"The Kiss,"** a story told, as its narrator claims, "in simple, geometric shapes and the bold colors of a child's box of crayons," romanticizes the unfulfilled dreams of Uzbek peasant women after the Russian Revolution. **"Peter and the Wolf"** revises the well-known symphonic folk tale as a young man's confrontation with his long-lost sister who grew up among the wolves in a pre-Fall wilderness. **"Overture and Incidental Music for *A Midsummer Night's Dream"*** recasts Shakespeare's play as "a midsummer's nightmare"—based on a feminist reading that disowns the 19th-century Mendelssohnian nostalgia that disinfected Shakespeare's wood, "cleansing it of the grave, hideous and elemental beings with which the superstition of an earlier age had filled it," and turned the play into an ethereal fairy tale. The penultimate tale, **"The Kitchen Child,"** pieces together its jaunty cockney narrator's own biological history as he searches for the mysterious stranger who sired him—and then disappeared while his mother (the head cook in an Edwardian kitchen) was busy with a lobster soufflé.

> **Angela Carter's agenda is to let down the hair of our received histories, to unfasten it pin by pin and coax its black sheep out of hiding, to shake out the strands of sexism, racism, and classism that have been woven into it.**
>
> **—*Jennifer Krauss***

The last piece in the collection, **"Black Venus,"** provides the perfect finish for *Saints and Strangers.* It revolves around Jeanne Duval, Charles Baudelaire's syphilitic Caribbean Creole mistress—the agent, so the story goes, of a "raped continent's revenge, perpetrating itself in the beds of Europe." But according to Carter's account, which is a play on the myth of the Fall, the reverse is true: it was Baudelaire, or the culture he epitomized, that gave Duval the disease. She "picked up the germ," as all of Carter's wronged heroines pick up their life sentences, "from the very first protector"—whether a historically specific colonialism or a more pervasive, insidious chauvinism. For Carter's purposes, then, Duval, as the sum total of all the good/bad girls that have gone before, is the supreme embodiment of the transpositions of *Saints and Strangers*: "She bent over backwards until the huge fleece of a black sheep, her unfastened hair, spilled on to the Bokhara. . . . She arched her back so much a small boy could have run under her. Her reversed blood sang in her ears."

Angela Carter's agenda is to let down the hair of our received histories, to unfasten it pin by pin and coax its black sheep out of hiding, to shake out the strands of sexism, racism, and classism that have been woven into it. These virtuosic tales that make strangers of saints and saints of strangers stretch backward beyond the traditional bounds of fiction toward a searing home truth that would emancipate the present—the small boy who runs through the hoop linking the old world and the new. (pp. 38-41)

Jennifer Krauss, "History and Histrionics," in The New Republic, *Vol. 195, No. 25, December 22, 1986, pp. 38-41.*

D. J. Enright   (essay date 1987)

[*Enright is an English critic, educator, poet, novelist, essayist, and editor. In the following excerpt, he provides a mixed assessment of* Saints and Strangers.]

Angela Carter has been described as "an addicted rewriter"; a rewriter, that's to say, of fairy tales, nursery stories, myths, and classical instances both real and fictitious. The title story of her earlier collection, *The Bloody Chamber,* concerning Bluebeard, that prime male chauvinist, illustrates her mode of operation at its brightest. Incorporating such gothic touches as vampirism, the larger part of the narrative unfolds in an expert reproduction of *fin de siècle* writing, French writing of course, for the Anglo-Saxons could never rise to such depths. "He stripped me, gourmand that he was, as if he were stripping the leaves off an artichoke." All the same, the author still contrives a satisfyingly happy ending, with the young bride rescued in the nick of time, not by her brothers, but by her brisk mother (as the daughter of a planter in Indochina, she has had experience in driving off junkloads of Chinese pirates), and subsequently setting up house with a blind and humble piano tuner.

In [*Saints and Strangers*], **"Our Lady of the Massacre"** is linguistically a pastiche of the Moll Flanders demotic. The Lancashire heroine, whose parents have died of the plague, takes to whoring, is transported to Virginia for stealing a client's gold watch, cuts off the ears of a brutal plantation overseer, and runs away to join the "red men," a distinctly more civilized race of beings. She marries a young brave and bears a child. When English soldiers kill her husband, she and her son are taken in by a childless minister and his wife. Little Shooting Star is duly given a respectable biblical name, but she refuses to call him by it. Thanks to the Indians, and no thanks to Christianity, she has become a good woman.

Angela Carter is at her most intemperate in **"The Cabinet of Edgar Allan Poe."** As Poe's future mother makes her stage debut,

> at this hour, this very hour, far away in Paris, France, in the appalling dungeons of the Bastille, old Sade is jerking off. Grunt, groan, grunt, on to the prison floor . . . aaaagh! He seeds dragons' teeth. Out of each ejaculation spring up a swarm of fully-armed, mad-eyed homunculi. Everything is about to succumb to delirium.

(The time scale, at any rate, can be trusted.) Poe's father dematerializes, not merely figuratively, but literally: "He said not one word to his boys but went on evaporating until he melted clean away, leaving behind him in the room as proof he had been there only a puddle of puke on the splintered floorboards." As is her wont, the author sprinkles into this witches' brew a spoonful of factuality, or of the down-to-earth. In connection with Poe's child-wife, Virginia Clemm, she remarks that in northern England "clemmed" means to be cold (or to be starving). The information may not signify much, but it acts as a braking device on fancy running riot.

Similar is her quasi-erudite relating of the name Puck to Dutch *"spook,"* in the story **"Overture and Incidental Music for *A Midsummer Night's Dream,"*** and the frisky realism whereby everybody is coughing and sneezing because of the contagious fogs with which Shakespeare cursed his Athenian wood. The Golden Herm—the changeling of the play, but *hermaphrodite verus* here, not "a lovely boy": that was just the patriarchal version of things—gives a grandly poetic account of himself: "Child of the sun am I, and of the breezes, juicy as mangoes, that mythopoeically caress the Coast of Coromandel far away on the porphyry and lapis lazuli Indian shore where everything is bright and precise as lacquer." And in the next breath he jeers coarsely at Titania, "she, the great fat, showy, pink and blonde thing, the Memsahib, I call her, Auntie Tit-tit-tit-ania (for her tits are the things you notice first, size of barrage balloons)." Polymorphous perverse is

what the fairies are, while Puck, who has fallen in technically difficult love with the Herm, is given to buggery, undinism, frotteurism, and scopophilia (voyeurism to us mere mortals), not to mention practices quite unmentionable. "Have *you* seen fairy sperm?" the reader is quizzed. "We mortals call it cuckoo spit."

Such fearful, deliberate coyness. A takeoff, we must suppose, of the nursery-tale formula, "Do you believe in fairies?" as *Peter Pan* enquires. A suspicion raises its horrid head that Angela Carter is addressing herself to the advanced primary schools found in some parts of London. And the keen interest young Peter evinces, in **"Peter and the Wolf,"** when he meets his wolf-fostered cousin and catches sight of "the crevice of her girl-child's sex" feeds the suspicion.

On the day of her celebrated deeds, Lizzie Borden, in **"The Fall River Axe Murders,"** is menstruating, a time when she is prone to headaches and trances, and the weather is stiflingly hot. Andrew Borden, a miser and a grinder of the faces of the poor, has a few weeks earlier taken a hatchet to Lizzie's pet pigeons, intending a treat for his gluttonous wife. So it's no mystery why she gave them both any number of whacks with the same implement.

"Black Venus" offers a more formidable heroine in the shape of Jeanne Duval, Baudelaire's Creole mistress. "Baby, baby, let me take you back where you belong," the poet proposes, romantically and unrealistically, "back to your lovely, lazy island where the jewelled parrot rocks on the enamel tree and you can crunch sugar-cane between your strong, white teeth." But there is little romance in Jeanne's heart. She would rather have a drink. Rum will do. "A slumbrous resentment of anything you could not eat, drink or smoke, i.e. burn, was her salient characteristic"; albeit she is willing to oblige "Daddy" with a sexy dance, and (which calls for some effort on her part) with sex. What this underprivileged colonial subject most resents is the linguistic richness of his poetry as compared with her poverty of utterance. After Baudelaire's death (and after a well-informed allusion to the last sighting of her recorded by the poet's friend, Nadar, as she limped along the street on crutches), she returns to Martinique, according to this account, where she "will continue to dispense, to the most privileged of the colonial administration, at a not excessive price, the veritable, the authentic, the true Baudelairean syphilis." That's one-upwomanship for you.

There is no one in these miniatures as endearing as Fevvers, the winged, deserving, and really quite sensible heroine of Angela Carter's novel *Nights at the Circus*. But **"The Kitchen Child"** is a lively, entertaining concoction with a good deal of flavor. You can smell the food. The child in question was mysteriously engendered while his mother, a cook in an English country house, was creating a lobster soufflé, the only other effect being that her hand shook and a little too much cayenne fell into the dish.

> The first toys I played with were colanders, egg whisks and saucepan lids. I took my baths in the big tureen in which the turtle soup was served. They gave up salmon until I could toddle be-

cause, as for my crib, what else but the copper salmon kettle?

Even more pleasing than downstairs getting the better of upstairs is when the two come together: by magical miscegenation the Yorkshire child becomes a French chef and the stepson of an appreciative *duc*.

Angela Carter's use of language, her large, eclectic, and glittering vocabulary, alternately lush and colloquial, is undeniably impressive. Whether you always admire the workings of her imagination is another matter; the new wine she puts in these old bottles can be peculiarly sour. Some readers will be ready to sink down on their knees in awed obeisance; others will feel like throwing up at times. It might be said of her—as Whitman said of Poe—that her place is "among the electric lights of imaginative literature, brilliant and dazzling, but with no heat." (pp. 15-16)

D. J. Enright, "Writers at Play," in The New York Review of Books, *Vol. XXXIV, No. 3, February 26, 1987, pp. 15-16.*

Clare Hanson   (essay date 1988)

[*In the following excerpt, Hanson explores Carter's portrayal of women as "other" in her short fiction.*]

Angela Carter has been called "the poet of the short story." She excels in the form and closely identifies with it: she has said that she finds it easier to deal with the issues which most concern her (the "shifting structures of reality and sexuality" by using "sets of shifting structures derived from orally transmitted traditional tales" rather than by using the form of the novel, which is more closely associated with myth. As with some other fiction writers such as Elizabeth Bowen, it can easily be argued that Carter's short fictions are finer than her novels, and that she has a special relationship with the form. The analogy with Bowen is particularly suggestive. Bowen once said that she found it impossible to incorporate her sense of the supernatural—a sense which was very important to her—into the novel form, whereas she could incorporate it into her short fiction, which made her short fiction in some way more truthful. Carter is similarly able to incorporate her sense of the fantastic into the short fiction form more easily than into the novel: she too uses the form to explore hidden or latent areas of experience.

I would like to concentrate on Angela Carter's most recent collection of short fiction, ***Black Venus*** (1985). The title story shows how far Carter has travelled . . . in her perception(s) of the woman as other. The story is about Jeanne Duval, Baudelaire's black mistress, and consists of a series of meditations and speculations interspersed with fragments of biographical fact. Jeanne serves for Carter as an image of all women. As a historical figure she is always defined against Baudelaire and subordinate to him. Carter attempts to reverse these priorities and places Jeanne at the centre of her story, as subject, while Baudelaire becomes Jeannes's object, viewed by her with affectional derision—"Daddy paid no attention to what song his siren sang, he fixed his quick, bright, dark eyes upon her decorated skin as if, sucker, authentically entranced." (But we might want to add a note of feminist criticism here, wondering who, after all, is the sucker? It is Carter who makes us ask the question, but she seems to collude in Jeanne's/all women's oppression when she writes of Jeanne's "reward"—"the eternity promised by the poet.")

Jeanne is actually described in the first pages of the story as a "tabula rasa." Carter makes the radical feminist suggestion here that Jeanne/woman exists only as she is defined in relation to men. Woman is the negative to man's positive, the other of society and culture. Because she exists only in relation to Baudelaire (to the onlooker) Jeanne can even become "less than nothing," for without the look, the regard, she does not even exist for herself:)

> She sulked sardonically through Daddy's sexy dance, watching, in a bored, fascinated way, the elaborate reflections of the many strings of glass beads he had given her tracking about above her on the ceiling. She looked like the source of light but this was an illusion; she only shone because the dying fire lit his presents to her. *Although his regard made her luminous, his shadow made her blacker than she was, his shadow could eclipse her entirely.* (my ital.)

Jeanne Duval offers an extreme image of the woman as other—she is trebly unknown to Baudelaire as a black woman from another continent. She fascinates because she seems to contain within herself all that is not known, all that is other.—

> He thinks she is a vase of darkness; if he tips her up, black light will spit out. *She is not Eve but, herself, the forbidden fruit,* and he has eaten her! (my ital.)

She is also of course obscurely threatening, associated with Eve and with the monstrous-feminine—"a woman of immense height." She is explicitly tarred with the misogynistic term "witch" traditionally used by men to distance themselves from the latent (unknown, again) power of women:

> Kids in the street chucked stones at her, she so tall and witchy and, when she was pissed, teetering along with the vulnerable, self-conscious dignity of the drunk which always invites mockery, and, always, she held her bewildered head with its enormous, unravelling cape of hair as proudly as if she were carrying upon it an enormous pot full of all the waters of Lethe.

If woman is unknown, the unknown is always feared. Venus in this sense is always black: the image of the loved woman in Western patriarchal culture is always a projected image in which the man's thought, to extend an image of Carter's, overtakes the woman's presence.

These themes recur obsessively in ***Black Venus***: in **"Our Lady of the Massacre,"** for example. Like **"Black Venus,"** this is a very literary text, or meta-text, parodying some of the themes and manners of Defoe's *Moll Flanders*. If *Moll Flanders* is, as Juliet Mitchell argues, concerned with changes in the role of women under bourgeois capitalism, then **"Our Lady of the Massacre"** is concerned to demonstrate still more clearly the ways in which a woman is defined by the particular society in which she lives. The woman at the centre of this story is protean, continually changing her character and nature to suit the circumstances in which she finds herself. She becomes, in turn, a hard-working servant girl, a prostitute, a slave, an Indian wife and repentant pilgrim, altering as the vagaries of life lead her from Lancashire to London and then to the colonies and beyond. She quickly attunes herself to any circumstance:

> 'Here is a morsel plucked from Satan,' says the one that widowed me to the Minister, who tells me to thank God that I have been rescued from the savage and beg the Good Lord's forgiveness for straying from His ways. Taking my cue from this, I fall to my knees, for I see that repentance is the fashion in these parts and the more of it show, the better it will be for me.

She has no name, or rather refuses naming and having a fixed identity pinned on her. "My name is neither here nor there" she says with literal truth at the opening of the story—she has different names for each geographical place she inhabits.

The central figure in **"Our Lady of the Massacre"** shares her protean nature with Lizzie Borden, of **"The Fall River Axe Murders."** Both women are literally fatal, the one involuntarily causing a massacre, the other being a murderess. It is this sense of the slippery and elusive nature of women and also of their awesome power which informs one of Carter's most revealing stories, **"The Cabinet of Edgar Allan Poe."** Again, this is a meta-text, a meditation on one of the figures whom we might expect to have influenced Carter most deeply, with his fine sense of the grotesque. The grotesque turns out, not surprisingly, to have a good deal to do with sexuality and with the construction of sexual identity.

For Carter, the most salient facts about Poe's early life are that his mother was an actress and his father died when he was young. Poe was thus exposed at a tender age to two seemingly irreconcilable sides of womanhood. He saw very clearly the *constructed* element in femininity and the feminine, watching his mother "making up" for innumerable feminine roles (she also played young men), seeing her "glass jewels" and "yellow wig." But he also saw the seemingly inescapable *biological* facts of female existence, watching his mother's "sore, milky breasts" as she struggled to feed her children, and seeing "a tit sucked in a green-room, the dug snatched away from the toothless lips as soon as her cue came." The circumstances of Poe's mother's life thus created in Poe an exacerbated sense of the duality of woman, made him acutely sensitive to the nature/nurture divide which continues to haunt and shadow our sense of female identity. For Poe himself in consequence woman becomes both infinitely desirable and infinitely horrifying. Woman *as an image* functions as a symbol of desire:

> *Item*: transformation. This is a more ambivalent relic. Something like this. . . Edgar would lie in prop-baskets on heaps of artificial finery and watch her while she painted her face. The candles made a profane altar of the mirror in which her vague face swam like a magic fish. If you caught hold of it, it would make your dreams

come true but Mama slithered through all the nets which desire set out to catch her.

On the other hand *as a real woman,* giving birth, the mother is a figure inspiring fear and horror. Poe retains a muted memory of the birth of his sister, which he and his brother witnessed. The memory becomes inextricably woven in with his feeling about his own mother and all women:

> *Item*: that women possess within them a cry, a thing that needs to be extracted . . . but this is only the dimmest of memories and will reassert itself in vague shapes of unmentionable dread only at the prospect of carnal connection.

From the complicated pathology of Poe's emotional life one strand can be singled out. The fear of the feminine, particularly of the body of the feminine, which he shows is shared, it has been argued, by many men. Julia Kristeva has analysed this response in her study of abjection. For Kristeva, the moment of abjection is that in which the child (not yet constituted as a subject) first begins to separate from its mother. If this process remains incomplete or compromised in any way, the child will remain locked in abjection, locked in the primary movement away from the mother. The child/adult will figure or displace this primary abjection/rejection unto other images inspiring fear or revulsion, in this way recalling the original feelings of abjection. This argument is clearly of crucial relevance for Poe, who seems almost the perfect example of Kristeva's theory of abjection. For her, the ultimate image of abjection is the corpse, and this is how Carter describes Poe's chosen bride, his chosen object of desire:

> For her skin was white as marble and she was called would you believe!—'Virginia,' a name that suited his expatriate's nostalgia and also her condition, for the childbride would remain a virgin until the day she died . . .

> For did she not come to him stiffly armoured in taboos—taboos against the violation of children; taboos against the violation of the dead—for, not to put too fine a point on it, didn't she always look like a walking corpse? But such a pretty, pretty corpse!

In **"The Cabinet of Edgar Allan Poe"** aspects of sexuality and sexual identity are explored in ways which transcend gender, and gender prejudice. Perhaps this is simply because Carter explores in this story areas of experience which pre-date our acquisition of a sexed, gendered identity. It would seem that it is only through an exploration of such areas of experience that we can hope to escape the constraints of sex and gender, to win free of those images of otherness. . . . (The term "women writers," incidentally, serves to justify Carter's claim that as women we are only defined *against* men. Male writers are just writers—women writers are. . . women writers.)

Julia Kristeva has asked, in her essay emblematically called "Women's Time."

> What can identity, even "sexual identity," mean in a new theoretical and scientific space where the very notion of identity is challanged?

Carter's movement back "before" sexual identity in her

recent fiction paradoxically works towards just such an entry into a new space and time.

It has been my premise . . . that women tend to be occupied with questions of identity in ways which men are not. . . . [Angela Carter takes up the question of power], demonstrating the disabling effects for woman of being characterised, always, negatively, in relation to men. It is almost impossible to find/imagine an image of women which escapes this masculine/feminine, positive/negative "violent hierarchy." Perhaps Carter herself achieves this with Fevvers in *Nights at the Circus* (1984) but this is "only" a novel, or as Carter might say, a myth. It is not a short fiction, representing the truth of this moment, in history—the short fiction being the art, as Nadine Gordimer says, of "the only thing one can be sure of—the present moment." (pp. 77-82)

> *Clare Hanson, "Each Other: Images of Otherness in the Short Fiction of Doris Lessing, Jean Rhys and Angela Carter," in* Journal of the Short Story in English, *No. 10, Spring, 1988, pp. 67-82.*

Maggie Anwell   (essay date 1988)

[*In the following excerpt, Anwell examines Carter's redefinition of femininity in "The Company of Wolves," noting that "the transformation of Perrault's faltering, passive figure into the 'strong-minded child' is crucial to the reclamation of the story." The unexcerpted portion of this essay discusses the film version of "The Company of Wolves" and its faithfulness to Carter's vision.*]

In the reception of her writing, even sympathetic critics [Such as Sandra Gilbert and Susan Gubar in their *The Madwoman in the Attic*] have at times portrayed Angela Carter as the inheritor of the 'infected sentence', the happy outlet for the feverish outpourings of the female imagination; a writer [as Carter herself notes] in the Gothic, Romantic tradition of women writers, 'erotic, exotic and bizarre' and open to the charge of keeping alive [what J. M. S. Tompkins calls in *The Popular Novel in England*] 'that superstition which debilitates the mind.' She is without doubt a determined fantasist, and fantasy, which seems to employ linguistic and imaginative excess, and moves uncomfortably close to the borders of insanity, has always had a mixed critical reception, by virtue of its capacity to subvert the stability of realism in order to describe alien psychic states and at the same time to give voice to censored female eroticism. But fantasy, suggests Mary Jacobus, can be seen as a textual strategy for escaping realist images of repressed female experience; it offers the possibility of a fictional transformation of material reality, and affirmation of women's ability to 'speak female desire as multiplicity, joyousness, pleasure, *jouissance—la mère qui jouit.*'

Angela Carter's 'territory' of dreams, surrealism and ambiguity makes a conscious use of fantasy to articulate a female gaze, which, with its 'bold and disciplined imagination and its power to perceive symbols' disturbs the everyday assumptions of patriarchy.

In this analysis of her retelling of the fairy story of Little Red Riding Hood [entitled **"The Company of Wolves"**] I shall aim to show how the transformation of Perrault's faltering, passive figure into the 'strong-minded child' is crucial to the reclamation of the story. Perrault's version was itself a falsification of the dynamics of the original folk tale, which offers an image of a girl who has to use wit and cunning to escape her fate, whereas Perrault's girl has to wait passively to be rescued. This enforces the patriarchal view that girls should accept their narrow sphere of action. The central character in the film version is another matter, and the reasons for the evident change of emphasis here lead us back to the feminist dilemma referred to above.

Close examination of Carter's short story reminds us that her original gaze at Red Riding Hood was not an 'obvious' feminist reclamation of a fairy story. Carter's heroine is undoubtedly the Wise Maiden cited by Propp in *Morphology of the Folktale,* who is able to outwit the villain by appearing to go along with his pretence until the truth is revealed, at which point she takes control of the action, insisting on her right to do as she thinks fit. Perrault's heroine, by contrast, gives no such indication of will or self-generated desire.

This change from passive victim to active protagonist is clearly a crucial textual strategy, and a feminist retelling might well be expected to follow Roald Dahl's assertion-trained Red Riding Hood in his *Revolting Rhymes,* who, at the critical moment, reacts in accordance with her Women's Self-defence Manual:

> Her eyelid droops, her eyelid flickers,
> She pulls a pistol from her knickers.

Female victim becomes female aggressor and beats the wolf at his own game. But this kind of mechanical retelling is just that: an obvious reversal of plot convention, dealing only with a realist analogy. A radical retelling must delve deeper than a simple manipulation of the familiar plot.

Carter's heroine is firmly within the folk tradition: she is the specially favoured youngest; she actively seeks her adventure; she has the wit, courage and cunning to save her skin. She understands the game more subtly than the wolf, who talks of death when she knows that his appetite can be assuaged in other ways. She acquiesces in the burning of her old clothes, for she knows that she won't be returning as the same person. She is apparently philosophical about her grandmother's fate—what's dead is dead and life must go on. She escapes her own fate as victim by asserting her own desires—for this little Red Riding Hood throws in her lot with the Big Bad Wolf.

Nothing could be further from the picture of female resistance in Roald Dahl's gun-toting heroine, who meets male aggression head on, than this willing acceptance of the wolf's advances. It is, indeed, an enigmatic ending, and if it is seen as a moral fable in the Perrault vein, then its message can only be that willing acceptance of male aggression is the best way to guarantee survival—hardly a message to gladden the hearts of women angered by the constraints put upon their freedom by aggressive masculine sexuality.

But it is in the form of the retelling, in the complexity of the inner world of the protagonist, that the story achieves its radical potential, and transcends this superficial reading—which is disturbingly present nevertheless.

Let us examine the depiction of this 'strong-minded child':

> Her breasts have just begun to swell; her hair is like lint, so fair it hardly makes a shadow on her pale forehead; her cheeks are an emblematic scarlet and white and she has just started her woman's bleeding, the clock inside her that will strike, henceforward, once a month.

With astonishing economy the girl is placed at the crossroads of female experience, when the vulnerability of childhood has to accommodate the visible signs of the unavoidable future. We are told that 'children do not stay young for long in this savage country', as if the gentle transition from childhood to adulthood is an unaffordable luxury. To survive one needs a strategy for dealing with the dangerous, hostile world; sentiment is of no use. And yet, 'she has been too much loved ever to feel scared.' More than this, she has been indulged—her mother cannot deny her and her grandmother has knitted her the red shawl. A sense of one's own power to deal with the danger is essential if one is to keep one's nerve. She sets off on her adventure with an unquenchable confidence and a pleasure in her own independence. She is already constituted as a whole person, and most important of all is the power of her virginity:

> . . . the invisible pentacle . . . She is an unbroken egg; she is a sealed vessel; she has inside her a magic space the entrance to which is shut tight with a plug of membrane; she is a closed system; she does not know how to shiver.

It is not new, this image of the power of virginity—a state set apart from the common lot, and in Christian folklore a prerequisite for female redemption. But this virgin is resolutely pagan; she has no intention of retaining her virginity once it is no longer useful to her. It is discarded then like the clothes which she will not need again. What *is* new in the description is the physical image of internal space, which of its essence can only be experienced by women. This is a theme which Angela Carter had explored at length in her novel *The Passion of New Eve,* in which the central male character's sense of physical self is transformed when he is given a womb.

The route to willing renunciation of this closed space is carefully laid out. It is not merely to appease the aggressor that she offers herself, but also to please herself. She had 'never seen such a fine fellow before'. She takes pleasure in his company, and in his desire for her:

> What would you like? she asked disingenuously.
>
> A kiss.
>
> Commonplaces of a rustic seduction; she lowered her eyes and blushed.

Significantly, the grandmother's vision of the werewolf is very different from the girl's perception of him as a handsome hunter. The first thing the grandmother sees is the redness of the eyes of a beast of prey—'devastating eyes red as a wound', then 'his feral muzzle' as 'sharp as a knife'. Where is the charming smile? His hunter's disguise is quickly removed, showing that his hair is thick with lice—he is less fastidious than the peasants of the village. It is the grandmother who first sees his naked sexuality, but a sexuality that can have no interaction with her age. He takes off his clothing only to transform himself into a carnivore, and she can do nothing to appease or placate him.

As the girl enters, she senses a difference—not one centred on her perception of the werewolf, but in her heightened awareness of the room around her: no indentation on the pillow, a closed Bible and the tick of the clock which affects her like the crack of a whip. She realises what has happened to her grandmother, and that she herself is 'in danger of death'. The girl who set out with such confidence ('she is a closed system; she does not know how to shiver') now shivers as she contemplates her fate. But the image is ambiguous: she fears the blood that she must spill, but will it be her lifeblood or the sign of her discarded virginity?

The dialogue between the girl and the wolf is written with the resonances of the original fairy tale and the tension of a plot reaching its fruition. It begins with the familiar hypnotic ritual, but then stops as she challenges him to tell her the truth—the truth she already knows from the evidence of her grandmother's hair in the hearth. His answer is evasive: 'There's nobody here but we two, my darling.' She abandons this line of questioning and, as if accepting his implied claim that they are now bound together, she asks: 'Who has come to sing us carols', and, as she looks at the wolves, she refutes their image as beasts of terror: 'It is very cold, poor things, she said; no wonder they howl so.'

Her interpretation of their demented howling as distress turns the tide: her death is now no longer inevitable, which suggests that her sympathetic innocence can indeed transform their natures. She trusts her own judgment and ceases to be afraid. Now she voluntarily sheds her clothes, including her shawl, 'the colour of sacrifices, the colour of her menses'. As the werewolf gives the standard reply, 'All the better to eat you with', she bursts out laughing. She knows far better than he that she is 'nobody's meat'. She has discarded the role of sacrificial victim along with her shawl, and is clear in her acceptance of her own sexuality. We may note that this is not an aggressive 'masculinised' sexuality: she is neither Justine, martyred by passive acceptance of her fate, nor Juliet, equating sexuality with violence. Instead, we are left with an image of her successful negotiation:

> See! sweet and sound she sleeps in granny's bed, between the paws of the tender wolf.

(pp. 76-81)

Maggie Anwell, "Lolita Meets the Werewolf: 'The Company of Wolves'," in The Female Gaze: Women as Viewers of Popular Culture, *edited by Lorraine Gamman and Margaret Marshment, The Women's Press Limited, 1988, pp. 76-85.*

Avis Lewallen   (essay date 1988)

[*In the following essay, Lewallen analyzes Carter's expression of female sexuality in* The Bloody Chamber.]

Wayward Girls and Wicked Women is the ironic title for a volume of short stories written by women, edited by Angela Carter, and published by Virago in 1986. The title, cover picture (sulky, seductive, tousled blond with pouting red lips, bare shoulders and plunging neckline) and editor's name (a writer with a reputation for polemic) signify sexuality as the subject under scrutiny. The back cover blurb does nothing to dispel this impression. In her Introduction to the volume Angela Carter explains the irony:

> To be a wayward girl usually has something to do with premarital sex; to be a wicked woman has something to do with adultery. This means it is far easier for a woman to lead a blameless life than it is for a man; all she has to do is to avoid sexual intercourse like the plague. What hypocrisy!

The majority of the stories, therefore, have little to do with sexuality *per se* and are about women facing their economic, social and sexual inequality with bravado, perseverance or at times perversity. The package promises something different from what it actually contains, and, though some of the stories are enjoyable, it is the cover, in what it reveals about the marketing practices of a feminist publishing house in relation to the supposed expectations of its readership, that is especially interesting. Sexy covers and titles sell books, even to women. Similarly, Angela Carter's own writing has a surface gloss and shimmer. Recently dubbed 'the high priestess of post-graduate porn', she has provocative ideas and a seductive style, but closer analysis reveals a dubious kind of sexuality for women.

The Bloody Chamber examines sexuality for women as victims within a misogynistic society, and in some ways this collection of tales is a fictional rendering of the ideas Carter expounds in her theoretical analysis of the works of the Marquis de Sade, *The Sadeian Woman*. In this she posits the notion of a 'moral pornographer':

> His business would be the total demystification of the flesh and the subsequent revelation, through the infinite modulations of the sexual act, of the real relations of man and his kind. Such a pornographer would not be the enemy of women, perhaps because he might begin to penetrate to the heart of the contempt for women that distorts our culture even as he entered the realms of true obscenity as he describes it. . . . And that is because sexual relations between men and women always render explicit the nature of social relations in the society in which they take place and, if described explicitly, will form a critique of those relations, even if that is not and never has been the intention of the pornographer.

Thus Sade, Carter argues, provides such a critique, exposing the political reality behind sexual mythology, while 'he declares himself unequivocally for the right of women to fuck'. Claiming and practising this right 'aggressively, tyrannously and cruelly' is, therefore, a historical process that has to be gone through before any kind of equalisation can be reached between the sexes. Perhaps the problem with this argument is that Carter herself does not have a sufficient historical perspective to recognise the sixties and the seventies as a period when women did claim their right to fuck. Such 'liberalisation' has partly resulted in a circumspect cynicism towards the notion of any sexual equality within the pervasive patriarchal system.

Ironically, Carter and one of her critics, Andrea Dworkin, both give supreme importance and power to this one aspect of sexual representation. I would not argue that pornographic representation is not important, but would say that it must be placed within the context of all forms of sexual representation. Some of these forms such as advertisements which utilise pornographic images, may, by the very fact of their seeming 'naturalness', be more pernicious. Pornography in Carter's and Dworkin's sense is the raw and extreme form of sexual representation and is underlined by more pervasive ideologies concerning female sexuality. It is hard to see that it can do more than perpetrate myths in a very obvious way, instead of, as Carter suggests, critically exposing the heart of misogyny.

Sade's dualism is simple: sadist or masochist, fuck or be fucked, victim or aggressor—never one and the same but always either/or. This is Sade's failure, claims Carter, because sex as described by him is always sequential and never mutually reciprocal. It is this dualism that pervades our thinking about sexuality and fits neatly into the schema of binary oppositions: subject/object, active/passive, and so forth. In *The Bloody Chamber* Carter is attempting to promote an active sexuality for women within a Sadean framework, and, therefore, within the logic of the world she creates, sexual choice for the heroines is circumscribed by Sadean boundaries. One wonders why, given her recognition of what she sees as Sade's failure, there is no attempt to address the question of these ideologically defined parameters.

The Bloody Chamber is mostly a collection of fairy tales rewritten to incorporate props of the Gothic and elements of a style designated 'magic realism', in which a realistic consciousness operates within a surrealistic context. The characters are at once both abstractions and 'real'. The heroine in **'The Tiger's Bride',** for example, bemused by surreal events, comments, 'what democracy of magic held this palace and fir forest in common? Or, should I be prepared to accept it as proof of the axiom my father had drummed into me: that, if you have enough money, anything is possible?' Symbolism is prevalent: white roses for sexual purity; lilies for sex and death; lions, tigers and wolves for male sexual aggression. Throughout the collection, specific attention is often drawn to the meaning of fairy tales themselves, and this has implications for the reading of Carter's stories.

In a perceptive but highly critical essay ["Re-Imagining the Fairy Tales: Angela Carter's Bloody Chambers," *Literature and History* 10, No. 1 (Spring 1984)] Patricia Duncker argues that the form of the fairy tale, along with all its ideological ramifications, proves intractable to attempted revision:

9.

my ~~too~~ heart well nigh stopped with apprehension when I ~~to~~ allowed ~~myself~~ to

exceedingly ~~f afriz~~ afraid, for every visitor, even the most

fleeting, soon heard some whisperings of the man they called

"La Bestia," ~~wh~~ whose passion for cards alone drove him out

of the absolute seclusion in which he lived, to whom, it seems,

I ~~must now play the whore for the sake of my father's raddled~~

~~reputation.~~ now, it seems, I must play the whore for the sake of my ~~father's raddled~~ reputation, a to a ~~man~~ who, in all his possess seemed ~~to have~~ no other name ~~but~~ the ~~but 'Beast'~~

My fat *Mrs B.'s old nurse, now dead, to whom she had lovely told me a boy*

~~My~~ English nurse once ~~told~~ me about *the* tiger-man she saw, in

London, when she was a little girl, (to scare me into good *my something* *I the M had been* *who loved* *he tamed* behaviour ~~x~~ for ~~x~~ I ~~was a~~ wild wee thing ~~and she could~~ not tame *charm* me into submission with the bribe of a spoonful of jam or a

pestering *sliding* ribbon or a frown.) If you don't stop ~~plag plaguing~~ the nursemaids, *down the bannisters, singing on a Sunday,* *den* my ~~beauty,~~ the tiger-man will come and take you away to his ~~cave~~ *my beauty.* in the mountains, They'd brought him from Sumatra, in the Indies,

she said; ~~and~~ his hinder parts were all hairy and only from the

head downwards did he resemble a man. And yet La Bestia goes *will a cannot cum.* always masked; ~~so~~ it ~~cannot~~ be his face that resembles mine.

But the ~~gix~~ tiger-man, in spite of his hairiness, could take a

glass of ale in his hand like a good Christian and drink it down.

Nana *sunk his pint,* Had ~~she~~ not seen him do ~~so~~, at the sign of "The George," by the *high* steps of Upper Moor-Fields, ~~when~~ she was just ~~as old~~ as me, ~~a lisped~~ *toddled, too* Then she would sigh, for ~~London, across the North Sea of seperation~~ *no higher than her marge, a lisped a toddled, too* ~~and~~ the lapse of years and ~~circumstance.~~ But, if this young lady *her boiled cabbage* was not a good little girl and ate up her crusts and ~~boiled~~ ~~bittxrx beetroot~~, the ~~fif~~ Tiger-man would put on his travelling *left wool,* coat of thick, black ~~wool~~, just like your daddy's, and ~~take~~ *jump astride* ~~ship at Tilbury across the Nxr waves until he stepped ashore at~~ *his raw black horse that was made* *the wind a ride through the night as fast as* ~~the harbour of Riga and hire~~ a ~~knxx horse to~~ ride through the night *the wind* as ~~fast as the Erl-king on his galloper~~ of wind and... come

straight to the nursery and —

Yes, my lamb, Gobble you up!

Carter is rewriting the tales within the strait-jacket of their original structures. The characters she re-creates must, to some extent, continue to exist as abstractions. Identity continues to be defined by role, so that shifting the perspective from the impersonal voice to the inner confessional narrative, as she does in several of the tales, merely explains, amplifies and reproduces rather than alters the original, deeply, rigidly sexist psychology of the erotic.

While I agree with Duncker's overall analysis, I think she significantly overlooks the use of irony, particularly the effect produced by the 'inner confessional narrative', which both acknowledges patriarchal structure and provides a form of critique against it. The ultimate position taken up may be politically untenable, but at the same time the ironic voice does not wholeheartedly endorse the patriarchal view. I think the use of irony can clearly be illustrated by the two contrasting versions Carter offers of 'Beauty and the Beast'.

Both **'The Courtship of Mr Lyon'** and **'The Tiger's Bride'** draw attention to the economic dependence of the daughter on the father/husband. **'The Courtship of Mr Lyon'** conforms in most respects to the traditional 'Beauty and the Beast' narrative. Beauty's father is bankrupt, but a chance meeting with the mysterious Mr Lyon, who is indeed a lion, provides a means of restoring his fortunes. The unspoken price for this benevolence is Beauty herself, but she is a price that can be exacted only through love, not through direct contract or guilt. Material exchange underlies the narrative, but it is somewhat obscured by Beauty's feelings of pity for Mr Lyon, tinged with unease about the sexuality in the beast which might also be sexuality within herself:

> How strange he was. She found his bewildering difference from her almost intolerable; its presence choked her . . . and when she saw the great paws lying on the arm of his chair, she thought: they are the death of any tender herbivore. And such a one she felt herself to be, Miss Lamb, spotless, sacrificial.

Mr Lyon's 'strangeness' —his sexual difference—repels, frightens but also attracts: 'It was in her heart to drop a kiss upon his shaggy mane but, though she stretched out her hand towards him she could not bring herself to touch him of her own free will, he was so different from herself '. With her father's fortunes restored, Beauty joins him in the city, which is in danger of corrupting her innocence, making her vain and causing her to forget her promise to return to Mr Lyon. She experiences contradictory feelings:

> she experienced a sudden sense of perfect freedom, as if she had just escaped from an unknown danger, had been grazed by the possibility of some change but, finally, left intact. Yet, with this exhilaration, a desolating emptiness.

Through a kind of oxymoronic yoking of feelings Carter conveys the hesitancy of burgeoning sexuality. We are reminded through style and structure of Mills and Boon romances. It is not until Beauty can feel love 'freely' and shed real tears that the beast can be transformed back into the man he is underneath. Her love will convert the potent sexuality into domestic bliss as in Mills and Boon, where male sexual aggression, usually exhibited by a moody, troubling indifference towards the heroine, will be tamed by love. Carter, therefore, consciously and ironically plays with the romance formula whereby troubling sexual difference is transformed through love into cosy domestication.

The heroine of **'The Tiger's Bride',** however, is a more knowing being both conscious and critical of her economic dependence on men:

> I watched with the furious cynicism peculiar to women whom circumstances force mutely to witness folly, while my father, fired in his desperation by more and yet more draughts of the firewater they call 'grappa', rid himself of the last scraps of my inheritance.

The ironic narrative stance gives us a heroine with a consciousness capable of recognising directly her economic and sexual lack of freedom in a patriarchal world. Her father loses her to a tiger in a games of cards and the connection between materialism and sexuality is directly drawn. In giving her father a white rose at their parting, the heroine pricks her finger— 'and so he gets his rose all smeared with blood'.

Ensconced in the tiger's palazzo, the heroine comes face to face with her own image in a 'clockwork twin'—a mechanical maid whom she will finally dress up in her own clothes and send back to her father to take her place. The tiger's only request is to see her naked, for which he will set her free and give her riches as a reward, but she refuses to subject herself to his gaze. It is not until he reveals himself naked to her that she complies, but simultaneously she realises she cannot be free within the patriarchal world her father inhabits:

> I was a young girl, a virgin, and therefore men denied me rationality just as they denied it to all those who were not exactly like themselves, in all their unreason. If I could see not one single soul in that wilderness of desolation all around me, then the six of us—mounts and riders, both—could boast amongst us not one soul, either, since all the best religions in the world state categorically that not beasts nor women were equipped with the flimsy, insubstantial things when the good Lord opened the gates of Eden and let Eve and her familiars tumble out. . . . I had been bought and sold, passed from hand to hand.

Therefore the heroine's choice is between a father who values her only in market terms and a tiger, representative of a sexuality that is seemingly free from all economic interest. This is illustrated in the *dénouement* when the logic of the real animal world of the palazzo reasserts itself. By recognising her own sexuality the heroine finds 'liberty', and she sees that the tiger's sexual 'appetite need not be my extinction'. The materiality of this world dissolves:

> And each stroke of his tongue ripped off skin after successive skin, all the skins of a life in the world, and left behind a nascent patina of shin-

ing hairs. My earrings turned back to water and trickled down my shoulders; I shrugged the drops off my beautiful fur.

The question of choice, or lack of it, is echoed throughout the tales, and this is the Sadean framework—fuck or be fucked, both in the literal and in the metaphorical sense. Within this logic, to choose to fuck, given the options, seems a positive step, but the choice in fact is already prescribed. As Patricia Duncker puts it, 'we are watching . . . the ritual disrobing of the willing victim of pornography'.

This comment is particularly applicable to the tale **'The Bloody Chamber'**, which begins,

> I remember how, that night, I lay awake in the wagon—lit in a tender, delicious ecstasy of excitement, my burning cheek pressed against the impeccable linen of the pillow and the pounding of my heart mimicking that of the great pistons ceaselessly thrusting the train that bore me through the night, away from Paris, away from girlhood, away from the white enclosed quietude of my mother's apartment, into the unguessable country of marriage.

The rhythm and language of this long sentence directly associates the movement of the train with the sexual anticipation of the adolescent heroine, with an imagination perhaps bred on Gothic horror stories. It is a tale full of Gothic motifs, and it plays with desire and danger, placing the reader, through the first-person narrative, in the heroine-victim position. This is the tale of one of Bluebeard's wives, and the heroine, seduced by wealth, power and mystery, skirts death in the quest for sexual knowledge. The narrative strategy, therefore, puts us the readers imaginatively within this ambivalent willing-victim position, and the tale attempts to illustrate not only the dangers of seduction, but also the workings of pleasure and danger seemingly implicit in sexuality for women. Again the narrative draws attention to the connection between material wealth and marriage. The heroine's mother has 'beggared herself for love' and thus tries to ensure her daughter's economic security by getting her a musical education. The heroine's corruption is threefold: material, as she is seduced by wealth; sexual, as she discovers her own sexual appetite; and moral, in the sense that 'like Eve' she disobeys her master-husband's command.

But this is a victim who is not only willing but also recognises that she has been bought:

> This ring, the bloody bandage of rubies, the wardrobe of clothes from Poiret and Worth, his scent of Russian leather—all had conspired to seduce me so utterly that I could not say I felt one single twinge of regret for the world of tartines and maman that now receded from me as if drawn away on string, like a child's toy. . . .

And, when she comes to pay the price, 'I guessed it might be so—that we should have a formal disrobing of the bride, a ritual from the brothels . . . my purchaser unwrapped his bargain'. Her slow recognition of the real essence of the bargain she has struck is ironically underlined by the associations with death: 'A choker of rubies, two inch-

es wide, like an extraordinarily precious slit throat'; 'funereal lilies'; and a husband with eyes 'dark and motionless as those eyes the ancient Egyptians painted upon their sarcophagi'.

Her own sexual potential is another form of corruption. Again this is conveyed through contradictory impulses, and there is a sensual, physical detail in the writing:

> The perfume of the lilies weighed on my senses; when I thought that, henceforth, I would always share these sheets with a man whose skin, as theirs did, contained that toad-like, clammy hint of moisture, I felt a vague desolation that within me, now my female wound had healed, there had awoken a certain queasy craving like the cravings of pregnant women for the taste of coal or chalk or tainted food, for the renewal of his caresses. . . . I lay in bed alone. And I longed for him. And he disgusted me.

The intermingling of disgust and desire is not so much fear of the husband as for the sexuality in herself:

> I seemed reborn in his unreflective eyes, reborn in unfamiliar shapes. I hardly recognised myself from his descriptions of me and yet, and yet— might there not be a grain of beastly truth in them? And, in the red firelight, I blushed again, unnoticed, to think he might have chosen me because, in my innocence, he sensed a rare talent for corruption.

The 'talent for corruption' is not only a willingness to be bought but also perhaps a willingness to participate in 'the thousand, thousand baroque intersections of flesh upon flesh', amply detailed in a connoisseur's collection of sado-masochistic volumes found in the library.

Of all the tales in the volume I found **'The Bloody Chamber'** most troubling in terms of female sexuality, largely because of the very seductive quality of the writing itself. As readers we are asked to place ourselves imaginatively as masochistic victims in a pornographic scenario and to sympathise in some way with the ambivalent feelings this produces. The heroine's own subsequent recognition of total manipulation does not allay my unease at being manipulated by the narrative to sympathise with masochism. The writing playfully equivocates between explanation of the victims position and condemnation of the sadistic perpetrator of atrocities.

The husband puts the heroine to the test. He ostensibly goes away on business leaving her the keys to the castle with strict instructions not to enter his private room, which of course she does. There she discovers not only the mutilated bodies of his three former wives, but also the fate that awaits her. It seems, however, that the moral of the tale—that wives should not disobey their husbands— gets lost on the way, since as this quotation shows she had no choice in the matter anyway:

> The secret of Pandora's box; but he had given the box, himself, knowing I must learn the secret. I had played a game in which every move was governed by a destiny as oppressive and omnipotent as himself, since that destiny was himself; and I had lost. Lost at that charade of inno-

cence and vice in which he had engaged me.
Lost, as the victim loses to the executioner.

The husband promptly returns to claim his victim and what saves her is not the presence of the blind piano-tuner—he is merely a comfort—but her mother's pre-science. Puzzled at her newly-wed daughter crying during a telephone call, she has intuitively recognised danger and flown to her rescue. Thus the *dénouement* gives us female revenge against male tyranny, but the heroine must wear the mark of her 'shame' on her forehead for ever. To be branded as guilty, despite recognition of the manipulation to which she has been subject, seems somewhat unfair. This is the only tale where the mother figure plays an important and positive role. In the others, as in their fairy-tale originals, mothers are either absent, insignificant or bad.

In the three tales described there is a foregrounding of the economic aspects of female sexuality in relation to patriarchy and thus an emphasis on the latent meaning of traditional tales. Patricia Duncker describes them in this way:

> The boys must be taught courage. The girls must be taught fear. For girls the critical metamorphosis is sexual, menstruation, puberty, marriage. For Sleeping Beauty the symbolic curse that comes upon her is puberty, the first shedding of blood, the curse that can only be redeemed by marriage, her rightful place. All women have to do is wait. She must not initiate sexual activity, a potential she now possesses that is fraught with danger. She must wait and sleep out the years until she is possessed.

In cultural terms, of course, virginity is the ultimate sign of female purity—it is a state with magical properties. Western civilisation has a religion founded on a miraculous virgin birth, and female sexuality defines female identity. This is outlined by Kirsten Hastrup:

> The first stage is that of the unspecified, yet creative virgin; the next stage is that of the sexually specified, child-bearing women, and the course is completed by a final return to unspecificity, this time of widowhood and of old women's impotence.

Older women, therefore, move into a nebulous space where their potential for evil, as witches and hags, predominates over their potential for good, as fairy godmothers. Virgins are always susceptible to preying males who, if the young women are not careful, will take from them the thing of value they possess. As the heroine of 'The Tiger's Bride' observes, 'my own skin was my sole capital in the world and today I'd make my first investment'. Sex outside marriage threatens the social order constructed through patriarchal fears over property and possessions, and fairy tales are very much concerned with the sexual economy. Most of the tales in *The Bloody Chamber* concentrate on the states of virginity and puberty. The only tale that deals specifically with a married female figure is 'Puss-in-Boots', which is a kind of Chaucerian fabliau told from the point of view of a salacious 'puss'. Here the female goes to adulterous fornication with gusto and with little concern for social niceties. Though amusing, the tale

does not have much to recommend it in terms of sexual politics.

Another beast that rears its sexual head in various guises is the wolf, which features in the three short tales that close the volume: **'The Werewolf'**, **'The Company of Wolves'** and **'Wolf Alice'**. **'The Werewolf'** is an appetiser for the others and is a variation on the story of Little Red Riding Hood. The moral is plain: 'The wolf may be more than he seems'—only in this case he is granny herself.

'The Company of Wolves' is another version of **'The Tiger's Bride'**. 'Strong minded' Red Riding Hood wilfully sets off to visit granny while 'the malign door of the solstice swings upon its hinges', but in the 'pentacle of her own virginity' she fears nothing. Meeting a handsome gentleman on the way, and failing to notice that 'gleaming trails of spittle clung to his teeth', she hopes he will reach granny's house first so that he can win the wager and gain a kiss. He does of course, treating granny as an *hors d'oeuvre* to Red Riding Hood's 'immaculate flesh'. She recognises the danger but refuses to be a sacrificial victim: 'The girl burst out laughing; she knew she was nobody's meat. She laughed at him full in the face, she ripped off his shirt for him and flung it into the fire, in the fiery wake of her own discarded clothing'. Thus, 'sweet and sound she sleeps in granny's bed, between the paws of the tender wolf'. The point again is the acceptance of animal sexuality, but with a choice between rape and death such acceptance might seem merely logical rather than natural.

The third tale, however, inverts the second inasmuch as the 'wolf' is a girl child nurtured by wolves. She is rescued from the litter. Nuns try to civilise her but fail, and she ends up as a domestic servant to a werewolf. With a canine consciousness she tries to unravel the meaning of menstruation and budding sexuality. This process is simultaneous with a recognition of self in the mirror—a sort of Lacanian mirror phase moved to puberty: hence the 'Alice' of the title. In effect menstruation brings both a consciousness of time and awareness of a sexual identity, which manifests itself in her desire to put on an old dress and wander out into the world. The nurturing instincts that seemingly come with female sexuality are put to good use when her master returns home one night wounded: 'she was pitiful as her gaunt grey mother; she leapt upon his bed to lick without hesitation, without disgust, with a quick tender gravity, the blood and dirt from his cheeks and forehead'. This tale suggests that sex and gender identity are one in the same. Even without cultural conditioning young women will want to put on dresses and minister to the sick in a maternal way. Nature has ascendancy over nurture.

Similarly, in **'The Erl-King'** desire is the product of nature—the Erl-King 'came alive from the desire of the woods'—but we deduce from the punch-line, 'Mother, mother, you have murdered me!', that the Erl-King is also the created child of desire in an Oedipal configuration, and therefore potentially dangerous: 'Erl-King will do you grievous harm'. Thus,

> A young girl would go into the wood as trustingly as Red Riding Hood to her granny's house but this light admits of no ambiguities and, here, she

will be trapped in her own illusion because everything in the wood is exactly as it seems.

Desire is dangerous because you may create out of it the cage of your own entrapment, like the young girls trapped as birds in the Erl-King's cages. I prefer **'The Snow Child'**, a short, sardonic piece on conflict between mother and daughter for the father's love, because, despite their story's reinforcement of the Electra complex and patent lack of sisterhood, the father's created child of desire literally melts away.

The elements of death and desire are also central to **'The Lady of the House of Love'**. The Countess is part Sleeping Beauty, part descendant of Vlad the Impaler: 'She hovers in a no-man's land between life and death, sleeping and waking, behind the hedge of spiked flowers, Nosferatu's sanguinary rosebud'. She has a 'horrible reluctance for the role' of vampire and desires to be human, to wake from her sleeping death like Sleeping Beauty woken by a single kiss. Here it is the virgin hero who is protected by his innocence. Patricia Duncker comments,

> In fact what the Countess longs for is the grande finale of all 'snuff' movies in which the woman is sexually used and ritually killed, the oldest cliché of them all, sex and death. She can abandon her predatory sexuality, the unnatural force, as her own blood flows, the symbolic breaking of the virgin hymen, the initiation into sexual maturity and then into death.

This seems to me apt but again ignores the irony: the Countess is the archetypal opposite of Sleeping Beauty and with a wistful pathos longs to be the fairy-tale figure she mimics, even though it will be the death of her. Desire yet again is dangerous.

In her 'Polemical Preface' to *The Sadeian Woman* Carter invokes history:

> But our flesh arrives to us out of history, like everything else does. We may believe we fuck stripped of social artifice; in bed, we even feel we touch the bedrock of human nature itself. But we are deceived. Flesh is not an irreducible human universal. Although the erotic relationship may seem to exist freely, on its own terms, among the distorted social relationships of a bourgeois society, it is in fact the most self-conscious of all human relationships. . . .

Therefore, Carter rightly argues, desire is a social construct and ideology shapes subjectivity but is itself subject to the historical process. In the 'wolf' tales, **'The Erl-King'**, **'The Snow Child'** and **'The Lady of the House of Love'**, the economics of sexuality are abandoned for a concentration on the nature of desire and sexual subjectivity itself. Carter wants to explore boundaries and taboos in an anthropological rather than sociological vein and perhaps challenge certain feminist orthodoxies. But, divorced from the economic in **'The Company of Wolves'**, sexual choice becomes a question of straightforward survival in a seemingly natural, brutally physical male world. In **'Wolf Alice'** sexual subjectivity becomes predetermined by sex alone, and in **'The Erl-King'** desire is dangerous but precisely how is open to question. Sex is always and every-

where heterosexual. Desire *is* dangerous for women, for very good material reasons, and the romances of Mills and Boon put across messages about the protection of those interests in much the same way as fairy tales. Desire does not just exist in an unspecified way, but, as Carter points out in *The Sadeian Woman*, is ideologically and historically constructed. That her tales leave the nature of that constructedness out of the picture is somewhat of a disappointment.

Carter's treatment of fairy tales themselves is similar. By foregrounding their significance within her own tales Carter provides another layer of meaning. David Punter, analysing her novel *Heroes and Villains*, comments, 'Carter ironically suggests that the Gothic visions is in fact an accurate account of life, of the ways we project our fantasies onto the world and then stand back in horror when we see them come to life.' This is also true of fairy tales. Thus, for the tiger's bride,

> Old wives' tales, nursery fears! I knew well enough the reason for the trepidation I cosily titillated with superstitious marvels of my childhood on the day my childhood ended. For now my own skin was my sole capital in the world and today I'd make my first investment.

> Nursery fears become made flesh and sinew; earliest and most archaic of fears, fears of devourment. . . .

The problem with Carter's attempts to foreground the relationship between fairy tales and reality, a productive exercise, is that the action for the heroines is contained within the same ideological parameters. So the actual constructedness of reality and the ideological premises of fairy tales remain intact. The tiger's bride, like the other heroines, realises the 'truth' of the 'nursery fears' and chooses a non-materialistic, animal sexuality, but she does not have the option of *not* choosing it. Within the framework of the tale her choice appears to be a liberating one, but in reality it is not, despite Carter's Sadean proposition that misogyny can be undermined by women's refusal to be sexual victims and by their adoption of a more sexually aggressive role.

Although there are dangers in comparing theoretical and fictional writing, I feel it is perfectly justifiable to argue that many of the ideas in *The Bloody Chamber* rest on Carter's interpretation of Sade, even if they do not fulfil her own analysis of the mechanisms of the historical process. It is possible to say that some of the tales 'render explicit the nature of social relations' as outlined in Carter's definition of the 'moral pornographer', but explanation is not always enough. Indeed, **'The Bloody Chamber'** tale, through its equivocation, borders on the reactionary. We do have to address questions of binary thinking as it affects gender and sexuality, but Carter's prescribed action for her heroines within stereotypical options is ultimately politically untenable. Her use of irony might blur the boundaries at times but it does not significantly attack deep-rooted ways of thinking or feeling.

I began this essay by mentioning the collection of short stories *Wayward Girls and Wicked Women*. Unfortunately, the 'girls' in the tales of *The Bloody Chamber* can most often be designated 'wayward' — they do not value their virginity more than their lives; they get seduced by wealth; they cynically weigh their chances in a world full of male predators — and 'wicked women', rather thin on the ground, remain stereotypically wicked. (pp. 144-57)

> *Avis Lewallen, "Wayward Girls but Wicked Women? Female Sexuality in Angela Carter's 'The Bloody Chamber',"* in Perspectives on Pornography: Sexuality in Film and Literature, *edited by Gary Day and Clive Bloom, Macmillan Press, 1988, pp. 144-57.*

Sylvia Bryant   (essay date 1989)

[*In the following excerpt, Bryant explores Carter's treatment of the Oedipus myth, the classic fairy tale "Beauty and the Beast," and sex roles in her "The Tiger's Bride" and "The Courtship of Mr. Lyon."*]

> Once upon a time, there lived a rich merchant who gave his three sons and his three daughters the best money could buy.... All the girls were very pretty, especially the youngest. When she was a baby, she was nick-named "Little Beauty," and the name stayed with her as she grew older....
>
> —"Beauty and the Beast"

The traditional narrative framework of the fairy tale has generated an ideologically potent mythology of moral exempla produced, as Angela Carter explains in her recent translation of some classic tales, especially for children who as "apprentice adults . . . will benefit from advice on how to charm, whom to trust, how to grow rich." For centuries, through oral and written narratives, these tenacious "parables of instruction" have inculcated into Western society absolute representative patterns for growing up which are both products and producers of a pervasive ideological system that is deceptively simple in its fantasy, for apparently "children need only be 'good' in order to deserve happy endings."

Film-maker Jean Cocteau, a translator like Carter of the traditional fairy tale narrative into not the textual medium but the filmic, envisioned fairy tale characters as "archetypes or stereotypes" which may be allowed "no subtle nuances between black and white, good and evil" [Jean Cocteau, *"Beauty and the Beast": Diary of a Film,* 1947]. And Cocteau's assessment is certainly historically accurate, for the narratives of these characters' lives have systematically codified socially acceptable parameters for individual behavior and experience, reinforcing essential sexual differences which are perpetuated by a cultural double standard of desire. Yet the seductively familiar, formulaic narrative repeatedly and successfully obscures the genre's inherent binarism of desire, glosses over the seemingly unself-conscious gender bifurcation, and denies, in fact, the presence of any narrative—any personal, individual story—to the characters at all. Both the moral of the tale and the fate of the girls and boys loom large—not just once, but upon every time.

This social scenario of reward based on essential goodness presents an essential problem, particularly for the "girls"

seeking their own stories and experiences other than those which literature and history has proffered to them. There is a heavy-handed evaluative double standard operating in the fairy tale, on the general level of representation and in regard to the specific level of that "moral" which positions the female character, and hence the subject-seeking female reader, at the definitional mercy of the dominant culture's inscribing pen. The central female of "Beauty and the Beast" manifests a particular brand of this essential prescriptiveness; as Carter explains it, "Beauty's happiness is founded on her abstract quality of virtue": the moral "is all to do with something indefinable, not with 'doing well,' but with 'being good.' " That "indefinable" quality of "virtue" is really quite clear, however, in the endless re-inscription of what has always already been: "The end of a fairy story is the end of a fairy story," as Cocteau explains the fate of his filmic heroine; "Beauty is docile."

> **To tell a different story, to imagine and construct otherness as positive not negative difference, and to offer positive positionalities for identification within that otherness, to disrupt the ideological status quo enough to disturb the heretofore complacent acceptance it has met among readers and viewers; such is precisely the work of Carter's fairy tale narratives.**
>
> **—Sylvia Bryant**

In *Alice Doesn't: Feminism, Semiotics, Cinema,* Teresa de Lauretis traces the "mapping of differences, and specifically, first and foremost, of sexual difference into each text" back to what has been a sort of Ur-story on which Western culture has built and bifurcated its society, and hence its fictions, of sexual differences—the myth of Oedipus. She summarizes this basic narrative paradigm of Oedipus as "a passage, a transformation predicated on the figure of a hero, the mythic subject"—"hero" being itself marked, in a sense, for gender and thus already excluding women from its central narrative position. Thus, the narrative fixity of women in fairy tales falls into peripheral positions which are either undesirable in their extremities or contradictory in their desirability. Or, as Ellen Cronan Rose has succinctly observed [in her "Through the Looking Glass: When Women Tell Fairy Tales," in Elizabeth Abel, Marianne Hirsch, and Elizabeth Langland's *The Voyage In: Fictions of Female Development,* 1983], the list of possible positionalities available to the female reader has been consolidated to only a select few: "madonnas and whores, saints and witches, good little girls and wicked queens."

Since the controlling narrative paradigm maps difference and desire, as de Lauretis describes it, predominantly "from the point of view of Oedipus . . . that of masculine desire," traditional narrative has literally en-cultured the sexual binary into restrictive, predetermined representations and positionalities of "acceptable" behavior and desire—for the female character/reader: goodness, purity, docility. And under the rubric of the Oedipal myth, woman's story is/can be only man's story—which is, after all, the same old story. In other words, no story. De Lauretis explains this woman's dilemma as Other in Oedipal narrative in, appropriately enough, a fairy tale frame of reference: "The end of the girl's journey, if successful, will bring her to the place where the boy will find her, like Sleeping Beauty, awaiting him, Prince Charming. . . . Thus the itinerary of the female's journey . . . so her story, like any other story, is a question of his desire."

That the narrative grip of Oedipus is difficult to break free from is evinced, certainly, by the tenacity of those revered fairy tales which have hooked into our cultural ideology, and also by what in the past has been a marked absence of narratives which work to disrupt the status quo. Yet such resistant, cross-grain re-writing is precisely the task of Angela Carter, whose feminist revisionary rewriting of some of those classic fairy tales is, as Lorna Sage has described her work [in "The Savage Sideshow: A Profile of Angela Carter," *New Review* 39-40 (1977)], more concerned with "myth-breaking" than "myth-making"— rewriting which "take[s] myths and turn[s] them inside out."

In *The Bloody Chamber,* Carter proffers two versions of the classic tale "Beauty and the Beast." One version, **"The Courtship of Mr. Lyon,"** a hip, contemporary '60s-style parody featuring a cigarette-smoking Beauty, is an overt expose of the contrived gender differences and positionalities that inform the original tale. In the companion piece, **"The Tiger's Bride,"** Carter takes her re-visioning a crucial step further, subverting "that old story" by re-positioning and redefining woman's desire on her own terms. Carter's imaginative conceptions and formulations of what sorts of possibilities are available to women through cultural myths are a far cry, certainly, from those of Oedipus, which are, as de Lauretis explains, "honed by a centuries-long patriarchal tradition." In fact, these iconoclastic, tradition-breaking tales—especially **"The Tiger's Bride"**—do precisely what de Lauretis argues feminist writing and re-writing must do to subvert the continued predominance of the pattern of the Oedipal narrative: Woman—Beauty—is imagined/imaged as "mythical and social subject" in her own right, providing her own referential frame of experience, writing her ending to her own story.

"To a certain extent," Carter acknowledges regarding the foregrounding of a political agenda in her work, "I'm making a conscious critique of the culture I was born to." And to the extent that we read her narrative revisions as critiques of the dominant culture's inscriptions of sexual difference and desire, it is interesting and illuminating to read Carter's "Beauty" stories against Jean Cocteau's classic 1946 film text, *La Belle et La Bête,* which has always been studied as an experimental, avant-garde venture into the possibilities of cinematic production, yet which is nevertheless as familiar a rendering of the fairy story as Carter's versions are de-familiar ones. Cocteau's film text is, obviously, a product of a different era than

Carter's texts; yet it can be and must be studied as an equally powerful and persuasive vehicle for the re-inscribing of the values of the dominant culture—those same gender positionalities represented in the original fairy tale. For, like written narrative, as de Lauretis has pointed out, (culturally) dominant cinema, too, "works for Oedipus." (pp. 139-42)

In *La Belle et La Bête,* the narrative tradition which inscribed, and which subsequently is inscribed by, the classic fairy tale remains unaltered in the end and is seemingly to be preserved at all costs; no questions asked. Angela Carter, however, sets out to count those costs and to ask some of those questions in her perverse, satirical versions of the classic fairy tale. **"The Courtship of Mr. Lyon,"** written from the same omniscient point of view as is her source, keeps the original plot more or less intact; hence, ostensibly Oedipus is still at work. But a principle deviation Carter makes from the original, and one which facilitates her breaking away from Oedipus, concerns the time frame of the story. The setting is twentieth-century England, and the tensions which Carter exposes as the modern Beauty confronts the archaic social systems still at work in her contemporary world construct a more overt critique of those systems—represented here more by the Beast even than by Beauty's father—than either traditional narrative or dominant cinematic versions have heretofore discovered.

In **"The Courtship of Mr. Lyon,"** Beauty replays the typical patterning of female roles—daughter, mother, even wife (her father calls home to say he'll be late for dinner)— until finally she accepts her allotted place at Mr. Lyon's side, thereby balancing a social system initially disrupted when "her birth killed her mother." As in the original version, male experience is privileged and the masculine domain is foregrounded; the title, in fact, is completely his, without the mention of her at all. The Beast's materialism bespeaks a certain luxury and camaraderie reserved, apparently, for the Masters of society; his estate, "a place of privilege," is "plainly that of an exceedingly wealthy man." And a certain duplicity exists between the Beast and Beauty's father, for both are indeed accustomed to being masters, possessors of beautiful and valuable things; the Beast, upon seeing Beauty framed in a photograph, recognizes and desires her because of a "certain look" that the camera had "captured." This proprietary conspiracy among masters is apparently nothing new to Beauty, and she acquiesces willingly yet ruefully, "with a pang of dread" but with little surprise that she is the token of barter offered to the Beast: "the price of her father's good fortune . . . on some magically reciprocal scale."

That the Beast and Beauty's father inhabit the same gender-privileged realm is reinforced throughout the narrative by the increasingly blurred lines of demarcation between animal and man. Mr. Lyon is distinguished perhaps most obviously from a mere animal by the socially stratifying title of "Sir" which precedes his name; and he is something of a gentleman's intellectual, able to converse with Beauty about "the nature of the moon . . . about the stars . . . about the variable transformation of the weather." Beauty's sense of obligation to this Beast is a familiar one: she is still passive, the virginal object of barter—a "young girl who looked as if she had been carved out of a single pearl"—who "stayed, and smiled, because her father wanted her to do so." And although she realizes her fate as "Miss Lamb, spotless, sacrificial," she herself expedites the process, offering herself to the Beast almost in desperation, as if she fears not being taken otherwise. Beauty returns to find this Beast dying not in nature but in his "modest bedroom" (which, with only "a nightlight on the mantlepiece, no curtains at the windows, no carpet on the floor" is, surely, in need of a woman's touch, the scene is replete with sexual overtones: "She flung herself upon him, so that the iron bedstead groaned, and covered his poor paws with kisses. 'Don't die, Beast! If you'll have me, I'll never leave you.' " Carter ironically and explicitly implies that, sans Beast, this Beauty, too, is somehow not completely Beauty, for she is not possessed of that desirable goodness: left on her own in London, for instance, Beauty's "pearly skin . . . was plumping out, a little, with high living and compliments . . . her face was acquiring, instead of beauty, a lacquer of the invincible prettiness that characterized certain pampered exquisite, expensive cats."

Beauty's fate is indeed that of a "kept," pampered woman; but her keeper must be, it seems, only the Beast and not merely herself. Her constructed space at his estate is comfortable and opulent but well-defined and artificial, a bedroom with "precious books and pictures and the flowers grown by invisible gardeners in the Beast's hothouse." She has everything she could possibly need, the narrative implies—everything but a sense of her own identity and a story of her own. The pattern of Oedipus emerges most fully in the closing scene, for although she has made the sacrifice, it is his desires that are fulfilled. And under the "soft transformation" of her silent tears, the Beast comes into his proper, formerly hidden, manly self: "a man with an unkempt mane of hair and, how strange, a broken nose, such as the noses of retired boxers, that gave him a distant, heroic resemblance to the handsomest of all the beasts." Ironically, Carter ascribes the last words of this text to Mr. Lyon, rapidly re-inscribing Beauty back into her womanly supporting role. The story ends, but the ideology of the narrative continues; and under the patronymic of the masterful Beast, "Mr. and Mrs. Lyon walk in the garden"—happily ever after.

"My father lost me to The Beast at cards." So begins **"The Tiger's Bride,"** which follows thematically on the heels of **"The Courtship of Mr. Lyon"** yet is a striking departure from—indeed a cross-grain re-reading of—**"Mr. Lyon."** By appropriating the personal voice, the girl in this second tale not only takes charge of telling the narrative of her life, and consequently of the narrative traditions of the fairy tale, but she also makes clear from the start that what blame there is to be assigned lies not with her but with the dominant systems to which she is only a bargaining chip. This Beauty has shaken both the name—she is referred to only as "the girl," "the young lady"—and the consequent sexually-specific images that are intertwined with it: she is not so delicate and feminine "a pearl" who easily capitulates but a darker, stronger, more resilient "woman of honor" who ably watches out after herself because no one

else will. And in carving out her own life-story, in resisting the story which literary and cultural traditions have patterned for her, her narrative becomes an alternative model for the female subject's desire, constructing what de Lauretis says feminist cinematic and written narrative must: "the terms of reference of another measure of desire and the conditions of visibility for a different social subject."

"The Tiger's Bride," like the original "Beauty and the Beast," is a narrative which is inherently voyeuristic; the terms of looking, however, are significantly altered, for the girl is subject of the [her] gaze as well as object of the [his, the tiger's] gaze. The girl's desires seem to hark back to a primal and natural state, literally and metaphorically—one that is pre-Oedipal, almost pre-ideological, prior to the time it became "not natural for humankind to go naked." And the tiger's request, "to see the pretty young lady unclothed nude without her dress," is so shocking and untenable to her because to comply she must throw off the familiar ideological constructs and patterns that have so comfortably clothed and covered over her own unexpressed sexual desires that she realizes not that she even possesses them: " 'Take off my clothes for you, like a ballet girl? Is that all you want of me?'. . . That he should want so little was the reason why I could not give it."

The transformation in **"The Tiger's Bride"** indeed centers on the girl, not The Beast, thus presenting a narrative challenge to the Oedipal myth that, as de Lauretis describes such re-patterning, "represent[s] not just the power of female desire, but its duplicity and ambivalence." This female subject is not so readily categorized as her fictional predecessors; she is, in fact, the antithesis of Mrs. Lyon who was "possessed of a sense of obligation" that subsumed her own will. The girl knows, moreover, what she does not want—to be passively passed, like her mother before her, from one player to another in the hegemonic power game: "My mother did not blossom long; battered for her dowry. . . ." Precisely what it is that she does want, however, she does not know, for like the white rose The Beast gives to her, she is herself "unnatural, out of season." And her ripping apart of the rose "petal by petal" portends the un-layering to which she will subject herself in order to discover the potential of her heretofore unconsidered, unexplored sexual self. Actively initiating herself into the dominant discourse, she bargains with the status quo to redeem her story and her subjectivity on her own terms. This time it is she who picks the rose at her father's request, implicating his carelessness in her fate: "When I break off a stem, I prick my finger and so he gets his rose all smeared with blood."

Not only is this girl not your typical Beauty; neither does she face the typical Beast. Just as she is entrapped in an unfamiliar land—demographically, and also socially, sexually—so he is encased in an unfamiliar skin; and, ill-fitted for traditional roles, both are outsiders because of their differences. Unlike his fictional predecessors, or the "tiger-man" of the old wives' tale who wore a " 'big black travelling cloak lined with fur, just like your daddy's,' " the Beast of this story is indeed more animal than man, bearing "an odd air of self-imposed restraint, as if fighting a battle with himself to remain upright when he would far rather drop down on all fours," and searching not for personal luxury or social status in the "vast-man trap" of his palazzo—but "solitude." He never desires to alter his nature permanently, and his temporary attempts at a false disguise cause him to appear a garish parody of the beast in humans that is so thinly and disingeniously covered: "I never saw a man look so two-dimensional. . . . He wears a mask with a man's face painted most beautifully on it. Oh, yes, a beautiful face; but one with too much formal symmetry of feature to be entirely human: one profile of his mask is the mirror image of the other, too perfect, uncanny." Never in complicity with the dominant, oppressive ideology, The Beast in fact stands directly opposed to it, taking issue against its double standards and short-sightedness and acquiring the girl not out of a selfish desire to save (or serve) himself, but because she, like he, is different, a rarity—to him, a thing unknown, a non-pearl of great price: "If you are so careless of your treasures," he growls at her father, "you should expect them to be taken from you."

The Beast's very otherness is what intrigues the girl in the first place. Like her, beneath the constructed facade of his social appearance, he seems to be seeking self-knowledge, self-fulfillment of some sort—a commonality she senses she shares with The Beast yet cannot name: "it cannot be his face that looks like mine." Her sympathy and inclination toward other than what society has dictated must be signals her own difference and surfaces explicitly in her natural affinity for the little black gelding, "the noblest of creatures": "I lirruped and hurrumphed to my shining black companion and he acknowledged my greeting with a kiss on the forehead from his soft lips." And it is when she recognizes that she and The Beast are (in their silence) "speaking" the same speech of difference—a relationship to which there are no ideological strings of social/sexual expectation attached—that she feels "at liberty for the first time in [her] life." In both bearing her gaze and forcing her to look upon his natural nakedness, The Beast consequently brings her to a clear seeing of herself—or at least, a clear seeing of her desire to better "see," to know, herself: "I felt my breast ripped apart as if I suffered a marvellous wound."

The sacrifice in **"The Tiger's Bride"**—if indeed there is a sacrifice at all—is his, for ultimately he asks her to do nothing for him that he has not done for her. Because "nothing about him reminded [her] of humanity"—physically, intellectually—she undresses for him, consummating the reciprocal relationship of desire and trust, not with words, but with the equal, non-differentiating, illuminating gaze that makes her subject, not just object, and makes a place for her desire—the multiple sexual subjectivity she has experienced and embraced: "[His tongue,] abrasive as sandpaper, ripped off skin after skin, all the skins of a life in the world, and left behind a nascent patina of shining hairs. My earrings turned back to water and trickled down my shoulders; I shrugged the drops off my beautiful fur." And her final act, the sleight-of-hand substitution of the maid, the "marvellous machine," marks a significant break with the past in favor of her emerging personal, female desires; for with this simulacrum of

woman, she effects both a deliberate completion of her own story on her own terms and handily interrupts the old story of female goodness and fidelity: "I will dress her in my own clothes, wind her up, send her back to perform the part of my father's daughter."

In "real life," the conflictive beast the woman must confront is, of course, not a representative tiger but the literal social/sexual limitations society ideologically imposes. In **"The Tiger's Bride,"** Carter does rethink social/sexual stereotypes and re-cast the direction fairy tales may take in our culture, but her heroine bucks a tremendous tradition of literary representation and cultural ideology—a tradition that does not lightly permit a ready escape, for Oedipus still looms large. Carter's re-routing of the same old narrative paradigm is remarkable in one sense, for if the trend of recent video productions is indicative, such tradition-breaking re-visioning of fairy tale myth is, to a large extent, apparently still culturally cross-grain, especially in media produced for popular audiences. (pp. 445-51)

Margaret Atwood has written in her *Circe/Mud Poems:* "It's the story that counts. No use telling me this isn't a story or not the same story. . . . The story is ruthless." And the continuing production and passive acceptance of the familiar stories in written and filmic narratives, especially through readily accessible popular cultural media models based on the traditional standards of sexual difference and masculine desire, are disturbing and motivating reminders that those traditions must be subverted, those stories must be retold. To tell a different story, to imagine and construct otherness as positive not negative difference, and to offer positive personalities for identification within that otherness, to disrupt the ideological status quo enough to disturb the heretofore complacent acceptance it has met among readers and viewers; such is precisely the work of Carter's fairy tale narratives. For from the simplistic level of the fairy tale to the material complexities of narrative cinema, the story of Oedipus and the narratives of his standard-bearers must be actively re-examined and openly challenged—as shown particularly both by Cocteau, in his reinscriptions of them, and by Carter, in her shattering of them. De Lauretis argues that the best work in and the acceptable agenda for re-writing and re-making contemporary narrative is and can only be "narrative and Oedipal with a vengeance," an argument which we in our readings and writings must extend, as Carter has done in her revisionary work, in order to set the socio-cultural stage for new narrative traditions, granting voice and place, subjectivity and desire to a different female social subject, according to other than the same old story. (p. 452)

Sylvia Bryant, "Re-Constructing Oedipus through 'Beauty and the Beast'," in Criticism, *Vol. XXXI, No. 4, Fall, 1989, pp. 439-53.*

Jill Matus (essay date 1991)

[*In the following excerpt, Matus analyzes Carter's innovative contribution to the historical treatment of the "Black Venus."*]

Angela Carter's **"Black Venus"** takes Jeanne Duval, the

Eurafrican mistress of Charles Baudelaire, as the subject of its subversive narrative. Baudelaire's letters and poems, as well as the accounts of Jeanne Duval offered by his biographers, provide Carter with material for this short narrative fiction. Engaging the "Black Venus" cycle of poems from *Les Fleurs du Mal* in a series of ironic allusions, Carter's text alternates imaginative, dramatic scenes of Jeanne and Baudelaire (and the cat) in his gloomy apartment with speculative commentary on such diverse matters as Jeanne's native land, the state of the colonies under Napoleon, Manet's representation of female nudity, and the evidence provided by Nadar (alias Felix Tournachon, photographer and friend of Baudelaire) about the fate of Jeanne as an old woman. Does Carter's story claim to be a substituting or superseding version, presenting a new and improved Jeanne Duval? The concerns raised in this question are perhaps allayed by the narrator's awareness of the problem, for the narrative voice continually dissolves the illusions it creates and disputes its own authority (along with that of Baudelaire, Nadar or anyone else) to tell the real story about this woman.

Yet even as it disclaims the truth of its own representations, and teases out the racist and colonialist assumptions that inform traditional versions of Jeanne Duval, Carter's

Jacket cover of The Bloody Chamber, and Other Stories *(1979).*

fiction appropriates and reconstructs Jeanne in its own politically-interested image. **"Black Venus"** is engaged and interested in challenging the politics of assumptions about the sexualized woman as dark, diseased and corrupting. The title of the story refers, therefore, not only to a cluster of poems Baudelaire wrote, and to the woman who inspired them, but to a wider context—the ironized discourse of Venus in nineteenth-century constructions of female sexuality. What informs and underscores Carter's story is a network of associations from nineteenth-century comparative anthropology, physiology and anatomy, as well as from art and literature, in which blackness, primitive sexuality, prostitution and disease are closely linked. This essay approaches the contexts in which such associations develop by considering, for example, how Baudelaire's poem on the anthropologist Cuvier relates to Cuvier's verdict on the Hottentot Venus; what derogatory connotations the term "steatopygia" has in nineteenth-century constructions of female sexuality, and how Angela Carter uses this term in celebratory description; what connection the Hottentot Venus may have with Zola's Nana and Manet's painting "Nana"; and what Carter's Jeanne has to do with Manet's portrait of Jeanne Duval or, strangely, Courbet's effacement of her from his painting "L'Atelier du Peintre."

Venus, goddess of love, has a long history as the signifier of feminine beauty and purity. Mythology, visual representation and literature show, however, that the figure of Venus has also been used to suggest whorish seductiveness and voluptuousness, narcissistic female self-absorption, and a variety of other denigrating versions of woman. The context for the label "Black Venus" is frequently colonial, where it reveals much about colonial perceptions of race and gender. Its range of associations is wide, from the virulence of Jef Geeraert's *Gangrene,* subtitled *Black Venus,* to the benign paternalism of Stephen Gray's poem "Black Venus," in which the speaker implores an island beauty not to yearn for the white man's world, sure to spoil her charms. Both idealization and denigration may be suggested by the term "Black Venus"—Baudelaire's friend Banville captures its quality when he describes Jeanne as both bestial and divine. But like "Hottentot Venus," the term is often employed in a bitterly ironic or oxymoronic way—as if to say, "How can what is black also be Venuslike?"

In a discussion of Zola's *Nana* [in *Critical Essays on Emile Zola,* edited by David Baguley, 1986] Roland Barthes uses the term "Hottentot Venus" in this way when he suggests that it would be ludicrous to imagine a woman like the Hottentot Venus possessing seductive power. Writing of Zola's capacity to objectify, he points out how the men and women of the Second Empire become a "piece of anthropology as strange as the life of the Papuans." Barthes likens Zola to an ethnologist studying a Kwakiutl tribe, so awesome is his detachment. We have an overwhelming sense of difference between ourselves and the people of whom he writes—we may even find it "difficult to understand the wholesale devastation that Nana brings about; affectively, it seems to us almost as improbable as the seductive power of the Venus of the Hottentots." Barthes's implication is that, as unbelievable as the seductive power of the Hottentot Venus may be, so improbable seems Nana's capacity for devastation. Just as Papuans and the Kwakiutl tribe are other, so are the Hottentot Venus as a seductive power, and Nana as man-eater. *Mangeuses d'hommes* is a common term for prostitutes in nineteenth-century France. But what Barthes's analogy does not make clear is that "the historically particular version of the eternal Man-eater," the Hottentot Venus, and a remote "primitive" tribe, have a specific kind of sexual otherness in common. To explore this further, we need to know more about the historically particular version of the Hottentot Venus.

In the second decade of the nineteenth century, a young African woman called Saartjie Baartman was exhibited in London and then Paris to show the peculiar and "typical" physiognomy of the African woman. She was known as the Hottentot Venus. About five years later she died in Paris and the renowned Georges Cuvier wrote up his observations on her cadaver. Cuvier's paper drew attention to the similarity of woman and ape and noted the distortions and anomalies of her "organ of generation." According to Cuvier, the highest form of ape—the orangutan—was comparable to the lowest form of man/woman, and more particularly, black woman. The Hottentot Venus was exhibited not as an incidental freak in a cheap circus, but as a type—the essence of woman's low position on the evolutionary ladder and the irrefutable evidence of her bestial and degenerate associations.

Sander Gilman's detailed study of the Hottentot Venus [*Difference and Pathology: Stereotypes of Sexuality, Race and Madness,* 1985] suggests that Cuvier was responsible for constituting the Hottentot Venus as the major signifier for the image of the Hottentot as sexual primitive in the nineteenth century. According to Gilman, the idea of primitive sexuality is also signified in images of size and grossness, particularly the steatopygia of the Hottentot woman. So, for example, Gilman argues that in a painting like Manet's *Nana*, the line of the exaggerated buttocks in the prostitute associates her with the Hottentot Venus and signifies her internal blackness and atavistic sexuality. (In nineteenth-century iconographies of the prostitute, steatopygia is a recurrent characteristic.) But the nineteenth-century association of the prostitute with the black was most readily compounded by the belief that prostitutes differed physiologically from ordinary women, that they were sexually primitive, even degenerate. Since the prostitute was also associated with disease, the link between blackness, primitive sexuality and corruption was further determined. In a complex variety of combinations, these characteristics could signal the grotesque and degenerate, as well as the exotic, forbidden and exciting. So, for example, Carter has Baudelaire, poet of decadence, look with fascination upon his dark mistress as "an ambulant fetish, savage, obscene, terrifying."

Baudelaire wrote a poem called "Cuvier's Verdict," in which Cuvier, questioned about where he would situate the Belgian on the chain of being, replies that this is indeed a problem since there is quite a gap between ape and mollusk. Another Belgian poem deals with the unsanitary habits of Belgian women, who surely use black soap since they always appear to be dirty. (Carter's Jeanne complains that Baudelaire will not pay for hot water for her bath and adds caustically that he probably thinks she does not need to bathe because her dark skin doesn't show the dirt.) Baudelaire's disparagement of Belgians, especially Belgian women, draws on the two categories that inform Cuvier's remarks about the Hottentot Venus—degeneration and blackness. Although Baudelaire did not write a poem about Cuvier's verdict on the Hottentot Venus, Carter's implication is that he nevertheless inscribed that verdict in the "Black Venus" poems.

Degeneration and blackness also define the white prostitute, such as Zola's Nana, celebrated in the novel as "la Blonde Vénus." In the opening scenes of *Nana* she takes part in an operetta called *La Blonde Vénus* at the Théâtre des Variétés. Although she is not able to move members of the audience with her artistic talents, she can certainly move its male members with the sight of her naked body. Zola describes her as a Venus in the true sense of the word, and as a force of nature. Although at first sight, La Blonde Vénus and the Hottentot Venus do not appear to have much in common, their association is closer and more complex than Barthes's analogy suggests. Though the former may arouse and seduce while the latter provokes curiosity and derision, they are both versions of female sexuality characterized as primitive and other, black and degenerate. It is, however, only when Zola's Blonde Vénus is dying, having contracted smallpox from her son, that her concealed inner blackness and rot are revealed. Smallpox, in this sense, is not so much small as it is merely pox—syphilis. Nana's demise is instructive in that her putrefaction is described as the rotting and decomposition of Venus. Since her son's contagion is the cause of her death, the text suggests that it is, of course, the produce of her thighs that eventually contaminates her. Those "snowy thighs" that corrupted Paris mock the association of snow and whiteness with purity, demonstrating that white as they are, hers are no different from the black ones overtly associated with corruption and disease. Nana reminds us of Nanahuatzin, the Aztec goddess, whom Carter mentions in **"Black Venus"** as the one blamed by Europeans for sending venereal disease from the New World to the Old—an erotic vengeance for imperialist plunder. Carter, however, mines the irony that Baudelaire's "black-thighed witch" (as his poem "Sed Non Satiata" styles her) may have contracted syphilis from him.

Carter's **"Black Venus"** situates itself squarely within the contexts of Venus mythology that I have been discussing, and confronts stereotypes with iconoclastic wit. The story displays qualities of much of Carter's work, which has been described by various critics as shocking, intoxicating, revisionist, abrasive. A characteristic procedure of Carter's is to seize upon some image, icon or bit of mythology and draw out its implications, making gorgeous what is denigrated or scorned, blaspheming against what is held sacred, and exposing what is usually kept covert. Carter's fiction relishes the so-called freaks excluded from the Western pantheon of Venuses and relegated to circuses and sideshows. Carter is interested in women larger than life, the giantesses of myth and history and fiction—Helen, Venus, Josephine Baker, Jeanne Duval and Sophia

Fevvers, the birdwoman in *Nights at the Circus,* in whom the association of gross size, deformity and sexual licentiousness, for example, are brought gloriously together. A poster advertises the attractions of the bewinged aerialiste Fevvers thus:

> The artist had chosen to depict her ascent from behind—bums aloft, you might say; up she goes, in a steatopygous perspective, shaking out about her those tremendous . . . pinions . . . powerful enough to bear up such a big girl as she.

Celebratory emphasis on the rear of this "Cockney Venus" seems to mock the association of grossness with female sexuality.

Although not specific about Jeanne in the way that she is about the "Cockney Venus," Carter emphasizes Jeanne's size, describes her as a "woman of immense height," and imagines Jeanne thinking of herself as a "great gawk of an ignorant black girl, good for nothing." In opposition to Jeanne's self-deprecation, Carter regards her as one of "those beautiful giantesses who, a hundred years later, would grace the stages of the Crazy Horse or the Casino de Paris in sequin cache-sexe and tinsel pasties, divinely tall, the color and texture of suede. Josephine Baker!" In contrast to the Hottentot Venus, exhibited in Paris as the butt of racist and misogynist humor, Josephine Baker exhibited herself at the Revue Nègre, commanding awe and capitalizing on her "savage" and "primitive" blackness. A recent biography, *Jazz Cleopatra,* describes how the dancer marketed herself in Paris by emphasizing her black animality, symbolized by the extraordinary life and power of her undulating buttocks. "The rear end exists," said Baker. "I see no reason to be ashamed of it. It's true that there are rear ends so stupid, so pretentious, so insignificant, that they're only good for sitting on."

Biographers of Baudelaire who write about Jeanne Duval concede her beauty, but in such a way as to suggest that she is an aesthetic object rather than a beautiful woman. She had that "enigmatic stylized black beauty which combines line and patina to produce an aesthetic effect, like a work of art in bronze or dark stone" writes Baudelaire's biographer, A. E. Carter [In *Charles Baudelaire,* 1977]. But he also says she was "a common slut, totally uncultivated and extremely stupid; and like most whores she lied with a deliberate compulsive mendacity which is close to paranoia." Rather than an exotic and fetishized *objet d'art,* she is, for Carter, a means to unsettle and parody canonical Western art. Carter asks us to imagine "The Birth of Black Venus," describing her (in terms of Botticelli's painting) aloft her scallop-shell, "clutching an enormous handful of dreadlocks to her public mound" while "wee black cherubs" blow her across the Atlantic. Artistic representations of Jeanne Duval by Manet and Courbet provide an interesting gloss on Carter's representation of Duval in the story. Courbet originally painted her next to Baudelaire himself in the "Atelier" but later removed her at Baudelaire's request. A close scrutiny of the painting reveals the ghostly traces of her effacement, which underscores Carter's suggestion in the story that Jeanne exists for Baudelaire as something on which he may feast his eyes, or that he may remove from sight, according to his

whim. Carter mentions Manet's *Le Déjeuner sur l'Herbe* in relation to a scene where Baudelaire sits impeccably dressed while Jeanne must be naked, clothed only in her skin, but she does not mention Manet's portrait of Jeanne (1862) in which she is positioned half-reclining, but very much clothed in full crinoline. Like Zola's Nana, Jeanne was reputed to be a bad actress and a good courtesan; however, Manet paints her very differently from the young and seductive Nana, in whom signs of degeneration are covert. In Manet's portrait of Duval, such signs are (at least in the eyes of some critics) more obvious. She is described as suffering the wages of her pathological sexuality: "stiff and half-paralysed, and her face . . . stupid and bestial from alcoholism and vice."

In **"Black Venus"** one of the problems confronting Carter is how to represent Jeanne without presuming to speak for her or know her mind. [Mikhail] Bakhtin's notion of dialogic interchange may help to explain Carter's sense of Jeanne, since Bakhtin emphasizes [in his *The Dialogic Imagination: Four Essays,* 1981] how the word in language is always half someone else's, "exists in other people's mouths." It becomes one's own only when the speaker populates it with intention and "expropriates" the word, adapting it to his or her own semantic and expressive needs. Jeanne's words, Carter suggests, have been more than half someone else's. A Francophone whose Creole patois made her feel in France as if "her tongue had been cut out and another one sewn in that did not fit well," Carter's Jeanne is without words, without country, without history. Noting that Baudelaire's eloquence has denied Jeanne her language, the narrator is concerned to make the silences of Jeanne's own narrative speak. Since her sugar daddy does not hear her, we should. As she dances for her "Daddy," Jeanne hums "a Creole melody . . . but Daddy paid no attention to what song his siren sang." As she does with other mythic ideas, Carter uses the notion of the irresistible song of the sirens to ironic effect. Baudelaire may call his mistress his siren, pose her as a seductress, but he is far too self-absorbed to hear any song but his own as irresistible.

Though Jeanne has been, in effect, silenced by Baudelaire's words and eclipsed by his shadow, Carter does not presume to appropriate Jeanne's story by knowing her mind; rather, she draws attention to other possible representations of her than those we already have by persistently imagining her as an ordinary down-to-earth woman concerned with her own immediate material conditions. Her language cannot speak for Jeanne, but it can compete with and challenge the languages that have sought to possess and exploit her. She attempts to formulate an alternative vocabulary to Baudelaire's and to expose the contingencies of his vocabulary. Carter's habit of unsettling ascriptions and projections manifests itself in making the reader scrutinize language closely and attend to the nuances of apparent tautology and the connotations that make a crucial difference. A good example hinges on how we understand "promiscuous": "Her lover assumed she was promiscuous because she *was* promiscuous." But Jeanne has her own code of honor. To her

> prostitution was a question of number; of being paid by more than one person at a time. That

was bad. She was not a bad girl. When she slept with anyone else but Daddy, she never let them pay. It was a matter of honour. It was a question of fidelity.

The passage draws attention to the misconstruction of Jeanne's actions from the point of view of the onlooker. Because she was promiscuous—took many sexual partners—does not mean in her terms that she was promiscuous (unable to discriminate among them).

One way in which Carter questions distorting versions of Jeanne is by challenging the poet's metaphoric power: "My monkey, my pussy-cat, my pet" he croons as he imagines taking her back to the island where the "jewelled parrot rocks on the enamel branch" and where she can crunch sugar-cane between her teeth. "But, on these days," the narrator counters, "no pet nor pussy she; she looks more like an old crow with rusty feathers in a miserable huddle by the smoky fire." Nor is there any romanticizing of her as the dispossessed child of the islands, yearning for her heritage: she doesn't know that she has a heritage, let alone that she has been deprived of it. Since the colony—white and imperious—fathered her, she is a child without history. The narrative suggests that traditional poetic tropes are inadequate and appropriating when they underscore Western constructions of motivation and desire.

As the poet's "agonised romanticism" transforms the homely Caribbean smell of coconut oil into the perfume of the air of tropical islands, his imagination performs an "alchemical alteration on the healthy tang of her sweat." "He thinks her sweat smells of cinnamon because she has spices in her pores." In place of the poet's "weird goddess, dusky as the night," "vase of darkness,"—a "black Helen" to his tortured Faust—the narrative shows us a woman who lights the smelly cheroots she smokes with his manuscripts, who tells him to let the cat out before it craps on the Bokhara, and who fears the syphilis she has contracted from her "first white protector"—Baudelaire.

Another strategy Carter uses is to challenge the mythical constructs that allow Jeanne to be represented as the exotic Eve, black temptress and queen of sin. The poet might like to believe she has come from an island paradise, but the narrator describes it as a "stinking Eden." Her fall, after she bites "a custard apple," is presented as a fall into the European—civilized—world. Later, however, the narrator offers another interpretation: if Jeanne is to occupy any position in the Genesis story, she would have to be the forbidden fruit—and Baudelaire has consumed her. (Felix Nadar once described her as a special dish for the ultrarefined palate.)

Baudelaire's biographers agree that Jeanne was a "mulatto" from the French Caribbean. Angela Carter writes:

> Where she came from is a problem; books suggest Mauritius, in the Indian ocean, or Santo Domingo, in the Caribbean, take your pick of two different sides of the world. (Her *pays d'origine* of less importance than it would have been had she been a wine).

What is important to Carter's story, whose ending envisages Jeanne's return to Martinique, is that her origins are colonial. Insofar as Jeanne's story is ever told it usually ends with Nadar's description of her hobbling on crutches, her teeth and hair gone. Carter, however, constructs a possible resurrection for her in the last pages of the story: "You can buy teeth, you know; you can buy hair." While Carter's narrator points out that the poet near death is so estranged from himself he is said to have bowed politely to his reflection in the mirror, Jeanne is pictured as having found herself. "She had come down to earth, and, with the aid of her cane, she walked perfectly well on it." A number of sources mention Duval's brother—a man she claimed was her brother—who lived off her and absconded with her possessions while she was in hospital. In Carter's closure this "high-yellow, demi-sibling" takes over her finances and, "a born entrepreneur," sets her back on her feet. She makes for Martinique and starts up a brothel.

The inclusion of this putative brother figure in the story preserves a bit of the biographical data, but what is the significance of this managing male? A self-directed female avenger might be thought more appropriate to the text's feminist politics, but Carter's text, besides challenging Western sexual stereotypes, is also a fable from a postcolonial perspective. Carter uses the brother figure to make a point about pimping, capitalist enterprise and colonial trade. Earlier the narrator tells us: "Seller and commodity in one, a whore is her own investment in the world and so she must take care of herself." Jeanne has not taken care of herself in this way, but under the management of this possibly demonic brother (we are told that for all Jeanne cares he could be Mephistopheles), who seems to be out for a cut of the profits, she gets a new lease on life dispensing pleasure and death to the colonial administrators of her native land. The last sentence of the story imagines her keeping in circulation the "gift" that Baudelaire had given her:

> Until at last, in extreme old age, she succumbs to the ache in her bones and a cortege of grieving girls takes her to the churchyard, she will continue to dispense, to the most privileged of the colonial administration, at a not excessive price, the veritable, the authentic, the true Baudelairean syphilis.

What goes around comes around. If Baudelaire's poems about Jeanne are often called the "Black Venus cycle," the name is apt, not least because they recycle a cluster of attitudes that govern the representation of sexualized woman, be she a Blonde, Black or Hottentot Venus. Angela Carter has, however, given that cycle a new turn. (pp. 467-75)

Jill Matus, "Blonde, Black and Hottentot Venus: Context and Critique in Angela Carter's 'Black Venus'," in Studies in Short Fiction, *Vol. 28, No. 4, Fall, 1991, pp. 467-76.*

FURTHER READING

Criticism

Gorra, Michael. "Fiction Chronicle." *The Hudson Review* XL, No. 1 (Spring 1987): 136-48.
     Brief, favorable review of *Saints and Strangers*.

Lokke, Kari E. "*Bluebeard* and *The Bloody Chamber*: The Grotesque of Self-Parody and Self-Assertion." *Frontiers* X, No. 1 (1988): 7-12.
     Compares Carter's version of the Bluebeard legend with Max Frisch's, noting that both authors use the grotesque as a method for exposing the brutality that informed traditional patriarchal views of women.

Additional coverage of Carter's life and career is contained in the following sources published by Gale Research: *Contemporary Authors*, Vols. 53-56, 136; *Contemporary Authors New Revision Series*, Vols. 12, 36; *Contemporary Literary Criticism*, Vols. 5, 41, 76; *Dictionary of Literary Biography*, Vol. 14; *Major 20th-Century Writers*; and *Something about the Author*, Vols. 66, 70.

André Gide

1869-1951

(Full name André Paul Guillaume Gide) French novelist, novella writer, playwright, diarist, critic, autobiographer, essayist, and poet.

INTRODUCTION

Credited with introducing modern experimental techniques to the French novel with such works as *Les faux monnayeurs* (*The Counterfeiters*), Gide is also highly esteemed for his novellas. Varying widely in content and form, his nine novellas range from a Symbolist prose-poem, *Le voyage d'Urien* (*Urien's Voyage*) to a retelling of a classical myth, *Thésée* (*Theseus*), and cover such subjects as religion, marriage, and the relationship between art and life. Critics have noted that the characters in Gide's works consistently reflect his own moral, intellectual, and philosophical concerns. Commentators on Gide's novellas therefore often attach as much significance to biographical detail as they do to artistic method.

Gide was born in Paris in 1869. His father, a professor at the University of Paris, died when Gide was eleven years old; afterward, Gide was raised by his domineering and highly protective mother, a strict Calvinist whose family background was Norman and Catholic. Gide's formal schooling was erratic, and he frequently required private tutoring at home because of his delicate health. Following the publication of his first novel, *Les cahiers d'André Walter* (*The Notebooks of André Walter*), Gide became associated with Stéphane Mallarmé's Symbolist literary coterie, which he would later satirize in the novella *Paludes* (*Marshlands*). In an attempt to escape the stifling Calvinist atmosphere of his home, Gide traveled to North Africa in 1893. There, he pursued previously denied sensual pleasures and discovered his bisexual inclinations for the first time. However, his early religious training remained a lifelong influence, and Gide became obsessed with resolving the struggle between the puritan and the libertine in his nature. This conflict is explicitly examined in two of his novellas, *Le Prométhée mal enchaîné* (*Prometheus Illbound*) and *La symphonie pastorale* (*The Pastoral Symphony*).

After returning to France in 1895, Gide married his cousin Madeleine. Despite their deep attachment to each other, their marriage was traumatic. Although Gide expressed an overwhelming spiritual need to share his life with his cousin, who provided him with a source of stability, Madeleine's strict Christian values often conflicted with his unconventional life style, which specifically separated love and sexual pleasure. Critics note that many of Gide's mature works were inspired by the difficulties he

experienced in this relationship. While he was well known and respected among his fellow writers, Gide remained unrecognized by the general public until the 1920s. His involvement as founder and editor of the prestigious *La nouvelle revue française* led to his discovery by a postwar generation of youth who rejected conventional social values and embraced both his restless search for spiritual truth and his belief that life should be lived to its emotional and intellectual fullest. The importance of Gide's examination of private morality and its effect on society was publicly recognized in 1947 when, after a lifetime of neglect by the literary establishment (due largely to his public confession of homosexuality), he was awarded the Nobel Prize for literature. Gide died in 1951.

A principal area of debate in interpreting Gide's imaginative work, particularly his short fiction, has been the question of genre. Throughout his literary career Gide displayed a self-conscious concern for genres by producing works which adhered to the structural and stylistic strictures of specific genres and by attempting to redefine and adapt their characteristics. Gide and his commentators have divided much of his work into three categories: récits, soties, and novels. Although critics agree that

L'immoraliste (*The Immoralist*), *La porte étroite* (*Strait Is the Gate*), and *The Pastoral Symphony* are clearly récits, that *Prometheus Illbound* adheres to the sotie model, and that *The Counterfeiters* is a novel, the categorization of *Isabelle*, *Marshlands*, and *Theseus* as well as the defining characteristics of Gide's genres has been a point of debate. Defined briefly, a Gidean récit is a psychological narrative in which the protagonist reflects on the past. As contradictory events and the principal character's self-justifying but facile interpretations accumulate, the narrator's beliefs and values are gradually discredited. In contrast, a Gidean novel attempts to create an objective portrait of reality by combining several points of view and focusing on characters moving toward an uncertain future. In his soties, Gide made extensive use of irony and absurdity to produce works which, as W. Wolfgang Holdheim has explained, "essentially constitute a self-persiflage of the artist and the work of art, specifically of the novelistic work of art, for the mainspring of their autocritique is their deliberate and visible refusal to 'imitate' reality."

In his short fiction, Gide addressed three principal concerns: the individual, religion, and the relationship between art and life. In *Marshlands*, Gide satirized the narrator—a novelist who is writing a novel called "Marshlands"—who vainly attempts, through discussion of his novel and the ideas behind it, to prompt his friends into carrying out social and individual reform. Commentators have observed that Gide's juxtaposition of the narrator's life and art suggests that the writer should be concerned with transforming life into art rather than promoting action in others through art. In *The Pastoral Symphony* and *Prometheus Illbound*, Gide treated religious themes. The former work satirizes the protagonist, a protestant pastor, for his failure to realize that his obsession with a blind girl is driven by sensual desire rather than Christian charity. In *Theseus*, Gide's last work of fiction, the title character narrates the story of his personal growth and development. Gide's version of the myth differs in several respects from the original; one of the most noteworthy differences is his reinterpretation of the labyrinth and the Minotaur. In the classical version, the Minotaur was a monster, half man and half bull, who ate youths and maidens, which Athens periodically sent as a tribute to King Minos of Crete, after they had become lost in the labyrinth's intricate complex of passageways. The labyrinth and Minotaur in Gide's retelling trap the victims by appealing to their longings for physical pleasure. Thus, critics analyzing Theseus's escape in Gide's version have observed that sensual desire and self-indulgence are depicted as forces which must be overcome because they subvert rationality and inhibit human progress—the inner development through which one transforms and transcends oneself. Critics today are divided in their assessment of Gide's works. While some see them as dated and of only minor interest for contemporary readers, others praise the perfection of Gide's style and the sincerity with which he set out to expose social, religious, artistic, and sexual hypocrisy. As reflections of his emotional struggles, commentators agree that part of the genius behind Gide's writing lay in his ability to translate the contradictions and complexities of his nature into art.

PRINCIPAL WORKS

SHORT FICTION

Le voyage d'Urien 1892
[*Urien's Voyage*, 1964]
Paludes 1895
[*Marshlands* published in *"Marshlands" and "Prometheus Misbound,"* 1953]
Le Prométhée mal enchaîné 1899
[*Prometheus Illbound*, 1919; also published as *Prometheus Misbound* in *"Marshlands" and "Prometheus Misbound,"* 1953]
Isabelle 1911
[*Isabelle* published in *Two Symphonies*, 1931]
La symphonie pastorale 1919
[*The Pastoral Symphony* published in *Two Symphonies*, 1931]
L'école des femmes 1929
[*The School for Wives*, 1929; also published in *The School for Wives. Robert. Geneviève; or, The Unfinished Confidence*, 1950]
Robert 1930
[*Robert* published in *The School for Wives. Robert. Geneviève; or, The Unfinished Confidence*, 1950]
Geneviève 1936
[*Geneviève* published in *The School for Wives. Robert. Geneviève; or, The Unfinished Confidence*, 1950]
Thésée 1946
[*Theseus*, 1948]

OTHER MAJOR WORKS

Les cahiers d'André Walter (novel) 1891
[*The Notebooks of André Walter*, 1968]
Les poésies d'André Walter (prose poems) 1892
Le traité du Narcisse (essay) 1892
Les nourritures terrestres (prose poems) 1897
[*The Fruits of the Earth*, 1949]
Philoctète (drama) 1899
Le Roi Candaule (drama) 1901
L'immoraliste (novel) 1902
[*The Immoralist*, 1930]
Prétextes (essays) 1903
[*Pretexts*, 1959]
Saül (drama) 1903
La porte étroite (novel) 1909
[*Strait Is the Gate*, 1924]
Les caves du Vatican (novel) 1914
[*The Vatican Swindle*, 1925; also published as *Lafcadio's Adventures*, 1928]
Dostoïevsky (criticism) 1923
[*Dostoevsky*, 1925]
Corydon (dialogues) 1924
[*Corydon*, 1950]
Les faux monnayeurs (novel) 1925
[*The Counterfeiters*, 1927; also published as *The Coiners*, 1927]
Si le grain ne meurt (autobiography) 1925
[*If It Die*, 1950]
Numquid et tu . . . ? (meditations) 1926
Voyage au Congo (travel essays) 1927
[*Travels in the Congo*, 1930]

Oedipe (drama) 1931
   [*Oedipus* published in *Two Legends: Oedipus and The-
      seus,* 1950]
Retour de l'U.S.S.R. (travel essays) 1936
   [*Return from the U.S.S.R.,* 1937; also published as *Back
      from the U.S.S.R.,* 1937]
Journal, 1889-1939 (journal) 1939
Journal, 1939-1942 (journal) 1946
The Journals of André Gide, 1889-1949. 4 vols. (jour-
      nals) 1947-51
Journal, 1942-1949 (journal) 1950
Et nunc manet in te, suivi de journal intime (journal)
      1951
   [*Madeleine,* 1952]
Le journal des faux monnayeurs (journal) 1951
   [*Logbook of the Coiners,* 1952]
My Theatre (dramas and essays) 1951
Ainsi soit-il; ou, Les jeux sont fait (memoir) 1952
   [*So Be It; or, The Chips Are Down,* 1959]
The Return of the Prodigal (essays and dramas) 1953

CRITICISM

André Gide   (essay date 1919)

[*In the following essay, originally published in the* Nouvelle revue française *in September 1919, Gide comments on the reasonableness and psychological truth of
the Greek myths, particularly the myth of Theseus.*]

The Greek fable is like Philemon's pitcher, which no thirst
can empty, if one drinks with Jupiter. (Oh! It is the god
whom I invite to my table!) And the milk my thirst draws
from it is assuredly not that which Montaigne drank, I
know—nor was the thirst of Keats and Goethe that of Racine or Chénier. Others will come like Nietzsche, whose
lips burn with a different fever. But he who, lacking respect for the god, breaks the pitcher, on pretext of seeing
the bottom and exposing the miracle, is left with shards
in his hands. Most often the mythologists offer us but the
shards of myth, bizarre bits in which we still admire here
and there, as on the fragments of a Etruscan vase, a chance
form, a gesture, a dancing foot, a hand stretched toward
the unknown, an ardent pursuit of some fleeing game, a
link detached from the perfect chorus of the Muses, whose
unbroken garland encircled the vase we recreate in our
imaginations.

The first condition for understanding the Greek myth is
to believe in it. I do not mean that one needs a faith like
that called for by the Church. The consent given the
Greek religion is of a quite different nature. It is strange
that a great poet like Hugo has understood that so little;
he took pleasure like so many others in stripping the divine figures of all sense so as to admire only the victory
over them of certain elemental forces and of Pan over the
Olympians. It was not smart of him, if I may say so, and
his Alexandrines suffer from it less than does our reason.

"How could anyone have believed in that?" Voltaire exclaims. And yet, it is to reason first and to reason alone
that each myth appeals: you have understood nothing of
the myth if you have not first accepted its reasonableness.
The Greek fable is essentially reasonable, and one can say,
without Christian impiety, that it is easier to believe in the
Greek fable than in the doctrine of Saint Paul, the characteristic of which is precisely to humble, supplant, stultify,
and shackle reason. It is for want of intelligence that Pen-
theus refuses to admit Bacchus; on the other hand, it is
Polyeucte's intelligence that at first interposes itself and
clouds his triumphant vision. I am not saying that intelligence does not eventually find in Christian dogma a supreme satisfaction, or that skepticism is of greater profit
for reason than faith; but the Christian faith is based on
renunciation of the intelligence; and if reason perhaps
emerges enhanced from this renunciation, it is in accord
with Christ's promise: All that you sacrifice for love of me,
you will recover a hundredfold—while he who here wishes
to save his reason shall lose it.

Strictly speaking, there are no mysteries in pagan mysticism: even those of Eleusis were but the whispered teaching of a few great natural laws. But the error is deigning
to recognize in the myth only the figurative representation
of physical laws, and to see in all the rest only the workings of *fatality.* With that frightful word we have given too
great an advantage to chance; it casts its blight wherever
we abandon explanation. But I maintain that the more we
reduce the role of fate in the fable, the more we learn from
it. In the absence of the physical law the psychological
truth comes clear, which speaks more compellingly to me.
What does fate teach us, whenever we let it appear? To
submit to what we can not resolve. But the great souls of
the legendary heroes were in point of fact unsubmissive
souls, and to allow chance to lead them is to misunderstand them. Doubtless they know this *amor fati,* which
Nietzsche admired, but the fatality here at issue is an inner
fatality. The fatality is in them; they bore it within them;
it was a psychological fatality.

Nothing has been understood about the character of Theseus, for example, if it is accepted that the bold hero *"Qui
va du dieu des morts déshonorer la couche"* ("Who to dis-
honor the couch of the god of the dead goes forth") left
quite inadvertently the black sail on the vessel bringing
him back to Greece, the "fatal" black sail which, deluding
his grief-stricken father, caused him to hurl himself into
the sea—thanks to which Theseus entered into possession
of his kingdom. An oversight? Come now! He forgot to
change the sail as he forgot Ariadne in Naxos. I understand full well that fathers do not teach that to their children; but if we wish to lift the story of Theseus above the
insignificance of an old wives' tale, we have only to see the
hero as fully conscious and strong-willed.

It gives me great pleasure to find this inner fatality that
leads him, that drives him to his exploits, in the words:
"Compagne du péril qu'il vous fallait chercher" ("Companion of the peril you had to seek"). It is true that I bend
somewhat the sense of the words to my own purposes. I
admit it. And why not? The complete work of art has the
miraculous quality of offering to us always more than was

imagined by the author; it permits us continually a richer interpretation. Do you believe for a moment that Hugo writing his funeral song to the tune of *"Malbrough"* imagined all that Péguy, in his *Clio*, would find in it? And yet who will dare say that Péguy was not right in seeing what he saw?

I picture Theseus at the court of Crete, *"Charmant, jeune, traînant tous les coeurs après soi"* ("Young, charming, drawing all hearts after him"), with whom the eldest daughter of Minos will fall in love, but who will fall in love with the younger. He comes to triumph over the monster, son of the Queen and the bull (I have already given my opinion on the Minotaur: if Pasiphaë had heard any talk about Leda's amorous adventure, she might very well have imagined that the bull hid Jupiter himself. A certain school of critics deigns to see in the bull merely a certain Taurus, the King's gardener, or his general, but if you allow me, we will send this explanation packing to join that of the solar myths and the Totems).

Son of a king (I am speaking again of Theseus), he comes to fight a royal bastard; he comes, eager for adventure, muscles still taut from the efforts of lifting away the rocks—for it was under one of them, his father had let it be understood, that he would find his weapons. Admirable test of training. Each of these heroes has his own weapons, fitted to no one else. It is only when he had recovered from Philoctetes the bow of his father Achilles that Neoptolemus was able to kill Paris; and we know that the bow of Ulysses could be strung by Ulysses alone.

He embarks (I am speaking again of Theseus) with the band of twenty youths and twenty maidens which Greece paid in annual tribute to Crete to be devoured by the Minotaur, so says the old wives' tale; personally I think that the monster in the depths of the labyrinth counted on them for his seraglio. Why so? Simply because I do not see such carnivorous tastes as inherited from Pasiphaë or the bull progenitor—I see it as lust. Pasiphaë, Ariadne, the Minotaur—what a family! And at the head Minos, the future judge of Hades! I know not how Minos judged the conduct of his wife and his children; nor why, before being called to judge the dead, he was compelled to see in his own home examples of every crime. I know not why, but I do know that there is a reason for it. In the Greek fable there is always a reason.

I wonder, too, why—of all the Greek heroes that fought at the siege of Troy—Ulysses alone, tireless wanderer, whose return was so exasperatingly deferred, was the only hero who came home to conjugal peace? Calypso, Circe, Nausicaä, the Sirens detain him for ten years (is he not the son of Sisyphus?) while in Ithaca the faithful Penelope waits for her husband. But the others, so impatient to return, is it not to find on their abandoned hearths only disorder, terror, and ruin?

I do not know the answer, but there must be one. Agamemnon, Ajax son of Oïleus, Idomeneus, Diomedes, all, I say, thrown toward a peril *"qu'il leur fallait chercher"* ("they had to seek") are greeted upon their return by adultery, murder, betrayal, exile, and the most fearsome crimes; toward them they hasten. While Ulysses who

alone, of them all, is to find at his hearth fidelity, virtue, and patience, remains for ten years separated by many an obstacle, and, I believe, by his vagabond curiosity, the restlessness of his genius. There is something of Sindbad in Ulysses; I am well aware that he longs for Ithaca, but it is under the spur of ill-fortune and in the manner of Sindbad, which did not prevent the latter, once home, from setting out again. It seems that Ulysses had a presentiment that on his hearth there waited no food for his restlessness, that his energy would find there no employment. Is it his anticipation of the security and tranquillity of Ithaca that makes him thus delay his return?

I admire in Theseus an almost insolent rashness. No sooner is he at the court of Minos than he seduces Ariadne. There is no evidence that he loves her. But he allows himself to be loved by her as long as this love can be useful. Is the thread that she ties to his arm there solely to guide him? No. It is the "apron string" and straightway Theseus finds it a bit short: he feels it tugging at him at the moment when, with horror and delight, he advances into the unknown depths of his destiny. And doubtless, we have there the subject of an operetta. I should very much like to know if he was thinking already of Phaedra? On leaving the court of Minos, did he carry off the two sisters at the same time?

It is doubtless plausible and agreeable to recognize in the Augean stables a cloud-filled sky, swept clear by a solar Hercules. It is enough that it should not be irrational for it to be Greek. But how much more meaningful it is to me to consider, for example, the following:

That Hercules, of all the demigods, is the only *moral* hero of antiquity, the one who, before setting forth, finds himself momentarily hesitating between "vice and virtue"; he is the only uncertain hero, the one whom the sculptor will for that reason represent to us as a melancholy hero; and we remember that, true enough, he is the one child of Jupiter whose birth is not the result of a victory of instinct over modesty and propriety; in order to possess the virtuous Alcmene the god was compelled to take on the appearance of her husband. If, doubtless, the theory of the laws governing heredity is of more recent formulation than the myth, I admire all the more that the myth can offer us this exemplary interpretation. (pp. 227-33)

André Gide, "Thoughts on Greek Mythology," translated by Jeffrey J. Carre, in his Pretexts: Reflections on Literature and Morality, *edited by Justin O'Brien, Meridian Books, Inc., 1959, pp. 227-33.*

Malcolm Cowley (essay date 1929)

[*An American critic, editor, poet, translator, and historian, Cowley made valuable contributions to contemporary letters in his long literary career. In the following excerpt, he praises the diversity of Gide's literary works and comments favorably on* The School for Wives.]

An author who wishes to profit rapidly by his success is forced to specialize. Having once created a public for himself, he is thenceforth ruled by its tastes, which he has helped to form: in other words, he is limited by his past achievements to one mood, one medium, and usually to one group of subjects. He abandons the uncertain joys of discovery for the rewards of exploitation. On the other hand, an author whose ambitions are less immediate is more at liberty to experiment in different fields. He may write poetry and prose, novels and dramas, but it is very seldom that he attempts so many different subjects and treatments that we can speak of him as having adopted the whole world of literature for his province.

Such is the case, however, with André Gide. To mention only his translated works—less than a fourth of those published in France—one of them is a tightly written psychological novel, another is an impossible and delightful adventure story, a third and a fourth are respectively a long critical study and a volume of travels in the Congo, a fifth is a very great novel in the leisurely, inclusive manner of Dickens and Dostoievsky . . . This list does not yet include two books which are indispensable to the understanding of Gide's career as a whole: I mean *Les Nourritures Terrestres*, a sort of lyric miscellany in which he propounds his fundamental ideas, and *Si le Grain ne Meurt*, his dignified and alarmingly honest autobiography.

The School for Wives, the last book he has written and the sixth to be translated, belongs to still another classification: it is a story told briefly by means of a woman's diary. In technique, however, it is essentially dramatic, being the history of a conflict that progresses by a series of revelations and confrontations, almost like one of Racine's tragedies, toward its one possible conclusion.

The characters in conflict are the two Delabordes. Eveline, the wife, is an admirably conscientious woman who is struggling, not for self-expression, but for honesty and self-respect. Robert, her political minded husband, is full of resounding principles, but at the same time he is willing to cheat, lie, or abase himself to achieve any petty triumph. He is a man of pliant surfaces, a hollow man with the soul of a matinee idol or a lobbyist—in other words, no soul at all: merely a few fragments of vanity and ambition that rattle inside him like dried peas. It is even a sort of compliment to call him hypocritical: in reality he is not frank enough with himself to realize the distance between his actions and his professions of faith. Eveline is actually the hypocrite of the two: for the last twenty years, she has consented to live against her beliefs. As for the two children, they have followed their parents: Gustave is like his father, and Geneviève, though she belongs to a generation less willing to compromise, is in other respects like her mother. Her frankness precipitates the final scene in which Eveline confronts her husband, announces that she can no longer live with him, and then is conquered like one of Shaw's heroines by her own strength and by his lack of it.

The story as a whole is a curious contrast to Gide's last novel. *The Counterfeiters* was long, rich, complicated; it treated many characters from many points of view; it attacked problems of conduct in a new way and reached heights of tragic feeling which have not been equalled since Dostoievsky. *The School for Wives* lacks all these qualities, for which it partly compensates by other virtues: naturalness, directness, and a surface perfection which

conceals a good many subtleties of character and judgment. Its limpid style is well rendered by Dorothy Bussy, Gide's official translator. . . And yet, the novel will be disappointing to those readers who, unfamiliar with its author's versatility, were expecting something more ambitious.

How shall we answer their complaint? . . . We might say that the book is like Giotto's circle, and that its simplicity could be achieved only by a master craftsman. Or we might take a different analogy from music. During his later years, in the intervals between great symphonies, Beethoven produced a number of very simple compositions for the pianoforte. Now, I have no intention of comparing the author of *The School for Wives* with a man whose genius, after all, was of a different order, but Gide, too, is a matter of many effects; he has lately written a rich symphonic work, and now that he turns to a simple narrative, a sort of *Albumblatt*, we have no right to be disappointed. (pp. 5-6)

Malcolm Cowley, "Albumblatt," in New York Herald Tribune Books, *October 20, 1929, pp. 5-6.*

Angel Flores   (essay date 1931)

[*Flores is an American educator, translator, and critic. In the following review, he discusses the themes and style of* Isabelle *and* The Pastoral Symphony, *praising Gide for the diversity of his fiction.*]

When *Isabelle*, the first of these *Two Symphonies*, was printed in 1911, Gide had published already *The Immoralist* and *Strait Is the Gate*, and yet most critics dismissed it as a work of transition. This much-abused word falls flat when applied to a Gide, for this indefatigable explorer of techniques and themes is always on the alert, forever changing the perspectives of contemporary fiction. What the critics knew was that something "different" had appeared, and they lazily proceeded to conceal themselves in a misty tautology. Separated by a score of years from the publication date of *Isabelle*, one can now see this "narrative" as an isolated achievement, complete and vibrant.

It is a mystery story, somewhat similar to but of course more coherent and subtle than Mrs. Radcliffe's classics. It takes place in an antique setting: chateau almost in ruins, shady gardens, creaking gates and doors; mysterious, lunatic tenants, a murder and a beautiful lady in exile. While "preparing a thesis on the chronology of Bossuet's sermons," a bold student is forced into this castle and is soon engulfed by its dark intrigue. His findings make the story, and to re-tell them is to spoil the denouement. Gide has given us a very refined "hair raiser," free from melodramatic accidents and supernatural silliness. Written retrospectively, the story begins after everything has taken place. The demon of curiosity spurs on the hero into his detective work: gradually the fibers appear, and then the texture, and then the designs on it. Even the vocabulary, deliberately archaic, has been synchronized to the gray atmosphere and the foggy characters, lending the whole, what Jacques Riviere termed a "sweet heaviness."

The second story in the volume, **The Pastoral Symphony**, is a modern version of the dangerous parable of the lost sheep. An elderly Protestant pastor finds a destitute, ignorant blind girl (Gertrude) and takes her home with him. The pastor's wife, kept busy by five other children, is not at all pleased with this new responsibility. Gertrude is not only blind, but has no knowledge whatsoever of language, manners or cleanliness. Perhaps the very difficulty of the task stimulates the good pastor; he has in front of him Condillac's animated statue, and he decides to infuse into it ideas and sentiments. It is a tedious and laborious process of assimilation and maturation, but at last Gertrude wins conscious awareness, and becomes a rational being, sinless in her blindness. However, unknowingly the pastor falls in love with Gertrude, and he engages in a duel of ideas when his eldest son Jacques, a theological student who has won part of her affections, wishes to marry her. "Now an instinct as sure as the voice of conscience warned me that this marriage must be prevented," says the pastor to himself in typically Gidean language—an instinct as sure as the voice of conscience! And he goes on, searching the gospels, searching "in vain for commands, threats, prohibitions. . . . All of these come from St. Paul. And it is precisely because they are not to be found in the words of Christ that Jacques is disturbed. Souls like his think themselves lost as soon as they are deprived of their props, their handrails, their fences. And besides, they cannot endure others to enjoy a liberty they have resigned, and want to obtain by compulsion what would readily be granted by love." Therein lies the culminating movement of this perilous **Symphony**: St. Paul and Christ, Christianity and Christ, challenge each other, wage open war as love disintegrates into atoms, into what Lalou has so happily termed "the polygamy of sentiments."

After a successful operation, Gertrude wins her eyesight, witnessing then more clearly the ugliness of human events. Jacques and his father only bring her unhappiness with their love, and after trying to commit suicide, she dies in a quandary of ambiguities. Two religious attitudes failed, St. Paul and Christ failed, the heart and the mind and the Gospels failed—the "angels" sank into the abyss of sin. . . . "Except a corn of wheat fall into the ground and die, it abideth alone: but if it die, it bringeth forth much fruit."

Gide has attained in this novel what one of his earlier characters desired most: "the greatest transparency, the suppression of opacity." It is a most exciting experience to follow one after another these two very different **Symphonies**, for one enjoys Gide in two different moods, always surprising and challenging. The phantoms from the old castle, projected through the consciously archaic and hazy language of **Isabelle**, linger awhile as one enters the tormenting drama of the fervently warm, limpid **Pastoral Symphony**.

Angel Flores, "Two Moods of Andre Gide," in New York Herald Tribune Books, *May 24, 1931, p. 3.*

Irvin Stock   (essay date 1949)

[*Stock is an American critic, dramatist, and short story writer. In the following essay, he analyzes Gide's retelling of the myth of Theseus, noting that the principal theme of Gide's* Theseus *is humankind's perpetual transformation and transcendence of itself.*]

André Gide has often remarked that most writers produce too quickly, that serious work should be allowed to ripen. More than any of his tales, **Theseus**, the latest to be translated into English, provides an example both of the process and of its justifying result. The first mention of it in his journal was in 1911. It was not published in France until 1946. The result is, we have a retelling of the myth that is brief in compass and simple unto apparent casualness in style and that yet manages to be at the same time a spiritual autobiography and a complete summation of his thought, of his unique contribution to the wisdom of our time. This is what happens when a good writer waits. His means shrink and his meanings multiply. *Everything* is converted into symbol. The process could hardly go further than it has done in **Theseus**, of which every reading discloses the crucial significance of details the reader might at first have been quite content to regard as imposed by the original myth alone or intended merely to enliven the story surface. For this reason, what follows must be limited to the main line of meaning and the most important episodes. A really detailed examination would have to be much longer than its subject; perhaps indeed no single critic can yet aspire to the complete analysis of so packed and dazzling a work.

The theme of **Theseus** is human progress. "Humanity," says its hero, "can do more and deserves better." Needless to say, what is involved here is not the 19th-century faith in progress which is at present in well-merited disrepute. That faith was after all a faith that material progress alone would make all other kinds unnecessary. Without despising material welfare (demanding it, rather), Gide is concerned chiefly with the continuous inner development by which man transforms and transcends himself. But such progress, the realization of man's endless possibilities, is an endless struggle, in which literally everything and everybody in the world may on occasion become his enemy. Think of whatever you like that might seem man's certain ally in this struggle. Rule out in your sophistication those allies who wear deceitfulness like a sign, and turn to the others who have in fact brought you thus far. It is of *them* Gide says beware. The time may come when exactly these will be the subtle enemies of your further progress. This has been the central torment and insight of Gide's career. From the start he has been dedicated to personal development at any cost. But what are his successive works, and his journals too, if not a record of the dangers that lurk on every road toward such a goal? That direction is wrong, says *La Porte Etroite*. But *L'Immoraliste* replies, Look what happens when you take the other. (Hence, of course, Gide's insistence that his books be understood together, rather than individually.) Everything can fail you except one thing: the infinitely resilient and fertile spirit of man. Let this be your oracle, says Gide, and listening, shut out every conflicting whisper. Theseus, then, tells the story of that struggle, which is man's but which has been more particularly André Gide's, and of how the hero, Theseus-Gide, vanquished his enemies and escaped their traps.

The story is told as a rather chatty autobiography, of the kind to which a "man of action" (so Gide characterizes his hero) might turn his hand when the time of activity had died away into that of thoughtful reminiscence. There are no doubt many advantages to such a method. But the most obvious is that it solves at one stroke the problem of compression, selection and rearrangement that looms first when one approaches the myth. In the chief sources, Plutarch and Diodorus, there are of course numerous versions of every episode and their chronological order does not necessarily correspond to an order of meaning. (It goes without saying that the myth was selected because of the degree to which its events *were* meaningful and required simply, as it were, the proper lighting.) With the aged Theseus himself as our narrator, browsing over his life and remembering of each epoch only what is appropriate to a motivating idea, Gide makes everything in the crowded confused history available when and as needed, leaving himself free by the same device to omit the irrelevant.

That the story is not an autobiography of Theseus alone is suggested by the very character descriptions that appear briefly here and there. Theseus remarks, for instance, that others have been more intelligent than he. "But people give me credit for good sense. The rest is added with the determination to do well that has never left me. Mine, too, is the kind of courage which incites to desperate enterprises. On top of all this I was ambitious." Just so has Gide deprecated his own intelligence, but with a modesty more apparent than real, since it is less on intelligence than on what follows in this quotation that great achievement is generally based. To the latter "the rest" is added. Nor is it a contradiction of this that Theseus is described as a man of action. Gide too is a man of action, both as an artist whose works are acts, in which ideas are submitted to the ordeal of life, and as a man who has lived his ideas and suffered all their consequences.

Theseus begins, appropriately enough, with his education, his relations with his elders. Gide makes a slight change here in order to keep father and son in contact and the education of Theseus exemplary. In the myth Aegeus, after getting with child a daughter of Pittheus, hides his weapons under a great stone, tells her that if the child is a son and he grows strong enough to reach them, he is to bring them to him in Attica, and then leaves for good. In Gide Aegeus himself is in charge of the boy's education, of which the stone-lifting is a symbol. It is he who tells him of the hidden weapons (hidden, he says, by Poseidon), and who sets him to recover them by lifting the stones about the palace. But when Theseus, after overturning all the stones in the neighborhood, is about to attack the flagstones of the palace in his zeal, his father stops him. The story of the weapons, he explains, was only a fiction designed to develop his strength. Handing them to his son, he continues, "Before giving them to you I now was waiting to see you deserve them. I can sense in you now the ambition to use them and that longing for fame which will allow you only to take up arms in defense of noble causes and for the weal of all mankind." Now this speech might be

intended to be taken literally and the fact that the reader does not himself see that readiness for the "good fight" mentioned by the father might be regarded only as a vagueness in the story characteristic of myth. Not so: education and family have here received a characteristic and savage thrust. It is by lies that the father has stimulated his son's development. This development, however, following its own laws, gets out of hand, until at last the father's very palace, the world which warms and shelters him and in which he reigns a king, stands suddenly in danger. At this, hastily, his smile surely rather forced, the father calls a halt and says it was all a joke. He gives his son the weapons (the freedom and strength he has in fact already won for himself) and with an unction and a flattery typical of the frightened elder, tries to bamboozle the powerful youth into turning his strength in another, a socially acceptable, direction. The thrust, as I say, is characteristic. It is Gide who declared, "Families, I hate you!" and whose development was forever overturning the flagstones, and not only the flagstones, of the palace of intellectual and moral conventions in which his elders uneasily slept.

That this episode is indeed seen as conflict is borne out by the fact that immediately after it, Gide anticipates his narrative by some years, and as if in passing, mentions how Aegeus died. Theseus, as Gide's predecessors have also informed us, was to have announced his safe return from the encounter with the Minotaur by replacing his vessel's black sail with a white one. He neglected to do this, disturbed by thoughts of Ariadne according to Diodorus, and according to Plutarch distracted by joy. As a result Aegeus, seeing the black sail, was maddened by grief and flung himself from a cliff into the ocean. According to Theseus-Gide, he simply forgot. "One can't think of everything. But to tell the truth, and if I cross-question myself, a thing I never much care to do, I can't swear that it was really forgetfulness. Aegeus was in my way." One begins to see with what delighted recognition Gide must have read the original fable.

Our hero's next struggle is with the monsters and criminals who make the highways of life a place of terror to our elders and against whom they feel it their duty to warn us. He has, of course, refused their advice to take the safe route to Attica, fired by the example of Hercules, as talented youth is forever stimulated by his great predecessors to feats of intellectual and moral daring and self-assertion, self-discovery. Is this Theseus talking or Gide? "No one can deny it. I think I have performed some notable services; I've purged the earth once and for all of a host of tyrants, bandits, monsters. I've cleared up certain dangerous byways on which even the bravest could not venture without a shiver." What are these tyrants, if not the ideas and conventions, outworn but still reigning, which prevent our free movement along the road of self-development? And much more is signified than the sexual convention which figures in Gide's most spectacular tyrannicide. His hero's adversaries are not all secular. "Whatever was inexplicable was put on to the gods. Terror and religion were so nearly one that heroism often seemed an impiety. The first and principal victory which man had to win was over the gods."

We learn from Plutarch and Diodorus that Theseus delighted to seize his opponent's own weapon and turn it against him. So he handled Corynetes, the club-bearer, Sinnis, the bender of pines, Procrustes, for whose bed all seekers of polemical metaphors must forever be grateful. When Gide repeats this information, adding that only by such tactics can we be sure of final victory, the mythic fact suddenly fills with meaning. Whether in matters of sexual ethics or philosophical debate, one can properly meet a challenge only by accepting the problem as presented, the realm of discourse in which it is stated and exists. To shrink from one's adversaries' weapons, terms, problems, is to leave the challenge not truly faced and the enemy never truly bested.

We come next to the most elaborately treated episode in the brief tale, that of the adventure in Crete. Here are embodied and dramatized the most basic and subtle opponents of man's development. Like the scene of its climax, it is a labyrinth of meanings in which it seems possible, if one relaxes, for the mind to wander endlessly. As Plutarch and Diodorus have told us, Theseus refuses the protection of his status, and volunteers as one of the seven young men, who, with seven maidens, must periodically be offered to the Minotaur. Gide's Theseus explains his volunteering in a statement which is also to be found in some form in Gide's journal. "I care nothing for privilege and claim that merit alone distinguishes me from the rest." For Gide too renounced the safety his wealth and position might have afforded him and threw in his lot with the outcasts, the victims and the explorers of culture. Many versions of this adventure are given by his predecessors. In some Theseus overcomes not a bull-man, monstrous issue of Pasiphaë, the queen of Crete, and a bull, but a surly athlete named Taurus in the athletic games held by King Minos. In Gide the animal-man remains, but he takes the fact of such games and places Theseus before them as a spectator. There the Grecian observes the effeminate sensual culture of Crete; there he is seen and loved by Ariadne and sees and is struck by the child Phaedra, her sister. Every detail now begins to contribute to a meaning which emerges fully later on. The meaning is this: Crete is the realm of self-indulgence, chiefly but not only sensual, with all its nourishment for growth and all its traps and curbs for it. As such, it is also the realm of art, whence costly and beautiful objects had long flowed into Attica, exciting our hero's youthful curiosity.

After the games, Theseus, as a young prince, has dinner at the palace. Here, in a private dialogue with Pasiphaë, he is introduced to the endless rationalizations which rise to sanction fleshly or any kind of self-indulgence, and which, sympathetically heard by one who should judge and restrain—in her case, Minos—corrode his certainty and render him impotent to perform his duty. Pasiphaë, whose history, appearance and manner proclaim her the arch-slut, declares herself, fondling Theseus' pectorals, to be a lover of heavenly things alone. "The difficulty, you see, is one never can tell exactly where the god begins and where he ends." If admonished by Minos on the subject of her peculiar tastes, she asks, "What about your mother?"—Minos himself being the son of Europa. Moreover, Minos believes with a "praiseworthy" tolerance which

Gide thus audaciously questions that one can't be a good judge until one has experienced everything, either oneself or through one's family. And so his family is only furthering his career by its various errors of conduct. That Gide is not a puritan we know. Here we see that when the *enemy* invites to license, he can become one. In conclusion, she pleads with the young man not to harm the Minotaur, but to become friendly with him, "and so end a misunderstanding which has done great harm to our two countries." If the Minotaur, as will soon become clear, is the heart of the symbol which is Crete—that is, the seductive flesh—then this friendship she desires may well have a meaning deeper than a mother's solicitude. (Gide often gives his adversaries good arguments.) It is the fruitful union of flesh—Crete—with spirit—Greece (or use any terms that are more congenial and up-to-date), where exclusive devotion to either cripples both.

Throughout this dialogue, Ariadne has been waiting impatiently for our hero on the terrace. When he appears, she fastens herself upon him with a promptness and a volubility that fill him with misgivings. Ariadne is the eternal feminine in her most irritating aspect and a most delicious satire. Possessive, practical, keeping her aspiring man's two feet on the ground by her mere clamorous existence, it is she who will save him in his struggle with the Minotaur. But her narrowness! And the enormous price she exacts! A man like Theseus can only begin at once, while he uses her, to figure out ways of welching in his suffocating bargain. Listen to her: she has warned him against trying to fly out of the maze like Icarus: "That I don't dare to recommend to you; it's too risky. You'd better get it into your head at once that your only hope is to stick close to me. We shall be together, you and I, from now on in life and death." Etc. Etc. Later Theseus tells us she was always saying, "You promised."

Granted that one must be practical and careful as it is Ariadne's eternal role to inform us, there is such a thing as being too much so and failing to reach one's proper limit. Sure enough, Theseus, allowing her her usefulness by putting one end of the famous thread in her hand, takes himself the spool, lest, if she had it, she refuse to unwind it as far as he wishes to go.

But the fact is, this type of woman is not really capable of being responsible for the hero's salvation, except as an instrument. Indeed, she yields so readily that Theseus can hardly believe himself "to have done the work of a pioneer." It is not in this particular hero and his salvation she is interested, in other words, but in a man, the fulfilment of her own destiny. Not she, but Dedalus instructs him in the dangers he faces and how to overcome them.

Gide ignores what his predecessors mention of Minos' anger with Dedalus for helping Pasiphaë consummate her perverse passion, as well as the flight of father and son caused by this. Dedalus is here as symbol of the pedagogue and scientist, and his son, whom we briefly meet, is a victim of the labyrinth, whose attempt to escape it by flying was a failure. The jealousy-murder of his rival Talos, as Dedalus here tells the story, becomes only a "difference" due to a significant philosophic conflict. Talos' images of the gods kept them in rigid hieratic posture; Dedalus—

and this is borne out by Diodorus—preferred to bring them closer to men by showing them with their limbs in motion and their eyes open. At the same time, by science he wished to bring men closer to the gods.

What follows is Gide's extraordinarily rich illumination of the two chief symbols of his tale: the labyrinth where the hero undergoes his most profound ordeal, and the thread which is his salvation. The labyrinth is a place difficult to escape from because—happy notion!—it affects the *will* to escape. Moreover, it is filled with vapors which "not only act on the will and put it to sleep; they induce a delicious intoxication, rich in flattering delusions, and provoke the mind, filled as this is with voluptuous mirages, to a certain pointless activity; pointless, I say, because it has merely an imaginary outcome in visions and speculations without order, logic or substance. The effect of these gases is not the same for all of those who breathe them; each is led on by the complexities implicit in his own mind to lose himself, if I may so put it, in a labyrinth of his own devising." Which of us, shrinking from the terrible labor of realizing some cherished purpose, has not also wandered in this labyrinth, where "without order, logic or substance," we could dream its accomplishment? And as we wander thus, our very strength becomes our weakness. For each of us, to use another metaphor which Gide is fond of, the devil assumes a different disguise, the one most congenial and seductive. Indeed, the very thirst for progress, for self-development and fulfilment, which is the condition of all that is best in life and culture, may, unanchored, send us soaring away from the earth on which all real progress is made.

How, then, can we guarantee to our aspiring thought order, logic and substance? To return to our drama, how is the hero to escape a labyrinth so ingenious? Hear Dedalus:

> Your will alone may not suffice . . . and so I have thought of this plan; to link you and Ariadne by a thread, the tangible symbol of duty . . . Be always determined not to break it, no matter what may be the charms of the labyrinth, the seduction of the unknown, or the headlong urging of your own courage. Go back to her, or all the rest, and the best with it, will be lost. The thread will be your link to the past. Go back to it. Go back to yourself. For nothing can begin from nothing, and it is from your past, and from what you are at this moment, that what you are going to be must spring.

Thus we see that the reality with which we must keep contact for all actual progress has two faces: one is tradition and the other is duty. These alone, however they may seem at times to slow us down, can save us from dissolution in self-indulgence. For the past is our earth, and like any plant, to grow upward we must have roots in the earth beneath us, the deeper and stronger indeed, the higher we would reach. And those roots are duty, by which the past at once restrains and nourishes, teaching us what we are and what the world is, with and from which we are to build. And thus we are shown too (as Gide has long since warned us) how dangerous it would be to understand our author too quickly. As the pursuer of every sensual fulfil-

ment became before our eyes the acid judge of sensuality unbridled, sensuality corrupting, using for its own purposes the resources of the spirit, so the arch-rebel, the adventurer, drawn always toward and over human boundaries, emerges here as the justifier of precisely those forces against which rebellion would seem necessarily and ever to struggle.

Moreover, is not Gide's tale itself a living demonstration of this insight from which it flows? That the completion of such a work—and all its fellow—was an enchaining and laborious duty by even means of which a fertile mind was prevented from dissipating its seed need not be insisted upon. It is also a lesson in the meaning and uses of tradition for the human spirit, devoted as it may and should be to the unknown that is the future. By thrusting hard against an ancient myth, Gide has been able to leap to his own new meanings. For what is myth? And here we must drop our metaphor of the past as the earth beneath us, for in fact it is more than this, it is also the air we breathe and the heaven of our aspiration. It seems beneath or behind us as we struggle away from it toward the truth that lies beyond, but when at last the truth is reached and we hear its voice, what it utters is always an echo. And perhaps what it chiefly echoes will be myth. Dedalus has called his son into the room, and Icarus, lost in the anguished theological speculation which was the inner labyrinth of *his* devising, gives Theseus an example of the danger he runs and then withdraws. Theseus is surprised to learn that Icarus is dead. "There is another truer plane on which time does not exist," Dedalus explains. "On this plane the representative gestures of our race are inscribed, each according to its particular significance. What happens in the case of a hero is this: his mark endures. Poetry and the arts reanimate it and it becomes an enduring symbol."

One word more about the invaluable Dedalus. Gide sees around him too, sees, as with other things, the defects of his virtues. Like so many teachers with their theories, and scientists with their instruments, he has a respect for his tool that Gide regards as excessive. "Man's personal strength can effect nothing," he says. "Better a good tool than a strong forearm." But men like Theseus—or Gide—have a kind of pride which such a remark is likely to irritate. Precisely because of it, Theseus determines to enter the maze without weapons and to fight the monster with his bare hands. For Gide, it is man that counts, and all theories, like other tools which restrict us to *their* way of conceiving and solving problems, are expendable on behalf of the new possibilities of which man is the inexhaustible reservoir.

Theseus follows the above instructions, finds and conquers the Minotaur and then, hated for it at the time by his intoxicated fellow Grecians, forcibly rescues them from their delicious captivity. The struggle with the Minotaur is left peculiarly vague. The monster himself is—surprisingly—beautiful. Far from leaping to devour them, he is found lying languorously amid flowers, while the eye he sleepily opens at the approach of Theseus is completely witless. Like that of the labyrinth in which he dwells, his power lies in attraction rather than force. How Theseus conquered him he cannot or will not recall. He mentions only that there was something voluptuous about the victory, and to leave the garden in which it occurred hardly bearable. But we may ask, how has Gide in his own life conquered such enslaving seduction? Why, by *yielding* to it. The symbol is surely apt: we know how hunger of the flesh can enslave the minds of those who keep it forever unsatisfied. To yield is at least one way to set oneself free. It has certainly been Gide's—and not as easy a way as it sounds to one brought up like Gide to Protestant self-restraint. He has remarked in his journal how he had to drive himself toward pleasure, long after he had realized its essential innocence and fruitfulness, as another might toward self-denial.

In the events that follow Gide slightly alters the myth, in which Phaedra is given to Theseus in marriage much later by her brother Deucalion. Here Theseus takes her with him, stealing her away by trickery, on the voyage back which results in Ariadne's abandonment on the island of Naxos. The question may arise why our hero prefers the unripe child to the mature woman. Perhaps, though Theseus in fact disavows the fondness for boys which is precisely a Cretan custom, his choice of one who is not yet a woman keeps his image a faithful one of his author. Perhaps too we are here being told, as Gide has told us elsewhere, that the pleasures of sex are purest when unadulterated with other considerations. An Ariadne would force recognition and acceptance of more than her body, whereas his delight in the childish Phaedra could be undistracted, and leave his mind equally undistracted in the pursuit of its own ends. This is a peculiarity of Gide's thought that may be less general than private in its validity. Whether it is so is a problem that would carry us far afield. The episode does, however, yield a meaning clearly general, and a meaning that seems at first glance wholly repulsive. Theseus found it rather disagreeable to have thus to deceive his host Minos, who, after the adventure in the labyrinth, had given him his entire confidence. Gide spares no inflection to make this episode appear unworthy of his hero. And how is it justified? Flatly, thus: "But it was not, and indeed it is never a part of my character to allow myself to be stopped by scruples. The voices of gratitude and decency were shouted down by the voice of desire. The end justifies the means. What must be must be." Then even decency can become our adversary in the struggle—even cunning and duplicity our necessary allies, as well as, on pleasanter occasions, the courage in which we can take pride? Alas, yes. When desire is strong and sure, it may be fatal to withhold fulfilment until one can elaborate a structure of justifications or find sanctioned means. (*Desire*, remember, not some cold-blooded theory of social welfare.) For after all, the inner life is of a complexity that may make it impossible anyway to know all that is involved in the relation of a cause and an effect, all the steps of a human process. Without knowing why, we may *know* that health and safety demand behavior it would be impossible to explain and justify on the rational conscious level. All this is dangerous—granted. At this level we play with dynamite. But it can't be helped. We must simply try to be careful. And we must remember on behalf of Gide that in admitting the occasional validity of a principle, he by no means gives it his total and permanent allegiance.

We come next to Theseus as a statesman. In Plutarch he is shown to have unified the many small quarreling city-states of Attica into one: Athens, containing three classes, nobility, husbandmen, and artisans, all equal in the dubious sense that each excelled the others in some one respect. Athens becomes a democracy in that the nobility govern it as equals instead of a single tyrant. Finally, its stock of human wealth is wisely increased by an invitation to foreigners to settle there and enjoy the rights of Athenians. Gide's Theseus simply destroys all privilege entirely and brings about complete equality among the citizens of Athens. When his friend Pirithous warns him that inequality is inevitable and will reestablish itself, he says he knows it well. But the new state will be an aristocracy not of wealth but of intellect. Gide's hero too invites foreigners to Athens "to increase her power and importance." All were to have the same rights as Athenians to begin with. "Any necessary discrimination could await the proofs of experience." What we get here is not simply a model state, it is a description of the proper conditions for the flowering of culture, for growth toward intellectual "power and importance" on the part of individuals. There must be an initial equality, not only among men, but among ideas and ethical codes. There must be receptivity toward foreign influences. "Any necessary discrimination could await the proofs of experience." In fact, Gide's Theseus does finally admit differences, a hierarchy, because it helps the state to function better. That is to say, for proper functioning both social and intellectual processes will demand such organization (consider the means by which we attain to inner unity), though it may conflict with some ideal of the perfectly just and rational. But by his efforts to make human values the principle of organizations, Theseus—as Plutarch too informs us—won for Athenians the name of "people," that is, raised them to full humanity.

There follows a brief mention of the ill-fated love of Phaedra for his son Hippolytus, and their deaths—here Gide takes his cue from Racine—and then the story closes with an episode for which the *Oedipus at Colonnus* seems to be Gide's precedent. Theseus is "surprised," however, that so little has been said of it. It is a meeting with Oedipus, a "moment at the crossroads when our two careers confronted each other." In this magnificent section Gide poses against his hero, triumphant, a hero of the opposite kind, the defeated, against his idea of man's proper destiny its classic adversary, and thus finds an opportunity of summing up in conclusion the meaning of his fable. Faced with the blind wanderer, Theseus expresses a faint sense of his possible inferiority. "No doubt I had triumphed everywhere, but on a level which, in comparison with Oedipus, seemed to me merely human—inferior, I might say." It puzzles him, moreover, that Oedipus was not only defeated by life, but seems actually to have contributed to his defeat by putting out his eyes. Why? he asks. The answer is that, as Theseus is a kind of humanist, devoted to tangible triumph as a man and on earth, Oedipus is one whose life has taught him that the spiritual and the earthly are in conflict and that the former demands for its fulfilment the renunciation of the latter. He blinded himself to shut out "the falsehood in which I no longer believed . . . and this so as to break through to reality . . . And at the moment when the blue of the sky went black before me, my inward firmament became bright with stars."

Theseus is ready to agree that the non-temporal world is important, but why, he demands, place it in opposition with the one "in which we live and act"? Because, Oedipus replies, what was dramatized in his own life, and now in the unhappy lives of his sons, is the truth that man is stained from birth, that he can break away from evil, the inevitable fruit of his original sin, only with divine aid—grace. And the chief road to this is through suffering and renunciation. It is by such means that Oedipus himself has attained grace in spite of his overwhelming sins. This is for Gide the great *other* idea, which he understands and for which he even feels a haunting sympathy, but which his whole life and work have opposed. For man is his absolute, in all his fecundity and variety—not one part of him or another—and none of the great ideas by which he has in the past enabled himself to advance, is large enough or strong enough to contain him forever. "I remain a child of this world," says Theseus, "and I believe that man, be he what he may, and with whatever blemishes you believe him to be stained, is in duty bound to play out his hand to the end." It is this faith that makes Gide a truer heir of Goethe, that supreme apostle of man's divinity, than his contemporary, and indeed his peer, who consciously wears the Goethe mantle: Thomas Mann. Both Goethe and Gide have found life good—on the whole—and considered it man's chief duty to make the most of himself, never to linger, but always to "pass on" along the road of his own endless realization. We have seen that for Gide this is far from being the road of self-indulgence. What it amounts to, rather, is a call never to come to rest in any fixed structure of ideas, attitudes, beliefs, to remain forever open to the new experience or insight which may break up an old pattern, to keep to *oneself* the responsibility to judge and evaluate. In a time when many are reacting to the world's undoubted horrors with an abdication of this responsibility, a responsibility which is a condition of growth and which is man's ennobling opportunity as well as his cross, this is a faith it is good to have so greatly reaffirmed.

In conclusion, it must be pointed out that nothing that has here been said can convey the wondrous delicacy with which these ideas have been dramatized in their truest human context. Gide's style would seem to be the perfection of its type: a clean spare line drawn about his ripened meanings. There has surely never been economy like this. To try to paraphrase a passage of his for the sake of brevity is madness. One can only use more words, never less. Indeed, the author of **Theseus** is not merely a philosopher, a seer, he is a great artist, which is to say his wisdom emerges always as charm, wit, grace—entertainment in the highest sense—in a single word: beauty. (pp. 202-14)

Irvin Stock, "André Gide: Apostle of Progress," in Accent, *Vol. IX, No. 4, Summer, 1949, pp. 202-14.*

W. G. Moore   (essay date 1950)

[*In the following excerpt, Moore analyzes the structure and theme of* The Pastoral Symphony *and investigates the connections between Gide's life and the ideas expressed in the novella.*]

A complete study of the conception of [**La Symphonie Pastorale**] is not possible since its actual source cannot be traced. We do not know whether the first suggestion came from a tale told to the author or was invented by him. Had he remembered where or how he came by it, he would probably have recorded the fact, as he has done for other themes of his writing. We only know that the original tale was in his mind at least twenty-five years before the writing of the book. His friend Paul Laurens, a Catholic, remembers having heard the tale from Gide at La Simiane, near Toulon, before embarking for Algiers in October 1893. Serious work on the composition seems to have begun on February 16th, 1918. In October of the same year the Journal mentions the difficulties of the final stages. The original title seems to have been simply *L'Aveugle*; the present one first occurs in an entry of June 8th, 1918.

The theme may be simply stated. Against the advice and inclination of his more practical wife and children a Protestant pastor takes into his home a blind orphan, whom he has found neglected and abandoned in a Swiss farmstead. Assuming entire care of her, he discovers that his eldest son has fallen in love with her and forbids any further meetings between the two. Not realizing that he is himself in love with her, he is troubled by the estrangement of his wife. An operation which succeeds in restoring sight to the blind girl opens her eyes also to the fact that she really loved the son and not the father. She attempts to drown herself in the river. In a final visit after her death the son breaks the news that both he and the girl had been secretly received into the Roman Church.

Detailed study of the composition shows this simple story to be developed and conveyed with an art which can only be called classical. The events, like the style, remain simple and seem to be less important than four conversations. The book is arranged, like *Werther*, in two parallel and complementary Cahiers. Two conversations with Gertrude (the blind girl) are given in each of these Cahiers. The attitude of the wife (Amélie) is given before and after each conversation.

The story is transmitted by the device of a private Journal, which ensures that all events and reactions are conveyed to the reader in the pastor's own words and even more significantly in his private thoughts. The interest clearly lies in the psychological processes of the pastor's conscience, not in the events as they might appear to other people. But this transmission through a private diary would seem to be much more than an artistic device. It is the key to the author's conception of the subject. He himself has suggested that his work was ironical. This transforms the subject at a stroke. What would be a story ironical only in its outcome, that a man's good idea turns against him, thus becomes a Freudian case of magnanimity as a cloak to the gratification of the sexual impulse. But close study reveals that Gide has presented more even than a Freudian case. A Journal implies honesty. A pastor conscientiously exercising a care of souls is committed to self-examination. It is precisely in his effort to be honest and to unravel hidden motive that the pastor reveals his ignorance of his true motive. He is in fact imprisoned within his religious formulae. The delicacy of the procedure is thus apparent. As Professor Hytier has written [in *André Gide*]: 'La maîtrise de Gide me paraît avoir précisément consisté à utiliser tous ses pouvoirs de sympathie et d'antipathie.' The pastor is portrayed as naive and ignorant of reality. He touches it unawares and in the end he awakes to it. Not only the pastor, but the story, lends itself to this ironical treatment. It is a living case of the blind leading the blind. In this story the blind see; the spiritual director is blind. To be blind is an advantage. Light means sin. To quote M. Hytier once more, 'l'ironie gît dans l'écart des paroles naïves du pasteur et des sentiments inavoués qu'elle recouvre, entre sa conscience et son inconscience; elle en fait le jouet pitoyable du lecteur.' The case presented is, as Archambault says, one of 'quasi innocent hypocrisy' and fits the apt definition in *Les Faux Monnayeurs* of an 'esprit faux' as 'celui qui éprouve le besoin de se persuader qu'il a raison de commettre tous les actes qu'il a besoin de commettre.'

The delicacy of the irony implies no softening of the satire, rather the reverse. The whole religious tradition and affection of the pastor is exposed with relentless logic. It presents a picture of Protestantism so unflattering, and indeed annihilating, that the book has caused great resentment among Protestants: Pastor Roland de Pury, writing in *Réforme*, claims that Gide's picture is so one-sided as to be cruel and unfair. Such critics resent the suggestion that Protestant pastors are short-sighted and hypocritical, covering their ignorance and vanity with neat quotations from Scripture, and that they are more blind than most men to the realities of life and the moral pitfalls which await the high-principled. This story, say such critics, is the caricature of the communion in which its author grew up.

In order to examine the justice of these criticisms we must ask whether the book was intended as a satire. There is no direct evidence of this, but it may nevertheless be the case. Such references as we do find made by its author do not suggest that Gide wished either to portray the spirit of Protestantism or to attack it (this does not say that the casual reader, and still more the spectator of the film which has been made from the story, may not take the pastor for a typical Calvinist). In a letter to a Jesuit, Gide called his book a warning ('livre avertisseur') denouncing the dangers attendant upon free interpretation of Scripture. It is difficult to see how this could have been done without showing the chief protagonists of such interpretation in a severe light; but the Protestant theme may be little more than the occasion for displaying certain features fundamental in modern life.

If we follow the clue given by the author in the letter quoted above we shall not be surprised that the interpretation of Scripture plays so important a part in the book. Gide's pastor is conscious of the danger of sheltering his acts behind Scripture:

> Quelques paroles du Christ me remontèrent du coeur aux lèvres, que je retins pourtant, car il me paraît toujours malséant d'abriter ma conduite derrière l'autorité du livre saint.

Yet he clearly applies to his ward not only the parable of the Lost Sheep but that of the Prodigal Son. He gives her to read selected portions of Scripture only; the Gospels, the Psalms and the Epistle of St. John, not those of St. Paul whom he holds to be responsible for many errors in current Christianity. He thinks that his son is deaf to the 'uniquely divine accent of the least word of Christ'. He rejects his son's defence of St. Paul as a sophisticated defence, and gives thanks that it is to those who become as little children that the Kingdom is promised. The Gospel he understands as a method of arriving at happiness; sin is anything that is opposed to the happiness of the soul. This attitude leads to sharp contention; his son and even blind Gertrude reproach him for not telling her what the world is really like; her happiness, she says, is consequently based on ignorance. As he becomes conscious that he loves her, he resists the idea that it is sinful to do so. When he prays for guidance it seems to him that the light which the doctors are about to restore to her is being removed from him. She recovers her sight, and with it the consciousness of sin, of their sin in loving, of her sin in taking another's place. She has discovered, independently of him, St. Paul's saying: 'I was alive apart from the law once, but when the commandment came, sin revived and I died' (Romans, vii, 9).

The student is sure to ask why Gide has worked out his story in such a way as to include so much beside its human interest, for this theological discussion is woven into the fabric of the story.

The theme of that story would at first sight appear to be the love of a pastor for a lost soul and the unconscious hypocrisy which it implies. But this is in reality only one of several themes. They include the attitude to Scripture and the discussion of the Protestant-Catholic conflict. For this pastor bases his conduct on an attitude to Scripture; the result of that conduct is to drive into the Roman Church his own son.

The most recent discussion of Gide's religious thought assumes that the attitude to Scripture was Gide's own attitude and that the book is therefore his answer to the orthodox Protestantism of his day. Since the matter seems more complicated than that, it is necessary to present the evidence in order and in detail.

The author has himself encouraged study of his own thought by publishing (under the title *Numquid et Tu*) a part of his *Journal* kept during the First World War. This contains significant references to his meditations on the meaning of the Gospel. We can watch him think over the very points in St. Paul which he later puts into the mouth of the pastor. These passages are all carefully dated and all occur in the course of the year 1916. The parallel passages in the **Symphonie Pastorale** we know to have been written in the central months of 1918. Clearly, therefore, the *Journal* gives not only the first form but the more direct and genuine form of Gide's thought. It must be read as the sincere record of what he actually thought. But the **Symphonie Pastorale** cannot so be read, for therein the thought is distorted to fit a story and it is put into the mouth of a character described to us ironically. The thought is an integral part of the allegory. It is both cause and effect of the disastrous presumption of the pastor, of the blindness of spirit which brings bitterness to himself, death to his ward and anguish of soul to his wife and son. In the light of all this, it would seem dangerously uncritical to accept, as Miss Pell does [in *André Gide: L'évolution de sa pensée religieuse* (1936)], the pastor's words as direct evidence of the author's views.

With this caveat in mind let us examine the parallels. In the *Journal* Gide wrote (March 12th, 1916: 'La parole du Christ est toujours nouvelle, d'une promesse infinie.' His pastor remarks that 'L'instruction religieuse de Gertrude m'a amené à relire l'Évangile avec un oeil neuf'. Christ, he says in the *Journal*, reveals in the Gospel the secret of supreme happiness, and again: 'Je sais que le secret de votre Évangile, Seigneur, tient tout dans ce mot divin: Joie'. These views are echoed by the pastor:

> Est-ce trahir le Christ, est-ce diminuer, profaner l'évangile que d'y voir surtout une méthode pour arriver à la vie bienheureuse? L'état de joie, qu'empêchent notre doute et la dureté de nos coeurs, pour le chrétien est un état obligatoire. Chaque être est plus ou moins capable de joie.

In 1916 Gide notes that the Gospel offers neither a recipe, nor a command, but the secret of happiness. The pastor also seeks in vain throughout the Gospel for any command, threat or prohibition. These things are found, he says, in the New Testament—but in St. Paul. He complains that various modern notions of Christianity come, not from Christ but from St. Paul. When reproached with picking and choosing his texts, he replied: 'Mais je ne choisis pas telle ou telle parole du Christ. Simplement, entre le Christ et saint Paul, je choisis le Christ'. This is very much what Gide had actually thought some years earlier:

> Mon Christianisme ne relève que du Christ. Entre lui et moi, je tiens Calvin ou saint Paul pour deux écrans également néfastes. Ah! si le Protestantisme avait aussitôt su rejeter saint Paul'.

This was written in 1910, but in 1916 the attitude is much the same:

> Ce n'est jamais au Christ, c'est à saint Paul que je me heurte, et c'est en lui, jamais dans l'évangile, que je retrouve tout ce qui m'avait écarté.

The origin of such views might well be sought in French Protestant sermons and treatises. Light will probably be shed on the question with the publication of a thesis by D. R. Haggis on *French Protestantism and Literature after 1870*.

More significant than any of these parallels, however, are the quotations from Paul's Epistles. After his son has absented himself from the Holy Table, the pastor leaves in his room the verse from Romans xiv, 2, and says that he might well have continued the quotation:

> Évidemment il s'agit ici d'aliments; mais à combien d'autres passages de l'Ecriture n'est-on pas appelé à prêter double et triple sens? ("si ton oeil . . .."; multiplication des pains; miracle aux noces de Cana, etc. . . .) Il ne s'agit pas ici d'ergoter;

la signification de ce verset est large et profonde: la restriction ne doit pas être dictée par la loi, mais par l'amour, et saint Paul, aussitôt ensuite, s'écrie: "Mais si, pour un aliment, ton frère est attristé, tu ne marches pas selon l'amour." C'est au défaut de l'amour que nous attaque le Malin. Seigneur! enlevez de mon coeur tout ce qui n'appartient pas à l'amour . . . .

All this is textually found in Gide's own *Journal* for February 21st and October 22nd, 1916. The former entry continues in these terms:

> Et Paul continue, et ceci entre en moi comme un glaive: "Ne cause pas, par ton aliment, la perte de celui pour lequel le Christ est mort".

The previous quotation from the **Symphonie Pastorale** continues thus:

> Car j'eus tort de provoquer Jacques: le lendemain je trouvai sur ma table le billet même où j'avais copié le verset: sur le dos de la feuille, Jacques avait simplement transcrit cet autre verset du même chapitre: "Ne cause point par ton aliment la perte de celui pour lequel Christ est mort" (Romans xiv, 15).

Close comparison of these passages sheds light on the composition of a work of art. The author has copied the actual words and passages which he had entered in his *Journal*, but he now attributes them to his misguided pastor. The *Journal* contains many more quotations; the artist has taken what he needed for his fiction.

Finally both *Journal* and novel quote Romans vii, 9, the latter putting it into the mouth of the dying girl, the former adding this significant comment:

> Certainement il n'est que trop aisé de détourner de son sens cette parole extraordinaire et de prêter ici à saint Paul une intention qui n'a jamais été la sienne. Pourtant si l'on accorde que la loi précède la grâce, ne peut-on admettre un état d'innocence précédant la loi? Étant autrefois sans loi je vivais. Cette phrase s'illumine et se gonfle malgré saint Paul d'une signification redoutable . . . Étant autrefois sans loi, je vivais. Oh! parvenir à cet état de seconde innocence, à ce ravissement pur et riant.

Are not these words suggestive of the whole artistic conception of Gertrude? For in her we find repeated precisely that state of innocence which precedes the law. What Gide thought in 1916 to have 'terrible meaning' has been moulded into the tragic figure of his story. Here as elsewhere the *Journal* is a source of the novel. The former, and not the latter, gives the actual thought of the author. The latter gives something quite different and clearly important: what the artist could make of it. Comparison of the two suggests that Gide the artist had a deeper and truer view of Christianity than Gide the thinker. His Protestant critics would have much more reason for complaint about the *Journal* than about the novel, for the attitude to Scripture in the *Journal* is more superficial and partial than in the novel.

We have not yet done with the parallels, however, since Gide has left valuable evidence of his own attitude to

Roman Catholicism, which must be compared with what he says in the novel. Some ten years after writing the novel he confessed that at one period he had been himself nearly converted to Catholicism. The pastor's son actually is so converted, for a specific reason: he has been warned by the error of his father. What prevented Gide from entering the Roman Church was, he said, the reasoning of his converted friends: none of them would ever know how he had profited by their example. He said to Claudel in 1926 that what kept him out of the Roman Church was not free thinking but the Gospel: 'Les catholiques ne connaissent pas l'Évangile.' The conversion of Jacques, therefore, cannot, any more than the views of the pastor, represent Gide's own view. Again the novel proves to be not autobiography but fiction. The true parallel would seem to be that the pastor's errors send Jacques to Catholicism just as the errors of Catholics kept Gide away from it. In each case it is faulty profession and not positive principle that is effective.

All this may seem to have taken us far from the human interest of the story. It has allowed us to establish certain conclusions as to artistic composition, but it must not obscure the fact that the central feature of the story is neither an attitude to Scripture nor the Protestant-Catholic debate. It is rather the spectacle of a man thinking he is right, and assuming that he is guided by God, when all the time he is guided by his all-too-human instinct. The confidence in his illumination is in the early pages radiant: 'Béni soit le Seigneur pour m'avoir confié cette tâche', and again: 'Il m'apparut soudain que Dieu plaçait sur ma route une sorte d'obligation'. He blames his wife for seeing nothing unreasonable or above reason in the Gospel. He prays for her in all sincerity. Yet he confesses that he has tried to keep all sin from Gertrude in order that she may remain pure. She asks several more awkward questions and even remarks one day that all the happiness she owes to him seems to rest upon ignorance. This is tragically verified when she at last recovers sight. He becomes increasingly caught in the toils of her innocent questions, such as: 'Est-ce par charité que vous m'aimez?' Since she thinks their love is guilty, he comes to dread her recovery of vision, he fears that without her love he can no longer love God. He is finally to hear from her lips her tragic interpretation of the word of Christ which he had interpreted so rashly: 'If ye were blind ye would have no sin, but now ye say, we see, your sin remaineth' (John ix, 41). The effect of the story clearly depends largely on this association between the giving of sight to the blind and the spiritual blindness of the pastor.

We see in this pastor a guilty man who only gradually becomes conscious of his guilt. This is a final feature of the story which the author himself has allowed us to study more fully than is usually possible in a work of art. For Gide, in the very weeks that he was writing the *Symphonie Pastorale*, was concurrently writing *Corydon* and was in his personal life alternately enchanted and tormented by his own passion. Comment on such intimate personal history would be out of place in a literary study, were it not for the fact that Gide's own ardent desire for sincerity has made much of that history public. To the careful reader of his *Journal* there is no doubt of the close parallel be-

tween fact and fiction. The discussions of Joy in the pastor's diary correspond to the affirmation of Joy in Gide's own *Journal* for September and October of 1917. Yet the same *Journal* records also his 'immense joy' at being alone with his wife, his complete inability to break the new attachment and his growing jealousy. In December 1917 we find this entry: 'La pensée de M. me maintient dans un état constant de lyrisme que je ne connaissais plus depuis mes *Nourritures*.' If it was, as he says, this state which enabled Gide to complete *Corydon*, may we not see in it the motive force behind the *Symphonie Pastorale*, written at the same time? The entries which span the following months, that is, the period of writing the story, are as poignant as anything in the *Symphonie Pastorale*. 'Ah, je brame après cette santé, cet équilibre heureux que je goûte auprès de M. et qui fait que près de lui même la chasteté est facile'. Such repose the pastor found in visits to his ward. May it not be Gide's own *malaise* which has sent him back to a story that had lain dormant for twenty-five years?

The attachments of the work to the life and passions of its author are probably more close than we could ever, without M. Gide's aid, have guessed. Yet perhaps the distinctive mark of his story is the delicacy with which its elements are fused and blended. The views on the Bible seem to be those of the author, but they are objectively and ironically expressed, that is, in a way that the author seems never to have held them. The study of this 'amour défendu' is closely related to the author's experience, yet at the same time generalized and focused by a true artist. Is it fanciful to suggest that the delicacy of tone and felicity of perspective are due to long meditation of the theme by an artist who worked in the tradition of the great French moralists? This artist lived in the atmosphere of La Rochefoucauld. He knew Molière's vivid pictures of Agnes, the young girl kept from reality by the watchful egoism of a lover, just as he knew Rousseau's *Émile*, and its aura of blessed innocence. He knew, and brought into his own story, Condillac's animated statue. Above all he was familiar with, and deeply appreciative of, the classical Racinian technique of Nuance.

Such a study as the foregoing is rendered easier by the author's revelation of facts usually withheld from the student, but we must beware of thinking that in explaining something of the genesis of the work we have fully explained what was created. The most interesting result of the investigation is perhaps the parallel between *Numquid et Tu* and the *Symphonie Pastorale*. Both works contain the same material, which means that the difference in presentation is most significant. The views of the pastor have been taken for Gide's own views because they were so much like what he thought; indeed they were what he had comparatively recently thought. Might we not say that they were what in another mood he might still think? But this difference of mood makes all the difference. The *Symphonie Pastorale* presents ironically what the *Journal* presents enthusiastically. In more general terms, the work of art uses plastically what the *Journal* reveals subjectively. The force of the one depends on the force of the other. Just as Gide had felt the pastor's view strongly, so his irony is thereby enriched. In fact the work illustrates a principle, formulated thus by M. Hytier: 'L'ironie est le contraire de la ferveur, mais très souvent l'ironie suppose la ferveur. Elle en procède' (*André Gide*). This principle, applied to *La Porte Étroite* and *L'Immoraliste*, as we have here applied it to the **Symphonie Pastorale**, might yield fruitful reinterpretation of Gide's art.

La Symphonie pastorale appears to be a critique of contemporary Protestantism. This aspect fades as the book is progressively studied, and in the end one can say no more than that it is so, if at all, only because it is a critique of a modern tendency exemplified in Protestantism.

—W. G. Moore

However that may be, the range of intention of this slight story emerges only after its connections with reality have been explored. At a first reading it appears to be a critique of contemporary Protestantism. This aspect fades as the book is progressively studied, and in the end one can say no more than that it is so, if at all, only because it is a critique of a modern tendency exemplified in Protestantism, but going beyond it at all points. It is a critique of the 'mensonge' inherent in the activity of modern man. The French moralists and artists of the seventeenth century explored certain hypocrisies which seemed inseparable from life in society. Their modern disciple follows the trail further. To him, as to them, attitudes are the result of pressure, economic or professional or social. These attitudes lead to most tragic results in the case of the well-meaning or the high-principled, since they imagine that their principles allow them to escape from the common lot. This illusion is disastrous. It is no accident that its disasters are being exposed today, thirty years after the **Symphonie Pastorale** was written, in such a book as Sartre's *L'Etre et le Néant*. It is surely no coincidence that this thinker gives so important a place to 'mauvaise foi', by which he seems to understand the lie to oneself, so that one is taken in as much as other people are. Sartre writes: 'La mauvaise foi a donc en apparence la structure du mensonge. Seulement, ce qui change tout, c'est que, dans la mauvaise foi, c'est à moi-même que je masque la vérité'. A Spanish writer, working in the very different field of university problems, expresses this point in a form which might serve as a marginal comment on the **Symphonie Pastorale**:

> It is our privilege to try to be whatever we wish; but it is vicious to pretend to be what we are not and to delude ourselves by growing habituated to the radically false idea of what we are. When the habitual behaviour of a man or an institution is false, the next step is complete demoralization. And thence to degeneracy, for it is not possible for anyone to submit to the falsification of his nature without losing his self-respect (Ortega y Gasset, *Mission of the University*, Kegan Paul).

(pp. 16-26)

W. G. Moore, "André Gide's 'Symphonie Pastorale'," in French Studies, *Vol. IV, No. 1, January, 1950, pp. 16-26.*

J. Robert Loy   (essay date 1951)

[*Loy is an American educator and critic. In the following essay, he addresses Gide's concept of morality as expressed in* Prometheus *and* Theseus.]

> Puis on a voulu expliquer; les livres ont amplifié les mythes;—mais quelques mythes suffisaient.
> —André Gide

The myth, as Plato knew so well, is not to be explained. Its very reason for being is that it suggests what the artist with a whole language at his disposal cannot say. In the **Prométhée** and in **Thésée**, Gide has called upon the myth to clarify moral issues which have ever been the motivating force of his life as a thinker and artist. Of the first he has said that he would not care to change "quatre phrases." The last—a work simmering so long in his mind—he has referred to simply and equivocally as "ce dernier écrit." The great span of life and experience between the two works (**Prométhée** is dated 1899; **Thésée**, 1944), the fact that he has twice chosen the myth as his medium, the many questions left with the reader in both works (but of which of Gide's works is this not true?) have all made very attractive this attempt to forget for a moment the aesthetic impact of the myth and bog down in the prosaic and the practical. M. Jean Hytier is certainly Gide's most perceptive critic when he insists that the aesthetic method is the most rewarding in understanding such a careful artist. But there are unfortunately some earth-bound minds, restless for meanings, who will not find peace until they can answer such a simple question as "What is an eagle?" Gide, himself, has justified such impertinence. For he never ceases to warn that the author knows least what he says, and that without the work of the reader and the critic, literary creation is a one-legged affair.

That the basic problem of all of Gide's production is a moral one cannot be denied. The point of attack may change slightly in various works, but it is usually what might be called the artist's approach to morality. Indeed, one must take Gide at his word when he suggests that the artist's *raison d'être* is akin to the philosopher's and that he should influence rather than act. It is in **Paludes** that the artistic conception and limitation of the moral problem are most patent. The outer world enters there only as do unwelcome visitors into a sick-room. Here, as in his earlier *traités*, Gide is writing propaganda for art as philosophy. But the futility of the hero's efforts, Gide's own feeling that this is a "satire de quoi?" show him the limitations of such an artistic and individual approach to what is in essence a common, social problem. He is clearly enmeshed in the age-old dilemma of the individual in society however much he might wish to solve personality on the plane of the individual artist. And so, in **Prométhée**, he has transcended the individual to arrive at social personality situated in a universal, metaphysical atmosphere. In **Thésée**, using an individual as his skillful *porte-parole*, he has come even farther from the individual to a kind of all-encompassing social commentary. That is why the two works become so interesting as an early and, perhaps, a final estimate of the same problem.

The difficulty from the outset of *Prométhée* is that the old plane (the salvation of the individual artist) remains very much present along with the broader metaphysical plane. There is a very perceptible remnant of *Paludes* and a clear announcement of the *Caves*. Thus the symbol, the meaning of the myth tends to suffer in communication from the very richness of interpretation. Might not Zeus represent equally the Lord of the Universe in general and the Lord of the Muses in particular; might not the café waiter represent Philosophy and Moral Values in general as well as Art in particular; might not Prometheus represent equally well the reformer in general and the artist in particular; might not the Eagle—but enough of conjecturing. That the general theme of the piece is one of moral values—whether on a personal or a social plane—becomes apparent as soon as all of the cascading anecdotes are cleared away. The second chapter is labeled "Chronicle of Public Morality." The only part of that chapter and of the rest of the work which is not anecdote is Gide's too rapid dismissal of the problem with a cursory: "I shall not speak of public morality; there is none." The rest of the *sotie*, however, is only a planned escape from the problem, an escape which in reality speaks of nothing except public morality, an escape introducing truths by an indirection dear to Gide and to the myth, and succeeding where exposition fails. If public morality by way of the artist's morality is the subject of *Paludes*, then *Prométhée* talks primarily of public morality with the artist reluctantly relegated to second place.

Such multi-plane interpretation is only part of the difficulty. For it is with *Prométhée* that the larger problem of the *acte gratuit*, so long present in Gide's mind, makes its official appearance. Doubtless much more is to be said of it later in the *Caves* and in the *Faux-Monnayeurs*, but nowhere have its ramifications been suggested so succinctly. From the limited salvation of the artist, the reader progresses in *Prométhée* through the larger salvation of mankind to the generative force of all moral consideration—human freedom. The world of *Prométhée* would seem to be a rather tight and enclosed hierarchy with an unmotivated Zeus at its head, a pseudo-unmotivated waiter as its first lieutenant, a reluctantly, confusedly, yet consciously motivated Prometheus as its chosen guinea pig par excellence, and with Coclès and Damocles, in descending order, its unrefined material, its common stuff. So it would seem, but there is the Eagle.

The eagle is the enigma and the key of the whole *sotie*. It is referred to variously and in, it would seem, ascending order as a "conscience", as "belief in progress," as a "raison d'être." The first conscience however plays a double semantic role. The first "consciousness" of man's being was of his beauty, but this soon changes to a more troubling "conscience" which demands more or better, i.e. a belief in progress. The progression to the *raison d'être* (with accompanying change in the beauty of the bird) entails a wearing on man's health which delights Prome-

theus. Actually, not many arrive to the last "state of eagle," for they have changed the belief in *well-being*, which is really progress, into a sickly hope for *more and better*. Prometheus plays a strange double role, a role between Zeus who has no eagle, and the rest of humanity, the others who have the eagle and comprehend it not.

It would be wrong to suppose, however, that Prometheus (unlike the waiter who has "arrived") is not confused somewhat by his double role, by his superior and refined knowledge of the eagle. Like the philosopher, like the artist, he tries to educate Coclès, Damocles and the Parisian public to his acceptance of things *sub specie aeternitatis*. On the other hand, he still rebels against his situation by reason of the Banker who refuses to explain, who has no eagle and less interest in clearing up Prometheus' questions, and by reason of the eagle itself who continually refuses to talk. The cardinal question thus becomes whether Prometheus has chosen the weaker or the stronger side of his character when he finally devours the bird with his Parisian friends.

The secret to Prometheus' capitulation and/or wisdom lies in the bad logic of his petition of principles; the very conclusion to his syllogism is lacking, although he assures us that it must follow from his first two propositions. The first propositions themselves, the very petition of principles are precarious enough. Why *must* one have an eagle? The categoric imperative fits badly here. Secondly, how does Prometheus know we all have an eagle save, as he admits, because he has induced as much from his own limited, personal experience. Yet the petition of principles (plus assorted fireworks and questionable pictures) was to have been his great resource in straightening out Coclès, Damocles and humanity in general. His reasoning is incapable of exposing what he "knows" as an individual and as an artist. But the truth remains nonetheless truth even if it cannot be proved. And that truth is best expressed in the contradiction which is at the basis of Prometheus' difficulty in the lecture hall. For, at first, he has defined his petition of principles as an "affirmation of temperament." Then he adds that "temperament is affirmed when the petition is lacking"—a somewhat incompatible addition. The eagle, Prometheus' equivocal position and the conclusion of the piece are all explained in that contradiction. The eagle is precisely what people have said it was, depending on the person talking and rising, as has been suggested, from the lowest plane of consciousness, through conscience, through a belief in progress to a *raison d'être* (comprehended by Prometheus), and beyond to the complete absence of eagle and problem for Zeus who, alone, is capable of the *acte gratuit*. Prometheus' embarrassing position is that he is torn between love for men and love for their eagle or what destroys them. He has even said he does not love Man, but, like Coclès, he is bound by his first devotion to them and he cannot deceive himself well enough to believe what he says. Humanity in its very broadest terms wins out over the aspirations of the perceptive, the more keenly sensitive man, over the philosopher and the artist. Touching, but essentially tragic is the final repast on the bird. Yet the rare individual, the artist, Prometheus, has kept something out of it all—the tail of the troublesome eagle, with which Gide has fashioned his masterful myth (an obvious identification of Gide with Prometheus). In short, since the free act is either impossible or exceedingly difficult for all but Zeus, man is determined, and, to assert himself, to save himself, he must create his own determinant, his own petition of principles, *a priori*. The seeming contradiction (that temperament and personality can be affirmed only when the petition is lacking) is but a further step, equally necessary—a "becoming" so close to Gide. Thus, one can and must have an eagle. Then one must transcend the eagle and "passer outre" to empirical morality, to a kind of belief in well-being which is far different from the sickly obsession with what is better. The tragedy is that so few will pass beyond and devour the self-created eagle; so many will delight only in helping to lick the bones of anyone's eagle so as to be rid of the painful and embarrassing bird.

As if Gide were not sure of suggesting sufficiently this difficulty of rising to experience as art and art as philosophy, he adds the anecdote of Tityre. Tityre has established his petition of principles and thus "found himself", in his debt to his growing community. Then Angèle tempts him away—not into the well-being which he sensed must come next, but into the empty search for anything better. That she in turn should be tempted away by the first passing stroller and that she should be going with him to Rome (Gide does not use the familiar *"Eo Romam"* merely for amusement) is not surprising. Like Prometheus' friends who help him eat his eagle, she is frightened by the uncertainty of the step beyond; she is too weak to "become," she can only fall back upon the attraction of the physical and on the comfortable, all-explaining organization of Rome. So Tityre is abandoned, as if Gide were underscoring the loneliness and the lone-ness of salvation. In any case, he strengthens the conclusion of the *Prométhée* proper: salvation is individual, abhors dogma, is humanist in the broadest sense. Only one point is somewhat unclear—whether Prometheus ought to have given in to his human pity for Damocles, or whether he should have gone on with his eagle when the bird refused to talk, explain and justify his devotion. Or has he surmounted the last frontier and can he now, Olympian, devour what has devoured him? Is the final scene a tragedy (as has been suggested), a triumph or, simply, a fact?

> If *Prométhée* is the story of a man who thinks, not necessarily first, but most of others, then *Thésée* is the recital of the life of a man who thinks, not necessarily first, but most of himself.
>
> —*J. Robert Loy*

If *Prométhée* is the story of a man who thinks, not necessarily first, but most of others, then *Thésée* is the recital of the life of a man who thinks, not necessarily first, but most of himself. Yet *Prométhée* has ended with the sudden change of its protagonist as he sits eating his eagle and

explaining that at least he has eaten well and saved the feathers; and *Thésée* ends with the altruistic warmth of Theseus as he remarks that for the good of future humanity he has lived. One wonders as he meets this metathesis whether Gide has not always vacillated helplessly between Christ and Nietzsche, whether he has even come to grips with the individual and with society at one and the same time. But a word or two first about Theseus.

Child of nature, blessed with physical charms and strength, product of an impressive background (be it Aegeus or Poseidon who sired him), Theseus thrills before all that the world can offer him in echo of the *Nourritures terrestres*. From his father, however, he learns that such orgasmic appreciation is not enough, that one achieves nothing without hard work and that the great man is he who shows to all the others what one man proposes and is capable of doing. Poor Aegeus! In such paternal counsel lie the germs of his own destruction. With the inadvertent yet frankly selfish forgetfulness about the sail, Theseus begins an existence which can be labeled only rugged individualism. Yet along with this obsession for arriving, there is a concern—artificial or otherwise—for others, for posterity. This man who pretends to set himself apart from the common man only because of his value, who hates to "stay" and thinks only of passing on, this same man justifies his everchanging interest in self into an obsession with the individual, any individual, then into Man, "because it is not enough to be, then, to have been; one must leave a legacy so as not to finish up in oneself." The problem of *Thésée*, much less involved than *Prométhée*—thanks to the prerequisite work which that latter piece represents and particularly thanks to an older Gide who is drawing a life-time of experience and detailed examination into a final (or near-final) statement—is to find out to what extent Theseus is to be judged the moral man by Gide and by his serious reader.

Like *Prométhée*, *Thésée* has its symbols. Daedalus is, properly speaking, the scientist; his son, Icarus, the philosopher and metaphysician: Ariadne conjures up simple physical attraction; Phaedra, the physical added to the sentimental. Yet through all these personalities, Theseus walks with complete confidence and aplomb, finding them all amusingly limited and somewhat inferior to his own singleness of purpose and self-sufficiency. Contrasted with the other transient characters, Theseus seems strangely and yet consistently the tyrant, the democrat, the communist commissar and the humanitarian all molded into one. He is working, he tells himself, for the future progress of mankind whose advice he never takes into consideration. "There is a time," he says, "to liberate men from fear, a time to curtail their liberty with planned occupation, to bring their leisure to gain and blossom. And all that cannot be done without discipline." (Theseus' discipline, naturally). He cannot allow the individual to hold himself, to be satisfied with a mediocre happiness. He thinks that man is not free, will never be free and that it is not good for him to be free, for then he introverts everything to himself and does not think of the beyond-self. Humanity (how strange the word sounds in this context!) is capable of and worth more. His great virtue, and he declares it shamelessly and sincerely, is believing in progress—the same progress which figured so secondarily in *Prométhée*.

Perhaps the highest point in the récit is the meeting between Theseus and Oedipus. These last two along with Prometheus have always figured prominently in Gide's artistic imagination. However great the sympathy with which Gide has treated Oedipus in his theatre, the king of Thebes seems a weak second to Theseus in the conclusion of the more recent *Thésée*. For Theseus, surprised that so little has been said of their meeting, the conversation at Colonus represents a crowning glory, and he seems to gloat over the favorable comparison he makes of himself with his "equal." Yet there is an ill-hidden regret when he sees Oedipus' daughters still at his side: his Hippolytus is irretrievably lost. Oedipus causes him to hesitate in his complacency. For Oedipus has opposed the Sphinx and dared to stand against the Gods. Why, then, his admission of defeat as he puts out his eyes? Theseus admits that either he cannot accept Oedipus' explanation or that, perhaps, he has understood him badly. And as Oedipus tries to make clear that, blind, he has finally grasped or glimpsed a well-being of another order, far removed from this earth, and that he has found a new kind of peace in daring the Gods on a grandiose scale, finally losing but losing somehow gloriously, Theseus hastens to assure the reader in his last paragraph that, compared to Oedipus' life, his own life suits him well. He has left behind him Athens, he has left his renown and, he assures himself, he has left a posterity of better men. He has lived, he concludes simply. As he had early known, the first and most important struggle of man is against the gods. Let Oedipus pretend that he has found well-being in his approach to the godhead; Theseus is glad to have lived this life, on this earth and, most particularly, on Attic soil. But this apology for his life—so sincere and happy superficially—could only come after his meeting with Oedipus. Gide knew that meeting had to happen and had long planned it. Theseus represents the man of action, the self-centered dictator (for here the terms are synonymous). The man of action is what Gide, the artist, has so many times admired physically, spiritually and even mentally—the *Übermensch*. Oedipus, like Prometheus, falls into the embarrassing middle category, half artist-philosopher, half man of action. Christ and Superman, the suggestion and the action, the renunciation and the freedom of which Gide has so often talked are here met as squarely as they have ever been since *Philoctète*.

The temptation is to suppose that in *Thésée*, "ce dernier écrit", he has made his choice and presented a final judgment on what he had written into *Prométhée* so many years before about man and his freedom and his moral responsibility. Should all pertinent passages from the *Journal* alone be arranged chronologically, one might substantiate a change from the young artist to the old man of wisdom, of practicality and of resignation. The limits of this study permit no such picture. Even a random glance at the *Journal*, however, from its beginning to the period of *Thésée* indicates a change in preoccupation. The young Gide, the solemn artist had said in 1892,

> Morality consists in substituting for the natural creature (the old Adam) a fiction that you pre-

fer. But then you are no longer sincere. The old Adam is the sincere man.

> This occurs to me: the old Adam is the poet. The new man, whom you prefer, is the artist. The artist must take the place of the poet. From the struggle between the two is born the work of art. . .

thus reducing natural man and moral man to sheerly artistic symbols. The old and the new Prometheus are here, but no hint of the administrator Theseus. The pseudo-hierarchy of the *Prométhée* is already apparent shortly afterwards in Gide's great respect (which continues unabated) for Goethe. Coclès-Damocles, Prometheus, Oedipus and Theseus are all clearly represented in the following:

> *Morality*
>
> Originality—first degree.
>
> I omit the lower degree which is mere banality, in which man is merely gregarious (he constitutes the crowd).
>
> Therefore: originality consists in depriving oneself of certain things. Personality asserts itself by its limitation.
>
> But above all this there is still a higher state to which Goethe achieves, the Olympian. He understands that originality limits; that by being personal he is simply anyone. And by letting himself live in things, like Pan, everywhere, he thrusts aside all limits until he no longer has any but those of the world. He becomes banal but in a superior way.

Is Theseus, then, the 'superior' banal, while Prometheus succeeds only in affirming his 'deprived' personality? In 1895, Gide will repeat of Goethe that nothing in life has calmed him so much as contemplating that great figure, yet in the very same entry he concludes: "The greatest nobility of life is obtained not through love of others but through love of duty." Does not this smack rather of the limitation level? In any case, duty for Goethe and for Theseus has not certainly the same meaning as for Prometheus. Undated *feuillets* for 1896 speak rather admiringly of the great "sickly unrest" of Prometheus, Orestes, Ajax and Oedipus, but make no mention of Theseus, who seems free from *Angst* and perfectly healthy. Is Theseus then superior or inferior to these others? In the *feuillets* between 1918 and 1919, Gide speaks at once of two sides of Theseus when he says:

> I consider liberty as a fearful and disastrous thing that one must try to reduce or suppress in oneself first—and even, if one can, in others. The frightening thing is imposed slavery; and for the lack of something better: the slavery to which one submits. Oh, voluntary slavery!

or again, in the *feuillets* after 1925:

> And I admit that man is never free; but the simplest and most honest thing is to act as if he were.

In the same general period he admits that he has taken most time and found it most painful to learn duties toward the State. All of this somehow suggests that Theseus, who has lived the practical if somewhat artificial life of the free individual, who pays only lip service to duty toward others, and who is devoted to his State, is right. And yet, at about the same time, one suddenly finds: "Oedipus, or the triumph of ethics!"—the same Oedipus who, so similar in many ways to Theseus, finally capitulates and thus negates all of Theseus' contentment in having simply lived. Or is one to read an irony into the word triumph?

There is a kind of explanation of this duality of Christlike humanitarianism and restraint, and Nietzschean ruthlessness and license (neither of which must be confused with the bourgeois good life) some ten years later, at the time of Gide's flirtation with communism. Humanity and progress (Prometheus' progress)—yes, but. . .

> . . . today we rate humanity much too high. . . What invites humanity to progress is precisely not to consider itself. . . as an end but rather as a means through which to achieve and realize something. This is what made me say, through the person of my Prometheus: "I do not love man; I love what devours him," and made me put my wisdom in this: knowing how to prefer to man the eagle that feeds on him.

But Prometheus has devoured his eagle ostensibly because his progress has hurt men. The kind of progress spoken of here fits Theseus much better. In 1931, Gide hesitates at leaving humanity out of art and decides that art is but artifice "if what is closest to the artist's heart is banished from it." In 1934, he suggests both Prometheus and Theseus, as well as Oedipus, when he says:

> You were told: fear of God is the beginning of wisdom; then, with God missing, the fear remained on your hands. Understand today that wisdom begins where fear ends, that it begins with the revolt of Prometheus.

In 1941, he attacks himself in the pseudo-person of the devil:

> Didn't you say yourself: "The family and religion are the two greatest enemies of progress?" . . . Didn't you even write, at a time when your thought was daring: "I do not like man; I like what devours him?" Doubtless a paradox, but not so much as you think. If I understand you, you meant that nothing great or beautiful is obtained save through sacrifice, and that the worthiest representatives of this miserable humanity are those in whom sacrifice is voluntary.

In 1942, he finishes the long-pondered *Thésée* and recaptures some of the thrill of the *Caves* and *Prométhée*, a common thrill perhaps for common subjects nicely treated. In 1947, after *Thésée*'s publication, comes the latest commentary:

> Take things, not for what they seem, but for what they are.
>
> Play with the cards you have.
>
> Demand of yourself what you are.

—a rather obvious picture of resignation, far from the difficult devotion to ideals of Prometheus and close to the practicality of Theseus.

Were one to hear only a résumé of *Thésée* along with certain selected passages, one could only assume that Gide has returned in his final thinking to the idea that excellence must be encouraged at the expense of mediocrity, that the seeming cruelty and inhumanity thus involved is but prudence. Thus, the action gained by the gifted strong man as he follows his bent, ascending, is worth more than infinite human charity and more desirable than profound thinking, however much closer such thinking may come to the Truth. There are times when the atmosphere of *Thésée* is frankly fascist and dictatorial, times when one must assume that the superior state of morality can produce only the Machiavellian prince. Such a conclusion is not only disillusioning, but would pass over Oedipus in *Thésée* and the recurring allusions to Prometheus in Gide's other writings with unwarranted haste. Two world wars have obviously left their mark on Gide's thinking; the fifty years from *Prométhée* to *Thésée* have necessarily changed the brash young artist of *Paludes*—particularly in a writer and thinker who takes care to ever renew himself. Is there none of the artist-moralist which remains? Is there none of the compassion of *Numquid et Tu?* Is there none of Promethean striving for well-being *sub specie aeternitatis*, none of the accompanying preaching of the fuller life which remains in this Theseus who has made adjustment with practicality at the expense of the artist, the philosopher and the individual? One must then assume that Theseus idealizes the administrator, the order out of chaos at any expense. Or perhaps one might plead that *Thésée* is but another facet of Gide and must be given no importance of finality. The rest of the facets of Gide turn up too clearly in *Thésée* to justify that argument. Then, too, granted it is but a facet, why has Gide, thinking so long and talking for so many years about his Theseus waited for the end of his career to write it?

Thésée is definitely a summing-up, and more than the superficial re-echoing of André Gide, from *les Nourritures terrestres* on, which strikes every reader instantly. Gide for all his classicism of style, for all his subtle intellectualism is essentially a realist. The outcome of *Paludes*, of *Prométhée* and particularly of *Thésée* could so easily have been tragic. But the whole Gide is always present to add to the very real pathos of the short-comings of his artist, the short-comings of his humanitarian philosopher, the shortcomings of his administrator, the irony which rises from the ideal as compared to the real. *Thésée* comes last because it represents Gide's fondest dream and the last rung on his ethical scale. But Theseus as the reader sees him is too ridiculous at times to be taken literally. Oedipus would never have strayed onto the scene of so careful and experienced a writer if Theseus were to be taken at face-value. The safer estimate is to assume that the artist, the humanitarian philosopher, the *ideal* superman are all present in Theseus, as they should be in Gide's ideal of the man of action—the highest degree of his ethical system. They are but overlaid momentarily by the cleverness, by the inhuman, egotistical superman—the man of action as he really exists. Certainly the writer in *Paludes* does take himself too seriously, certainly Prometheus does bring about the collapse of his eagle by his own insistence. Theseus is triumphant as a summing-up in this sense, that he is perhaps less ridiculous and, except for his hesitation with Oedipus, more satisfied with his life than the others as he states simply: "I have lived." But such simple-minded acceptance and resignation (although tempting to Gide) are accompanied by the very real regret for Prometheus and his eagle, for Oedipus and his powerless blind triumph, for Daedalus and his science, for Icarus and his torturing questions. *Thésée* tells of the price we pay for action just as *Prométhée* had told of the price, we pay in this world as it is for the higher aspiration of the philosopher and the artist. And *Thésée* had to come last, had to sum-up, for action is experience and art and philosophy are timeless. Gide has been all the while painting his own *Comédie humaine;* he is still the artist who goads and stirs but does not act. Morality with Gide still ends in the aesthetic, and *Prométhée* and *Thésée* are two cruelly realistic parts of the artist's moral man. The extent of the disillusionment from *Thésée* is that the whole Olympian moral man does not exist. Gide has only traced the limits, the outlines, the exaggeration. That is why the irreverent tone and the wit (which shocks Archambaut into seeking nothing serious in a mere *sotie* like *Prométhée*). For "the work of art is an exaggeration." That is why the myth.

"Ce traité n'est peut-être pas quelque chose de bien nécessaire: Quelques mythes d'abord suffisaient." Its conclusion is not astounding. With tongue in cheek and wanting to believe it himself, only half, Gide recalls that "the point of morality for the artist is not whether the Idea which he exposes be more or less moral and useful to the great number; the point is that he should expose it well." (pp. 32-43)

J. Robert Loy, "Prometheus, Theseus, The Uncommon Man and an Eagle," in Yale French Studies, *No. 7, 1951, pp. 32-43.*

Albert J. Guerard   (essay date 1951)

[*Guerard is an American educator, novelist, and critic. In the following excerpt, he comments on* Urien's Voyage *and* Marshlands (Paludes), *noting their relation to Gide's other works and their relation to such literary movements as Surrealism, Symbolism, and Existentialism.*]

Le Voyage d'Urien (1893) has had few readers and almost no commentators; it demands a much fuller analysis than Gide's other early works. For this earnest prose-poem is one of the most tantalizing of Gide's works, psychologically, and its literary and historical interest is much greater than that of *André Walter*. One notable advance is that Gide can now look at his aspirations to purity with an occasional ironic smile. The twelve pilgrims who resist the seductions of Queen Haiatalnefus are a little ridiculous, their chastity somewhat pompous: "Slowly then the twelve of us, in state and symmetry, hieratic in our sumptuous apparel, descended toward the sun, even unto the last step where the broken waves drenched our robes with foam . . . Nobility of spirit constrained us to make no gesture, to keep silent . . ." And the change from the diary of an adolescent in a solitary room to a symbolist journey

to the North Pole and its divine city already shows some progress toward objectivity. The voyage is a "voyage du rien" (Mallarmé had feared it would be the account of a real trip), yet contains everything. It is a Homeric *Pilgrim's Progress*, replete with sirens and other perils of the sea: a dream of life as a series of embroidered and sensuous dreams, and as the puritan rejection of those dreams. A verse palinode admits that the author might have resisted all Urien's temptations, but had been subjected to none of them. His book nevertheless comes as close to being a novel as anything French symbolism would produce. It represents the extreme limit to which Gide would go to satisfy the symbolists who had adopted him, and writing it perhaps hastened his sharp reaction—to the irony of *Paludes*, to the earthy hedonism of *Les Nourritures terrestres*. Yet even the student of Gide's later style must take *Le Voyage d'Urien* into account: its luxuriant rhythms and exotic descriptive riches, its nebulous appeal to the fringes of the reader's consciousness. These vague harmonies and uninhibited translations of soul into landscape had to be exploited, before the progressive chastening of style could begin.

As a Symbolist novel, *Le Voyage d'Urien* stands somewhere between the occult reality of *Arthur Gordon Pym* and the cloudy philosophizing of Novalis's *Lehrlinge zu Sais*, which Gide had recently read. The voyage of the "Orion" is a dream adventure through desire; an "invitation au voyage" of which the first condition is that the pilgrims leave their pasts and their books behind. These young men, wearied by fruitless studies, set out on an unpremeditated journey. Yet they dimly understand their "valor" will be tested, and vaguely long for heroism. The sirens are encountered early enough in the voyage, and before the first month is out some of the sailors have deserted. To go ashore and there be led astray is of course the obvious temptation. But the obscure temptation to bathe beside the ship or elsewhere soon seems more dangerous. The pilgrims who remain on board, or who watch the others but abstain, eagerly question them concerning the forbidden joys, until these others have a right to say: "Here are bold chevaliers! Are you afraid even to taste the fruit? And does your barren virtue consist only in abstinence and doubt?" After the obvious sensuous enticements and pestilential languors of "The Dolorous Ocean" comes the ennui of "The Sargosso Sea": the ennui which follows not upon surfeit but upon the annihilation of desire. Here the pilgrims casually encounter Ellis (Urien's destined soul-mate) or at least a woman who resembles her, and the ship passes over a submerged city. The same day they observe the first blocks of ice. A few, sick with ennui, must be left behind, but the eight who remain embark on the "Voyage to a Glacial Sea."

The goal proves to be a disappointing, "apathetic," and unfrozen little lake. The pilgrims wonder then whether it is perhaps better not to attain one's goal, but decide that the joy of effort and satisfied pride is reward enough. What then has been the voyage's and the book's meaning? That it is impossible to achieve genuine peace without having led the will through evil, through the temptations of passion and sluggish indifference? "The hard trials are past. Far away are the gloomy shores where we thought we should die of ennui; farther still the shores of illicit joys; let us count ourselves fortunate to have experienced them. One cannot come here except through them. To the loftiest cities lead the straightest ways; we are going to the heavenly city." This statement, which may be attached so easily to Gide's total meaning, comes at the beginning not the end of the "Voyage to a Glacial Sea," and is almost the only one to offer such a comforting explicitness. It is perhaps better to avoid all intellectual paraphrase; to admit that any ethical summary of *Le Voyage d'Urien* falsifies the impression it makes.

For the adventures seem truly gratuitous, unless interpreted psychologically. And here precisely lies the historic interest of *Le Voyage d'Urien*, which has never been fully recognized: it is a distinct and important episode in the transition from symbolism to surrealism; from the mysterious but somber soul-voyages of symbolism to the free absurdity of surrealist nightmare. Some of the gratuity reminds us vaguely of *The Ancient Mariner* and directly of *Arthur Gordon Pym*. The mysterious ship of the dead which appears and disappears could have been borrowed from either work, or borrowed simply from legend. Gide's Paride disintegrates as easily as Poe's Peters, one losing an arm and the other a leg. Gide's Eskimo community is more sophisticated and less cruel than Poe's; at a crucial hour his pilgrims find a warning message written blazingly on ice, as Poe's find a message in stone. Poe's water gets

warmer as we near the South Pole, and at Gide's North Pole we find an unfrozen lake. The mysterious sheep-woman of *Le Voyage d'Urien* recalls the numerous sheep lost in Maeterlinck's marshes, but also the white luminous deity at the end of *Arthur Gordon Pym*. Most interesting of all, in both works, is the gratuitous menace of water. "I felt a numbness of body and mind," Poe's narrator tells us, "a dreaminess of sensation . . ." He watches an animal float by. "I would have picked it up, but there came over me a sudden listlessness, and I forbore. The heat of the water still increased, and the hand could no longer be endured within it. Peters spoke little, and I knew not what to think of his apathy." [In a footnote, Guerard states: "These similarities are not offered as proof that Gide was influenced by *Arthur Gordon Pym*, which he may or may not have read by 1892. They merely help us to 'locate' *Le Voyage d'Urien* in a general literary movement."]

It takes no psychiatric bias to see that *Arthur Gordon Pym* also dramatizes preconscious longings and fears. There is nevertheless a great difference between the two works, which brings Gide's much closer to surrealism. Except in the final pages, Poe is as careful to prepare and justify his mysteries as any Gothic novelist. Gide, on the other hand, does not even bother to explain how his pilgrims happened to set out. There is no logic in the connection of events, other than an inner logic of psychological necessity. Streams may flow backward; the *Orion* may "become" a felucca in an instant; a monument—"for some unknown reason"—may suddenly rise out of a plain. The mysterious child of the sixth chapter is perhaps borrowed from Novalis, but Ellis is borrowed from no one. The pilgrims' first meeting with her is a midpoint, as is were, between the revery of Poe or Baudelaire and the dense inconsecutiveness of Roussel's *Impressions d'Afrique*; the meeting is completely unprepared. We may even see the transition between the two modes, in successive paragraphs. The first paragraph is in the symbolist manner, the second in the surrealist.

> The fourth day on the banks some smoke-colored herons hunted worms in the ooze; beyond them a level lawn extended. At night beneath reflected clouds pallid in the lingering day, the river appeared to run in a straight line, for the banks were hidden in shadow. The oars of the felucca, as they turned, caught in the reeds of the bank.

> The seventh day we met my dear Ellis, who was awaiting us on the lawn seated under an apple tree. She had been there a fortnight, having arrived before us by the overland route. She wore a polka-dot dress and carried a cerise parasol. Behind her was a little valise with toilet articles and some books; a Scotch shawl was over her arm; she was eating a salad of escarole and reading *The Prolegomena to All Future Metaphysics*. We had her climb into the boat.

It is difficult to argue the influence of *Le Voyage d'Urien* or of *Les Chants de Maldoror*, alike unread at the time, against the influence of Rimbaud and Laforgue. But in terms of Gide's own development, the absurdity of the second part of *Le Voyage d'Urien* certainly led to *Paludes*, *Le Prométhée mal enchaîné*, and *Les Caves du Vatican*. And these, we know, had a real influence on surrealism.

The major interest of *Le Voyage d'Urien* is nevertheless a personal and psychological interest. The "objective psychic content" would be inviting under any circumstances: the transparently homosexual reactions, the accumulated images of dissolution, the unexplained fears of water and submersion in water. This psychological interest becomes compelling—dangerously compelling—when we consider the circumstances under which the book was written. It is the last of Gide's books to precede his discovery of his homosexual nature, and immediately preceded that discovery. It is therefore only too easy to find—in the increasing homosexual language—a literal and dramatic breaking of submerged forces to the troubled surface of consciousness. The danger is that we should infer too much about the creativity of the preconscious from this single instance, where many instances would be needed for proof. But beyond this we know, from *Si le grain ne meurt*, that *Le Voyage d'Urien* accompanied that same struggle with masturbation which affected *André Walter*:

> At La Roque, the summer before the last, I thought I would go mad. There I spent nearly all my time cloistered in the room where only work should have kept me, trying in vain to work (I was then writing the *Voyage d'Urien*) . . . haunted and obsessed. Hoping perhaps to find some escape through excess itself, and to recover equanimity beyond it; hoping to debilitate my demon (I see there his advice) and debilitating only myself—I spent myself obsessively until exhausted; until there awaited me only imbecility and madness. [*Si le grain ne meurt*]

Given such a forthright statement, it would be amusing to demonstrate that the richer imagery and freer revery of *Le Voyage d'Urien* was due to the fact that it was written during a period of excessive self-indulgence, while *André Walter* was written during a period of attempted self-control. But the fact that *André Walter* was a first book, an exercise in learning to write, makes any such inference dangerous. The biographical background of *Le Voyage d'Urien* is unquestionably significant. But we will lose that significance if we try to define it minutely.

"Souls are landscapes," says Gide's Preface to the second edition, and the landscapes of *Le Voyage d'Urien* are fluid and dissolving. Longing for fixity, the pilgrims travel past transforming shores evanescent as "insincere actions." They explore floating islands, and are lost among shifting dunes and moving knolls. Crossing an ambiguous plain they come upon a valley of mists, and then a prodigious city of hanging gardens and fantastic minarets. But "the voices were dying away; and as they fell, lo! the city faded, evanesced, disintegrated on a strophe; the minarets, the slender palms vanished; the flights of stairs crumbled; sea and sand became visible through gardens on fading terraces." Some of the imagery of dissolution and putrefaction must be discounted as symbolist and decadent commonplace. This is perhaps least true where the dissolving agent is water—warm water, the recurrent menace on this voyage of the Puritan will. In the queen's grotto air and

diaphanous water merge, and solid objects seem magically displaced. Icebergs melt in warm water at significant moments in the story. Can we not see in the corpse, imprisoned in a solid ice wall, a wishful image of fixity and unmenaced purity?

If we are to believe *Si le grain ne meurt*, Gide did not yet know where the real menace lay. The homosexual images and reactions, so curiously uncensored, must be accepted as undeliberate too. Like Huxley's noble savage, Angaire fears that even the slightest tenderness will cause women to take off their clothes, and he admits preferring solitary pleasure. The pilgrims walk away from a performance by whirling dervishes when their flowing robes become too revealing. That evening the sailors bathe in the warm water and then lie down on deck, "writhing with desire." But the pilgrims do not bathe, nor do they dare even lie down. On another occasion the sailors return from their sexual exploits, bringing fruits which bleed like wounds. In Queen Haiatalnefus' realm the native men have long since retired to live by themselves. There remain on the streets boys with women's faces, or women with the faces of boys, "admirable creatures." And significantly enough, Ellis must dissolve before Urien can unite either with her or with God.

In one remarkable chapter, we shall see, an almost uncensored homosexual imagery supports the binding symbol of water. More obvious and less interesting is the explicit disgust with normal sexual experience—yet not entirely normal, since through one fevered night the sailors and native women engaged in "incomplete embraces." The equation could not be simpler: those who traffic with the native women vomit, contract the plague, and die, while those who abstain survive. The three crucial expeditions into narrow, sheltered yet dangerous places suggest no such conscious meanings. The queen's grotto is a lovely place, approached through calm canals overhung by creepers and trees; the second grotto is a shadowed place of stagnant waters, where lethargic bats hang from the ceiling. The narrow fiord of the third part is "gloomy" and with somber depths. The invitation is pressing to see in all three only the trauma of birth—yet still more evident seems the imaged fear of normal sexual penetration. The pilgrims find no difficulty leaving these narrow places but great difficulty entering them. In the first grotto they refuse to bathe because of the crabs, sea nettles, and "cruel" lobsters. Ellis contracts swamp fever in the second, and there first causes Urien to doubt her identity. Auks nest on the cliffs of the fiord. Frightened, the females abandon their eggs, which roll down the rocks and shatter in "horrible streaks of white and yellow." Is there not some significance in the fact that Eric's wanton destructiveness, in hurling rocks at the birds, occurs at this particular point in the story?

The water, in any event, is "polluted" by the eggs—and we may want to take the actual consistencies of water into account when we consider the pilgrims' attitude toward bathing. Only "water born of ice" seems wholly pure and invigorating. Yet the saffron-skinned men who bring snow from the icehouses of the original port have "bloody loincloths," and the blue water of the harbor is stained by bales of purple and dissolving dyes. Plague-stricken for their orgies, the sailors and native women "pollute" the water of the washhouses with their "defiled tunics." "With long poles they stirred the slime at the bottom; clouds of sediment arose; bubbles came to the surface and burst. Bent over the rim, they inhaled these odors of the fen without revulsion; they laughed, for they were already stricken." The significance of these sentences derives from the fact that they are wholly gratuitous.

Water is yet the attractive as it is the destructive element, and the temptation to bathe is a more real one than any encountered on land. On the fifth day the pilgrims swim in the ocean and are penetrated by the "languor" of the waves. Later they refuse to bathe out of fear of the sirens whom their less courageous shipmates have visited. On a third occasion the sailors, bathing after sexual indulgence, are beautiful yet "gleam with unwonted pallor." A single sentence concludes the sixth chapter: "We did not bathe that day." The effect "is of a statement in code"—and the obvious inference is that bathing is simply equated with sexual indulgence, which is both ruinous and beautiful. A full census of the baths taken by pilgrims and sailors supports this equation, which may even have been an intentional one. Tepid water is the property which debilitates, which dissolves will and energy. But it is also the obscure source of riches and dreams. The longing to bathe may also be a longing to dissolve the personality, to rejoin the healing depths of the unconscious, to achieve Jungian integration. When Queen Haiatalnefus drops one of her rings into the sea, Urien refuses to join the other pilgrims in diving after it—"not through ennui, but on the contrary through a desire too great, so fascinated had I always been by the mysterious depths of the waves." His companions remain long under water, and on their return fall into a deep sleep. "A numbing torpor at first drugged my senses," Clarion says on awaking, "and I thought only of the pure slumber I could have in that cool water, couched on the soft seaweed." Later, the submarine city beneath their ship is an azured vision of repose; it fills Urien with a "lyric ecstasy." In unconsciousness and in death, in water, the miserable self may be dissolved.

The desire to dissolve the self thus seems to take on several forms in *Le Voyage d'Urien*, and to have a multiple meaning. A verbalized and conscious longing for fixity is affronted by the spectacle of a dissolving universe. But what does this longing for fixity really signify, and does it not cover a less conscious longing to be one of the dissolving forms? And what would dissolution itself bring, if accomplished in these tepid waters: escape from the "miserable personality," or the riches of restored energy, or sexual release and expense? A passage from the *Lehrlinge zu Sais* suggests that these impulses may be, at a given moment, inextricably connected: "He felt his miserable personality melt, submerged beneath waves of pleasure, and that nothing remained but a home for the incommensurable genetic force—a whirlpool in which everything is swallowed by the vast ocean. What does the flame ubiquitously offer? An intimate embrace, from which the sweet liquid trickles in voluptuous drops."

Compared with the diffuse *Lehrlinge zu Sais*, *Le Voyage*

d'Urien has the density and economy of the most conscious art. Yet the fifth chapter of the first part—which conveys both the latent homosexuality and the fear of dissolution—must certainly have escaped any rational "intention" and all but the most rudimentary of unconscious censorship. It forces upon us not merely the equivalence of water, indulgence and dissolution, but also the very physical terms of the homosexual embrace. The pilgrims go to a coral islet, and there watch fishermen dive for coral, sponges, and pearls. "The men had saffron-colored skin; they were naked, but around their necks hung bags to be filled with shells." They must cut away with knives the tentacles which attach to their bodies; when they come to the surface their lungs contract, and a thread of blood— "sumptuous on their golden skin"—almost makes them faint. The pilgrims are "diverted" by seeing the ocean floor and the blood of these men. They then bathe themselves in pools which are too warm and in which children are playing. At the bottom of a pool are mosaic figures and two statues that spout perfume into basins. The pilgrims allow the perfume to flow over their arms and hips. And soon a torpor comes over them, as they breathe "this tepid mist—immobile, floating, abandoned; in vain swooning in the marvelous water, green and blue, where glowed only the dimmest light, where the arms of the slender children were tinted blue by the light, and drops falling from the ceiling plashed in monotone." That evening the sailors and the weaker of the pilgrims go on shore in search of women, and those who remain on board are tormented by the thought of their embraces. There is an enormous red moon; there are fires on shore; the night is unbearably hot over the phosphorescent sea. And now we learn, abruptly, that the pilgrims have been watching the sleeping fishermen: "And out of the forest wide-winged vampires, prowling near the sleeping fishermen, sucked the life from their naked feet, from their lips, and overwhelmed them with slumber by the silent beating of their wings."

All this is conveyed in a little more than five hundred words. It should be emphasized that there are no logical connections between the four "episodes": the observation of the fishermen, the swim in the magic pool and subsequent torpor, the evening restlessness on the ship, the coming of the vampires. There are no transitional phrases, yet not a single word breaks the prevailing and complex mood. Mere revery—which normally results in such diffuseness—has here imposed rather than destroyed unity by the very urgency of its demand: by its longing for a nevertheless dreaded relaxation, by its "selection" of particular and revealing imagery. However florid some of its pages, *Le Voyage d'Urien* already shows Gide's ability to record feelings exactly; to penetrate—more successfully than he knew—beneath the level of full consciousness.

Between *Le Voyage d'Urien* and *Paludes*, finished during the winter of 1894-95, lies the partial self-discovery of Gide's first voyage to North Africa; his sickness and his attempt to "normalize" himself, his crucial confession to his mother that he had escaped her control. His first impulse was to preach the gospel of liberation; to persuade others to break their bonds. He was already planning *Les Nourritures terrestres*. Returning to France, he was astonished to find the literary salons unchanged—and that none of his friends, bound by their miserable and routine lives, suspected the importance of his message. How could he save these friends from a misery of which they were wholly unaware? Even a partial liberation had alienated him completely. "Such a state of *estrangement* (which I felt especially when with those closest to me) could well have led me to suicide, had it not been for the escape I found in describing it ironically in *Paludes* "[*Si le grain ne meurt*]. Gide's own escape from routine and habit would not come until the second trip to North Africa in 1895, and perhaps not even then. *Paludes* is not merely the satire of comfortable and resigned stagnation. It is also self-satire: the ironic portrait of a convention-bound writer who preaches against conventions. It could even be described as a satire on the seriousness of the existential revolt against seriousness, half a century before literary existentialism. It could also be called a satire on the books Gide would later write, and on his famous "attitude": on the desire to rescue readers from complacency by disturbing them.

Paludes is another book within a book. Gide is writing a *Paludes*, but so too is his ridiculous hero. (This double, incidentally, has already thought of the "acte gratuit"—which a philosopher quickly reduces to absurdity.) By describing the monotony of Tityrus, starting at his marshes, the apostle of freedom hopes to demonstrate to his friends the vanity of their lives. He preaches against comfortable resignation and habit, against routine and bourgeois complacency, against a timid refusal to live, against everything that reduces the individual to a function or social role. "If one knew he was imprisoned, he would at least have the desire to get out." Who is Bernard? The person one sees Thursdays at Octave's. Who is Octave? The person who receives Bernard on Thursdays. Our personalities have been reduced to the masks society compels us to wear. What will such men have accomplished in the only life that is given them? "They will have fulfilled their role." The author of "Paludes" is asked why he complains, since everyone is content in his servitude. "But precisely because nobody complains! The acceptance of the evil aggravates it. It becomes a vice, gentlemen, since one ends by enjoying it." One charm of *Paludes* (Gide's and not the story of Tityrus) lies in the fact that its rebel is more bound by habit, memoranda, and convention than anyone else. He argues the necessity of deracination, and finally takes a one-day trip outside Paris with the sensible Angèle. But only the unrebellious Hubert and Roland have the courage to go to Biskra. (The one-day trip fell by ill-chance on a Saturday, and of course one had to return to Paris for Sunday-morning worship.) The author of "Paludes" is also trapped by the "revolutionary" book he is writing; it stands between him and the enjoyment of "life," from which he is compelled as a writer to profit. His function is to be the person who writes "Paludes"; after finishing it, he begins at once on "Polders."

The *saugrenu* of *Paludes* derives from the second part of *Le Voyage d'Urien*; Ellis has become Angèle. The calculated formlessness and sprightly playing with ideas take us much closer to *Le Prométhée mal enchaîné*, however; souls are no longer landscapes, except for purposes of ridicule. Even *Les Caves du Vatican* would be no freer of sensuous detail and surface subjectivity. The liveliness of the satire and coolness of the humor almost totally conceal the personal compulsion under which *Paludes* was written. The fact remains that though Gide makes fun of the unliberated liberator, he fully approves his doctrine. The self which we must now dissolve is no longer the frustrating and unseen superego, nor the perceived sense of guilt. It is rather the self formed by habit and custom, by inertia, by the docile logic of everyday civilized living. But this impulse to awaken from a complacent somnambulism is not treated subjectively at all. Sartre would dramatize these problems more massively in *L'Age de raison*, and *Paludes* is beyond doubt an anticipation of literary existentialism—though the revolt preached by Sartre and Camus seems an inevitable and recurrent reaction to a mechanized age, and to a society as conservative and restrictive as the French. In terms of Gide's own development, the self-satire of *Paludes* marks an important progress toward the critical, detached subjectivity of *L'Immoraliste*. It is indeed hard to conceive how Gide could have written, after such a cool book, the uninhibited *Nourritures terrestres*. In many ways *Paludes* seems a more mature work than the famous testament which followed it. (pp. 58-71)

Albert J. Guerard, in his Andre Gide, second edition, *Cambridge, Mass.: Harvard University Press, 1969, 287 p.*

Germaine Brée   (essay date 1963)

[*Brée is a French-born American critic and translator. Her critical works are devoted to modern French literature and include* Marcel Proust and Deliverance from Time *(1955) and* The French Novel from Gide to Camus *(1962). In the following excerpt from* Gide, *her comprehensive study of Gide's works, Brée examines theme and style in* Marshlands, Prometheus Misbound, Isabelle, *and* Theseus.]

Marshlands (1895)—a "satire of what?"—is an impertinent, rather contemptuous glance backward at the "path of dreams," the "submissive gestures," and the limited horizons of Gide's early work.

> I know that a soul implies a gesture
>
> From which a certain sonority radiates.

In 1893 Gide had made the gesture. His first two trips to North Africa, where he spent the winters of 1893-1894 and 1894-1895, were not merely touristic forays. His *Journal* and writings show that by 1893 he had surreptitiously become detached from the strict tenets of religious and social orthodoxy which his mother had so firmly instilled in him. These first of many journeys released in Gide a streak of restlessness, a taste almost for vagabondage which was eventually to take him far afield: all over Western Europe, several times to Africa, from Algeria to the Congo, to Egypt, to Greece and to Russia. They did not entirely break the shackles of a certain asceticism in Gide's way of life, as reflected in his persistent indifference to any luxury or beauty in his surroundings and to the lack of concern for comfort, even for conveniences, which his acquaintances often mention. But in contact with the vitality of people living in primitive conditions Gide divested himself of the strait jacket of repression which had so hampered him. At last he succeeded in coming to grips with the outside world.

First his voyage, then a long convalescence in Algeria following his bout with tuberculosis, opened to him a larger vision of existence and new worlds of feeling. The new joys that beckoned him awoke a sensuous appetite which Gide indulged freely though somewhat self-consciously. Still with some posing, to be sure, he seems to have discovered that life was infused with inexhaustible delights. For the first time he appears to have tasted the irresponsible joys of a schoolboy on a long, sunny summer vacation. His new freedom, from both family and literary friends, and his convalescence seem to have introduced him to manifold phenomena of existence and accustomed him to thinking of the joys of the senses as a laudable source of pleasure rather than of sin. His long-repressed sexual desires began to seem legitimate: flesh and spirit then were perhaps not necessarily enemies? With alacrity Gide began to accustom his senses to pleasures he had hitherto reproved. The whole mood of his writing changes, illuminated, sometimes rather fatuously still, by these newly found pleasures.

With Gide, however, literature is never very far in the background. His African journeys could hardly have been better timed. The brilliant coterie of talented young men— Valéry and Claudel among them—who had gravitated around Mallarmé were showing signs of restlessness. Although still respected, sometimes adulated, Mallarmé was not their only master. Symbolism was on the wane and its succession was open. The ephemeral school of "naturism" had appeared with its "back to nature" slogan. Whitman, Dostoevsky and Nietzsche were the new constellations in the French literary sky. Everything challenged an ambitious young writer—and Gide was ambitious—to try himself in new directions. Gide moved from his symbolic tales to the satirical *Marshlands* and to the direct lyricism of *Fruits of the Earth* with apparent ease.

"I had demanded from my mind such a denial of the reality of appearances," Gide wrote of his symbolist stage, "that the variegated pattern and diversity of the outer world and the veil of the Maya had lost all importance for me, which is extremely dangerous for an artist." The veil of the Maya (the shimmering beauty of appearances) was greatly to preoccupy him in the next phase of his work. For a while he put aside problems of being and appearance, image, symbol and idea. With many of his contemporaries he turned to the living world he had previously scorned.

His emancipation favored the release of latent creative forces. Almost all Gide's later work took shape in his mid-twenties, between 1893 and 1896. Writing to his friend Marcel Drouin, during the winter of 1894-95, Gide outlined his program:

> Aside from work add my correspondence with my mother, and you will see what is left for the terribly tough translation of Novalis, for *Marshlands* which isn't getting done, and for all the rest I'm trying to do at the same time: *Philoctetes*, which I finished *preparing* in Engadine,

and of which some passages are written; *Proserpine* the novel I told you about in La Roque . . . the volume "of pure lyricism" on which I am working more particularly. . . .

He referred here to *Fruits of the Earth*, and already he had in mind *The Immoralist, Strait Is the Gate*, and **The Pastoral Symphony**, and mentioned *Bathsheba*, **Theseus**, and *Saul* in *Fruits of the Earth*.

Returning briefly to Paris between his first two trips, Gide looked with dismay and detachment at the narrowness of the horizons that had previously encircled him:

> I brought back with me, on returning to France, the secret of a man resurrected, and suffered at first the same kind of abominable anguish that Lazarus must have felt after he rose from the grave. Nothing that had occupied me earlier seemed important any more. How had I been able to breathe in the stifling atmosphere of the salons and coteries, where all their vain agitation . . . stirred up a dusty smell of death. This state of "estrangement" (which I suffered from particularly when I was with my own family) might very possibly have led me to suicide, were it not for the relief I found in describing it ironically in **Marshlands**.

"Estrangement" in the literary salons, but even more at home. . . . Gide-Lazarus was never again to feel in harmony with that milieu outside which his cousin Madeleine Rondeaux was never to venture. The curtain had now gone up on the intimate conflict which *Et nunc manet in te (Madeleine)* eventually disclosed, hence the gravity of the crisis and the temptation of suicide. **Marshlands** reduces these feelings to a kind of absurdity.

What Gide attacked in **Marshlands** was the suffocating atmosphere of the literary coterie, the disintegration of "days into little elusive hours," the sense of stagnation and his own feelings of bewilderment.

> I had new things to say, yet it was impossible now to speak to them [his former friends]. I wished I could persuade them and give them my message, but none of them stopped to listen. They went on living; they kept on going, and the things that satisfied them seemed to me so paltry that I could have cried out in despair at not having been able to persuade them.

Holding his new message in reserve for *Fruits of the Earth*, Gide made an all-out attack on literary life in Paris through the thinly disguised figure of a not very Vergilian Tityrus in **Marshlands**.

At the center of his tale is an unnamed author involved in the writing of a book, *Paludes (Marshlands)*, whose message he tries vainly to communicate in an ever-rising hubbub of inane comment and argument. Gide tells us that three factors merged to give him the idea for his story: his own mood, one of Goya's sketches, and a few lines in Vergil's first eclogue. Goya's sketch portrayed a harassed intellectual, head in hands, surrounded by a tormenting circle of hostile people. Vergil's Tityrus, in words familiar to all schoolboys who studied Latin, claimed that, although he possessed only a small stretch of marsh, it was his and he was content with it. Gide's writer is quite clearly in the position of Goya's intellectual; as for Tityrus, he symbolizes everything that irritated Gide in Paris. In addition, *Marshlands* is a semifacetious, semibitter parody and satire of Gide's own previous literary endeavors. Gide's hero, or rather antihero, is a narrator-writer who keeps an agenda, writes notes with his novel in view, and writes a novel concerning a hero who keeps an agenda—the height of complexity. He works with Gide's former landscape of mud, moors, swamp and stagnant waters, but now it characterizes not Gide himself but the "woeful soul" of the writer's hero, Tityrus. Even the paradisiac and crystalline forms of which the *Narcissus* speaks are parodied in a fable about salt mines, peopled with slaves. Gide later remarked:

> I had the greatest difficulty in getting a new foothold on reality and in relinquishing the theories of that school (I mean the one formed by Mallarmé's followers) which tended to present reality as an accidental contingency and wanted the work of art to escape from its grip.

"*Urien's Voyage* made it possible for me to laugh in *Marshlands*," he wrote. Parodying himself, Gide attacks by indirection, pushing the literary processes of the symbolists to their most absurd consequences: in his marshes Tityrus angles for nothing, swallows earthworms with relish; the would-be author loads his text with rare words and elaborate epithets, he takes trips to the botanical gardens—all to give a concrete content to a most dismal inner landscape. Having finished *Marshlands*, Gide's author begins *Polders*. Pretty openly Gide is accusing his symbolist friends of going around in circles in their own little worlds. In fact, everything in *Marshlands* goes in circles: events, characters, objects. Everything is "small"; the "little pondweeds" in the Aquarium; the "little Aquarium"; the "little ventilator" in the "little salon" of Angela, the writer's patient friend, who runs a small literary salon; the "little journey" he and Angela undertake: "Toward evening I felt a little tired and, after dinner I went over to sleep at Angela's. . . . She was alone. As I entered she was playing a Mozart sonatina with precision on a newly tuned piano. . . . She had lit all the candles in candlesticks and put on a dress with a small check pattern."

Marshlands is the story of a writer disgusted with the petty monotony of his life who, to express his disgust, hits upon the symbol of Tityrus in his marsh. During a short, incomplete week running from Tuesday evening to Sunday evening we see the man struggling with his projected book and, because of it, waging a hopeless antistagnation campaign with everyone around him. The fight culminates at Angela's dinner party where the narrator finds himself in the position of Goya's figure. All eyes are upon him, jarring voices pick up the word "Marshlands," throwing it at him like a sort of accusation: "*Marshlands*, what is *Marshlands*?" "You should put that into *Marshlands*."

Gide gives his story a rapid circular movement, introducing an amazingly mechanical device of repetition, a framework from which he draws his more obvious comical effects:

> Tuesday: At six o'clock in came my great friend Hubert; he was on his way from riding school.
>
> He said: "I say! Are you working?"
>
> I replied: "I am writing *Marshlands*."
>
> Thursday: At six o'clock in came my great friend Hubert; he was on his way back from a business committee meeting . . .
>
> . . . At this moment someone came up the stairs; it was Martin. He said: "I say! Are you working?"
>
> At this moment someone came up the stairs; it was Alexander, the philosopher. He said: "I say! Are you working?"
>
> Sunday: At six o'clock in came my great friend Gaspard. He was on his way from fencing school. He said: "I say! Are you working?"
>
> I replied: "I am writing *Polders*."

The same small mechanical patterns with the same slight variations characterize the narrator's life as he solemnly records it in his agenda:

> In my agenda there are two parts: on one page I write what I am going to do, and on the opposite page I write every evening what I have done. Then I compare. I subtract and what I have not done, or the deficit, becomes what I ought to have done.

This, he notes, introduces the "unexpected" into his life. Thus Wednesday's page reads:

> Try to get up at six o'clock. . . .
>
> Write to Gustave and Leo.
>
> Feel astonished at not having received a letter from Jules. Call on Gontran.

And here comes the announced play of the unexpected:

> Wednesday: I opened my agenda to the coming Saturday, and on the page for that day I read: "Try to get up at six"—I crossed it out.
>
> Friday: On the agenda, as soon as I got up, I read "Try to get up at six." It was eight o'clock; I took up my pen; I crossed it out.

Since even in a short week the unexpected is monotonously repeated, the hero revolts against the insignificant round of habits that circumscribes his life, a small revolt but an anguished one. His protest rises like a monotonous leitmotif throughout the tale, becoming increasingly violent:

> Our lives, Angela, I assure you, are a good deal duller and more mediocre [than Tityrus'].
>
> Really, we must try to put a little variety into our lives.
>
> We ought to try to stir up our lives a little.
>
> Angela . . . we ought to try to put a little variety into our lives.

When the narrator describes the lives of his friends, Richard and Hubert, summarizing them in a few lines, he reduces them to a Tityrus-like marsh: Hubert's exciting panther hunt becomes an anecdotal demonstration of Hubert's inane activity. The touching story of the nightwork secretly undertaken by Richard and his wife is an anecdotal form of Richard's inane virtue. The narrator's own account of his duck-hunting expedition and his little journey with Angela are only other examples of their symbolically aquariumlike existence. By repeating his parody in this manner on various levels and through diverse techniques Gide produced in **Marshlands** a kind of literary version of the "mobile," an infinitely amusing abstract and airy structure, which showed considerable technical mastery and a new flexibility.

Marshlands, the book the hero is writing, is as strange an object as the cuttlefish egg in *The Amorous Attempt*, and far more elusive as it develops and begins to impose itself. To the questions: What is *Marshlands*? and Who is Tityrus? the narrator at first gives a simple answer. *Marshlands*? . . . a book. Or again, "It is primarily the story of those who are not able to travel." Or, "It is the story of a bachelor who lives in a tower, entirely surrounded by marshes." At first Tityrus is mostly the narrator's friend Richard, happy in his mediocrity. The subject of *Marshlands*? "What I wanted to express is *the* emotion my life has given me: the boredom, the emptiness, the monotony." But once the book is on its way it retroacts and something unforeseen occurs. Tityrus comes alive and begins to change. Like his creator, he starts to think about his marsh. "I am Tityrus!" the writer exclaims, forgetting that Tityrus is supposed to be odious, and he writes: "Tityrus smiles." From that point on, fascinated by his symbol, the narrator sees everything in its light; Tityrus shows up all the marshlike sides of life. Tityrus gathers strength and substance: now he is Hubert, Angela, everyone. He becomes an exemplary figure, man, in one of his fundamental attitudes toward life. He is man "recubans," lying down. From symbol he has become myth—a burlesque myth around which everything revolves.

The narrator's relation with his hero also changes. As soon as Tityrus becomes more complex than a mere symbol he escapes from his creator. At Angela's dinner party all speak of Tityrus in various ways: psychological, ethical, metaphysical. He raises all the problems of man's fate. And suddenly, harassed and perspiring, the narrator has a kind of illumination, an *idea*, which turns on the word "retrospection." Up to now, as his agenda showed, he has lived backwards. Each day his agenda marked what he did not do and this becomes his program of action for the next day. He is always in deficit with regard to the past. Hence his boredom and his unchanging marshland. In contrast, now, he hits upon the idea of the "free act," the spontaneous act, the act not written down in advance, the act "to come." In the heat of the ensuing discussion the obsessive theme of stagnation is pushed into the background. The arguments revolve around the concept of the free act. Is it possible? Is it ethical? Here Tityrus stalls and the narrator's book halts with him. But, breaking the round of routine, the theme of travel asserts itself: the hero and Angela go on their unsuccessful little journey, as Hubert and Roland leave for North Africa. At least the narrator has

transmitted his feelings for a short while, if only to Angela. As for the rest, as he has said throughout the book, "I don't mind it myself, because I am writing *Marshlands*." But he comes back and as he sits down to write *Polders* one of his "great friends" drops in and the merry-go-round begins again.

Complex, full of fun and humor, economical in its devices, Gide's **Marshlands** is a little masterpiece; it stirs up a world of ideas. It is a kind of manifesto too, and an act of independence which was not greatly appreciated at the time. Gide's little satire—or sotie, as he called it, using a medieval term—has its serious side. It describes the genesis of a work of art as Gide conceived it at the time. Tityrus is to the fictional author of *Marshlands* what Urien had been to Gide. Both are symbols of a mood. Tityrus and all his activities offer a consistent image of stagnation. But a mood is a shifting thing. As Gide's writer struggles along with his narrative, notes, agenda, discussions, he becomes detached from his initial symbol. Now he uses it as one might use a pair of glasses to examine a heterogeneous number of unrelated aspects of his everyday existence. And so the mood, which had produced the image, now moves from image to idea as the writer begins to interpret in its light both the inner and outer implications with which he is grappling. Tityrus now begins to grow, to embody all that stagnates; now it is about Tityrus, his attitude in life and his significance that everyone argues. The image of stagnation has moved away from its limited, subjective origin. The fictional *Marshlands* will now express the writer's temporary point of view, but with a detachment which allows him to raise any number of general questions concerning human living. But, since Tityrus is a character, living in his own world, however simplified, the interpretations he elicits will forever be a matter for argument. Tityrus raises questions; Gide does not resolve them.

Gide's *Marshlands* contains a theory of creativity. Instead of being a "denial of the reality of appearances," the work of art is the temporary unification and interpretation of appearances, organized through an interplay of image and idea.

—Germaine Brée

By a dynamic dialectical process the character Gide imagined can retroact upon the writer and produce within the work complementary new ideas which in the beginning it did not contain. The idea of stagnation in itself excludes the idea of adventure. But in **Marshlands** both the desire for adventure and its need arise from the anguish with which the narrator envisages stagnation. The two contradictory ideas are there, though indirectly, pulling at his little tale, inciting the restlessness which is the source of his writing.

Gide's **Marshlands** contains a theory of creativity. Instead of being a "denial of the reality of appearances," the work of art is the temporary unification and interpretation of appearances, organized through an interplay of image and idea. As it had been for poets since Baudelaire, the image is the core of this work. It is still pre-eminently literary in its origin, emanating from the classics Gide knew well, and so lends itself to a certain intellectualization, suggesting, rather than other images, an idea. The idea suggests certain limits within which to work and, in turn, becomes a factor of expansion. A work of art in this sense is a proposition, as Gide said, which by a kind of autogeneration suggests its antithesis. The narrator in *Marshlands* may sit down again to write *Polders*. Gide, for his part, has finished with his marshlands. Menalcas, the man of free acts and adventure, follows Tityrus. *Fruits of the Earth* is in the offing.

The Gidian dialogue is now in operation as a creative process. Each of Gide's literary works answers the preceding one, illuminating what the other left in shadow. In the sense that each is "critical," as Gide said, and voluntarily organized to disclose in depth one chosen aspect of life, it is also, by indirection, ironical. Momentarily proportions are distorted, life is stylized, until finally the forces waiting in the dark rise once more to the surface and Gide, having carried us along in his adventure, returns us to a reality newly grasped. Without returning to the realism he detested, Gide had moved away from the dead end of symbolism. Finally, *Marshlands* formulates the two closely related ideas—the free act and the open future—which apply to all Gide's future novels. (pp. 54-65)

. . . . .

Gide's *Prometheus Misbound* . . . deals with the human lot, but in [an] . . . amusing and devious way. In its blending of disparate tones *Prometheus* recalls *Marshlands*. To the reader's surprise it starts with the matter-of-factness of a police report, in spite of the ominous background suggested by the title:

> In the month of May, 189-, at two o'clock in the afternoon, the following incident was seen which might have appeared odd.

> On the boulevard which leads from the Madeleine to the Opera, a stout middle-aged gentleman, whose unusual corpulence alone distinguished him, was accosted by a thin gentlemen, who smilingly, and, in our opinion, without ill intention, handed to the first a handkerchief which he had just let fall. The stout gentleman thanked him briefly and was about to continue his way, when, changing his mind, he leaned toward the thin person, and must have asked him for some information . . .

A banal anecdote whose sequel is still "odder." For the stout gentleman hands an envelope to the thin one who writes an address, then:

> The thin gentleman . . . had not had time to smile a goodbye, when the stout gentleman, to express his thanks, slapped his hand abruptly on the other's cheek . . . and disappeared. . . .

In spite of the prosaic, factual tone, a dozen questions are raised by this curious anecdote: Why the slap? To whom is the envelope addressed and what is its content? What happened next? A slight shock is in store for the reader, with the casual remark concerning the stout man: "I learned afterwards that it was Zeus, the banker." A little later Prometheus walks into a café on the same boulevard. Zeus and Prometheus, on a Paris boulevard? What connection can there be between the incongruous behavior of the banker and the grandeur of those Aeschylian adversaries?

In the circumscribed setting of the café at the intersection of the two Paris boulevards, Gide introduces a strange set of people. There it is whispered that Zeus, the banker or "Miglionaire," the giver of the slap, is God Almighty:

> —Do you know what people say? the waiter asked the banker.

> —What do they say?

> —That you are God Himself.

> —Let them say it, he answered.

The mythical hero Prometheus soon drops in, singularly transformed:

> When, on the top of the Caucasus, Prometheus had fully realized that his chains, fetters, strait jackets, parapets and other scruples were all in all making him feel very stiff, in order to change position he rose on his left side, stretched out his right arm, and, between four and five o'clock in autumn, walked down the boulevard which leads from the Madeleine to the Opera.

Out of another realm come two characters familiar to all schoolboys who struggled with Latin: the one-eyed Cocles, defender of his country, and Damocles, the courtier seated for all eternity at a banquet with a sword held by a hair dangling over his head. Fresh out of Gide's own *Marshlands* appear Angela and Tityrus, joined soon after by another character, Meliboeus, the flute-player taken, like Tityrus, from Vergil's *Eclogues*: a curiously anachronistic group with whom the waiter in the café enjoys chatting. By its very absurdity so burlesque a situation destroys any preconceived notion the reader may have had of Gide's purpose, and whets his curiosity.

After the initial anecdote, Gide's *Prometheus* proceeds by leaps and bounds through dialogues and speeches, each more startling than the one before. Ideas spark in all directions: What is a gratuitous act? An idiosyncrasy? Are eagles to be cherished? The brilliant profusion and baffling incongruity of realistic details, the rapid tempo of the action, the disparities and contrasts in style, and the nonchalant tempo of the whole are the complex ingredients which Gide uses in order thoroughly to mystify his reader.

As each character in turn moves to the front of the stage, caught as if by a moving spotlight, it may seem at first as if Gide is focusing his attention entirely on the events and the dialogue. At this point the satire seems droll, somewhat frivolous, and rather superficial. The narrator entitles the first part of his tale "A chronicle of Private Morality": "I shall say nothing about public morality," he warns, "because there's no such thing." He exploits the rather facile comic effects that arise from the unexpected transformation of a serious myth into prosaic modern reality. Prometheus, asked to state his profession, declares himself to be a manufacturer of matches. Sometimes Gide indulges in sheer impertinence: since Prometheus can give no satisfactory account of his occupations, the waiter classifies him as a man of letters. Sometimes he plays with the legend allowing Prometheus to set aside his self-imposed chains or reversing the laws of perspective for the descent of Prometheus's eagle among the café habitués:

> A bird, which seemed enormous from a distance, was seen at close quarters to be not so large after all.

And there are many witty exchanges in the dialogue in the best tradition of the boulevards. The most comical and at the same time disruptive element in the satire is the precariously ambivalent seriousness with which each of the motley crew of characters insists on playing the role assigned him, however incongruous it may seem in relation to the situation as a whole.

Is there any other purpose to Gide's novel-sotie? All Gide ever said about it when he re-edited it much later was that he had hardly had to change a word. Should it be read as an arbitrary and somewhat haphazard improvisation? Everything suggests, rather, that the complex and funny superstructure of the work is built on very solid foundations, that it has unity and makes sense.

Three seemingly unrelated stories are told in the course of the tale, from various points of view: the story of Cocles and Damocles; the story of Prometheus and his eagle, and, related by Prometheus himself, the story of Tityrus, Angela and Meliboeus. The first part of the sotie focuses mainly on Cocles and Damocles; the second on Prometheus; the third on Tityrus. Each part concludes with a marked change in the relationship of Prometheus with his eagle. At the end of the first part the eagle, descending upon the Parisian café, smashes its glass front and accidentally puts out one of Cocles's eyes. "Prometheus took leave of the waiter and of Cocles, and as he slowly made his way back to the Caucasus he pondered: 'Shall I sell it?—wring its neck? . . . or tame it, perhaps?'"

At the end of the second part the eagle triumphs: "Gentlemen," Prometheus proclaims, "you must love my eagle." As the *sotie* ends, with total disregard for his legend, Prometheus has killed his eagle and is eating it for dinner with his friends. The eagle, clearly, has a leading part in the whole. But exactly how is it connected with the story of Tityrus? And what did Gide mean by his title describing Prometheus as neither bound nor unbound, but illbound or misbound? The facts in the case are the following:

Zeus drops a handkerchief. He asks Cocles, who picks it up by chance, to give him an address, any address. Zeus carries an envelope containing 500 francs—a meager sum today but quite considerable at the time—which he sends to the address chosen at random by Cocles, whom he then slaps. Zeus' activity amounts to just this; it is quite trivial. Cocles and Damocles meet by chance in a café near the Madeleine, ruled over by a bustling and officious waiter.

Prometheus chances to come by. The waiter quite gratuitously brings the three characters together:

> The restaurant here is very well arranged; with tables for three. . . . Tables for three, yes, I've found very convenient. Three gentlemen arrive; we introduce them . . . Then they sit down . . . they talk. . . . I set relationships going; I listen, I scrutinize, I direct the conversation. When dinner is over I know three inner beings, three personalities! But they don't. As for me, you understand, I listen, I relate; they undergo the relationship.

This is all the waiter ever does. His role, like that of Zeus', is strictly limited.

In contrast Cocles and Damocles have a story to tell for which Zeus is, in part, responsible. "I have led a perfectly ordinary life," says Damocles, "and made a duty of this formula: to resemble the commonest of men." The mystery of the 500 francs, coming out of the blue, makes him unique among men. Consumed with anxiety, Damocles first looks in vain for his benefactor and then dies, worried to death by his unresolved problem. Cocles, an average, moderately good, nondescript man was strolling down the boulevard in search of some opportunity to distinguish himself from other men. Kindly, he picks up the handkerchief. The blow he receives undeservedly revolts him by its injustice so that when, accidentally, the eagle later puts out his eye, he is transformed into a man with a grievance, hence a cause.

Zeus moves and acts in the most irresponsible way, and admits it:

> I am rich, richer than anyone can imagine. You belong to me; he belongs to me; everything belongs to me. . . . My influence on Paris is hidden, but it isn't any the less important. It is hidden because I don't follow through. Yes, above all I have a spirit of initiative. I launch. Then, when some affair is launched, I leave it; I don't touch it again.

> The Waiter: Isn't it true that your actions are gratuitous?

> The Miglionaire: I alone, he alone whose wealth is infinite, can act with absolute disinterestedness; man, no. Thence my love of gambling; not of gain, understand, of gambling. . . . I gamble by lending to men. . . . I play but I hide my cards. I experiment. . . what I lend to Man, what I plant in him, it amuses me to see that it grows; it amuses me to see it growing.

Amoral and absurd, he plants anxiety or revolt, gives eagles, plays with man, all to no purpose. The waiter, on his level, despite what Zeus says, is equally irresponsible.

But neither Cocles nor Damocles can accept Zeus' irresponsibility and the random nature of the circumstances that have affected them. Moral and rational themselves, they insist upon introducing moral evaluations and logic everywhere. Damocles, having received an unexplained gift, feels indebted to the giver—an idea quite foreign to Zeus. Damocles must find a reason for what occurred: "I pondered a great deal, in accordance with the best methods of inquiry: *Cur, unde, quo, qua?*—whence, wherefore, how, why?"

Whereas Damocles searches for a cause, Cocles concentrates on consequences: reparation for the injustice done him. Damocles dies and Cocles prospers in line with his own, more aggressive temperament.

> Gentlemen, declares Prometheus, whatever we do, we shall never escape from begging the question. What does it mean, to beg the question? Gentlemen, if I may venture to say so, begging the question is always an assertion of temperament; for where principles are lacking, assertion of temperament steps in.

There is no way out of the *petitio principii*, the logical fallacy here described by Prometheus, which consists in disguising in a premise the proposition to be proved. Why does Prometheus propose that every man have an eagle? Because he himself has an eagle. Why does Zeus perform gratuitous acts? Because it is in his nature so to do. Why do Cocles and Damocles react so violently to Zeus' gratuitous act? Because it is in their natures to establish rational links of cause and effect. They and we are all exactly in the position of the Parisians in Prometheus's final tale: having seen the nude flute player, Meliboeus, walk down the boulevard with Angela, they grabbed the evening papers "and suddenly everyone learned that the woman was Angela, and this Meliboeus was someone without any clothes on who was going to Italy."

Gide brought together his heterogeneous group of characters in a kind of fable to suggest to his readers, or perhaps even more to explain to himself, the new world view which he now held and of which they are the "givens." "I would like to be able to consider the works of an artist as a complete microcosm," Gide wrote at that time, "entirely *strange* but including the whole complexity of life." **Prometheus** is just such a microcosm. In Gide's world neither Zeus nor Prometheus has supernatural powers. They did not create Cocles and Damocles nor do they control them. All the characters exist on the same level of equality. Zeus may drop his handkerchief, but he obliges no one to pick it up. Prometheus proposes that men should adopt eagles; he cannot order them to do so. There is a very clearheaded and reasonable point of view behind Gide's allegory. Zeus symbolizes the elements of a determinism which man can neither understand nor explain because it *is* his very existence. Zeus creates the random situation, which in itself has no sense and need have no further consequence. Cocles and Damocles are drawn into his game only by chance. He has no hidden fate specifically in store for them.

But Zeus does, unwittingly, challenge something basic in the two men: their need to make sense. Since this is impossible, the very existence of Zeus will be felt by them as absurd, as a sickness. Zeus' role is discussed from five points of view, within the framework of the sotie, and never yields anything further. Like the existentialists, Gide had come to accept the notion of the incomprehensibility, in human terms, of man's position in the natural world. Zeus has lost his power on the human level, and the questions

man asks have no value other than human; Zeus has no use for them.

The waiter's café is the place where, already troubled by Zeus, Cocles and Damocles meet, on the initiative of the waiter. Here social connections are established and idiosyncrasies revealed, but nothing more happens until Prometheus, who after all is the hero of the tale, enters the game.

Prometheus is a very disruptive character. Even his voice, in spite of himself, is disturbing: "his voice, after that of the others, immediately seemed so deep that everyone realized that until then he had been silent." He alone is not limited to the drab, small world of the café. He has had a long and varied past history and, in the course of the story, goes back and forth from the Caucasian Mountains to the boulevard; he is at one moment confined in a prison that "was isolated from the rest of the world and from which nothing could be seen but the sky," where he enjoyed an ecstatic solitude. Like the waiter, he speaks with Zeus; he is the only character to sympathize with Damocles's misfortune; he gives lectures and makes speeches. His eagle smashes windows, puts out eyes, and the pair cause considerable trouble wherever they appear.

Although he doesn't realize it, Prometheus is a stranger among men, a Gulliver in a world of Lilliputians. What is more, unlike the other characters, he freely and constantly changes. First, by his own choosing, he was tied to the Caucasus; tired of this posture, he decided to take a look at Paris. He calls forth his eagle more or less at will and when he decides to do so he kills it. His convictions change as much as he does: he first says he loves men; then that he loves only what devours them; he did not always have an eagle. With pathetic eagerness, before he kills his own, he insists that all men must have an eagle. Then he makes obscure and facetious remarks, quite varied in tone. He spends his time freeing himself—from his chains, from his prison, from his eagle. The Gidian Prometheus, with the inner depth of his voice, seems to embody man's inner drive to transcend his fate.

For Gide, all human possibilities, adventures and tragedies seem to originate from the ever-present and eruptive power of Prometheus, restricted though it be by the flat and rigid limitations of human existence. In the satire Prometheus acts out some of these adventures: the chains, the eagle, finally the carefree irresponsibility suggested by Meliboeus.

Like Zeus and the waiter, Prometheus is amoral and irresponsible. But, each time, he is himself involved in his own game, undergoing an inner metamorphosis. What is more, he feels he must draw all men into the game. From his own relations with his eagle he draws a gospel which he preaches most pathetically: all men must have eagles. He offers them a highly schematic form of the Nietzschean *amor fati*: Cocles must cherish his wound, in fact deepen it; Damocles must delve deeper into his anguish. But a short while before, feeling a sense of "great expectation," he had preached with equal conviction a doctrine of progress, and later he produces Meliboeus, the carefree nude flute player on his way to Rome.

Prometheus is a dangerous character, persuading Damocles, for example, to cultivate an inner anguish for which Damocles pays with his life. He is the great deceiver, the only deceiver in fact in the microcosm in which he moves, disregarding the limits imposed on human beings by the chance circumstance of the human lot. The Prometheus in us, Gide suggests, is always "misbound," and ready to teach us how to play with fire. It is he, not Zeus, who cultivates chains and eagles. At the instigation of Prometheus, nondescript human beings start out along dangerous paths, and in so doing test out their possibilities. But somewhere along the way they must, they will, encounter Zeus.

So, the freedom of human beings can of necessity be maintained only by a precarious equilibrium. For Gide, man's ethical freedom is analogous to the artist's: he must create a harmonious whole out of separate, incongruous "givens," of which one at least will always be unique, his own idiosyncrasy.

In his subsequent work Gide takes up his characters at the point where Prometheus abandons them. Had Zeus been a writer, he would no doubt have written a naturalistic novel; the waiter would have composed a drama of psychological analysis and Prometheus would have created a problem novel. Gide with his flexible point of view will write the story of men who attempt to live coherently in an incoherent world, who commit themselves to absolutes in a universe of shifting variables and relativity. "Man serves one or several gods in himself," wrote Gide, "before he projects his faith into the skies."

Brilliant and significant in Gide's development as this sotie is, it is too stylized, too complicated perhaps to attain any great intrinsic value of its own. Gide, incidentally, was quite willing more or less transparently to make fun of himself in his own sotie. Prometheus, shackled by his own scruples to his Caucasian rock, a melancholy preacher to whom no one listens; Damocles, on whom Zeus bestows a sum of money; Cocles, who devotes himself to good works—in a mock-heroic vein, all seem aspects of Gide himself. The story of Tityrus, with which the book ends, is a kind of allegorical summation of young Gide's own life. Tityrus, in his marshland, plants a seed; it turns into a tree which calls for a garden, gardeners, a whole organized city, until at last, devoured by the ensuing responsibilities, Tityrus gives up the tree, as Prometheus gave up his eagle.

Gide was no longer a man to allow eagles, trees, books or prophets to devour him; he intended to follow his own path and keep his freedom. But Prometheus also touches lightly upon another matter of great importance to Gide: the strenuous effort he was making, along with others in his generation, to solve to his own satisfaction such literary problems as those of vision and form, the adaptation of traditional forms to changing intellectual perspectives. The writer is a kind of Prometheus too, but a Prometheus whose own work commits him as Prometheus can never be committed. Gide suggests that the very writing of the work and its completion gives limits to the idea that fashioned it—"informed" it, as Gide would say—those very limits that Prometheus cannot be bound by. (pp. 86-97)

. . . . .

Isabelle is a first-person narrative, told by a young historian and would-be novelist, Gérard Lacase. Gide starts off the tale by making use of a "true story" technique, recalling the real circumstances that inspired the tale: a visit he and his friend Francis Jammes had made several years before to a Norman estate, Formentin, near Gide's own home. Formentin becomes the "Quartfourche" of the story. The abandoned estate had fascinated Gide when he was an adolescent as had the story behind its ruin: family discord, a daughter who squandered family revenues, a child abandoned to servants, the estate burdened with debt, the ruin and final disintegration of a once-prosperous landed family. What the young historian Lacase makes of these facts entirely "taken from outside" is the crux of the Gidian tale.

Gide himself cannot, for once, be confused with the narrator, whom he views with an amused irony and detachment far removed from the underlying emotional involvement which sustains his two preceding récits. The tale is written with a certain briskness, free from most of the mannerisms of style Gide was still cultivating in *Strait Is the Gate*, as he himself recognized.

In line with the oldest conventions of the mystery story, Gide introduces himself and Jammes, along with the fictional Lacase, in the position of listeners to a tale they beg Lacase to tell, thus focusing the reader's attention on the true-story atmosphere and masking the complete artificiality of the device. No man could speak a story with such finished perfection, quoting without hesitation from a letter or reproducing verbatim whole dialogues. But this matters little, for the procedure is used with a quiet deftness and mastery.

The facts Gérard recalls are straightforward and simple. He first came to Quartfourche to do some scholarly research. There he fell among the strangest set of characters: the owners, M. and Mme. de Saint-Auréol; their in-laws, M. and Mme. Floche; a housekeeper, Mlle. Verdure; an abbé; a sullen servant, Gratien; and a young boy, Casimir. Slowly he began to uncover signs of an underlying drama: the portrait of a beautiful girl, an unsent letter written by Isabelle de Saint-Auréol when she was twenty-two to the lover with whom she was to elope that night; the story of the "accidental" death, on that very night, of the young Viscount Blaise de Gonfreville; a nocturnal visit and family scene. . . . The mystery centers on the enigmatic Isabelle and her tragic love affair.

Through Lacase, Gide handles his tale with the skill of a seasoned detective-story writer. Various interpretations are suggested as the story progresses, always on the brink of melodrama, until the very end when unexpectedly Lacase comes face to face with the real Isabelle. In this tale, for the first time, Gide provides a vigorous, realistic setting. The château and its inhabitants are seen with a clarity that contrasts sharply with the vague aura of mystery that finally envelops his bizarre characters as they slowly take on human consistency and depth.

Lacase's arrival seems at first to animate a world of Balzacian grotesques. During the first four chapters each of the strange persons among whom he is staying is scrutinized in turn, and successive keys to the Quartfourche enigma tantalizingly suggested. Are they all mad, as gentle M. Floche suggests? Are they lifeless mechanical puppets who merely exist automatically? Are they sinister and criminal? Which are good, which are bad? Where is the Isabelle of the title? The seriousness with which Lacase tells his story, in which he is deeply involved, is a subterfuge which dissimulates the fun Gide is having with his all-too-naïve historian.

Characteristically, in chapter four, the central chapter of the seven, Gide at last introduces his heroine, but indirectly through a medallion which fascinates Lacase. She is the enigma of the château incarnate. When, in the last chapter, the mystery is dispelled by a set of hard facts, the characters seem to the reader all the more puzzling for their humanization. *Isabelle* leaves our imagination at a "Quartfourche," a crossroads, leading in many directions. Gide successively plays on all kinds of emotions: curiosity, suspense, fear, pity, indignation, moral sense, the need to find out the truth. Casimir, the poor abandoned child, is there to draw a few tears. His transformations in Lacase's eyes are typical of what happens to all the characters. Suspect at first, and morally black, they turn to gray and finally tend to appear white, with the exception of poor Isabelle, who, through a truly Dickensian reversal, moves from pure white to black.

Gide, obviously, knew how to tell a good story and *Isabelle* can be read as such. Yet, as one might expect, his intent was not so simple: "Finished my novel the night before last with too much ease," he noted in his *Journal*, "and this makes me fear that I did not put into the last pages all that it was *incumbent upon me* to put there." The subtitle he had in mind for his tale, "The Pathetic Fallacy," casts light on his intentions, and on his contention that the hero of the story is Lacase rather than Isabelle.

Young Lacase, before he even sets foot at the Saint-Auréols', dreams of participating in the romantic rituals of "château society." The grumpy coachman and rundown carriage sent to meet his train soon warn him of his mistake. Two days with the family prove so utterly boring that, to his hosts' consternation, he plans to leave. Gide is obviously playing with a Pirandellian theme: if Lacase should leave, what would become of the Floches, Saint-Auréols and company, who have just "found an author"? There would be no novel. How would all the fragments Lacase observes and that Gide has taken as data be "related," made into a story? Isabelle is the bait that arouses Lacase's curiosity because Lacase is a sentimental young man. The minute his imagination has settled on this one center of interest, his boredom is dispelled and his curiosity awakened. Item by item he compels the hidden fragments of the puzzle to appear. Though a budding scholar, he had wanted to experience adventure and find material for a novel. Given his heightened sensitivity, a subterranean network of relationships begins to be apparent. But the covert life of Quartfourche that Lacase senses corresponds in reality to his own predilection for the romanesque. Isabelle herself, until the very end, is only seen by him at night. Lacase's secret pursuit of a truth hidden in

shadow is very similar to the task Gide had set himself as a novelist.

For the first time Gide makes use of such hackneyed novelistic devices as hidden letters, secrets pried out of locked writing desks, false-bottomed cabinets—all of which reappear in *Lafcadio's Adventures* and *The Counterfeiters*. They have a double function, suggesting clandestine activities which barely ripple the apparently even surface of life, and, concurrently, marking definite stages in the story, each discovery adding one more link to the chain.

Lacase, of course, falls in love with Isabelle. Historian that he is, on the lookout for all relevant information, he nonetheless singles out only those facts which support his hypothesis and thus fabricates the most ethereal and victimized Isabelle and the most romanesque of love stories. He can make sense of the facts only as they satisfy his own conventional sentimentality.

Later he finds himself face to face with the true Isabelle. The park is now devastated; the owners have died, the child Casimir has been abandoned to the gruff and sullen care of Gratien, the servant. A hard-boiled and discontented Isabelle stares out at Gérard, neither the mechanical doll of one of his dreams nor the sweet and inconsistent Isabelle of his imagination, but a real, impenetrable woman. The pathetic fallacy which had "informed" Lacase's interpretation of the Quartfourche mystery becomes apparent. Lacase immediately loses interest in the real Isabelle. But the reader does not. What is Isabelle really like? Is she really a murderer? A nymphomaniac? A woman who in true Gidian style has ruined her chance for happiness and brought about her lover's death because she feared to live? Isabelle's face, at any rate, as she at last looks out at the reader, is the hard and disconcerting face of reality. Until this point each of the other characters—Lacase, the abbé, Gratien, the Floches, Mlle. Verdure, Mme. de Saint-Auréol—has quite simply interpreted Isabelle according to his or her own idea of what motivates human beings, thereby introducing into the story a human content not inherent in the bare facts and which expresses only their own inner sensitivity. The theme of pathetic fallacy is repeated at all levels, giving Gide's story—as distinguished from Lacase's—its meaning without requiring either explanation or symbol.

Lacase's story in *Isabelle* illustrates the elusive, Protean aspect a set of events assume as soon as one tries to find rational explanations for them from the outside.

—*Germaine Brée*

On the surface *Isabelle* may seem to illustrate only the very commonplace idea that dreams lose their poetry when confronted with reality. In fact, what the tale conveys is that no dream is equal to a reality it can only impoverish or disguise, but never grasp. Lacase's story illustrates the elusive, Protean aspect a set of events assume as soon as one tries to find rational explanations for them from the outside.

The path that Lacase follows as apprentice-novelist is Gide's own. Life, Gide suggests, yields to the novelist's attention only fragmentary, unrelated data. Only when some avid, inner feeling orients the novelist-observer's attention does he begin to relate the facts observed, to grasp their hidden relationships. The "figure in the carpet," as it emerges for Gide, derives its substance from reality but its organization and meaning from the subjective inner impetus that guides the writer's search.

Isabelle emphasizes the twofold relation between the facts objectively observed and the young novelist's subjective mood. A fictional world emerges when the outer and inner worlds are momentarily in equilibrium, a temporary state in a doubly dynamic process which can never be halted. The novelist's work, like Lacase's story, will thus perpetually evolve. As he probes more deeply into the hidden dynamics of human destiny and motivation, the modalities they assume change in his eyes and so will the tale he tells and the perspectives he establishes. Each tale will assume its own form, a form which cannot be repeated. The story told, the writer is free to start again. Lacase is no novelist in Gide's eyes. Like the would-be writer of *Marshlands*, he will only write other stories which mirror his own inner sensitivity.

Isabelle greatly clarifies the place in Gide's work of the two more ample and far more impressive tales, *The Immoralist* and *Strait Is the Gate*. In a way both Michel and Alissa resemble Lacase, pursuing, as he does, an elusive and shadowy face—their own. But the harsh reality Michel and Alissa discover hurts them far more irremediably than the discovery of the real Isabelle could ever hurt Lacase. At least, all three went beyond the insignificant and boring surface that life offers the unthinking. What each perceives is one point of view only, but a point of view that opens on a vast and turbulent Protean reality. The writer, by maintaining unchanged throughout the story the particular nature of the characters' relation to the world about them, their pathetic fallacy, rounds out and completes what in real life can only be tentative, temporary, incomplete. Gide seems to hint that the perfect organization and tonal unity of his own récits derive from a form of pathetic fallacy, literary rather than sentimental. He was now impatient with the limitations imposed upon the récit by the tonal unity it required and the tremendous effort it demanded of the writer. To write as Jerome might, in a rather dull, pedestrian way, had proved one of the major difficulties he encountered when working on *Strait Is the Gate*. In *Isabelle*, with Lacase's descriptions of the novel's rather burlesque set of characters, Gide was experimenting with certain deliberate breaks in tonality, juxtaposing satire and pathos. (pp. 169-75)

. . . . .

Theseus is made to order for Gide: his successes and trials, his amorous adventures and devotion to the public cause, his tolerance, and the freedom and strength of his life and personality. Gide had first been charmed by the less edifying sides of his hero's life. In *Fruits of the Earth* Theseus is cited among the famous lovers who have known how not to be faithful. Theseus' impertinent good luck in his love affairs and his infidelities become, in Gidian language, the refusal to "get stuck." The slight connotation of vulgarity in the expression suggests the almost imperceptible vein of indecency with which Gide handled the erotic episodes in the tale. He lingered perhaps a little insistently on the voluptuous pleasures of Crete, taking an altogether too special joy in depicting a heterosexual Theseus, a barbarian in Cretan eyes, who, instead of falling in love with the King's son Glaucus, as expected, prefers the charms of the young princess, Phaedra: a completely gratuitous episode invented by Gide for his own delight. But the legendary Cretan atmosphere authorized the nonchalant eroticism with which he endowed his story.

At the time when he was thinking of his "Treatise on the Dioscuri," Gide had already expressed his preference for the benevolent Theseus over the more heroic Hercules. Daedalus, in the récit, explains to Theseus that same preference, inherited from Gide:

> At one time I saw quite a lot of your predecessor, Hercules. He was a stupid fellow, and I could never get anything out of him but heroics. What I did appreciate in him, and what I appreciate in you, is a sort of absorption in the task at hand, an unrecoiling audacity, a temerity even, which thrusts you forward and destroys your opponent. . . . Hercules took greater pains than you do; was more anxious, also, to do well; and was rather melancholy, especially when he had just completed a great exploit. But what I like in you is your joy; that is where you differ from Hercules.

Theseus, as compared to Oedipus, is an entirely sane and healthy hero. The parallel Gide established between the two men is rather amusing: Theseus and Oedipus are both kings' sons, whose births are shrouded in mystery. Both, as young men, start out on the road to adventure and both, at first, perform the same acts: they rid the earth of monsters. Both succeed to the thrones of their fathers under rather ambiguous circumstances. Here Gide gave the legend a slight Freudian twist: On his way back from Crete, the legend tells us, Theseus "forgot" that he had promised Aegeus, his father, to put up a white sail if he had vanquished the Minotaur; the shock of the black sail kills Aegeus—a revealing incident in Gide's eyes. Theseus, therefore, is less innocent than Oedipus, who kills his father Laius by chance, without knowing who he is. Oedipus marries his mother, to be sure, but Theseus is responsible for the death of his son Hippolytus. The two heroes reigned successfully for many years, each over his own city. The balance of crime, ambition, self-sacrifice, service and success is just about even for both. But at this point their fates diverge. Oedipus plunges into disaster and his people undergo a cruel war. Theseus' kingdom prospers and develops in peace. Oedipus is the destroyer of Thebes, Theseus the founder of Athens.

It was particularly pleasing to Gide's imagination that the two legendary heroes lived during the same years, that their paths crossed, that Oedipus died peacefully under the protection of Theseus and that, because of this, Athens obtained the special favor of the gods. Actually Gide saw in the two myths two récits. Theseus and Oedipus could complement each other as had Tityrus and Menalcas in Gide's youth, Michel and Alissa a little later. Gide's Oedipus helped to create Theseus, just as Theseus in turn, when he came into being, modified the figure of Oedipus, which Gide treats much more sympathetically in the récit than he had in the play.

To think of Theseus merely as a projection of Gide himself would limit the scope of the tale. Yet the comparison at times is both pertinent and amusing, as when Theseus declares, surely with Gide in mind:

"No one can deny it: I have, I think, performed some notable services. . . . I've cleaned up certain dangerous byroads on which even the bravest could not venture without trembling; and I've cleared up the skies in such a way that man, his head less bowed, may be less afraid of the unexpected." But Theseus is not Gide, nor is the story a Gidian apologia. Brought up in the manner of Lafcadio, but in a fabulous age, Theseus with his fine equilibrium and limited good sense is no more Gide than are Daedalus and Icarus, whom Theseus encounters in the récit. Gide was particularly fond of this last of his heroes, but treated him with the same affectionate irony as any of his earlier creations.

For **Theseus** Gide used the spoken narrative he had adopted for *The Immoralist*. The Athenian king speaks in a warm, engaging voice for which Gide easily found the right tone, re-creating his own myth for his listeners. The juxtaposition of the mythical universe of ancient Greece and Theseus' familiar matter-of-fact vocabulary is a rich source of poetry and humor. Theseus is as at home in his world as we are in ours, and his feelings, very similar to our own, give our everyday contemporary world a kind of poetic extension into the fabulous. The directness and musicality of Theseus' language acts as a sort of charm and touches the imagination. He comes to life immediately with his first sentence: "It was for my son Hippolytus that I had wanted to tell the story of my life so that he would benefit from it: but he is no more, and I shall tell it just the same." For this storytelling Gide forged a deceptively simple style, rich in controlled modulations. Theseus' description of his arrival at Cnossos, for example, combines the wonder of what he saw with the simple reality of what he felt. For the first, Gide used the long incantatory sentence he had tried out fifty years before in *El Hadj*; for the second, in brilliant contrast, the flat declarative statement with a strong anachronistic flavor:

> I was so overwhelmed by fatigue that I could hardly feel due astonishment at the great courtyard of the palace, or at a monumental balustraded staircase and the winding corridors through which attentive servants, torch in hand, guided me to the second floor, where a room had been set apart for me. All but one of its many lamps were snuffed out after I arrived. The bed was scented and soft; when they left me, I fell at once into a heavy sleep which lasted until the evening of the following day, although I had already slept during our long journey; for only at

> dawn, after traveling all night, had we arrived at Cnossos.

> I am by no means a cosmopolitan. At the court of Minos I realized for the first time that I was Greek, and I felt very far from home.

Theseus uses to good purpose all the resources of style Gide had mastered over the years.

His narrative falls into three parts: the hero's childhood, his journey to Crete and victory over the Minotaur, and the founding of Athens. All Gide's themes appear successively in the various episodes—the sensuous plenitude of childhood, the disciplines necessary to adolescence, the struggle against monsters, and so forth—but are condensed and nourished by the wisdom of a now elderly Theseus, the wisdom of Gide's old age. And it is Gide's voice that breaks through directly in the conclusion with no trace of irony or doubt:

> If I compare my lot with that of Oedipus, I am content. I have fulfilled my destiny. Behind me I leave the city of Athens. It has been dearer to me even than my wife and son. My city stands. After I am gone, my thought will live on there forever. I draw near to a solitary death willingly. I have enjoyed the good things of the earth, and I am happy to think that after me, and thanks to me, men will find that they are happier, better and freer. I worked for the good of those who are to come. I have lived.

All Gide's thought leads to Theseus, and it was a Theseus within himself that he had striven so long to perfect. "I remain a child of this world," says Theseus, "and I believe that man, be he what he may, and whatever his faults, is duty-bound to play out his hand to the end." Many others contribute to this wisdom of Theseus: Aegeus, Minos, Pasiphaë, Ariadne, Daedalus, Icarus, Pirithoüs, and Oedipus all in turn talk with him as a young man, revealing something of importance for him to learn. But the meetings with Daedalus, placed in the center of the story, and the last conversation with Oedipus, at the end, are the two great "moments of truth" for Theseus.

Daedalus, a sculptor, has freed the gods from their traditional hieratic positions, representing them in motion and thereby bringing Mount Olympus down to earth. A man of science like Prometheus, Daedalus has tried to penetrate the secrets of the gods so that, "with the aid of science" he could "mold mankind to the likeness of the gods." Such a two-fold ambition to realize a meeting of gods and men had, in fact, presided at the birth of Theseus, who is himself half-god, half-man. Daedalus thus formulates the idea that Theseus illustrates: man fashioned in the image of humanized gods.

Among all the voices that merge in Theseus' without ever diverting him from his task of founding the city of Athens, there is one that differs from all the others, Oedipus's. Theseus tolerates and even welcomes the man whom Gide had treated so harshly some years before. But he does not understand him, hence the irony and yet the respect in his account of their conversation:

> I am surprised that so little should have been

said about the meeting of our destinies at Colonus, about that moment at the crossroads when our two careers confronted each other. I consider it the summit and crown of my glory. Till then I had forced all life to do obeisance to me, and had seen all my fellow men bow in their turn (excepting only Daedalus; but he was my senior by many years. Besides, even Daedalus gave me best in the end). In Oedipus alone did I recognize a nobility equal to my own.

At the very end of his life Gide thus gave the mystical, even Christian Oedipus entrance into his world, though a little reluctantly and only under the aegis of Theseus. Gide had come a long way since *The Notebooks of André Walter.*

It was Theseus' resolution to carry through his task to the very end without getting lost in any labyrinths. This had also been Gide's task as a writer. Like his hero, he had gone his way, conversing with many others yet pushing ever forward on his own. What his own work could not encompass someone else's might, someone whom he would welcome with the same respect that Theseus offered Oedipus. For Gide, an artist, is committed, like any other man, only to *his* own work, as Theseus was to his, or Daedalus and André Gide to theirs. What is most engaging perhaps about Gide's writing is the Theseus-like manner through which he "obtained," as he would say, the writer he became, molding him a little more with each work, from the tormented *André Walter* to a serene and tranquil *Theseus.* (pp. 265-70)

> *Germaine Brée, in her* Gide, *Rutgers University Press, 1963, 302 p.*

W. Wolfgang Holdheim   (essay date 1968)

[*Holdheim is a German-born American educator and critic. In the following excerpt from his* Theory and Practice of the Novel: A Study on André Gide, *Holdheim defines the distinguishing characteristics of a Gidean récit, sotie, and novel.*]

[All Gidean works written in more or less narrative prose] may be divided into four distinct groups:

1. The early works, written under the impact of German romanticism and French symbolism. This group comprises *Les Cahiers d'André Walter* (1891), some symbolist treatises (the last of which, *El Hadj*, appeared as late as 1899), and the *Voyage d'Urien* (1893).

2. The *récits*, short first-person narrations, of a classical clarity of form and sometimes strongly autobiographical. These are, in chronological order: *l'Immoraliste* (1902), *La Porte étroite* (1909), *Isabelle* (1911), *La Symphonie pastorale* (1919) and the trilogy *l'Ecole des femmes* (1929), *Robert* (1929), *Geneviève* (1936, unfinished).

3. The three so-called *soties*, a typically Gidean genre which intermingle reality and fantasy with a grotesque humor (usually described as "*saugrenu*"). They are *Paludes* (1895), *Le Prométhée mal enchaîné* (1899) and *Les Caves du Vatican* (1914).

4. *Les Faux-Monnayeurs* (1926), the only one of Gide's writings which he finally acknowledged as a "roman."

Two other works could be added to this list. One is *Thésée* (1946), technically more or less a return to the *récit* tradition. The *Thésée*, however, is Gide's humanistic testament, a kind of didactic summary of his ideas and experiences in the guise of a retelling of the Theseus myth—a late and special case without real importance for the problem of the novel. As for *Si le Grain ne meurt. . .*, it has . . . some bearing on that problem, but as an autobiography it falls outside our scope. It is justifiable that these two writings are usually excluded from studies on Gide as a novelist.

This also applies to the symbolist treatises, which could not be called "novels" by any standard. The matter is less clear for *Les Cahiers d'André Walter* (lyrical more than narrative in tone) and the *Voyage d'Urien*, which were conceived, respectively, as a romantic and a symbolist novel. Both, and even a treatise like *La Tentative amoureuse*, have technical procédés that will be developed in Gide's later narrative writings. Moreover, the bizarre humor of the *Voyage d'Urien* makes it a precursor of the *soties*, and much in its general atmosphere and technique already points toward surrealism. But the procédés in question are more skilfully handled in later works.

This leaves us with the *récits*, the *soties* and the "novel," three narrative genres on whose distinction Gide has insisted with more emphasis than exhaustiveness. But his remarks, few as they are, cannot be high-handedly dismissed. (p. 151)

"Pourquoi j'eus soin d'intituler 'récit' ce petit livre? simplement parce qu'il ne répond pas à l'idée que je me fais du roman; non plus que la *Porte étroite* ou que l'*Immoraliste*; et que je ne voulais pas qu'on s'y trompât. Le roman, tel que je le reconnais ou l'imagine, comporte une diversité de points de vue, soumise à la diversité des personnages qu'il met en scène; c'est par essence une oeuvre déconcentrée." . . . [This passage of 1914 from a projected preface for *Isabelle*] is the best known of the few Gidean statements (in fact there are only two) which emphatically distinguish the *récit* from the novel. Opposing vitalistic deconcentration to artistic declaration is important despite its briefness. It is underplayed or misinterpreted by those who affirm the basic homogeneity of the two genres. Thus [in *André Gide romancier* (1954), Pierre] Lafille relativizes the distinction by reducing it to purely psychological terms: the road from the *récit* to the novel is simply Gide's own road from the Self to the Other, from solipsism to the reality of the outside world. Form is made an epiphenomenon of the author's extra-literary subjective processes—a type of reductionism which is a survival of the nineteenth-century biographical approach. This interpretation also ignores the fact that the question of the *récit* and the novel is not an individual quirk of Gide's but a symptom of a general preoccupation. It is surprising that even Ramon Fernandez, who shares this preoccupation, does not judge very differently where André Gide is concerned. He concludes [in *André Gide* (1931)] that Gide considers the *récit* as a transition between the "inner monologue" and the novel. Built upon the interaction of two characters only one of whom is fully illuminated, it corresponds "au moment où l'écrivain éprouve le besoin de communiquer au lecteur une aventure personnelle qui exige la présentation d'au moins une autre personne que lui." The novel, a depiction of many persons all of whom are equally illuminated, will be the final step away from egocentricity. If we thus present the question from the exclusive point of view of the writer's inner need, we indeed get a perfect continuity of genres, a steady and gradual line of transition that runs via the *récit* to the novel. This continuity, however, disappears as soon as we consent to examine the two genres in their own right and to give primary importance to the question of form. The *Isabelle* preface explicitly does both, it declares the novel "par essence" to be formally decentralized. True, Fernandez' interpretation finds some support in Gide's vitalistic views on self-projection. His schema as it were depicts Gide in the process of realizing that he can only express himself fully through many characters. On the other hand, it not only ignores the entire artistic aspect of Gide's theorizing but also minimizes the realistic criterion, that other component of Gidean vitalism, which plays a major part in this particular statement: is not the deconcentration of the novel meant to be a replica of the deconcentration of objective reality?

It is little wonder that Fernandez, having unduly limited Gide's view, considers it insufficient and offers a supplementary *récit* theory of his own [in *Messages* (1926)]. Its key criterion is time: whereas the *récit* views events from the angle of the past, the novel is the genre of the present. The latter presents thoughts and feelings as they arise, events as they come about, its order is determined by their natural genesis and succession. The *récit*, on the other hand, narrates events that are terminated, arranging them according to the logic of demonstration and exposition. Its world is not living but intellectually reconstructed, and the presentation of the concrete is often replaced by abridged accounts and abstract schemas. The creative genesis of the two genres parallels this intrinsic distinction. The novel springs from immediate aesthetic syntheses of perception, its characters are apprehended by an aesthetic intuition which resembles that by which we perceive living persons: their reality imposes itself directly, without the mediation of reasoning. In the *récit*, however, everything is intellectually conceived and explained, its syntheses are not immediate but construed. Proving and persuading rather than presenting concretely, it is essentially oratorical rather than aesthetic.

Many elements of this theory are recognizably Gidean. There is the stress upon (and the doubt concerning) overall intellectual control, so symptomatic of a period of unrest and transition. Ancient forms and values are crumbling, and the Western mind must somehow assimilate a swiftly changing reality by which it threatens to be submerged. For the French writer, the heir of a rationalistic and classical tradition, this problem is bound to be particularly acute. François Mauriac writes in 1928 that the French novelist's paradoxical task is to write works that have the teeming and mysterious richness of Dostoevsky's and are nevertheless logical and reasonable. Fernandez' entire distinction between the genres corresponds to the Gidean opposition between classicism and vitalism, art and life. His shortcoming is that he evades the crucial problem (how can the novel be vitalistic and still artistic?) by mere sleights-of-hand in verbal definition, principally by a questionable use of the term "aesthetic." In fact he denies this qualification to the architectural, classical elements of a work of art and insists that the novel is "le plus artistique de tous les genres, précisément parce que son équilibre esthétique est plus intérieur, plus indépendant de règles apparentes et fixes." Supposedly this equilibrium comes about by means of an aesthetic intuition and through the use of aesthetic procédés. What procédés, and how can their inevitable mediacy be reconciled with the synthetic immediacy of perception and presentation? All this is too vague and contradictory to lead to a genuine aesthetics of the novel. If the novelist's "intuition" (we recognize Bergson's influence) is analogous to direct everyday perception, why then is it particularly "aesthetic?" Fernandez probably thinks of inherently meaningful poetic moments (which are a very different thing); but then we revert to the familiar question whether the novel can and should be a succession of privileged fragments of time—quite apart from the fact that the equation of the "aesthetic" and the "poetic" is more than doubtful. Such juggling with words cannot conceal the fact that the novel, far from being essentially and unequivocally aesthetic, is artistically a problematical genre.

This fact is brought out clearly by another leading critic of that period, whose views fruitfully supplement those of Fernandez. Albert Thibaudet, however, does not oppose the novel to the *récit* but rather to the drama, that classical genre *par excellence*. Under the influence of Bergsonian ideas, he defines it [in *Réflexions sur le roman* (1938)] as a work which is not composed but naturally "déposé à la façon d'une durée vécue qui se gonfle et d'une mémoire qui se forme." Deposition as against composition: like Gide the vitalist (and like Fernandez), he emphasizes the immediacy of the creative process, the novelist's immanence in the temporal flux and his renunciation of overall control. But Thibaudet does not commit the imprudence of classifying this type of creativity as "aesthetic." Still a good classicist at heart, he in fact impugns the artistic purity of the novel by defining it as anti-genre rather than a genre, a composite form that developed by assimilating the substance and techniques of the traditional genres as they dissolved. For him, the essence of the "aesthetic" lies precisely in the mediate process of composition, which is not a product of nature but of art. Pointing out that composition is equally necessary to rhetoric (which wants to persuade) and to the theater (which wants to attain dramatic effects), Thibaudet transcends Fernandez' one-sided tendency to relegate it to the "non-aesthetic" realm of oratory. True, his conception of "composition" is far too narrow. Unlike Gide, he still sees it as the application of a predetermined order, a pre-established formal schema. Of course the problem of form in literature can no longer, on any level, be reduced to the schema of the French school composition or the rules of Aristotle and Boileau. But Thibaudet's doctrinal exaggeration can be ignored. His merit lies in insisting on the *spatial* character of all composition. It is indeed wrong to take Lessing's distinction between space-arts and time-arts too seriously. Literature also tends to be spatial, it overcomes the basic temporality of its medium and often (as in the drama) that of its subject. Weaving a story into a closed and coherent configuration, the writer in effect transforms succession into juxtaposition and balance in space, he spatializes time itself. Moreover, he usually (as in a poem) imprisons his subject in a web of images and reflexive references, in a system of meaning that cuts across and neutralizes its temporality and makes it completely *there* all at once. Gide recognized that composition is essentially detemporalization when he said that it aims for "un équilibre hors du temps." All finished form is intrinsically spatial.

The difference between the classical work (be it *récit* or drama) and the novel is pictured by Thibaudet as one between space and time, by Fernandez as one between the past and the present. The two views are far from irreconcilable, and it is indeed Fernandez' chief contribution that he has formulated the more traditional polarization as an intratemporal distinction. Yet even here his view requires a correction, for he is wrong in treating the novel as the genre of the present. To be sure, he knows (and states) that the novel is shaped by the development of events, that it follows the rhythm of lived duration, but he does not clearly draw the consequences. If he speaks in terms of the present, it is because he wants to emphasize the novelist's dependence on what is happening as it happens, his immanence in the temporal flux. But he forgets that this is not a pure present, in which the self entirely coincides with the emotion of the moment, but a *projective* one that is pregnant with a future it ignores—*praesens de futuris* rather than *praesens de praesentibus* (to borrow St. Augustine's terms), not *contuitus* but *expectatio*. This is why Fernandez tends to confuse the novelist's "intuition" with that of the lyrical poet, for the present is the temporal dimension that presides over the lyrical experience. The novel, then, is governed by the future. The point has since been made by other theoreticians, notably by Sartre. Already Rivière, however, in his remarkable essay on the novel of adventure, defines "adventure" as "the unexpected" (Gide's cherished *imprévu*!) and demands that both reader and author should be inside the characters to the point of sharing their ignorance of the future.

The novel's supposed association with the future is one reason for its leading position among modern genres: in much of modern philosophy, the future has become the primary dimension of temporality, in fact the very essence of time. The first philosopher who has clearly established this primacy is Schelling, and it is he who shows us how Thibaudet's space-time polarization can be meaningfully equated with the opposition between past and future of Fernandez (in the corrected version). What follows will naturally not be a philosophical analysis of Schelling's theory of time, but merely a simplified schema which can be applied by analogy to this literary problem and thus serve as a conceptual aid and illustration. Schelling's starting point is Kant's recognition of space and time as the two transcendental forms which shape our experience of reality. Pure time would be intensity, sheer activity, dynamism, whereas pure space may be defined by such terms as extension, rest, and Being. But both in themselves are abstract ideal limits, in fact they only appear through an interaction in which they mutually limit and determine one another. Intensity (representable by a point) expands into space, resulting in a line. Viewed statically, this line is a geometric figure representing spatial simultaneity, but viewed dynamically it is a moving point that engenders the experience of temporal succession. Intensity is primary in this interaction, and extension is merely the ground which time needs to realize itself concretely. This original hierarchy, however, can be inverted (falsified, as it were) by our perspective. We are free to view reality under the aspect of time (dynamically or "intuitively," in the Bergsonian sense) or under that of space (in the mode of reflective prehension and eidetic representation). Each perspective will in its turn furnish us with the two dimensions of space and time, but their character and relation will be different. Let us put it schematically:

I. Temporal perspective,

a) Time in time (the future).

b) Space in time (the past).

II. Spatial perspective.

a) Time in space (the line).

b) Space in space (the plane).

In the mode of time, the *future* (the domain of becoming, of the possible) is primary and determining, the past is merely the presupposition for its dynamic realization. Viewed in the mode of space, both dimensions are frozen into geometric figures. The whole spatial perspective, however, is none other than that of the past (which is precisely "space in time") if it acquires primacy. Then the past (the realm of the given, of Being, of events that are terminated once and for all) is determining, whereas the future is mere negativity, non-being—that which does not yet exist and is meaningful only insofar as it is determined by the past and destined to become a past in its turn. It is evident that we here have a perfect conceptual tool for reducing the space-time polarity to an intra-temporal one: temporality is transformed into spatiality by the perspective that is governed by the past. Space is time fixed, finished, coagulated—it is the symbol of the perfected self (says the philosopher Otto Weininger), whereas time is the symbol of the self that wills. Perfection is also the artistic ideal, and so our schema permits us to restate the difference between life and art. Life is the natural domain of immanence where time (the future) reigns supreme. Art is the "artificial" realm of transcendence and Apollonian distance—of a reflective purpose that is based upon a stance of retrospective observation, of a spatialization of time that is essentially its reduction to a finished past. The classical genres, tending toward a formal perfection resting in space, express the essential nature of art—a nature which the novel will somehow try to overcome.

The anti-vitalistic character of classical art can therefore be described as specifically anti-temporal. This raises a problem with regard to the drama. . . . [The drama is] non-vitalistic by virtue of its refusal of episodism and empiricism, its rejection of contingency, its stress on the hero's intelligible essence. But does it not unfold in time? Goethe and Schiller point out that the action of the drama is always completely present, in contrast to that of the epic which is completely past. This definition is justified in its own terms, which are not ours. It bears on the drama's method of presentation rather than on its structural essence. Brought about by the play's visibility, its immediate appeal to the eye which creates an effect of liveliness rather than reflecting a substance of vitality, this *nunc* is really a *hic*, a "presentness" rather than an authentic present. Its evolution in time would rather make the drama the genre of the future. This is the thesis of Emil Staiger, who defines the "dramatic style" (which may appear in genres other than the drama) as one that is essentially oriented toward the future. One of the many valuable aspects of Staiger's analysis is that it acknowledges and illuminates the parallel with the rhetorical argument (and even with the logical demonstration) which Fernandez held against the *récit*. The whole dramatic work is built up in view of a final event (the *dénouement*) towards which the hero projects himself. The will is futuristic, and so is pathos, as an extreme form of intentionality. The same holds true for the solution of a problem or a persuasive statement. A logical or rhetorical argument is entirely structured by and towards the final point that is to be proved. This close correspondence between the dramatic and the demonstrative, incidentally, goes far toward explaining the success of the intellectual (ideational) drama of our time. Especially in Sartre's case we see how dialectical tension can be aptly transformed into dramatic tension. The question is, however, whether we here have to do with genuine futurity. Both for the drama and the demonstration, the answer must be negative. Actually the conclusion of an argument is previously known, for it is contained in all its steps and controls its entire structure. The conclusion is that which is implicit in the beginning so that it may be explicit at the end: existentially, a logical demonstration is always circular. The same can be said of the drama, pervaded and shaped as it is by its inherent purpose. Oedipus' search for the murderer is only the demonstration and exposition of something which he somehow knew at the outset. In the same way Nietzsche (in Gide's "heroic" interpretation) embarked on a tragic game against himself and his own reason at the *beginning* of his life. Events merely give the hero the occasion to work out his destiny—and destiny is not freedom, it is pre-determinative and anti-temporal. The drama is the genre where essence precedes existence, its *dénouement* has something of a *quod erat demonstrandum*. This is why Lukács rightly says that it does not know the concept of time. The "unity of time" in the classical drama properly aims at the abolition of temporality. So does the perfect contrapuntal economy of the action, and its completed and closed character (with a beginning, a middle and an end)—that Aristotelian plot structure which is so reminiscent of the divisions of a rhetorical argument. Even the "present" of presentation stressed by Goethe and Schiller is in the last analysis a transformation of duration into plastic visibility, of the Dionysian into the Apollonian, of time into space. And when (in the French classical tradition and in that of the Greeks) the dramatic method of visual presentation is occasionally abandoned in favor of the epic narration of past events, is it not then as if the perspective of the past, which governs tragedy in secret, momentarily bursts forth into full evidence?

A logical objection might be made: the *dénouement* which shapes the drama is not an efficient but a final cause and therefore in league with the future. The distinction is logically justified, but here lie its limits. Let us return to the analogy of discursive reasoning. In the elaboration of new scientific laws, logicians distinguish between the "context of discovery" and the "context of justification." The former is not logical but psychological, not necessary but in varying degrees contingent. The discovery may be largely due to chance, the scientist may even happen upon it while he is in quest of something else. For this "lived" process, the justification must substitute another one which observes the strict rules of rational proof. Logically, the point to be proved is at the end of the process of justification—but in fact it is at the beginning, for the justifier knows it before he embarks upon his argument. Existentially, the difference between final and efficient causes is not one of essence but only one of modality, for all causation is predeterminative. The context of discovery alone, with its component of faltering uncertainty, has the characteristics of true duration. As for tragedy, the chorus of Anouilh's *Antigone* points out that it is clean, unsullied by "dirty hope" (which deals with an uncertain future), independent of contingent reality. On the other hand, the experience of duration needs external reality (in all its opacity) as an obstacle and a foil. Genuine succession does not exist without genuine confrontation. We may will or desire a particular thing, plan for a specific purpose, but we are never sure if and when it can be obtained. We are always to some degree at the mercy of events. The future is never unfailingly inscribed in the present: finalism is an overstatement and therefore a travesty of intentionality. Time is the domain of the unforeseen, not the foreseeable, of dispersion and not concentration. Graphically, it should perhaps after all be represented by a zigzag rather than a line. The drama is a *tour de force*, for it detemporalizes time in the very process of going through its motions. It imitates its dynamic movement, marshals and even accents its intensity, while actually stylizing it into spatiality. The zigzag becomes a straight line without deviations, the shortest geometrical road to a given point. And that geometrical point, that given "future" toward which everything moves and whose foreknowledge fills the whole action with a sense of "time running out," is in reality something that already is, i. e., a *past*. How then to account for the drama's extraordinary intensity? This is not the place for an aesthetics of the drama. Perhaps the power of spatial concentration is added to the sweep of dynamic movement. Mechanically the secret push of the efficient cause may be added to the manifest attraction of the final cause. And in the midst of all this dynamism, do not we often have the feeling that we are really not advancing? Then we catch a glimpse of the pseudotemporality of a genre which operates a veritable "defuturization of the future."

If the drama is classicism in its purity, what is the exact place of the *récit*? We may consider it as the triumph of classical form in the domain of narration, but this definition is far too broad. Above all, the *récit* should be distinguished from another narrative subgenre, the novella. The French *nouvelle* culminated with Maupassant, and twentieth-century French critics have given it little attention. In 1943, Jean Fougère describes it as a genre of formal perfection and economy that "frappe juste" and (unlike the novel) "ne joue pas sur la durée." We are not far from the definition of the drama, to which indeed the novella is closest of all literary forms. Told as the story of a crisis, towards which the whole action projects itself and which is the formal principle of its unity, it brings about the same detemporalization of the future. This is clear in *La double Méprise*, the work by Mérimée which Gide briefly considered a model for the "pure novel," and even clearer in the short stories of Kleist, which Staiger cites as perfect examples of dramatic style. The chief difference from the drama lies in the method of presentation, which is here of course primarily narrative. But the distinction is not essential. The narrator is the omniscient author, often as hidden as the playwright and pretending that the story moves to its inevitable conclusion all alone. The representational limitations of the narrative method seem here to be overcome. Actually "tout récit est par définition récit du passé," which is why Thomas Mann aptly calls the teller of stories: "dieser raunende Beschwörer des Imperfekts." But in the *nouvelle*, the theatrical fiction of the author's absence helps to neutralize this epic element. Seemingly the story tells itself as it is happening, and we go along with it. It tends to be a story told by nobody, an absolute narration as it were, which has overcome its allegiance to the obvious narrative past (the "once upon a time") and has instead substituted the dramatic past (which is a false future). The *nouvelle* is a dramatization of narration itself.

This is a sweeping generalization, to be sure, but then definitions are. In practice, genres and subgenres have an irritating way of overlapping, and nothing is more fluid than the frontier between the *nouvelle* and the *récit*. Thus the author's absence and the absolute narration are not doctrinaire requirements but ideal limits toward which the novella tends. This does not mean, for example, that the story cannot be told in the first person singular, thus moving closer to the more openly narrative character of a reminiscence. But even if there is such an "I," it is as it were a surface phenomenon: the unity of the work lies in its finalism, in the culminating event which gives it form. Conversely, a *récit* is not necessarily a first-person story, though this technique most clearly expresses its essential tendency. For here the *I* (or if there is none, the central *point of view* which is focussed on one central hero) becomes the formal principle of unity. There may be many important events spread over a long period of time and even if one of these is crucial thematically, it is not so formally: what holds the work together is the centrality of perspective allied with the centrality of the hero. In the *nouvelle* we have a foreshortening of time and external reality, both of which merge in one single fateful crisis. In the *récit* time and reality are extended instead of merging in one focal point. As in autobiography (of which the *récit* is the fictional counterpart), subjective essence and objective factuality develop side by side, in a reciprocally determinative stylization. As for the unifying perspective, we will see that it need not be subjective: the important thing is that a narrator is palpably there. For there is no attempt to dramatize narration by endowing it with immediacy and presentness. The *récit* is frankly narrative, a tale told by one who reflectively looks back upon the past. Finalism is replaced by retrospectivity, instead of a narration that

tries to deny its essential character we have one that exposes it, the hidden past masquerading as a future becomes a past that is openly displayed. We are one step further away from the drama and one step closer to the epic—and yet dramatic elements are still there. They reside in the strongly unified, architectural character of the *récit*, which differs sharply from the anecdotic decentralization of the epic.

We see that the Gidean distinction between novel and *récit* in terms of centrality is fundamental. Despite its sketchiness, it at least implies what Fernandez says on the matter and is ultimately more precise. But Gide does not view the vitalistic novel as a mere return to the episodic looseness of the epic. Let us note that French classical doctrine, despite its prejudice in favor of tectonic structure, still considered the epic one of the major genres. This attitude is partly but not exclusively explained by the historical eminence of that form: it should be added that the epic is still (and even more obviously than other genres) oriented toward a finished past. Its narrator is a universal controlling presence, its decentralization is spatial and not at all incompatible with form. In fact it is the nonchalant expression of a basic indestructible order in the universe. We can say, with Lukács, that the ancient epic simply does not need the strait jacket of architectural structurization to escape from fragmentation. Each of its episodes reflects both an ever-present indestructible totality and a fundamental organicity, each of its fragments partakes in an objectivity that is given once and for all. The novel, however, which is the "epic" of Fichte's period of "complete sinfulness," can only reflect (or try to organize) the chaos of modernity. Totality, objectivity, order are no longer given, they are at best the doubtful fruit of a demiurgic effort. And the decentralization of the Gidean vitalistic novel is post-chaotic rather than pre-chaotic, as it were, and therefore more essential than the epic's. It is more than a spatial autonomy of separate parts, it is in the last analysis the inherent multiplicity of becoming, the dispersion of the temporal process. Time is the true domain of subjectivity and relativity. Forsaking the epic past, the novel thus comes to seek the modern experience of intratemporality, marked by the primacy of the future. Not the false predetermined "future" of the drama but a lived future with its infinite and uncontrollable contingencies. Later theoreticians may have stated this more unequivocally than Gide, but it is really quite explicit in his theorizing. What is the desired immanence of the author in his work, the "perpetual emergence" of his creation, except an ignorance of the future—in Edouard's words a refusal "to foresee?" And when Gide wishes that his novel should not "se boucler, mais s'éparpiller, se défaire. . . ," he is describing a temporal process. This entire temporal perspective is nothing else than a restatement of Gide's vitalistic theory of the novel. Time, governed by futurity, is the essence of life in the process of being lived. Already in the *Traité du Narcisse*, the breaking of the branch was the act of vital spontaneity (*l'imprévu*) which marked the genesis of time and fragmentation. And the identity of "life" and "time" once more underlines the basic problem of novelistic vitalism: the novel is committed to an unknown future and rejects the finished past, its determined intratemporality excludes all spatialization—how then can it be a work of art?

"Pourquoi j'appelle ce livre *Sotie*? Pourquoi *récits* les trois précédents? Pour bien marquer que ce ne sont point là des romans. . . *Soties, récits*, je n'ai jusqu'à présent écrit que des livres ironiques—ou: critiques, si vous préférez—dont sans doute voici le dernier." This extract from a projected but omitted preface to *Les Caves du Vatican*, cited in the Journal of 12 July 1914 (Gide had already reported a slightly different version on 30 June), is the second important Gidean statement on narrative genres. Its criterion is the vitalistic immediacy of creation. However, we know that this tenet is not only going to be belied by the practice, but that it is only a limited aspect of the theory. Both Gidean theorizing and the Gidean novel end up by tending toward a kind of super-irony. This means that *récits* and *soties* in principle regain the right to be considered as precursors of *Les Faux-Monnayeurs*. We ask which of the two is the more authentic candidate for this position.

What is the exact difference between the *récit* and the *sotie*? Gide describes both forms as "critical" or "ironic"; the question is how they differ within the framework of this common definition. It is generally known in what sense Gide's *récits* are critical: they expose the dangers of certain existential tendencies that are usually the author's own. *L'Immoraliste* criticizes a quasi-Nietzschean superman immoralism, *La Porte étroite* a quasi-Jansenist cult of spiritual heroism, **La Symphonie pastorale** a quasi-evangelical ideal of passivity. But this does not suffice to distinguish them from other Gidean writings, for there is hardly a work of his that is not critical in this way. Thus the drama *Saül* castigates an excessive propensity toward receptivity, and even the *soties* attack many human (and often Gidean) attitudes. What should be determined is the exact nature and modality of the critique as it appears in the *récit*, i.e., the manner in which the critical substance is related to the formal characteristics of the genre.

We found the *récit* to be built around a unified point of view which is often (and in Gide always) personified in a first-person narrator. The historical origin of this form is the romantic *Icherzählung*, the tale told in the guise of a confession. The central "I" is the principle of structural concentration, and especially in France this procedure was soon bound to be utilized by a classical urge for strict formalization and control. The clearest case in point is Benjamin Constant's *Adolphe*, which is perhaps the first truly modern French *récit*. Adolphe tells his own story, but is this the genuine confession of a subjective ego? The detached author becomes a narrator who is (or was) involved in the events, but this does not mean that he has lost his author's privileges. The contrary is true: Adolphe, the committed narrator, comes to share in them. Here lies the source of his much-discussed objectivity and lucidity. The fact is that Adolphe is not an individual subjectivity at all, he is nothing less than the omniscient writer who has been smuggled into the work. And it is precisely this fake immanence of the transcendent, this deceptive intramundanity of the extramundane, which creates the impression that the story is completely transparent—that it happened just like that and for the reasons given, that everything is understood and resolved once and for all. Through a clever reversal, the subjective ego is actually the objective focus of interpretation, the individual per-

spective is a covert invasion of absolute truth. This is artistic concentration masquerading as existential subjectivity! The "point of view," then, is not necessarily subjective. The "I" of Gide's *récits*, however, is deliberately subjectivized, even though it retains its power of formal integration. Michel's reminiscences in *l'Immoraliste*, Jérôme's in *La Porte étroite* present an individual deformation of reality rather than an absolute reality. Does this mean that Gide returns to romantic subjectivism? By no means, and not only because of the difference in atmosphere between his works and (for example) Chateaubriand's *René*. That atmospheric distinction merely reflects a radically different conception of subjectivity. The romantic subjectivity is positive. Although it bewails its misfortunes and accents its isolation from the world, it really affirms itself triumphantly in its effusions. Its attitude toward itself is fundamentally uncritical. Far from being experienced as a lack, subjectivity becomes an absolute in its own right. On the other hand, Gide's narrative point of view is subjective by virtue of its limitations. Subjectivity is presented critically as a deprival of objectivity, a failure to see things "as they are." It goes with an existential flaw, a fault in character which renders it clearly visible. Jérôme's want of lucidity is caused by (and serves) his fatal weakness, Michel's limitation is a result of (and panders to) his anarchic tendencies, and the minister's blindness in **La Symphonie pastorale** is both the reason and the tool of his inadmissible desires. The character flaw helps to bring about the catastrophe which permits the hero to realize his shortcomings and turn the critical light upon himself. The ultimate and triumphant criterion of value is the author's objectivity, the absolute perspective of the transcendent literary intelligence, but it is indirectly introduced as an existential autocritique of the narrator which gradually arises and moves from implicitness to explicitness.

The Gidean *récit*, then, can be defined as a critique of existential attitudes, brought about by means of a progressive negativization of the unifying point of view. **Isabelle** is very much a *récit* according to this recipe. Here as elsewhere, we have the deforming refraction of events through the mind of a central character who finally sheds his illusions. Critics have been severe, and not quite unjustly, in their judgment on a book which seems to exhibit a cold technical perfection without personal involvement. However, this much-maligned little work is quite important for a special reason: there is a duality in its critique which is a deflection towards the *sotie*.

Let us briefly recall the story. The narrator, Gérard Lacase—just as Michel in *l'Immoraliste*—moves in an atmosphere of death and seeks a breakthrough toward life. By "death" I here mean everything that is fixed, constrictive and not living. In *l'Immoraliste* it is bourgeois morality (especially its culmination in marriage and the family), property, tradition, and the entire world of the past which Michel studies with the dry methods of objective historical scholarship. In **Isabelle**, the depiction of death is suffused with a kind of haunting negative intensity. Gérard too is a scholar (a literary one, not a historian), and the subject of his study is Bossuet, that most severe representative of a millenary tradition, that most extreme exponent of a court frozen in formalism. He visits the old castle la

Quartfourche, inhabited among others by M. Floche, who owns unpublished Bossuet documents. The house with its inhabitants (the old Floches, the senile Saint-Auréols, and an unbearable abbé who judges everything by immovable moral standards) is a deadly evocation of a past that has invaded the present and kills all life. The inmates of this atemporal enclave lead a mechanical, an almost reified existence. Or rather they behave like bizarre plants more than human beings. Gérard, overcome with anguish in this stifling atmosphere where time has stopped, clutches for the scarce signs of a life that seems deeply buried beneath the apparent immobility. Avid to extract this hidden substance, he discovers the family secret: the daughter of the Saint-Auréols, Isabelle, years ago had been involved in an unsuccessful elopement that had caused her lover's violent death. Gérard falls in love with the mysterious maiden: she becomes the image of life which will permit him to escape from his *ennui*, on her he projects his desire for vital commitment.

Isabelle is usually treated as a critique of the romantic illusion, and so it is, as witness the very setting of the story with its ancient castle full of Gothic mystery. When Gérard finally meets Isabelle, he realizes that this presumed incarnation of a romantic dream is a vulgar woman, egoistical and sensual, who had herself been responsible for her lover's death. For a mediocre reality, he had substituted a figment of his imagination. But the romantic illusion here takes on a specifically Gidean coloration: it becomes associated with the ideal of vitality. As a symbol of vital intensity to which the hero attaches himself in his quest for the fullness of existence, it plays the same role which the dissipated life of the barbarous Athalaric played for Michel. But while the Gothic king's biography was a historical (although idealized), example, the ideal of the passionate and misunderstood Isabelle is purely literary. And the confusion of life and literature is here a fundamental theme. His very field of study exposes Gérard to the literary temptation, but it is even more important to note that he is a would-be novelist. The writer of novels, in his view, has two distinct and equally crucial tasks. On one hand he seizes "life" in its pulsating freshness and variety, in its fascinating plenitude. On the other hand he discovers "the truth" beneath appearances: "Romancier, mon ami, me disais-je, nous allons donc te voir à l'oeuvre. Décrire! Ah, fi! ce n'est pas de cela qu'il s'agit, mais bien de découvrir la réalité sous l'aspect. En ce court laps de temps qu'il t'est permis de séjourner à la Quartfourche, si tu laisses passer un geste, un tic, sans pouvoir t'en donner bientôt l'explication psychologique, historique et complète, c'est que tu ne sais pas ton métier." Vital intensity and the realist's demand for truthfulness: these are the two aspects of Gide's vitalistic theory of the novel, although Gérard still sees them in their limited traditional form. Vitality appears as a story both beautiful and "interesting," acted out by "interesting" persons. And the ideal of truthfulness is conceived as a closed system of total explanation that leaves no room for *l'imprévu*. There seems to be a mysterious harmony between truth, interest, beauty and intensity, a real coincidence of life and art. At first Gérard indeed believes that truth and interest go together, not knowing "avec quelle malignité les événements dérobent à nos yeux le côté par où ils nous intéresseraient davantage, et com-

bien peu de prise ils offrent à qui ne sait pas les forcer." But soon he realizes how hard the interesting side must be sought, and he begins to force events, transforming them to make them correspond to a literary convention. His speculations are nothing but "psychological lyricism." The "deeper reasons" he discovers are not truthful explanations but constructions of a novelist who is doing his job, expressions of a traditional novelistic view of reality.

The critique clearly has a dual impact. On one hand it is indeed directed against the idealistic falsification of reality. When he understands the truth, Gérard adopts an attitude of disabused melancholy and no longer understands how he could have sought "life" with such impatience. In this respect, *Isabelle* is in the tradition of the romantic literature of disillusionment. But the critique is also specifically literary, almost technical, bearing in particular on a certain all-too-familiar construction of plot and character. Here it is less concerned with romanticism as such than with that stale and stereotype conception of the "interesting" which the realistic novel had inherited from the romantic tradition, less with *le romantisme* than with *le romanesque*. In this sense, *Isabelle* is in the line of certain naturalistic developments and makes us think of the implicit critique which is found in a work like Henri Céard's *Une belle Journée*. All this sounds very old-fashioned indeed, but in its wider implication Gide's work goes beyond this particular context and questions the novelistic imagination as such, with its specific falsification of reality. Do we not here already have a novelist who catches himself red-handed in the process of fabulation? Something in *Isabelle* reminds us (very distantly, I admit) of Henry James' difficult late work *The Sacred Fount*.

The critique, then, is both existential and literary. However, the existential aspect retains primacy, as is proper for a *récit*. In the last analysis Gérard wants to be a lover rather than a novelist, and if he ends up by writing no novel, it is because of his vital disillusionment. But his fabulizing activity does emerge as a theme in its own right. His subjectivity is among others expressly a creative subjectivity, the autocritique of the "I" is also one of the novelist qua novelist and (by implication) of the novel as a novel. This makes *Isabelle* in a sense a transition between a *récit* and a *sotie*, for the displacement of emphasis which is here sketched constitutes the distinction between the respective critical essences of these genres. What is secondary in *Isabelle* becomes primary in the *soties*: they turn on themselves as a literary creation, they essentially constitute a self-persiflage of the artist and the work of art. Specifically of the novelistic work of art, for the mainspring of their autocritique is their deliberate and visible refusal to "imitate" reality. If they conjure up worlds of fantasy that they do not take seriously themselves, it is because they refuse the illusion that the novel can be an image of reality. Already Maupassant had recognized in his famous preface to *Pierre et Jean* that the realists should really be called "illusionists." But this very self-consciousness quite obviously makes Gide's *soties* not only the best commentaries on and illustrations of the complex Gidean theory of the novel but the most authentic precursors of the final Novel, *Les Faux-Monnayeurs*. Let us add that the *soties* also experiment with structural deconcentration, that vitalistic and ultimately technical requirement which remains active in the ironic novel sought by Gide. For the distinction between *récit* and novel on the basis of decentralization retains its validity: *Les Faux-Monnayeurs* strives for centrifugality, it does not try to be a well-made classical work of art. (pp. 154-70)

> *W. Wolfgang Holdheim, in his* Theory and Practice of the Novel: A Study on André Gide, *Librairie Droz, 1968, 269 p.*

Kurt Weinberg   (essay date 1976)

[*Weinberg is a German-born American educator and critic. In the following excerpt from his book-length study,* On Gide's Prométhée: Private Myth and Public Mystification, *Weinberg speculates on Gide's concept of faith and grace through an examination of the religious crises faced by the characters Coclès and Damoclès.*]

The Meaning of the **Prométhée** logically derives from an exposition which precedes it in the form of a prologue. A sort of slapstick prelude, it is narrated dispassionately, dryly reported without commentary like a *fait divers*: "On the boulevard which leads from the Madeleine to the Opéra," a fat gentleman drops his handkerchief. A lean man picks it up, runs after the fat one and returns it to him. The fat gentleman gives the lean one a flask with "portable ink," a pen, and an envelope, inviting him to address it to a "name" he knows. After having put a five hundred franc note into the envelope, the fat gentleman slaps the lean one so powerfully that he falls down. The fat gentleman leaves the scene in a cab. Bleeding heavily, the lean man rises again and testily tells the worried audience that he barely felt anything, and asks them if they will please leave him alone. Now the author intervenes with the casual remark that he subsequently learned the fat gentleman was Zeus, the banker. The identity of the ill-treated lean man and that of the "elect" so whimsically chosen is slowly revealed in the *sotie*'s first part ("La moralité privée"); the former is Coclès, the latter Damoclès.

The complex structure of part I, "Chronique de la moralité privée," introduces, one by one, the characters of the *sotie*. The scene is a Parisian café on the *grands boulevards*. Chance and necessity are intertwined in the meeting of the *garçon*, Prometheus, Damoclès, and Coclès. Each character, with the exception of the transcendent "Miglionnaire" Zeus, is given his turn in the limelight: "Histoire du garçon et du Miglionnaire"; told by the *garçon*; "Histoire de Damoclès"; "Histoire de Coclès"; "Prométhée parle"; "Histoire de l'aigle." To this perspectivism corresponds the precipitous action of a farce of errors, interspersed with the protagonists' "stories" or speeches, within the framework of the sections numbered one to four: a dual web of structures illustrating by their very nature the incommunicability of a nigh Kafkaesque morality authored by the "Miglionnaire" Zeus. Part I ends in the midst of confusion and misunderstandings with apocalyptic overtones which will be analyzed in the course of this exegesis.

The intricacies of the **Prométhée**'s dual structure, studied in detail by W. W. Holdheim [in *Theory and Practice of the Novel* (1968)], are carried over into parts II, III and

IV. Part II, "La Détention de Prométhée," Prometheus, denounced by the *garçon* and imprisoned, receives the *garçon*, who informs him about the changing fortunes of Damoclès and Coclès. Prometheus feeds his eagle, demonstrating its "morality," in the chapter headed "Il faut qu'il croisse et que je diminue." Prometheus escapes by means of his eagle. He then gives his lecture on everyone's eagle, ultimately begging the question in the chapter entitled "La Pétition de principes." Damoclès catches a cold when leaving the lecture hall.

Part III, "La Maladie de Damoclès," shows the rise of Coclès (who had lost one eye to the eagle at the end of Part I) and the decline of Damoclès (who on that same memorable occasion had thought that he had paid for all and everything). Damoclès dies and is buried. The whole sequence of events is enigmatically punctuated by an "Interview du Miglionnaire," given to Prometheus and the *garçon*.

Part IV, "Histoire de Tityre," is a parable told by Prometheus in lieu of a funeral oration for Damoclès. The story of Tityre's fixed idea, implanted by Ménalque, which grows together with a tree planted by Ménalque in Tityre's swamp so that both become an overpowering obsession, illustrates the futility of human efforts to decipher transcendent messages. The parabolic truth of "Histoire de Tityre" (and of the **Prométhée** as a whole) is confirmed by the joyful consumption of the eagle (by Prometheus, Coclés, and the *garçon*), and by the author's cryptic postscript, in the form of an epilogue, on the inscrutability of acts and creations which go beyond human intentions.

The four parts of the **Prométhée** demonstrate the disquieting consequences of the dramatic prelude in numerous episodes in which Prometheus and the *garçon* act as intercessors. By telling his eagle's story (and history) and the parable of Tityre's tree, Prometheus shows in a glass darkly the *moralité privée* of the central fable. The sober objectivity of the prelude, the "realist" narratives of absurd and grotesque circumstances, and the naturalism and gothic humor of the strange happenings burlesque themselves, testifying to loss of innocence in novelistic narcissism by way of the irony which now permeates the novel's aesthetics and structure. Three features of the **Prométhée** are in flagrant contradiction with objectivity, the mimetic "realism," and the "naturalistic" sobriety of its style. First, there are the alienated characters, a strangely eclectic group assembled from Sicilian and Roman legendary history (Damoclès and Coclès), Greek mythology (Zeus, Prometheus, the eagle), modern finance and even restaurants (Zeus, the banker and "Miglionnaire," and the *garçon* who ministers to the culinary needs of his guests). Protagonists emerging at the same time from Gide's previous works **Paludes**, *Les Nourritures terrestres*) and Virgil's *Eclogues* (Tityre, Moelibée, Ménalque), these characters allude to the economic, medical, and alimentary vocabulary of the Christian doctrines of salvation. Secondly, there is the hidden supernaturalism of the "happenings," which are narrated in "naturalistic" terms or occur as dialogues in trivial everyday language. And thirdly, time and place (May 189-, the Parisian *grands boulevards*, the *salle des nouvelles lunes*) incorporate *hic et nunc*, here and now, the grotesque episodes of the *sotie*, and yet convey the timelessness of myth as well as the real scene, which is transformed by it.

In the themes of the ***Prométhée*** Gide stages mystery, sacrament, self-denial, martyrdom, and the secret of sacrifice in the form of a farcical mystification of matters of faith, grace, predestination, and Eucharist. Originally mystification represented the typological correlation between sensuous symbol and the object it symbolized. Mystery equals sacrament ("sacramentum vel mysterium"); a sacred act is almost the equivalent of sacrifice in Augustine's definition ("quasi sacrum facere"); and, according to Isidore of Seville, it corresponds to "secret" ("sacrum = secretum").

Mystery and mystification begin with the very title of the ***Prométhée***, with the ambiguities hidden in the words **mal enchaîné**. First, they suggest that the ***Prométhée*** is logically poor (*mal enchaîné*) in its formal structure, as at first glance it may appear with its confusing *tiroirs*, its anecdotes within episodes and narratives, its dual structure of chapters overflowing from one numbered section into the next one. Secondly, logically poor (*mal enchaîné*) too is Prometheus's prescience regarding the unpredictable reactions which the "banker's" playful *acte gratuit* produces in the meditative Damoclès and Coclès, the man of works, owing to their (rather limited) free will. Finally, *mal enchaîné*, "poorly bound," Prometheus descends from the Caucasus, proving his ubiquity by appearing incognito in a Parisian café. Although he can free himself of Zeus's gift, for a long time he prefers to his freedom the eagle that feeds on his vital substance, the devouring beast that is his cross, his suffering, his love—his passion. Ambiguously the eagle is at the same time the divine side that consumes his humanity and the human congregation gnawing at his divine substance. "Il faut qu'il croisse et que je diminue," Prometheus reflects on his bird of prey, using (like Tityre, the author-hero of ***Paludes*** the words of John the Baptist at the baptism of Christ, "He must increase, and I must decrease" (John 3: 30). As long as the eagle remains external, Prometheus's divinity is unfulfilled; it is actualized in the Eucharist, the banquet of life in the company of Coclès and the *garçon* where the eagle is eaten in Holy Communion, *et nunc*, bringing eternal life to the body of the community. As so often in nineteenth-century literature (and already in Goethe's *Prometheus* fragment of 1774), the redeemer of mankind appears as a synthesis of Lucifer and Messiah, impotent in his intercession with a jealous God who scorns, persecutes, and punishes him with the vindictiveness of a suspicious superego. Prometheus, the redeemer-tempter, prefers to man that which devours man: "Je n'aime pas les hommes; j'aime ce qui les dévore." In this he resembles Zeus, who shows a sardonically clinical interest not in Damoclès the man but in his fatal disease. By what is man devoured? By his quest for self-fulfillment and identity, not by his pursuit of happiness. As the *garçon* explains to Prometheus, the crowd is searching for its personality on the "boulevard qui mène de la Madeleine à l'Opéra"—the broad road of sin which from the church of the forgiven sinner (Madeleine symbolizing Mary Magdalene) leads to operative grace, and where in the prelude Coclès, too, had tried to find happiness—"Ce qu'ils cherchent, c'est leur personnalité . . . ce que nous appelons ici,

idiosyncrasie." They have "no continuing city" here "but . . . seek one to come" (Heb. 13: 14). What the crowd seeks cannot be obtained by external means of grace: it is that *gratia operans* ("operative grace") which in mysterious ways effects a person's innermost self, working through his idiosyncrasies which he may never fully discover. The descent of the (lifted up) Prometheus ("The Son of Man must be lifted up," John 3: 14) takes place outside time, or rather in pagan cyclic time, seasonally: "entre quatre et cinq heures d'automne." Coclès and Damoclès, however, are situated in time, in history: Coclès, *natural* man, good *before* the fall, enters historical time after the fall when he reflects for the first time on good and evil: "Et si ce n'est pas par erreur—pensai-je, car pour la première fois je pensais; si ce soufflet m'était bien destiné!" Coclès with his temporal, linear existence can ask himself whether he owes his fall to *predestination* or rather to a *mistake* (a sin), just as Damoclès during the remainder of his earthly life can doubt his "call" since it merely came to him as a matter of chance (*fortuitement*). Prometheus alone can proclaim his extemporality, his existence outside history: "Vous avez chacun votre histoire; je n'en ai pas." Only when the time is ripe and harvest at hand does he appear symbolically, at the hour of the last supper whose reenactment connects the old Adam with the new man. In his sacramental concealment Prometheus remains incognito, unrecognizable.

"Chronique de la moralité privée," the subheading of the ***Prométhée***'s first part, ambiguously hints at the sacral farce of the arcana of predestination and free will: the "private morality" of the *acte gratuit* as the Augustinian *gratia gratis data*, a free act of divine grace which—undeserved and whimsical—goes counter to the expectations of public morality. Canceling out the concept of grace as the effect of good works, it deprives morality of its rewards, of its meaning. Hence, *la moralité privée* reveals a second hidden sense: it is "bereft of morality," or "morality abolished." Where an arbitrary act of grace predetermines before birth who will be among the elect, there too begins a mysterious and mystifying (*privée*) morality which is no longer justifiable by reason. It is the Pauline "il faut s'abêtir" of Pascal, stagnation in a pool of bad conscience, feelings of guilt and unfulfilled duties; it is self-hatred counteracting that continuous renewal of the self which for Gide is the true meaning of the Christian doctrine of redemption *et nunc* (John 6, *passim*) and which he still understands a quarter of a century later as the promise of a state of paradisiacal joy, here and now: "L'état de joie dont nous parle le Christ est un état, non point futur mais immédiat" [*Dostoïevsky: Articles et causeries* (1923)].

Mystery and mystification: To Prometheus (whom he does not recognize) the *garçon* explains the mystery of the *acte gratuit*, Coclès's rather unpleasant encounter with Zeus: a sort of pentecostal happening (it takes place in May) on the broad road between sin and operating grace; a descent of the Holy Spirit which at first seems to work against natural man (Coclès) in favor of the apparently "chosen" (but only "called") Damoclès, but which subsequently seems to reverse its action; a mystery which the *garçon* fails to comprehend although he attempts to explain what little he understands of it. In the *garçon*'s description this *acte gratuit* only admits a fideist interpretation. It must be accepted as a matter of faith and escapes rational cognition. In the *garçon*'s own terms, it occurred "without a motive," "irrationally" (*sans motif, sans raison*, "born of itself " (*né de soi*), a truly "disinterested act" (*l'acte désintéressé*, "without finality" (*l'acte aussi sans but*) and hence without a master (*donc sans maître*). Spontaneously generated, the *acte gratuit* is "free" (*l'acte libre*), an unrequested gift (*l'Acte autochthone*). Autochthonous in its allegorical divinity (implied by its capitalization), it potentially has the power of an entelechy which may or may not actualize potential grace in some one "called" but not necessarily "chosen." "J'étais quelconque, je suis quelqu'un," and "cette aventure me détermine," declares Damoclès most unhappy about the course of events which determines his unbidden "idiosyncrasy" as well as his fate. He misunderstands the possible salvation which his new state of unfreedom might bring him; likewise he fails to comprehend the decisive role of his will to resist, his *posse resistere*, his willful ingratitude (born of ignorance and annihilating grace), which too was a free gift of operative grace bestowed upon him by a divine irony cruel in its mystifying mysteries. One begins to see why Zeus is a banker: his gifts are illusory, they are merely *loans*— "Mon jeu c'est de prêter aux hommes . . . je prête, mais c'est avec l'air de donner." The owner of a banking establishment to which all mankind consciously or unknowingly is indebted, Zeus is also the banker at the cosmic gambling-table of grace where he keeps a bank that no one can break. Zeus's omnipotence, the sadistic cat-and-mouse game of his impenetrable acts of grace which destroy the skeptic Damoclès (who has no reason to believe himself "chosen" or even "called"), Zeus's cynical gambler's nature, capable only of winning, seem like a parody of the almost monotheistic Zeus of Aeschylus. Simultaneously his agnomen "le Miglionnaire" with its pseudo-Italian beginning ("Miglion-") points to ultramontane (Roman) origins, while its ending ("-naire") hints on one hand at the vernacular French, the language of the Reformed cult, and on the other hand at the four Gallican articles drawn up by Bossuet in 1682, the third of which insisted that the ancient privileges of the Gallican Church were inviolable: dark allusions which bring to mind the Bossuet quotation in Gide's diary [*Journal 1889-1939* (1951)] —so close to Calvinism—which we have cited as a text correlated with the morality of the ***Prométhée***. The word (or nonword) "Miglionnaire," derived from "million," an augmentative form of "mille," also puns upon "millénaire," the "millennium," while Zeus's uncommon corporeal substance (*sa peu commune corpulance*) and his indefinite age (*entre deux âges*) metaphorically indicate this god's role between two aeons. "Je suis riche, bien plus que l'on ne peut l'imaginer. Tu es à moi," he prides himself, speaking to Prometheus, and pointing to the *garçon*: "Il est à moi; tout est à moi." His infinite riches and health, his dubious monetary gift which like a sword hangs over Damoclès's head tormenting him unto sickness and death, the correlations between duties, debts (*dettes, devoirs*) and failing health correspond to the medical and economic vocabulary of Christian salvation.

Mystery and mystification: the *garçon* understands as little about the nature of Zeus and the supernatural prob-

lems of grace and predestination as Coclès and Damoclès, who are made to suffer through them; yet he humbly admires and accepts them as inscrutable matters of faith. Throughout the ***Prométhée*** the *garçon* plays the role of a mediator between the natural and the supernatural. In fact he holds the office of a minister. As such he remains anonymous. It is not his name, but his office alone that is important: *garçon* "waiter," in Latin, *minister*—a priest of the Reformed cult. He administers the three Calvinist sacraments: the Last Supper baptism and absolution (to the dying Damoclès). *Minister verbi Dei*, as minister of God's word he propagates the good word, talks to Zeus and intercedes with him, vaguely divines the nature of this *Deus ignotus*, the unknown God who does not reveal himself to reason and whose medical and financial services save only the believer, bringing damnation to the infidel. Although during Damoclès's fatal illness Zeus daily asks the *garçon* for news about the patient's health, he does not answer this minister's fervent prayers to make himself known to the anguished sufferer. "Damoclès guérirait pourtant s'il connaissait son bienfaiteur," the worried *garçon* confides in Prometheus. "Je le lui dis [à Zeus], mais il persiste, veut garder son incognito." "Zeus incognito, Deus ignotus": like Calvin's God, Zeus is interested in evil, in Damoclès's sin, not in the creature who is suffering from evil, from sin. "C'est, non Damoclès, mais bien sa maladie qui l'intéresse," the *garçon* comments, reporting Zeus's attitude of scientific detachment. Gide's God is the God of the Romantics, who condemns because he has made man's moral life impossible ("la moralité privée" par Dieu!). Zeus is touched neither by Coclès's anxiety nor by Damoclès's agonies. Like Blake's "Nobodaddy," a sardonic and unmoved mover, he plays the experimentalist who calmly watches the effects of his gratuitous act. The *garçon* imitates Zeus the observer: "Si vous croyez que tout ça le tourmente [Zeus]!! C'est comme moi: il observe . . . ." "To observe" at the same time implies for Zeus the observance of his own laws for predestination and grace, and for the *garçon* that of the rites of his cult. In an interview, Zeus reveals his protean nature to the "observing" and "observant" *garçon*. He first appears as the occult force of finance capital—the ***Prométhée***'s action falls into the period of the Dreyfus affair, and Gide seems to avail himself of an opportunity to express his discretely *Dreyfusard* attitude, deriding the *anti-Dreyfusards*' professed fear of a conspiracy of "international Jewish finance capital." "Vous me croyez banquier; je suis bien autre chose," Zeus tells the *garçon*. "Mon action . . . est cachée, mais n'est pas moins considérable." But he immediately changes into the Leibnizian watchmaker God: "Oui, j'ai surtout l'esprit d'initiative. Je lance. Puis, une fois une affaire lancée, je la laisse; je n'y touche plus." He distributes those eagles which, as conscience and consciousness, devour all vitality. He himself has no eagle. "Pas plus que dans le creux de la main," he asserts, alluding to his omnipotence as that of a Lord who hath measured the waters "in the hollow of his hand" and whose Spirit has not been "directed" by any "counsellor" (Isa. 40: 12-13). Zeus, the "*garçon*'s friend," is humbly told by this minister, "[On dit] que vous êtes le Bon Dieu"; and he answers with truly Gidean coquetry, "Je me le suis laissé dire . . . ."

Mystery and mystification: the problems of free will, predestination, and grace—or determinism. The doctrinary *garçon* as propagator of the divine Word speaks of his long hesitation between belief and disbelief in man's freedom of action: "J'ai longtemps pensé que c'était là ce qui distinguait l'homme des animaux: une action gratuite." The feminine form *action gratuite*, its gender implying passivity, seems here to contrast a fallible human action with the creative *acte gratuit*, the divine act of grace. "J'appelais l'homme: l'animal capable d'une action gratuite." The sentence twists Aristotle's definition of man as an *animal rationale*, suggesting the hubris involved in any attempt to liken man's supposed freedom of rational action with the irrational mystery of the divine act of grace. Faced with this inscrutable matter of faith, the *garçon* resists the temptation of determinism: "ça n'est pas pourtant que je sois déterministe" by professing belief in the paradoxical coexistence of free will and predestined grace. He also accepts the absurdity of a "calling" that does not necessarily result in the "choosing" of the elect: "Il s'agit de trouver quelqu'un sans le choisir." In these words he explains the deceptive call which goes out to Damoclès by way of the banker's *acte gratuit*. The fate of Gide's Damoclès resembles in fact that of his legendary namesake at the court of the tyrant Dionysius I: "Destrictus ensis impia / Cervice pendet" ("over whose impious head the drawn sword hangeth," Horace *Carmina*), or as Cicero, who tells the anecdote, comments, "Satisne videtur declarasse Dionysius nihil esse ei beatum, cui semper aliqui terror impendeat?" ("Does not Dionysius seem to have said plainly that there was no prosperity for a man perpetually threatened by terror?" Cicero *Disput. tuscul.*). Just as the knowledge of the sword suspended over his neck by a horsehair destroys the Syracusan courtier's joy in his lord's gift, so Gide's Damoclès is unable to enjoy the money sent him by Zeus: he is devoured by his lack of faith (his particular "eagle"); his bad conscience about the undeserved grace bestowed upon him makes of him a desperate seeker for his creditor to whom he wants to return the five hundred franc note. It was given him to deprive him of his peace, and for the amusement of Zeus. As in Calvinist doctrine, the "call from without" must be complemented by an "inner call" which Damoclès cannot experience. He lacks the primary condition for listening to the potential call from within, namely faith ("The wicked man travaileth with pain all his days. . . . A dreadful sound is in his ears: in prosperity the destroyer shall come upon him. He believeth not that he shall return out of darkness, and he is waited for by the sword," Job 15: 20-22). Zeus experiments, playing his deceptive game at Damoclès's expense: "J'aime qu'on ne sache pas que je prête. Je joue, mais je cache mon jeu. J'expérimente. . . . Ce que je prête aux hommes, ce que je plante en l'homme, je m'amuse à ce que cela pousse; je m'amuse à le voir pousser. L'homme sans quoi serait si vide!" This passage anticipates the essence of Prometheus's parable of Tityre and his tree. Efficient grace is without us and can enter into us only through faith. Not the means of grace, not faith, not freedom, not redemption are planted here, but servitude, suffering, malicious joy at the damnation of others. "Je suis descendu dans la rue," Zeus explains his intentions, "cherchant le moyen de faire souffrir quelqu'un du don que j'allais faire à quelque autre; de faire jouir cet autre du mal que j'allais faire à cet un":

for Coclès the slap in the face (which he hardly feels at all); for Damoclès the five hundred francs, a carte blanche of pardon which painfully weighs on his conscience as a debt heavier to bear than the sins it is supposed to wipe out. The means of grace are clearly perceptible; the principle of their distribution, "la façon de les donner" remains unclear and unintelligible. Prometheus, who has every reason to believe that he knows this principle, is grouchily put into his place by Zeus with a crude "Et quoi! vous connaissez." Zeus wants to keep his prestige: prestige not only literally but in the primitive sense of the word (still current in the age of the Reformation), i.e., a sorcery, an illusion, a deception, a magician's trick ("Je ne veux pas perdre mon prestige"), a major reason why he does not make himself known to Damoclès. The secret of the illusion must be kept to the bitter end, and possibly beyond. Hence too the *acte gratuit* does not make apparent precisely who is redeemed, in whose person, under whose mask. Is it the Cyclops-like Coclès, the "natural" man, who gives his eye for an eye (of glass) which he wears "not without grace" (*pas sans grâce*), a man of faith, gratitude, and works? Coclès who (in vain) offers the other cheek (Luke 6: 29)—"il tend en vain son autre joue"—and cautiously seeks and "researches" Zeus, only to avoid him, without knowing why, and without ever seeing him again ("je recherchai bien mon giffleur; oui, mais ce fut pour l'éviter, . . . et si je l'évitai, ce fut sans le savoir,")? (The *passé simple* indicates the uniqueness of this search and research which took place once, in the past.) In short, is Coclès redeemed by the sacrifice of Damoclès the Jansenist or Calvinist pessimist who, graceless, *ingrate*, simply cannot believe in "sufficient grace"? Or is Damoclès saved despite his ungracious ingratitude and his sickness unto death, healed after death because of Zeus's *acte gratuit*, his capricious and disturbingly ambiguous gift of grace? Does Damoclès's fleshly death precede his spiritual rebirth? Impenetrable, the "banker's" *acte gratuit* illustrates the mystery of Christ's deputyship, the interchangeability of guilt and expiation (II Cor. 5: 18-21), and Joseph de Maistre's doctrine of the reversibility of guilt and punishment, according to which in the plan of divine love the seemingly guiltless are made to suffer and expiate for the guilty. From the divine viewpoint, *sub specie aeternitatis*, the question of who suffers for whom is indifferent. All of Zeus's experiments are admissible since original sin has affected all mankind with collective guilt. "Car parce que l'acte est gratuit, il est ce que nous appelons ici: *réversible*," explains the *garçon*: "Un qui a reçu cinq cents francs pour un soufflet, l'autre qui a reçu un soufflet pour cinq cents frances." This grotesque commentary in the circus style of clowneries underlines the indifference—i.e., the *equivalence*—of reward and punishment: there is nothing to choose between Coclès, and Damoclès, *l'un vaut l'autre*. The *garçon*'s pious gloss stresses the one-sidedness of free grace (*gratia gratis data*). Zeus may give or lend as much as he likes; the recipient of his unwanted gifts or loans, however, is not allowed to refuse or return his gracious grants. Coclès, in the spirit of Jansenism and the Reformation, is drastically taught the Pauline doctrine that without deserving it he is "justified freely by his [God's] grace through the redemption that is in Christ Jesus" (Rom. 3: 24). Neither participation in the sacraments nor good works can be of assistance; free grace alone, *l'acte gratuit*, is efficient; and free grace, at first glance, does not seem to be bestowed upon Coclès. Free grace is radically opposed to salvation through the obedient observance of the law (Rom. 5: 21; 6: 14; Gal. 5: 4). It precludes in Paul's teachings the very tokens of obedience to the law: good works (Coclès's eagerness in the prelude, his establishment of a hospital for the one-eyed) and "fleshly wisdom" (II Cor. 1: 12), i.e., Coclès's natural goodness. But the redemption of Damoclès too remains dubious, in spite of his calling: he failed to be justified by faith (Rom. 5: 1f.).

Mystery and mystification: as soon as the *garçon* attempts to apply reasoning to the complex problems of this situation, all categories become tangled. The incomprehensible mystery of the *acte gratuit* is confused with the human rationality of the *action gratuite*. The *garçon* gets lost in the labyrinth of the inscrutables while there emerge simultaneously the demoralizing aspects of predestination and grace which seem to render superfluous, useless, redundant all moral efforts and behaviour: "Et puis on ne sait plus . . . on s'y perd—Songez donc! une action gratuite! il n'y a rien de plus démoralisant." Faced with the insoluble mystery, all "knowledge" comes to an end. Seen from the vantage point of human reason and reduced to the level of an impulsive and free action (*l'action gratuite*), the divine act of grace appears to be little more than a disinterested yet absurd game, a sort of first prize won in the lottery of providence—a winning ticket for which the winner did not pay, which won *sans raison* and, taken at face value, does not seem to benefit the winner; altogether a puzzling happening, totally devoid of morality (*la moralité privée!*), profitless, a game for game's sake to which Zeus alone holds all the clues. "Moi seul, celui-là seul dont la fortune est *infinie* peut agir avec un désintéressement absolu; l'homme pas. De là vient mon amour du jeu; non pas du gain, comprenez-moi—du jeu; que pourrais-je gagner que je n'aie pas d'avance? Le temps même. . . ." The disinterested game with grace and predestination reveals itself as the impulsive pastime of a God who has exiled himself from time, taking refuge in eternity. The sporadic experimentation with which he passes away the time resembles a parody of the positivistic *Zeitgeist* of the 1890s, the spirit of scientific observation which overlaps that of Zola's naturalist manifesto on *Le Roman expérimental* (scorned by Gide) and where the ills of man in society are seen *à travers un tempérament*, but with a clinical detachment similar to Zeus's attitude toward the dying Damoclès. Viewed in this fashion, there seems to be a common denominator of farce and disinterested gambling—conscious on the divine level, unsuspected on that of the creature—between *l'acte gratuit*, the capricious act of grace, and *l'action gratuite*, the free, rational, "scientifically correct" action by which Man in search of salvation (theological, scientific, or novelistic) is unknowingly led into a grotesque impasse.

Revelation can be given through the casting of lots (Josh. 18:6; Acts 1:26). "Sortilege" is *sortes legere*, reading the outcome of events from sacred lots, as practiced by Homer's Greeks and by Mopsus when the Argonauts embarked. *Fatum* is the oracular word, the word as fate, and soothsaying an attempt to influence the course of future

happenings, to force fate into a mold. In the Virgilian lots (*sortes Vergilianae*) the future is foretold by opening at random a volume of Virgil: Virgil the necromancer whose fourth *Eclogue* was believed to be typological, a prophecy of Christianity; Virgil, who was glorified in Dante's *Divina Commedia* as a prophet of Christianity and regarded throughout the Middle Ages and the Renaissance as *anima naturaliter Christiana*, a Christian soul by nature. The *sortes Vergilianae* are a rite piously performed by medieval Christians. A prophecy is captured by pricking a needle into the haphazardly opened New Testament or the Virgilian codex. The word caught, in more than one sense a "catchword," foretells and influences the future. Augustine called this type of white magic *de paginis evangelicis sortes legere* ("soothsaying from the pages of the Gospels"). As literal interpretation of biblical passages, *sortes Vergilianae* are a sortilege practiced to the present day by fundamentalists.

The lots of Damoclès and Coclès—their respective conscience and consciousness, their "eagles"—are determined by the casting of lots, by a divine "coup de dés [qui] jamais n'abolira le hasard." Damoclès "called" dies while doubting his potential redemption. Coclès, "fallen" under a divine blow and deprived of an eye by a blow of the divine eagle's wing, Coclès, severely tried by Zeus, survives and participates with Prometheus and the *garçon* in the banquet of life: the divine casting of the dice has not abolished chance.

The lots of Damoclès and Coclès picked by a needle in God's creative Word are objects, played into their hands by Zeus as matters of chance: for Coclès the *mouchoir*, the sudarium; for Damoclès the five hundred franc note. The sudarium might be that of Lazarus risen from the dead (John 11:44), a dark prophecy of salvation for Coclès ("Non est ad astra mollis a terris via"; "Does not the road to heaven lead through new-turned earth?" Seneca *Herc. fur.*). Or it might be the sudarium of the wicked servant, who hoards in it his master's pound without accumulating interest. It is taken away from its idle keeper, "For I say unto you, That unto every one which hath shall be given; and from him that hath not, even that he hath shall be taken away from him" (Luke 19:11-26); or, Matthew 25:27, "il te fallait donc remettre mon argent aux banquiers." A prophecy of Coclès's damnation and Damoclès's redemption? God's word picked by lot for Damoclès? In the parable of the two debtors (Luke 7:41), one owes "five hundred pence," and the other fifty; "And when they had nothing to pay, he frankly forgave them both" (Luke 7:42). Coclès and Damoclès likewise have nothing to pay, for everything belongs to the "Miglionnaire," to Zeus who allows himself to be called "le Bon Dieu" and who can frankly forgive his debtors by free grace, *l'acte gratuit*. "Nullus enim potest per seipsum a debito peccati liberari, nisi divina gratia veniam consequatur"; "No one can be freed from the debt of sins, unless divine grace will follow mercy" (Pope Gregory the Great, XXXIIIa *Homelia in evang*). The moral: the debtor whom the creditor loves most is the one whom he has forgiven most (Luke 7:42-43), provided, of course, that the borrower show "gratitude." This latter grace depends on his knowledge of his master's forgiveness. Zeus, worried about his "prestige," does not let himself be loved. Damoclès is allowed to feel his "guilt," the burden of his fated and fateful "debt," but he will never know his creditor's name; his life-destroying doubts prevent *fides* (both "faith," and, in its Latin meaning, "monetary credit"). Lacking faith and *gratia praeveniens* ("anticipatory grace" which enlightens understanding), he cannot believe in forgiveness of his "debt." He is unable to curb his impious curiosity to know a creditor who wants to remain incognito, *Deus ignotus*, the unknown God. Grace is withheld from him; he cannot be grateful for a "debt" which he had no desire to contract. Hence he lacks the two primary conditions for "forgiveness": faith and the inner grace of gratitude. His "humiliation," quite literally a "lowering" (conveyed by way of a medical image, *"un rétrécissement de la colonne,"*) occurs after Prometheus's speech exhorting all men to love their devouring eagles in order to ensure the beauty of these birds of prey. Damoclès's irredeemable ills increase while Coclès (for whom he worries) painfully attempts to sacrifice himself: "Il [Coclès] ne parle plus que de se dévouer et passe tout son temps à chercher partout dans les rues une nouvelle gifle qui vaille quelque argent à quelque nouveau Damoclès. Il tend en vain l'autre joue." The *garçon* suggests to Prometheus that only a "brusque and miraculous salvation" could help Damoclès: "A moins d'un salut brusque et miraculeux, le mal ne peut que s'aggraver. Il est très bas, je vous assure"—an ambiguous hint at Damoclès's "humiliation" in the scriptural sense of the word. The creditor avoids any contact with Damoclès and even with Coclès, to whom he had shown himself once. For Damoclès he remains *deus absconditus*, the hidden God, never manifesting himself as *deus revelatus*, the revealed God, in the spirit of *gemina praedestinatio*, twin predestination, as Augustine, Luther, and Calvin had taught. For both Coclès and Damoclès, this hidden God without revelation has staged an eschatological joke without apocalyptic significance. In a Calvinist sense, Damoclès cannot believe in grace offered him without revelation; nor can Coclès by his eager devotion, by "passing all his time in the streets looking for a new slap," find that "free grace" which "is not of him that willeth nor of him that runneth, but of God that showeth mercy" (Rom. 9:16). Damoclès lacks *gratia efficax*, efficient grace which alone can enlighten, Augustine's *crede ut intelligas* ("believe"—but also in an economic sense, "lend," "loan"— "so that you may understand"). Where there is no efficient grace, there can be no answer to questions even if the questioning follows the best scholastic order of *cur, unde, quo, qua* "Votre gain prenait sur ma misère," Coclès reproaches Damoclès. But the treasure which, thanks to Coclès's suffering, fell into Damoclès's lap oppresses Damoclès; he is tormented at the idea that "c'est grâce à la gifle d'un autre que je tiens là ces cinq cents francs!" These undeserved riches are useless to him but he is incapable of parting with them. He does not dare to consider them as a "reward," a salary earned for his salvation (*salus* meaning health). Consequently he does not deposit this money in "the savings bank" (*la Caisse d'épargne*) as savings which bring interest (*oeconomia*, in the patristic vocabulary of salvation). The result is that altogether the worries about his "debt," the unrestituted five hundred francs, poison his life. They are his Promethean eagle, his "idiosyncrasy";

inalienably rooted in his conscience and consciousness, they keep him out of the kingdom of heaven ("Verily I say unto you, That a rich man shall hardly enter into the kingdom of heaven" [Matt. 19:23]). Neither for Coclès nor for Damoclès do the prophecies of the *sortes Vergilianae* abolish chance. Instead of bringing health and freedom (*franchise, affranchissement*) to Damoclès, the "hated, execrated" five hundred francs seem to enslave him toward everyman, toward all and no one in particular: "Ces cinq cents francs, haïs, exécrés, je croyais les devoir à tous et n'osais les donner à aucun—j'en aurais *privé tous les autres*." The impasse of charity and grace is one of choice and cruelty, the privilege of the powerful, the mystery of the Almighty, inaccessible to Damoclès whose moral scruples keep him within that limbo of indecision where dwell *le genti dolorose / C'hanno perduto il ben dell'intelletto* ("the suffering race / Who have lost the wealth of intellect," Dante, *Inferno* III). Once each week he brings the worthless means of grace back into circulation without being able to cast it off: he changes the banknote into coins, the coins again into a banknote. "C'est une folie circulaire," the vicious circle of an ever-repeated exchange without redemption that encompasses and stifles his life; the whole process is economically unsound, and does not lead to salvation. The moral dilemma produced by Zeus's immoral gift of grace ruins his health; the interplay of Damoclès's lack of merit, his feelings of indebtedness and duty (*dettes* and *devoir*), as well as the concealed and impenetrable identity of his creditor and "benefactor," undermine his vital substance: "Seigneur! Seigneur!" he cries out, "à qui devais-je? . . . Le devoir, Messieurs, c'est une chose horrible; moi, j'ai pris le parti d'en mourir." The guilt feeling that drives him freely to choose death deprives him of free actions (*les actions gratuites*). He is literally possessed by his "possession," the obsessive five hundred francs which weigh on him so that he cannot be supernaturally uplifted by *gratia elevans*, uplifting grace. "Denarios quingentos," five hundred francs, those *fata* (oracular and fatal words) determining his lot, also point to the fact that redemption was lost on the "boulevard qui mène de la Madeleine à l'Opéra" (Coclès's broad road of Damascus, leading from sin to operative grace) where the passing crowd (*massa perditionis*, "the masses of the damned"—but also "the bankrupt"!) in vain seek their salvation, their personalities, their idiosyncrasies, and where Coclès had earned for his good deed the brutal reprobation of Zeus. The grateful sinner who in the house of Simon the Pharisee had washed with her tears and anointed Christ's feet (Luke 7:36ff.) is traditionally confused with Mary Magdalene ("la Madeleine"). "Therefore I tell you that her sins, her many sins, must have been forgiven her, or she would not have shown such great love" (Luke 7:47). "Your faith has saved you" (Luke 7:50). In the medicoeconomic vocabulary of salvation faith and love have saved and enriched the sinner. They are precisely those gifts of grace which Damoclès lacks in order to be healed and freed of his debts; their absence drives him to his death.

In their eagerness to fulfill the law, their *devoir*, and to follow the voice of reason, Coclès and Damoclès are incapable of understanding that self-humiliation and unquestioning faith are prerequisites for efficient grace. Opposed to the rationality of the law (Rom. 5:21; 6:14; Gal. 5:4), efficient grace precludes rewards for good works (Rom. 4:4; 11:5f.; 3:24) and frustrates the "fleshly wisdom" (II Cor. 1:12) of reasoning. Seeking their salvation on the broad road "where sin [abounds]" without knowing that "there [does] grace much more abound" (Rom. 5:20), they want to obtain redemption by performing their duty. They remain unredeemed as long as they fail to comprehend the christological miracle of redemption from the law. It is true that Damoclès, through the five hundred francs, has an epiphany, an Easter experience of sorts; they give him his *nouvelles pensées*, uplifting him from the triviality of his *anciennes pensées*. The old Adam seems to give way to the new man: "Je menais une vie parfaitement ordinaire et me faisais un devoir de cette formule: ressembler au plus commun des hommes." The observance of the law (*devoir*) is now replaced by Damoclès's discovery of his uniqueness, a distinction bestowed upon him by Zeus's *acte gratuit* through which Damoclès feels that he has been chosen: "Or, . . . depuis trente jours, je sens que je suis un être original, unique, répondant à une singulière destinée." Thirty days of the new and unique life, the new month or moon (*lune*) of a singular destiny, of spiritual rebirth in an idiosyncrasy at last found, stand in a cryptic relationship to Prometheus's discourse in the *salle des nouvelles lunes*, that sort of auditorium and hall of a new age, a new aeon where the revelation of the Incarnate Word ("le Discours de Prométhée") appears to cause Damoclès's fatal disease and Coclès's conspicuous restoration to health: "Le secret de leur vie est dans le dévouement à leur dette; toi, Coclès, à ta gifle; toi, Damoclès, à ton billet." Damoclès fails to understand Prometheus's warning: "[il te fallait] garder tes cinq cents francs, continuer de les devoir sans honte, d'en devoir plus encore, de devoir avec joie." Damoclès's fears, his life-devouring conscience, his joyless ingratitude for the free gift of a new personality, an idiosyncrasy, demonstrate his inability to recognize the signs of grace mysteriously bestowed on his person which could not have been attained by external means (*ex opere operato*, "by grace worked through the sacrament"). By refusing his lot in the lottery of grace, he throws away his life. He cannot redeem the five hundred francs which he does not allow to redeem him. Without blind acceptance and love of his fate (the Nietzschean *amor fati*), the sortilege cast upon him by his fate must needs become fatal to him. For he tries to rid himself of that which the passersby in vain attempt to find on the sinful road of the law, the "boulevard qui mène de la Madeleine à l'Opéra." Neither the unexpected letter with the five hundred francs nor Prometheus's discourse is interpreted by Damoclès as the revelation of his redemption: both give him the painful awareness of a debt unwittingly contracted and for which nonetheless he must assume full responsibility. Zeus's gift of grace, freely played into his hands by the stupidity of chance, ignites in him a fervor not of belief but of desperate longing for some sign of life from his creditor.

Zeus's letter to Damoclès contains the five hundred franc note, a material gift (or loan) but no spiritual message. Not knowing what to make of it, Damoclès takes the envelope with its address "d'une écriture inconnue"—*écriture* meaning "handwriting," but also "scripture"—to a number of graphologists for a minute analysis. In these graphologists one easily recognizes a modern metaphor for the Sopherim, the Biblical scribes, learned in the Scriptures and in the exposition of the law, but always presented in the New Testament as myopic jurists deeply concerned with the letter of the law, blind and deaf to the spirit, and devoid of any understanding for the mysteries of grace. The spirit of this *écriture*, this Scripture, remains unknown to the scribes as well as to Damoclès. According to the judgment of some graphologists, it testified to the great bounty (*d'une grande bonté*) on the part of the writer; others saw in it signs of weakness (*plutôt de la faiblesse*). Damoclès concludes: "Le manque complet de caractère qu'elle [l'écriture] m'a révélé dans la suite par l'entremise des graphologues consultés ne m'a permis de rien apprendre." The writer, of course, was Coclès; his "manque complet de caractère" points to the absence of a personality, of an "idiosyncrasy" of his own. As writer of the unknown scripture, the *écriture inconnue* addressed to Damoclès which so badly upsets the latter, he seems to reveal a second identity: that of a scriptural writer of epistles containing a message of grace, incomprehensible to human reason. In other words, Coclès is at the same time the "old Adam" (Saul) and the "new man" (Paul); his encounter with Zeus on the *grands boulevards* represented Saul's conversion into Paul on the road to Damascus as well as Adam's fall. His persecution of the Lord turned into the pursuit of the Lord: in the grotesque language of the *sotie*, the handkerchief dropped (and picked up) as a coquettish token of erotic intentions ("love") and the blow given to Coclès represent Saul's fall and subsequent rise on the way to Damascus, his rebirth as Paul which makes him oblivious to the suffering inflicted upon him by Zeus, the threefold God (Zeus, the Father; the banker, $\sigma\omega\tau\eta\rho$, the savior; the "Miglionnaire," the Holy Spirit—cast out to the millions of believers as the promised riches of the millennium).

By having the mere envelope of Zeus's gift analysed by dubious graphologists, Damoclès proceeds like the scribes of the new Testament, but also like Protestant exegetes and textual critics whose rationalist literal-mindedness enables them to realize the human origins of the *écriture*, the scriptural manuscript (the "bounty" or "weakness" of Coclès-Saul-Paul). What they all fail to see is its spirit, the symbolism of the mystery, Zeus's *acte gratuit* which, in the form of the trivial five hundred franc note, was concealed underneath the human handwriting—mysterious in itself and hidden in its envelope—in vain awaiting Damoclès's confession of faith, which alone could have activated its liberating gift of grace. But Damoclès is not redeemed, for he follows Coclès in his footsteps on the road to Damascus without understanding the sign which is sent him. He only knows of his guilt, and this rational knowledge of his debt causes him to fulfill his *devoir*, to live up to the demands of the law by the use of external means of grace (*ex opere operato*, on the way to the Opéra): "Reconnaissant, je voudrais l'être—mais je ne sais pas envers qui." He feels enslaved to Zeus's banknote, not realizing that it is his free ticket, his pass for redemption: "Avant j'étais banal mais libre. A présent j'appartiens à lui [billet]." Shortsightedly he cannot see beyond the present moment. Damoclès's unrecognized passport for salvation turns into chagrin, shagreen, a Balzacian *peau de chagrin*, a property of which the owner cannot rid himself and which rapidly shortens his life. Coclès too refuses the gift of grace for purely legal reasons; he is careful not to pass on Zeus's slap to Damoclès—preventing him from having a "road to Damascus" experience—for he fears "Si je vous avais rendu la gifle vous eussiez cru devoir me rendre ce billet, et . . . il ne m'appartient pas." Having only written the address on the envelope, he remains in the dark and fearful as to the meaning of its contents.

The chance of predestination determines the receiver of the fateful gift of grace. Coclès fortuitously (*fortuitement*) knew Damoclès by his name, by a strange hazard which however approached a mysterious and mystifying illumination: "Le nom que j'inscrivis, et qui vint je ne sais comment dans ma tête, était pour moi celui d'un inconnu!" Arbitrarily, Coclès had become the instrument of revelation (in his own way, a myopic "scribe" of providence to whom the spirit of the "letter" he inscribed remained unknown). Arbitrarily, Damoclès had misunderstood the meaning of this revelation. He had seen his only salvation in the remote possibility of redeeming his mysterious and unrecognized pass to redemption by returning it to his unknown creditor. Obviously, Zeus's offer of grace had not been a serious one, for predestination refused Damoclès the receiving grace of faith without which he could not have received salvation. Finally, chance had determined the fall of Coclès as the punishment *and* reward of someone who has persecuted, and (without knowing it) pursued, sought the Lord and seen the hidden God, *Deus absconditus*: Coclès, the receiver of the burning blow dealt him by a god, of the Promethean fire, of ardent illumination, and of Gidean *ferveur*—Coclès-Saul-Paul on the road to Damascus; and Coclès, the narrow-minded, who loses one eye to the Promethean eagle, to the descending Holy Spirit—Coclès-Paul, the myopic Pauline tradition (as seen by Gide), one-eyed in its lacking of depth-perception. Limited, and full of good will, Coclès is always ready for external grace: "Mon désir n'étant point de me soustraire à une motivation extérieure, je me soumis." For a Christian, his behavior is at least externally correct. He begins his *histoire* with repeated assertions that he has no great relations on earth: "Je n'ai pas grandes relations sur la terre." He proves his missionary zeal, his piety. As the founder of a hospital for the one-eyed (a refuge for those suffering from literal-mindedness) he shows his charity; and he even follows the command of the Sermon on the Mount by offering (however vainly) his other cheek. But everything points to the fact that Coclès-Saul-Paul remains until Damoclès's death a figure not of the present but of the Mosaic law, even of Moses himself: his face's burning from Zeus's slap gives witness to his vision of God; what Coclès brings back is the law and the Messianic promise. Even in the hospital which he directs, the one-eyed inmates seem to owe their condition to the survival of the "old law" of "an eye for an eye." And the *garçon*, with Christian anti-Semitism, accuses Coclès of being crafty in his business dealings: "C'est un roublard. Avec l'argent que lui rapporte la collecte, il songe à fonder un hospice. . . . Un petit, oui; rien que pour les borgnes. Il s'en est nommé directeur." As the Church was founded with secular means, and upon the doctrines of Paul, so, in a Nietzschean sense, he founds a hospital for those who are failing, shady, suspicious (*borgnes!*), kings among the blind. In sum,

nothing has changed since the days of the law, nothing will change until the death of Damoclès and the protean Coclès's redemption from the shackles of Pauline teachings at the banquet of life where, in the company of the *garçon* and Prometheus, the Promethean eagle is eaten. (pp. 35-62)

Kurt Weinberg, in his On Gide's "Prométhée:" Private Myth and Public Mystification, *Princeton University Press, 1976, 145 p.*

Dennis J. Spininger   (essay date 1975)

[*In the following essay, Spininger examines Gide's juxtaposition of his* sotie *and* récit *modes in the novella* Marshlands (Paludes).]

It has been generally acknowledged that André Gide's early work, **Paludes**, written in the years 1893-94 and published in 1895, constitutes a departure from the writings which preceded it. It can be read as a satirical commentary on the artificial earnestness and *préciosité* not only of literary cults, the Symbolistes in particular, but of Gide's own prior range of emotional expression and ideological limits. It also offers a crucial perspective on the generic terms later devised by Gide himself (in 1914) to classify and describe so much of his prose fiction—the *sotie* and the *récit*—for it is a mixed and complex variant of both. When Gide revived the term *sotie* (from the medieval drama, where it was used to describe a satire of the burlesque kind) to baptize three of his works, **Paludes, Le Prométhée mal enchaîné**, and *Les Caves du Vatican*, he underlined the satiric thrust which these works have in common. He also provided a potentially false restriction which has prevented many critics from perceiving the formal complexity of **Paludes**, whose fundamental nature is that of the mixed mode.

Actually Gide himself employed two other generic terms for this work, long before he sought to differentiate between the *sotie*, the *récit*, and the novel as the three main divisions of his prose. **Paludes** was originally subtitled the "Treatise on Contingency," and in the dedication Gide declares that the work is a satire, but refuses to specify the targets of his ironic commentary by calling it a "satire de quoi" ("a satire on—what?"). But just as treatise and satire are not mutually exclusive terms, and in their way unite the apparently opposing possibilities of serious persuasion and burlesque, so the corresponding terms *récit* and *sotie* define generic modes, potentially disparate in that the emphasis of each tends to work in opposite directions, but capable of successful union. The richness of **Paludes**, in fact, derives from such a successful union.

The unnamed narrator-protagonist of the work is a writer who creates an exaggeratedly serious *récit* called "Paludes," which is only one, though a major, element of Gide's *sotie*, also ironically called **Paludes**. The combination was Gide's masterstroke; it established at once the intricate weaving of distance and sympathy, of absurdity and pathos, a complex *chiaroscuro* of neatly balanced double effects. Like the title, the generic form is double. The formal procedures by which Gide shaped this into a coherent single work is the topic of this study.

Nor are the double effects limited to formal elements. The combination of burlesque irregularities and satiric whimsy on the one hand and a serious critique on the other has thematic correlatives. The work is informed by a playful contrast of the apparent and the real, of the ludicrous and the serious, and constantly raises the distinction between fiction and life in ways appropriate to the mixed generic mode. The genre is a mutation, and crucial distinctions and similarities between the *sotie* and the *récit* can be exposed by an examination of how the one is organically grafted onto the other in this work.

[In *The French Novel from Gide to Camus* (1962)] Germaine Brée once sought to illuminate the two modes by referring to common ingredients, but arranged in different proportions and with differing objectives: "in both cases he [the Gidean hero] is pathetic and absurd; explicitly pathetic and implicitly absurd in the *récit*, explicitly absurd and implicitly pathetic in the *sotie*." When the two modes are successfully combined, as they, are in *Paludes*, this tenuous balance of pathos and absurdity is complicated and enriched. One formula of this combination is that the comic strands of the *sotie* operate from the outer shell as both mirror and critique of the interior *récit*.

The first and last of the formal gestures in *Paludes*, the dedication and the "Table des phrases les plus remarquables de *Paludes*" ("List of the most remarkable phrases in *Paludes*"), which invites the reader (out of consideration for "personal idiosyncrasies") to fill in his own additions to the list, form an overt parody of the collaboration theory. Yet we know that Gide took this theory rather seriously. Long before discussion of the "intentional fallacy" was brought into critical vogue, he indicated his awareness of possible meaning distinct from his own intentions. In the preface to *Paludes*, he postulates a separation of the creative and the critical faculties, which are to be reunited through collaboration of the author and the reader:

> Avant d'expliquer aux autres mon livre, j'attendis que d'autres me l'expliquent. Vouloir l'expliquer d'abord c'est en restreindre aussitôt le sens; car si nous savons ce que nous voulions dire, nous ne savons pas si nous ne disions que cela.

> [Before explaining my book to others, I am waiting for others to explain it to me. To want to explain it beforehand would immediately restrict its meaning; for if we know what we wanted to say, we do not know whether we were saying only that.]

In other words, Gide both affirms the theory of collaboration and criticizes it through parody. Gide's genuine desire to make contact with his readers sometimes led to superficial devices, but here he establishes an artistic equilibrium. His control is demonstrated by this ability to see an absurd dimension even in a theory he holds to be true.

His narrator also proposes a theory of collaboration, but he does not possess the sense of humor by which he can detach himself from the comic consequences to which the theory is liable when the possible revealed meanings are not at least tied down to textual evidence. It is an act of

intelligence to allow that one's results may be different from one's intentions; it is the height of absurdity to suppose, as the narrator seems to, that the range of interpretations can be as unlimited as the individuals who make them. Gide's refusal to proscribe specific limits in his dedication of this "satire" may be a serious extension of his desire not to restrict meaning for the reader in advance. The blank page that follows the two items Gide himself placed on the list of remarkable phrases, "pour respecter l'idiosyncrasie de chacun" ("in order to respect the idiosyncrasy of each [reader]"), is deliberately comic.

There are many links between Gide and his artist-narrator, especially as the narrator develops an aesthetic from the process of writing itself. Among the many lucid statements about art, which in their totality constitute an impressive *ars poetica*, the narrator claims that

> l'art est de peindre un sujet particulier avec assez de puissance pour que la généralité dont il dépendait s'y comprenne. . . . Il suffit qu'il y ait possibilité de généralisation, la généralisation c'est au lecteur, au critique de la faire.

> [Art consists of painting a particular subject with power sufficient to contain the generality on which it depended. . . . It suffices that there should be the possibility of generalization; it is for the reader, the critic, to make the generalization.]

As different as Gide's *Paludes* is from the narrator's "Paludes," they share an identical conception here.

But Gide can see the comic vulnerability of this theory, whereas the narrator cannot. When an acquaintance, Nicodème, remarks upon the story of "Paludes," he misconstrues the evidence to discover an irony not present in the text. The narrator realizes that Nicodème has misunderstood, but the humor is heightened because he cannot appreciate that the whole scene is a comic version of reader collaboration. Again, when Angèle comments on the beauty of a poem he has improvised, he is perplexed and says:

> Puis, vous avez peut-être raison;—il se peut en effet qu'ils soient bons. L'auteur ne sait jamais bien lui-mème. . . .

> [Then, perhaps you are right;—it is quite possible that they (the verses) may be good. The author himself never really knows. . . .]

Both Angèle's demonstrable stupidity concerning aesthetic matters and the narrator's reduction of the collaboration theory to the ridiculous proposition that the author cannot tell if a judgment is correct, even after it is made, line out the understated humor of this passage.

It is Gide's sense of humor, not the narrator's, that provides the comic treatment which exposes the absurdity of the situation. There is nevertheless an internal collaboration between them. The author of the *sotie* (Gide) and the author of the *récit* (the narrator) overlap at the point where there is genuine pathos in the work. The most serious aspect of the *sotie*, the wisdom that is dissimulated beneath the folly, is conducted by and large through the narrator. The folly that is disclosed "under the simulacra of wisdom" in the narrator's *récit* is exposed by Gide. The burlesque surface of **Paludes** reflects something absurd at the very heart of the narrator's tale and situation. In turn, however, the narrator anchors the delightful whimsy of the *sotie* in his own serious concerns.

Gide's transcendence of his narrator's commitments is witnessed not only in the fact that his **Paludes** includes the other, but in his ability to go beyond the narrator's earnestness and to achieve a simultaneous comic perspective. Gide can relax his own serious attitudes toward the thematic and situational pathos of **Paludes** precisely because his character is so consistently vocal and dogmatic about it. The satirical thrust of "Paludes" is wholly serious; **Paludes** is a fantastic burlesque with the serious at its center, but covered in layers of a comic perspective that serve to correct the narrator's overserious view. One must also observe, however, that the relationship is mutually corrective.

One of the critical attempts to define the *sotie* and *récit* as generic terms is of help to us here: "The 'récits' he [Gide] saw as concentrated critical studies of a single character or a single problem. . . . The 'soties' by contrast are ironic adventures in the absurd, pre-surrealistic fantasies. These are not merely stories of 'sots' or fools; the word has some of its medieval connotation of irresponsibility" [Albert J. Guerard, *André Gide* (1951)]. If the whimsical devices of the *sotie* prevent the moralizing of the narrator from becoming ponderous and overbearing by inserting a sense of lightness and airiness, the reiterated insistence by the narrator upon his anguished message also prevents the comic whimsy from dissipating into the air altogether or from becoming wholly irresponsible. From the point of contact or agreement, Gide moves outward toward comic distance while his narrator moves inward toward overserious involvement. It is in the finely orchestrated juxtaposition of these two positions that the sense of absurdity resides. They do not cancel each other out like positive and negative charges in equal proportions. Rather, they create the field of tension in which the central pathos is dramatized. Gide's technical strategies, proceeding from the nature of the mixed generic mode, ultimately illuminate and refine the serious matter beneath his comic surface.

As one might expect in a book largely concerned with the process of writing a book within the book, much of this serious matter has to do with art itself and its relation to life. The narrator's journal records for us the progress of his writing "Paludes" and the events of his daily existence. Even when he seems not to be fully aware of all the interrelationships between these two progressions, they are clear to the reader because of the perpetual juxtaposition. He does realize that the same anguish, which is the source of his creative power, however limited, and which motivates his bitter satire against stagnation, is also the source of his vain proselytizing among the circle of his acquaintances. He hopes at first that they will understand and oppose the spiritual marshlands from engulfing them. We never learn what first prompts his own recognition of the paludal atmosphere of his life and the lives of his friends, but we see him engage in a battle on two fronts. The attempt to stir others to action is pretty much futile. The ludicrous conse-

quences create scenes appropriate to the *saugrenu* of the sotie. The more important struggle is an artistic one: his attempt to distil and to concentrate his recognition into a viable aesthetic form. From our established distance as readers, we are able to see process and product and even a transitional phase of "unfinished notes."

The format of **Paludes** also contributes to this examination of the contrast and the connection between the narrator's "real life," or that part of it which he records in his journal, and the way he reshapes it and ultimately objectifies it in his fiction. Since the narrator's journal already constitutes a transitional phase—he is typical of Gide's artist-characters, whose lives are never wholly separate from the potential representation of them artistically—we cannot claim to glimpse unselected reality in a direct way. Limited as we are to the point of view inherent in the journal form, the problem of sincerity (always an acute one for Gide himself and raised consciously by the narrator here) is crucial. We can on the other hand distinguish several phases of the process of life as it is channeled into art.

There are six chapters, corresponding to the six days of recorded time from Tuesday to Sunday, a deliberate allusion to the six days of the creation in *Genesis* and a parallel to the six days enumerated for Tityre, the character whose diary provides the structure of the narrator's "Paludes." The chapters are not arranged to give increasing evidence of either "life" or "art" in an extreme form, although we begin with the information that the narrator is at work on "Paludes" and we learn that on the sixth day he finishes it. Each chapter contains evidence of both the narrator's social life and of his endeavor to shape this into effective artistry. This device produces a special kind of depth, whereby the action of writing is seen in the context of other experiences, acting upon and reacting reciprocally to these.

The titles given to each chapter do reveal some deliberate arrangement, however. In the first three we move from "Hubert" (Tuesday) to "Angèle" (Wednesday) to "Le Banquet" (Thursday). This last is the scene of a literary symposium at Angèle's home. In the second three-day group we move once more from Hubert ("Hubert ou la chasse au canard"—Friday) to Angèle ("Angèle ou le petit voyage"—Saturday) and then to "Dimanche." By the third day he struggles toward the most explicit aesthetic defense of his writing. On the sixth day he completes the text. Elements of his social activity and artistic action, never wholly autonomous, cross most dramatically in the two middle chapters, in fact at the end of chapter three and the beginning of chapter four, i.e., at the very center of the work. If we follow the line of his attempt to make art work socially, as an instrument to generate action (*faire agir*), these central portions illustrate his worst failures. When we follow the more important attempt to focus his personal life in art (*agir*), there is a discernible and positive climax in these same scenes. The narrator quite early defines writing as action, but he himself confuses this with producing action in others until the signal failures at Angèle's salon permit him to reassess this position.

Thus the two lines of the "plot" move forward together toward this core section, but become more distinct thereafter. In one part of this center (the end of chapter three), we have a half-waking nightmare in which the experiences of the past three days, his desires and frustrations, are capriciously, even surrealistically mixed in apparent disarray, following the illogic of dreams. His anxiety is never again so clear or so lucid as at this point:

> je me sens prendre peu à peu, à measure que je les dépeins, par toutes les maladies que je reproche aux autres, et je garde pour moi toute la souffrance que je ne parviens pas à leur donner . . . .—Mais alors, ils ont raison de ne pas souffrir—et je n'ai pas raison de le leur reprocher;—pourtant je vis comme eux, et c'est de vivre ainsi que je souffre . . . Ah! ma tête est au désespoir!—Je veux inquiéter—je me donne pour cela bien du mal—et je n'inquiète que moi-même.

> [I feel myself seized gradually, as I describe them, by all of the maladies with which I reproach others, and I keep for myself all the suffering that I cannot manage to give them. . . . —But then, they are right not to suffer—and I am wrong to reproach them with it;—I live the way they do, however, and living in that way makes me suffer . . . Ah! my head is in despair.—I want to disquiet (others)—I give myself considerable trouble for that—and I disquiet no one but myself.]

The shift from *vouloir inquiéter* to *s'inquiéter* reproduces at another level that from *faire agir* to *agir*.

We have in this nightmare the most apparently unselected material in the whole work (it is, of course, meticulously arranged by Gide). At the beginning of the next chapter, we immediately see the narrator "calmly" transpose some of this material into art, as he writes another and the best passage we ever see of "Paludes," that in which Tityre discovers a cure for fever, presumably marsh fever, "la fièvre paludienne." This centered juxtaposition of the capricious and the carefully selected, life and art, is also the best example of the overlap of *sotie* and *récit*. It is noteworthy that the serious use of juxtaposition complements the use of juxtaposed incongruities as a source of humor. The same device serves both the comic and the serious purpose of the work.

In the chapters which follow, the narrator gradually withdraws from his crusade to bring his acquaintances out of the marshlands. The rest of chapter four is taken up by two kinds of artistic representations of "true" stories, one by Hubert, the other by the narrator. Chapter five describes the anticlimactic "little" journey with Angèle, screened by a deliberate and announced selection process, since the narrator begins this entry with:

> ne noter du voyage rien que les moments poétiques—parce qu'ils rentrent plus dans le caractère de ce que je le désirais.

> [Note nothing but the poetic moments of the journey—because they conform more to the character which I desired.]

In the last chapter we return to a process of discontinuous transcription, very like the entries in the first chapter. We seem to have come full circle and, in terms of the narrator's social life, we have.

The circle and the circular patterns of behavior dominate much of *Paludes* and much of the important criticism about this work. It is not necessary here to re-examine the round symbolic objects, the circular arguments, the recurring circular patterns in social situations which contribute to this domination. Nor is it necessary to analyze the battery of comic techniques Gide uses to achieve the ludicrous and burlesque elements that pertain to the nature of the *sotie*, thanks to William W. Holdheim's acute discussions of this material [in *Theory and Practice of the Novel: A Study on André Gide* (1968)]. But it is also with Holdheim that we must take issue. He picks up Germaine Brée's suggestion that "to the general circular movement in *Paludes*," the narrator's critique "adds a straight-line movement of revolt." He argues, however, that the linear motion is deflected into another circle and that the attempt to bring circularity and linearity into accord collapses into failure.

I think that while the *sotie* is there to weave incongruous and humorous circles around even the most serious concerns of the narrator, and despite the fact that he is a creature who participates in circular nonsense, the creative action of writing "Paludes" constitutes and remains a linear movement of some force. At the point where the component ingredients of the *sotie* and the *récit* coalesce, there is a kind of vector movement generated, derived precisely from the accord between the circle and the line, which results in a spiral motion upwards. Nor is this a curve on one plane only. The circling around a point or center in curves that increase or decrease but do not shift planes would simply be another form of the deflected line. But if one conceives of the coiling in constantly changing planes, we can obtain a three-dimensional image of the motion, for the spiral is helical.

In the climactic nightmare scene of fever and anguish, the narrator perceives how an idea, once engendered, comes to possess its own autogenerative power of propulsion: "Il semble que chaque idée, dès qu'on la touche, vous châtie . . ." ("It seems that each idea, as soon as you touch it, punishes you . . ."). Later, to Angèle, he repeats this notion: "Il faut porter jusqu'à la fin toutes les idées qu'on soulève . . ." ("One must carry to the very end every idea that one stirs up . . ."). His book is like that, too; unlike the preplanned items in his journal, it develops in an authentically unforeseen way, fed by the experiences from day to day, feeding these activities in its turn, passing from a simple allegory of physical for spiritual stagnation to a complex symbol with psychological and moral ramifications. Once, when he admits that he always carries "Paludes" with him so that it even bores him, and Angèle suggests he give it up, he tells her:

> Vous ne comprenez pas. Je le laisse ici; je le retrouve là; je le retrouve partout; la vue des autres m'en obsède et ce petit voyage ne m'en aura pas délivré.

> [You don't understand. I leave it here; I find it again there; I find it again everywhere; the sight

of other people obsesses me with it and this little journey will not have delivered me from it.]

The need is imperious and internal, he has to follow its consequences and he does.

As he constantly redefines the meaning of his "Paludes," answering the repeated questions concerning its nature (usually "*Paludes?* Qu'est-ce que c'est?"), he consistently enlarges it and extends the area of its application. His very obsession is "aesthetically efficacious" since it enables him to translate everything that is useful to his conception into the language of the marshlands. His first simple response, that "Paludes" is a book, is replaced by an increasingly precise description, and one that is constantly adapted to terms suitable to each questioner. To Hubert he claims that "Paludes" is particularly the story of one who cannot travel, he who possesses the field of Tityre and makes no effort to leave it, who on the contrary is content to stay where he is. He rattles off the "plot":

> Le premier jour, il constate qu'il s'en contente, et songe à qu'y faire. Le second jour, un voilier passant, il tue au matin quatre macreuses ou sarcelles et vers le soir en mange deux qu'il a fait cuire sur un maigre feu de broussailles. Le troisième jour, il se distrait à se construire une hutte de grands roseaux. Le quatrième jour, il mange les deux dernières macreuses. Le cinquième jour, il défait sa hutte et s'ingénie pour une maison plus savante. Le sixième jour. . . .

> [On the first day he ascertains that he is satisfied and muses on what to do. The second day, a migratory flight passing, in the morning he kills four scoters or teal, and towards evening he eats two of them which he had cooked on a meagre fire of scrubwood. The third day, he distracts himself by building a hut of tall reeds. The fourth day, he eats the last two scoters. The fifth day he takes his hut apart and contrives a more skillful house. The sixth day. . . .]

Hubert interrupts to say he understands; he has not understood at all. The catalogue of Tityre's activities is ironic in itself, a kind of bustle to fill in time, but lacking any coherent purpose, as the building and the tearing down of the hut aptly illustrate. A few paragraphs later, when Angèle offers a catalogue of Hubert's activities that parallels Tityre's for inanity and self-complacency, we realize that the narrator had worked out an insidiously ironic commentary about "his great friend." Angèle introduces her praise of Hubert by saying, "Lui du moins fait quelque chose . . . il s'occupe" ("He at least does something . . . he keeps himself busy"), and concludes it by noting that on Sundays, he hunts. So does Tityre, and the subsequent story of the duck hunt in chapter four ratifies the parallel.

The narrator realizes that Hubert did not perceive the mirror image he had held up to him:

> Hubert n'a rien compris à *Paludes* . . . il ne comprend pas un état qui n'est pas un état social; il s'en croit loin parce qu'il s'agite.

> [Hubert understood nothing of *Paludes* . . . he does not understand any condition which is not

a social condition; he believes he is different because he is busy.]

He decides to make Tityre despicable because of his resignation; in a later installment this character is forced to eat mudworms and comes to enjoy them. Hubert judges that Tityre's contentment makes him a happy man, and does not see that the ability to adapt to anything can be a negative adjustment power.

With Angèle, the narrator concentrates upon the monotony of a life that is repetitive and never examined with proper attention. He admits that this includes himself, but insists that it is even more applicable to Angèle. Her contentment, like Tityre's, rests upon false premises. She only thinks she is happy, "parce qu'elle ne se rend pas compte de son état" ("because she does not realize her own condition"). Our lives, he assures her, "sont encore bien plus ternes et médiocres" ("are even more dull and mediocre").

It is never precisely the same story in any of his subsequent explanations. The changes are always slight, the versions are always compatible, but the area of satiric coverage is continually amplified. The name of his character comes from a literary precedent, Virgil's first *Eclogue*, but the model is drawn from life, his friend Richard. The landscape and the character are also revised to accord with the experiences of the narrator's life, especially at the literary banquet, where he even discusses and justifies the changing emphasis in his explanations:

> la seule façon de raconter la même chose à chacun . . . c'est d'en changer la forme selon chaque nouvel esprit.—En ce moment, *Paludes* c'est l'histoire du salon d'Angèle.

> [the only way to tell the same thing to everyone . . . is to change its form according to each new mind.—At this moment, *Paludes* is the story of Angèle's salon.]

> *Paludes*— . . . c'est l'histoire du terrain neutre, celui qui est à tout le monde . . . —mieux: de l'homme normal, celui sur qui commence chacun;—l'histoire de la troisième personne, celle dont on parle—qui vit en chacun, et qui ne meurt pas avec nous.

> [*Paludes*— . . . is the story of neutral ground, that which belongs to everyone . . . —better: of the normal man, that on which everybody begins;—the story of the third person, he of whom one speaks—who lives in each of us, and who does not die with us.]

To a physiologist he claims that "Paludes" is the story of "animaux vivant dans les cavernes ténébreuses, et qui perdent la vue à force de ne pas s'en servir" ("animals living in dark caverns, and who lose their sight by not putting it to use").

Tityre ceases to be an allegorical representation in a parable; he gains some of the potency of myth or, rather, of a symbol in a universalized mythic landscape. He is the symbol of man's perpetual relapse, of his fear of action, and of monotonous recurrence. This suggests a pattern of growth in the narrator's writing, influenced by his life style and the contacts with his acquaintances, but not inclusive of them. In other words, his daily routine remains stagnant and circular in a way that his writing does not. At the level of social action he fails miserably, except perhaps in one or two instances. But the success of his writing cannot be measured by its ability to function as propaganda, even though he himself tries to force this function upon it, any more than Gide's *Nourritures terrestres* can be evaluated by the number of trips to Africa it instigated. The narrator is constantly being asked what he is *doing*. His answer is consistently that he is *writing* "Paludes." The strength of this implicit equation between writing and action even works through as a direct statement: "probablement que c'est pour agir" ("probably in order to act").

The identification of writing as a form of action is a key idea in **Paludes**. That the narrator forgets for a time that it is or should be disinterested action leads to several comic episodes where he tries to use his "Paludes" or the themes which are central to it as an instrument by which to recommend particular forms of authentic action in others. He will succeed in getting Angèle to cry and to admit that Hubert's bustling ways do not necessarily indicate a more vital life ("Vit-il plus parce qu'il s'agite?") ("Is he more alive because he busies himself?"). And when Hubert leaves for Africa with Roland, the narrator is correct to assert that he helped to promote the voyage. But the real form of authentic action for the narrator is writing, even though, paradoxically, writing automatically involves artifice. Some of the diversity of real life must disappear as the artist cuts away the unselected diffusion to get at the essential truth. As the narrator informs Angèle, "J'arrange les faits de façon à les rendre plus conformes à la vérité que dans la réalité" ("I arrange the facts in a manner that makes them conform to truth more than they do in real life"). The narrator's discoveries of increasingly more expressive ways of telling "Paludes," while they fail comically as propaganda, provoke significant successes at the level of his internal creative life. The linear movement is here and that is why it is so essential to notice that the initial failures to get Hubert and Angèle to revitalize their lives is followed by a meditation after which he transposes the opening lines of his work into verse. This typifies the advance his conception undergoes, allied, though in a minor key, to the major shift in poetic realization, from allegory to symbol, from external to internalized landscape, and from the satiric object as a state of things to the satiric object as a state of mind, one which adjusts to, resigns itself to, and, at worst, actually enjoys the perniciously circumscribed conditions.

His sense of plight is obsessional. While he is writing "Paludes," he can scarcely think of anything else, or can think of them only in relation to its premises:

> Il suffit qu'elle puisse être différente et qu'elle ne le soit pas. Tous nos actes sont si connus qu'un suppléant pourrait les faire et, répétant nos mots d'hier, former nos phrases de demain.

> [It is enough that it might be different, and isn't. All of our actions are so well known that a surrogate could do them, and by repeating our words of yesterday, form tomorrow's phrases.]

Because he takes his *récit* so seriously he would like to

demonstrate his own exemption from the criticism launched at the complacency of a Tityre, but knowing that he shares so many of the negative attributes of his character, he is forced to admit he has himself sat for the portrait as much as Richard, Hubert, Angèle, or any member of the salon. "Tityre, c'est moi et ce n'est pas moi;—Tityre, c'est l'imbécile; c'est moi, c'est toi—C'est nous tous . . ." ("Tityre is me and not me;—Tityre is the imbecile; he's me, he's you—he's all of us . . ."). When he withdraws himself from the identification, it is always because of his writing: "Moi cela m'est égal, parce que j'écris *Paludes*" ("It's all the same to me, because I am writing *Paludes*"). This statement recurs like an ironic refrain, but although it is ironic, it does designate the means by which the narrator attains a double status, one part in relation to his *récit*, another in relation to Gide's *sotie*. He is at once both the agent and the object of satire.

Like all of the other characters, and sometimes more than the others, he is a target of the burlesque humor. He resists variety and his planned *imprévu* is trivial and scarcely preferable to Tityre's sloth. He slips easily into overstatement and pretentiousness. Like Tityre, his thoughts are gloomy, he wanders through "étangs sans sourires" ("unsmiling pools"). He overinclines toward the serious, lacking a sense of humor. Thus he is so conscious of his note that "Tityre smiles" as a poetic thought, for it never occurs in reality. But Gide smiles through a good part of **Paludes** and rescues us from the narrator's overseriousness. The narrator admits that all of his jokes are serious. Gide uses the *sotie* to assert that all serious things are also jokes, i.e., susceptible to comic treatment.

In so many of the details of the journal report there are ambivalent meanings, one of which is inevitably in ironic repercussion to the narrator's stated preferences, expectations, anxiety with mechanization, or supposed superiority to the narrow circumstances of other lives. The narrator is quite alert to conditions of oppression and suffocation, but when he is reminded of how stifled he feels at gatherings, he decides to go to Angèle's soirée anyway, in order to point out to some acquaintance that it is stifling. The absurdity of this partially weakens the otherwise real anxiety he feels. He is so blindly serious and grave about his proselytizing efforts with one friend that he fails to comprehend the burlesque nature of the incident in which the two of them exchange notes opposite in content, but nearly identical in form. The mirror inversion suggests comic ineffectuality. His horror of repetition and of circular movement (*e.g.*, Angèle's ventilator) does not prevent us from seeing that he is a creature of repetition, ironically involved in several concentric movements.

When Tityre acts in an inverted way, looking for a disease only because he has discovered a cure, the ludicrousness of it may be applied to the narrator's backward living according to the deficits in his agenda. And when he comes to write how Tityre is *always* lying down, so as to fix his character's negative moral position, it is ironic that he himself is reclining in bed at the time, and, after recording the notation, immediately goes back to sleep.

His resolutions are normally short-lived or fragile. Each time he opens a window, he invariably closes it again. His expectations of liberation from the trip with Angèle are comically disappointed. His attachment to Angèle in general resembles that between Molière's Alceste and Célimène; she is the high priestess of all he renounces and despises. She is the primary object of his propagandist endeavors and consequently his worst failure. Once, he too hastily thinks he can break their routine by announcing it is too late for church, to which she replies that they can attend a later service—"et tout retomba de nouveau" ("and everything collapsed once again").

The cumulative effect of these ironies is to create a governing comic tone along the surface of *Paludes*, a sense of the absurd. It is the product of juxtaposing contrarieties in a particular way. The serious perspective which the narrator adopts for the patently comic situation of the exchanged notes, for instance, simultaneously increases and modifies the comic. In a reversal of this procedure, Gide's comic tone heightens by contrast, even as it undermines, the serious quality of the narrator's thoughts and actions. Despite the ironic system in which it is set, and despite the negative power of the burlesque techniques employed against it, some of the narrator's pathos survives. In their turn, Gide's satiric devices are offset, so that they have the force of reservation or of modification rather than negation. The narrator's propagandist attempts to arouse the society around him are foolish and ineffectual, but the sheer persistence of his trying is somewhat heroic. His suffering is concentrated, perhaps overblown in its dependence upon a narrow area of interest, but it is real.

The force of the first-person narration is to make us, not accomplices of the narrator, since the devices of the *sotie* promote a certain amount of distance, but rather sympathetic observers. Of necessity we come to know more of him than any other character. Indeed, each of the others, even Hubert and Angèle at the "real" level and Tityre at the fictional one, finally loses his clarity of outline. Most of them never possessed any, being a range of mere two-dimensional types, caricatures with bizarre names covering many nationalities (thus a technique of generalization); and those who are granted more detail and observation time blur increasingly, until they have only representational value. They fall back, as it were, into the paludal morass.

If the narrator's obsessional idea—"Elle est pesante comme Dieu" ("It is as heavy as God")—becomes a method of apprehending him, it is still his idea, and his suffering because of it, which unifies all the other elements, and by which each of the other characters is evaluated and dismissed with a judgment of guilty. The very persistence of his constant attention to it focuses our interest there, too:

> A présent que j'ai commencé de chercher les équivalents des pensées, pour les rendre aux autres plus claires—je ne peux cesser. . . .
>
> [Now that I've begun to look for the equivalents of thoughts so as to make them clearer to others—I cannot stop. . . .]

The irregularly formed but lucid statements that emerge from the troubled state of mind during his night of fever and nightmare, his dark night of the soul, is the highest level of consciousness and integrity achieved in the work. None of the other characters is capable of it, and not even the burlesque elements of his self-created suffering can remove its power to bind the reader's sympathy. The lapses into imperception and the pauses to record "in a phrase" may undercut it, but they cannot and do not destroy it. This unnamed narrator has some of the heroic as well as the comic features of Molière's Alceste. He is occasionally more convincing perhaps, for the moderating power of Philinte is present in no character, but only in the battery of ironic devices employed by Gide. To be sure he is narrow in many respects, but among the morally infirm midgets of his social and literary circle, the narrator stands out like a giant, or a protagonist.

Everything and everyone not only revolves around his conscious attack against moral apathy and spiritual stagnation in his own mind; they do, in fact, have no other frame of reference. We only know of them what we see through the refracting prism of his governing idea. It is Gide who measures the narrator, but it is the narrator who determines the register of measurement for everyone else.

> **Writing *is* a form of action, and within the context of Gide's *Paludes* the only effective one. The narrator achieves artistically what he fails to accomplish socially.**
>
> **—*Dennis J. Spininger***

He is disappointed in the reactions to his *récit*. His audience cannot see beyond the surface and, at that, cannot see their own faces in the surface reflections. They consistently accept Tityre's contentment at mask value, and the shallowness of their aesthetic perception corresponds perfectly to the paucity of their moral understanding. They refuse or are unable to perceive the implicit absurdity of Tityre's position, and it is not because the narrator's artistic powers are deficient, but simply because they share in Tityre's blindness. That is why the question of happiness upon false premises arises in connection with Angèle as well as Tityre, and why the constant redefinition of the satirized object takes on the vocabulary of each interlocutor: the parallels are thereby solidified. They are the animals who live in dark caves, "who lose their sight from not making use of it."

Writing *is* a form of action, and within the context of Gide's work the only effective one. The narrator achieves artistically what he fails to accomplish socially. Just as his real experiences react upon the nature of his fictional objectification of them, so his writing is itself an experience and an action, reacting upon and transcending all the other aspects of his life. "Paludes" is his inward revolt.

Whatever one may personally feel about the cathartic nature of the creative process, about its efficacy for releasing the author from extremes to which his characters are vulnerable, Gide believed it. He felt indeed that his writing of *Paludes* was curative in this manner. The estrangement he felt after returning from his African journey might possibly have led to suicide had he not found relief, describing it ironically in *Paludes*. And there is something of an equation also in this sense between Gide's *Paludes* and the narrator's. The latter's claims to be removed from the problems he satirizes objectively—"I don't mind it myself, because I am writing 'Paludes' "—ironically contrast with the noticeable degree of mechanization and stagnation in his own life, and the honest report of shared maladies during his more perceptive moments confirms this. But a certain amount of his self-distinction remains valid; he is not content with the vices, even if he finds them in his own person. It is his lone voice, charged with anguish, that is raised against the vicious acceptance of stagnation. If it is a voice in the marsh-desert, it is nonetheless a satisfactory artistic expression of the problem and the anguish which accompanies recognition of the problem.

He really does confront the unforeseen in his writing of "Paludes." It develops in a way he could not and did not suspect beforehand. In his own words, from a note to Angèle: "La perception commence au changement de sensation; d'où la nécessité du voyage" ("Perception begins where sensation changes; hence the necessity for travel"). The failure of his little trip with her does not disprove his premise, but only his conclusion. He learns that travel is not an automatic escape route. He carries "Paludes" with him, always; it has wearied him and bored him. The past prolongs itself, like the mosses under the water:

> Nous n'usons pas notre mélancolie, à refaire chaque jour nos hiers nous n'usons pas nos maladies, nous n'y usons rien que nous-mêmes, et perdons chaque jour de la force.
>
> [We don't wear down our melancholy, we don't wear away our maladies by remaking our yesterdays each day, we wear out nothing but ourselves and each day we lose some of our force.]

He never quite walks on his hands, which is his expression for the *acte libre* he desires, but that he walks at all is a measure of heroism in a world where "Tityre *semper* recubans."

When the narrator speculates that he had perhaps not gone far enough in his trip with Angèle, he is mistaken. He gives temporary credence to the possibility of Hubert's success as he leaves for Biskra in the final chapter, but we already have an indirect rejection of that possibility before it is entertained:

> Je vous assure que, quant à nous, si nous envions ces habitants si libres, c'est parce que, chaque fois que nous avons bâti dans la peine quelque toit pour nous abriter, ce toit nous a suivis, s'est placé dès lors sur nos têtes; nous a préservés de la pluie, il est vrai, mais nous a caché le soleil.
>
> [I assure you that, as for ourselves, if we envy these dwellers who are so free, it is because each time we have built, painfully, some roof to shelter us, this roof has followed us, has placed itself ever since over our heads; has saved us from the rain, it is true, but has hidden the sun from us.]

Hubert has his house, too, and it is very narrow indeed; we can be sure that the roof of it follows to hide the sun, let him distribute his charities and responsibilities however he will. The image of Hubert submerged wilfully in the bog (in the story of the duck hunt) is fitting at once to the narrator's jealousy of him and to his actual position in the marshland register.

It is not spatial but temporal distance that one must achieve:

> Ne pourrons-nous jamais poser rien hors du temps—que nous ne soyons pas obligés de refaire?
>
> [Shall we never be able to place anything outside time—that we won't be obliged to do again?]

The narrator is not aware of all the ramifications of this statement when he makes it, but it is an essential truth that had come to him during his fever. He is the only one who realizes that we must confront our responsibilities, carry the idea to the end. So long as an idea is left incomplete, we are compelled to repeat it again and again. On the day following this feverish awareness, the narrator is able to translate some of his fever conceptions into the last installment of "Paludes" we ever get to see. Immediately afterwards there is the incident of his uncivil dismissal of a pesky visitor, Alcide. The event is comically trivial, especially relative to his subsequent pride in it. He calls it a "great change," as he always calls his acquaintances "great" friends. The exaggeration is mild burlesque, but the change is genuine.

Perception *does* begin where sensation changes; and all of the changes his conception of "Paludes" undergoes do sharpen his sensibility and, to a degree, finally release him. We must look below the comic surface of Gide's *sotie*, just as we are expected to look beyond the surface gravity of the narrator's *récit*. The journal entry by which we learn that "Paludes" will be completed is typically unsmiling: "Finir *Paludes*.—Gravité." We smile, at Gide's invitation, but we also acknowledge that the narrator performs his authentic act. It is extra-temporally, through an assertion "outside time" and, in this work, that means through art, that valid action occurs. As one returns, the concentric circles gather around once more.

The final entry in the journal reproduces the mechanics of the first one. The variation is seemingly slight; instead of Hubert, it is "my great friend" Gaspard who enters at six o'clock to ask "Tiens! tu travailles?' " ("Well! Are you working?") And now that the narrator has completed "Paludes," he is working on "Polders." Whether or not the decision to begin a work, whose topic is not far removed from the one he has just concluded, invalidates the suggestion about successfully carrying his idea to the end must be approached cautiously. Most critics have scoffed at the change, especially as Gide himself went on to *Les Nourritures terrestres*. Yet the word *polders* is not a precise synonym for *paludes*; it can be seen as an extension to a new perspective. For *polders* is a Dutch-derived term for reclaimed swampland or marsh, conquered by human effort, dried out and made to furnish a fertile landscape. To the extent that the external landscape illustrates the internal one, the difference may be salutary. It is only, true to the nature of the *sotie*, trivial on the surface. If there is an upward spiral movement, as I have claimed, the return is at a higher plane of consideration.

Another example of cross-purposes or apparent contradictions on different levels of relevance may illuminate the problem. Several times the narrator opens a window as a symbolic act of deliverance. He is motivated by his sense of stifling distress. Invariably he closes the window again out of fear of catching cold. The practical concern for his physical well-being contradicts the gesture as symbol. Of Gide's many techniques for undercutting with a sense of the absurd and the ludicrous, this is the most interesting. What is performed at a "real" level, but with the intention of symbolic reference, has nevertheless real conditions to contend with: to open a window, as a dramatic illustration of freedom, makes one liable to chill. This is a model of retroactive influence in miniature. The different meanings pertain to different levels of appreciation for the same single act. These modify one another in a humorous way, but do not negate one another. At the point of overlap, there is both absurdity and pathos.

"Polders" is not a radical point of departure from the work just completed, and we know that the narrator hopes not to contradict himself in his new work, but it is certainly not mechanical repetition either, and some of the associations are positive. It remains true that the narrator's artistic creativity reverses the impotence of his personal relations and the general ineffectuality of his social life. Beneath the supreme rhetorical irony that the narrator's "Paludes" is only a portion of another and better work, called by the same name, we can still perceive the aesthetic alliance between Gide and his narrator.

The use of the book within a book allowed Gide to produce a dimension of depth not only along the horizontal plane, where a theme or a situation can be variously graphed through different characters, but also a depth through a vertical arrangement of levels of consciousness in his major protagonist. Since this, in turn, reacts and is reacted upon by each of the other characters, we get a series of vertical-horizontal relationships pushed down through several internal levels and superimposed upon one another. As Jean Hytier writes [in *André Gide* (1962)]: "In fact *Paludes* has this strong point, that the object of its satire inevitably reappears not only externally, in all the forms of life, but internally, in all the manifestations of consciousness." The controlling device for these complex modulations of depth is the mixed generic mode itself. A figure of parody when seen from one optic, the narrator is the recognized creator of significant myth from another. No one but the narrator (and, of course, Gide and the collaborative reader) understands his organic conception of the work of art, which is, like the egg of his metaphor, born full:

> Un livre . . . est clos, plein, lisse comme un oeuf.
> On n'y saurait faire entrer rien, pas une épingle,
> que par force, et sa forme en serait brisée.

> [A book . . . is closed, full, smooth as an egg. One couldn't contrive to get anything else into it, not

even a pin, except by force, and its form would be shattered by it.]

On the list of remarkable phrases at the end, Gide places two lines, before he turns over the blank page to the caprice of his readers. These are: "Il dit: 'Tiens! Tu travailles,'" and "Il faut porter jusqu'à la fin toutes les idées qu'on soulève" ("He says: 'Well! Are you working,'" and "One must carry to the very end every idea that one stirs up"). In capsule form this is the essence of the serious concern yoked to the center of the book which is like an egg, "closed, full, smooth."

The delightful aspect of the *sotie* is analogous to painting the shell of the egg in variegated burlesque colors. This process neither deforms nor punctures the egg; instead it appropriates the organic form to art. In the "Postface" for the second edition of **Paludes**, Gide submitted a comment that assists in explaining the aesthetic utility of the mixed generic mode.

> J'aime aussi que chaque livre porte en lui, mais cachée, sa propre réfutation et ne s'assoie pas sur l'idée, de peur qu'on n'en voie l'autre face. J'aime qu'il porte en lui de quoi se nier, se supprimer lui-même; qu'il soit un tout si clos qu'on ne puisse le supprimer que tout entier. . . .

> [I would also like each book to bear within itself, but hidden, its own refutation, and not rest upon the idea, lest one not see its other aspect. I would like it to bear within itself the means by which it denies itself, cancels itself out; that it be a whole so closed that one could suppress it only in its entirety. . . .]

By fusing two genres in **Paludes**, Gide achieved this objective. (pp. 3-25)

Dennis J. Spininger, "The Complex Generic Mode of André Gide's 'Paludes'," in Twentieth Century French Fiction: Essays for Germaine Brée, *edited by George Stambolian, Rutgers University Press, 1975, pp. 3-26.*

Anne L. Martin (essay date 1977)

[*In the following essay, Martin interprets* Isabelle *as a transitional work between Gide's three principal genres: the* récit, sotie, *and novel.*]

Isabelle is a curious little tale which somehow never seems to have found its place in Gide's *oeuvre*. From the outset, no one, not even its author, seemed able to decide what it was meant to be, or what its true significance was.

Conceived outside the strictures of Gide's own highly subjective theory of literary creation, **Isabelle**, written in 1910 and published early the following year, was shortly thereafter dismissed by its auth... as "un intermède semi-badin entre deux oeuvres trop ...ieuses". Gide later expanded on this to Charles Du ...s:

> J'ai eu très jeune le sentiment d'avoir devant moi une série de volumes de papier blanc: mes oeuvres complètes. J'écris le tome VII ou le tome XII selon la longueur de la gestation ou le degré de perfection de mon métier. Il n'y a qu'un de

mes livres qui ait été fait, pour ainsi dire de l'extérieur. C'est *Isabelle*. J'avais vu l'histoire du livre et je l'ai écrit un peu comme un exercice pour me faire la main. Cela se sent.

But before taking the notoriously Protean author at his word, it might be advantageous to paraphrase Juste-Agénor de Baraglioul's admonition to Lafcadio in *Les Caves du Vatican*, on which Gide was already at work when he disowned *Isabelle*: "Mon enfant, les oeuvres complètes sont une grande chose fermée; vous ne serez jamais qu'un bâtard."

That Gide's sympathies — in life and in art — lay on the side of illegitimacy is by now axiomatic. Accordingly, it is not unreasonable to suspect that this alleged piece of "comic relief" had greater significance for its author than the general neglect into which he encouraged it to fall would indicate. Like Lafcadio, *Isabelle* has the immediate charm and romantic appeal of a natural child, and it is these very qualities which conceal its serious purpose. For all its apparent frivolity, *Isabelle* was neither carelessly nor accidentally conceived. Rather, it marks a pivotal point in the evolution of Gide's theory of literary genres, more particularly of the novel, and if its author subsequently sought to disown it in the face of critical rejection, his account of his reasons for so doing bears closer scrutiny.

Isabelle is, according to its author, an ironic work, "la critique d'une certaine forme de l'imagination romantique". Gidean irony (or criticism, for he used the terms quasi-synonymously) consists in the discrediting of an idea through its systematic exaggeration and distortion. In his early *récits*, this exaggerative process was channelled towards one goal: personal catharsis through the creation of a fictional clone whose life was an ironic criticism of a specific, narrowly-defined ethical or psychological dilemma faced by Gide. Thus *La Porte étroite* "est la critique d'une certaine tendance mystique" and *L'Immoraliste*, "d'une forme de l'individualisme".

By the time of *Isabelle*, however, it can be shown that the focus of this exaggerative process had become aesthetic, its critical irony directed toward a particular literary tendency rather than a moral or existential problem. The ironic exaggeration of an aesthetic theory necessarily means the exaggeration of its component parts — treatment of plot, of character, or chronology; narrative techniques, style, structure and tone — with an emphasis on the theme which runs through virtually all Gide's works: the conflict between art and reality. But the concern is with the entire process and not just the underlying ideas. To produce an aesthetic critique, Gide uses narrative form ironically to deform the theories which he sets out to criticise. In defining the irony of *Isabelle*, it may therefore be argued that Gide might more accurately have spoken of "la critique d'une certaine forme de l'imagination *romanesque*".

Why *romanesque*? *Isabelle* is one of Gide's most "situated" works, albeit neither socio-politically, as were the later —*dipe* or *Ecole des femmes* trilogy, nor psychologically or ethically, like the works which had preceded it. *Isabelle*'s situation is quite simply literary, and it is from the unfashionable perspective of the work's historical context that it must first be approached.

This context was particularly complex. It was created on one hand by heated battles over the redefinition of the novel which were being waged by turn-of-the-century Parisian *literati*: xenophobic nationalism versus literary cosmopolitanism; the eclipse of the *roman d'analyse* and the short-lived *naturiste* novel in the face of the meteoric ascent of the *roman d'aventure*; and the first stirrings of the revolution which was to sweep progressively through all the arts, Surrealism.

On the other hand, it was a reflection of a more personal artistic crisis. The systematic ironic criticism of psychological and ethical preoccupations had served to free Gide from his artistic solipsism of the 1890s. But in so doing, it had also exhausted the inspiration which had produced his early works. The ideas which had hitherto animated Gide's writings dated, for the most part, from the period 1885-1895; the Symbolist aesthetic which informed them was scarcely more recent, and had in any event already been dealt a lethal blow by *Paludes*. The essentially moral fervor which had carried Gide through the rapid-fire production of the 1890s seemed suddenly to give out — before all the books which he intended to derive from it had been written.

In 1902, unnerved by the critical failure of *Le Roi Candaule* and of *L'Immoraliste*, Gide abruptly plunged into a period of creative impotence. It was not until October 1908 that he was able to finish *La Porte étroite* under the dual impetus given him by the unexpected inspiration for *Le Retour de l'Enfant prodigue* (1907) and a forcible reanimation of his earlier state of mind. But when, the day after the *récit* was completed, Gide reports in his *Journal* that he had shaved off his André Walterian moustaches, his tonsorial action appears symbolic: the past had ruthlessly to be dispensed with. He was beginning to realize what he much later admitted to Henri Drain, that he had up until now systematically been presenting himself not as an artist, but as a moralist. At present, it was time to return the emphasis to art, and to develop the technical means of dealing with his as yet undecided future works.

He had already begun to resurvey the theoretical boundaries of his art in the late 1890s. In 1898 he had started to contribute critical "Lettres à Angèle" to *L'Ermitage*, and by 1900 he was regularly reviewing books for *La Revue Blanche*. During the first decade of the new century, he firmly established his importance as a literary critic and theoretician of a new school. He soon found himself at the centre of the group of writers and critics with whose help he was to launch the *Nouvelle Revue Française* in 1908. Concurrently, he was developing new literary contacts both in France and abroad, and entering into a series of important literary correspondences. From 1900 to 1904 he delivered lectures on literature and on the theatre in Belgium and Germany, and published two volumes of collected critical essays, *Lettres à Angèle 1898-1899* (1900) and *Prétextes* (1903). Important articles on Oscar Wilde appeared in *L'Ermitage* in June 1902 and August 1905, and a first study on Dostoievsky was printed on 25 May 1908 in *La Grande Revue*. Undated excerpts from his *Journal*, dealing for the most part with ongoing literary quarrels, began to appear regularly in the fledgling *N.R.F.* the following year. At the same time, he was caught up in the literary cosmopolitanism of the period; he never would recover from the impact of Dostoievsky and of such English novelists as Defoe, Fielding, Dickens, Stevenson and Conrad, whom he was soon reading in the original.

Thus at the turn of the century Gide, like many of his contemporaries, found himself at an artistic crossroads, and, in a gesture which was inimitably his own, he seized hold of this image of his dilemma and turned it into a metaphor for his new aesthetic. "L'artiste n'est ni d'un camp ni de l'autre," he wrote prophetically in 1901; "[il est à tout point de rencontre;] il est à tout point de conflit." In the years which preceded the cataclysm of the First World War, those meetings and conflicts were to focus more and more insistently for Gide on the renewal of the novel, a genre which had, by the end of the last century, entered into decline. The new works of which Gide had earlier only dreamed began to take form, passing through the permutations which, he fervently hoped, would result in a revitalization of that genre, transforming it, according to his now-famous formula, into "un carrefour, un rendez-vous des problèmes".

Isabelle is a first step in this experimentation, and as such, a revealing intersection on the road to the novel. Like *L'Immoraliste*, it is the story of a story, the transcription of a tale told by Gérard Lacase to two of his friends. In August 189—, Francis Jammes and an unnamed companion, the narrator *je*, visit the abandoned château of La Quartfourche in the company of Gérard, at whose neighbouring property of La R . . . they are guests. The visit manifestly affects Lacase, and that evening, upon their return to La R . . ., his friends prevail upon him to recount the story of the abandoned house. It is his oral narration (introduced and presumably written down by *je*) which constitutes the central text of *Isabelle*.

Gérard recounts that as a young doctoral candidate he had accepted an invitation to visit La Quartfourche in order to consult manuscript documents of Bossuet, on whom he was preparing a thesis. But although he presented himself to M. Floche, his host, as a student, Gérard actually considered himself to be a novelist, and it was as a novelist and not as a scholar that he reacted to La Quartforche and the strange collection of people who lived there. Introduced into a bizarre waxwork environment which differed radically from his expectations of life among country aristocracy, endowed moreover with a hyperactive imagination for which Bossuet provided scant nourishment, Gérard decided to amuse himself and to exercise his artistic skills by concocting novelistic descriptions of the château and its inhabitants. This artistic transposition would, he believed, crystalize his superficial impressions into authoritative representations, permitting him to arrive at a more profound understanding of La Quartfourche's reality:

> Romancier, mon ami, me disais-je, nous allons donc te voir à l'oeuvre. Décrire! Ah, fi! ce n'est pas de cela qu'il s'agit, mais bien de découvrir la réalité sous l'aspect. En ce court laps de temps qu'il t'est permis de séjourner à la Quartfourche, si tu laisses passer un geste, un tic, sans pouvoir t'en donner bientôt l'explication psychologique, historique et complète, c'est que tu ne sais pas ton métier.

But although his descriptions of the park, of the doddering Floches and their eccentric relatives, the Saint-Auréols, his observations of the behavior of their crippled grandson, pathetic Casimir de Saint-Auréol, and his tutor, the unsavory abbé Santal, sustain the reader's interest through their skilful parody of most of the main novelistic techniques of the late 19th century, it becomes increasingly clear that the psychological and historical explanations they provide are not only incomplete, but also incorrect. Rather than revealing reality underlying appearance, Gérard's observations create a factitious appearance which, if it does not entirely falsify reality, at least distorts it badly. Gérard's naïve confidence in art as a means of getting at truth is in this way undercut, and in the process, several decades of French aesthetic theory are neatly and ironically discredited.

The reader is not particularly surprised therefore when, upon discovering a miniature of an "angelic" young woman, Gérard exclaims: "Quel est ce conte où le héros tombe amoureux du seul portrait de la princesse?" and promptly falls in love. He abandons his desultory caricaturization of his hosts to devote himself to an impassioned reconstruction of the biography of this mysterious beauty, whom Casimir identifies as his mother, Isabelle de Saint-Auréol. Caught up in the excitement of his pursuit, Gérard quite forgets that he is supposed to be an objective, investigative novelist; indeed, he forgets about being a novelist at all, and so is unaware that the story which he is so lovingly piecing together belongs more to the realm of fiction than of fact. The Dickensian-*cum*-Balzacian novel peopled by the solid, if grotesque Floches and Saint-Auréols gives way to a fantastically romanticized tale about the tragic love affair of bored and beautiful Isabelle. Caught up in the spell of his own fabulation, Gérard systematically misinterprets the facts which he gathers, weaving them into a romantic illusion in his own image rather than a realistic portrait of the absent heroine. Even a glimpse of the real Isabelle during one of her rare midnight visits to the château does not shake his fiction; rather the theatricality of the entire episode only serves to blind him further to her true nature.

It is not until the reappearance of a daylight Isabelle at the end of the story (in a chapter which Gide maintained he did not originally intend even to write) that Gérard's illusions are dispelled. The "novel" which he had created about the fairy-tale princess is replaced by the sordid reality of her actual existence; Isabelle is not the ethereal angel of his dreams, but a venal and perhaps criminal profligate, who plunders and auctions off La Quartfourche to settle her ill-gotten debts. In the end, Gérard, turning his back on both his dream and the deception of its underlying reality, impulsively buys the farm on which Casimir has taken refuge with the gardener, Gratien. And although it is never specified, the reader is left with the impression that Gérard has become neither a scholar nor a novelist, but that he has abandoned the chimeric world of books for the secure and tangible reality of life as a country squire.

Gérard's account is thus first of all an illustration of the unreliability of art, or more particularly, of a novelistic aesthetic which purports to be able to investigate and reveal "la réalité sous l'aspect". Two permutations of the written word (and by extension, two novelistic aesthetics) are systematically discredited during the course of the tale. Historical documents (the Realist tradition) repeatedly prove to be uninteresting if not incomprehensible, and the possibility that they may lead to a clear comprehension of "fact" is discarded. Gérard cannot keep his attention on the Bossuet bible and manuscripts, which in any event are of only "mediocre interest" to his thesis. Casimir, whose education consists in producing fair copies in quadruplicate of his teacher's study on Averrhoès, does not understand what he is copying, and when he asks questions is told by the abbé that he may understand when he is older.

Imaginative (romantic and adventurous) writings, however, solicit both interest and misplaced confidence. Casimir, who spends his evenings literally drooling over popular accounts of "grands voyages", has developed an almost mystical faith in the power of the written word to transform dream into reality: if he can persuade Gérard to sign a note promising to return to La Quartfourche the following year, then Gérard will indeed return. The child is convinced that, by entrusting his desire to paper, he is assuring his wish will come true. Gérard, who should know better (and who indeed considers the note to be "une simagrée"), suffers nevertheless from a more sophisticated version of Casimir's confidence in fictional causality. When he accidentally discovers an old love letter written by Isabelle, Gérard sees only the romance of a passionate girl preparing to flee with her lover, and not the reality of a selfish young woman who plans to steal her aunt's jewels to finance her *fugue*.

The fault, of course, is shared. The written word is illusory only to those willing to be deluded. Casimir, weak-minded and virtually illiterate, is the innocent victim of a distinction which he cannot understand. But Gérard is not. He has deliberately chosen to ignore the written word's capacity for getting at fact by identifying himself not as a scholar concerned with the reality beneath the words, but as a novelist, interested only in the romance of the words themselves. His is the "pathetic illusion" which Gide had originally intended to mock in the story's abandoned subtitle, *L'Illusion pathétique*. His reconstruction of Isabelle's story is an artistic illusion, an idealized fiction based upon a wilful misinterpretation of the relationship between art and reality, a deliberate confusion of factual representation and fictitious misrepresentation arising from Gérard's pathetic fallacy that Isabelle's story must necessarily conform to his own imaginative wishes. Happily for him, Gérard eventually realizes that he is in love with a dream and, deceived, rejects his imaginary attachment to Isabelle in the world of fiction in favor of concrete commitments to Casimir and Gratien in the real world. It is because he has realised that he was mistaken in preferring fiction to fact that, when he is called upon to reconstruct that mis-

take for his friends, Gérard is able to demonstrate a partial awareness of the irony of giving his version of Isabelle's story even orally artistic form. He deliberately prejudices the veracity of his account by introducing his earlier self as a *romancier*, that is as a purveyor of romance, a fictionalizer, a naive young man who saw reality through exclusively literary eyes:

> A vingt-cinq ans je n[e] connaissais à peu près rien [de la vie], que par les livres; et c'est pourquoi sans doute je me croyais romancier; car j'ignorais encore avec quelle malignité les événements dérobent à nos yeux le côté par où ils nous intéresseraient davantage, et combien peu de prise ils offrent à qui ne sait pas les forcer.

The failure of Gérard's attempts to "force" events to reveal their secrets to him, guided by his "pathetic illusion" that art can reveal reality, is rendered doubly ironic for the reader by the fact that the events with which he is confronted are actually real, and not merely in the novelistic world of La Quartfourche. With the debatable exception of *La Porte étroite*, **Isabelle** is the least fictitious of Gide's fictions. It is based upon the true story of the demise of the Floquet family, whose property Formentin bordered La Roque-Baignard, the Gide family estate in Calvados. R.-G. Nobécourt and Pierre-Jean Pénault have discussed in detail the history of Formentin and its inhabitants, and have more than adequately documented the surprising extent to which **Isabelle** is a faithful transposition of fact. Pénault especially has shown that Gide was not merely spinning imaginary edifices from a simple *fait divers*, as he was subsequently to do in *Les Caves* and in *Les Faux-Monnayeurs*. Rather it appears that he actively researched the details of Formentin's ruin in much the same way that Flaubert is purported to have verified the history of Delphine Couturier. Yet **Isabelle** is deliberately not *Madame Bovary*, and it is precisely for this reason that the fidelity with which Gide kept to his factual sources is of more than anecdotal interest.

If Gide chose to give his story such extensive bases in fact, it was not merely to parody Flaubertian Realism, nor was it because he lacked the imagination to stray from the facts. It was because of the opportunity for aesthetic criticism provided by a story which would so obviously "make a good novel". Gide's concern was not so much with the facts about Formentin as with the obsessive fascination which such a history can have for an artist, and the multiple ways in which what he called "poetic imagination" can distort reality. **Isabelle** is not so much a fictionalization of a real story as a critique of the psychological and aesthetic processes involved in such a fictionalization, as well as of the illusion that art can reveal the mysteries of life: "l'illusion romantique" ("pathétique") and "l'illusion romanesque".

Insofar as Gérard is concerned, Gide's interest in his romanticizing imagination seems specifically self-corrective. Like the story which Gérard is about to tell, the narrator's introduction is also a fictionalization of fact. Francis Jammes was, of course, a real person, and he was truly a guest at La Roque-Baignard in the autumn of 1898. He and Gide, in the company of Henri Ghéon, actually did visit mysterious Formentin, and the lines from Jammes' "Elégie quatrième" with which *je* concludes his transcription of Gérard's narrative were indeed written at Gide's suggestion to commemorate their trip to the château. In this way the introduction to *Isabelle* invites the reader to equate Gide with *je* and, more importantly, with Gérard, who thus stands in the same ambiguous relationship to his creator as do the protagonists of the moralistic *récits*, with the unique difference that, unlike Alissa or Michel, Gérard is a novelist, and the relationship is therefore not ethical but artistic. He is not blinkered by the obsessively subjective and unimaginative vision which prevents Michel or Saül from seeing the world and themselves as they really are. Rather, Gérard suffers from the conflict between his investigative objectivity and his "illusion pathétique", whose scintillating mirages blind him to the reality he seeks to reveal. His flaw is not existential, but merely artistic. Gérard ultimately fails not as a man but as a novelist, becoming the victim of Gide's aesthetic irony by becoming a parody of the moralistic heroes, whose cathartic function he nevertheless assumes. Gérard is a novelist Gide did not become, a fictional double who relieves Gide of an aesthetic rather than an ethical temptation.

Thus the thrust of *Isabelle*'s criticism is artistic and more specifically novelistic — "romanesque" — and the problems posed by the text bring us back to the question of genre. Most early reviewers assumed *Isabelle* to be a novel, although there was no consensus as to just what kind of novel. Rachilde saw in it a *roman d'aventure*, a gothic tale reminiscent of those by Anne Radcliffe; to Marcel Ray it was a detective story in the Sherlock Holmesian vein; to others it was merely a romance. All were accordingly deceived when the "novel" abruptly ended shortly after the first meeting between Gérard and Isabelle. "L'action ne s'engage jamais!" wailed Jean-Marc Bernard in *Le Divan*. ". . . Le roman cesse à l'instant où l'on s'attendait à le voir commencer. Après de multiples péripéties, on n'aboutit nulle part."

Alone in supporting *Isabelle* were Lucien Maury and Jacques Rivière, both of whom wisely decided that the book was not a novel. Maury considered it a sort of baroque variation upon the *récit*. Rivière declared it an experiment which Gide had undertaken to prove to himself that he was capable of dealing with non-subjective plots and characters. As such, Rivière argued, it must be viewed as a transitional work between the extant *récits* and the true novels to come. "*Isabelle* . . . donnera peut-être plus tard quelque embarras aux faiseurs de classifications. A la fois elle s'attarde et elle ouvre une ère nouvelle," he concluded.

And in fact Gide himself was the first to suffer such an "embarras". *Isabelle* belongs to that transmigratory period during which Gide, hypersensitive to questions of genre, rebaptized "*récits*" and "*soties*" his earlier "novels". This generic redefinition seems to have occurred while Gide was actually writing *Isabelle*, for if he had at first referred to the work as a *roman*, by the time it was published, Gide had changed his mind. His "Projet de Préface" designates *Isabelle*, together with *L'Immoraliste* and *La Porte étroite*, as a *récit* because its form no longer corresponded to Gide's evolving ideas on the novel:

Pourquoi j'eus soin d'intituler "récit" ce petit livre? Simplement parce qu'il ne répond pas à l'idée que je me fais du roman; non plus que la *Porte étroite*, ou que l'*Immoraliste*; et que je ne voulais pas qu'on s'y trompât. Le roman, tel que je le reconnais ou l'imagine, comporte une diversité de points de vue, soumise à la diversité des personnages qu'il met en scène; c'est par essence une oeuvre déconcentrée. Il m'importe du reste beaucoup moins d'en formuler la théorie que d'en écrire. Je ne sais point si j'y réussirai; mais ce que je trouve plaisant c'est de reprocher, comme l'ont fait quelques critiques, à ces récits de ne point être ce que précisément je voulais qu'ils ne fussent point.

Isabelle, then, is not a novel. Yet everything about it points to the novel. Its hero aspires to be a novelist; the story which it tells is nothing if not *romanesque*; and it is certainly more than coincidental that it is set in the mysterious property of "la Quartfourche, qu'on appelait plus communément: le Carrefour," by its very name the physical embodiment of Gide's metaphor for the kind of books he longed to write: "un carrefour, un rendez-vous des problèmes."

But is it, as Gide insists, a *récit*? True, the story of *Isabelle* is related by a single, retrospective narrator, and set within an extrafictional frame peculiar to the *récits*. But whereas in *L'Immoraliste* or *La Symphonie pastorale* the narrator's point of view does not change (hence the tragic dénouement), the narrator of *Isabelle* himself proceeds through a tripartite movement of demystification which the *récits* reserve for the reader. There results a deliberate disruption of the linear chronology of the *récit* form, and a displacement of the story's point of view. This formal evolution is announced by Gérard in the introduction:

Je vous raconterais volontiers le roman dont la maison que vous vîtes tantôt fut le théâtre, commença Gérard, mais outre que je ne sus le découvrir, ou le reconstituer, qu'en partie, je crains de ne pouvoir apporter quelque ordre dans mon récit qu'en dépouillant chaque événement de l'attrait énigmatique dont ma curiosité le revêtait naguère . . .

—Apportez à votre récit tout le désordre qu'il vous plaira, reprit Jammes.

—Pourquoi chercher à recomposer les faits selon leur ordre chronologique, dis-je; que ne nous les présentez-vous comme vous les avez découverts?

—Vous permettrez alors que je parle beaucoup de moi, dit Gérard.

—Chacun de nous fait-il jamais rien d'autre! repartit Jammes.

Although *Isabelle* does not achieve the sort of novelistic "deconcentration" engendered by the use of multiple narrators, the chronological dislocations of the narrative succeed in loosening up the *récit* structure by refracting Gérard's individual viewpoint through a prismatic succession of discoveries. In this way Gide creates a novelistic diversity of points of view antithetical to the unremitting subjectivity of the existential *récits*, but without having to sacrifice the unifying continuity of a first person narrative.

But although the *récit* is conducted from a single viewpoint, that point of view is no longer interior to the narration. Gérard stands outside Isabelle's story; the tragedy is not his, but hers. A linear *récit* might very well have been constructed out of the history of Isabelle, as Gide himself remarked in his letter to Bernard, although this would necessarily have meant the suppression of Gérard. Or *Isabelle* could have been enlarged into a novel by freeing the other characters from the control of the narrator and permitting them to speak for themselves; in this case, Gérard could have remained, but at best could only comment upon, rather than control, the story, as Edouard comments in *Les Faux-Monnayeurs*. But Gide chose to do neither, and by centring his story on a would-be novelist and not on a morally reprehensible heroine, shifted its centre of gravity from an ethical to an aesthetic axis. The pattern of dominance established by Jérôme and Alissa, by Gertrude and the Pastor, is reversed, and *Isabelle* is split in half, not "vertically" (as in *La Porte étroite* or *La Symphonie pastorale*, in which the transition from Jérôme's narrative to Alissa's journal or the passage of the Pastor's journal from a retrospective to a contemporaneous account of the action, divide the *récits* into "first" and "second" halves without shifting their focus), but "horizontally", so that a virtual *récit* invisibly parallels the actual narration, creating a double image which the reader is never entirely able to tune out.

On one level *Isabelle* is the story of a story which Gide never wrote. The mystery of Formentin was obviously inspirational, as the existence of Jammes' elegy testifies. But while Jammes wrote his poem on the night of their visit to the property, Gide allowed the inspiration to mature for a dozen years before committing it to paper, and then when he finally tapped it, he wrote not the story of "Isabelle", but an account of a romantic young artist's reaction to the story of Isabelle. Gérard's "disorganized" narration is haunted by the ghost of the artistically organized tale which both Gide and Gérard might have written. Gérard did not write the *récit* "Isabelle", presumably because his disillusionment with the heroine extended to his confidence in art. Gide did not write it because by writing about Gérard he purged himself of the temptation to give in to the "pathetic illusion" of Formentin.

Thus *Isabelle* becomes an ironic comment not only upon those traditional realistic and naturalistic avatars of the novel which substitute illusion for reality while purporting to do just the opposite, but also upon the techniques and pretentions of Gide's own morally critical works. Despite its masquerade as a *récit*, *Isabelle* is in the lineage not of *La Porte étroite*, but of *Paludes* and of *Les Caves* and *Les Faux-Monnayeurs*, for which it clears the way. *Paludes* appears in retrospect, to have been a kind of aesthetic roundabout: at its centre is the fictional "Paludes", about which Gide's novelist-hero endlessly circles because he lacks the imagination to break free of the centripetal force of his Symbolist theories. *Isabelle*, on the other hand, is an extrageneric crossroads. Gérard, as an aspiring novelist, is repeatedly hurtled away from the virtual "Isabelle"

at its centre by the centrifugal impetus of his undisciplined (and uncodified) "novelistic" imagination.

It is interesting to note that at an early stage in *Isabelle*'s composition, Gide had proposed to entitle the work "La Mivoie", from the name of his maternal grandparents' property. That he changed his imagery en route is significant, and sheds light on his later rejection of the work as "un exercice pour me faire la main". *Isabelle* is a reticent work. It does not, as Gide had obviously hoped, move his art further along the road he wanted to travel, leaving him, perhaps, midway to the novel. Rather, it simply demonstrates that he was not yet on the right track. It provides no answers to the problem of revitalizing the novel, proposes no new aesthetic techniques for conflating art and reality. Its importance to Gide's evolution at the turn of the century lies not in what *Isabelle* is, but in what it is not: it is not a 19th century novel, nor a Gidean moralistic *récit*, nor even, as Jean Hytier suggests, a *sotie*, although it contains elements of each. But, most emphatically, it is no dead end. It stands consciously and rather courageously at the intersection of all three genres, turning ironically away not only from those roads down which Gide himself had already journeyed, but also from all the well-beaten paths of his predecessors. Through this process of elimination *Isabelle*, as an artistic crossroads, suggests the possibility of an as yet untravelled route, and thus becomes a new point of departure in Gide's search for the novel. (pp. 34-45)

Wallace Fowlie on Gide's *récits*:

[Gide's] *récits* are constructed on the opposing theme of sentiment and intelligence. The sentimental theme is the romantic quest for passion, for the absolute of passion. And the intellectual component is both the criticism of this passion and the will to construct clearly the composition of the book which itself will be a liberation from all passionate entanglements and all deliberate choices.

It would be more accurate to look upon the *récits* of Gide, not as easily identifiable transcriptions of his own life, but as exercises in self-rehabilitation. The writing of each book represented for him a cure, a means of moving beyond a personal problem or dilemma. The form of the writing is sparse because Gide, unlike a Balzac, does not amplify. He retraces the story succinctly, and almost always, at the end, feels and makes the reader feel, impatience to bring to an end what he is considering. But if there is a personal need in the writer which motivates the writing, Gide comes to the task of writing, as an artist, as a man for whom an aesthetic triumph is more important than the analysis of a moral problem, and for whom the intrinsic beauty of the literary work is in itself the solution of a moral problem. Even within a given *récit*, as in *La Symphonie pastorale*, one story offsets the other, as a theme in a musical composition enriches another theme.

Wallace Fowlie, in his André Gide: His Life and Art, *1965.*

Anne L. Martin, " 'Isabelle' or André Gide at the Crossroads," in Essays in French Literature, *No. 14, November, 1977, pp. 34-47.*

Emily S. Apter   (essay date 1986)

[*An American educator and critic, Apter is the author of* André Gide and the Codes of Homotextuality (1987). *In the following essay, she analyzes and assesses Gide's attempt to write from a feminine voice in* The School for Wives, Robert, *and* Geneviève.]

> "Lesbianisme de Michelet." Pour Michelet, les rapports de l'homme et de la femme ne sont donc nullement fondés sur l'altérité des sexes; le mâle et la femelle, ce sont des figures morales, destinées à juger conventionnellement des faits ou des états historiques: l'Histoire est mâle, la Syrie est femelle. Mais, érotiquement, il n'y a qu'un spectateur et son spectacle; Michelet lui-même n'est plus ni homme ni femme, il n'est que Regard; son approche de la femme n'oblige à aucun caractère viril. Au contraire: puisque, d'ordinaire, c'est le mâle qui est le premier tenu éloigné, par une sorte de tabou génétique, de la crise sanguine de la Femme, Michelet s'efforce de dépouiller en lui le géniteur; et puisque cette même crise n'est livrée en spectacle qu'à d'autres femmes, à des compagnes, mères, soeurs, ou nourrices, Michelet se fait lui-même femme, mère, soeur, nourrice, compagne de l'épouse. Pour pouvoir mieux forcer le gynécée, non en ravisseur, mais en spectateur, le vieux lion revêt la jupe, il s'attache amoureusement à la Femme par un lesbianisme véritable et ne conçoit finalement le mariage que comme une sorte de couple sororal.
>
> Roland Barthes, *Michelet*

Speaking here of Michelet's writing persona as "femme," as "lesbian" voice and finally, as "language wet-nurse" ("langage-nourrice"), Barthes sets out the entire narratological problem of "female impersonations"—that is, the recitation by male authors of female roles. What was the norm on the Greek and Elizabethan stage emerges in both modern fiction and historiography as a rather rare occurrence. To be sure, illustrations abound of third-person or omniscient narrators who record the dialogue of women or, through either "style indirect libre," or interior monologue succeed in simulating a woman's thoughts. But in French literature there exist relatively few cases of first-person narratives written by men that endeavor to authenticate themselves as replicas of the feminine "je." Though epistolary examples may be identified (*Les Liaisons dangereuses, Julie ou La Nouvelle Héloïse,* Balzac's *Mémoires de deux jeunes mariées*), they lack the sustained psychological autonomy of a first-person diegesis. Indeed, in the transition within Gide's own oeuvre from epistolary dyad (*La Porte étroite*) to first-person triad, or to use Gide's term, to first-person "triptych" (*L'Ecole des femmes, Robert, Geneviève*), one observes Gide's attempt to perform what few writers before him had ever tried—the narrative transvestism of a woman's fictive "je." If Barthes' Michelet can be figured as a "Michelet-femme," ventriloquist for the mute statue of a far-off Joan of Arc, then so the author of this trilogy of récits may be

figured as a "Gide-femme," singing the as yet unwritten song of some Nouvelle Nouvelle Héloïse.

Gide, in fact, signalled *La Nouvelle Héloïse* as an intertext of his *Geneviève* in response to Madame Théo Van Rysselberghe's inquiry as to whether this work would be a novel. "Oui et non, vous allez voir," he had replied: "ce sera tout autre chose, une manière de roman genre *Nouvelle Héloïse*, avec de longues dissertations qui n'empêcheront pas le pathétique." Referring here to *Geneviève*'s bifurcated generic status as both tragi-comic family romance and "récit à thèse" (a problem to which we will return shortly), this seemingly casual reference to Rousseau's masterwork provides interesting grounds for speculation as to the origins of Gide's feminism; his possible sources of inspiration for the experiment of writing the feminine voice. On one side there emerges an obvious parallel to Rousseau insofar as *Geneviève* may also be read as a modern continuation of the Héloïse legend. A martyr to her passion (with passion later refined into courtly love, according to Denis de Rougement) this medieval heroine motivated Rousseau's bourgeois rewriting of her story just as Rousseau's version prompted Gide's anti-bourgeois rewriting of a bourgeois rewriting. A rebel like Abelard's Héloïse, Gide's Geneviève (whose name recalls another medieval prototype of feminism, the enterprising patron saint of Paris), disregards the standards of conventional behavior to which women were subject at the end of the nineteenth century. Her only resemblance to her eighteenth-century prototype Julie lies in her crisis of sublimation, when, as a girl she is barred by her parents from pursuing a latent lesbian obsession with an exotic, alluring schoolmate. Implicitly posing Geneviève's homosexual longing for Sara against Julie's chaste veneration for Saint-Preux, Gide thus travesties the eighteenth-century bourgeois (Platonic) paradigm at the same time as he dramatizes a historic revolution in the mores of women in his own century.

But in its twentieth-century feminism *Geneviève* also seems to have derived its doctrine obliquely from Héloïse by way of a chain of personal relationships that joined Gide in the thirties to an Anglo-French circle of feminist writers and thinkers, including Dorothy Bussy, Gide's translator, and the English historian Enid McLeod, author of an important biography of the original Héloïse and close friend of Elisabeth Van Rysselberghe, daughter of "la petite dame" and mother of Catherine Gide. The interlocking relationships between Gide, Elisabeth, Enid McLeod, and Ethel Whitehorn (called "Whity" in Madame Théo's *Cahiers*, and also an English schoolfriend of Elisabeth) have not yet been unravelled in detail, but it is clear that they are reflected on a number of levels in *Geneviève*. After her parents withdraw her from school so as to break her infatuation with the artistic Sara, Geneviève, in recompense, receives English lessons from the mother of another schoolgirl, Gisèle Parmentier, who rivals Geneviève for the affections of Sara. Madame Parmentier, herself a highly-educated English woman, provides the example of a moderated feminism to both daughter and pupil, who in turn recall Whity and Elisabeth. Further, the feminist Geneviève imitates Elisabeth's resolution to bear a child out of wedlock as a testimonial to the importance of women's independence. The substitution of a sororal support system for the nuclear family (in many ways the exact counterpart of the fraternal associations portrayed in *Paludes*, *L'Immoraliste* or *Les Faux-monnayeurs*), to which Geneviève commits herself as one of the founding members of the "Ligue pour l'indépendance féminine," reinforces the hypothesis that Gide's "gynotextuality" was profoundly influenced by the quasi-feminist ideology defined by Elisabeth and her friends. Like Enid McLeod, whose career was devoted to making the lost voices of women speak anew from Héloïse and Christine de Pisan to Colette, or Michelet's legendary "sorcières" who perished as victims of popular suspicion towards those of the weaker sex intrepid enough to take up the sword, Gide's Geneviève carries the suppressed chivalric heritage of women into modern middle-class society, leaving behind Rousseau as a kind of parenthetical reminder of a Héloïse forever bound.

Though these intertexts for Gide's feminism are only possible to project rather than verify (he himself left few clues either in his *Journal* or reported conversations), they nonetheless guide us towards the trilogy's generic status as "récit à thèse;" to its *thetic* (in the Greek sense of positioned or posed) rhetoric. Applied to the problem of gender-coding in relation to narrative voice, this thetic aspect focuses attention on the ideological identity of a homosexual voice that stands in for that of a lesbian feminist. It was precisely the prospect of creating a feminist complement to *Corydon* that aroused Gide's interest in the first place, as he confided to "la petite dame:"

> Je pense beaucoup à Geneviève . . . je voudrais faire dire à Geneviève des pensées extrêmes que je n'ai pas encore dites et auxquelles elle arrive à travers ses expériences: (. . .) Si j'arrive à dire tout ce que je veux ça pourrait être bien, je vous assure, bien plus hardi que *Corydon*, un vrai livre de combat comme je n'en ai, en somme, pas encore écrit, un livre qui serait à la fois vivant et plein de théorie . . .

The difficulty of writing a "combat book," a work of theory animated by the life blood of fiction, became apparent to Gide as he began composing **Geneviève**, particularly when it came to the task of crafting a feminine voice. Confessing in his *Journal* that he found it awkward and unrewarding to write "fémininement," he doggedly persevered only because he believed in the trilogy's value as exemplum in the ongoing political struggle for sexual freedom:

> Mais je n'éprouve aucune satisfaction à écrire fémininement, au courant de la plume, et tout ce que j'écris ainsi me déplaît. Je doute que ce style sans densité puisse avoir quelque valeur et crains parfois de m'aventurer dans une entreprise désespérante indigne de les autres propos, que je me reproche dès lors de délaisser pour elle.

Though the complaint here was of a primarily stylistic order—Geneviève's voice lacked density—Gide nonetheless refused to allow the thetic qualities of his normative program to predominate through simplistic, undigested polemics. As Albert W. Halsell, following Susan Suleiman's theory of the ideological novel has indicated, Gide's rhetorical strategies were consistently more refined. They included "des appels à l'authorité du texte extradiégé-

tique," (Molière's *Ecole des femmes*, *Jane Eyre*, *Clarissa Harlowe*, *Adam Bede*); the favoring in number and quality of female voices (Eveline, Geneviève) over male voices (Robert); and the use of preterition (roughly, "Robert was wonderful/brilliant/perfect etc. but . . .") as an understated means of casting Robert's words and gestures in a negative light.

The last of these techniques is also particularly prevalent on what might be characterized as the *mimetic* level of discourse; the level on which Gide as male (rather than homosexual) voice tries to imitate directly the tones and cadences of a female narrator. Here we are led to investigate the presence, absence or distortion of what might be identified as classic feminine tropes. Eveline's literary self-effacement, her silences, withheld inferences, and quotation of male discourse all form a coherent pattern of figures conventionally attributed to the female voice. Alternatively, Geneviève's curious description of an Oedipal fixation in place of the expected Electra complex (as in Proust's *La Confession d'une jeune fille*), points to a lapse in the sustained mimesis attempted by the male author; a moment where psychological and textual verisimilitude predictably fail.

Intercalated almost imperceptibly within the structures of female impersonation, following the *thetic* and the *mimetic*, is a third level of *parody*, where questions of narrative transvestism most clearly emerge. Is Eveline's voice comparable to an effeminate male voice; that of a Gide in woman's costume? Or, to move in the opposite direction, do the pompous, histrionic, Tartuffian antics of Robert constitute a full-scale travesty of classic stereotypes of masculine behavior—vanity, domination and castration anxiety? On yet another plane, is Gide, the homosexual male, masquerading as Geneviève, the homosexual female, and if so, can we detect an attitude of derision towards the feminist protagonist that also suggests a trace of auto-pastiche on Gide's part? Is finally the dissonance established between all three voices a parody of marital discord, secretly ensconcing a scathing indictment of the entire institution of marriage?

Though the three récits form a chronological sequence starting with **L'Ecole des femmes** (published in 1929) and ending with **Geneviève** (1936), their fictive frames establish the narratrice, Geneviève, as the proleptic reader of the entire trilogy. It is she who, acting as literary executor, forwards her mother's manuscript to the editor, "Monsieur André Gide," as if anticipating that **L'Ecole des femmes** will prompt the counter-récit of her father, thereby creating a sympathetic climate for the reception of her own autobiography. Mediator of the récits which precede hers, purveyor of a progressive social vision, and of the three narrators, the most firm in her convictions, Geneviève is naturally the most appropriate vehicle for the thetic dimension of the trilogy.

To a striking extent **Geneviève** illustrates the requisites of the paradigmatic "roman à thèse" as defined along general lines by Susan Suleiman [in *Authoritarian Fictions: The Ideological Novel as a Literary Genre* (1983)]. Positing the genre's "essentially teleological" nature—its reference to and resolution in "a doctrine that exists outside the novel," Suleiman prompts us not to underestimate the relationship between *Geneviève* as novel and *Corydon* as extra-textual credo; itself culled from writers as diverse as Hirshfeld, Krafft-Ebing, Bohn, Perrier, Ward, Plato, Goethe, Wilde, Whitman, Rémy de Gourmont, and Léon Blum. According to Suleiman, doctrine is textually transmitted through techniques that include "redundancy" (Barthes' "surplus of communication"), and the "reduction of ambiguity," with the latter frequently the result of "a dualistic system of values"; a self-evident, incontrovertible "right" versus "wrong." In *Geneviève*, the privileging of feminist values (right) over sexist values (wrong) is guaranteed (just as in *Corydon* homosexual values are privileged over anti-homosexual attitudes) with the assistance of a dialogical model of apprenticeship. Corydon is to his recalcitrant pupil (the narrator) as Sara and Gisèle Parmentier are to Geneviève—the "donors" of enlightenment. As Suleiman, departing from Greimas, has observed, the apprenticeship dynamic often involves three actants or three roles, that of "donor," "helper" and "opponent."

Following this model, Eveline and Madame Parmentier emerge as "helpers" who aid the donors (Sara and Gisèle) in positioning Geneviève against the "opponent" Robert. Here, however, we discover an interesting quirk resulting from the Gidean reversal of gender perspective, for if, as Suleiman argues, "the archetypal donor (or helper) is a paternal figure," then *Geneviève* furnishes the counterexample of donor-helper as *maternal* figure.

Eveline's journal, which goes only part way in outlining a feminist platform (it recounts the coming to consciousness of a woman formerly content to live in submission to her husband's volition), may be seen as a partial maternal donation, in need of supplementation by the more daring tenets of IF (the acronym, with pun on the English meaning intended, for the "Ligue pour l'indépendance féminine"). A number of IF's precepts appear to derive from *Corydon*: the idea that what society condemns as sexual aberration must be understood, defended with pride, and normalized within a protected, vanguard community; the belief that misogyny is culturally alleviated by homosexuality; the commonplace that women are more practical, more down to earth, and thus better equipped to deal with material problems; or the notion that heredity can be selected for with beneficial results to society. Several of these ideas reveal a difficulty in conversion from the homotextual to the gynotextual code. The misogyny argument, for example, is carried over clumsily and inferred only implicitly. Corydon maintains that:

> la décadence d'Athènes commença lorsque les Grecs cessèrent de fréquenter les gymnases; et nous savons à présent ce qu'il faut entendre par là. L'uranisme cède à l'hétérosexualité. C'est l'heure où nous la voyons triompher également dans l'art d'Euripide et avec elle, comme un complément naturel, la misogynie.

The underlying logic, farfetched though it seemed to Gide's friend Charles du Bos, is that the institution of pederasty in ancient Greece enabled men to preserve an image of women as unbesmirched by masculine desire, and thus worthy of the highest respect. In *Geneviève* this attitude finds its correlary in the heroine's commitment to maintaining her distance from the male sex: ("Quant à moi," Geneviève proclaims, "je ne puis accepter de me donner toute à quelqu'un. Je me révolte à l'idée de devoir soumettre ma vie à celui qui me rendra mère"). Her resolve to preserve self-respect by remaining aloof from men is facilitated by the fact that her passion is only aroused by women. When Gisèle asks her whether, if their beloved Sara was born a man, Geneviève would wish him/her to sire her children, Geneviève replies in the negative with, by way of explanation, the admission that "physical attraction" is not sufficient when choosing a mate. This exchange is significant not only because it openly confirms Geneviève's hitherto unspoken lesbian proclivities, but also because it indicates that father-figures constitute such a threat, that to render them benign requires transforming them into female surrogates; figuratively speaking, emasculating them.

On one level these subtexts allow Gide, as homosexual narrator, to be acknowledged as the courageous forerunner of a lesbian feminist "je"; he, who successfully translates a dualistic (albeit unconventional) set of values from one gender-code into the other. On another level, by implying that paternity sanctified by love and sanctioned by matrimony leads inevitably to some kind of symbolic castration for both sexes, the narrator of *Geneviève* may be suspected of eclipsing legitimate alternatives to the homosexual alliance. It is perhaps no accident that the only happy marriage of the entire trilogy—between Doctor Marchant and Yvonne, a close friend of Eveline's—is marred by her sterility and the existence of an unfulfilled yet undeniable sympathy between the Doctor and Eveline.

If infelicitous marital situations serve the thetic objectives of this gynotextual récit, they fail to facilitate the mimetic representation of a woman's authentic desire for a man. Eveline's rhetoric of esteem for Robert in the early days of their courtship is on all accounts unconvincing. With affirmations clouded by qualifiers, "mais, bien que, quoique, même" and so on, Eveline, as narrator of *L'Ecole des femmes* forfeits all semblance of genuine love for Robert: "Cette extraordinaire distinction de tout son être et de ses manières," she gloats, "je pense qu'il ne la doit qu'à lui-même, car il m'a laissé entendre que sa famille était assez vulgaire." The false naiveté of her observation rings forth in the rhetorical antithesis, for what is offered to Robert by way of a compliment to his manner is immediately subtracted with the information that, despite allegations to the contrary, he is ashamed of his "vulgar" origins. In another context, Robert astonishes his fiancée, shortly after returning from his mother's funeral, with his "stoic" determination to settle the terms of the legacy:

> Je l'ai revu. Comme sa douleur est digne et belle! Je commence à le comprendre mieux. Je crois qu'il a horreur des phrases toutes faites, car il a pour me parler de son deuil la même réserve qu'il avait pour me déclarer son amour. Et même, par crainte de laisser paraître son émotion, il évite tout ce qui pourrait l'attendrir. Il n'a même été question entre nous que de questions matérielles, et avec maman que de règlement de

succession et de la vente que Robert veut faire
de la propriété qui lui revient.

Here, Eveline plays the role of imperceptive narrator, fatuously asserting what we as readers see through effortless-
ly. As a narrator, she fails to communicate genuine erotic
attraction to her future spouse, and her apparent unaware-
ness of his opportunism and avarice is belied by repeated
preterition. When, for example, Eveline remarks: "Je lui
ai demandé de ne me présenter que ses amis véritables;
mais il est difficile, dès qu'on le connaît un peu, de ne pas
devenir son ami . . ." the covering phrase, "mais il est difficile," though intended to prevent the reader from discern-
ing Robert's superficiality, is ultimately de-negated by her
own depictions of his comportment with others. Eventually such feeble excuses and efforts at rationalization, induce
reader disbelief towards her claim of happy marriage. In
this respect, the attempt on the part of a male author to
simulate the monological, confessional voice of a young
girl in love emerges as fundamentally flawed.

More successful, though somewhat mechanical and stilted
in construction and tone, is the projection of lesbian desire
in *Geneviève*, for clearly Gide, as homosexual author,
found it easier to produce a compelling facsimile of lesbian
affection than its heterosexual analogue. In Geneviève's
portrait of Sara, there is an uncanny resemblance to Gide's
description of Donatello's David (with the equivalent of
his arresting gaze displaced to Sara's mesmerizing voice)
or to Michel's rendering of Bachir and Moktir. Just as Michel, in the presence of these Arab youths, blushes with
pleasure and shame as he seeks to overcome their indifference, so Geneviève, "rougissant beaucoup," endeavors to
obtain the merest sign of recognition from her schoolmate.
Here, in the first impression of Sara's "Oriental" beauty
and strangely seductive mien, we discover the gynotextual
body grafted onto the homotextual model as presented in
Les Nourritures terrestres or *L'Immoraliste*:

> De peau brune, ses cheveux noirs bouclés,
> presque crépus, cachaient ses tempes et une par-
> tie de son front. On n'eût pu dire qu'elle était
> précisément belle, mais son charme étrange était
> pour moi beaucoup plus séduisant que la beauté.
> Elle s'appelait Sara et insistait pour qu'on ne mît
> pas d'h à son nom. Lorsque, un peu plus tard,
> je lus *Les Orientales*, c'est elle que j'imaginais,
> "belle d'indolence", se balancer dans le hamac.
> Elle était bizarrement vêtue, et l'échancrure de
> son corsage laissait voir une gorge formée. Ses
> mains rarement propres, aux ongles rongés, étai-
> ent extraordinairement fluettes.

Though there is nothing overtly incongruous in this en-
semble, one discerns what seems almost to be an excess of
metonymical symmetry in the substitution of feminine for
masculine traits. From the darkness of complexion, to the
"not quite pretty" overall effect of lazy, quizzical sensuality, the description is virtually androgynous, and when
parts of the body are specifically noted, it is as if their selection were based on their contiguity or opposition to corresponding parts of the male anatomy. Where the rounded
shoulders and naked feet of young boys magnetize the
erotic attention of Michel, it is the formed throat and
graceful, if unkempt, hands, that similarly function for the

woman's body. Nor do the comparisons necessarily stop
at the appreciation of physique. As Geneviève is careful
to observe, Sara insists that her name be spelled in the Biblical way, with the letter "h" suppressed. This mark of her
"difference" can be variously interpreted as the badge of
her Jewish identity (branding her as exile and outcast, but
also as "bohemian," sexually and artistically free); or as
the sign of her destiny as a latter-day incarnation of Lot's
wife, for like the Biblical spouse, changed into a pillar of
salt for looking back, she too has leanings towards Sodom,
that "astral" city of inversion. Similar imprimaturs of difference had been even more developed in Gide's male gender code, with North Africa operating in the place of Israel as a mytheme of cultural otherness and an Oscar Wilde
prototype used to evoke aesthetic and erotic marginality.

Some feminist critics might argue that because the Sara
figure is fundamentally entrenched in homoerotic stereotypes; her features broken into isolated fragments more
characteristic of the fetishistic masculine gaze than the
feminine, (which tends perhaps more towards organic,
syncretic, emphatic appraisal), she should be read as a parody rather than as a mimetic characterization of a
woman's woman. This of course implies that a trade-off
in gender investment has occurred: the feminization of the
male narrator has dictated in return the masculinization of
female characters. Undoubtedly, Geneviève, Sara, Gisèle, and to some extent Eveline, conform to caricatures
of phallic women, those who, according to Sara Kofman's
revisionist interpretation of Freud, surpass men in resolving the Oedipal complex. Whereas adolescent males relinquish their libidinal attachments to the mother as they
gain confidence in the phallus (developing their super-egos
as they overcome castration anxiety), women are "already
castrated," and therefore must develop their egos through
sheer determination. ". . . loin d'abandonner alors sa
masculinité antérieure," Kofman says [in *L'engime de la
femme* (1980)] of the phallic woman, "elle s'y maintient
obstinément, l'exagère même, (. . .) cherche son salut dans
une identification avec la mère ou le père: bref, cette voie
est celle d'un 'puissant complexe de masculinité' où la fille
fantasme qu'elle est malgré tout un homme." Certainly
Geneviève manifests a "masculinity complex" as defined
by Freud and ratified by a feminist theorist, especially in
her strength of will and "identification with the mother."
Moreover, her type, as analyzed by Kofman, is even more
profoundly confirmed by a lesbianism that itself may be
interpreted as surrogate homophilia:

> Le choix d'objet homosexuel qui caractérise sou-
> vent ce type de femmes est pensé non comme le
> désir d'une femme pour une autre femme, mais
> bien comme le désir d'un homme pour un autre
> homme (pour une femme qu'elle pense, à son
> image, comme porteur de pénis, puisqu'elle-
> même s'identifie à la mère phallique ou au père).
> Son homosexualité serait simplement une consé-
> quence de son complexe de virilité.

If Gide's homoerotic portrayal of Geneviève's lesbianism
and *maternal* surinvestment may be read in one sense as
an Oedipal travesty (featuring Electra as patricidal Amazon), in another sense, it can be seen as an example of
Freudian verisimilitude. In this respect it should be noted

that Gide himself had become increasingly aware of
Freud's work from the early 1920's. When, in 1922, he
wrote in his *Journal*: "Freud, le freudisme . . . Depuis dix
ans, quinze ans j'en fais sans le savoir," he articulated the
striking predisposition of even his earliest writings towards psychoanalytical interpretations of sexual development. Moreover, in *Geneviève* he alludes directly to Freud
through his heroine who attributes her illness to psycho-
sexual neurosis: "Sitôt après ce que j'en ai dit, je tombai
malade. La scarlatine où, comme dirait Freud, se réfugiait
le désarroi de tout mon être." The open recognition of
Freud's impact would imply Gide's knowledge of the
Freudian theory of female sexuality, as he seems to have
based his typology of the masculine woman on research
that was beginning to be popularized in the literature of
the thirties. Seen in this light, the apparent satire of gender
roles—feminine masquerading as masculine, lesbian masquerading as homosexual—emerges instead as psychoanalytical realism; a mimetic rather than parodic order of
characterization.

But where, in this case, does mimesis end and parody
begin? Certainly an element of high farce is injected into
L'Ecole des femmes and *Robert* as Gide dons the costumes of beleaguered wife and injured husband, propelling
a kind of Punch and Judy show into the narrative arena.
Using similes such as "une comédie," "un tableau vivant,"
or the phrase: "Il me rappelle ces marionnettes à tête
légère qui d'elles-mêmes se redressent toujours sur leurs
pieds," to capture the hypocritical poses assumed by Robert, Eveline prepares the way for that consummate moment of grotesque inversion where she will appropriate
Robert's role and he will be delegated hers. This gender
reversal is presented from Eveline's perspective shortly
after she avows that she no longer loves him:

> Alors il se passa quelque chose d'extraordinaire:
> je le vis brusquement prendre sa tête dans ses
> mains et éclater en sanglots. Il ne pouvait plus
> être question de feinte; c'étaient de vrais sanglots
> qui lui secouaient tout le corps, de vraies larmes
> que je voyais mouiller ses doigts et couler sur ses
> joues, tandis qu'il répétait vingt fois d'une voix
> démente:
>
> "Ma femme ne m'aime plus! Ma femme ne
> m'aime plus!. . ."

The spectacle of male tears, paralleling Arnolphe's mask
of outraged despair at the discovery of Agnès' unwitting
infidelity in Molière's comedy, invites interpretation as a
kind of mock castration scene.

In Robert's narrative, the fear of castration is parodied as
he bemoans the maternal role that, due to her own laxity,
his wife has forced him to play in the moral education of
their children: "Que de fois j'ai senti que la position prise
par Eveline retenait le vrai progrès de ma pensée en me
forçant d'assumer dans notre ménage une fonction qui
aurait dû être la sienne." But if the exchange of gender
here provokes petty resentment and unease, later it precipitates full-fledged paranoia as Eveline's visage becomes a
"book" on which is printed the sign of the lost phallus—a
"vertical, double bar:" "Je lisais au pli de son front," Robert reveals, "à cette double barre verticale qui commençait

de se dessiner entre ses sourcils, une obstination grandis-
sante." As if to further reinforce the underlying graphic
image of castration anxiety, Robert receives Eveline's penetrating gaze like the knife that is used in the ritual sacrifice of the phallus: ". . . ce regard opérait sur moi *à la manière d'un scalpel*, détachant de moi cette action, cette parole ou ce geste, de sorte qu'ils parussent non plus tant nés
vraiment de moi qu'adoptés." (My emphasis) The surgical
separation of self from self-image (diminishing the male
ego as it emasculates the body) is unmitigated even by
Robert's appeals for her salvation: "ma prière, . . . *pareille
à la fumée d'un sacrifice non agrée*, retombait misérable-
ment sur moi-même." (My emphasis) If before, gender inversion were presented as the stuff of light comedy, it now
gives way to the macabre carnivalization of what Lamartine, glossing on the tragic episode of Abelard's castration,
said of the philosopher and his courageous lover Héloïse:
"Ici, comme toujours, le coeur de la femme fut viril, le
coeur de l'homme fut féminin."

If one stands back to consider the interplay of the three
levels of discourse hitherto discussed—the thetic, mimetic
and parodic—there is certainly no single voice articulated
in either gender or kinship role, that projects the domin-
iant chord, thereby privileging one level over the other. In
this sense the trilogy, taken as a medley of four fictive narrators (Eveline, Robert, Geneviève, and the "editor"
André Gide) and at least six transsexual meta-narrators:
the male author as wife (Gide-Eveline); the patriarch as
matriarch (Gide, father of Catherine-Eveline); the matriarch as patriarch (Eveline as object of Oedipal fixation and
"masculine woman"); the homosexual as patriarch (Gide-
Robert); the male sexist as woman (the emasculated Robert); and the homotextual voice as gynotextual voice (Gide
alias Corydon-Geneviève), affords an example of what
Barthes characterized as both "un neutre," or sexually indeterminate, and "le neutre," associated with "white writing" or "writing without style." In *Roland Barthes* he defined "le neutre" through a now familiar chain of evocative figures:

> Figures du Neutre: l'écriture blanche, exemptée
> de tout théâtre littéraire—le langage ad-
> amique—l'insignifiance délectable—le lisse—le
> vide, le sanscouture—la Prose (catégorie poli-
> tique décrite par Michelet)—la discrétion—la
> vacance de la "personne", sinon annulée, du
> moins rendue irréparable—l'absence d'imago—
> la suspension de jugement, de procès—le dé-
> placement—le refus de "se donner une conte-
> nance" (le refus de toute contenance)—le princi-
> pe de délicatesse—la dérive—la jouissance: tout
> ce qui esquive ou déjoue ou rend dérisoires la pa-
> rade, la maîtrise, l'intimidation.

Serving as intuitive index to an entire spectrum of deriva-
tions that range themselves behind the omnibus designation of "degree zero" or the rhetorical utopia of "neutrali-
ty," this entry commemorates the disappearance of a mas-
ter-narrative—that supreme Romantic fiction anchoring
history in the authoritative voice of its narrator. Not only
has the modern narrator lost a fixed sexual identity, but
his neutered, anonymous voice has been misplaced or displaced into a dystopia of conditional silence. Barthes'
analogy: "La voix est, par rapport au silence, comme

l'écriture (au sens graphique) sur le papier blanc," points to what remains of authorial identity after the post-Symbolist ascension to silence and white paper—it is, simply, "le grain de la voix,"—an expression that Gide himself, with his fondness for the music of the voice as well as for the image of the "grain" as inseminating particle and floating, personal signifier, could have easily ceded to Barthes. This ineffable, glottalized utterance, "un mixte érotique de timbre et de langage," is treated by Barthes [in *L'obvie et l'obtus* (1982)] as the originary sign of the subject; a carrier of the primordial "Ecoutez!" motivating the infant to its mother, the confessor to the priest, the patient to his analyst. "L'originalité de l'écoute psychanalytique," Barthes maintains, "tient à ceci: elle est ce mouvement de va-et-vient qui relie *la neutralité et l'engagement*, la suspension d'orientation et la théorie". (My emphasis). On one level seen as the purest locutionary agent of mediation between the zero degree threshold of communication ("neutralité") and the point of spoken interaction with the Other, "le grain de la voix" is also conceived by Barthes as an "écriture"—a kind of "writing out loud." Defined in contradistinction to the *actio* of ancient rhetoric—the codes governing the physical exteriorization of expression in the art of oratory, "l'écriture à haute voix," according to Barthes [in *Le plaisir du texte* (1973)] articulates that "forgotten," "censored" part of speech that provides the essential liaison to the hidden, erotic source of expression:

> . . . 'l'écriture à haute voix' n'est pas phonologique, mais phonétique; son objectif n'est pas la clarté des messages, le théâtre des émotions; ce qu'elle cherche (dans une perspective de jouissance), ce sont les incidents pulsionnels, c'est le langage tapissé de peau, un texte où l'on puisse entendre le grain du gosier, la patine des consonnes, la volupté des voyelles, toute une stéréophonie de la chair profonde; l'articulation du corps, de la langue, non celle du sens, du langage.

Barthes' alliterative rendering of this graphically invisible, incantatory, gutteral, phonetically abrasive, sexual vibrato recalls the abstract ideals of the Symbolist sign, particularly the emphasis placed by Baudelaire and Mallarmé on the imprecision of sense and corresponding refinement of musical tonality, respiration and stress. It is this prelinguistic, proto-Symbolist instrumentation that, significantly enough, rings out in the voice of Geneviève's Sara, who, like her namesake Sarah Bernhardt, is gifted with the powers of transforming the "récit" (as genre of spoken writing) into a sensual, vocably self-referential "récitatif." Not surprisingly, the literary intertext in the scene which stages Sara's "écriture à haute voix" is Baudelaire's sonnet, *La mort des amants*. In the poem's second stanza, the motif of doubling—woman to woman, mirror to mirror, flame to flame, assonance to assonance—mimes the enunciation and echo of pure sound as it travels from the speaker to the enraptured auditor:

Usant à l'envi leurs chaleurs dernières,

Nos deux coeurs seront deux vastes flambeaux,

Qui réfléchiront leurs doubles lumières

Dans nos deux esprits, ces miroirs jumeaux.

This verse, with its Saphhic innuendos and sonoric repetitions "enabyme" awakens in Geneviève (just as it had awakened in the young post-Symbolist Gide whose *Traité du Narcisse* is "quoted" in Geneviève's response to the poem), the beginnings of a secret longing for "jouissance:"

> Je ne suis pas très sensible à la poésie, je l'avoue, et sans doute serais-je restée indifférente devant ces vers, si je les avais lus moi-même. Ainsi récités par Sara, ils pénétrèrent jusqu'à mon coeur. Les mots perdaient leur sens précis, que je ne cherchais qu'à peine à comprendre; chacun d'eux se faisait musique, subtilement évocateur d'un paradis dormant; et j'eus la soudaine révélation d'un autre monde dont le monde extérieur ne serait que le pâle et morne reflect.

In its evocation of a "dormant paradise," the brilliance of which reduces the real world to the status of a "pale and dull reflection," Sara's voice, like Narcissus' gaze, produces a visionary object of desire that necessarily remains distant. But this strange, unearthly music of the human voice, as far as Sara is concerned, waits only to be translated into gestures by those whom it has sensually and spiritually stirred: "Mais il ne tient qu'à nous d'y vivre," she remonstrates to the dubious, romantically resigned Geneviève. In her confidence in the authenticity of "le grain de la voix," or what Barthes would later call "le bruissement de la langue," Sara acts as a cover for the counterfeit nature of the "Gide-femme," with its at times uncannily believable impersonation of the feminine voice. (pp. 264-78)

> *Emily S. Apter, "Female Impersonations: Gender and Narrative Voice in Gide's 'L'Ecole des femmes', 'Robert' and 'Geneviève'," in* The Romanic Review, *Vol. LXXVII, No. 3, May, 1986, pp. 264-78.*

Winifred Woodhull (essay date 1988)

[*In the following essay, Woodhull examines Gide's depiction in* Theseus *of gender relations and the proper ordering of society.*]

Thésée, a text Gide had dreamed of writing since his youth and had alluded to and made notes for in his *Journal* since 1931, is finally completed and published only in 1946 when the writer, like his narrator Theseus, is an old man who has finished his work in life. Though the first notes on the project date from the period in which Gide wrote his "triptych" *L'Ecole des femmes*, *Robert*, and *Geneviève* (1929-36), *Thésée* emerges as a work that tends to close the questions raised in the earlier texts concerning the significance of gender identity in the writing and reading of literature. If, as Emily S. Apter has argued [in "Female Impersonations: Gender and Narrative Voice in Gide's L'ecole des femmes, Robert, and Geneviève," *Romanic Review* (1986)], Gide's triptych is important as an "experiment of writing the feminine voice" in accordance with feminist values—an experiment which challenges not only the male writer's social privilege but also the security of his masculine identity—his récit on the Greek hero, lawmaker, and ladies' man is above all an exercise in writing out the female voice and inscribing the primacy of the homosocial bond among men as the basis for cultural stability and vitality.

Theseus's psychosocial development follows a path leading from a polymorphously perverse relation to the outside world governed by the pleasure principle to a firm sense of his masculinity and mastery, illustrated in the narrative by his numerous conquests of women. Though in the main adventure—the labyrinth episode—Theseus finds himself in a relation of dependence with Ariadne and is momentarily tempted by homosexual desire for the Minotaur, he is "saved" by the woman whose thread leads him back out of the maze, where he regains his self-possession and position of dominance. At that point, true to form, he conceives a plot to abandon Ariadne—after all, it was she who had thrown herself at *him*, so he was in no way committed—in favor of her younger sister Phaedra. Having dressed his child bride in her brother Glaucos's clothes (the girl just happens to be the spitting image of her sibling), he escapes from Crete, deposits Ariadne on the island of Naxos where she is said to become Dionysos's wife, and returns to Athens to reign. As my summary of events suggests, the social order he establishes there is founded on the victory of self-mastery over the vagaries of desire, and the symbolic neutralization of women.

Insofar as Gide is still experimenting with problems of voice and identity in *Thésée*, he elaborates a reflection on textuality as a labyrinth from which the male author, whose writing practice puts his identity into question, must emerge safe and sound in order to rejoin his fellows. Yet at first glance *Thésée* reads more like a *récit à thèse* proclaiming, on the one hand, the primacy of the autonomous individual over the social group and, on the other, the superiority of "meritocracy" over other political systems. Its unequivocal declaration of an ideology that exists outside the text and its reduction of ambiguity using the technique of redundancy make it an overtly ideological récit which conforms to the model elaborated by Susan Suleiman. The words of wisdom imparted to Theseus by Daedalus in the Minotaur episode ("seul compte, parmi les hommes, l'individu. . . . Il te reste à fonder Athènes, où asseoir la domination de l'esprit") carry a clear message which is echoed later in the hero's characterization of the new social order he has founded: "Je ne fais cas de rien que du mérite personnel et ne reconnais pas d'autre valeur. . . . [C]ette aristocracie nouvelle . . . [sera] celle non de l'argent, mais de l'esprit."

The corollary to the liberal political doctrine expressed in the lines just quoted is the affirmation of secular humanism over a religious world view. "Les premières et les plus importantes victoires que devait remporter l'homme, c'est sur les dieux" says Theseus of his early exploits. This idea is stated repeatedly throughout the tale and is emphasized again at the end when the founder of the first democracy asks rhetorically "Eh! de quoi s'occuper, que de l'homme?" Gide's text thus openly espouses a particular ideology and seeks to persuade readers to adopt it by designating Theseus as an *exemplum*. "Sache montrer aux hommes," his father tells him, "ce que peut être et se propose de devenir l'un d'entre eux."

Yet, because *Thésée* articulates contradictions within the

doctrine it is promoting and thus avoids presenting it as a monolithic entity, the récit meets a necessary, though not sufficient, condition for being deemed a "work of art" rather than "vulgar propaganda." Upon arriving at the court of King Minos, for instance, the uncouth Theseus realizes that until this point he has lived like a savage and must learn to adapt to the customs of the refined society in which he now finds himself. The first scenes set in Crete suggest, then, that it is not enough to perform heroic deeds; to a limited extent, even a hero must respect society's definition of a civilized person.

Likewise, Theseus is obliged to curb his rugged individualism; rather than entering into relationships with others only as adversaries to be defeated, one by one, by brute force, he must "please" the company he keeps. This development implicitly challenges the liberal conception of society as an assembly of people who are *essentially* individualist, but agree to form a social contract for negative reasons, that is, in order to limit others' infringements on what is taken to be the liberty of the individual. Despite the fact that the refinement of the Minoan Empire is associated with the decadence that will cause its downfall, Theseus's personal development is favorably influenced by his encounter with the Cretans, whose culture impresses upon him the need for a positive social bond based on shared values and cooperation with others. This is borne out by the hero's decision, once he succeeds to Aegeus's throne, to abandon his father's political strategy of dividing his subjects in order to strengthen his authority as ruler, and to try instead to establish harmony among them. "Par un partage égal des terres," he says, "je supprimai d'un coup les suprématies et les rivalités qu'elles entraînent."

This last statement points to another way in which the doctrine of liberalism is problematized in *Thésée*. Not only does it suggest that individualism can be exploited by rulers to disempower the ruled, it also affirms the confiscation and redistribution of private property by the representative of the state—a socialist measure—as an acceptable means to [an] end of establishing economic equality among citizens. The text thus marks liberalism's guarantee of formal political equality as inadequate to ensure social justice, since it fails to curb entrepreneurial power and unscrupulousness. If the rich have sometimes acquired their fortunes by honest means and hard work, Theseus maintains, they have more often done so "par injustice et par abus."

In *Thésée*, social justice is by no means synonymous with the absolute equality of all citizens. On the contrary, as we saw above, Theseus envisages the development of a new aristocracy based on will and intellect. On this point he is in agreement with his friend Pirithous, who states bluntly, "Il est bon que les meilleurs dominent la masse vulgaire de toute la hauteur de leur vertu." This overt dismissal of the majority of the people as vulgar masses, though uncharacteristic of 20th-century liberalism, comes as no surprise to the reader since Theseus has consistently presented himself as a superior being who is to set an example for the morally and intellectually feeble creatures he meets everywhere he goes. Part of his strength resides in his contempt for social convention, which needlessly constrains the appetites and inclinations of the vigorous individual while seeming to satisfy them. The stultifying effect of convention is figured, for example, in the artifice of Cretan society, which is sharply contrasted with Theseus's "naturalness." The "corridors tortueux" of Minos's palace, like the labyrinth itself, are associated with intoxicating drinks and perfumes that disorient and threaten to trap the hero. "Oppressé par l'atmosphère factice de ce lieu," Theseus twice affirms his need to be in the open air and, upon returning to Athens, proclaims, "Je prétends vivre en roi tout aussi simplement que j'ai vécu jusqu'à ce jour, et sur le même pied que les humbles." Unlike the decadent Cretans and the Athenian youths who succumb to the charms of the labyrinth (in Gide's version the labyrinth is a figure for seduction rather than for physical confinement), Theseus resists the anesthetization of the will, repeatedly reminding the reader of the need to remain one's own master.

The intertext for Theseus's celebration of the "overman" is Nietzsche's *Thus Spake Zarathustra*. Echoing the Zarathustrian notion of self-overcoming, Gide's hero repeatedly pronounces the watchword "passe outre." Theseus is enjoined to beware of the seductive charms of both social convention and women in order to pursue his life of conquest, and to resist the temptation to abandon his life of adventure and hard work on the pretext that he has already accomplished enough. In this, he closely resembles Zarathustra, to whom life confides the secret of self-overcoming: "I am *that which must always overcome itself.* Indeed, you call it a will to procreate or a drive to an end, to something higher, farther, more manifold: but all this is one "[Friedrich Nietzsche, *Thus Spake Zarathustra*]. And like the wanderer Zarathustra who observes that "What returns, what finally comes home to me, is my own self and what of myself has long been in strange lands and scattered among all things and accidents," Theseus associates his wanderings with the rediscovery of the self. For example, he learns from Daedalus that Ariadne's thread will lead him out of the labyrinth of subjective dissolution by linking him to his past. "Reviens à toi. Car rien ne part de rien, et c'est sur ton passé, sur ce que tu es à présent, que tout ce que tu seras prend appui."

Finally, the Gidian and Nietzschean heroes share disdain for religion, which is said to fetter and mystify humanity. In contrast to the saint who tells him, "Man is for me too imperfect a thing. Love of man would kill me," Zarathustra declares, "I love man." Similarly, Theseus is contrasted with Oedipus, who in Gide's tale is cast as a saint who affirms the "grandeur" of suffering, claiming that "[l'homme] n'est nulle part plus valeureux que lorsqu'il tombe en victime, forçant ainsi la reconnaissance céleste et désarmant la vengeance des dieux." Theseus, for his part, refuses to admit of an opposition between the eternal realm that Oedipus locates in inner life and the outside world in which men live and act; like Daedalus, he affirms the complementarity of the two spheres. In a rewriting of some lines from Hesiod's *Theogony*, Gide formulates the problem in these terms:

> Dans le temps, sur un plan humain, [chacun] se développe, accomplit son destin, puis meurt.

> Mais le temps même n'existe pas sur un autre plan, le vrai, l'éternel, où chaque geste représentatif, selon sa signification particulière s'inscrit. . . . Ainsi en advient-il des héros. Leur geste dure et, repris par la poésie, par les arts, devient un continu symbole.

This observation of course functions as a *mise en abîme* of Theseus's first-person narrative relating his own heroism, and of Gide's récit as well.

In view of the cataclysmic events of World Wars I and II . . . and the consequent political, economic, and intellectual upheaval in Europe, Gide's *Thésée* may be read as an attempt to reaffirm the soundness of Western institutions through the time-honored, human-centered vehicle of Greek myth.

—*Winifred Woodhull*

As the passage just quoted suggests, Gide's text relies upon a notion of cultural continuity linking modern Western civilization to antiquity. It is the presumed status of Theseus's story as a "continous symbol" that both guarantees the hero's greatness and ensures his story's relevance to 20th-century readers. Indeed, in view of the cataclysmic events of World Wars I and II, the unprecedented slaughter of human beings in the concentration camps, the annihilation of large populations by the atomic bomb, and the consequent political, economic, and intellectual upheaval in Europe, Gide's récit may be read as an attempt to reaffirm the soundness of Western institutions through the time-honored, human-centered vehicle of Greek myth.

In light of this, the existence of a clear intertextual link between *Thésée* and *Zarathustra* is somewhat ironic because the Nietzschean text, by emphasizing historical and psychic discontinuity, radically unsettles the foundations of European culture. In *Thésée* on the other hand, the figure of the "overman" ultimately functions to promote bourgeois liberalism—including the notion of the autonomous human subject—and to conceal the contradictions within that doctrine. For instance, Gide assimilates Nietzsche's notions of "self-overcoming" and the will to power to the liberal ideal of "progress," an ideal which, at least until the post-war period, often does less to encourage social change than to mask the perpetual reproduction of the same mode of production, the same class relations, the same sex-gender arrangements. Despite the similarity in the *content* of certain declarations made by Zarathustra and Theseus, the textual figurations of their views are very different. Gide achieves a certain dialogism, to be sure (for example, in the exchange between Theseus and Oedipus on the role of religion in social life), but always privileges Theseus's voice in the end and makes of the self-possessed male hero the primary agent of social transformation. Nietzsche, on the other hand, refracts Zarathustra's vision through a "hundredfold mirror" and has his hero say that "whoever guesses what is my will should also guess on what *crooked* paths it must proceed" (emphasis Nietzsche's). These "crooked paths" stand in marked contrast to the straight one followed by Theseus once he emerges from the labyrinth and arrives in Athens, where he commits himself to heterosexual monogamy and the construction of a lasting monument to humanity. "J'épousai la femme et la cité à la fois. . . . Le temps de l'aventure est révolu, me redisais-je; il ne s'agissait plus de conquérir, mais de régner." Significantly, he dedicates his city to Pallas Athena, the chaste goddess whose hand "knows the art of controlling and guiding straight."

The ideologically charged notions of progress and of the "great man" as exemplum tend, then, to mask instabilities within subjects and discontinuities within and between civilizations. As a result, they produce an effect of harmony and resolution at the conclusion of the récit. Theseus's self-possession and accomplishment seem to have laid the basis for a more just and stable society. But more important, the example the tale provides for modern readers holds out the possibility of reconstructing post-war Europe on its old foundations, denying the need to invent radically new artistic and social forms.

Nonetheless; Gide's resurrection of the Theseus myth does not effectively conceal the contradictions within liberal humanism. Though in the last lines of the récit, Theseus congratulates himself on the greater happiness and freedom he has bequeathed to his fellow men, the reader remembers his declarations a few pages before regarding the necessarily "illusory" nature of the freedom enjoyed by the masses, whose deception was the condition for their betterment. The instrumentalization of human activity characteristic of Theseus's "new" city is manifested in the description of the Athenians as "bons instruments" and of Athenian social life as "le fonctionnement générale de la machine." Part of the interest of *Thésée*, then, is that while purporting to edify and instruct readers by exemplifying individual accomplishment and social improvement, it simultaneously discloses some of the ways in which modern culture frustrates those goals. In an important sense, Theseus's Athens, as presented in Gide's récit, is not a city we should strive to build, but rather one we already live in and ought to change.

This last point comes clearly into focus if we consider the treatment of gender relations in *Thésée* and the ways in which gender is shown to inform interpretive acts. A key issue in Gide's text is the link between sex-gender arrangements and the strength or weakness of a civilization. Particularly in its handling of the opposition between the Minoan Empire and Greece, *Thésée* associates cultural vitality with heterosexuality, the domination of women by men, and the symbolic construction of femininity as nothing more than a negative version of masculinity. In Crete, men's homosexual inclinations and insufficient control over women are depicted as the main sources of weakness and vulnerability in the culture at large. Theseus distances himself from the pederastic practices of both the Cretans and his fellow Greeks, saying "bien que Grec, je ne me sens aucunement porté vers ceux de mon sexe . . . et diffère en cela d'Hercule." This claim foreshadows his victory over the Minotaur, and thus over Cretan hegemony, since the battle with the monster involves exposing himself to, but ultimately resisting, homosexual desire. Reflecting on his experience in the labyrinth, Theseus acknowledges his temptation, saying "Je ne gardai de ma victoire sur lui qu'un souvenir confus mais, somme toute, voluptueux," but thanks to Ariadne, he manages not to give in to it.

Pederasty, however, is not the only weakness displayed by the Cretan men, for they are effeminate as well—scarcely distinguishable from women. "Les hommes . . . portaient aux mains, aux poignets, au cou, presque autant de bagues, de bracelets, et de colliers que les femmes." Only Minos stands out in the sexually undifferentiated crowd at Knossos; his jewelry is not "vulgar" like the other men's but is finely crafted from gems and gold, and his dress is similarly distinctive. "Tous les hommes avaient le torse nu. Minos seul, assis sous un dais, portait une longue robe."

Yet Minos, too, despite his status as king, judge, and legislator, resembles a woman in his inability—or really, lack of resolve—to judge things rationally and, above all, to rely on his own judgment. Not only does he indulge his lascivious wife Pasiphae by believing the ridiculous tales she tells—she claims to have taken the bull who sired the Minotaur to be divine—but worse, he allows himself to experience the world through her by *taking her word* for things. In one of the most sharply ironic passages of the récit, Pasiphae explains to Theseus why Minos listens to what she has to say about the conception of the Minotaur. "[Il] pense qu'il ne sera bon juge qu'après qu'il aura tout éprouvé, par lui-même ou dans sa famille. . . . Ses enfants, moi-même, chacun dans sa diversité, nous travaillons, par nos écarts particuliers, à l'avancement de sa carrière." More is at stake here than the familiar association of women with uncontrollable sensuality and irrationality. For what are presented as "feminine" weaknesses are marshalled to disqualify Pasiphae's testimony in the eyes of a self-respecting judge, that is, Theseus and, by extension, the reader. This symbolic disqualification effectively silences Pasiphae, because though she may chatter endlessly, her words are not to be taken seriously in public debate; unlike Minos, Theseus knows not to be taken in by Pasiphae, not to take her word for anything.

Still, despite his wisdom in this matter, Theseus *is* somewhat vulnerable to Pasiphae's sexual appetites and irrational behavior. In fact, as the following passage illustrates, all the female members of the Cretan royal family arouse the hero's desire—and dread. "Durant tout le repas, Ariane me pressa du genou sous la nappe; mais c'est surtout la chaleur que dégageait la jeune Phèdre qui me troublait. Cependant que Pasiphaë, la reine, en face de moi, me dévorait tout cru de regard, Minos, à côté d'elle, souriait inaltérablement." In this compromising situation, Theseus at least has an advantage over Minos in being aware of the danger. As he notes in the first pages of the récit, what is important where women are concerned is to avoid being taken with them, "de ne point se laisser appoltronner par aucune, ainsi qu'Hercule entre las bras d'Omphale."

But how is it that Theseus associates women's desire—and his desire for women—with domination by women? We find an important clue in the descriptions of Pasiphae and her daughters, which call to mind the Mountain Mother of Crete and the cthonic religion that is eventually displaced by the Greek worship of male sky gods. The depiction of Pasiphae, for instance, is clearly modeled on statues of the mother goddess found in Crete. "Ses bras et le devant de sa poitrine étaient nus. Sur ses seins opulents s'étalaient perles, émaux, et pierreries. . . . Une sorte de diadème d'or la couronnait." Both the queen's and Ariadne's dresses are embroidered with flowers and animals which point to the goddess's function as mother and protector of nature. Only Phaedra's dress differs, for it is decorated with figures of children playing. As we shall see, it is no accident that Theseus prefers Phaedra ("sensiblement plus jeune") to her older sister, since the younger girl evokes less powerfully the imposing figure of the Great Mother.

Ariadne—before Greek myth reduces her to the status of thread-bearer—is a Cretan goddess of the sky and underworld. As such, she is associated with the mother goddess-son god dyad characteristic of cthonic cults. Theseus's dependent relation to Ariadne in the labyrinth scene thus obliquely recalls, for example, that of Dionysos to Semele, Attis to Kybele, and Adonis to Aphrodite—a relation in which the son (often also a consort) is subordinate to the mother. This interpretation of Theseus's tie to Ariadne makes it possible to read the adventure of the labyrinth as a staging of the mother-son relation as it is symbolically constructed *before* the worship of patriarchal sky gods becomes hegemonic; that is, before the mother is subordinated to the father *and* to the son. In this light, the adventure can also be seen as an inscription of experience from the boy's early childhood, when the boundaries between the self and the other are unstable, and the infant attributes his helplessness to his mother's overpowering strength. Of course, Gide's récit allows the reader to glimpse these archaic psychic and social experiences only to cover them over again. In fact, it is precisely the inversion of the son's relation of dependence that ensures Theseus's victory not only over the Minotaur, but over Minos and his empire. The key is to dominate women.

As we might suspect, however, Theseus does not manage this alone. He is counseled and given practical assistance by Daedalus, the architect of the labyrinth, who anticipates and appropriates every function assigned to Aridane in less patriarchal versions of the myth. In *Thésée* it is Daedalus who comes up with the scheme of using a thread to get in and out of the maze, and Daedalus who provides the thread. Clearly Ariadne, the woman who weaves, is displaced by the hero's mentor both where practical skill and cunning intelligence *mêtis* are concerned. Her role henceforth will be merely the passive one of holding the thread, and even that troubles Theseus, who insists on holding the skein so as to be able to control his distance from her by raveling and unraveling it. What is more, the coding of Daedalus as a paternal figure—for instance, he addresses Theseus as "fils de la Grèce, mon cousin"—functions to displace Ariadne in her role as a powerful and revered mother. In this context, the thread acquires significance as a link between father and son; an embodiment of the law of the father, which guarantees the subordina-

tion of women, the thread is a bond that assures Theseus of his place in the social order, and requires that he return to that place upon emerging from the labyrinth. "Ce fil te permettra, te forcera, de revenir," says Daedalus.

Theseus, then, must come back not only to his proper place but also to Ariadne ("Reviens à elle"), whose subordinate position ensures the hero's dominance. But Ariadne is a guarantor of Theseus's power in other respects as well. Not least of all, as his heterosexual lover (provisional though she may be), Ariadne deflects Theseus's homosexual inclination, which is apparent in his reaction to the Minotaur. "Le monstre était beau. Comme il advient pour les centaures, une harmonie certaine conjugait en lui l'homme et la bête. De plus, il était jeune, et sa jeunesse ajoutait je ne sais quelle charmante grâce à sa beauté; armes, contre moi, plus forte que la force." Ariadne's thread ("figuration tangible de devoir") prevents the force of the father's law from being overcome by illicit desire and thus ensures the stability of paternal authority. In the adventure of the labyrinth, it is the structure of Theseus's tie to woman that enables the hero to differentiate himself from the Cretan pederasts, who give in to homosexual desire, and from Pasiphae, who succumbs to the charms of a beast. This same tie accounts for his superiority over Minos, who condones the errors of his countrymen and allows his wife to deceive and manipulate him. Theseus's victory thus marks the triumph of male supremacy and symbolically reaffirms the law of the father.

Beyond this, though, the figure of Ariadne lends credence to Theseus's fantasy of unified subjectivity and stable gender identity, a key element in his "victory." Ariadne, in opposition to whom the male hero defines himself, remains at the threshold of the labyrinth and guarantees that Theseus will emerge from the scene of subjective undoing with his masculine identity intact.

That the labyrinth figures subjective undoing is manifested in Theseus's encounter with Daedalus's son Icarus, who has fallen victim to the spells of the maze. The boy's monologue reveals that his madness consists in an inability to set masculinity and feminity in fixed relation to one another; hence his anxious queries regarding origins and sexual difference.

> Qui donc a commencé, l'homme ou la femme? L'Eternel est-il féminin? Du ventre de quelle grand Mère êtes-vous sorties, force multiples? Et ventre fécondé par quel engendreur? Dualité inadmissible. Dans ce cas, le dieu, c'est l'enfant. Mon esprit se refuse à diviser Dieu. Dès que j'admets la division, c'est pour la lutte. Qui dieux a, guere a.

Here again we encounter, more explicitly than before, the problem of the mother goddess as the primary power fecundated by the son god. The structure of this hierarchy alone is apparently enough to drive a sane man mad. But there is more. The problem for Icarus is not simply the structure of the relation between masculinity and femininity, but the very existence of a dichotomy. The duality is "inadmissible" because, in order for him to remain anchored psychically, his mental life must appear to be as indivisible as he imagines God to be.

For Icarus, the awareness of sexual difference and irreducible psychic division produces unbearable tension which leads him to seek transcendance of earthly existence. The boy's desire to escape from a human dilemma through union with God is mocked in a parody of symbolist rhethoric: "L'azur m'attire, ô poésie! Je me sens aspiré par en haut. . . . Je ne sais quel est cet attrait qui m'engage; mais je sais qu'il n'est qu'un terminus unique: c'est Dieu." Needless to say, Icarus is fated to fall from the heights to which he aspires and, like Oedipus, to meet with defeat by virtue of seeking an other-worldly solution to the problems of this world.

Theseus, on the other hand, finds a practical solution to these problems. By entering into a homosocial relation with Daedalus mediated by a domesticated Ariadne, he lays the basis for a social order that effectively excludes women from the symbolic field. In effect, their society recognizes only one sex, and consists in an assembly of what are assumed to be stable male subjects. Thanks to Ariadne's thread, Theseus is able to enter the maze in which his gendered subjectivity is ravelled and unravelled—and thus to summon a return of the repressed—with the assurance of emerging again as a conqueror.

In Gide's *récit à thèse*, then, the adventure of the labyrinth functions as a figure for the instabilities that are repressed in the sex-gender arrangements of the social order it is promoting. Yet it could also be said that this episode provides a model of reading, one which reinforces the gender hierarchy in our culture while seeming to undermine it. As Nancy K. Miller has demonstrated [in "Arachnologies: The Woman, the Text, and the Critic" in *The Poetics of Gender* (1986)], the labyrinth figures prominently in contemporary literary criticism as a figure for textuality, just as the metaphorics of weaving and femininity informs male critics' discussions of the making and unmaking of writing and reading subjects. Male readers can jubilantly affirm their subjective undoing because, like Theseus, they are tied to a domesticated woman who, like Ariadne, remains on the threshold of the maze, ensuring that they will emerge unscathed from their exposure to the instabilities of psychosexual constitution. The metaphoric web of the labyrinth scene in Gide's *Thésée* thus invites a practice of reading and interpretation characteristic of the work of Barthes, Derrida, and the American deconstructionists in which, as Miller has said, "the discourse of the male weavers stages 'woman' without in any way addressing women."

What follows the labyrinth scene bears out my claim that *Thésée* stages the instabilities of gender relations and subjective division only to repress them again more effectively. It is no accident, for example, that Ariadne, once she has served her purpose, is deceived and abandoned on a remote island, for her situation at the confines of civilization marks the marginality of her position in the social and symbolic order her faithless lover founds. Since Ariadne is reported to be in the company of a new consort, Dionysos—a foreigner whose status as son god and association with cthonic cults have not been entirely forgotten—one is tempted to interpret this inscription of her fate as one which preserves at least a trace of her earlier grandeur.

But Gide is quick to write over this inscription by having Theseus interpret the report of her marriage to Dionysos as "une façon de dire qu'elle se consola dans le vin." Thus, though he does not choose to end Ariadne's story with the account of her suicide—the alternative ending is that she hangs herself with her own thread—he nonetheless disempowers her and effaces her almost completely as a marker of instability in his own identity.

Before we leave Ariadne, it is worth noting that she is rendered innocuous in *Thésée* not only by being discredited as a powerful mother figure and a woman endowed with cunning intelligence, but also, like her mother, by being disqualified as a speaker. Significantly, she announces to Theseus, point by point, what Daedalus will tell him the next day regarding the dangers of the labyrinth, but what she says carries no authority; she explicitly defers to the architect of the maze, saying "Demain, je te présenterai à Dédale, qui te dira." If her words are not to be taken seriously, it is in part because Ariadne is cast as one who speaks inauthentically, just as her father Minos lives inauthentically. Theseus's claim that the princess is "trop férue de littérature" implies that she is in love with love as presented in books rather than with the hero himself. It matters little whether her model of love comes from classical drama or lyric poetry, for in either case, she is merely quoting rather than living—hence the presentation of her speech as pastiche. "Tu triompheras [du Minotaure], j'en suis sûre," says Ariadne, "il suffit de te voir pour n'en pouvoir douter. (—Tu ne trouves pas que ça fait un beau vers? Tu es sensible?)." Interestingly, though, as we saw above, Theseus himself continually quotes Zarathustra, just as his mentor Daedalus quotes Hesiod (though the citational character of their discourse is not identified as such), so the criterion of authenticity does not seem to be "originality" but rather reference to the "right" sources, namely sources which celebrate the solitary male hero and downplay love.

Small wonder, in any case, that the garrulous Ariadne is abandoned in favor of Phaedra, who never says a word. As passive and compliant as her older sister is willful and sexually forward, she promises to be the perfect partner for our hero—the very model of womanhood in the new Athens. Yet Theseus no sooner sets sail for Attica than the nagging questions of gender identity and desire resurface. Theseus's means of escaping with Phaedra is to disguise her as her brother Glaucos and pretend to abduct him. Minos is thereby led to believe that Theseus is acting in accordance with the Cretan pederastic code, which requires that a boy's beauty in body, mind, and heart be confirmed in the eyes of the community by an adult who takes him as a lover. To be sure, the labyrinth scene marked the pederastic code as "wrong," and Theseus's feigned adherence to it here, on one level at least, tacitly upholds the heterosexual norm precisely because of the feint involved. However, the abduction of Phaedra in the guise of her brother also replays the transgressive moment of the labyrinth episode, namely the encounter with the Minotaur as object of desire. So when Theseus asserts that "sur toutes les voies de la reconnaissance et de la décence, celle de mon désir l'emportait," it is open to question which desire he is referring to—the homosexual attraction, or the wish for a silent and compliant wife.

The text does not oblige us to decide one way or the other—indeed, it invites a reading that affirms the coexistence of these apparently contradictory forms of desire. In wedding a girl who looks just like a boy, Theseus forms a conjugal bond that discloses the homoerotic and homosocial basis of the city he founds, a city he dedicates to Pallas, the phallic virgin who is born not of woman but of man. Still, however well-suited the institution of marriage may be to the establishment of a society of men, it does not successfully contain women's desire. For it turns out that Phaedra harbors a desire of her own—one which, by definition in this context, is illicit and results in disaster. Phaedra falls in love with Theseus's son Hippolytus but is spurned by the young man, who is a devotee of Artemis (another virgin guardian of manhood). Phaedra's revenge is to accuse Hippolytus of incestuous love for her and bring Theseus's curse down upon him, a curse which brings death to the innocent youth. Filled with remorse, Phaedra then commits suicide. Theseus's apparent largesse in declaring Phaedra's love for Hippolytus understandable seems to confirm his approval of all authentic passion and to suggest that, even for women, the constraints imposed by monogamy are difficult to tolerate. The force of this judgment is severely undercut, however, by the fact that Theseus makes it only after both his wife and son have died violent deaths and been punished for their actual or potential challenge to his authority.

In considering the twin deaths of Phaedra and Hippolytus, the reader may be struck by the fact that they are the last two in a series of symbolic or "real" murders and suicides that punctuate the narrative. Indeed, by the end of the récit most of the main characters have been killed off one way or another. On the one hand, there are the female lovers, Ariadne and Phaedra, whose desires and powers are incompatible with the social order Theseus establishes, and the potential male lover, the Minotaur. On the other, there are a number of Oedipal rivals whose stories frame those of the lovers: Theseus's father Aegeus, his son Hippolytus, and Oedipus himself, a paternal figure who is at odds with the hero ideologically. In each case, Theseus acknowledges that he gains something from the rival's death—a throne; freedom to tell his story as he pleases without having to censor it for the prudish Hippolytus's sake; and the advantage of having King Oedipus die on Athenian soil—a blessing in the eyes of the superstitious, whom the enlightened Theseus is happy to humor.

To be sure, the hero's good-natured response to these deaths marks both his awareness and acceptance of unconscious aggressive impulses (as we know Gide applauds the work of Freud) and his irrepressible enthusiasm for life, even in the face of great sorrow. Yet one cannot help noticing the link between the death of all the people for whom Theseus cared and the peace of mind he expresses at the end of his narrative: "Derrière moi, je laisse la cité d'Athènes. Plus encore que ma femme et mon fils, je l'ai chérie. . . . Pour le bien de l'humanité future, j'ai fait mon oeuvre. J'ai vécu." Undeniably, Theseus's sense of satisfaction is tied to his solitude, a state which takes on signifi-

cance at the end of the récit not just because the hero's own death is approaching, but also because it characterizes a social ideal embodied in the city of Athens; it is the complement to the homosocial bond among men, each of whom paradoxically imagines himself to be singular, a man apart. Even Theseus's friendship with Pirithous is sacrificed to this ideal, for "Il est un point passé lequel on ne peut avancer que seul."

The protagonist is thus very far from where he started in his youth, when he entertained an intimate and eroticized (albeit narcissistic) relationship with everything around him. "J'étais le vent, la vague. J'étais plante; j'étais oiseau. Je ne m'arrêtais pas à moi-même, et tout contact avec un monde extérieur ne m'enseignait point tant mes limites qu'il n'éveillait en moi de volupté." By the end of his life Theseus has not only purged himself of unruly desires and distanced himself from what he experiences as compromising contact with others, but has elevated this state of solitude and privation to the status of a social principle. It is doubtful, then, that the version of liberal humanism embodied in Theseus's Athens can bring the happiness it promises; indeed Gide's récit weakens its own thesis by articulating—and momentarily affirming—the multiple forms of pleasurable attachment that humanism enjoins us to give up. (pp. 1-12)

Winifred Woodhull, "Out of the Maze: A Reading of Gide's 'Thésée'," in Journal of the Midwest Modern Language Association, *Vol. 21, No. 1, Spring, 1988, pp. 1-14.*

Wendy B. Faris   (essay date 1988)

[*Faris is an American educator and critic. In the following excerpt, she investigates Gide's variations on the labyrinth motif in* Theseus.]

Two groups of texts that employ the labyrinth as a symbolic landscape illustrate the two predominant meanings of labyrinthine journeys in modern literature. The category of the voyage toward the self includes novels by André Gide, Lawrence Durrell and Anaïs Nin; the rubric of the voyage toward the text encompasses an essay by Albert Camus, and novels by Julio Cortázar, José Donoso, and Umberto Eco. It is easy to predict, however, that while the first category is more psychologically oriented, the second of a more metafictional nature, the lines of these two journeys—toward the integrated self and toward the artistic text—will tend not only to intersect but to converge. In any case, in their employment of the labyrinth as symbolic landscape, both groups should be imagined as falling under the general heading of the world-as-labyrinth that permeates all uses of the image. Furthermore, the works resist even the categorization of two kinds of voyages for a more general reason; this is because . . . the labyrinth's greatest strength is its polyvalence, its capacity to represent different areas of experience and thus to suggest the interdependence of diverse phenomena. This quality of semiotic indeterminacy is itself conceptually a labyrinth, one path of interpretation leading inevitably to another. (pp. 121-22)

[Gide, Durrell, Nin, and Camus] use the labyrinth in such

a way that it forms part of the geography of romance. The voyage in the labyrinth is accomplished in a realm that is more primitive than the habitual dwelling place of the explorer, and at some distance from it. . . . [In narratives by Cortázar, Donoso, and Eco] the labyrinths of city, house and library are explored daily by their occupants. The first group of explorers returns with some sense of renewal, of discovery, or of growth. The second does not. The first group's narrative use of the labyrinth thus remains closer to the old initiation pattern of a single ordeal, endured and left behind. In the second case, the process of renewal suggested by the labyrinth pattern, though desired, is not completed, for in them the labyrinth expands into all time and space.

As in Ovid's original description of the labyrinth, and in other symbolic uses of the design, during the journeys in these modern texts the labyrinth mediates between natural and constructed forms and spaces, and between man's different imaginative capacities. Similarly, symbolic treatments of the labyrinth in the twentieth century, as earlier in its history, often set the pattern in opposition to another image. In Camus's "The Minotaur or the Stop in Oran," Oran as labyrinth is contrasted with the sea beyond it, and also with European towns. In Nin's *Seduction of the Minotaur*, two labyrinths—city and jungle—oppose each other. In Cortázar's *Hopscotch* the labyrinth contrasts with heaven. This kind of opposition frequently establishes an interplay between two concepts, between a labyrinthine space and a nonlabyrinthine space, between a real or imagined journey and a subsequent place of rest, between postponed and satisfied desire. It thus suggests the possibility, or the problematic nature, of movement between them.

In all cases, the image of the labyrinth in the twentieth century reflects man's confrontation with a world no longer perceived as mapped out by God. It still functions as a structure of quest, though of course the object of the quest differs from work to work. As I have just suggested, most frequently the quest represented by the labyrinth is a journey of self-discovery; ostensibly a voyage out, it is symbolically a voyage within. In developing the correlation between labyrinthine physical environments and labyrinthine thoughts, and between setting and psychological and artistic development, these texts . . . point up the complex and puzzling interdependence of the world and the mind, the perceived and the perceiver. The labyrinth in these works thus suggests a parallel with modern physics, where the medium of perception alters the entities perceived, and vice versa. (pp. 122-23)

> Each is led on by the complexities implicit in his
> own mind to lose himself, if I may so put it, in
> a labyrinth of his own devising.

Theseus stands out from other uses of the labyrinth pattern in our times because it is an explicit retelling of the classical story. However, within this classical framework, Gide departs in significant ways from the original narratives. [In *André Gide: A Critical Biography* (1968)] George Painter traces Gide's interest in Theseus and his adventure in the labyrinth back to a passage in *Fruits of the Earth*: "The memory of the past had only such power over me as was needed to give unity to my life; it was like the mys-

terious thread that held Theseus to his past love, yet did not prevent him from travelling through the newest of landscapes." He also records Gide's later notes in his journal that lead toward his interpretation of the myth in *Theseus*: "Ariadne, after he has slain the minotaur, makes Theseus return to the point from which he set out. . . . In the Theseus this must be brought out—to put it vulgarly, the thread is . . . the apron-string" ("le fil à la patte"). We see here that the labyrinth serves Gide as a model for the integration of past and present selves, of old and new experiences, but also—in the discrepancy between the statements, the first from 1897 and the second from 1927 and 1940—for the problems involved in achieving such an integration. Gide's version of the myth thus engages the labyrinth as a symbol for the mind, and builds imaginatively and explicitly on that idea. (p. 123)

Gide retains the familiar resonances of youthful initiation in his labyrinth, for the Theseus who journeys to Crete is clearly a young man. Yet we hear of his exploits from the mature Theseus, and so the diachronic/synchronic duality of the image, the difference between the wanderer and the designer or the surveyor, is thus inherent in the narrative technique itself, for we continually sense the distance between the young Theseus as actor, exploring the labyrinth of his own youthful desires, and the mature Theseus as narrator, placing, explaining, surveying, and designing his discourse about those desires.

In contrast to this distinction between wanderer and designer, Gide also prefigures a modern tendency to merge Daedalus and Theseus, the artisan and the explorer . . . by having the two men meet to discuss the labyrinth. Daedalus tells Theseus that he has planned the labyrinth around the individual's consciousness rather than around exterior forces. Since he believes that desire is the essential factor in controlling a man, or the minotaur, the jailer must work on his captive's desires. As a result, he calculates that the best way of keeping someone in a labyrinth is to make it so that he doesn't want to leave; therefore he has constructed a labyrinth that the minotaur will enjoy. In this labyrinth, then, heavy vapours put the will to sleep and induce "a delicious intoxication, rich in flattering delusions, and provoke the mind, filled as this is with voluptuous mirages, to a certain pointless activity," devoid of logic or substance. Daedalus has converted the task of building the labyrinth into the construction of an entire aesthetic universe, which subverts rational, purposeful activity. The labyrinth is art for art's sake rather than art that leads to or away from anything. It is Gide's version of Daedalian ingenuity overextending itself, ingenious artistry gone wild. Although its pleasurable environment appears as a reversal of the fear usually associated with winding corridors and unknown egress, this labyrinth is dangerous precisely because it is so pleasant. It works like a drug. The aesthetic world of Gide's labyrinth is magical and chameleon-like, for it lures and entraps people in many ways, according to their various desires and designs: "Each is led on by the complexities implicit in his own mind to lose himself, if I may so put it, in a labyrinth of his own devising." (The original French uses the anatomical word *cervelle—brain*, recalling that a labyrinth has the same convoluted shape as the brain.) In this clear and cogent interiorization of the myth, it is evident that it is not only the minotaur's desires that must be satisfied, but also those of his pursuers.

Theseus is saved, as usual, by Ariadne's thread, but the thread here represents not love but reality, duty, an antidote to the pure and pleasurable art of the labyrinth itself. For Theseus and his youthful companions, the sensual labyrinth embodies the danger of forgetting themselves; escape from this labyrinth therefore represents an affirmation of individual identity.

The sexual dimensions of achieving this identity provide intriguing complications for Gide's labyrinth. Here let us recall first that early labyrinths in the form of ritual dances sometimes served to symbolize a process of amorous initiation; in psychological interpretations the maturity to love someone other than the suffocating mother is often the goal of a labyrinthine journey, the achievement of which is signaled by the rescuing of a youthful female partner. R. F. Willetts reminds us [in *Cretan Cults and Festivals* (1962)] that "the youths and maidens who accompanied Theseus underwent an ordeal" and that after this ordeal Theseus married the king's daughter. He concludes that the labyrinthine "Knossian dance in her honour was part of the ritual of collective marriage, following on the graduation of the initiates: it was a love dance." In his interpretation of the myth, Gide takes on these resonances and turns them about, presenting Ariadne's love as an additional danger, a constraining force. Theseus is cooped up by Ariadne as he might have been in the labyrinth, both temptations of the flesh. Her holding of the thread is distinct from the thread itself, which is a thread of practicality, "the tangible symbol of duty [,] . . . your link with the past. Go back to it. Go back to yourself. For nothing can begin from nothing, and it is from your past, and from what you are at this moment, that what you are going to be must spring." As the thread represents responsible integration of his past, it is constructive; as it transmits Ariadne's powers of sensuality and coercion, it is simply entangling, taking on qualities of the labyrinth it is intended to conquer. In a half-comic, half-serious bit of misogyny, Gide explicitly rejects the idea that a man's rite of passage toward his adult self requires a woman's aid. He conflates the enveloping mother and the liberating anima figures, working against the tradition that sees the latter as a helpmate and a reward for differentiating oneself from the former. Gaston Bachelard detects a similar fear of female power in the novel *Philae's Death* by Pierre Loti. There the narrator explores the crypt of an Egyptian temple whose corridors, which seem about to close in and bury him, are filled with a thousand sculptures of a large-breasted goddess, which the explorer must brush as he passes. Bachelard asks [in *La terre et la rêveries du repos* (1948)] if it is not "symptomatic that the fear of brushing a breast and the fear of being buried are united on the same page." Here it is also useful to recall that the church emphasized Ariadne's string as a symbol of grace, of the help man required to extricate himself from the labyrinth of worldly entanglements. Again, Gide recognizes the dangers of remaining in the labyrinth, but he rejects both this symbolic force of Ariadne and the feminine form it takes, advocat-

ing instead man's independent strength. The labyrinth of this particular life does not lead to the paradise of the female heart or to God but rather to individual force.

The battle at the center of Gide's labyrinth is never revealed, for as Theseus has told us, the labyrinth's mystery is different for each individual; the vapours will cause him to create his own particular prison and his own minotaur as well. Theseus's brain is his labyrinth and ours is ours. Although Gide leaves us to imagine exactly how the conquest takes place, we do get a few hints. After his return, Theseus says that the monster even appeared beautiful— another reversal of traditional visions of terror at the center of the labyrinth and an indication that Theseus's victory over the minotaur may have been sexual. These hints about the struggle at the heart of the labyrinth indicate that in addition to his rejection of the feminine, Gide also distances himself a bit from his own youthful sexual exploits, for in making Theseus express a preference for young men and in having him tell us on his return from the labyrinth that the minotaur was a young man, and beautiful, we realize that this dream of voluptuousness— this minotaur—was the one the vapours caused Theseus to imagine for himself, the one most dangerous for him, the one that he must finally subdue if he is to return to the world.

In the philosophy the narrator expresses, Gide integrates the classical ideal of the middle way into his treatment of the labyrinth, emphasizing that the task of conquering this particular labyrinth, representative of youthful excesses, requires a steady, reasonable man. This labyrinthine trial, narrated by an older man, represents less a coming of age that is a break with the past than an initiation into consciousness of continuity with the past. Ariadne's thread in this context represents the line of Theseus's life story, a line which is to remain unbroken and inclusive. Nevertheless, in addition to his responsibility, Theseus is also "disponible," or open to all kinds of experience. In addition to praising him for devotion to the task at hand, Daedalus also commends him for audacity and temerity, and finally says that what he loves in him is his joy. Theseus is able to conquer the minotaur and the labyrinth because he meets them on their own terms, even uses their own weapons against them. At the same time that Theseus holds onto the string of reality, of rational perspective, he conquers the minotaur in a manner consistent with his sensual surroundings. (pp. 124-27)

In contrast to Theseus, of course, Icarus represents a defeated sensibility. As with Theseus, Icarus's labyrinth is located within himself, but he cannot free himself from it—from the danger of too much abstract reasoning, but also of too much poetry: "Icarus was . . . the image of man's disquiet, of the impulse to discovery, the soaring flight of poetry." Icarus represents extremes, Theseus the middle way. Icarus describes from the grave the prelude to his flight and fall in a parodic résumé of what appear to be some of Gide's own intellectual stages. He reveals his attraction to God, whose kingdom "is peace. All is absorbed, all is reconciled in the Unique Being"; his discontent with the merely horizontal plane of logic where he is tired of wandering: "Ah, how sick I am [therefore] of 'therefore,' and 'since,' and 'because'! Sick of inference, sick of deduction"; and his attraction to pure poetry: "to lose my shadow, to lose the filth of my body, to throw off the weight of the past! The infinite calls me!" The ignominious nature of his death clashes with the high-flown quality of his rhetoric. His failure and Theseus's success demonstrate that the world of the sensual imagination, of the vaporous labyrinth, must be tempered with the heavier weight of one's past, one's duty, and an aesthetic based on a rational as well as an intuitive relation to the world; in literary terms, poetic flight is to be combined with prosaic exploration.

Near the end of the *récit*, Theseus confronts Oedipus at Colonnus. The confrontation, through the contrast of the two men, further defines Theseus's character and the nature of Gide's labyrinthine space. Theseus pays homage to the older man's spirit as he tells of their meeting, saying that he recognized his own achievements to be merely human, whereas Oedipus had "stood man upright before the riddle of life, and dared to oppose him to the gods." Theseus knows that his conquest of the labyrinth has required steady labor, and his victory constitutes not flight into a higher realm but passage through the vapours into another stage of life on earth. It stands for action in the world and confrontation with a dangerous part of the self, whereas Oedipus's activity figures an opposing side of man's activity, his union with the divine. This meeting of Theseus with Oedipus after Theseus has conquered the labyrinth exemplifies Eliade's distinction between two kinds of initiations, the normal human variety and the shamanic or esoteric one. The first is often symbolized by a labyrinthine structure, on the ground, and represents exploration of the earth and the human mind; the second is frequently symbolized by a pole or a tree that rises toward the heavens, and represents assumption of superhuman powers.

Typical of the twentieth century in his use of the labyrinth, Gide both recalls and denies allegiance to the ancient religious resonances of the pattern. On the one hand, with his imaginary vaporous labyrinth that represents every person's psyche, Gide, like Durrell and Nin, transfers the traditionally sacred space at the center of the labyrinth and the knowledge it represents to the psychological domain, and also locates the heroic myth in human experience. The labyrinth is thus divested of religious overtones; Oedipus and the superhuman realm are located outside it. On the other hand, Gide's use of this part of the classical plot, where Theseus confronts Oedipus's supernatural realm after narrating his own ordeal in the labyrinth, preserves the traditional kind of labyrinthine path that leads to a sacred center. (pp. 127-29)

Wendy B. Faris, "Symbolic Landscapes," in her Labyrinths of Language: Symbolic Landscape and Narrative Design in Modern Fiction, *The Johns Hopkins University Press, 1988, pp. 121-66.*

FURTHER READING

Bibliography

Brosman, Catharine Savage. *An Annotated Bibliography of Criticism on André Gide, 1973-1988*. New York: Garland Publishing, 1990.

Annotated bibliography of works by and about Gide organized according to critical approach and topic.

Biography

Fowlie, Wallace. *André Gide: His Life and Art*. New York: Macmillan Co., 1965, 217 p.

Critical biography with individual chapters on *Marshlands, The Pastoral Symphony,* and *Theseus.* Fowlie contends that "no matter what form of literature [Gide] used. . . each work turns out to be a portrait of André Gide or at least the examination of some moral problem central to his very existence."

Mann, Klaus. *André Gide and the Crisis of Modern Thought.* New York: Creative Age Press, 1943, 331 p.

Emphasizes the relationship between Gide's philosophy and the human condition. Mann maintains that Gide's "work is a microcosm that involves the complete scope of modern man's experiences and obsessions. . . . His biography mirrors, and in part anticipates, the tremendous crisis we are passing through."

March, Harold. *Gide and the Hound of Heaven.* Philadelphia: University of Pennsylvania Press, 1952, 421 p.

Examines Gide's "literary continuity" in contrast to his "underlying moral discontinuity" in an attempt to explain the significance of Gide's career and the hidden motivation and reason for his life and work.

Painter, George D. *André Gide: A Critical Biography.* New York: Atheneum, 1968, 147 p.

Explores the connections between Gide's life and works. Painter explains that he has "tried to approach Gide's works through the living mind that created them, to describe not only their actual nature and content, but their organic growth from the history of that mind and heart."

Criticism

Ames, Van Meter. *André Gide.* 1947. Reprint. New York: Kraus Reprint Co., 1971, 302 p.

Critical examination of Gide's life and works in which Ames briefly discusses Gide's shorter works of fiction.

Bettinson, Christopher. "*La symphonie pastorale.*" In his *Gide: A Study*, pp. 53-66. Totowa, N. J.: Rowman and Littlefield, 1977.

Argues that like *Strait Is the Gate* and *The Immoralist*, "*La symphonie pastorale* explores the tension between the conflicting impulses towards physical fulfilment and religious exaltation."

Cordle, Thomas. *André Gide.* New York: Twayne Publishers, 1969, 183 p.

Chronological study of Gide's fiction with each work receiving a separate commentary. Cordle "seeks to interpret [Gide's] stories and plays as representations of the latent forces of his personality."

Garzilli, Enrico. "The Myth of the Labyrinth and the Self."

In his *Circles Without Center: Paths to the Discovery and Creation of Self in Modern Literature*, pp. 89-117. Cambridge, Mass.: Harvard University Press, 1972.

> Discusses Gide's *Theseus* as well as works by Jorge Luis Borges and Alain Robbe-Grillet, arguing that "the energy underlying the myth [of Theseus] and its retelling comes from the fact that man's search for self becomes labyrinthine as he proceeds."

Holdheim, William W. "Gide's 'Paludes': The Humor of Falsity." *The French Review* 32 (April 1959): 401-09.

> Argues that the irony in *Marshlands* extends well beyond a simple parody of Symbolism and that the novella's significance to the history of ideas derives from its stance "halfway between rationalism and twentieth-century nihilism."

Horn, Pierre. "*Isabelle*: A Detective Novel by André Gide." *Romance Notes* XVIII, No. 1 (Fall 1977): 54-61.

> Contends that Gide employed most of the devices and methods commonly associated with the detective genre in *Isabelle*.

Hytier, Jean. "The *Récits*." In *Gide: A Collection of Critical Essays*, edited by David Littlejohn, pp. 73-92. Englewood Cliffs, N. J.: Prentice-Hall, 1970.

> Examines Gide's *récits*—*The Immoralist, Strait Is the Gate, Isabelle,* and *The Pastoral Symphony*—noting their relation to Gide's *soties* and arguing that they have been misunderstood and that critics have failed to discern their hidden irony.

Pasinetti, P. M. "Fiction from Three Languages." *The Sewanee Review* LVIII, No. 3 (July-September 1950): 547-62.

> Comparative book review in which Pasinetti classifies *Isabelle* and *La symphonie pastorale* as "special types of novels" that "show the author's stress on the aesthetic values of his work both in general structure and in specific technical details."

Pollard, Patrick. "Gide's *Thésée*: The Diary of a Moralist." *French Studies* XXVI, No. 2 (April 1972): 166-77.

> Examines *Thésée* as Gide's "legacy of teaching for pos-

terity" and as a romanticized account of Gide's moral development, maintaining that neither interpretation is entirely valid.

Rinsler, N. S. "Gide and Symbolism: The Evidence of *Paludes*." *Essays in French Literature*, no. 13 (November 1976): 62-76.

> Contends that *Marshlands* is not, as many critics have argued, "a simple condemnation of Symbolism" but rather an investigation of the limitations and possibilities of the Symbolist novel.

Rossi, Vinio. *André Gide*. New York: Columbia University Press, 1968, 48 p.

> General overview of Gide's major works with separate discussions of *Marshlands, Prometheus Illbound, The Pastoral Symphony,* and *Theseus*.

Turnell, Martin. "The Protestant Cell: I. The Three *Récits*." In his *The Art of French Fiction*, pp. 245-62. London: Hamish Hamilton, 1959.

> Compares *Strait Is the Gate, The Immoralist,* and *The Pastoral Symphony* in the context of Gide's religious concerns and his relations with his mother and wife. Turnell notes that in each work "the woman is sacrificed to the weakness or the depravity of the man who kills the thing he loves."

Watson-Williams, Helen. *André Gide and the Greek Myth: A Critical Study*. London: Oxford University Press, 1967, 200 p.

> Traces the development of Gide's interest in Hellenism. Watson-Williams maintains that through his choice of myths and manner of presentation, Gide reveals the problems that most concerned him and "explores the central problem of man's relationship with his surrounding world."

Additional coverage of Gide's life and career is contained in the following sources published by Gale Research: *Contemporary Authors*, Vols. 104, 124; *Dictionary of Literary Biography*, Vol. 65; *Major 20th-Century Writers*; *Twentieth-Century Literary Criticism*, Vols. 5, 12, 36; and *World Literature Criticism*.

Charlotte Perkins Gilman

1860-1935

(Full name Charlotte Anna Perkins Stetson Gilman) American short story writer, essayist, novelist, and autobiographer.

INTRODUCTION

Gilman was a prominent social activist and the leading theorist of the women's movement at the turn of the century. While examining the role of women in society and propounding social theories in her nonfiction works, she depicted the realization of her feminist ideals in her novels and short stories. Gilman is best known today for her short story "The Yellow Wallpaper," in which she portrayed a young woman's mental breakdown.

Gilman was born in Hartford, Connecticut, to Frederick Beecher Perkins, a noted librarian and magazine editor, and his wife, Mary Fritch Perkins. Although Gilman's father frequently left the family for long periods during her childhood and eventually divorced his wife in 1869, he directed Gilman's early education, emphasizing study in the sciences and history. During his absences, Perkins left his wife and children with his relatives, thus bringing Gilman into frequent contact with her independent and reform-minded great-aunts: Harriet Beecher Stowe, the abolitionist and author of *Uncle Tom's Cabin* (1852); Catherine Beecher, the prominent advocate of "domestic feminism"; and Isabella Beecher Hooker, an ardent suffragist. Their influence—and the example of her mother's own self-reliance—were instrumental in developing Gilman's feminist convictions and desire to effect social reform. Early in her life Gilman displayed the independence she later advocated for women: she insisted on remuneration for her household chores, and later she paid her mother room and board, supporting herself as a teacher and as a commercial artist. At twenty-four, she married Charles Walter Stetson, who was also an artist. Following the birth of their daughter in 1884, Gilman suffered from severe depression. She consulted the noted neurologist S. Weir Mitchell, who prescribed his "rest cure": complete bed rest and limited intellectual activity. Gilman credited this experience with driving her "so near the borderline of utter mental ruin that I could see over." She removed herself from Mitchell's care, and later, attributing her emotional problems in part to the confines of marriage, she left her husband.

After her separation, Gilman moved to California, where she helped edit feminist publications, assisted in the planning of the California Women's Congresses of 1894 and 1895, and was instrumental in founding the Women's Peace Party. She spent several years lecturing in the United States and England on women's rights and on labor re-

form, and in 1898 she published *Women and Economics: A Study of the Economic Relation between Men and Women as a Factor in Social Evolution*. In 1900 she married George Houghton Gilman, who was supportive of her intense involvement in social reform. From 1909 through 1916 Gilman published a monthly journal, *The Forerunner*, for which she wrote nearly all of the copy. As a vehicle for advancing social awareness, *The Forerunner* has been called her "single greatest achievement." In 1935, having learned that she suffered from inoperable cancer, Gilman took her life, writing in a final note that "when one is assured of unavoidable and imminent death, it is the simplest of human rights to choose a quick and easy death in place of a slow and horrible one."

In her nonfiction works Gilman argued that women's secondary status in society, and especially women's economic dependence on men, is not the result of biological inferiority, but rather of culturally enforced behavior. She further emphasized this belief in her short stories, once declaring that she wrote fiction to illustrate her social ideas. Portraying women struggling to achieve self-sufficiency or adapting to newfound independence, Gilman's short stories frequently provide models showing women how to change their lives or redesign society. In "Making a Change," for example, Gilman relates the experiences of Julia, a female musician who has little time, patience, or ability for domestic chores. Realizing that she is miserable without her music and that her husband and baby are also suffering, Julia establishes a day-care center on the roof of her apartment building, with her mother-in-law being the chief caregiver. Gilman further advocates social reform in such stories as "The Cottagette" and "Her Housekeeper," in which the male characters take on traditionally female responsibilities, including cooking, cleaning, and caring for children.

"The Yellow Wallpaper," considered Gilman's best work of short fiction, is also one of her least typical. Rather than an optimistic vision of what women can achieve, the story is a first-person account of a young mother's mental deterioration, based on Gilman's own experiences. Gilman herself has stated the "real purpose of the story was to reach Dr. S. Weir Mitchell, and convince him of the error of his ways. . . . Many years later, I met someone who knew close friends of Dr. Mitchell's who said he had told them that he had changed his treatment of nervous prostration since reading 'The Yellow Wallpaper.' If this is a fact, I have not lived in vain." Gilman initially had difficulties getting "The Yellow Wallpaper" published; Horace Scudder of *The Atlantic* refused to print it, stating that "I could not forgive myself if I made others as miserable as I have made myself!" Eventually, however, "The Yellow Wallpaper" won the attention of William Dean Howells, who later included it in his *The Great Modern American Stories: An Anthology* (1920). Early reviewers generally classified "The Yellow Wallpaper" as a horror story, with most commenting on Gilman's use of Gothic conventions. It was not until Elaine R. Hedges's afterword to a 1973 edition of "The Yellow Wallpaper" that the story won scholarly attention. Most modern commentators now interpret "The Yellow Wallpaper" as a feminist indictment of society's subjugation of women and praise its compelling characterization, complex symbolism, and thematic depth.

Some critics have dismissed Gilman's short stories as mere vehicles through which she explicated her feminist and socialist beliefs, noting that Gilman herself once admitted that "if I can learn to write good stories it will be a powerful addition to my armory." Others, however, have acknowledged that these works are realistic, accessible, and thought-provoking. Commentators have also lauded Gilman's short fiction for presenting heroic female characters and for offering practical solutions to everyday problems. Ann J. Lane has observed: "Many Gilman enthusiasts do not much like her fiction. They consider it too ideological, too didactic. . . . Her work is ideological, but she implies that all literature is ideological, only its familiarity, its 'naturalness' to us, makes it appear to reflect all possible world views. Although she does not challenge all the conventions of her day, she introduces a new sense of intellectual play when she poses her 'What if' questions in the arena of traditional male-female relations, thereby exposing the absurd pieties embedded in domestic life."

PRINCIPAL WORKS

SHORT FICTION
*"The Yellow Wallpaper" (short story) 1892; published in journal *New England Magazine*; also published in book form as *The Yellow Wallpaper* in 1892
"The Rocking Chair" (short story) 1893; published in journal *Worthington's Illustrated*
*"The Cottagette" (short story) 1910; published in journal *The Forerunner*
*"Making a Change" (short story) 1911; published in journal *The Forerunner*
*"Turned" (short story) 1911; published in journal *The Forerunner*

OTHER MAJOR WORKS
In This Our World (poetry) 1893
Women and Economics: A Study of the Economic Relation between Men and Women as a Factor in Social Evolution (essay) 1898
Concerning Children (essay) 1900
The Home: Its Work and Influence (essay) 1903
Human Work (essay) 1904
The Punishment That Educates (essay) 1907
Women and Social Service (essay) 1907
What Diantha Did (novel) 1909; published serially in journal *The Forerunner*; also published in book form in 1910
The Crux (novel) 1911
The Man-Made World; or, Our Androcentric Culture (essay) 1911
Moving the Mountain (novel) 1911
Benigna Machiavelli (novel) 1914; published in journal *The Forerunner*
Herland (novel) 1915; published serially in journal *The Forerunner*; also published in book form in 1978
With Her in Ourland (novel) 1916; published in journal *The Forerunner*
His Religion and Hers: A Study of the Faith of Our Fathers and the Work of Our Mothers (essay) 1923
The Living of Charlotte Perkins Gilman (autobiography) 1935

*These works were later reprinted in *The Charlotte Perkins Gilman Reader*.

CRITICISM

William Dean Howells (essay date 1920)

[*Howells was the chief progenitor of American realism and the most influential American literary critic during the late nineteenth century. The author of nearly three dozen novels, he successfully weaned American literature away from the sentimental romanticism of its infancy, earning the popular sobriquet "the Dean of American Letters." Howells's inclusion of "The Yellow Wall-*

paper" in his 1920 anthology The Great Modern American Stories, *from which this excerpt was taken, provided Gilman with her first broad exposure as an author.*]

Horace Scudder (then of *The Atlantic*) said in refusing [Mrs. Gilman's story **"The Yellow Wall Paper"**] that it was so terribly good that it ought never to be printed. But terrible and too wholly dire as it was, I could not rest until I had corrupted the editor of *The New England Magazine* into publishing it. Now that I have got it into my collection here, I shiver over it as much as I did when I first read it in manuscript, though I agree with the editor of *The Atlantic* of the time that it was too terribly good to be printed. (p. vii)

> *William Dean Howells, "A Reminiscent Introduction," in* The Great Modern American Stories: An Anthology, *edited by William Dean Howells, Boni and Liveright, 1920, pp. vii-xiv.*

Charlotte Perkins Gilman   (essay date 1935)

[*In the following excerpt from her autobiography, Gilman discusses critical reaction to "The Yellow Wallpaper" and explains why she wrote the story.*]

Besides [the poem] "Similar Cases" the most outstanding piece of work of 1890 was **"The Yellow Wallpaper."** It is a description of a case of nervous breakdown beginning something as mine did, and treated as Dr. S. Weir Mitchell treated me with what I considered the inevitable result, progressive insanity.

This I sent to Mr. Howells, and he tried to have the *Atlantic Monthly* print it, but Mr. Scudder, then the editor, sent it back with this brief card:

> Dear Madam,
>
> Mr. Howells has handed me this story.
>
> I could not forgive myself if I made others as miserable as I have made myself!
>
> Sincerely yours,
>
> H. E. Scudder

This was funny. The story was meant to be dreadful, and succeeded. I suppose he would have sent back one of Poe's on the same ground. Later I put it in the hands of an agent who had written me, one Henry Austin, and he placed it with the *New England Magazine*. (pp. 118-19)

I never got a cent for it till later publishers brought it out in book form, and very little then. But it made a tremendous impression. A protest was sent to the Boston *Transcript*, headed "Perilous Stuff"—

> To the Editor of the Transcript:
>
> In a well-known magazine has recently appeared a story entitled **"The Yellow Wallpaper."** It is a sad story of a young wife passing the gradations from slight mental derangement to raving lunacy. It is graphically told, in a somewhat sensational style, which makes it difficult to lay aside, after the first glance, til it is finished, holding the

reader in morbid fascination to the end. It certainly seems open to serious question if such literature should be permitted in print.

> The story could hardly, it would seem, give pleasure to any reader, and to many whose lives have been touched through the dearest ties by this dread disease, it must bring the keenest pain. To others, whose lives have become a struggle against an heredity of mental derangement, such literature contains deadly peril. Should such stories be allowed to pass without severest censure?
>
> M. D.

Another doctor, one Brummel Jones, of Kansas City, Missouri, wrote me in 1892 concerning this story, saying:

> When I read 'The Yellow Wallpaper' I was very much pleased with it; when I read it again I was delighted with it, and now that I have read it again I am overwhelmed with the delicacy of your touch and the correctness of portrayal. From a doctor's standpoint, and I am a doctor, you have made a success. So far as I know, and I am fairly well up in literature, there has been no detailed account of incipient insanity.
>
> (pp. 119-20)

But the real purpose of the story was to reach Dr. S. Weir Mitchell, and convince him of the error of his ways. I sent him a copy as soon as it came out, but got no response. However, many years later, I met some one who knew close friends of Dr. Mitchell's who said he had told them that he had changed his treatment of nervous prostration since reading **"The Yellow Wallpaper."** If that is a fact, I have not lived in vain.

> **"The Yellow Wallpaper" is a description of a case of a nervous breakdown beginning something as mine did, and treated as Dr. S. Weir Mitchell treated me with what I considered the inevitable result, progressive insanity.**
>
> **—*Charlotte Perkins Gilman***

A few years ago Mr. Howells asked leave to include this story in a collection he was arranging—*Masterpieces of American Fiction.* I was more than willing, but assured him that it was no more "literature" than my other stuff, being definitely written "with a purpose." In my judgment it is a pretty poor thing to write, to talk, without a purpose. (p. 121)

> *Charlotte Perkins Gilman, in her* The Living of Charlotte Perkins Gilman: An Autobiography, *1935. Reprint by Arno Press, Inc., 1972, 341 p.*

Elaine R. Hedges   (essay date 1973)

[*An American educator, editor, and critic, Hedges has*

contributed to numerous feminist works. In the essay below, she provides the first lengthy analysis of "The Yellow Wallpaper." She employs a highly biographical form of criticism, inferring that the events in the story closely parallel the facts of Gilman's own breakdown.]

"The Yellow Wallpaper" is a small literary masterpiece. For almost fifty years it has been overlooked, as has its author, one of the most commanding feminists of her time. Now, with the new growth of the feminist movement, Charlotte Perkins Gilman is being rediscovered, and **"The Yellow Wallpaper"** should share in that rediscovery. The story of a woman's mental breakdown, narrated with superb psychological and dramatic precision, it is, as William Dean Howells said of it in 1920, a story to "freeze our. . . blood."

The story was wrenched out of Gilman's own life, and is unique in the canon of her works. Although she wrote other fiction—short stories and novels—and much poetry as well, none of it ever achieved the power and directness, the imaginative authenticity of this piece. Polemical intent often made her fiction dry and clumsily didactic; and the extraordinary pressures of publishing deadlines under which she worked made careful composition almost impossible. (pp. 37-8)

"The Yellow Wallpaper" has resurfaced in several anthologies. However, tucked away among many other selections and frequently with only brief biographical information about its author, the story will not necessarily find in these anthologies the wide audience it deserves.

Yet it does deserve the widest possible audience. For aside from the light it throws on the personal despairs, and the artistic triumph over them, of one of America's foremost feminists, the story is one of the rare pieces of literature we have by a nineteenth-century woman which directly confronts the sexual politics of the male-female, husband-wife relationship. In its time . . . the story was read essentially as a Poe-esque tale of chilling horror—and as a story of mental aberration. It is both of these. But it is more. It is a feminist document, dealing with sexual politics at a time when few writers felt free to do so, at least so candidly. (p. 39)

[The story] was greeted with strong but mixed feelings. Gilman was warned that such stories were "perilous stuff," which should not be printed because of the threat they posed to the relatives of such "deranged" persons as the heroine. The implications of such warnings—that women should "stay in their place," that nothing could or should be done except maintain silence or conceal problems—are fairly clear. Those who praised the story for the accuracy of its portrayal and its delicacy of touch, did so on the grounds that Gilman had captured in literature, from a medical point of view, the most "detailed account of incipient insanity." . . . [However], no one seems to have made the connection between the insanity and the sex, or sexual role, of the victim, no one explored the story's implications for male-female relationships in the nineteenth century. (p. 41)

By the time she was in her late teens Charlotte Perkins had begun seriously to ponder "the injustices under which women suffered." Although not in close touch with the suffrage movement (with which indeed she never in her later career directly associated herself, finding its objectives too limited for her own more radical views on the need for social change), she was becoming increasingly aware of such current developments as the entrance of some young women into colleges—and the ridicule they received—of the growing numbers of young women in the working population, of a few books being written that critically examined the institution of marriage. . . . She began to write poems—one in defense of prostitutes—and to pursue her own independent thinking. (pp. 43-4)

A year after [her] marriage she gave birth to a daughter and within a month of the birth she became, again in her own words, "a mental wreck." There was a constant dragging weariness. . . . "Absolute incapacity. Absolute misery."

It would seem that Charlotte Perkins Stetson felt trapped by the role assigned the wife within the conventional nineteenth-century marriage. If marriage meant children and too many children meant incapacity for other work; if she saw her father's abandonment and her mother's coldness as the result of this sexual-marital bind; if she saw herself as victimized by marriage, the woman playing the passive role—then she was simply seeing clearly.

It was out of this set of marital circumstances, but beyond that out of her larger social awareness of the situation of women in her century, that **"The Yellow Wallpaper"** emerged five years later. (p. 46)

[**"The Yellow Wallpaper"**] is narrated with clinical precision and aesthetic tact. The curt, chopped sentences, the brevity of the paragraphs, which often consist of only one or two sentences, convey the taut, distraught mental state of the narrator. The style creates a controlled tension: everything is low key and understated. The stance of the narrator is all, and it is a very complex stance indeed, since she is ultimately mad and yet, throughout her descent into madness, in many ways more sensible than the people who surround and cripple her. As she tells her story the reader has confidence in the reasonableness of her arguments and explanations.

The narrator is a woman who has been taken to the country by her husband in an effort to cure her of some undefined illness—a kind of nervous fatigue. Although her husband, a doctor, is presented as kindly and well meaning, it is soon apparent that his treatment of his wife, guided as it is by nineteenth-century attitudes toward women is an important source of her affliction and a perhaps inadvertent but nonetheless vicious abettor of it. Here is a woman who, as she tries to explain to anyone who will listen, wants very much to *work*. Specifically, she wants to write (and the story she is narrating is her desperate and secret attempt both to engage in work that is meaningful to her and to retain her sanity). But the medical advice she receives, from her doctor/husband, from her brother, also a doctor, and from S. Weir Mitchell, explicitly referred to in the story, is that she do nothing. The prescribed cure is total rest and total emptiness of mind. While she craves intellectual stimulation and activity, and at one point poignantly expresses her wish for "advice and companion-ship" (one can read today respect and equality) in her work, what she receives is the standard treatment meted out to women in a patriarchal society. Thus her husband sees her as a "blessed little goose." She is his "little girl" and she must take care of herself for his sake. Her role is to be "a rest and comfort to him." That he often laughs at her is, she notes forlornly and almost casually at one point, only what one expects in marriage. (pp. 48-50)

[He chooses] for her a room in the house that was formerly a nursery. It is a room with barred windows originally intended to prevent small children from falling out. It is the room with the fateful yellow wallpaper. The narrator herself had preferred a room downstairs; but this is 1890 and, to use Virginia Woolf's phrase, there is no choice for this wife of "a room of one's own."

Without such choice, however, the woman has been emotionally and intellectually violated. In fact, her husband instills guilt in her. They have come to the country, he says "solely on [her] account." Yet this means that he must be away all day, and many nights, dealing with his patients.

The result in the woman is subterfuge. With her husband she cannot be her true self but must pose; and this, as she says, "makes me very tired." Finally, the fatigue and the subterfuge are unbearable. Increasingly she concentrates her attention on the wallpaper in her room—a paper of a sickly yellow that both disgusts and fascinates her. Gilman works out the symbolism of the wallpaper beautifully, without ostentation. For, despite all the elaborate descriptive detail devoted to it, the wallpaper remains mysteriously, hauntingly undefined and only vaguely visuable. But such, of course, is the situation of this wife, who identifies herself with the paper. The paper symbolizes her situation as seen by the men who control her and hence her situation as seen by herself. How can she define herself?

"The Yellow Wallpaper" deserves the widest possible audience. For aside from the light it throws on the personal despairs, and the artistic triumph over them, of one of America's foremost feminists, the story is one of the rare pieces of literature we have by a nineteenth-century woman which directly confronts the sexual politics of the male-female, husband-wife relationship.

—Elaine R. Hedges

The wallpaper consists of "lame uncertain curves" that suddenly "commit suicide—destroy themselves in unheard-of contradictions." There are pointless patterns in the paper, which the narrator nevertheless determines to pursue to some conclusion. Fighting for her identity, for some sense of independent self, she observes the wallpaper and notes that just as she is about to find some pattern and

meaning in it, it "slaps you in the face, knocks you down, and tramples upon you."

Inevitably, therefore, the narrator, imprisoned within the room, thinks she discerns the figure of a woman behind the paper. The paper is barred—that is part of what pattern it has, and the woman is trapped behind the bars, trying to get free. Ultimately, in the narrator's distraught state, there are a great many women behind the patterned bars, all trying to get free.

Given the morbid social situation that by now the wallpaper has come to symbolize, it is no wonder that the narrator begins to see it as staining everything it touches. (pp. 50-2)

[But this woman] never does get free. Her insights, and her desperate attempts to define and thus cure herself by tracing the bewildering pattern of the wallpaper and deciphering its meaning, are poor weapons against the male certainty of her husband. . . . (p. 52)

It is no surprise to find, therefore, that at the end of the story the narrator both does and does not identify with the creeping women who surround her in her hallucinations. The women creep out of the wallpaper, they creep through the arbors and lanes and along the roads outside the house. Women must creep. The narrator knows this. She has fought as best she could against creeping. In her perceptivity and in her resistance lie her heroism (her heroineism). But at the end of the story, on her last day in the house, as she peels off yards and yards of wallpaper and creeps around the floor, she has been defeated. She is totally mad.

But in her mad-sane way she has seen the situation of women for what it is. She has wanted to strangle the woman behind the paper—tie her with a rope. For that woman, the tragic product of her society, is of course the narrator's self. By rejecting that woman she might free the other, imprisoned woman within herself. But the only available reaction is suicidal, and hence she descends into madness. Madness is her only freedom, as crawling around the room, she screams at her husband that she has finally "got out"—outside the wallpaper—and can't be put back.

Earlier in the story the heroine gnawed with her teeth at the nailed-down bed in her room: excruciating proof of her sense of imprisonment. Woman as prisoner; woman as child or cripple. . . . These images permeate Gilman's story. If they are the images men had of women, and hence that women had of themselves, it is not surprising that madness and suicide bulk large in the work of late nineteenth-century women writers. "Much madness is divinest sense . . . Much sense the starkest madness," Emily Dickinson had written some decades earlier; and she had chosen spinsterhood as one way of rejecting society's "requirements" regarding woman's role as wife. One thinks, too, of Edith Wharton's *The House of Mirth,* with its heroine, Lily Bart, "manacled" by the bracelets she wears. (pp. 53-4)

Such suicides as that of Lily, or of Kate Chopin's heroine [in *The Awakening*], . . . as well as the madness that descends upon the heroine in **"The Yellow Wallpaper,"** are all deliberate dramatic indictments, by women writers, of the crippling social pressures imposed on women in the nineteenth century and the sufferings they thereby endured: women who could not attend college although their brothers could; women expected to devote themselves, their lives, to aging and ailing parents; women treated as toys or as children and experiencing who is to say how much loss of self-confidence as a result. (pp. 54-5)

The heroine in **"The Yellow Wallpaper"** is destroyed. She has fought her best against husband, brother, doctor, and even against women friends (her husband's sister, for example, is "a perfect and enthusiastic housekeeper, and hopes for no better profession"). She has tried, in defiance of all the social and medical codes of her time, to retain her sanity and her individuality. But the odds are against her and she fails. (p. 55)

> *Elaine R. Hedges, in an afterword in* The Yellow Wallpaper *by Charlotte Perkins Gilman, The Feminist Press, 1973, pp. 37-63.*

Beate Schöpp-Schilling   (essay date 1975)

[*Below, Schöpp-Schilling attacks what she terms "the intentional and biographical fallacy" that some critics, including Elaine R. Hedges, utilized in their criticism of "The Yellow Wallpaper." Schöpp-Schilling discusses the story in relation to the principles of Adlerian depth psychology. Alfred Adler (1870-1937) was an Austrian psychiatrist who theorized that human behavior stems from an attempt to compensate for feelings of inferiority caused by physical, psychological, or social deficiencies.*]

Most of Charlotte Perkins Gilman's rather didactic literary productions were written between 1890 and 1916 and can be characterized as "realistic" in the sense defined by literary critics of that period. **"The Yellow Wallpaper,"** however, a short story written in a highly expressionistic manner, can be seen within the framework of a specific kind of "psychological realism" that so far has not been sufficiently appreciated. With the help of an interdisciplinary combination of Adlerian depth psychology and literary criticism, I want first to give an interpretation that explores the relationship between Gilman's life and this specific literary work from a psychological point of view. In a second step, I will evaluate the story as a psychologically realistic account of the causes and the progressive stages of mental illness.

Published in 1892 and read by contemporary readers and reviewers as an effective tale of incipient insanity, the story is seen today by feminist scholars primarily in the light of Gilman's own life. Ann Douglas Wood and Gail Parker accept Gilman's motives for writing the story as expressed in her autobiography, where she speaks of her desire to convince Dr. S. Weir Mitchell, famous for his rest-cures, of the errors of his medical treatment, which she herself had to undergo. . . .

Elaine Hedges, who has written the most detailed critical discussion of the story so far, also sees it partly as an indictment of the medical advice Gilman received from Mitchell. But beyond that she praises it as a feminist document "which directly confronts the sexual politics of the male-female, husband-wife relationship." She, too, has recourse to Gilman's autobiography. (p. 284)

[These] critics do not avoid two pitfalls of literary criticism, i.e., the intentional and the biographical fallacy. Especially in the case of Hedges the method of reading Gilman's life into her story is particularly deceptive since she relies exclusively on Gilman's own interpretation of her life. This sort of information can never be taken at face value for autobiographical statements combine fact *and* fiction, the latter being an expression of the individual's unconscious need to justify his lifestyle.

After having decoded the autobiography with the tools of Adlerian depth psychology, one has to disqualify Gilman's own interpretation of her breakdown as just this sort of rationalization. Beneath the self-sacrificing attitude which places her work, "the elevation of the race," above her "more intimate personal happiness," one senses an extreme fear of entering into close personal relationships due to her utter lack of confidence in her ability to succeed in them. When confronted with the demands of marriage and motherhood, she helplessly escaped into a serious depression, using the role-conflict as a convenient cover. Seeing her breakdown in these terms allowed her to ask for the freedom to realize herself in the realm of work, where she felt more secure, though even there she was plagued by feelings of inferiority. Viewed in the light of these psychic processes, a more complex connection between author and work than the usual *l'homme et l'oeuvre* approach achieves is established: Gilman's gruesome relentlessness in depicting the sado-masochistic relationship between husband and wife can be explained as her unconscious attempt to cope with her fears and to justify her decision to leave her husband.

If looked at aside from Gilman's life and interpreted with the help of Adlerian depth psychology, the story itself reveals an intuitive grasp of psychological processes which so far has not been sufficiently acknowledged by the critics. The story's heroine, after having been forbidden by her husband to exercise her creative powers in writing, defies him by turning to a different kind of paper, the hideous wallpaper with which he forces her to live. Through her exclusive preoccupation with its design, she descends into madness, which ultimately enables her to creep triumphantly over her husband. Here Gilman reveals a fundamental truth about interpersonal relationships, hinting at the active, protest-like characteristics of mental illness, which represents the continual though completely perverted attempt of a human being to overcome his feelings of inferiority.

Beyond this, Gilman succeeds with high artistic perfection in the realistic depiction of the progressive stages of her heroine's psychic disintegration, which starts with depression and feelings of guilt and aggression, then develops into increasing withdrawal from reality, a persecution complex, odor hallucinations, synaesthesia and ends in the complete breakdown of her ego. She objectifies this through her ingenious use of the image of the wallpaper with its multiple function as part of the setting, as objective correlative to the heroine's repressed emotions, and finally as the symbol of her life. (pp. 284-85)

Beate Schöpp-Schilling, " 'The Yellow Wallpaper': A Rediscovered 'Realistic' Story," in American Literary Realism 1870-1910, Vol. 8, No. 3, Summer, 1975, pp. 284-86.

Loralee MacPike (essay date 1975)

[*In the following essay, MacPike examines the psychopathological symbolism in "The Yellow Wallpaper."*]

Charlotte Perkins Gilman's short story **"The Yellow Wallpaper,"** first published in 1892, is a study of social degeneration into madness. As such it may seem an unlikely focus of American literary realism; yet it is a very fine illustration of realist symbolism. The furnishings of the narrator's room become a microcosm of the world that squeezes her into the little cell of her own mind, and the wallpaper represents the state of that mind.

The story line is deceptively simple. The narrator, a writer, finds herself increasingly depressed and indefinably ill. Her husband John (a physician), her brother, and her doctor all concur that she needs complete rest and a cessation of her work if she is to "recover," by which they mean "appear as a normal female in a world created by and for men." Gilman is not speaking in any militant feminist terms; she merely shows how her narrator needs to work in order to feel at ease with herself and the self's potential. Instead, she is hustled off to the country into a life of enforced idleness of body and mind. Although she would have preferred a room opening on the garden, her husband consigns her to the upstairs room, a former nursery, whose major features are ancient yellow wallpaper, bars on the windows, and a huge bedstead nailed to the floor.

The fact that the narrator's prison-room is a nursery indicates her status in society. The woman is legally a child; socially, economically, and philosophically she must be led by an adult—her husband; and therefore the nursery is an appropriate place to house her. The narrator's work threatens to destroy her status as a mere child by gaining her recognition in the adult world; this is reason enough for her husband to forbid her to work. Her work is, as he suggests, dangerous; but its danger is for him, not her, because it removes her from his control. The nursery, then, is an appropriate symbol for the desired state of childlikeness *vis-à-vis* the adult world that her husband wishes to enforce.

The nursery's windows are barred, making the setting not only a retreat into childhood but a prison. The narrator is to be forever imprisoned in childhood, forbidden to "escape" into adulthood. She instinctively feels that, just as only her work can transport her out of the world of childhood, so too can it alone free her from her dependence upon her husband in particular and the male-created world in general. Emergence from the chrysalis of childhood would also free her in the larger sense, making her a responsible member of society rather than merely a cloistered woman. It could provide for her a physical movement out into an active life, but the bars in the unchosen

room of her existence effectively prevent such an emergence.

The bedstead is the third symbol of the narrator's situation. A representation of her sexuality, it is nailed to the floor, ostensibly to prevent the former youthful occupants of the room from pushing it about. As the nursery imprisons her in a state of childhood, so the bedstead prevents her from moving "off center" sensually—not merely sexually—in any sort of physical contact with another human being. Her inability to care for her own child is but another fixity in her life, and the immovable bedstead symbolizes the static nature of both the expression and the product of her sexuality, thus denying her this outlet for her energies just as the bars deny her physical movement and the nursery her adult abilities.

These three items—the nursery, the bars on the windows, and the bedstead—show not only the narrator's mind but the state of the world that formed that mind. Her dilemma is not strictly personal, for the forces that shaped her, cutting off all possibility of personal realization, movement, or sexuality, are the processes that shape many women's lives. Gilman shows, through the normality of the narrator's life, the sources of her frustrations. The apparently unusual circumstances of bars, a nailed-down bed, a nursery for a bedroom are all explained as possible occurrences in a normal household. Although unusual perhaps, they are not extraordinary in the way Hawthorne's settings or Wilkie Collins' plots can be said to be extraordinary. It is not necessary for Gilman to give any background whatever, neither social comment nor history; for her use of the stuff of the narrator's life as symbolic of her state of mind and its causes suffices.

The three symbols of the narrator's existence coalesce in the yellow wallpaper, which is the primary symbol of the story which not only represents the narrator's state of mind but *becomes* that state of mind. As she grows increasingly fond of the wallpaper, the narrator realizes that it may well be the only part of her life she can control. She learns to use it on an intellectual level to replace the adult intellectual activity forbidden her. Seeking a human with whom to interact, she finds heads in the wallpaper, sees them move as if behind undulating, almost-imperceptible bars. At first she becomes angry with the heads' "impertinence" and "everlastingness," not recognizing that these are the two qualities she herself exhibits: the impertinence of trying to achieve humanness against all restrictions and the everlastingness of her own stubborn core of self which can never fully yield to outside expectations. Her refusal to accept the wallpaper as either ugly or meaningless is a representation of the tenacity of her own character, which can yield to such outside constraints as a prison nursery but will never surrender its right to remain outside interpretation, as does the wallpaper. In relation to the "principle of design" imposed by the masculine universe, both the wallpaper and her mind refuse to follow any logic other than their own.

Slowly, the wallpaper becomes something more than an object for the narrator. She begins to see in it a movement and a purpose she has been unable to realize in her own life. As her madness develops, she shifts her own desire for escape from the limitations of her husband's expectations onto the figure behind the undulating bars of the wallpaper, the figure of a woman, "stooping down and creeping about" behind the pattern as she herself creeps behind her restricted life. The rescue of that woman becomes her one object, and the wallpaper becomes at once the symbol of her confinement and of her freedom. The disparate symbols of Gilman's story coalesce in the symbol of the wallpaper, itself imprisoned in the nursery, with the humanoid heads, behind their intangible bars, denied the sexuality of bodies.

If realism is to be defined, as Wellek has defined it, as "the objective representation of contemporary social reality," Gilman's story is indeed realism; but her realism, like Henry James's, is a representation of what is real *to the author.* There can be no "objective reality" as such because it is always seen by subjective observers. Gilman was such a subjective observer insofar as she was a member of a group (women) viewed as external to integral (male) society. Her reality she presented not directly, but through the objects comprising the backdrop of her narrator's life—objects which symbolize her assigned status in the world but which, paradoxically, also give her the opportunity to achieve complete freedom. In a world where half the human race must be rendered non-entities in the most radical sense of the word, insanity is the only creative act available to those doomed to be defined as subhuman by submission to society's standards. In this sense Gilman anticipates R. D. Laing, who says that in an insane world only the mad are sane. (pp. 286-88)

> *Loralee MacPike, "Environment as Psychopathological Symbolism in 'The Yellow Wallpaper',"* in American Literary Realism 1870-1910, *Vol. 8, No. 3, Summer, 1975, pp. 286-88.*

Sandra M. Gilbert and Susan Gubar   (essay date 1979)

[*Gilbert and Gubar are American critics who have coedited such works as* Shakespeare's Sisters: Feminist Essays on Women Poets *(1979) and* The Norton Anthology of Literature by Women: The Tradition in English *(1985). In the following excerpt, taken from their* The Madwoman in the Attic: The Woman Writer and the Nineteenth-Century Literary Imagination, *Gilbert and Gubar offer a feminist analysis of "The Yellow Wallpaper." After identifying the effects of the social restrictions placed on such nineteenth-century women writers as Christina Rossetti, Emily Brontë, and Charlotte Perkins Gilman, the authors conclude: "It is not surprising . . . that spatial imagery of enclosure and escape, elaborated with what frequently becomes obsessive intensity, characterizes much of their writing."*]

[Women have often] been described or imagined as houses. Most recently Erik Erikson advanced his controversial theory of female "inner space" in an effort to account for little girls' interest in domestic enclosures. But in medieval times, as if to anticipate Erikson, statues of the Madonna were made to open up and reveal the holy family hidden in the Virgin's inner space. The female womb has certainly, always and everywhere, been a child's first and most satisfying house, a source of food and dark security, and

therefore a mythic paradise imaged over and over again in sacred caves, secret shrines, consecrated huts. Yet for many a woman writer these ancient associations of house and self seem mainly to have strengthened the anxiety about enclosure which she projected into her art. Disturbed by the real physiological prospect of enclosing an unknown part of herself that is somehow also not herself, the female artist may, like Mary Shelley, conflate anxieties about maternity with anxieties about literary creativity. Alternatively, troubled by the anatomical "emptiness" of spinsterhood, she may, like Emily Dickinson, fear the inhabitations of nothingness and death, the transformation of womb into tomb. Moreover, conditioned to believe that as a house she is herself owned (and ought to be inhabited) by a man, she may once again but for yet another reason see herself as inescapably an object. In other words, even if she does not experience her womb as a kind of tomb or perceive her child's occupation of her house/body as depersonalizing, she may recognize that in an essential way she has been defined simply by her purely biological usefulness to her species.

To become literally a house, after all, is to be denied the hope of that spiritual transcendence of the body which, as Simone de Beauvoir has argued, is what makes humanity distinctively human. Thus, to be confined in childbirth (and significantly "confinement" was the key nineteenth-century term for what we would now, just as significantly, call "delivery") is in a way just as problematical as to be confined in a house or prison. Indeed, it might well seem to the literary woman that, just as ontogeny may be said to recapitulate phylogeny, the confinement of pregnancy replicates the confinement of society. For even if she is only metaphorically denied transcendence, the woman writer who perceives the implications of the house/body equation must unconsciously realize that such a trope does not just "place" her in a glass coffin, it transforms her into a version of the glass coffin herself. There is a sense, therefore, in which, confined in such a network of metaphors, what Adrienne Rich has called a "thinking woman" might inevitably feel that now she has been imprisoned within her own alien and loathsome body. Once again, in other words, she has become not only a prisoner but a monster.

As if to comment on the unity of all these points—on, that is, the anxiety-inducing connections between what women writers tend to see as their parallel confinements in texts, houses, and maternal female bodies—Charlotte Perkins Gilman brought them all together in 1890 in a striking story of female confinement and escape, a paradigmatic tale which (like *Jane Eyre*) seems to tell *the* story that all literary women would tell if they could speak their "speechless woe." **"The Yellow Wallpaper,"** which Gilman herself called "a description of a case of nervous breakdown," recounts in the first person the experiences of a woman who is evidently suffering from a severe postpartum psychosis. Her husband, a censorious and paternalistic physician, is treating her according to methods by which S. Weir Mitchell, a famous "nerve specialist," treated Gilman herself for a similar problem. He has confined her to a large garret room in an "ancestral hall" he has rented, and he has forbidden her to touch pen to paper until she is well again, for he feels, says the narrator, "that with my imaginative power and habit of story-making, a nervous weakness like mine is sure to lead to all manner of excited fancies, and that I ought to use my will and good sense to check the tendency."

The cure, of course, is worse than the disease, for the sick woman's mental condition deteriorates rapidly. "I think sometimes that if I were only well enough to write a little it would relieve the press of ideas and rest me," she remarks, but literally confined in a room she thinks is a one-time nursery because it has "rings and things" in the walls, she is literally locked away from creativity. The "rings and things," although reminiscent of children's gymnastic equipment, are really the paraphernalia of confinement, like the gate at the head of the stairs, instruments that definitively indicate her imprisonment. Even more tormenting, however, is the room's wallpaper: a sulphurous yellow paper, torn off in spots, and patterned with "lame uncertain curves" that "plunge off at outrageous angles" and "destroy themselves in unheard of contradictions." Ancient, smoldering, "unclean" as the oppressive structures of the society in which she finds herself, this paper surrounds the narrator like an inexplicable text, censorious and overwhelming as her physician husband, haunting as the "hereditary estate" in which she is trying to survive. Inevitably she studies its suicidal implications—and inevitably, because of her "imaginative power and habit of story-making," she revises it, projecting her own passion for escape into its otherwise incomprehensible hieroglyphics. "This wall-paper," she decides, at a key point in her story,

> has a kind of sub-pattern in a different shade, a particularly irritating one, for you can only see it in certain lights, and not clearly then.
>
> But in the places where it isn't faded and where the sun is just so—I can see a strange, provoking, formless sort of figure, that seems to skulk about behind that silly and conspicuous front design.

As time passes, this figure concealed behind what corresponds (in terms of what we have been discussing) to the facade of the patriarchal text becomes clearer and clearer. By moonlight the pattern of the wallpaper "becomes bars! The outside pattern I mean, and the woman behind it is as plain as can be." And eventually, as the narrator sinks more deeply into what the world calls madness, the terrifying implications of both the paper and the figure imprisoned behind the paper begin to permeate—that is, to *haunt*—the rented ancestral mansion in which she and her husband are immured. The "yellow smell" of the paper "creeps all over the house," drenching every room in its subtle aroma of decay. And the woman creeps too—through the house, in the house, and out of the house, in the garden and "on that long road under the trees." Sometimes, indeed, the narrator confesses, "I think there are a great many women" both behind the paper and creeping in the garden,

> and sometimes only one, and she crawls around fast, and her crawling shakes [the paper] all over.... And she is all the time trying to climb through. But nobody could climb through that

pattern—it strangles so; I think that is why it has so many heads.

Eventually it becomes obvious to both reader and narrator that the figure creeping through and behind the wallpaper is both the narrator and the narrator's double. By the end of the story, moreover, the narrator has enabled this double to escape from her textual/architectural confinement: "I pulled and she shook, I shook and she pulled, and before morning we had peeled off yards of that paper." Is the message of the tale's conclusion mere madness? Certainly the righteous Doctor John—whose name links him to the anti-hero of Charlotte Brontë's *Villette*—has been temporarily defeated, or at least momentarily stunned. "Now why should that man have fainted?" the narrator ironically asks as she creeps around her attic. But John's unmasculine swoon of surprise is the least of the triumphs Gilman imagines for her madwoman. More significant are the madwoman's own imaginings and creations, mirages of health and freedom with which her author endows her like a fairy godmother showering gold on a sleeping heroine. The woman from behind the wallpaper creeps away, for instance, creeps fast and far on the long road, in broad daylight. "I have watched her sometimes away off in the open country," says the narrator, "creeping as fast as a cloud shadow in a high wind."

Indistinct and yet rapid, barely perceptible but inexorable, the progress of that cloud shadow is not unlike the progress of nineteenth-century literary women out of the texts defined by patriarchal poetics into the open spaces of their own authority. That such an escape from the numb world behind the patterned walls of the text was a flight from disease into health was quite clear to Gilman herself. When **"The Yellow Wallpaper"** was published she sent it to Weir Mitchell, whose strictures had kept her from attempting the pen during her own breakdown, thereby aggravating her illness, and she was delighted to learn, years later, that "he had changed his treatment of nervous prostration since reading" her story. "If that is a fact," she declared, "I have not lived in vain." Because she was a rebellious feminist besides being a medical iconoclast, we can be sure that Gilman did not think of this triumph of hers in narrowly therapeutic terms. Because she knew, with Emily Dickinson, that "Infection in the sentence breeds," she knew that the cure for female despair must be spiritual as well as physical, aesthetic as well as social. What **"The Yellow Wallpaper"** shows she knew, too, is that even when a supposedly "mad" woman has been sentenced to imprisonment in the "infected" house of her own body, she may discover that, as Sylvia Plath was to put it seventy years later, she has "a self to recover, a queen." (pp. 88-92)

> *Sandra M. Gilbert and Susan Gubar, "Infection in the Sentence: The Woman Writer and the Anxiety of Authorship," in their* The Madwoman in the Attic: The Woman Writer and the Nineteenth-Century Literary Imagination, *Yale University Press, 1979, pp. 45-92.*

Ann J. Lane (essay date 1980)

[*Lane is an American historian, editor, and essayist who specializes in feminist scholarship. In the essay below,*

*she surveys the principal themes in Gilman's short fic-
tion and discusses the structures, plots, and characters
Gilman employs to illustrate her iconoclastic ideas.*]

Gilman's fiction is part of her ideological world view, and
therein lies its interest and its power. We read her books
today because the problems she addressed and the solutions she sought are, unhappily, as relevant to the present
as they were to her time. Several themes appear persistently. (p. xiv)

In Gilman's stories, certain characters break out of limiting places with the help of intervening others. There is a
formula and there are stock characters who work out the
formula. The young girl-woman, restricted by her traditional view of parental obligation or social place, or endangered by an innocence that does not protect her from a
cruel libertine, is offered the model of an older woman, frequently a doctor, who presents her with options she never
knew existed and knowledge she did not have. Middle-
aged and older women, having done their service to husband and children, often extract from their own previously unexamined experience possibilities for new opportunities that point out the pleasures and powers available in
our last years. Support for the young does not usually
come from within the immediate family, neither from parents nor from siblings. Indeed, the young frequently need
to reject their immediate families to seek help from others,
sometimes a grandfather or an aunt, more often not a relative at all. Men who are redeemable, and Gilman does
offer many such examples, are decent, sensitive, and well-
meaning, though conventional; but they are capable, when
pressed, of changing, a quality of conversion without
which they are lost.

Although Gilman was a socialist, and identified herself as
such, and although her utopian fiction creates an ideal socialist society, the strategies she offered in her realistic fiction were often strangely conservative. There were many
cooperative ventures scattered throughout the nation; yet
her short-term, immediate suggestions for individual or
social reform took women out of the home and into capi-
talistic business activities, not into producer or consumer
cooperatives. Gilman evaded the issue of class by examining women's issues alone and resolving women's problems
without reference to class. Most of the employed women
of her time were servants, and yet Gilman's solutions, for
individuals or projected onto a larger social screen, very
rarely addressed the concerns or needs of a servant class
in a way that could be expected to win them over to her
point of view.

Gilman gave little attention to her writing as literature,
and neither will the reader, I am afraid. She wrote quickly,
carelessly, to make a point. She always wrote fiction to
meet a deadline. Still, she had a good ear for dialogue, was
adept at sketching within a few pages a familiar but complicated set of relationships, and knew well the whole
range of worries and joys women shared. She wrote to engage an audience in her ideas, not in her literary accom-
plishments. (pp. xv-xvi)

[In her] entire body of published and unpublished fiction
. . . , Gilman examines, clearly and pointedly, a variety of
problems women share and a variety of proposed ways of

dealing with those problems. Although Gilman later ascribed a didactic reason for writing it, **"The Yellow Wallpaper"** came from a deep and private part of her that she
ordinarily kept well protected from the public, and perhaps from herself. She may have taken the risk with the
hope that writing **"The Yellow Wallpaper"** would purge
her of the demons she so feared would one day claim her
permanently. However, the debilitating depressions never
did disappear entirely and for many years neither did the
frightening specter of insanity. Never again did she publicly plumb her emotions with the intensity and honesty that
permeate **"The Yellow Wallpaper."** (p. xvii)

Gilman used fiction as a device to offer an answer to the
question she always posed: "But what if. . . ?" What if she
wants a family and a career, and her husband-to-be objects? What if her children are grown up and she is bored?
What if her husband is abusive and she wants to leave him,
but she does not know how? What if her vacuous life
causes her to make impossible demands upon her caring
husband? . . . Except in **"The Yellow Wallpaper,"** there
is always a feasible, positive alternative, and there is always a happy, or at least a moderately happy, ending. The
questions, in one form or another, came from Gilman's
own experience, either because she had herself come to a
satisfactory resolution or, more often, because she had not
and suffered the consequences, which she wished to spare
subsequent generations. If there were not many models
after which young women could fashion a new way of life,
then Gilman would create them in fiction. (pp. xvii-xviii)

Many Gilman enthusiasts do not much like her fiction.
They consider it too ideological, too didactic. Gilman mis-
chievously used the commonly shared forms and structures of her day—farces, domestic novels, mysteries, adventure stories—and infused them with her own brand of
feminism and socialism. Her work is ideological, but she
implies that all literature is ideological, only its familiarity, its "naturalness" to us, makes it appear to reflect all
possible world views. Although she does not challenge all
the conventions of her day, she introduces a new sense of
intellectual play when she poses her "What if" questions
in the arena of traditional male-female relations, thereby
exposing the absurd pieties embedded in domestic life. (p.
xviii)

Gilman was determined to package her social vision in
ways persuasive to a general audience. [Her] short stories
are written in the style and with the simplicity common
to women's magazines of the day. Each story is a lesson.
Each focuses on a specific problem, usually but not always
a problem shared primarily by women, and each has a
happy resolution. The happy ending, however, comes
about as a result of a good deal of intelligence, resourcefulness, and, most important, a willingness to defy convention, to look afresh at an old situation. What each story
requires is the shaking off of traditional ways of doing
things, especially as they relate to accepted male or female
behavior. (p. xix)

"When I Was a Witch" has a wishes-come-true technique
that is used, not to turn everything touched to gold, but
to improve the quality of collective life. . . . But what do
you imagine would happen to our cities if the homilies to

which we pay lip-service were acted upon with sincerity: if people told only the truth in their pulpits, in their newspapers, in their stockholders' meetings? What would happen if the pain we inflict on others we felt in their place? The point she makes is droll, because we, in fact, would be astonished if truth, decency, courtesy, and generosity ruled our public life.

"If I Were a Man" applies the same sport to a husband-and-wife switch. When Mollie Mathewson, a "true woman," suddenly finds herself Gerald Mathewson, she discovers what it feels like to be a man: the quiet superiority; the pleasure of his large size; the comfort of his sensible clothing and shoes; the sense of power from controlling his own, earned money. In the body and mind of a man with the "memory of a whole lifetime," Mollie sees the world as a big place, a place of business and politics and action. Most startling of all, she learns what men really think about women.

Gilman felt strongly that innocence was a device through which girls and women were victimized, so innocence is the moral villain of **"The Girl in the Pink Hat."** An effort to seduce an innocent is foiled, partly because the young lady, though naive is not without courage and determination, and partly through the interference of a woman who is a combination of Nancy Drew and Miss Marple. . . . In this story the villain can be recognized by the smell of his breath and by his attempts to "assert a premature authority" over the woman he claims to love. Gilman frequently created a particular kind of man who is successful in winning women and then mistreating them. Trust, if not rooted in knowledge and experience, is dangerous, we learn.

In **"The Cottagette"** we see how to catch a man and how (almost) to lose one, if we accept without thinking the standard canons of female wiles. Malda follows the advice of her friend Lois because Lois, who is thirty-five and divorced, claims to know the real route to marital success. . . . [Malda is prepared] to sacrifice her time, her pleasures, her work, to make that home for the man she loves, who, fortunately wants her the way she was, "wild and sweet . . . truly an artist" not a household drudge. We discover that gratifying and beautiful work need not be esoteric; that there are men who value women as individuals, not as domestic servants. . . . (pp. xix-xx)

"The Unnatural Mother" comes out of Gilman's private pain, for it was a phrase often used against her in the press. In this story the mother is considered unnatural because she willingly sacrifices her own child to save the community, Ironically, the child survives, the town inhabitants survive, and only she and her husband perish. . . .

The tension between career and family, a problem in Gilman's time as in ours, is a frequent theme in her fiction. **"Making a Change"** is a typical piece on the subject. Julia, a wonderful musician and an exalted beauty, has neither the patience for unrelieved mothering nor the abilities for household management. She tries only because it is her duty. Everybody is miserable: the baby cries, the wife is distraught, the husband sulks, and the mother-in-law wrings her hands. Then the women conspire to change it all. On the roof of the apartment house they set up a baby-

garden with fifteen babies, run by Julia's mother-in-law. Julia returns to her music and thus relieves Frank of his obligation to be sole breadwinner. Everybody does what he/she is best suited for, and the children are happy because they are with other babies while being cared for by a competent person, who is not their mother.

"An Honest Woman" is a "fallen" woman who gets up. Deserted by the man she loved and lived with (though he could not marry her), Mary Cameron puts her life together, defying the conventional notion that, as one person observes, "you can't reform spilled milk." She is Gilman's answer to Nathaniel Hawthorne. Unlike Hester Prynne, who carries her humiliation with dignity, Mary Cameron refuses to carry it at all. She feels grief but no shame, for she is an honest woman. . . . (p. xxi)

> Many Gilman enthusiasts do not much like her fiction. They consider it too ideological, too didactic. Gilman mischievously used the commonly shared forms and structures of her day—farces, domestic novels, mysteries, adventure stories—and infused them with her own brand of feminism and socialism.
>
> —*Ann J. Lane*

Adultery was a subject genteel folk avoided talking about, except to denounce the women who engaged in it. In **"Turned,"** Mrs. Marroner (a Ph.D. formerly on a college faculty) discovers that her husband has seduced and impregnated their docile, trusting servant girl, Gerta. Initially enraged at the girl's disloyalty, Mrs. Marroner soon turns her fury on the husband who took advantage of the girl's innocence without even loving her. . . . It is the seduction she cannot forgive, the use of power against a helpless victim. It is an "offense against all women and against the unborn child." The two women unite and together confront the villainous man. . . . (p. xxii)

In **"The Widow's Might"** the mature woman, having spent her adult life devoted to husband and children, decides it is time to go off and play, to run her own business, to do whatever she chooses. Not a helpless, broken, distraught woman after her husband's death, she discovers resources within herself never before explored.

Mr. Peebles in **"Mr. Peebles' Heart"** is a fiftyish, grayish, stoutish man who has spent his life doing his duty, which meant essentially supporting women—his mother, his wife, his daughters—by running a store that he detested. He is persuaded by his sister-in-law, who is a doctor and a "new woman," to take off and travel. He does, and returns "enlarged, refreshed, and stimulated." His wife, left to take care of herself, also changes and grows in his absence. As a result, a tired and conventional marriage, built on unarticulated assumptions that did not help either party develop, gains a new life when the people involved learn that their possibilities are limitless.

Gilman's message is essentially just that: our possibilities for change are limitless, if we want them. How to achieve those changes is examined on a small scale in the short stories, and in a considerably more complicated way in the novels. . . . (pp. xxii-xxiii)

> Ann J. Lane, "The Fictional World of Charlotte Perkins Gilman," in The Charlotte Perkins Gilman Reader: The Yellow Wallpaper and Other Fiction *by Charlotte Perkins Gilman, edited by Ann J. Lane, Pantheon Books, 1980, pp. ix-xlii.*

Juliann E. Fleenor   (essay date 1983)

[*Fleenor is an American educator and critic who has published essays on Alice Munro and nineteenth-century American female writers. In the following essay, she compares the Gothic elements found in Gilman's autobiography to those in "The Yellow Wallpaper," "The Rocking Chair," and "The Giant Wistaria."*]

Fictional forms can sometimes pervade the manner in which women shape their autobiographies. A case in point is the Gothic, a literary genre popular with female readers and authors for nearly two centuries. Identified as women's fiction and analyzed by feminist critics for evidence of women's experiences, it has been suggested that the Gothic has been used to voice rebellion and anger over the status of women; its themes of madness and disintegration have been analyzed for proof of women's victimization. The female experience, it has been suggested, is that of victim in an androcentric society, and the Gothic form with its ambivalent female symbolism and its psychological effect has been congenial for expressing that ambivalent experience for both readers and writers. In particular, the Gothic has been a form which has expressed women's need for and fear of maternity. Women writers have used the Gothic to convey a fear of maternity and its consequent dependent mother/infant relationship as well as a fear of the mother and a quest for maternal approval.

I would like to propose in the following discussion that the Gothic form is one framework through which Charlotte Perkins Gilman shaped her autobiography as well as generalized about the female experience. Its use is both limiting and yet revealing—limiting in that it reduces Gilman's life to that of a victim; revealing in that its use suggests that the major conflict in Gilman's life was with her female self, with her mother, and with the very act of creation. Nancy K. Miller has suggested [in her "Emphasis Added: Plots and Plausibilities in Women's Fiction," *PMLA* (January 1981)] that women's fiction has been about the plots of fiction and not about life. Might it also be possible that women's autobiography, at least in this instance, is about the plots of fiction *and* about life? In an attempt to answer that question, let me first discuss the nature of autobiography and the nature of women's autobiographies.

Whatever division existed between fiction and autobiography has been disappearing for some time, if it ever existed

at all. Once, autobiography was commonly assumed to be real and fiction unreal. Increasingly, critics of autobiography have been seeking form, shape, and unity, all common to literary forms. But that literary basis has been difficult to discover or define. Some critics have suggested that autobiographical form is determined by the writer's desire to discover one identity based on one facet of the personality. Reality is simplified, and a pattern is imposed on the writer's life with a coherent story. On the other hand, Francis Hart [maintained in his "Notes for an Anatomy of Modern Autobiography," *New Literary History* (1970)] that writers have complicated and shifting intentions which account for autobiography as a changing and varied form within the same work. William Spengemann has attempted to synthesize these two poles by asserting that:

> . . . we must view autobiography historically, not as one thing that writers have done again, and again, but as the pattern described by the various things they have done in response to changing ideas about the nature of the self, the ways in which the self may be apprehended, and the proper methods of reporting these apprehensions.

In his study, *The Forms of Autobiography*, Spengemann examines fiction and autobiography by men, claiming that autobiography has been found "to assume fictive forms in the modern era." The questions Spengemann asks about autobiography are, how does the self know the self, and how is the self to be reconciled with the absolute. He concludes: "What makes *Sartor Resartus* and *David Copperfield* autobiographies . . . is not the inclusion of autobiographical materials but their efforts to discover, through a fictive action, some ground upon which conflicting aspects of the writer's own nature might be reconciled in complete being."

Spengemann's conclusions have only limited application to women's autobiographies. Estelle Jelinek suggests that women's autobiographies differ generally from those written by men. She points out these three characteristics: an emphasis in male autobiographies on the public life, while women write about their personal lives; understatement in women's autobiographies as women camouflage their feelings and distance themselves from their lives; and irregular narratives in women's autobiographies rather than an orderly linear chronology. The first two appear contradictory; the emphasis upon the personal leads a reader to expect that women would reveal their feelings; yet distancing occurs. Gilman's autobiography only partially fits these general characteristics. She writes consistently about her public life, stressing her commitment to the social welfare rather than the private. She writes of her personal experience; but it is always generalized to the plight of other women. Finally, her narrative is linear, beginning with her early life and proceeding chronologically to her death.

Spengemann has suggested that fiction and autobiography seek a reconciliation of the writer's nature into what might be construed as an absolute, a quest for completeness. Women's autobiographies have for the most part ignored that quest by keeping to the private sphere, not the public one. Thus, the female identity has been defined through

Gilman and her brother, about 1862.

its relationships with others, not by its own dimensions. Gilman's autobiography fits this definition.

Spengemann's approach to fiction through autobiography, however, is intriguing. I would suggest that if fiction can be analyzed through autobiography, then autobiography might in turn be analyzed through a literary form, the Gothic. The Gothic paradigm has been and continues to be an important vehicle for women writers. If he is correct, and if autobiography is the thing that writers "have done in response to changing ideas about the nature of self," then the form might not be so fluid and changing in relation to women's autobiographies. The Gothic form can be used to suggest that the nature of the female self has not been fluid and changing, but limited within a patriarchal culture. Women's autobiography could be described as the Gothic has been, as ambivalent and concerned with women's lives in the private sphere. In this instance *The Living of Charlotte Perkins Gilman* offers a unique opportunity to relate Gilman's puzzling autobiography to her Gothic stories. This analysis also reveals that she wrote in response to the ideas of the nature of woman and woman as mother. Such a study gives an opportunity to move between fiction and autobiography and perhaps further define the nature of women writers and the nature of the mother-author conflict women face.

Moving between Gilman's short story, **"The Yellow Wallpaper,"** and her autobiography is not a novel suggestion.

Readers have consistently connected Gilman's story and her life. Perhaps the popularity of the Gothic itself has also prepared women readers for this connection, for the story graphically describes the nervous breakdown of a woman after she is confined to her country home by her physician-husband and told not to work but to rest. Since Gilman herself experienced a similar breakdown, readers have generally accepted her assertion that the story was a literal transcription of her life. She writes in her autobiography that:

> . . . the real purpose of the story was to reach Dr. S. Weir Mitchell, and to convince him of the error of his ways. I sent him a copy as soon as it came out, but got no response. However, many years later, I met someone who knew close friends of Dr. Mitchell's who said he had told them that he had changed his treatment of nervous prostration since reading **"The Yellow Wallpaper."** If that is a fact, I have not lived in vain.

Ann Douglas, Gail Parker, Patricia Meyer Spacks, and Elaine Hedges have all accepted Gilman's statements and have interpreted the story accordingly as "the form of her life," as the story of Gilman's "blighted, damaged" yet "transcendent" life, and as the story of "a woman who is denied the right to be an adult." These feminist critics move, as Gilman intended, from the story to the autobiography and back again. Her journals and letters support this interpretation as well. Sandra Gilbert and Susan Gubar have recently suggested [in their *The Madwoman in the Attic: The Woman Writer and the Nineteenth-Century Literary Imagination* (1979)] that Gilman's story is a tale of all literary women trapped in a house which rapidly becomes the narrator's own body.

Although it is not generally known, Gilman wrote at least two other Gothic stories around the same time as **"The Yellow Wallpaper."** All three were published in *The New England Magazine.* At the time that **"The Rocking Chair"** and **"The Giant Wistaria"** were written, Gilman and her young daughter, Katherine, were living in the warmth of Pasadena, separated from her husband, Charles Walter Stetson. Gilman later noted in her papers: "**'The Yellow Wallpaper'** was written in two days, with the thermometer at one hundred and three in Pasadena, Ca." Her husband was living on the east coast, and, perhaps coincidentally, all three stories appear to be set in a nameless eastern setting, one urban and two rural. All three display similar themes, and all three are evidence that the conflict, central to Gilman's Gothic fiction and later to her autobiography, was a conflict with the mother, with motherhood, and with creation.

In all three stories women are confined within the home; it is their prison, their insane asylum, even their tomb. A sense of the female isolation which Gilman felt, of exclusion from the public world of work and of men, is contained in the anecdote related by Zona Gale in her introduction to Gilman's autobiography. After watching the approach of several locomotives to a train platform in a small town in Wisconsin, Gilman said, " 'All that, . . . and women have no part in it. Everything done by men, working together, while women worked on alone within their four walls!' " Female exclusion, women denied the opportunity to work, or their imprisonment behind four walls, led to madness. Her image, interestingly, does not suggest a female subculture of women working together; Gilman was working against her own culture's definition of women, and her primary antagonists were women like her own mother.

"The Rocking Chair" perhaps suggests conflict with an androcentric society. A beautiful, golden-haired girl sits in a clumsy, brass rocking chair, "something from the old country." She is visible to two young men, but only from a distance. They describe her in terms of a feminine enigma: "Hers was a strange beauty, infinitely attractive, yet infinitely perplexing." They can never see her while they too are in the house, only while they are outside. The chair and its origins represent the effect that an androcentric tradition has upon women and men. The fact that she cannot be seen except from a distance indicates how the man relates to the woman. In this case she is in a rocking chair rather than on a pedestal. Originally the story was called "Inanimate," with the adjective modifying perhaps the girl, perhaps the chair. Her existence is created by the two men. They are doubles of each other, together since childhood, at school, as college roommates, and now as hack journalists. They "are organisms so mutually adapted that they never seem to weary each other." But that is not true of their relation to the unnamed girl.

The chair the girl occupies is described by Maurice, the narrator: "I never saw a chair so made to hurt as that one. It was large and heavy and ill-balanced, and every joint and corner so shod with brass." When asked about its origin, the landlady, whom they call Mrs. Sphynx, replies, "It is Spanish . . . Spanish oak, Spanish leather, Spanish brass, Spanish—." Maurice describes it in detail:

> It was a strange ill-balanced thing that chair, though so easy and comfortable to sit in. The rockers were long and sharp behind, always lying in wait for the unwary, but cut short off in front; and the back was so high and so heavy on top that what with its weight and the shortness of the front rockers, it tipped over forward with an ease and a violence equally astounding.

> This I knew from experience, as it had plunged over upon me during some of our frequent encounters with it. Hal also was a sufferer, but in spite of our manifold bruises, neither of us would have had the chair moved, for did not she sit in it, evening after evening, and rock there in the light of the setting sun?

Each man sees the other in the chair with the girl in his arms, and each claims to be sitting in the chair alone. Consequently, each grows suspicious of the other; they quarrel and end their friendship. Gilman appears to be satirizing the male proclivity to worship of a non-existent woman.

In the manuscript the landlady is identified as the girl's mother. There is also the assertion that the mother/landlady keeps the girl away from the two men and the neighbors. The neighbors pity the daughter because the mother refuses to be sociable and keeps the daughter from being so. Neither leaves the house; the narrator notes: "Of course we made covert inquiries in the neighborhood, but nothing new could be elicited. That there was a pretty daughter, often seen in the window, that the mother was reserved and disagreeable neither calling nor returning calls, and that everybody pitied the daughter—that was all." The implication is that the mother imprisoned the girl. However, this description is eliminated from the published story, leaving it much tighter in focus. The omission of the neighbors' account makes the existence of the girl and the mother less possible.

Gilman could not or would not draw the mother/daughter relationship with any sense of reality. There are no conversations between them in either the manuscript or the published version. The narration is restricted to the male point of view. In fact, although the landlady is identified as the mother, at one point she denies it. All this takes place in an empty house in an unnamed city, where the light is usually shut out. The narrator describes the scene: "A waving spot of sunshine, a bright signal light, that caught the eye at once on a waste of commonplace houses and all the dreariness of a narrow city street. Across some low roof that made a gap in the wall of masonry, shot a level brilliant beam of the just setting sun, and struck directly on the golden head of a girl in an upper window." Nature is kept out of this place, except when it enters through one "brief signal light" which ends on the non-existent girl.

There are similarities between **"The Rocking Chair"** and **"The Yellow Wallpaper"** other than those mentioned above. The men beg at the door for the young woman to open it, as does the husband in **"The Yellow Wallpaper."** They search for her:

> Door after door I knocked at, tried and opened; room after room I entered and searched thoroughly—in all that house, from cellar to garret, was no furnished room but ours, no sign of human occupancy. Dust, dust and cobwebs everywhere—nothing else.

The house is empty, actually having never been occupied and they discover they are the only occupants. The girl here becomes one of the figures behind the wallpaper in the later story, and the landlady/mother becomes the woman outside of the wallpaper.

The friends are separated by this vision, one dies, killed with the same kind of slashes left by the rocking chair. The narrator returns to his room:

> The room was empty, both rooms utterly devoid of all life. Yes all, for with the love of a whole lifetime surging up in my heart I sprang to where Hall lay beneath the window and found him cold and dead.

> Dead, and most horribly dead—those heavy merciless blows—those deep three-cornered gashes—I started to my feet—even the chair had gone.

> And again that whispered laugh!

With that nearly comic image of the rocking chair inflicting mortal wounds Gilman ends her Gothic tale, one which combines satire with horror, as she satirizes the male need to create charming young women to pursue even when that pursuit leads to the death of a best friend, or perhaps a part of themselves.

The setting in **"The Rocking Chair"** is the city; in **"The Giant Wistaria,"** it is the country: **"The Giant Wistaria,"** however, is similar to **"The Yellow Wallpaper"** in that both have as a theme the punishment of women, by both women and men, for being women. In fact, women are punished for having babies because doing so imprisons them in the social structure symbolized by the house. The house is again employed as a major symbol; it is haunted, as is the manor house in **"The Yellow Wallpaper,"** by female vulnerability and the sin of maternity.

The young woman in **"The Giant Wistaria"** has had an illegitimate child, given to a servant by her parents. The woman wears a carnelian cross, one of agate, which could be either flesh colored or deep red. Like Hester Prynne, she wears a symbol of her adultery. Unlike **"The Rocking Chair,"** however, the maternal conflict is explicit here: the mother tells the daughter "Meddle not with my new vine child! See! Thou hast already broken the tender shoot! Never needle or distaff for thee, and yet thou wilt not be quiet!" The parents even lock her in her room, binding her to keep her there.

A hundred years later, after the death of all those involved, four young people—two women and two men—visit the house and find a huge wistaria vine covering the house. Nature now runs wild:

> The old lilacs and laburnums, the pires and syringa, nodded against the second-story windows. What garden plants survived were great ragged bushes or great shapeless beds. A huge wistaria covered the whole front of the house. The trunk, it was too large to call a stem, rose at the corner of the porch by the high steps, and had once climbed its pillars; but now the pillars were wrenched from their places and held rigid and helpless by the tightly wound and knotted arms.

> It fenced in all the upper story of the porch with a knitted wall of stem and leaf; it ran along the eaves, holding up the gutter that once supported it; it shaded every window with a heavy green; and the drooping, fragrant blossoms made a waving sheet of purple from roof to ground.

Like the house in Shirley Jackson's novel, *We Have Always Lived in the Castle,* nature has reclaimed the house. Like **"The Yellow Wallpaper,"** the four visitors begin to see female figures throughout the grounds, even though the house is unoccupied. A group of trees look like "a crouching, haunted figure" of a woman picking huckleberries. For one of the visitors the vine itself takes on human form and appears as " 'a writhing body—cringing—beseeching!' " One of the men begins to dream of the young mother, and soon they discover that she has been buried under the porch in the roots of the giant wistaria. The woman, through the vine has held the house in her arms, and her baby—dead at the age of a month—lay in the old well in the basement. Thus, pregnancy leads first to ostracism and then to death for both mother and child.

This fate might be construed as apt punishment for illegitimacy, but no such confusion exists in **"The Yellow Wallpaper."** Diseased maternity is explicit in Gilman's third Gothic story. The yellow wallpaper symbolizes more than confinement, victimization, and the inability to write. It suggests a disease within the female self. When the narrator peels the wallpaper off, "It sticks horribly and the pattern just enjoys it! All those strangled heads and bulbous eyes and the waddling fungus growths just shriek with derision." This passage describes more than the peeling of wallpaper: the "strangled heads and bulbous eyes and waddling fungus" imply something strange and terrible about birth and death conjoined, about female procreation, and about female physiology. Nature is perverted here, too. The narrator thinks of "old foul, bad yellow things." The smell "creeps all over the house." She finds it "hovering in the dining-room, skulking in the parlor, hiding in the hall, lying in wait for me on the stairs." Finally, "it gets into my hair."

The paper stains the house in a way that suggests the effect of afterbirth. The house, specifically this room, becomes more than a symbol of a repressive society; it represents the physical self of the narrator as well. She is disgusted, perhaps awed, perhaps frightened of her own bodily processes. The story establishes a sense of fear and disgust, the skin crawls and grows clammy with the sense of physiological fear that Ellen Moers refers to as the Female Gothic.

My contention that one of the major themes in the story, punishment for becoming a mother (as well as punishment for being female), is supported by the absence of the child. The child is taken away from the mother, almost in punishment, as was the child in **"The Giant Wistaria."** This differs from Gilman's experience; she had been told to keep her child with her at all times. In both the story and in Gilman's life, a breakdown occurs directly after the birth of a child. The narrator is confined as if she had committed a crime. Maternity—the creation of a child—is combined with writing—the creation of writing—in a way that suggests they are interrelated and perhaps symbiotic, as are the strange toadstools behind the wallpaper.

The pathological nature of both experiences is not surprising, given the treatment Gilman received, and given the fact that maternity reduced women to mothers and not writers. Childbirth has long been a rite of passage for women. But the question is, where does that passage lead? Becoming a mother leads to a child-like state. The narrator becomes the absent child.

All three of these stories have similar themes related to the Gothic as it is used by women. All depict women trapped and driven insane in a patriarchal society. They illustrate a conflict with the mother or with maternity itself, for all are about the act of creating a narrative; they are all processes of discovery. In **"The Rocking Chair"** the young man pieces together the story for the reader; in **"The Giant Wistaria"** the two couples discover through intuition, dreams, and finally the removal of the old porch, the secret of the house; and in **"The Yellow Wallpaper"** the narrator—this time nameless—reads the wallpaper, creating figures and a diseased nature from its faded surfaces.

Imagination is diseased in these stories, like the overgrown gardens in **"The Giant Wistaria,"** like the abandoned garden in **"The Yellow Wallpaper,"** and like the darkened city street where one beam of sunlight reaches the head of the young woman. In two of these stories the creation of an infant is related to the creation of the narrative. In both the infants are conspicuous by their absence, further evidence of a diseased female imagination. In the hands of a female writer, diseased imagination and madness become diseased maternity; for literary creation is directly related to the creation of a child. (pp. 227-35)

> *Juliann E. Fleenor, "The Gothic Prism: Charlotte Perkins Gilman's Gothic Stories and Her Autobiography," in* The Female Gothic, *edited by Juliann E. Fleenor, Eden Press, 1983, pp. 227-41.*

Mary Jacobus   (essay date 1986)

[*An English educator and critic, Jacobus has contributed to such works as* Women Writing and Writing about Women *(1979). In the essay below, she discusses the validity of Freudian and feminist readings of "The Yellow Wallpaper."*]

> I May Here be giving an impression of laying too much emphasis on the details of the symptoms and of becoming lost in an unnecessary maze of sign-reading. But I have come to learn that the determination of hysterical symptoms does in fact extend to their subtlest manifestations and that it is difficult to attribute too much sense to them.

Freud's footnote to *Studies on Hysteria* amounts to saying that where hysteria is concerned it is impossible to over-read. The maze of signs, his metaphor for the hysterical text, invokes not only labyrinthine intricacy but the risk of self-loss. What would it be like to become lost in the subtleties of sign reading? Charlotte Perkins Gilman's short story, **"The Yellow Wallpaper,"** provides an answer of sorts. It would be like finding one's own figure replicated everywhere in the text; like going mad. This tale of hysterical confinement—a fictionalized account of Gilman's own breakdown in 1887 and the treatment she underwent at the hands of Freud's and Breuer's American contemporary, Weir Mitchell—could almost be read as Anna O.'s own version of "Fräulein Anna O." The flower of fiction reproduces herself, hysterically doubled, in the form of a short story whose treatment by feminist readers raises questions not only about psychoanalysis, but about feminist reading.

Freud had favorably reviewed a German translation of Weir Mitchell's *The Treatment of Certain Forms of Neurasthenia and Hysteria* in 1887, the year of Gilman's breakdown, and himself continued to make use of the Weir Mitchell rest-cure alongside Breuer's "cathartic treatment." Gilman later wrote that after a month of the Weir Mitchell regimen ("I was put to bed and kept there. I was fed, bathed, rubbed, and responded with the vigorous body of twenty-six") she was sent home to her husband and child with the following prescription: " 'Live as domestic a life as possible. Have your child with you all the

time. . . . Lie down an hour after each meal. Have but two hours' intellectual life a day. And never touch pen, brush or pencil as long as you live.' " Not surprisingly, she "came perilously near to losing [her] mind" as a result. Mitchell, who apparently believed that intellectual, literary, and artistic pursuits were destructive both to women's mental health and to family life, had prescribed what might be called the Philadelphian treatment (a good dose of domestication) rather than the Viennese treatment famously invoked by Chrobak in Freud's hearing (*"Penis normalis dosim repetatur"*).

Gilman, by contrast, believed that she only regained her sanity when she quit family life—specifically, married life—altogether and resumed her literary career. "The real purpose of the story," according to Gilman herself, "was to reach Dr. S. Weir Mitchell, and convince him of the error of his ways." Hearsay has it that he was duly converted: "I sent him a copy as soon as it came out, but got no response. However, many years later, I met someone who knew close friends of Dr. Mitchell's who said he had told them that he had changed his treatment of nervous prostration since reading 'The Yellow Wallpaper.' If that is a fact, I have not lived in vain." Weir Mitchell figures in this autobiographical account from *The Living of Charlotte Perkins Gilman* (1935) as a surrogate for the absent father whom Gilman also tried to "convert" through her writing. As Juliet Mitchell puts it, "Hysterics tell tales and fabricate stories—particularly for doctors who will listen." But to read **"The Yellow Wallpaper"** as a literary manifestation of transference reduces the figure in the text to Gilman herself; recuperating text as life, the diagnostic reading represses its literariness. Gilman's is a story that has forgotten its "real purpose" (conversion), becoming instead a conversion narrative of a different kind—one whose major hysterical symptom is an unnecessary (or should one say "hysterical"?) reading of the maze of signs.

John, the rationalist physician-husband in **"The Yellow Wallpaper,"** diagnoses his wife as suffering from "temporary nervous depression—a slight hysterical tendency" and threatens to send her to Weir Mitchell. This hysterical tendency is shared not only by a story whose informing metaphor is the maze of sign reading figured in the wallpaper, but by the readings which the story generates. If Gilman creates a literary double for herself in the domestic confinement of her hysterical narrator, her narrator too engages in a fantastic form of re-presentation, a doubling like that of Anna O.'s "private theatre." Just as we read the text, so she reads the patterns on the wallpaper; and like Freud she finds that "it is difficult to attribute too much sense to them." Hers is a case of hysterical (over)reading. Lost in the text, she finds her own madness written there. But how does her reading of the wallpaper differ from readings of the story itself by contemporary feminist critics?

Two pioneering accounts of the assumptions involved in feminist reading have used as their example **"The Yellow Wallpaper"**—by now as much part of the feminist literary canon as Freud's *Dora*. Both Annette Kolodny's "A Map for Rereading: Or, Gender and the Interpretation of Literary Texts" and Jean E. Kennard's "Convention Coverage or How to Read Your Own Life" focus on the feminist deciphering of texts which are seen as having deeper, perhaps unacceptable meanings hidden beneath their palimpsestic surfaces. Kolodny's argument—that interpretative strategies are not only learned, but gender inflected—emphasizes the unreadability of texts by women embedded in a textual system which is controlled by men. Her own reading of **"The Yellow Wallpaper"** repeats the gesture of Gilman's narrator, finding in Gilman's story an emblem of women's dilemma within an interpretive community from which they are excluded as both readers and writers. For Kolodny, the doctor-husband's diagnosis anticipates the story's contemporary reception; male readers thought it merely chilling, while female readers were as yet apparently unable to see its relevance to their own situation. The "slight hysterical tendency" turns out to be, not that of Gilman's narrator or even of her story, but the hysterical blindness of Gilman's contemporary readers.

As Kolodny points out, John (the husband) "not only appropriates the interpretive processes of reading," determining the meaning of his wife's symptoms ("reading to her, rather than allowing her to read for herself"); he also forbids her to write. Kolodny's retelling of the story involves the selective emphasis and repression which she views as normative in any attempt to make meaning out of a complex literary text:

> From that point on, the narrator progressively gives up the attempt to *record* her reality and instead begins to *read* it—as symbolically adumbrated in her compulsion to discover a consistent and coherent pattern [in the wallpaper]. Selectively emphasizing one section of the pattern while repressing others, reorganizing and regrouping past impressions into newer, more fully realized configurations—as one might with any complex formal text—the speaking voice becomes obsessed with her quest for meaning. . . .

"What [the narrator] is watching . . . is her own psyche writ large," Kolodny concludes. But whose obsessive quest for meaning is this? Surely that of the feminist critic as she watches her interpretive processes writ small, finding a figure for feminist reading within the text. The result is a strange (that is, hysterical) literalization; the narrator, we are told, "comes more and more to experience herself as a text," and ends by being "totally surrendered to what is quite *literally* her own text." The literalization of figure (a symptom of the protagonist's hysteria) infects the interpretive process itself. Read as the case which exemplifies feminist reading, just as "Fraulein Anna O." exemplifies hysterical processes for Breuer and Freud, **"The Yellow Wallpaper"** becomes, not the basis for theory, but the model on which it is constructed. Ostensibly, Kolodny emphasizes the need to re-learn interpretive strategies. But her reading ends by suggesting that re-vision is really pre-vision—that we can only see what we have already read into the text. Meaning is pre-determined by the story we know; there is no room for the one we have forgotten.

As Kennard points out, surveying approaches such as Kolodny's, or Gilbert and Gubar's in *The Madwoman in the Attic*, readings that stress the social message of **"The Yellow Wallpaper"** (assuming both that the narrator's madness is socially induced and that her situation is common to all women) have become possible only as a result of "a series of conventions available to readers of the 1970s which were not available to those of 1892." Kennard summarizes the concepts associated with these conventions as: *patriarchy, madness, space,* and *quest.* Feminist interpretations of **"The Yellow Wallpaper"** have tended, inevitably, to see the story as an updated fictional treatment of Mary Wollstonecraft's theme in her novel, *The Wrongs of Woman: or, Maria* ("Was not the world a vast prison, and women born slaves?"); mental illness replaces imprisonment as the sign of women's social and sexual oppression. But how justifiable is it to read into Gilman's story a specifically feminist tendency of this kind? And what is the tendency of such thematic readings anyway? We have learned not only to symbolize (reading the narrator's confinement in a former nursery as symbolic of her infantilization) but to read confinement itself as symbolic of women's situation under patriarchy, and to see in madness not only the result of patriarchal attitudes but a kind of sanity—indeed, a perverse triumph; the commonsensical physician-husband is literally floored by his wife at the end of the story. As he loses consciousness, she finds herself in the madness whose existence he has denied.

The "feminist" reading contradicts the tendency to see women as basically unstable or hysterical, simultaneously (and contradictorily) claiming that women are not mad and that their madness is not their fault. But a thematic reading cannot account for the Gothic and uncanny elements present in the text. The assumption of what Jacqueline Rose calls "an unproblematic and one-to-one causality between psychic life and social reality" not only does away with the unconscious; it also does away with language. In the same way, the assumption of a one-to-one causality between the text and social reality does away with the unconscious of the text—specifically, with its literariness, the way in which it knows more than it knows (and more than the author intended). Formal features have no place in interpretations that simply substitute latent content for manifest content, bringing the hidden story uppermost. A kind of re-telling, feminist reading as Kennard defines it ends by translating the text into a cryptography (or pictograph) representing either women in patriarchal society or the woman as writer and reader. If we come to **"The Yellow Wallpaper"** with this story already in mind, we are likely to read it with what Freud calls "that blindness of the seeing eye" which relegates what doesn't fit in with our expectations to the realm of the unknown or unknowable.

The "feminist" reading turns out to be the rationalist reading after all ("the narrator is driven mad by confinement"). By contrast, signs that might point to an irrationalist, Gothic reading ("the narrator is driven mad by the wallpaper") are ignored or repressed. Kennard admits that although the "feminist" reading is the one she teaches her students, "Much is made in the novella of the color yellow; feminist readings do little with this." The color of sickness ("old foul, bad yellow things"), yellow is also the color of decay and, in a literary context, of Decadence (although the *Yellow Book* was not to appear until 1894). In

America, it gives its name to "the yellow press" and to the sensationalism ushered in during the mid-1890s by color printing. Gilman's wallpaper is at once lurid, angry, dirty, sickly, and old: "The color is repellent, almost revolting; a smouldering unclean yellow, strangely faded by the slow-turning sunlight . . . a dull yet lurid orange . . . a sickly sulphur tint"). The sensational ugliness of yellow is an unexplained given in Gilman's story. Yet the adjectival excess seems to signal not just the narrator's state of mind, but an inexplicable, perhaps repressed element in the text itself.

If feminist readings do little with the color of Gilman's title, they do even less with the creepiness of her story. Both Kolodny and Kennard ignore the uncanny altogether. Like the yellowness of the wallpaper, it is unaccountable, exceeding meaning; or rather, suggesting a meaning which resides only in the letter. The uncanny resists thematization, making itself felt as a "how" not a "what"— not as an entity, but rather as a phenomenon, like repetition. A symptom of this uncanny repetition in the letter of the text is the word "creepy," which recurs with a spectrum of meanings spanning both metaphorical and literal senses (seeming to remind us, along with Freud, that figurative expressions have their origin in bodily sensations). Gilman's contemporary readers (to a man) found the story strange, if not ghostly. Her own husband thought it "the most ghastly tale he ever read." The editor of *The Atlantic Monthly*, rejecting it, wrote that "I could not forgive myself if I made others as miserable as I have made myself!" and when he reprinted it in 1920, William Dean Howells called it a story to "freeze . . . our blood." The *OED* reveals that the word "creepy" starts as "characterized by creeping or moving slowly," only later taking on the sense of chill associated with the uncanny ("creeping of the flesh, or chill shuddering feeling, caused by horror or repugnance"). Toward the end of the nineteenth century, the term came to be used especially in a literary context (*OED*: "A really effective romance of the creepy order"; 1892—the year in which **"The Yellow Wallpaper"** was finally published in the *New England Magazine*). If Gilman wrote a minor classic of female Gothic, hers is not only a tale of female hysteria but a version of Gothic that successfully tapped male hysteria about women. What but femininity is so calculated to induce "horror or repugnance" in its male readers?

The story's stealthy uncanniness—its sidelong approach both to the condition of women and to the unspeakably repugnant female body—emerges most clearly in the oscillation of the word "creepy" from figurative to literal. The link between female oppression, hysteria, and the uncanny occurs in the letter of the text; in a word whose meaning sketches the repressed connection between women's social situation, their sickness, and their bodies. A reading of the "slight hysterical tendency" displayed by **"The Yellow Wallpaper"** involves tracing the repression whereby the female body itself becomes a figure for the uncanny and the subjection of women can surface only in the form of linguistic repetition. A necessary first move would be to recover its lost literary and political "unconscious." The setting for Gilman's story is "a colonial mansion, a hereditary estate, I would say a haunted house, and reach the

height of romantic felicity—but that would be asking too much of fate!" The trouble with the narrator is that her husband doesn't believe she's sick: the trouble with the text is its refusal of "romantic felicity." The narrator is no Jane Eyre (though the sister-in-law who is her "keeper," or "housekeeper," is named Jane) and her husband no Rochester ("John is practical in the extreme,"); yet she must play the role of both Jane Eyre, who at once scents and represses a mystery, and Bertha Mason, who explodes it while refusing all attempts at sublimation—"I thought seriously of burning the house," the narrator confesses at one point.

In this prosaic present, romance can only take the form of hallucination (like Anna O.'s daydreaming); or perhaps, the form of a woman deranged by confinement. Female oppression has been de-eroticized, making the woman's story at best merely creepy and at worst sensational, just as the colonial mansion has been emptied of its romantic past. The empty house evokes romantic reading ("It makes me think of English places that you read about"), with its hedges and walls and gates that lock, its shady garden, paths, and arbors, and its derelict greenhouses. The rationalist explanation ("some legal trouble . . . something about the heirs and co-heirs") "spoils my ghostliness," writes the narrator; "but I don't care—there is something strange about the house—I can feel it. I even said so to John one moonlight evening, but he said what I felt was a *draught*, and shut the window." Like the coolly rational Dr. John in *Villette*, who diagnoses Lucy's hysteria as "a case of spectral illusion . . . resulting from long-continued mental conflict." John comes to stand not only for unbelief ("He has no patience with faith") but for the repression of romantic reading. His *"draught"* is a literary breeze from *Wuthering Heights* ("the *height* of romantic felicity"?), and his gesture a repetition of Lockwood's in the nightmare that opens Emily Brontë's book. Indeed, like Lockwood confronted with the ghost of Cathy in his dream, John has "an intense horror of superstition" and scoffs at intangible presences ("things not to be felt and seen") as a way of shutting them out of house and mind. Hence his horrified loss of consciousness at the end of the story, when the narrator confronts him in all her feminine otherness.

Madness—the irrational—is what Doctor John's philosophy cannot dream of, and his repressive refusal of the unconscious makes itself felt in the narrator's inconsequential style and her stealthy confidences to the written page. But the same rationalist censorship also makes itself felt in Gilman's authorial relation to the uncanny. An age of doctors had made the tale of supernatural haunting a story about hysteria; no one dreamed of taking Anna O.'s death-head hallucinations seriously or believed that her *"absences"* or "split-off mind" were a form of demonic possession. As Freud points out, literature provides a much more fertile province for the uncanny than real life. A deranged narrator is licensed to think irrational thoughts and confide the unsayable to her journal ("I would not say it to a living soul, of course, but this is dead paper and a great relief to my mind"). Gilman herself only differs from the insane, in the words used by Alice James to describe the recollected torments of her own hysteria, in having imposed on her "not only all the horrors and sufferings of insanity but the duties of doctor, nurse, and straight-jacket." Medical knowledge, in other words, straight-jackets Gilman's text as well as her narrator: "I am a doctor, dear, and I know," John tells his wife. It is as if Gilman's story has had to repress its own ancestry in nineteenth-century female Gothic, along with the entire history of feminist protest. The house in **"The Yellow Wallpaper"** is strange because empty. An image of dispossession, it points to what Gilman can't say about the subjection of women, not only in literary terms, but politically—imaging the disinherited state of women in general, and also, perhaps, the symptomatic dispossession which had made Gilman herself feel that she had to take her stand against marriage alone, without the benefit of feminist forebears. Lacking a past, privatized by the family, all she had to go on was her personal feeling. *"Personally,"* the narrator opines near the start of the story ("Personally, I disagree with their ideas. Personally, I believe that congenial work . . . would do me good")—the subjection of women is also the enforced "subjectivity" of women, their constitution as subjects within an economy which defines knowledge as power and gives to women the disenfranchizing privilege of personal feeling uninformed by knowledge ("I am a doctor, dear, and I know"). In other words, an economy which defines female subjectivity as madness and debases the literature of the uncanny to the level of the merely creepy.

Mary Wollstonecraft's invective against the infantilization of women through sensibility and ignorance in *The Rights of Woman* becomes Gilman's depiction of marriage in terms of a disused attic room that has formerly been a nursery ("It was nursery first and then play-room and gymnasium, I should judge; for the windows are barred for little children, and there are rings and things in the walls"). But where Wollstonecraft had taken an enlightenment stance in her polemic (if not in her novel), Gilman is compelled to assume an irrationalist stance which she has no means of articulating directly; in her story, the irrational inhabits or haunts the rational as its ghostly other, hidden within it like the figure of a mad woman hidden in the nursery wallpaper. The site of repression, above all, the family is also the place that contains both strangeness and enslavement (as Engels reminds us in *The Origin of the Family, Private Property and the State,* the word "family", derives from "famulus," or household slave). For Freud, *"Heimlich"* and *"Unheimlich"* are never far apart; what is familiar returns as strange because it has been repressed. John may shut out the "draught," but the strangeness he fears is already within the home and creeps into the most intimate place of all, the marital bedroom—creeps in as both woman's estate and woman's body; at once timorous, stealthy, and abject; and then, because split off from consciousness, as alien.

The figure whom the narrator first glimpses in the wallpaper "is like a woman stooping down and *creeping* about behind that pattern," and by the light of the moon which *"creeps* so slowly" she watches "that undulating wallpaper till I felt *creepy"* (my italics). The meaning of the word "creep," according to the *OED*, like that of "creepy," starts from the body; and it too ends by encom-

passing a figurative sense: "1. To move with the body prone and close to the ground . . . a human being on hands and feet, or in a crouching posture"; "2. To move slowly, cautiously, timorously, or slowly; to move quietly or stealthily so as to elude observation"; and "3. fig. (of persons and things) a. To advance or come on slowly, stealthily, or by imperceptible degrees. . . . b. To move timidly or diffidently; to proceed humbly, abjectly, or servilely, to cringe." As "creepy" becomes "creep" we are reminded of Freud's formulation about the language of hysteria: "In taking a verbal expression literally . . . the hysteric is not taking liberties with words, but is simply reviving once more the sensations to which the verbal expression owes its justification." "Creepy" and "creep"—the female uncanny, the subjection of women, and the body—are linked by a semantic thread in the textual patterning of Gilman's story; only by letting ourselves become "lost in an unnecessary maze of sign-reading" like the narrator herself (and like Freud) can we trace the connection between female subjection and the repression of femininity; between the literature and the politics of women's oppression.

The narrator of **"The Yellow Wallpaper"** enacts her abject state first by timorousness and stealth (her acquiescence in her own "treatment," and her secret writing), then by creeping, and finally by going on all fours over the supine body of her husband. If she was Anna O., her creeping would be read as hysterical conversion, like a limp or facial neuralgia. At this point one can begin to articulate the relationship between the "feminist" reading, the hysterical reading, and the uncanny. The story is susceptible to what Kennard calls the "feminist" reading partly because the narrator herself glimpses not one but many women creeping both in and out of the wallpaper. But like the inconsequential, maddening pattern in the wallpaper—like a hysterical symptom—the repressed "creeping" figure begins to proliferate all over Gilman's text:

> It is the same woman, I know, for she is always creeping, and most women do not creep by daylight.
>
> I see her on that long road under the trees, creeping along, and when a carriage comes she hides under the blackberry vines.
>
> I don't blame her a bit. It must be very humiliating to be caught creeping by daylight!
>
> . . . . .
>
> I often wonder if I could see her out of all the windows at once.
>
> But, turn as fast as I can, I can only see out of one at one time.
>
> And though I always see her, she *may* be able to creep faster than I can turn!
>
> I have watched her sometimes away off in the open country, creeping as fast as a cloud shadow in a high wind.

And finally: "I don't like to *look* out of the windows even—there are so many of those creeping women, and they creep so fast."

As the creeping women imprisoned both in and out of the wallpaper become the creeping woman liberated from domestic secrecy ("I always lock the door when I creep by daylight") into overt madness ("It is so pleasant to be out in this great room and creep around as I please"—as the "creeping" figure is embodied in the narrator's hysterical acting out—there emerges also a creeping sense that the text knows more than she; perhaps more than Gilman herself. At the culmination of the story, the rationalist husband tries to break in on his wife's madness, threatening to take an axe to her self-enclosure in the repetitions of delusion and language. The story's punch line has all the violence of his attempted break-in:

> "What is the matter?" he cried. "For God's sake, what are you doing!"
>
> I kept on creeping just the same, but I looked at him over my shoulder.
>
> "I've got out at last," said I, "in spite of you and Jane. And I've pulled off most of the paper, so you can't put me back!"
>
> Now why should that man have fainted? But he did, and right across my path by the wall, so that I had to creep over him every time!

The docile wife and compliant patient returns as a defiant apparition, her rebellious strength revealed as the other of domesticated invalidism. This time it is the doctor who faints on the floor. But the story leaves us asking a creepy question. Did she tear and score the wallpaper round her bed herself, or has her madness been pre-enacted in the "haunted" house? Who bit and gnawed at the heavy wooden bed, gouged at the plaster, splintered the floor? What former inmate of the attic nursery was confined by those sinister rings in the wall? As readers versed in female gothic we know that Bertha Mason haunts this text; as readers of the feminist tradition from Wollstonecraft on, we know that the rights of women have long been denied by treating them as children. The uncanny makes itself felt as the return of a repressed past, a history at once literary and political—here, the history of women's reading.

"Now why should that man have fainted?" The narrator's question returns us to male hysteria. The body of woman is hystericized as the uncanny—defined by Freud as the sight of something that should remain hidden; typically, the sight of the female genitals. The woman on all fours is like Bertha Mason, an embodiment of the animality of woman unredeemed by (masculine) reason. Her creeping can only be physical—it is the story that assumes her displaced psychic uncanniness to become "creepy"—since by the end she is all body, an incarnation not only of hysteria but of male fears about women. The female hysteric displaces her thoughts onto her body: the male hysteric displaces his fear of castration, his anxiety, onto her genitals. Seemingly absent from **"The Yellow Wallpaper,"** both the female body (female sexuality) and male hysteria leave their traces on the paper in a stain or a whiff—in a yellow "smooch" and a yellow smell that first appear in metonymic proximity to one another in Gilman's text:

> But there is something else about that paper—

the smell! I noticed it the moment we came into the room. . . .

It creeps all over the house.

I find it hovering in the dining-room, skulking in the parlor, hiding in the hall, lying in wait for me on the stairs.

It gets into my hair.

Even when I go to ride, if I turn my head suddenly and surprise it—there is that smell!

Such a peculiar odor, too! I have spent hours in trying to analyze it, to find what it smelled like.

It is not bad—at first, and very gentle, but quite the subtlest, most enduring odor I ever met.

In this damp weather it is awful, I wake up in the night and find it hanging over me.

It used to disturb me at first. I thought seriously of burning the house—to reach the smell.

But now I am used to it. The only thing I can think of is that it is like the *color* of the paper! A yellow smell.

There is a very funny mark on this wall, low down, near the mopboard. A streak that runs round the room. It goes behind every piece of furniture, except the bed, a long, straight, even *smooch*, as if it had been rubbed over and over.

At the end of the story, the narrator's own shoulder "just fits in that long smooch around the wall." The mark of repetition, the uncanny trace made by the present stuck in the groove of the past, the "smooch" is also a smudge or smear, a reciprocal dirtying, perhaps (the wallpaper leaves "yellow smooches on all my clothes and John's"). In the 1890s, "smooch" had not taken on its slangy mid-twentieth-century meaning (as in "I'd rather have hooch/And a bit of a smooch" [1945]). The "smooch" on the yellow wallpaper cannot yet be a sexual caress, although dirty rubbing might be both Doctor John's medical verdict on sexuality and the story's hysterical literalization of it. As such, the dirty stain of smooching would constitute not just the unmentionable aspect of the narrator's genteel marital incapacity, but the unsayable in Gilman's story—the sexual etiology of hysteria, certainly (repressed in Gilman's as in Breuer's text); but also the repression imposed by the 1890s on the representation of female sexuality and, in particular, the repression imposed on women's writing.

And what of the "yellow smell"?—a smell that creeps, like the figure in the text; presumably the smell of decay, of "old foul, bad yellow things." *Studies on Hysteria* provides a comparable instance of a woman "tormented by subjective sensations of smell," the case of "Miss Lucy R.," an English governess secretly in love with the widowed father of her charges. Since, in Freud's words, "the subjective olfactory sensations . . . were recurrent hallucinations," he interprets them as hysterical symptoms. Miss Lucy R. is troubled first by "a smell of burnt pudding," and then, when the hallucination has been traced back to its originating episode, by the smell of cigar smoke. The episode of the burnt pudding turns out to be associated not only with her tender feelings for her employer's children but with tenderness for her employer ("I believe," Freud informs her, "that really you are in love with your employer . . . and that you have a secret hope of taking their mother's place"). The smell of cigar smoke proves to be a mnemonic symbol for a still earlier scene associated with the disappointing realization that her employer doesn't share her feelings. Here, hysterical smells function as a trace of something that has been intentionally forgotten—marking the place where unconscious knowledge has forced itself into consciousness, then been forcibly repressed once more. Freud does not pursue the question of smell any further in this context, although he does so elsewhere.

Jane Gallop's *The Daughter's Seduction* intriguingly suggests not only that smell is repressed by Freud's organization of sexual difference around a specular image ("sight of a phallic presence in the boy, sight of a phallic absence in the girl") but that smell in the Freudian text may have a privileged relation to female sexuality. The female stench, after all, is the unmentionable of misogynist scatology. Two disturbing or "smelly" footnotes in *Civilization and Its Discontents* seem to argue, according to Gallop, that prior to the privileging of sight over smell, "the menstrual process produced an effect on the male psyche by means of olfactory stimuli" and that "with the depreciation of his sense of smell . . . the whole of [man's] sexuality" fell victim to repression, since when "the sexual function has been accompanied by a repugnance which cannot further be accounted for." In other words (Gallop's own), "The penis may be more visible, but female genitalia have a stronger smell"; and that smell becomes identified with the smell of sexuality itself.

Gallop connects Freud's footnotes with an essay by Michèle Montrelay associating the immediacy of feminine speech and what she terms, italianately, the "*odor di femina*" emanating from it. Montrelay is reviewing *Recherches psychoanalytiques nouvelles sur la sexualité féminine*—a book which, combining theory with case histories like *Studies on Hysteria,* "take[s] us to the analyst's: there where the one who speaks is no longer the mouth-piece of a school, but the patient on the couch. . . . Here we have the freedom to follow the discourse of female patients in analysis in its rhythm, its style and its meanderings." "This book," Montrelay concludes, "not only talks of femininity according to Freud, but it also makes it speak in an immediate way. . . . An *odor di femina* arises from it." For Montrelay, feminine immediacy—predicated on the notion of an incompletely mediated relation between the female body, language, and the unconscious—produces anxiety which must be managed by representation; that is, by the privileging of visual representations in psychic organization. Or, as Gallop explicates Montrelay, "The '*odor di femina*' becomes odious, nauseous, because it threatens to undo the achievements of repression and sublimation, threatens to return the subject to the powerlessness, intensity, and anxiety of an immediate, unmediated connection with the body of the mother." The bad smell that haunts the narrator in **"The Yellow Wallpaper"** is both the one she makes and the smell of male hysteria emanating from her husband—that is, fear of feminini-

ty as the body of the mother ("old, foul, bad yellow things") which simultaneously threatens the boy with a return to the powerlessness of infancy and with anxiety about the castration she embodies.

"The Yellow Wallpaper," like the Freudian case history or the speech whose immediacy Montrelay scents, offers only the illusion of feminine discourse. What confronts us in the text is not the female body, but a figure for it. The figure in the text of **"The Yellow Wallpaper"** is "a strange, provoking, formless sort of figure, that seems to skulk about behind that silly and conspicuous front design." A formless figure? "*Absences*" could scarcely be more provoking. Produced by a specular system as nothing, as lack or absence, woman's form is by definition formless. Yet both for the hysteric and for Freud, figuration originates in the body—in "sensations and innervations . . . now for the most part . . . so much weakened that the expression of them in words seems to us only to be a figurative picture of them . . . hysteria is right in restoring the original meaning of the words and depicting its unusually strong innervations." The hysterical symptom (a smell, a paralysis, a cough) serves as just such a trace of "original" bodily meaning. Figuration itself comes to be seen as a linguistic trace, a "smooch" that marks the body's unsuccessful attempt to evade the repressiveness of representation.

What is infuriating (literally, maddening—"a lack of sequence, a defiance of law, that is a constant irritant to a normal mind") about the yellow wallpaper is its resistance to being read: "It is dull enough to confuse the eye in following, pronounced enough to constantly irritate and provoke study, and when you follow the lame uncertain curves for a little distance they suddenly suicide—plunge at outrageous angles, destroy themselves in unheard-of contradictions." A hideous enigma, the pattern has all the violence of nightmares ("It slaps you in the face, knocks you down, and tramples upon you. It is like a bad dream"). But perhaps the violence is really that of interpretation. The "figure" in the text is at once a repressed figure (that of a woman behind bars) and repressive figuration. Shoshana Felman asks, "what, indeed, is the unconscious if not—in every sense of the word—a *reader*?" Like the examinations undergone by Lucy Snowe and Anna O., interpretive reading involves the specular appropriation or silencing of the text. Only the insistence of the letter resists forcible translation.

In Gilman's story, the narrator-as-unconscious embarks on a reading process remarkably like Freud's painstaking attempts, not simply to unravel, but, more aggressively, to wrest meaning from the hysterical text in *Studies on Hysteria*: "by detecting lacunas in the patient's first description . . . we get hold of a piece of the logical thread at the periphery. . . . In doing this, we very seldom succeed in making our way right into the interior along one and the same thread. As a rule it breaks off half-way . . ."; and finally, "We drop it and take up another thread, which we may perhaps follow equally far. When we have . . . discovered the entanglements on account of which the separate threads could not be followed any further in isolation, we can think of attacking the resistance before us afresh." The language of attack entangles Freud himself in a

Thesean fantasy about penetrating the maze to its center ("I *will* follow that pointless pattern to some sort of a conclusion," writes Gilman's narrator, with similarly obsessional persistence).

The meaningless pattern in the yellow wallpaper not only refuses interpretation; it refuses to be read as a text—as anything but sheer, meaningless repetition ("this thing was not arranged on any laws of radiation, or alternation, or repetition or symmetry, or anything else that I ever heard of"). Attempts to read it therefore involve the (repressive) substitution of something—a figure—for nothing. At first the pattern serves simply to mirror the narrator's own specular reading, endlessly repeated in the figure of eyes ("the pattern lolls like a broken neck and two bulbous eyes stare at you upside down. . . . Up and down and sideways they crawl, and those absurd, unblinking eyes are everywhere"). But as the process of figuration begins to sprout its own autonomous repertoire of metaphors ("bloated curves and flourishes—a kind of 'debased Romanesque' with *delirium tremens*"; "great slanting waves of optic horror, like a lot of wallowing seaweeds in full chase"), it becomes clear that figures feed parasitically on resistance to meaning; the pattern "remind[s] one of a fungus. If you can imagine a toadstool in joints, an interminable string of toadstools, budding and sprouting in endless convolutions—why, that is something like it." The function of figuration is to manage anxiety; any figuration is better than none—even a fungoid growth is more consoling than sheer absence.

Learning to read might be called a hysterical process, since it involves substituting a bodily figure for the self-reproducing repetitions of textuality. Significantly, the narrator's sighting of a figure in the text—her own—inscribes her madness most graphically. As the "dim shape" becomes clearer, the pattern "becomes bars! The outside pattern, I mean, and the woman behind as plain as can be. I didn't realize for a long time what the thing was that showed behind, that dim subpattern, but now I am quite sure it is a woman." The figure of bars functions in Gilman's text to make the narrator's final embodiment as mad woman look like a successful prison break from the tyranny of a meaningless pattern: "The woman behind shakes it! . . . she crawls around fast, and her crawling shakes it all over . . . she just takes hold of the bars and shakes them hard. And she is all the time trying to climb through." The climax of Gilman's story has her narrator setting to work to strip off the paper and liberate the figure which by now both she and we—hysterically identified with her reading—recognize as her specular double: "As soon as it was moonlight and that poor thing began to crawl and shake the pattern, I got up and ran to help her. I pulled and she shook, I shook and she pulled, and before morning we had peeled off yards of that paper." And finally, "I've got out at last . . . so you can't put me back!"

The figure here is the grammatical figure of chiasmus, or crossing (*OED*: "The order of words in one of two parallel clauses is inverted in the other"). "I pulled and she shook, I shook and she pulled" prepares us for the exchange of roles at the end, where the woman reading (and writing) the text becomes the figure of madness within it. Gilman's story hysterically embodies the formal or grammatical figure; but the same process of figuration dimly underlies (like the "dim shape" or "dim sub-pattern") our own reading. By the very fact of reading it as narrative, hysterical or otherwise, we posit the speaking or writing subject called "the narrator." "*Figure*" also means face, and face implies a speaking voice. In this sense, figure becomes the trace of the bodily presence without which it would be impossible to read **"The Yellow Wallpaper"** as a first-person narrative, or even as a displaced form of autobiography.

The chiastic figure provides a metaphor for the hysterical reading which we engage in whenever the disembodied text takes on the aspect of a textual body. Since chiasmus is at once a specular figure and a figure of symmetrical inversion, it could be regarded as the structure of phallogocentrism itself, where word and woman mirror only the presence of the (masculine) body, reinforcing the hierarchy man/woman, presence/absence. Is there a way out of the prison? The bars shaken and mistaken by the madwoman might, in a different linguistic narrative, be taken for the constitutive bar between signifier and signified. The gap between sign and meaning is the absence that the hysteric attempts to abolish or conceal by textualizing the body itself. Montrelay writes of the analyst's discourse as "not reflexive, but different. As such it is a *metaphor*, not a mirror, of the patient's discourse." For Montrelay, metaphor engenders a pleasure which is that of "*putting the dimension of repression into play on the level of the text itself*"—of articulating or designating what is not spoken, what is unspeakable, yet incompletely repressed, about the feminine body. The ultimate form of this unmentionable pleasure would be feminine jouissance, or meaning that exceeds the repressive effects of interpretation and figuration. Montrelay's formulation risks its own literalness, that of (hysterically) assuming an unmediated relation between feminine body and word. But her story follows the same trajectory as Gilman's. The end of **"The Yellow Wallpaper"** is climactic because Doctor John, previously the censor of women's writing (as Felman demands, "how can one write *for* the very figure who signifies the suppression of what one has to say to him?"), catches the text, as it were, *in flagrante delicto*. The return of the repressed, in Freud's scenario, always figures the sight of the castrated female body. What we glimpse in this moment of figuration is the return of the letter in all its uncanny literalness to overwhelm us with the absence which both male and female hysteria attempt to repress in the name of woman. (pp. 229-48)

Mary Jacobus, "An Unnecessary Maze of Sign-Reading," in her Reading Woman: Essays in Feminist Criticism, *Columbia University Press, 1986, pp. 229-48.*

Gloria A. Biamonte   (essay date 1988)

[*Below, Biamonte provides a thematic and stylistic analysis of the short story "The Giant Wistaria," stating that the elements in this story anticipate many of those found in "The Yellow Wallpaper."*]

Many of Charlotte Perkins Gilman's theoretical works analyze the relationship of women to their society. Con-

An excerpt from "The Yellow Wallpaper"

I don't know why I should write this.

I don't want to.

I don't feel able.

And I know John would think it absurd. But I *must* say what I feel and think in some way—it is such a relief!

But the effort is getting to be greater than the relief.

Half the time now I am awfully lazy, and lie down ever so much.

John says I mustn't lose my strength, and has me take cod liver oil and lots of tonics and things, to say nothing of ale and wine and rare meat.

Dear John! He loves me very dearly, and hates to have me sick. I tried to have a real earnest reasonable talk with him the other day, and tell him how I wish he would let me go and make a visit to Cousin Henry and Julia.

But he said I wasn't able to go, nor able to stand it after I got there; and I did not make out a very good case for myself, for I was crying before I had finished.

It is getting to be a great effort for me to think straight. Just this nervous weakness I suppose.

And dear John gathered me up in his arms, and just carried me upstairs and laid me on the bed, and sat by me and read to me till it tired my head.

He said I was his darling and his comfort and all he had, and that I must take care of myself for his sake, and keep well.

He says no one but myself can help me out of it, that I must use my will and self-control and not let any silly fancies run away with me.

There's one comfort, the baby is well and happy, and does not have to occupy this nursery with the horrid wallpaper.

If we had not used it, that blessed child would have! What a fortunate escape! Why, I wouldn't have a child of mine, an impressionable little thing, live in such a room for worlds.

I never thought of it before, but it is lucky that John kept me here after all, I can stand it so much easier than a baby, you see.

Of course I never mention it to them any more—I am too wise—but I keep watch for it all the same.

There are things in that paper that nobody knows but me, or ever will.

Behind that outside pattern the dim shapes get clearer every day.

It is always the same shape, only very numerous.

And it is like a woman stooping down and creeping about behind that pattern.

I don't like it a bit. I wonder—I begin to think—I wish John would take me away from here!

Charlotte Perkins Gilman, in her "The Yellow Wall-Paper," reprinted in The Practical Imagination: Stories, Poems, Plays, *Harper & Row, 1987.*

cerned with the destructiveness of rigidly segregating women into sex-related functions, Gilman repeatedly asserted the need to realize women's potential for contribution to the human sphere. *Women and Economics* (1898) most fully expounds Gilman's theories, while it turned her into an idol for many radical feminists and contributed to her later renown as "the most original and challenging mind which the woman's movement produced." But, Gilman's theoretical writing tells only part of the story.

Complementing the excessive reliance on reason in her theoretical works, Gilman's fiction presents a panorama of female heroes—heroes whose visionary quests not only alter their reality but enable them to achieve a new power within it. These female characters vividly bring to life Gilman's theories, suggesting metaphorically the radical restructuring of society she advocated.

"The Giant Wistaria" published in June 1891 in the *New England Magazine* contains the seeds for the restructuring Gilman sought. Published one year before **"The Yellow Wallpaper,"** **"The Giant Wistaria"** anticipates many of the elements later found in the explosive story based on Gilman's own breakdown following her daughter's birth and, more importantly, following the devastating effects of Philadelphia neurologist S. Weir Mitchell's "rest cure." Gilman describes the treatment in her autobiography:

'Live as domestic a life as possible. Have your child with you all the time.' (Be it remarked that if I did but dress the baby it left me shaking and crying—certainly far from a healthy companionship for her, to say nothing of the effect on me.) 'Lie down an hour after each meal. Have but two hours' intellectual life a day. And never touch pen, brush or pencil as long as you live.'

Nearly going insane from a "cure" requiring extended bed rest, inactivity, isolation, and a totally domestic life, Gilman, not unexpectedly, chose to focus in her fiction on the concerns of motherhood, creativity, and confinement—concerns often accompanied by creative attempts at liberation. And, in the opening lines of **"The Giant Wistaria,"** these issues become obvious.

"The Giant Wistaria" presents two linked stories, the older one a painful tale of destroyed motherhood, the recent one a narrative of discovery and interpretation. In the recent narrative, Jenny (the name given to **"The Yellow Wallpaper's"** nameless narrator's sister-in-law), is convinced that the summer house she and her husband are renting is haunted:

But I'm convinced *there is* a story, if we could only find it. You need not tell me that a house like this, with a garden like this, and a cellar like this, isn't haunted!

Jenny, her husband, and her friends move toward uncovering a century-old tale of a woman and her child—a tale which we, as readers, have been partly told in the opening segment of the story.

Gilman's opening vignette takes place in the eighteenth century in the house that 100 years later is rented by Jenny and her husband George. In this early tale of "illegitimacy," grief, imprisonment, and suffering, a nameless young woman is breaking the tender shoots of her mother's wistaria vine, brought over on the boat from England by her father, and pleading for permission to see her child, a child born out of wedlock and now locked away in the attic with "a hard-faced serving woman" attending to it.

Though her mother refuses her wish, she tries to quiet her daughter's words before they are stopped by her father's hand. The mother is, however, too late. Infuriated by what he perceives to be her shamelessness, Samuel Dwining (the only character given a name in the opening sketch) has his daughter locked away in an upper room where we later see her gazing out of the window. After his initial outburst, the father informs his wife that they will be leaving the following day for England in order to save "our house from open shame." Expressing no feeling for his daughter's wishes, Samuel plans to marry her to her cousin, "a coarse fellow" whom, as her mother sympathetically observes, the daughter shuns. Thus, he hopes to separate her permanently from her child, and transplant her in a land where her "sin" will remain undiscovered.

Samuel feels his protesting wife is mad to think of their daughter's wishes, and since his desire to see her drowned remains an unfulfilled act of Providence, he will give her "a new life to cover the old." The prefatory sketch begins with Mistress Dwining's words to her daughter asking her not to meddle with the new vine (she instinctively desires to keep her daughter away from her husband's gift—a gift whose potency is later made evident), and closes with the daughter's white face gazing from the prison window of her upper room as her "eyes of wasted fire" peer through the shadows.

Gilman breaks the story's solemn tone as she moves us 100 years ahead into the nineteenth century with Jenny's excited words to her husband George:

> O, George, what a house! what a lovely house!
> I am sure it's haunted! Let us get that house to
> live in this summer! We will have Kate and Jack
> and Susy and Jim of course, and a splendid time
> of it!

The huge wistaria vine that covers the whole front of the house, wrenching the porch pillars from their place and holding them "rigid and helpless by the tightly wound and knotted arms" lets us know that this is, in fact, the same house, and that a good deal of time has passed. Like the "ancestral halls" in **"The Yellow Wallpaper,"** the wistaria-covered house has long been untenanted, except for a back apartment where the caretakers live. Easily rented for the summer, the house does not initially fulfill Jenny's desire for ghosts who will reveal its story. As George tells their friends who join them for a vacation, "she made up her mind at first sight to have ghosts in the house, and she can't even find a ghost story!"

But George's condescension will not last long. Now hav-

ing in Jenny a willing listener to hear her tale, the spirit of the imprisoned woman returns to leave wordless impressions of her history. After an evening of storytelling and imagining the horrors that might surround them—the trees that "for all the world [look] like a crouching, hunted figure" and the giant wistaria trunk looking "for all the world like a writhing body—cringing—beseeching"—the six friends wander off to bed with Jenny's words ringing in their ears: "We shall all surely dream." And, of course, they do.

But the similarity in their dream-like experiences frightens them into action. While the shadows of the wistaria leaves crawl over her moonlit bedroom floor, Jenny hears the rattling and creaking of the chain on the well, dragging across the cellar floor. Jack, it seems, has seen the shadow of a "crouching, hunted figure . . . wrapped up in a shawl, and [carrying] a big bundle under her arm." Frantic with terror, the crouching figure rummages through one of the bureau drawers, but before she glides noiselessly away, Jack notices the little red cross around her neck. Grounding these tales in a frightening reality, George tells how, after giving Jenny bromides for her nerves, he went to the cellar in search of burglars only to see "a woman hunched up under a shawl," holding the well's chain, and wearing a red cross around her neck. But when he reaches down to touch her, she is not there.

So, after discussion over breakfast, off they go to the basement, and though we fear what they will discover in the well bucket, it is not until they return to the sunlight in front of the house that Jenny asks: "How old should you think it was, George?" Unsure whether she means the age of the found infant or how long it was there, George answers both questions, letting her know that the one-month old baby preserved in the lime in the well water had been there for "all of a century." But the silence that follows George's revelation is soon broken by the cry of the workmen, who are rebuilding the uprooted porch, for beneath it, in the cellar and held "in the strangling grasp of the roots of the great wistaria, lay the bones of a woman, from whose neck still hung a tiny scarlet cross on a thin chain of gold." And so the story ends.

Rich in images and themes that abound in Gilman's later fiction, **"The Giant Wistaria"** begins Gilman's examination of a female world, not as simply a world inhabited by women and filled with the experiences of their lives, but a world that communicates its stories in its own unique way and needs a receptive and knowing audience to be heard. The unnamed young mother of the opening segment deplores her father's brutal separation of her from her child; nor does she give into his attempt to place her within the confines of a forced marriage that would "cover" her chosen life with one of *his own making*. She appeals to her mother, who as a mother and a woman might understand her perspective, unlike her father who considers her motherhood a "blot" and "stain" that casts "shame" on their house. Though she does understand her daughter's plea, the mother is powerless to help, her words only causing her husband to question: "Art thou mad, woman?" But in the end, the young woman's refusal to participate in a tale not of her own making proves fatal in a world that will not allow her *to create her own story,* choose her own identity, mother the child she has borne regardless of her society's sanction of her actions.

Left by her parents who return to England (and we can only imagine her mother's suffering as she becomes the second woman to be forced by her husband to leave a child behind), the young woman does not survive. An impenetrable silence surrounds her relationship with the father of her child. No words remain to express her pain. We do not know whether she found her way out of her room; nor do we know who placed her child in the well. Did her father upon hearing her refusal to return to England kill the child? Did he, in fact, kill her? Or, was the horror of that decision left to the young mother, who, deserted by family, locked away in her chamber, and without a supportive community to turn to, saw death as the only answer to a life she could not recreate, or using a metaphor that Gilman vividly brings to life in **"The Yellow Wallpaper,"** could not rewrite?

However, this woman's story does not remain unheard. The cellar becomes her grave, and the tree that grasps her in its roots disrupts the foundation of the "haunted house." The giant wistaria which gives the story its name not only covers the entire front of the house, it runs "along eaves, holding up the gutter that had once supported it." Supporting the house after destroying its human-made foundation and replacing it with a natural one, the

Gilman in 1876.

"ghost" of this woman creates a different sort of "text" for her story. Her text becomes the place of her imprisonment in the same way as the yellow wallpaper becomes the nameless narrator's new medium of expression once her "loving" husband prohibits her from writing.

And so, this giant wistaria, throwing "moving shadows, like little stretching fingers," calls out for a reader, and finds one in another woman a century later.

Jenny, though her husband mocks her, knows right away that the house is haunted and has a tale to tell. Unable to interpret the signs around them, the men gently ridicule the women's perception that something is strange in the house. Jack, the reporter, will make up a ghost if they do not find a real one, attempting like Samuel Dwining to place his version of the ghost's story over an alternative reality he cannot perceive, for "it's too good of an opportunity to lose!" But, Kate won't allow him to make fun of the women's perceptions, for she is sure "this is a *real* ghostly place." Where she perceives "a crouching, hunted figure," Jim sees "a woman picking huckleberries," as he, like Jack, is unable to conceptualize the world these women perceive. Kate and Jenny's perceptions are also validated by Susy, who sees a "writhing body" in the wistaria vine, one that calls out to them. But Jim also mocks her words with his condescending retort:

> 'Yes,' answered the subdued Jim, "it does, Susy. See its waist,—about two yards of it, and twisted at that! A waste of good material!"

Playing with Susy's words, Jim denies her perceptions, but Jenny's closing prediction for a night of ghostly dreams comes horrifyingly to life for both the men and the women.

What Jenny, Kate, and Susy, or George, Jack, and Jim will do with the fragments left of this woman's tale remains unclear. The women's willingness to acknowledge the spirit felt in the house has turned a long-time emptied dwelling into an unexpected text—a text of suffering inflicted on a woman unable to gain control over her own life; a text that vividly paints the destructiveness of male control in defining women's lives—a destructiveness that in **"The Giant Wistaria"** perverts the realm of motherhood into one of sin, into a tale of death and oppression rather than one of life and growth; a text that suggests the different conceptual and perceptual worlds that men and women live in, and that paves the way for a female community that will hear, transmit, and create more liveable tales for future women.

In the fictional works that follow this short story, Gilman continues to explore the worlds women can create and the power they can develop. Envisioning a power that grows once women remove themselves from the destructive confines of the patriarchal home, Gilman creates female heroes who free themselves of the external and often internalized negative stereotypes of femininity, find the work that will fulfill them and bring the economic independence necessary for further growth, create a network of supportive female friends, and, in many of the novels and short stories, metaphorically and literally rename themselves and learn a new language, giving name and voice to the woman left strangled beneath the cellar a century before. (pp. 33-37)

> Gloria A. Biamonte, "'. . . There Is a Story, If We Could Only Find It': Charlotte Perkins Gilman's 'The Giant Wistaria'," in LEGA-CY, Vol. 5, No. 2, Fall, 1988, pp. 33-8.

Polly Wynn Allen   (essay date 1988)

[*In the following excerpt from her* Building Domestic Liberty: Charlotte Perkins Gilman's Architectural Feminism, *Allen identifies Gilman's short stories as effective vehicles for the writer's ideas on female autonomy, self-identity, and nonsexist living arrangements.*]

Charlotte Gilman did not agonize over the writing of her realistic short stories and novels as she did over her social ethics. Instead she wrote them casually, almost in sport. Even so, she was mindful of their educational potential. She recognized the capacity of strong fiction to move people, confiding to her diary in 1893, "If I can learn to write good stories it will be a powerful addition to my armory."

In spite of this awareness, Gilman consistently judged her philosophy to be of much greater social significance than her fiction. Except for **"The Yellow Wallpaper,"** she scarcely mentioned her story writing in her autobiography except to say that she had written tales to help support herself and her family. In the *Forerunner*'s first year, she expressed the modest hope that her stories would provide "interest and amusement" to her readers.

The realistic story, more than the utopian one, was Gilman's forte. In it she typically portrayed an ordinary white middle-class woman (or group of women) wrestling with common dilemmas that pit family obligations against individual ones. Convinced that such conflicts could best be resolved architecturally, she conjured up settings in some stage of feminist transformation for about one-third of her stories.

Gilman wanted her fiction to reinforce the individual aspirations of women. She hoped that the struggles of her imaginary heroines would encourage her female readers to take themselves seriously as autonomous actors on the stage of history. Through her stories, she tried to communicate the unfamiliar notion that women's efforts to achieve personal independence were full of moral significance.

Gilman could have said about all her fiction what she said of **"The Yellow Wallpaper"**: "I wrote it to preach. If it is literature, that just happened." Stating her aims in 1926, she wrote: "One girl reads this, and takes fire! Her life is changed. She becomes a power—a mover of others—I write for her." Gilman planed her feminist ideas in fictional gardens, the artistic quality of which was only an incidental concern. Her guiding hope as storyteller was to cultivate the soil, to enlarge the common woman's sense of what was possible.

In an explicit way, the central point of Gilman's realistic fiction was to juxtapose woman's old morality of minding the domestic sphere with her new morality of responsible self-fulfillment in the world. She aimed to demonstrate conclusively both the superiority and the rightness of the new morality. She accomplished this by creating contrasting characters living by the two codes as well as characters struggling to move from the domestic code to the higher one. She was forthright about treating the moral dilemmas of women, using such titles as **"Turned," "A Cleared Path," "Making a Change," "Mary Button's Principles," "Mrs. Powers' Duty,"** and **"Mrs. Merrill's Duties."**

In an implicit way, many of Gilman's stories testified powerfully to the liberating potential of nonsexist spatial design. By means of architectural backdrops, much of her fiction portrayed very tangible ways of solving the problems of isolated, overworked women. Being able to move into a more socialized dwelling or to join forces with other women in common spaces were opportunities she encouraged every woman to pursue.

Gilman created four types of feminist environment in her realistic fiction. In one, she portrayed apartment hotels or boardinghouses as the setting for progressively liberated life styles. In a second cluster of tales, she depicted groups of neighboring residences, linked to central facilities for laundry, child care, food delivery, and cleaning services. Women form alliances in a third group of stories, associations that meet in clubhouses to foster sisterly cooperation both in the conduct of domestic life and in training for employment outside the home. A fourth set of stories celebrates the existence of recuperative spaces, most often located in the country, run by women and for women.

In **"Forsythe and Forsythe,"** four professional people find romance and supportive simplicity in an apartment hotel in Seattle, Washington. The name of the story refers to a man and woman, George and Georgiana Forsythe, who are husband and wife as well as cousins. Equal partners both at work and at home, they find respite from their joint practice of law in two adjoining (and distinctively decorated) apartments. Whereas George's flat is "undeniably bachelorish," there is "a wholesome femininity" in the decor of Georgiana's. Among the amenities available in the building are a restaurant on one of the lower floors and a child-care center on the roof.

In the story's rather thin plot, George's old friend Jim Jackson comes to visit Forsythe and Forsythe, at home. With a reputation for being "Rigidly conservative, even reactionary," Jackson is highly skeptical at the outset about such unorthodox living arrangements. But gradually two factors bring him around. First, "He grew used to the smooth convenience of the apartment very rapidly, even tacitly approved of the steady excellence of the food and service." Second, he can't resist the charms of the strongly independent, "mischievous" Clare Forsythe, who is George's sister and Jackson's former sweetheart. In the nine years since they have seen each other, Clare has established herself as a prominent "sanitary engineer" (plumber?), living in her own apartment in the same building as her brother and sister-in-law. Jackson finds the attraction of Clare much "greater than the repulsion caused by her limitless progressive views." Conveniently, Jackson's estranged wife mails him divorce papers just as the story ends, freeing the former skeptic to declare his love for Ms. Forsythe and to embrace her liberated life style wholeheartedly.

Gilman wanted her fiction to reinforce the individual aspirations of women. She hoped that the struggles of her imaginary heroines would encourage her female readers to take themselves seriously as autonomous actors on the stage of history.

—*Polly Wynn Allen*

In **"Her Housekeeper,"** an unusual domestic environment is instrumental in winning the heart of a beautiful actress. Widowed after an unhappy marriage, Mrs. Leland is determined never to wed again. Committed to pursuing her promising career as well as protecting her freedom, she sees marriage as profoundly threatening to both. Above all, she wants to avoid domestic drudgery. "I hate—I'd like to write a dozen tragic plays to show how much I hate—Housekeeping!" she exclaims to Arthur Olmstead, a would-be suitor and fellow resident of a flourishing boardinghouse.

Slowly but surely, over a period of several months, Olmstead persuades Mrs. Leland that marriage to *him* would not involve any such dreary entrapments. As a matter of fact, he demonstrates that he has the means, the skill, and the temperament to relieve her forever of housewifely chores. He often entertains Mrs. Leland and her five-year-old son, Johnny, charmingly, in his apartment. One day he tells her that his real estate business (about which he had been purposefully vague) consists of running apartment hotels such as the one both he and she occupy. In fact, he owns their very residence as well as several others.

For as long as she had lived there, Mrs. Leland had reveled in the building's excellent cooked-food service, patronizing both the downstairs restaurant and the room-service delivery made possible by an automatic dumbwaiter attached to her flat. Furthermore, she had marveled at Mr. Olmstead's nurturant manner with children, as expressed toward Johnny. One day she complimented this remarkable man as follows: "Do you know you are a real comfort? . . . I never knew a man before who could—well leave off being a man for a moment and just be a human creature." Convinced at last that she and Mr. Olmstead could make a very positive, unconventional marriage while maintaining (and even enhancing) their spatially supportive environment, Mrs. Leland marries "Her Housekeeper" and proceeds to live happily ever after. (pp. 145-48)

In a second group of Gilman's short stories, the liberated domestic environment consists of systems of linkages between households. In three of the stories, an enterprising heroine takes responsibility for establishing a domestic service and/or business in a particular neighborhood. (p. 151)

Mary Watterson, the twenty-eight-year-old heroine of **"A Cleared Path,"** owns and runs a small, diversified business in Los Angeles. Among the domestic services her "marvelous little shop" offers to the surrounding community are a small laundry, a sewing and mending bureau, and a sales outlet for children's ready-made clothing. Having been built up over an eight-year period, Watterson's business is a "model" both of exemplary labor relations (her employees, who are partners in a system of "profit sharing," have "charming work-rooms" in which to sew, mend, launder, or sell) and of "honesty, accuracy and efficiency." Spurred by the "phenomenal growth" in the city of Los Angeles, the business has done exceedingly well. As a result, the owner has branched out a bit, investing her surplus in a few pieces of real estate.

A feminist love story ensues, involving Ms. Watterson and Ransome Woodruff, a New Englander-turned-Montana-rancher, who is visiting his sister in southern California. After meeting Mary, Woodruff repeatedly extends the length of his sojourn in Los Angeles. His fascination with her proceeds from respect to passionate attraction and total commitment. Ms. Watterson's feelings for Woodruff are perfectly equivalent.

Throughout the story, Woodruff struggles to overcome his old-fashioned convictions about marriage. He believes that in circumstances like theirs the wife is the one who must relocate. This would mean that Watterson would have to give up her business and move to Montana. She wants none of that. After much soul searching, conversation, and consciousness raising, Woodruff sees the light and decides to sell his ranch so he can move to Los Angeles. He apologizes to Mary for having been "just a plain pig," and the story ends with the news that "in truth they were married the next day." Gilman thus made her point dramatically that a woman's work in the world is "a higher duty" than following her heart, especially when the work involves such "distinctly social" service to the world as a central housekeeping business.

The housekeeping service that gets reorganized communally in **"Making a Change"** is child care. Like many of Gilman's female characters, Julia Gordins is frustrated to the point of impending insanity by the conflicting claims of her family's care and the expression of her life work. A gifted musician who had taught piano and violin before her marriage, Gordins is afflicted by the notion that a married woman must take personal responsibility for all the needs of her family. In particular, the round-the-clock demands of her newborn son, Albert, have exhausted her to the point of derangement. Julia's mother-in-law, Mrs. Gordins, who resides with the young family, has repeatedly offered her services as nursemaid. But Julia's sense of duty, pride, and wifely devotion will not permit her to accept them. And so she suffers, as do her sleepless husband and frustrated mother-in-law.

The combination of internecine hostility and chronic fatigue weighs so heavily on Gordins that one day she decides to end her life. As her husband leaves for work, she is feeling heavily despondent, but he fails to perceive it. After bumbling through the baby's bath, she uncharacteristically asks the senior Mrs. Gordins to mind the baby and proceeds to her room. After a short time, the older woman smells gas, quickly looks for its source, and, having found it, nimbly enters the transom window to rescue Julia.

In the aftermath of this crisis, the generation gap disappears. Mrs. Gordins comes to cherish the young woman as her very own daughter. As the trust between them grows, they devise a plan for starting a neighborhood child-care center on the roof and top floor of their building. The grandmother happily assumes the role of "baby garden" coordinator, furnishing the rooftop with sandpile, seesaws, swings, floor mattresses, and a shallow pool. The threefold purpose of this establishment is to allow Julia Gordins to resume her musical career, to employ the underutilized talents of the senior Mrs. Gordins, and to provide a much-needed social service. Gilman frequently suggested in her stories that women's intergenerational needs for self-expression, like those of the older and the younger Mrs. Gordins, should be approached simultaneously, in a complementary, mutually supportive manner.

"Old Mrs. Crosley" is another story in which a felicity of matched needs is found. Here Gilman expressed concern for the middle-aged woman facing the "empty nest" syndrome. Written when Gilman herself was fifty-one, it is a morality tale about a fifty-two-year-old woman who decides there can be meaningful life after her last baby marries and becomes a father.

In the first part of the story, Mrs. Crosley is depressed because of her age and her lost raison d'être. Her three children are living their own lives in three distinct cities. Mr. Crosley, her fifty-four-year-old husband, has entered a new phase of his life by taking up politics, which he loves. Mrs. Crosley feels apathetic, unskilled, and lonely. Although her home runs smoothly and comfortably, she does not take pride in that fact because she believes she owes it all to her two servants, a cook and a maid.

One evening when she is feeling particularly old and worthless, Mrs. Crosley receives a visit from John Fairmount, the young minister of her church. Expressing his sympathetic concern for her as a fellow human soul, the Reverend Mr. Fairmount assists Mrs. Crosley in identifying an important skill she possesses but has never acknowledged. She is a great personnel manager. She has had extraordinary success in hiring household workers, training them, and maintaining their morale. She is the only woman in town with "excellent servants." He urges her to turn this unusual ability into a community venture.

Over the objections of her husband and children, Mrs. Crosley starts a business that trains and furnishes household help on either an hourly or a permanent, full-time basis. Her "Newcome Agency" offers centralized services as well as a labor bureau. She puts some of her well-trained laborers to work running a laundry and a cooked-food shop. In addition to getting her started, John Fairmount continues to give her support and encouragement, drumming up business for her agency wherever he goes. (pp. 151-53)

Gilman told several stories about what women could do collectively to augment their individual powers. Pending

the development of domestically integrated neighborhoods, she advocated the establishment of women's alliances everywhere so that women could meet together regularly for recreation and collaboration. Since there were not many socialized residential areas with shared services at the time she wrote, these tales were aimed to show readers how they might get such facilities started.

Gilman set two of these stories in England: **"A Council of War"** and **"A Surplus Woman."** Though neither has as much dramatic vitality as the best of her stories, these two British tales set forth in succinct fashion Gilman's sense of feminist political strategy.

Although **"A Council of War"** is very diffuse, this earlier story contains some tough realism about the bitter conflicts aroused by women's struggle for empowerment. In it a group of "between twenty and thirty" women meet in London for a conversation about their frustrations and their strategic options for overcoming them. They discuss sexism, antifeminist backlash, their abstract sense of idealistic purpose, and their concrete goals for "the enlargement of women." Considering the possibility of a long-term strike to achieve higher wages, the vote, and gender equality throughout society, these trade unionists and suffragists brainstorm about political tactics.

The wide-ranging "war" that results exemplifies Gilman's penchant for global analysis and her weakness as a practical tactician. Within a few minutes of conversation, the women decide to establish a "great spreading league of interconnected businesses" owned and faithfully patronized by women. They also resolve to acquire halls in which to speak, and paper mills, printing shops and publishing offices, which will help spread their message of liberation. Accepting no limits on their entrepreneurial ambitions, they agree in addition to start "a perfect chain of Summer boarding houses," a laundry business, and an employment agency connected to a "Training School for Modern Employment." A committee of three, appointed at the close of the story, is instructed to consult "widely" on these far-reaching schemes and to report back at the next meeting. The story ends on an expectant note: "and the women looked at one another with the light of a new hope in their eyes."

"A Surplus Woman," though similar in format, shows how Gilman refined the enthusiasms expressed in the earlier story. The emerging organization here is less militantly confrontational and considerably more focused.

Susan Page, a young British woman whose father, brother, and lover have all been killed in the World War, bravely faces the social implications of the war's liquidation of a "whole generation of masculine youth." Determined that women make the best of their necessary singleness, she envisions new opportunities for female bonding which would not exist if young women like herself were all starting families.

Page calls a meeting of five women to propose that they form a "Women's Economic Alliance" with branches throughout England. The WEA's underlying purpose would be to enable single women to become productive members of society. Her plan calls for a strong emphasis on training, with "employment agencies" in every locale. Each local branch would conduct an "economic census" of women and then proceed to establish appropriate classes and eventually a "high grade vocational college" with traveling lecturers and libraries.

After persuading them to join her and then actually training large numbers of women, Page and her new colleagues organize domestic service businesses, run by the newly trained women, all over the country. Like the women in the first story, these look forward in the long run to the establishment of residential clubhouses with shared facilities. But in this second tale of British sisterhood, Gilman showed a more mature sense of what was possible, a more restrained sense of agenda, a greater realism. Its increased sense of political strategy makes for a better story, too. (pp. 155-57)

In another group of stories, Gilman featured special places where women (and sometimes men) could go for rest, recreation, and healing. A number of summer resorts like the ones portrayed here were actually built, incorporating Gilman's specifications for connected, kitchenless facilities. Apart from their ordinary lives, women find here both new forms of therapeutic togetherness and opportunities for refreshing solitude.

"Girls and the Land" is the story of Dacia Boone, a young woman living in Seattle, Washington. Like the novel *What Diantha Did,* this story is a detailed set of directions on how to create a Gilmanesque space.

With a very shrewd business sense and a sturdy contentment with her life style as a single woman, Dacia Boone is impervious to her mother's worries about her homeliness; she turns a deaf ear to Mom's frequent exclamation, "If only you had been a man!" She sets out to accumulate enough wealth both to assist her stepfather in a development project and to build a "Vacation Place" in the country where groups of "working girls" from clubs throughout the state can go for two weeks of wholesome camping. Along with many fiscal details about how she accomplishes this, the story shows Dacia making a stunning success of both building projects. In the course of her enterprising activity, she also meets a talented carpenter/designer, Olaf Pedersen, with whom she starts a furniture business and falls in love.

"Maidstone Comfort" is a "rambling summer settlement" at the seashore. It comes into existence as the result of a timely collaboration orchestrated by a "quiet, adaptable, middle-aged" character by the name of Benigna MacAvelly.

Sarah Maidstone Pellett owns a considerable amount of remote, beach-front property, which her domineering husband will not let her develop. MacAvelly introduces Pellett to Molly Bellew, a floundering twenty-year-old rebel who is on the threshold of inheriting millions of dollars. Together Pellett and Bellew build and manage a beautifully restorative seaside compound which is also handsomely lucrative.

Maidstone Comfort, like Gilman's utopian places, combines natural beauty with architectural integration. A whole village of small, brightly colored cottages is built along curving streets beside the shoreline; luxuriant flowers, vines, and shrubs adorn the areas between them. Convenient to all of the houses is a hotel at which guests can take excellent meals. As an additional service, "a brisk motor-wagon" equipped with "neat receptacles" is primed, upon receipt of a phone call, to deliver outstanding food to a cottage's back door and to return later to pick up the dirty dishes. No one who comes to this place for recuperation has to give a single thought to the question of what to eat. (pp. 158-59)

In short, modest stories about white middle-class and upper-middle-class women, Gilman unselfconsciously made her most compelling argument for nonsexist architecture. To dwell imaginatively for a few moments in a landscape with connected domestic facilities suggests powerfully that such environments are both desirable and achievable.

As the backdrop for dozens of Gilman stories, socialized feminist spaces need no elaborate rationale. Their vitality is compelling in and of itself, representing the way the landscape will look when empowered women learn to look out for their own interests. In contrast to the distorting one-sidedness of her philosophical universe, here individuality is reassuringly secure, celebrated in the struggles of heroines to achieve personal autonomy. In the world of Gilman's realistic fiction, growth and conflict, individuality and connectedness, uncertainty and ambiguity are all experienced and taken into account. Except for the recurrent figure of Mrs. MacAvelly, no character is portrayed mothering other people endlessly without looking after her own needs.

Gilman's realistic fiction corrected for her theoretical excesses. She located its characters squarely in the familiar flux of history where decisions and actions were always conditioned by the necessities of space and time. Here no one gives any thought to the abstract normative considerations discussed in her formal ethics; the actors show no concern for conforming themselves to evolutionary laws. Nor are they obsessed with their duty to self-efface in deference to the ideal of social unity.

In recent years the humble narrative has come into its own as a bearer of ethical meaning. Recognized in women's consciousness-raising groups as a crucial mode of empowerment, its capacity to enliven moral principles has recently been noted by both activists and academics.

A contemporary philosopher, Stanley Hauerwas, has written appreciatively about the ethical significance of stories, recognizing in them a necessary complement to normative abstractions. He reminds moral theorists of their creative dependence on descriptive narrative, lest they forget and attempt to survive in the realms of "pure" cogitation. He writes, "If our lives are to be reflective and coherent, our moral vision must be ordered around dominant metaphors or stories." He discusses the everyday process by which we form our character and virtue, indeed the very story of our lives, in response to stories that have captured our imagination. At his most enthusiastic, he claims: "To be moral persons is to allow stories to be told through us . . . Our experience itself, if it is to be coherent, is but an incipient story." At times more aware of it than at others, Gilman's own life story as well as the rich produce of her literary imagination provided an invaluable grounding to her lifelong project of social ethics.

Gilman's realistic stories help reconstruct the heart of her vision for the built environment. More than anything else, she wanted to liberate women from solitary, burdensome housework. To that end she urged women to pursue as many strategies as they could think of appropriate to their particular location and circumstance. Where possible, they should live in socialized residences attached to commercialized domestic services. If there were none, they should consider starting one, even a very informal, small-scale service, with the hope that it would grow. They should talk to each other about what they need. They should meet in large and small groups and try to solve their problems collectively. They should form alliances.

Men are not without significant roles in Gilman's stories. Dozens of them see the light and choose to live in liberated households. A few even engage in domestic work themselves, most notably Ford Mathews in **"The Cottagette,"** who fixes a "perfect" picnic lunch and begs his fiancée to stop doing housework, and Arthur Olmstead in **"Her Housekeeper,"** who looks after children and develops admirable apartment hotels. Although the challenge of involving men equally in housework was not high on Gilman's agenda, a few of her stories suggest that she would appreciate the justice of such a campaign. (pp. 162-63)

> *Polly Wynn Allen, in her* Building Domestic Liberty: Charlotte Perkins Gilman's Architectural Feminism, *Amherst: The University of Massachusetts Press, 1988, 195 p.*

Catherine Golden   (essay date 1989)

[*Golden is an American editor and critic who has contributed to such publications as* Victorian Studies, Salmagundi, *and* The Journal of Aesthetic Education. *In the essay below, she comments on the intertextuality of* "The Yellow Wallpaper."]

The first-person narrative of **"The Yellow Wallpaper"** unfolds as a diary written by a woman undergoing a three-month rest cure for a postpartum depression. Judith Fetterley has argued that the wallpaper functions as a text through which the narrator expresses herself; its pattern becomes the dominant text and the woman behind the pattern the subtext with which the narrator identifies. To recall the terminology of *The Madwoman in the Attic*, the yellow wallpaper thus can be perceived as a "palimpsest." Similarly, Charlotte Perkins Gilman's story itself can be read as a palimpsest. The hallucinations and dramatic actions of tearing the wallpaper and creeping on the floor comprise the dominant text, but the writing comprises the second muted text, informing the narrator's final characterization. This muted text shows how the narrator fictionalizes herself as the audience of her story. Forbidden to write but continuing to do so in secret, the narrator comes to express herself by writing her own text. As she comes to see the wallpaper as a palimpsest, she presents

herself on paper in a way that suggests that, although mad, she is not completely "destroyed" by her patriarchal society. As the story unfolds, the narrator's writing ceases to match her thoughts and actions or to convey a cohesive characterization of a timid oppressed figure. The increased use of "I" and her syntactical placement of the nominative case pronoun within her own sentences demonstrate a positive change in self-presentation precisely at the point when her actions dramatically compromise her sanity and condemn her to madness.

The narrator records her stay in a country ancestral hall through ten diary-like entries, each undated and separated only by several lines of blank space. The separateness of these units can be seen as a spatial indication of the narrator's own fragmented sense of self. As Walter Ong notes [in "A Writer's Audience Is Always a Fiction," *PMLA* (1975)] the audience of a diarist is oneself "encased in fictions. . . . The diarist pretending to be talking to himself has also, since he is writing, to pretend he is somehow not there. And to what self is he talking? To the self he imagines he is? Or would like to be?" Although the narrator may in fact be writing for a fictional self, the way she imagines this self to be changes as the entries continue. The writing in her early entries matches the dominant text of her thoughts and actions. In the opening sentence the narrator introduces her husband before herself: "It is very seldom that mere ordinary people like John and myself secure ancestral halls for the summer." Rarely used for self-expression, the reflexive case more effectively emphasizes an antecedent rather than replaces a subject. The narrator who claims she wants very much to write also hides her own belief that writing is "a great relief to my mind" by placing this insight in parentheses. Punctuation marks eclipse the forcefulness of this belief, which directly confronts the opinion of those who prescribe her rest cure: her physician-husband, John, who "hates to have [her] write a word"; her physician brother; the socially prominent nerve specialist S. Weir Mitchell, who is "just like John and [her] brother, only more so!"; and even John's sister Jennie, an "enthusiastic housekeeper" who "thinks it is the writing which made [her] sick!" At this point in the story the self-consciousness displayed through punctuational subordination keeps the narrator in a subordinate place within her sentences. The muted text matches the dominant text of her actions, which at this point reveals the narrator as fanciful and fearful. Even though her room initially repulses her, she rests in the former nursery because John chose it for her. The narrator prefers a room "that opened on the piazza and had roses all over the window, and such pretty old-fashioned chintz hangings!", yet she does not pursue her softly expressed conviction: " 'Then do let us go downstairs." Asserting herself only through her secret act of writing, she hides her journal when she senses John's entry. Fear of detection restricts the amount she writes; she remains aware of her larger social reality at this point in the story and does not perceive of her private journal as a place for self-expression or a safe domain.

The dominant text of her actions and the muted text of her writing no doubt initially concur, in part, because the narrator is not only oppressed by those who forbid her to write but by language itself. The language through which the narrator writes is imbued with a social, economic, and political reality of male domination of the late nineteenth-century that governs the way the narrator perceives language. The doctors pronounce the narrator "sick!" There is no escaping the words through which the doctors deliver their diagnosis, their prescription of a rest cure, or the language the narrator must produce to maintain her sanity.

In the initial entry the narrator refers frequently to "Dear John" as well as what "John says." "John" appears four times on the opening page, the last three of which successively introduce a new paragraph:

> John laughs at me, of course, but one expects that in marriage. John is practical in the extreme. He has no patience with faith, an intense horror of superstition, and he scoffs openly of any talk of things not to be felt and seen and put down in figures. John is a physician, and *perhaps*—(I would not say it to a living soul, of course, but this is dead paper and a great relief to my mind)—*perhaps* that is one reason I do not get well faster.

Her husband appears ten times as "John" and eleven times as the forceful nominative "he" within the initial entry of thirty-nine short paragraphs. Reference and deference to her husband keep John firmly the subject of her sentences that describe how he "scoffs" and "laughs" at her and loses "patience" with her. Within her own journal of "dead paper" meant to be read by no "living soul" (except, of course, the narrator), she privileges the man who laughs at her, misunderstands her nature, and calls her, albeit affectionately, his "blessed little goose."

While she calls John by his proper name, the narrator elects to remain nameless until the very end of the story, where she hints that her name may be Jane. Moreover, she rarely presents herself through "I." To recall the opening sentence of the story, "It is very seldom that mere ordinary people like John and myself secure ancestral halls for the summer." Herein "like" functions as a preposition meaning "similar to." Usage favors "me" rather than "myself" after a preposition; the reflexive case is heavier and more cumbersome in English than in other languages. In introducing "myself" and "John," the narrator intensifies her awkward positioning in her sentence and society; she is not even on par with "ordinary people like John." Since the muted text of her writing initially concurs with her actions, it is not surprising that the narrator concludes at the end of the first entry: "There comes John, and I must put this away,—he hates to have me write a word." Using "I" becomes not an act of assertion but rather of acquiescence determined by John's authority. The blank space confirms that the narrator has put away her writing in compliance to John's prescription.

The narrator also elects to present herself anonymously as "one," "a kind of disguised *I*." The narrator disguises her autonomy when she begins to question John's authority: "You see he does not believe I am sick! And what can one do?" "One" dominates the second page of the first entry (it occurs three times in close proximity). The syntactic

positioning calls further attention to this pronoun. The expression "what is one to do" semantically conveys the narrator's helplessness and perceived inability to change her uncomfortable situation; the repetition of "one" creates a haunting echo of anonymity throughout this entry and the entire story.

As the entries unfold, the narrator comes to write for a different self hinted at one the opening page through her three-fold presentation of self as "I" (one time hidden in parentheses). To recall Ong once again, the narrator comes to write for the more forceful self she "would like to be." Simply by writing and exercising grammatical options within her patriarchal language, she writes in a way that questions and ultimately challenges the authorities that confine and oppress her. Her visible expansion on the sentence level shows the muted text diverging from the dominant text. Learning to read the subtext of the yellow wallpaper, the narrator gives way to fancy and loses sight of her larger social reality. However, she concomitantly fictionalizes an identity overriding the fragmentation inherent within the discrete units of language she produces and the fragmentation she feels as a woman within her society. The narrator's greater self-awareness, emerging through her self-presentation beginning in the third entry, undermines her original compliance to John's orders to "lie down ever so much now" and "to sleep all [she] can."

When the narrator begins to cry uncontrollably at "nothing," to obsess with her reading of the shapes of the wallpaper's dominant and muted pattern, and to perceive that the muted text "is like a woman stooping down and creeping about behind that [dominant] pattern," she begins to write for a forceful fictionalized self, beginning successive sentences with "I":

> I don't know why I should write this.
>
> I don't want to.
>
> I don't feel able.
>
> And I know John would think it absurd. But I must say what I feel and think in some way—it is such a relief !

The contents of the "I" sequence records the narrator's vacillation and questioning of her own prescription of writing to improve her nervous condition. Janice Haney-Peritz even suggests that "such contradictions . . . betray the narrator's dependence on the oppressive discursive structure we associate with John." But the clustering of "I," the italicized emphatic "must," and the exclamation point following "relief " convey an emerging sense of self and conviction precisely when she begins to have delusions leading to her final actions of tearing the wallpaper from the walls in order to free the woman and that part of herself trapped behind the restrictive bars of the dominant pattern of the wallpaper.

Appearing a total of seven times in this sequence, "I" introduces each of four consecutive sentences, three of which begin a new paragraph. No longer deferring to "John" or the social authority he represents, she conspicuously positions "I" in a configuration suggestive of a stronger albeit fictionalized self. The positioning and four-fold use of "I" most noticeably recalls the four-fold repetition of John on the opening page. However, in the third entry the narrator dramatically inverts her original pattern; by beginning the first three rather than the last three paragraphs with "I," the narrator gives heightened emphasis to self. The introductory positioning of the subject connotes power, and her use of "I" demonstrates a reversal of the dynamics of power between the narrator and John.

The narrator occasionally reverts to the reflexive case, such as within the fourth entry when she writes about solving the wallpaper's pattern: "I am determined that nobody shall find it out but myself!" In this sentence, however, the weight of the reflexive gives added force to her assertion, further accentuated through the surrounding words and the punctuation. A coordinating conjunction of contrast placed directly in front of the reflexive, "but" underscores her conviction and calls attention to "myself"; an exclamation mark reiterates this force. In the eighth, ninth, and tenth entries, the narrator uses "I" for self-presentation as well as to initiate short direct sentences, such as in the final entry when she tells John she cannot open the door to her room: "I can't,' said I." "I" becomes the first and the last word. The narrator syntactically occupies the two most powerful positions within her own sentence.

The choice and positioning of pronouns suggest a forceful sense of self complicating the narrator's final characterization. Independent of the muted text, the dominant text of her actions incrementally reveals her destruction. The later entries in which the narrator also comes to creep by daylight and to gnaw her bed in anger demonstrate her delusional actions, which become increasingly dominant. In fact, "a slight hysterical tendency" grows into eventual madness as she gets into the muted text of the yellow wallpaper. Given to fancy from the start, she begins to see the wallpaper come to life as she cries "at nothing . . . most of the time" and cannot sleep. Within the wallpaper she sees "strangled heads and bulbous eyes and wadded fungus growths." Personified midway through the second entry ("This paper looks to me as if it *knew* what a vicious influence it had!", the muted side of the wallpaper assumes a human shape as the narrator sees within it "a strange, provoking, formless sort of figure." The muted figure within the wallpaper increasingly gains more definition for her. Although in the third entry she qualifies that the figure looks "like a woman," she confirms this perception in the fourth entry when she claims "now I am quite sure it is a woman." As the muted pattern becomes dominant to the narrator, her delusions translate into actions of madness that become most apparent during the final four entries. She sees the woman behind the wallpaper creeping and begins to creep herself, at first secretively just as she begins her writing: "I always lock the door when I creep by daylight. I can't do it at night, for I know John would suspect something at once." The dominant wallpaper pattern becomes prison bars, and the woman locked behind "just takes hold of the bars and shakes them hard." Sympathizing with the muted text, she writes more forcefully but acts more madly. She begins to peel the wallpaper from the walls to release that part of herself trapped by her

own social condition as mirrored by the barred pattern of the wallpaper. The muted woman behind bars becomes a symbol and a message for women as the narrator sees outside the window "so many of those creeping women, and they creep so fast"; in fact, she begins to "wonder if they all come out of that wallpaper as I did?"

Born of an hallucination, her identification leads the narrator to free herself from the restrictive pattern of her own society, and this liberation is conveyed on paper through her pronoun choice. Particularly the opening of the tenth entry celebrates the narrator's fusion of identity with the subtext of the wallpaper: "I pulled and she shook, I shook and she pulled, and before morning we had peeled off yards of that paper." But following her dramatic freeing of the woman behind the wallpaper, the narrator emerges independent and forceful. Hiding the key to her room under a plantain leaf, she seals herself in her room so that she can "creep around as I please!" The narrator tells her husband where he can find the key. Unlike the initial entry in which she senses John's entrance and puts away her journal, she does not allow his intrusion to disrupt her creeping in the finale. The narrator, mad, is no longer timid in her action. Echoing her use of "one" to avoid self-confrontation, the narrator now speaks with detachment of her husband: "Now why should that man have fainted? But he did, and right across my path by the wall, so that I had to creep over him every time!"

More than the tone of writing or pronoun usage, the placement of pronouns in this closing paragraph reveals the narrator's growing sense of awareness of her former submissive state and a reversal of the power dynamics of gender. Relegating John to a modifying phrase following an intransitive verb, the narrator assumes the subject position within the final clause. This sentence, in fact, exchanges the grammatical positions the narrator originally elected for each to occupy in a grammatically similar sentence on the opening page of **"The Yellow Wallpaper"**: "John laughs at me, of course, but one expects that in marriage." In selecting an intransitive verb to convey John's abuse, the narrator in her early writing undeniably isolates herself from his emotional cruelty. The verb "to laugh" can only function intransitively and thus cannot possess or envelop the narrator, "me," as its object. But, in doing so, the narrator relegates herself (and later John) to a weak position within the formal bounds of the sentence. Not a basic or essential sentence part, the prepositional phrase "at me" functions as a modifier embellishing the sentence (in this case adverbially). Governed only by the preposition "at," the narrator in the first entry can be dropped from her sentence, which would thus read grammatically: "John laughs . . . , of course, but one expects that in marriage." With such a revision her presence would remain only through a disguised reference to self ("one"). However, by changing positions with John in the grammatically similar sentence in the tenth entry, the narrator now sends John—who has fainted to the floor—to a nonessential, powerless, syntactical place. Governed only by the preposition "over," John can be dropped from her final clause, which would thus read grammatically: "I had to creep . . . every time!" The narrator's actions are outside the realm of sanity, but the syntactic position she comes to occupy conveys her emerging sense of defiance against one of the forces in her patriarchal society that has fragmented her.

Other examples, particularly in the final four paragraphs of the tenth entry, join with this exchange of grammatical positions to affirm the narrator's newly imagined self:

> "What is the matter?" he cried. "For God's sake, what are you doing!"
>
> I kept on creeping just the same, but I looked at him over my shoulder.
>
> "I've got out at last," said I, "in spite of you and Jane. And I've pulled off most of the paper, so you can't put me back!"
>
> "Now why should that man have fainted? But he did, and right across my path by the wall, so that I had to creep over him every time!"

John's name seems conspicuously absent from these paragraphs. Four times the narrator substitutes the nominative case for John's name ("he cried" and "he did" within her narration and "you" twice in her dialogue). Within these paragraphs she thrice substitutes the objective case for John and further reduces his status by making each pronoun an object of a preposition ("at him," "of you," and "over him"). In the final paragraph she also uses the demonstrative pronoun "that" in "that man," a detached and generic reference to John. Unlike the demonstrative "this," "that" points the reader to something or someone who is respectively farther away in a spatial sense and thus works to distance the reader and the narrator from John and his authority, to which she once readily adhered. Used to direct the reader to a preceding rather than a subsequent reference, "that man" also orients the reader to the previous rather than the two future references to him, occurring in the final sentence; the wording anticipates John's disappearance from the final dramatic clause and close of **"The Yellow Wallpaper,"** which leaves the narrator creeping flamboyantly in the daylight as she desires.

The narrator presents herself as "I" six times in the final four paragraphs, twice forcefully beginning her own paragraphs. She displays her growing sense of self, power, and confidence at the point at which she has uncoded the text of the yellow wallpaper and liberated its muted side. In addition, an exclamation point at the end of both the last and the penultimate paragraphs gives emphasis to her final sentences, in which she moves into the subject place initially reserved for John. When referring to self, she uses the possessive case twice and the objective case once, but she no longer positions the objective case reference for self in a precarious place. Importantly, in the sentence "can't put me back," "me" functions as a direct object of the transitive verb "put." Securely positioned, "me" becomes essentially connected to the action verb. The use of negation in this sentence subtly undermines the contents of earlier sentences containing transitive verbs, such as "John gathered me up in his arms, and just carried me upstairs and laid me on the bed"; while in both sentences "me" carries the force of her male oppressor, the negation in the later sentence equally negates his force and matches the

writing in the finale, where the narrator is able to write a sentence that can function grammatically without "John."

Examining the muted text of the narrator's writing within this palimpsest in relation to the dominant text of her delusional actions permits the narrator a dubious victory. Her widening use of "I" and grammatical repositioning of "I" and "John" hint at a degree of personal liberation for her fictionalized self recorded within this tale of a woman's breakdown. The muted text of her writing comes to reflect her growing self-awareness as she moves beyond the prescription of healthy eating, moderate exercise, and abundant rest and chooses literal madness over John's prescription for sanity. As the narrator tears the paper to free the woman and that part of herself trapped within the story's mirrored palimpsest and creeps over her husband, she acts in a way that implies a cogent madness, rid of the timidity and fear that punctuate her earlier entries. Only at the point at which she acts out of madness does she find a place within the patriarchal language she uses, although not yet within her larger social reality. Creeping deeper into madness and her fictionalized self, the narrator writes in a defiant voice, circumvents John's force, and banishes "him" to the outer boundaries of her own sentence. (pp. 195-200)

Catherine Golden, "The Writing of 'The Yellow Wallpaper': A Double Palimpsest," in Studies in American Fiction, *Vol. 17, No. 2, Autumn, 1989, pp. 193-201.*

Susan S. Lanser   (essay date 1989)

[*Lanser is an American critic and educator whose works include* The Narrative Act: Point of View in Prose Fiction *(1981). In the following essay, she attempts to deconstruct traditional feminist readings of "The Yellow Wallpaper." Lanser asserts: "None of us seems to have noticed that virtually all feminist discourse on 'The Yellow Wallpaper' has come from white academics and that it has failed to question the story's status as a universal woman's text. A feminist criticism willing to deconstruct its own practices would reexamine our exclusive reading of 'The Yellow Wallpaper,' rethink the implications of its canonization, and acknowledge both the text's position in ideology and our own."*]

In 1973, a new publishing house with the brave name of The Feminist Press reprinted in a slim volume Charlotte Perkins Gilman's **"The Yellow Wallpaper,"** first published in 1892 and out of print for half a century. It is the story of an unnamed woman confined by her doctor-husband to an attic nursery with barred windows and a bolted-down bed. Forbidden to write, the narrator-protagonist becomes obsessed with the room's wallpaper, which she finds first repellent and then riveting; on its chaotic surface she eventually deciphers an imprisoned woman whom she attempts to liberate by peeling the paper off the wall. This brilliant tale of a white, middle-class wife driven mad by a patriarchy controlling her "for her own good" has become an American feminist classic; in 1987, the Feminist Press edition numbered among the ten best-selling works of fiction published by a university press.

The canonization of **"The Yellow Wallpaper"** is an obvious sign of the degree to which contemporary feminism has transformed the study of literature. But Gilman's story is not simply one to which feminists have "applied" ourselves; it is one of the texts through which white, American academic feminist criticism has constituted its terms. My purpose here is to take stock of this criticism through the legacy of **"The Yellow Wallpaper"** in order to honor the work each has fostered and to call into question the status of Gilman's story—and the story of academic feminist criticism—as sacred texts. In this process I am working from the inside, challenging my own reading of **"The Yellow Wallpaper,"** which had deepened but not changed direction since 1973.

My inquiry will make explicit use of six well-known studies of **"The Yellow Wallpaper,"** but I consider these six to articulate an interpretation shared by a much larger feminist community. The pieces I have in mind are written by Elaine Hedges, Sandra Gilbert and Susan Gubar, Annette Kolodny, Jean Kennard, Paula Treichler, and Judith Fetterley, respectively, and their publication dates span from 1973 to 1986. Reading these essays as a body, I am struck by a coherence that testifies to a profound unity in white, American feminist criticism across apparent diversity. That is, although Hedges is concerned primarily with biography, Gilbert and Gubar with female authorship, Treichler with textual form, and Fetterley, Kolodny, and Kennard with interpretation, and although each discussion illuminates the text in certain unique ways, the six readings are almost wholly compatible, with one point of difference which is never identified as such and to which I will return. I will also return later to the significance of this redundancy and to the curiously unchallenged, routine elision from nearly all the discussion of one of the story's key tropes.

The theoretical positions that **"The Yellow Wallpaper"** helped to shape and perhaps to reify may be clearer if we recall some of the critical claims with which U.S. academic feminist criticism began. In the late and early seventies, some academic women, most of them trained in Anglo-American methods and texts, began to take a new look at those works by men and a few white women that comprised the standard curriculum. The earliest scholarship—Kathryn Rogers's *The Troublesome Helpmate* (1966), Mary Ellmann's *Thinking about Women* (1968), Kate Millett's *Sexual Politics* (1970), Elaine Showalter's "Women Writers and the Double Standard" (in *Woman in Sexist Society,* 1971)—was asserting against prevailing New Critical neutralities that literature is deeply political, indeed steeped in (patriarchal) ideology. Ideology, feminists argued, makes what is cultural seem natural and inevitable, and what had come to seem natural and inevitable to literary studies was that its own methods and great books transcended ideology.

This conception of literature as a privileged medium for universal truths was defended by the counterclaim that those who found a work's content disturbing or offensive were letting their "biases" distract them from the aesthetic of literature. Feminist criticism was bound to challenge this marginalization of social content and to argue that literary works both reflect and constitute structures of gender and power. In making this challenge, feminist criticism was implying that canonical literature was not simply *mimesis,* a mirror or the way things are or the way men and women are, but *semiosis*—a complex system of conventional (androcentric) tropes. And by questioning the premises of the discipline, feminists were of course arguing that criticism, too, is political, that no methodology is neutral, and that literary practice is shaped by cultural imperatives to serve particular ends. Although the word "deconstruction" was not yet in currency, these feminist premises inaugurated the first major opposition to both (old) scholarly and (New) critical practices, generating what has become the most widespread deconstructive imperative in the American academy.

Yet the feminist project involved, as Gayle Greene and Coppélia Kahn have put it, not only "deconstructing dominant male patterns of thought and social practice" but also "reconstructing female experience previously hidden or overlooked." In the early 1970s, the rediscovery of "lost" works like **"The Yellow Wallpaper,"** Kate Chopin's *The Awakening,* and Susan Glaspell's "A Jury of Her Peers" offered not only welcome respite from unladylike assaults on patriarchal practices and from discouraging expositions of androcentric "images of women in literature" but also an exhilarating basis for reconstructing literary theory and literary history. The fact that these works which feminists now found so exciting and powerful had been denounced, ignored, or suppressed seemed virtual proof of the claim that literature, criticism, and history were political. The editor of the *Atlantic Monthly* had rejected **"The Yellow Wallpaper"** because "I could not forgive myself if I made others as miserable as I have made myself!" Even when William Dean Howells reprinted Gilman's story in 1920 he wrote that it was "terrible and too wholly dire," "too terribly good to be printed." Feminists could argue convincingly that Gilman's contemporaries, schooled on the "terrible" and "wholly dire" tales of Poe, were surely balking at something more particular: the "graphic" representation of " 'raving lunacy' " in a middle-class mother and wife that revealed the rage of the woman on a pedestal.

As a tale openly preoccupied with questions of authorship, interpretation, and textuality, **"The Yellow Wallpaper"** quickly assumed a place of privilege among rediscovered feminist works, raising basic questions about writing and reading as gendered practices. The narrator's double-voiced discourse—the ironic understatements, asides, hedges, and negations through which she asserts herself against the power of John's voice—came for some critics to represent "women's language" or the "language of the powerless." With its discontinuities and staccato paragraphs, Gilman's narrative raised the controversial question of a female aesthetic; and the "lame uncertain curves," "outrageous angles," and "unheard of contradictions" of the wallpaper came for many critics to symbolize both Gilman's text and, by extension, the particularity of female form. The story also challenged theories of genius that denied the material conditions—social, economic, psychological, and literary—that make writing (im)possible, helping feminists to turn questions like

"Where is your Shakespeare?" back upon the questioners. Gilbert and Gubar, for example, saw in the narrator's struggles against censorship *"the* story that all literary women would tell if they could speak their 'speechless woe.' "

"The Yellow Wallpaper" has been evoked most frequently, however, to theorize about reading through the lens of a "female" consciousness. Gilman's story has been a particularly congenial medium for such a re-vision not only because the narrator herself engages in a form of feminist interpretation when she tries to read the paper on her wall but also because turn-of-the-century readers seem to have ignored or avoided the connection between the narrator's condition and patriarchal politics, instead praising the story for its keenly accurate "case study" of a presumably inherited insanity. In the contemporary feminist reading, on the other hand, sexual oppression is evident from the start: the phrase "John says" heads a litany of "benevolent" prescriptions that keep the narrator infantilized, immobilized, and bored literally out of her mind. Reading or writing her self upon the wallpaper allows the narrator, as Paula Treichler puts it, to "escape" her husband's "sentence" and to achieve the limited freedom of madness which, virtually all these critics have agreed, constitutes a kind of sanity in the face of the insanity of male dominance.

This reading not only recuperated **"The Yellow Wallpaper"** as a feminist text but also reconstituted the terms of interpretation itself. Annette Kolodny theorized that emerging feminist consciousness made possible a new, female-centered interpretive paradigm that did not exist for male critics at the turn of the century. Defining that paradigm more specifically, Jean Kennard maintained that the circulation of feminist conventions associated with four particular concepts—"patriarchy, madness, space, quest"—virtually ensured the reading that took place in the 1970s. Furthermore, the premise that "we engage not texts but paradigms," as Kolodny puts it in another essay, explodes the belief that we are reading what is "there." Reading becomes the product of those conventions or strategies we have learned through an "interpretive community"—Stanley Fish's term to which Kolodny and Kennard give political force; to read is to reproduce a text according to this learned system or code.

These gender-based and openly ideological theories presented a radical challenge to an academic community in which "close reading" has remained the predominant critical act. A theory of meaning grounded in the politics of reading destabilizes assumptions of interpretive validity and shifts the emphasis to the contexts in which meanings are produced. A text like **"The Yellow Wallpaper"** showed that to the extent that we remain unaware of our interpretive conventions, it is difficult to distinguish *"what* we read" from *"how* we have learned to read it." We experience meaning as given in "the text itself." When alternative paradigms inform our reading, we are able to read texts differently or, to put it more strongly, to read different texts. This means that traditional works may be transformed through different interpretive strategies into new literature just as patriarchy's "terrible" and repellent

"Yellow Wallpaper" was dramatically transformed into feminism's endlessly fascinating tale.

It is, I believe, this powerful theoretical achievement occasioned by **"The Yellow Wallpaper"** that has led so much critical writing on the story to a triumphant conclusion despite the narrator's own unhappy fate. I have found it striking that discussions of the text so frequently end by distinguishing the doomed and "mad" narrator, who could not write her way out of the patriarchal prison-house, from the sane survivor Charlotte Perkins Gilman, who could. The crucial shift from narrator to author, from story to text, may also serve to wrest readers from an unacknowledged overidentification with the narrator-protagonist. For just as the narrator's initial horror at the wallpaper is mirrored in the earlier critics' horror at Gilman's text, so now-traditional feminist rereadings may be reproducing the narrator's next move: her relentless pursuit of a single meaning on the wall. I want to go further still and suggest that feminist criticism's own persistent return to the "Wallpaper"—indeed, to specific aspects of the "Wallpaper"—signifies a somewhat uncomfortable need to isolate and validate a particular female experience, a particular relationship between reader and writer, and a particular notion of subjectivity as bases for the writing and reading of (women's) texts. Fully acknowledging the necessity of the feminist reading of **"The Yellow Wallpaper"** which I too have produced and perpetuated for many years, I now wonder whether many of us have repeated the gesture of the narrator who *"will* follow that pointless pattern to some sort of conclusion" —who will read until she finds what she is looking for—no less and no more. Although—or because—we have read **"The Yellow Wallpaper"** over and over, we may have stopped short, and our readings, like the narrator's, may have reduced the text's complexity to what we need most: our own image reflected back to us.

Let me return to the narrator's reading of the paper in order to clarify this claim. The narrator is faced with an unreadable text, a text for which none of her interpretive strategies is adequate. At first she is confounded by its contradictory style: it is "flamboyant" and "pronounced", yet also "lame," "uncertain," and "dull." Then she notices different constructions in different places. In one "recurrent spot" the pattern "lolls," in another place "two breadths didn't match," and elsewhere the pattern is torn off. She tries to organize the paper geometrically but cannot grasp its laws: it is marked vertically by "bloated curves and flourishes," diagonally by "slanting waves of optic horror like a lot of wallowing seaweeds in full chase," and horizontally by an order she cannot even figure out. There is even a centrifugal pattern in which "the interminable grotesques seem to form around a common centre and rush off in headlong plunges of equal distraction." Still later, she notices that the paper changes and moves according to different kinds of light. And it has a color and smell that she is never able to account for. But from all this indecipherability, from this immensely complicated text, the narrator—by night, no less—finally discerns a single image, a woman behind bars, which she then expands to represent the whole. This is hardly a matter of "correct" reading, then, but of fixing and reducing possibilities, finding a space of text on which she can locate whatever self-projection will enable her to move from "John says" to "I want." The very excess of description of the wallpaper, and the fact that it continues after the narrator has first identified the woman behind the bars, actually foregrounds the reductiveness of her interpretive act. And if the narrator, having liberated the paper woman, can only imagine tying her up again, is it possible that our reading too has freed us momentarily only to bind us once more?

Most feminist analyses of **"The Yellow Wallpaper"** have in fact recognized this bind without pursuing it. Gilbert and Gubar see the paper as "otherwise incomprehensible hieroglyphics" onto which the narrator projects "her own passion for escape." Treichler notes that the wallpaper "remains indeterminate, complex, unresolved, disturbing." Even Fetterley, who seems least to question the narrator's enterprise, speaks of the narrator's "need to impose order on the 'impertinence' of row after row of unmatched breadths." Kolodny implicates all critical practice when she says that the narrator obsessively and jealously "emphasiz[es] one section of the pattern while repressing others, reorganiz[es] and regroup[s] past impressions into newer, more fully realized configurations—*as one might with any complex formal text.*" And Kennard states openly that much more goes on in both the wallpaper and the story than is present in the standard account and that the feminist reading of **"The Yellow Wallpaper"** is far from the final and "correct" one that replaces the patriarchal "misreading" once and for all. Still, Kennard's position in 1981 was that "despite all these objections . . . it is the feminist reading I teach my students and which I believe is the most fruitful"; although suggesting that a new interpretive community might read this and other stories differently, she declined to pursue the possibility on grounds of insufficient "space"—a term that evokes the narrator's own confinement. In light of these more-or-less conscious recognitions that the wallpaper remains incompletely read, the redundancy of feminist readings of Gilman's story might well constitute the return of the repressed.

I want to suggest that this repressed possibility of another reading reveals larger contradictions in white, academic feminist theories and practices. Earlier I named as the two basic gestures of U.S. feminist criticism "deconstructing dominant male patterns of thought and social practice" and "reconstructing female experience previously hidden or overlooked." This formulation posits as oppositional an essentially false and problematic "male" system beneath which essentially true and unproblematic "female" essences can be recovered—just as the figure of the woman can presumably be recovered from beneath the patriarchal pattern on Gilman's narrator's wall (a presumption to which I will return). In designating gender as the foundation for two very different critical activities, feminist criticism has embraced contradictory theories of literature, proceeding as if men's writings were ideological sign systems and women's writings were representations of truth, reading men's or masculinist texts with resistance and women's or feminist texts with empathy. If, however, we acknowledge the participation of women writers and readers in "dominant . . . patterns of thought and social prac-

tice," then perhaps our own patterns must also be deconstructed if we are to recover meanings still "hidden or overlooked." We would then have to apply event to feminist texts and theories the premises I described earlier: that literature and criticism are collusive with ideology, that texts are sign systems rather than simple mirrors, that authors cannot guarantee their meanings, that interpretation is dependent on a critical community, and that our own literary histories are also fictional. The consequent rereading of texts like **"The Yellow Wallpaper"** might, in turn, alter our critical premises.

It is understandably difficult to imagine deconstructing something one has experienced as a radically reconstructive enterprise. This may be one reason—though other reasons suggest more disturbing complicities—why many of us have often accepted in principle but ignored in practice the deconstructive challenges that have emerged from within feminism itself. Some of the most radical of these challenges have come from women of color, poor women, and lesbians, frequently with primary allegiances outside the university, who have exposed in what has passed for feminist criticism blindnesses as serious as those to which feminism was objecting. In 1977, for example, Barbara Smith identified racism in some of the writings on which feminist criticism had been founded; in 1980, Alice Walker told the National Women's Studies Association of her inability to convince the author of *The Female Imagination* to consider the imaginations of women who are Black; in 1978, Judy Grahn noted the "scathing letters" the Women's Press Collective received when it published Sharon Isabell's *Yesterday's Lessons* without standardizing the English for a middle-class readership; at the 1976 Modern Language Association meetings and later in *Signs*, Adrienne Rich pointed to the erasure of lesbian identity from feminist classrooms even when the writers being taught were in fact lesbians; in the early 1980s, collections like *This Bridge Called My Back: Writings by Radical Women of Color* and *Nice Jewish Girls: A Lesbian Anthology* insisted that not all American writers are Black or white; they are also Latina, Asian, Arab, Jewish, Indian.

The suppression of difference has affected the critical canon as well. In 1980, for example, *Feminist Studies* published Annette Kolodny's groundbreaking "Dancing Through the Minefield: Some Observations on the Theory, Practice, and Politics of a Feminist Literary Criticism" to which my own elucidation of feminist premises owes a considerable and respectful debt. In Fall 1982, *Feminist Studies* published three responses to Kolodny, criticizing the essay not only for classism, racism, and homophobia in the selection and use of women's texts but also for perpetuating patriarchal academic values and methodologies. One respondent, Elly Bulkin, identified as a crucial problem "the very social and ethical issue of *which* women get published by whom and why—of what even gets *recognized* as 'feminist literary criticism.'" Bulkin might have been speaking prophetically, because none of the three responses was included when "Dancing Through the Minefield" was anthologized.

All these challenges occurred during the same years in

which the standard feminist reading of **"The Yellow Wall-paper"** was produced and reproduced. Yet none of us seems to have noticed that virtually all feminist discourse on **"The Yellow Wallpaper"** has come from white academics and that it has failed to question the story's status as a universal woman's text. A feminist criticism willing to deconstruct its own practices would reexamine our exclusive reading of **"The Yellow Wallpaper,"** rethink the implications of its canonization, and acknowledge both the text's position in ideology and our own. That a hard look at feminism's **"Yellow Wallpaper"** is now possible is already evident by the publication in 1986 of separate essays by Janice Haney-Peritz and Mary Jacobus which use psychoanalytic theory to expose the limits of both the narrator's and feminist criticism's interpretive acts. I believe we have also entered a moment not only of historical possibility but of historical urgency to stop reading a privileged, white, New England woman's text as simply—a woman's text. If our traditional gesture has been to repeat the narrator's own act of *under* reading, of seeing too little, I want now to risk *over* reading, seeing perhaps too much. My reading will make use of textual details that traditional feminist interpretations have tended to ignore, but I do not propose it as a coherent or final reading; I believe no such reading is either possible or desirable and that one important message of **"The Yellow Wallpaper"** is precisely that. At the same time, I concur with Chris Weedon when she insists that meanings, however provisional, "have real effects."

One way back to **"The Yellow Wallpaper"** is through the yellow wallpaper itself: through what I mentioned earlier as the point of difference and the point of silence in the feminist interpretations I have been discussing here. I begin with the difference that occurs within and among otherwise consistent readings when critics try to identify just whose text or what kind of text the wallpaper represents. For Hedges and for Gilbert and Gubar, the wallpaper signifies the oppressive situation in which the woman finds herself; for Kolodny the paper is the narrator's "own psyche writ large"; for Treichler it is a paradigm of women's writing; and for Fetterley it is the husband's patriarchal text which, however, becomes increasingly feminine in form. Haney-Peritz alone confronts the contradiction, seeing the wallpaper as both John's and his wife's discourse, because the narrator "relies on the very binary oppositions" that structure John's text.

It seems, then, that just as it is impossible for the narrator to get "that top pattern . . . off from the under one" so it is impossible to separate the text of a culture from the text of an individual, to free female subjectivity from the patriarchal text. Far from being antitheses, the patriarchal text and the woman's text are in some sense one. And if the narrator's text is also the text of her culture, then it is no wonder that the wallpaper exceeds her ability to decipher it. If, instead of grasping as she does for the single familiar and self-confirming figure in the text, we understand the wallpaper as a pastiche of disturbed and conflicting discourses, then perhaps the wallpaper's chaos represents what the narrator (and we ourselves) must refuse in order to construct the singular figure of the woman behind bars: the foreign and alien images that threaten to "knock [her]

down, and trample upon [her]" images that as a white, middle-class woman of limited consciousness she may neither want nor know how to read. In avoiding certain meanings while "liberating" others from the text, in struggling for the illusion of a fully "conscious knowing, unified, rational subject," is the narrator going "mad" not only from confinement, or from the effort to interpret, but also from the effort to repress? In this case, are those of us who reproduce the narrator's reading also attempting to constitute an essential female subject by shunting aside textual meanings that expose feminism's own precarious and conflicted identity? If the narrator is reading in the paper the text of her own unconscious, an unconscious chaotic with unspeakable fears and desires, is not the unconscious, by the very nature of ideology, political?

If we accept the culturally contingent and incomplete nature of readings guaranteed only by the narrator's consciousness, then perhaps we can find in the yellow wallpaper, to literalize a metaphor of Adrienne Rich, "a whole new psychic geography to be explored." For in privileging the questions of reading and writing as essential "woman questions," feminist criticism has been led to the paper while suppressing the politically charged adjective that colors it. If we locate Gilman's story within the "psychic geography" of Anglo-America at the turn of the century, we locate it in a culture obsessively preoccupied with race as the foundation of character, a culture desperate to maintain Aryan superiority in the face of massive immigrations from Southern and Eastern Europe, a culture openly anti-Semitic, anti-Asian, anti-Catholic, and Jim Crow. In New England, where Gilman was born and raised, agricultural decline, native emigration, and soaring immigrant birth rates had generated "a distrust of the immigrant [that] reached the proportions of a movement in the 1880's and 1890's." In California, where Gilman lived while writing **"The Yellow Wallpaper,"** mass anxiety about the "Yellow Peril" had already yielded such legislation as the Chinese Exclusion Act of 1882. Across the United States, newly formed groups were calling for selective breeding, restricted entry, and "American Protection" of various kinds. White, Christian, American-born intellectuals—novelists, political scientists, economists, sociologists, crusaders for social reform—not only shared this racial anxiety but, as John Higham puts it, "blazed the way for ordinary nativists" by giving popular racism an "intellectual respectability."

These "intellectual" writings often justified the rejection and exclusion of immigrants in terms graphically physical. The immigrants were "human garbage": " 'hirsute, low-browed, big-faced persons of obviously low mentality,' " " 'oxlike men' " who " 'belong in skins, in wattled huts at the close of the Great Ice age,' " ready to " 'pollute' " America with " 'non-Aryan elements.' " Owen Wister's popular Westerns were built on the premise that the eastern United States was being ruined by the " 'debased and mongrel' " immigrants, " 'encroaching alien vermin, that turn our cities to Babels and our citizenship to a hybrid farce, who degrade our commonwealth from a nation into something half pawn-shop, half-broker's office.' " In the " 'clean cattle country,' " on the other hand, one did not find " 'many Poles or Huns or Russian Jews,' " because pioneering required particular Anglo-Saxon abilities. Jack London describes a Jewish character as " 'yellow as a sick persimmon' " and laments America's invasion by " 'the dark-pigmented things, the half-castes, the mongrel-bloods.' " Frank Norris ridicules the "half-breed" as an "amorphous, formless mist" and contrasts the kindness and delicacy of Anglo-Saxons with " 'the hot, degenerate blood' " of the Spanish, Mexican, and Portuguese.

Implicit or explicit in these descriptions is a new racial ideology through which "newcomers from Europe could seem a fundamentally different order" from what were then called "native Americans." The common nineteenth-century belief in three races—black, white, yellow—each linked to a specific continent, was reconstituted so that "white" came to mean only "Nordic" or Northern European, while "yellow" applied not only to the Chinese, Japanese, and light-skinned African-Americans but also to Jews, Poles, Hungarians, Italians, and even the Irish. Crusaders warned of "yellow inundation." The California chapter of the Protestant white supremacist Junior Order of United American Mechanics teamed up with the Asiatic Exclusion League to proclaim that Southern Europeans were "semi-Mongolian" and should be excluded from immigration and citizenship on the same basis as the Chinese; Madison Grant declared Jews to be "a Mongrel admixture . . . of Slavs and of Asiatic invaders of Russia"; and a member of Congress announced that " 'the color of thousands' " of the new immigrants " 'differs materially from that of the Anglo-Saxon.' " The greatest dangers were almost always traced back to Asia; in a dazzling conflation of enemies, for example, Grant warned that " 'in the guise of Bolshevism with Semitic leadership and Chinese executioners, [Asia] is organizing an assault upon Western Europe.' " Lothrop Stoddard predicted that " 'colored migration' " was yielding the " 'very immediate danger that the white stocks may be swamped by Asiatic blood.' " Again and again, nativists announced that democracy "simply will not work among Asiatics," that "non-Aryans," especially Slavs, Italians, and Jews, were "impossible to Americanize." The threat of "Yellow Peril" thus had "racial implications" much broader than anxiety about a takeover of Chinese or Japanese: "in every section, the Negro, the Oriental, and the Southern European appeared more and more in a common light." In such a cultural moment, "yellow" readily connoted inferiority, strangeness, cowardice, ugliness, and backwardness. "Yellow-belly" and "yellow dog" were common slurs, the former applied to groups as diverse as the Irish and the Mexicans. Associations of "yellow" with disease, cowardice, worthlessness, uncleanliness, and decay may also have become implicit associations of race and class.

If **"The Yellow Wallpaper"** is read within this discourse of racial anxiety, certain of its tropes take on an obvious political charge. The very first sentence constructs the narrator in class terms, imagining an America in which, through democratic self-advancement, common (British) Americans can enjoy upper-class (British) privileges. Although the narrator and John are "mere ordinary people" and not the rightful "heirs and coheirs," they have secured "a colonial mansion, a hereditary estate," in whose queerness she takes pride; this house with its "private wharf"

stands "quite alone . . . well back from the road, quite three miles from the village" like "English places that you read about, for there are hedges and walls and gates that lock, and lots of separate little houses for the gardeners and people." I am reminded by this description of another neglected "gentleman's manor house" that people "read about"—Thornfield—in which another merely ordinary woman "little accustomed to grandeur" comes to make her home. Charlotte Brontë's Jane Eyre is given a room with "gay blue chintz window curtains" that resemble the "pretty old-fashioned chintz hangings" in the room Gilman's narrator wanted for herself; Jane is not banished to Thornfield's third floor, where "wide and heavy beds" are surrounded by outlandish wall-hangings that portray "effigies of strange flowers, and stranger birds, and strangest human beings,—all of which would have looked strange, indeed, by the pallid gleam of moonlight"—and where, if Thornfield had ghosts, Jane tells us, these ghosts would haunt. Like Gilman's narrator, Jane longs for both the freedom to roam and the pleasures of human society, and her "sole relief " in those moments is to walk around the attic and look out at the vista of road and trees and rolling hills so much like the view the narrator describes from her nursery in the writing that is her own sole "relief." It is from her attic perch that Jane feels so keenly that women, like men, need "exercise for their faculties" and "suffer from too rigid a restraint," as in her attic Gilman's narrator lies on the "great immovable bed" and longs for company and exercise.

But the permanent, imprisoned inhabitant of Thornfield's attic is not Jane; she is a dark Creole woman who might well have been called "yellow" in Gilman's America. Is Gilman's narrator, who "thought seriously of burning the house" imagining Bertha Mason's fiery revenge? Does the figure in the paper with its "foul, bad yellow" color its "strange, provoking, formless sort of figure" its "broken neck" and "bulbous eyes" resemble Bertha with her "bloated features" and her "discoloured face"? Surely the narrator's crawling about her room may recall Bertha's running "backwards and forwards . . . on all fours." And like Brontë's "mad lady," who would "let herself out of her chamber" at night "and go roaming about the house" to ambush Jane, the "smouldering" yellow menace in Gilman's story gets out at night and "skulk[s] in the parlor, [hides] in the hall," and "[lies] in wait for me." When the narrator tells John that the key to her room is beneath a plantain leaf, is she evoking not only the North American species of that name but also the tropical plant of Bertha's West Indies? When she imagines tying up the freed woman, is she repeating the fate of Bertha, brought in chains to foreign shores? Finally, does the circulation of Brontë's novel in Gilman's text explain the cryptic sentence at the end of the story—possibly a slip of Gilman's pen—in which the narrator cries to her husband that "I've got out at last. . .in spite of you and Jane."

Is the wallpaper, then, the political unconscious of a culture in which an Aryan woman's madness, desire, and anger, repressed by the imperatives of "reason," "duty" and "proper self-control" are projected onto the "yellow" woman who is, however, also the feared alien? When the narrator tries to liberate the woman from the wall, is she trying to purge her of her color, to peel her from the yellow paper, so that she can accept this woman as herself? If, as I suggested earlier, the wallpaper is at once the text of patriarchy and the woman's text, then perhaps the narrator is both resisting and embracing the woman of color who is self and not-self, a woman who might need to be rescued from the text of patriarchy but cannot yet be allowed to go free. Might we explain the narrator's pervasive horror of a yellow color and smell that threaten to take over the "ancestral halls," "stain[ing] everything it touched," as the British-American fear of a takeover by "aliens"? In a cultural moment when immigrant peoples and African Americans were being widely caricatured in the popular press through distorted facial and bodily images, might the "interminable grotesques" of **"The Yellow Wallpaper"**—with their lolling necks and "bulbous eyes" "staring everywhere," with their "peculiar odor" and "yellow smell" their colors "repellent, almost revolting," "smouldering" and "unclean" "sickly" and "particularly irritating" their "new shades of yellow" erupting constantly—figure the Asians and Jews, the Italians and Poles, the long list of "aliens" whom the narrator (and perhaps Gilman herself) might want at once to rescue and to flee?

For if anxieties about race, class, and ethnicity have inscribed themselves as a political unconscious upon the yellow wallpaper, they were conscious and indeed obsessive problems for Gilman herself, as I discovered when, disturbed by my own reading of **"The Yellow Wallpaper,"** I turned to Gilman's later work. Despite her socialist values, her active participation in movements for reform, her strong theoretical commitment to racial harmony, her unconventional support of interracial marriages, and her frequent condemnation of America's racist history, Gilman upheld white Protestant supremacy; belonged for a time to eugenics and nationalist organizations; opposed open immigration; and inscribed racism, nationalism, and classism into her proposals for social change. In *Concerning Children* (1900), she maintains that "a sturdy English baby would be worth more than an equally vigorous young Fuegian. With the same training and care, you could develop higher faculties in the English specimen than in the Fuegian specimen, because it was better bred." In the same book, she argues that American children made "better citizens" than "the more submissive races" and in particular that "the Chinese and the Hindu, where parents are fairly worshipped and blindly obeyed," were "not races of free and progressive thought and healthy activity." Gilman advocated virtually compulsory enlistment of Blacks in a militaristic industrial corps, even as she opposed such regimentation for whites. In *The Forerunner*, the journal she produced single-handedly for seven years, "yellow" groups are singled out frequently and gratuitously: Gilman chides the "lazy old orientals" who consider work a curse, singles out Chinatown for "criminal conditions," and uses China as an example of various unhealthy social practices. And she all but justifies anti-Semitism by arguing, both in her "own" voice and more boldly through her Herlandian mouthpiece Ellador, that Jews have not yet "'passed the tribal stage'" of human development, that they practice an "'unethical'" and "'morally degrading'" religion of "'race egotism'"

and "'concentrated pride,'" which has unfortunately found its way through the Bible into Western literature, and that in refusing to intermarry they "'artificially maintain characteristics which the whole world dislikes, and then complain of race prejudice.'"

Like many other "nativist" intellectuals, Gilman was especially disturbed by the influx of poor immigrants to American cities and argued on both race and class grounds that these "undesirables" would destroy America. Although she once theorized that immigrants could be "healthier grafts upon our body politic," she wrote later that whatever "special gifts" each race had, when that race was transplanted, "their 'gift' is lost." While proclaiming support for the admission of certain peoples of "assimilable stock," she declared that even the best of "Hindus . . . would make another problem" like the existing "problem" of African Americans, and that an "inflow" of China's "'oppressed'" would make it impossible to preserve the American "national character." This "character," it is clear, requires that "Americans" be primarily people "of native born parentage," who "should have a majority vote *in their own country*." Surprisingly perhaps for a socialist, but less surprisingly for a woman whose autobiography opens with a claim of kinship with Queen Victoria, Gilman seems to equate class status with readiness for democracy. Repeatedly she claims to favor immigration so long as the immigrants are of "better" stock. In her futurist utopia, *Moving the Mountain*, for instance, a character remembers the "old" days when "'we got all the worst and lowest people'"; in the imaginary new America, immigrants may not enter the country until they "come up to a certain standard" by passing a "microscopic" physical exam and completing an education in American ways. It is surely no accident that the list of receiving gates Gilman imagines for her immigrant groups stops with Western Europe: "'There's the German Gate, and the Spanish Gate, the English Gate, and the Italian Gate—and so on.'"

Classism, racism, and nationalism converge with particular virulence when Ellador, having established her antiracist credentials by championing the rights of Black Americans, observes that "'the poor and oppressed were not necessarily good stuff for a democracy'" and declares, in an extraordinary reversal of victim and victimizer to which even her American partner Van protests, that "'it is the poor and oppressed who make monarchy and despotism.'" Ellador's triumph is sealed with the graphic insistence that you cannot "'put a little of everything into a melting pot and produce a good metal,'" not if you are mixing "'gold, silver, copper and iron, lead, radium, pipe, clay, coal dust, and plain dirt.'" Making clear the racial boundaries of the melting pot, Ellador challenges Van, "'And how about the yellow? Do they 'melt'? Do you want them to melt? Isn't your exclusion of them an admission that you think some kinds of people unassimilable? That democracy must pick and choose a little?'" Ellador's rationale—and Gilman's—is that "'the human race is in different stages of development, and only some of the races—or some individuals in a given race—have reached the democratic stage.'" Yet she begs the question and changes the subject when Van asks, " 'But how could we discriminate?' "

The aesthetic and sensory quality of this horror at a polluted America creates a compelling resemblance between the narrator's graphic descriptions of the yellow wallpaper and Gilman's graphic descriptions of the cities and their "swarms of jostling aliens." She fears that America has become "bloated" and "verminous," a "dump" for Europe's "social refuse," "a ceaseless offense to eye and ear and nose," creating "multiforeign" cities that are "abnormally enlarged" and "swollen," "foul, ugly and dangerous," their conditions "offensive to every sense: assailing the eye with ugliness, the ear with noise, the nose with foul smells." And when she complains that America has "stuffed" itself with "uncongenial material," with an "overwhelming flood of unassimilable characteristics," with "such a stream of non-assimilable stuff as shall dilute and drown out the current of our life," indeed with " 'the most ill-assorted and unassimilable mass of human material that was ever held together by artificial means,' " Gilman might be describing the patterns and pieces of the wallpaper as well. Her poem "The City of Death" (1913) depicts a diseased prison "piped with poison, room by room,"

> Whose weltering rush of swarming human
>   forms,
> Forced hurtling through foul subterranean tubes
> Kills more than bodies, coarsens mind and soul.
>
> . . . . .
>
> And steadily degrades our humanness . . .

Such a city is not so different from the claustrophobic nursery which finally "degrades" the "humanness" of **"The Yellow Wallpaper's"** protagonist.

The text of Gilman's imagining, then, is the text of an America made as uninhabitable as the narrator's chamber, and her declaration that "children ought to grow up in the country, all of them," recalls the narrator's relief that her baby does not have to live in the unhappy prison at the top of the house. Clearly Gilman was recognizing serious social problems in her concern over the ghettos and tenements of New York and Chicago—she herself worked for a time at Hull House, although she detested Chicago's "noisome" neighborhoods. But her conflation of the city with its immigrant peoples repeats her own racism even as her nostalgia about the country harks back to a New England in the hands of the New English themselves. These " 'little old New England towns' " and their new counterparts, the " 'fresh young western ones,' " says Ellador, " 'have more of America in them than is possible—could ever be possible—in such a political menagerie as New York,' " whose people really " 'belong in Berlin, in Dublin, in Jerusalem.' "

It is no accident that some of the most extreme of Gilman's anti-immigrant statements come from the radical feminist Ellador, for race and gender are not separate issues in Gilman's cosmology, and it is in their intersection that a fuller reading of **"The Yellow Wallpaper"** becomes possible. For Gilman, patriarchy is a racial phenomenon: it is primarily non-Aryan "yellow" peoples whom Gilman

holds responsible for originating and perpetuating patriarchal practices, and it is primarily Nordic Protestants whom she considers capable of change. In *The Man-Made World: or, Our Androcentric Culture*, Gilman associates the oppression of women with "the heavy millions of the unstirred East," and the "ancestor-worship[ping]" cultures of the "old patriarchal races" who "linger on in feudal Europe." The text singles out the behaviors of "savage African tribes," laments the customs of India, names the "Moslem" religion as "rigidly bigoted and unchanging," and dismisses "to the limbo of all outworn superstition that false Hebraic and grossly androcentric doctrine that the woman is to be subject to the man." Elsewhere, Gilman declares that except for "our Pueblos," where "the women are comparatively independent and honored," nearly all "savages" are "decadent, and grossly androcentric." In one of two essays in *The Forerunner* attacking Ida Tarbell, Gilman identifies Tarbell's "androcentrism" as "neither more nor less than the same old doctrine held by India, China, Turkey, and all the ancient races, held by all ignorant peasants the world over; held by the vast mass of ordinary, unthinking people, and by some quite intelligent enough to know better: that the business of being a woman is to bear and rear children, to 'keep house,' and nothing else." "The most progressive and dominant races" of the present day, she claims, are also "those whose women have most power and liberty; and in the feeblest and most backward races we find women most ill-treated and enslaved." Gilman goes on to make clear that this is an explicitly Aryan accomplishment: "The Teutons and Scandinavian stocks seem never to have had that period of enslaved womanhood, that polygamous harem culture; their women never went through that debasement; and their men have succeeded in preserving the spirit of freedom which is inevitably lost by a race which has servile women." That the "progressive and dominant races" Gilman lauds for not "enslaving" women were at that very moment invading and oppressing countries around the globe seems to present Gilman with no contradiction at all; indeed, imperialism might provide the opportunity, to paraphrase Gayatri Spivak, to save yellow women from yellow men.

In this light, Gilman's wallpaper becomes not only a representation of patriarchy but also the projection of patriarchal practices onto non-Aryan societies. Such a projection stands, of course, in implicit tension with the narrative, because it is the modern-minded, presumably Aryan husband and doctor who constitute the oppressive force. But for Gilman, an educated, Protestant, social-democratic Aryan, America explicitly represented the major hope for feminist possibility. The superiority of this "wider and deeper" and "more human" of religions is directly associated with the fact that "in America the status of women is higher," for example, than in "Romanist" Spain. Not all people are equally educable, after all, particularly if they belong to one of those "tribal" cultures of the East: "you could develop higher faculties in the English specimen than in the Fuegian." And Gilman's boast that **"The Yellow Wallpaper"** convinced S. Weir Mitchell to alter his practices suggests that like Van, the sociologist-narrator of two of Gilman's feminist utopias, educated, white Protestant men could be taught to change. The immigrant "invasion" thus becomes a direct threat to Gilman's program for feminist reform.

As a particular historical product, then, **"The Yellow Wallpaper"** is no more "*the* story that all literary women would tell" than the entirely white canon of *The Madwoman in the Attic* is *the* story of all women's writing or the only story those (white) texts can tell. **"The Yellow Wallpaper"** has been able to pass for a universal text only insofar as white, Western literatures and perspectives continue to dominate academic American feminist practices even when the most urgent literary and political events are happening in Africa, Asia, and Latin America, and among the new and old cultures of Color in the United States. We might expand our theories of censorship, for example, if we read **"The Yellow Wallpaper"** in the context of women's prison writings from around the world—writings like Ding Ling's memoirs and Alicia Partnoy's *The Little School: Tales of Disappearance and Survival in Argentina* and some of the stories of Bessie Head. We might have something to learn about interpretation if we examined the moment in Partnoy's narrative when her husband is tortured because he gives the "wrong" reading of his wife's poems. We might better understand contemporary feminist racial politics if we studied the complex but historically distanced discourses of feminists a century ago. Perhaps, like the narrator of Gilman's story, white, American academic feminist criticism has sought in literature the mirror of its own identity, erasing the literary equivalent of strange sights and smells and colors so that we can have the comfort of reproducing, on a bare stage, that triumphant moment when a woman recognizes her self. Perhaps white, American feminist practice too readily resembles that of Gilman, who deplores that historically "we have cheated the Indian, oppressed the African, robbed the Mexican," and whose utopian impulses continue to insist that there is only "one race, the human race," but for whom particular, present conditions of race and class continue to be blindnesses justified on "other"—aesthetic, political, pragmatic—grounds.

"The Yellow Wallpaper" also calls upon us to recognize that the white, female, intellectual-class subjectivity which Gilman's narrator attempts to construct, and to which many feminists have also been committed perhaps unwittingly, is a subjectivity whose illusory unity, like the unity imposed on the paper, is built on the repression of difference. This also means that the conscious biographical experience which Gilman claims as the authenticating source of the story is but one contributing element. And if we are going to read this text in relation to its author, we may have to realize that there are dangers as well as pleasures in a feminist reading based on a merging of consciousnesses. Once we recognize Gilman as a subject constituted in and by the contradictions of ideology, we might also remember that she acknowledges having been subjected to the narrator's circumstances but denies any relationship to the wallpaper itself—that is, to what I am reading as the site of a political unconscious in which questions of race permeate questions of sex. A recent essay by Ellen Messer-Davidow in *New Literary History* argues that literary criticism and feminist criticism should be recognized as fundamentally different activities, that feminist criti-

cism is part of a larger interdisciplinary project whose main focus is the exploration of "ideas about sex and gender," that disciplinary variations are fairly insignificant differences of "medium," and therefore that feminist literary critics need to change their subject from "literature" to "ideas about sex and gender" as these happen to be expressed in literature. I suggest that one of the messages of **"The Yellow Wallpaper"** is that textuality, like culture, is more complex, shifting, and polyvalent than any of the ideas we can abstract from it, that the narrator's reductive gesture is precisely to isolate and essentialize one "idea about sex and gender" from a more complex textual field.

Deconstructing our own reading of the wallpaper, then, means acknowledging that Adrienne Rich still speaks to feminist critics when she calls on us to "[enter] an old text from a new critical direction," to "take the work first of all as a clue to how we live . . . how we have been led to imagine ourselves, how our language has trapped as well as liberated us . . . and how we can begin to see and name—and therefore live—afresh," so that we do not simply "pass on a tradition but . . . break its hold over us." Feminist critical theory offers the deconstructive principles for this continuing revision, so long as we require ourselves, as we have required our nonfeminist colleagues, to look anew at what have become old texts and old critical premises. Still, the revision I am proposing here would have been impossible without the first revision of **"The Yellow Wallpaper"** that liberated the imprisoned woman from the text. Adrienne Rich has addressed the poem "Heroines" to nineteenth-century white feminists who reflected racism and class privilege in their crusades for change. It is both to Gilman herself and to all of us whose readings of **"The Yellow Wallpaper"** have been both transformative and limiting, that, in closing, I address the final lines of Rich's poem:

> How can I fail to love
>   your clarity and fury
> how can I give you
>   all your due
>   take courage from your courage
> honor your exact
>   legacy as it is
> recognizing
>   as well
>   that it is not enough?
>
>   (pp. 415-36)

Susan S. Lanser, "Feminist Criticism, 'The Yellow Wallpaper,' and the Politics of Color in America," in Feminist Studies, *Vol. 15, No. 3, Fall, 1989, pp. 415-41.*

Greg Johnson (essay date 1989)

[*In the essay below, Johnson discusses "The Yellow Wallpaper" as an example of a Gothic allegory, noting in particular its themes of rage and regression.*]

In the autumn of 1830, shortly before Emily Dickinson's birth, her mother made an unusual request. At a time when her pregnancy—or as it was then called, her "confinement"—might have been expected to absorb her attention, Mrs. Dickinson abruptly demanded new wallpaper for her bedroom. Apparently dismayed by this outburst of feminine whimsy, her stern-tempered husband refused, prompting Mrs. Dickinson to her only recorded act of wifely defiance. Though "the Hon. Edward Dickinson would not allow her to have it done," a neighbor's descendant recalled, "she went secretly to the paper hanger and asked him to come and paper her bedroom. This he did, while Emily was being born."

To place this incident in context, we should be note that Mrs. Dickinson, aged twenty-six, had just moved into her father-in-law's Amherst mansion and now faced the grim prospect of living with her husband's unpredictable relatives, along with the even grimmer perils of early nineteenth-century childbirth. Although Mrs. Dickinson was by most accounts a submissive, self-abnegating, rather neurasthenic woman—in short, the nineteenth-century ideal—it is tempting to read the wallpaper incident as a desperate gesture of autonomy and self-assertion. Emily Dickinson's most recent biographer, Cynthia Griffin Wolff, suggests that "The little explosion of defiance signaled fear and distress, and it was the prelude to unhappy, silent acceptance."

Though the color of Mrs. Dickinson's wallpaper went unrecorded, the anecdote forms a striking parallel to Charlotte Perkins Gilman's **"The Yellow Wallpaper,"** first published in 1892 but, like Emily Dickinson's work, underappreciated until decades after her death. Both the domestic incident and the terrifying short story suggest the familiar Gothic themes of confinement and rebellion, forbidden desire and "irrational" fear. Both include such Gothic staples as the distraught heroine, the forbidding mansion, and the powerfully repressive male antagonist. If we focus on the issue of the Gothic world and its release of imaginative power, however, the stories form a dramatic contrast. A woman of ordinary abilities, the unimaginative Mrs. Dickinson would later represent the nadir of female selfhood to her brilliant, rebellious daughter. "Mother does not care for thought," the poet remarked dryly in 1862; and by 1870, she could issue this blunt dismissal: "I never had a mother." But Dickinson surely would have admired the unnamed heroine of **"The Yellow Wallpaper,"** who willingly accepts madness over repression, refusing a life of "unhappy, silent acceptance." The poet would have especially responded to the woman's identity as a writer, and to the way in which her story adroitly and at times parodically employs Gothic conventions to present an allegory of literary imagination unbinding the social, domestic, and psychological confinements of a nineteenth-century woman writer.

Rather than simply labeling the narrator a madwoman at the story's close, we might view her behavior as an expression of long-suppressed rage: a rage which causes a temporary breakdown (like those actually suffered by both Dickinson and Gilman) but which represents a prelude to psychic regeneration and artistic redemption. This reading accounts for two elements of the story usually ignored: its emphasis upon the narrator as a writer, who is keeping a journal and putting forth her own text—**"The Yellow Wallpaper"**—as an antithetical triumph over the actual wallpaper that had nearly been her undoing; and its brit-

tle, macabre, relentlessly satiric humor that suggests, in the story's earlier sections, her barely suppressed and steadily mounting anger. As in many of Poe's tales, this seemingly incongruous humor serves only to accentuate the Gothic terror of the narrator's situation.

In their pioneering study, *The Madwoman in the Attic*, Sandra Gilbert and Susan Gubar have examined the ways in which nineteenth-century women writers—Charlotte Brontë in *Jane Eyre*, for instance—express forbidden emotions in powerful but carefully disguised forms. Just as that other Mrs. Rochester, Bertha Mason, may be read as a raging doppelganger whose burning of Thornfield Hall expresses her alter ego Jane Eyre's forbidden anger and allows her the Victorian redemption of blissful marriage, so are the maddening frustrations of Gilman's heroine allowed their fearsome release, resulting in her triumph over her husband in the story's unforgettable final scene. (At one point in **"The Yellow Wallpaper,"** too, the narrator has fantasies of burning the house down.) Unlike Jane Eyre, however, Gilman's heroine identifies wholly with the raging "madness" of the double she discovers locked within the tortured arabesques of the wallpaper. Her experience should finally be viewed not as a final catastrophe but as a terrifying, necessary stage in her progress toward self-identity and personal achievement. Four years after her breakdown, Gilman is clearly allegorizing her own rage and justifying her defiant choice of art and activism over conventional feminine endeavors.

The narrative focus of **"The Yellow Wallpaper"** moves relentlessly inward, detailing the narrator's gradual absorption into the Gothic world of psychic chaos and imaginative freedom; but Gilman controls her heroine's deepening subjectivity through repetition, irony, parodic humor, and allegorical patterns of imagery. The two worlds of the story—the narrator's husband and sister-in-law's daylight world of masculine order and domestic routine, and her own subjective sphere of deepening imaginative insight—are kept clearly focused and distinct. Most important, Gilman reminds the reader frequently that her narrator is a habitual writer for whom **"The Yellow Wallpaper"** is a kind of diary, an accurate record of her turbulent inward journey. Drawing on Gilman's experience of post-partum depression and breakdown, the story is far more than an indictment of nineteenth-century attitudes toward women and an account of one woman's incipient psychosis. Gilman made her heroine a writer for purposes of art, not autobiography, and the story as a whole describes a woman attempting to save herself *through* her own writing, to transform what she calls "dead paper" into a vibrant Gothic world of creative dreamwork and self-revelation.

Two of the story's major structural devices are its contrasting of the husband's daylight world and his wife's nocturnal fantasy, and the religious imagery by which she highlights the liberating and redemptive qualities of her experience. When the story opens, she acknowledges that the idea of their rented summer house as a Gothic setting is laughable, a romantic fancy of the kind her husband wishes to repress. The allegorical opposition is quickly established: her husband (named John, suggesting a male prototype) is a "physician of high standing," a figure of dominance in every sense—social, domestic, intellectual, physical. He is a thoroughgoing empiricist who "scoffs openly at any talk of things not to be felt and seen and put down in figures." Throughout the story John, along with his like-named sister and housekeeper Jane, is associated with the rigidly hierarchical and imaginatively sterile daylight world that ridicules Gothic "fancies" and represses in particular the "hysterical tendency" of women. Before the story opens, the narrator had abandoned her own social responsibility of motherhood, and the object of this summer retreat is a "rest cure" (of the kind made popular by Dr. S. Weir Mitchell, the famous Philadelphia neurologist who treated Gilman during her own depression, and against whom the story enacts a brilliant literary revenge). That her husband exerts his tyrannical control in the guise of protectiveness makes the narrator feel all the more stifled and precludes outright defiance. As she remarks sarcastically in the opening section, "He is very careful and loving, and hardly lets me stir without special direction."

It is the daylight consciousness of late-Victorian America, of course, which has designed the flamboyantly hideous yellow wallpaper that the narrator initially finds so repulsive. Even John wants to repaper the room, but after his wife complains about the wallpaper, he benevolently changes his mind, since "nothing was worse for a nervous patient than to give way to such fancies." Associating her nervous illness with her "imaginative power and habit of story-making," he forces his wife into daily confinement by four walls whose paper, described as 'debased Romanesque,' is an omnipresent figuring of the artistic degeneration and psychic chaos she fears. It is here that John makes a significant error, however, as he underestimates the very imaginative power he is seeking to repress. By placing his distraught wife in a nursery, he is merely following the nineteenth-century equation of non-maternal women—that is, spinsters and "hysterics"—with helpless children. Yet he is unthinkingly allowing her the free play of imagination and abdication of social responsibility also characteristic of children. Thus as the story progresses, the narrator follows both her childlike promptings and her artistic faith in creating a Gothic alternative to the stifling daylight world of her husband and the society at large.

The story's terrific suspense derives from the narrator's increasingly uncertain fate and from the considerable obstacles blocking her path from one world to the other, not the least of which is her own self-doubt and debilitating psychic exhaustion. Near the end of the next section, she glimpses a subpattern in the wallpaper, which can be seen only "in certain lights, and not clearly then"; beneath the "silly and conspicuous front design" is a figure she describes as "strange, provoking, formless." These three adjectives suggest a notably ambivalent attitude toward her own inchoate, slowly emerging selfhood; but significantly, she notes that she is viewing the pattern by sunlight. Near the end of the next section, at sunset, she can "almost fancy" a coherent design in the wallpaper. Yet immediately after using her husband's forbidden word, she feels an emotional and psychological depletion that is emphasized by a series of brief, depressed paragraphs:

> It makes me tired to follow [the pattern]. I will take a nap, I guess.

> I don't know why I should write this.

> I don't want to.

> I don't feel able.

> And I know John would think it absurd. But I *must* say what I feel and think in some way—it is such a relief!

> But the effort is getting to be greater than the relief.

This passage describes the narrator's spiritual nadir, and may be said to represent her transition from conscious struggle against the daylight world to her immersion in the nocturnal world of the unconscious—or, in other terms, from idle fancy to empowering imagination. The nature of Gilman's allegory becomes especially clear when, for the first time, the narrator watches the wallpaper by moonlight and reports with childlike glee: "There are things in the paper that nobody knows but me, or ever will." Yet the transition is incomplete and puzzling. While John sleeps, she lies awake "trying to decide whether that front pattern and the back pattern really did move together or separately," noting that "by daylight" the pattern is a constant irritant to a "normal mind." Then comes the moment of terrified but thrilling revelation:

> By moonlight—the moon shines in all night when there is a moon—I wouldn't know it was the same paper.

> At night in any kind of light, in twilight, candlelight, lamplight, and worst of all by moonlight, it becomes bars! The outside pattern, I mean, and the woman behind it is as plain as can be.

The remainder of the story traces the narrator's gradual identification with her own suppressed rage, figured as a woman grasping the bars of her prison and struggling frantically to get free. Sleeping during the day, since "By daylight [the woman] is subdued, quiet," the narrator comes to life at night, struggling past the stifling outer pattern of the wallpaper to free the sister, the twin, the mirror image, the lost self. "As soon as it was moonlight and that poor thing began to crawl and shake the pattern, I got up and ran to help her." In this process of ecstatic reciprocity—"I pulled and she shook. I shook and she pulled"—the narrator destroys the wallpaper and expresses her desperate rage, finally integrating herself and the woman trapped in the paper into a single triumphant "I." Yet instinctively she recognizes that her access of power has its source in the unconscious (she had once called the wallpaper "a bad dream") and that she is temporarily confined to the Gothic world of her own making: "I suppose I shall have to get back behind the pattern when it comes night," she exclaims, "and that is hard!"

But the writer's own patterns—especially her imagery of liberation and redemption—suggest otherwise. In a story focused upon a woman's enforced dependency, for instance, it's not surprising that the narrator takes special note of the Fourth of July. As the holiday approaches, she begs her husband to invite her cousins Henry and Julia, lively people who are presumably supportive of her writing, to visit her; but he refuses, instead inviting "Mother and Nellie and the children," a group which suggests conventional domesticity. As for Henry and Julia, she reports her husband's saying that he "would as soon put fireworks in my pillow-case as to let me have those stimulating people about." This startling phrase, "fireworks in my pillow-case," is a brilliantly concentrated figure for the imaginative "independence" soon to begin as the narrator lies watching the wallpaper by moonlight beside her sleeping husband.

Because such independence represents her personal salvation, the narrator images her intense suffering in terms suggesting a religious allegory and recalling Dickinson's self-assertion as "Queen of Calvary." Although it is John who has "no patience with faith" and the wallpaper which commits every "artistic sin" it is the narrator who endures hellish pain while confined by her husband and his punishing walls. The windows of her room are barred, and just outside the door is a gate at the head of the stairs, as though to separate an Edenic green world ("full of great elms and velvet meadows") from her infernal cell. Her bed, nailed to the floor, suggests a sexual crucifixion, while inside the wallpaper, its color a "lurid orange in some places, a sickly sulphur tint in others," she sees suicide victims with broken necks and bulbous eyes, and senses in the paper's general effect of horror an "everlastingness." And the narrator underscores her own sense of guilt (is it possible that she deserves this torment?) when she mentions that the woman caring for her temporarily abandoned baby is named "Mary," imaging the spiritual and maternal perfection which the narrator so conspicuously lacks. The narrator, her identity in turbulent flux, fits nowhere inside this theologically and socially determined allegory and is appropriately nameless.

Despite the demonic forces marshaled against her, the narrator continues to rebel; it is important to stress to extent to which she chooses to suffer rather than accept the artistic sin of the wallpaper. Clinging to the faith her husband disavows, she instinctively attempts to save herself, as it is her visionary penetration of the paper's menacing reality that locates her own long-suppressed rage and allows its redemptive expression. But, as William Patrick Day notes in his comprehensive study of Gothic literature, the function of imagination in such works is not only therapeutic; it also initiates an analytic resolution: "the Gothic fantasy can localize imagination. It cannot be a complete escape, only the prelude to an understanding of the links between the imagined and real worlds." Since both the daylight world and the Gothic world are "mad" when experienced in terms of the other, it is the narrator's own text which represents her potential triumph, not the ghastly, merely rhetorical gloating of the final scene in which, lost in fantasy, she crawls repeatedly over the body of her prostrate husband. If we focus upon the competing texts offered by the story—that of the wallpaper itself and of the revived "dead paper" the narrator uses to inscribe her powerful vision—we can see Gilman wrestling with the ambivalence toward imaginative power that is central to the American Gothic tradition and is particularly intense in the case of a woman who denied throughout her life that her work possessed any genuine literary value. In the text of **"The Yellow Wallpaper,"** in short, she allows her

heroine a furious and uncompromising rebellion that she could never acknowledge fully as her own.

As Gilman's narrator begins surreptitiously writing the text eventually to be titled, triumphantly, **"The Yellow Wallpaper,"** she stresses its value as simple therapy, "a great relief to my mind." The first two sections end abruptly with statements emphasizing both the immediacy and covertness of her writing: "I must put this away,— [John] hates to have me write a word" and "There's sister on the stairs!" Despite her outward acceptance of her rest cure, the text has already assumed the character of a subversive document. An experienced writer, she understands the healing power which inheres in the act of writing and recognizes intuitively that her physician husband's rest cure can lead only to her psychic degeneration. After describing the wallpaper, she recalls her own imaginative power as a child, when she needed only "blank walls" (just as now she needs only "dead paper") to empower her imagination: "I used to lie awake as a child and get more entertainment and terror out of blank walls and plain furniture than most children could find in a toy store." The phrase "entertainment and terror" suggests, of course, a child's version of Gothic—the imaginary ghosts, bogey men, and other invented horrors populating a typical child's bedroom. In adulthood, however, her blank childhood walls have become inscribed with what represents, essentially, an unchosen fate demonically opposed to her childlike imaginative freedom; simply put, this fate is her psychological confinement and torture as a woman desiring creative autonomy in nineteenth-century America. As Annette Kolodny writes, the narrator begins " 'reading' in the wallpaper the underlying if unacknowledged patterns of her real-life experience" and "discovering the symbolization of her own untenable and unacceptable reality."

Rejecting this text and its meaning, the narrator continues doggedly with her own antithetical text, constantly fighting—as we have already seen—the debilitating exhaustion of her struggle. In a key phrase, she notes that "I don't feel as if it was worth while *to turn my hand over* for anything" (my italics). This recalls Sylvia Plath's famous poem "Tulips," whose speaker has become an invalid in circumstances not unlike the narrator's and who wants "to lie with my hands turned up and be utterly empty." Gilman's narrator, however, refuses the passivity of those upturned hands; whenever she can avoid the watchful eyes of John and Jane, she does turn her hand over and continue writing. Her short paragraphs and clipped, declarative sentences—in such marked contrast to the rolling, baroque periods and effusive style of a more typical Victorian Gothic—suggest the frantic intensity not only of her experience but of her writing process itself. An obsessive writer, she gradually confronts in her own text the threatening, demonic text inscribed upon the wallpaper.

Before examining that text, we should note that the narrator's frequent sarcasm and macabre humor also suggest her developing anger and the effective, opposing power of her own writing. The caustic tone is especially apparent when the story is read alongside Gilman's non-fictional and autobiographical writings. Shortly after finishing

"The Yellow Wallpaper," for instance, she wrote her friend Martha Lane: "When my awful story **'The Yellow Wallpaper'** comes out, you must try & read it. Walter says he has read it *four* times, and thinks it the most ghastly tale he ever read." She added dryly: "But that's only a husband's opinion." At times the narrator's sarcasm is equally patent, as when she remarks that "John is a physician, and *perhaps* . . . that is one reason I don't get well faster"; or when she calls herself "unreasonably angry" and "basely ungrateful" as a wife and patient; or when she mocks her husband's empiricism by developing her own "scientific hypothesis" about the wallpaper; or when, contemplating suicide, she says that "to jump out the window would be admirable exercise" but that "a step like that is improper and might be misconstrued." Likewise the central symbol of the story ironically equates her crisis with an item of feminine frippery—mere wallpaper—that is far beneath serious male consideration. More subtly, she also takes an ironic view of the Gothic conventions she is employing, revealing anger at her own role as a helpless and distraught Gothic heroine. In one of several passages verging on parody, she mocks both her husband's extreme condescension and her own "feminine" dependency. They're lying in bed, and John has just expressed optimism about her improved appetite and health:

> "I don't weigh a bit more," said I, "nor as much; and my appetite may be better in the evening when you are here but it is worse in the morning when you are away!"
>
> "Bless her little heart!" said he with a big hug. "She shall be as sick as she pleases! But now let's improve the shining hours by going to sleep, and talk about it in the morning!"
>
> "And you won't go away?" I asked gloomily.

But if Gilman parodies the conventional Gothic in such scenes, it is only to underscore her narrator's isolated confrontation—once John has fallen asleep—with the very real terrors of the wallpaper.

When she first begins "reading" the paper, she notes that the children who once occupied the nursery had stripped it off in great patches around the head of the bedstead, as if instinctively preserving their healthy imaginative autonomy. Clinging to her own autonomy as an artist, she first judges the wallpaper on aesthetic grounds; it not only contains "one of those sprawling, flamboyant patterns committing every artistic sin," but also embodies "unheard-of contradictions." Its color is "repellent, almost revolting." Here she is reading the text objectively, in essence, as an artist confronted by bad art. But as the story proceeds, aesthetic distaste turns to outrage: "I know a little of the principle of design, and I know this thing was not arranged on any laws of radiation, or alternation, or repetition, or symmetry, or anything else that I ever heard of." (These are precisely the laws, it should be noted, that govern her own artistically successful text.) Gradually the wallpaper becomes nightmarishly unreadable, with its "great slanting waves of optic horror," and the narrator begins to hallucinate menacing toadstools, fungus, and other unspecified "old, foul, bad yellow things." In her fear and panic, she endures a synaesthetic disorientation

From left to right: Dorothy Stetson Chamberlin, Gilman, Walter Stetson Chamberlin, and George Houghton Gilman. Pasadena, California, 1927.

in which she can smell the paper and see it rub off onto her clothes. The more confused she becomes, however, the clearer her vision of an emerging "subtext," in which her imprisoned double is frantically shaking the bars of her prison.

As we witness the narrator in the final scene, creeping along the floor, we might recall once again that her bedroom is actually a nursery. The fact that she is crawling on all fours—as opposed to lying still and docile under her husband's "rest cure"—suggests not only temporary derangement but also a frantic, insistent growth into a new stage of being. From the helpless infant, supine on her immovable bed, she has become a crawling, "creeping" child, insistent upon her own needs and explorations. (The parallel with Bertha Mason in *Jane Eyre*, who likewise crawls on all fours and exhibits similar destructiveness, is surely deliberate.) To the daylight world, of course, this transition is terrifying; poor John, in Gilman's witty inversion of a conventional heroine's confrontation with Gothic terror, faints dead away. Seizing rather than surrendering to power, the narrator is thus left alone, the mad heroine of her own appalling text.

Although Gilman's Gothic allegory so powerfully demonstrates that writing is her only salvation, the poignant facts of her own biography point to her internalization of the restrictions enforced by John in her story and by Dr. S. Weir Mitchell in her life. A compulsive writer who produced scores of volumes and earned a worldwide reputation as an eloquent advocate of women's rights, Gilman discredited the value of her imaginative writing throughout her career; she wrote to William Dean Howells, who asked to reprint **"The Yellow Wallpaper"** in a collection of American masterpieces, that the story was "no more 'literature' than my other stuff, being definitely written 'with a purpose' "—that purpose being to demonstrate to Dr. Mitchell the cruelty and inefficacy of the rest-cure. (She sent him a copy of the story upon publication, but received no response.) Patricia Meyer Spacks, in an incisive discussion of Gilman's curiously impersonal autobiography, *The Living of Charlotte Perkins Gilman,* notes that although Gilman's breakdown led her to abandon marriage and motherhood, become a professional writer, and devote herself to social causes, this self-determination was limited strictly by her continuing need to be "good" and necessarily precluded the acknowledged use of her own imaginative power.

Thus Gilman's life story became, as Spacks asserts, "a paradigm of feminine anger," what Gilman herself called "a lifetime of limitation and wretchedness." Denied the artistic redemption that Emily Dickinson had achieved by renouncing the world, as well as the conventional satisfactions of nineteenth-century housewifery and motherhood, Gilman uneasily compensated for her denial of creative selfhood with the fulfillment of useful work. Committing suicide not because her inoperable cancer caused her pain but because she felt her "usefulness was over"—the phrase comes from her suicide note, a poignant last text of self-effacement—Gilman stayed true to her own daylight world of feminism, social commitment, and constant hard work. Still under-read, still haunting the margins of the American literary canon, Gilman and the full scope of her achievement await their due recognition. Reading **"The Yellow Wallpaper,"** we can only guess at the furious effort, and the constant bargaining with her own demons, by which that achievement came into being. (pp. 521-30)

> *Greg Johnson, "Gilman's Gothic Allegory: Rage and Redemption in 'The Yellow Wallpaper',"* in Studies in Short Fiction, *Vol. 26, No. 4, Fall, 1989, pp. 521-30.*

Lisa Kasmer   (essay date 1990)

[In the essay below, Kasmer offers a symptomatic reading of "The Yellow Wallpaper."]

When Charlotte Perkins Gilman attempted to publish her short story **"The Yellow Wallpaper"** in 1892, she met with the consternation of disapproving males. Horace Scudder, then editor of *The Atlantic Monthly,* declared himself repelled by the morbid nature of the tale. He explained that he could not publish the story as he "could not forgive" himself if he made others as miserable as he had made himself by reading it. Ironically, these remarks echo the words of the domineering husband within Gilman's story. John is unable to appreciate the seriousness of his wife's illness. Instead he insists that as a physician and her husband, he knows her fears about her illness are merely morbid.

Dismissed by most critics when the story finally appeared in *The New England Magazine* in May 1892, it was virtually ignored for fifty years. In 1982, Elaine Hedges, editing for the Feminist Press, articulated the irony inherent in Scudder's reaction. The critics had not examined a theme inherent in the "morbid" tale—woman's oppression—dismissing Gilman's own commitment to feminist issues. Gilman, in fact, wrote the story in hopes of pointing out the dangers of the "rest cure," developed by Dr. S. Weir Mitchell, a nerve specialist, a treatment Gilman herself underwent. According to Gilman, "the real purpose of the story was to reach Dr. S. Weir Mitchell, and convince him of the error of his ways." This treatment, commonly prescribed to women diagnosed with hysteria, attempted to help the patient through reintegrating her into her "proper" position as wife by forcing her to focus only on her home and children. When Gilman underwent this treatment, she came perilously close to having a nervous breakdown. In contrast to Mitchell's seemingly self-serving theory, Gilman felt she had only regained her health when she left her marriage and returned to her literary career.

Since this (re)emergence of the story, which Hedges declares a "feminist document," feminist critics have embraced the story as fervently as Gilman's male contemporaries shunned it. Three prominent critical works have recently discussed **"The Yellow Wallpaper"**: *Madwoman in the Attic, The Writer and the Nineteenth Century Imagination* by Susan Gilbert and Sandra Gubar; "A Map for Rereading: Or Gender and the Interpretation of Literary Texts," by Annette Kolodny; and "Convention Coverage or How to Read Your Own Life," by Jean Kennard. These critics have raised the story to the level of a parable for feminist readings—the work becomes a tale extolling the value of feminist readings or "revisionary readings." This type of reading, which Adrienne Rich calls for and defines in "When We Dead Awaken: Writing as Re-Vision," entails "a radical critique, feminist in its impulse, that would take the work first of all as a clue to how we [as women] live, how we have been living, how we have been led to imagine ourselves, how our language has trapped as well as liberated us; and how we can begin to see—and therefore live—afresh." Taken together, these recent interpretations of the story draw two parallels. First, they align the inability of the narrator's husband to understand his wife's condition, in effect to read her text, with the difficulty Gilman's contemporaries had in understanding the work itself. Second, they associate the narrator's forging her own independence, and by "extension the independence of all women," through her interpretation of the wallpaper, with their own re-readings of the text.

Using as a foundation the laudatory piece Hedges wrote on **"The Yellow Wallpaper,"** Gilbert and Gubar proclaim that **"The Yellow Wallpaper"** is the story all "literary women would tell if they had the voice." They explain that when the narrator, through a "revisionary reading" of the symbols in the wallpaper, "discovers her double and enables this double to escape from her textual/architectural confinement," by ripping down the wallpaper, she effects her own liberation. The authors extend this act of liberation to the "progress of nineteenth century literary women out of the texts defined by patriarchal poetics into the open spaces of their own authority."

In her article, Kolodny continues along the same lines, affirming that it is "unfortunate that Gilman's story was so quickly relegated to backwaters of our literary landscape because, coming as it did at the end of the nineteenth century, it spoke to a growing concern and American women who would be serious writers." She extends Gilbert and Gubar's critique, yet she is primarily interested in understanding the lack of attention given to the story's feminist theme up to that time. She explains that Gilman's contemporaries lacked the foresight to view a middle-class housewife's life as oppressively maddening. As Kolodny points out, nineteenth century readers familiar with Poe's macabre tales of madness were unable to "transfer their sense of mental derangement to the mind of a comfortable middle class wife and mother." She elaborates upon this idea of the untransmittability of the narrator's condition by juxtaposing the unpenetrable quality of the text to the narrator herself, who is a "text which can neither get read or recorded," since her husband "will not heed what she says of herself" and forbids her to write. According to Kolodny, then, the narrator "gives up her attempt to record her reality and instead begins to read it" by attempting to decode her own meaning, just as contemporary critics must try to re-interpret the story. And in this double act of re-interpretation, like Gilbert and Gubar, Kolodny sees truth and triumph: the narrator discovers, even in madness, liberation and the critics discover the "true" hidden meaning of the text.

In her article published in 1981, Jean Kennard explores more fully the origin of this re-interpretation of the story initially illuminated by Hedges. She explains that since literary conventions change with social and political changes, current feminist novels and feminist politics have shaped the way feminist scholars as an "interpretive community" see literary symbols. For example, the room, or in the story the narrator's confinement to her room, has become symbolic of the situation of women in patriarchal society. More important (and strange, as Kennard acknowledges), madness has become a "higher form of sanity" within this society: within **"The Yellow Wallpaper,"** the narrator's descent into madness is seen as a "way to health, as a rejection of and escape from an insane society."

In attributing a revisionary reading to the narrator at the end of the story, these critics assume that the narrator, in being able to critique her own situation, is using a discourse, which can express her desires. This assessment fails since it becomes clear within the story that the narrator is trapped in patriarchal discourse. She, therefore, cannot consciously understand her situation: her madness can only be a parodic from of liberation. In a recent article, "Monumental Feminism and Literature's Ancestral House: Another Look at 'The Yellow Paper,'" Janice Haney-Peritz faults these works, based on this notion of the narrator's lack of access to language. She points out that these critics wrongly make the story into a "feminist monument" or a memorial to feminist triumph as she feels the narrator only acts out her husband's desires. Haney-

Peritz views the narrator's entrapment as inescapable, making the entire story a "repetition," only a reflection of patriarchal desires. She states, "Indeed it may be the case that in reading 'The Yellow Wallpaper,' we are reading the story of John's demands and desires rather than something distinctively female. If so, then the assurance that the identification [of the feminine in the text] as liberating becomes highly problematic. . . .'"

These critics incorrectly define the feminine as a feminist "truth" which encompasses the condition of all women. They do not seek (or like Haney-Peritz dismiss) the feminine within the text. Instead, I define the feminine as those moments in the text that disrupt the male desire, allowing the desires of the woman to emerge. Even though the narrator is entrapped in her husband's discourse, I propose that her desires can be clearly seen in the symptomatic points, or the impasses of meaning, in her journal. Moreover, her desire points toward a liberating and disruptive force which at once mirrors and contains her unconscious—the yellow wallpaper itself. This force allows the narrator to begin to surpass her husband's language and desires and to establish her own.

In **"The Yellow Wallpaper,"** the narrator records her impressions in a series of journal entries during a summer stay with her husband in a colonial mansion they have let. Responding to his wife's complaints that she is ill, her husband, John, takes her away that summer for a rest. His object is to combat her illness, which he dismisses as a "temporary nervous depression." Ignoring her complaints that she is really ill, he sets her on a program modelled on the "rest cure," consisting of air and complete rest. The narrator disagrees with his diagnosis and the treatment but follows the program anyway. As part of the treatment, she must stay in her room, and as she spends more and more time there, she becomes increasingly agitated and obsessive about the "horrid" wallpaper decorating it. She imagines the figure of a woman moving about behind it. Ultimately, she sinks into madness, entering the imaginary world of the wallpaper and acting upon this image of her own imprisonment within her marriage by tearing down the wallpaper and "releasing" this woman.

Initially, the narrator does react to her husband's diagnosis with pained uncertainty. She bemoans her husband's insistence that she is not sick and disagrees with his treatment for curing her: "Personally I disagree with his methods. I believe work and congenial company would do me good." It becomes clear within her journal writings, however, that she has accepted her husband's diagnosis, acknowledging that "when one's husband is a physician and of high standing, what can one do?" She understands that the authoritative opinion of her husband will be taken as law. In fact, he constantly lords his status as a doctor over her, using the reasoning, "I am the doctor," to squelch her fears.

With no other choice, she takes the medication which he has prescribed and adheres to his regimen. Her taking the medication orally takes on monumental metaphorical significance, however. It becomes clear that she has swallowed John's language as well. Indeed, she "mouths" her husband's very words, only speaking of her illness in his terms. When she attempts to say aloud that she feels she is not well mentally, she stops because John looks at her with such a "stern reproachful look."

On one level, the narrator's husband has taken away his wife's ability to speak her own thoughts by reassuring her friends that there is "really **nothing** the matter" with her. Any complaint of hers is **halted** before she can speak. But more insidiously, she has lost her ability to accept this thought which contradicts her husband's. As Haney-Peritz points out, in order for the narrator to accept her husband's ideas concerning her health, she cannot merely incorporate the content of her husband's language. She must also take on the form of his discourse: "The narrator's writing not only recounts John's prescriptive discourse but also relies on the very binary oppositions which structure that discourse." For the narrator to accept that she is well, as her husband believes, although she knows that she is not, she must follow her husband's thought-patterns.

Symbolically, she has been inserted into this system of discourse, which the family situation that John has created within the summer house emphasizes. His re-creation of the family involves placing his wife in the position of the absent child to whom she has recently given birth. He allows his sister, Jennie, whom the narrator describes as the "perfect housekeeper," to watch over her in his absence. In his actions toward his wife, John reinforces the idea that she is the child, forcing her to sleep in the room that used to be a nursery, making her take naps, reading to her before bed-time, and calling her his "little girl." In this way, he mimics the original insertion of the child into a system of language. This point is illuminated by Jacques Lacan's theory of language. In Lacanian terms, language does not arise within the individual, but outside her, constituted under a general law on which the language is founded. The child submits to that law as she enters the symbolic realm—a pre-existing structure of social and sexual roles.

The child, then, can no longer see herself as a unified self-generating subject; she is now limited by the discourses which cannot completely represent her.

The law on which John's language is founded, and to which the narrator has submitted, is the phallus or the patriarch, a first principle, which his thought-system holds as inarguable, and from which all other meanings are constructed. This principle is based on the logic of binary opposition, a hierarchy of meanings determined by their difference from their opposite. The hierarchical system within his language, created by a male-dominated society and placed on the founding principle of man necessarily excludes woman and makes other rigid distinctions between what is acceptable and what is not, for example, between truth and falsity, sense and nonsense, reason and madness. His language consistently reasserts this system, so the narrator can intone like a mantra: "John is practical in the extreme. He has no patience with faith, an intense horror of superstition and he scoffs openly at any talk of things not to be felt and seen and put down in figures."

His diagnosis of his wife, which dominates the story as the

catalyst that creates all action within it, exemplifies his pattern of thinking as grounded in phallocentric logic and patriarchal culture. In diagnosing his wife as having a "slight hysterical tendency," he subscribes to the medical profession's view within the nineteenth century of woman as inferior and in need of moral training. In the nineteenth century, hysteria was attributed to a woman's inability to exercise self-control or to curb her emotions and desires. As one late-nineteenth century physician asserted: "Young persons who have been raised in luxury and too often in idleness, who have never been called upon to face the hardships of life, who have never accustomed themselves to self-denial, who have abundant time and opportunity to cultivate the emotional and sensuous, to indulge the sentimental side of life. . . . These are the most frequent victims of hysteria." John frequently admonishes his wife to control herself because lack of control is so "dangerous to a temperament like [hers]."

John's assertion that his wife's sickness is a "false and foolish fancy" must necessarily negate her assertions that she is not well, maintaining his authority within this hierarchy at her expense. Moreover, his prescription of complete rest, not only overrules her desire to write and to have company, but on a symbolic level, takes away her ability to communicate. Within his diagnosis, just as he establishes male above female, he also distinguishes between the real and things that cannot be seen. In the nineteenth century, hysteria was found to have no organic origin and consequently not viewed as a physical illness. To most nineteenth century doctors, hysteria was viewed as a "false and foolish fancy" of emotional women.

The narrator, initially trapped within her husband's discourse, is unable to find her own words, or to articulate her feelings. These feelings do exist, however. They surface in her journal as symptomatic points, the impasses of meaning where John's system of logic fails. They lead her to make ironical statements: "He [John] is a physician and perhaps that is one reason I do not get well faster." His position as a doctor—a healer—in essence, becomes a deterrent to her health, as his diagnosis cannot encompass her real problem. As Luce Irigaray explains, "The rejection, the exclusion of a female imaginary certainly puts woman in the position of experiencing herself only fragmentarily, in the little-structured margins of a dominant ideology, as a waste, an excess. . . ."

This schizophrenic vision contained in the narrator's writing makes it nearly impossible for her to create. Her writing has become exhausting, not because she writes against her husband's wishes, as Kolodny suggests, but because she can only write her husband's wishes. Navigating her thoughts through John's phallocentric discourse is debilitating, making her writing the "dead paper" she refers to it as. Helene Cixous, a French feminist, suggests that the patriarchal language that woman must use forces her to defer to the "male perspective," and "annihilates" the "specific energy" of her thought (*The Newly Born Woman*).

At the moment when the narrator is stopped from speaking as she makes the final attempt to tell John she does not think she is getting any better, the narrator is forced to realize that she has lost her last means of communication. Tellingly, at that point, she turns to the wallpaper, "laying for hours trying to decide whether . . . [the] front pattern and back pattern really . . . [do] move together or separately." And it is through this study of the wallpaper that she attempts to understand her situation. Current scholarship asserts that the paper, which the narrator describes as "horrid" and "vicious," comes to represent for the narrator her oppressive marriage. Haney-Peritz elaborates this point by suggesting that the wallpaper symbolizes the oppressive discourse in which she is trapped. She refers to the following description the narrator gives of the wallpaper: "The pattern is dull enough to confuse the eye in following, pronounced enough to constantly irritate and provoke study, and when you follow the lame uncertain curves for a little distance they suddenly commit suicide—plunge off at outrageous angles, destroy themselves in unheard of contradictions." For Haney-Peritz, the word "pronounced" as well as the phrase "unheard of contradictions" suggest that the "specific oppressive structure at issue [within this passage] is discourse."

These descriptions of the wallpaper, along with the narrator's progressive vision of a symbolic order contained in it, make clear that the wallpaper does suggest a discourse. However, the oppressive nature of the wallpaper stems from the narrator's entrapment in patriarchal discourse. Since she must use this oppressive discourse to describe the wallpaper, her feelings about it can only be detectable in the interstices of her descriptions. Thus, on the surface the wallpaper is horrid as her descriptions of its yellow color make clear: "It is the strangest yellow, that wallpaper! It makes me think of all the yellow things I ever saw . . . but . . . old foul, bad yellow things." This shade of yellow, "revolting and smouldering," suggests a "yellowing" of paper so that on the surface, the wallpaper represents her stifling entrapment in John's language. On the surface, the wallpaper seems to represent a parchment containing the "ancient law" on which John's language is founded. However, within her descriptions of the wallpaper appear glimpses of the wallpaper as a potentially liberating force.

Although Haney-Peritz describes the wallpaper as an oppressive structure which represents "man's prescriptive discourse about a woman," the terms "lack of sequence" and "defiance of law" which the narrator uses in describing the pattern suggest that the discourse, which this pattern represents, is symbolically opposed to the hierarchical binary logic of phallocentric discourse. The narrator goes on to say, "I know a little of principle of design, and I know this thing was not arranged on any laws of radiation, or alternation or repetition, or symmetry or anything else that I ever heard of," and she has certainly "heard" the discourse of John. Instead, the "defiance of law" within the pattern, which makes it undefinable, anticipates Helene Cixous' description of *ecriture feminine,* writing that inscribes femininity by surpassing patriarchal representations of woman. Cixous says of *ecriture feminine:* "It is impossible to define a feminine practice of writing . . . for this practice can never be theorized, enclosed, coded. . . . It will always surpass the discourse that regulates the phallocentric system" ("The Laugh of the Medusa").

Moreover, as it is described by the narrator, the design of the wallpaper contains a surplus that suggests its ability to exceed and overspill the constraints of her husband's language. It is impossible for the narrator to follow the pattern of the wallpaper because within the design, pattern is placed on top of pattern: "Each breadth stands alone; the bloated curves and flourishes—a kind of 'debased Romanesque' with delirium tremens—go waddling up and down in isolated columns of fatuity. But on the other hand, they connect diagonally, and the sprawling outlines run off in great slanting waves of optic horror, like a lot of wallowing sea-weeds in full chase . . . They have used a horizontal breadth for a frieze, and that adds wonderfully to the confusion." Cixous says that for woman's writing to overcome patriarchal representations, this writing must "dislocate [patriarchal language], explode it, turn it around" (*The Newly Born Woman*).

Within the story, Gilman makes clear that the source of this dislocating structure is the narrator herself. Gilman establishes a physical connection between the narrator and the wallpaper, which suggests that this wallpaper can act as a medium for her desire. For example, the narrator mentions her need to touch the wallpaper to see if it is moving, and it becomes evident that she often touches it as Jennie scolds her for getting yellow "smooches" from the wallpaper on her clothing. In this way, the wallpaper has left its mark on the narrator, yet it is the narrator who initially "marked" it. This bodily contact with the wallpaper symbolizes the narrator's inscribing the wallpaper with her desire by allowing her to surpass the words of her husband and release her desire directly. This "writing the body," then involves the imaginary as the narrator has direct access to reality. In her interaction with her family, the narrator stresses this belief that she possesses the wallpaper and, more importantly, that it contains her. She becomes jealous of anyone who looks at the wallpaper. She says, "I have watched John when he did not know I was looking . . . and I've caught him looking at the paper! And Jennie too. I caught Jennie with her hand on it once. . . . I asked her in a quiet, a very quiet voice, with the most restrained manner possible, what she was doing with the paper. . . ."

The narrator's description of the paper reinforces the notion that it mirrors her desire. She insists that the paper has a smell: "It is not bad—at first, and very gentle, but quite the subtlest, most enduring odor I ever met." This description of the smell clearly links it to female sexuality, an idea Mary Jacobus explores in her article "An Unnecessary Maze of Sign-Reading." She quotes Jane Gallop as saying, "The penis may be more visible, but female genitalia have a stronger smell." Thus, for Jacobus, that smell becomes identified with the smell of "sexuality itself." This sign of sexuality that entrances the narrator permeates the whole house: "I find it hovering in the dining-room, skulking in the parlor, hiding in the hall, lying in wait for me on the stairs. It gets into my hair." Her sexuality becomes a pervasive and enduring force within the household, disrupting the image John has created of his wife as a little girl.

More important, using her imaginative power and "habit

of storymaking," the narrator allows her emotions to surface within the pattern of the wallpaper. For example, she attributes qualities to the pattern that allude to certain personality traits John warns she must use her "will and self-control" to contain. The following excerpts from her analysis of the pattern reveal intense emotions of anger, violence, and provocation;

> It is dull enough to confuse the eye in following, pronounced enough constantly to irritate and provoke study, when you follow the lame uncertain curves for a little distance they suddenly commit suicide—plunge off at outrageous angles, destroy themselves in unheard-of-contradictions. The color is hideous enough and unreliable enough and infuriating enough, but the pattern is torturing. . . . You think you have mastered it [the pattern] and then it knocks you down, slaps you.

Tellingly, these emotions parallel the feelings she refers to in describing her physical condition. For example, the narrator often mentions the anger and uncertainty she feels toward John: "I get unreasonably angry with John sometimes. . . . But John says if I feel so I shall neglect proper self-control, so I take pains to control myself—before him, at least, and that makes me very tired."

A comparison of the descriptions of anger, though, shows the restrictions on her when she attempts to define herself within John's exclusionary hierarchy. In speaking of her anger, even though she has acknowledged that John does not believe she is sick and will not listen to her, she defines this emotion as "unreasonable," and asserts that she must control it. For the narrator, emotions that must be relegated to marginalia in her own journal writings overspill in this structure outside binary logic.

She also sees in the wallpaper the "mysterious" aura that she feels within the house. She insists she feels something "strange" within the house they are staying in. She goes on to say she would describe the house as haunted and reach the height of "romantic felicity," but John would dismiss her curious notion. This wallpaper, which changes with the light and seems to move, holds that mysterious, unrepresentable quality.

The structure of this new discourse is made tangible in the narrator's own writing in her journal. Just as to her the pattern of the wallpaper has a "lack of sequence" and a "defiance of law," her sentences begin to contain "defiant" structures and words. Before the narrator becomes interested in the wallpaper, her narrative is over-laden with sentences which are short and simple. These sentences maintain the binary logic of John's language by paralleling and prioritizing contradictory statements. Within these sentences, she brings up her feelings in an initial statement and then immediately negates those same feelings with a statement based on John's beliefs. For example, she says, "John does not know how much I really suffer. He knows there is no reason to suffer, and that satisfies him," but then goes on to say, "Of course it [the narrator's illness] is only nervousness." In contrast, when she begins to describe the wallpaper, her sentences become convoluted and complex with phrase piled upon phrase, suggesting

emotion and excitement. For example, she says of the paper: "The outside pattern is a florid arabesque, reminding one of a fungus. If you can imagine a toadstool in joints, an interminable string of toadstools, budding and sprouting in endless convolution—why that is something like it. That is, sometimes."

Through studying the wallpaper and experiencing this new pattern of thinking, the narrator surmounts her stifling condition. She says that she's "getting really fond of the room in spite of the wallpaper. Perhaps because of the wallpaper." Once she begins to study the wallpaper, she says, "I must say what I feel," even though she has mentioned earlier that she has not felt like writing.

Moreover, the shift of the margins of her own text to the forefront of the "text" of the wallpaper and her writing allows the narrator to begin to deconstruct the false text of contentment she has created so far in her journal. Slowly, the narrator sees figures appear within the wallpaper, representing her condition, which is "unrepresentable" within John's discourse. Slowly the "strong, provoking, formless figure" that seems to skulk about behind "the front design" of the paper becomes clearer and emerges as "a woman stooping down and creeping about behind the pattern" and the outside pattern becomes "bars" representing her own stifling condition in her marriage. This promises a moment of liberation for the narrator; she has found a symbolic representation of her condition.

However, as soon as she grasps this symbolic representation of her true feeling, she begins to repress any connection of this symbol to herself. Instead, she begins to see the symbols not as abstractions, but as reality. Therefore, she shifts from the symbolic realm to what Lacan calls the imaginary. She begins to view the woman behind the wallpaper as real. In her descriptions of the woman she writes: "I pulled [the wallpaper] and she shook." She has regressed to the position of a child, in Lacanian terms, who in not distinguishing between subject and object, has no need for language.

It is her inability to leave behind her husband's vision, her insistence on applying the rigid logic of her husband's thought-patterns to the pattern in the wallpaper, that forces her to reject this representation as symbolic. She is only able to approach the pattern according to her husband's logic, demanding, in her analysis, a pattern that she is familiar with. In studying the pattern, she calls "the lack of sequence" and "defiance of law" "infuriating" and insists she "will follow that pointless pattern to some sort of a conclusion." Thus, she echoes her husband's sentiment that fanciful thoughts are "dangerous."

Upon entering the imaginary realm and leaving the symbolic realm completely, the narrator believes that the woman behind the wallpaper is literally trapped, and she rips down the paper. In tearing down the paper, she destroys her only access to symbol, through which she can consciously understand her own thoughts. Once she has destroyed this access, she takes on the symbols of her oppression with the only medium she has left—her body. This entering into the imaginary completely, without access to symbol, is disruptive to the family, but ultimately dangerous to the narrator as she can only be "interpreted" by those around her.

The narrator does not triumph at the end as Gilbert and Gubar, Kolodny, and Kennard suggest. Instead, she loses the ability to communicate and surmount her situation. In effect, the final image of her is that of her creeping like a child, having to move over her husband who has fainted in her path.

Within their interpretations, the critics' desire to define the narrator and the story completely overshadows the very power of the story—its intricacies and mysteries. They seek the "feminist" truth within the story as rigidly as they claim male critics have sought their truth. They ignore the deeper structure of patriarchal power—language—and the complexities of that structure. Under the narrator's descent into madness resides complications and uncertainties, the most basic being: who is really speaking in the story—is the narrator speaking of her desires or her husband's? In fact, in probing the prone, delusional body of the narrator at the end of the story and naming her "liberated," they mimic the narrator's husband, who says the narrator must get well for "his sake," and then claims she is getting better. Once again the narrator is left to be "read," yet they insist their act is different in that they have the capability to read her correctly.

Haney-Peritz asserts that these critics have failed in declaring as feminine and liberating what seems to be a reflection of John's desire. However, Haney-Peritz concludes that all searches for the feminine in a text must be deluded, since we can never really know who is speaking, and can never be liberating because they involve a sense of the imaginary—a misrecognition to her. I feel I have shown that the identification of the feminine within the text is not only possible, because desire inheres in words, but also favorable. It involves a recognition of difference, a force different from the patriarch. This force points toward liberation. The wallpaper, as a symbol of *ecriture feminine,* makes clear the possible release of the narrator's thoughts. And it is this possibility that allowed Gilman herself to express on paper these feelings about her own nervous breakdown and to have the courage to pursue it to publication. Ultimately, her writing triumphs by avoiding "repetition of patriarchal language," which Cixous names as essential to liberation. (pp. 1-13)

Lisa Kasmer, "Charlotte Perkins Gilman's 'The Yellow Wallpaper': A Symptomatic Reading," in Literature and Psychology, *Vol. XXXVI, No. 3, 1990, pp. 1-15.*

Conrad Shumaker   (essay date 1991)

[*In the following essay, Shumaker discusses the elements of realism and reform in "The Yellow Wallpaper."*]

The History of Charlotte Perkins Gilman's **"The Yellow Wallpaper"** clearly illustrates problems of canon and audience in American literature. Published in 1892, the work was virtually ignored by readers, despite efforts by William Dean Howells, probably the most influential Ameri-

can critic of his time, to convince editors and audiences of its excellence. Though the story is now read as a brilliant and artistically innovative exploration of woman's role, Gilman herself chose to defend it, not in terms of its "literary" merit or feminist theme, but as an attempt to show S. Weir Mitchell the potential dangers of the "rest cure," his remedy for "nervous diseases." After publishing **"The Yellow Wallpaper"** she wrote no more fiction for nearly twenty years, and then wrote stories for *The Forerunner* much more conventional in form (and less striking to a modern audience) than her first work.

There is, of course, a seemingly logical and simple explanation for Gilman's reaction and for the difference between **"The Yellow Wallpaper"** and the stories that appeared later. Gilman saw herself above all as a reformer dedicated to improving society by showing how the forced dependence of women threatened not only women themselves but society as a whole. **"The Yellow Wallpaper"** failed to reach an audience and, despite its rumored effect on Mitchell's treatment of "nervous" women, did not really make a significant contribution to that effort. Indeed, the general neglect of the story has led recent commentators such as Annette Kolodny and Jean E. Kennard to suggest that the audience failed to read the work in terms of woman's role at all, since readers lacked a tradition of women's literature or a set of conventions which would enable them to recognize its feminist perspective. Gilman, who already had a New Englander's distrust of "art" (as opposed to "work"), turned to lecturing and to writing *Women and Economics*; when she returned to writing fiction, she wrote the kind of purposeful fiction that could not be misunderstood. She was to defend the earlier story, denying the charge that she had been trying to drive women crazy, and claimed that she simply meant to call attention to the problems posed by the "rest cure." **"The Yellow Wallpaper,"** then, was useful, a tool of practical reform instead of a misunderstood literary artifact.

But in a sense to explain things in this way is simply to restate the question in a different form. In *Women and Economics* Gilman argues long and persuasively that the characteristics women share with male human beings are far more numerous and important than the differences between the sexes. Therefore women should have all the economic and social freedom that belongs to them as human beings, most importantly, the freedom to work. **"The Yellow Wallpaper"** seems to be the perfect fictional complement to this argument: to a modern audience, at least, the story presents a powerful and haunting picture of a woman robbed of her humanity (and her ability to work) and treated as just a woman. Besides offering a realistic depiction of mental breakdown, it gives us one of the most striking characters in our literature. In the terms that William Dean Howells used in his arguments for realism, the narrator is a character, not a type—that is, she is not a simple creature designed to illustrate an idea imposed on us by the author but a complex being who reacts to her situation in believable and interesting ways. Indeed, as I have argued elsewhere, there is reasonably clear evidence that Howells himself recognized that the story challenged the conventional role of women, since he first wrote to Gilman to praise a poem that attacked women's role quite directly. Why, then, was Gilman's audience—and perhaps even Gilman herself—apparently unwilling to acknowledge that **"The Yellow Wallpaper"** addressed the problem of women's lost humanity in marriage?

This formulation of the question will take us eventually into the story itself, which anticipates the misunderstanding in a very interesting way, but in order to grasp more fully Gilman's predicament we must look first at a more general problem that faces anyone who attempts to combine realism and reform. According to Howells, who helped Gilman publish her story in the 1890s and included it in his collection of *The Great Modern American Stories* in 1920, the realist differs from the idealist or the romantic in attempting to give us life as it is, "human feelings and motives, as God made them and as men know them" (*Criticism*). The realistic writer will take his work "into the public square and see if it seems true to the chance passer." Howells's model ultimately owes much to the scientific approach to describing experience. Rejecting the ideal grasshopper, "evolved . . . out of the grasshopper in general," the realist, like the scientist or the photographer, simply presents the commonplace individual grasshopper—life as it is. When it comes to characters, he will give us humans rather than types, just as the scientist or photographer will give us the real grasshopper rather than the wire and cardboard ideal.

Equating what "seems true to the chance passer" and "life as it is" looks quite naive, of course, but in a sense it accords with what proponents of speech-act theory, among others, assert about the relationship of linguistic "truth" to extra-linguistic authority. A statement about the way humans behave in society is "true" when the institutions that govern society (for the writer's audience) lend it force. In the words of J. L. Austin:

> It is essential to realize that "true" and "false," like "free" and "unfree," do not stand for anything simple at all; but only for a general dimension of being a right or proper thing to say as opposed to a wrong thing, in these circumstances, to this audience, for these purposes and with these intentions.

Without getting involved in the question of whether this applies to all statements under all conditions, we can see that, to the aspiring reformer in a more or less democratic society, Howells's definition is a very practical one. If she wishes to move her audience to reform sexual relationships, for example, the realist writer must seem to be presenting "life as it is." As Michel Foucault points out, " 'truth' is linked in a circular relation with systems of power which produce and sustain it, and to effects of power which it induces and which extend it." To have any social effect, a writer's description must enter this circular relation or "regime" of truth. Her writing must be granted the authority of "truth" by the society she wishes to influence before it can partake of the power of extension that the system affords. Theoretically, the social authority that must validate the American writer's portrait of society is indeed the "chance passer" in the "public square," or, to be more precise, the middle-class reader of fiction, the audience to whom she must appeal if her description of injustice is to provoke action. For the purpose of the reformer,

then, a thing is real if the author can convince the audience—"the chance passer"—that it is.

At the same time, if we look more closely at what Howells says and at realism as it is practiced, a number of tensions arise. First, the distinction between "characters" (or humans) and "types" quickly breaks down. In attempting to explain Balzac's violations of the realist aesthetic, for example, Howells says in *Criticism and Fiction* that as a human being Balzac was necessarily not "a type, but a character; now noble, now ignoble, now grand, now little; complex, full of vicissitude." Later in the same work, though, he approvingly quotes Armando Palacio Valdés's criticism of "effectism" in the works of such writers as Bulwer and Dickens. These writers, Valdés says, "begin by deliberately falsifying human feelings, giving them a paradoxical appearance completely inadmissible." How are we to know the difference between a character who is "complex, full of vicissitude" and one whose feelings are falsely "paradoxical"? According to Valdés, one should "study humanity," presumably in the way the scientist studies the grasshopper. Leaving aside for now the tricky question of how much our perception of human reality in literature depends on our previous experience of literary conventions themselves, we are still faced with a problem here, since what Howells seems to be suggesting when he quotes Valdés is that the writer must extract from experience in dealing with other human beings certain principles governing the portrayal of humans in fiction. Characters will be, then, representative or typical from the start. If they are too singular, too full of vicissitude or paradoxical, they will not accord with the generalized picture of "man" or "woman" the reader has derived from his experience. This tendency toward generalization, is, of course, already built into the scientific model that Howells begins with; an insect is "a grasshopper" only insofar as it resembles the generalized grasshopper that scientific consensus has created. The scientist begins with the assumption that "the grasshopper" will behave in consistent and predictable ways in its natural habitat, and he studies the behavior of an individual grasshopper only in order to make general statements about the characteristics or behavior of grasshoppers as a species. If the behavior of an individual is shown to be anomalous, that individual becomes irrelevant, except perhaps as an illustration of the way in which unusual conditions can pervert the behavior of grasshoppers. Thus, as Walker Percy points out, the scientist can tell us nothing about the characteristics that make the individual an individual.

And then people tend to be harder to study than grasshoppers. Since man's natural habitat is society, our judgment of a character's "reality" will also depend on the social circumstances under which we view the specimens of humanity we're studying. Photographing a grasshopper in its "natural" state, for example, is relatively simple because of the way we choose to define the term natural: we call an insect's state natural if, as far as we can tell, it hasn't been significantly affected by human action. As soon as we try to photograph a human, on the other hand, all kinds of questions about artifice and convention (dress, pose, background, for example) necessarily come into play. Since such conventions are obviously part of the human habitat yet—like romantic ideals—created by humans, how does the photographer or the writer distinguish between the real or natural and the conventional? Or is there any distinction to be made? And to what extent will the chance passer in the public square accept as real variations from the conventional? The male reader's view of women's feelings, for instance, might be based on the women he has known in the social roles of mother, wife, sister, lover, etc., and, of course, on his own feelings about those individuals and their roles. But since those roles are governed by conventions (including literary conventions), what he is likely to accept as "real" is a fleshing out of those conventions, combined, perhaps, with modifications of the conventions that echo his own hopes or fears. At the same time, his fear that women might not be what convention says they are could cause him to reject any portrait of a woman that threatens to reinforce that fear. In a time when women are showing signs of discontent with their traditional role, his fears might lead him to dismiss as "effectism" the drawing of Gilman's narrator crawling over her prostrate husband which illustrates **"The Yellow Wallpaper"** in the *New England Magazine*, but accept one of a mother smiling down at her child in the exact pose of a Raphael Madonna as an example of commonplace reality. In a story or novel he might accept a woman who is restless within the confines of her role, since his own fears and experience may give him some basis for believing in her, but a woman who openly or even privately denies that women are what their conventional roles proclaim them to be will probably either strain his credulity or threaten his sense of the way things should be. After all, don't all the women he has "studied" in his social relations (and read about in other literary works) behave more or less as convention dictates? And doesn't that make the world a comfortable place in which to live? As we will see as we look more closely at Gilman's story, the situation is even more complex when the reader is a woman, since in some ways her very identity as a social being is at stake.

The problem is complicated further when the writer is attempting to promote social reform, for then she must necessarily convince the audience that the human being presented is indeed a type or representative of a larger group. If a character is too clearly an individual, then she creates no impulse to reform the situation that has made her what she is. A good example of this principle is Jacob Riis's *How the Other Half Lives*, published in 1890, the year that **"The Yellow Wallpaper"** was written. Riis's realism is even purer in a sense than Howells's, since Riis does not intend to present a fiction at all but documents New York tenement dwellers' living conditions through photographs and descriptive text, most of which simply present (often quite "unartistically") the individuals that Riis sees and talks to. Yet the stereotyping that the book has been criticized for is also an inevitable part of the effort, for in a sense it is only by denying that the people he sees are individuals that he can move his audience to consider reform. A photograph of a child sleeping in a littered doorway may arouse sympathy for that child as an individual, but if we are led to see him as an "Italian street Arab," typical of a group which represents a danger to society in its present condition, then we might be inclined to act to change that condition.

To summarize briefly, then, the realist writer, and especially the realist reformer, must present types in order to be seen as presenting "real" human beings. Obviously, realistic characters will differ from, say, Hawthorne's Richard Digby: we can accept Digby's petrification in the dark forest without believing that bigoted people really turn to stone, but we expect characters who are presented as realistic portraits of "life as it is" to coincide with our view of what humans usually are, which means that they will largely be governed by social conventions if they are middle-class characters, or stereotypes if they belong to the lower classes. They may pressure or stretch some conventions to an extent, but if they deny that the conventions or stereotypes reflect "reality," they are likely to be seen as unrealistic themselves. If they are to promote reform, characters must seem to be representative of the group whose situation needs reforming.

There is thus a tension between the feminist writer's role as realist and her role as reformer. As a practitioner of realism as defined by Howells (that is, as someone who proposes to show us "life as it is" in order to show why it must be changed), the writer must respect the conventions that make up a large part of what the audience will accept as "reality." Yet if women's role is what the writer wants to reform, then those very conventions are what must be attacked. In effect, the writer must hope that a significant portion of her audience already feels enough doubt about those conventions to accept her unconventional portrait of reality. As Sandy Petrey argues, literary realism had its beginnings in a time when large numbers of people disagreed about which statements and descriptions made sense and which did not. In his attempt to describe "life as it is" in the face of such disagreement, the realist writer is led to focus on the way in which social authority determines the authority of language and attempts to "embody particular ideologies so as to make them appear universal." At some level, in other words, realist fiction is about the way in which social authority silently determines which statements we will accept as descriptions of "life as it is" and which we will reject as nonsense.

Turning to **"The Yellow Wallpaper,"** we find that Gilman has tried to make her narrator typical. In her own explanation of the story, she implies that the narrator is representative of women who have suffered from the "rest cure," but the fact that the doctor is also the narrator's husband suggests that the narrator represents married women in general. Indeed, her husband is first introduced by the sentence, "John laughs at me, of course, but one expects that in marriage." The shift from "me" to "one" and the concluding "in marriage" show that the narrator is referring to the experiences of a larger group, that wives expect to be laughed at by husbands. Throughout the story, Gilman strengthens this implication that the relationship between physician and patient is really a metaphor for the relationship between husbands and wives by having John mix his professional and domestic duties.

After telling his patient (his wife) that she is not strong enough to go visiting, for example, the doctor "gathered me up in his arms, and just carried me upstairs and laid me on the bed." Later he asks her to trust him "as a physician" while they lie in bed together. Finally, the narrator's brother is also a doctor, but his wife needs no treatment: she is "a perfect and enthusiastic housekeeper" who thinks the narrator got sick from trying to write.

The symbols in the story reinforce this identification. The central fixture in the room is a huge and immovable bed; there are bars on the windows and a gate at the head of the stairs; the wallpaper is described as an entangling "pattern" which strangles the women who try to escape from it. It takes a certain willful blindness, I think, not to see that the story is, on some level at least, about woman's loss of freedom and humanity within the institution of marriage.

Why did the audience apparently have such a hard time reading it that way, then? We get our first hint in the fact that the narrator in the story cannot read her own journal.

Indeed, in a sense the story is about the impossibility of reading such a story. The narrator's journal represents her attempt to tell the truth about John and her own state of mind, in a form that will never be read. She can commit to the "dead paper" thoughts that she could never tell a human listener, she says. But in spite of this apparent freedom, she can't affirm directly that John and the conventions he represents have imprisoned her behind an entangling pattern. At some level she knows that she has been made a prisoner, and in the terribly comic ending she acts out the infantile role that John has forced her into when she creeps around the room. But she cannot say such things directly, and, more importantly, she cannot read the description of herself that emerges from her own narrative. To the very end of the story, the figure behind the bars must be some other woman, an individual who does not represent women like her.

One striking example of this inability to read occurs when she asks John to change the wallpaper. He refuses, saying that "after the wallpaper was changed it would be the heavy bedstead, and then the barred windows, and then that gate at the head of the stairs, and so on." When she asks to move to one of the "pretty rooms" downstairs, he uses his role of husband to make her request seem childish: "Then he took me in his arms and called me a blessed little goose, and said he would go down to the cellar, if I wished, and have it whitewashed into the bargain." She concludes her description of the conversation by saying, "I would not be so silly as to make him uncomfortable just for a whim." In this passage, as in several others, she reveals that the room is literally a prison. We can see that her request to move to a nicer room is reasonable and that John is trying to make her feel childish in order to impose his will and keep her within the barred room and the "entangling pattern" of their conventional marriage. Her reading of the scene, however, insists on the conventional view of husband and wife that has imprisoned her in the first place: John is right and she is silly. To read the scene otherwise would be to destroy the conventions that give her identity. If the picture of a woman behind bars—which she sees when she looks at the wallpaper and we see as we read her journal—is a realistic portrait of her relationship to John, then her conventional view of her husband and her own identity as cherished and protected wife must be

fictional. To put it another way, the image of a woman behind bars is to us a realistic portrayal of her situation, but to her it must remain a real picture of another woman, and to John it would be the most fantastic of fictions. He continually warns his wife about creating dangerous "fancies" which will interfere with her perception of reality.

In fact, John sees the whole problem in terms of his wife's flirtation with "fancy," i.e., her failure to accept completely his physical, social, and linguistic authority to describe reality. When she shows the smallest tendency to question his view of her, he combines physical (and sexual) gestures—carrying her upstairs to bed—linguistic descriptions—she is a "silly goose"—and reminders of his role as a physician to reinforce that authority.

This strategy produces an extremely interesting effect in the scene in which the narrator attempts to hint that his treatment is now working and is affecting her mental health. When his wife says that she isn't getting better, John flatly denies her authority to describe herself and asserts his own: "I am a doctor, dear," he says, "and I know." When she persists, he gives her "a big hug." "Bless her little heart," he says, "She shall be as sick as she chooses." Her illness, he implies here, is a result of her childish choice of fantasy over reality. This belief is made explicit when the narrator suggests that John's treatment is making her sicker: that notion is "a false and foolish fancy," he says. "Can you not trust me as a physician when I tell you so?" Since, as Paula A. Treichler points out, John's role as male physician means that his "representational claims are strongly supported by social, cultural, and economic practices," the narrator/wife has no choice but to accept his description of her condition. After this conversation, the narrator pretends to sleep, but she is actually lying there "trying to decide whether that front pattern and the back pattern really did move together or separately." The "front patterns" represents, among other things, the conventions that imprison her. It is silly, contradictory, and aesthetically repulsive, but it is also powerful, covered with the bulbous eyes of those who have been strangled attempting to escape. (Significantly, both the bars and the heads of those who fail to escape are part of the pattern. Prison and prisoner—or stereotype and self—are identical here.) The "back pattern" will become the shape of a woman who crawls and shakes the bars of the front pattern, trying to get out. Symbolically, then, the narrator is wondering whether there is a self behind the conventions, a back pattern which is somehow independent of the "silly and conspicuous" facade and potentially capable of escaping from it. Does she exist apart from John's conventional description of her and the extra-linguistic authority that supports that description?

The answer to this question is complicated. To be sure, the back pattern does become separate from the front, and the narrator eventually helps the creeping woman escape. But the status of this woman is problematic. For one thing, the narrator can't decide whether the creeping woman is an individual or a type. At one point she sees a woman creeping outside every window she looks through, but she decides that they must all be the same woman, since "most women do not creep by daylight." "I always lock the door," she adds, "when I creep by daylight." At the very end of the story, however, the narrator sees "many" women creeping in the garden outside her window and then unlocks the door to show John her own creeping in the light of day. The question of how many women creep by daylight is in effect a question about audience and authority. To creep by daylight is to acknowledge and demonstrate one's infantile condition, but it is also to reveal the dishonesty of the conventional "front pattern." If many women creep by daylight, then the narrator's description might be seen as realistic. If, on the other hand, other women do their creeping in secret, isolated from each other as the narrator is at the end of the story, the conventional view of woman's identity with (and happiness within) the front pattern will remain intact.

There is a further problem in that the creeping woman isn't really freed—the narrator remains in the room with a rope around her waist, still creeping and detouring around the immovable bed. She does force John to accept her linguistic authority at one point. When he wants into the room, she tells him that the key is outside near the front door, and when he won't listen to her, she "said it again, several times, very gently and slowly, and said it so often that he had to go and see. . . ." Here the roles are momentarily reversed—she treats him as a child and forces him to respond to her statement. But when he comes in, all she can do is demonstrate the infantile condition to which she has been reduced. John's speechlessness doesn't bring her to her feet, since she is free only to "creep by daylight." She can recapitulate the pattern in a way that forces John to see its effect, but she hasn't really made herself independent of it. The narrator is simply acting the role John has imposed on her, but without the "front pattern" which disguises the true relationship between husband and wife.

Moreover, even the freedom to creep by daylight is dearly bought. Recognizing herself as the woman who was behind the bars of the wallpaper, the narrator loses all social identity. At that moment she ceases to be the wife that she was and becomes nameless and isolated. When she views the picture of the imprisoned woman as realistic, she not only becomes separate from "Jane," the loved and protected wife of John (who becomes simply "that man" as she crawls around the room); she also loses her relationship to everyone else and her ability to act in a social context. To put it another way, "Jane" cannot read a story that describes her as a creeping woman. She turns away from her own narrative, leaving her now authorless character to repeat endlessly the action that reveals and defines her.

Gilman's audience was faced with a similar problem. To admit that the narrator was "realistic" in Howells's sense—typical or representative—was to admit that the conventional view of sexual relationships was a fiction. It would have required seeing creeping women everywhere. The hostility and depression that the story apparently provoked suggests that readers felt threatened by the way in which the story challenged conventional roles which they accepted as real but which were proving to be suspiciously unsatisfactory in a number of ways.

Women had complained about creeping just enough to raise fears that the pattern might crumble. Thus, physicians could praise the story as a realistic portrait of individual madness, but Howells, even in 1920, had to couch his praise in vague terms that hinted of its "terrible" qualities without specifying just why it was terrible or why he was praising it as realist fiction if it was so terrible. Ultimately, the readers who accused Gilman of trying to drive women crazy were perceptive in their own way. If read carefully, the story would leave women beside themselves, threatening the peculiar realist fiction that they had to accept as reality. Having taken realism into territories where her audience couldn't follow, Gilman had to wait until more women were prepared to see themselves creeping by daylight. In the meantime she turned to other ways of demonstrating the dangers she perceived in woman's conventional role. (pp. 81-92)

> *Conrad Shumaker, "Realism, Reform, and the Audience: Charlotte Perkins Gilman's Unreadable Wallpaper," in* Arizona Quarterly, *Vol. 47, No. 1, Spring, 1991, pp. 81-93.*

E. Suzanne Owens (essay date 1991)

[In the following essay, Owens discusses Gilman's use of Gothic conventions in "The Yellow Wallpaper."]

In 1885, Charlotte Perkins Gilman suffered severe post partum depression followed by complete emotional breakdown. By 1890, she had been treated for her condition by the leading specialist in women's "hysteria," Dr. Silas Weir Mitchell. She had also divorced her husband, moved alone to California, and begun a writing career. Soon after, she transformed her personal experience into fiction as the brilliant short story, **"The Yellow Wallpaper,"** published in 1892. In the Afterword to the Feminist Press reissue of the story in 1973, Elaine Hedges calls attention to Gilman's neglected masterpiece as "one of the rare pieces of literature we have by a nineteenth-century woman which directly confronts the sexual politics of the male-female, husband-wife relationship." Predating Kate Chopin's novel *The Awakening* by three years, **"The Yellow Wallpaper"** evidences Gilman's early critique of "the crippling social pressures imposed on women in the nineteenth century and the sufferings they thereby endured," a theme later writers, including Edith Wharton, would address.

Gilman's tale is acknowledged by feminist critics as a study of psychology and sexual politics grounded in autobiographical realism. It is a significant work in nineteenth-century literature because of these features. But a second story exists beside the story of repression and madness we read today—a supernatural tale drawn from the best nineteenth-century Gothic conventions, particularly from Edgar Allan Poe and Charlotte Brontë. Recently, Eugenia C. Delamotte has noted the story's Gothic elements, yet Gilman's first readers reacted to **"The Yellow Wallpaper"** as a ghost story, a narrative combining the supernatural with aberrant psychology framed by sexual politics.

Gilman's response to the events of her own life mirrors her narrator's confused assessment of her situation in the story. In a 1935 autobiography, Gilman traced the events of her first marriage to painter Walter Stetson in 1884, a period of genuine happiness mixed with increasing depression that Gilman could neither understand nor dispel. Her diary for 1884 recorded bouts of sleeplessness, sinking spirits and "hysteria" preceding her daughter's birth in March of 1885:

> We had attributed all my increasing weakness and depression to pregnancy, and looked forward to prompt recovery now. All was normal and ordinary enough, but I was plunged into an extreme of nervous exhaustion which no one observed or understood in the least. Of all angelic babies that darling was the best, a heavenly baby. My nurse, Maria Pease of Boston, was a joy while she lasted, and remained a lifelong friend. But after her month was up and I was left alone with the child I broke so fast that we sent for my mother. . . . and that baby-worshiping grandmother came to take care of the darling, I being incapable of doing that—or anything else, a mental wreck.

Even after moving to "a better home" and securing the help of a servant to assist her mother and her "loving and devoted husband," Gilman "lay all day on the lounge and cried."

Like the narrator she would later create, Gilman found the cure for her condition to be worse than the condition itself. A family friend intervened with money to allow Gilman to visit nerve specialist S. Weir Mitchell in Philadelphia. The "rest cure" prescribed included a prohibition of prolonged intellectual stimulation or writing, a regimen that exacerbated Gilman's condition. Her return to family life under these restrictions cost her her sanity: "The mental agony grew so unbearable that I would sit blankly moving my head from side to side—to get out from under the pain. Not physical pain, not the least 'headache' even, just mental torment, and so heavy in its nightmare gloom that it seemed real enough to dodge. . . . I would crawl into remote closets and under beds—to hide from the grinding pressures of that profound distress. . . ." Gilman felt she had no choice but to separate from her husband and daughter, allowing him to remarry and arranging for his new wife to take custody of the child. As she began life over in California, she regained her health, but her bouts with depression continued on and off for nearly forty years.

"The Yellow Wallpaper" was produced during a burst of creative energy in 1890, along with numerous articles and poems. Gilman considered the story "a description of a case of nervous breakdown beginning something as mine did, and treated as Dr. S. Weir Mitchell treated me with what I considered the inevitable result, progressive insanity." She had received from William Dean Howells a letter of appreciation for a poem and article she had published that year, so she forwarded the short story to him, hoping that Howells could get it published in the *Atlantic Monthly*. The *Atlantic*'s editor, Horace E. Scudder, rejected the piece with the stunning reply, "I could not forgive myself if I made others as miserable as I have made myself!" Gilman thought his reaction was "funny" because she intended for her tale to be "dreadful"; she comments in her autobiography: "I suppose he would have sent back one of

Poe's on the same ground." **"The Yellow Wallpaper"** was eventually published in the *New England Magazine* in January of 1982, to immediate reader reaction. A letter of protest was sent to the *Boston Transcript* recommending the "severest censure" of such a graphic depiction of "mental derangement," but a physician in Kansas City wrote to praise Gilman for offering the first "account of incipient insanity" he had found in literature, speculating that her tale followed some experience with opium addiction. Gilman had hoped the story would influence Mitchell and his colleagues in their treatment of other women's "cases"; she discovered some years later that he had, in fact, read it and changed his consideration of women's hysteria.

"The Yellow Wallpaper" was published again in 1920 as part of Howells's collection, *The Great American Short Stories,* although, as Elaine Hedges points out in her Afterword to the recent Feminist Press edition, it was the "chilling" quality of the tale to which Howells apparently responded. Even in 1920, Hedges claims, "no one seems to have made the connection between insanity and the sex, or sexual role, of the victim, no one explored the story's implications for male-female relationships in the nineteenth century." In keeping with Howells's characterization of the tale as a story that would "freeze our . . . blood," Hedges summarizes the work's initial reception: "In its time . . . the story was read essentially as a Poe-esque tale of chilling horror—and as a story of mental aberration." That is, the horror story is what Gilman's first readers reacted to, apart from evidence that at least a few physicians, including Mitchell, learned from it something of the sexual politics that framed Gilman's own experience and that of her fictional character. Gilman's implied comparison of the story to one of Poe's, together with her expressed hope for its impact on physicians, indicate the complexity of her intentions for this story. A close reading of the story in the context of nineteenth-century Gothic conventions illuminates its dual nature.

Gilman's unnamed narrator begins her tale not with descriptions of the story's setting—a colonial house—but with her impressions and expectations about such a setting. A series of questions and suppositions begins the story, an opening that indicates the troubled mood of the woman who spins her own tale and establishes the disturbed aura of her surroundings. She and her husband, John, are "mere ordinary people" in a "hereditary estate," a structure of indeterminate history, but speculates: "I would say a haunted house and reach the height of romantic felicity—but that would be asking too much of fate!" The narrator's expressed desire to find the house haunted may serve to put the reader on notice that subsequent events are to be mediated by a heightened or unstable imagination, but we cannot immediately say whether the narrator's gleeful expectancy reflects mental illness or that lesser condition ascribed to so many women—an imagination excited by overindulgence in novel reading. She goes on, in fact, to "proudly declare that there is something queer about it," and is led to ask two questions concerning the house which commonly appear in ghost stories: "Else why should it be let so cheaply? And why have stood so long untenanted?" To readers familiar with the ghost story genre, the questions affirm the narrator's rationality, since characters in ghost stories usually turn out to have good reason to wonder about these very conditions.

The narrator's husband, John, laughs when she reports her impressions, but she calls him "practical in the extreme." In fact, the reader is given an important clue for judging the validity of the narrator's speculations when she claims that John has "an intense horror of superstition, and . . . scoffs openly at any talk of things not to be felt and seen." The opening of the story draws attention to ambiguous circumstances viewed by one character as queer if "romantic" and appealing, and by the other character, a man of extremes in practicality and a horror of the intangible, as laughably trivial.

This estate is isolated three miles from the closest village and commands a view across an expanse of landscape towards a river. The house itself is never clearly described in layout or scale, but its grounds are sketched. The narrator notes the garden more than once, "large and shady, full of box-bordered paths, and lined with long grape-covered arbors with seats under them." And she responds to this setting by comparing it to "English places that you read about," a reference that will become clearer later in the story. Although the narrator generally refrains from evaluating the setting outside the house, her descriptive details speak for themselves: "There are hedges and walls and gates that lock, and lots of separate little houses for the gardeners and people." The maze-like garden is at once "*delicious*" and foreboding. Walls and hedges are cells that enclose and partition, while the "gates that lock" add an odd detail that reinforces a sense of the garden as prison. And despite the attraction of "grape-covered arbors," the grounds are in disrepair with greenhouses that, the narrator says, "are all broken now." The narrator repeats the explanation that "the place has been vacant for years" because of what she had heard—but never verified—was "some legal trouble . . . about the heirs and co-heirs," all evidence, she claims, that "spoils my ghostliness." That evidence is far from convincing, however. Again, the reader is confronted by a mixture of impressions and suggestions. First, the narrator holds to an initial feeling for the queerness of the estate: "There is something strange about the house—I can feel it." Second, she attempts to rationalize her first impressions, to accept John's practicality over her own intuition. This clash between her own propensities and John's is depicted in a brief incident when the narrator apparently tries once more to describe her uneasiness to John "one moonlight evening": "but he said what I felt was a *draught,* and shut the window."

This pattern of details creates a conventionally Gothic setting. Gilman begins with an isolated estate of uncertain but troubled history and surrounds it with extensive shaded, labyrinthine grounds in decay. Even rumored trouble among the heirs is a stock situation. Before Gilman's narrator ever begins her description of the fateful yellow-papered room at the top of the house, she, an emotionally charged woman, has entered what the reader should understand as recognizable territory for ghosts, hauntings, and possessions. Furthermore, the tale has barely begun

---

"The Yellow Wallpaper" is acknowledged by feminist critics as a study of psychology and sexual politics grounded in autobiographical realism. But a second story exists beside the story of repression and madness we read today—a supernatural tale drawn from the best nineteenth-century Gothic conventions, particularly from Edgar Allan Poe and Charlotte Brontë.

—E. Suzanne Owens

---

when the moon rises and a character's uneasiness is dismissed as "a draught": the stage is set for supernatural manifestations in accordance with ghost story conventions. Understandably, the narrator is unable to dispel the "ghostliness" she feels.

If she is psychologically unstable, these signs alone might indicate projections of the woman's deterioration from the moment she enters the scene. When she tries to describe the bedroom, she cannot escape a sense of her own peculiarity, confessing, "I used to lie awake as a child and get more entertainment and terror out of blank walls and plain furniture than most children could find in a toystore." The reader is supposed to understand that she has always been highly imaginative and perhaps predisposed to terror: "I remember what a kindly wink the knobs of our big, old bureau used to have, and there was one chair that always seemed like a strong friends. . . . I used to feel that if any of the other things looked too fierce I could always hop into that chair and be safe." She checks her "fancy" throughout the tale, however, for John "says that with [her] imaginative power and habit of story-making, a nervous weakness like [hers] is sure to lead to all manner of excited fancies." Are her intuitions and perceptions, then, mere manifestations of personality rather than reliable clues to the strangeness of the estate?

But this imaginative predisposition, too, follows conventions of the Gothic tale. For example, Edgar Allan Poe's classic tale of doubling, "William Wilson," published in 1839 and already a classic American tale by Gilman's time, introduces the narrator on the first page: "I am the descendant of a face whose imaginative and easily excitable temperament has at all times rendered them remarkable; and, in my earliest infancy, I gave evidence of having fully inherited the family character." Gilman's narrator is, in turn, a literary descendant of a race of highly imaginative Gothic narrators. Gilman's setting would also have sounded familiar to readers of "William Wilson," with its suggestive description of a boys' school: "The house, as I have said, was old and irregular. The grounds were extensive, and a high and solid brick wall, topped with a bed of mortar and broken glass encompassed the whole. . . . At an angle of the ponderous wall frowned a more ponderous gate. It was riveted and studded with iron bolts, and surmounted with jagged iron spikes." Here is another walled and imprisoning landscape, yet despite its frightening appearance, Poe's narrator expresses his pleasure in the place: "To me how veritably a place of enchantment!"

In addition to the American Gothic tradition that Poe represented, Gilman drew upon British tradition as well, and in particular from a masterpiece of Gothic terror framed by sexual politics, *Jane Eyre* (1847). Charlotte Brontë's Thornfield Hall—literally one of those "English places that you read about"—is isolated approximately six miles from the village of Millcote, a distance noted by Jane Eyre as she records her first impressions of her new home: "About ten minutes after [passing a church] the driver got down and opened a pair of gates; we passed through, and they closed behind us." Like Gilman's narrator, Jane Eyre passes from familiar ground into isolation and enclosure, an enclosure symbolized by the gates that close behind her. Housekeeper Mrs. Fairfax greets Jane with a brief description of the estate, noting, "Thornfield is a fine old hall, rather neglected of late years perhaps, but still a respectable place." Jane will discover that Thornfield has, like the house in Gilman's story, been virtually "untenanted" for years due to Mr. Rochester's frequent absences. The foreboding setting has been established.

The focus of Gilman's story is, of course, the bedroom at the top of the house where her narrator reluctantly retreats for "rest" and solitude. She had preferred a room "downstairs that opened onto the piazza and had roses all over the window," but is not permitted a choice in the matter: "John would not hear of it." She enters, instead, a peculiar room that, at first impression, belies its history: "It is a big, airy room, the whole floor nearly, with windows that look all ways, and air and sunshine galore. It was nursery first and then playroom and gymnasium, I should judge, for the windows are barred for little children, and there are rings and things in the walls." Indeed, her judgment is mere speculation. Added to the barred windows and rings are the shredded wallpaper, a "heavy bedstead," which the reader later learns is nailed to the floor, and a "gate at the head of the stairs." The narrator's first reference to the wallpaper suggests another reference to Poe's "William Wilson": "The paint and paper look as if a boys' school had used it." But more specifically, Gilman's attic-level room recreates the symbolic spaces of *Jane Eyre*: Jane's second-floor room and its third-floor counterpart, the prison-room for the madwoman, Bertha Mason Rochester. Gilman's room is no nursery, but a cell designed for physical and psychological restraint.

Sandra Gilbert and Susan Gubar's study of nineteenth-century women's literature takes its title, of course, from Brontë's Bertha: *The Madwoman in the Attic*. They too emphasize the Gothic conventions evident in Brontë's setting, including the ambiguous architecture of Thornfield itself. And Jane Eyre, while not physically confined either to her bed chamber or the house, as Gilman's narrator is through the strictures of her husband's "rest cure," moves, nevertheless, within ambiguous enclosures. Gilbert and Gubar note: "These upper regions [Thornfield's second and third stories], in other words, symbolically miniaturize one crucial aspect of the world in which [Jane Eyre] finds herself. Heavily enigmatic, ancestral relics wall

her in; inexplicable locked rooms guard a secret which may have something to do with *her*." Gilman's narrator is denied the smaller piazza room with "such pretty old-fashioned chintz hangings" and moves instead to the isolation of the large yellow-papered, barred-windowed room at the top of the house. Jane Eyre is led to her room by Mrs. Fairfax past a central staircase window which was "high and latticed," a variation of the barred window, and into a smaller enclosure on the upper floor: "A very chill and vaultlike air pervaded the stairs and gallery, suggesting cheerless ideas of space and solitude; and I was glad when I was finally ushered into my chamber to find it of small dimensions, and furnished in ordinary modern style."

Jane associates the smaller space with comfort, as Gilman's narrator does by implication when she calls the larger room "as airy and comfortable a room as anyone need wish," after expressing her own wish for the smaller one. The two rooms Gilman's narrator describes suggest Jane's room in other ways as well; when she first sees her room in the light of day, Jane says, "The chamber looked such a bright little place to me as the sun shone in between the gay blue chintz window curtains, showing papered walls and a carpeted floor, so unlike the bare planks and stained plaster of Lowood [Jane's boarding school] that my spirits rose at the view." Jane is given a room like the one Gilman's narrator longs for, with chintz curtains and walls presumably papered in something more appealing than the yellow wallpaper, but Jane is also drawn to the mysterious third floor, where Bertha Rochester lives in a room like Gilman's narrator's, a room large enough to have areas of "deep shade," a room not barred but "without a window." Nor is Jane's small room secure against encroachment: it is in this room that Jane Eyre receives the nocturnal visits of Bertha Rochester. So, too, Gilman's narrator will be "visited" nightly by a figure (or figures) in the wallpaper, a woman who eventually "breaks out" and, the narrator claims, steals beyond the confines of the imprisoning bedroom. On the night of Bertha's attack on Mason, Jane will be locked in the third-floor room adjoining Bertha's, imprisoned as Bertha is imprisoned. On Gilman's narrator's last day in the house, she will lock herself in her room in order to claim the space as her own.

Gilman's narrator passes most of her days alone in the bedroom, writing secretly. Gradually, she introduces the yellow wallpaper that becomes her ultimate obsession, and its significance for her changes as she claims its appearance changes: "[It is] one of those sprawling flamboyant patterns committing every artistic sin." She describes the color as "repellent, almost revolting; a smouldering unclean yellow, strangely faded by the slow-turning sunlight," and then "hideous," "infuriating," and "torturing." Her attempts to describe the pattern itself fail each time to form a coherent picture, for the pattern is "pointless," with "bloated curves and flourishes—a kind of 'debased Romanesque' with *delirium tremens*." Moreover, she says of the paper that it "changes as the light changes," and finds it most disturbing by moonlight: "I kept still and watched the moonlight on the undulating wall-paper till I felt creepy," a curiously appropriate choice of terms for a character who will end the story by "creeping."

The wallpaper frightens her, and she tries to convince John that they should leave the estate:

> There are things in that paper that nobody knows about but me, or ever will.
>
> Behind that outside pattern the dim shapes get clearer every day.
>
> It is always the same shape, only very numerous.
>
> And it is like a woman stooping down and creeping about behind that pattern. I don't like it a bit. I wonder—I begin to think—I wish John would take me away from here!

What does she think? She had sensed "strangeness" from the beginning and had tried to reason away the "ghostliness" of this place. Now she sees movement across the patterns on the wall, a movement confined to nighttime until the end of the story: "at night in any kind of light, in twilight, candlelight, lamplight, and worst of all by moonlight." In daylight, she adds, the figure she sees in the paper is still: "By daylight she is subdued, quiet." The narrator's perceptions of the strangeness of the place, combined with her perception of nocturnal movements, suggest that what she fears is a ghost, and like sensitive characters in many ghost stories, she asks to be taken away from the haunted house. As she discovers, it is one thing to wish for a ghost; it is quite another to be haunted by one.

As the visitations continue and, in fact, increase, Gilman's narrator begins to pick up a penetrating odor in the bedroom, a smell that she assumes comes from the wallpaper although it follows her throughout the house and even outside:

> But there is something else about that paper—the smell! I noticed it the moment we came into the room, but with so much air and sun it was not bad. Now we have had a week of fog and rain, and whether the windows are open or not, the smell is here.
>
> It creeps all over the house.
>
> Even when I go to ride, if I turn my head suddenly and surprise it—there is that smell!
>
> Such a peculiar odor, too! . . .
>
> In this damp weather it is awful. I wake up in the night and find it hanging over me.

Readers familiar with ghostly conventions will recognize in this odor a conventional indicator of a ghostly visitation. The narrator's fear of that presence in her bedroom and her suspicion that she is confronted by the supernatural frame her description. Her response at this point in the story comes during a period of relative composure and control, yet it identifies her with Brontë's madwoman, who burns down Thornfield Hall: "I thought seriously of burning the house—to reach the smell." If the break in the narrator's sentence signals an unwillingness to associate the smell with the supernatural, it may also prevent her

from revealing motives more closely aligned with Bertha's: revenge and liberation from captivity.

Like many of her predecessors in ghost stories, what the narrator resists is her own identification with the haunting presence, the woman or women trapped behind the wallpaper. But if she is, in fact, suffering from the gradual and cumulative effects of a haunting, her final deterioration comes with the ghost's possession of her body, thus leading her to "creep" by daylight. The narrator reports seeing the woman from the wallpaper "on that long road under the trees" just before the narrator admits that she locks her bedroom door and creeps by daylight around the room. To a reader familiar with the Gothic, the events of the story suggest possession as much as they do hallucination: the narrator watches a figure appear in the pattern of the wallpaper, witnesses increased agitation in the menacing rattling of the pattern's "bars," follows this figure's movements as it appears to break loose from the bars on the wall, and finally takes on that figure's form as she begins to crawl about the bedroom floor. As Gilbert and Gubar note: "Eventually, as the narrator sinks more deeply into what the world calls madness, the terrifying implications of both the paper and the figure imprisoned behind the paper begin to permeate—that is, to *haunt* the rented ancestral mansion." By the end of the story, the narrator can do nothing but "creep," a verb she uses six times in the last thirty lines. Her identification with the woman in the wallpaper is explicit and complete; she worries, "I suppose I shall have to get back behind the pattern when it comes night."

The narrator's cry of triumph has puzzled many critics: "I've got out at last . . . in spite of you and Jane." Elaine Hedges suggests that the intrusion of the name could be a result of a printer's error, a misprint of either "Julia" or "Jennie," the housekeeper and sister-in-law residing in the house, or a reference to the narrator's real name. In the latter case, Hedges takes the line as an indication of "the narrator's sense that she has gotten free of both her husband and her 'Jane' self: free, that is, of herself as defined by marriage and society." Alternatively, if we assume that the narrator's madness accounts for the events, "Jane" is the rational self giving way to the irrational. But if this is an account of supernatural possession, the voice speaking that sentence is the voice of a ghost announcing its victory over the narrator/victim, now revealed to be "Jane."

In any case, the connection to Jane Eyre is inevitable. Gilbert and Gubar read Brontë's novel as a tale of splitting psyches personified by Jane and Bertha, acknowledging the supernatural frame of the story: "In view of [the] frightening series of separations within the self—Jane Eyre splitting off from Jane Rochester, the child Jane splitting off from the adult Jane, and the image of Jane weirdly separating from the body of Jane—it is not surprising that another and most mysterious specter, a sort of 'vampyre,' should appear in the middle of the night to rend and trample the wedding veil of that unknown person, Jane Rochester." Furthermore Jane Eyre's "splitting" is incited, as is Gilman's Jane's, by a scene in which she looks out across the grounds surrounding the house. Jane Eyre's fragmentation is complicated by her doubling with Bertha, whom Gilbert and Gubar call "Jane's truest and darkest double," "the angry aspect of the orphan child, the ferocious secret self Jane has been trying to repress ever since her days at Gateshead." Like the ghostly double that finally possesses Gilman's narrator, Bertha is an angry captive, intent upon breaking free. She is finally revealed as a wild, though indistinguishable, figure running back and forth in the attic cell, where, "[she] grovelled, seemingly, on all fours," just as Gilman's narrator does at the end.

Gilman's narrator vents her destructive rage only on the wallpaper in her room, while Bertha burns Thornfield Hall to the ground. Whereas Bertha dies and Rochester lives on, however, the ending may be reversed in Gilman's story. John is said to have "fainted" at the end, as the narrator says: "so that I had to creep over him every time!" Perhaps, however, he has died from shock, a classic consequence of confronting a ghost—a fitting end for the disbeliever. The ambiguity of the ending suits the ambiguity of the story as a whole. Has the narrator merely succumbed to madness, or has something more uncanny occurred? Clearly, late nineteenth- and early twentieth-century readers, who were more familiar with the ghost story tradition, read it in those terms. But if **"The Yellow Wallpaper"** is truly a story of ghostly possession, are we to rejoice in the ghost's victory, or only to lament the limitations of the combined force of female worldly and otherworldly power, which can only be expressed by creeping? (pp. 64-78)

> *E. Suzanne Owens, "The Ghostly Double behind the Wallpaper in Charlotte Perkins Gilman's 'The Yellow Wallpaper'," in* Haunting the House of Fiction: Feminist Perspectives on Ghost Stories by American Women, *edited by Lynette Carpenter and Wendy K. Kolmar, The University of Tennessee Press, Knoxville, 1991, pp. 64-79.*

FURTHER READING

Bibliography

Scharnhorst, Gary. *Charlotte Perkins Gilman: A Bibliography.* Scarecrow Author Bibliographies, No. 71. Metuchen, N.J.: Scarecrow Press, 1985, 219 p.
　　Comprehensive primary and secondary bibliography which also cites selected biographical sources.

Biography

Black, Alexander. "The Woman Who Saw It First." *The Century Magazine* CVII, No. 1 (November 1923): 33-42.
　　General overview of Gilman's life and career. Black discusses in particular how Gilman's unhappy youth influenced her feminist writings.

Hill, Mary A. *Charlotte Perkins Gilman: The Making of a Radical Feminist, 1860-1896.* Philadelphia: Temple University Press, 1980, 362 p.

The first of a planned two-volume biographical study. In this volume Hill traces Gilman's feminist convictions and explains "some of the patterns of her early life." By contrasting excerpts from Gilman's private letters and journals with her published works, Hill suggests that Gilman's idealistic, intellectual goals conflicted with her personal needs and the practical demands of her life.

Criticism

Ammons, Elizabeth. "Writing Silence: 'The Yellow Wallpaper'." In her *Conflicting Stories: American Women Writers at the Turn into the Twentieth Century,* pp. 34-43. New York: Oxford University Press, 1991.
　　Feminist analysis of "The Yellow Wallpaper." Ammons maintains that the theme of "mother-loss that permeates [the text] foretells a major concern of women writers in America at the turn into the twentieth century as, collectively and individually, they faced the issue of leaving the old century."

Chandler, Marilyn R. "*The Awakening* and 'The Yellow Wallpaper': Ironies of Independence." In her *Dwelling in the Text: Houses in American Fiction,* pp. 121-47. Berkeley: University of California Press, 1991.
　　Comparative study of "The Yellow Wallpaper" and Kate Chopin's *The Awakening.* Chandler states: "Taken together the stories present the old, tragic double bind of female fate pushed to its extremes and ending in suicide or madness."

DeKoven, Marianne. "A Different Story: 'The Yellow Wallpaper' and *The Turn of the Screw.*" In her *Rich and Strange: Gender, History, Modernism,* pp. 38-63. Princeton: Princeton University Press, 1991.
　　Comparative analysis of "The Yellow Wallpaper" and Henry James's *The Turn of the Screw.* DeKoven asserts: "I will read both these works as incipiently modernist expressions of profound ambivalence concerning the radical changes in society and culture promised by the 'revolutionary horizon' of socialism and feminism, changes overtly desired by Gilman and overtly feared by James."

Delamotte, Eugenia C. "Male and Female Mysteries in 'The Yellow Wallpaper'." *Legacy* 5, No. 1 (Spring 1988): 3-14.
　　Examines the Gothic conventions of "The Yellow Wallpaper" from a feminist perspective.

Gornick, Vivian. "Twice Told Tales." *The Nation* 227, No. 9 (23 September 1978): 278-81.
　　Examines the similarities between "The Yellow Wallpaper" and David Reed's *Anna.* Gornick explains: " 'The Yellow Wallpaper' was a brilliant metaphor for the fatal suffocation of spirit that commonly lay behind a 19th-century woman's happily married life. The eerie sensation that *Anna* duplicates the metaphor is inescapable. And never more so than in the fact that in both cases the husbands are decent men who, standing on the edge, suffer intensely as they gaze down into the pit that has swallowed the women they love."

Kennard, Jean E. "Convention Coverage or How to Read Your Own Life." *New Literary History* XIII, No. 1 (Autumn 1981): 69-88.
　　Suggests that modern interpretations of "The Yellow Wallpaper"—particularly feminist ones—differ from

early interpretations because literary conventions have changed.

King, Jeannette, and Morris, Pam. "On Not Reading between the Lines: Models of Reading in 'The Yellow Wallpaper'." *Studies in Short Fiction* 26, No. 1 (Winter 1989): 23-32.

Uses Lacanian psychoanalysis to interpret "The Yellow Wallpaper," concluding that "in pursuit of a view of herself which is an ideological formation, the narrator misreads the yellow wallpaper, her other self, and in this way seeks to limit the play of its signifiers."

Kolodny, Annette. "A Map for Rereading: Or, Gender and the Interpretation of Literary Texts." *New Literary History* XI, No. 3 (Spring 1980): 451-67.

Discusses "The Yellow Wallpaper" as a story which "anticipated its own reception." Kolodny indicates that the uncomprehending husband of the story symbolizes male readers who would not understand the depth of meaning in "The Yellow Wallpaper."

Lewis, Peter. "Herland and Ourland." *The Times Literary Supplement*, No. 4074 (1 May 1981): 484.

Brief favorable review of *The Charlotte Perkins Gilman Reader* in which Lewis asserts that "The Yellow Wallpaper" suggests that Gilman "could have turned out to be a fiction writer of considerable significance if she had not channelled most of her creative energy into the women's movement from the mid-1890s on."

Lovecraft, Howard Phillips. "Introduction" and "The Weird Tradition in America." In his *Supernatural Horror in Literature*, pp. 12-16, pp. 60-75. New York: Ben Abramson, 1945.

Early standard interpretation of "The Yellow Wallpaper." Lovecraft mentions "the impulse which now and then drives writers of totally opposite leanings to try their hands at [horror stories]," and cites "The Yellow Wallpaper" as an example of such a story.

Massé, Michelle A. "Gothic Repetition: Husbands, Horrors, and Things That Go Bump in the Night." *Signs* 15, No. 4 (Summer 1990): 679-709.

Freudian analysis of the Gothic elements in "The Yellow Wallpaper."

Pringle, Mary Beth. " 'La poétique de l'espace' in Charlotte Perkins Gilman's 'The Yellow Wallpaper'." *The French-American Review* III, Nos. 1-2 (Winter-Spring 1978-1979): 15-22.

Relates "The Yellow Wallpaper" to Gaston Bachelard's 1957 phenomenological study *La poétique de l'espace*. Pringle maintains that Bachelard's theory is a "valuable critical tool for interpreting literature because it emphasizes the subjectivity of the fictional, physical setting as presented by the narrator."

Shumaker, Conrad. " 'Too Terribly Good to Be Printed': Charlotte Gilman's 'The Yellow Wallpaper'." *American Literature: A Journal of Literary History, Criticism, and Biography* 57, No. 4 (December 1985): 588-99.

Discusses the conflict between "feminine imagination" and "masculine rationality" in "The Yellow Wallpaper."

Treichler, Paula A. "Escaping the Sentence: Diagnosis and Discourse in 'The Yellow Wallpaper'." In *Feminist Issues in Literary Scholarship*, edited by Shari Benstock, pp. 62-78. Bloomington: Indiana University Press, 1987.

Analyzes "The Yellow Wallpaper" as a demonstration of the conflict between patriarchal language and feminine discourse.

Veeder, William. "Who Is Jane? The Intricate Feminism of Charlotte Perkins Gilman." *Arizona Quarterly: A Journal of American Literature, Culture, and Theory* 44, No. 3 (Autumn 1988): 40-79.

Provides a character analysis of the protagonist of "The Yellow Wallpaper." Veeder incorporates into his essay an explication of Gilman's feminism, including her views on female victimization and marriage.

Wiesenthal, C. S. " 'Unheard-of Contradictions': The Language of Madness in C. P. Gilman's 'The Yellow Wallpaper'." *Wascana Review* 25, No. 2 (Fall 1990): 1-17.

Challenges critics who have tried to link the narrative form of "The Yellow Wallpaper" to a "determined historical structure or condition." Wiesenthal states: "Instead, by holding the concept of the principle of madness as the variable which problematizes the narrative form, I will attempt to show that the apparent sacrifice of psychological realism entailed by Gilman's narrative mode—far from constituting any sort of 'defect'—actually involves a highly creative displacement of the actual signifying process of madness, processes Michel Foucault refers to as a form of 'delirious discourse.' "

Additional coverage of Gilman's life and career is contained in the following sources published by Gale Research: *Contemporary Authors*, Vol. 106; and *Twentieth-Century Literary Criticism*, Vols. 9, 37.

E. T. A. Hoffmann

1776-1822

(Born Ernst Theodor Wilhelm Hoffmann) German short story writer, novelist, composer, and critic.

INTRODUCTION

One of the most important figures in nineteenth-century European literature, Hoffmann is best known for his bizarre and fantastic short fiction. In these works he created a world where everyday existence is infused with the supernatural. Hoffmann's combination of realism and fantasy is often cited as a major influence on the work of many authors, including Edgar Allan Poe, Fedor Dostoevski, and Charles Dickens.

A child of estranged parents, Hoffmann was born in Königsberg and raised by his maternal grandmother and uncle. He studied law and accepted a low-level bureaucratic position in Berlin, struggling to earn a living while at the same time pursue his primary ambition to compose music. This conflict between his artistic endeavors and his career became a recurring theme in his short fiction. Hoffmann joined the Bamberg Theater as musical conductor and stage director in 1806. Biographers speculate that Hoffmann's frustration over his stalled music career and an unrequited love for one of his students inspired his early works of short fiction. In 1814 Hoffmann accepted a judicial post in Berlin and rose from unpaid court councillor to judge on the supreme court of appeals. He died in 1822.

Hoffmann's most representative stories are typified by a detailed realism in character portrayal and setting description combined with outlandish, frequently satirical plots. These works often feature elements of fairy tales and occultism, psychopathological phenomena such as hallucinations and somnambulism, and an array of grotesque concepts that includes lifelike automatons and doubles. "Der goldene Topf " ("The Golden Pot") is often designated by critics as characteristic of Hoffmann's fiction. In this story an awkward and poetically inclined student, Anselmus, is torn between his art and his pragmatic, bourgeois fiancée Veronica. Sitting outside a cafe one afternoon, he meets and falls in love with a snake named Serpentina, who encourages him to abandon his mundane existence and to write poetry with her in the mythical land of Atlantis. "The Golden Pot," like other stories by Hoffmann, satirizes middle-class values, which are viewed as inimical to the pursuit of art. Hoffmann's most frequently discussed story is "Der Sandmann" ("The Sandman"). In an early essay Sigmund Freud used "The Sandman" to exemplify the literary representation of the uncanny, and critics have since focused on the nightmarish qualities of this tale. Much of the story is related through the letters of the protagonist, Nathanael, whose recollections of a bedtime story about a sinister figure called the Sandman become confused in his mind with actual events in both his childhood and adult life. His inability to distinguish imagination from reality leads him to fall in love with a beautiful woman who, he later realizes, is only an automaton. Following this revelation he commits suicide by throwing himself from a tower. Such far-fetched and melodramatic storylines have become closely identified with Hoffmann, and to many critics his works epitomize the extravagance of the Romantic imagination. At the same time Hoffmann's stories display qualities that are considered more typical of modern than of Romantic writing. In reference to Hoffmann's fiction, Glyn Tegai Hughes has asserted that "the exploitation of the subconscious, the examination of the alienated self, the attempt to show creatures of the imagination placed in the real world and, above all, the holding of these in balance by irony, by narrative point of view, by the resources of art, are a major contribution to modern literature."

PRINCIPAL WORKS

SHORT FICTION

Fantasiestücke in Callots Manier. 4 vols.   1814-15
Nachtstücke. 2 vols.   1817
Klein Zaches gennant Zinnober   1819
  [*Little Zack* published in *Fairy Tales*, 1857; also pub-
    lished as *Little Zaches, Surnamed Zinnober* in *Three
    Märchen of E. T. A. Hoffmann*, 1971]
Die Serapions-Brüder. 4 vols.   1819-21
  [*The Serapion Brethren.* 2 vols., 1886-92]
Prinzessin Brambilla   1821
  [*Princess Brambilla* published in *Three Märchen of E.
    T. A. Hoffmann*, 1971]
Meister Floh   1822
  [*Master Flea* published in *Three Märchen of E. T. A.
    Hoffmann*, 1971]
Die Letzten Erzählungen. 2 vols.   1825
Hoffmann's Strange Stories   1855
Hoffmann's Fairy Tales   1857
Weird Tales. 2 vols.   1885
Three Märchen of E. T. A. Hoffmann   1971

OTHER MAJOR WORKS

Die Elixiere des Teufels   (novel)   1815-16
  [*The Devil's Elixir*, 1824; also published as *The Devil's
    Elixirs*, 1963]
Lebens-Ansichten des Katers Murr   (unfinished novel)
  1820-22
  [*The Educated Cat* published in *Nut-Cracker and
    Mouse-King, and, The Educated Cat*, 1892; also pub-
    lished as *The Life and Opinions of Kater Murr* in *Se-
    lected Writings of E. T. A. Hoffmann, Volume 2*,
    1969]
Gesammelte Werke. 5 vols.   (short stories, novels, and
  criticism)   1960-65

CRITICISM

Sir Walter Scott   (essay date 1827)

[*A Scottish author of historical romances, Scott was one
of the leading proponents in the early nineteenth century
of verisimilitude and historical accuracy in literature.
Perhaps more than any of his contemporaries, he clearly
represents the increased tolerance of the Romantic age
toward all literature, so much so that many later critics
and scholars have severely criticized him for his habit of
praising nearly everyone and for his lack of discrimination in critical matters. Scott never truly formulated a
guiding or central theory to his work, but his criticism
was usually based on a high regard for realism and the
desire to assess an author's place in literary history. In
the following excerpt, he criticizes Hoffmann's stories as
unnecessarily extravagant and grotesque.*]

The author who led the way in [the Fantastic style] of lit-

erature was Ernest Theodore William Hoffmann; the peculiarity of whose genius, temper, and habits, fitted him
to distinguish himself where imagination was to be
strained to the pitch of oddity and bizarrerie. He appears
to have been a man of rare talent,—a poet, an artist, and
a musician, but unhappily of a hypochondriac and whimsical disposition, which carried him to extremes in all his
undertakings; so his music became capricious,—his drawings caricatures,—and his tales, as he himself termed
them, fantastic extravagances. (p. 74)

We do not mean to say that the imagination of Hoffmann
was either wicked or corrupt, but only that it was ill-
regulated and had an undue tendency to the horrible and
the distressing. Thus he was followed, especially in his
hours of solitude and study, by the apprehension of mysterious danger to which he conceived himself exposed; and
the whole tribe of demi-gorgons, apparitions, and fanciful
spectres and goblins of all kinds with which he has filled
his pages, although in fact the children of his own imagination, were no less discomposing to him than if they had
had a real existence and actual influence upon him. (p. 81)

It is no wonder that to a mind so vividly accessible to the
influence of the imagination, so little under the dominion
of sober reason, such a numerous train of ideas should
occur in which fancy had a large share and reason none
at all. In fact, the grotesque in his compositions partly resembles the arabesque in painting, in which is introduced
the most strange and complicated monsters, resembling
centaurs, griffins, sphinxes, chimeras, rocs, and all other
creatures of romantic imagination, dazzling the beholder
as it were by the unbounded fertility of the author's imagination, and sating it by the rich contrast of all the varieties
of shape and colouring, while there is in reality nothing
to satisfy the understanding or inform the judgment. Hoffmann spent his life, which could not be a happy one, in
weaving webs of this wild and imaginative character, for
which after all he obtained much less credit with the public, than his talents must have gained if exercised under
the restraint of a better taste or a more solid judgment. . . . [Notwithstanding] the dreams of an overheated imagination, by which his taste appears to have
been so strangely misled, Hoffmann seems to have been a
man of excellent disposition, a close observer of nature,
and one who, if this sickly and disturbed train of thought
had not led him to confound the supernatural with the absurd, would have distinguished himself as a painter of
human nature, of which in its realities he was an observer
and an admirer.

Hoffmann was particularly skilful in depicting characters
arising in his own country of Germany. Nor is there any
of her numerous authors who have better and more faithfully designed the upright honesty and firm integrity
which is to be met with in all classes which come from the
ancient Teutonic stock. (pp. 81-2)

Unfortunately [Hoffmann's] taste and temperament directed him too strongly to the grotesque and fantastic,—
carried him too far "extra moenia flammantia mundi," too
much beyond the circle not only of probability but even
of possibility, to admit of his composing much in the better
style which he might easily have attained. The popular ro-

mance, no doubt, has many walks, nor are we at all inclined to halloo the dogs of criticism against those whose object is merely to amuse a passing hour. . . . But we do not desire to see genius expand or rather exhaust itself upon themes which cannot be reconciled to taste; and the utmost length in which we can indulge a turn to the fantastic is, where it tends to excite agreeable and pleasing ideas. (pp. 92-3)

Hoffmann has in some measure identified himself with the ingenious artist by his title of **Night Pieces after the manner of Callot [Phantasiestüeke in Callots Manier],** and in order to write such a tale, for example, as that called **"The Sandman,"** he must have been deep in the mysteries of that fanciful artist, with whom he might certainly boast a kindred spirit. We have given an instance of a tale in which the wonderful is, in our opinion, happily introduced, because it is connected with and applied to human interest and human feeling, and illustrates with no ordinary force the elevation to which circumstances may raise the power and dignity of the human mind. [The narrative **"The Sandman"**] is of a different class:

> half horror and half whim, Like fiends in glee, ridiculously grim.

This wild and absurd story is in some measure redeemed by some traits in the character of Clara, whose firmness, plain good sense and frank affection are placed in agreeable contrast with the wild imagination, fanciful apprehensions, and extravagant affection of her crazy-pated admirer.

It is impossible to subject tales of this nature to criticism. They are not the visions of a poetical mind, they have scarcely even the seeming authenticity which the hallucinations of lunacy convey to the patient; they are the feverish dreams of a lightheaded patient, to which, though they may sometimes excite by their peculiarity, or surprise by their oddity, we never feel disposed to yield more than momentary attention. In fact, the inspirations of Hoffmann so often resemble the ideas produced by the immoderate use of opium, that we cannot help considering his case as one requiring the assistance of medicine rather than of criticism; and while we acknowledge that with a steadier command of his imagination he might have been an author of the first distinction, yet situated as he was, and indulging the diseased state of his own system, he appears to have been subject to that undue vividness of thought and perception of which the celebrated Nicolai became at once the victim and the conqueror. Phlebotomy and cathartics, joined to sound philosophy and deliberate observation, might, as in the case of that celebrated philosopher, have brought to a healthy state a mind which we cannot help regarding as diseased, and his imagination soaring with an equal and steady flight might have reached the highest pitch of the poetical profession. (p. 97)

[Hoffmann's] works as they now exist ought to be considered less as models for imitation than as affording a warning how the most fertile fancy may be exhausted by the lavish prodigality of its possessor. (p. 98)

> *Walter Scott, in an originally unsigned essay titled "On the Supernatural in Fictitious Com-*

position," in The Foreign Quarterly Review, *Vol. 1, No. 1, July, 1827, pp. 61-98.*

Sigmund Freud   (essay date 1919)

[An Austrian neurologist, Freud was the father of psychoanalysis. The general framework of psychoanalytic thought, explained in his seminal work The Interpretation of Dreams *(1900), encompasses both normal and abnormal behavior and is founded on the tenet that one's early experiences profoundly affect later behavior. Freud's interrelated theories of the unconscious (primitive impulses and repressed thoughts), the libido (sexual energy that follows a predetermined course), the structure of personality (id, ego, superego), and human psycho-sexual development (sequential stages of sexual development) have been widely used in the treatment of psychopathy. Freud was sometimes harshly criticized for his innovative theories, especially his insistence that sexual impulses exist in very young children and his definition of the Oedipus and Electra complexes. Nonetheless, he was for the most part greatly respected as a thinker and teacher. In addition, Freudianism has had significant influence on various schools of philosophy, religious and political ideas, and artistic endeavors such as surrealism in art, atonal music, and stream of consciousness in literature. Thus, along with such important thinkers as Karl Marx, Friedrich Nietzsche, and Albert Einstein, Freud is considered one of the most important shapers of modern thought. In the following excerpt from his essay "The Uncanny," which was originally published in* Imago, *Vol. 5, he analyzes Hoffmann's "The Sandman."]*

It is only rarely that a psycho-analyst feels impelled to investigate the subject of aesthetics even when aesthetics is understood to mean not merely the theory of beauty, but the theory of feeling. . . . But it does occasionally happen that he has to interest himself in some particular province of that subject; and then it usually proves to be a rather remote region of it and one that has been neglected in standard works.

The subject of the 'uncanny' is a province of this kind. (p. 368)

[The] 'uncanny' is that class of the terrifying which leads back to something long known to us, once very familiar. (pp. 369-70)

In proceeding to review those things, persons, impressions, events and situations which are able to arouse in us a feeling of the uncanny in a very forcible and definite form, the first requirement is obviously to select a suitable example to start upon. (p. 378)

[In his paper 'Zur Psychologie des Unheimlichen,' E. Jentsch says]: 'In telling a story, one of the most successful devices for easily creating uncanny effects is to leave the reader in uncertainty whether a particular figure in the story is a human being or an automaton; and to do it in such a way that his attention is not directly focussed upon his uncertainty, so that he may not be urged to go into the matter and clear it up immediately, since that, as we have said, would quickly dissipate the peculiar emotional effect of the thing. Hoffmann has repeatedly employed this psychological artifice with success in his fantastic narratives.'

This observation, undoubtedly a correct one, refers primarily to the story of **'The Sand-Man'** in Hoffmann's *Nachtstücken*. . . . But I cannot think—and I hope that most readers of the story will agree with me—that the theme of the doll, Olympia, who is to all appearances a living being, is by any means the only element to be held responsible for the quite unparalleled atmosphere of uncanniness which the story evokes; or, indeed, that it is the most important among them. Nor is this effect of the story heightened by the fact that the author himself treats the episode of Olympia with a faint touch of satire and uses it to make fun of the young man's idealization of his mistress. The main theme of the story is, on the contrary, something different, something which gives its name to the story, and which is always re-introduced at the critical moment: it is the theme of the 'Sand-Man' who tears out children's eyes. (pp. 378-79)

[There is] no doubt that the feeling of something uncanny is directly attached to the figure of the Sand-Man, that is, to the idea of being robbed of one's eyes; and that Jentsch's point of an intellectual uncertainty has nothing to do with this effect. Uncertainty whether an object is living or inanimate, which we must admit in regard to the doll Olympia, is quite irrelevant in connection with this other, more striking instance of uncanniness. It is true that the writer creates a kind of uncertainty in us in the beginning by not letting us know, no doubt purposely, whether he is taking us into the real world or into a purely fantastic one of his own creation. . . . But this uncertainty disappears in the course of Hoffmann's story, and we perceive that he means to make us, too, look through the fell Coppola's glasses—perhaps, indeed, that he himself once gazed through such an instrument. For the conclusion of the story makes it quite clear that Coppola the optician really is the lawyer Coppelius and thus also the Sand-Man.

There is no question, therefore, of any 'intellectual uncertainty'; we know now that we are not supposed to be looking on at the products of a madman's imagination . . .; and yet this knowledge does not lessen the impression of uncanniness in the least degree. The theory of 'intellectual uncertainty' is thus incapable of explaining that impression.

We know from psycho-analytic experience, however, that this fear of damaging or losing one's eyes is a terrible fear of childhood. . . . A study of dreams, phantasies and myths has taught us that a morbid anxiety connected with the eyes and with going blind is often enough a substitute for the dread of castration. In blinding himself, Oedipus, that mythical lawbreaker, was simply carrying out a mitigated form of the punishment of castration—the only punishment that according to the lex talionis was fitted for him. We may try to reject the derivation of fears about the eye from the fear of castration on rationalistic grounds, and say that it is very natural that so precious an organ as the eye should be guarded by a proportionate dread. . . . (pp. 382-83)

[But] I would not recommend any opponent of the psy-

choanalytic view to select precisely the story of the Sand-Man upon which to build his case that morbid anxiety about the eyes has nothing to do with the castration-complex. For why does Hoffmann bring the anxiety about eyes into such intimate connection with the father's death? And why does the Sand-Man appear each time in order to interfere with love? He divides the unfortunate Nathaniel from his betrothed and from her brother, his best friend; he destroys his second object of love, Olympia, the lovely doll; and he drives him into suicide at the moment when he has won back his Clara and is about to be happily united to her. Things like these and many more seem arbitrary and meaningless in the story so long as we deny all connection between fears about the eye and castration; but they become intelligible as soon as we replace the Sand-Man by the dreaded father at whose hands castration is awaited. [Freud elaborates in a footnote: In the story from Nathaniel's childhood, the figures of his father and Coppelius represent the two opposites into which the father-imago is split by the ambivalence of the child's feeling; whereas the one threatens to blind him, that is, to castrate him, the other, the loving father, intercedes for his sight. That part of the complex which is most strongly repressed, the death-wish against the father, finds expression in the death of the good father, and Coppelius is made answerable for it. Later, in his student days, Professor Spalanzani and Coppola the optician reproduce this double representation of the father-imago, the Professor is a member of the father-series, Coppola openly identified with the lawyer Coppelius. Just as before they used to work together over the fire, so now they have jointly created the doll Olympia; the Professor is even called the father of Olympia. This second occurrence of work in common shows that the optician and the mechanician are also components of the father-imago, that is, both are Nathaniel's father as well as Olympia's. I ought to have added that in the terrifying scene in childhood, Coppelius, after sparing Nathaniel's eyes, had screwed off his arms and legs as an experiment; that is, he had experimented on him as a mechanician would on a doll. This singular feature, which seems quite out of perspective in the picture of the Sand-Man, introduces a new castration-equivalent; but it also emphasizes the identity of Coppelius and his later counterpart, Spalanzani the mechanician, and helps us to understand who Olympia is. She, the automatic doll, can be nothing else than a personification of Nathaniel's feminine attitude towards his father in his infancy. The father of both, Spalanzani and Coppola, are, as we know, new editions, reincarnations of Nathaniel's 'two' fathers. Now Spalanzani's otherwise incomprehensible statement that the optician has stolen Nathaniel's eyes so as to set them in the doll becomes significant and supplies fresh evidence for the identity of Olympia and Nathaniel. Olympia is, as it were, a dissociated complex of Nathaniel's which confronts him as a person, and Nathaniel's enslavement to this complex is expressed in his senseless obsessive love for Olympia. We may with justice call such love narcissistic, and can understand why he who has fallen victim to it should relinquish his real, external object of love. The psychological truth of the situation in which the young man, fixated upon his father by his castration-complex, is incapable of loving a woman, is amply proved by numerous analyses of patients whose story, though less fantastic, is hardly less tragic than that of the student Nathaniel.]

[We] venture, therefore, to refer the uncanny effect of the Sand-Man to the child's dread in relation to its castration-complex. (pp. 384-85)

> *Sigmund Freud, "The 'Uncanny',," translated by Alix Strachey, in his* Collected Papers, *Vol. 4, translated by Joan Riviere, The International Psycho-Analytical Press, 1925, pp. 368-407.*

Harvey W. Hewett-Thayer   (essay date 1948)

[In the following excerpt, Hewett-Thayer examines the diverse influences on Hoffmann's short fiction.]

During the brief period of Hoffmann's literary activity he was a prolific author, responding both to the call of the in-dwelling "demon" and to the urgency of financial need. Many of his tales do not fall readily into any rubric of clas-sification. Though certain perpetual interests may appear in them—such as the problem of the artist or the phenom-ena of occultism—these elements are subordinate to the mere telling of a story. Some of these tales, as stories, are to be reckoned among his major achievements, but many of them also are the product of a lively imagination, work-ing under the stimulus of a contract with a publisher.

To the former class **"Das Majorat" ("The Entail")** indubi-tably belongs. It is not only one of the best of Hoffmann's stories but an outstanding work of German fiction. **"Das Majorat"** has also the distinction of being, together with **"Der Sandmann,"** the work upon which Sir Walter Scott based his one sided appraisal of Hoffmann, and it offers perhaps the most plausible evidence for the influence of Hoffmann on Edgar Allan Poe (*The Fall of the House of Usher*). The autobiographical elements are especially sig-nificant, perhaps more directly derived from Hoffmann's life than in any other story except *Kater Murr*. The narra-tor, Theodor, accompanies his great-uncle V—as Hoff-mann often did—to the estate of a nobleman whose legal affairs were under the supervision of the great-uncle; Theodor is a young lawyer with pronounced musical gifts, and he falls in love with the wife of another man, a remi-niscence of Hoffmann's passion for "Cora" Hatt. (p. 313)

In **"Das Majorat"** Hoffmann has met squarely the two chief obligations which rest upon the storyteller, to create characters both convincing and interesting, and to con-struct a well-knit plot. Each character in the story is a firmly rounded, carefully developed individual. In some of his stories, it may be admitted, haste in fulfilling obliga-tions to an editor led to careless methods and the inclusion of figures taken from stock, so to speak; but this is not the case in **"Das Majorat."** The Justiciary is an example of the novelist's character drawing at its best. Presumably his great-uncle stood in part as model for the character but with what modifications none can tell, for almost nothing is known of him beyond the love and reverence with which Hoffmann regarded him. He develops the character grad-ually and for the most part according to the epic tradition. through action: there is no general analysis of his qualities. Theodor mentions him first simply as the "splendid old

uncle." Epithets are brought into direct connection with acts: he is vehement and irascible and hence is about to utter an oath when it seems that no proper preparation has been made for their reception at the castle: but he has him-self under control and turns his wrathful oath into a ring-ing laugh, for he saw the humor of the situation. The phrase "inclined to merrymaking of all sorts" (zu allem Lustigen aufgelegt) introduces the amusing scene where the old man presents his nephew to the two eccentric old aunts of the Baron and then entangles them in an intricate web of ironical jesting. The support of religious faith gives him both courage and consciousness of power to face the dread phenomena of the unseen world without flinching: "like a commanding hero" he stands there, and there is something more than human in his mien after his triumph over the specter. Theodor's boyish love for the Baroness he opposes with good-humored ridicule or with blunt and telling sarcasm. He deflates Theodor's pride in his some-what accidental slaying of the great boar; he laughs in his nephew's face: "God is mighty in the weak," he says. Whatever is sturdy, solid, and balanced in the young man he evidently owes to the old man's training. The Baron treats the Justiciary with almost childlike reverence, even with awe. The novelist develops a character through what others in the story think and say of him.

The mystery story, from Hoffmann's day to this, depends upon the skill of the author, first in presenting an enigmat-ic situation, the weaving of a complicated web of circum-stances, and then the unraveling of the web through the ingenuity of the investigator. Hoffmann's story fulfills these conditions only in part, for **"Das Majorat"** is much more than the mere detection of Daniel's crime. As al-ready noted, Hoffmann's eye is fixed on the fated family whose career of gradual disintegration he follows to its final doom. It is thus not a forerunner of the modern de-tective story in the same sense as **"Das Fräulein von Scuderi."** Yet the technique of the detective story may be observed. The mystery story thrives through the creation of suspense—not only an initial sensation, but by frequent pinpricks of later stimuli. Most of Hoffmann's tales show a sovereign mastery of the technique of suspense. For ex-ample in **"Das Majorat"**: Old Franz leads the Justiciary and Theodor into the apartment which is to serve as the hall of justice—the room with the walled-up door. There is a bright fire on the hearth, and Theodor on entering feels cheered: "Yet my great-uncle remained standing in the middle of the room, looked about him and said in a very serious, almost solemn, tone: 'So here, this is to be the courtroom?' Franz, holding the candle high so that a bright spot on the broad dark wall, the size of a door, struck one's eye, said in a muffled and pain-filled voice, 'Here judgment has already been given once,' " and to the query of the Justiciary he replies that the remark "only just slipped out." The question of the Justiciary was of course purely rhetorical; he knew what the old servant meant. When Wolfgang returns to find his father lying dead, he takes a piece of paper from his pocket and burns it by one of the great candles that stand at the four corners of his father's bier. This scene the reader holds in mind until he learns the content of the letter and why the new Baron burned it. Usually Hoffmann observes quite rigidly the rule that should govern the telling of a mystery tale;

Theodor, as author, tells all he knows at the time—a feeling of suspense may be communicated to the reader of which the personal narrator is not conscious. **"Das Majorat"** was published in the second volume of the *Nachtstücke*, 1817. (pp. 317-19)

"Meister Martin der Küfner und seine Gesellen" ("Master Martin the Cooper and His Assistants") is a story so worth-while in itself that one might resent the undue prominence sometimes given it simply as a source for Wagner's *Meistersinger*; it does not need to shine by reflected light. Hoffmann's love for southern Germany, halfway to Italy, the land of his longing, has found its expression in this little tale of Nuremberg in the latter part of the sixteenth century. Like other members of the Romantic brotherhood, he found in the old Bavarian towns a beauty, a lingering medieval charm, as nowhere else in German lands. During his stay in Bamberg he visited Nuremberg and here he has incorporated the memories of his enchantment. It is the city of Albrecht Dürer, of painters, sculptors, silversmiths, goldsmiths, and of the Meistersinger, and with loving devotion and the carefulness of a scholar Hoffmann recreates the past. Hoffmann's Nuremberg is, admittedly, a romanticized version of the sixteenth century German town, but the reader surrenders to his magic, and refuses to consider any possible inaccuracy in the focus of his picture. In the larger sense, perhaps such evocations of the past are more real than the labored and learned studies of the social historian, even as Velasquez' *Breda* and Rembrandt's *Night Watch* are essentially more eternally true than a photograph could have been. Hoffmann is indeed not entirely blind to matters that interest the historian of society. There are some hints of a period of transition in the old free city, more than a hint indeed of increasing self-confidence in bourgeois ways and bourgeois virtues, such as Hebbel in *Agnes Bernauer* portrayed in the Augsburg of an earlier century. But Hoffmann does not stress the point; it is all incidental to his narrative.

To Meister Martin's cooper shop orders come from far and near, for his workmanship is unrivaled. The accumulated wealth of his coffers might have enabled him to challenge the patricians of the old city or the neighboring noblemen in elegance of living. Though he maintained the old patriarchal system and housed some of his workers in his own spacious dwelling, he was still a patron of the arts and acquired things of beauty for his home. He was also an enthusiastic supporter of the Meistersinger. To him the craft of the cooper ranked with the noblest occupations of man, for the casks and hogsheads of his making were works of art comparable with other products of artistic genius in his own city. His love of his work was an obsession, and he had sworn to bestow his fair daughter only upon a cooper; in this resolve he was fortified by the cryptic prophecy of his dying grandmother, which he arbitrarily interprets according to his own prepossessions. The beauty of Rosa is such that the sons of patrician families or even of noblemen in the vicinity look upon her with favor—Hoffmann has not forgotten the first act of his beloved *Käthchen von Heilbronn*.

The story centers in the efforts of three suitors, the "Gesellen" of the title, to win the hand of Rosa. Each has abandoned, temporarily at any rate, the career in life already indicated for him, learned the trade of the cooper, and obtained work in Meister Martin's workshop; each intends to desert the fashioning of vats, barrels, and hogsheads as soon as the prize is won. Conrad, the nobleman's son, quits the workshop after a violent altercation with Meister Martin, in which pride of birth contends with pride of workmanship. Reinhold the painter, who has already gained a considerable reputation in Italy, wavers in his devotion to the "base" handiwork, and his devotion to Rosa he incorporates in a portrait at which he works secretly; when it is finished, his experiment is at an end—an idea that Hoffmann has employed elsewhere. Friedrich alone remains, but feigns illness, absents himself from the cooperage, and works with untold delight in the atelier of his former master, a goldsmith. The superb goblet which he makes as a present for Rosa is discovered to satisfy the wording of the great-grandmother's prophecy as well as a cask for bubbling wine.

For **"Der Kampf der Sänger"** one may reverse the statement made above concerning **"Meister Martin der Küfner"**; its share in the creation of Wagner's *Tannhäuser* is of greater interest than the story itself. Hoffmann has failed to conjure up even a romanticized picture of the Middle Ages which is satisfying. He could not follow in Fouqué's footsteps, though there are traces of Fouqué's style. The vision of the procession at the beginning of the story was evidently suggested by Tieck's "Aufzug der Romanze," and there is an echo of Tieck ("Der Runenberg") in the episode of the mysterious stranger whom Ofterdingen meets in the forest and the stranger's gift of a book that is missing when Ofterdingen awakes in the morning. It is clear that Hoffmann could enter more understandingly and more sympathetically into the bourgeois world of late sixteenth century Nuremberg than into the age of chivalry. The story proves also that the supernaturalism of medieval tradition lay largely outside of Hoffmann's domain. Though he makes quite abundant use of it in the necromancy of the great minstrel Klingsohr and in the diablerie of his demon representative Nasias, his interest is only halfhearted—he has come by it secondhand. The type of supernaturalism which Hoffmann correctly enough associates with medieval superstition was too bare-faced, forthright, and crude, and it lacked the tantalizing mystery of the borderland where the natural and the supernatural are indistinguishable.

Hoffmann provides a charming introduction to his tale of medieval love and song. While the rude winds of the spring equinox roar and bluster outside, the author sits in his lonely room with Wagenseil's treatise on the Meistersinger open before him. To the tempest he pays no heed, but, closing the book, he gazes raptly into the fire on the hearth, lost in the magical picture of times long passed. In the vision that follows he finds himself in a flowery meadow, surrounded by the twilight gloom of a dense forest; "the streams murmured, the bushes rustled as if in secret whisperings of love, and sounding in the midst of it all a nightingale lamented his sweet woe." Presently from a distance the joyful sound of hunting horns is heard—the stags and roes peep out of the wood—and then the music of harps and human voices blending in heavenly melody.

From the forest a train emerges, at the head huntsmen with shining horns; then a stately gentleman in princely mantle, on a palfrey at his side a lady of wondrous beauty; on six steeds of varied colors six riders follow, playing on harp and lute and singing in wonderful, clear tones; richly clad pages and servants bring up the rear of the procession. A stranger appears and accosts the dreamer; it is old Professor Wagenseil himself, and he points out the figures in the train one by one, the Landgraf von Thüringen, the Gräfin Mathilde von Falkenstein, and the six minstrels whom the Landgraf has gathered at his court. These opening paragraphs arouse keen anticipation in the reader which unhappily the author does not completely satisfy. To the story of Heinrich von Ofterdingen that Hoffmann found in Wagenseil and in other accessible sources, he made substantial additions, particularly in a closer definition of the hero's character. At the beginning Heinrich von Ofterdingen is a youth of extraordinary promise in the world of minstrelsy, sharing with the other singers the purity of purpose and the exalted conception of the minstrel's spiritual message. But he is moody and passionate, in love with the beautiful widowed Countess Mathilde von Falkenstein, whose favor he seeks through the power of song; he disappears from the court, despairing and defeated, in perceiving that his lady looks with greater favor upon his closest friend, the minstrel Wolframb von Eschenbach. He turns away from the high ideals of his companions, seeking the more robust but profane art of Klingsohr to raise his powers above his fellows, and returns to court in pride and boastful arrogance, scorning the petty achievements of his old friends. For a time the Countess falls under his spell, but again he meets defeat, for however transcendent his skill, the evil he has learned creeps into his song. Again he flees from his old home but this time for remorse and spiritual regeneration.

That Hoffmann himself was doubtful of the story's merit may be inferred from the comment of the Serapion Brothers. To be sure, the tale is the work of Cyprian, one of the three Hoffmanns, but it is severely criticized by Theodor, Hoffmann's more essential self. Concretely, however, his criticism is beside the mark—that Cyprian's story has ruined for him the picture of Heinrich von Ofterdingen in Novalis' novel, that the minstrels, though ever making ready to sing, still never really sing. In reality Novalis' Heinrich von Ofterdingen has virtually nothing in common with the legendary minstrel except his name and his birthplace in Eisenach, and Ottmar demolishes the second objection by remarking that it was unreasonable to expect Cyprian to insert verses of his own as specimens of Wartburg minstrelsy. But Ottmar's own criticism is pertinent: Cyprian should guard himself against looking into old chronicles, since reading of this sort might easily entice him into an alien territory, in which an outsider with no special sense of direction would waver about on every false pathway, without ever being able to find the right one.

Hoffmann's longing to visit Italy was never fulfilled, but through ceaseless poring over books on Italy and views of Italian scenes he recreated Italy in his mind and heart as if he had really been there. . . . [He] used Italian backgrounds repeatedly in his stories—in **"Prinzessin Brambilla,"** and in parts of **"Die Fermate"**, **"Das verlorene**

Spiegelbild", **"Die Jesuiterkirche in G."**, **"Der Artushof "**, **"Ignaz Denner"**, *Die Elixiere des Teufels,* and *Kater Murr,* an amazing list for one who never saw the country. The scene of two other stories, **"Signor Formica"** and **"Doge und Dogaressa"**, is laid entirely in Italy.

That the "Signor Formica" of Hoffmann's tale is Salvator Rosa, the Italian artist, musician, and poet, would seem to offer him a peculiarly congenial theme. In the range of his professional and avocational activities, Salvator Rosa resembled Hoffmann, but the resemblance goes deeper. Not only in their versatility were they akin, but in their temperaments. Maassen quotes at length a passage from Lady Morgan's life of Salvator Rosa characterizing the artist as a man and remarks that it could be applied word for word to Hoffmann. In the work of the Italian, Hoffmann found something not dissimilar to the qualities that he admired in Jacques Callot—for example, the small, grotesque, and agitated figures which Rosa placed against a background of mountain and forest. Despite the title, which refers to Salvator Rosa, Hoffmann is not writing a study of his artistic kinsman in seventeenth century Italy, and the specific problems of the artist are only incidentally touched upon. The story concerns two young people who are in love and Salvator Rosa's benevolent and intricate plotting to overcome the obstacles to their union. The title is justified since Rosa pulls the strings that control the action of the tale. One might say that Hoffmann's thinking on the problems of the artist passed over into *Kater Murr,* the first part of which was written at the same time. **"Signor Formica"** is a sprightly and diverting tale, and it is perhaps presuming to ask more of a storyteller.

Salvator Rosa has escaped from Naples to Rome after the insurrection of Masaniello. Desperately ill, he finds shelter in the home of a widow, where he had lodged years before when he was an unknown painter. His illness forms the novelist's scheme for introducing Antonio Scacciati, a young barber-surgeon, and the worthy Doctor Splendidiano Accoromboni, nicknamed the Pyramid Doctor because so many of his patients lie buried in the cemetery beside the pyramid of Caius Cestius. When summoned the Pyramid Doctor names one hundred and twenty diseases that Rosa did not have, but off-hand he is unable to find a name for his present malady; he returns, however, a few hours later, has found a nice name for it, and brings medicines that smell as if drawn from the River Acheron. Rosa continues to grow worse until he rises from his bed and throws the bottles out of the window upon the head of the doctor who happens to be entering. Dr. Accoromboni is hand and glove with the aged Pasquale Capuzzi, an eccentric miser, with whose niece Mariana the young barber-surgeon is in love; Capuzzi is a ridiculous fop, and regards himself as an illustrious composer and matchless singer. Accoromboni, only four feet tall and amply paunched, Capuzzi, tall and thin as a riding whip, with long pointed nose and chin, together with Capuzzi's dwarf servant Pitichinaccio, form an incomparable trio and should alone rescue the story from the disdain with which some critics regard it.

Antonio, though only a barber and blood-letter, is in secret an artist, has even been a pupil of Annibale Carracci and Guido Reni, but has been unable to gain any recognition from the hidebound guild of Roman painters. Rosa plays a trick on these arch-conservative critics; having conceived a warm liking for the young man, he exhibits one of his paintings, a Magdalen, as the work of a promising young Neapolitan artist, recently deceased. All Rome flocks to see the picture; critics and artists are unanimous in declaring it a masterpiece. The leading guild of artists, the Accademia di San Luca, elects the painter to posthumous fame as a member—all this when Salvator Rosa gleefully and sarcastically reveals the identity of the painter.

Capuzzi is in love with Mariana himself and obtains papal dispensation for the marriage in spite of the relationship. She is virtually a prisoner in his house, guarded by the dwarf Pitichinaccio. Plot and counterplot—Salvator Rosa and Antonio on the one side and Capuzzi and his two companions on the other—form an intricate and amusing, indeed often hilarious, pattern in Hoffmann's narrative. Eventually Mariana is abducted, and the young lovers flee to Florence. Involved in the plot is the establishment of a new theater in Rome where Rosa functions as manager and actor. The historical Rosa was an exceedingly clever actor; actually his participation in more or less impromptu street performances was well-known, but Hoffmann alters this and uses the mystery of Signor Formica's identity as a telling element in the plot. In this part of the story the novelist touches on conditions in the Roman theater that he portrays more brilliantly and effectively in **"Prinzessin Brambilla."** He has in mind something of the scenery and the technique of the "Commedia dell' Arte" and visually perhaps some of Callot's little sketches called "Balli."

A painting by Wilhelm Kolbe in the Berlin exhibition of 1816 provided the initial stimulus for the story **"Doge und Dogaressa"**: the gray-bearded Doge Marino Falieri and his young bride are standing, accompanied by several attendants, before a balustrade, with a view of Venice as a background. The sordid story of Falieri's conspiracy to gain sovereign power in the Venetian state was fused with romantic glow by the marriage of the eighty-year-old Doge to a beautiful girl of eighteen; it has stimulated the imagination of Byron, Otto Ludwig, and others, though before Hoffmann's story there is record of only one use of the theme in literature. Presumably Kolbe heard the story in Venice; perhaps he could say with Byron that the Scala dei Giganti where Falieri was "crowned, discrowned, and decapitated struck forcibly my imagination." Hoffmann saw something in the painting that interested him, and he sought sources of information. It can be shown that he transcribed the historical facts of the story from Le Bret's history of Venice, often with striking verbal correspondence.

But Le Bret's factual and rather pedestrian narrative supplied only a limited amount of raw material out of which the novelist was to fashion a beguiling and tragic story. The story is, indeed, Hoffmann's own; he takes historical events, develops a hint here and there in his source, adds material entirely his own, and thus in complete mastery builds up the structure of his tale. A comparison of Hoffmann's text with this one source illustrates the novelist's

Hoffmann's self-portrait.

deft and fertile methods of transforming his source into a work of art. There is space for only a glimpse of all this.

Of the conspiracy itself in a political sense Hoffmann naturally gives only a somewhat cursory account—only what is required; he is telling the tragic story of two young lovers. That the beautiful wife of the Doge had many admirers, that the Doge himself was "beside himself with jealousy" he found in Le Bret; further, that Michael Steno, a young man of patrician family and a member of the Council of Forty, was said to be one of these admirers, though other reports, among them the source that Lord Byron used, maintained that Steno's attentions were directed toward one of her ladies in waiting. Hoffmann, however, weaves Steno's love for the Dogaressa into the plot of his story. Le Bret does not mention the name of the Doge's bride; Hoffmann calls her Annunziata; Byron uses the name Angiola. The hero is entirely Hoffmann's invention—a mere gondolier, who nevertheless raises his eyes to the wife of the ruler. In his source Hoffmann read the simple statement that one of the conspirators was a German, Antonius Dalebinder; since he is writing a story for German readers, he takes the hint and makes his hero a German, though Antonio has lived all his life, at all events since earliest childhood, in Italy. As a humble gondolier he is obviously not one of the conspirators, though at the end, after discovering the circumstances of his father's death, he seeks personal vengeance through a brief participation in their activities.

The bare fact that the Bucentoro, bringing the newly elected Doge home to Venice, is imperiled by a rising tempest, is noted in Le Bret. Hoffmann turns the historian's bald record into an impressive picture: the gondolier rows his frail vessel out to the huge but unseaworthy ship of state and rescues the Doge from death. The rich reward that the Doge bestows upon him enables Antonio to play another role than that of a gondolier. On the occasion of a great procession Antonio and Annunziata see one another, and again on the following day when he uses an audacious stratagem to approach her, for he recognizes in her a playmate of his childhood days; the love that was then a mere seed in the soil is now by sudden miracle brought to full bloom.

The old beggar woman Margareta is an original and characteristic addition. She had been Antonio's nurse, and he is strongly drawn to her before his memories of the past are awakened. She has knowledge of secret remedies, precious salves, simples, and herbs, and had carried on her unofficial art of healing among the Venetian populace until ecclesiastical authority intervened; and she has strange mesmeric and prophetic powers. The novelist employs her to reveal something of Antonio's past and by her cryptic prophecies and warnings to foreshadow coming events, and thus bind the story together.

On the night when the Doge is executed Antonio finds his way into the palace; in the turmoil of that fatal night the lovers make their escape to a boat that a friend of Antonio's is holding in readiness for them, and they put out to sea, old Margareta with them. But a fierce storm arises and they are drowned: "The sea, the jealous widow of the beheaded Falieri, stretched up its foaming waves like giant arms and snatched them down into the bottomless deep."

The composition of **"Das öde Haus" ("The Deserted House")** illustrates Hoffmann's response to a different type of stimulus. Although the material assembled by Hans von Müller and developed further by Harich is in part conjectural, it forms a neat and more than merely plausible pattern. In the very center of metropolitan life, on Unter den Linden, stood a house that was apparently deserted, its windows closed and the blinds drawn; rumors were indeed current that a woman lived there in mysterious seclusion. Such a house naturally excited Hoffmann's interest. During these days Hoffmann, who was occasionally invited to the houses of the socially prominent, even to the palace of Chancellor Hardenberg, was once seated at table beside the beautiful Helmina (Wilhelmina) Lanzendorf, who lived in the house of Chancellor Hardenberg as a protégée of Countess Pappenheim, the Chancellor's daughter. As noted above, the parentage of this famous figure in Berlin society has remained a mystery to this day. During the dinner she complained of a headache, and Hoffmann proposed the curious remedy of sipping the foam from a glass of champagne; in a letter to Graf Pückler he describes this incident as occurring "on a desert island," a characteristically satirical designation for a formal dinner party. As Hoffmann brings into his story both a Graf P. and a Dr. K., which patently stand for Graf Pückler and Dr. Koreff, it is not an unreasonable conjecture that the three participated in fanciful speculations as to the identity of Helmina Lanzendorf and the mystery of the deserted house, perhaps advancing the diverting possibility that she was the illegitimate daughter of the unknown lady of Unter den Linden No. 9. Thus **"Das öde Haus"** may have come into being. The material is promising, but unfortunately Hoffmann tells his story in a rather awkward fashion.

The personal narrative of Theodor occupies about two-thirds of the story. He is drawn by a morbid fascination to the deserted house, which is popularly regarded as haunted, watches its sightless windows from a park bench, once sees a woman's hand place a crystal vase on the window ledge, and later catches a glimpse of a face that in beauty corresponds to the arm and hand he has seen. A mirror that he purchases from an itinerant peddler has, as he accidentally discovers, the magic power, when breathed upon, to reproduce this face; that this is no mere hallucination is shown by his physician's astonishment in seeing the face himself. Eventually Theodor forces his way into the house and is met by an aged woman in bridal array who greets him as her bridegroom.

Later at a dinner party an incident occurs corresponding to Hoffmann's adventure with Helmina Lanzendorf. At dinner Theodor is paired with a young lady, who, as Graf P. informs him, is a niece of the insane woman in the deserted house; the latter is said to be recovering from her madness under the ministrations of Dr. K. Then from Dr. K. Theodor hears the story. This explanatory sequel, a technical device that dogged Hoffmann's footsteps, is here singularly ineffective. It does not explain all that the reader has a right to learn, even allowing for inexplicable mysteries. The novelist has really told his story and his interest slackens; even the style becomes factual and colorless. The woman of the deserted house is Gräfin Angelika von Z., who became insane when her lover Graf S. deserted her for her younger sister, and retired to the long-untenanted family house in town. In developing the narrative the novelist calls to his aid secret connections between Angelika and members of a gypsy band, especially with a tall and horrible old hag in a blood-red shawl; from them she had apparently gained the telepathic power whereby she lures her former lover to death in the deserted house. Hoffmann seeks to mystify the reader as to the parentage of Edmonde, Theodor's companion at dinner; she had been secretly stolen by the gypsies but when she had been as mysteriously returned, Angelika claimed her as her child. In the first part of **"Das öde Haus"** Hoffmann runs more or less true to form; he succeeds admirably in endowing the mysterious, silent house with a ghostly fascination, in presenting the morbid, nervous state of a sensitive youth who allows the mystery of the house to enthrall him to the verge of mental unbalance. But in the explanatory sequel one sees the author too plainly at work manufacturing the antecedent circumstances to correspond to the eeriness of the house. Hoffmann himself thought the story an inferior work.

The predilection for the mysterious, even for the fearful, did not as a rule extend to "charnel-house horrors." The power of suggestion is more effective than a bald presentation of the horrible; to hint that there is something mysterious or terrible behind a closed door or one slightly ajar, works more potently on the nerves than to present the door wide open. Hoffmann's chief excursion into the field of the revolting is the short narrative embedded in the conversations of the Serapion Brothers to which editors have given such names as **"Der Vampyrismus"**, **"Eine Vampyrgeschichte,"** or **"Die Hyänen"**; the French translation calls it simply **"Comte Hippolit."** It is the story of a man whose wife has a morbid appetite for human corpses, and the awful climax of the tale is reached in the scene where he finds her with several old hags in a cemetery devouring a body which they have exhumed from a newly filled grave.

Otherwise the closest approach to the horrible for its own sake is in the story **"Ignaz Denner."** Hoffmann resented Kunz's rejection of the tale as unworthy of a place in the *Fantasiestücke* and later with pardonable malice called Kunz's attention to the publication of the story in the *Nachtstücke*. The scene of most of the story is the lonely cottage of Andres, a forest warden. Unwittingly Andres, though upright and God-fearing, falls into the toils of an infamous scoundrel, Ignaz Denner, who is possessed of mysterious and sinister powers. Denner is the head of a robber band, and Andres is actually on the scaffold, the arm of the executioner already raised, to suffer the penalty for participation in a robbery, when a witness provides an alibi. Denner escapes from prison, and though it was on Denner's false testimony that Andres was accused, Andres plays the part of the Good Samaritan to the outwardly repentant malefactor, but later, when he comes upon Denner in the very act of murdering Andres' nine-year-old son, he shoots him. The explanatory sequel is here inserted before the final events of the story. Ignaz is the son of a Neapolitan doctor who was in league with the devil; this doctor had murdered in succession one wife after another, then murdered each child she had borne him, taking out the heart of the child and preparing from the blood a secret life-giving elixir; the child must be nine weeks or nine months old for the blood to have the proper potency. The mother of Ignaz had succeeded in saving his life. The doctor's crimes are revealed and he is condemned to death, but the flames do not consume him and he disappears; the boy Ignaz escapes equally miraculously from his father's burning house. The subsequent activities of father and son as heads of robber bands extended over wide regions in Italy and Germany. All this the novelist fails to inform with any real significance. At times he piles up the gruesome with heavy hands. But the youth in the fairy tale who went out into the world to discover what shuddering meant would not experience it from Hoffmann's story.

"Die Brautwahl" (**"The Choice of a Bride"**) contains stuff out of which Märchen are made—Hoffmann's own Märchen—but this material is on the whole so irrelevant that the story belongs rather among the "Berlin Novellen." When **"Die Brautwahl"** was placed in the setting of a meeting of the Serapion Brothers—in volume three—Theodor himself criticizes sharply the role of the two "rev-

enants" who really lived in the sixteenth century but like the two magicians in **"Meister Floh"** are still quite humanly alive; their share in the story is forced, he says. Though they are often mildly entertaining, Hoffmann's imagination quite as often limps along without its characteristic swing: Tusmann, after an evening in a tavern with the two "revenants," has a series of fantastic adventures on the way home, spins about in a dizzy dance, sees himself standing before the door of his own house, and on coming to himself discovers that he is seated on the bronze horse of the Great Elector in Schlüter's famous equestrian statue. Leonhard the goldsmith moves from place to place with magical speed; Albertine sees him in her room, where she had previously seen only the stove; the streaks of green paint which the irate artist has smeared on Tusmann's face can be removed only by Leonhard's magic handkerchief.

The story contains the germ of a companion piece to **"Der goldene Topf,"** but the author was either too much in haste or too weary to work it out. Edmund Lehsen is a promising young artist in Berlin. His awkwardness on first meeting Albertine Vosswinkel at an art exhibition might well have been one of the misadventures of Anselmus: he stoops to pick up Albertine's handkerchief, the two heads crash together, he starts back, and at the first step treads on the pug dog of an elderly lady and at the second on the gouty foot of a professor. Aroused by the tumult, people rush from the neighboring rooms and level their lorgnettes at Edmund. He is temporizing with his artistic equipment, which is as yet insecurely grounded; he longs to visit Italy, the "homeland of art," but still does not go. He falls in love, or thinks he does, with the pretty face of Albertine Vosswinkel, who is Veronika or Candida in a slightly different version. Leonhard the goldsmith, a pallid follower of the Archivarius Lindhorst or of Prosper Alpanus, has known Edmund from babyhood and concocts a plan to defeat Edmund's two rivals for Albertine's hand—the Geheimer Kanzlei-Sekretär Tusmann, a former schoolmate of her father, bald-headed and ugly, and Baron Dümmerl, the son of old Manasse, the other "revenant." He fills the Kommissionsrat Vosswinkel with abject terror by showing that Vosswinkel's pocketbook will be seriously endangered if he refuses his daughter's hand to either of these suitors, and thus induces the perplexed parent to approve of a solution of the problem taken directly from the casket scene in *The Merchant of Venice*.

All of this could have been accomplished without the use of supernaturalism. Obviously Edmund wins in the choice of the caskets, but the marriage is to be delayed until after Edmund has returned from a year in Italy. It is, however, plain that the separation will cure the young painter of his infatuation, and he will devote himself entirely to art. In the case of Edmund Lehsen, Hoffmann was more transparent than usual when introducing contemporary characters into his tales; the name "Lehsen" is obviously an anagram for Hensel (Wilhelm), whose sketch of Hoffmann is perhaps the most satisfactory likeness of the author; he was a brother of Luise Hensel, the poetess, whom Brentano loved in vain.

In **"Die Brautwahl"** Hoffmann has created several figures

which at the beginning give promise of a high place among his most memorable characters, but his creative powers became sluggish, and he failed to develop them into well-rounded portraits. Undue emphasis upon a single trait leads to "flat characters" or caricatures. Vosswinkel, the Kommissionsrat, is a businessman who with all his pretensions to cultural interests thinks only of money. When his portrait is to be painted, the artist suggests—in view of the somewhat grim likeness of him painted earlier—that he be portrayed in the happiest moment of his life, when his wife accepted his suit or when his beloved daughter was born. Vosswinkel is enthusiastic about the general principle, but chooses rather the hour when he received notice from Hamburg that he had won a large sum in the lottery, and insists on being painted with the letter in his hand, so displayed that its contents can be read. In Tusmann the novelist presents an inveterate pedant; his pockets are always filled with books, but it is a matter of indifference what they are, an algebra or cavalry exercise rules; in anticipation of marrying Albertine, he is studying a treatise on political wisdom translated from the Latin of Thomasius and published in 1710. In the casket he receives, not the portrait of Albertine, but a blank book which has the magic property of turning itself into any book he may wish to read.

Hoffmann had been for some years at home in Berlin, and he filled the story with local coloring and contemporary references; streets are mentioned familiarly—Friedrichstrasse, Königsstrasse, Spandauer Strasse; Albertine is studying the piano with Herr Lauska, a contemporary teacher, and sings in Zelter's Academy; Devrient has been playing Shylock, and Tieck's "Sternbald" is cited as an example to the young painter.

At their meetings the members of the Serapion Club related anecdotes, some of which, as already noted, have been given names by editors of Hoffmann's works; others contain germs perhaps that Hoffmann never worked out into stories. Though **"Aus dem Leben eines bekannten Mannes,"** sometimes called **"Der Teufel in Berlin,"** was written and read aloud by its author, the manner in which the story is introduced indicates that Hoffmann intended it to be judged somewhat informally. Theodor has found a copy of Hafftitz' *Microchronicon berolinense* on Lothar's desk, open at the point where one could read: "In this year the Devil walked openly on the streets of Berlin, followed funeral processions, behaving in a very sad manner, etc." Beside the book he found a manuscript in Lothar's hand which he confiscated, and now at the meeting of the club produces it to the dismay of Lothar himself. Lothar had supposed that he had long since destroyed this unsuccessful product of a jocular mood, and charges Theodor with playing a malicious joke upon him, but eventually he consents to read his story. This amusing trifle was published first in *Der Freimüthige* (May 1819), the same magazine in which sixteen years before Hoffmann had first seen his work in print.

A stranger, well-dressed and of stately mien, appears suddenly in Berlin and through his charming manners, his extraordinary gallantries, makes himself popular in society in spite of some odd habits: he is slightly lame, but if one extends a helping hand, he is likely to leap several yards in the air with his helper and descend twelve paces away; he knocks at night on the doors of his acquaintances, dressed in white grave clothes and the next day excuses himself by saying that he merely wished to remind people of the transitoriness of life. Even the Elector becomes interested in him and offers him a place in the government. Apart from the general description, the single anecdote that makes up the story concerns the relations of the stranger with old Barbara Roloffen, a midwife, and he disappears in the form of a huge black bat when she is burned as a witch.

In the same year *Der Freimüthige* published another slight sketch by Hoffmann, **"Die Haimatochare,"** in which he contrives an amusing comedy about the jealousies of two rival scientists who hitherto have been devoted friends. Two entomologists, Menzies and Broughton, visit the island of O-wahu to study insect life there. Menzies, seeking a rare butterfly, finds "a dweller of the isles" (Insulanin) who becomes the entrancing object of his devotion. By use of the word "Insulanin" the storyteller reserves the point of his satire for a final disclosure, though he supplies hints enough for the nimble-minded. Broughton is insane with jealousy and lays claim to the treasure. A duel results in which both scientists are slain. The letter of Captain Bligh of the "Discovery," the ship on which the expedition was made, to the governor of New South Wales gives an account of the duel and the causes of it. The two scientists had quarreled over the possession of an insect which Davis, one of the ship's crew, called a louse, but from its bright colors the captain thinks it different from any known species. One of the scientists had shot the pigeon on whose wing (called "the carpet" in the correspondence of the scientists) the insect was concealed, but it was the other who discovered it there. In reply to Bligh's inquiry, the governor directs that "Haimatochare" should not be sent to a museum but buried at sea. This ceremony takes place with great pomp. The story is composed of letters which, Hoffmann says, were entrusted to him by Chamisso after his voyage around the world. Most of the letters are written by the two entomologists and develop both in brevity and fury as the altercation advances.

"Das steinerne Herz," published in the **Nachtstücke**, contains nothing to justify its inclusion under the title; there is not a solitary whiff of the uncanny. The chief character is an eighteenth century "original" such as adorned a multitude of novels, particularly those written under the influence of Lawrence Sterne. His early eccentricities had broken up a youthful love affair, and the lady in question had married a more reliable man. Reutlinger, the melancholy nobleman, incorporated his grief in a heart-shaped wood in the center of which he built a heart-shaped pavilion, and in the marble floor he set a red stone in the form of a heart. Now in the early nineteenth century he gives a great party, all the guests appearing in eighteenth century costume. The events of this festival, together with the necessary preliminaries, make up the story. The happenings of the day bring about a reconciliation between Reutlinger and his nephew, whom years before he had cast out into the rude world for a childish offense, and the union of the nephew and a daughter of Reutlinger's former loved one. Hoffmann's treatment of this rather trivial theme is appropriately lighthearted, and the story is lengthened by obvious padding—such as the account of the tailor's wedding and the nephew's misadventures with a caricature, an echo of Hoffmann's indiscretion long ago in Posen.

The short story **"Spielerglück" ("Gambler's Luck")** is chiefly interesting for the fictional use of an incident in Hoffmann's early years, which was the origin of a curious vagary that he maintained through life. On his journey from Glogau over the mountains to Dresden, Hoffmann stopped for the night at a watering place where there were gaming tables. Under the influence of his traveling companion he took a hand at the play, and with amazing success; every venture on his part brought in golden returns. He became terrified—was some malign power taking possession of him?—and from that time on he never touched a playing card. This experience is the basis for **"Spielerglück."** In the case of the gambler in question, whose first experience follows Hoffmann's very closely, the passion for gambling, though once satisfactorily resisted, becomes deeply ingrained. In the end, having lost all material possessions, he consents to play for his wife as a final stake, not knowing that his opponent had once been in love with her.

In Richer's *Causes Célèbres* Hoffmann found the story of **"Die Marquise de la Pivadière,"** the account of an alleged crime together with the detailed testimony of various witnesses, the opinions of magistrates and judges, and quotations from French laws of the time covering legal procedure. He supplied an introductory narrative, carried the story farther back into the past, and deepened the psychological problems involved. The Marquise and her father confessor are tried for the murder of her worthless and faithless husband. Though the circumstances and the seemingly incontrovertible evidence of eyewitnesses point to their guilt, the body of their victim cannot be found. Even after the Marquis comes forward alive and well, with plausible reasons for his disappearance, there are certain subtle legal questions calling for solution, such as the testimony of the eyewitnesses and the investigation of illegitimate influences behind their falsified evidence. That the identity of the man now claiming to be the missing Marquis is called into question complicates the case still further. In view of Hoffmann's interest in "doubles" and his use of the motif in his tales, it may seem odd that he makes little of this aspect of the case. He was particularly concerned with the psychology of the heroine, building up her character as determined by the peculiar upbringing of an austere and eccentric father. To enhance the interest of the story he invents an episode in the early life of the Marquise and Charost, now her priest and confessor. As young people they had fallen in love with one another at first sight, and intrigue on the part of the Marquise's father had separated them. The story is one of the novelist's minor performances, but more than any other of his stories it shows the intrusion of his professional interests as a lawyer into his literary work. (pp. 323-40)

Harvey W. Hewett-Thayer, in his Hoffmann: Author of the Tales, *Princeton University Press, 1948, 416 p.*

Wolfgang Kayser   (essay date 1957)

[*Kayser's study* The Grotesque in Art and Literature *was the earliest attempt to compose a critical history of the grotesque as a distinct category of aesthetics. Kayser traces the evolution of the term "grotesque" from its first application to an ornamental style in Roman architecture through its various manifestations in the works of nineteenth- and twentieth-century authors and artists, among them Edgar Allan Poe, Franz Kafka, and the Surrealist painters. Kayser defines the grotesque as "the estranged world"; by choosing the modifier "estranged," Kayser intends to distinguish a merely non-naturalistic world, as in the traditional fairy tale, from one in which once familiar objects, characters, and situations are altered in some demonic and uncanny way. While Kayser manages a precise description of the nature and function of the grotesque in art and literature, he concludes that its sources and ultimate meaning are unknown. The grotesque, he concludes, "is primarily the expression of our failure to orient ourselves in the physical universe," and the motive behind the artistic creation of the grotesque is the "attempt to invoke and subdue the demonic aspects of the world." In the following excerpt from a translation of* The Grotesque in Art and Literature, *Kayser discusses the role of the grotesque in Hoffmann's short fiction.*]

Hoffmann's *Nachtgeschichten* appeared in 1817. It was preceded by the *Phantasiestücke in Callots Manier,* the title of which, as well as the author's preface, in paying homage to Callot suggests its appropriateness in the present context [of the grotesque]. Actually, even those of Hoffmann's stories which were composed before the *Nachtgeschichten* are full of grotesque elements. . . . Callot's and Bruegel's names are repeatedly mentioned, and occasionally they appear side by side. "Don't drink—look at her closely!" people are warned of beautiful Julia in **"Abenteuer in der Sylvesternacht" ("Adventures on New Year's Eve"),** "Haven't you seen her before on the warning signs put up by Bruegel and Callot?" This admonition is given in a dream which contains a perfect grotesque; in it trees and plants become disproportioned, the "little one" turns into a squirrel, and the other figures are transformed into candy creatures that come to life and creep about in an ominous manner—until the dreamer awakes with a cry. Whereas in this instance Hoffmann employs motifs from Callot and the ornamental grotesque, a dream from *Die Elixiere des Teufels (Elixirs of the Devil)* reads like the literary equivalent of certain of Bosch's or Bruegel's infernal visions:

> I wanted to pray, when I became aware of a bewildering whispering and rustling. Persons whom I knew to be gentle were distorted into the wildest caricatures. Heads moved along on crickets' legs attached to their ears and sneered at me. Strange fowl—ravens with human faces—whirled in the air. I recognized the concertmaster from B. with his sister, who danced madly to the tune of a waltz which her brother played on his chest, which served as a violin. Belcampo, with an ugly lizard's face and mounted on a ghastly winged worm, violently approached me and wanted to comb my beard with

a red-hot iron comb. . . . Satan stridently laughs,
"Now you are wholly mine."

While Aurelia is here transformed into Satan, the grotesquely drawn figure of Dr. Dapertutto in **"Die Abenteuer"** turns out to be the devil, and Giulia his creature. As
soon as the reader is certain of this fact, the grotesque
scenes in which the world was alienated lose part of their
strangeness, and some of the grotesque has disappeared
since it ceases to puzzle us. If the devil himself appears,
we are prepared for all sorts of infernal tricks. What at
first reading struck us with the full force of the grotesque
seems milder or different in retrospect. When the stranger
in the novella **"Aus dem Leben eines bekannten Mannes"**
(**"From the Life of a Well-known Man"**) favorably impresses the inhabitants of Berlin by his politeness, but
jumps six feet high and twelve feet wide across the street
when offered help by a compassionate pedestrian; when at
night, dressed in a white shroud, he knocks at doors; when
he acts most strangely but explains his actions (though
never satisfactorily)—the world begins to be alienated.
But when we are informed that it was the devil (for Hoffmann is retelling a Berlin chronicle of 1551), we are so-
bered and loath to reread the story. Expressions like "Callot's and Bruegel's warning signs" and Hoffmann's preface to his ***Phantasiestücke*** indicate that the German author wanted to see the works of these painters interpreted
in a special manner, namely—in spite of his fascination
with the grotesque—as a Christian mode of indoctrina-
tion. This confirms an observation derived from certain
traits of the ***Phantasiestücke*** as well as some of Hoffmann's earlier stories: that a full interpretation and organization of the "secret realm of spirits" weakens the force
of the grotesque, no matter how much Hoffmann likes and
manages to portray the ominous alienation of the world
in other places. There are sufficient genuinely grotesque elements still remaining in these stories; Hoffmann is much
too preoccupied with this phenomenon not to use it even
in passages totally unrelated to the infernal sphere and
which are in no way illuminated by it when seen in retrospect.

In the opening section of **"Sylvesternacht,"** Victor Hugo
could have found an excellent illustration for the clash between the grotesque and the sublime, a clash which becomes abysmal through grotesque exaggeration. The excited narrator has rediscovered his lost sweetheart, whom
he finds to be more angelic than ever. Music from Mozart's "sublime E Flat Major Symphony" is heard. "I shall
never let your go, your love . . . inspiring higher life in art
and poetry . . . but didn't you return in order to be mine
forever?—Precisely at that moment, a clumsy, spider-
legged figure with protruding frog's eyes came stumbling
in, laughed foolishly, and shrieked: 'Where the devil has
may wife gone?' " With a few precise strokes Hoffmann
has drawn a grotesque figure composed of human and animal traits, whose models could easily be found in Callot's
engravings. But the grotesque is further heightened by the
fact that this monster is the beautiful woman's husband,
who appears at the very moment when the narrator thinks
that he will never be separated from her. We would not
be surprised if he were to go mad on the spot, but all he

does is to rush out of the house, leaving his hat and coat
behind.

Ornamental grotesques, Bosch, Bruegel, and Callot—all
these manifestations of the grotesque reappear in Hoffmann's writings. . . Almost all of Hoffmann's stories yield
examples of the eccentric gestic style of eccentric figures
which we derived from the *commedia dell'arte*. Take the
following passage: "The innkeeper covered the mirror,
and immediately afterwards a little thin fellow dressed in
a coat of a strange, brownish hue came rushing into the
room. He moved with an awkward speed, clumsily, quickly, I am tempted to say. As he hopped about in the room,
his coat with the oddest folds and wrinkles moved around
his body in such a peculiar way that in the candlelight it
almost looked as if many figures were moving toward, and
away from, each other." This example is taken from **"Sylvesternacht,"** which also contains a caricature that is on
the point of becoming grotesque. The reader had just witnessed a hellish grotesque, in which the infernal tempters
appeared to the narrator and almost persuaded him to sell
his wife and child to the devil—an act that would damn
his soul forever. But his wife's good graces have saved him
at the very last moment. He now steps up to her bed in
order to listen to her farewell speech, which begins as a
caricature of the pedantic housewife but ends grotesquely:
" 'When you reach Nuremberg, however, add a brightly
colored hussar, and a piece of gingerbread, as a loving father. Fare thee well, my dear Erasmus!' The woman
turned over and went to sleep." This passage is obviously
not only intended to satirize the mixture of common sense
and insensitivity but also is designed to render the world
strange and ridiculously ominous in the face of such inhuman, puppet-like behavior.

In E. T. A. Hoffmann's works we thus encounter the various types of the grotesque which emerged in the three centuries . . . Hoffmann is a master in the composition of grotesque scenes; still we get the impression that the grotesque effect is usually weakened by the conclusions of his
works. The novellas so far discussed ultimately turned out
to have a meaning, since the intruding hostile and alienating forces were mostly seen as infernal temptations. The
figures rose out of hell, and not out of the void. Some of
the ominous qualities of the grotesque are lost, no matter
how vaguely defined the hellish mythology. This is also
true of **"Der goldene Topf "** (**"The Golden Pot"**), in which
certain scenes are models of the grotesque (the name of the
Hell Bruegel is significantly mentioned). Seen as a whole,
however, the novella turns out to be a fairy tale illuminated by allegory. The good and evil powers which struggle
for the artist's soul are carefully delineated, and once
again the question concerning the relation of part to whole
becomes appropriate. It is apparently quite easy to enter
the realm of the grotesque, but outside help is needed if
one wants to leave it. The grotesque pushes one into an
abyss, and if the story is to be continued, another level is
needed for its enactment. Hoffmann likes to present grotesque scenes in the form of dream experiences. The
dreamer wakes with a piercing cry but, getting out of bed,
moves on to a different level of existence. We recall that
Gottfried Keller wove the web of the grotesque around his
combmakers in the brighter and ironically satiric world of

Seldwyla. It was a satire also which provided the frame for the grotesque scenes in Goethe's *Satyros* as well as in certain of Lenz's plays. Klinger used the recognition and reconciliation of two feuding families as a foil for the grotesque world of his eccentric characters and thereby reached a satisfactory conclusion. In these instances, the ties between the grotesque scenes and the whole of which they form part are obviously looser than in the case of an all-encompassing satire. Hoffmann was fond of countering the horizontal movement of a story of temptation—or, in **"Der goldene Topf,"** of a story of temptation and salvation—with the vertical movement of the grotesque scenes. But the meaning inherent in the story of temptation detrimentally affected the grotesque in retrospect.

The question as to whether the grotesque itself can furnish the structural basis for a more extended work of literature or, to put it more cautiously, whether it can appear within a larger context having a greater affinity to it than the didactic story or even satire, has been answered by certain works written prior to the twentieth century, by the plays of Schnitzler, Pirandello, Beckett and others, as well as by Kafka's stories. Bonaventura had been the first to use the loosely patterned type of the sequential, spatial novel for the grotesque. If the author of the *Phantasiestücke* still put up warning signs, Bonaventura did in no way suggest an over-all meaning.

"Der Sandmann" concludes with Nathanael's fall into the abyss. The hostile power which enters his life is not a devil but the dealer in barometers Coppola, who appears to be identical with the lawyer Coppelius, who had acted so hostilely toward the boy (it is typical of Hoffmann's art that the doubts concerning their identity are never fully resolved). In Nathanael's description, Coppelius himself, however, again appears as a Callot grotesque composed of human and animal traits and merges with the sandman. His nurse had told him that this creature visits children "who don't want to go to bed and throws handfuls of sand into their eyes, causing them to fall bleeding out of their sockets. He then throws the eyes into his sack and takes them to the half-moon as food for his children, who sit in their nest with crooked owl-like beaks." A nursery tale, to be sure, but one that seems to have a hidden meaning. For Coppelius, whom Nathanael's parents called a sandman, aims at the boy's eyes during the fatal encounter when he catches him spying. He wants to throw "red-hot grains" into his eyes and afterwards tear them out. The eyes are a leitmotif of the novella, often in conjunction with the motif of the doll. The eyes of Clara, Nathanael's fiancée, are like a lake "in which the pure azure of the cloudless sky is mirrored." In a dream Nathanael sees himself standing with Clara before the altar, when Coppelius touches the latter's eyes and causes them to fall like bloody sparks into the dreamer's breast. The mechanical doll Olympia has everything—limbs, gait, and voice; only her glance lacks the "ray of life." The barometer dealer offers Nathanael a pair of sharply ground spectacles, that is, an artificial means of improving his vision; Nathanael finally buys a telescope, which he will always carry about him, and which symbolizes his dimmed and alienating glance. Or is it that he sees more sharply than other people? With the telescope he will finally identify the strange

bush—which, as Clara puts it, "seems to move in our direction"—as the approaching Coppelius, whom he tries to meet by jumping from the tower. This remarkable emphasis on realistic details is typical of the style of the grotesque and reminds one of the cold and wiry strokes in the etchings of Callot or Goya. Taken by itself, the isolation of the eyes has an ominous and alienating effect. It forces us, moreover, to acknowledge the full meaning which they have here assumed: the eyes as an expression of the soul, as a link with the world; the eyes as the actual seat of life.

One of the most grotesque scenes in the novella is Nathanael's encounter with the doll Olympia. While everybody else regards this mechanized image of life as both ridiculous and sinister (the solution of the puzzle is not furnished by the narrator but by the events themselves), Nathanael, who has fallen in love with her after seeing her through the telescope, is blind. He disregards the mechanical aspects and is ecstatic in the doll's presence. When he finally learns the deception, madness takes hold of him, since the excitement was too great and his contact with reality too tenuous. Once again he seems on the point of being cured when he opens his eyes, "as if from a heavy and terrifying dream," to recognize Clara, bending over him. But on the tower, in the presence of the approaching bush, his wits desert him forever.

Madness is the climactic phase of estrangement from the world. The whole novella is an account of the triumph of the inner life of a highly gifted, imaginative, artistic individual (Nathanael is a poet)—a process set in motion by the author and accelerated through repeated encounters with an ominous power. And this in spite of the fact that this power (Coppola, Coppelius) does not directly interfere with the action but merely functions as a catalyst—just as Züs Bünzli acted as a catalyst for the estrangement of the world around the combmakers. The stories are also similar insofar as in both a certain amount of guilt is involved. An ounce of justice too much and in the wrong place (the narrator speaks of the journeyman's "inhuman" plan), and an ominous force immediately answers the provocation. Little Nathanael, too, offends when he desires to see the sandman and hides behind the curtain in order to achieve his goal. In both instances the punishment is out of proportion to the guilt, and, basically, these ethical categories cannot encompass the events depicted in the story, for the "guilt" was in each case performed in the nature of the protagonists. Nathanael's character, moreover, merely enhances certain traits of his father, whose alchemistic experiments—which drove him into Coppelius' arms and, finally, into death—resulted from the urge to gain access to the secret forces behind reality. The abysmal nature of Hoffmann's story consists in the very fact that the artist, whose existence rests on his rich imagination, is in danger of being exposed to other forces which estrange the world for him. Time and again in Hoffmann's stories it is the artist who provides the point of contact between the real world and the ominous forces, and who loses hold of the world because he is able to penetrate the surface of reality.

In the story of such an estrangement of the world Hoffmann has found the horizontal action which enabled him, or rather forced him, to compose grotesque scenes. There was no need for him to produce devils or infernal monsters. It is a sign of Hoffmann's gradually acquired mastery that even those aspects of Coppelius' and Coppola's appearance and behavior which seem unnatural and improbable, permit a doubt or encourage the reader to seek an explanation within the limits of verisimilitude. At the very beginning of the novella, he makes Clara write a letter in which she describes Nathanael's youthful experiences and his harrowing encounter with the weathermaker in so reasonable a fashion that the reader is led to trust her. He feels she is justified in stating that the dark powers are victorious only if man's soul receives them willingly and grants them authority over the Self. Following this, the soul projects these phantoms into the outer world and is constantly attracted by the fatally deceptive images which it created or at least enhanced. A serene soul, on the other hand, does not give access to such dangers. By putting these words into Clara's mouth Hoffmann causes his readers to believe, like her, in the existence of the "dark powers" and thereby increases the horror stemming from Nathanael's experiences. Let Nathanael exaggerate the ominousness of Coppola's character; his doing so is in itself a symptom of the estrangement which leads him toward what goal? It is possible to give comic expression to the fact that he mistakes a doll for a human being, thinks that she loves him, and confesses his love to her, but Hoffmann's presentation of the matter is so genuinely grotesque that its effect upon us is humorous and horrible at the same time. Hoffmann gains still another advantage by leaving the reader in doubt as to how things are in reality: who Coppelius is, whether he returns in Coppola, what is wrong with the telescope, etc.; a satisfactory explanation of these matters is not provided. The narrator, whose task begins after the presentation of the opening letters, initially seems to adopt a familiar attitude. He claims to be poor Nathanael's friend and appears to know his entire story. But gradually he abandons this bird's-eye view, moves very close to the events themselves, occasionally fuses with the other characters (and adopts their perspective) or turns into a deeply affected eyewitness of the events—an example of the new narrative point of view, the perfection of which is one of Hoffmann's great and lasting achievements. But since this narrator, when he began to speak, introduced himself as one of those people whose excitable soul leads to conflicts and causes them to be at odds with the outside world (he is an "author"), and since, at the same time, he appeals to the highly imaginative reader, we tend to identify ourselves with Nathanael and regard his fate as a latent possibility of our own existence. (pp. 68-76)

Wolfgang Kayser, "The Grotesque in the Age of Romanticism," in his The Grotesque in Art and Literature, *translated by Ulrich Weisstein, Indiana University Press, 1963, pp. 48-99.*

Marianne Thalmann   (essay date 1961)

[*In the following excerpt from a translation of her* Das Märchen und die Moderne: zum Begriff der surrealität im Marchen der Romantik, *Thalmann discusses the defining characteristics of Hoffmann's short fiction.*]

There is no need to repeat the theories on dualism, Schelling's theosophy, and G. H. Schubert's philosophy of nature. Studies in the field have given us ample information concerning the influences on E. T. A. Hoffmann, his reading, his sources, and his exchange of ideas with the Bamberg doctors. It is a fact: Hoffmann is as eclectic as a lending library; this is borne out by his beseeching notes to Kralowsky, the librarian. He threw himself into his reading with as much gusto as his whole generation. His avid interest in the occult and in the esoteric sciences, not found anywhere else to this degree except in French literature, reflects his need for artificial magic. By combining the urban reality of gaslights with the oriental pomposity of cheap literature, he produces a world of grotesque obscurities in which the foreground of life ceases to be real. (p. 88)

[Hoffmann's "Serapion principle, for which *Serapion-Brüder* is named, demands that the material for fiction] be taken from our actual environment, in which, one must admit, there is something inherently theatrical, but that this material then be separated from the objective world so that we are filled with consternation. This means that these stories must condition themselves to a definite pace and, what is more, to a definite content. Until now such subject matter had not necessarily been fairy-tale material, and when it was used that way, it was received with a sceptical shake of the head. The usual and commonplace in Hoffmann does not merely contain the wonderful and strange; it has become unfathomable. (p. 90)

E. T. A. Hoffmann was greatly influenced by the *opera buffa*. "Poet and Composer" ("Dichter und Komponist") in the *Serapion Brothers* sheds light on this subject. In addition to the everyday events which Tieck required for the fairy tale, Hoffmann demands something decidely contemporary, the fairy tale "in tails," so to speak. In doing so, he affirms his dual Berlin existence, those experiences which can be given a specific date, and actual events which he as an examining magistrate can no longer escape. He knows what it is to fear the reality of a bureaucratic century. What he loves about the *opera buffa* is the wild leaps and bounds of his neighbor "in his familiar cinnamon-colored Sunday suit with the gold-covered buttons" in which there is no trace of tragedy. Here the strange combines with the banal, the comical with the grotesque. The realism of a Breughel and a Callot has taken hold of him. This leads him to a strikingly modern confession: he recognizes in the tragicomical a legitimate form of expression for his time, one hundred years before it avowedly became that for us. But he states theoretically that "only in the truly romantic" do the comic and tragic blend so completely "that they dissolve to become one in the total effect." Here "the adventurous [enters] everyday life; in the conflicts which result, I believe, the essence of the true *opera buffa* is to be found"—a Hoffmannesque variation on Novalis' "coincidence and chaos." What Hoffmann introduces into romanticism is the buffoonish fairy tale where, out of the adventurous flight of individual figures, out of the bizarre game of chance, the fantastic is born which "propels" our daily lives "at the top and at the bottom." In limiting himself to "the serious people, senior court judges, archivists, and students," who are given a ghostlike quality, he makes resounding laughter a new indispensable note in the fairy tale. The fairy tale has changed over from the monotony of daily life in Tieck to the major events of the official calendar in Hoffmann, who singles out from contemporary society a particular titled group of the middle class to play the leading roles.

Even H. v. Müller, the most profound commentator on Hoffmann's fairy tales, is of the opinion in his epilogue to the *Fairy Tales of the Serapion Brothers (Märchen der Serapions-brüder)* that the ironic tone is not commendable in the fairy tale. One would have to agree with this in respect to the folk fairy tale, but that is not the salient point here. In the "literary fairy tale," which evolves on a different plane of narrative writing, the material itself has merely relative value, and irony naturally appears as a means of showing that everything is relative. The ironic tone paves the way for the grotesque, which Hoffmann adopts in his later works. Hoffmann has also deviated from the early romantic fairy tale in rejecting "little verses in the story," and he condemns the mixing of forms, a must for the Schlegel circle, because this is, in his view, an attempt to conceal "some weakness of the material." There is nothing lyrical about Hoffmann. Even in his comical little verses that occasionally crop up he is leftish. He is only interested in narrating.

By combining the urban reality of gaslights with the oriental pomposity of cheap literature, Hoffmann produces a world of grotesque obscurities in which the foreground of life ceases to be real.

—*Marianne Thalmann*

Hoffmann made use of the fairy-tale form in works other than the *Serapion Brothers,* for he considered it the ideal receptacle for the fantastic. From the very start he is not only an author, but also a storyteller. More than anyone else, he holds all the strings in his hand. He candidly shoves aside the pretense that someone is reading the story aloud and establishes direct contact with the reader himself. He is always the author who tries to fascinate his audience. From the standpoint of art, this becomes sensationalism, but at the same time, a capricious form of irony. He sets up his figures in front of us and with us like a complicated chess problem. We know that we are playing, and we know, too, that it is a game for experts. The significant moves of the game are prepared for in each instance below the title of the chapter by means of an informative table of contents. Hence a typographical image is created for the eye which has the power of suggestion, puts us in contact with the author, and also puts us at his mercy. This, too, belongs to the ironic tone of the Hoffmann fairy tale.

The "well-beloved, kind, gracious reader" is taken along on a visit to the house of the fairy-tale hero where Ännchen (**"The King's Bride"—"Königsbraut"**) serves him

bread and butter and raw ham, where he and the Brakel family (**"The Strange Child"—"Das fremde Kind"**) wait for their uncle, the count, and the stork on the roof instructs him quite explicitly about the friendly innocence of the house. Hoffmann introduces his main characters before the first move is made. He describes their clothing, their appearance, and the young man "who pleases you so much at first sight, dear reader, is none other than the student Balthasar" (**"Klein-Zaches"**). They are introduced in their character masks as lovers, schoolmasters, and magicians. He lets us look in every direction. We see how he controls the game, how he moves the figures back and forth, dismissing them and conjuring them back again. The remarks, "it can no longer be kept secret," "it has already been said," "it suffices to say," keep the author-director in constant contact with his reader. Countless times he addresses the reader directly: "The kind reader already knows" (**"Master Flea"—"Meister Floh"**), "it seems absolutely necessary to keep the kind reader from the worst possible misunderstandings" (**"Flea"**), or he asks the reader a question: "What will happen now?" (**"Nutcracker"**). He calls his reader by name: "I appeal to you, most gracious reader or listener—Fritz—Theodor—Ernst—or whatever your name is" (**"Nutcracker"**). He takes the reader into his confidence about technical matters: "It is a long established custom that the hero of a story, when he is seized by a powerful emotion, runs out into the woods or at least into the lonely thicket" (**"Flea"**), or "It is seldom good when the author ventures to describe to the kind reader exactly how this or that beautiful person . . . looks" (**"Flea"**), or "Once upon a time—what author today can presume to begin his little story that way" (**"Flea"**). He addresses his reader intimately: "Perhaps you, oh my reader, like me are of the opinion that the human mind itself is the most wonderful fairy tale of all.— What a magnificent world lies buried in our breast" (**"Brambilla"**). Such excursuses often assume an unusual length, particularly at the beginning of the fairy tales, continuing for several paragraphs. This form of ironic textual interpolation increases precariously in the later fairy tales. As a result the material is to a large extent taken out of the carefree atmosphere of the fairy-tale past and moved up into the loquacious yesterday of realism.

The same narrative devices also serve Hoffmann in staging the conclusion of his fairy tales. With the skill of the professional director, which he has, he sets up a final tableau. There must be weddings at the end. It must be a gay ending in which the tricks of fate and the bizarre complications of life dissolve in laughter. What else can save us? We, government officials and would-be poets, are no longer made of tragic wood. We are difficult people with many impediments, without fulfillment, and at best only a privy councilor. The checkmate of the opponent is thoroughly discussed, and the last moves are made with bravura. Even in **"The Golden Pot" ("Der goldene Topf")** the ending is an artificially posed problem. The entire final chapter is devoted to a consideration of the difficulties of the material, rather than to the story-telling. The author sympathizes with Anselmus. We all presumably do the same. But how to express this? He doubts that he will have the opportunity to add a twelfth chapter. He makes us fear that we will never learn what happens to Anselmus. It is no longer so easy to write things as it once was. A letter to Lindhorst, an evening with him over a glass of exquisite punch—and then, in the presence of the reader, this long awaited ending is written. It happens this way, too, at the end of **"Klein-Zaches,"** where Hoffmann ceremoniously takes leave of the reader. He is overcome with "melancholy and anxiety," and he asks, "Is it not more pleasant if there is a gay wedding at the end instead of a sad funeral?" And after Klein-Zaches' funeral he stages the gala wedding of Balthasar and Candida, a finale which is carefully considered in every detail. Moreover, he achieves a decorative effect. The last sentence of the fairy tale reads: "And so the fairy tale of Klein-Zaches, called Zinnober, now really has a completely happy ending." And he puts the word "ending" like a self-satisfied scroll somewhat lower on the page as a last decoration for the eye. In **"Master Flea,"** where the author's interjections almost surpass the tolerable limits of a suggestive game, Hoffmann turns to the reader—for whom he surely need not describe the wedding feast—and particularly to the beautiful female readers who may plan the parade of the brides to suit their fancy. (pp. 91-95)

[In **"The Golden Pot,"** Subtitled **"Fairy Tale of our Times,"** Hoffmann] touches upon the fundamental substance of all his fairy tales—the sidewalk and coffeehouse character of their plot. What does this "of our times" imply? It is not a "once upon a time" in the old-fashioned sense of smug memories. It is the news item from yesterday's paper, an accident, a club announcement, fireworks in the Linkisch Bad in Dresden. It is built on a love story taken from bourgeois circles of inferior officials, where the men have a specific rank and corresponding pension, and the women and girls have their secure place in the home. Thus, the romantic fairy tale began with the Wackenroder version of "our day," made its way to Tieck's commonplace experiences, and with Hoffmann it then went from the curious days to the timely and even sensational happenings of the big city.

Consequently, every plot follows the church calendar of feast days and week days—in this particular case, from Assumption Day to Veronica's birthday. The days themselves are carefully divided into office hours, hours for coffee, strong beer, and punch, and finally hours for sleep. The events also have their geographic reality in the Koselschen Garten in Dresden, at the Rossmarkt in Frankfurt, at the Porta del Pòpolo in Rome. The people occasionally have "nervous outbursts," but that passes. They may be noisy, they may get sentimental, they may do more than just quench their thirst, but they sleep it all off and everything falls back into place.

The hero of the story, the student Anselmus, comes from the same middle-class stratum of society. He lacks logic, is a Philistine, a genius, and a hypochondriac all in one. He has his mark of Cain. And every Anselmus is a Hoffmann. Hoffmann does not scorn the middle class with its vulgarities. He, too, would like to take out his sweetheart, call the waiter, and order coffee with the air of the connoisseur. He, too, would like to have a title, and the golden watch and steady income of a privy councilor. He is unquestionably loyal to life as it is. He is no saint. Unlike

Wackenroder, ascetics were not his meat. He is much closer to the victim of misfortune. He is never lucky enough to find the prize, he never arrives on time, his bread and butter always falls face down, a button always pops off at the last minute. And in presenting this figure, Hoffmann goes far beyond the instability of Tieck's heroes. He stands much closer to the outer edges of experience; he is not afraid of approaching the margins of sanity. His hero is not merely a dreamer; he is already inwardly impaired: he exhibits schizophrenic traits, he lives in hallucinations, and experiences reality on different levels of consciousness, making a grotesque impression on the people around him.

The action of **"The Golden Pot"** begins with a mischievous intervention of fate. A ridiculous tumble, a collision with a basket of apples, and the chiding voice of the apple woman fills the young man with "imperceptible fear." The hostile powers do not attack him from the depths of his person, but from outside, and they draw him into a whirlpool of visions, deceptions, and failures. From then on, everything has two faces: it can be a doorknocker or a grimace, a red dressing-gown or a clump of tiger-lilies. The paradoxical has become a vacillating balance, a classification receiving the legal protection of the authorities. The fluctuation of the action between Veronica, the tangible little daughter of Schoolmaster Paulmann, and the voices of Serpentina in the lilac bush constantly confuse the game.

And here in true Schikaneder style the traditional plot of the trivial novel begins. Anselmus is imperceptibly guided from outside. Strange things take him by surprise; they assail him. He does not expect them, nor does he actually conjure up this enchanted world, as Tieck's heroes do. He is afraid of it even before it appears. His fear can already be clinically defined. He becomes clay in the hands of older men who have overcome their taste for folly and are acquainted with the wounds of life, although they themselves have remained unscarred. In these figures Hoffmann has translated the heroes of the Masonic novel into wise and attractive personalities. The emissaries of the order as they are found in the cheap literature of the eighteenth century have developed into bourgeois characters who have acquired a certain mastery over the pain of daily life and, at the same time, radiate the light of their humorous relationship to it. They know the inadequacies of the Philistine, the tears it costs to be young and to want to be gifted. They laugh with the bureaucrats, and they make fun of the tormented, something that Hoffmann himself could never do. We realize that both sides are ridiculous. Like Lindhorst they enjoy putting a ducat into the vest pocket of these awkward students. Like Drosselmeier they build for dreamy children a castle with moving figurines for Christmas and slip them a bag of candy. They perform clever little tricks for them, and they know how to tell stories about dragons, salamanders, mouse kings, and magicians, so that their listeners forget the time. They are men with experienced and flexible faces, of unimposing stature, lean and advanced in years with the keen eye and the creaking voice of the old emissary. If Dr. Alpanus is the clever Brahmin among them, then Herr Dapsul is the grotesque mysterymonger, dressed all in gray, who finally becomes a gray mushroom. And Hoffmann also cannot re-sist the temptation of having an exciting Master Flea who wears beautiful golden boots with diamond spurs on his last pair of legs and who has a fine, scornful laugh, speaks in an undertone, and slaps his front hands together to ap-plaud. And whoever follows them with his eyes and sees how they whisper to each other in the dark and how the rings on their fingers sparkle, almost believes that he is see-ing a phantom prince.

They are not geniuses and they are not ladies' men, either. They are senior councilors, archivists, and physicians, who carry out the duties of their office with tact and intel-ligence. They know all about the unhappy love of a night-ingale for a crimson rose which occupies the young, but they have pushed it out of their mind in order to gain their manhood. They are bachelors who live for their work, as-cetics out of conviction. They, therefore, have an Olympi-an quality about them; their wisdom and humor give them a serenity that Hoffmann himself does not possess. These men at work experience once again, one may well say, the happiness of an integrated personality, hardly known to romanticism and never to appear again. The Archivist Lindhorst can make a fairy tale out of any antique manu-script and entertain his friends at the tavern, with it keep-ing a close eye on the fellows who down their liquor on an empty stomach. He employs Anselmus as a copyist, supports him in his speculations and dreams, and even plays the role of a phantom prince in them. As a transcrib-er of oriental writings, Anselmus undergoes a period of ac-tual apprenticeship when he is charged with silence and steadfastness. Lindhorst builds bridges for him between reality and the texts. The story of Phosphorus which he copies becomes reality for Anselmus. He rewrites it and makes it his own story: he boldly takes up the fight against the hostile powers who are pursuing the descendants of Phosphorus; he goes through fire and water; Serpentina steps out of the temple to meet him; Lindhorst-Sarastro gives him the princess in marriage and a manor in Atlan-tis. A happy ending for a person on the border line, who is no longer able to find a place in a world of upright offi-cials.

For Paulmann and Heerbrand, Anselmus is a closed case. It was clear to them from the start that something was ba-sically wrong. The people around him are not only deaf to him, they break out in resounding laughter. Veronica marries her Heerbrand, becomes the wife of a privy coun-cilor, and gets her bourgeois security in the corner apart-ment of a new house on the Neumarkt. Such people some-times lose their balance, it is true, but they never lose the ground from under their feet.

All the Hoffmann fairy tales are constructed on this prin-ciple. After **"The Golden Pot"** he tries to assume the same tone in fairy tales which are scarcely suitable for children, although they were written for Hitzig's children. At least children figure as the main characters in **"Nutcracker"** and **"The Strange Child,"** and the natural surroundings of the child, the toy chest and the grove, furnish the set-ting. There is no doubt about it, these fairy tales have their origin in the overheated rooms of the burghers and in the scenery of the Sunday stroller. And nothing is more re-

mote from Hoffmann than the secret of childhood. Even Mariechen is merely "a little sleep-walker," as the reader must agree. The country children remain exaggerated in-nocence and the city children a biting caricature. Both are a Rousseau cliché, unconvincing as childhood. The Papa-geno-Tamino character of the hero is neatly divided here between brother and sister. Fritz **("Nutcracker")** is the re-alist, Marie the dreamer. Felix **("The Strange Child")** is the more languishing one, his sister Christlieb the more prosaic. The role of the hostile powers falls to the parents, whose maturity has an alienating effect. In both cases the woman, the mother of the children, is the sceptic for whom daydreaming represents something unhealthy and unauthentic. In both cases it is the ingenious toy with its mysterious mechanism which confuses the children. It be-longs to the world of the clever sophist, and oppresses chil-dren for whom abstraction and technology are still charged with hostility. From this toy they experience the first shattering of their naive world.

In these two fairy tales it is again a master who takes them in hand: the godfather Drosselmeier **("Nutcracker")** and the fairy child **("The Strange Child")**. Both love what is childlike: they love the time of life when one may still dream, when one quite naturally imagines and even sees a wonderful world behind the objects of reality. Both the godfather and the fairy child tell a story which associates children's lives with strange happenings in distant places and casts the first shadows over their childhood. What they tell is another Phosphorus fairy tale, translated into a youthful language so that children feel involved in it. These fairy tales within fairy tales, a play within a play, so to speak, represent a continuation of a romantic struc-tural concept, and are part of every one of Hoffmann's fairy tales. In them the battle between powers and oppos-ing powers is so intensified that they become fantastic. By portraying the conditions that undermine the Philistine world, Hoffmann briefly exposes his own time. He alien-ates the world of the petty bourgeoisie by implicating it in a past which presupposes a very different kind of reality.

As a result of the fairy tales, these children, too, begin to experience the visions of a restless sleep, as well as the transformation of the day and of everyday phenomena into something mysterious. Mariechen's dreams on Christmas night involve her in the battle of hostile powers: the Mouse King marches to war against Nutcracker whom she loves. This leads to tests and dangers which she bravely endures and which signify that she, almost over-night, has been touched by the pain of growing up. Having experienced this, she may go with Nutcracker through the fairy-tale woods, over the candy meadows, and enter the marzipan castle—the Anselmus fate of a little girl ending in the children's Atlantis. And in Schoolmaster Ink (Ma-gister Tinte) Felix discovers the evil Pepser who dirties the fairy kingdom of his Serpentina. The boy bravely attacks him with a flyswatter, defeats him, and then may live hap-pily ever after. It is a stronger ending than in **"Nutcrack-er,"** but is out of the same can of paint.

After these two children's fairy tales, Hoffmann approach-es the middle class with growing sarcasm in his question-able fairy tales about success and politics. Balthasar, the hero of **"Klein-Zaches,"** is an Anselmus whom life treats some-what more kindly, even though he was "not worth much" as a poet. From the very beginning he is head over heels in love with a Candida in whom he sees a Serpentina. But Zaches, the hostile element, enters his life, a repulsive little fellow who has been assured of blind success by a sentimental fairy because of her piously protective feeling toward dwarfish ugliness. Wherever Zaches goes, he takes the light out of people's faces and the ideas out of their heads, while the creative person loses name and success. All around this empty automaton, Klein-Zaches, reigns the witchery of the snobs into whose hands society has fallen. We find in the Hoffmann fairy tale the beginnings of a future army of misfits: the tormented person, Burgher Schippel, Professor Unrat, the Tesmanns, and Ejlerts. His need for amassing such figures grows. The hero is reflected in his friend, powers and adversaries are doubled, even the figure of the master doubles: Alpanus supports Balthasar who is endowed with "an inner music," and Rosabelverde supports Klein-Zaches, whose loathsomeness she finds touching. Men look to see how the mechanism works, while women become the prey of their own sentiment. The game of influence and success, truth and deception, goes back and forth between these two figures. Balthasar also must endure the trials of inner conflict and doubt and must risk the battle with Klein-Zaches before he wins his Candida in a now prosaic world and may call Dr. Alpanus' estate his own. With tongue in cheek, Hoffmann lets morality win: young married couples are generously remembered by good uncles, everyone receives his title at the right time, and every virtuous girl of the suburbs finds her well-to-do Peregrinus Tyss. There is nothing so lasting as these vulgarities. Hoffmann does not deny that such a world still exists. It is becoming more and more difficult, however, for the unusual person to live in it.

The story inserted in **"Klein-Zaches"** is more concise than the others. It consists only of a letter of the scholar Professor Pholomäus Philadelphus to his friend Rufin about the conditions in an enlightened country. The malicious portrayal of particularism and the antics of red tape left behind misgivings in the minds of the responsible authorities so that Hoffmann was prosecuted after the publication of **"Master Flea."** The legal proceedings in the fourth adventure of that fairy tale were interpreted as a persiflage of the judicial commission. Since the *Magic Flute* all ridicule had come under political suspicion. Hoffmann was prosecuted on the grounds of having exposed official information and having been disrespectful of His Majesty and his own superiors. **"Master Flea"** is of all these fairy tales, however, the fairy tale of Bohemianism which Hoffmann understood so well. Its characters drink their nights away in restaurants, run through the sidestreets, boisterously climb iron fences and peer into lighted windows. They are arrested by mistake, beat each other up, tell horror stories, and amuse the tavern guests with their feats of legerdemain so that their audience is dumbfounded. Whereas Registrar Heerbrand (**"The Golden Pot"**) committed every sort of foolishness under the influence of punch for one evening, the arch-conservative Peregrinus Tyss, the respectable heir to a business fortune, loses himself completely for a while before returning to his honorable intentions of marriage. The hero is Georg Pepusch, the wildest student in

Jena, and his sweet-heart is Dörtje, the most fickle of girls who is traveling with her uncle, the owner of a flea circus. If the circus does not attract, the girl does. Hoffmann has almost exceeded the tolerable limits with his main characters. Pepusch is the thread-bare poet at the height of exaltation, where he feels nothing but scorn for society, Dörtje is a circus Serpentina with incredibly modern ways, the master is an animal philosopher who is enormously fond of talking, and the hostile powers are cunning traveling comedians. On the surface, man has become a questionable creature in an environment whose standard of value has lost all sense for the transparent. **"Master Flea"** is an outstanding example of motif-juggling, but in the juggling the lengthy story falls apart and Hoffmann noticeably exhausts himself. Each meeting means a new danger and a new test for Pepusch. Hoffmann accumulates them as Münchhausen accumulates his tall tales (Lügenmärchen). The characters meet each other under true and assumed names, and as Bohemians they play an inserted oriental fairy tale to the end which, as usual, has no conclusion. In their dual existence as traveling comedians on the one hand and princes and princesses on the other, the bourgeois world is distorted to the point of absurdity. They perform mock duels, threaten each other with wooden pistols, fight with telescopes, enlarge and reduce objects to grotesque proportions, and fool the police with their pranks. They all experience a happy ending after weathering the chaos. The bachelor Peregrinus Tyss finds his way back to his humdrum routine and marries Bookbinder-Röschen who will keep all the naughty dreams away from him in the future. Pepusch and Dörtje also find each other, and in the form of flower magic, their wedding turns out to be a new version of the old temple magic from the *Magic Flute*. Here Hoffmann chooses the night-blooming cereus whose blossoms wither in the morning light as he mates with a lavender-and-yellow-striped tulip—a both sentimental and grotesque motif.

"Nutcracker and Mouse King," the fairy tale about the doll, stands at the end of the first volume of the *Serapion Brothers*. **"The Strange Child,"** the fairy tale about the fly, concludes the second volume, and **"The King's Bride"** is the fairy tale about the carrot, the last volume. **"The King's Bride"** is the fairy tale of fairy tales. The Schikaneder pattern is grotesquely exaggerated from the beginning to the end. It treats the theme of the alienation of man and object throughout, and hence it becomes "le comique absolu," as Baudelaire said, who greatly admired this fairy tale. The leading lady is a Veronica without a bit of imagination. For her only things with names exist, commodities, her household, yet from the lettuce, beans, and carrots in her garden, from the independence of these plants as they go through the world conforming to human beings, she experiences enchantment, for not even the dullest wit can escape it completely. A ring on a carrot which she pulls out of the ground suddenly slides onto her finger. And who could resist such a pretty little harmless thing?

The master who sees through the hostility between objects and wants to control it is Herr Dapsul, Ännchen's father. But even the mask of the emissary has become grotesque. He schemes, observes, conjures, he knows the mysteries of all the constellations without being able to cope with a single one. He also contributes the curious story about the salamanders, gnomes, and Undines as well as the story about the sylph who has loved him for twelve years and whom he hopes to marry. But the master is no longer the lord of creation as before. The adversaries trip him; he slips, he falls on his bottom, he is thrown into the frying pan along with the chopped eggs, he is transformed into a mushroom. The machinery of magic of the Masonic novel has become independent, and human existence now merely evokes laughter. Herr Dapsul of Dapsulheim is the dilettante of dilettantes and, as a master, he is a clown who royally entertains his audience.

Ännchen experiences all the dangers which a country wench can encounter, all the intrigues of the vegetable King Carota, all the horror of insects and plague, all the temptations of her suitors, all the trials that befall her as a result of the lyrical bombast of her fiancé, Amandus. But steadfast and faithful to the end, Amandus rescues her from the clutches of the hostile powers and the cunning of King Carota, and along with her, her father, Dapsul, who having been transformed into a mushroom is in danger of being eaten.

It is above all in the grotesque form of this plot where E. T. A. Hoffmann gains full control over the traditional trappings of magic without sacrificing the artistic, something that cannot always be said of him. **"The King's Bride"** is the fairy tale of an expert who delights his audience at the end by even giving it a glimpse into his studio. It is a grotesque of boorish existence, and what could be more ridiculous than that at a time of crisis for man and society. After being hit over the head with a space, the lyrical fiancé, Amandus, finally becomes a true family man whose greatest worry in life is finding the finest tobacco for his pipe. Herr Dapsul has found his peace and is waiting for his sylph who never comes. The wedding of these two unimaginative country bumpkins puts an end to the uncanny, forever. The happy ending is not only in harmony with fairy-tale practice, but also with the ironic tone of a story whose aim is to amuse. It needs this game with the pretty tableau at the end, and for this Hoffmann could scarcely have found a better model than the *Magic Flute*.

The basic plot of his fairy tales and the oriental extravagance of his insertions, as far as they stem from the trivial novel of the eighteenth century and its sources, are things inherited from the past behind which the enlightened world hides its fright. Hoffmann makes this material grotesque by including in it a sense of the unfathomed deeps of life and his horror of middle-class hierarchies. It is in this grotesque element that the unity of his work and his greatest achievement as a writer is to be found. We can trace its development in all Hoffmann's stories: in the ironic tone of the presentation, in the capricious way in which the author guides us from episode to episode, in the distorted proportions of our reality, in the loathsomeness and ugliness of his characters, in the buffoonish and tragicomical nature of everything middle class and mediocre. The paradoxical consequently loses its sacral character, still found in Wackenroder and Novalis to such a high degree. In Hoffmann it becomes something for which there is no cure, no divine grace. To speak of him, therefore, as a "thoroughbred romanticist," as has been done, is untenable. He always wanted to be the thoroughbred but never possessed that quality, and furthermore, he knew it. F. Schultz includes him among the supplementary voices of romanticism. Within this category he became the arsonist of romanticism who, in the final analysis, saturated it with the oil of mystery and destroyed it. For that very reason, however, he has been known outside Germany as the epitome of romanticism.

Hoffmann came to literature by way of the opera and the theater and hence, he loved scenery. Indeed, even the staging of the action imbibed Schikaneder's talent to make the ending of every act a hit and to sanction jokes. That means rich scenery, many stage settings, and a good deal of equipment. In this respect, too, Hoffmann was naturally closer to the trivial novel than any other romanticist, for there he found a superabundance of mysteries from which he merely had to choose.

Time takes its natural course. That we live in time is part of that mediocrity which Hoffmann tries to capture in his work, and he therefore gives substantially more importance to news items than heretofore. His people attach as much value to an accurate clock as to their Sunday roast. Misfortune seeks out the hero because he does not yet have a watch in his pocket. And the surroundings in which people live also become much more important. Houses watch us right and left. Street corners trip us. Something giggles in the vegetable bed, and there is whispering in the lilac bush. We wander with Hoffmann into crowded libraries with gilded palm trees and emerald leaves behind which sinister parchment rolls lie, into studies with sky-blue drapes and a mysterious floor made of worn talismans. Pictures jump out of their books, strange animals are busily reading and writing, and magic mirrors reflect distorted faces instead of our own. The whole ferocious seriousness of the studios in Herr Dapsul's tower room with its dusty books, curious instruments, and astronomical charts, becomes a parody on the scholar. Even the mirror playchest of the Stahlbaum children expands to a Callotian fantasy of dolls and figures. By taking us on a tour of bourgeois living rooms and studios, the fairy tale "of our times" attempts to show how space has alienated itself from man. The tangible rooms with their sofas, dining-room tables, and sewing baskets, which feign a certain closeness because everything in them is correctly labeled and deciphered, become both comical and malicious because Hoffmann feels that his own surroundings are absurd. He is sceptical about this reality with its gaping background behind which one senses the sinister lurking. But the fact that the technique of presentation seems realistic probably explains why he has almost been numbered among the realists who castigate the bourgeoisie for their sins. The truth is, however, that it was more Hoffmann's horror of bourgeois virtues which pursued him through life.

We return from romantic flights into space to the narrow confines of the living room, cluttered with objects and figures. Hoffmann has a preference for small intimate rooms, as was so often true of the painters of the grotesque. His people live uncomfortably close to each other but set in motion, the walls burst and the room is extended to fantas-

> **Hoffmann makes his material grotesque by including in it a sense of the unfathomed deeps of life and his horror of middle-class hierarchies. It is in this grotesque element that the unity of his work and his greatest achievement as a writer is to be found.**
>
> *—Marianne Thalmann*

tic dimensions. The parade of the toy figures in **"Nutcracker"**—the brave gardeners, Tirolese, Tungus, barbers, harlequins, tigers, long-tailed monkeys, and apes, the crowds in the capital of Fairyland, all the figures of sugar and tragacanth, the shepherds and lambs, mailmen and dancers, enlarge the play room to a playground of terrifying proportions. The little showcase of the flea circus with its tiny cannons, powder cases, armored cars, rifles, cartridge pouches, and sabers, takes on the size of Napoleonic battlefields. And the shadows on the wall that march toward the visitors at Leuwenhoek's command, beetles, spiders, slime mold, interspersed with vinegar eels and eelworms, are a grotesque Inferno. The fantastic entrance of Princess Brambilla remains unsurpassed as a spectacle of this type with its enormous numbers of figures and spatial effects. There we find musicians, unicorns, Moors, apes, and pages, who throw the Roman street into a turmoil, as well as the lettuce and melon princes, the cucumber barons, the bean princesses, the onion and beet generals of King Carota, who snap to attention in front of ännchen, under fire by the bean artillery and the carrot guard. Hoffmann creates the most oppressive kind of fear in these grotesques of overcrowded rooms. (pp. 97-109)

But inasmuch as a fairy tale also needs some room to breathe, Hoffmann likes to turn to the capital of a small principality, to a narrow little provincial city where the dignitaries, petty princes, and their bureaucrats, live together in security. This locale also has an uncomfortable closeness. It is filled to the bursting point with rushing, laughing, stumbling, pushing. And even where Hoffmann goes beyond the street corner to the village, the woods, the pond, or the cliff, it does not become real, but remains scenery in which the decorative element, the frosting on the cake, so to speak, is the most important thing. Without going far astray, one may say that Hoffmann does not invent nature symbols, but simply uses the ready-made landscape terminology gained through his wide reading. It is a collapsible scenery which can be set up in a flash. He is not a lover of nature, as Hitzig confirms. He needs company and people; he comes to life in overcrowded restaurants; he is at home in the streets. He has no affinity to nature and compensates for this lack by overcrowding his sets. He sees with the eyes of the Sunday stroller: pretty slender birch trees, tall dark fir trees, lovely flowers, flowery fields, charming villages, golden clouds, golden beetles, golden harps, golden purple. There is no skimping when it comes to gilding. Hoffmann is not a master of spir-

itual coloring, but an expert on brilliant gloss, and he therefore prettifies his scenes to the point of distortion. Mountains are omitted. Occasionally, a cliché suffices. The "Waldeinsamkeit" ("forest solitude") seems to him to be a scene complete in itself that just needs to be set up. It has lost its mystery. By now it is nothing more than an instrument to create emotional perspectives.

The landscape adapts itself to his purposes in a profusion of verbs. It rustles, hums, rocks, whispers, and murmurs. The wind joins in like the strains of a harp. Streams sigh with longing, the waters moan, the birds and insects dance capers and entrechats in the ballet of the landscape while they send forth little sparks from their costume wings and soar aloft and dip again. Swans with golden necklaces pass by; diamonds have the fragrance of lilies, carnations, and roses. Objects and color, fragrance and thing, part company and realign themselves to produce new effects. Shrubs sparkle like "green-glowing carbuncles," the water of the rivers is "dark-yellow," fish are "rose-red" and mingle "with gold-scaled dolphins" and "silver soldiers." Language and content scarcely coincide anymore; however, this is less apt to lead to something spiritual than to something ostentatious and cheap.

It is in the nature of this theatrical tinsel that given scenes have a given setting. Weddings, for example, with which the fairy tales regularly close, have a prescribed scenery. What is modestly implied in **"Nutcracker"** with its golden carriage drawn by silver horses and followed by 22,000 figures adorned with pearls and diamonds who dance at the wedding, becomes more and more a mass mobilization of figures and frills. The old *Magic Flute* ending becomes a gigantic display of fireworks which the enlightened Mosch Terpin [in **"Klein Zaches"**] justly calls the work of that "devil of a fellow, the opera director and firework-maker of the prince." Trees and bushes rustle, springs and birds rejoice, insects dance, diamonds twinkle, odors "float through the air with rustling wings" (**"The Golden Pot"**). In **"Klein-Zaches"** the "flaming rainbows" and the "piercing chimes of the bells" are added. What Hoffmann has in mind is the scenery of the opera buffa.

At the end of **"Master Flea"** the garden scenery, which is strange from the start with its flowers and birds, takes on an oriental character. Even that must be given a try. Cedars rustle, birds of paradise soar by, a cactus bursts into bloom. Yet of all his elaborate landscapes, none can surpass the confectioner's landscape in **"Nutcracker."** Marie is led by Nutcracker along the orange brook, over the candy meadows, through the almond gates, past the cake trees to the marzipan castle. It is a landscape in which everything smells sweet, glistens, and gushes, and the little villages are made of grade A chocolate. Just how much Hoffmann has chosen all this for its exterior effect is revealed in Fabian's comment about Balthasar's poems: "It is just the same old song again about melancholy and bliss and talking trees and forest streams. All your verses teem with these pretty things which sound quite acceptable to the ear and are consumed to advantage so long as one does not look any deeper" (**"Zaches"**). One cannot help but think that this is Hoffmann's way of giving his reader a gentle rap on the knuckles for having gullibly swallowed such enormous quantities of poetic sweets without noticing how grotesquely they were dished out.

Delighting as he did in elaborate scenery, E. T. A. Hoffmann makes use of far more absurd formations than did the early romanticists with their abstract thinking. He resorts to Callotian compositions, to figures that are part plant, part animal, and part man, to malicious objects, to transformations which keep destroying the identity of the person. He makes us marvel and shudder at a world in which people and things no longer are what they seem. Little snakes with dark blue girlish eyes sing in the lilac bush; Schoolmaster Ink, in the shape of a fly, nibbles on a piece of bread with butter and honey; the porter ruffles up his feathers as an ostrich; Lindhorst's ceremonious messenger has a bird nose with glasses and a wig like a feather cap; the podgy frog beside the garden walk turns out to be a gardener. Magic combs dress Klein-Zaches' hair; the sleeves of a dress coat shrink while coattails become trains; coffeepots maliciously hold back the coffee; carrots sigh and giggle; rings send out magic rays. Hoffmann's voluminous reading furnishes him with an inexhaustible number of examples of hostile powers appearing in human life, and through them he shows us the grotesque mechanism of our existence. He transforms what is dull in the writings of the past so that they reflect the condition of his own day, a condition between laughter and fear, in which the spiritual person is destroyed and the bourgeois form of life becomes a caricature. An alienation of reality appears, because what is behind this reality, the surreality of dreams, fears, and abysses, becomes significantly more important. The caricature is not a criticism of society. Hoffmann has a natural talent for it, and in it he expresses his fear of the deformation which is taking place all around him and which is also corroding him.

With equal artistic skill Hoffmann also gives his language a grotesque turn. Nouns are strung together so that his scenes become oppressively overcrowded and each individual object takes on a threatening life of its own. A vegetable garden can become an uncanny mirror world "of many-colored plumage, rapuntika, English turnips, little green-heads, montrue, big mogul, yellow prince-heads, etc., so that you are dumbfounded, especially if you do not know that what is meant by these distinguished names is nothing more than cabbage and lettuce" (**"The King's Bride"**)—or their counterpart in the loathsome things of the garden underworld. ännchen looks down into the muddy vegetable beds "and in this mud all kinds of ugly creatures were stirring and creeping out of the womb of the earth. Fat earthworms were slowly twining around one another while beetle-like creatures were awkwardly creeping along stretching out their short legs in front of them. On their backs they were carrying large onions, but these had ugly human faces and grinned and stared at one another with sad yellow eyes and tried to grab one another by their long crooked noses with their little claws and pull one another down into the mud." The march of horrors in **"Master Flea"** is still more intensified by the mirror battles of Leuwenhoek: "Plant-lice, beetles, spiders, slime mold, which had grown to incredible sizes, stretched out their proboscises, walked along on their long hairy legs, and with their jagged maxillae the grayish ant robbers

seized and crushed the gnats who defended themselves and struck out with their long wings, and in the midst of it all, vinegar eels, eel worms, polyps with a hundred arms, wound in and out among one another, and Infusoria peered out from all the gaps with distorted human faces." And yet it is not the language which makes Hoffmann's fairy tales. It is not a question of artistic language here. Even words are merely a means of transforming the world into grotesque proportions and relationships. These things were already conceived as an aesthetic principle of form in Tieck's "Sternbald," where Ludovico speculates about "exceedingly strange forms," and speaks of figures "which would be a combination of all sorts of animals and would finally take on the form of plants down below: insects and reptiles on which I would imprint an amazing resemblance to human characters, so that they would express attitudes and passions in a comical, and yet terrifying way."

When we consider the figures which E. T. A. Hoffmann includes in his fairy-tale repertoire, we find that every fairy tale has a young pair whom he endows with the eccentric agility of the commedia dell'arte. The hero stands in the midst of a society of older people who have respectable titles and serious faces, yet who can become playful and malicious without provocation. But one of them exudes an unusual charm. That means that Tamino/Papageno, Pamina/Papagena, and Sarastro from the *Magic Flute* pattern continue on in their leading roles. Tamino/Papageno are combined in one modern figure possessing greater instability and dangerously explosive tendencies. For his heroes Hoffmann chooses reckless young people who are full of music and wild dreams, who have a touch of genius, but who never fully mature. Their prototype is the poor deformed Nutcracker in whom Hoffmann's own face is grotesquely immortalized. All of these heroes are full of dissonances and, like Kreisler, would sometimes like to stab themselves with an "extravagant quinte." They are poets of poems that are not yet written and, in most cases, will never be written. They are "an intrigue on two legs . . . an adventure which has jumped out of the book into life," as Giglio Fava calls himself and people like him (**"Brambilla"**). They are neurotics with lots of unfinished plans. The jubilant sounds of the day, conjured up by the romanticists, disintegrate in atonal music in E. T. A. Hoffmann. To call the life of such people "a mystery of pure artistic genius," as has been said of Anselmus, and to imagine that every other crazy lad is potentially an artist, won't do. Here one cannot avoid an only too familiar word. The spiritual person begins to experience a painful "alienation of the world" ("Weltverfremdung"), and, therefore, the artist is of a different substance. The early romanticists are still consecrated: Novalis has his belief in Paradise, Tieck knows the strength of being able to believe, Brentano makes his escape to orthodox Christianity, but Hoffmann has only his "corner window" through which he observes the marketplace, the bargaining of the women and the buffoonery of the men. In the artistic person's now incurably disturbed condition the human being alienates himself through his own doing. His neighbors call this insanity, but this kind of insanity is not a clear-cut clinical case. It has its origins in the basic human experience of the grotesque, and it is in this form that Hoffmann completes the deformation of the bourgeoisie.

The Hoffmann heroes love pretty blond blue-eyed girls with roguish smiles whose only fault is that they are too tightly laced, like Candida, and eat too much cake at tea. They have read their *Wilhelm Meister* and Fouqué's *Magic Ring* (*Zauberring*) and then have merrily forgotten them both. They play the piano fairly well, sing a little, never end a letter without a P.S., and never sigh. They know all about the latest hat, and like Röschen, they are terrified of a flea. They shed a tear over a wilted tulip, and dream, like ännchen, of young carrots and sausages. As Herr Dapsul puts it, they are artless children "blest with ignorance" (**"The King's Bride"**) who get engaged over the steaming soup and become good housewives. They will never be fooled by a fairy tale! Their pots will never boil over, they will never spoil a meal, they will never break a glass, and they will always have perfect weather on washday, "even though it rains, thunders, and lightnings, everywhere else." The boys see heavenly traits in their girlish faces and make goddesses of them, but the girls, alas, find these heroes lacking in full-blooded masculinity. Hoffmann translates the *Magic Flute* couple into "our times," in other words, into something grotesquely buffoonish.

None of the fairy tales is named after these figures. Hoffmann puts into his titles everything which is ludicrous and bizarre and which, therefore, intervenes in the action: **"Nutcracker and Mouse King,"** powers and adversaries; **"Klein-Zaches,"** the bureaucratic demon; **"Master Flea,"** the animal philosopher. Where in Tieck it was simply The Goblet, it is now **"The Golden Pot"** with the accent on golden; instead of The Elves it is now **"The Strange Child"** with the emphasis on strange, and **"The King's Bride"** ironically puts the stress on the king whom every girl would like to marry, even if he turns out to be only a vegetable king. No matter what insight these people gain, it always has a ridiculous effect because it ends with a question mark. Hoffmann is no Villon with the courage to live in opposition to society. He knows what life costs, but he is no longer in a position to pay the price. He is himself a member of the middle class who will never experience the return of a golden age. Like a graphic artist, he sits bent over his drawing board and with a certain lack of objectivity, he depicts our world behind which there is neither heaven nor hell, because it contains both in itself.

Hoffmann dims the lights of his Sarastro-figures since he cannot refrain from amassing powers and adversaries and playing with magic tricks, so abundant in the Masonic novel. He includes, however, all those who pass by outside, the secretaries, schoolmasters, and councilors, all those whom Schopenhauer called "the manufactured goods of nature" and whom Nietzsche condemned to destruction as the "many too many." And it is Hoffmannesque, not romantic, that these people who are always respectable and also determine what is to be considered respectable are a hostile world which has only a smirk for the gifted person, since it is the maneuverable and dashing journalist whom they need for their Sunday paper. They constitute a tightly knit clique which has shamelessly

taken over the world. In such an environment the spiritual person must remain hopelessly alone. Going out from **"The Golden Pot"** as the prototype of the Hoffmann fairy tale, there are the intolerable, yet indispensable citizens with their official uniforms and their graduated incomes, and along with them the boys who no longer can cope with such things as office hours, for they are more pliable and of softer wood. The effects of yesterday's punch, which the deputy schoolmaster and the secretary can bravely sleep off, plunge the student Anselmus into daydreams and disturb his balance, things in which the respectable official does not want to be involved. They have many faces: they are Christian clergymen who coddle a loathsome child, schoolmasters who cannot distinguish between a linden and a chestnut tree, red-pencil bureaucrats, physicians who cautiously feel for a pulse, city children who can say the names of all the rivers and cities backward and forward. They go to bed at exactly ten o'clock. They press their thumb and forefinger together to take a pinch of snuff before asking their superior for the hand of his daughter in marriage. They know how to mix arrack, lemons, and sugar perfectly, and they always celebrate their ceremonious holidays with the same menu and the same wine.

What evolves as a natural result of Hoffmann's analysis of this hazy world of mediocrity where the usual and the unusual clash with such force, is the grotesque of a tragicomical world in which an exalted mood is a delusion and a declaration of love merely ridiculous. With that the new image of man has entered a precarious border zone. Hoffmann himself, to be sure, is not at home there, but he can already look into it from a distance. The breach in society between the well-balanced person who can always snap back into what has been certified as balance, and those who are less balanced, as Hoffmann no doubt felt deeply with respect to himself, appears in his fairy tales as the fundamental enmity between the Philistine and the genius. What results is the distortion of the burgher as the Philistine who has freed himself from the sublime and the tragic. In his devotion to the Nutcrackers, moreover, Hoffmann begins to justify the man of genius and the dark side of life outside the bourgeois sphere by means of exhaustive effects. In any tragicomical situation, which has its greatness but no nobility, the bohemian takes the place of the poet. He has left the romantic behind and has become the product of a deformed society, so that no God can bring solace any more. Brentano, who certainly admired Hoffmann and was also indebted to him, understood this situation well. In a letter to Hoffmann of January 1816 he writes: "For a long time I have had a horror of all poetry which reflects itself and not God." Because of the inadequacies of current values and because of the absence of God, people are seized by a fear of the world. They laugh at its strangeness, to be sure, but they can no longer find a constructive order and meaning in life. Hoffmann no longer sees transitions. The battle between the extremes which gives rise to his ironic tone is so bitter that objects and machines take up the fight. Not even they can remain aloof from it.

All the fairy tales get their life from the transformations of one thing into another. Toys and kitchen utensils come alive. The demarcation lines between animal, plant, and man collapse; microscopes and mirrors destroy the natural proportions of things. If we take dragons and salamanders as they are used in **"The Golden Pot"** to be the principle underlying the evil magic which befalls people, if we accept the malicious and fiery as elements which can never unite in peace, then we find them in all of the Hoffmann fairy tales: the gnawing mice and the brave Nutcracker; Schoolmaster Ink and the shining fairy child; Alpanus, the noble Brahmin, and Rosabelverde with her mandrake; Herr Dapsul, the salamander-clown, and Carota, the malicious vegetable king. There is no longer any meeting of the minds between the right and the left. Hoffmann, who is more a graphic artist than a painter of the grotesque, sticks strictly to black and white. Everything has more than only one mask, but it no longer has a face which we could easily recognize. The wicked apple woman fills Anselmus with fright when she appears to him as a door knocker and a snake, only to end as a dried-up carrot. To Veronica she is the old Rauerin, or Liese, or the coffeepot. And Lindhorst goes around the corner like a vulture in flight, he climbs down into the punch bowl, he flares up out of the goblet in the shape of a flame, and as a clump of tiger lilies he parades through the garden in his red silk dressing gown. In **"Klein-Zaches"** these metamorphoses take the form of clever pranks played by the rivals, Alpanus and Rosabelverde. As a butterfly, a Camberwell Beauty, Rosabelverde soars to the ceiling, pursued by Alpanus, the stag beetle, or she runs across the floor as a little mouse, chased by a gray tomcat, and at the end they both appear for the finale—she in a white dress with a diamond belt, he in a robe with gold embroidery and wearing a crown on his head. In **"Master Flea"** there are immense numbers of hostile powers around Dörtje-Gamaheh: two magicians, Swammerdam and Leuwenhoek, both of whom claim an ancient lineage and make rings and microscopes sparkle; two traveling comedians, the genius Ethel and Prince Leech (Prinz Egel); the two lovers, Pepusch and Tyss. Shots are fired from wooden pistols, intrigues are contrived with magic mirrors, until the marriage and love-death of Cactus Zeherit and the yellow- and lavender-striped tulip, Gamaheh, bring the fairy tale to a close.

After **"The Golden Pot"** the ironic tone increases in the fairy tales to the point where it is grotesque. In this first fairy tale one cannot help hearing the human overtones of a poet who has come late to literature, and everywhere one looks one still finds something of human dignity. **"Nutcracker and Mouse King"** and **"The Strange Child,"** fairy tales with children as their heroes, move in a world which Hoffmann knows only on the surface. He is incapable of portraying children. His fireworks do not really start until **"Klein-Zaches,"** the fairy tale of bureaucracy, which he despised and yet wanted. There he takes us along with him on his strange adventures in the bohemian world, where even the respectable people like Peregrinus Tyss occasionally get off the track. But **"The King's Bride,"** in which he perfects this type of grotesque fairy tale and arrives at the irony of irony, in his masterpiece. A surplus of wit, laughter that does not offend, this is Hoffmann's highest trump. The unhappiness one feels over the people of means and the inflationary values of society dissolve in this laughter and become something which in the last

analysis no longer hurts. An artistic solution presents itself here which spiritualizes, even though it is not a story of redemption. It is not a plot that is governed by reason, it is not about a Satan, a Cain, or a Wandering Jew, but simply about the horror of the most common everyday things in which the tragicomical and the grotesque unite in a natural bond. They stand there before us, all those respectable people, and each one has a screw loose in his head. The girl is so prosaic that she can marry the vegetable king so that the white cabbage will thrive, and the father, a mad mystery-monger and dilettante in the occult, who never forgets to take out his white beard and put on his high pointed cap when it comes to speculating, and the bridegroom, Amandus, who is so sentimentally poetic that he would consider an estate in Atlantis lowly prose. And all that is necessary is a blow on the head with a spade for the entire household to regain its senses and tick in time with the clock. Herr Dapsul is once again the untroubled dilettante, Amandus the respectable head of a family who swears by the classicists and Virginia tobacco, and Ännchen becomes a lady who lets the maid pull up the carrots. The irony with which Hoffmann portrays these simple people who have accidently slipped over into the realm of the fantastic has a charm no longer mixed with bitterness. The fairy tale has become a work of artistic subtlety. E. T. A. Hoffmann did not write another **"Golden Pot,"** it is true, but in the **"The King's Bride"** he finally wrote the grotesque without tears. (pp. 109-20)

> *Marianne Thalmann, "The Hoffman Fairy Tale," in her* The Romantic Fairy Tale: Seeds of Surrealism, *translated by Mary B. Corcoran, The University of Michigan Press, 1964, pp. 88-120.*

René Wellek   (essay date 1967)

[*Wellek's* A History of Modern Criticism *(1955-86) is a major, comprehensive study of the literary critics of the last three centuries. Wellek's critical method, as demonstrated in* A History *and outlined in his* Theory of Literature *(1949), is one of describing, analyzing, and evaluating a work solely in terms of the problems it poses for itself and how the writer solves them. For Wellek, biographical, historical, and psychological information is incidental. Although many of Wellek's critical methods are reflected in the work of the New Critics, he was not a member of that group, and rejected their more formalistic tendencies. In the following essay, he offers a reevaluation of Hoffmann's works.*]

E. T. A. Hoffmann is today hardly more than a name in the English-speaking world. The opera *Les Contes d'Hoffmann* (1882), by Jacques Offenbach, is rarely performed, though it is still fairy well known. It uses three of Hoffmann's stories: **"The Sandman," "The Lost Reflection,"** and **"Councillor Krespel,"** ascribing these adventures to Hoffmann himself, who tells these tales in a tavern while drinking himself into a maudlin stupor.

Students of literature will have come across his name in many contexts: Hoffmann has been claimed as an important source of motifs and plots for Edgar Allan Poe (and Washington Irving); for the early Balzac, and Prosper Mérimée; for Gogol and Dostoevsky; and for many German writers from Heine to Kafka. Hoffmann seems like a forgotten well from which many have drunk, but which has dried out today. When we go back to it, we soon discover that it, in turn, was fed by many sources: the older Germans, particularly the enormous, shapeless imagination of Jean Paul; the English Gothic romance, such as the work of "Monk" Lewis; the Italian eighteenth-century fairy comedy of Carlo Gozzi; the occult, mystical, or pseudo-mystical philosophies of the time; the beginnings of psychiatric investigations of abnormal behavior and the life of dreams; and, dimly in the background, the world of Shakespeare: fairies, goblins, witches, melancholy philosophers such as Jaques, and fools.

There is no question of Hoffmann's immense historical importance. The student of the main trends of nineteenth- and twentieth-century literature must know him. The mystery and detective novel, the figure of the artist in conflict with society, the theme of split personality, the use of fantastic dreams, and many other motifs can be, at least in part, traced back to him.

But there is, as Matthew Arnold pleaded long ago, a difference between the historical and the "real" estimate. The real estimate inevitably asks what a work of art may mean today, not only to myself but to my contemporaries and the future. It is a question which assumes that there are permanent values in literature which transcend the ephemeral and temporal. Often, in an act of imaginative sympathy, we have to remove the obstacles laid in our path to reach them. Our ignorance of former times or our difficulties in understanding vanished manners of feeling, expression, and convention set up formidable barriers. We cannot deny that in the case of Hoffmann these barriers may be of considerable height for some of us.

Much of Hoffmann's writing is couched in an almost formulaic sentimental diction which may be hard to take, though Hoffmann is obviously laughing at himself. Much of the satire is directed against an extinct society: the petty courts of tiny German principalities, the pompously stolid burghers, and the weepy, ethereal girls of the German middles classes of the time. Much of the technique of narration will strike us as old-fashioned: the addresses to "dear reader," the insertion of letters, the opportune coincidences, the substitutions of children at birth, and other paraphernalia of romance.

We must not, however, be deterred by this. If we applied standards which precluded such conventionalities, we could not read Poe or much of Dostoevsky's intricate novels, such as *The Possessed,* and we would have to avoid a good deal of Balzac and Dickens, who also indulge in sentimental rhetoric and devise creaky plots and unexciting mysteries. Still, to make the effort to read Hoffmann leads to rich rewards.

Hoffmann has a complex vision of the world. It is, at first, easiest to think of it simply as a scale which extends from brute matter to supernal beauty—"supernal" in the vague, mystical sense in which Poe spoke of it. Many of Hoffmann's stories revolve around a conflict between mind and matter, soul and body, art and life. His writings are per-

vaded by a nostalgia for a happier world in which the artist and all spiritual men must find consolation for the failure of life. The conclusion of **"The Golden Pot"** puts it memorably: the estate on the island Atlantis and the hand of the fairy Serpentina, with which the student Anselmus is rewarded, are none other but "the life of poetry in which the sacred harmony of all beings is revealed as the deepest secret of Nature." The artist is a visitor from this other world—misunderstood and even persecuted by the cloddish world of the Philistines. He can never make his peace with them. Even in his love for a woman he must remain resigned and pure. His love of are must be disinterested, all-absorbing. Music is the highest art; it takes us into the upper world most quickly.

Hoffmann, who composed a romantic opera, *Undine,* wrote much good criticism of Gluck, Mozart, and Beethoven, and for some years earned his living as a conductor and music teacher, shared his German contemporaries' view of music being not only an emotional release and exaltation but a secret language of the beyond, a door to the supernatural and the divine. Music is only one of these means; the other (or is it the same?) is imagination, the creative imagination of the poet and the unconscious workings of our dream-life. The dream, as with so many poets of the time—from Novalis to Nerval—is the ivory gate through which we enter the realm of truth and beauty.

This almost Neo-platonic vision in Hoffmann remains, however, only a private hope; there is nothing Messianic or Utopian about it. Rather, one suspects it to be a consolatory scheme which he imbibed from the German romantic surroundings while, existentially, most personally, this radiant vision is denied or distorted by his profoundest experience: the horror behind the surface of the world, a sense of the malignity of fate, of the powers which dispose of us arbitrarily and make life rather a nightmare than a hope or, at best, a silly and inconsequential dream.

There is much in Hoffmann which is merely sinister and weird, and this earned him the reputation of "spooky" Hoffmann—though he rarely introduces ghosts into his stories and deals rather with phenomena explainable by telepathy, hypnosis, or hallucination. But there is much more in Hoffmann which shows a profound sense of the precariousness of our existence, for which he found unforgettable symbols and myths ever since he professed to have heard the Devil's voice as a boy on the seashore in East Prussia: a weird sound which filled him with profound terror and piercing compassion. This other world is not the Atlantis of **"The Golden Pot."** It is a world of demons who govern us and even enter into us. We hand helplessly between this and the other world or are ourselves divided between them. Thus, many of Hoffmann's most interesting characters are split personalities, even physical "doubles," alternatingly good and evil men, eccentrics, criminals, even madmen. Hoffmann had studied what was then accepted psychiatry—Mesmerism, magnetic and electric explanations of the mind—and he often describes the symptoms of division and self-alienation with almost clinical accuracy. The double is for him the question mark put to the concept of the human self, a symbol of the doubt we have of human identity and the stability of our world. The automatons, puppets, and even the stock figures of the Italian *commedia dell' arte* so prevalent in his tales represent the sense of man's dependence on superior powers, the determinism in which Hoffmann believes. It is a macabre world peopled by grotesque figures: sinister scientists, or *revenants* from a former age, or malicious goblins living in the musty corners of old German cities.

There is much in Hoffmann which is merely sinister and weird, and this earned him the reputation of "spooky" Hoffmann—though he rarely introduces ghosts into his stories and deals rather with phenomena explainable by telepathy, hypnosis, or hallucination.

—René Wellek

This whole contradictory world, almost Manichean in its division into good and evil, light and darkness, even within an individual, rarely is allowed to degenerate into melodrama or farce because it is seen with a sense of detachment and irony, viewed with a feeling of superiority. The rapid changes of mood, the piquant mixture of tears and laughter, the whole tragicomedy of life is pointed up by a technique of telling in which the teller of the tale is always present and prominent. A sense of make-believe and play is never absent. (pp. 49-52)

[Hoffmann's] tales were collected in several volumes during his lifetime. One of these volumes, *The Serapion Brothers,* provided a loose framework which need not be taken too seriously, for many of the stories were published independently and are hardly related to the persons of the tellers. Ignoring the distinctions of the volumes and making allowances for overlappings between the types, we can distinguish three main groups of stories: retellings of traditional stories elaborated to suit Hoffmann's moods and taste, fantastic fairy tales, and grotesques of his own invention. The first group contains some of Hoffmann's most successful writing, if we judge in terms of traditional construction, formal story line, and adherence to the conventions of realism. The sources in a memoir or history provide some restraint and an anchorage in the world of concrete things. **"Mlle de Scudéry,"** among our examples, is the more effective because Hoffmann controls the method of telling the story superbly. The cutback describing the events of some twenty-three years is dramatized by the situation of telling: the murder charge against Olivier, the despair of Madelon, and the change which Mlle de Scudéry experiences in listening to the story, her growing conviction of Olivier's innocence preparing for the happy ending.

The fantastic fairy tale, best represented by **"The Golden Pot,"** breaks completely with the world of cause and ef-

fect. In a riot of capricious fancy, everything comes to mean everything else: a rhetoric of metamorphoses changes man into plant, plant into animal, an applewoman into a doorknocker, a turnip into a king. One can see in these stories anticipations of the irresponsible dream world of the surrealists, a stream of free association, a melting of all the senses, colors, sounds, and perfumes (long before Rimbaud). One may even look for deeper meanings in the symbolism drawn from Masonic rites—sometimes suggested by Mozart's *Magic Flute*—from alchemy, from the world of sylphs and gnomes best known to us from Pope's *Rape of the Lock,* or from the stock figures of the Italian Pantalone, Scaramuccia, Brighella, etc. But it may be wiser to enjoy these fairy tales simply as gorgeous capriccios, as the kind of spectacle the Russian ballet provided. It is not accidental that Tchaikovsky's *Nutcracker* ballet is based on one of Hoffmann's children's tales.

The third group is probably closest to Hoffmann's heart and mind: The horrifying and grotesque world of his eccentrics, automatons, mad scientists, and wild musicians clashing with dreamy students and unsophisticated girls. **"Councillor Krespel"** is possibly the most impressive story of its kind. It is only seemingly disjointed. The hero is introduced, at first, in the comic episode of the building of his house, but then he slowly assumes a sinister meaning in the mind of the student telling the story. Only at the end do we discover that the teller completely misinterpreted Krespel's character and that Krespel sincerely wanted to preserve the life of his beloved Antonia. He is a kind-hearted father who puts on an "antic disposition" to scare off the suitors. But the solution is not as predictable as we might guess form the scene in which Krespel expels the betrothed of Antonia with terrible threats. We assume that Antonia will die as soon as she is again seduced into singing. You pay, we seem to be told, with your life for the perfection of art. But nothing of this sort happens: Antonia dies in Krespel's dream, in which, with supernatural perception, he hears her sing. The three parts of the story, though unrelated in tone, move easily from the oddities of the house being built to the weird dissecting of ancient violins, from the comic dispatch through the window of Krespel's Italian *prima donna* wife to the funeral procession, and are nevertheless balanced with consummate art. They yield the propitious mixture of grotesquerie, lyrical rapture, and sinister menace.

Ultimately, Hoffmann should be judged as an artist who created a unique world of the imagination. His art should appeal to us because of its ingredients which are, in many ways, kindred to the art of our time. Hoffmann, one must say, is hardly a committed writer, though he detests the stifling atmosphere of post- Napoleonic Germany. Unconcerned as he may be with a social utopia, he nevertheless has something in common with our time: a sense of the absurd, of the tragicomedy of life. A single mood, a single tone, is unknown to him. He mixes his colors deliberately, insistently. He comes up to T. S. Eliot's conception of the artist. He composes poetry, falls in love, reads Spinoza, smells cooking—all at the same time. He attains a tense though precarious equilibrium of opposites: dark and light, mad and sane, grotesque and nostalgic, tragic and comic. A time which appreciates Gogol and Kafka, Dostoevsky and Beckett, might well go back to Hoffmann, not primarily because of historical curiosity but for the enjoyment of the spectacle of an artist struggling to define a world of the imagination which is akin to the world of our most admired and representative writers. (pp. 54-6)

René Wellek, "Why Read E. T. A. Hoffmann?" in Midway, Vol. 8, No. 1, June, 1967, pp. 49-56.

Leonard J. Kent and Elizabeth C. Knight   (essay date 1969)

[*In the following excerpt from an essay originally published in 1969, Kent and Knight examine Hoffmann's characteristic themes and techniques as represented in his major stories.*]

In the introduction to his collection *Fantasy Pieces in the Style of Callot,* Hoffmann says of Jaques Callot, a French engraver and etcher of the seventeenth century:

The irony which mocks man's miserable actions by placing man and beast in opposition to each other only dwells in a deep spirit, and thus Callot's grotesque figures, which are created from man and beast, reveal to the penetrating observer all the secret implications that lie hidden under the veil of the comical.

Shakespeare's plays, beautifully translated by A. W. Schlegel, were a revelation to the Germans—who lacked the advantage of a Shakespeare tradition—not least of all because they felt a strong affinity to his use of supernatural elements and to his view of man as an actor. Hoffmann, perhaps at least as much as any of his contemporaries, admired Shakespeare. He was extremely sympathetic to the view expressed by the melancholy Jacques in *As You Like It:* "All the world's a stage and all the men and woman merely players." (pp. xvii-xviii)

["Ritter Gluck"] is one of Hoffmann's very best tales and contains many elements which reappear again and again in his works.

Very clearly, Gluck is the musician-hero whose art has removed him from the vulgar realm of the bourgeois and has raised him to the level where the mystery of the world and of his soul are known to him, as they are not to the narrator—if there really is a narrator separate from the musician. A host of questions arises: Is this "chance" acquaintance really not predetermined? Is the musician merely a madman who sees himself as Gluck? Is the "madman" really Gluck? Is he perhaps a reincarnation of Gluck? Is it possible, after all, that the narrator and Gluck are one and the same and hence exist in two worlds simultaneously, the external world of reality and the inner romantic world of the spirit? But what is this "reality"? We are told in the beginning of the story that what follows took place in 1809; however, we know that the composer Gluck died in 1787. How could Gluck, according to our standards of reality, find himself in Weber's Café, in Berlin, twenty-two years after his death? Perhaps, one could argue, there is no Gluck; it is the narrator who is insanely imagining that

he exists. But Hoffmann convinces us that this man is Gluck, for he tells us as much himself, in the very last line of the story, with the italicized *"I am Ritter Gluck."*

All in all, as in much of Hoffmann, we are left with one satisfactory conclusion: the world itself has more than one reality, and different realities may coexist at exactly the same moment; this being so, the world we thought we knew so well is undermined.

This is a seminal story: the fantastic takes place in an accurate and contemporary setting; the whole question of "doubleness" is raised; through music, the spirit is seen as communicating with the Divine; the attack upon the premise that there is but one reality is made; the imaginative, gaining strength because it overlays the prosaic, is already in full power.

This story may also be, as a German critic maintains, the key to an understanding not only Hoffmann but of many of the literary works to follow, because we see in "Ritter Gluck" what he calls "the abandonment of duration," which implies no less the abandonment of place and, making possible any and all combinations, projects an "absurd" and frightening, completely open-ended existence.

"The Golden Pot" is a masterpiece, one which Hoffmann considered his best story. In it, the various ingredients which make up Hoffmann's fictional world are blended with amazing success. It is, at least on one level, the story of an artist who rejects Philistia, not only because fantasy promises escape and greater rewards, but also, concomitantly, because the destitute and overwhelmed student Anselmus hardly belongs to this "comfortable" world at all; he is a pariah who rips his coat on a nail, loses his hat while bowing, is forever late, and is always breaking things because, he tells us, he "walks straight ahead, as if he were a lemming." The simile is well-chosen. Like a lemming, he is headed for total destruction. The world he ultimately flees to is one of green-gold snakes and salamanders, of bronze-gold palm trees, and marvelous tropical birds who make music as they fly—the stunning "wonderland of Atlantis." On this level Anselmus may be seen as strongly autobiographical, for he represents Hoffmann as he wrestled with the problem of the artistic soul meeting the gross realities head on and suggests that the world of Philistia can be conquered by the poet, that the denigration and pressure of Philistia recede and disappear under the marvels conjured up by the poetic imagination, and that the poet reaches salvation.

But there are other interpretations, the most obvious one being much blacker; for if the prosaic world is so enervating and destructive and intolerable to the poet, he must retreat to the Atlantis he needs for survival. Having retreated, he has renounced his claim to reality and exists only in Atlantis, which, of course, does not exist at all. Unlike **"Ritter Gluck,"** it may not here be a question of simultaneous realities; rather, it may be one in which the very identity of the poet is threatened with extinction.

Given Anselmus's condition as he barely survives in Dresden, perhaps one can agree that the madness of Hoffmann's artists results primarily from their estrangement from the world and symbolizes the very suffering of the world as it, in turn, torments those most sensitive to its pain. Or, it has been argued that the story is simply a metaphoric depiction of the development of the artist in which some of the characters represent various projections of mind, the apple-woman being fear, and so on.

Perhaps Anselmus is himself merely a projection of the registrar, a projection which disappears when the registrar marries Veronica and, therefore, no longer has a need to exist in a world of fantasy. Or is it that parts of a single character assume individual identities so that Veronica and Serpentina are one, even as Anselmus and the registrar are one?

The story contains allegorical possibilities and may well have imbedded in it ironical elements which expose to ridicule some contemporaneous German philosophy; but these elements are nebulous and arcane. There are mythic elements as well, at least one of which deserves some mention.

The German romantics, were concerned with a synthesis, with a conception of man living in perfect harmony and unity with nature. Atlantis perhaps suggests the Biblical Eden and Paradise before the fall of man (which resulted because "thought" overcame spirit and soul). Restoration of harmony and Paradise may, after all, only be possible through the triumph of faith and, ultimately, poetry.

This is the only one of Hoffmann's many stories dealing with artists which has a happy domestic ending. It may even be said that the bourgeois life depicted in **"The Golden Pot"** is not without its rewards, if Veronica is any measure. Yet the ending itself may well be ironical, for even when many of the almost limitless possible interpretations are considered and the story is read again and again, the final impression is that this world is simply no place for the poet:

> Be calm, be calm, my friend. Do not lament so! Were you not yourself just now in Atlantis, and do you not at least have there a nice little farmstead as a poetic possession of your inner mind? Is the bliss of Anselmus anything else but life in poetry, the poetry to which the sacred harmony of all things is revealed as the most profound secret of Nature?

However it be interpreted, **"The Golden Pot"** is a wondrous product of the romantic imagination. The soft and teasing haze drifting over it is fully in keeping with a time and an author dedicated to illusion.

"Der Sandmann" ("The Sandman") is at once one of the more perplexing and successful stories Hoffmann wrote. An interestingly constructed work, it is one of the surprisingly few stories in which evil seems unequivocally to win.

The exchange of letters at the beginning is artistically successful in that the reader gains an "unobstructed" view of Nathanael and Klara—of Nathanael as the archetypal romantic, and of Klara as the embodiment of love and domestic virtue. But as the story progresses, the mental deterioration of Nathanael is only sometimes depicted from his point of view. A narrator supplies additional information, but not always evenly, for the narrator is alternately sensitive and sympathetic, and critical and even sardonic.

Here the narrative technique supports the questionmarks imbedded in the fabric of the story because it precludes a clear determination as to how much is happening and how much is imagined.

The story may be seen as the projection of a madman's fantasies. Nathanael's description of his childhood—and there is no reason not to believe him—supplies adequate "evidence" of several experiences which could have, given his temperament, led to psychosis. Thus viewed, the fantastic events described support the contention that here a childhood trauma, which may have been temporarily suppressed in the subconscious, finally asserts itself and results in distortion and death.

Hoffmann seems to have been aware of organic and functional psychoses long before modern science defined them and twentieth-century literature exploited them; but, of course, his interest was primarily esthetic and not scientific.

—Leonard J. Kent and Elizabeth C. Knight

Possibly more in keeping with Hoffmann is a reading which sees Coppelius-Coppola—if, indeed, they are one and the same—as a malicious agent of a hostile fate which exists both in Nathanael's mind and in external reality. Nathanael is, then, powerless to ward off this evil, this implacable horror which corrupts and destroys. Is it not this evil force which pushes Nathanael into irreversible madness when he discovers that the woman he loves is in fact what he is only metaphorically, an automaton? Created by Coppelius, she is no less fate's evil emissary.

This may be, at least in part, an archetypal revenge story, for Nathanael as a child had looked upon what was forbidden and had seen the secrets of the soul. An eye motif runs through the story: there are eyes during the forbidden experiments; Coppelius threatens to remove Nathanael's eyes; when Olympia is destroyed, her eyes fall out; "coppola" is the Italian world for "eye-socket," and so on. Are the eyes all symbols of Nathanael's punishment for trespassing? Are they rather merely a symbol for the occult, for magic?

It is difficult to determine the degree of Hoffmann's satiric intentions in this story, primarily because the attitude lacks consistency or full development; yet it is unmistakably present. Nathanael, on the one hand a tragic victim of fate, is an absurd romantic as well, not because he would reach for Atlantis, but because his fervent speeches and his soulful poetry are directed at an automaton who can only respond to "How profound is your mind. Only you, only you understand me" with a literally mechanical "Ah."

A critic has written perceptively that

It is possible to give comic expression to the fact that he mistakes a doll for a human being, thinks that she loves him, and confesses his love to her, but Hoffmann's presentation of the matter is so genuinely grotesque that its effect upon us is humorous and horrible at the same time. [Wolfgang Kayser, *The Grotesque in Art and Literature*]

Nathanael is no less estranged from reality than Anselmus, and even as in **"The Golden Pot,"** there is some objective basis for understanding what may be viewed as a flight from reality—in Anselmus' case, his marginal existence in Dresden; in Nathanael's, his traumatic experiences as a child. But one should keep in mind that in Hoffmann objectified material serves well because it enriches the range of potential interpretations but does not exhaust them. There is nothing in **"The Sandman"** which explains, for example, Coppelius' uncanny power over Nathanael; nor should there be.

On any level, Nathanael is in mortal turmoil: he is a poet possessed by a demon, whether it be internal or external, or both. He is a romantic who carries within himself his own destruction. He must try to reach beyond reality, but having once done so, he may have reached too far ever to be able to return. Besides, Coppelius stands ever ready to block his way.

"Rat Krespel" ("Councillor Krespel") is particularly noteworthy because Krespel is one of Hoffmann's great characters. Humorously and affectionately depicted at first as merely a charming eccentric whose physical appearance is comic rather than sinister, as one "who waltzed a little with the builders' wives and then sat down with the town musicians, took up his fiddle, and conducted the dance music until daybreak," he is yet the artist who invariably finds the ordinary stifling and restrictive. His eccentric, "crazy," behavior is here most effectively depicted as his only way of avoiding madness. In many ways, what so shocks one about Krespel at the conclusion of the story is the realization that he may be the most sane of any of Hoffmann's artists; hence, his estrangement from the everyday world has about it a condemnatory power less obvious and convincing in other depictions of the artist as one who truly seems on the brink of madness. That Hoffmann may see Krespel as sane suggests, quite aside from its other implications, that the viewed him as strongly autobiographical.

It is a dark story from which the supernatural has been excluded but in which the occult functions, especially in the implication of prenatal influence and Antonia's fatal connection and the singular violin. Antonia is destined to die: dedicating herself to art with her lover means death, but abandoning art to remain with her father is also a form of death.

The tragedy, however, is Krespel's, for he, hostile to all interference, still desires to interfere and manipulate, and ultimately he comes to recognize this for the evil it is. He twice accuses himself of having tried to play God, the Father, and once accuses the narrator of considering himself to be God, the Son. Both Krespel and the narrator have interfered in Antonia's life—Krespel by treating his daughter as a mechanical object, another violin, which he can dissect and direct; the narrator by wishing to save Antonia from her father. The evil involved is identical to that of which Kapellmeister Kreisler accuses Meister Abraham in *Kater Murr*.

It is again impossible to determine where Krespel's dream begins and how much of what we read is to be taken as having happened; but one of the major themes can here be isolated, and what it tells us as pessimistic as anything in Hoffmann: art and love cannot coexist.

"Die Bergwerke zu Falun" ("The Mines of Falun") is a marvel of the fantastic and an expression of the German romantic's conception of the miner as a man of almost superhuman quality because he has access to secrets hidden from others. The very secrets of creation are his because he works deep within the bowels of earth and is, hence, by virtue of his intimacy, heir to her mysteries and treasures.

The story opens with sunshine and gaiety, but the tone shifts, first when Elis discovers that his mother is dead, then, immediately following, when an old miner excoriates him for despising the mines—"an enchanted garden"—which he has never known. Significantly, the old miner concludes, "I have uncovered for you, Elis Fröbom, all the glories of a calling Nature did truly intend for you . . . do as your judgment dictates." It is at this point that Elis, enticed by a surpassingly lovely dream, enters a fantastic world which ultimately claims him as a victim.

Like Nathanael in **"The Sandman,"** who "sees" with his spy glass what others cannot, Elis "sees" in the mines metals which are hidden from others. For both Nathanael and Elis the bourgeois world of love and marriage becomes the determining factor that drives them to the world of fantasy and to their doom (in neither story is fantasy equated with the world of art). There is no reconciling Atlantis.

Hoffmann is here interested in revealing the agony of the split personality, and he achieves this not only through the description of events, but also through a particularly marvelous dream that foreshadows the action and reveals Elis's inner dissension, the cause of which Hoffmann typically ascribes to an occult power operating outside the individual and controlling him mercilessly. In the end, Elis succumbs, as does Nathanael, imminent marriage precipitating catastrophe.

"Mademoiselle de Scudéri" is one of Hoffmann's greatest stories, not primarily because it is an early example of detective fiction, or because it contains a splendidly exciting plot and is set in a Paris which is described in wonderful and accurate detail, but because, along with the magnificent Madeleine de Scudéri, it also contains René Cardillac, one of Hoffmann's most sinister artists because he unites in his person the artist and the criminal (a motif later to be developed by Thomas Mann).

Cardillac carefully plans and commits numerous murders, each time plunging a dagger into the heart of a victim for whom he has created a masterpiece of the jeweler's art. Why does he commit such crimes? Because art has become a curse and creativity has become the ultimate selfishness. Councillor Krespel destroys his violins and silences his daughter's voice to keep her for himself; Cardillac cannot give up his masterpieces, and when he must, he murders to retrieve them. This is a self-conscious, uncontrollable drive, for he refuses to make jewelry for those whom he admires, and it is this that creates great suspense when Mademoiselle de Scudéri neglects to rid herself of the mysterious jewels that come into her possession.

This is one of Hoffmann's best-constructed stories; it is also one of the few works in which suspense is so intense and into which it is directly and quickly introduced. The opening scenes are masterful and, from the first knock on the door at midnight until the resolution of the crimes, Hoffmann manages to resist the dreamlike atmosphere so typical of him and to proceed with sharp and deft strokes.

Mademoiselle de Scudéri is surely, in several ways, one of the most admirable "detectives" in all fiction, not because of her skill—it is her "bungling" which is so endearing—but because of her humanity and nobility of character. Further, she is an especially effective character because she is Cardillac's foil. Her steps are determined but sometimes wavering, in marked contrast to the fixed and mechanical movements of Cardillac. Hoffmann is able in this story to exploit his strength at characterization as he quickly fills in details that individualize and give life to his cast.

Perhaps because this story is less dreamlike than many of the others, we may find the love affair between Madelon and Olivier less acceptable in its details than we would were it transferred to a fantastic setting. Hoffmann's depiction of love tends to be so highly romantic and stylized that one wonders whether the pearly tears staining a white bosom are intended ironically, as Nathanael's professions of love to the automation Olympia in "The Sandman" may be. But one rejects that idea in this story and concludes that it was impossible for the romantic Hoffmann to see this aspect of life any more realistically than he could see other aspects.

But the "tear-stained white bosom" aside, this is a splendidly provocative and sympathetic story in which goodness triumphs in a manner as disarming as it is convincing. As with no other story by Hoffmann, one is left with a feeling that madness may not be the only answer to the world, that evil spirits can be exorcised by virtue. "Mademoiselle de Scudéri" suggests that the "power of blackness" may yet be overcome.

"Die Doppeltgänger" (**"The Doubles"**) is one of Hoffmann's final stories and was not published until the year of his death. Here again there are puppets; but, interestingly and crucially, they are not metaphors but exist within the reality of the story. Hoffmann not only conceives of his leading characters as puppets, but sees himself as their master, as perhaps the dark fate to which he so often alludes.

Thus, not only does George Haberland, a puppeteer, inject himself onto the stage, where he appears as a monstrous, grotesque, and disembodied head, but the puppets actually discuss him. Hoffmann, in the person of Haberland, is able to inject himself into the story by making his characters

motionless, by freezing them in the scene in the seventh chapter when the doubles confront each other: they "stopped in horror and remained rooted to the floor." Hoffmann goes back in time to supply the reader with what he considers necessary information, then suddenly releases his characters with a powerful "So!" The action then continues.

Nowhere else in Hoffmann do we so clearly see the arbitrariness of life. On the stage of life, action begins of stops according to the whim of some irrational power which controls us even as it mocks and is unresponsive to us. Man is seen as a manipulated puppet who dances to the pull of strings he neither sees nor can begin to understand.

This is not a supernatural story. Untypically, no battle rages for the very soul of man. The outside forces are mute. The doubles, the two young men who look alike, are not doubles in the sense that Ritter Gluck and the narrator of his story may be. They look alike because they were fathered by the same man at the same instant, one physically, the other spiritually. Further, their resemblance is only superficial, for they are different in taste and temperament and perception. One is truly a *Fürst* (prince), a man of affairs, a man of the world—hardly a desirable calling from Hoffmann's point of view. The other, more positively portrayed, is a maturing artist. Both carry in their imaginations the same dream of Natalie, a notion so horrifying to her that she commands them to renounce her and then retreats to a nunnery; and neither Schwendy, the true *Fürst*, nor Haberland, the true artist, finds this difficult to accept. The former will find happiness in reigning; the latter will find his inspiration in his art. Woman, Hoffmann seems to be saying, has no place in either life.

If the supernatural is absent from this story, the occult is not; for Hoffmann, as suggested by **"Rat Krespel"** and **"Mademoiselle de Scudéri,"** believed in prenatal influence, even to the extent that it would produce a child physically identical to one produced by means more traditional than spiritual love.

There is much about **"The Doubles"** which is humorous and satirical. The innkeepers are marvelously drawn as absurd men who spend much of their lives arguing and fighting, primarily because it has become a delightful habit which each finds indispensable. The world they inhabit is no less entertaining and comprehensible. They and their world serve as effective relief until the problem of the doubles is "solved." Typically in Hoffmann, it is the human quality of these men and their existence which give to the raven and all it represents a very special veneer of the mysterious and of potential horror.

The question of influence is rarely so clear and direct as it may seem; and one must be cautious, always aware that a host of circumstances and coincidences may conspire to make one author appear to be much indebted to another. Yet, this said, Hoffmann's strong historic importance seems very firmly established.

The artist in conflict with society, alienated man, the detective novel, the theme of split personality, the full exploitation of the subconscious and its striking manifestations,

---

Hoffmann's fictional world is incredibly rich; it is one in which anything can happen, where dream and reality, the conscious and the unconscious, the prosaic and the fantastic may occur simultaneously and reflect each other.

—*Leonard J. Kent and Elizabeth C. Knight*

---

the particular use of the fantastic and the grotesque, the use of automatons and puppets, a peculiar vision of a deterministic world, the detachment of the author—these are only some of the elements that can, at least partially, be traced back to Hoffmann.

Without going into a prolonged and unnecessarily detailed analysis, it should be noted that, outside of Germany, Hoffmann's influence on literature was most strongly felt in the United States, Russia, and France.

Irving, Hawthorne, and Poe were among those in America who were acquainted with his works (Irving had spent some time in Germany and knew the language; Hawthorne and Poe could, if necessary, have read Hoffmann in English, for translations of his stories were serialized in *Blackwoods* magazine as early as 1824). In Irving the influence seems essentially general, though specific legends used by Hoffmann can be identified. Hawthorne's use of the ancestral curse stems from Hoffmann's **"Das Majorat" ("The Legacy")**. Poe, in whom the Hoffmann influence seems pronounced, wrote a very good story, "William Wilson," which seems singularly indebted to Hoffmann's use of the double.

In Russia, Hoffmann seems to have had an all-pervasive influence and, by 1830, to have been the object of something like a "cult." Pushkin, Turgenev, Gogol, and Dostoevsky were among those who strongly admired him. In Dostoevsky this influence is most consistent and clear, especially in Dostoevsky's use of the subconscious. It is hardly surprising, therefore, that Dostoevsky, in a letter to a friend, wrote that he and a companion "talked of Homer, Shakespeare, Schiller, and Hoffmann—particularly Hoffmann."

In France, Hoffmann's fame was such that Sainte-Beuve, George Sand, and Baudelaire were among those who either directly or indirectly reflect something of Hoffmann's works or ideas. Interestingly, Hoffmann's influence in France seems to have diminished after 1855, at which time Baudelaire's translation of Poe appeared.

Hoffmann appears to have had less luck across the Channel, where Scott's essay "On the Supernatural in Fictitious Compositions and Particularly on the Works of E. T. A. Hoffmann" may have further poisoned a climate already somewhat hostile by creating the impression that Hoffmann was a superficial teller of gruesome tales; and despite the fact that Carlyle saw fit to translate Hoffmann's

"Der goldne Topf," a superb story, his introduction to it is rather condescending and less than enthusiastic. But "Teutonic romanticism" left its mark—on the Brontës, for example, and, in Scotland, on Robert Louis Stevenson, whose *Dr. Jekyll and Mr. Hyde* and *Markheim* are very Hoffmannesque.

In Germany, for many years following Hoffmann's death, the critical estimate of his work was hardly more positive than it was on the other side of the Channel. Goethe, for one, agreed with Scott and wrote that he had been saddened to see "that the morbid works of this sick man for many years had had an influence in Germany and [that] such aberrations have been inoculated upon healthy spirits as highly beneficial innovations." But the advantage of distance allows one to understand this. The pendulum of taste, always in movement, had already swung away from romanticism before Hoffmann's death; and some critics argue that in Germany Hoffmann and romanticism probably died simultaneously. At any rate, many of the literary works that immediately followed in Germany were imbued with a social and political consciousness that can perhaps be appreciated through this comment made in 1853, directed at the German romantics in general and at Hoffmann in particular: "One lived in an artist's world of dreams; one did not even read the newspaper." But this taste or course, would change too.

Ultimately, we think it is not pushing too hard to suggest that, specific influences aside, the whole literary world of psychological fiction owes Hoffmann an inestimable debt. Hoffmann shifted the scene of man's incessant conflict from the external world to the mind, where the struggle for identify and survival takes place on a level and with a consistency and intensity absent from earlier literature, and where its significance is greatly increased. There is no question but that Hoffmann anticipated much of what psychologists were later to uncover. Hoffmann seems to have been aware of organic and functional psychoses long before modern science defined them and twentieth-century literature exploited them; but, of course, his interest was primarily esthetic and not scientific.

Hoffmann had a divided allegiance. On the one hand, his pursuit of the irrational and the mysterious, his preference for the enigma rather than the solution, suggests that he was a true romantic; but there is more than a hint that he was not unaffected by the Enlightenment, for the seemingly miraculous is sometimes explained—on one occasion, much to the chagrin of Kapellmeister Kreisler in *Kater Murr*, who is peeved at Abraham for a rational explanation of what he preferred to think of as supernatural. The occult attracted the romantic Hoffmann because it satisfied him emotionally and because it enabled him to exercise his imagination to the limits of its potential, thus exorcising the detestable world of the philistine. For Hoffmann, the occult and the fantastic seem to have meant nothing less than the ultimate emancipation from mediocrity, from what he called "too much reality."

Hoffmann's fictional world is incredibly rich; it is one in which anything can happen, where dream and reality, the conscious and the unconscious, the prosaic and the fantastic may occur simultaneously and reflect each other. It is a world where the virtuous and the criminal, the mediocre and the brilliant, the charlatan and the scientist, the merchant and the artisan, the philistine and the artist all live, sometimes in a single body. It may be a sinister and terrorizing world, but it is often one that is animated by brilliant humor and satire too.

Above all, Hoffmann's fictional world is worth knowing because in it is to be found his complex vision of humanity, of man engaged in an archetypal struggle to establish identity in a hostile, absurd, and remarkably modern world. (pp. xxvii-xxxix)

> *Leonard J. Kent and Elizabeth C. Knight, in an introduction to* Tales of E. T. A. Hoffmann, *edited and translated by Leonard J. Kent and Elizabeth C. Knight, The University of Chicago Press, 1972, pp. ix-xxxix.*

Horst S. Daemmrich   (essay date 1973)

[*In the following excerpt, Daemmrich argues that Hoffmann's stories ultimately convey a pessimistic vision which gives them a strong affinity with twentieth-century literature.*]

[The major themes and motifs in Hoffmann's work] form a dynamic structural pattern which constitutes the basis for a grand design of man in search for identity. In his design Hoffmann captured the struggle between man's yearning for self-transcendence and the will to self-assertion as well as the clash between visions of beauty and the atavistic forces of evil. By identifying the feeling of fear with man's existence and the image of the cage with the structure of the world, Hoffmann portrayed the disintegration of the individual in a world of uncontrolled forces. The grand design is of singular importance because it embraces Hoffmann's literary work as a whole and sheds light upon the aesthetic structure of his narratives. The originality of the conception demanded a new artistic technique and a total transformation of old values. Hoffmann recognized the problem and looked into the chaos. But it was left to philosophers to continue his thinking and to modern existentialism to search for a completely new basis for man's existence. (pp. 9-10)

No judgment of Hoffmann's achievement seems possible without considering the existential situation of his heroes. The most persistent view expressed by scholars rests precariously upon the tenet that Hoffmann's fictional characters yearn for a spiritual harmony which can be attained only in an ethereal realm of beauty and truth. The energy which sustains them springs from the unwavering faith in this ideal. Their mode of existence is judged as a relentless struggle in which they seek to free themselves from the wheel of life. Consequently, critics have not only underscored the inevitably dualistic world view of the protagonists in Hoffmann's narrations but have also distinguished between their momentary tragedy and their eventual salvation. This assessment has a seductive charm, because it is essentially optimistic in emphasizing the vision of a cosmic harmony which consoles man for the ordeals of life and promises to redeem him.

But does not this optimism, largely derived from interpretations of **"The Golden Pot"** [**"Der goldne Topf"**, 1814] and those fairy tales in which Hoffmann seems to resolve metaphysical contradictions in a myth of transcendence, overlook the profound pessimism pervading most of his works? Do not his transcendental speculations indicate also a disturbing awareness of man's ontological insecurity? Is it not true that Hoffmann's heroes are destined to live in a threatening world even though they may dimly perceive or even experience in a clairvoyant moment a universal harmony? (pp. 22-3)

The reader who looks for a sublimation of life in Hoffmann's works will instead frequently find the exposition of evil, an affinity for death and self-destruction, the projection of semi-consciousness, primitive emotions, and the tyranny of fear and anxiety. Not surprisingly, scholars who recognized that the literature of romanticism tended not only toward transcendental speculation but also toward pessimism, nihilism, and a "myth of evil" have always pointed to Bonaventura, Jean Paul, and Hoffmann as authors who succeeded best in capturing the spirit of negation and evil. The cipher of an inexplicable fate was interpreted as the expression of man's inability to master forces in life which were apparently beyond his control, and alter ego projections were regarded as the first indication of the modern crisis in man's identity. Yet, as long as the view persists that two distinct spheres, reality and a transcendental realm, clash in Hoffmann's writings, the basic structure and the intent of his work will be misunderstood.

Indeed, the contrast between sublime vision and primeval fear, reinforced by the themes of self-transcendence and self-realization, forms an essential part of a grand design. Against the background of an apparently stable bourgeois society Hoffmann paints a picture of man trapped in a cage from which he tries in vain to break out. Primitive instincts that previously seemed tamed suddenly overwhelm individuals, and demonic, unexplainable forces seem to rule the lives of persons who are caught in a deep identity crisis. Included in the design are metaphors which seem to rise straight out of the darkness of the unconscious alter ego projections, such as the motif of drinking blood, pictures of incest, murder, and human sacrifice, and the preference for masks noticeable in the frozen eerie smile of many characters.

Admittedly, it is more rewarding for the humanistic scholar to point to revelations of beauty and goodness than to those of ugliness and evil. Yet, to do justice to Hoffmann's works one must observe the prevailing ideological and structural tension between self-transcendence in a sublime vision of cosmic consciousness and self-realization in a harsh adverse world. . . . [In Hoffmann's grand design there is a] basic clash between the yearning for innocence and the intense fascination with evil and destruction. . . . [The] grand design of man's existential plight structurally unifies Hoffmann's writings. Its basic features include vistas of beauty and of nature animated by friendly spirits together with visions of horror and a demonic world. It reveals a part of man's nature which we prefer to overlook: the ruthless assertion of the will, the desire to inflict pain, and the lust for destruction. With his design of the tortured self Hoffmann broke with the conventions of his day and anticipated a major concern of modern existential literature. (pp. 22-4)

In the tales **"Automata"** [**"Die Automate,"** 1814], **"Ignaz Denner"** (1816), **"The Vow"** [**"Das Gelübde,"** 1817], **"The Mines of Falun"** [**"Die Bergwerke zu Falun,"** 1819], and **"Mademoiselle de Scudery"** [**"Das Fräulein von Scuderi,"** 1820] . . . Hoffmann probes into the dark forces confronting man from within, portrays the profound discord of fallen man, and explores the psychology of evil. (p. 73)

What fascinates Hoffmann is the ugliness of a world which has rejected all ethical norms as well as man's deep seated fears, his thoughts, drives, and the desires which are repressed by civilized society. The will to portray man's unconscious motivations and thoughts manifests itself in several stylistic features such as a stream of consciousness technique which records thoughts, dreams, and the perception of real occurrences without distinction. The description of reality becomes less precise and charged with emotional qualities. Repeatedly used linguistic clichés point not only to a devaluation of reality but also to some of the characters' stereotyped barren conceptions of the

Drawing by Hoffmann.

world. Different levels of awareness are mirrored in different experiences of time; for instance, while the monk Medardus [in *The Devil's Elixirs (Die Elixiere des Teufels,* 1815/16)] suffers in a preconscious, sometimes insane condition, his world, like that of Benjy in Faulkner's *The Sound and the Fury*, becomes timeless. Past and present occurrences fuse into an eternal now. When he seems conscious, his perception of time corresponds to the imaginary course of events. Ideas and thoughts assume representational shapes in alter ego projections, in figures stepping out of paintings, and in concrete descriptions of martyr scenes or the loss of one's shadow. But above all Hoffmann succeeds in symbolizing man's terror in scenes of sudden arrest or torture, scenes in which children are stabbed, the bones of victims crushed, their flesh torn, and in which the pain becomes unendurable. The stories that convey to the reader an intensified perception of man's unconscious form part of a development in literature which began with romanticism and is still in process, a development in which man's unconscious, psychological processes, his primitive instincts, and every thought no matter how trite or ridiculous become subjects for artistic representation. Whether Hoffmann felt that such art would free man and increase his consciousness of himself or limit his vision cannot be ascertained. The "psychological narrations" give the impression of an absurd rather than a tragic view of existence, because the characters either passively await their fate or suffer a senseless, arbitrary doom.

"Automata" contains the most detailed discussion and explicit rejection of machines and marionettes. In contrast to Kleist, Hoffmann sees no gracefulness in any life imitating mechanism. To him machines lack soul and will. Since their actions are completely predetermined, Hoffmann employs mechanical figures to symbolize a life which is manipulated by forces beyond human control. "I could imagine that it might be possible to enable figures to dance quite graciously by means of a secret mechanism within them. They also should dance with people and execute difficult movements so that a live dancer holds a wooden lady and swings with her back and forth. Could you watch this for one minute without horror?" Hoffmann singles out intricate musical machines for his most vitriolic attack, whereas he seems rather intrigued by the possibility of electronic music. The events and the theoretical discussions prompted by such mechanisms show how he abhors and yet is strangely fascinated by a human existence of passive acquiescence to fate.

In the story Hoffmann interweaves a dream sequence with the rational debates of two friends. Swept along with everyone else in the city, Ludwig and Ferdinand go to see a machine which mysteriously seems capable not only of answering the most difficult questions but also of predicting the future. It seems as if "young and old, rich and poor" throng to the oracle because they lack inner security and look for support in the machine's mysterious and alarming revelations, the truth of which is half-hidden, half-revealed. When Ferdinand fearfully and hesitantly approaches the machine and inquires whether he will ever see his beloved again, he hears that he will lose her. Wounded to the core, he tries to decipher the meaning of the ominous prediction. All efforts to find an answer to the riddle in the intricate mechanism of the machine have to be abandoned. Even the suggestion that it might be manipulated by a person possessing extrasensory powers proves erroneous.

The reader slowly becomes aware that Ferdinand is looking for an answer which is deeply embedded within himself. He has encountered the woman he loves only once in a dream vision and then painted an idealized miniature portrait of her that he carries on an amulet around his neck. To him the picture has become a symbol of inspiration; to find the girl in the actual world would mean to lose an essential part of himself; therefore he fears such an encounter and is ultimately relieved when he realizes the nature of his ideal. That the machine only echoes man's secret hopes and fears, that the whisper of the automaton is in fact the voice of the questioner's own unconscious finally begins to dawn upon Ludwig after his friend's deeply disturbing experience.

Fragmented pieces of observation, projections of unconscious fears, dreams, and conscious reflections blend into a dynamic sequence of events in **"A New Year's Eve Adventure"** [**"Die Abenteuer der Sylvester-Nacht,"** 1815]. In this story Hoffmann warns his readers, moreover, that the narrator-protagonist cannot cut the web spun by his unconscious and does not distinguish between actual and imaginary events. Haunted by the fear of being alone, by memories of lost happiness, and by the recognition of his mortality, the narrator rushes through the streets. As he hastens from party to winecellar and from there to a hotel room, momentary impressions call forth associations in his mind. Inspired by a painting of temptation or a vision of his ideal, he first experiences moments of bliss with his "love" Julie. The dreamlike quality of the encounter is several times briefly disrupted by her glance which frightens, almost terrorizes him. Suddenly music—he holds her hand—he knows for his good she must stay, for she alone inspires his creativity—her husband calls—and a strange woman leaves him. He rages on, descends into the winecellar, and is inspired by literary motifs. Soon he converses with Peter Schlemihl whom he has never "seen but frequently imagined" and with a stranger who has lost his mirror-image.

The three recognize their disharmony, suffering, and finally each other: the narrator who sacrificed his self, Schlemihl who lost his shadow, and Erasmus Spikher who gave away his image. Soon fear disrupts their conversation. Again the narrator hurries away, takes a hotel room where he meets Spikher in bed, has visions of him writing, and then either imagines or consciously recognizes that everything he has seen was a beautiful arrangement of candy figures in a window. When he awakens he finds a manuscript which purports to explain the disaster that befell Spikher, but which really mirrors his own fate, giving the reader a renewed insight into the protagonist's shattered self. In the account, "The Story of the Lost Reflection," Spikher travels to Italy, meets Giulietta, an angelic woman, and is overpowered by the feeling that she is the incarnation of his yearning for beauty. Seized by an insane passion for her and willing to risk his soul, he is confronted by visions of evil. Satan offers help. Spikher murders

an admirer of Giulietta and, forced to flee, cannot tear himself away from her until he has left his image in her arms. Later he is terror-stricken by the idea that his loss will be discovered and tempted to murder wife and child for Giulietta. The visions disappear when he finally conquers his lust.

Spikher's emotions, excesses, and suffering parallel those of the narrator. Indeed Spikher's exclamation upon first seeing Giulietta characterizes the emotions of both: "Yes, it is *you*, I have always loved *you*, *you* angel! I have seen you in my dreams, *you* are my happiness, my salvation, my ideal!" As a result of their love, their "shimmering dream-ego" becomes independent and they experience a loss of an essential part of the self. To view the resulting identity crisis only in the light of Spikher's fate would be misleading. He sacrificed himself to a phantom without experiencing a truly redeeming love. The narrator offers himself to a vision of beauty which continues to inspire him and to give him a ray of hope in the darkness of his turmoil.

The compulsion which endangers the free development of man's potential assumes demonic proportions in **"The Primogeniture"** [**"Das Majorat,"** 1817], **"The Vow,"** and **"The Mines of Falun."** In **"The Primogeniture"** Hoffmann presents two distinct actions: the events experienced by Theodor, the narrator, and the chronicle of Count Roderich's family which Theodor's great-uncle relates to him. Aside from the external connection which is established when Theodor falls in love with the countess, the two stories have the same focal point in the thematic juxtaposition of enslavement versus self-determination. The question raised is whether man is completely in the hands of demonic forces or capable of making just and right decisions. Several events, such as the tragedy which befalls the family, the death of Seraphine, and Theodor's love which almost leads to a catastrophe, would support the view that an inscrutable power rules man's destiny. The great-uncle, a powerful figure who counsels the members of the family and actually saves Theodor, concludes upon contemplating the destruction of the people he served so well that the mystery remains unsolved: "It is the essential point that I cannot explain, that no one can express." The family chronicle, however, proves to be an extensive account of man's weakness, of hate and primitive passion. Hoffmann's characterization of the old count and his two sons is certainly not designed to awaken the reader's compassion. Their failure in life springs from their own obsessions and evil deeds which reach a climax when Hubert conspires with the old servant Daniel to kill his brother. The final chapter in the chronicle is written when Roderich, the last heir of the estate, and his wife Seraphine meet Theodor.

In contrast to their ancestors, Roderich and Seraphine are depicted as noble characters who suffer a fate which they cannot understand. They fear the past and the atmosphere of the castle in which the crime has been committed. As soon as Theodor arrives he too is strangely affected by the surroundings. As he reads Schiller's "Geisterseher" that night, he suddenly feels a ghost moving through the room. The scratching sounds, the steps, and the breeze cannot simply be attributed to his vivid imagination, for his great uncle not only believes his story but also succeeds the following night in banning the ghost of Daniel, who had killed his master and later died of shock in that room. However superior the reader may feel to the experience, it enables him to participate in the fictional events and, above all, to comprehend Hoffmann's intention. For the ghost, both real and imagined, assumes fateful proportions in Seraphine's fantasy. Her fear reminds Roderich of the past and the unresolved question whether he is morally responsible for Daniel's death, despite the fact that the man had been a murderer.

The final disaster occurs when Seraphine is killed in an accident. The picture of the sled pulled by the shying horses conveys the impression of speeding life which flings Seraphine out of the cage into the bright open field. Her cry, "The old man—the old man is chasing us," and the great-uncle's remark, "Evil fate, an awesome power, has reached even her, the lovely lady" would indicate that she was trapped. How ardently she desired to break out of her castle-prison becomes most evident in the brief moments of joy she experienced with Theodor. Sensitive, interested in poetry and music, an accomplished singer and pianist, he has fallen in love with her. But his romantic, "knightly love" soon becomes a compulsion. She responds to his yearning; while he plays the piano and she sings, a vision of beauty opens before her eyes. One evening she confides to him her fears of the curse that seems to hang over her life. By relating his own experience and by softly playing a canzone of St. Steffani, Theodor conveys to her the feeling of freedom. The evening ends with a scene in which reality and imagination blend into a vision of love: "How did it happen that I knelt before her, that she yielded to me and while I embraced her a long, radiant kiss burned my lips?" Yet fear and intoxication prove more powerful than the aesthetic love experience. She begins to be haunted by the vision of Daniel, perhaps an indication of her guilt feeling. Theodor, driven to the brink of madness, rages in the forest. He escapes disaster when his great-uncle, realizing the danger, departs with him the next morning. Though we are encouraged by the great-uncle's decisive action and the recognition that the old count, his sons, and Daniel were responsible for their misfortunes, we suffer with Seraphine and Roderich. They face an incomprehensible world and gripped by an apparently implacable fate seek in vain to fulfill themselves.

A study of the structure of the narrative, the major motif and themes, discloses that in this tale Hoffmann uses the traditional elements of the fairy tale but in an inverted form. He obfuscates the stark contrast and separation between good and evil. Instead of the anticipation of a happy ending he arouses a feeling of impending disaster. The motif of Prince Charming who comes to awaken Sleeping Beauty is transformed: Theodor cannot free Seraphine but intensifies her fear instead. Finally, the theme of liberation is reversed to one of enslavement. Thus Hoffmann has actually created the "infernal fairy tale" which deals with man's existential anguish and the suffering of those who face a wretched, absurd world. (pp. 74-81)

The themes of love and destruction as well as the image

of the cage recur in **"The Vow."** The story has invited comparisons with Kleist's "Die Marquise von O. . . ." and has been judged as inferior. Despite the many parallels a comparison is not revealing, because the two works differ in basic conception. Kleist's heroine rises above the events that seem to destroy her and thus masters her destiny. Hoffmann's heroine is totally shattered and destroyed by the incongruity between her vision and reality. The plot is stark and clear: after the insurrection following the first partition of Poland, Stanislaus, a freedom fighter, returns to the girl he plans to marry. Hermenegilda, a girl of great beauty and intellect who is impulsive to the point of being irrational, rejects him because he and his friends did not succeed in liberating Poland. After he has left, she deeply regrets her action and her yearning for him soon becomes obsessive. At this moment a younger cousin of Stanislaus arrives. Their resemblance is so startling that Hermenegilda mistakes him for Stanislaus. Affected by her feelings, Xaver develops a love for her which becomes an insane passion. One evening, while she envisions being married to her faraway friend, Xaver takes advantage of her. She becomes pregnant, still convinced that she had been with Stanislaus. Xaver explains his deception, offers his love, and begs her to marry him, but the truth completely shatters her confidence in man. "She leaped up with a heart-rending cry, a cry no longer human but resembling the piercing wail of a wild animal and while her body writhed in agony, stared at the count with blazing eyes."

She renounces the world and secludes herself in a room resembling a cell to give birth to a child. As if she had not suffered enough, Xaver returns after the child is born and in a singularly horrifying confrontation tears the boy from his mother's arms. In the ensuing struggle Xaver rips the veil from Hermenegilde's face and looks at a white mask. The scene clearly reveals the poet's intentions. Hermenegilda, through her vow never to show her face again, has actually become a symbol for Everyman and her cries of pain reflect the suffering of man. Though she had originally become a victim of her own emotion, the outrageous betrayal gives universal significance to her despair. Again the story focuses on the by now familiar themes and motifs, but is unsurpassed as a stark picture of betrayal.

In the representation of compulsion, however, Hoffmann succeeds far better in **"The Mines of Falun."** Like many of his narrations this story can be interpreted as portraying a central conflict between man's demonic vision and reality. According to this view the hero Elis Fröbom is driven into a mine by the romantic yearning to discover the mystery of earth only to find death on his wedding day. But **"The Mines of Falun,"** like most of the narratives considered so far, can be read on more than one level. Structurally, it is once again an infernal fairy tale: Hoffmann inverts the motif of the young hero who climbs to the top of a mountain of glass, gains his princess, and lives happily ever after. In Hoffmann's version, the hero descends to the core of the mountain in search of the secret of life, the mysterious red almandine, but discovers the ultimate truth—death. Indeed, the themes of love and compulsion, self-realization and captivity are woven into a symbolic narration of man's confrontation with death on his journey into his unconscious. (pp. 81-3)

René Cardillac is the most memorable and, judging by the critical attention he has received, one of the most complex characters created by Hoffmann. Many interpretations of "Mademoiselle de Scudéry" have focused on Cardillac as a type of demonic artist. Hoffmann's characterization of other artists lends little credence to this view, however. Indeed, the only artists to whom meaningful parallels can be established are Klingsohr and Heinrich (**"The Contest of the Minstrels,"** [**"Der Kampf der Sänger,"** 1819]) and the stranger (**"Kreisler's Certificate"**). The reader who is not familiar with the subtleties of criticism concerning the nature of the artist will more likely be reminded of a fairy-tale figure: the evil dwarf who hordes a treasure and destroys everyone who comes to take it. The almost mythic stature of Cardillac derives from his demonic obsession and the fact that he becomes a visible figure for all the evil that has been cancerously spreading through society. For this reason Hoffmann captures in great detail not only the atmosphere that breeds a succession of crimes but also the fear of a court that condemns as many innocent as guilty persons.

But while the action revolves around the sustained concealment and final disclosure of Cardillac's crimes, each stage adds importance to Olivier Brusson's fate and the question whether Madeleine de Scudéry, who holds the key to Olivier's release, can save him. The poetess also introduces to the narrative the major theme of unselfish love. Pressured to establish a new court with extraordinary powers to search for the criminals who have robbed and murdered lovers on their way to a rendezvous, the king turns to Madeleine de Scudéry for advice. Though Hoffmann does not state the fact, she replies in the spirit of gallantry and idealized love expressed in her novels. Her reply that "a lover who fears thieves is not worthy of love" has the following consequences: it induces Cardillac to send her his most precious jewels, an act which strains his will power to overcome his compulsion to the breaking point; Olivier's fear that Cardillac will kill the poetess forces him to warn her; the poetess who has looked at the world with great serenity is shocked into awareness of the dark forces in man and is confronted with a heroic love which seems to surpass her imagination.

Contrasted and interwoven with the theme of love is that of compulsion which harms not only those possessed by it but also those confronted with it. Hoffmann introduces the theme when he depicts the fear which seized Paris when first Captain de Sainte Croix and the Marquise de Brinvillier, later la Voisin and others, turn to poisoning their victims out of sheer pleasure after they have killed for profit. Cardillac's compulsion, in contrast, provides him little joy. Characterized as the unfree man *kat-exochen*, he has become totally enslaved to his obsession for which he holds a malevolent fate responsible. By giving an explanation which seems rational to Cardillac but superstitious to the reader, Hoffmann accentuates the man's weakness and inability to free himself from his demon. After the first murder he feels peace for the first time in his life. "The specter had disappeared, the voice of Satan was silent. Now I knew the intentions of my evil star; I had to obey or perish!" To be sure, Cardillac does not blindly follow his drive. Fully aware that his demon will force him

to seize the jewelry from the poor victim, he struggles, refuses to deliver it, even declines to work for people he respects. Nevertheless, by consciously designating some to be murdered and others to be robbed, he proclaims himself master over life and death. Since he has no philosophical basis for his action, he fails to achieve Alban's amoral independence. Though Cardillac never regrets his crimes, he has moments of fear for his soul. In such a mood and prompted by Scudéry's verse, he decides to give her the jewels. By giving this present to a lady known for her virtue and piety he hopes to find a spokesman for his soul. But his compulsion soon proves the stronger. Raging against himself and Madeleine de Scudéry, he gives in to his demon and finds his own death while attacking a new victim.

The person with whom we identify, whose struggle arouses our pity, and whom we would like to see pardoned, if not legally at least in the spirit of compassion and forgiveness, is Olivier Brusson. From the tale's beginning, he suffers serious misfortunes. Basically good, he is forced into an insoluble dilemma by his conviction that the disclosure of Cardillac's crimes will destroy Madelon's faith in mankind, by the fact that the administration of justice has been undermined in the state, and by his unfailing love for Cardillac's daughter. "Trapped in this labyrinth of crime, torn by love and revulsion, by joy and horror, I was like the condemned soul, beckoned by a beautiful, softly smiling angel but held fast by Satan's burning claws, and the holy angel's loving smile that reflects all the bliss of heaven becomes the most agonizing pain. I thought of flight, even of suicide—but Madelon!" Olivier's inner torment certainly equals, perhaps even surpasses, Cardillac's. Every crime committed by Cardillac flings him deeper into a hell of self-accusation and intensifies his suffering. He sees no solution until he puts his fate into the hands of Madeleine de Scudéry. Fully conscious of the disasters wreaked by his silence, he is willing to accept any punishment but, all-too-humanly, hopes for a miracle.

His anguish reaches a climax when he loses the good will of the poetess. Henceforth his actions are dictated solely by the attempt to convince her that he was a victim both innocent and guilty but not a murderer. As the scene with La Regnie shows, she cannot succeed in freeing Olivier as long as she views the world in the light of her own artistic creations. And she cannot help him after her faith in man has been destroyed: "Never before in her life deceived so bitterly by her emotions, mortally wounded by the hellish power on earth in whose existence she had never believed, Madeleine de Scudéry despaired of all truth." Only after the poetess finally comprehends Olivier's ordeal does she have the power to save him. For through his story she begins to see that while there is room for the high ideals she envisioned, the world contains more evil, human suffering, and ambiguities than she imagined. This awareness is critical for Olivier's rescue since only the full force of her conviction can move the king's heart. By presenting the monarch with a vivid tableau of the events in the form of a work of art that sways him through its poetic truth, she is able to capture his attention and avert disaster for Olivier. The scene and the tale's happy ending for the two lovers seem to contain a promise that there is hope almost beyond hope for the victims of life. (pp. 87-91)

Each age, we are told, rewrites the literature of the past in its own image. E.T.A. Hoffmann, as he appears in my appraisal, seems to reflect modern distinctions and preferences. . . . Perhaps he seems very modern to us only because his deep concern with the quest for self-realization is as timeless as his account of the internal tensions and external conflicts besetting man. His view of the world lacks all shallow optimism. Atlantis beckons, but it seems to be the desperate cry of a tormented artist who knows that the infernal cage exists here and now. Even the dreams of fairyland prove to be illusions because the beautiful glitter cannot hide the anguish of its people. And while lonely artists battle a soulless, dehumanized world, Hoffmann seriously questions the mission of art and the artist in *Nutcracker and the King of Mice.* Not surprisingly, the themes of self-assertion and negation, love and compulsion, angelic and satanic vision, freedom and enslavement and the motifs of the cage, the consuming circle, and the shattered self form the basic constellation of his design.

Though many struggle almost beyond endurance for self-realization, they discover that their road leads into a confining circle which they can transcend only in dreams or death. . . . Hoffmann presents a picture of man in the process of development whose struggle for self-knowledge is played out against the background of a gigantic dance of masks and shattered selves who are convinced that an "unknown, sinister fate" has bound them to the wheel. While some risk their souls to free themselves and others follow their compulsion, while true heroes struggle in tragic isolation and unsung victims of evil are destroyed in an incomprehensible world, the modern anti-hero has already entered the stage. Caged, torn in inner conflict, isolated, schizophrenic, absurd, and utterly fantastic, he tumbles from cell to cell or ends his life in a hallucinatory nightmare. (pp. 117-18)

> *Horst S. Daemmrich, in his* The Shattered Self: E. T. A. Hoffmann's Tragic Vision, *Wayne State University Press, 1973, 141 p.*

A. Leslie Willson   (essay date 1977)

[*Willson is an American educator and author. In the following essay, which is a revised and enlarged version of an essay originally presented at a conference on literature and the occult in April 1975, he explores the role of the occult in Hoffmann's short fiction.*]

The piercing and melodic sound of a voice like a singing crystal goblet, the susurrus of wind caressing the grasses (or was that the slither of an enormous snake?), the steady, solemn, and inevitable tolling of a clock at midnight that evokes the constancy of time and the omnipresence of death and the spirits that hearken to the summons of the powers of darkness, the sudden flash of cognition that permeates the race of man and calls up scenes from an immemorial past, the aura of a presence from the nether world of darkness that prickles the spine—these attest to a faculty of man that lies mostly dormant and unused; these phe-

nomena of the here-and-now animate man's awareness of the there-and-then, whether reaching into the past or projected into the future.

Magic is deeply entrenched in the heart and mind of man—from the sympathetic antics of the stone-age shaman, who was a storyteller too, to the spoon-bending exertions of the mind of a contemporary initiate into powers that lie mostly untapped in the reservoir of the human spirit. That which lies hidden and latent in the sources of the soul seems to rise most readily at the call of the imaginative writer whose power of will may be greater than his affirmation of reality, so that when his perception—which is an intentional act, whether the mind realizes it or not—of the unknown reaches into another realm of being, he may himself become ambivalent about what he is able to evoke.

When he was a boy E.T.A. Hoffmann played at magic with his friend Theodor Hippel; and as an adult Hoffmann occasionally awakened an unsympathetic wife from her sound sleep because the creations of his own mind frightened him so that he required the company of a more mundane intelligence. From his boyhood prestidigitations on the edge of the arcane to his adult absorption with the profounder aspects of the esoteric, Hoffmann never lost contact with the nightside of nature and the precipitous depth of the subconscious.

The age in which Hoffmann lived was fascinated with the inventive folk mind, with the supernatural, with superstition, with witchcraft, with the new science that had grown out of alchemy, with the phenomena of dream and of hypnotism, with the uncanny performance of automatons, and with the modes of divination that reached back into antiquity. Other authors of the age—Schiller, Novalis, Goethe, Kleist, Eichendorff, Fouqué, Chamisso—joined hosts of others from former ages to evoke experiences of man that seem beyond the pale of rational explanation. Hoffmann's particular contribution to this tradition is no secret: he mixed the world of the dark occult with the world of glaring day, and though he was skeptical he could nonetheless state that the age of the miraculous and marvelous continued to hold sway over the affairs of men.

In some of Hoffmann's tales the skeptic and the disbeliever is hence fair game for the adept in arcane mysteries. In **"Die Automate"** the whole town is atwitter about the Talking Turk, an automation that answers any question put to him. The clicking wheels and rasping levers amply testify to the artful construction of the figure, but the source of the multi-lingual voice and the secret of the Turk's ability to penetrate into the mind of the questioner remains a mystery. Ferdinand, a skeptic, who with his friend Ludwig tests the Turk's divinatory talent, is profoundly struck with the ability of the automaton. He speaks of forces that dominate the thoughts of man through magical powers, that can divine in the thoughts of man the germ of future events.

Ferdinand's question to the Turk is of so personal and private a nature that no trick of the automaton's maker could have divined an answer: he had asked about a delectable singer whom he had met in a dream—the customary astral emanation—but whom he had then seen in person. His question to the Turk had been: "Werde ich künftig noch einen Moment erleben, der dem gleicht, wo ich am glücklichsten war?" The Turk had answered: "Unglücklicher! In dem Augenblick, wenn du sie wieder siehst, hast du sie verloren!" Though he is shaken by the automaton's answer, Ferdinand resists the explanation of his friend Ludwig, who truly believes in some penetrating power, though not in the precise power of the Turk himself. He believes that the operator of the automaton is able to set up a psychic communication with the questioner, so that he who asks the question reveals the answer himself through some alien principle of thought transference.

Ferdinand is willing to accept the explanation of his friend, but the song of his dream-beloved that sounded at the instant he asked the question remains inexplicable. He cannot expunge from his heart the conviction that the prediction of the Turk will come true—as it does when he happens upon a chapel wedding and sees the woman of his dream before the altar. Upon noticing him, she faints; but despite the evident fulfillment of the prophecy, Ferdinand claims that the Turk was wrong, since the image of his beloved remains inviolable in his heart. Ludwig, who knows that the bridegroom had not journeyed to the chapel, recognizes the shattered psychological state of his friend but believes the Turk's prediction avoided a more tragic consequence for Ferdinand.

"Die Automate" dwells on the marvel of automatons and the mystery of prognostication and of powers that penetrate the secret thoughts of men; but in **"Der Sandmann"** an automaton's influence is horrifying and tragic. Nathanael is the victim of a horrible sequence of events that stretches from his childhood to his suicidal leap from a town hall tower. The malevolent twelfth hour makes its force felt at once in the story, whether it be at midnight or at midday: it is at high noon that a knock on Nathanael's door reveals a peddler of barometers whose scruffy exterior reminds him of a horrifying childhood experience.

On certain evenings, at nine o'clock—a significant though unorthodox hour is several of Hoffmann's tales—Nathanael's mother had hurried the children to bed, and they had scurried to avoid the advent of the dreaded Sandman, who stole children's eyes and carried them off to the moon. No sooner had the children fled to their beds than Nathanael heard heavy, thumping steps climb the stairs and the door to his father's study flung open loudly. The boy's fantasy, drawn already to kobolds, witches, and sprites, centers on the Sandman, whose curious and repulsive shape he sketches on tables, cupboards, and walls with chalk and charcoal.

Moved by insuperable curiosity, despite his fright, Nathanael peeps out one evening at the Sandman and discovers to his astonishment that the dreaded monster is none other than the lawyer Coppelius, a strong-willed family friend. Subsequently the boy flees his hiding place in his father's study, from which he has been watching the eerie alchemistic experiment of their search for the elusive alkahest, only to hear Coppelius cry out: "Augen her, Augen her!" The boy's fright is compounded by the taunts and threats of Coppelius about children's eyes and the articulation of limbs. When not long afterwards an explosion destroys the study and kills the boy's father, Coppelius vanishes from the town. Now Nathanael has presentiments of doom when he recognizes the visage of Coppelius in the face of the barometer peddler.

Up to this point in the story Hoffmann has made use of a variety of occult paraphernalia: creatures that inhabit childhood terror, utensils and practices of alchemy, and the presentiments of doom evoked by a burning stare in a satanic face. Nathanael's friend Clara, who innocently intercepts his letter to her brother Lothar, tries to reassure him that he is himself the source of his fear: "Es ist das Phantom unseres eigenen Ichs," she writes. Nathanael holds Coppelius to have been the essence of evil, but Clara insists that can be so only if he believes it: "Nur dein Glaube ist seine Macht." Nathanael writes a love poem for Clara, but it turns into a terrible vision in which at the end Death stares at him amicably through Clara's eyes. Her consternation at the poem results in his thrusting her away with the epithet: "Du lebloses, verdammtes Automat!"

Lothar writes Nathanael about Olimpia, the lovely daughter of Professor Spalanzani, whose beauty is uncanny in part because her eyes seem blind, as though she were sleeping wide-eyed. When Nathanael's apartment burns down, he moves into one located adjacent to the house of Professor Spalanzani and the stage is set for disaster. A soft knock at his door brings the peddler Coppola again, who denies he wants to sell a barometer but rather "schöne Oke"—that is, "schöne Augen," which turn out to be eye glasses. Coppola—whose very name means "eye" (*coppo*) in Italian—transfixes Nathanael with an array of flashing, glittering eyepieces, and to be rid of this double of the detested Coppelius, Nathanael buys a spyglass. He had been enchanted, that is, mesmerized, by the glittering eyepieces; and quite in the tradition of geloscopy, the divination of the future through laughter, he is not encouraged by the loud cackle of the departing Coppola.

Though he reflects that Clara would consider him a tasteless voyeur, he is driven by an irresistible urge to look at the house adjacent, where he observes Olimpia through the spyglass. Her figure seems strangely bent and angular, and her eyes are sightless, but his rapture is uncontrollable. Spalanzani gives a ball, and Nathanael attends and gravitates immediately to Olimpia, whose cold hands seem to pulse with warmth as he holds them, who answers his chatter monosyllabically with, "Ach, ach," and whose lips are ice cold. Though she seems stiff and soulless, as though she moved because she had been wound up, and though she sings at a mechanical tempo, he cannot restrain his adoration of her. When sometime later he hears the sounds of a struggle in Spalanzani's study and discerns Coppelius's voice, he rushes to intervene and sees the two men struggling over Olimpia, who is tossed and brandished by Coppola-Coppelius before he runs away with her dangling from his arms. Nathanael sees her empty eye sockets and realizes she was a life-sized puppet. When Spalanzani flings her eyes at him, he loses his senses, throws himself on the professor, and is dragged away to an insane asylum.

Nathanael begins to doubt the reality of the human figure, but soon he seems to regain his right mind under the care of Lothar and Clara. On an excursion he and Clara climb the town hall tower and from that lofty edifice look over the town. He peers down through his spyglass and is seized again by his madness, shouting "Püppchen dreh dich, Püppchen dreh dich," whereupon he seizes Clara and tries to throw her over the parapet. Lothar rescues his sister, and Nathanael takes up the insane cry he had uttered in Spalanzani's study: "Feuerkreis dreh dich." Down below in the stunned crowd Coppelius says: "Wartet nur, der kommt schon herunter von selbst," and with the cry "Sköne Oke" Nathanael jumps over the parapet and falls to his death. Coppelius disappears into the throng.

"Der Sandmann" is a tragic tale of a youth who falls victim to a necromancer with mesmeric powers, but the later story "Der Elementargeist" involves a human protagonist in a struggle with minions of the Devil and with elementary spirits, particularly with a hellish Irish major and with a combination succubus-salamander. Viktor is led by the powers of darkness to a confrontation with the succubus that the major had invoked for him—though she now is a fat, absurdly inappropriate baroness. Told to his friend Albert in a flashback, Viktor's story makes use of an assortment of occult phenomena: an invocation of elementary spirits at midnight by the light of flickering firebrands in an abandoned castle dungeon, a galvanic mirror to enchant the target victim into a state of submission, a doll-like homunculus, an imaguncula that represents a salamandrian maiden who is to entice Viktor's soul to the dark recesses of the spirits of Hell. When the major invokes the salamander to appear and Viktor falls in a faint, his lieutenant friend carries him out while the major carries out the ill-fated captain at whose urging the invocation had taken place. The lieutenant then turns Viktor over to the major, who returns, and then he quails with fright when he sees the major ahead, carrying the captain as before, and sees the major at his side, carrying Viktor: a double, the dreaded *Doppelgänger*, has entered the scene to assist after the nefarious midnight conjuration. This is a rare example of the bilocation of the physical and astral body in adjacent space.

Paul Talkebarth, a military orderly and simple male malaprop, had consulted with a reincarnation of an earlier Hoffmann figure—the scurrilous applewife Liese of "Der goldne Topf"—who reads the future in coffee grounds and who is able to pour leaden figurines for magical purposes. She had told Talkebarth that a young gentleman was in danger of his life because of a salamander, "die schlimmsten Dinge, deren sich der Teufel bediene." While being visited in recurring dreams by the discarnate succubus, whom the major had conjured with an absurd recitation of practice phrases from a French grammar, Viktor begins to resist the wiles of the cabbalistic teraphim. But when he orders her to leave, calling her a "verführerische Ausgeburt der Hölle," an enraged major appears, his eyes spewing the fires of Hell, and Viktor loses consciousness. But Paul shoots his gun and the demons vanish. When Viktor confronts the baroness with the question of whether she had ever been in the town where he had his visita-

tions, she admits it circumspectly with the remark: "Ein düstres Schicksal [verdammt] mich dazu, beständig ein anderes Wesen zu scheine, als ich wirklich bin." Viktor cries out the word of conjuration he had heard the major use: *Nehelmiahmiheal,* and the baroness falls senseless to the floor. At the end of the story Viktor mourns that it had all been "ein langer, böser Traum," and that he had been denied the love and delight of a higher being.

The salamander of "Der goldne Topf" is quite a different creature, as is the applewife-witch Liese. Instead of being a succubus in league with the Devil, Lindhorst is a prince dethroned from his high position among the elementary spirits, condemned to spend ages on the earth among common men. She, instead of being a fortune-teller on the edge of town, is a denizen of the Underworld, bent on the destruction of her arch-enemy. Caught in the middle of this super- and subterranean strife is Anselmus, the clumsy initiate, whose fate is spun from the skeins of day and the web of night into the gossamer world of Atlantis. Hoffmann intentionally mixes the romantic world and the mundane world in the fairy tale. No hour is spared the infernal machinations of the witch, whether it be midday—when her doorknocker visage causes Anselmus to cringe and collapse in a scary wrestling match with a venomous, hissing, discarnate viper—or whether it be midnight, when Liese spirits Veronika to a crossroads incantation, complete with all the hardware of occult rites, including the spade to dig the pit for charcoal, the pot to brew the foul potion that will bind Anselmus to Veronika, and the tripod to set it on—not to forget the constant familiar of the witch, the lurking, circumambulating cat. Veronika's astral body accompanies the witch on her midnight excursion, which the salamander—in the form of a lunging, screeching vulture—disrupts with hideous cries. The fairy tale has a happy and harmonious Atlantean ending, but not all of Hoffmann's tales end on a light note. Often as not they end with abrupt insanity, when the mind is stretched beyond its breaking point.

Hoffmann mixed the world of the dark occult with the world of glaring day, and though he was skeptical he could nonetheless state that the age of the miraculous and marvelous continued to hold sway over the affairs of men.

—A. Leslie Willson

Cyprian, one of the Serapion brethren, tells an untitled tale that has variously been called "Der Vampyrismus" and "Eine Vampyrgeschichte" or—by one editor—"Die Hyänen". The tale comes about because the friends are discussing the use of horror in stories, which in the hands of an imaginative writer can stir the mysteries and fears that dwell in the heart of every human being. Horror should not degenerate into what is repulsive and offensive, but an author should have the right to use the lever of fright, of horror, and of terror to achieve his purpose. So Cyprian illustrates such a flight of fancy with his tale of the vampire. As in many of Hoffmann's tales Count Hyppolit is met with a penetrating, burning gaze when he admits into his castle a baroness, whose exterior mien belies the satanic glow in her eye. The father of the count had hounded the baroness during his life for reasons that are better not mentioned, it is said. The count hastens to apologize for his father's deeds, and he takes the hand of the baroness in his own:

> Er fühlte seine Hand von im Tode erstarrten Finger umkrallt, und die grobe knochendürre Gestalt der Baronesse, die ihn anstarrte mit Augen ohne Sehkraft, schien ihm in den hässlich bunten Kleidern eine angeputzte Leiche.

The daughter of the baroness, Aurelie, claims that her mother is often stricken with catalepsy, and the count twists his hand free with some effort. When the baroness has recovered, the count invites her to stay for a while in his castle, suppressing an admission that he has become enamored of her daughter.

He grows accustomed to the deathly pale face of the baroness, to her ghostly figure, and he blames her affliction for her odd behavior, which seems to lead her nightly to stroll through the park to the church cemetery. The count asks for and receives Aurelie's hand, but on the morn of the wedding day a mishap spoils all plans: the baroness is found lifeless in the park, and all efforts to revive her are futile. Aurelie reacts with mute tearlessness, and the wedding is postponed for a few weeks. But a nameless dread seems to have gripped Aurelie: she turns pale suddenly without cause, as though she were about to be jerked into oblivion by a nameless, invisible, and inimical power.

When the marriage has at last been celebrated, the count feels it would be indiscreet to interrogate Aurelie about what bothers her, though he hints at it gently. She confesses that her mother's death had ushered in a dread that she could not rid herself of, a dread that her mother would rise from the grave and tear her out of the arms of her husband. She then tells the count about the death of her own father in her childhood, the appearance of the baroness, whose life style included daily visits by a man who brought wealth to a shabby household. Though the man must have been forty, he looked much younger, had a fine figure, and could be called handsome—but his glances filled Aurelie with terror. When in a half-drunken state he embraced her, she fled into her room but was admonished by her mother, who insisted that she must submit to the man. But her mother and the suitor had a monstrous fight during which the police were summoned and discovered that they had captured Urian, a hunted criminal, the son of an executioner.

Now the count seems unable to console Aurelie, and her state of mind is not improved when she becomes pregnant and hears the doctor comment on the odd appetites that sometimes afflict pregnant women, such as that of the wretched woman who had butchered her husband for a taste of his flesh. The countess becomes paler and paler, eats less and less, and seems to have a particular aversion for meat. Because she eats nothing finally, the doctor says

that something is going on that is beyond his ability as a medical man to explain.

At this point a castle servant tells Hyppolit that the countess leaves the castle every night and returns at dawn. The count believes that she, like her mother, has entered upon an adulterous relationship. Having noticed that he sleeps very soundly after his bedtime drink, he forgoes the drink and follows his wife out into the night. She goes through the park to the church cemetery, where he loses her momentarily, then:

> Da gewahrte er im hellsten Mondesschimmer dicht vor sich einen Kreis furchtbar gespenstischer Gestalten. Alte halbnackte Weiber mit fliegendem Haar hatten sich niedergekauert auf den Boden, und mitten in dem Kreise lag der Leichnam eines Menschen, an dem sie zehrten mit Wolfesgier.—Aurelie war unter ihnen.

The count runs off in horror and sinks down at his castle gate in a stupor. The next morning, in his wife's chamber, he finds her sleeping peacefully. At breakfast, when she recoils before the meat, he mentions the horror of the past night and calls her a hyena, whereupon she throws herself upon him and tears at his breast with her teeth. He flings her away and she dies twitching spasmodically on the floor, whereupon he goes mad.

The bifurcation of the world in Hoffmann's tales is truly a reflection of the dichotomy in the world familiar to man, a world that has on its fringes the frightening figures of a realm just beyond the edges of man's ratiocination, a realm accessible to the imagination and even more dreaded and deadly because of its inchoate form. The fantasms of the fancy torture and torment man, who is caught on the ambivalent rack of belief and disbelief. Hoffmann himself was in that predicament. He made full use of the split personality of Everyman, knowing full well that horror resides more in the imagination than in reality but that it is no less powerful for all that. What is hidden and arcane is both transfixing and menacing. The crystal voice that sings in a goblet may have its source in a mantic sphere, and the clock that tolls may be a summons for you. (pp. 264-71)

> *A. Leslie Willson, "Hoffmann's Horrors," in* Literature and the Occult: Essays in Comparative Literature, *edited by Luanne Frank, The University of Texas at Arlington, 1977, pp. 264-71.*

Glyn Tegai Hughes   (essay date 1979)

[In the following excerpt, Hughes provides an overview of Hoffmann's short fiction.]

Only in recent years has Hoffmann's work been partly freed from his biography. Interpretations may still take account of, but are not now dominated by, his alcoholism (doubtful), his schizothymic states (occasionally miscalled insanity), his ill-health (not now thought to have been syphilitic), or the tension between his professional and artistic selves. Hoffmann was a lawyer, a very competent and conscientious one and, as far as he could be, a reforming civil servant. He was also a musician of great talent, composing many works that almost fought their way into the permanent repertory, and a draughtsman and caricaturist of skill and dash. He became a known writer slightly late in life, though he had completed a three-volume novel by the time he was nineteen and was writing another before the end of that same year, 1795. Neither has survived and they are known only by their titles, *Cornaro* and *Der Geheimnisvolle.* It is therefore an exaggeration to claim that his literary talent was fired by his passion for his young music pupil Julia Mark (he had also published **"Ritter Gluck"** before meeting the then thirteen-year-old girl), though the emotional upheaval in the years 1811 and 1812 was certainly acute. The experience, in any case, came at a period of great difficulty for Hoffmann. When Warsaw fell to the French in November 1806 the Prussian civil service in the city was disbanded, and he had found himself out of work. The next few years were therefore spent in attempts to earn a living, as a portrait painter, music critic and teacher, musical director of a theatre (in Bamberg, Leipzig and Dresden) and, eventually, writer. He started mainly with articles on music, but by the time he returned to the service of the Prussian state in 1814 he was an established general author.

Yet, though none of this is decisive, there is no doubt that there are many autobiographical correspondences in the work. The idealized form of Julia Mark does recur in many of the female figures; friends and relations are pictured, often named, sometimes caricatured, in the fiction; and the locale (restaurant, theatre, picnic spot) frequently springs from personal reminiscence. The correspondences must, however, all be treated with some caution, as may be illustrated by comparing the dates of birth of Hoffmann himself and of Johannes Kreisler in *Kater Murr.* Hoffmann was born on 24 January 1776; Kreisler grudgingly reveals that he was born 'on St John Chrysostom's day, that is to say on the twenty-fourth of January of the year one thousand seven hundred and something.' But St John Chrysostom's day is 27 January, which is also the birthday of Mozart, whose name Amadeus had been adopted by Hoffmann instead of his own third name of Wilhelm. Some mystification, not to say fooling, is at work. We are, in fact, dealing with a fiction. What is really misleading in Hoffmann's case is any attempt to reduce the fictions to exemplars of some autobiographical pathological state. For Hoffmann is the great storyteller of the Romantics and his meanings are as much in how he tells as in what is told. Indeed it is telling, creating, that represents the core of life.

Hoffmann's two main definitions of his narrative theory are linked to the titles of two of his collections of Novellen and Märchen, and it makes little difference to the underlying principles that the introductory material containing the theory postdated some of the individual pieces, or that in the **Serapionsbrüder** the framework was something of an afterthought added for publicity purposes. The first two volumes of *Fantasiestücke in Callots Manier* appeared for Easter 1814, with a preface by Jean Paul, and they were followed by a third volume at the end of that year and a fourth at Easter 1815. Hoffmann had considered calling them 'Bilder nach Hogarth' (Pictures after

Hogarth) but decided eventually on Jacques Callot (1592-1635), the French engraver, eighty or more of whose prints were to be seen at Bamberg. Hoffmann admired in Callot the great technical ingenuity, the thousands of figures and details in a confined space and yet each individualized, the audacity, power, life and naturalness of the depiction. (Towards the end of Hoffmann's life the sketch *Des Vetters Eckfenster,* 1822, gives a comparable and very moving picture of the dying man's loving gaze at the richness and variety of life as he looks through his window onto the market square.) Yet Hoffmann was equally attracted by the strangeness of the prints, by the way the most ordinary feature takes on a romantic, fantastic quality, by the grotesque deformations that allow mysterious allusions. For the writer the analogy with Callot lies in his receiving into his 'inner romantic imagination' all the myriad detail of the phenomenal world, and reproducing it in strange attire.

The procedure seems, at first sight, to be reversed in the 'Serapion principle'. *Die Serapions-Brüder. Gesammelte Erzählungen und Märchen* appeared in four volumes between 1819 and 1821, and the loose conversational links were certainly inspired by the regular informal gatherings of Hoffmann and his friends: the publisher Hitzig; Karl Wilhelm Contessa, a popular and not untalented narrative writer; David (Johann) Ferdinand Koreff, fashionable doctor and enthusiast for magnetism; and, less regularly, Chamisso and Fouqué. The opening tale is that of the supposed hermit Serapion whose fancies are so vivid and objective that they entirely replace reality for him. This becomes the 'Serapion principle' (das serapiontische Prinzip), according to which the more powerful the imagination, the more realistic the product. One can only bring effectively to life what one has seen within oneself; and one is reminded of Caspar David Friedrich's prescription that 'the painter should not just paint what he sees before him, but also what he sees within himself. (pp. 112-14)

The Callot and Serapion principles are both aspects of the same aesthetic conviction: sensory observation is fired by imagination, and imagination must express itself concretely in the world of the senses. This productive tension between Hoffmann's capacity for myth-making and his evidential observation of the everyday ensures that an aesthetic echoing Novalis and Schelling does not lead to bloodlessness and insubstantiality. Creative energy in its unconscious working throws up images and forms (perhaps it is more than a soothing ploy when he keeps assuring his publisher that the next work is well on the way—in his imagination it no doubt is). Hoffmann's head one might irreverently describe as a nourishing compost-heap hot with speculatory novelties from magnetism to cabbalism, with frenzied personal griefs and disappointments, with raucous comedy—where else in Romanticism would one find an Irish joke? All this is then exteriorized in a much more deliberate way than has often been thought. The juridical mind creates its own patterns of witnesses' statements, of written and oral evidence, of logic and counter-logic, all within the courtroom, all safely in a frame. Thus, though Hoffmann's subject may be the irreparable dualism or heterogeneity of existence, his art-forms offer a reconciling prospect, somewhere on the edge of the real world.

Hoffmann's exploitation of the subconscious, the examination of the alienated self, the attempt to show creatures of the imagination placed in the real world and, above all, the holding of these in balance by irony, by narrative point of view, by the resources of art, are a major contribution to modern literature.

—Glen Tegai Hughes

We see this in his first published story **"Ritter Gluck"**, which prefigures much of his later work. The narrator, in an exactly described Berlin in late August 1809, meets a stranger of unusual appearance and obvious musical gifts. The story ends with the stranger playing and singing from a blank score of Gluck's *Armida,* with embellishments that intensify the original; Gluck himself had died in 1787 but the stranger solemnly announces 'I am the Chevalier Gluck.' Much ingenuity has gone into speculating whether the musician is mad, a reincarnation, a dream, an incorporation of the spirit of music, an expression of the duality of existence, of the coexistence of two realities. Two points may be more worth our attention: the ambivalent position of the narrator and the primacy of the realm of art. Doubt is the narrator's chief characteristic; we are never sure of his position and it seems more than just idiomatic that at the end he should be 'beside himself' (außer mir). He is standing at some strange point which is and is not the Berlin of 1809, and is caught up in the creative power of an artist, who in a sense is also his creature. This creative power torments Gluck, his dreams unfit him for bourgeois life even as they break down the barriers between reality and illusion. Any harmony comes in the final artistic product, symbolized by Gluck's soft clasp of the narrator's hand and his strange smile.

Hoffmann's Märchen pursue the theme of the disjointed world and the possibility of aesthetic reconstruction, of redemption within the sphere of art. They are, in his new formulation, ideal vehicles in which to link the everyday and the supernatural, as implied indeed in the title of **"Der goldne Topf. Ein Märchen aus der neuen Zeit,"** written between July 1813 and February 1814 (a period, incidentally, during which he was presenting Mozart's *Magic Flute* at Dresden, but also a time of great personal unhappiness and stress).

The locale is modern Dresden, the student Anselmus's notion of happiness is a visit to the pleasure gardens outside the town ('the bliss of the Linke paradise'); we should note the term 'paradise' and perhaps also the apples he upsets and the curse placed upon him as a consequence: 'into the crystal thou shalt soon fall'. . . . This is quickly followed by an awakening of the poetic, magical instinct in him

through the crystal bells by which the little fire-snakes first call to him. Misleadingly his bourgeois love Veronika has a voice like crystal; but when Anselmus has blotted the magic hieroglyphs of nature that Archivarius Lindhorst has given him to copy, he finds himself stoppered in a crystal bottle. One ingenious commentator also suggests that Anselmus's lengthy absence from Dresden was caused by his suicide, plunging into the icy, and thus crystalline, waters of the Elbe; but Hoffmann is perhaps inventive enough without such aid.

Precious stones, crystalline forms, have a fascination for the Romantics (one thinks of the carbuncle in **"Heinrich von Ofterdingen"** and in **"Meister Floh"**,) as being on the frontier of organic life; but they represent also a threat to man in their cold perfection or their daemonic attraction, like the 'cherry-red sparkling almandine' of **"Die Bergwerke zu Falun"**. In **"Der goldne Topf"** crystal is one motif of many through which the everyday world is penetrated by the energy of the poetic world. But the motifs are, until late on in the story, presented in an ambiguous light, so that the reader is kept puzzled as to the nature of reality. What Anselmus had taken for a fire-lily bush turns out to be Archivarius Lindhorst's dressing gown; when he seems to see the Archivarius fly away into the darkness a large bird of prey rises screeching before him— that is what it must have been, and yet how *did* the Archivarius disappear? Changes of perspective, half-concealed shifts of the narrative point of view, rationalizations by the characters themselves, matter-of-fact accounts of the inconceivable, all deliberately serve to confuse the reader. Archivarius Lindhorst's brother has not gone to the dogs but to the dragons, as he relates, taking a pinch of snuff; he adds that he is in mourning for his father who died quite recently, three hundred and eighty-five years ago. This naturally contributes to the comic effect which, in Hoffmann, has many facets other than the often cited grotesque and ironic; indeed in his letter to Kunz on 19 August 1813 giving a first outline of the Märchen he invokes the spirit of Gozzi with the buffooneries of the recreated *commedia dell'arte*. **"Der goldne Topf"** satirizes elements in contemporary philosophy, uses bureaucratic style for incongruous communications, sets the most philistine objects and professions alongside mythic projections, makes play with clumsiness and with other peculiarities of physique, teases the reader with hints or obfuscations, follows an impassioned argument about whether Lindhorst really is a salamander with a knock about description of a morning-after hangover. Hoffmann's comedy often reminds one of a grimace, a desperate manic grin. The surprise is that he generally brings it so well under control; well enough, for instance, to eliminate the original intention that the golden vessel should be a chamber-pot (though **"Klein Zaches"** reverts to the motif).

In **"Prinzessin Brambilla"** Hoffmann makes an explicit allegorical defence of humour as a reconciling force, summing up the dramatic context of the 'capriccio', as the work is called. Looking into the crystal prism (symbolic of the purity of nature) that is the Urdar lake—as one might look at a stage comedy—the characters in an interpolated Märchen see the antics of their own mirror-image, recognize the nonsense of all existence here below, and are amused. Reversing the order of things is a releasing experience; when the self is exteriorized at the same time as the rest of the world a degree of harmony is achieved, and one finds autobiographical confirmation of this in a diary entry about the Julia Mark agonizing: 'found, that it is possible to abstract oneself from Kth [the code for Julia]', 8 January 1812.

The mythic elements in the Märchen are reminiscent of Novalis, whom Hoffmann greatly admired; but the unusual feature is that the mythic is now itself viewed ironically. Both in **"Der goldne Topf "** and **"Prinzessin Brambilla"** the interpolated or interwoven Märchen derive from G. H. von Schubert, and present the disruption of a golden age (a paradisal garden) by the intrusion of reflective consciousness. Themes from astrology, Indian and Nordic mythology, folk magic, demonology, mesmerism and contemporary psychiatry fill out the mythic structure. Anselmus, in **"Der goldne Topf,"** escapes from the world of philistinism to the aesthetic realm of Atlantis where love reveals the harmony of all things; he has become a poet.

The visionary content is, however, dampened down by the fictional framework, within which Archivarius Lindhorst has had to show the narrator how to finish and interpret his story. The narrator (and we are to think of the artist's position in the real world) bemoans his fate in having to return to his garret and the uncertainties of life, when Lindhorst taps him on the shoulder and reminds him that he has at least 'an agreeable tenant-farm as a poetic possession in Atlantis.' The poetic imagination, the inner world of dreams, provides a link between reality and the supersensual world, even if only a tentative and discontinuous one.

"Klein Zaches, gennant Zinnober. Ein Märchen" can be said to continue the contrast between the bourgeois world and that of the imagination, but in less exalted terms and with much bizarre complication. The philistine, rationalistic world, in which much contemporary thought and many aspects of society are satirized, shows itself to be a world of a appearance; reality is found only in the aesthetic experience. In the context of the fiction this resides in the humour, the dominating experience in this Märchen. Later, indeed, Hoffmann expressly insists that its chief purpose is fun and resists allegorical interpretations (preface to **"Prinzessin Brambilla"**).

Hoffmann's last work, **"Meister Floh. Ein Märchen in sieben Abenteuern zweier Freunde,"** written between August 1821 and February 1822, resulted in his being charged with defaming senior civil servants. As a member of a commission investigating alleged crimes against the state, mainly by liberal and revolutionary students, he had very honourably stood out against illegalities committed by the powerful chief of police, von Kamptz, whom he now caricatured in the so-called Knarrpanti episodes of **"Meister Floh."** The result was that the Märchen appeared in censored form little more than a month before Hoffmann's death on 25 June 1822, and it was not published in its entirety until 1908. In the course of the proceedings against him Hoffmann prepared a defence that has recently been interpreted as an important affirmation of his artistic purposes.

This is perhaps pitching it a little high. As a poetological statement it amounts to not very much more than a defence of heterogeneity, of the interrelationship of all the parts (in itself a disingenuous defence of the Knarrpanti episodes, which have a very proper function but were also, in all probability, an afterthought). Nevertheless it does show Hoffmann again expounding a theory of aesthetics, this time resting on the base of Carl Friedrich Flögel's *Geschichte der komischen Literatur*, which allows the bringing together of the most disparate elements.

"Meister Floh" is, if anything, even more marked by grotesque inventiveness than its predecessors, though there is at times an air of contrivance or of downright muddle. Those critics, particularly Hans-Georg Werner, who are concerned to stress the realist in Hoffmann, see in it a fading of commitment to the suprasensual world, and link this to his return to public life and to the political climate of the post-Napoleonic period. A juster appreciation, at least of the content of the Märchen, may however be provided by the satire on the exact sciences, especially in the persons of Leuwenhöck (Leeuwenhoeck) and Swammerdamm, the seventeenth-century Dutch scientists still apparently alive in Frankfurt in the 1820s; Leuwenhöck indeed calls attention to this mythic abolition of time and space when he says to Pepusch, 'you are the only one in Frankfurt who knows that I have been lying in my grave in the old church at Delft since the year 1725.' The two are 'crazy retail dealers of nature' and are condemned because they seek to examine nature's secrets microscopically and competitively instead of lovingly, reverently. Inner, organic, unifying growth, allegorized here in plant life, passes them by. And it is unity with the organic whole that Peregrinus finds at the end of the Märchen through fidelity and love.

The richness of Hoffmann's themes, from spookery to gnosis, from opera buffa to high tragedy, from alchemy to Naturphilosophie, from folk demonology to exploitation of the subconscious, is to be found not only in his Märchen but also in his Novellen. These, after all, are the Tales of Hoffmann on which much of his reputation was founded, and it should be remembered that he was, for the whole of the nineteenth century, must the best known of the German Romantics, read by Pushkin, Turgenev, Gogol, Dostoevsky, Gorki Herzen and many others in Russia, by Balzac, Musset, Huysmans and Baudelaire in France, by Irving, Hawthorne and Poe in America, and by Heine, Immermann, Raabe, Kafka and Thomas Mann in Germany.

The related themes of Doppelgänger and automata are to be seen in **"Die Automate"** and **"Der Sandmann"**. Hoffmann's fascination with automata and mechanical marvels was, no doubt, fed by viewing mechanical musicians constructed by the Kaufmanns of Dresden or by reading Johann Christian Wiegleb's *Die natürliche Magie*, particularly the second volume published in 1786. Their fictional impact, however, goes far beyond trickery; they raise questions about the nature of personality and of knowledge, about the relationship between the inner creative core in man and the dead mechanical construct without; gravest of all they question the necessity of the self. It is not, as some critics claim, that these automata are meant to induce feelings of mystery and horror in us; for the modern reader their implausibility would prevent this. What Olimpia in **"Der Sandmann"** does to us she does through Nathanael, for in him we see a descent into madness that a shifting narrative perspective enables us to accept as purely pathological or as accompanied by incursions from some fatal magic realm, some dark creative unconscious. The motif of the eye and the fear of losing one's eyes, which Freud equated in this story with the fear of castration, suggests more strongly the loss of identity, the destruction of the mediator between self and world. The feeling of alienation, of metaphysical abandonment is strong.

An allied theme is the dualism in human personality. **"Die Bergwerke zu Falun"** is based on Schubert's account in *Die Nachtseite* of the recovery of a miner's body totally preserved after fifty years, a story used by Hebel, by Arnim in a ballad in *Gräfin Dolores* and, based on Hoffmann's account, by Hugo von Hofmannsthal and by Trakl (in the 'Elis' poems). The stress in Hoffmann is on the rift in Elis Fröbom's nature and his withdrawal into the dangerous regions of the subconscious mind and into the mythic, undifferentiated realm of nature. Elis has fled from love, in his search for unattainable knowledge and perfection; he is, literally, petrified (as in his dream of 'his very being melting into the gleaming rock', and finally crumbles into dust.

"Das Fräulein von Scuderi" pursues the theme of the split personality, but here it is apparently associated with the problem of artistic creativity. Cardillac, who murders to regain the jewelry he has wrought, seems behind his bourgeois façade to show a wild possessiveness, a projection of himself into his own creation, that allows of no limits. Ellis has convincingly shown that sexual neurosis must be added to this; Cardillac has an unconscious desire to protect his mother's virtue and to punish her lover. The overt explanation that his ungovernable lust for jewelry arises from pre-natal influences is so far distanced by narrative point of view that we are to understand it as unconscious camouflage.

The moral authority of Fräulein von Scuderi herself, the detailed descriptions, of Paris as of Falun, the criminological interest (we are here dealing with one of the earliest detective stories) all serve to anchor the story in everyday life. This is characteristic of Hoffmann; whatever the excesses of the imagination, the real world remains vividly at hand. (pp. 116-22)

There is a good deal to criticize in Hoffmann: an often cliché-ridden and overblown style, an over-ready commitment to the modish tricks of his day's best sellers, an uncritical dabbling in fashionable ideas, a willingness to let theatrical props invade his fiction. Yet the exploitation of the subconscious, the examination of the alienated self, the attempt to show creatures of the imagination placed in the real world and, above all, the holding of these in balance by irony, by narrative point of view, by the resources of art, are a major contribution to modern literature. The very structure of the literary work itself is to serve to create harmony between reason and imagination, by sharing the artist's dominance over both. (p. 125)

Glyn Tegai Hughes, "The Risks of the Imagination: Hoffmann, with Chamisso, Fouqué and Werner," in his Romantic German Literature, Holmes and Meier Publishers, Inc., 1979, pp. 112-26.

Leo Schneiderman   (essay date 1983)

[*In the following excerpt, Schneiderman analyzes psychological and autobiographical aspects of Hoffmann's short fiction.*]

Ernest Theodor Amadeus Hoffmann is not well known to American readers; yet he is one of the great representatives of late romanticism in literature in the early nineteenth century. Hoffmann's many tales and novellas are often extraordinarily rich and show unusual psychological penetration. Written at white heat, partly satirical, often lyrical, his short stories assert the claims of the ideal world. Hoffmann was born in Königsberg in 1776 and came from a long line of civil servants and lawyers. . . [He] lost his father through divorce; but the latter, a lawyer with the temperament and interests of an artist, exercised a strong influence on Hoffmann's imagination, and served as Hoffmann's ego-ideal. As a boy, Hoffmann received careful training in music from his uncle and excelled at an early age in both music and drawing. Although his uncle saw to it that Hoffmann was trained as a lawyer and entered the civil service, Hoffmann's youthful ambition was to become either an artist or a composer. At age of eighteen, Hoffmann had a scandalous love affair with an older married woman. Hoffmann's uncle shipped him off to another set of relatives and Hoffmann's subsequent career, until his early death at age 45, consisted of wandering from one city to another, sometimes supporting himself as a lawyer and sometimes as a musical director. At the age of 26, Hoffmann married an attractive local girl in Posen, where he was serving as a minor official. That same year—1822—Hoffmann was banished to a small Polish village as punishment for circulating caricatures of high military officers. During the two years of his exile, Hoffmann composed numerous musical compositions and published his first essay, a literary piece on Schiller. Hoffmann was subsequently transferred to Warsaw where, in addition to working as a government lawyer, he organized a variety of musical activities and composed operas, ballets, and his first symphony. Expelled from Warsaw by Napoleon's armies, Hoffmann made his way to Bamberg and Dresden, where he supported himself and his wife (their only child, a daughter, had died earlier) from 1807 to 1814, earning a scant living as musical conductor, music critic, and writer of short stories for magazines. In 1809, Hoffmann fell in love with a 15-year old music pupil, Juliane Mark. Although this "affair" was never consummated and the girl was quickly married off to a Hamburg banker, Hoffmann was deeply affected by this episode, as he had been by his earlier love affair with the young married woman, Dora Hatt. Before he relinquished Juliane, Hoffmann brought the scandal out into the open, humiliating his devoted wife. After 1814 and until his death in 1822, Hoffmann occupied a secure and prestigious position as a judge in Berlin, thanks to the efforts of his lifelong friend, Theodor

Hippel, a politically influential official. As a judge, Hoffmann was singularly fair-minded and defended freedom of expression during a period of intense political witch-hunting.

In sum, Hoffmann achieved a wide and appreciative audience for his short stories during his lifetime even though his legal career was demanding and his musical activities occupied a special place in his heart. Hoffmann's musical career never brought him the recognition he sought as a composer, despite his high level of productivity, including music for the opera, *Undine.* Ironically, Hoffmann's fictional works inspired a multitude of musical productions long after his death. These adaptations embrace operas, such as Offenbach's *Les Contes d'Hoffmann* and his less well-known *Le Roi Carotte,* as well as Stern and Zamara's *Der Goldschmied von Toledo,* Hindemith's *Cardillac,* etc. Among ballets inspired by Hoffmann's tales are Delibe's *Coppélia* and Tchaikovsky's *Nutcracker.* Hoffmann's literary ancestors undoubtedly were Rousseau and Goethe, whose nature-loving, melancholic, and unconventional heroes are the prototype of Hoffmann's sensitive, unworldly male protagonists. Curiously, several years before Hoffmann's tales came to the attention of a wide European audience outside Germany, a number of his stories were translated into Russian and appeared in Russian literary magazines. There is even evidence that Hoffmann's influence extended to Pushkin, especial in "The Queen of Spades," and also to Dostoevsky [Charles E. Passage, *The Russian Hoffmannists*]. Hoffmann's significance for the modern reader rests in no small part in his ability to deal forthrightly with destructive aspects of the human psyche, as well as with human aspirations toward transcendence, a theme that has been explored insightfully by H. S. Daemmrich [*The Shattered Self: E. T. A. Hoffmann's Tragic Vision*].

When a writer such as Hoffmann invents uncanny and often bizarre events it is all too easy for the psychologically-oriented critic to argue that the author is not fully in control of his materials and that primary process thinking has taken the place of creative regression in the service of the ego. As I have argued elsewhere in regard to the fictional works of H. H. Munro ("Saki"), this may in fact be the case when the writer is under the influence of deeply repressed longings, fears, or hatreds. Although Hoffmann undoubtedly wrote out of powerful emotional needs, he was a self-conscious artist and literary pioneer, eager to explore the farthest limits of emotional sensibility in the then current spirit of romanticism.

To illustrate the complexity of the problem of separating conscious from preconscious or unconscious forces affecting the creative process it might be useful to look at a brief but crucial phase of Hoffmann's life. I refer to his love affair with Dora Hatt, married and ten years his senior, when Hoffmann was scarcely 18. Dora, who was married to a man 19 years her senior and, moreover, one who neglected her to pursue his business as a wine-merchant, fell in love with Hoffmann, who was her music teacher. Since Dora and Hoffmann lived in the same house, their relationship quickly turned into a clandestine affair, and as soon as it was discovered by Hoffmann's uncle, his guard-

ian, the romantic youth was sent away. Hoffmann's involvement with Dora did not end once and for all, because he carried on a secret correspondence with her from 1794 to 1797, when he returned to Königsberg and tried unsuccessfully to get Dora to obtain a divorce.

> **Although Hoffmann undoubtedly wrote out of powerful emotional needs, he was a self-conscious artist and literary pioneer, eager to explore the farthest limits of emotional sensibility in the then current spirit of romanticism.**
>
> **—Leo Schneiderman**

There is no doubt that this unhappy affair left a lasting impression on Hoffmann. The question arises: Did Hoffmann use this episode to provide a loose framework for his story of Oedipal-type love in **"Datura Fastuosa"** (1818), in which an 18-year-old student enters a marriage of convenience with a 60-year-old widow? The young student in the story, Eugenius, loved his elderly wife—his professor's widow—like a son, but ultimately came to resent her for standing in his way when he became infatuated with a seductive adventuress, also older and more experienced than the protagonist. A few observations about this story may help clarify the relative influence of primary and secondary thought processes in the construction of the plot, and may throw some light, as well, on the author's ambivalent attitude toward his ego-ideal.

On the symbolic level, **"Datura Fastuosa"** concerns itself with problems of transition from innocence, i.e., latency, to sexual maturity. To be sure, the protagonist is already 24 years old when he marries the professor's widow. But the youth, who appears to have no parents, living or dead—a significant omission by Hoffmann—has lived his entire life under sheltered conditions. His student days, in fact, have been spent working in the professor's greenhouse, to the exclusion of almost all other activities. Except for one devoted friend, Sever (modeled after Hoffmann's friend, Hippel), Eugenius is presented as one who has had no previous human involvements, to say nothing of romantic attachments. Parenthetically, a gentle and attractive teenage girl, Gretchen, the adopted child of the late professor and his wife, is secretly in love with Eugenius, who hardly notices her until the last page of the story, when he suddenly declares his love for her and asks her to marry him. Eugenius, then, at 24 is described as a total naif, an unworldly idealist, pure of heart, and inexperienced in the ways of the world. Hoffmann shows us that Eugenius is the sort of person who easily becomes an object of derision because ordinary people cannot understand him or appreciate his spiritual nature. Although Hoffmann's intention is to present an exemplar of the romantic type, i.e., the sensitive, misunderstood artist-dreamer, he is no less concerned with surrounding his hero with symbols of innocence, namely, the pale flowers and herbs of the professor's greenhouse. These passionless flora are contrasted with the lush tropical vegetation of the garden in which Eugenius is overcome with passion for the exotic adventuress, literally a magic garden of temptation symbolized by the scented plant, *Datura fastuosa* (gorgeous thornapple), which grows just inside the garden gate. This plant is a favorite of the professor's widow but it only grows in all its lush splendor in the magic garden, which belongs to a confederate of the adventuress; in the professor's greenhouse the plant is hardly more than an insignificant bush. The sexual symbolism of the enchanted garden is unmistakable, especially since it is the setting in which the adventuress and her sinister accomplice, a monk named Fermino, hatch their plot to ensnare the sexually awakened Eugenius. In the end, happily, the evil machinations of the plotters are frustrated and a chastened, but wiser hero rests content with a colorless, but adoring "Gretchen."

On the manifest level, this is a story about a youth's mimesis of marriage, his emancipation from a maternal woman, his loss of innocence with a sexually provocative, but evil woman, and his belated discovery of true love with a young girl who makes no demands on him. If we move slightly beyond the manifest level, it becomes apparent that Eugenius, obscurely laboring in the professor's garden, is still fixated at the pregenital level, and that his tender and solitary ministrations to the plants have onanistic overtones. Eugenius' flower-preoccupation also seems to serve the purpose of binding anxiety in conjunction with the youth's defensive withdrawal from his peers.

The latent content of **"Datura Fastuosa,"** involving Eugenius' marriage to a 60-year-old widow, is evidently Oedipal, signifying the fulfillment of a forbidden wish. At the widow's behest, Eugenius even dresses in the late professor's old-fashioned clothes, decorated with pictures of plants, thereby replacing the dead man in every sense except the sexual, insofar as the marriage is entirely platonic. There is in all this a distinct suggestion of unconscious seduction by a mother-figure. Moreover, the late professor is clearly a "good-father" image and positive ego-ideal, beloved by his erstwhile pupil, but contributing to Oedipal temptation by his sudden removal (like Hoffmann's father). By contrast, Hoffmann has provided a "bad father" (but positive ego-ideal symbolizing freedom and bold manhood) in the shape of the insidious monk, Fermino, who, acting like a procurer, tempts Eugenius with a beautiful and sensual woman, the adventuress, Gabriela. That this temptation is essentially Oedipal is indicated by Eugenius' discovery of Fermino and Gabriela locked in a sinful embrace in the magic garden. It was for the sake of Gabriela's love that Eugenius, at Fermino's instigation, had planned to kill the professor's widow by placing a poisonous powder in the calyx of the *Datura fastuosa,* whose sweet perfume the woman was in the habit of inhaling each day. In effect, Eugenius had come full circle with the intended destruction of his wife-mother, having freed himself from her control.

If we study the elements of this highly dramatic story, with its rich sexual symbolism (the powder in the calyx of the widow's favorite flower is but one example) and compare these features with Hoffmann's love affair with Dora Hatt, we can see certain basic similarities. The real-life mistress and the fictional wife-mother alike involve the male in a situation of extreme danger. The threat of discovery was obviously very real in the case of Dora, and in fact soon led to the loss of the valued love-object. On the face of it, Hoffmann should have had no negative feelings toward Dora during their love-affair. But we know that a few years later, a still enamoured Hoffmann failed to persuade Dora to break with her husband. Is it possible that Hoffmann reacted to this disappointment with mixed emotions of grief and anger? A letter written by Hoffmann to Hippel in August, 1797 (only four months after returning emptyhanded from his trip to Königsberg to see his beloved Dora), combines positive and negative emotions in a curious way, referring either to Dame Fortune or possibly Dora as "this false woman player who now wants to toss me bad cards forever." If this remark really refers to Dora—I am by no means certain this interpretation is correct—it would be consistent with the story-line of **"Datura Fastuosa,"** where there are a number of clues that the young student was ambivalent toward his wife-mother.

The most obvious sign was Eugenius' attempt, while under the evil influence of Fermino, to poison Frau Helms. As it turned out, he changed his mind at the last minute after learning of Fermino's and Gabriela's treachery. A second clue is provided by Eugenius' initial infatuation with Gabriela, who personified everything that the wife-mother was not—youth, beauty, and the attraction of illicit sex. A third clue takes us to the heart of the storymaking process. It consists of the splitting off of the "bad" woman from the wife-mother image. Gabriela, the temptress, represents the "dangerous," i.e., sexual component of the incestuous love-object. It is legitimate to turn against her, as Eugenius does at the story's end, but it is inadmissible that after all the wife-mother has done for Eugenius, he should feel hatred toward her. The author, in his letter to Hippel, had not revealed the full depth of his feeling toward Dora Hatt, but in **"Datura Fastuosa,"** written in 1821 and published posthumously in 1822, Hoffmann succeeded at last in imposing artistic form on the unfinished emotional business of his ardent youth. Parenthetically, the general idea for composing **"Datura Fastuosa"** was suggested to Hoffmann by his friend, the writer Adelbert Chamisso, as noted in a letter from Hoffmann to a botanist whom he asked for help in supplying botanical details. It is worth noting that in Chamisso's version, the young student marries the professor's elderly widow in order to obtain access to a rare, exotic plant in her locked greenhouse, which would otherwise have remained off-limits to him. The Oedipal theme in Chamisso's nuclear plot is interesting in its own right, but is not elaborated.

The use of flora as sexual symbols is conspicuous not only in **"Datura Fastuosa"** but is even more pervasive in **"The King's Bride."** The ambience of this thoroughly surrealistic story is entirely that of magical gardens, of flourishing turnips and cabbages, of "Kale ladies, lavender pages, and lettuce princes." Presiding over this world of exuberant nature, at least nominally, is a Herr Dapsul, an eccentric old man absorbed in Cabbalistic studies, astrological observations, and other occult matters which he pursues atop an old tower on his estate. The actual cultivator of the productive fields and vineyards is Dapsul's earthy, buxom daughter, Anna, who, spade in hand, is never far from her beloved vegetables. Anna is presented as a kind of latterday vegetation goddess whose affinity for plants and vines, and whose ecstatic love of her kitchen garden bespeak an almost libidinal attachment to the soil: "And it really seemed as though the carrot children in the earth rejoiced over ännchen's joy, for the thin laughter that rang out clearly rose from the soil."

Appropriately, this Kore of the vegetable patch is courted by a powerful but repulsive sorcerer-gnome who is called King Daucas Carota, and who possesses the shape and coloring of a giant carrot. At first Anna is repelled by the sight of the three-foot tall creature, but when the latter convinces her that he is the royal ruler of a vast domain filled with luxuriant greenery, she begins to see him in a new light. In short, Anna falls in love with her saffron-yellow admirer, realizing that by marrying the gnome she will become the queen of nature. Warned by her father that the gnome king intends to deprive her of her human form and to drag her underground, like Persephone, Anna discovers too late that she has started to turn into a carrot. Her father tries in vain to destroy the carrot king, but Anna's true redeemer turns out to be her poet-sweetheart, the rather unmanly Amandus von Nebelstern. Amandus makes the evil gnome diminish in size and finally disappear by singing an unbearably sentimental song of his own composition, accompanying himself on the guitar. Anna subsequently recovers her human form and her beauty by slipping her ring onto a carrot sticking out of the ground.

Apart from the transparent symbolism of Anna's ill-starred affair with a carrot and the manner of her redemption, the ending of this story throws a special light on Hoffmann's use of symbolism for literary and psychological purposes. In the final scene Anna throws away her spade and agrees to stay out of the garden evermore. Her future husband, Amandus, brought back to his senses by an accidental blow from the discarded shovel, resolves to stop writing poetry, which, he concludes, is a "silly and pretentious" activity. Hoffmann appears to have used nature symbolism and sentimental, ethereal poetry as metaphors for pregenital sexuality. His message is: It is as unlawful and fruitless for a maiden to cultivate her garden on her own as it is for a healthy young man to waste his time writing bad poetry. It is interesting that sexual awakening cannot occur in the world of flora as depicted in **"The King's Bride,"** but that in **"Datura Fastuosa"** a distinction is made between Professor Helms' plain garden and the libidinized, exotic garden of Fermino and Gabriela, the shameless lovers. Hoffmann has clearly recognized the evocative power of vegetation and has expressed it admirably in different contexts. He has also given us an archetypal morality play in **"The King's Bride,"** warning against the disastrous consequences of narcissistic love.

"Datura Fastuosa" and **"The Golden Pot"** share a common motif: adolescent identify crisis centering on the conflict between the lure of adult sexuality and the habit of dependence based on a symbiotic relationship with an ide-

alized mother-figure. In **"Datura Fastuosa"** the 24-year-old protagonist permits himself to be talked into a platonic marriage with a 60-year-old woman so that he can prolong his botanical studies, i.e., his pregenital mode of life. In **"The Golden Pot"** we are at first misled because the place of the nurturent mother-figure is taken by a magical snake, Serpentina, who inspires the boyish hero, Anselmus, with an unearthly kind of love and becomes his poetic muse. In each story the adolescent hero is loved by a beautiful young girl who longs for marriage and a settled life. In **"Datura Fastuosa"** the death of the older woman frees the youth to marry a suitable partner. In **"The Golden Pot,"** written when Hoffmann was 38, the outcome is quite different because Anselmus rejects Veronika, his beautiful, but hopelessly bourgeois sweetheart, thereby recovering his lost powers of poetic invention. He also awakens once more to the overpowering beauty of nature, of which the snake Serpentina is the embodiment. On the manifest level, the hero of **"The Golden Pot"** may be said to have chosen the ideal over the real world. In fact, Hoffmann employs the image of Anselmus-confined-to-a-bottle to symbolize the boy's fear of entrapment by the workaday world. On the psychological plane, however, it appears that a regressive choice—even an onanistic one, in light of the phallic character of Serpentina—has been made, eschewing the genital mode for a vaguely sensual "festival of love" centered on earth, water, insects, and birds.

The nature symbolism, whatever else it might have meant to Hoffmann, seems to have been his metaphor for "otherness," that is, everything that is innocent and lies outside the orbit of the crass world of reality. Evidently, even as a married man approaching middle-age Hoffmann could still fantasize what might have been had he chosen to detach himself from the ties of human intimacy, including the demands of marriage. It will be recalled, in this connection, that **"Datura Fastuosa"** posited the centrality of the Oedipus complex with respect to a boy's struggle to find his identity as a mature man. Paradoxically, though Hoffmann describes nature in the lushest terms, it becomes for him the zone of non-human or non-social vitality; in this region nature provides a setting within which a boy can remain an innocent, united with his mother in a relationship antithetical to his growth.

Just as the mother, the platonic love-object, stands for an alternative to mature love, so, too, Hoffmann uses the images of a beautiful but inaccessible woman to symbolize an ethereal ideal, as in **"The Artus Exchange."** In this story, a young merchant who would rather be an artist, falls in love with the portrait of a girl. Although he tries to find the girl he eventually gives up and becomes reconciled to thinking of her as his deathless inspiration to become a great creative artist. There is perfection in the portrait of the unknown girl because, like the mother-figure in **"Datura Fastuosa,"** the painting permits of no carnal knowledge. Hoffmann has carried this strategy a step further in **"The Sandman"** by creating a love-object in the form of a mechanical doll, the beautiful Olimpia. The young protagonist, Nathanael, faced with a choice between a flesh-and-blood girl, Clara, who loves him, and the minimally responsive robot, Olimpia, finally chooses the doll. As a consequence, he commits suicide, having entirely lost the ability to separate reality from illusion. But again, one must not be thrown off the track by Nathanael's erotic attraction to the mechanical woman. The doll is no more than a passive mirror for the youth's self-love, as Hoffmann clearly indicates, and is not a sex-object in the same sense as a real girl. The doll's "father" is the evil Coppelius, who had earlier threatened to deprive Nathanael of his eyes, i.e., to castrate him. Even though Nathanael was never in any danger of committing a sexual offense against a mere robot, he had reason to fear retribution because the doll was an onanistic love-object belonging to the sphere of regressive fantasy. The pyschodynamic formula would appear to be: He who loves narcissistically is guilty of the sin of onanism and must be punished. Ultimately, Nathanael destroys himself in a psychotic rage, only moments after fusing the image of the robot with that of Clara in a final hallucination.

The syncretic Olimpia/Clara image reveals an underlying confusion. In effect, Nathanael was unable to move beyond narcissism because the guilt and fear associated with his infantile sexuality had generalized to real women. The imagined consequences of making love to a real woman were just as terrifying to him as the penalties for allowing himself to cling to an erotic obsession centered on a fantasy-figure. "The Sandman" is not only a fictional treatment of the Oedipal motif, but illuminates an episode in the life of Hoffmann. I refer to Hoffmann's deep emotional involvement as a man in his mid-thirties with his 16-year-old musical student, Juliane Mark. By this time Hoffmann's marriage to his devoted, but unartistic wife had settled into a rut and his nightly drinking bouts at the local tavern, alternating with periods of depression, had come to be symptomatic of his unhappiness. The object of Hoffmann's love was married off by her parents in 1812 and the relationship with Hoffmann evidently was never consummated. Returning to "The Sandman," it may be supposed, on one level, that the beautiful robot Olimpia with whom Nathanael had become infatuated, corresponds to Juliane, and that the boy's forgotten fiancée, the sensible but unimaginative Clara, is modeled on Hoffmann's wife. If this supposition is correct we can feel justified in concluding that Hoffmann has indeed combined unconscious conflicts rooted in childhood with thematic materials drawn directly from adult experience. Such a synthesis would be in keeping with a view of the creative process that recognizes the interplay of conscious and unconscious forces, with the latter influences reflecting day-to-day problems confronting the artist, as well as pointing to the role of artistic discipline and craftsmanship.

There is also a folkloric dimension to "The Sandman." The frightening figure of Coppelius, the "Sandman," with his horrible face and his powerful, menacing figure, is probably the lineal descendant of a timeless array of masked tormentors and initiators. The katchinas of the Pueblo Indians, or the Black Peter who figures in the St. Nicholas Day customs of the Netherlands are members of the same fraternity. As an archetypal bogey-man who threatens children with unspeakable punishments, the masked initiator represents the father in his malevolent aspect. The fact that the masked initiator is also an instructor in the tribal mysteries does not cancel out his primary function: By inspiring extraordinary fear the masker's aim is to force the novice to identify himself with the adult norms of the tribe and with its ancestral totem. Coppelius is not an instructor, of course, but he is an initiator who gives the young Nathanael to understand that he must abandon the illusionary zone of infantile safety and security that is symbolized by his mother and his loving, but prosaic betrothed, Clara. Instead, Nathanael has no choice but to take his chances in the seemingly hallucinatory but paradoxically real world of cruel and destructive men. In this deadly realm, adults such as the "good" father perish because they are driven by greed or maybe even intellectual curiosity. And the "bad" father, Coppelius, unscrews Nathanael's arms and legs and rearranges them arbitrarily in a demonstration of the demonic power of the extra-familial world, in which human beings can be reduced to puppets.

Freud focused on the "bad" father as the much-feared castrator in his pioneering analysis of "The Sandman" in his essay, "The Uncanny." In this guise, Coppelius threatens to put out Nathanael's eyes, as I have mentioned, thereby administering the prescribed punishment for Oedipal sinners, that is, boys and men who remain incestually attached to the mother. As Freud pointed out (on the advice of Mrs. Rank), the very name Coppelius (from *coppella*, meaning crucible in Italian) links that sinister figure with the father and his secret alchemical experiments. But the name Coppelius is also connected with "coppo," or eye-socket and points to an important use of symbolism by Hoffmann. Imagery pertaining to the eye and the function of seeing occurs in a number of Hoffmann's works, but is especially prominent in "The Sandman."

For example, the child Nathanael *spies* on his father and Dr. Coppelius while they are engaged in their experiments. When Coppelius discovers the child, an hallucinatory scene unfolds in which Coppelius threatens to burn out Nathanael's eyes with glowing coal dust. This threat seems to be the horrible fulfillment of a tale Nathanael had heard from his nurse, to the effect that the Sandman steals children's eyes and feeds them to his brood of owls. Coppelius himself is described as having a large head with a beaklike, frightening face. Only the intervention of Nathanael's father—the "good" father—saves the boy from being blinded. Years later, Coppelius, now calling himself Coppola and posing as a seller of barometers, calls on Nathanael and sells him a pair of binoculars which will figure in the young man's undoing in the story's dénouement.

As a university student, Nathanael is smitten with Olimpia, as I have indicated, and *spies* on her day after day as she sits motionless across from his window. There is also the terrifying scene, not long after, in which Coppelius and Professor Spallanzani, who helped Coppelius build Olimpia, engage in a furious struggle over the mannequin, tearing out her blood-specked eyes in the process. A moment later Spallanzani informs Nathanael, who has just arrived on the scene, that the eyes were really Nathanael's and that Coppelius had stolen them from the youth. He then flings the eyes at Nathanael's breast, as Hoffmann puts it, and Nathanael tries to strangle the professor. Overcome by frenzy, Nathanael is taken away to a "madhouse," from which he is soon released as cured.

In the final climatic scene, Nathanael, beside himself with rage, tries to throw Clara from a tower, while "streams of fire glowed and spurted from his eyes." A few seconds later, he spies Coppelius through his binoculars and leaps to his death from the tower, shouting: "Circle of flames, spin—circle of flames, spin!"

Did Hoffmann unconsciously employ eye-symbolism to represent the trauma and fascination of the primal scene as witnessed by his young protagonist? Is the eye-symbolism also a metaphor for castration-anxiety? To say that Hoffmann has merely employed a literary device is not satisfactory, given the dramatic power and ubiquity of the eyemetaphor, with it voyeuristic implications. For example, in **"Master Floh,"** a housekeeper, Aline, peeps through a keyhole and sees two men pulling and twisting George Pepusch's body and trying to push it through the keyhole—surely a scene replete with sexual symbolism. In **"Gluck,"** a frustrated and despairing composer finally has an hallucinatory experience in which he sees a vision of a sunflower opening and a "radiant eye" within its calyx inspiring him to create beautiful music immediately. He is suddenly drawn into the calyx and encircled by flames, awakening to discover that he has not written a single note. Ultimately, the composer becomes psychotic, imagining that he is the composer Gluck. In this case as well, the opening of the "eye" inside the flower and the protagonist's absorption into it suggest a sexual motif. But Hoffmann has made it clear that we are in the zone of wishful thinking and has provided us with images that connect sexuality either with cruelty or failure, indicating the failure of the wish.

In a remarkable parallel to **"The Sandman,"** Hoffmann's **"Cremona Violin,"** the author has painted a portrait of a bizarre old man who appears to "control" a beautiful, but mysterious young woman who can sing with extraordinary sweetness. Like Coppelius in **"The Sandman,"** this wizard-like old man, Councillor Krespel, is undoubtedly the "creator" and the captor of his fair charge; in reality, he is her father. The narrator, who takes it upon himself to rescue the captive maiden, stands in a peculiarly Oedipal relationship to the old man, who is a rather terrifying, hypermanic individual. Councillor Krespel collects rare violins and is a violin-maker in his own right. However, he never allows anyone to hear or see his renowned collection of violins. Krespel resembles the evil monk Vallies in **"Datura Fastuosa"** insofar as both men own or control a beautiful woman who sings bewitchingly. Krespel's rare violins, which he is in the habit of taking apart and putting together again—seemingly in search of some musical secret of perfection—also remind one of Coppelius' mechanical doll, and even of the boy Nathanael, whom Coppelius takes apart limb from limb in a nightmarish sequence in **"The Sandman."** The common element in these comparisons is the master-creature relationship in which a powerful and fearful male adult manipulates a helpless child or young woman. When the creature is a woman, she appears to be, in one instance, the good-bad mother, who, like Vallie's accomplice, the beautiful Gabriela, betrays the young

man who loves her. In the case of the mechanical doll, Olimpia, the good-bad mother role is less obvious because the doll clearly does not withhold herself from the young protagonist, Nathanael, of her own free will, but is rendered inaccessible to the hero by the destructive rage of her two creators, Spallanzani and Coppola (Coppelius). Nevertheless, we are obliged to think of Olimpia as a temptress because she is perceived as an irresistible love-object by Nathanael. In **"The Cremona Violin,"** the good-bad female is the fair singer, Antonia, whom the narrator loves, but he is denied the opportunity of hearing his beloved's voice by her eccentric guardian, old Krespel. Antonia is also an ambivalent love-object because she is accessible on the level of platonic friendship, but not otherwise.

It is Antonia who provides us with an important lead as to the symbolic meaning of "singing" in Hoffmann's stories. The reason the young narrator of **"The Cremona Violin"** is prevented by Krespel from hearing Antonia sing is because singing is filled with sexual meaning in the context of this story. It is more than a prelude to romance or its accompaniment. For Hoffmann, singing—like playing the violin, like constructing a mechanical doll, like dabbling in alchemical experiments, like raising hot-house flowers—is quintessentially erotic, but in a perverse, pregenital way. For this reason, Hoffmann's master-creature relationships are sexual in character, with strong overtones of dominance and submission, and with an undertone of destructive rage. Although Hoffmann creates many character sketches of lovable and approachable young women— Gretchen in **"Datura Fastuosa"** is as good an example as any—he cannot refrain from introducing an element of danger when he turns his attention to romantic themes. The danger to the hero is greatest when the love-object is the "creature" of an older and more powerful man, i.e., when she belongs to the "bad" father. The Oedipal theme in such cases is too obvious to be overlooked.

Further insight into Hoffmann's conception of Oedipal conflicts is provided by his story **"Mademoiselle de Scudéry."** Why, for example, does Hoffmann insist on casting the elderly and distinctly maternal heroine of this tale in the role of a spinster? Why is she not, at the very least, a widow? But to ask this question is to reveal that one does not grasp the significance of the Oedipal drama in Hoffmann's writings. There can be no *Madame* de Scudéry because the "good" mother, as far as Hoffmann is concerned, has to be pure and virginal. And Mlle. de Scudéry is indeed the "good" mother in relation to the unfortunate Olivier de Brusson, for did she not help to rear him as an infant, even before he was orphaned in childhood? It is also true that the kindly, aristocratic lady believes in the innocence of the young man, who has been accused of murdering his death-dealing master, Cardillac, the quintessential "bad" father. Cardillac belongs to Hoffmann's extensive gallery of "bad" fathers because he stands between young Brusson and the object of his love, Cardillac's beautiful and tender-hearted daughter.

But Cardillac is the "bad" father in a more general sense. He has a compulsion to lie in wait in order to slay amorous cavaliers on their way to keep an assignation. At the same time Cardillac robs them of the jewels they invariably carry as a gift to their mistresses. In this way the castrating "bad" father punishes a multitude of errant sons by preventing them from consummating their unlawful love affairs. In addition, Cardillac seizes the jewels, Jung's archetypal symbol of the *anima,* and takes back what he believes to be his own. After all, did he not, in his capacity as goldsmith, manufacture the jewels in the first place? In other words, was not the feminine love-object his own from the start? So reasons Cardillac on the unconscious level, and his creator, Hoffmann, as well. Strangely enough, it is not clear whether Cardillac kills his lustful victims in his familiar capacity as the "bad" father—the enemy of love—or in the more novel role of incestuous jealous son! The latter possibility, however startling, is supported by Cardillac's strange explanation of his compulsion to steal jewels. In a revealing conversation with his assistant, Olivier, the old goldsmith recalls that his pregnant mother had been assaulted sexually by a Spanish cavalier wearing a flashing jewelled necklace. In the act of resisting her would-be seducer, Cardillac's mother grabbed at the beautiful pendant which had dazzled her only moments earlier, filling her with a "desire for the sparkling gems." The Spaniard thereupon fell to the ground, and the woman with him, but the excitement had proven too much for the cavalier and he died on the spot. Cardillac went on to relate:

> My mother sought in vain to extricate herself from the dead man's rigid arms. With his hollow eyes, whose light had gone out, directed upon her, the dead man tossed this way and that with her upon the ground. Her shrill screams for help finally reached some people passing in the distance, who hurried to her aid and released her from the arms of her terrible lover.

If this is not a description of a primal scene, it is a fair facsimile! Seen through the eyes of his fetal son, the father /Spaniard was committing an outrage upon the mother. He deserved to die, and did indeed expire. So, too, must all those other cavaliers with sex on their mind, whom Cardillac stabs to death, one by one, not even allowing them to "sin" beforehand. But I will not insist on this interpretation. Let us say that Cardillac is more convincing as the rival-father vis-à-vis young Oliver, all the more so because Cardillac has so much in common with the Sandman, who also exists only to frustrate the sexual wishes of the vulnerable Nathanael. It is instructive to note that Cardillac professes to admire the elderly Mlle. de Scudéry and says to her: "Have pity on me Mademoiselle, and take the jewelry. You have no idea what veneration for your virtue and your high merits I carry in my heart! Regard my meager gift as simply an attempt to prove to you my most heartfelt admiration."

The dignified old woman is not unmoved by Cardillac's impassioned plea. The worldly Marquise de Maintenon, who observes her reaction to the goldsmith, remarks: "And are you not acting like a bashful young thing who longs for the sweet fruit that is offered her, if only she could take it without a hand and without fingers?" We seem to be witnessing a flirtation that appears to be of no consequence for the main story line, and which, at any rate, leads nowhere. And yet, precisely because it is an apparently gratuitous component of the story, it must not be allowed to pass unnoticed. Mlle. de Scudéry is, after all, the "good" mother and Cardillac is the "bad" father. Of course she must rebuff the man and his jewels. Hoffmann's scenario requires that, at 73, Mlle. de Scudéry continue a stranger to carnal love, but the astute Marquise de Maintenon says to her tauntingly: "Now we know, Mademoiselle, Master René (Cardillac) is desperately in love with you and is beginning according to the proper and ancient customs of true gallantry, to assail your heart with costly gifts."

Hoffmann then goes on to say that the two women jest merrily about how it would be if Mlle. de Scudéry were really to become the bride of Cardillac. Their thoughts then turn to more "serious" matters as they try to decide what to do with the jewels which Cardillac has pressed upon the old noblewoman. Nevertheless, Cardillac's admiration for Mlle. de Scudéry, like his admiration for King Louis IV, is not without significance. In fact, Cardillac refuses to make jewelry for either Mlle. de Scudéry or the King because he fears they might become the object of his homicidal rage and of his compulsion to take back his jewels once he has sold them to a customer. But why should this classically anal-sadistic character spare anyone? The old lady must remain beyond the reach of either lust or violence because she is the virginal "good" mother, even though Cardillac is strongly drawn to her and at one point even falls to his knees and kisses her skirt and her hands and then runs from the room, knocking over furniture and breaking china and glasses. The juxtaposition of love and violence in this scene reflects Cardillac's ambivalence, or more precisely, the author's unconscious delineation of Cardillac and Mlle. de Scudéry as "bad" father and "good" wife /mother. As for the King, Hoffmann spares him the enmity of the savage goldsmith because, paradoxically, the womanizing King is the "good" father who absolves Olivier Brusson of all guilt in connection with the death of Cardillac when the latter is killed by one of his would-be victims. Stated in psychoanalytic terms, the "good" father pardons the son for having harbored murderous intentions toward the "bad" father, the sexual rival, and allows himself to be convinced that the "bad" father was slain by someone else.

As was stated earlier, Hoffmann was a devoted champion of romantic idealism. He fulfilled the esthetic requirements of romanticism by affirming in his fictional works the primacy of imagination over crass reality, of heartfelt emotion over crabbed reason, and of innocent faith over skepticism. These were difficult demands for Hoffmann because he was a deeply pessimistic man with a cyclical temperament (not unlike that of his contemporary, the French ideologue, Henri Saint-Simon). On the psychological plane idealism cannot be viewed simply as a philosophical or artistic position that one selects freely from among many others solely on the basis of its intrinsic merits. It is necessary to ask, "What is the ontogenesis of idealism and why does it take certain symbolic forms in literature, and not others?"

If we examine Hoffmann's stories closely, it becomes apparent that the realm of the ideal is psychologically linked with the imagery of the "good" parent, be it father or mother. The real world, which Hoffmann perceived as filled with violent, insensitive, mocking self-servers, is most often symbolized by a "bad" parent figure, sometimes in the form of a powerful wizard—Coppelius in **"The Sandman"**—or, in the guise of a witch, the evil old apple-woman in **"The Golden Pot."** Examples of "good" parents are the wizard, Archivarius Lindhorst in **"The Golden Pot,"** the widow, Mrs. Helms, in **"Datura Fastuosa,"** or the magical Herr Dapsul von Zabelthau in the fairy tale, **"The King's Bride,"** to name only a few in each category.

Of special interest is the way in which Hoffmann interweaves his sexual motifs with his recurring symbols of the ideal and the real. Invariably, Hoffmann's young heroes must choose between spiritual love and physical love in resolving the identity crisis of adolescence and young manhood. Sometimes the spiritual love-object is literally a spirit, as in **"The Golden Pot"** or a platonic love-object, as in **"Datura Fastuosa."** Although such de-sexualized love-objects are predominantly benevolent, their very nurturance is at times resented because Hoffmann's protagonists sense that it is an impediment to growth and self-assertion, including sexual freedom. In **"The Sandman,"** the idealized love-object is the alluring mechanical woman, Olimpia. Her positive qualities (she is programmed to be an attentive and seemingly adoring listener in her lover's presence) are outweighed in the end, however, by the fact that she can be taken apart and destroyed by her evil designers, Coppelius and his partner, Professor Spallanzani. Hoffmann's flesh-and-blood heroines stand for the real world, with its necessary limitations and humdrum routines, although the author consistently portrays them as beautiful and kind-hearted. Despite their attractive qualities, these heroines are usually ignored or resisted by Hoffmann's heroes until the very end because, as in the case of the idealized heroine, they are perceived as an obstacle to complete freedom.

Thus, the "ideal," as treated by Hoffmann in fiction, is represented by unavailable, platonic love-objects just as reality is symbolized by sexually responsive women. Both the real world and the idealized, magical dream-world (such as Atlantis in **"The Golden Pot"**) contain rewards and snares, although Hoffmann makes it clear in almost every story that the realm of fantasy is far superior to the ordinary world. This predilection is announced in one of Hoffmann's earliest letters to Hippel, written when Hoffmann was only 19: ". . .we must not banish daydreaming. Daydreaming is to us what color is to a painting. It enhances every idea that occupies our intellect, and it spreads over our every thought of happiness a beneficent sense of gentle delight. Only through daydreams do friendship and love (not love and friendship) gain their worth. And tell me, furthermore, wasn't it always daydreams that prompted every great deed ever done. . . .?"

As if to underscore the centrality of fantasy in Hoffmann, he surprises us at every turn by investing his idealized, magical settings with sensuous, distinctly libidinized qualities. As a result, his de-sexualized heroines, such as the muse Serpentina in **"The Golden Pot,"** always appear in a context of thinly disguised sexual arousal and emotional intensity on the part of the male protagonist, whereas the nubile, but prosaic heroines (Clara in **"The Sandman,"** Madelon in **"Mademoiselle de Scudéry,"** Gretchen in **"Datura Fastuosa"**) are presented in low-keyed situations, the ambience of domesticity. When an idealized woman is imbued with sexual powers by Hoffmann (the seductive, but unattainable Gabriela in **"Datura Fastuosa"** is an example), she automatically falls into the category of the "bad" woman, even though she belongs to the domain of wish-fulfillment. It is clear from Hoffmann's treatment of the idealized woman that she must be identified with spiritual forces that contend with the norms of bourgeois life. In those instances where Hoffmann's magical characters are tainted with worldly greed or cruelty, as in the case of Coppelius, they do not cease to belong to the spirit world, but are treated as malevolent entities.

The ontogenesis of Hoffmann's interpretation of the ideal can be traced to the loss of his father (through divorce) when Hoffmann was only two. The ideal came to signify the realm of irretrievable loss, a never-never land where the "good" father resides like a remote wizard or benevolent demi-god in the clouds. The dead father, and the stricken mother, entirely sealed off from her young son by chronic, possibly psychotic depression, stand for perfect love, perfect innocence, perfect nurturance—in short, the ego-ideal—in contrast to the sordid real world, presided over by Hoffmann's cold, tyrannical bachelor uncle, Otto Doerffer, and the strict spinster aunt, Sophie. Hoffmann's wizards in their enchanted workshops, his magical "salamanders" and gnomes, and his many fantastic, comical creatures belong with the dead ancestors. They are spirits of the noble and beneficent dead, and one communes with them by entering the zone of daydreams and hallucinations. Sometimes they appear as vengeful ghosts or bad genii who are anti-sex and anti-life, but this defect is a side-effect of their virtue, which is that they transcend the forces of everyday, profane life.

Hoffmann fulfilled the esthetic requirements of romanticism by affirming in his fictional works the primacy of imagination over crass reality, of heartfelt emotion over crabbed reason, and of innocent faith over skepticism.

—*Leo Schneiderman*

Hoffmann suggests to us that the romantic frame of mind, which ever sees the ideal as being in opposition to the actual, is a form of homage to the idealized memory of a past that never was. Whether that past is one's own childhood or the childhood of the human race—the Golden Age—it is a myth born of psychological necessity, like all myths. By believing in and feeling the goodness of our parents and ancestors we not only internalize their positive traits, but become capable of projecting the ego-ideal onto the larger world. Hence, we look for ideal alternatives to the actualities of life. If we are story-tellers like Hoffmann, we find these alternatives in the dream-world of make-believe, just as contemporary science-fiction writers locate "the other place" in another galaxy. Reformers and revolutionaries locate the fulfillment of their hopes in the future, and conservatives look to the past. Romanticism is closely associated with the rise of 19th and 20th century nationalism and political reaction, both forms of ancestor worship.

Hoffmann was essentially apolitical; but it is well known that he was a champion of political freedom and, indeed, in his capacity as a supreme court judge, bravely defended human rights. In this way, Hoffmann distinguished between the ideal in fiction, which was to be found only in fairyland, and the ideal in everyday human affairs, which can be approached only by struggling realistically against cruelty and injustice. It can be said by Hoffmann, finally, that he was faithful to the romantic spirit in his art as well as in his life, partly concealing life's failings in his art in the name of the ideal, to be sure, but only to provide a dramatic vehicle for communicating his ethical concerns in an entertaining way, without bitterness. It can also be said that in real life, Hoffmann lacked a mother capable of giving him security, and a father to prepare him for the challenges of the objective world. He attempted to create a fictional world in which the terror of life was offset by the healing power of love and compassion. (pp. 288-310)

> Leo Schneiderman, "E. Th. A. Hoffmann's 'Tales': Ego Ideal and Parental Loss," in American Imago, Vol. 40, No. 3, Fall, 1983, pp. 285-310.

Thomas A. Kamla   (essay date 1985)

[*In the following excerpt, Kamla examines psychoanalytical aspects of Hoffmann's "Vampirism."*]

Since Hoffmann's vampire story was written expressly for volume four of *The Serapion Brothers,* it was, as with several other tales, not assigned a title and has been variously labelled **"Vampirism," "Cyprian's Narrative," "Tale of a Vampire," "The Hyena,"** etc., depending on which biography or critical edition of the author's works one might happen to consult. The theoretical discussion of this theme by members of the Serapion circle before and after the story and the sources they mention indicate that Hoffmann was more than casually familiar with the myth of the bloodsucking undead, which had been garnering interest among European writers of Dark Romanticism since the turn of the nineteenth century. From these discussions, it becomes apparent that Hoffmann wishes to avoid explicit portrayal of the incredible, horrific trappings associated with vampirism, preferring to exercise "poetic tact" in order that "the gruesome does not degenerate to the level of the disgusting and loathsome."

During the debate preceding the story, Hoffmann seems more concerned with the underlying idea of vampirism, that is, with the psychological implications of its gruesome elements, and regards the "dread" and "horror" it evokes not as an aesthetic confirmation of the sublime but as a manifestation of all too human aberrations which, as the narrator Cyprian states, reside "within our own breast," indeed which originate "more often in thought than in appearances." It is not Cyprian who places emphasis on the supernatural content of the vampire myth but other members of the literary circle. Thus, we hear from Sylvester: "To my knowledge a vampire, you see, is nothing more than a living corpse who sucks the blood of those still alive," and Lothar: ". . . that a vampire is nothing more than a cursed chap who has himself interred as a corpse only to rise shortly thereafter from the grave and suck the blood of the people asleep, who then become vampires as well." Cyprian takes the position that the unexplained supernatural is not a necessary concomitant of vampiric fantasies, and that such fantasies are indeed rooted in human behavior, as evidenced by the factual account upon which he bases his narrative: ". . . that the story really did take place and [Cyprian] named the Count's family and the parental estate where everything had occurred." Since Cyprian discards a purely fantastic perception of vampirism in favor of a realistic one, the theme would then seem to bear metaphoric significance in terms of psychological maladjustment, in which case we would be dealing with a very genuine, albeit disguised, instinctual content.

From the outset, the title **"Vampirism,"** or any of its variants, needs to be qualified, as it conveys an inadequate message for the kind of pathological behavior portrayed in the story. This is especially so when one considers that the oral aggression exhibited by the leading character Aurelie extends beyond the early infantile urge to suck or, as the title suggests, to bite simply in order to draw blood, and instead combines the urge to bite with that of tearing and devouring. It is really the tendency toward ghoulish cannibalism, a pathological condition in which a living person visits the body of the dead, that illustrates the story's main concern, and not the unrealistic suggestion of nocturnal visitations by a revenant. Commenting on Cyprian's narration at its conclusion, Lothar perceives this necessity of shifting thematic emphasis when he exclaims: "Compared to your story vampirism is a real child's game, a funny Shrovetide play that would make you die laughing." Since vampirism, more precisely ghoulism, does not pervade the story as an explicit thematic component, this remark can only refer to those final events in which such content is manifest, namely the graveyard scene depicting Aurelie feeding on the flesh of an exhumed corpse, and the concluding episode in which she attacks and bites her husband after he exposes her abnormal craving.

Compared with the predominant sections of **"Vampirism,"** which comprise interior story and frame and focus on the dynamics of human interaction, these closing scenes might appear incongruously shocking to those readers who fail to see Aurelie's pathological degeneracy as a logical outgrowth of the events recounted. Owing doubtless to the dehumanized instinctual impact of the conclusion, the story, since its appearance in 1821, has had to suffer as a work of literature, being regarded by most critics—and a number of the Serapion Brothers, for that matter—as a popular contribution to Gothic horror. It is no wonder, then, that serious, in-depth investigations of the story are virtually nonexistent.

Hoffmann's novella is deserving of such concerns, however, if for no other reason than that a latent content informs the text which makes the closing scenes—the visual presentation of this content on the manifest level—psychologically (per Cyprian) explainable. With the exception of the end, the story, to the extent that one apprehends its surface meaning, is not at all about the undead or grave robbers. Yet, in his portrayal of the heroine, the author alludes precisely to those prototypical stages of emotional life (infantile orality, maternal dependence and incorporation, parent-provider as narcissistic complement, self-object differentiation, and puberty) which, if frustrated in their development, may eventually awaken in the subject an inclination toward the kind of aggressive behavior suggested by the vampire-ghoul syndrome. Such prototypical forms of experience are essential components in Aurelie's flashback, as she proceeds to relate events of her past life to her newly wedded husband, Count Hyppolit. Her story within a story, seen by some readers as a structural inconsistency because it impedes the flow of the narrative proper, is important in a psychoanalytic interpretation, for it allows us to establish the unconscious motivation underlying the heroine's oral fixation and instinctual perversion in the frame.

From Aurelie's account, it becomes clear that her formative years had been disrupted by a series of traumatic experiences involving perverted love on both the narcissistic and object-related levels of childhood and puberty. Understandably, her early recollections have ebbed with time; what she does recall from her childhood, though, is an incident so emotionally painful that its latent meaning, repressed in her unconscious, must perforce resist articulation. Only certain details are recounted:

> During her early youth Aurelie indistinctly recalled that a terrible ruckus occurred one morning in the house. When things finally quieted down, the governess picked Aurelie up and carried her into a large room where several people were assembled. In the middle of the room lay, outstretched, the man who had often played with Aurelie, fed her sweets, and whom she had called "Papa." Her little hands reached out to him and she wanted to kiss him. The customarily warm lips were ice cold, however, and Aurelie, without knowing why, broke out in uncontrollable weeping.

However sketchy this recollection, a repressed content still seems to suggest itself through images of love and food which point to the interdependence of narcissism and orality in an undifferentiated self-object relationship. Her lecherous mother constantly away (hence the need of a governess), Aurelie's only parental relationship is with a man whose demonstrations of affection and supplies of sweets have earned him the name "Papa." The fact that he is not Aurelie's natural father is incidental as long as he fulfills the narcissistic function of supplier. Since the autoerotically inclined infant does not distinguish between love and food, this man serves as Aurelie's narcissistic complement, her provider and lover, so to speak; oral in-

corporation ("sweets") is thus a function of paternal love. And with the mother absent—to the young daughter's mind, out of the way—the child need not be concerned about competing demands on the father's time and can claim exclusive possession in its striving for uninterrupted instinctual gratification.

These observations are, or course, based on assumptions that antedate the actual course of events in Aurelie's flashback. What is implied in her account is not narcissistic reinforcement through the gratification of oral instinct, but narcissistic dispossession and perversion through the withdrawal of supplies and the kissing of a corpse. Kissing, like food, is also linked with oral incorporation: subject and object merge as long as this form of autoeroticism remains pleasurable. And it was through kissing and sweets that Aurelie was able to identify, merge with, her narcissistic complement, her "Papa."

With Aurelie's provider laid out on the table, lifeless, oral pleasure is withdrawn and the child experiences narcissistic frustration. Add to this the displeasure of kissing ice cold lips that had been customarily warm, and we approach that familiar, yet strange realm of Freud's uncanny which, on returning in repressed form in Aurelie's behavior later on, reveals a transgressive function in bringing to light desires which should have remained concealed. That Aurelie is unable to explain to her husband why she had wept so bitterly back then merely indicates that deepseated psychological issues are at work which defy conscious explanation. The expectation of a pleasurable response through kissing had been subverted by a disturbing sensation, so that the oral activity of kissing itself became ambivalent, encompassing on the unconscious level both pleasure and pain. Aurelie's narcissistic identification with the parent-provider thus experienced a split, producing a perversion of the love instinct in which the child's desire to possess orally fuses with the desire to inflict pain.

Critics of a nonpsychoanalytic persuasion might argue that Aurelie's childhood account constitutes such an isolated, momentary phase of her earlier life that to infer the kind of latent presuppositions outlined above is untenable even in the psychoanalytic approach. In their peculiar configuration, however, the images evoked in Aurelie's account do not suggest merely an innocuous preoccupation with orality, but focus instead on that stage of infantile autoeroticism in which the pleasure of incorporation had passed from sucking to biting with an object other than the mother, namely her rival in the oedipal triangle, and with that, a cannibalistic component comes into play. It is this component that ultimately establishes the nature of the heroine's oral fixation.

As Aurelie continues her account, we see her as a girl of sixteen who becomes the victim of the most depraved kind of sexual exploitation at the hands of her mother, with whom she had been living since the onset of puberty, and the mother's lover, an escaped convict and voluptuary posing as a rich baron. The ambivalent autoerotic experience of Aurelie's childhood prefigures at this later level of emotional development a self-object relationship that inhibits healthy sexual awakening. In both instances, the experience of perversion—the one occurrence narcissistic, the other ego-related—constitutes the sadistic alternative to normal instinctual development. Now, as a young girl, Aurelie witnesses not only a revolting sexual act between mother and suitor; she in turn becomes the target of an attempted rape by this same adult male. The mother then attempts to arrange a marriage of convenience between the daughter and the man who, at the unconscious oedipal level, represents the father figure as the third element in the sexual triangle. What might be only unconsciously wished for in a childhood relationship (the daughter replacing the mother) ought to have been superseded by the reality principle at the ego stage (the daughter reserving to the mother the right, within the bounds of propriety, to intimacy with a potential, surrogate father); instead, Aurelie is forced into a relationship that has the appearance of confirming a traumatic childhood fantasy, one in which the Papa figure turns into a source of displeasure. Aurelie's horror at her mother's design stems from the dualism between unconscious oedipal drives and ego-perception, the one desiring incestuous union, the other repressing it with the knowledge that this later "Papa" figure embodies displeasure in the form of sexual domination and sadistic aggression. Once the mother's scheme fails and the daughter observes her being beaten by her paramour, the impact on unconscious desire and ego-formation becomes even more compelling: the greater the shock to Aurelie's moral sensibilities, the greater the intensity of instinctual drives bent on sadistic possession.

The manifest content of the story indicates that Aurelie's emotional state and moral character are not seriously impaired when she marries, despite the privation and maltreatment she had been subjected to at the hands of a lewd mother. Her love for Count Hyppolit seems perfectly normal, at least initially, so that one is led to believe that an ego-directed sense of decency has prevailed after all over any oral-sadistic identification with love. And so it has—on a conscious level. During the turbulent years of puberty and the early period of her marriage, Aurelie's ego was more receptive to the moral demands of the superego than to the instinctual ones of the unconscious. Yet any suggestion of a link between sexual love and aggression, however much rejected by Aurelie consciously, could only act as an additional stimulus to her unconscious, inasmuch as this region of her psyche was vulnerable to, indeed conditioned by, intimations of instinctual perversion originating with the displeasure experienced in the infantile, autoerotic phase and, subsequently, the "shocking loathsomeness of the stranger and the depraved mother," behavior which, as we discover, "made a mockery of moral sensibilities and caused Aurelie to react with horror." Aggressive libidinal drives that unconsciously strive for narcissistic gratification remain, if only briefly, repressed, allowing a self-object fusion between wife and husband to be achieved at the height of marital love. It is at this point in **"Vampirism"** that the present action resumes, and we are faced with the question as to what actually triggers the repressed desire of Aurelie's unconscious, producing transgressive impulses toward sadism, necrophilia, and necrophagia.

Once again, the primary motivator is Aurelie's mother, the baroness. Critics who interpret literally the statements of the Serapion Brothers concerning vampirism assume that she, like her daughter, also embodies this myth, although little textual evidence can be adduced that would support this view. Certainly Aurelie's actions throughout the novella invalidate any such claim, and only at the beginning does the baroness betray behavior which might be construed—not as vampiric—but, like that of Aurelie at the end, ghoulish: after she arrives at Hyppolit's castle with her daughter, she is reported to have taken nocturnal walks toward the cemetery, in which vicinity she is found dead, without explanation, on the morning Aurelie and Hyppolit are to wed.

What lends itself more readily to textual analysis and in turn helps to shed light on the baroness's apparent ghoulism is her almost demonic proclivity for evil and a witch-like appearance that instills horror in those she encounters. Thus we read that her initial impression on Hyppolit was "repugnant" and that she "penetrated . . . [him] with a glowing stare". Deceived into believing that her motives for visiting him harbor no ill will, he shakes the baroness's hand, whereupon "ice cold trembling ran through him. He felt his hand grasped by fingers frozen in death, and the large, bony figure of the baroness, who glared at him with eyes that lacked vision, seemed like a dolled-up corpse in her ugly, gaily-colored clothes". A witness to this scene, Aurelie laments the fact that catalepsy is the cause of this cadaverlike behavior, a physical impediment full of sexual-aggressive overtones that will have severe psychic repercussions for the daughter once she discovers she is to become a mother. Finally, we hear: "The Count had grown accustomed to the strangely furrowed, deathly pale face, the ghostly figure of the old woman, and attributed everything to her sickliness as well as her propensity for dark, morbid longings, as she often went on nocturnal walks [as indicated above] through the park to the cemetery".

It is characteristic of Hoffmann to interweave opposing realms of existence in his works, obfuscating the borderline between reality and fantasy so that the reader is often unsure to which realm he is to orient himself. In the scene just described the fantasy content of folklore (witches) conjoins with medical explanation (catalepsy) to evoke fear and horror (here the reader would be expected to identify with Hyppolit's reaction) while still remaining rooted in reality. In psychoanalytic criticism, however, the structural irony created by the two realms is obviated when we locate the source of fantasy, not in the supernatural domain of myth, but in the human unconscious. We know it is common practice in folklore for witches to torment and place curses on the good and innocent (the evil mother's treatment of Aurelie) and to revel in sexual excesses with the Devil (suggested by her catalepsy and "dark, morbid longings"). Such actions impact psychologically on unconscious desire. Thus, in the figure of the baroness, Hoffmann is not actually portraying a witch (**"Vampirism"** is no fairy tale), but adopting its metaphor to illustrate a problematic relationship between mother and daughter, one that is only exacerbated by the mother's apparent ghoulish cravings—and herein lies the connection with the biting and corpse imagery of Aurelie's childhood experience.

When we consider the portrayal of the baroness in this extended context, it becomes all the more difficult to envision her in the maternal role of a loving, caring mother. The natural instinct of the daughter to identify maternally with the mother is frustrated by a motherly image more evocative of the abnormal. Once Aurelie reaches puberty, she knows that the woman who has come for her is her real mother, a role that really had been fulfilled by a kind of surrogate mother, the governess, up to that point. Since the baroness never proved herself worthy of this role by demonstrating the same attention and care, her relationship with Aurelie can only produce a conflicting mother image, the one caring, the other threatening. At the "heillose Treiben der Mutter," "unsavory escapades" ranging anywhere from wantonness to suspicious graveyard activity, Aurelie senses only revulsion, an emotion that can, even with one's mother, turn to hate. Thus, on revealing her past to her husband, she asks whether there is anything more horrible than having to abhor one's own mother ("Gibt es . . . etwas Entsetzlicheres, als die eigne Mutter hassen, verabscheuen zu müssen?"), an attitude that gives affirmation to an unnatural feeling, Aurelie's horror at this realization being proof that maternal love is the natural bond. The unconscious implication of so ambivalent a reaction is that the maternal instinct itself appears unnatural and thus must be repressed if the daughter is to maintain ego stability. On witnessing a sexually abominable act between her mother and the stranger, Aurelie's "delicate, maidenly feelings" had been "dealt a deadly blow," a sign that disgust for the vulgar and a sense of shame cannot tolerate such a perception of womanhood. Consequently, she must repress any thoughts about her mother that conflict with maternal expectations that derive from normal interpersonal relationships. When these thoughts do invade Aurelie's conscious, her reaction is instinctively one of horror: the long familiar ties that bind mother and daughter are transformed into the unfamiliar by the alienating experience of hate, which accounts for Aurelie's later fear—vampiric in content—that her mother will one day return from the dead and restore the instinctual bond through exclusive possession.

Just as Aurelie had experienced instinctual frustration as a child, so does she experience obstacles at the level of ego-preservation; in neither case do needs and expectations agree. The autoerotic desire for gratification had met with displeasure at the infantile level; at the level of ego-perception the need to channel impulses and control environment had also been thwarted. The crucial phase of emotional development is rooted, of course, in the molding experience of childhood, for it is here that the ramifications of self-other relationships establish themselves as driving impulses within the unconscious psyche. And if these relationships are traumatic at the infantile level and remain unhealthy at the later, ego-oriented stages, then it is only a question of time before the repressed pleasure-pain principle holds sway over the reality principle.

So it is with Aurelie. A daughter's relationship with her mother presupposes an instinctual identity in terms of maternal fusion. A disruption of this fusion already suggested itself at the earlier stage of infancy when Aurelie, since birth, had been given over to the care of a governess. Thus,

of the two levels underlying a girl's identification with her mother, the affectionate pre-oedipal attachment and oedipal hostility, Aurelie ostensibly never benefited by the first; and the phase of the tender pre-oedipal attachment is, as Sheila Baker has pointed out, "the decisive one for [a girl's] acquisitions of those characteristics which are necessary for her later femininity to be successful" ["Activity-Passivity: Masculinity-Femininity," in *Basic Psychoanalytic Concepts on the theory of Instincts,* Humberto Nagera, ed.]. Aurelie might still have been able to assert a sense of feminine esteem at the later pubertal level if, by her actions, the baroness had demonstrated that instinct and desire can be transformed into socially acceptable forms of behavior, rather than into impulses that are sexually aggressive and perverted. Then Aurelie would have been better able to master unconscious desire later, owing to a healthy perception of interpersonal relationship. Libidinal energy as it concerns the maternal and sexual instinct might then have developed in a normal way from the self to the object, and those other prototypical phases of human experience that Aurelie passes through—adulthood, marital love, pregnancy, and childbirth-might also have proceeded normally. Needless to say, this is not the case.

Aurelie's hate and fear of her mother, and her corresponding estrangement from reality, intensify when the baroness places a curse on her on hearing of Aurelie's love for Count Hyppolit:

> Aurelie had to feel overjoyed at the thought that she was now free of all her worries. How deeply terrified she became, though, when in this blissful state she spoke to her mother about the merciful providence of heaven, whereupon the baroness, infernal flames in her eyes, screeched: 'You are my misfortune, you vile, unholy creature. At the height of your dream of bliss, however, revenge will strike you in the event I am snatched away by an unexpected death. In catalepsy, the price I am paying for having born you, the cunning of Satan'—at this point Aurelie stopped and, throwing herself at the Count, implored him not to make her repeat everything her mother had said in her insane rage.

What Aurelie chooses not to repeat, or to repress, is the suggestion in this passage of the mother having sexual relations with the Devil. The baroness entertains just such a delusion in her demonic hysteria, and sees Aurelie's birth as the link that binds her with Satan. At work here is a psychological meaning of catalepsy, which in demoniacal possession points to a hysterical symptom symbolizing coitus. The baroness regards her condition not merely as a physical impediment, induced by pregnancy and birth, but as the workings of Satan which—and this is what Aurelie is unable to repeat—will ostensibly extend to the mother's offspring. The revenge referred to implies that the daughter will inherit, indeed incorporate, the instinctual inclinations of the mother when she dies, the most prominent of which are aggressive possession and sexual excess.

As the story unfolds, it becomes apparent that the seemingly separate experiences of childhood narcissism and maternal identity, more specifically of oral and sexual aggression, are really coextensions of an all-inclusive instinctual perversion. The mother's mysterious demise near the castle graveyard (a manifestation of the death instinct resulting from a fusion of oral-sexual aggression and cataleptic attack), her curse, her intimate involvement with the sadistic stranger, and the almost devilish delight she had taken in depriving Aurelie of the basic necessities (living environment, clothing, sustenance—thus a reinforcement, by analogy, of narcissistic deprivation) have activated Aurelie's fantasy to the point where anxiety, fear, and morbid dread overpower the defenses of shame, disgust, and morality, permitting a hitherto repressed childhood traumata exert a dynamic influence on her behavior at the end. Since Aurelie's infantile orality is bound up with the impression of eating, kissing, biting, provider, and the dead, it follows from the story's latent content that this kind of incorporation, once all ego-defenses have broken down and the unconscious becomes reality, will spawn a sadistic hunger of rather extreme proportions, one, as with Aurelie, that seeks to sate the appetite of love by fusing necrophilia with necrophagia.

Not surprisingly, Aurelie's regression to the infantile stage of oral sadism occurs at the moment she realizes she is pregnant. Viewed psychoanalytically, pregnancy itself is a kind of incorporation; it is a time when unconscious fantasies around introjection become mobilized (the child's identification with its narcissistic complement), when the revival of receptive demands and oral-sadistic strivings take place. This explains Aurelie's depressed mental state on learning of her condition, a state that signals an incipient obsessional neurosis that will degenerate into the kind of pathological behavior noted above. Indications of a personality disorder are already evident from the following:

> A short time had passed when a noticeable change came over Aurelie. While the deathly pallor of her face and her weary eyes seemed to indicate illness, her confused, unstable, indeed shy behavior pointed to some new secret which disturbed her. Even her husband she avoided, at times locking herself in her room, at other times seeking the most remote areas of the castle grounds. And when she did show up, her tearful eyes and distorted features gave testimony to some kind of horrible torment that she was suffering.

Aurelie's "new secret" and "horrible torment" anticipate a surfacing of the concealed from origins that are different and yet related: on the one hand, a kindling of repressed morbid cravings traceable to childhood; on the other, revulsion and fear of motherhood resulting from the baroness's actions. The element linking the two, as noted earlier, is instinctual perversion. Aurelie's apprehension, suggested by her inner torment, about destructive instinctual urges is rooted in the same apprehension, owing to the association of motherhood with the demonic (the baroness's curse), about pregnancy being instinctually unnatural. Add to this Aurelie's unconscious fear (implied in her inability to repeat the mother's curse in its entirety) that, on her mother's death, aggressive possession will be transferred to the daughter, and pregnancy becomes associated with a Satanic, and thus sexually perverse, act. Aurelie is

also gripped by the terrifying presentiment that her mother will rise from the grave "and tear her from the arms of her beloved down into the abyss." That she entertains a fantasy that ascribes to the mother a supernatural, "vampiric" power is an extension of a growing psychological preoccupation with aggression and possession, and gives evidence of a deepening estrangement from the reality principle. Such a terror-stricken fantasy, underscored by hate of the mother, points up the ambivalence of Aurelie's actions at the end: her ghoulish cannibalism is not only oral but anal, constituting a defense against, and thereby release of, her presentiment.

A striking characteristic of oral aggression is that it represents a perversion of love and, on returning in repressed form, interferes with a normal love relationship between husband and wife. Aurelie's pregnancy is a natural outgrowth of such a relationship; but it also marks the event that activates her repressed oral fixation, as seen in her refusal to eat ordinary food. Her preference for the flesh of deceased bodies (like her mother, she makes nocturnal sojourns in the cemetery) underscores the pathological implications of the sadistic-cannibalistic character of frustrated infantile orality. The cannibalistic nature of sensual love, because it is necrophagous, is thus displaced to an object (exhumed body) that does not represent the recipient of normal affections (Aurelie's husband).

One might view Aurelie's physical condition and refusal of food in various ways. Pregnancy itself, as we had observed, can connote a kind of pleasurable incorporation of the subject's unconscious experience of childhood had been narcissistically intact. In Aurelie's case, however, the experience of pregnancy is not so clearly definable. Not only are the unconscious oral fantasies it evokes ambivalent (the trauma of childhood being both pleasurable and painful), but the maternal instinct underlying it is disturbing. Owing to the baroness's curse and its emotional impact on the daughter, pregnancy is at once a maternally perverse and guilt-producing experience since it suggests the incorporation of a foreign body that is the base, instinctual product of an unnatural union which would almost appear adulterous, given the heroine's state of depression and anxiety. To allay this guilt, Aurelie rejects all human food, the idea being that the instinctual sensations caused by internalized objects should not be nurtured by incorporating still other objects.

Aurelie's refusal of food, however, does not necessarily represent a repression of eating cravings; she rejects specific foods because they are not the desired ones. Thus, as Otto Fenichel has noted [in his *The Psychoanalytic Theory of Neurosis*], "it is not the drive that is refused but the acceptance of a substitute." Although the physician attending Aurelie admits that cravings in some pregnant women assume abnormal, even sadistic proportions, he is at a loss to diagnose the cause of his patient's unusual reaction to this phenomenon. On hearing the anecdote of a woman who experienced such an uncontrollable craving for the flesh of her husband that she literally hacked him to pieces, Aurelie reacts in a manner inconsistent with her enthusiastic one prior to the anecdote, in which she had been captivated by the topic of the "strange cravings" felt

by pregnant women and had implored the doctor to elaborate further. Now we read of her reaction: "Hardly had
the doctor spoken these words when the Countess sank
fainting into the chair. Not without difficulty was she able
to be saved from the nervous fits which set in." An apparent contradiction between motive and behavior, intent and
action, emerges in this scene, so that unconscious impulses
must be inferred. When we read that this emotional crisis
"seemed to have a salutary effect on the Countess," then
we suspect a latent, erotic reaction to the anecdote, one in
which the sadistic hacking of human flesh ("zerfleischte,"
elicits a mixture of unconscious sexual responses (excita-
tion, orgasm, release of tension).

When hacking is supplanted by biting, pathological tendencies become still more compelling. Aurelie's reaction
to food is decidedly ambivalent: both anorexia (loss of appetite) and bulimia (abnormal hunger) characterize this
instinct. Indeed, it is precisely because her craving is
pathological that she experiences a lack of appetite for ordinary food. Aurelie's refusal of the food eaten by others,
especially meat, has the effect of creating a continuous, abnormal hunger which strives for incorporation through
oral-sadistic aggression. The unconscious meaning of
pathologically craved food may be represented by feces,
or the babies supposed to have arisen from them, and any
kind of decomposing material, particularly human
corpses. Aurelie's behavioral response to pregnancy is
thus to activate this meaning through the appropriate incorporation.

Conflicting with this unconscious striving for violent instinctual gratification is the moral component in Aurelie's
behavior, which of course rejects any perverted connotation of sensual love in favor of one based on mutual affection. Prior to Aurelie's pregnancy, the sensual aspect of
marital love was presumably shared freely, without inhibition, so that one may indeed speak of a self-object merger
that was not onesidedly narcissistic, this being a precondi-
tion for any kind of instinctual perversion. As a result of
her pregnancy, however, Aurelie's instinctual nature extends from the sexual to the maternal, and she is suddenly
confronted with a fantasy of motherhood which, psychologically conditioned by the perverse actions of the baroness, is incompatible with the fruit born of a normal sexual
union between husband and wife.

The security and affection that Aurelie finds in her beloved
signify, at the surface level of meaning, that motherhood
will be the natural fulfillment of a relationship based on
mutual devotion. Her behavior on becoming pregnant,
however, hints at impulses and motives incongruous with
such an assumption. It is at this point that Aurelie's fear
of the mother, even at death, is most intense, and the way
to cope with this fear is by introjection of the threatening
parent. Related fantasies, then, must also be assumed. If,
by this identification, the idea of motherhood is incompatible with a pregnancy resulting from a normal marital
union (owing to the mother's curse), then we reconstruct,
at the level of unconscious fantasy, a projection of the be-
getter to a source that is compatible with this idea, namely
to the Satanic kind suggested in the baroness's assessment

of her own pregnancy, in which Aurelie was really a pre-
figuration of the child she herself is now carrying.

Aurelie's repressed oral and maternal fantasies begin to
dictate her actions once the fear and dread underlying
them are internalized and supplant rational motivation.
Following the logic of such fantasies in their extreme
form, we interpret Aurelie's uncharacteristic behavior
subsequent to pregnancy to mean that the child she has
incorporated symbolizes an ill-conceived, foreign body engendering a morbid craving for food which can only be
foul, unnatural, something incorporated by an act—
aggressive biting and tearing—that befits the dehumanized content. The inclination to necrophilia, which implies
a confusion of the pleasure-producing sensations of love
(the tender kiss turned into the devouring bite), degenerates in Aurelie's case to the preconscious, animalistic level
of necrophagia. Aurelie's cannibalistic savoring of the
flesh of an unknown corpse thus signifies the nadir of a
psychopathological regression to a most primitive form of
infantile oral sadism.

The quality of endearment inherent in a self-object love relationship between two people yields, with the return of
the repressed on the blind, instinctual level, to a narcissistic striving for self-object fusion, a state of undifferentia-
tion of self from other. At work here is Aurelie's unconscious childhood impulse, frustrated by a lifeless, un-
responding corpse, to equate the pleasure of eating with
that of kissing, as well as a frustrated maternal instinct
which retards normal development toward motherhood,
creating in the subject the fantasy that pregnancy is a
symptom of insatiable oral craving. The infantile identification of food as an erotic, pleasurable feeling had been
dealt a traumatic blow when Aurelie, as a child, experienced the death of her provider. Her refusal of normal
food as an adult, an unconscious reenactment of this earlier experience, suggests that pleasure through nourishment
is to be sought not among familiar, human providers, but
in an unnatural, lifeless realm in which incorporation
through necrophagia underscores an instinctual need to
reestablish a narcissistic equilibrium that had been disrupted in childhood.

When Count Hyppolit suddenly reveals to Aurelie the reason for her refusal to eat ordinary food, stating that "out
of graves you drag your food, devilish woman!" the heroine actually becomes the embodiment of animal instinct:
"As soon as the Count uttered these words the Countess,
howling loudly, lunged at him and bit him in the breast
with the fury of a hyena. The Count hurled the raging
woman to the floor and, convulsing horribly, she died."
Repressed in Aurelie's unconscious had been an instinctual existence that experienced both pleasure and displeasure, so that in social behavior any one of the inclinations
could turn into affectionate or hostile impulses, depending
on the history of the subject's emotional development. The
propensity to love had characterized Aurelie's disposition
up to a certain point; now it is the instinct for hate and cruelty that is the determinant of her behavior up to the very
end. (pp. 235-51)

Thomas A. Kamla, "E. T. A. Hoffmann's
Vampirism Tale: Instinctual Perversion," in

American Imago, *Vol. 42, No. 3, Fall, 1985, pp. 235-53.*

Shelley L. Frisch   (essay date 1985)

[*In the following essay, Frisch analyzes the narrative structure of "The Sandman."*]

[In his essay "The Uncanny"] Sigmund Freud defined the "uncanny" as "that class of the frightening which leads back to what is known of old and long familiar." He illustrated this conception of the uncanny by analyzing E. T. A. Hoffmann's **"Sandman,"** which comprises the first of Hoffmann's *Night Pieces,* written in 1816. Hoffmann's **"Sandman"** explores the increasingly schizophrenic world of a young man, Nathanael, who cannot shake his obsession with a childhood fairy tale, and who reacts hysterically to a salesman who seems to be the Sandman come to life. Readers share Nathanael's mounting distress and find themselves, like Nathanael, ultimately incapable of distinguishing between the fantasy of fairy tales and the reality stressed by other characters in the story.

The story begins in epistolary format. In a letter from Nathanael to his friend Lothar, Nathanael reflects on his recent encounter with a barometer salesman-optician, whom he identifies with the Sandman. From a flashback we learn that when Nathanael was a boy, his father had associated with a dreadful alchemist named Coppelius, and during the experiments the two conducted together, Nathanael's father died. On the evenings that Coppelius came to visit, Nathanael was always sent to bed early, with the warning that the Sandman was coming. Upon questioning his nurse Nathanael discovered that the Sandman plucks out the eyes of children who do not obey their parents' orders to go to bed; he then transports the eyes to the "half-moon" to feed his children. Curious to see the dreaded Sandman for himself, Nathanael hides in the closet of his father's study one night and is discovered by Coppelius, who attempts to harm the boy: but Nathanael is saved by the intervention of his father.

We then return to the present and to Nathanael's encounter with an Italian optician named Giuseppe Coppola, who exclaims in faulty German that he has eyes to sell. Nathanael draws back in terror, both at the similarity of the optician's name to the alchemist Coppelius's and to the mention of eyes as the product for sale. Memories of the Sandman come flooding back, and Nathanael reels in panic until he realizes that Coppola is selling spectacles and telescopes, not eyes. Still, he is struck by these uncanny similarities and remains haunted by the possibility of their identity.

Nathanael buys a telescope from Coppola and with its aid discovers a neighbor of whom he was hitherto unaware, a beautiful but strangely immobile woman named Olimpia. He pursues her, only to discover that she is an automaton, whose eyes have been implanted in her by Coppola. At this discovery Nathanael goes mad and falls into a long illness, during which he produces eerie, fantastic poetry. Upon recovering he returns to the "rational" world of his correspondent Lothar and his girlfriend Klara, who, he now believes, are right in dismissing the extraordinary

events he has experienced. Nathanael is disappointed that they reject his poetic ventures but agrees that they are irrational. Finally, though, he spies Coppola / Coppelius once again, through his telescope, and jumps to his death from a tower.

This short summary provides the essentials of the material from which Freud drew in his essay to explain how events become uncanny. Freud noted that Nathanael's fear of losing his eyes represents a castration complex, akin to Oedipus' self-blinding when he discovers that he has killed his father and slept with his mother. Nathanael may harbor a secret wish to kill his father, Freud explained, and finds his wish fulfilled in the figure of the Sandman / Coppelius, the instrument of his father's death. Because he then wishes to repress that fulfilled wish, Nathanael buries the memory of the Sandman. When he encounters the optician Coppola and notices in him two uncanny resemblances (similarity of name and business of selling "eyes"), Nathanael succumbs to a temporary madness. The "un-" prefix of *uncanny*, Freud explained, denotes a confrontation with that which is familiar but until that moment successfully repressed. Repeated encounters with Coppola / Coppelius, in which the motif of eyes continues to play an important role, reinforce the feeling of the uncanny, in which repetition constitutes an important factor.

Freud isolated the Sandman as the focal point of interest in the story, thereby countering the view of other critics who attributed the presence of the uncanny to the mechanical doll Olimpia. Freud considered it irrelevant to debate the humanity of Olimpia, because establishing whether she is in fact living or a mere automaton does not address the *effect* of the uncanny on Nathanael. It is through his perceptions of the uncanny, maintained Freud, that we can best understand the meaning of the story. Freud concentrated in part on the biographical background of E. T. A. Hoffmann himself, whose father abandoned the family when Hoffmann was young, and on Freud's own case studies; both of these factors are said to bear out the verisimilitude of Nathanael's experiences.

Freud's dissection of Nathanael's psychoses illuminates the character of Nathanael and the relationship of Hoffmann to his main character. Freud followed Nathanael's increasing madness with a shrewd explication of how Nathanael's feelings of the uncanny escalate. He accurately noted the central role of the Sandman and the subsidiary role of Olimpia in unleashing long-repressed anxieties, which may be connected to an ambivalent feeling of Nathanael (and perhaps of Hoffmann) toward an inattentive father. Most important, Freud stressed that the uncanny involves something long familiar and yet unfamiliar, which by its reappearance at unexpected moments disconcerts an unwary victim.

Overall, however, Freud's interpretation of **"The Sandman"** fails as a literary interpretation of the fantastic. Freud admitted that the uncanny in literature differs from the uncanny in life; yet he treated the confusion of Nathanael, in which fantasy and reality intermingle, more as a case study of schizophrenia than as a work of literature. Freud even underscored the psychological "truth" of Nathanael's visions by describing similar personality disorders among his own patients. Freud once remarked to a friend that he was not fond of reading and commented: "I invented psychoanalysis because it had no literature." He viewed the story through the perspective of the protagonist's neuroses and constantly judged its truth value. Freud thereby committed the error that Jonathan Culler called "premature foreclosure—the unseemly rush from word to world" [in his *Structuralist Poetics*].

It is within the German Romantic circle itself that we discover a more pertinent analysis of the literary creation of the uncanny. Ludwig Tieck's "Shakespeares Behandlung des Wunderbaren" of 1976 lays a theoretical foundation for the manner in which the illusion of the supernatural is created in the comedies and tragedies of Shakespeare. Tieck's discussion of comedies treats the *Wunderbare* ("marvelous") in much the same manner as Tzvetan Todorov's recent *Fantastic: A Structural Approach to a Literary Genre* the supernatural events described provoke no definitive reaction of anxiety in either the characters or in the implicit reader. According to Tieck the supernatural world is moved so close to the reader (or viewer) that it becomes accepted as part of the fictional premise. His examination of tragedies demonstrates how fear and anxiety can be induced in the reading or viewing audience by the use of particular fictional techniques.

The characteristics of the tragedies that compel the viewer both to accept and to be repelled by the supernatural are three, according to Tieck. First, the world of the supernatural is presented as distant and incomprehensible and is always subordinated to the "real" world; consequently, the passions and events concerning the major characters attract the attention of the viewer and are of more interest than the ghosts themselves. Thus we yearn to understand Hamlet's dilemma but care little for his father's apparition. Second, the supernatural must be prepared in some way. If the appearance of Hamlet's father's ghost were to open the play, Tieck explained, we would not have developed a necessary fear of him; instead, we would simply accept the ghost as part of the fictional frame-work.

We must be convinced that it is both possible and frightening for him to appear, so as to share the characters' dismay when we must formally face him. Therefore, *Hamlet* opens not with the ghost himself but with the frightened sentries who ponder his reality. Third, a natural explanation of the supernatural increases our intellectual uncertainty and thus augments our suspense. In the case of Hamlet we can attribute his vision of the ghost in part of Hamlet's proclivity to melancholy and superstition.

All three of these characteristics accurately describe the evocation of the supernatural in Hoffmann's **"Sandman."** First, the "real" character Nathanael commands our attention far more than the Sandman Coppelius or the automaton Olimpia. The fantastic characters remain abstractions for us, but Nathanael's raptures and fears seem close and comprehensible. Second, the Sandman does not appear in the story until the reader has heard of the evil he can perpetrate and how great Nathanael's fear of him is, and so we are prepared to experience with the sympathetic character Nathanael the uncanny similarity he draws to the optician Coppola who sells "eyes." Finally,

although we identify with Nathanael we have just enough reason to doubt the reliability of his perceptions that we cannot shake a nagging doubt about the actuality of the Sandman throughout much of the story.

Recent "reader-response" criticism has called for a renewed interest in this type of poetics. Like Tieck reader-response critics examine the means by which readers' reactions are encoded into texts. However, their analyses go further than those of Tieck by showing that the reader is *addressed* directly and indirectly within the text. Walker Gibson spoke of the "mock reader" in texts, Stanley Fish of the "informed reader," Gerald Prince of the "narratee," Walter J. Ong of the "fictionalized audience," Wolfgang Iser of the "implied reader," and Christine Brooke-Rose of the "encoded reader." None of these "readers" is identical to the "real" reader who peruses a book in his living room. These *narratees* (to use Prince's apt term) are the fictional counterparts of "narrators": they exist within the fictional framework itself. Although the critical literature on Hoffmann has nowhere recognized the role that the narratee plays in his works, I will demonstrate that this role is crucial in creating the uncanny effects of **"The Sandman."**

The story opens with a letter from Nathanael to his friend Lothar, which he begins by exclaiming: "You certainly must be disturbed." The exclamation sets the narrative tone for the tale as a whole. Second-person narration, addressed to a sympathetic narratee, appears not only in the introductory letters but in the subsequent interpretation of them by an additional narrator whose reliability is even more questionable than Nathanael's. The second narratee is told by this narrator that he has experienced similar encounters with the fantastic: "Have you, gentle reader, ever experienced anything that possessed your heart, your thoughts, and your senses to the exclusion of all else? Everything seethed and roiled within you; heated blood surged through your veins and inflamed your cheeks. Your gaze was peculiar, as if seeking forms in empty space invisible to other eyes, and speech dissolved into gloomy sighs". We, the "real" readers, are thus allied with the anxieties of Nathanael, with an equally nervous narrator who continually apologizes to us for needing to set down Nathanael's experiences in a story, and with two narratees in whom Nathanael and the narrator explicitly attempt to instill feelings of the uncanny. Our uncomfortable intimacy with all of these figures forces us to confront the fantastic along with them and heightens our personal horror of each appearance of the dreaded Sandman.

The narrator overtly states his intention to make his narratee, whom he calls the "gentle reader" and the "sympathetic reader," receptive to the supernatural occurrences of the story: "my dear reader, it was essential at the beginning to dispose you favorably towards the fantastic—which is no mean matter." He expresses the hope that his narratee will picture the characters as vividly as if he had seen them with his own eyes. Nathanael pleads for understanding and acceptance of the supernatural from his narratee Lothar.

The "real" reader is left with the question of whether he ought to accept the role assigned to both of these narratees and thereby declare its events uncanny. Christine Brooke-Rose's article "The Readerhood of Man" suggests that a text with an apparent overencoding of the reader gives rise to the truly ambiguous text:

> The clearest type is the truly ambiguous text. . . . [It] seems to overdetermine one code, usually the hermeneutic, and even to overencode the reader, but in fact the overdetermination consists of repetitions and variations that give us little or no further information. The overdetermination functions, paradoxically, as underdetermination.

Hoffmann's **"Sandman"** provides us with two narratees after whom we may model our own interpretation of events. The "real" reader thus becomes an overencoded reader, who is told repeatedly that he ought to accept the uncanny. That this text remains nonetheless fundamentally underdetermined is attested to in the ample critical literature on **"The Sandman,"** which debates and redebates the question of the relative reliability of the narratees and the story's other characters.

In the end the "real" reader must dismiss as inconsequential any attempt to distinguish between "actual" supernatural events and "mere" products of Nathanael's and the narrator's imaginations. The production of uncanny effects in literary texts rests precisely on the intellectual uncertainty built into the text. Freud's study of the uncanny concentrates on removing stories from the literary sphere and ascertaining their degree of psychological truth. Tieck directed his attention to the manner in which responses to the supernatural events are incorporated structurally into a text and thereby addressed the specifically literary conventions that separate fact from fiction. In applying reader-response critical theory of Hoffmann's **"Sandman,"** I hope to have demonstrated that the tale's narrators continually force an identification of their narratees with the unnerving events of Nathanael's life, so that the narratees

adopt their own anxieties and fear of the uncanny. Remarks addressed in the second person to these narratees necessarily draw in the "real" reader as well. We become the "gentle" and "sympathetic" reader about whom the narrator exclaims: "Everything seethed and roiled within *you.*" (pp. 49-54)

> *Shelley L. Frisch, "Poetics of the Uncanny: E. T. A. Hoffmann's 'Sandman'," in The Scope of the Fantastic—Theory, Technique, Major Authors: Selected Essays from the First International Conference on the Fantastic in Literature and Film, edited by Robert A. Collins and Howard D. Pearce, Greenwood Press, 1985, pp. 49-55.*

Malcolm V. Jones   (essay date 1986)

[*Jones is an English educator and critic who specializes in Slavonic studies. In the following essay, he responds to Sigmund Freud's reading of "The Sandman" (see excerpt dated 1919) and offers an alternative perspective.*]

Freud's study of **'Der Sandmann'** enjoys a privileged position among psychoanalytical works on Hoffmann's story. That is not to say, of course, that it dominates all critical analyses. Nor do all its admirers find it uncontroversial. Quite the reverse. [In her *Psychoanalytic Criticism*, 1984] Elizabeth Wright mentions 'at least nine recent readings of Freud's essay, all showing the unmistakable imprint of Lacan and Derrida. The general view is that it would indeed be a mistake to let Freud's analysis of Hoffmann be the last word on the uncanny. What is interesting is precisely the inadequacy of his interpretation, and how this inadequacy has produced a whole series of after-effects.' Quite apart from Lacan, Derrida, Foucault and others who have had a major impact on critical theory, Freud modified his own views after writing his article and psychoanalysis itself has moved on since Freud's day. Some of his most treasured and controversial ideas no longer have the same central explanatory function in the work of his successors. Some concepts about which he was hesitant and uncertain—for instance the crucial idea of the aggressive instinct which had long been the major source of his disagreements with Adler—have in the work of some of them come again to prominence. Other ideas which are central to Freud's reading of **'Der Sandmann'**—for example the castration complex—underwent modification in his later work. All this creates a situation of such complexity that no attempt will be made to encompass all the problems and readings which have resulted. My aims are more modest.

[My first task] will inevitably be to examine again briefly Freud's own study of **'Der Sandmann'**. Freud's account is, of course, that of a psychoanalyst looking at a work of literature. So, in effect, have been most of the recent discussions mentioned by Wright: Freud's essay is held up as 'a prime example of the return of the repressed, because what is left out of the story returns to haunt the essay. What follows, by contrast, will be the account of a literary critic making use of psychoanalytical concepts in attempting to produce a richer reading of the text.

Victor Lange on Hoffmann's achievement:

If magnetism, somnambulism, hypnotism, and other such states beyond rational consciousness are among Hoffmann's favorite metaphors, they represent not so much the improbable machinery of Gothic fiction as a record, poetically illuminated, of experiences in which Hoffmann himself seems to have shared. His strength as a writer was not any excellence in the style of his prose but his ability to render elusive figures in action, platitudinous characters suddenly made transparent by the perception of intensely felt and unsettling forces. These figures seem abruptly to move from one state of mind to another, from familiar behavior to outrageous actions, from idyll to savage satire. It is at just such moments of shifting gestures and performances, such changes in levels of involvement, that the irrepressible force of the most powerful human impulses—hope and desire, love and hatred, beauty and horror—can be given presence and shape.

Victor Lange in his introduction to E. T. A. Hoffmann: Tales, 1982.

A final series of questions and proposals will be about the concept of the uncanny itself, which remains a highly controversial area in which there is nothing approaching agreement.

Freud begins his account with a synopsis of **'Der Sandmann'**, which has been criticized for its significant omissions. There is no mention of narration, plot and figuration on the level of literature, and various features of interest to psychoanalysis itself are ignored both in the synopsis and the article as a whole: for example, the relation between perception and desire; the return of the repressed in the form of Clara and Olimpia; the repeated images of death. Narcissism is consigned to footnotes. And it is curious that the repetition compulsion, which plays a central part in Freud's contemporaneous work in *Beyond the Pleasure Principle* and figures so prominently in Hoffmann's story, should receive so little (systematic) attention in the essay on **'Der Sandmann'**. Such questions have been dealt with elsewhere and are well summarized by Wright; they will not be pursued in detail here. Omissions aside, we may remind ourselves that Freud makes two principal points. The first is that the effect of the uncanny is directly related to the figure of the Sand-Man and to the idea of being robbed of one's eyes and not, as Jentsch would have it, to intellectual uncertainty of any sort. There is no uncertainty in the narrative: we know we are not supposed to be looking on at the products of a madman's imagination. The second point is that psychoanalysis has shown that dread of losing one's eyes is often associated with the fear of being castrated and this story is a particularly compelling illustration of the thesis:

> For why does Hoffmann bring the anxiety about eyes into such intimate connection with the father's death? And why does the Sand-Man always appear as a disturber of love? He separates the unfortunate Nathaniel from his betrothed and from her brother, his best friend; he destroys the second object of his love, Olimpia, the lovely doll; and he drives him into suicide at the moment when he has won back his Clara and is about to be happily united to her. Elements in the story like these, and many others, seem arbitrary and meaningless so long as we deny all connection between fears about the eye and castration; but they become intelligible as soon as we replace the Sand-Man by the dreaded father at whose hands castration is expected.

Freud applies his theory to the detail of the story in a long footnote which follows the passage quoted above. Here is a brief extract:

> In the story of Nathaniel's childhood, the figures of his father and Coppelius represent the two opposites into which the father-imago is split by his ambivalence; whereas the one threatens to blind him—that is, to castrate him—the other, the 'good' father, intercedes for his sight. The part of the complex which is most strongly repressed, the death-wish against the 'bad' father, finds expression in the death of the 'good' father, and Coppelius is made answerable for it. This pair of fathers is represented later, in his student days, by Professor Spalanzani and Coppola the opti-

> cian. (. . .) they have jointly created the doll Olimpia (. . .)

In spite of Wright's claim that Nathanael is afraid of castration as a real event, Freud does not in fact seek to explain Nathanael's experience as paranoid projection ('we know now that we are not supposed to be looking on at the products of a madman's imagination'). The psychoanalytic account is, as Neil Hertz points out [in *Textual Strategies: Perspectives in Post-Structuralist Criticism*, 1979], latent in the story and is held to account for its uncanny effect on the reader, while the account of Nathanael's being driven to suicide by an evil external power is manifest (We may defer discussion of the view that 'the conclusion of the story makes it quite clear that Coppola the optician really is the lawyer Coppelius and also, therefore, the Sand-Man'. Even though this reading may be naive, and the more sophisticated reader, like, for example, Hélène Cixous, may prefer a pluralist reading, it is still open to defenders of Freud to insist on the uncanny effect of the story on the reader and to advance the same explanation for it.) Freud's principal claim is that the sensation of the uncanny which the story arouses derives from 'the anxiety belonging to the castration complex of childhood'. He warns any opponent of the psychoanalytic view against selecting this particular story to support the argument that anxiety about the eyes has nothing to do with the castration complex. Some readers, Samuel Weber for instance, have thought that Freud actually underplays this connection [in his "The Sideshow, or: remarks on a canny moment," in *Modern Language Notes*, 1973]. It will become clear that my view, by contrast, is that it is possible to give a perfectly satisfactory account of the story which relegates the castration complex to a marginal position.

Freud does not claim that his reading provides the simplest possible model to account for the maximum number of significant features of the text. Indeed he allows for the possibility that although the text could in principle be explicated in this way, Hoffmann's imaginative treatment of his material might in practice have made such wild confusion of its elements that it was no longer possible to 'reconstruct their original arrangement'. The fact that it is possible to effect the reconstruction here does not mean that the untutored reader could be expected to do so, or that there is no other model to be found with greater explanatory power for the actual text. Still, Freud does find the story particularly suitable for his type of reading and the possibility of its being an exceptionally rich one should not be dismissed out of hand by those who consider Freudian theory far-fetched or outdated (or its anachronistic, lurking presence in Hoffmann's story uncanny). Even with this proviso, there are problems about the status of Freud's reading. He disarms all common-sense or 'rationalistic' objections to the centrality he gives the castration complex by reference to his experience with neurotic patients. But although the positivist in Freud appeals to clinical experience, there is no doubt that he considers that the text offers independent confirmation of his reading. Elements of the story which he wishes particularly to emphasize (e.g., the role of the Sand-Man as disturber of love, his driving Nathanael to suicide and 'many others') 'seem arbitrary and meaningless so long as we deny all connection between fears about the eye and castration'. Is this really the case? And, if in general terms it is, has Freud necessarily got the connection right?

Let us take the example of Olimpia. Could it not be plausibly argued along Freudian lines that Olimpia is a materialization not of 'Nathanael's feminine attitude towards his father in his infancy' (than which, according to Freud, she can be 'nothing else') but of Nathanael's incestuous feelings towards his youngest sister? The old woman who frightens Nathanael with her terrifying story of the Sand-Man is his youngest sister's nurse. Moreover, it is his mother, the primary object of incestuous feelings, who seeks to reassure him. If Nathanael's erotic feelings are fixated from an early age on his sister this would explain his difficulties in sustaining a 'normal' relationship with Clara. It would also help to explain the character of his affection for her. She and her brother Lothar were taken in by Nathanael's mother soon after Nathanael's father's death, when they too became orphans. Not only was Clara, so to speak, an adopted sister, but both she and Nathanael had recently lost their fathers, thus removing the primary external censors to an incestuous relationship. It is interesting to note in this connection that one careful and intelligent reader, Rosemary Jackson in her book on fantasy, mis-remembers Clara as Nathanael's sister. Of course, Clara's position in this respect is ambiguous. As 'sister' she is taboo. Hoffmann's narrator makes this ambiguity clear by the very fact of mentioning that there could be no objection to their mutual affection. Further, if we accept Freud's view that there is a split father-imago ('whereas the one threatens to blind him—that is, to castrate him—, the other, the "good" father, intercedes for his sight'), it requires no special ingenuity to perceive that here 'sight' is to be equated with sexual awareness of the other and that the eyes are the principal organs for the transmission of such awareness. If this interpretation is valid and Freud is right in seeing Spalanzani and Coppola as 'reincarnations of Nathanael's pair of father's, it is hardly surprising that they should also be perceived as joint fathers of Olimpia. In other words, Nathanael and Olimpia, according to this reading, have the same father/s: they are 'brother and sister'. Whether Olimpia is a doll or a stupid girl, it is clear that Nathanael has projected his incestuous feelings for his sister onto her. The significance of the eye-glass in this reading is that it heightens and intensifies both Nathanael's sexual awareness and his dread of being punished /castrated by his father—a classic Freudian situation. It is one of his 'fathers', Coppola, who sells him the eye-glass, at a cost which he later dimly suspects may have been excessive. 'Spalanzani's otherwise incomprehensible statement that the optician has stolen Nathanael's eyes, so as to set them in the doll', which Freud sees as 'evidence of the identity of Olimpia and Nathaniel's is surely comprehensible, without recourse to this explanation, as a way of saying that his (and Olimpia's) father/s have in this curious 'allegory' equipped Olimpia with the same sexual awareness regarding Nathanael as he has regarding her, or that, in reality, 'Olimpia's eyes' as Nathanael sees them, are, like the identification of Spalanzani and Coppola with the Sand-Man and Nathanael's father, projections of his own incestuous desires. The plausibility of such a reading weakens the

claim of Freud to furnish a definitive (though as his critics would maintain, an incomplete) psychoanalytical account, even though it preserves a connection between sexual experience and the eyes, together with the central role, in both the plot of Hoffmann's story and Freud's reading of it, of the father-imago. Indeed, without wanting to claim too much for it, we may note that this alternative Freudian version has a slight advantage over Freud's in that it accounts for a larger number of significant features of the text, including all those to which Freud himself alludes.

Freud does not attempt to apply psychoanalytic theory on the level of the surface structure of the text. This is because he holds that it is to be read as a tale of the supernatural which cannot be made to accord (on this level) with what Todorov calls 'reality as it exists in the common opinion'. However, he is surely wrong in claiming that Hoffmann has entirely abandoned his initial ambiguity or that the story is wholly resistant to a naturalistic reading. We can note, without embarking here on a detailed analysis of narrative focus in **'Der Sandmann'**, that the narrator of the story makes it clear that his fundamental organizing principle is the telling of a good story, a story moreover which he appears greatly excited about. Hertz refers to a 'likeness between the unfolding of Nathanael's fate and the elaboration of a narrative, between the forces driving Nathanael and whatever is impelling the narrator'. The telling of the story involves, in this case, a shift from the point-of-view of 'reality as it exists in the common opinion' to a point-of-view not unlike that of Nathanael convinced that he is involved in supernatural events. Whether this is to be read as confirmation of the supernatural nature of the events themselves or whether Hoffmann is employing a form of *erlebte Rede* (free indirect speech) is not the sort of question which interested Freud. It may, however, interest a modern reader, who can assume that the latter thesis is at least worth examining, and who will note the narrator's own admission of how his heart and mind and thoughts were completely possessed by the story of Nathanael to the exclusion of everything else, how everything seethed and boiled within him, how he was completely captivated by the elements of marvel and alienness in Nathanael's life and racked his brain for a way of commencing his story in an original manner to predispose the reader to the idea of the fantastic. This is not the voice of a narrator with serious pretensions to 'objectivity' and detachment. It is legitimate then to enquire whether Nathanael's conduct and experience (as distinct from the reader's response) can be accounted for adequately in psychoanalytical terms, and whether the centrality which Freud gives to the Oedipus complex is the best basis for such an account. This task . . . will involve asking whether subsequent developments in psychoanalysis can provide simpler models with equal or superior explanatory power and, if so, whether these can be grafted on to Freud's model or necessitate a radically different one. (pp. 77-82)

The central explanatory function of sexuality in Freudian psychology was one of the principal factors behind the early schisms in the psychoanalytic movement. Another, closely related to it, was disagreement about the nature of aggression. By 1919, when 'The Uncanny' was published,

Freud had already been grappling for some years with both these questions, latterly in ways forced upon him by experience of the First World War. Freud had always recognized aggressive behaviour, but not a primary aggressive instinct. By 1920, in *Beyond the Pleasure Principle*, he had tentatively developed a new theory according to which the term 'aggressive instinct' was principally used to designate the activity of the death instinct turned outwards. In 'The Uncanny' Freud refers the reader to *Beyond the Pleasure Principle*, but he clearly believed that he had discovered the basis for the uncanny effect of **'Der Sandmann'** in the Oedipus complex and he offers no other explanation for Nathanael's experiences. It has been common in recent critical assessments for Freud's ideas in *Beyond the Pleasure Principle* and later works (notably those on the repetition compulsion and the castration complex) to be grafted on to his discussion of **'Der Sandmann'** and the uncanny. A summary of these can be found in Elizabeth Wright's book, already cited. But his newly developing views, radical though they were and pivotal though this 1920 text turned out to be, were at this stage expressed with an extreme degree of hesitancy and reticence and the connections between phenomena which gave rise to the repetition compulsion (which Freud used to justify his introduction of the idea of the death instinct) and aggressive behaviour were extremely tenuous. The fundamental idea of the death instinct and the place accorded to aggressive behaviour within the new theory did not win widespread acceptance among psychoanalysts then, nor have they done so since. Other accounts of aggression were clearly necessary and Freud's successors were not slow to provide them. It is arguable, moreover, that it is an adequate account of aggressive behaviour which is lacking in both Freud's account of **'Der Sandmann'** and his conception of the uncanny. Possible biographical reasons for this omission (or repression) will be considered later. Rather than complicate the issue further by reference to the theories of Adler, who had introduced the idea of an aggressive instinct as early as 1908 and with whom Freud was at loggerheads, I refer below, somewhat arbitrarily, to the eclectic position of Anthony Storr whose relatively recent books on human aggression and destructiveness are well known and easily accessible.

Storr grants that there is no agreement among psychoanalysts about aggression and that Freud's influence has been so powerful that it must be taken into account. Particular attention may be drawn to three points in his critique of Freud by way of sketching his general stance. (I) 'Although the acceptance of a death instinct is in one sense an admission of a primary aggressive drive, yet the concept still implies that aggression directed against the external world is a secondary phenomenon which would not exist unless the primary instinct was blocked or interfered with (. . .) there is nothing in Freud's later work which would support the idea of a positive, primary aggressive drive; and hence nothing which is obviously opposed to the idea that some kind of frustration is always antecedent to aggression.' (2) In man, as in animals, there is a physiological mechanism which, when stimulated, gives rise to subjective feelings of anger and to physical changes which prepare the body for fighting. Such evidence suggests that aggression is as much an innate drive as sexuality. (3) If

we can bring ourselves to abandon the pleasure principle, it is not so difficult to accept the idea that the achievement of dominance, the overcoming of obstacles, and the mastery of the external world, for all of which aggression is necessary, are as much innate human needs as sexuality or hunger.

Aggression, *qua* destructive hostility, may be closely connected with sexuality but is not necessarily secondary to it. In Storr's opinion, Freud's tardy recognition of the will to power is still bedevilling our thinking: 'the establishment of a place in the dominance hierarchy chronologically *precedes* the attainment of sexual satisfaction; and if efforts at attaining a place fail so that the individual is graded near the bottom of the pecking order the penalty is that he remains unmated.' 'Children (. . .) have little idea of sexual pleasure; but they have a lively concept (sic) of dominance-submission relations, since they are engaged perpetually in struggles to establish status in relation to their parents, rivalry with siblings and contemporaries, and all the manifold phantasy activity of childhood which is concerned with being as big, as strong, as powerful as the feared and envied adults who surround them.'

According to Storr, then, the primary difficulty experienced by children is in establishing a sense of their own power and a place in the human hierarchy, and their sexual difficulties, upon which Freudian psychoanalysis places so much emphasis, are secondary to this.

Like Freud before him, Storr in *Human Aggression* draws attention to the ubiquitous nature of terrifying fantasies of an aggressive kind among people of varying cultures:

> When Red Riding Hood visits her grandmother she finds that a wolf has usurped the grandmother's place. The protective, kindly figure has been replaced by a dangerous and destructive creature. It is this exchange of figures which makes the story particularly alarming. To encounter a wolf is frightening enough, but to find that one's loving grandmother has turned into this terrifying beast is to add to the situation that basic insecurity which springs from a sudden loss of trust in a person upon whom one relies. (. . .) So long as the good and the bad are separated, children can tolerate violence, death and other things which might be expected to disturb them. But to discover that the person one believed was on one's side is actually malign, is to enter so unpredictable and unsafe a sphere of experience that children become alarmed, just as an adult might if he discovered that the injections which his doctor was giving him were poisonous rather than therapeutic.

One of the most devastating threats to a child's attempts to locate himself in the hierarchy structure occurs when a trusted member of the family circle—that stable, reassuring world in which he is orientating himself—is suddenly perceived as unreliable or even hostile, or in an ambiguous relationship to hostile and unsympathetic forces from an unknown world outside.

Nathanael's discovery that his father is in league with, or the prisoner of, the terrifying Sand-Man, is an experience of the same order as that which Storr describes. If we turn back to the text we shall find that not only in his childhood, but also in later life, Nathanael's relations with others (apart from Olimpia whom we shall consider separately) seem to be based on two distinct sets of emotions and perceptions of reality. The first may be characterized as protective, reassuring, common-sense, and sees reality 'as men commonly perceive it'. In this world talk of the supernatural appears marginal and unthreatening. The second is terrifying, hostile, incomprehensible, fantastic. In it the common-sense world is swallowed up in and subordinated to a supernatural realm hostile to the individual self and governed by unknown and unfathomable laws. The opposition nature/supernatural, in which these terms subsume all the characteristics listed above and in which the latter than term is subordinate and dependent, is subverted and reversed. Nathanael's relationships with his mother (apart from a brief but perhaps significant moment of doubt), Clara, Lothar and Siegmund (apart from his paranoid interludes) for the most part belong to the first category. To the second category (apart from periods of common-sense lucidity) belong his relationships with Coppelius, Spalanzani, Coppola. It is in the ambiguous relationship with his father (the grandmother/wolf figure) that Nathanael discovers the terrifying trap-door from one world of relationships and perceptions to the other, the uncanny moment when the opposition natural/supernatural seems about to be reversed. On the one hand his father represents domestic contentment in the family circle with his pipe, beer, wonderful stories, amusements and picture-books. On the other his father's stories have introduced him to tales of goblins, witches and dwarfs. He has opened his imagination to the realm of the Sand-Man.

By his own account the first threat to domestic contentment comes with the sound of heavy steps on the stairs at night. The process of alienation (from the hearth) is taken a stage further with the discovery that the Sand-Man 'sends us away from papa'. Thirdly, he decides that his mother is lying when she tries to reassure him, thus introducing ambivalence into even this relationship. Although the principal breach is and remains that between Nathanael and his father, we perceive here a threat to his relations of trust with his mother too. It is the youngest sister's nurse, as we have already remarked in another connection, who confirms his terror with her blood-curdling account. He torments himself with the terrible apparition— an alien in the bosom of the family—whenever he hears noise on the stairs at night. This goes on for years until he yields to the temptation to *look at* the fabulous Sand-Man on one of his visits, to peer into the other realm. The famous scene takes place: the Sand-Man is revealed as the lawyer Coppelius and his father as his accomplice. Nathanael's mother hates Coppelius as much as the children do, whereas his father treats the lawyer as a higher being. But such is Coppelius's behaviour and Nathanael's state of terror, that, instead of being reassured by the discovery that the Sand-Man is after all only the lawyer Coppelius, Nathanael's terror is redoubled by the realization that the terrible Sand-Man has found his incarnation in the lawyer. Here, subtly but unmistakably (though not at this stage irrevocably), the fateful reversal has taken place in Nathanael's consciousness, and this reversal, once it has occurred, leaves a deep and indelible trace. Certainly Nathanael's

image of the Sand-Man has changed, but his threatening, supernatural character is unimpaired: 'I no longer conceived of the Sand-Man as the bug-bear in the old nurse's fable, who fetched children's eyes and took them to the half-moon for food for his little ones—no! but as an ugly spectre-like fiend bringing trouble and misery and ruin, both temporal and everlasting, everywhere he appeared.'

Finally Coppelius brings about the father's death.

Freud, of course, insists that the Sand-Man is an alternative father-imago, representing Nathanael's fear of castration. But, unless one is prejudiced in favour of Freudian theory, there is nothing here to compel such a reading. A more obvious one would be that the Sand-Man represents Nathanael's infantile dread of hostile forces external to the security of the family circle, a dread which, as Storr intimates, is never intenser than when a member of that trusted circle himself seems in some way to be implicated in that threat. It is natural that the father, who has to live in and deal with the hostile external world, should attract this role to himself.

It might be objected that this does not explain the intensity of Nathanael's experience. But it is not so unusual as it appears at first sight. Many children have bad dreams and, if Melanie Klein is to be believed, they also suffer in early infancy from aggressive fantasies which they project onto others [Antony Storr, *Human Aggression*, 1968]. Some have hyperactive imaginations and many, if not all, sometimes confuse 'reality' with 'fantasy', as both Nathanael and Hoffmann's narrator seem to do. Even in Nathanael's first letter it becomes evident that his experiences are unusually intense and also that they have persisted into adolescence and adulthood. Clara, with Lothar's help, makes a brave attempt to give them a common-sense explanation in her letter to Nathanael, referring to dark and hostile powers which can be thwarted by firmness and cheerfulness. She continues:

> It is also certain, Lothar adds, that if we have once voluntarily given ourselves up to this dark physical power, it often reproduces within us the strange forms which the outer world throws in our way, so that thus it is we ourselves who engender within ourselves the spirit which by some remarkable delusion we imagine to speak in that outer form. It is the phantom of our own self whose intimate relationship with, and whose powerful influence upon, our soul either plunges us into hell or elevates us to heaven.

Clara does not altogether understand these last words, but suggests to Nathanael in her letter that if he convinces himself that these foreign influences have no power over him, they will cease to endanger him, for it is only belief in their hostile power that makes them dangerous.

In psychoanalytical terms, what Clara and Lothar are pointing to is the power of paranoid projection. As Storr says, paranoid traits can be detected in most of us and many analysts, following Melanie Klein, now refer to the earliest stage of emotional development as the paranoid—schizoid position. 'Projection' is generally taken to be the mechanism by which human beings disown what is unacceptable in themselves and attribute it wrongly to someone else, though it can also relate to pleasant experience (such as those characteristic of infatuation)—as both Clara and Freud were aware.

According to this view, Nathanael is projecting onto Coppelius, and in part onto his father, his own unacceptable aggression, and this projection is given extra intensity by a sudden loss of trust in a person and an environment upon which he relies for his sense of security, a loss experienced first in early infancy in the traumatic fashion described and given added colour by the Sand-Man motif. This motif is associated with a sudden reversal of the oppositions natural/supernatural, secure/insecure, etc. It is re-experienced throughout childhood and adolescence whenever key associations trigger it off.

It may perhaps seem odd for an adult to project a delusional system based upon the materials out of which fairy-tales are made. Yet two things should be remembered. The first is that Nathanael's delusions have their origin in infancy and have since been modified to accord with Romantic literary motifs—he even composes a poem on the subject. The second is that delusional beliefs, no less fantastic, are to be found not only in primitive societies but have been accepted throughout history by persons of high intelligence, about witches, Jews and other outsider groups. Embryonic delusions are to be detected in virtually everyone. Of course Nathanael's delusions are not commonplace. But nor are they so greatly exaggerated.

Independently of Freud's thesis, there is evidence in the text for a connection between the eyes and emotionally charged perception. When Coppola first visits Nathanael he is trying to sell him thermometers and weather-glasses. Shortly afterwards the narrator describes the state of Nathanael's mind, asking the reader if he has ever experienced anything like it: 'All was seething and boiling within you; your blood, heated to fever pitch, leaped through your veins and inflamed your cheeks. Your gaze was so peculiar, as if seeking to grasp in empty space forms not seen by any other eye, and all your words ended in sighs betokening some mystery.' Thermometers are instruments for measuring temperature and weather-glasses for perceiving details not seen by the naked eye. Coppola, like Spalanzani and Coppelius, has on Nathanael the effect of 'raising the temperature' and 'sharpening the perception'. Put another way, they help to trigger off Nathanael's paranoid delusions. The threat to the eyes can therefore be seen much more simply as a threat to Nathanael's capacity for orientating himself within the real world as men commonly perceive it and finding a secure place in the structure of a world ordered on the principles of common-sense. The fear of the theft of the eyes (and bodily dismemberment) seems to represent what Laing calls a 'primary ontological insecurity', the fear of the great unknown, ultimately fear of spiritual and physical death or transfer to a world where common-sense, emotional security and natural law have no purchase. Paranoid projection is not the only way in which Nathanael deals with his aggressive impulses, perceived as external threat. He is also prey to explosions of rage (e.g. against Clara) and to bouts of depression which lead eventually to his suicide (aggression turned inwards).

But why should the eyes especially be associated with the capacity for finding a secure place in the structure of a world ordered on the principles of common-sense? One answer is that it is the eyes that are threatened in the nurse's story which makes such an impact on Nathanael. An arbitrary association is therefore established in early infancy between security, daytime, the family circle and waking vision on the one hand and insecurity, night-time, banishment, sleep and the mutilation of the eyes on the other. According to Nathanael's mother's version, the expression that the Sand-Man is come simply means that Nathanael feels sleepy, as if someone had thrown sand in his eyes, but he already associates the phrase with sinister footsteps and being sent away from his father, which he does not want. According to the nurse's version, this feeling sleepy is a sign that the wicked Sand-Man is punishing Nathanael for not wanting to go to bed, by stealing his eyes to feed his beaked children. It is hardly surprising that the threat to the eyes should take on a key role in his psychological economy. But there is another answer which finds a repeated echo in the tale: it is in the eyes that one reads character, the soul, through which one establishes relationships with others and discerns their disposition towards oneself. To lose one's eyes deprives one of the means for forming such relationships. To have one's vision distorted, for example by the use of 'weather-glasses', is to have one's relationships with others distorted.

The symbolism of the eyes in relation to the castration complex is central to Freud's reading, and it might, if space permitted, be worth tracing this motif in the story together with other motifs which characterize Nathanael's delusions. The system of delusions associated with the Sand-Man becomes more complex at every stage with the accumulation of new motifs. To the motifs of the transference of the eyes, the manipulation of limbs and the selling of weather-glasses is added that of the circle of fire and the confusion of real girls and automata. That there is a sexual element in Nathanael's experiences is undeniable. It is even possible, as I have tentatively suggested, that the incest motif is to be traced back to early childhood. But that the sexual factor must be considered primary and the dominance factor secondary is extremely doubtful. That the motif of the eyes cannot be explained satisfactorily apart from fear of castration is evidently false, though the sexual motif intensifies and lends added colour to the emotions. According to my alternative thesis the threat to the eyes represents a threat to the ability to form relationships within the dominance hierarchy of the family, and by extension in the world of 'reality as men commonly perceive it' as a whole. Paranoid projection is only the most dramatic of Nathanael's strategies for displacing his aggression, but it is the one that leads to his ruin.

This was clearly not Freud's view, but the fact that Freud was at precisely this time radically revising his own theories about the relationship between aggression and sexuality, and in the view of most commentators—not only Adler—did not do so satisfactorily, is a factor which we may wish to keep in mind. Storr suggests that Freud allocated relatively little importance to aggression as compared with sexuality because of the necessity for advancing his theories of infantile sexuality against a current of almost universal obloquy, and also, after 1908, by the necessity of resisting Adler's view of a primary aggressive instinct. In other words, Freud too was involved in establishing his own place in the hierarchy and preserving his position of dominance in the world of psychoanalysis. The first involved a determined and single-minded struggle to establish the principle of infantile sexuality even at the cost of undervaluing other drives; the second involved resisting his former disciples and current rivals at similar cost. Hence, perhaps, the related facts that he did not himself fully incorporate the theory of aggression implicit in *Beyond the Pleasure Principle* into his reading of **'Der Sandmann'**, that the theory was not fully worked out and was presented very tentatively, and that in the view of most of his successors it remains one of the least satisfactory aspects of his later psychoanalytic theory. (pp. 82-90)

Freud disputes Jentsch's view that Olimpia is the source of the feeling of the uncanny because of the uncertainty about whether she is living or inanimate. Who or what is Olimpia? Most commentators accept the view that she is actually a doll, an uncannily life-like one to be sure, manufactured jointly by Spalanzani and Coppola, who fool not only Nathanael but the other students and citizens as well, until Nathanael's misadventure with her reveals the imposture. But there are several problems with a naive acceptance of this interpretation. The first is that in his current state of mind Nathanael seems just as capable of *imagining* the scene in which the two creators of Olimpia pull her apart (as a punishment for incest?) as he is of falling in love with a doll. Moreover the 'discovery' of the fraud is entirely a matter of gossip. The Professor of Poetry and Eloquence writes the whole story off as 'an allegory, a continuous metaphor'. Not only were the citizens unable to tell that Olimpia was 'really' a doll when she was around (though in retrospect they 'remember' all sorts of peculiar things about her) but afterwards some of them find themselves unable to tell whether their own mistresses are really dolls or not, and everyone goes to comical extremes to prove to others that they are real. Where does the truth lie in all this, where the truth may be defined as the point of view of a Clara or a Siegmund? To avoid this question by concentrating on the satirical, 'feminist' tone of the passage is to fail to take Hoffmann's text seriously at this point. Clara does not witness these events, but Siegmund's view is conveyed to the reader. Olimpia is singularly statuesque and soulless. If her eyes were not so utterly devoid of life she might pass for a beauty. Her movements seem like clockwork, and so on. She seems only to be acting *like* a living creature. In other words she creates an impression of the 'uncanny' on Siegmund and his friends. Clara would almost certainly tell Nathanael not to be silly: Olimpia was just a stupid girl, with whom Nathanael was infatuated until his paranoid delusions supervened, triggered off by the association of Spalanzani and Coppola with the dreaded Sand-Man. In fact Nathanael himself shows a progressive tendency to confuse real girls with dolls. It begins with his indignant riposte to Clara when she has rejected his poem: 'You damned lifeless automaton!' It continues with the Olimpia episode and concludes with the attempt to hurl Clara off the tower, yelling 'Spin round, wooden doll! Spin round, wooden doll!' Freud holds that we know that we are not supposed to be looking on at the products of a madman's imagination.

But such a view is surely based upon a naive trust in the reliability of the narrator's voice and, what is more, undermines the basis of the experience of the uncanny. Not only is the narrator concerned with telling a good story, which makes his 'objectivity' suspect, and not only is there in his narrative as well as in Nathanael's experience a confusion and a blurring of the line between the real and the illusory, but it is at least arguable that there is a transition from third-person narrative to *erlebte Rede* precisely at the point where he discovers Spalanzani and Coppola struggling over Olimpia. The difficulty of distinguishing between 'objective' narrative and free indirect speech leaves the question shrouded in ambiguity. It appears that the narrator got the story, together with the opening letters, from his 'friend' Lothar. But in what form? In the style of the letters, or has Lothar changed his views about the Sand-Man? And how did Lothar get hold of the story and how was it told to him? There is no way of telling. On the evidence of the text these questions must remain open, and so they must for the experience of the uncanny to persist. There are further problems here about narrative focus which deserve to be examined in detail. But it is enough now to expose the ambiguities. What matters in the end is not whether Olimpia was 'in reality' a doll or a stupid girl, but that she, as much as the incarnations of the Sand-Man, is a product of Nathanael's imagination, stimulated by the use of Coppola's weather-glass, and that her existence in Nathanael's imagination is situated on the margins of the natural and the supernatural. It would be entirely in keeping with Nathanael's perception of the Sand-Man to assume that she is indeed real and that the opposition natural/supernatural is compulsively deconstructed as soon as he catches an uncanny glimpse of the possibility of its deconstruction. As I remarked earlier, infatuation may also be seen as a type of paranoid projection. It is Nathanael's attempt to legitimize this system of delusions by giving Olimpia his mother's ring that triggers off the other system, that of the Sand-Man. Nathanael can no more legitimize Olimpia by invoking his mother than he can neutralize the 'bad projection' of the Sand-Man with the 'good projection' of Olimpia. Within the hierarchy Nathanael—Sand-Man—Olimpia, where the Sand-Man threatens to usurp Nathanael's place, there is no question that the Sand-Man is prior to Olimpia, in spite of Nathanael's wish to establish a direct relationship with her and exclude him. In the first place she is Spalanzani's daughter and Nathanael comes to fall in love with her through the use of Coppola's glass. In the second, it is this pair that wreaks revenge by destroying her and Nathanael's sanity.

Nathanael has tried before to legitimize his delusions through a member of the family circle when he tries out his poem on Clara. But she uncompromisingly rejects it. His violent reaction almost leads to a duel between him and Lothar. There can be no compromise between the world of reality as men commonly perceive it and the world of paranoid delusions, between the world of the natural and the world of the supernatural. One has to subsume the other. The question is which subsumes which. (pp. 90-2)

What then of the concept of 'the uncanny'?

Freud's concern is not to psychoanalyse Nathanael and it is only incidentally to give a psychoanalytical account of the principal motifs in the story. He selects **'Der Sandmann'** as a suitable of 'the uncanny' in literature, and has no doubt that in this story the feeling of something uncanny is directly attached to the figure of the Sand-Man, that is, to the idea of being robbed of one's eyes, which he equates with the dread of castration. To avoid going over old ground, we may regard this as a special case, and any doubts arising from earlier discussion need not deter us from looking further at Freud's views about the uncanny in general.

More generally the uncanny is related to what is frightening. The uncanny constitutes 'that class of the frightening which leads back to what is known of old and long familiar', repressed desires or surmounted modes of thinking belonging to the prehistory of the individual and of the race. An uncanny effect, says Freud, 'is often and easily produced when the distinction between imagination and reality is effaced, as when something that we have hitherto regarded as imaginary appears before us in reality, or when a symbol takes over the full functions of the thing it symbolizes, and so on. It is this factor which contributes not a little to the uncanny effect attaching to magical practices. The infantile element in this, which also dominates the minds of neurotics, is the over-accentuation of psychical reality in comparison with material reality—a feature closely allied to the belief in the omnipotence of thoughts.'

The general theory as expressed here is quite consistent with the alternative reading of **'Der Sandmann'** which I have proposed. So is Freud's interesting account of the etymology of the German words 'heimlich' and 'unheimlich'. According to this, 'das Heimliche' is ambivalent in its meaning. It has associations of the familiar, friendly, cheerful, comfortable, intimate and of 'being at home in the world', as well as associations of 'that which is hidden, secreted, obscured, so that its negation means to disclose, to discover, reveal, expose areas normally kept hidden'. The uncanny embraces both these levels of meaning and transforms the familiar into the unfamiliar. Rosemary Jackson, in her account of Freud's treatment of the uncanny, summarizes: 'what is encountered in this uncanny realm, whether it is termed spirit, angel, devil, ghost or monster, is nothing but an unconscious *projection*' [*Fantasy, The Literature of Projection*, 1981]. [In *Poétique*, 1973] Hélène Cixous argues that the uncanny exists only in relation to the familiar and the normal. It 'only presents itself, initially, on the edge of something else' or, as Weber has it, from a position *abseits*. For Cixous the unfamiliarity is not merely displaced sexual activity, but a rehearsal of an encounter with death, whereas for Freud the association with death is but an instance of the uncanny along with, for example, epilepsy and madness or the fear of being buried alive.

Freud additionally mentions the role which repetition and the 'double' in all its many cultural manifestations have in the production of the sensation of the uncanny, though he does not develop the idea and refers the reader to the work of Otto Rank and his own *Beyond the Pleasure Principle*. Hertz in his brilliant essay on Freud and the uncan-

ny makes great play with the idea of intertextual repetition: 'The feeling of the uncanny would seem to be generated by being-reminded-of-the-repetition-compulsion, not by being-reminded-of-whatever-it-is-that-is-repeated. It is the becoming aware of the process that is felt as eerie, not the becoming aware of some particular item in the unconscious, once familiar, then repressed, now coming back into consciousness. [It is my view that this is one but not the only basis for the experience of the uncanny.]

That a footing in the world of the familiar, the world of reality as men commonly perceive it, is the starting point for any experience of the uncanny is a matter on which all seem to agree and may be regarded as axiomatic. A world that knows only the fantastic (such as the world of fairytales) does not elicit such sensations. The story of Red Riding Hood is not uncanny but the little girl who knows it may get uncanny glimpses of her own grandmother which remind her of the story. Within this context of normality the experience of the uncanny is a momentary glimpse of (or a sensation of seepage from) another world governed by different and unknown laws, usually though not always terrifying. Once this alternative world takes over the imagination, once the hierarchical opposition is reversed, the experience of the uncanny as such has passed, and something else has taken its place. The uncanny is an experience of the *threshold*.

The second point on which there is general accord is that repetition or likeness seems to characterize most forms of the uncanny. Freud argues that it may be repetition itself, not the thing repeated, which produces the sensation. Likeness, or convergence, can be observed in many of those experiences which commonly prompt us to use the word 'uncanny': an 'uncanny coincidence', an 'uncanny resemblance' (the double, plagiarism, perhaps also the sensation of the presence of the strong poet, *pace* Bloom, at the shoulder of the successor). Yet for the word 'uncanny' to seem appropriate it is essential that the likeness or convergence seem to defy the laws of reality as commonly understood. We are not inclined to speak of an 'uncanny resemblance' between twins, for example, not, at least, if we know they are twins, because the experience is one which everyday reality allows for. But we may speak of an 'uncanny resemblance' between individuals less alike than twins, because our experience of reality does not allow for such a degree of resemblance between individuals unrelated by blood. The *déjà vu* experience is a good example of a sensation of repetition which cannot be confirmed within the world of everyday reality. Other examples of temporally spaced likeness include precognition of various kinds.

Thirdly, all seem agreed that the experience of the uncanny must be infused with dread deriving from the unconscious projection of infantile or primitive fears. No doubt the perception of degrees of likeness or convergence not sanctioned by the laws of reality as men commonly perceive it triggers off the mechanism of projection. That displaced hostility is common to all such negative projections seems evident, as is the fact that death is the ultimate expression of such projections. In Hoffmann's story, Nathanael's experiences are several times associated with death, to which his paranoid delusions ultimately lead him. But can one also conceive of the uncanny in connection with positive projections, such as those involved in infatuation? The English language does not seem to encourage such usage. Yet it is not impossible that a lover should say, for instance, that the way his friend seems to anticipate his thoughts or the way he repeatedly intuits her presence without seeing her is 'uncanny', without there being any suggestion of dread but rather of pleasurable elation. Whatever usage may dictate, the psychological mechanisms involved seem to be similar. Siegmund's reaction to Olimpia provides us with one of the most interesting examples of the uncanny experience: 'We felt quite afraid of this Olympia, and did not like to have anything to do with her; she seemed to us to be only acting *like* a living creature, and as if there was some secret at the bottom of it all' ('Uns ist diese Olimpia ganz unheimlich geworden . . . '). That is a splendid expression of the experience of the uncanny. Not, let it be noted, 'she seems to behave like a doll', but 'she seems to be acting *like* a living creature'. Momentarily, another dimension has insinuated itself into Siegmund's awareness. His statement only makes sense if that is assumed. That she might *be* a doll does not seem to have occurred to him, though that would be unnatural enough. The phrase he uses betrays the fact that he has assumed the reversal of the opposition natural/supernatural, while not apparently being aware of it. He is poised precariously in that eerie region where radical discontinuity threatens to sever permanently his links with the world of normality, if once he should peer into the abyss.

The word 'unheimlich' occurs only rarely in Hoffmann's text. The first time is in Clara's letter to Nathanael where she refers to Coppelius's 'mysterious labours along with your father' ('unheimliche Treiben mit Deinem Vater') and quotes Lothar on 'that mysterious power' ('jene unheimliche Macht', not 'Nacht' as Weber has it). Another is when Nathanael first notices the strangely fixed look about Olimpia's eyes: 'I felt quite uncomfortable' ('Mir wurde ganz unheimlich. . .'). Further examples are Siegmund's remark on Olimpia, quoted above, and Nathanael's rebuttal of this remark.

A fourth point seems not to have been explicitly formulated elsewhere, though it follows naturally. I have been speaking for the most part of the 'horizontal' factors in the experience of the uncanny (convergence, repetition, likeness, etc.). I have also broached the 'vertical' ones: the projection of infantile hostility; the experience of a supernatural dimension deriving from primitive superstition. If the basic trope underlying the horizontal relationships here is *metaphor*, then the basic trope underlying the vertical is *metonymy*, or, more exactly, synecdoche. These momentary experiences *stand for* another realm where other, mysterious, and usually terrifying laws hold sway, laws against which no man can hold out, the very possibility of which reminds him of his radical vulnerability and 'ontological insecurity'. No reader of James Frazer's *Golden Bough* will be entirely surprised by this discovery, since Frazer delineates two types in what he calls Theoretical Magic (magic 'regarded as a system of natural law, that is a statement of the rules which determine the sequence

of events throughout the world'): homeopathic magic and contagious magic. 'Homeopathic magic is founded on the association of ideas by similarity; contagious magic is founded on the association of ideas by contiguity (. . .) But in practice the two branches are often combined'. Frazer does not describe the particular combination I have discussed. Since he is writing about the practice of magic there is no reason why he should. It is nevertheless interesting that the structure of magic conceived of theoretically on the basis of a study of its practice should display parallels with the structure of the experience of the uncanny, the threshold between the natural and the supernatural. As Freud says: 'As soon as something *actually happens* in our lives which seems to confirm the old, discarded beliefs we get a feeling of the uncanny; it is as though we were making a judgement something like this: "So, after all, it is *true* that one can kill a person by the mere wish!" ' (pp. 92-96)

Although he concedes that they are not always sharply distinguishable in reality, Freud makes a distinction between experiences of the uncanny based upon repressed infantile complexes and those based upon surmounted primitive beliefs. The former are 'not of very frequent occurrence in real life'. But Storr reminds us that the two are not so far removed from each other:

> it is easy to demonstrate, from legend and myth, that terrifying phantasies of an aggressive kind are so ubiquitous amongst peoples of varying cultures that they cannot possibly be considered exclusive to neurotic or psychotic persons. For example, the figure of the witch who eats children and who threatens the virility of the male occurs in such a variety of guises all over the world that it is obvious that she is an expression of an archetypal phantasy which is common to all mankind. For we have all, as infants, been at the mercy of a female figure possessed of absolute power over us: and although we may hope that, during most of our babyhood, she appeared as tender, protective and compassionate, it is not difficult to recognize that she might also, when angry or rejecting, have taken on a different and more sinister aspect.

Of course Freud knew this quite well, though, having chosen not to 'psychoanalyse' Nathanael, he did not discuss as such the links between the fairy-tale image of the Sand-Man and Nathanael's infantile complexes. Clearly such links are not necessary to the experience of the uncanny, but where they exist are not difficult to perceive, whether or not one abandons the central explanatory role of the castration complex and accepts the priority of aggression.

Storr's particular eclectic type of psychoanalytic theory is of help therefore not only in reading **'Der Sandmann'** but also in the more general study of the uncanny. Where does this leave Freud's analysis. . .?

That the feeling of something uncanny in this story is directly attached to the figure of the Sand-Man is certainly true, though it is also directly attached to the figure of Olimpia. That the figure of the Sand-Man is associated with the fear of losing one's eyes is also a statement of fact. Where the present account differs from Freud's is in its view of the significance of this motif. It is not necessary to put Freud's clinical experience in question to doubt the centrality of the castration complex in arousing the sensation of the uncanny. We have seen that the eye motif can be quite well explained on other grounds which seem to offer a richer and more satisfying account of the text as a whole.

Freud's thesis that there is no intellectual uncertainty in **'Der Sandmann'** is itself virtually indefensible, and his conclusion that this cannot therefore be the explanation for the experience of the uncanny is therefore based on very shaky foundations. Intellectual, and emotional, uncertainty would appear after all to have something to do with the effect, though doubt as to whether an object is living or inanimate awakens a sense of the uncanny not because of intellectual uncertainty as such, but because the posing of this kind of question arises out of a situation where the 'natural' is threatened with subversion by the supernatural. The fact that the uncertainty may be easily resolved by means of a naturalistic explanation does not necessarily prevent the feeling of the uncanny occurring. (The appearance on television of a person whose death has recently been announced would be a case in point.) In Nathanael's case the 'realization' that Olimpia is a doll not only does not forestall the feeling but does nothing to prevent a further descent into the realm of the supernatural. Dolls, after all, are not 'normally' equipped with the eyes of living persons which lie all bloody on the ground.

Finally, Freud's application of the Oedipus complex to the problem of the uncanny puts fear of the father at the very centre of Nathanael's emotional world. According to the present reading, fear of the father is secondary and stands for terror in the face of a hostile, seemingly incomprehensible and radically threatening environment. That is not to say that oedipal factors may not enter into and colour the picture, according either to Freud's own reading or the alternative reading which we have suggested. It is to insist that they have no primacy in relation to outwardly directed aggression. Similarly, other factors which according to Freud turn something frightening into something uncanny—animism, magic, sorcery, 'the omnipotence of thoughts', death, involuntary repetition, epilepsy, madness, dismemberment, being buried alive—only do so when they accompany or trigger off a glimpse of that same abyss in which reality as men commonly perceive it and make themselves at home is radically subverted by an alternative, supernatural order of things.

In my view it is possible, then, to give a post-Freudian psychoanalytic account of **'Der Sandmann'** which does less violence to Hoffmann's text than Freud's, does more justice to aggression and gives less prominence to sexuality (in accordance with subsequent ethnological research and a broad consensus in post-Freudian theory and clinical experience) and in some respects at least yields a richer reading. At the same time these adjustments offer a fruitful approach to a redefinition of the uncanny. Whether they can be successfully grafted on to an otherwise unmodified Freudian account is doubtful and it therefore seems preferable to regard them as the basis for an alternative reading.

Freud's article has given rise not only to further discussions of **'Der Sandmann'** and the experience of the uncanny, but to classification of types of literary theory. Jonathan Culler discusses J. Hillis Miller's view that:

> Already a clear distinction can be drawn, among critics influenced by these new developments, between what might be called (. . .) Socratic, theoretical, or canny critics, on the one hand, and Apollonian/Dionysian, tragic, or uncanny critics on the other.

Of the latter, he writes, 'the thread of logic leads (. . .) into regions which are alogical, absurd. (. . .) Sooner or later there is the encounter with an "aporia" or impasse. In fact the moment when logic fails in their work is the moment of their deepest penetration into the actual nature of literary language, or of language as such.'

A rather better account of the uncanny in the work of contemporary criticism and critical theory (better, that is, in terms of the present discussion) might lay emphasis on the point where the text hangs, as it were, over the abyss of deconstruction, or the alogical, the absurd, where from a firm footing in logocentric reality as men commonly perceive it (say, criticism in the liberal tradition), we tread unwarily on the trap-door which leads to a radical, terrifying reversal of 'normal' priorities and a world whose laws, at first at least, we only dimly apprehend.

There is the uncanny moment. (The moment perhaps where one senses this article beginning to slip back into the Freudian orbit from which it aimed to escape.)

Where does this leave us? **'Der Sandmann'** is undoubtedly an example of the uncanny in literature. The uncanny can sometimes be sensed in critical theory and practice as well. But **'Der Sandmann'** and Hoffmann as a whole can also be said (have also been said) to exemplify the 'carnivalization of literature', that realm of discourse in which the ancient categories of the carnival are 'reincarnated', where the hierarchies and relationships of non-carnival 'everyday life' are temporarily reversed and held up to renewing carnival laughter (in Hoffmann's case laughter with a sinister ring, reminiscent of the 'carnival of Hell'). 'Carnival celebrates the shift itself, the very process of replaceability, and not the precise item that is replaced. Carnival is, so to speak, functional and not substantive. It absolutizes nothing, but rather proclaims the joyful relativity of everything.' 'In death birth is foreseen and in birth death, in victory defeat and in defeat victory, in crowning a decrowning. Carnival laughter does not permit a single one of these aspects of change to be absolutized or to congeal in one-sided seriousness.' Freudian theory has performed in our time a carnival function, reversing everyday hierarchies, offending against the seemly, the decorous and the common-sense, challenging, subverting and mocking in the public square what others have seen as centres of logocentric truth, presenting, as Bakhtin has it, 'le monde à l'envers'. (Recent times have seen numerous other examples of what may be called 'the carnivalization of literary theory'.) A 'carnivalized' reading of Hoffmann, Freud and the many critical accounts of them would therefore revel in the enthroning and the dethroning of common-sense or the Sand-Man within the story and of Freud outside it, in the 'eccentricity' of an alternative Freudian or latter-day psychoanalytic reading, in the displacing and reaffirmation of the world of common-sense. The carnival does not itself experience the uncanny, but may act it out. Perhaps it is in this context that the present debate best makes sense. (pp. 96-9)

Malcolm V. Jones, " 'Der Sandmann' and 'The Uncanny': A Sketch for an Alternative Approach," in Paragraph: The Journal of Modern Critical Theory Group, *Vol. 7, March, 1986, pp. 77-99.*

Neil Hertz on Freud's interpretation of "The Sandman":

An interesting and, I think, serious objection can be raised to Freud's reading of Hoffmann, and that is that Freud has overstabilized his first account of the story, that there is, indeed, more cause for doubt and uncertainty as one moves through **"The Sandman"** than Freud allows. Looking back at his paraphrasing of the story we can see one way in which this overstabilization has been accomplished. Freud retells the story, occasionally quoting from the text, but what is remarkable is that everything he includes within quotation marks has already appeared within quotation marks in **"The Sandman"**: that is, he quotes nothing but dialogue, things said by Nathanael or by some other character; the words of the narrator have completely disappeared, replaced by Freud's own, and we have the illusion of watching Nathanael's actions through a medium considerably more transparent than Hoffmann's text. For Hoffmann's narration is anything but unobtrusive: it is, rather, vivid, shifty, and extravagant, full of assonances, verbal repetitions, literary allusions and startling changes in the pace, in the mood, and in the quasi-musical dynamics of its unfolding. What is more, this narrative exuberance is, at certain moments, rendered thematically important within the story in ways that make Freud's decision to set it aside seem more puzzling. For it may be that what is unsettling, if not uncanny, about **"The Sandman"** is as much a function of its surface as of the depths it conceals.

Neil Hertz in Textual Strategies: Perspectives in Post-Structuralist Criticism, *ed. by Josué V. Harari, 1979.*

Clayton Koelb   (essay date 1988)

[*Koelb is an American educator and critic with a special interest in German literature. In the following excerpt, he examines the figurative language in "The Sandman."*]

At the close of **"The Sandman,"** its hero is described as a person with a "lacerated soul" ("im Innern zerrissen"). The metaphor of internal dismemberment is a common one, and the phrase would pass without notice if it did not come at the end of this particular story. **"The Sandman"** so forcefully presents a fantasy of dismemberment or the anxiety of dismemberment that it has become, at least since Freud's essay on the uncanny, the central text for almost any discussion of "Zerrissenheit." Focusing on powerful images of bodies torn apart—the latest, the description of Nathanael's shattered head (*zerschmetterter Kopf*), occurs only two sentences earlier—the text does not allow

the reader to accept the notion of being "im Innern zerrissen" as easily as one ordinarily might. In other circumstances we would read this as a metaphor of a troubled psyche and nothing more. In this case, however, the vehicle does not allow itself to be submerged by the tenor of the figure. The picture of Nathanael's corpse, quite "zerrissen" in its own right, is too fresh in the reader's mind, the physical reality of dismemberment too graphically present, to permit the signifier "zerrissen" to pass harmlessly out of the realm of the literal. The juxtaposition in the text of the description of Nathanael's shattered head and his dismembered psyche forces a question as to the relation between tenor and vehicle, between the literal and figurative readings authorized by rhetorical construction. Common usage suggests that we read the word "zerrissen" here as the vehicle in a metaphor of psychic disruption, but the context of the story, especially the immediate context, would authorize us to read it as a metonymic extension of the physical sunderings occurring throughout the tale. Where is the rhetoric, where the reality? Is the physical dismemberment presented by the body of the narrative to be seen as the figure for the reality of Nathanael's psychic trauma (as, for example, Freud would have it), or is that psychic trauma with its language of internal dismemberment a figure, a metonymic supplement brought into being by the power of the grisly reality just described?

Hoffmann's story is centrally concerned with this question, with spinning out the many possibilities inherent in a rhetoric of "Zerrissenheit." It makes its beginning out of this problem and finds its imaginative space in the area between the literal and the figurative. The very word "zerrissen," in its apparently figurative extension, is explicitly introduced at the commencement of the tale, in the very first paragraph. Nathanael excuses his tardiness in writing letters on the grounds of his "Zerrissenheit": "Alas, how could I write to you in the tormented frame of mind which has disrupted all my thoughts!" At this early stage in the narration, though, the reader has no reason to pause over the commonplace expression "zerrissene Stimmung des Geistes"; it passes as an innocuous trope. So too does the related expression "pull myself together" ("fasse ich mich zusammen") by which Nathanael signifies his efforts to counteract the internal "Zerrissenheit" preventing his writing. This rhetoric of coming apart and pulling back together can work here only proleptically, anticipating the many scenes of dismemberment that will follow.

The reader is quickly introduced to one of these scenes, the explanation of the concept of the "Sandman" demanded by the young Nathanael, first from his mother and then from the nursemaid. The mother explains in a simple and direct way that there is no actual Sandman: "When I tell you that the Sandman is coming, it only means that you are sleepy and can't keep your eyes open any longer, as though someone had sprinkled sand into them." The Sandman, in other words, is a metaphor. But Nathanael cannot accept the notion that the Sandman is only the vehicle in a figure conveying sleepiness, just as the reader at the end of the story cannot simply take "zerrissen" as the vehicle in a figure conveying psychic disruption. At the end of the story, the reader's mind is too occupied with descriptions of actual dismemberment to accept the figure as nothing but figure, and here at the beginning Nathanael's mind is conditioned similarly by what he considers his experience of the "real" Sandman: "I had surely always heard him coming up the stairs." Prejudiced as he is in favor of a more literal reading, it is no wonder that the nursemaid's picture of a monster Sandman, implausible as it might otherwise be ("I was old enough to realize that the nurse's tale of the Sandman . . . couldn't be altogether true"), strikes Nathanael as intuitively correct:

> He is a wicked man who comes to children when they refuse to go to bed and throws handfuls of sand in their eyes till they bleed and pop out of their heads. Then he throws the eyes into a sack and takes them to the half-moon as food for his children, who sit in a nest and have crooked beaks like owls with which they pick up the eyes of human children who have been naughty.

By accepting the nursemaid's version of the Sandman and rejecting his mother's, young Nathanael is exchanging one form of "Zerrissenheit" for another. For it is clear that the boy would far prefer a world in which his physical body is threatened with being torn apart by an actual, horrible Sandman to one in which meaning is forced so far apart from the apparent intuitive clarity of the signifier. The nursemaid's story preserves the notion that language means what it says, whereas the mother's explanation makes a rift between what is said ("The Sandman is coming") and what is meant ("There is no Sandman. You are sleepy."). It also proposes a gap between the boy's experience (hearing the "Sandman") and language ("There is no Sandman"). Nathanael chooses to preserve the unity of language both with itself and with the world of experience even though it means also accepting the threat of personal dismemberment. The latter seems somehow the lesser evil.

Of course, the mother's explanation of the Sandman as metaphor cannot be entirely erased from the child's mind. His desire to dispel lingering doubts about the reality of the Sandman motivates his wish to see what one might suppose he would never want to see, the "horrible Sandman" himself. This wish to "investigate the mystery" ("das Geheimnis zu erforschen") prompts him to hide in his father's room one night and to discover thereby that the Sandman, "the horrible Sandman, was the old lawyer Coppelius who frequently had dinner with us!" This discovery would seem to solve Nathanael's difficulty: here was a real person who could plausibly fit the role of Sandman while at the same time banishing the bogeyman of the nurse's story. Nathanael relates that in this moment of discovery "the Sandman was no longer the hobgoblin of the nurse's tale, the one who brought the eyes of children for his brood to feed upon in the owl's nest in the half-moon." But if that were so, Nathanael would have to reinterpret the nurse's story as itself somehow figurative and thus reinstate the linguistic rift he has labored so hard to deny. To validate his faith in the unity of words and meanings, Nathanael has to find a way to fit this new piece of information, that Coppelius "is" the Sandman, into the nurse's text.

Part of the solution to this difficulty lies ready to hand in the linguistic material of Coppelius's name. Since Nathanael, at the time he writes his letter, believes that Coppelius

is identical to the Italian barometer dealer Giuseppe Coppola, it is evidently significant that the Italian word "coppo" means "eye socket." Since an eye socket is something that wants an eye, the bearer of the name Coppelius (or Coppola) would be at least linguistically equivalent to the nursemaid's Sandman. Nathanael's experience (real or imagined) then confirms this identification: Coppelius is presented as a kind of demon sorcerer at work on a project involving making eyes for automatons. His cry of "Give me eyes!" ("Augen her!") terrifies Nathanael into revealing his presence, and Coppelius threatens to carry out the nurse's script for the Sandman: "Pulling glowing grains from the fire with his naked hands, he was about to sprinkle them in my eyes." Nathanael's father intervenes to save his son's eyes, but Coppelius acts out the role of the dismembering Sandman in another way: "He thereupon seized me so violently that my joints cracked, unscrewed my hands and feet, then put them back, now this way, now that way."

The introduction of the theme of automatons in this scene—a theme that will play such an important role later in the story—serves to consolidate and reinforce the correctness of the nurse's picture of the Sandman. Since her story proposes the separability of body parts from the living body, its (nonfigural) interpretation requires some kind of framework for understanding human beings as assemblies of parts. Such a framework is readily available in the child's world in the form of the doll, a toy that often loses and regains eyes or limbs in the course of its lifetime. That Coppelius treats Nathanael like a doll, removing and rearranging his body parts, comes as a "logical" extension of the Sandman story, as does the implied scene of body part manufacture upon which Nathanael intrudes. The "Zerrissenheit" the child suffers at the hands of Coppelius is the price he pays for avoiding the dismemberment of the linguistic sign. It is a price he seems always ready to pay.

Other characters in the story, however, take up the role originally played by the mother, that of asserting that "there is no Sandman." Nathanael's fiancée Klara advocates this view forcefully, proclaiming that "in my opinion all the fears and terrors of which you speak took place only in your mind and had very little to do with the true, external world." This realistic and down-to-earth position annoys Nathanael to such a degree that he begins to resent her and to suspect that she is devoid of all human emotion. When she refers to a poem he has written on the subject of Coppelius as a "mad, insane, stupid tale," he calls her a "damned, lifeless automaton." The insult is a hyperbolic metaphor. Like the other figures in **"The Sandman,"** however, this too become the locus of a confrontation between tenor and vehicle. It is clear enough that Nathanael utters the phrase with a figurative intent, that he does not mean to suggest that Klara is actually a mechanical artifact; but it is also clear that Nathanael's perspective on metaphor cannot allow the concrete vehicle to be obliterated by the intended meaning. If language has proclaimed Nathanael's beloved an automaton, then she must really be one. Nathanael's affections stray from Klara to Olympia, who turns out indeed to be (as far as the reader can determine) a wooden doll, an "Automat." When it is discovered that Professor Spalanzani has been passing off a mechanism as his daughter Olympia, the ladies and gentlemen of society are shocked and are not at all comforted by the explanation given by the professor of rhetoric that "it is all an allegory, an extended metaphor." They, like the young Nathanael, can no longer accept the denial of the literal, the assertion that "there is no Sandman."

But if the existence of the "literal" *Automat* Olympia is a response to and validation of the vehicle of the metaphor applied to Klara, it is also in the event a validation of the view of the world that allows for the existence of a Sandman. Nathanael's preference for the literal over the figurative, for the vehicle over the tenor, implies the dismemberment of the self by the Sandman. Nathanael's way of thinking, carried to its logical end, envisions a world in which the self, in contemplating objects in the world, is always in danger of discovering that those objects are in fact parts torn out of that very self. This possibility, while in one sense deeply disturbing, is in another also highly attractive: it holds out the hope that the world is not filled with alien objects but also contains elements actually belonging to the self.

The figure of Olympia actualizes both the buoyant delight in self-recognition and the abject despair at the discovery of one's personal dismemberment. At first only the former comes into play. Nathanael is enchanted with the recognition that in this creature he can find a reflection of himself: "You deep soul [*Gemüt*], in which my whole being is reflected," he tells her. And to Siegmund he confesses, "I discover myself [*mein Selbst*] again only in Olympia's love." The reader will certainly detect in these pronouncements a certain irony: to some degree the self that Nathanael discovers in Olympia is indeed nothing more than his own voice, his own interpretation of her silences. But in another sense she does double Nathanael's self, to the degree that we understand that self as the product of the elaborated myth of the Sandman, for she is always and only what he was in the memory/story/dream of his experience in his father's study: a collection of separable parts, something whose limbs can be "unscrewed." In particular one set of Olympia's parts, the eyes, are alleged by the narrative to belong to Nathanael: "The eyes—the eyes stolen from you!" confesses Spalanzani when Nathanael discovers the truth about Olympia.

The discovery that Olympia is in fact a "lifeless doll" is what turns Nathanael's joy in self-recognition into horror. What had formerly seemed to be the reflection of living spirit in her now seems rather to be the reflection of her lifeless objecthood in him. Where before he has seen the two of them as parts of the same living organism, now he must see them both as pieces of one dismembered, dead body. When Nathanael calls upon the "wooden doll" ("Holzpüppchen") to "whirl around" ("dreh dich"), he is invoking himself as well as Olympia. More precisely, he is invoking the *trope* ("turn," "Wendung") by which language turns a person (Klara, Nathanael) into a wooden doll, a doll into a person. Such tropes, such "turned" phrases that insist on saying "Sandman" and "there is no Sandman" all at once, are the agents controlling Nathanael's existence: they are the things that make him what he is, but also the things that make his life impossible.

Nathanael's death itself (or at a minimum the madness that causes his death) is brought about by his last attempt to recover the literal level, the vehicle, from its metaphorical significance. The final scene takes place on a tower that Nathanael and Klara climb at her suggestion: " 'Let us climb to the top once more and look at the distant mountains!' No sooner said than done." After all that has happened in this story, with its emphasis on the movement from what is purely linguistic (*gesagt*) to what exists in reality (*getan*)—as for example the transformation of the pejorative epithet "Automat" into a genuine automaton—we are obliged to hesitate for an instant over this otherwise innocuous commonplace, "gesagt, getan." The common significance of this phrase, one that applies here also, stresses the speed with which a proposal is put into action. This is the aspect that is made explicit in the English expression "no sooner said than done." The German version, however, implies by juxtaposition the replacement of speech by action, the transformation of speech into action: what was "said" is now "done." Nathanael's story, especially the stories of his "madness," focuses attention precisely upon the process of turning something that is, ordinarily, only "gesagt"—"The Sandman is coming"—into a description of what is actually "getan." By introducing the scene at the top of the tower with the words "Gesagt, getan!" the narrator signals proleptically the return of the principle that allows the Sandman to exist and that makes Nathanael "mad."

Klara herself then, at the summit of the tower, provokes the return of the Sandman's perspective by calling Nathanael's attention to a "strange little grey bush" ("sonderbaren kleinen grauen Busch") that she says appears to be coming toward them. In doing so she conjures up a piece of language, a metaphor, that the narrator uses to describe Nathanael's preoccupation with Olympia. When he is prevented by a set of curtains from viewing Olympia throught the window,

> Nathanael, in despair, driven by longing and an ardent passion, rushed out beyond the city gates. Olympia's image [*Gestalt*] hovered before him in the air, emerged from the bushes, and peered up at him with great and lustrous eyes from the shining brook. Klara's image [*Bild*] had completely faded from his soul.

According to the narrator, then, bushes [*Gebüsch*] are things out of which Olympia's form [*Gestalt*] might emerge—though the narrator means this only figuratively. His trope is meant to tell us that, no matter what Nathanael actually experienced in the world, his thoughts were occupied with Olympia. The narrator's trope, though, also belongs somehow to Nathanael's consciousness—whether we understand this as a function of the narrator's "omniscience" or of the power of figurative language to infect every level of the story makes little difference—so that the mention of the bush immediately causes Nathanael to rediscover the Sandman's point of view ("er fand Coppolas Perspektiv") and to take up the spyglass. Taking up the spyglass in turn causes Nathanael to reenact the earlier psychic process by which Klara's image (*Bild*) was replaced by Olympia's form (*Gestalt*). When he accidentally looks at Klara through the "Perspektiv" ("spyglass/point of view") belonging to the Sandman, he sees Olympia, or more specifically the "turn" that makes the two women equivalent, and he once again goes mad. After trying to throw Klara off the tower, he jumps off himself and is "shattered" ("zerschmettert").

The transformatory power of Nathanael's perspective on figurative language is taken up by the narrative; it infects the story and its telling. If a perspective can bring about the metamorphosis of a living girl into a wooden doll (Klara into Olympia), then a "Perspektiv" ("spyglass") can bring about the reverse. To the same degree that Nathanael and his story force the reader to find the literal in the figurative, so too do they encourage us to find the figurative in the literal. When the narrator relates that Nathanael "egriff Coppolas Perspektiv," we know that the statement is to be read literally: Nathanael seized the spyglass he had bought from Coppola. But how, given the context, can we avoid hearing at the same time a figurative indication that Nathanael is here "taking up" the "point of view" belonging to the Sandman (in his incarnation as Coppola)? For, as we know, it is the (nurse's) Sandman whose point of view requires that there be no difference between human bodies and assemblies of parts. The world *Perspektiv* hovers undecidably between tenor and vehicle, between physical object and abstract idea.

Over and over again, the narrative presents figurative language in such a way as to put into question the unity of signifier and signified in the rhetorical sign. The possibility of literal reading intrudes upon the language used to describe even ordinary events. After a description in which we are asked to understand as literally true the phrase "he unscrewed my hands and feet," how can we fail to pause at a sentence saying "the detestable and loathsome Coppelius stood before me with fiery eyes, laughing at me malevolently"? Although the sentences immediately surrounding this one make it clear that this is a metaphor for young Nathanael's obsessive concern with the image (*Bild*) of Coppelius, the larger context makes one uncertain. A sentence of this form might very well be meant as literally true. When Klara writes to Nathanael that "the horrid barometer dealer Giuseppe Coppola followed my every step," our uncertainty must return. This is the down-to-earth Klara speaking, for whom metaphors are entirely figurative and for whom "there is no Sandman," so we can rest assured that she was not actually followed by anyone. But we need that contextual assurance.

Even the narrator's own discourse becomes suspect in this way. What does he mean when he says that "even at this moment Klara's face [*Bild*] is so vividly before me that I cannot avert my eyes"? Can we really be absolutely confident that this is a metaphor, when just a few lines earlier, in Nathanael's second letter to Lothar, a character (Spalanzani) is described by reference to an actual picture in a Berlin pocket almanac? A few lines later Klara is described again in terms of pictures: she has "Magdalenenhaar," and her coloring is "Battonisch," while her eyes are compared to a "lake by Ruisdael." This language suggests that Klara is not so much a person as a "Bild," a picture (or a metaphor). Indeed, the narrator suggests in this same passage that the whole of his narration is a "picture [*Ge-*

bild] to which I will endeavor to add ever more color as I continue with the story." If "picture" is taken as a figure for the narrative **"The Sandman,"** then we can reinterpret the narrator's sentence about Klara's "Bild" being before him as, in this new sense, almost literally true. The "image" of Klara is directly in front of the writer who writes that image.

The entire story becomes subject to the mutual contamination of literal and figurative language. It is as if language itself, which we think of as our servant and subject, had staged a rebellion and taken over the position of mastery. When the storyteller explains the problem he had in beginning his story and gives some examples of the alternative openings he rejected, he includes this one: " 'Go to hell!' the student Nathanael cried, his eyes wild with rage and terror, when the barometer dealer Giuseppe Coppola—." This opening was rejected because "I thought I noticed something humorous [*etwas Possierliches*] in Nathanael's wild look—but the story is not at all comic." Does the narrator mean that *his description* of Nathanael's wild look had something comic about it? Or was that description so vivid that it came to life before him (like Klara's "Bild"), allowing him to discover far more information in that "wild look" than the words suggest? Did he reject this sentence because it was unsuccessful or because it was all too successful? Is the phrase "wild look" to be understood, in the second instance, as the figure of the discourse containing the first instance (a metonymy), or is it a reference to an actual wild look, indeed that very look mentioned in the previous sentence? Does this image promote or prevent the continuation of the narrative?

These same questions arise when we look again at the declaration that "even at this moment Klara's face is so vividly before me that I cannot avert my eyes." On the one hand, there seems to be the suggestion that this image of Klara is actually preventing the narrator from getting on with his story: "I could now confidently continue with my story, but even at this moment. . . ." The continuation of the "story" ("Erzählung") is apparently interrupted by the narrator's effusive and highly figured description of Klara, or at any rate of that image of Klara that stands before the narrator's eyes. On the other hand, though, the story is itself a "Bild," one to which Klara certainly belongs; and the preoccupation with Klara's "Bild," far from hindering the progress of the "Erzählung," actually serves as its beginning, as its point of departure.

The reader is constantly pushed by the rhetoric of the story into the position of trying to adjudicate an undecidable confrontation between the literal and the figurative. Every time the reader makes a decision—"Yes, *this* is certainly a figure, while *that* has to be taken literally"—the text presents material that forces one to reverse the earlier ruling. The reader is thus in the middle of the story's action, construing that action, as I do, as a conflict between two modes of reading. This central position is exactly where the narrator expressly places both himself and his reader, though of course he does so figuratively. In the same passage I have been discussing—the point of transition between the epistolary opening and the narrator's continuation of the tale—Hoffmann's narrator tries to explain the technical problem he faced in beginning his story and his solution of it by means of the three letters. The problem, he says, is one that must be familiar to his reader, whom he asks—rhetorically, of course: "Have you, gentle reader, ever experienced anything that totally possessed your heart, your thoughts, and your senses to the exclusion of all else?" The narrator then goes on to describe the difficulties one has in trying to communicate to others such an experience, which he describes as a "picture in your mind" ("das innere Gebilde"). Words are inadequate: "Yet, every word, everything within the realm of speech, seemed colorless, frigid, dead." The solution to the problem could come only through the assistance of some kind of framing outline:

> If, like an audacious painter, you had initially sketched the outline of the picture within you in a few bold strokes, you would have easily been able to make the colors deeper and more intense until the multifarious crowd of living shapes swept your friends away and they saw themselves, as you see yourself, in the midst of the scene that had issued from your soul.

The three letters which begin **"The Sandman"** are to be understood, we are told, "as the outline of the picture [*den Umriß des Gebildes*] to which I will endeavor to add ever more color as I continue the story."

This metaphor (*Bild*) of the picture (*Bild*) proposes that the most desirable place for both teller and hearer of a story is "in the midst of the scene" ("mitten im Bilde"), where the word *Bild* is a manifest figure of narration and a literal expression of figuration. Whether or not the narrator succeeds in achieving the ideal of communication figured by the phrase "mitten im Bilde," he has certainly succeeded in putting both himself and his reader in the middle of his narration, since here, at the joint between the letters and the narrative proper, the attention of the story suddenly swerves away from Nathanael, Klara, and the others to the narrator and reader themselves. Nathanael's problems are for the moment forgotten while the text concentrates on the problem of the author, which he presents as also belonging to a hypothetical reader. This problem of author and reader is essentially rhetorical in the classical sense: that is, it is concerned with the adequacy of verbal expression, with how to make a verbal structure as vivid as the structure of experience. This experience belongs to an inner psychic realm (*deine innere Glut*) but it cannot be communicated unless it can be brought outside. The figure of the painting proposes that the transfer from inside to outside can be accomplished by making an outline or boundary (*Umriß*) around the internal picture (*inneres Bild*) and "throwing" this piece of inner experience "forth" (*hinwerfen*). The German idiom for making a sketch (*einen Umriß hinwerfen*) suggests both this act of throwing and another of making a tear (*Riß*) around something. The text foregrounds the notion of tearing (*reißen*) by using in the same sentence forms of the verbs *umreißen* and *fortreißen* containing the morpheme *riß* (*Umriß, riß die Freunde fort*). The process of externalizing the inner picture, then, requires that the unity of the inner self be sundered.

That same process also obliges the narrator to sacrifice the

unity of his text. In order to create the "Umriß" that he deems necessary for making his story of Nathanael a vivid and accurate depiction of his supposed experience, the narrator must resort to something that does not belong to his narration, the three letters: "There were no words I could find which were appropriate to describe, even in the most feeble way, the brilliant colors of my inner vision. I resolved not to begin at all" (perhaps better translated here as "I concluded not to begin at all"). The inadequacy of language—of his own language at any rate—forces the narrator to abdicate his office at the very outset of his story. He comes to a conclusion ("Ich beschloß") before he even begins—the conclusion that he must not begin at all but rather must leave the task of beginning to others. The very power he wishes to communicate, the "Farbenglanz des innern Bildes," is the thing that necessitates importing something not belonging to that "inneres Bild." The image described as residing within the self is somehow greater than the self that contains it. The narrator must have recourse to materials that are not narrated; that is, the story opens in the absence of the self whose experience it purports to depict. The body of the narrative is split apart (*zerrissen*) by the device, the outline (*Umriß*), that allows it to come into being.

The narrator's problem is, as Neil Hertz was perhaps the first to point out, directly analogous to that of his hero Nathanael. Both are equally taken up with the problem of trying to preserve the integrity of inner experience, and both discover that this act of preservation calls for the dismemberment of the self. The matter of the plot and its narration thus form a solidarity that becomes at times almost impossible to disentangle. For just as the narrator wants to depict Nathanael, Klara, and so on, as vividly as possible, so does Nathanael want to give a lively image of his experience of Coppelius:

> Nathanael was forced to confess to himself that the ugly image [*Gestalt*] of Coppelius had faded in his imagination, and it often cost him a great deal of effort to present Coppelius with adequate vividness in his writing where he played the part of the sinister bogeyman. Finally it occurred to him to make his gloomy presentiment that Coppelius would destroy his happiness the subject of a poem.

The same metaphor of painting, of filling in the vivid colors of a picture, that governed the narrator's presentation of his narrative problem figures in this presentation of Nathanael's waning power of imagination. In this case, though, storytelling is not so much the problem as the solution to the problem, for in writing Nathanael is overwhelmingly successful in restoring the image of Coppelius to its full power in his mind. He finds it so successful, in fact, that "when he read the poem aloud to himself, he was stricken with fear and wild horror and he cried out: 'whose horrible voice is that?'"

Nathanael's story is like the narrator's in another way. The result of a successful narration, it was proposed, would be that the story would sweep the audience away ("riß die Freunde fort"). Nathanael the author succeeds in having just this effect on Nathanael the listener: "Nathanael was carried away inexorably by his poem." The repetition of the verb *fortreißen* reinforces the imagery of "kolorieren" invoked before to characterize Nathanael's poem as a successful example of "sketching the outline of an internal image" ("den Umriß eines innern Bildes hinwerfen"). What formerly dwelled within him has been cast out, torn free from its original place, and now belongs completely to the world outside himself. The sentence that he himself uttered now seems to belong entirely to another, to demand the question, "Whose horrible voice is that?"

Nathanael finds his own narration of his version of the Sandman story so vivid that he takes it for reality, just as he had earlier taken the nursemaid's version as correct. This story of which Nathanael is the author and audience takes on a certain life and power of its own, such that it begins to govern Nathanael's actions and thus to contaminate the narrator's story. One of the details Nathanael invents for his poem is the "Feuerkreis" ("circle of fire") into which Coppelius flings Nathanael and which takes him away from Klara, whirling "with the speed of a whirlwind" ("mit der Schnelligkeit des Sturmes"). This whirling circle of fire returns, first in the scene in Spalanzani's study where Nathanael discovers the professor and Coppola fighting over the doll he knew as Olympia, then at the very end of the tale, when Nathanael suddenly attacks Klara at the top of the tower. In both cases Nathanael, apparently overcome by his terror of the Sandman, suddenly begins to shout "Feuerkreis dreh dich" or "dreh dich Feuerkreis" and to behave in a violent, deranged manner. According to the narrator, Nathanael is indeed mad on both occasions, and in the first instance he describes in vivid metaphors the onset of this madness: "Then madness racked Nathanael with scorching claws, ripping to shreds his mind and senses."

Once again Nathanael is made to experience "Zerrissenheit" at the hands of the Sandman, but again this dismemberment seems to be the price paid for an attempt to preserve unity. Nathanael here, just as earlier, attempts to make his experience conform to the text of the Sandman story, though this time it is his own version rather than that of the nurse that serves as the controlling text. The movement proposed by the earlier imagery of "den Umriß eines innern Bildes hinwerfen" is here reversed: what was formerly torn out of Nathanael's inner self now tears its way back in, creating a second "Riß" in the already severely ripped "Inneres" of the hero. The story tears him apart—his own story—both going and coming.

At the same time, the need to tell the story is performing a similar operation on both the narrator and his narration. The necessity of discourse ("I was most strongly compelled to tell you"), requiring the internal to be made external, forces the creation of a "Riß" within the speaker. Such a person is, like Nathanael, "im Innern zerrissen."

The turn of the tale's attention away from Nathanael's problem to that of the author has not been much of a turn after all: the issue remains basically the same. Both author and character confront the dilemma of preserving the unity of experience-in-language and solve the problem by sacrificing the unity of the self. In both cases the "Bild"

is preserved intact at the cost of allowing the self to be dismembered.

Both the character(s) identified with the Sandman and the story **"The Sandman"** participate fully in the problematic of unity and disunity. While the name belonging to Coppelius and Coppola seems on the one hand to suggest (by way of *coppo,* as mentioned above) the loss of eyes and thus a dismemberment, the same name also points, by way of *copula,* to an act of joining. To a German speaker, whose language contains the verb *koppeln,* this latter sense would in fact be more prominent. In his incarnation as Spalanzani (whose name might suggest *spalten* ("splitting") to a German speaker), the Sandman is in fact more concerned with joining than with sundering: not only does he put Olympia together out of lifeless parts, but he also encourages the joining of his "daughter" to Nathanael:

> Professor Spalanzani appeared to be most pleased by the intimacy which had developed between his daughter and Nathanael, and he gave Nathanael many unmistakable signs of his delight. When, at great length, Nathanael ventured to hint delicately at a possible marriage with Olympia, the professor's face broke into a smile and he said that he would allow his daughter to make a perfectly free choice.

This act of "putting together" is at the same time, of course, a taking apart, since Nathanael's interest in Olympia so takes over his mind that he "had completely forgotten that there was in the world a Klara whom he once loved." It is also in a very real sense superfluous; Spalanzani has already united Nathanael and Olympia in the most intimate way possible, since he claims to have assembled his automaton daughter using Nathanael's own eyes. The professor has already made them "one flesh" without benefit of clergy or of sexual intercourse. This sort of joining is, however, the most unsettling imaginable, particularly for Nathanael, since it is predicated on the possibility of the body's disassembly. The relationship between Olympia and Nathanael, as it stands revealed in Spalanzani's study, puts into question the opposition between joining and sundering: the proper word for it might be "cleave"—both "cleave together," as in the old wedding ceremony, and "cleave apart," as with a cleaver. The implications of this rhetorical construction are consoling and terrifying at the same time.

The body of the story, its formal presentation, is implicated in this same rhetorical process, since it must divide itself formally (between "letters" and "narrative") in order to preserve the integrity of the experience it purports to represent. At the same time, it questions the opposition between inside and outside, claiming as a guarantee for the authenticity of any experience its place "inside" the self, while acknowledging both the need to bring out the piece of inner experience, in a communicative act, and the impossibility of doing so successfully without the intervention of an agency whose origin is in fact "outside" (e.g., the opening letters). More important than these rhetorical maneuvers (though of course deeply interconnected with them) is the text's insistence on maintaining an opposition that both characters in the tale and readers of it would prefer to dissolve: that is, the opposition between tenor and vehicle. As readers, we have learned to understand the tenor of metaphorical language as by far more important than the vehicle. The vehicle exists, we learn, only for the sake of the tenor, as a kind of helping hand on our way to understanding. When we read that "Hector is a lion," we are supposed to think only about Hector's valor and strength and not about actual lions with all their nonhuman characteristics. Klara and Nathanael's mother are figures in the story who represent this position. Nathanael, on the other hand, wants to see the lion and hear its roar. For him "Hector" is the name of a lion, a creature with a mane and a tail, and "Sandman" is the name of a person who divides children from those they love and destroys their happiness.

Nathanael has something in common with Kleist's Penthesilea, for like her he defines himself in large measure by his insistence upon reading literally. To be sure, he does not announce this insistence to the world as candidly as does Penthesilea, but he does not have to. He inhabits a very different sort of world, one in which the boundary between literal and figurative is not so rigid. Penthesilea dwells in a society that firmly rejects her equation of kissing and biting (*Küsse/Bisse*) and allows her to carry out the full literal enactment of tropes only within the confines of her own mind and body. Nathanael on the other hand inhabits a world in which society is quite prepared to accept a mechanical doll as a human being and thus to ratify the equation of person and automation proposed by the trope Nathanael uses against Klara. Nathanael's refusal to accept his mother's figurative interpretation of the Sandman does not go against the grain of his interpretive community. On the contrary, the universe he lives in seems prepared to accept, even to adjust itself physically, to the demands of a mode of reading in which the vehicles of metaphorical expressions efface their tenors.

The reader inhabits this same world, at least while reading the story, and finds it a very interesting but also intellectually uncomfortable place. Over and over again, the story's language puts the reader in a position of not being able to decide (at least for an instant) whether the sentences of **"The Sandman"** are to be read in the manner of Nathanael or Nathanael's mother. When we first begin the story, there is little question that we are expected to read tropes in just the way Nathanael's mother does: Nathanael's description of his spiritual condition as "zerrissen" encourages us, by the use of abstract terms like "Stimmung" and "Geist," to proceed directly and unimpeded from vehicle to tenor, from material signifier to psychic significance. By the story's close, however, we are no longer able to make such an easy choice. Nathanael's figurative and literal "Zerrissenheit" confront each other, and in that confrontation hangs suspended the essential issue of the story: " 'Who is this nasty Sandman . . .?' 'There is no Sandman.' "

The reader has to face up to the unresolvable uncertainty of rhetorical discourse and is left in a position quite different from that of the principal characters in the story. Klara, who tames the rhetoricity of figures by letting the tenor efface the vehicle, lives happily ever after. Nathanael, who sought to have the vehicle overwhelm the tenor,

succumbs to the literal reading of the story's master trope and is shattered by the Sandman. The only figure within the fiction faced with a problem analogous to the reader's is the figure of the fiction itself, which struggles to present itself as unified and whole by an act of radical self-division. The story's characters all confront the problem of rhetorical language by trying in one way or another to eliminate it. If either tenor or vehicle could definitively suppress the other, figurative language would lose its rhetoricity. Only the narrative itself, which is in this case the figure of a character and not a genuine character, tries to accommodate itself to the absolute uncertainty of rhetorical reading. If the story itself, as figure, were a genuine character faced with the dilemma of reading its own rhetorical discourse, it would be able to dramatize the experience of its readers. (pp. 114-34)

> *Clayton Koelb, "The Stuff of Rhetoric," in his* Inventions of Reading: Rhetoric and the Literary Imagination, *Cornell, 1988, pp. 114-49.*

Doris T. Wight   (essay date 1990)

[*In the following essay, Wight presents a Freudian interpretation of "The Mines of Falun."*]

Like all doomed heroes of classical tragedy before him, Elis Fröbom seems to betray masochistic compulsion as he marches inexorably towards his fate in the E. T. A. Hoffmann's tale **"The Mines of Falun."** Elis may seem an unlikely tragic hero at first. No highborn individual, he is merely a sailor, the son of a sailor. Yet Elis Fröbom has managed by a stroke of fate to elevate himself to the status of an Oedipus, having, like Oedipus, achieved the unconscious wish that Freud attributed to every son, victory

Self-portrait of Hoffmann.

over the father for possession of the treasured mother, and this has marked the humble sailor for tragedy.

The guilt of having survived the accident that killed his father must have left severe Oedipean repercussions in Elis's soul, but before the death of his mother our protagonist has successfully repressed them by making the possession of his mother a burden as well as a satisfaction. Busy earning money to care for his dear burden and refusing himself the sexual indulgence that his freer fellow-sailors enjoy, Elis has kept in check the demands of a primitive spirit deep within calling for retribution for the death of his father and older brothers. Had the son desired his father's and brother's deaths, and realized that ambition by omnipotence of thought? Clearly, the ghost of the senior males, particularly the father, rumbles below, deep in the son's psyche. When the shocking blow of the loss of the precious mother occurs in the life of an innocent young man "scarcely twenty," his latent guilt surfaces. The distress exploding within the youth is so painful that natural urges toward life natural in one only twenty years old are overthrown, and our tragic hero's masochistic march towards death commences.

The story will end with emphasis on death beneath the earth on St. John's festival begins artfully with the stress on life upon the surface of the earth on another festival. Hoffmann's joyous opening scenes show the crew of a newly returned rich East Indiaman happily disembarking for the joyous *Hönsning*:

> The Swedish flags waived gaily in the azure sky while hundreds of boats of all kinds, overflowing with jubilant seamen, drifted back and forth on the crystal waves of the Götaelf, and the cannon on the Masthuggetorg thundered forth resounding greetings towards the sea . . . Musicians in curious, gay-colored costumes led the way with violins, fifes, oboes, and drums which they played with vigor while singing all kinds of merry songs. The sailors followed them two by two, some with gaily beribboned jackets and caps from which fluttering pennons streamed, while others danced and leaped and all shouted with such exuberance that the sound echoed far and wide . . .

A climax of bonhomie is reached in the paragraph just before Elis Fröbom makes his first appearance:

> The finest beer flowed in rivers, and mug after mug was emptied. As is always the case when seamen return from a lengthy voyage, all sorts of pretty girls soon joined them. A dance began; the fun grew wilder and wilder, and the rejoicing louder and madder.

Our first glimpse of Elis Fröbom is in dismal, ominous contrast to all the scenes of happiness; as we will learn, Elis, rushing home to bring his beloved mother the gold he has earned on his voyage has just learned of her death three months earlier:

> Only one lone seaman, a slim handsome youth scarcely twenty years old, had slipped away from the turmoil and was sitting alone on a bench by the door of the tavern.

A couple of happy fellow sailors approach and scold the solitary lad, delineating to him and to us the gloomy side of his personality and its dangers:

> Elis Fröbom! Are you being a wretched fool again and wasting these lovely moments with silly thoughts? Listen, Elis, if you are going to stay away from our *Hönsning,* then keep away from our ship. You will never be a decent, proper sailor. You have courage enough and are brave in times of danger, but you don't know how to drink and would rather keep your money in your pockets, than throw it away on landlubbers. Drink, boy, or may the sea devil, Näck, that old troll, take you!

One of the sailors attributes Elis' gloom to his heritage, telling him, "I know you are a Neriker man, and they're all sad and dreary and don't really enjoy the good life of a seaman." This is our first hint of the compulsive masochism which will in time doom our hero, the first hint that his natural mourning for his mother will, because of guilt operating on his inborn temperament, become a punishing melancholia. Elis' joyous sea companions, trying their best to save the young lad from his dark threat, tell him that they will sent him a remedy, and soon a sweet young girl comes to the silent and withdrawn Elis as he sits outside the tavern. However, after pressing the maiden's hand to his breast longingly, Elis can only give her some of the bright ducats and a beautiful East Indian scarf he had evidently brought for his recently deceased mother and send her away, after which he sinks into melancholy reverie so deep that he expresses aloud an open death-wish: "If only I laid buried at the very bottom of the sea! There is no one left in this life with whom I can be happy."

As if conjured up by Elis' own grief and depression, an old miner now appears, a being "strangely familiar" to the sailor, who sympathizes with the lad, seemingly attempting to console him. Their conversation, to which I shall return in a moment, will have fateful consequences for Elis Fröbom; first, however, a brief look at Freud's ideas concerning masochistic grief will be profitable.

Freud explains in his paper on "Mourning and Melancholia" why some succumb to melancholia instead of suffering normal grief. The distinguishing characteristics of both are deep dejection, abrogation of interest in the outside world, loss of the capacity to love, and inhibition of activity. However, there is another trait found in melancholia: a fall in self-esteem. Here the component of masochism makes its entry. In melancholia there is "a lowering of the self-regarding feelings to a degree that finds utterance in self-reproaches and self-revilings, and culminates in a delusional expectation of punishment."

However much Elis must have loved his mother, the severity of his reaction to her death indicates the onset of a morbid pathological disposition. Freud discusses the obsessional states of depression which may follow the loss of a love-object. Ambivalent feelings can surface and give rise to sadism which, when self-directed, gives rise to suicide impulses. If Elis not only loves his mother but unconsciously hates her as well because of the buried guilt he feels at possessing her, he is thrust beyond the state of mourning into melancholia; and perhaps this is what Hoffmann makes us sense through Elis' behavior and situation in those first few pages of the tale.

If the ghost of his father, or the devil of some old religious or superstitious fears, appears to Elis in the guise of the old miner immediately upon the voicing of Elis' death-wish, one may correctly read that the devilish father ghost has itself caused that death-wish by unremitting internal accusations, the shock of the death of his mother having reactivated the earlier shock to Elis of the death of his father. Elis believe that he owes not only an unpaid debt to that father ghost but a second debt as well as to the ghost of his mother, who he fears died in poverty. Guilt is the key to why Elis cannot experience merely grief at the death of his mother, but is doomed to suffer melancholia and to suffer, as we will see, masochistic compulsions, including suicide urges.

In *Beyond the Pleasure Principle* Freud discusses the problem of trauma, stating that the organism in striving to maintain control of itself constantly sets up barriers against disruptive stimuli. Had Elis' father never died, or had he died in another way—from common illness, say, rather than from the sudden sea storm that miraculously spared Elis—Elis might have been spared. Again, had the second sudden blow not occurred: had Elis' mother not died before he had a chance to alleviate her poverty, or had she died from some cause that Elis had been aware of, so that he might have been not so unprepared at the sudden loss of this treasured person, then Elis might have escaped his doom. As Hoffmann has set forth his character and his character's situation, however, Elis, made the victim of two devastating shocks and their attendant calls to guilt feelings, is doomed. For, according to Freud, apprehension of danger can safeguard us from its attendant wounds. It is the surprise attack on the psyche, the blow coming to strike the nervous system with its guard down, that wreaks such mental havoc. Even a physical wound attending a surprise injury, says Freud, helps defend the victim from a subsequent illness, perhaps because one has a sense of having paid off any possible guilt debt incurred. Elis, however, escaped the storm that killed his father unscathed and escaped, in full health and vigor, the poverty and illness that destroyed his mother.

When a trauma has occurred, the victim grievously strains to cope. He or she tries belatedly to develop the apprehension that was absent when the trauma occurred. The way to do this is to reenact the trauma, and in the replay hopefully to develop the desirable apprehension. Thus dreams, by which one enacts events through the imagination, are the way in which victims of traumatic neurosis strive to cure themselves, and Freud has differentiated carefully between the wish-fulfillment dreams of minds not suffering from traumatic neurosis and those like Elis' which are. By this theory, Elis Fröbom's dreams should be a reenactment of the shock of his learning of the death of his mother. Analysis of Elis' first long dream, which can be called his Basic Dream since it is the prototype for all the later dreams described in the tale, should illustrate this idea. Note in the bracketed comments how Elis' mind constantly expresses its schizophrenic problem, its seeing every-

thing in rigid opposites, including the all-important oppositions of life and death

III The Basic Dream

(Part 1: Elis alone and then with metal female forms.)

Elis is in a ship on a clear sea with dark clouds above. Looking down into the waves he sees a crystal floor [down is up] into which the ship dissolves [opaque is clear]. Looking up, he sees a dome of dark minerals instead of clouds [up is down].

Elis walks, but suddenly metal flowers and plants [confusion of inorganic and organic] spring up around him with parts both above, blossoms, and beneath roots, intertwined.

The metal flowers deeper down show themselves not to be female forms [inorganic is organic], for which Elis feels pain and rapture [confusion of pleasure and pain].

Elis throws himself down onto the crystal ground, but he finds himself up in the air [down is up].

(Part 2: Elis with miner, Queen, mother, beloved as a girl)

Elis hears a hearty voice and sees the old miner beside him, but the miner suddenly becomes huge [ordinary size is extraordinary] and is cast of glowing metal [organic is inorganic].

A sudden flash of lightning from the depths [light from dark] allows Elis to see the solemn face of a majestic woman [inorganic-the depths-is organic].

The old miner seizes Elis, telling him that this is the Queen [inorganic is organic] and that he may look up now [looking down permits looking up].

Elis looks up and sees a crack in the dark dome with stars shining through [dark is light]. He hears his mother's gentle voice calling his name, but the figure merges with that of a young girl [the old love is a new love].

Elis asks the old miner to take him to the upper world with its friendly sky [request that down be made up], where he feels he belongs [request that the strange be made familiar]. The old man warns him, calling him by surname, that he must be faithful to the Queen to whom he has given himself [denial follows former permission].

Elis looks down into the majestic woman's rigid face and feels himself dissolving into its minerals [organic becomes inorganic].

Elis awakes screaming in mingled fear, horror, and rapture [pain is pleasure].

That Elis wakes screaming is proof that this Basic Dream, with its constant proof of the split feeling in Elis, all those insistences on contradiction, is a desperate attempt at the regaining of mental health, for Elis has managed to develop a fear of the Queen of the depths, who is here set up in opposition to the figure of the loving dead mother with the gentle voice who belongs to the world up above, perceived through a crack in the dome, who like the lovely young girl calls Elis to save him from metallic maidens and the terrible Queen. By willing himself to awaken in the world of reality at the end of the dream, Elis has denied his masochistic yearning for death itself which lurks behind the queen.

This dream will appear again and again, and as long as apprehension of the rigid majestic queen does occur, Elis seems to have a chance to avoid his doom—his longing for death. When, however, later on apprehension can no longer occur within Elis at the idea of death in the figure of the Queen of the lower depths, Elis' madness and imminent death obviously triumph.

This is to anticipate the course of events, however. Elis' Basic Dream was elaborately set forth here because Hoffmann uses the dream occurrences and variations so crucially in psychological depiction of Elis' fatal march towards his doom. Elis' plight in its resemblance to that of Shakespeare's Hamlet should be noted. Early in Hoffmann's tale, as well as in Elis' dream, the old miner does not seem hostile to Elis' escape. In Elis' dream, although he warns him that he must be faithful to the Queen (as the dead King adjures the young prince not to harm Gertrude in the play), the old man does let the lad look up briefly at the old gentle mother and at the young beloved, a life figure. This again testifies to the sane part of Elis' mind early in the story resisting delusory ideas.

Before leaving the subject of his dreams as part of Elis' fight to hold on to sanity and life, one should state that the interpretation of the Basic Dream given above is reinforced in credibility by the old helmsman's dream which Elis recalls when he first looks into the gigantic entrance to the mine at Falun. This dream is surely the basis for Elis' own Basic Dream:

> When Elis Fröbom looked down into the monstrous abyss, he thought of what the old helmsman on his hip had told him long ago. Once, when he was lying in bed with a fever, it had suddenly seemed to the helmsman that the waves of the sea had receded and that the immeasurable abyss had yawned beneath him so that he could see the frightful monsters of the depths in horrible embraces, writhing in and out among thousands of strange mussels and coral plants and curious minerals until, with their jaws open, they turned rigid as death. Such a vision, the old seaman said, meant imminent death in the ocean, and he actually fell from the deck into the sea accidentally shortly thereafter and vanished.

Elis is reminded of the helmsman's story because, as Hoffmann explicitly tells the reader, the abyss that the door of the mine appears seems like the ocean depths, its black minerals and bluish red metallic slag like monsters reaching for him.

The frightful monsters of the depths whose tentacles serve for the capture of prey have become in Elis' own Basic Dream the metal flower-females with twining arms or roots. Interesting indeed is the evocation by those writhing

appendages of the snaky hair of the mythological Gorgon or Medusa who turns those who look upon her to stone. Snaking inorganic flower females and rigid terrifying Queen are one, a primordial female figure beyond the recently-dead mother whom Elis must confront, perhaps a signifier for the earlier forbidden beloved incest figure of childhood, now demanding the retribution of Elis' death itself.

There are, of course, more than dreams to Hoffmann's tale. What else goes on in Elis as he struggles through his days? Is there a surfacing of repressed material in ways other than through dreams? As one reads **"The Mines of Falun"** one is struck over and over by descriptions of compulsive sensations and sensations of the uncanny experienced by Elis. Again and again the tenuous hold of Elis' conscious self over his unconscious processes gives way; one might be dealing with a sleepwalker.

As was previously noted, a deep rough voice sounds behind Elis at the very instant when Elis expresses his masochistic death-wish. That some part of Elis knows that he himself has compulsively called for this old man can be guessed from Hoffmann's description of Elis' reaction:

> As Elis continued to look at the old man, it seemed to him as if a familiar figure were approaching him offering friendly comfort in the wild loneliness in which he believed himself lost.

Stronger yet is the sense of *deja vu* that the melancholic Elis experiences as the old man begins to give his feverish account of the beauty of the metals down in the mine.

> Elis listened intently. The old man's strange way of talking about the marvels under the earth as if he were in their midst engaged his whole being. He felt oppressed. It seemed to him as if he had already descended to the depths with the old man and that a powerful magic was holding him fast so that he would never again see the friendly light of day. And then it seemed to him again as if the old man had opened up to him an unknown world in which he belonged and that all the enchantment of this world had long ago been revealed to him in his earliest boyhood as strange, mysterious presentiments.

After returning to the harbor, Elis has to be pulled away by his comrades from a dream as he looks into the water at the harbor—clearly a hint at a compulsive suicide urge. Elis' hold on consciousness is so weak that now even in his waking states material constantly erupts from the unconscious. A voice whispers ceaselessly in his ear that he must go to Falun, "your home." This voice pursues him for three days as he roams the streets of Göteborg, and even takes visual form on the fourth day when the old miner passes visibly before Elis, beginning to lead him to Falun. And in some uncanny way Elis knows that he is on his way to Falun.

> On and on Elis went without stopping. He knew very well that he was on the road to Falun, and it was this knowledge that calmed him in a special way, for he was certain that the voice of destiny had spoken to him through the old miner

who was now leading him towards his true vocation.

When Elis actually sees the goal of his journey, Falun, in the distance, he somehow knows that he is at the correct spot; and here amid lakes and mist and towers he sees the same old miner of Göteborg standing in front of him, a giant, pointing toward Falun in the mist and then vanishing.

Elis is appalled at the tremendous entrance to the mine and its appallingly dead interior, but it is when he sees miners creeping out of the depths that he again experiences hair-on-end terror as he recognizes what his unconscious is driving him towards. Trembling with horror, a giddiness that he had never known seizing him, Elis feels as if invisible hands were pulling him down into the abyss, into the huge jaw of hell, where no tree, no blade of grass lived in the barren, crumbled, rocky waste that seemed nothing less than Dante's inferno, from which the miners crept out like doomed black earthworms.

After so many negative experiences, Elis' positive reaction when first he sees Ulla Dahlsjö, the lovely young daughter of the chief official of the district. Momentarily he blesses his fate that has led him to Falun. Yet the compulsive behavior continues as he finds himself telling Ulla's father Pehrson Dahlsjö that he dislikes the sea now and that his deepest wish is to become a miner, a surprising statement, for it was not what he had been thinking at all. Yet he feels that he could not have told the manager Dahlsjö anything else: it was "as if he had expressed his innermost desire, of which he had till now been unconscious."

The narrative moves rapidly as the once-successful sailor is transformed, apparently, into a successful miner. Yet although he is liked by Pehrson Dahlsjö and loved by the radiant Ulla, all is not truly well with Elis, for he is afraid to really speak up and ask his beloved to marry him. His hesitation warns us that his melancholia, with its deep-seated guilt and need for punishment and the denial of happiness in life is not really overcome. Worse, an incident showing how alive still is Elis' fantasy figure of the old miner. When he is down in the deepest bore of the mine, being subjected to deadly sulphur fumes, Elis now hears a knocking, and not only mysteriously but impossibly, Elis encounters the old miner of Göteborg again. The old fellow begins to revile him, accusing him of being "insincere" as a miner. His threats and warnings to Elis are terrible to hear:

> You despicable, miserable rogue . . . Down here you are a blind mole whom the *Metallfürst* (Metal Prince) will never favor, and up above you are unable to accomplish anything . . . Oh yes, you want to win Pehrson Dahlsjö's daughter Ulla for your wife . . . Beware, you cheat, that the *Metallfürst,* whom you mock, doesn't seize you and hurl you into the abyss so that all your bones are smashed on the rocks. And never will Ulla be your wife, that I say to you.

Elis' need for punishment is warning him that he is overreaching himself when he dreams of life with Ulla. When the chief foreman sees Elis emerge from the mine depths with ghastly pallor, he first assumes that Elis has been a victim of the sulphur fumes, but then he has a second explanation for Elis' deadly pallor. Perhaps, says the foreman, Elis has seen the ghost of old Tobern, a solitary and obsessed miner who supposedly had had secret connections with the very bowels of the earth. This strange figure had met his death in an apocalyptic cave-in of St. John's day one hundred years earlier.

At this revelation that he may have been meeting with a ghost, Elis rushes to his employer Pehrson Dahlsjö's house, where the third great shock of his life occurs: he receives the false impression that he has lost his beloved Ulla Dahlsjö. This supposed loss of the woman who had been leading him back to life and health unhinges Elis completely: he dashes back to the mines, surrendering incoherently to his masochistic guilt-feelings, to the father-surrogate ghost Tobern and to the earth below. "Tobern!" he cries, "You were right. I was a vile fellow to yield to the foolish hope of life on the surface of the earth." Dreaming a dream in which for the first time the death-Queen does not cause apprehension in him, he succumbs and is found in a rigid, catatonic state, his face pressed against the cold rock.

Although Elis is found and the mistaken idea that his beloved Ulla will wed another is cleared up and Elis himself is hailed as the bridegroom-to-be, the lad's hold on reality has been fatally undermined, as the following lines so clearly reveal: "In the midst of all his bliss it sometimes seemed to Elis as if an icy hand were gripping his heart and a dark voice were speaking, 'Is this your highest ideal, winning Ulla? You poor fool! Have you not seen the Queen's face?' "

In his paper "The Economic Problem in Masochism" dealing with the three types of Masochism, including the moral type, the condition from which apparently Elis Fröbom suffers, Freud discusses the "heightened sadism of the super-ego to which the ego subjects itself." In this, the accent falls "on the masochism in the ego itself, which seeks punishment, whether from the super-ego within or from parental authorities without . . . in both cases there is a craving which is satisfied by punishment and suffering." Freud states that the danger of moral masochism— and this surely has significance for Elis Fröbom—"lies in its origin in the death-instinct and represents that part of the latter which escaped deflection on to the outer world in the form of an instinct of destruction." Even more telling may be Freud's next, final sentence in his essay which seems so significant to our understanding of the character and behavior of Elis Fröbom. "But since, on the other hand, it has the value of an erotic component, even the destruction of anyone by himself cannot occur without gratification of the libido."

The erotic component in Elis' death wish is so powerful that it sweeps aside life-surrogates for primeval love objects and harks back to the original parental figures, in the story **"The Mines of Falun"** given form as the dead mother, with behind her the Queen, and as the dead father, with behind him the old miner and, deeper still, the *Metallfürst,* the Metal Prince. The Queen and Metal Prince belong to the inner world of the earth—the mine—and to the inner world of Elis himself—his childhood unconscious. The dutiful sailor son, barely twenty, cannot survive the shocks to his sensitive nature of the deaths of his older brothers, father, and mother. Projecting his father and mother in particular from his unconscious into his super-ego, where they become menacing fantasy figures of eroticism and longing which can be satisfied only by Elis' death, Elis' urge towards the depths of the mines is irresistible. These sadistic parents, the majestic Queen whose heart is the blood red carbuncle without which Elis will never have a peaceful moment and the Metal Prince who claims one's total dedication to the task of grubbing in the earth, these are Hoffmann's representations of the divine pair next to the fates that parents pose to children. In the following paragraph Freud explains why Hoffmann in his narrative has instinctively created these powerful figures:

> In the course of development through childhood which brings about an ever-increasing severance from the parents, their personal significance for the super-ego recedes. To the imagos they leave behind are then linked on the influences of teachers, authorities, of self-chosen models and heroes venerated by society; these persons need no longer be introjected by the ego, which; has now become much more resistant. The last figure the series beginning; with the parents is that dark supremacy of Fate, which only the fewest among us are able to conceive of impersonally . . . All those who transfer the guidance of the world to Providence, to God, or to God and Nature, rouse a suspicion that they still look upon these farthest and remotest powers as a parent-couple- mythologically-and imagine themselves linked to them by libidinal bonds. *In Das Ich und das Es* I have made an attempt to derive the objective fear of death in mankind also from the same sort of parental conception of Fate. It seems to be very difficult to free oneself from it.

In **"The Mines of Falun"** E. T. A. Hoffmann has created a tale that lends itself astonishingly to a Freudian interpretation. Many other Hoffmann tales have been previously cited by others as showing intuitive psychological insights prefiguring those that Freud would subsequently reach analytically.

The final grotesque ending of the tale, with Ulla Dahlsjö, the cheated bride of fifty years ago, at last reunited with the long-buried corpse of Elis Fröbom, her almost immediate death upon his body, and the burial of the pair together in the church where fifty years earlier they were to have been wedded—this is surely the ultimately romantic death-wish for lovers, with Eros and Thanatos merged, however fruitlessly, in perfect union and fulfillment. (pp. 49-55)

> *Doris T. Wight, "Masochism, Mourning, Melancholia: A Freudian Interpretation of E. T. A. Hoffman's Tale, 'The Mines of Falun'," in* Germanic Notes *Vol. 21, Nos. 3 and 4, 1990, pp. 49-55.*

FURTHER READING

Elardo, Ronald J. "E. T. A. Hoffmann's Klein Zaches, the Trickster." *Seminar* XVI, No. 3 (September 1980): 151-69.
    Maintains that "Hoffmann's attention to detail in his depiction of Zaches is an indication of his fascination with the negative component of the unconscious and his dread of contact with this sphere."

——. "The Maw as Infernal Medium in 'Ritter Gluck' and 'Die Bergwerke zu Falun'." *New German Studies* IX, No. 1 (Spring 1981): 29-49.
    Traces the influence of Dante's *Inferno* on Hoffmann's "Ritter Gluck" and "The Mines of Falun."

Ellis, John M. "Hoffmann: 'Rat Krespel'." In his *Narration in the German Novelle: Theory and Interpretation*, pp. 94-112. London: Cambridge University Press, 1974.
    Asserts that Hoffmann's story has such a strong appeal "because its theme of an obsession which is defensive in nature but destructive in effect is bound to strike a familiar chord in any reader."

Grimm, Reinhold. "From Callot to Butor: E. T. A. Hoffmann and the Tradition of the Capriccio." *MLN* 93, No. 3 (April 1978): 399- 415.
    Contends Hoffmann's use of the literary form of the capriccio makes him "the founder of this genre in German literature" and that he brought it "to a point of perfection which is later never equalled."

Hertz, Neil. "Freud and the Sandman." In *Textual Strategies: Perspectives in Post-Structuralist Criticism*, edited by Josué V. Harari, pp. 296-321. Ithaca, N.Y.: Cornell University Press, 1977.
    Examines Freud's analysis of "The Sandman."

Hewett-Thayer, Harvey W. *Hoffmann: Author of the Tales.* New York: Octagon Books, 1971, 416 p.
    Survey of Hoffmann's life and works.

Kamla, Thomas A. "E. T. A. Hoffmann's 'Der Sandmann': The Narcissistic Poet as Romantic Solipsist." *Germanic Review* LXIII, No. 2 (Spring 1988): 94-102.
    Analysis of "Hoffmann's portrayal of narcissism within an epistemological context befitting the age in which he lived and wrote, namely, Romantic idealism with its focus on the attainment of truth and knowledge through subjective perception."

Kontje, Todd. "Biography in Triplicate: E. T. A. Hoffmann's 'Die Abenteuer der Silvester-Nacht'." *German Quarterly* 58, No. 3 (Summer 1985): 348-60.
    Examines how Hoffmann's relationship with his music student Julia Mark influenced his work.

Lange, Victor, ed. Introduction to *E. T. A. Hoffmann: Tales*, pp. vii-xvii, New York: Continuum, 1982.
    Brief overview of Hoffmann's career.

McGlathery, James M. *Mysticism and Sexuality: E. T. A. Hoffmann, Part One: Hoffmann and His Sources.* Las Vegas, Nev.: Peter Lang, 1981, 191 p.
    Determines how sexual repression and sublimation were manifested in Hoffmann's life and work.

Morse, David. "The Folktale." In his *Romanticism: A Structural Analysis*, pp. 191-227. Totowa, N.J.: Barnes & Noble Books, 1982.

Maintains that Hoffmann was obsessed with the role of the artist and "inserts that tale of the artist into . . . a central position in the literature of Romanticism."

Negus, Kenneth. *E. T. A. Hoffmann's Other World.* Philadelphia: University of Pennsylvania Press, 1965, 183 p.

Discerns a private mythology underlying Hoffmann's work, which is "untarnished by any worn-out tags and epithets of the commonly known, ancient mythologies, yet [has] much of their cosmic import."

Nock, Francis J. "E. T. A. Hoffmann and Nonsense." *The German Quarterly* XXXV, No. 1 (January 1962): 60-70.

Asserts that, because it contains an element of "fun" seldom found in German literature, Hoffmann's humor is misunderstood by his compatriots.

Pavlyshyn, Marko. "Interpretation of Word as Act: The Debate on E. T. A. Hoffmann's 'Meister Floh'." *Seminar* XVII, No. 3 (September 1981): 196-204.

Places "Master Flea" within a historical context and insists that it "is an early and successful exercise in literary activism."

Siebers, Tobin. "Absolute Laughter and the Fantastic: Baudelaire, Hoffmann, and Gogol." In his *The Romantic Fantastic*, pp. 78-103. Ithaca, NY: Cornell University Press, 1984.

Contends that "Little Zaches, Surnamed Zinnobar" is both hideous and hilarious "because Hoffmann costumed Zinnobar so effectively in the garb of caricature that we overlook the genuine brutality of the story."

Slessarev, Helga. "E. T. A. Hoffmann's 'Prinzessin Brambilla': A Romanticist's Contribution to the Aesthetic Education of Man." *Studies in Romanticism* IX, No. 1 (Winter 1970): 147-60.

Argues that Hoffmann's tale "is the poetic expression of his hope for the betterment of mankind through the influence of the arts, a hope which he shared with so many of his contemporaries."

Stanley, Patricia. "Hoffmann's *Phantasiestücke in Callots Manier* in Light of Friedrich Schlegel's Theory of the Arabesque." *German Studies Review* VIII, No. 3 (October 1985): 399-415.

Explores the literary concept of the arabesque in Hoffmann's short fiction.

Tatar, Maria M. "Blindness and Insight: Visionary Experience in the Tales of E. T. A. Hoffmann." In her *Spellbound: Studies on Mesmerism and Literature*, pp. 121-51. Princeton, N.J.: Princeton University Press, 1978.

Discusses the role of mesmerism in Hoffmann's short fiction.

Taylor, Ronald. *Hoffmann.* London: Bowes & Bowes, 1963, 112 p.

Critical overview stressing the importance of Romanticism and music to Hoffmann's work.

——. "Music and Mystery: Thoughts on the Unity of the Work of E. T. A. Hoffmann." *Journal of English and Germanic Philology* LXXV, No. 4 (October 1976): 477-91.

Discusses the influence of music on Hoffmann's literary works.

Weiss, Hermann F. "The Labyrinth of Crime: A Reinterpretation of E. T. A. Hoffmann's 'Das Fräulein von Scuderi'." *Germanic Review* LI, No. 3 (May 1976): 181-89.

Places Hoffmann's story within a historical context.

Additional coverage of Hoffmann's life and career is contained in the following sources published by Gale Research: *Dictionary of Literary Biography*, Vol. 90; *Nineteenth-Century Literature Criticism*, Vol. 2; and *Something about the Author*, Vol. 27.

Norman Maclean

1902-1990

(Full name Norman Fitzroy Maclean) American essayist, critic, novella and short story writer, and nonfiction writer.

INTRODUCTION

A professor of English literature, Maclean wrote his only works of fiction when he was in his early seventies. These were collected in *A River Runs Through It, and Other Stories*, which consists of two novellas and a short story that center on life in Montana in the early and mid-twentieth century. The title story of this volume, an amalgam of fiction and autobiography, is considered a classic of modern American literature.

The son of an immigrant Scottish Presbyterian minister, Maclean was born in Clarinda, Iowa. In 1909 his family moved to Missoula, Montana, where Maclean spent the better part of his childhood learning to hunt and fish along the Big Blackfoot River. He was educated at home until the age of ten when he was apprehended by truant officers and enrolled in elementary school. Although both his parents encouraged Maclean's love of poetry, he often felt a conflict between the expectations of his affectionate mother and his disciplinarian father. Maclean later told an interviewer: "[My mother] and my father fought for my soul when I was young, my father wanting me to be a tough guy and my mother wanting me to be a flower girl. So I ended up being a tough flower girl." In 1924 he graduated from Dartmouth College and went on to teach literature at the University of Chicago, where he remained until his retirement in 1973. Three years later he published *A River Runs Through It, and Other Stories*. A second book, *Young Men and Fire*, is a painstakingly researched account of a devastating 1949 forest fire that exhibits Maclean's knowledge of and fascination with the American West. This work was unfinished when Maclean died in 1990 and was published posthumously two years later.

Maclean's most acclaimed work, the novella *A River Runs Through It*, is a semifictionalized account of his experiences fly-fishing on the Big Blackfoot River in 1937. Critics have pointed out that the story is also a tribute to Maclean's father and an elegy for his brother Paul, who was beaten to death in 1937 for reasons still unclear. Commentary on *A River Runs Through It* often focuses on the version of the American western myth that Maclean presents in this work. At the center is Paul, Maclean's charming but reckless younger brother who is a master fly fisherman—"an artist," Maclean calls him. Asking help from no one, even when he is in serious trouble, Paul is the typical western hero who says little and dies valiantly. Ma-

clean's narrative is also typical of American western fiction in giving little attention to women characters, who usually are treated as outsiders and threats to male solitude. Helen Lojek commented that reading *A River Runs Through It* "is . . . to enter a world shaped by an unexamined and probably unconscious masculinity." Critics almost unanimously praise the novella for its engaging prose style and its probing of the deepest implications of family ties.

PRINCIPAL WORKS

SHORT FICTION

A River Runs Through It, and Other Stories   1976

OTHER MAJOR WORKS

Norman Maclean (criticism, essays, and interviews) 1988
Young Men and Fire   (nonfiction)   1992

CRITICISM

John G. Cawelti   (essay date 1976)

[*Cawelti has written several studies of American popular culture and formula fiction, including* The Six-Gun Mystique *(1971) and* Adventure, Mystery and Romance: Formula Stories as Art and Popular Culture *(1976). In the following review of* A River Runs Through It, and Other Stories, *Cawelti praises Maclean as an important writer of American western fiction.*]

Both the pulp Western with its heroics and the serious Western novel in its attempt at an epic statement of the confrontation between man and nature or between White and Indian are expressions of the myth of the West as otherness, as the expression of something unique to human experience and history which must be treated in an appropriately grand and distinctive fashion. The importance of this myth to American culture has been often indicated by scholars, most recently in Richard Slotkin's superb *Regeneration Through Violence.* Yet, there is also an important truth in discovering the universal constants of human experience which lie beneath that distinctive landscape of mythical action. This is the discovery that flashes through many of the most memorable writings about the West—it is there in Twain's *Roughing It,* in Stephen Crane's two great Western stories, "The Blue Hotel," and "The Bride Comes to Yellow Sky," in Andy Adams' *Log of a Cowboy,* in the best parts of Wister's *The Virginian,* in the stories of H. L. Davis, in Walter Van Tilburg Clark's *The Ox-Bow Incident,* in Thomas Berger's *Little Big Man* and, most recently, in Norman Maclean's *A River Runs Through It and Other Stories.*

Maclean's stories are semi-autobiographical and told in the form of reminiscences: an older man looks back on some central experiences of his youth: how he learned to fish and how fishing was entangled in his relations with his father and younger brother (*A River Runs Through It*); how he worked with a superhuman logger who turned out to be a pimp during the winter season (**"Logging and Pimping and 'Your Pal, Jim' "**); and how he became part of a Forest Service crew's summer-end ritual of "cleaning out the town" and learned something about life and art in the process (***USFS 1919: The Ranger, The Cook and a Hole in the Sky***). But the stories are conceived as fictions. Instead of being primarily attempts to remember and state the exact particulars of a past time and place, they use the particular to express, through the devices of art, some general truths about human nature and life. They are like memories which have been revolved in the mind throughout a lifetime until their hidden truths have been brought to the surface and revealed. Thus there is a wonderful interplay between the consciousness of the old man telling us the stories and the perspective of the boy of over half a century ago. We see not only what the boy thought or failed to think, but how he began to understand his life and something of what that boy, as a man in his 70s, has made of it since:

> I was young and I thought I was tough and I knew it was beautiful and I was a little bit crazy but I hadn't noticed it yet.

So begins ***USFS 1919,*** which becomes a wide-open Western anecdote about a comic-heroic trek across the Bitteroot Mountains, an encounter with a whore who cursed in iambic pentameter, and a climactic fight in a saloon over a crooked card game. The story even contains a Western-style hero, one Ranger Bill, who rides off into the sunset, as it were, at the end. Yet these Western elements are not deployed for the sake of creating an epic mythos or telling of high adventure but to explore what Maclean sees as one of the most profound human discoveries:

> I had as yet no notion that life every now and then becomes literature—not for long, of course, but long enough to be what we best remember, and often enough so that what we eventually come to mean by life are those moments when life, instead of going sideways, backwards, forward, or nowhere at all, lines out straight, tense and inevitable, with a complication, climax, and, given some luck, a purgation, as if life had been made and not happened.

These stories have that magical balance of the particular and the universal that good literature is all about and that so many attempts at Western fiction miss completely. Indeed, it would be more just to say that these are not Western fictions at all, but stories about life as it happened and was created by one man who lived through his formative years in western Montana and who has the gift of words and the shaping imagination to make it possible for us to share some of that experience. Maclean gives us the West in full measure. His stories are permeated with the monumental landscape of the "Big Sky Country" observed with a keen documentary eye as well as a sense of the awesome beauty of mountains and rivers. He writes brilliantly about work and sport. His pages describing logging, packing, mule-skinning, trail-cutting and fishing are full of precise images which convey as rich a sense of the spiritual form of these activities together that bear comparison with such classics as Adams' *Log of a Cowboy.* Humor of the tall-tale variety abounds, side by side with an extravagant comedy of manners detailing the peculiar social rituals of loggers, fishermen and other Western types. Yet underneath the richness of particular details, there runs a wise and compassionate understanding of life and art forged through a lifetime of experience and learning and embodied in a prose that is richly colloquial yet highly controlled and which sometimes rises to extraordinary eloquence. Perhaps nothing conveys the rich and deep sense of human life which runs through this book than the beautiful words which conclude the title story:

> Now nearly all those I loved and did not understand when I was young are dead, but I still reach out to them.
>
> Of course, now I am too old to be much of a fisherman, and now of course, I usually fish the big waters alone, although some friends think I shouldn't. Like many fly fisherman in western Montana where the summer days are almost Arctic in length, I often do not start fishing until the cool of the evening. Then in the Arctic half-light of the canyon, all existence fades to a being with my soul and memories and the sounds of

the Big Blackfoot River and a four-count rhythm and the hope that a fish will rise.

Eventually, all things merge into one, and a river runs through it. The river was cut by the world's great flood and runs over rocks from the basement of time. On some of the rocks are timeless raindrops. Under the rocks are the words, and some of the words are theirs.

I am haunted by waters. (pp. 24-6)

> *John Cawelti, in a review of "A River Runs Through It and Other Stories," in* The New Republic, *Vol. 174, No. 18, May 1, 1976, pp. 24-6.*

Roger Sale   (essay date 1976)

[*In the following excerpt from a review which originally appeared in 1976, Sale states that while experience as a fly fisherman is helpful when reading* A River Runs Through It, *it is not necessary for a full appreciation of the work.*]

[Norman Maclean] retired a few years ago from the University of Chicago, where he had won a number of awards for distinguished teaching. Before now, he was known to me only as the author of two essays in the neo-Aristotelian collection *Critics and Criticism,* on *Lear* and the Augustan lyric, both sound, nicely written, and a bit dull. For years, he says at the beginning, he told his children stories of things that had happened to him, and they finally asked him to write them down. Which he did, though the result is clearly the work of the current, retired Maclean, not of a father trying to interest young children in woods and water.

There are three stories in *A River Runs Through It;* two are long enough to qualify as short novels. The short one is inconsequential, and the long one about being seventeen and in the Forest Service is flawed by its becoming a variation on the familiar Western tale of a rite of passage. But the 100-page-long title story, about fly fishing, one might call perfect except that it makes no pretense to be shapely or artful. At the end [the protagonist's] father says, "Why don't you make up a story and the people to go with it? Only then will you understand what happened and why. It is those we live with and love and should know who elude us." Maclean, though, does not care about making up a story in which he will understand what happened; he wants to write about those he lived with and who eluded him: "Now nearly all those I loved and did not understand when I was young are dead, but I still reach out to them." The story is his reaching out.

Mostly to his brother, younger by three years, who did not move away or become a professor of English. He stayed home, became a reporter on a newspaper in Helena, Montana, drank too much, and became a great fly fisherman. At the heart of the story are the two brothers, Norman and Paul, on the trout streams of western Montana, loving and eluding each other, fishing. They are the sons of a Scottish Presbyterian minister: "In our family," is the first

line, "there was no clear line between religion and fly fishing."

As the boys were raised, so we are instructed,

> . . .if you have never picked up a fly rod before, you will soon find it factually and theologically true that man by nature is a damn mess. The four-and-a-half-ounce thing in silk wrappings that trembles with the underskin motions of the flesh becomes a stick without brains, refusing anything simple that is wanted of it. All that a rod has to do is lift the line, the leader, and the fly off the water, give them a good toss over the head, and then shoot them forward so they will land in the water without a splash in the following order: Fly, transparent leader, and then the line—otherwise the fish will see the fly is a fake and be gone.

The first point, then, is that it is simple, though of course the boys did not conclude, as others have, that it was really simple.

> But what's remarkable about just a straight cast—just picking up a rod with line on it and tossing the line across the river? Well, until man is redeemed he will always take a fly rod too far back, just as natural man always overswings with an ax or a golf club and loses all his power somewhere in the air; only with a rod it's worse, because the fly often comes so far back it gets caught behind in a bush or rock. . . . Then, since it is natural for man to try to attain power without recovering grace, he whips the line back and forth making it whistle each way, and sometimes even snapping off the fly from the leader, but the power that was going to transport the little fly across the river somehow gets diverted into building a bird's nest of line, leader, and fly that falls out of the air into the water about ten feet in front of the fisherman.

One has to quote such passages, or else the story is reduced to effects, conveying nothing of Maclean's care.

Being a true Presbyterian, Maclean can know about fishing without making us feel outsiders for not knowing, even though most of us are in fact outsiders. Not having recovered grace, haunted by the mysteries of fishing, he would not dream of trying to imply that he has solved the mysteries. A still better fisherman, like his brother Paul, would dream of this even less. So after the rod and the cast came the rivers, and the fish:

> One great thing about fly fishing is that after a while nothing exists of the world but thoughts about fly fishing. It is also interesting that thoughts about fishing are often carried on in dialogue where Hope and Fear—or, many times, two Fears—try to outweigh each other.

Thus one fear may be that there is a rock the fish will have to be taken past when hooked, and the line must be pulled so tight if he is taken past the near side he will probably fight free of the hook, especially since the weather has been warm and the fish's mouth will therefore be soft. But the other fear is that if the fish is taken on the far side of the rock the line will get caught under it.

The world narrows, and all one has are the questions one asks, the hopes and fears, and a river running through it all.

> In the arm, shoulder, or brain of a big-fish fisherman is a scale, and the moment the big fish goes into the air the big-fish fisherman, no matter what his blood pressure is, places the scale under the fish and cooly weighs him. He doesn't have hands and arms enough to do all the other things he should be doing at the same time, but he tries to be fairly exact about the weight of the fish so he won't be disappointed when he catches him.

Then, after Maclean weighs this fish at a most satisfying seven or eight pounds, and the fish jumps into the bushes hanging over the water, tying a different knot on every branch he passes, comes disaster:

> The body and spirit suffer no more sudden visitation than that of losing a big fish, since, after all, there must be some slight transition between life and death. But, with a big fish, one moment the world is nuclear and the next it has disappeared. That's all. It has gone. The fish has gone and you are extinct, except for four and a half ounces of stick to which is tied some line and a semitransparent thread of catgut to which is tied a little curved piece of Swedish steel to which is tied a part of a feather from a chicken's neck.

It is an enchanted tale. Paul instructs Maclean a few times, in the sign language of fishers who are also reticent Scots, and once Maclean catches a fish in a hole where his brother cannot because he carries with him special flies, which Paul scorns. There is Maclean's brother-in-law from the West Coast, who fishes with bait, and whom the brothers discover one afternoon, on an island in the river, horribly sunburned, because he and the prostitute with him have made love and fallen asleep in the August sun. There is Paul's drinking, for which there is no explanation other than that to him nothing in life measures up to fly fishing. On the day Maclean learns his brother has been beaten to death in a fight, Maclean and his father talk quietly, mostly about the way all the bones in Paul's casting hand were broken. The story, having a river running through it, generally follows its own path, meandering here and rushing there, but it has to stop at this point.

I have read the story three times now, and each time it seems fuller. Necessarily, I wonder. . . if the very source of the enchantment, its way of being "about" something, must restrict its audience. I have never fished, but I go with a friend who does, to a river only somewhat less wonderful than the big Montana rivers. I have stared at that river, and at others throughout the West, not with the eye of a fisherman, but enchanted nonetheless. I simply don't know what I would make of Maclean's story if I knew no fishers, had never been entranced by trout streams, but I find it hard to believe it would matter as much to me if I knew about none of these things.

There is always something wonderful in reading a book by someone who is absorbed in what he or she does. And that absorption must extend beyond matters of technique and skill. In his Forest Service story Maclean describes a ranger who can pack a whole string of horses and mules so they can walk and climb for days without the packs slipping or the animals becoming hobbled. It must be a rare skill, but then, that is all it is, which is why this story lacks the magic of *A River Runs Through It.* (pp. 88-92)

> *Roger Sale, "Bradley & Maclean," in his* On Not Being Good Enough: Writings of a Working Critic, *Oxford University Press, 1979, pp. 84-93.*

Maclean on his early education:

My father did not allow me to start elementary school but taught me himself. Most everything crucial that happened to me since has been influenced by his teaching. He was a very stern teacher, very harsh. He put me in a room across from his, where he worked every morning on his sermons while my mother ran the church. I'd study for forty-five minutes and then I'd recite to him for fifteen. He might start me off in the morning by telling me to write a theme on such and such. All I got was writing and reading, nothing else. So I would write this thing and three-quarters of an hour later I would bring it in to him and he'd tear it apart and say take it back and write it half the length. So I'd take it back with tears in my eyes. It was rough, this kind of treatment, learning economy of style when kids my age were learning their ABC's. So I'd give it back to him, and he'd say, "O.K., now do it half as long again," so I'd take it back and do it again and by that time it would be a quarter of twelve, and he'd say, now throw it away.

Norman Maclean, in an interview from TriQuarterly, *Spring 1984.*

Walter Hesford (essay date 1980)

[*In the following essay, Hesford compares* A River Runs Through It *to the piscatory writings of Henry David Thoreau and Izaak Walton.*]

"In our family," writes Norman Maclean, "there was no clear line between religion and fly fishing." In *A River Runs Through It,* he is faithful to family tradition. As he pays tribute to the art of fishing, especially as practiced by his younger brother Paul, he fishes with words for the words of life that his father, a Presbyterian minister, heard beneath the river's current. In so doing, Maclean is also faithful to the tradition of piscatory prose as established by Izaak Walton's *The Compleat Angler.* It is a generous prose, one that reflects and fosters a love for its subject, one that will not be hurried as it circles toward the synthesis of contemplation and action, piety and practice, and beauty and power which, both Maclean and Walton suggest, is the hallmark of genuine art and genuine religion.

This is not to say that *A River Runs Through It* strives to imitate *The Compleat Angler* in either stance or substance. Indeed, Maclean's father warned his teen-age sons against its influence: "Izaak Walton is not a respectable writer. He was an Episcopalian and a bait fisherman." One suspects or hopes that this was intended to be humorous, though bait fishermen are consistently castigated in the story as unredeemably fallen mortals. Perhaps a more devastating criticism of Walton came from brother Paul, age thirteen or fourteen: "The bastard doesn't even know how to spell 'complete.' Besides, he has songs to sing to dairymaids." Norman, the future professor of English and writer, defends Walton: "Some of those songs are pretty good." Paul, unimpressed, asks, "Whoever saw a dairymaid on the Big Blackfoot River?"

Clearly, western Montana, where the Big Blackfoot runs and where the Macleans grew up, sponsors a different aesthetic from Walton's seventeenth-century English countryside (though this countryside was torn by civil war, and not likely to give unmediated birth to piscatory pastorals). *A River Runs Through It* does not shy away from the rough realities that encompass the author and eventually overcome his brother. As "preacher's kids," they seemed to find it necessary to play rough, to adopt a tough, irreverent stance in order to achieve independent status, a stance still evident in the style of the mature author, but tempered with wit, generosity, and wisdom. Maclean's witty assertion that his father "told us about Christ's disciples being fishermen, and we were left to assume, as my brother and I did, that all first-class fishermen on the Sea of Galilee were fly-fishermen and that John, the favorite, was a dry-fly fisherman" would certainly have shocked Walton, who took devout pride in his holy precursors. The reader, however, should not be misled into taking lightly Maclean's discipleship. His irreverence ultimately does reverence to his brother, whose keeper he proves, and keeps alive the faith of his father. He is thus truly pious, and as seriously committed as Walton was to exploring the religious significance of his subject.

To give this significance a broader context, I would like to claim the privilege of all writers tracing piscatory themes and meander a bit. Maclean is not the first American to fish with words for the words of life. It seems worthwhile to look at the synthesis of contemplation and action worked out by an earlier American disciple in the brotherhood of anglers. It is a select brotherhood. Washington Irving, perhaps the first noted American writer to attempt to cast himself as a compleat angler, acknowledges his complete failure in his humorous essay, "The Angler," included in *The Sketch Book*. He can no more put Walton to use along the Hudson highlands than Maclean's brother can along the Blackfoot. After tangling himself up in the recommended gear, Irving abandons the art and treats himself and the reader to various recollections, culminating in a loving portrait of a Cheshire fisherman, a true follower of Walton. There is difficulty, it seems, in imagining such a man in an American setting. Ernest Hemingway's Nick Adams might, in the "Big Two-Hearted River" stories, fish with the requisite dedication, but his aims are solipsistically therapeutic rather than spiritual, and Hemingway's prose is informed by a limiting, ritualistic intensity which militates against piscatory meditation.

Maclean's efforts, I think, may most fruitfully be compared with those of Henry David Thoreau, who combines the receptiveness of an Irving and the involvement of a Hemingway. Thoreau's first book, *A Week on the Concord and Merrimack Rivers,* is replete with a Waltonian ca-

talogue of fish that inhabit Concord waters, and with portraits of anglers who inhabit Concord, the most complete of whom, fittingly, is an Englishman by birth. In Walden, Thoreau portrays himself as a complete angler who, obeying higher laws and an ascetic sensibility, finally transcends the practice altogether.

There are three strains in Thoreau's piscatory prose that also achieve significance in *A River Runs Through It.* The first is an antinomian strain. I am taking the liberties with this old heresy-tainted term usually taken by Americanists, and applying it to the celebration of the truth of the individual heart or consciousness as opposed to the laws of an established religion or society, to the cultivation of inner laws which may supplant the laws of the land. It comes as some surprise that there is even a hint of antinomianism in Walton, the conservative Anglican—though perhaps it shouldn't, when we remember that in his day the Puritans were establishing the law. Walton's true anglers love to be quiet and stay clear of noisy legal affairs. They also follow in the footsteps of the holy fishermen who preached *"freedom from the incumbrances of the Law, and a new way to everlasting life"* (emphasis Walton), who preached a gospel of religious and social deliverance. It may seem paradoxical that Walton schools his disciples in the tradition and discipline of his art, and at the same time suggests that their traditional predecessors spread freedom. The paradox may be resolved if one believes that the gospel liberates as it fulfills rather than violates the law, that freedom is discipline transfigured. This seems to be the unheretical belief of true anglers, including Thoreau and Maclean.

Thoreau compares with pleasure the free, natural life of the fisherman with the cramped "civil politic life" of a judge; the former, though, perhaps, a social outcast, is wiser, Thoreau implies, than the arbiter of social justice (*A Week*). The fishermen Thoreau honors are "wild men, who instinctively follow other fashions and trust other authorities than their townsmen. . . ". What authorities these wild men follow is not clear, but no doubt they are more conductive to their discipline and freedom than are the laws of the land—especially such as might attempt to regulate where and how they should conduct their business. Thoreau spoofs distant legislators who "regulate the number of hooks to be used" at Walden Pond, but "know nothing about the hook of hooks with which to angle for the pond itself, impaling the legislature for bait." Thoreau, one gathers, does know about such a hook. It is his art, with which he has caught forever Walden, and through which he has put to death the old law, establishing for himself and his readers a new law and gospel.

We might expect a romantic like Thoreau to be an antinomian, but we expect to find a taint of the heresy even less in a Presbyterian than in an Anglican. Yet when he gave his sons catechism lessons Sunday afternoons as prelude to a walk on the hills, the Rev. Maclean tried to arouse their hearts rather than their fears: "he never asked us more than the first question in the catechism, 'What is the chief end of man?' And we answered together so one of us could carry on if the other forgot, 'Man's chief end is to glorify God, and to enjoy him forever.' This always seemed to satisfy him, as indeed such a beautiful answer should have, and besides he was anxious to be on the hills where he could restore his soul and be filled to overflowing for the evening sermon."

Though he enjoyed himself in nature, the Rev. Maclean did not believe that man could *naturally* achieve his chief end, either in religion or fly fishing. He held the orthodox position "that man by nature was a mess and had fallen from an original state of grace," a state not easily regained: "all good things," he felt,"— trout as well as eternal salvation—come by grace and grace comes by art and art does not come easy." Art meant "picking up God's rhythms" (for the fly fisherman, this was a "four-count rhythm between ten and two o'clock"). These rhythms enabled man "to regain power and beauty." The poor sinner and poor fisherman were likely "to attain power without recovering grace," and their performance was thus, according to the minister, lacking in the beautiful. "Unlike many Presbyterians," reports his son, "he often used the word 'beautiful'."

It is Maclean's brother Paul who comes to embody the beautiful. He may be a doomed sinner in the judgment of the world and in the judgment of his father's congregation, but in the eyes of both father and brother he seems redeemed by his beautiful fishing. Early on Paul decided that "he had two major purposes in life: to fish and not to work, or at least not allow work to interfere with fishing." When he became a reporter, writes his brother, "he had come close to realizing life's purposes, which did not conflict in his mind from those given in answer to the first question in *The Westminster Catechism.*" Paul could enjoy God by perfecting his chosen art, even while, as a natural man, he entangled himself in affairs and in gambling debts. Within his art, he disciplines himself, lives by the rhythm preached by his father, makes himself worthy of grace.

After he is brutally beaten to death because, it appears, he failed to pay his debts, Paul's father and brother derive some ultimate solace from remembering him as a fisherman. When the father pushes Maclean for more information about Paul's death, the author replies,

> "I've said I've told you all I know. If you push me far enough, all I really know is that he was a fine fisherman."
>
> "You know more than that," my father said. "He was beautiful."
>
> "Yes," I said, "he was beautiful. He should have been—you taught him."
>
> My father looked at me for a long time—he just looked at me. So this was the last he and I ever said to each other about Paul's death.

Paul's beauty may not count much toward heaven in orthodox circles, but it is informed with God's rhythm, if he has been pious in his art, he may be said to enjoy God forever. It seems the intention of his brother so to say.

A second strain common to the piscatory prose of Thoreau and Maclean reflects an involvement with the natural world befitting anglers. Both men try to synthesize the

Maclean's brother Paul.

natural and the supernatural; both consider the possibilities of a natural religion. Walton in his quiet way also celebrates the natural kingdom, wherein "the goodness of the God of *Nature* is manifest" (emphasis Walton). He would not, of course, take nature for God, nor therein ground his faith. His complete angler would be apt to carry his Bible with him to read in solitude by a stream whereas Thoreau's would be more likely to substitute his natural activity for Bible study. The Walton of the Concord River fishes as "a sort of solemn sacrament," without biblical sanction or benefit of clergy whereas Thoreau's would be more likely to substitute his natural activity for Bible study.

Fishing has a part in Thoreau's own sustained sacrament at Walden, in his incorporation of the natural and the supernatural. He tells of dark nights in which his "thoughts wandered to vast and cosmogonal themes in other spheres" until a "faint jerk" on his line in the water linked him once more to the natural sphere. "It seemed," he concludes, "as if I might cast my line upward into the air, as well as downward into this element which was scarcely more dense. Thus I caught two fishes as it were with one hook." His whole life at Walden became one artful hook with which to catch experience, body and soul, to enjoy God forever right now, to attain a perfection in space and time that breaks the boundaries of space and time.

Maclean as well as Thoreau takes seriously Christ's command, "Be ye therefore perfect, even as your father which is in heaven is perfect" (Matt. 5:48). Like Thoreau, he looks to nature for perfection, seeks high moments of integration with a world "perfect and apart" from the messy affairs of men. He achieves identity with the river, feels, incorporates its past, future, and present. He experiences romantic "spots of time" in which "eternity is compressed into a moment," in which all time and space are now and here. One such spot concludes when a big fish he has been trying to land disappears or is transfigured into a bush. "Even Moses," asserts Maclean, "could not have trembled more when his bush blew up on him." His tone suggests that he thinks this episode more comic than romantic or sacramental, but by casting himself as a Montana Moses standing before the natural turned supernatural, Maclean wittily testifies to the religious dimensions of his life and art.

Maclean's aesthetic quest for perfection in nature, for a purely natural religion such as Thoreau sustained himself with, is tempered and qualified by two sets of circumstances, of realities. The realities of fishing often leave him with a tangled line and an empty hook, cutting short those spots of time that should have culminated in a big catch, and confirming the Presbyterian notion of the world of men as a mess. More importantly, the circumstances of human life, the realities, especially, of his brother's story, compel Maclean to look at perfection—and nature—more humanistically. In doing so, he explores the ultimate religious significance of his subject, a significance to be considered in the conclusion of this paper.

The third strain present in Thoreau's writing and *A River Runs Through It* is elegiac. The authors pay tribute to past or passing cultures and to loved ones they have lost. Walton also memorializes old friends, old habits, and an old faith. (Some of the "how to" content common to piscatory prose reflects, I think, the desire to honor and keep alive dying skills.) Thoreau's wild fishermen are a dying breed, remnants of less civilized, populated, and propertied times. Moreover, they remind him of his freer, more natural youth. In elegizing them, he, in a sense, elegizes himself. Maclean too honors scenes and skills dear to him as a young man. With rough tenderness, he describes a time when one could leave some locally brewed beer in the Blackfoot and some clothes on its shore without worrying about marauding hordes (of, needless to say, bait fishermen) from Great Falls, not to mention the West Coast. Montana is presented in this story as, paradoxically, violent and pastoral, rugged and innocent—all in all, a "beautiful world" if one could survive.

There is not much religious significance to this aspect of the elegiac strain, except in that it seeks to keep old ways and values vital, to keep the faith. The strain runs deeper, however. Thoreau's *A Week* is his elegy for his brother John, with whom he took his river journey, and who now, Thoreau assures himself, ascends "fairer rivers." The death of his brother was a shattering experience for Thoreau, complicated by guilt over not being open enough in his love for him in life, and not being able to rescue him from the grip of lockjaw. Thoreau works out his guilt in his writing, overcomes his doubts about the efficacy of love, and sustains through art his brother's life.

A River Runs Through It is an elegy for brother Paul. It tests the efficacy of brotherly love. Brotherly love is a tradition among anglers; Walton traces it back to the broth-

erhood of fishing disciples surrounding Jesus. Maclean centers his concern on a belief or instinct that precedes the gospel, one which reflects a common situation: "I knew there were others like me who had brothers they did not understand but wanted to help. We are probably those referred to as 'our brothers' keepers,' possessed of one of the oldest and possibly one of the most futile and certainly one of the most haunting of instincts. It will not let us go." His concern as his brother's keeper will not let him go as he tries to enter the perfect world fishermen and other artists like to immerse themselves in. It eventually fosters a richer understanding of perfection and love, but it fails to keep his brother alive. It appears, indeed, to be one of the most futile of instincts.

Much of Maclean's story deals with his failure to help his brother, who drinks and gambles too much, always desperate, it seems, to prove himself, to stake himself. He won't accept money or advice; the best Maclean can do is go fishing with him, share in an art which Paul has perfected, in which his essential beauty is manifest. A fishing trip provides a "momentary stay against confusion," but it does not settle his gambling debts or bring order out of the confusion of the world beyond the river. A subplot of the story, which has Maclean trying to help a brother-in-law, a prodigal son of Montana turned West Coast debauchee and bait fisherman, appears to reconfirm the failure of brotherly concern: all the brother-in-law gets out of the fishing expedition his sister (Maclean's wife) and mother hope will help him is a lot of whiskey and beer, a bad sunburn, and a whore. Believing Maclean to be in trouble with his wife and mother-in-law over the condition of their burnt-up and burnt-out baby, Paul becomes, in a change of roles, *his* brother's keeper. He organizes a family fishing trip. It is this trip, the last the brothers and their father take together, that, as recollected by Maclean, provides him and the reader with the assurance that brotherly love does have its efficacy, that neither this nor any love is in the long run futile. This trip, furthermore, completes his and our religious education.

It would be helpful, I think, to set the lessons of this, the climactic scene of the story, in the context of the story's genesis. Maclean traces its beginnings to a hot afternoon on the river:

> As the heat mirages on the river in front of me danced with and through each other, I could feel patterns from my own life joining with them. It was here, while waiting for my brother, that I started this story, although, of course, at the time I did not know that stories of life are often more like rivers than books. But I knew a story had begun, perhaps long ago near the sound of water. And I sensed that ahead I would meet something that would never erode so there would be a sharp turn, deep circles, a deposit, and quietness.

Waiting for his brother, he senses the patterns and sounds of the river stimulating and shaping his responses and making available a model for his art. He might have found in Thoreau or elsewhere the conventional analogy between the course of a river and the course of a life, but he could not find in any book, nor did he yet know, the realities of life that do not lend themselves, any more that rivers do, to neat and happy aesthetic or philosophic formulations. Waiting for his brother, he does not have the human realities to work with. When his brother arrives, in love and in death, he does. In one sense, Paul's death is that "something that would never erode," thereby determining the shape of his life and the shape of his brother's story. In another sense, it is love that never erodes, that informs life with significance, that fosters any story worth telling.

Love does not depend on understanding. Father and son agree on this when, after Paul's death, they struggle to explain what happened: " 'Are you sure you have told me everything you know about his death?' he asked. I said, 'Everything.' 'It's not much, is it?' 'No,' I replied, 'but you can love completely without completely understanding.' 'That I have known and preached,' my father said." The father does not need to be educated in the gospel—that is his profession. In a later conversation which still reflects the presence of Paul, the father, however, prods his story-telling son toward an easier profession:

> "You like to tell true stories, don't you?" he asked, and I answered, "Yes, I like to tell stories that are true."
>
> Then he asked, "After you have finished your true stories sometime, why don't you make up a story and the people to go with it?
>
> "Only then will you understand what happened and why.
>
> "It is those we live with and love and should know who elude us."

Maclean, however, follows his father's practice rather than his advice. He fishes with words for those real and elusive people he has lived with and loved. The result is *A River Runs Through It.*

The last family fishing trip is filled with complete acts of love: Paul bringing the family together; Paul hugging his mother, who loves best the son she understands least; Paul rising early to make breakfast after a night on the town; Paul suggesting that he and Maclean fish close together; and Paul wading across the river to give his brother the fly to catch the last fish his brother ever caught in his company. Maclean thinks of these as his finest fish, the fruit of brotherly love. Through Paul, Maclean achieves a new definition of "finest," a more humanistic understanding of perfection which humanizes his art.

The author is satisfied with his day's catch. While waiting for Paul to fish his limit, which he always does as if to fulfill the law, Maclean searches out his father, whom he rightly suspects is finished fishing and reading the gospel. When the preacher comments on the biblical passage he has been pondering, a dispute ensues:

> "In the part I was reading, it says the Word was in the beginning, and that's right. I used to think water was first, but if you listen carefully you will hear that the words are underneath the water."
>
> "That's because you are a preacher first and then a fisherman," I told him. "If you ask Paul, he will tell you that the words are formed out of water."
>
> "No," my father said, "you are not listening carefully. The water runs over the words. Paul will tell you the same thing."

The father affirms the assertion of the first verse of John: Logos, the Word—Reason, Spirit—precedes and informs the material world, is its life, its rhythm, its significance. He has come to believe in the primacy of meaning. We are not told what meaning he discerns in the words underneath the water. That is left to our imagination and religion.

The young Maclean feels his father is biased because he lives by words, and thinks Paul, a man of action, who lives most fully when fishing the water, will support the liberal, empiricist, naturalistic position he himself apparently holds. The father thinks not. We never hear from Paul on the subject; his last words in the story announce his not-to-be-honored wish for three more years to perfect his ability to think like a fish, to perfect an art which his father and brother already see as perfectly beautiful. Why is the father sure that his younger, somewhat prodigal son shares his faith? Perhaps the key is "carefully," a word the father emphasizes through repetition. A man who carefully, religiously devotes himself to his natural sphere of action, as Paul does when fishing, concludes, or knows without concluding, that within this sphere there is a rhythm, a rightness, a Word which comes to inform his art.

The conclusion of *A River Runs Through It* suggests this, and suggests that Maclean has listened carefully for a long time, heard the words, and been converted to the faith of his father and brother:

> Now nearly all those I loved and did not understand when I was young are dead, but I still reach out to them.
>
> Of course, now I am too old to be much of a fisherman, and now of course I usually fish the big waters alone, although some friends think I shouldn't. Like many fly fishermen in western Montana where the summer days are almost Arctic in length, I often do not start fishing until the cool of the evening. Then in the Arctic half-light of the canyon, all existence fades to a being with my soul and memories and the sounds of the Big Blackfoot River and a four-count rhythm and the hope that a fish will rise.
>
> Eventually, all things merge into one, and a river runs through it. The river was cut by the world's great flood and runs over rocks from the basement of time. On some of the rocks are timeless raindrops. Under the rocks are the words, and some of the words are theirs.
>
> I am haunted by waters.

Maclean leaves us reaching and fishing, fishing and writing. He leaves us in hope and he leaves us haunted. He has explored the basement of time and found timeless raindrops. As timeless as the raindrops are the words under the rocks.

Whose words? There is some difficulty in catching the antecedent of "theirs." Logical antecedents are "rocks" and "raindrops"; they make natural sense. It is, however, human sense that Maclean has been making. I propose leaping up two paragraphs to those he loves, to those he has been trying to reach. Some of the words, I think, are theirs. More especially, it is his father and brother to whom he has been listening carefully. They offer him the words of life. Not the Word, but the words. Like the waters that haunt Maclean, the Word assumes a multitude of forms, including human. Men and women contribute their own words, help bring the world into significance. The author, a sign broker by profession, is fundamentally humanistic, as is his art. Nevertheless, reaching out to loved ones and reaching out to readers, he follows a high religious calling: Maclean is a fisher of men. (pp. 34-45)

> *Walter Hesford, "Fishing for the Words of Life: Norman Maclean's 'A River Runs through It'," in* Rocky Mountain Review, *Vol. 34, No. 1, Winter, 1980, pp. 34-45.*

Harold P. Simonson (essay date 1982)

[*Simonson is an American educator and critic who has written several books on American literature and history. In the following essay, he examines the religious symbolism and imagery in* A River Runs Through It.]

"In our family, there was no clear line between religion and fly fishing." With this arresting opener, Norman Maclean begins his novella, *A River Runs Through It* (1976), the first work of original fiction ever published by the University of Chicago Press in its long history. It is also Maclean's own first work of fiction, written after his return to Montana following retirement as William Rainey Harper Professor of English at the University of Chicago. Remarkable in many ways, his novella deserves recognition as (I believe) a classic in western American literature. As for the analogy between religion and fly fishing, Maclean hooks it, plays and fights it, and finally lands it with masterful form. In short, the analogy works artistically. Moreover, the river (Montana's Big Blackfoot River) takes on intriguing dimensions, which I will argue include both symbolic and typological significance. For the author, his closing sentence says it all: "I am haunted by waters."

Christ's disciples were fishermen, those on the Sea of Galilee were *fly* fishermen, and Maclean's favorite, John, had to be a *dry-fly* fisherman. This was the logic Maclean as a boy learned from his father's Presbyterian sermons. Yet for all the sermons preached and heard, and all the hours the boy and his brother Paul studied *The Westminster Shorter Catechism,* what really restored their souls, including that of their clergyman father, was to be in the western Montana hills where trout rivers run deep and fast. Ernest Hemingway had said in "Big Two-Hearted River" that swamp fishing was a "tragic adventure"; for Maclean, fishing the Big Blackfoot River was a redemptive one, thanks not only to divine grace but to self-discipline. The theology is sound Calvinism: God does all, man does all.

As for human nature, theologically speaking, just try to use a fly rod for the first time and, says the author, "you will soon find it factually and theologically true that man by nature is a damned mess." Calvin couldn't have said it better. Only the "redeemed" know how to use it. Until such time, a person "will always take a fly rod too far back, just as natural man always overswings with an ax or golf club and loses all his power somewhere in the air." Natural man does everything wrong; he has fallen from an original state of harmony. And he will continue to be a mess until through grace and discipline he learns to cast "Presbyterian-style." The great lesson the father taught his two sons was that "all good things—trout as well as eternal salvation—come by grace and grace comes by art and art does not come easy."

All this theological business isn't as heavy-handed as it sounds. Indeed, Maclean transforms it into characterization, metaphor, humor, and fine detail. He also transforms memories of his father and brother into Rembrandt portraiture edged in darkness and tragedy but also pervaded by a haunting presence, a prelapsarian truth associated with sacred origins, the divine *logos*. Maclean would have us see fishing as a rite, an entry into "oceanic" meanings and eternities compressed into moments, epiphanous "spots of time," the *mysterium tremendum*. Entering the river to fish its dangerous waters is to fish eternity, and to unite in love with those few persons who also obey the exacting code. No one obeyed the code more religiously than brother Paul who, when entering the river, made fishing into a world perfect and apart, a place where joy comes first in a perfect cast, then in a strike that makes the magic "wand" jump convulsively, and finally in a big rainbow trout in the basket—in all, a performance of mastery and art.

Narrator Maclean remembers his brother Paul as a master dry-fly fisherman, indeed as a true artist when holding a four-and-a-half ounce rod in his hand. But more, Paul was one for whom the river in its sacrality held answers to questions, and for whom fly fishing was the search for those answers. That, Paul said, was what fly fishing was, and "you can't catch fish if you don't dare go where they are." Paul dared, and he showed his brother and his Presbyterian father, both expert fishermen too, how to dare. On what was to be their last fishing trip together, before Paul's murder and the father's later death, all things seemed to come together—the river, the fishing, the father and two sons. Sinewing the union was love, and in the union the powerful Big Blackfoot River spoke to them.

It is truly a redemptive moment, caught and held secure in Maclean's memory and in his narrative art. I find it difficult to restrain my admiration; I find Maclean in this story equal to anything in Hemingway and a good deal more courageous, theologically.

In order for this assertion to sink in, I need to emphasize that Maclean's theology includes a doctrine of man. To reiterate, Maclean says that man is a "damned mess." Maclean's courage comes not in asserting this doctrine, which Hemingway and numberless other twentieth-century writers have had no trouble with, but in juxtaposing it with a doctrine of salvation. Without the juxtaposition, damnation is no less a bromide than is salvation. The courage comes in one's affirming a larger context of reality in which the juxtaposition both is and is not reconciled. To change the image, we might imagine a world where a river runs *through* it but is not *of* it. The test of courage is to embrace the paradox.

As for the messiness unto damnation, Maclean's story does not equivocate. The world is a fallen one, people are liars and cheats, family entanglements ruin the most blessed vision. When the narrator's brother-in-law steps off the train at Wolf Creek, we see in Neal the genus, *phonus bolonus,* dressed in white flannels, a red-and-white-and-blue V-neck sweater over a red-and-white-and-blue turtleneck sweater, and elegant black-and-white shoes. At Black Jack's Bar his big talk with oldtimers and the town's whore, Old Rawhide, shows him in his true element. The family picnic the following day on the Elkhorn River shows him disgustingly out of it. He fishes not with flies but worms and gets nothing; he whimpers from his hangover and feigns sickness to avoid picnic chores. A genuine bastard, he doesn't deserve the solicitude he gets, and he wouldn't get it except for family loyalty. The two brothers know he doesn't even deserve Montana. Neal violates everything that is good, including the code of fishing. On a subsequent trip he violates a trust by stealing beer that the two brothers have left to cool in the river—and in *this,* the Big Blackfoot River. Even worse, he has brought not only a coffee can of worms for bait but also Old Rawhide, and has screwed his whore on a sand bar in the middle of "our family river." The brothers find the two asleep, naked and sunburned. On the cheeks of her ass they see the tattooed letters: LO / VE. The river sanctuary has been defiled; never again will the brothers throw a line here at this hole.

Close as narrator Maclean appears to be to his brother Paul, both reverencing the river whose secrets only the best dry-fly fishermen can hope to touch, a vast gulf nevertheless separates them. If they both find the river an oceanic enigma where answers lie hidden in watery shadows, the narrator finds his brother an enigma as well.

That Paul seeks answers in fishing leaves his brother wondering about the questions being asked. Somewhere deep in Paul's shadowy inner world is chaos that the four-count rhythm of casting has not disciplined, a hell that grace has not transformed. Yet Paul seeks no help either from brother or father. Only the visible things show—namely, that he drinks and gambles and fights too much, that gambling debts translate into enemies, that his job as reporter on a Helena newspaper confirms a world full of bastards, and, finally, that he wants no help, asks for none, expects none except what the hard-driving river can bring. Clearly, Paul lives in a world more profoundly fallen than that represented even by Neal's damned messiness. Confirmation of this fact comes in the manner of Paul's death: beaten by the butt of a revolver, nearly all the bones of his right hand (his fighting hand) broken, and his body dumped in an alley—this, the death of a dry-fly fisherman whose rod was a wand of magical power and beauty, and who, when inhabiting this river-world, embodied laughter and discipline and joy.

Wherein, then, is saving grace? In the water? In the words that the father reads in his Greek New Testament? In the Word, the *logos,* from the Fourth Gospel that the father seeks to interpret as the two of them, father and son, wait on the riverbank to watch Paul catch his final big fish? "In the part I was reading," the father explains, "it says the Word was in the beginning, and that's right. I used to think water was first, but if you listen carefully you will hear that the words are underneath the water."

Now comes the crucial distinction.

"If you ask Paul," the son says, "he will tell you that the words are formed out of water."

"No," the father replied, "you are not listening carefully. The water runs over the words. Paul will tell you the same thing."

Of course, Paul never tells, and we suspect he never found out. Neither his brother nor his father knows the truth about him. Yet the distinction deserves close attention together with the images that Maclean allows to arise from his memory, images that come out of the past to bear new meanings, joining the past and the present in the image and the image bearing the truth.

Watery images bring forth fish seen sometimes as "oceanic," with their black spots resembling crustaceans. The river itself flows from origins shaped by the ice age, the rocks by more elemental forces emanating "almost from the basement of the world and time." The rain is the same as "the ancient rain spattering on mud before it became rock . . . nearly a billion years ago." Whereas in the sunny world where the river-voice is "like a chatterbox, doing its best to be friendly," in the dark shadows where the river "was deep and engaged in profundities" and where it circled back on itself now and then "to say things over to be sure it had understood itself "—in these primal depths the voice issues from a "subterranean river" where only the most courageous ever venture and where only *real* fishing takes place.

Through such imagery Maclean takes us to foundations antecedent to water. From these foundations the father in the narrative hears words—words beneath the water, words before the water. The distinction between words formed out of water and words formed out of foundations beneath the water is the distinction between mystical pantheism and the Christian *logos.* The distinction is between the *unity* of creator and creation on the one hand and their *separation* on the other. Again, the distinction is between the saving grace found in one's merging with nature, and that found in one's belonging to the God antecedent to nature, the God in nature but not of nature, immanent yet transcendent. And whatever the word spoken in the pantheistic unity, it is not the same as that spoken in the separateness, spoken in the *logos,* spoken from under and before the timeless rocks.

I am not suggesting that Maclean, the author, is involved in mere theological dialectic. What he is saying is not what comes from such abstractions but from memory and images, from time past when he and his father and brother were one in love if not in understanding. And now those he loved but did not understand are dead. "But," he adds, "I still reach out to them." Something of this love he still hears in the waters of the river and in the foundations beneath. Perhaps he hears the Word itself as did John of the Fourth Gospel. This is what the father must have heard too and what his brother Paul did not. Whether the words come from water or from the deeper foundations, they are words his memory translates into those of father and brother, words that spoke of love. In their words he has his epiphany, yes his redemption, and thus he can say, "I am haunted by waters."

I said earlier that Maclean's story is a classic, deserving a place in the pantheon of western American literature. Putting aside such matters as structure and tone, characterization, imagery, and a hundred other elements that subtly harmonize (whether the art be that of Maclean's fiction of his fishing), I find something else, something identifying the river as *symbol* and *type*.

As for symbol, all the age-old meanings associated with living waters—one immediately thinks of purification, fertility, and renewed life—are predicated upon a perceiving mind and a symbolic mode of perception. I'm concerned here more with the act of perception than with the object, more with the perceiver than the perceived or percept. In short, the perceiver as symbolist finds significance through the interaction of experience and imagination, whereas the perceiver as typologist finds significance through a sacred design that is prior to, and independent of, the self. The mode of perception makes all the difference, and in this analysis the two modes are radically different. Symbolism eventuates in a direct interpretation of life, whereas typology relates to history, prophecy, teleology. The symbol is created in the womb of the perceiver's imagination, whereas the type is revealed within the perceiver's faith. Again, the symbolist possesses a special quality enabling him to fuse object and meaning; the typologist possesses a special but different quality enabling him to see what has already been fused and now revealed but is separate from, and independent of, him. Finally, the symbolist enters the river, as it were, and is redeemed by the waters which his imagination transforms into purification and renewal. But the typologist enters what has already been transformed or, more accurately, what flows from a sacred design, purpose, or destiny, made visible through the regenerate eyes and ears of faith.

In Maclean's story the two modes of perception show the river as both symbol and type. When attention is upon Paul's marvelous artistry, validating the halo of spray often enclosing him, we see by means of the narrator's imagination not only a transformed fisherman but a river metamorphosed into a world apart. Fishing becomes a world apart, a world perfect, an imagined and sinless world fusing person with vision. For Paul, when he steadied himself and began to cast, "the whole world turned to water." The narrator shares in the imagined oneness of his brother's world.

But the narrator does not lose himself in it. He also hears his father's words bespeaking a separate design, revealed as the *logos* or Word that was in the beginning—before the river and before human imaginings. More than speech, this Word is divine action—creating, revealing, redeeming. That the father carries his Greek New Testament

along with his fishing rod is a fact not lost upon the author as narrator. Through his father's faith the son reaches out to hear this other Word. No wonder he is haunted by waters.

In truth, the river runs through his mind and consciousness and language and life. But something also runs through the river itself, something that is in it but not of it, something more elemental than water. (pp. 149-55)

Harold P. Simonson, "Norman Maclean's Two-Hearted River," in Western American Literature, *Vol. XVII, No. 2, August, 1982, pp. 149-55.*

Maclean on Chicago literary figures of the 1930s:

We came in and Sherwood Anderson just stopped and froze and looked at Carl Sandburg. Sandburg is engaged in one of his monologues. Conversation was not possible with him. He was a monologist. So he's mooning along about Emerson, the first really great true American. And Sherwood listens for a while. Finally he stops Sandburg right in the middle of a sentence. He says, "Emerson was the first great Rotarian." Boom. The place just froze. There we stood, up on the platform like actors, with a stunned audience beneath us. Well, there was no more to the evening at all. Nobody could get anything started after that.

So, a couple of days later, I'm going to Chicago and Ferdinand Schevill takes me down to Michigan City, and I got on the Yellow Peril. Who's sitting in the Yellow Peril but Sandburg. You know, with his snap-brim hat and his long thin cigar. So I go over and sit by him and he looks at me for a while and he doesn't say a word. Then he says, "That sorry...that son of a bitch!" he said, "What does he mean? What does he mean about Emerson being the first great Rotarian?" He pulled the brim of his hat down until it touched his cigar and never said another word to me all the way to Chicago. All was not quiet on the Chicago literary front in those days.

Norman Maclean, in an interview from TriQuarterly, *Spring 1984.*

Wallace Stegner   (essay date 1988)

[*Stegner was an American novelist. In the following essay, he examines style and theme in* A River Runs Through It.]

The writing career of Norman Maclean is a phenomenon. A retired English professor from the University of Chicago at the age of seventy begins, secretly and almost shamefacedly, to write down the stories of his youth that he has told his children. He produces three stories of such unfashionable length and kind—among other defects, "they have trees in them"—that no magazine or trade publisher is interested. Through the influence of friends, they are finally brought out by the University of Chicago Press, which never published any fiction before that and so far as I know has published none since.

This slim book, virtually without reviews or advertising, finds its way into hands that pass it on to other hands. Fly fishermen discover it first, with delight, but others besides fishermen respond to it. A little group of admirers forms and spreads. A second printing is needed, then a third, then a paperback edition. By word of mouth a reputation is born. Now, ten years after his first and only fictions saw print, this author of three stories is an established name, an authentic western voice, respected and imitated, and books are being written about him.

Why? How? Every writer and publisher wishes he knew. The usual channels of publicity and criticism had virtually nothing to do with it. Neither did literary fashion, for that, along with the orthodoxies of contemporary short story form, is simply ignored in these stories.

For one thing, they are "realistic," and realism, as everyone knows, was long since left to the second-raters. For another, they are about the West, an environment of broad hats and low foreheads, a place traditionally short of thought and with only rudimentary feelings. For still another, they are about a *historical* West, Montana in the years during and just after World War I, a West that was less a society than a passing phase of the frontier; and they contain some of the mythic feeling and machinery, the crudeness, the colorful characters, and the ox-stunning fist fights made all too familiar by horse opera.

Don't look here for the economy and precision that have marked the short story at least since Joyce and in some ways since Poe. The characteristic modern short story starts as close to its end as it can. It limits itself to a unified action, often a single scene, and to the characters absolutely essential to that action. It covers the time and space required, no more, and picks up the past, insofar as it needs it, in passing. Ibsen perfected that "uncovering" technique in his plays a hundred years ago, rediscovering for both drama and fiction Aristotle's three unities.

But two of Maclean's stories spread across whole summers, and the third contains an entire life. In all three the action moves around—mountains to town, town to the Big Blackfoot to Wolf Creek, camp to cafe, cafe to bar. Instead of a rigidly limited cast of characters, whole communities inhabit these tales: rangers, cooks, dynamiters, packers, pimps, whores, waitresses with and without freckles, bartenders, barflies, family, in-laws, small-town doctors, horses, and coyote-killing dogs. Around their discursive actions a world grows up. Inclusion, not exclusion, is the intention; amplitude, not economy, is the means.

Furthermore, this writer talks to his readers, guesses at the motivations of characters, sums up, drops one-liners of concentrated observation and wisdom. He is garrulous and personal. The puppeteer shows his hands and feet. No wonder he couldn't find an orthodox publisher.

It is instructive to note what is not here, but more so to note what is. All three of these stories, even **"Logging and Pimping,"** the first-written, shortest, and least-satisfying, grow on re-reading. The two longer ones grow a great deal. Things missed or only half seen edge out into the open. Things that looked only reported turn out to have been *rendered.* Throwaway lines reveal unexpected perti-

nence, discursiveness that we first forgave as naivete has to be reappraised as deep cunning. Maybe Maclean knew fully what he was doing, maybe he only moved by instinct sharpened through years of studying literature, maybe his hand was guided by love and nostalgia for places and people long left behind. However he did it, he made a world.

The Montana of his youth was a world with the dew on it. Perhaps the time of youth always has dew on it, and perhaps that is why we respond to Maclean's evocation of his. But I lived in Montana, or close to it, during those same years, and it was a world younger, fresher, and more touched with wonder and possibility than any I have since known. After seventy years, I still dream it; and when it is revived by these stories it glows with a magical light, like one of those Ansel Adams photographs that are more magnificent than the scenes they pretend to represent.

The remembered and evoked world of barely-touched wilderness and barely-formed towns has, for all its primitiveness, violence, and freedom, an oddly traditional foundation. A raw society, it offers to growing boys mainly a set of physical skills—riding, shooting, fishing, packing, logging, fire-fighting, fist-fighting—and a code to go with them. The hero, the admired and imitated person, is one who does something superlatively well. To fail at a skill, if you try your best, is unfortunate but respectable; to fail in nerve or trying is to merit contempt.

It is absolutely right that the seventeen-year-old Norman Maclean of *USFS 1919* should model himself on Bill Bell, the best ranger, best packer, best all-around mountain man, and best fighter in the Bitterroot country. It is right that in **"Logging and Pimping"** a grown-up Norman Maclean should half kill himself keeping up with the sadistic logger-pimp Jim. It is right that in *A River Runs Through It* he and his brother, trained by their father in fly fishing and its mysteries, should reserve their deepest contempt for bait fishermen. Skill is both competitive and proud. As the basis of a code, it can be harshly coercive on attitudes and conduct. Also, it is not enough. Unaccompanied by other more humane qualities, skill can produce a bully like Jim or a tinhorn like the cook. The code goes beyond skill to character; for those who subscribe to it, it defines a man. A man for young Norman Maclean is neither mouthy nor finicky; he is stoical in the face of pain; he does not start fights but he tries to finish them; he does what his job and his morality tell him to do. But he cannot get by on mere skill. He needs something else, some decency or compassion that can only be learned from such sources as the boys' preacher father. In the beginning, he reminds his son, was the Word.

I knew a few P.K.'s in my youth. Most were Scottish. All had to learn to reconcile the harsh, limited, demanding code of their frontier society with the larger codes in which grace and personal salvation ultimately lie. Norman Maclean learned that. His brother Paul, with more skills, with every advantage except the capacity to transcend the code of his place and time, did not.

I speak as if the stories were about real people. I think they are. Maclean gives us no reason to make a distinction between real and fictional people. The stories are so frankly autobiographical that one suspects he hasn't even bothered to alter names. The only thing that has happened to young Maclean's experience is that it has been recollected in tranquillity, seen in perspective, understood, and fully felt. The stories are a distillation, almost an exorcism.

The Maclean boys grew up in a world "overbearing with challenges" and dominated by the code. Sent to the firewatch station on Grave Peak, sure that he has been sent off as punishment for his dislike of the cook, young Maclean responds by trying to do the job so well, in spite of rattlers, grizzlies, and lightning storms, that Bell will have to admit he has been unjust. (Bell doesn't; he takes the performance for granted.) Pulling all day on the end of a seven-foot crosscut whose other end is in the hands of a bully determined to put him down, Maclean would die on the saw rather than admit he was even tired. Told to go for the money if a fight breaks out, he goes for it, though he knows he will get his face busted. Commanded to take his impossible brother-in-law fishing, he and Paul do, though they would rather drown him.

In every case the reward for faithfulness is acceptance. The logger-pimp Jim learns enough respect for Maclean to make him a "pal." Bill Bell, making up for the whole unsatisfactory summer, asks him to join the crew again next year. And the women caretakers of the impossible brother-in-law let him know without saying it (they are no more mouthy than their men) that he has done his duty, that the failure is not his.

These rites of passage through observance of the code, these steps toward a simplistically-understood manhood, dominate both **"Logging and Pimping"** and *USFS 1919*, and are present in *A River Runs Through It.* But they are not enough to account for the astonishing success of Maclean's little book. The fact is, the title story contains everything that the other two do, and far surpasses them, transcends them. It flies where they walk. Where they are authentic, humorous, ironic, observant, and much else, *A River Runs Through It* is both poetic and profound.

In the other stories the skills under discussion are work skills from a half-forgotten time. They are recreated as lovingly as Melville recreates the boats, the gear, the try-works, and the rest of his cetology. They pack the crevices of the narrative with a dense exposition of *process*. Getting up from reading, we could make a pass at fighting a forest fire or balancing the load on a mule.

But fishing with a dry fly, which is the skill that gives both meaning and form to *A River Runs Through It,* is not labor but an art, not an occupation but a passion, not a mere skill but a mystery, a symbolic reflection of life.

Fly fishing renounces the pragmatic worms and hardware of the meat fishermen. It is truly an art, "an art that is performed on a four-count rhythm between ten and two o'clock." It calls for coordination, control, and restraint more than for strength. To do it right you need not only skill but the imagination to think like a fish. It has its rituals and taboos, and thus is an index to character like the code, but far subtler. There is no clear distinction between it and religion. It takes place in wild natural places, which

for Maclean mean awe, holiness, respect; and in water, which he feels as the flow of time.

Like the lesser skills, fly fishing has its arrogance. Witness Paul's response to Izaak Walton's *Compleat Angler*: not only is Walton a bait fisherman but the sonofabitch can't even spell "complete." The pride of a supreme artist, plus an unswerving adherence to the code, is a recipe for disaster, a fatal flaw. Despite his artistry and his grace, Paul is one who cannot be helped because he will not accept help. Some saving intelligence, a capacity to see beyond or around the code, saves Paul's brother, but his brother cannot save Paul.

So is this a story of *hubris* in the Bitterroots, of a young god destroyed by pride? If it is, why all that other stuff the story contains—all that tawdry story of looking after the incompetent, mouthy brother-in-law, all that bawdy farce of the whore Old Rawhide and the sunburned backsides? If this is a story of pathetic or tragic failure, why is it cluttered up with so much exposition of the art of fishing, so many stories of fishing expeditions, so many homilies from the preacher father, so many hints about the relations of Norman Maclean with his wife's family? An impressive story as it stands, would this be even more impressive if it were cleaned up, straightened up, and tucked in?

I will tell you what I think. I only think it, I don't know it; but once when I suggested it in Norman Maclean's presence he didn't deny it. Perhaps, like Robert Frost, he thinks a writer is entitled to anything a reader can find in him. Perhaps I persuaded him of something he hadn't realized. More likely, he knew it all along.

The fact is, or I think it is, that this apparently rambling yarn is made with the same skill that Paul displays while fishing the Big Blackfoot, the same deliberation and careful refusal to hurry, the same reading of the water. "It is not fly fishing if you are not looking for the answers to questions," the author says, and this is big water demanding every skill.

Listen to how Paul fishes—(this is early in the story, and may be taken as a forecast of what is to come):

> The river above and below his rock was all big Rainbow water, and he would cast hard and low upstream, skimming the water with his fly but never letting it touch. Then he would pivot, reverse his line in a great oval above his head, and drive his line low and hard downstream, again skimming the water with his fly. He would complete this grand circle four or five times, creating an immensity of motion which culminated in nothing if you did not know, even if you could not see, that now somewhere out there a small fly was washing itself on a wave. Shockingly, immensity would return as the Big Blackfoot and the air above it became iridescent with the arched sides of a great Rainbow.
>
> He called this "shadow casting," and frankly I don't know whether to believe the theory behind it—that the fish are alerted by the shadows of flies passing over the water by the first casts, so hit the fly the moment it touches the water. It is more or less the "working up an appetite" theo-

ry, almost too fancy to be true, but then every fine fishermen has a few fancy stunts that work for him and for almost no one else. Shadow casting never worked for me. . . .

But if shadow casting never worked for the fisherman Norman Maclean, it works marvelously well for the fictionist. He fills the air with flies that never really settle, he dazzles us with loops of glittering line, he keeps us watching Old Rawhide, who does not matter at all, and the brother-in-law, who matters only in that he demonstrates the lack of everything that makes Paul special, and he keeps us from watching Paul, who does matter. Then, on page 102 of a 104-page story, the fly settles, and we strike at what we have been alerted to but have not been allowed to anticipate.

Bluntly, brutally, in a few hundred words, the important part of the story is ended with Paul's life; the shadow falls suddenly on a tale that has been often sunny, even farcical. Time comes down like a curtain, what has been vibrantly alive is only remembered, we are left hollow with loss, and we end in meditation on the Big Blackfoot in the cool of the evening, in the Arctic half-light of the canyon, haunted by waters.

The ending is brought off with such economy only because it was earlier obscured by all the shadow casting. A real artist has been fishing our stream, and the art of fishing has been not only his message but his form and his solace. An organ should be playing Bach's *Es Ist Vollbracht.*

A River Runs Through It is a story rooted in actuality, in known people and remembered events. But it is a long way from a limited realism. It is full of love and wonder and loss, it has the same alternations of sunshine and shadow that a mountain stream has, and its meaning can be heard a long way from its banks. It is an invitation to memory and the pondering of our lives. "To me," Maclean remarks in his introduction, "the constant wonder has been how strange reality has been."

Fisherman or not, who is not haunted by waters? (pp. 153-60)

> *Wallace Stegner, "Haunted by Waters," in* Norman Maclean, *edited by Ron McFarland and Hugh Nichols, Confluence Press, Inc., 1988, pp. 153-60.*

Gordon G. Brittan, Jr.   (essay date 1988)

[*Brittan is an American educator and critic. In the following excerpt, he analyzes how Maclean's use of language in* A River Runs Through It *gives meaning to the events of the narrative.*]

A River Runs Through It is Maclean's memoir, unsentimental and moving, of days some 50 years ago or so spent in and around fly-fishing some streams in western Montana with his brother Paul and his father, a Scot and Presbyterian minister in Missoula who drew no clear line between fly-fishing and religion. But it is also a great deal more.

In the attempt to say what more, allow me to look with you at a couple of passages.

The river that runs through it is the Big Blackfoot. In some sense it is both the center and the image of their lives, a symbol of time, of change, but also something permanent. Maclean is sitting on its banks, a young man, finished with his fishing, looking at the river, trying to forget the brother-in-law and his dubious woman friend who have tagged along, drunk the beer, and almost ruined the day.

> I sat there and forgot and forgot, until what remained was the river that went by and I who watched. On the river the heat mirages danced with each other and then they danced through each other and then they joined hands and danced around each other. Eventually the watcher joined the river, and there was only one of us.

To which Maclean adds humorously, "I believe it was the river."

At least it was a selfless moment.

With all content removed, he begins to reflect on the river's form.

> Not far downstream was a dry channel where the river had run once, and part of the way to come to know a thing is through its death. But years ago I had known the river when it flowed through this now dry channel, so I could enliven its stony remains with the waters of memory.

In death, the form is fixed, whether of a thing or of a person, as it is of the past, which is also dead and gone. But the past can be recovered. reconstituted, and brought to life in memory.

> In death it had its pattern, and we can only hope for as much. Its overall pattern was the favorite serpentine curve of the artist sketched in the valley from my hill to the last hill I could see on the other side. But internally it was made of sharp angles. It ran seemingly straight for a while, turned abruptly, then ran smoothly again, then met another obstacle, again was turned sharply and again ran smoothly. Straight lines that couldn't be exactly straight and angles that couldn't have been exactly right angles became the artist's most beautiful curve and swept from here across the valley to where it could be no longer seen.

We can only hope for pattern or form because nowhere else is there coherence or significance. But this pattern is not simply found; it is also imposed. The smooth serpentine curve of the artist is contrasted with the crooked lines and sharp angles of the river itself. There are no perfect forms in nature. We derive them only by an effort of abstraction.

Maclean doesn't so much *tell* us there's a pattern as *show* us the pattern. The pattern is in his sentences, of course, but more especially in their rhythm and their sound. Notice how the rough rhythm of "Straight lines that couldn't be exactly straight and angles that couldn't have been exactly right angles" (it's difficult to read these words without stumbling) gives way, mid-sentence, to the smooth and flowing "became the artist's most beautiful curve and swept from here across the valley. . . ." To say that Maclean is a great story-teller is to suggest many things, but it is first to insist that the stories be read with the ear. At one point, we are told about how fishermen "read" the water. But mainly we are supposed to listen to the river, to the words, and more especially to the voices and their cadences.

Story-telling is also teaching, Maclean likes to say, and here as elsewhere he draws on his knowledge of geology to take us inside the river and to deepen our understanding and appreciation of its form. For what is knowledge but knowledge of form?

> The Big Blackfoot is a new glacial river that runs and drops fast. The river is a straight rapids until it strikes big rocks or big trees with big roots. This is the turn that is not exactly at right angles. Then it swirls and deepens among big rocks and circles back through them where big fish live under the foam. As it slows, the sand and small rocks it picked up in the fast rapids above begin to settle out and are deposited and the water becomes shallow and quiet. After the deposit is completed, it starts running again.

Finally, Maclean rejoins the river, generalizing this pattern to include his own:

> As the heat mirages in front of me danced with and through each other, I could feel patterns from my own life joining with them. It was here, while waiting for my brother, that I started this story, although, of course, at the time I did not know that stories of life are often more like rivers than books. But I knew a story had begun, perhaps long ago near the sound of water. And I sensed that ahead I would meet something that would never erode so that there would be a sharp turn, deep circles, a deposit, and quietness.

This is an important moment in the narrative. Life for the first time within it begins to take on the coherence of literature. For it is, after all, only in telling a story, about our own lives and those of others, that form begins to emerge, that events follow one another with a certain inevitability, that there is a beginning and an end; and that we start to see significance. Such story-telling is always after the fact; lived experience is for the most part formless and without meaning. Only later do we begin to discover patterns, unities, but only as we begin, in this case as an old man, to recover that experience in memory and order it in words.

I've spent a long time with this passage, quoting much of it. For it seems to me to be a perfect example of the patterns about which Maclean is speaking, moving symmetrically from the initial thoughtless merging of writer and river, observer and observed, to reflections on ways in which the writer's forms are and correspond to the river's to a thoughtful re-merging of writer and river through the discovery of a new pattern, a story, that embraces both of them. (pp. 184-86)

A second passage, toward the end of the story, has more

Maclean's father, John Norman Maclean.

to do with the Calvinist than the Aristotelian Maclean. Again we're on the banks of the Big Blackfoot. Maclean and his father are sitting together at the end of another day, watching Paul demonstrate all his power and artistry in the catching of one last big fish, a copy of the Greek New Testament by their side. It's too deep for Paul to wade across, so tucking his cigarettes and matches in his hat, he starts to swim:

> My father and I sat on the bank and laughed at each other. It never occurred to either of us to hurry to the shore in case he needed help with a rod in his right hand and a basket loaded with fish on his left shoulder. In our family it was no great thing for a fisherman to swim a river with matches in his hair. We laughed at each other because we knew he was getting damn good and wet, and we lived in him, and were swept over the rocks with him and held his rod high in one of our hands.

We're swept along too. That's the gift of the great story-teller, to bring his listeners into the story, especially when he's trying to teach them something, even something difficult like the 4-beat rhythm of a cast. This is the Paul they understand, in whom they do not merely live but exist. But there is another Paul whom they do not understand, a son and brother who is a creature of passion and can't come to terms with his own violence and is found beaten to death in an alley. Maclean gives us to understand that Paul had somehow fallen from grace and was beyond salvation by anyone, though not beyond their love. At the same time, although grace can never be recovered much less earned, Paul is a figure of grace, at least standing in the Big Blackfoot with a fly rod in his hand. "To him," Maclean says of his father, "all good things—trout as well as eternal salvation—come by grace and grace comes by art and art does not come easy." This, I suppose, was the riddle, some form of the problem of evil: Paul was graceful and could be understood and Paul was damned and beyond all human comprehension. The most that could be made of his life was to find or create a pattern that, even if it left some things, as it must, incomprehensible, restored Paul's grace by an art that is effortless and did not come easy. (pp. 187-88)

> *Gordon G. Brittan, Jr., "Common Texts," in* Norman Maclean, *edited by Ron McFarland and Hugh Nichols, Confluence Press, Inc., 1988, pp. 182-89.*

Wendell Berry   (essay date 1988)

[*Berry is an American novelist, poet, and critic. In the following essay, he compares* A River Runs Through It *with Ernest Hemingway's "Big Two-Hearted River."*]

Works of art participate in our lives; we are not just distant observers of *their* lives. They are in conversation among themselves and with us. This is a part of the description of human life; we do the way we do partly because of things that have been said to us by works of art, and because of things that we have said in reply.

For a long time, I have been in conversation with "Big Two-Hearted River," and with myself *about* "Big Two-Hearted River." I have read the story many times, always with affection and gratitude, noticing and naming its virtues, and always seeing clearly in imagination the landscape and all the events of Nick Adams' restorative fishing trip. It is this clarity with which Hemingway speaks his story into the reader's imagination that is his great and characterizing virtue:

> The river made no sound. It was too fast and smooth. . . . Nick looked down the river at the trout rising. . . . As far down the long stretch as he could see, the trout were rising, making circles all down the surface of the water, as though it were starting to rain.

There is a moving courage in this plainness, freeing details, refusing clutter.

But that is not what my conversation with this story has been about. It has been about the ending, when Nick has fished down the river to where it leaves the sunlight and enters a heavily wooded swamp. At that point Nick turns back because "in the fast deep water, in the half light, the fishing would be tragic."

The story ends: "There were plenty of days coming when he could fish the swamp." I assume that such days were indeed coming, but they do not come in this story. And I have asked myself what it means that the story ends where it does, and what Hemingway meant by "tragic."

So far, I have been unable to believe that he meant the word literally. The swamp seems to be a place where one might hook big fish and then lose them. But tragedy is not a name for the loss of fish. Or it may be that Nick fears that fishing in the swamp would make him sad, a dark swamp inevitably suggesting or symbolizing what is mysterious or bewildering. But the correct name for such sadness (in anticipation, at least) is melancholy, not tragedy. It is hard to escape the feeling that Hemingway uses "tragic" more seriously than a casual speaker would use "awful" or "terrible," but not much more. If he means the word seriously, then he is talking about a tragedy that he knows about but the reader does not.

At any rate, the story receives a challenge at the end that it does not accept. It refuses to go into the dark swamp. I think that what it calls "tragic" is really messiness or unclarity, and that it refuses out of a craftsmanly fastidiousness; it will not relinquish the clarity of its realization of the light and the river and the open-water fishing. It is a fine story, on its terms, but its terms are straitly limited.

Similarly, the burned town and countryside at the beginning might have been felt as tragic, suggestive as they are of the war-damage in Nick's past—but they are felt, in fact, only as a kind of cleansing away of all that is past, leaving Nick in isolation: "He felt he had left everything behind." That sentence sets the story in its bounds: it cannot be tragic because it is about a solitary man in an unmemoried time. So far as we can learn from the story itself, the man comes from nowhere, knows and is known by nobody, and is going nowhere—nowhere, at least, that he cannot see in full daylight.

"Big Two-Hearted River" seems to me, then, to be a triumph of style in its pure or purifying sense: the ability to isolate those parts of experience of which one can confidently take charge. It does not go into dark swamps because it does not know how it will act when it gets there. The problem with style of this kind is that it is severely reductive of both humanity and nature: the fisherman is divided from history and bewilderment, the river from its darkness. Like the similarly reductive technical and professional specializations of our time, this style minimizes to avoid mystery. It deals with what it does not understand by leaving it out.

Lately, my conversation with "Big Two-Hearted River" has been joined and a good deal clarified by Norman Maclean's long story, *A River Runs Through It,* also a story about fishing, not so neat or self-contained as Hemingway's but just as fine, on its own terms, and far more moving.

Fishing, in Mr. Maclean's story, is not a rite of solitary purification, a leaving of everything behind, but a rite of companionship. It is a tragic rite because of our inevitable failure to understand each other; and it is a triumphant rite because we can love completely without understanding. Fishing, here, is understood as an art, and as such it is emblematic of all that makes us companions with one another, joins us to nature, and joins the generations together. This is the connective power of culture; sometimes it works, sometimes it fails; when it fails, it fails into tragedy, but here it is a tragedy that confirms the completeness, and indeed the immortality, of love.

Though the river of *A River Runs Through It* is the Big Blackfoot which, so far as we are told, enters no swamp, the whole story takes place in a dark swamp of sorts: the unresolvable bewilderment of human conflict and affection and loss. The style is confident enough, for Mr. Maclean accepts fully the storyteller's need to speak whole-heartedly however partial his understanding, but it is not pure or self-protective. It is a style vulnerable to bewilderment, mystery, and tragedy—and a style, therefore, that is open to grace.

This story is profoundly and elatedly religious—though it is untainted by the doctrinal arrogance and the witless piety that often taint "religion." Reading it, we are not allowed to forget that we are dealing with immortal principles and affections, and with the lives of immortal souls. "In our family," the first sentence reads, "there was no clear line between religion and fly fishing." And one is inclined at first to take that as a little family joke. The sentence states, however, the author's conviction of the doubleness, the essential mysteriousness, of our experience, which presides over the story to the end, and gives it imaginative force of the highest kind.

The theme of fly fishing and (or as) religion is developed masterfully and with exuberant humor in the first few pages, which give the story its terms and its characters, its settled fate and its redemption. These pages sketch out the apprenticeship served by the writer and his younger brother, Paul, to their father, who was a Presbyterian minister and a fly fisherman:

> As a Scot and a Presbyterian, my father believed that man by nature was a mess and had fallen from an original state of grace.... I never knew whether he believed God was a mathematician but he certainly believed God could count and that only by picking up God's rhythms were we able to regain power and beauty.

"Our father's art" of fly fishing is seen, then, as a way of recovering God's rhythms and attaining grace—no easy task for "if you have never picked up a fly rod before, you will soon find it factually and theologically true that man by nature is a damn mess." Before he is "redeemed," "it is natural for man to try to attain power without recovering grace." These are sentences that we celebrate, reading them, because they are themselves celebrations of their own exact insight. "Power comes not from power everywhere, but from knowing where to put it on." The boys' father believed that "all good things ... come by grace and grace comes by art and art does not come easy."

By the end of page six, not only have these connections been made between fishing and religion, art and grace, but our attention has been brought to focus on Paul, the brother, and we know that Paul is a superb fly fisherman and a compulsive gambler. By the end of page eight, we know also that he has a high temper, that he is inflexibly self-ruled, and that he is a street fighter. The story by then has its direction, which is as unbending as Paul's character. It is a story of the relentlessness of tragedy, and it is told with

the relentlessness of the grace that comes by art. The story is relentlessly painful, and it relentlessly causes one to read on rejoicing to the end.

This is tragedy pretty much in the old Greek sense: a story of calamity and loss, which arrive implacably, which one sees coming and cannot prevent. But the relentlessness of the tragedy is redeemed by the persistence of grace. The entrances of grace come at moments of connection of man and fish and river and light and word and human love and divine love. If we see Paul drunk, defeated, jailed, and finally beaten to death, we also see him in glory. In the passage which follows the writer has sat down to watch his brother fish. Paul has swum out through dangerous water to a rock and climbed up on it and begun casting. There is no minimizing here:

> Below him was the multitudinous river, and, where the rock had parted it around him, big-grained vapor rose. The mini-molecules of water left in the wake of his line made momentary loops of gossamer. . . . The spray emanating from him was finer-grained still and enclosed him in a halo of himself. The halo of himself was always there and always disappearing, as if he were candlelight flickering about three inches from himself. The images of himself and his line kept disappearing into the rising vapors of the river, which continually circled to the tops of the cliffs where, after becoming a wreath in the wind, they became rays of the sun.

The story is not in that, of course; that is only a glimpse that the story affords of the truest identity of the man it is about. The story is about the failure of the man to live up to his own grace, his own beauty and power, about the father's failure to be able to help, and about the writer's failure as his brother's keeper. And yet it is this glimpse and others like it that give the tragedy and the story their redemption and make possible the painful and triumphant affirmation at the end. This Paul, who failed, was yet a man who had learned the art of participating in grace. After his death, his brother and his father spoke of him, acknowledging their failure to help and to understand. The father asked:

> "Are you sure you have told me everything you know about his death?" . . . . I said, "Everything." "It's not much, is it?" "No," I replied, "but you can love completely without complete understanding." "That I have known and preached," my father said. . . .

> "I've said I've told you all I know. If you push me far enough, all I really know is that he was a fine fisherman."

> "You know more than that," my father said. "He was beautiful."

This story's fierce triumph of grace over tragedy is possible, the story "springs and sings," because of what I earlier called its vulnerability. Another way of saying this is that it does not achieve, because it does not attempt, literary purity. Nor does one feel, as one reads, that Mr. Maclean is telling the story out of literary ambition; he tells it, rather, because he takes an unutterable joy in telling it and therefore *has* to tell it. The story admits grace because it admits mystery. It admits mystery by admitting the artistically unaccountable. It could not have been written if it had demanded to consist only of what was understood or understandable, or what was entirely comprehensible in its terms. "Something within fishermen," the writer admits, "tries to making fishing into a world perfect and apart. . . ." But this story refuses that sort of perfection. It never forgets that it is a fragment of a larger pattern that it does not contain. It never forgets that it occurs in the world and in love.

I will not, I hope, be taken to be downgrading the literary art or literary value. This story is the work of a writer who has mastered his art, and I am fully aware that it would not be appreciable otherwise. I am only trying to make a distinction between two literary attitudes and their manifestation in styles.

Hemingway's art, in "Big Two-Hearted River," seems to me an art very considerably determined by its style. This style, like a victorious general, imposes its terms on its subject. We are meant always to be conscious of the art, and to be conscious of it as a feat of style.

Mr. Maclean's, on the other hand, seems to me a used, rather than an exhibited, art, one that ultimately subjects itself to its subject. It is an art not like that of the bullfighter, which is public, all to be observed, but instead is modest, solitary, somewhat secretive, used, like fishing, to catch what cannot be seen. (pp. 213-19)

> Wendell Berry, "Style and Grace," in Norman Maclean, *edited by Ron McFarland and Hugh Nichols, Confluence Press, Inc., 1988, pp. 213-19.*

Helen Lojek (essay date 1990)

[*In the following essay, Lojek criticizes aspects of the "western American myth" apparent in* A River Runs Through It.]

To read Norman Maclean's 1976 story *A River Runs Through It* is to enter a world in which tight, rhythmic prose (sentences flowing together like molecules of the Big Blackfoot River they describe) yields much comprehension of the joys and difficulties of family love. It is also, however, to enter a world shaped by an unexamined and probably unconscious masculinity. In large part, that masculinity is linked to elements of western American myth, and Maclean seems too much of a western insider to be fully aware of the limitations of that myth. To recognize the joys and beauties of *A River Runs Through It* without recognizing the restrictions of its masculine myth is to miss the complex, often ambiguous, ways in which the work continues patterns commonly found in writings about the American West.

There are, of course, several mythic American Wests: the frontier, the cattle range, the mining fields, to mention a few of the broadest categories. But heroes in fictional portrayals of all of these Wests have generally shared a cluster of personal characteristics. Tight-lipped, powerful, independent loners governed by a "code" of fair but assertive

behavior, they are uncomfortable with the strictures and conventions of encroaching civilization. It is that category of western hero into which Maclean's brother Paul fits, and recognizing Maclean's recasting of elements of the western myth into a tale of fly fishing in Montana in the 1930s reveals continuities and connections between his story and a long literary tradition.

Maclean himself envisioned his tales as western. "I started reading western stories kind of to refresh myself on them before going very far with [my own stories]," he [said in an interview in 1985]. And he has twitted publishers for their hesitancy about accepting his works. "Then, to add further to their literary handicaps, these stories turned out to be Western stories—as one publisher said in returning them, 'These stories have trees in them'."

Critics too have pointed to the work's regional nature. Harold Simonson calls it "a classic in western American literature." Wallace Stegner contrasts the popularity of Maclean's stories with the fact "they are about the West . . . they are about a *historical* West . . . and they contain some of the mythic feeling and machinery . . . made all too familiar by horse opera." And Kenneth Pierce fulminates about the "pigfuckers in the East" who refuse to render Maclean's "dazzling achievement" its due.

There are, of course, westerns and westerns. Or, as John Milton puts it, there are westerns and Westerns. The small *w* western "deals in stereotyped characters and stock patterns of action; it exploits the myths of the frontier, it depends upon a two-sided morality of good and evil . . . ." The upper case Western, on the other hand, "is of high literary quality . . . is sensitive to human behavior as well as to meaningful qualities of the land, is conscious of the relationship between the historical past and the present, is engaged in defining western man (in both senses of the term Western). . . ." As a whole, I think, Maclean's tale is in fact a Western. But it is not as unambiguously in that category as readers often assume, and a primary reason for its tenuous categorization is Maclean's perpetuation of aspects of western myth which allow him to slip into stereotyped characters and prevent him from fully exploring the relationship between past and present.

It is in his casting of Paul as a mythic western hero that Maclean's indebtedness to western myth is most clearly visible. At thirty-five and the "height of his power," Paul is noticeably superior to other Montanans (who are, of course, generally superior to the rest of us). Standing on the top of a cliff, putting "all his body and soul into a four-and-a-half-ounce magic totem pole," Paul casts his line rhythmically out over the water, making loops and circles designed to convince the fish that a hatch of flies is out.

> The mini-molecules of water left in the wake of his line made momentary loops of gossamer, disappearing so rapidly in the rising big-grained vapor that they had to be retained in memory to be visualized as loops. The spray emanating from him was finer-grained still and enclosed him in a halo of himself. The halo of himself was always there and always disappearing, as if he were candlelight flickering about three inches from himself. The images of himself and his line

kept disappearing into the rising vapors of the river, which continually circled to the tops of the cliffs where, after becoming a wreath in the wind, they became rays of the sun.

To the strangers who pause to watch, says Maclean, Paul "must have looked something like a trick rope artist at a rodeo, doing everything except jumping in and out of his loops." These observers find Paul's physique and skill so awe-inspiring that they can only watch and murmur "Jesus."

The canyon where Paul is fishing is a worthy opponent for such a fisherman. It is where the Blackfoot "roars loudest," so powerful that even Meriwether Lewis skirted it, "no place for small fish or fishermen." Yet Paul swims it casually, in his clothes, with one hand holding his rod high and his fish basket hung on his shoulder. So sure are his instincts, in fact, that he does not even pause to study the river before plunging in.

If we postpone momentarily a consideration of why this mythic western hero has come to be fly fishing, there is no doubt that Paul is another in a long line of such heroes. The hero's superiority is immediately evident to the admiring observer—especially to the observer/narrator, a figure whose previous incarnations include an easterner in *The Virginian* and a child in *Shane*. Paul is almost godlike, ringed by a halo and holding a magic totem pole. And the patterns of his casts merge with the patterns of the vapor and the wind and the sun, creating a mystical unity of man and nature—a momentary unity also achieved by western heroes from Deerslayer to the Virginian to (later in this story) Norman Maclean himself.

Paul is also the sort of loner idealized by American literature in general and idolized in lower case westerns. He never marries, knows he will never leave Montana, seeks neither wealth nor status, and refuses all offers of help. He neither puts his problems into words nor acknowledges their severity. This insistence on reticent self-sufficiency ranges from a refusal to borrow flies to a refusal to accept a loan which might save his life, since his eventual murder apparently stems from unpaid gambling debts. At the same time that he refuses to accept aid, however, he renders it with unself-conscious generosity, swimming the river in order to lend flies to the brother from whom he refused to borrow them, and taking time off to go fishing when his brother needs that escape. The twin strands of Paul's character—his willingness to help those less capable plus his adherence to a credo of tightlipped "toughing it out"—are lineal descendants of the western code perpetuated by authors from James Fenimore Cooper to Louis L'Amour.

Maclean never uses the word *code* to describe Paul's beliefs, but he hardly needs to. The credo is described with such precision, and its elements are so familiar, that we recognize it instantly for what it is—witness Wallace Stegner's constant use of *code* in discussing Maclean's work (which he links to the Montana of his own youth). Paul's firm code includes a determination never to be bested, and absolute fidelity to his word—having given it, he never "kicks" about keeping it. Most of all, however, Paul's code centers around the ritual of fly fishing, mandating that "real" fishermen be on time, despite pains of morning fatigue or hangover, and that they not steal each other's beer. Paul never drinks while fishing (beer is not "drink") but reaches for a bottle as soon as he is finished. And he reserves his greatest scorn for those who "fish" with worms—especially worms collected in a red Hills Brothers coffee can.

The westerner's desire to die with his boots on is reflected in the consolation which Norman and his father take in the fact that Paul, beaten to death in a back alley, has not died before breaking every bone in his right hand (his fishing hand) fighting back. And the westerner's favorite object of scorn, the tenderfoot who will never understand the code, is reincarnated in Neal, an offensive brother-in-law who, though born in Montana, has moved to California—which Paul describes as the migratory destination for failed fly fishermen—and returns wearing tennis sweaters. When Neal decides to go fishing he remembers the worms in the red can but forgets his rod. Because he is *not* in fact an easterner, but a failed westerner, there is no chance Montana can make a man of Neal. He has had his chance, and he has failed to learn the lessons the West has to teach. For such an individual there can be no salvation.

Maclean's recasting of the western myth into fly fishing terms affords opportunities for spiritual examination and growth, as commentators like Glen Love and Wendell Berry have pointed out. But it also involves him in more problematic aspects of the myth. Like every classic western hero before them, Maclean and his brother prefer a world without women, and the masculinity of the fly fishing domain is one of its prime attractions.

In Maclean's world women do not fish. That in itself is not a problem, given the right of individuals to select their own activities. But the implications of this masculine narrative are more far-reaching than may at first appear. Fly fishing is clearly the most desirable activity in this imperfect world, but it is an activity unavailable to women, who if they visit the river at all go there to pick huckleberries or to fix sandwiches for the men who fish. Before what turns out to be Maclean's last fishing trip with his father and brother, his mother (who has not been invited to accompany them) helps to locate the gear his father has not used in years. She knew, the narrator tells us, "nothing about fishing or fishing tackle, but she knew how to find things, even when she did not know what they looked like." His mother-in-law has an equally carefully defined role.

> She knew how to clean fish when the men forgot to, and she knew how to cook them, and, most important, she knew always to peer into the fisherman's basket and exclaim "My, my!" so she knew all that any woman of her time knew about fishing, although it is also true that she knew absolutely nothing about fishing.

The women in Maclean's family are bonded in a female community which nurses and supports and loves—but which knows nothing about the heroic, meditative activity of fishing. They, however, have sense enough not to try to participate in the true significance of fishing. A passing stranger is not so wise. Having impressed Maclean initially with her bulging "motherly breasts," she inquires whether he will stay to see Paul land his fish. Maclean's reply seems designed to emphasize her inability to comprehend the true significance of fishing.

> "No," I answered, "I'd rather remember the molecules."
>
> She obviously thought I was crazy, so I added, "I'll see his fish later." And to make any sense for her I had to add, "He's my brother."

The deliberate riddling, the implication that important sense is beyond this woman, and the fact that the young Norman's emotional and verbal distancing are addressed to her, not to her equally present (but more appropriately reticent) husband, reveal his protectiveness of fishing as an exclusively masculine preserve. And it is fishing which, properly undertaken, is most likely to yield genuine understanding.

So clearly linked are fishing and masculinity, in fact, that Maclean and his brother (like Huck and Deerslayer and Shane before them) are often fleeing the troubling world of women when they light out for the river. At the same time, of course, the brothers are motivated by awareness that "To women who do not fish, men who come home without their limit are failures in life"—an analysis oddly similar to the one which suggests that men go to war because women are watching. In either case, the story clearly presents what Simone de Beauvoir first identified as Woman as Other.

In describing this gender-divided world, Maclean the author often seems unaware of the implications. "We regarded [the Big Blackfoot] as a family river," he admits, obscuring the fact that only the male part of his family knew the river well. And "each one in our family considered himself the leading authority on how to fish the Blackfoot," The masculine pronoun *himself* is more than a grammatical convention here, since it accurately reflects the reality that no woman in his family presumed any authority about fishing. But Maclean's easy assumption that "each one in our family" is a *himself* is revealing.

Asserting that Maclean is generally unaware of the implications of such word choices is, of course, a tenuous proposition, one dependent on what is *not* included. What is not included in passages revealing the gender division of this world is the balance of voices Maclean achieves in much of the rest of the narrative, where younger and older selves are regularly juxtaposed so that the tale takes full advantage of the gain in perspective which comes with age. That faintly ironic tone about the foolishnesses of youth cannot be heard when Maclean is using elements of the western myth.

This absence of awareness in the narrative is illustrated if two similar passages from Maclean's other works are juxtaposed. First, a section from a 1978 speech **"Teaching and Story Telling."**

> In our family, men folk did not go around saying they loved each other. In our family, nature was a medium of our love, a carrier of it, an object of it, a cause of it. We loved each other because we loved the same sights and sounds and rivers,

because we recognized, not only that we were part of it but that all of us in some ways were masters of it—swinging an axe, building our log cabins, leading ducks on the wing, noting Caddis flies hatching from the bottom of shallow water in early September, and just leaning on the oars at sunset. And we knew that nature was often the master of us, and we loved both nature and ourselves because of that. Any description of nature in this story has something to do about family love.

This passage is very close to the one quoted earlier from *River.* In it, *family* clearly means *male family. Men* don't say they love each other. Further, though some women may indeed have mastered nature, Maclean's mother—judging by everything he has ever written about her—never swung an axe, built a cabin, or fly fished. "Family love" is too broad a term for what Maclean is describing. "Fraternal love" would be closer.

Second, a snippet from a 1984 interview.

> My family . . . didn't talk much about how much we loved each other. Fishing is where we all opened our hearts, including my mother. (**"Two Worlds"**)

In this second passage Maclean's phrasing hints at a greater degree of awareness about the gender-specific nature of his approach. In the interview's relatively full three-paragraph passage about "family love," every example refers to his relationship with his father or his brother. The phrase "including my mother" stands out awkwardly, an assertion unsupported by evidence, but a brief reminder (to us? to himself?) that Maclean knows that the twenty-five per cent of his immediate family represented by his mother should be included in a discussion of "family love."

The self-conscious inclusion of his mother in the passage is doubly odd because it contrasts with the entire body of Maclean's work: stories, essays and interviews all suggest that if his mother went on fishing trips at all, it was only to sit on the bank and make sandwiches. Perhaps her inclusion (however brief) in this discussion of fishing's more significant spiritual aspects indicates a heightened awareness on Maclean's part of the restrictive masculinity of his memories of fishing.

In any case, one thing is clear in *A River Runs Through It*: fishing is masculine. Fishing is also an indication of virility, and handling a rod well is important in more than one sense. Explaining why the tennis-appareled brother-in-law wants to go fishing, the character Norman observes: "he doesn't like to fish. He just likes to tell women he likes to fish. It does something for him and the women."

Neal may be eager to impress women, but the narrative as a whole indicates that women constantly threaten emasculation. Mary Clearman Blew has convincingly identified in Paul's Northern Cheyenne girl a descendant of "the sensual and destructive Dark Women out of the mainstream of American fiction." The Cheyenne girl is also, as Clew notes, a descendant of a great-grandmother who "helped cut the testicles off Custer's still living troops," and she clearly represents a danger to Paul—both in her own right and because she allows him to act on his own most self-destructive impulses. But "good" women as well as "bad" are a threat in this Montana world. Denied admittance to the covered truck bed which shelters the others from the rain, for example, Maclean (who had offended the women by failing to take adequate care of the brother-in-law) pokes his head through the sheltering canvas and sees the glitter of slashing cutlery: "When the women weren't using their hardware to make sandwiches . . . they were pointing it at me." The instruments of nurture are simultaneously instruments of threat, and although Maclean says he's worried about his *throat,* one wonders.

In one of the funniest episodes of the story, Neal manages to violate all elements of the fly fishing code. He forgets his rod, brings his worms, drinks whiskey, and steals beer. Worst of all, however, he brings a woman with him and conducts a minor orgy which leaves them lying on a sandbar, sunburned in embarrassing places. The woman, Old Rawhide, is a particularly unattractive version of the western whore, lacking any semblance of the mythic heart of gold (possession of which might have made her understand why she should not go fishing). Old Rawhide is in sharp opposition to the "virgin" family women who have sense enough to remain at home. But the heightened, tall-tale elements serve unintentionally to underscore what seems to be the real crime—the intrusion of any woman into this masculine idyll.

Neal's actions are described as a "violation" of the fishing ritual, and when Paul disposes of Old Rawhide by kicking her right between the LO and the VE tattooed on her buttocks, it is clear that he is disposing of more than one particular whore. That, no doubt, is why he does not kick Neal as well: the violation may have been masculine, but it is the woman who needs to be disposed of. The narrator suggests that Old Rawhide is a surrogate for Neal, who can't be touched because his sister (Norman's wife) and his mother (Norman's mother-in-law) have asked Norman to look out for him. That explanation leaves the basic situation unchanged. The fault is woman's—good women ask what they should not; bad women go where they should not; and even mythic heroes are hapless when the frontier gives way to Petticoat Junction.

The confrontation between Paul, laconic representative of the real West, and Old Rawhide, the whore whose presence threatens to rob fly fishing of its spiritual value, begins, Maclean informs us, at high noon, "Just as if the scene had been taken for a Western film." And one sign of Paul's heroic stature is his ability to deliver this dismissive kick in the ass, a feat which Norman, who tries it later, cannot manage. Old Rawhide's defeat, however, is not without ironies. The Maclean brothers have difficulty dislodging her from Neal's side, where she clings with a tenacious insistence that "I'm your woman. I'll take care of you." And it is Old Rawhide who helps the sunburned, drunken Neal back across the water from the sandbar to the shore, even though she is not in much better shape than he is. This sturdy individual, whose name indicates her toughness and durability, has partially assumed the

role usually reserved for the heroic male protector. The Maclean brothers are not amused by the inverted relationship between Old Rawhide and Neal.

Popular western myth, with its simplistic distinction between good guys and bad guys and its innately virtuous hero, has always had parallels with the Calvinism so deeply ingrained in much of American life. Paul's vulnerability to sexual women—to the Indian woman who tempts him and to the white woman who challenges him—reminds us of another link between western mythology and Calvinism, for both distrust women, especially sexual women. Paul's Cheyenne girl and Old Rawhide do not cause his failure (at least not entirely) but his inability to deal with them signals a fatal weakness in his character and women in general threaten his world. The Emersonian responsiveness to the healing power of nature which is also part of western mythology is finally not enough to save Paul.

A disturbing aspect of Maclean's exclusion of women from the world of fly fishing and spiritual quest goes beyond its apparent denial of these opportunities to women. Ultimately the implication is that such heroic ventures are impossible for *either* sex in a heterosexual world. And so the preferences which show in Paul Maclean's life patterns and in Norman Maclean's language choices continue increasingly anachronistic patterns of disconnection between men and women.

Maclean's use of mythic western patterns may stem from his conception of story telling as a male activity—both teller and listeners are male. He originally told these stories to his children, for whom he set out to create "pictures of how *men and horses* did things in Western parts of the world" (*River*, emphasis added). But his first public presentation of autobiographical material, in the mid-1970s, was to an all male club, Stochastics (the Thinkers), who refer to the yearly meeting at which wives are allowed as their "heterosexual meeting" (*River*). Maclean has identified his storytelling models as the bunkhouse story in which "a lot happens" (**"Teaching"**) and the tale told next to a Forest Service campfire (**"Hidden Art"**). Western storytelling seems not in fact to have been an exclusively male activity, but the models Maclean cites are all masculine. In his Montana there are no Scheherazades and the EEOC has not yet encountered the bunkhouse or the USFS—and so his tales naturally take on overtones of male bonding or male rites of passage. The readings for the Stochastics and the regular appearance in *Esquire* of articles by and about Maclean seem natural extensions of the male storytelling models.

Ordinarily, the typical western hero Paul so clearly resembles duplicates the actions of his mythological folk hero precursors and battles the forces of evil to a standstill. But Paul is ignominiously defeated when he should have been righteously triumphant. This is a tale of Paradise Lost, and the nostalgic tone is unsurprising. "What a beautiful world it was once," when no one stole beer, and when "unselected inhabitants of Great Falls and the Moorish invaders from California" had not usurped the Blackfoot. Like Deerslayer and Jeremiah Johnson and the Brave Cowboy before them, the Macleans are forced to realize that their world is doomed by the very American spirit and culture which opened it originally. And that doom, as was the case in other losses of Paradise, is linked with the coming of women. What Walker Percy, in another context, has called the "nomadic, bachelor West" gives way to the "housed, married West." Fly fishing is where western masculinity makes its last stand.

From one point of view it seems odd to make of fly fishing an activity whose significance looms so monumentally. Does it really make sense for men casting into the waters of Montana's Blackfoot to envision themselves as rightful heirs of the skills and prerogatives of generations of western folk heroes? Is not the very notion of a code oddly diminished when it prohibits Hills Brothers cans and tennis sweaters but allows the "hero" to kick a woman and drop her off partially naked on the edge of town? Used in this context, the idea of a code too often seems foolish, a case of life imitating art and men attempting to assert significance for their actions by casting them in heroic modes. These questions remain not just unanswered, but also unexplored in Maclean's story. Similarly unexplored is the possibility that what really destroys Paul is not a corrupt world, but Paul's own unthinking adherence to an outmoded myth.

As Maclean presents it, Paul's experience matches that of Deerslayer and Jeremiah Johnson and Huck Finn in many ways. Not the least of those ways is that all these males find that the greatest dangers in life lie not in the power and vagaries of nature, which they can master, but in the ugliness of society which—if they do not flee it—will first corrupt and then destroy them. Paul, the master of the river, is mastered by the town. Drink, gambling, back alley brawling, and the attractions of a dark woman with beautiful legs join forces to corrupt his heroic status. He is an American Adam without a Virgin Land to which to flee—or so Maclean would have us believe.

There is, however, another possibility suggested by the evidence Maclean presents. Paul's difficulties may in fact be a result not just of the corruptions of civilization, but also of his own adherence to a credo which no longer matches his world. Paul refuses to accept help from his father and brother, or even to discuss his problems. He adheres to an ideal of self-sufficient male behavior, going it alone without admitting difficulties or accepting help (an ideal now frequently labeled "macho"). At one point Maclean begins to explore the implications of Paul's choice.

> [T]he Greeks . . . believed that not wanting any help might even get you killed. Then I suddenly remembered that my brother was almost always a winner and often because he didn't borrow flies. So I decided that the response we make to character on any given day depends largely on the response fish are making to character on the same day.

That, however, is as far as Maclean pushes his thinking on the subject, shifting "rapidly back to reality" and concentrating on his fishing.

There are considerable ironies in Maclean's failure to explore fully the possibilities that Paul's code may be his major problem. Maclean admires his brother (sometimes excessively), and his dominant tone in describing Paul is

reverential. Yet Norman Maclean himself, the brother who is "saved," does not observe the rigidities of the code which shapes his brother's life. He marries, he actually talks to his father, he both asks for and accepts help when he needs it. One of the story's most important moments comes when Norman, repenting the difficulties caused when he and Paul leave Neal to burn (literally and metaphorically) in the sun, is reconciled with the women in his family. One by one they come out of the sickroom and embrace Norman, each in her separate way letting him know that he is forgiven and that all is well between them. It is a scene involving mutual respect, love, and support which crosses gender barriers. It is also a scene in which it is impossible to imagine Paul.

In the 1930s the western myth of independent masculinity no longer matched, if it ever had, even Montana, last outpost of the "real West." Paul's adherence to a frontier pattern, in the absence of a new territory to escape to, seems the greatest tragedy of all. Had he been able to reach out to those who were reaching out to him, to accept their support and perhaps their help, he might not have been overwhelmed by his difficulties. But that is a possibility Norman Maclean considers only in his passing hint that fish are responding differently to character these days, and Paul's is a tragedy he never directly confronts. The contrast between Paul's experience and Norman's experience is not one Maclean analyzes. It speaks only between the lines of his tale.

In tracing the beginnings of his story to his feeling that the patterns of his life joined the patterns of the river, Maclean voices his understanding "that stories of life are often more like rivers than books." He goes on, however, to describe his sense that "ahead I would meet something that would never erode so there would be a sharp turn, deep circles, a deposit, and quietness." It is Paul's death which will never erode. And one reason that it will not erode—for writer or for reader—is that Maclean fails to analyze the inadequacy of the western myth as a pattern for his brother's life.

A River Runs Through It, then, perpetuates a worldview which has strict limitations. An insider, accepting the framework of the myth, Norman Maclean never steps outside his world long enough for significant analysis of its limitations. Making such a charge about a work I find deeply moving always leaves me with a nagging sense that I am being ungracious (and ungracious is the most gracious term male colleagues have used in protesting my analysis). But I believe these things need to be said. Like the loops of gossamer formed by Paul's fishing line, the loops of western myth, with its gender-divided world, are often difficult to see. And like those fishing-line loops, the myth's restrictions as well as its values have been retained in our memories and continue to shape American life and American literature. We need to recognize the restrictions as well as the values. (pp. 145-56)

Helen Lojek, "Casting Flies and Recasting Myths with Norman Maclean," in Western American Literature, *Vol. XXV, No. 2, August, 1990, pp. 145-56.*

FURTHER READING

Foote, Timothy. "A New Film About Fly Fishing—and Much, Much More." *Smithsonian* 23 (September 1992): 121-22, 124-34.
> Discusses Robert Redford's film adaptation of *A River Runs Through It.* Foote traces the project from the initial bargaining between Redford and Maclean to the final film version and gives a detailed comparison of the film and the novella.

Kazin, Alfred. "Frontiers of True Feeling: Norman Maclean's Montana Classic." *Tribune Books* (6 August 1989): 1, 9.
> Review of a new edition of *A River Runs Through It.*

McFarland, Ron, and Nichols, Hugh, eds. *Norman Maclean.* Lewiston, Idaho: Confluence Press, 1988, 226 p.
> Includes interviews, essays by Maclean, and critical studies of Maclean's fiction.

Morrow, Patrick D. Review of *A River Runs Through It, and Other Stories,* by Norman Maclean. *Western American Literature* 11, No. 4 (Winter 1977): 358-59.
> Favorable review.

Seán O'Faoláin

1900-1991

(Born John Francis Whelan) Irish short story writer, novelist, biographer, nonfiction writer, editor, and playwright.

INTRODUCTION

O'Faoláin is best known for his compassionate, humorous, and ironic short fiction depicting life in twentieth-century Ireland. Commentators have noted that, like his countrymen James Joyce and Frank O'Connor, O'Faoláin imbues his work with a romantic idealism that is tempered by intense disillusionment with both Irish politics and the strict tenets of the Catholic church. Summarizing O'Faoláin's short stories, Bruce Allen observed that they reveal "a remarkably skillful and sophisticated technician who can render a small private world in such evocative, echoing detail that its universal relevance is instantly suggested."

Born in Cork, O'Faoláin was the son of parents loyal to the British government. For many years O'Faoláin shared his parents' political beliefs until, as an adolescent, he witnessed the Easter Rebellion of 1916. Abhorring the brutality of the British military, he soon aligned himself with the proponents of an independent Ireland. He studied Gaelic, altered his name to its Gaelic cognate form, and joined the Irish Volunteers, an organization that later produced some members of the militant Irish Republican Army (IRA). His subsequent experiences in the Irish revolution of 1919-21 and as director of publicity for the IRA during the Irish civil war intensified his patriotism. After the defeat of the IRA in 1923, O'Faoláin resolved to leave Ireland. He attended Harvard University and, while earning his master's degree in comparative philology, he began to write short stories based on his experiences and his disappointment with the IRA and its inability to achieve its ideals. He returned to Ireland in 1929 and established himself as a prominent literary and cultural critic. O'Faoláin enjoyed a long, distinguished career as a prolific author in several genres and as editor of the Irish literary journal *The Bell*. He died in 1991.

O'Faoláin's short fiction often reflects his disenchantment with Irish politics and the Catholic church, which he perceived as rigid and unforgiving. His early stories frequently deal with the effects of the Irish civil war on the country's people. "The Bombshop," for example, focuses on three IRA members who make bombs in a tiny apartment above a clothes shop owned by a kind, elderly woman named Mother Dale. Fearful of being discovered and frustrated with their confinement in a cramped space, the three rebels quarrel violently and exchange gunfire. When they discover that a stray bullet has hit and killed Mother Dale, the revolutionaries attempt to atone for their actions in a local church, but instead encounter a funeral service

in progress for another casualty of the insurrection. Critics praise the story for its poignant depiction of all the victims of the Irish civil war, regardless of their status as soldiers or civilians or their political affiliation. O'Faoláin's later stories depict interpersonal relationships and the effects of what he considered inflexible religious doctrines and social conventions on his characters' lives. In "A Born Genius," Pat Lenihan abandons a promising operatic career in New York City and returns to Ireland when he discovers his estranged father has committed bigamy. While attempting to resuscitate his singing career in Ireland, he is tormented by guilt over his desire for a married colleague. Fearing the eternal damnation that is accorded as punishment for adultery by Catholicism, he forsakes his operatic career to avoid succumbing to temptation and spends the rest of his life as a clerk in a vinegar factory. Critics cite Lenihan's unquestioning adherence to his religion, inability to forgive, and lack of tenacity as representative of O'Faoláin's own perception of the Irish temperament. Gordon Henderson has remarked that by focusing on his perception of Ireland's national character, O'Faoláin "took the short story as he received it from Maupassant and Chekhov and transformed it into something uniquely his own and uniquely Irish."

282

PRINCIPAL WORKS

SHORT FICTION

Midsummer Night Madness, and Other Stories   1932
A Purse of Coppers   1934
Teresa, and Other Stories   1947; also published as *The Man Who Invented Sin, and Other Stories,* 1948
The Finest Stories of Seán O'Faoláin   1957; also published as *The Stories of Seán O'Faoláin,* 1958
I Remember! I Remember!   1961
The Heat of the Sun   1966
The Talking Trees, and Other Stories   1971
Foreign Affairs   1976
The Collected Stories of Seán O'Faoláin   1983

OTHER MAJOR WORKS

A Nest of Simple Folk   (novel)   1934
Bird Alone   (novel)   1936
She Had to Do Something: A Comedy in Three Acts (drama)   1937
DeValera   (biography)   1939
Come Back to Erin   (novel)   1940
An Irish Journey   (travel)   1940
The Great O'Neill: A Biography of Hugh O'Neill, Earl of Tyrone, 1850-1916   (biography)   1942
The Short Story   (criticism)   1948
Vive Moi!   (autobiography)   1964

CRITICISM

John V. Kelleher   (essay date 1966)

[*In the following excerpt, Kelleher favorably reviews O'Faoláin's* The Heat of the Sun, *praising the collection's depth of meaning.*]

Seán O'Faoláin must have walked away from this job with more than one backward glance of satisfaction, or so I would guess from the tone of his new book. There are a couple of somber stories in *The Heat of the Sun,* and human pain and sorrow are present and accounted for, but over all there is an openness in the writing and a gaiety which, if by no means unprecedented in his work, are here sustained much longer and with greater ease than ever before. With greater dexterity, too. Like Yeats, the master at 66 is performing feats of agility and skill that would have been impossible to his less nimble youth. Hence, no doubt, the communicated exhilaration.

The best feat is the newly mastered tale. He has written single examples before, but here are a number in succession, all successful. In the foreword, he discusses how they differ from short stories. The story he compares to a kite, so difficult to get into the air, always tied to its base point, but capable of such color and play once it is up. The tale is like a small plane "that carries a bit more cargo, roves farther, has time and space for more complex character-

ization, more changes of mood, more incidents and scenes, even more plot." Though the reader may prefer the tale because it is less difficult, for the same reason it is less likely to give the writer pleasure.

He ought to know, but I wonder. O'Faoláin's short stories usually carry a lot more cargo than appears. They are loaded with meaning. Not the sort that is wired to a symbolic substructure removeable for classroom demonstration, but the kind that results from intense thinking and feeling and from fascinated observation of normal psychology with all its quirks and abysses. The meaning is inseparable from the style; it is pulled into the fabric, and you never know when or if you have got it all. As the years have gone by, he has had more and more of it to convey. As a result, a few of his kites have lumbered a bit. But these tales, every cranny freighted, fly like birds.

They are elegantly written, read delightfully, and are as clear as crystal. Or they are till you start thinking and go back for another try. Then you realize that that theme was not the only theme; there is also . . . For example, in the opening tale, **"In the Bosom of the Country,"** O'Faoláin is obviously dealing with male and female religions as they compounded and confused in the one church. But then there are also love, pity, marriage, honor, discipline, reason, endurance, and friendship (all mind you, also male and female and therefore full of mutual necessity and exasperation) and of course there are also lay and cleric, English and Irish, and Ireland itself. State the theme? The tale itself is the most economical possible statement, and every word of it is true.

There are 11 tales and stories in all, the whole flock airborne and darting about. (pp. 64-5)

> John V. Kelleher, "Irish Portraits," in The New York Times Book Review, *October 16, 1966, pp. 64-5.*

Maurice Harmon   (essay date 1966)

[*An Irish educator and critic, Harmon has written several critical studies on Irish authors and literature. In the following excerpt, he analyzes technical and thematic aspects of O'Faoláin's early short fiction.*]

The theme of self and society is clearly related to O'Faoláin's interest in the writer's struggle to achieve and maintain an equilibrium between his personality and his environment. His approach to the whole question of the artist and his world is an acknowledged reflection of Flaubert's statement that the secret of masterpieces lies in the concordance between the subject and the temperament of the author. A good short story, he believes, is produced by "punch" and "poetry," a combination of reality (plausibility) and the personal voltage of the writer that lights up the material in a distinctive, ultimately indefinable way [*The Short Story*]. His definition of personality is like that expressed by the priest in **"A Broken World"**:

> All we can do is to state a personal feeling that the distinctive mark of personality is harmony

in the internal art of the individual, the whole *compositum* as a Thomist would say, moving in a unity of being, with an undivided force of energy, towards its own ends.

The constant task of the writer, therefore, is to establish a rapprochement between himself and the circumstances that condition his life so that his literary personality may flourish intact.

The evidence that a particular sensibility has discovered a subject uniquely suited to itself is an important element in evaluating a story. O'Faoláin's view of the relationship between subject and temperament is that the writer imagines the subject into his own likeness. He can, therefore, very often be identified in relation to particular situations and types of character. Their presence defines the nature of the literary personality to which they have appealed and through which they have emerged as distinctive creations. A writer's work can be said to have imaginative integrity when it contains a pattern of recurrent situations and characters. It can be judged in the light of the nature and the quality of the particular view of life they express. Through them one may discern a writer's faith. "A faith," O'Faoláin explains [in his *The Vanishing Hero, Studies in Novelists of the Twenties*], "for literary purposes, means any feeling for life or any way of seeing life which is coherent, persistent, inclusive, and forceful enough to give organic form to the totality of a writer's work." *Purse of Coppers* treats the question of self and society in various ways and with a distinctive bias; failure and frustration are endemic. The response is predominantly negative: Lenihan in **"A Born Genius"** broods in defeat, totally unable to come to terms with the conditions that hamper his freedom; O'Sullivan in **"The Old Master"** chooses the escape route of phantasy and self-deception that lead to a *folie de grandeur*; Hanafan in **"Admiring the Scenery,"** the most rational and sensitive of the three, with the most balanced response to life, suffers from the knowledge that his environment cannot satisfy his imaginative needs. External marks of frustration prevail but the artist himself is not defeated. Out of the negative factors that appeal to him, and despite the general feeling of hopelessness, he continues to create ordered and disciplined work.

The successful manipulation of the self for an artistic purpose is primarily an internal struggle; it is discernible in the technical struggle through which the writer gains mastery over the methods of his forms. *Purse of Coppers* besides being an allegory of the internal struggle, is also a revelation of the development in technical skill; it shows the writer adjusting to his materials, seeing how they can reflect his environment and his own distinctive relation to it. The development is away from the romanticism of *Midsummer Night Madness,* from the overdescriptive to the concise, from an emphasis on the impact of the subject to a smoother, detached style. The ornamental and scientific use of detail is found in earlier stories in *Purse of Coppers*—**"My Son Austin," "A Born Genius,"** and even **"A Broken World"**—but O'Faoláin gets away from the naturalistic style. He prefers the kind of meaningful compression that allows the reader's imagination to dilate with suggestion. Thus instead of giving a full description of a character, he gives a few details that suggest the whole man. Weaker and earlier stories constantly exceed the limitations of the short story form; they try to include the perspective, scope, and relative casualness of the novel. From 1936 on, however, he faces up successfully to the limitations and the challenges of the shorter form. Stories such as **"Sinners," "Discord,"** and **"Admiring the Scenery"** are masterly in technique.

"Sinners" is controlled throughout by a disciplined dialogue that quietly and carefully represents the varying shades of feeling and thought emerging through the Canon's interrogation of the frightened servant girl in the confessional. Her employer has told him the girl has stolen a pair of boots, and he remembers he refused the girl absolution the previous Saturday because she did not seem sorry enough for being away from confession for five years. This foreknowledge complicates his approach, since he is bound under the *sigilium* not to make use of such information.

> "My poor child," he said, ever so gently, dutifully pretending to know nothing about her, "tell me how long it is since your last confession."
>
> "It's a long time, Father," she whispered.
>
> "How long?" To encourage her he added, "Over a year?"
>
> "Yes, Father."
>
> "How much? Tell me, my poor child, tell me. Two years?"
>
> "More, Father."
>
> "Three years?"
>
> "More, Father."
>
> "Well, well, you must tell me, you know."
>
> In spite of himself his voice was a little pettish. The title "Father" instead of "Canon" was annoying him, too. She noted the change of voice, for she said, hurriedly:
>
> " 'Tis that, Father."
>
> " 'Tis what?" asked the Canon a shade too loudly.

Descriptive material in this passage is minimal yet the dramatic interplay, kept in a minor key, shifts gradually and perceptibly. The Canon's losing battle for self-control and his well-meant intention undermined by his scrupulous conscience are balanced humorously against the increasing fear of the main. As his defenses weaken, hers strengthen. Later, leading her through the ten commandments, in growing irritation at his own stupidity for using this approach, he finally reaches an area of relative certainty:

> "Stealing?" prompted the Canon, and he waited for her to say that she had stolen Mrs. Higgin's boots.
>
> "I never in my life, Father, stole as much as the head off a pin. Except when I was small I once stole an apple in the nuns' orchard. And they

caught me and gave me a flaking. And they took the last bite out of my mouth."

"You never stole articles of dress?" threatened the Canon, and he suddenly realized that there were only three very unlikely commandments left. "Clothes? Hats? Gloves? Shoes?"

"Never, Father."

There was a long pause.

"Boots?" he whispered.

The opening paragraph of this story also shows the economical and oblique manner in which O'Faoláin now uses words:

> The Canon, barely glancing at his two penitents, entered the confessional. From inside he looked wearily across at the rows of penitents on each side of Father Deeley's box, all still as statues where they sat against the wall, or leaned forward to let the light of the single electric bulb, high up in the windy roof, fall on their prayer books. Deeley would give each about ten minutes, and that meant he would not absolve the last until near midnight. "More trouble with the sacristan," sighed the Canon, and closed the curtains and lifted his hand towards the slide of the grille.

This comes to terms at once with the situation. The main character is introduced and unobtrusively much of his character appears. There is the contrast between his curate's popularity ("rows of penitents") and his own lack of appeal ("two penitents"). There is the fact that he notices it and that it has an effect on him ("barely glancing . . . looked wearily across"). There is the suggestion of lack of electrical fittings and the implication that the Canon is economizing on small things. His petulance appears in his reflection on the length of time Father Deeley gives to each penitent and implies his own mechanical nature, which favors efficient frugality rather than time-consuming human contact and sympathy. Characteristically, he sees people as statues, a point of view that reflects his own inability to attain life. Weariness, petulance, defeat, a concentration on trivial rules and regulations, all these prepare us for his failure in the confessional, for his authoritarianism, his irritation, his vanity, his misunderstanding, his cruelty, his disgust with human nature that will not fit in with his suppositions.

"Discord" resembles **"Admiring the Scenery"** in that it is a meeting of three characters who do not form a background for each other. Two young people on their honeymoon in Dublin visit a priest. His laughter and enjoyment are incongruous against the background of slums, broken lives, madness, and death that surrounds his life. Basically, he wants a quiet parish in the country. However, custom has diminished the ugliness of his familiar inferno but for the lovers the descent into the underground crypt leads them uncomfortably close to the knowledge of death and age for which they are altogether unprepared. The story is developed through juxtaposition of these contrasting attitudes.

. . . Suddenly they saw a wild-bearded, hollow-faced man standing away back in the nave, praying devoutly. His beard was soft but tangled; his hair was to his shoulders; he held his two arms aloft as he prayed; his eyes shone. Curiously they watched him, a little frightened.

"Who is he?" asked the girl of the priest.

"He's daft," whispered the priest. "An ex-soldier. He sometimes preaches to the empty church. Come this way."

"He'd terrify me," said the girl.

Peter laughed again as he led them down another flight of stairs through an old trap door.

. . . Somehow, since they had met the priest, several years had been added to both of them. They had come upon one of those moments of life when, like the winter butterflies in the high corners, they felt the hurt of cold. Breezily the priest returned, coated, buttoned, slapping his hands.

"Admiring the Scenery" is perhaps the most successful of these stories from O'Faoláin's point of view, since it combines a gentle, poetic atmosphere with a realistic or plausible situation. It represents the emergence of a balanced approach made up of a realistic use of detail and a romantic sensibility. The revelation of character is carried out by an unconscious unmasking of the narrator, Hanafan, by himself. The familiar device of the story within a story is presented with a skillful juxtaposition of present and past, or outer story and inner story, so that the setting, the responses it produces, the characterization, and the themes fuse and correspond. The setting of the outer story, the beautiful evening, is similar to the setting of the inner story, the beautiful night. Hanafan, responding to the present scene, sets out to relate the loneliness of the stationmaster on the former occasion and how this was momentarily transcended; at the same time, Hanafan reveals his own loneliness and the dissimilarity of the present occasion; the inability of these three people to form a background for each other heightens the sadness. On both occasions Hanafan quotes poetry: on the present, the first two stanzas of Gray's "Elegy in a Country Churchyard;" on the former, a section from Sir Thomas Browne's "The quincunx of heaven runs low and 'tis time to close the five ports of knowledge. . . ." The contrast here also relates to the different emotions aroused by the two scenes. The elegiac tone of Gray's poem, its weariness and regret, contrasts subtly with the wonder and imaginative delight of the Browne passage and sets off the two occasions exactly.

This contrast is also made in the description of the setting; the present scene, "before sunset in early spring, a soft evening of evaporating moisture and tentative bird song;" the former, "one hard, moonlight night in December. . . . The snow was white on the hills. It was blazing. . . . A deep, rich night, and no harm in the winds, but they puffing and blowing." Both descriptions set the mood for the occasion: the softer gentler tone for the present, its tentative quality; the harder, more joyous quality of the former, its successful integration of personality and mood. The act of admiring the scenery is not an intellectual one, not a projection of the idea of the beauty into one's consciousness. It is, as Hanafan shows by his narrative and his own behavior, an emotional, sensory response. The mood of the story is muted and soft, a reflection of the evening. The communication of a distinct personality subsumes the whole work so that the relationship between the punch and the poetry is evenly and effectively maintained.

The emphasis in **Purse of Coppers** moves away from the social context and centers on human nature instead. **"Admiring the Scenery"** and **"Discord"** illustrate this change. This shift in perspective becomes more evident in later stories and indicates an increasing ability of the author to separate his reactions to uncongenial circumstances from his literary activity. A greater detachment is the reward of such self-discipline, and it is surprising to find an author who is capable of much polemical writing and much hard social commentary becoming so gentle. His sensitivity to the context of human behavior, his warm sympathy for his own people and his understanding of the conditions of their lives predominate.

His understanding of the technical aspects of the short story developed rapidly after 1936. It may have been that his growing realization of the difficulty of handling his material in the novel form led him to regard the shorter length with more interest and a more critical awareness of its techniques. His first writings on the short story appeared in *The Bell* (1944) and were later expanded and incorporated into *The Short Story*. In this work he formulates some of the theories that are evident in his writings. He understands, for example, the function of conventions and the various ways in which writers try to make fiction seem plausible: the device of the preamble in which the writer tells how he came into possession of the facts; the device of the first person narrative, overused by O'Faoláin in the early stories in **Purse of Coppers.** Maupassant, as O'Faoláin points out, had shown how these various introductory remarks and other references to time, place, or occasion could be avoided simply by coming to terms with the situation. Later stories in **Purse of Coppers** consistently avoid the elaborate introductory approach. *The Short Story* also comments on the kind of technique favored by Chekhov, which had been influential in improving the quality of these later stories. This is the method of informing by suggestion or implication, the most important of the shorthand conventions used by modern short story writers. It makes for compression and for the pleasure of discovery and imaginative dilation. The excitement of this genre lies in its compression. The writer searches for language that will suggest; he avoids excessive detail and prefers implication to explanation.

In **"Discord,"** for example, the young lovers have come to visit Father Peter. "Always awkward with the newly wedded, he had led them straight to the window immediately [when] they entered the room," and there "his black arm pointing between their heads, led their eyes over the aerial plain." The discord between the young people and the priest is introduced here with slight touches: the black arm dividing them, the phrase "led their eyes" suggesting compulsion and restraint, and the repetition of the word "led" reinforcing the idea of mutual uncertainty and embarrassment. These imply the character of the priest. All his subsequent cheeriness does not overcome this initial insecuri-

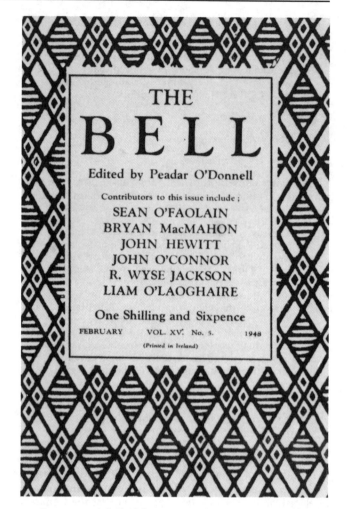

Front cover of the Irish literary journal founded by O'Faoláin.

ty, and the sense of a forced situation—forced cheeriness, forced kindness—becomes increasingly evident until the image of discord is inclusive of a whole way of life and the character of the man. His compulsive pattern of speech and behavior signifies an attempt to survive, to retain individuality, amid the misery and decay, the sin and frustration, the loneliness and compression of his life. His natural good nature has been corroded by his environment, but the lovers neither understand nor want to understand the tragic nature of their friend; they dismiss him as a comic caricature and, like the lovers in **"The Patriot,"** seek for happiness and forgetfulness in love.

O'Faoláin's stories after 1936 are full of gentle, humorous scenes in which character is revealed against a careful counterpoint of idea and imagery. His very personal fusion of realistic observation with romantic sensibility is expressed in this method. In **"Teresa"** the two nuns are returning from an unsuccessful pilgrimage to Lisieux. Teresa, the young postulant, has discovered that she is unfitted for the hardship of her order but now in the presence of her comfortable, chocolate-chewing companion and looking across at the worldly delights of Dinard she announces a new decision. The intense feelings of the older nun are reflected by the sounds and movements of the waves, by her controlled whisper, by her tightly shut eyes, and by her final exclamation:

> "I have decided to join the Carmelites," said the novice.

> They halted. They looked across the sea wall into the blue of Dinard. A few lights were already springing up over there—the first dots in the long golden necklet that already they had come to know so well. A lone sea gull squawked over the glassy water. The sunset behind the blue pinnacles of the resort was russet.

> "And what's wrong with our own order, Sister dear?" asked Patrick of the vacancy before her.

> "I feel, dear Sister Patrick," judged the novice staring ahead of her, "that it is too worldly."

> "How is it too worldly?" asked Patrick in a whisper.

> "Well, dear Sister Patrick," pronounced the novice, "I see, for example, that you all eat too much." The little wavelets fell almost inaudibly, drunken with the fullness of the tide, exhausted and soothed by their own completion.

> "I shall tell Mother Mary Mell that you think so," whispered the old nun.

> "There is no need, dear Sister, it will be my duty to tell her myself. I will pray for you all when I am in the Carmelites. I love you all. You are all kind and generous. But, dear Sister, I feel that very few nuns really have the right vocation to be nuns." Patrick closed her eyes tightly. The novice continued: "I will surrender to the divine love. The death I desire is the death of Love. The death of the Cross."

> They heard only the baby tongues of the waves. The evening star blazed in the russet sky. The old nun saw it, and she said, in part a statement, in part a prayer, in part a retort:

> "Sweet Star of the Sea!"

The ironies here are almost too subtle to explain: the worldly shallow Teresa; the good-natured, disciplined old nun; the parable of the gay life across the water; the religious connotations of the evening star; the too polite manner of address; the natural calm of the ocean and the beauty of nature contrasted with the enforced restraint of the old nun and her charity in the face of attack; the clichés of the young nun's adolescent religious intentions associated with the baby tongues of the waves and the final triumph of the old nun over her silent inner conflict, her struggle for self-control associated with the blaze, the purity, and the radiance of the symbolic star. Over all O'Faoláin moves with a gentle, warm, and compassionate understanding, controlling the emotional nuances, expressing the growth of shades of feeling and decision, sure of his judgment which he reveals implicitly. In such sequences his technical mastery is superb; situation and construction merge into a single movement.

The Short Story also discusses the conventions by which writers suggest that the endings are not disjunctions but continuities; they seek to provide an illusion of permanence. There are a number of ways in which this can be done; O'Faoláin makes use of at least three. There is the poetic ending that floats the narrative into a "poetic" continuity of place whose image remains after the conclusion:

> The dawn moved along the rim of the mountains and as I went down the hill I felt the new day come up around me and life begin once more its ancient, ceaseless gyre.

The last sentence of **"Sinners"** leaves a similar impression of place: "He turned towards the dark presbytery deep among the darkest lanes." Such a conclusion corresponds also to those endings which merge the episode into a general moral picture. In **"The Old Master"** John Aloysius has been treated as a figure of amusement to his contemporaries, but the final sentence places his activities and their response to them in a moral perspective. For, as O'Faoláin writes, it was only after his death that people began to think of him as a human being. "I wonder," he adds, "is there any wrong or right in that? Or is it, as John would have said, that one kind of life is just the same as another in the end?"

> **The varied nature of O'Faoláin's stories attest to his artistry; he knows when to follow the principles he has learned and when to modify them to suit the requirements of a particular story.**
>
> **—Maurice Harmon**

Most modern writers, he observes, do not use such easy or obvious devices. Chekhov was able to invoke the "poetic" mood of place and to imply a general moral or idea, but he also developed the method of using transitions from one tense to another to suggest life going on as before, from the past to the present with the suggestion of continuity in the future. Even as early as **"A Broken World"** O'Faoláin had absorbed this practice:

> The train could be heard easily, in the rarefied air, chugging across the bridges that span the city, bearing with it an empty coach. In the morning, Ireland, under its snow, would be silent as a perpetual dawn.

But he is not tied by such conventions. Modern writers do not always take care to provide a sense of continuity. As the short story form has become more widely read the conventions have needed less and less concealment. For not only does the reader share knowledge of these devices with the writer but also by tacit agreement he suppresses it, or some of it, and the writer relies on the sophistication and intelligence of the reader, his sensitivity to suggestion and implication, his ability to distinguish nuances of observation and revelation. "Every writer appeals therefore to a complex mass of emotions, of sensory experiences, of accepted, or acceptable ideas whose existence he presumes." As a result, writers often make no effort to save the story from a sense of disjunction; many of O'Faoláin's good stories are like this, **"The Fur Coat,"** for example. But the ability of modern writers to be so free may be a result of the older conventions remaining implicit: "That 'so it goes on' (though there is now no need to say so); or that it is a moral tale, or a comment (though now there is no need to be explicit about it); or that it is 'typical', i.e. that it is a tale of, perhaps Java or Italy, but that it is a microcosm of everywhere" [*The Short Story*].

Characterization, O'Faoláin also observes, can be no more than assumed in a short story; there is no time for development, no time for unnecessary details or elaborate description. In place of detailed characterization there may be a situation that expresses character or temperament; or conversation that reveals it; or gesture that expresses it. Thus **"The Fur Coat"** expresses the natural human desire of a woman for some luxury in a life that has been full of privation and her consequent inability to accept the luxury without guilty feelings. **"The Trout"** uses the discovery of the fish in the dark and terrifying wood to express the young girl's transcendence of childish fears and her first radiant discovery of courage. **"Sinners"** and **"Teresa"** are examples of the controlled use of dialogue to reveal character. In **"The End of a Good Man"** Larry Dunne shoots his favorite but intractable pigeon and in that gesture expresses his anguish and hurt pride. In **"Childybawn"** Benjy goes back to Angela and becomes engaged but then keeps her waiting five more years until his mother dies, thereby expressing his lasting failure of human sympathy and his deeply rooted selfishness.

The Short Story gives some indication of the technical aspects of O'Faoláin's work. In practice he was able to exceed or surpass many of these principles. His best early stories tend to follow a concise, restrained, and economical manner as in **"Admiring the Scenery"** or **"Discord."** But many of his later ones, **"One True Friend," "The Silence of the Valley," "Childybawn,"** or **"Lovers of the Lake,"** extend far beyond the limitations of form and method outlined in this book. The varied nature of his stories as a whole, their tendency to go beyond his own principles of conciseness and lack of full characterization, their ability to dilate into philosophical, moral, and social considerations, and their lack of similarity in length may indicate that he has never found any particular scale within which to express himself completely. But they also attest to his artistry; he knows when to follow the principles he has learned and when to modify them to suit the requirements of a particular story. (pp. 81-92)

· · · · ·

[O'Faoláin's] work now shows his achievement of an inner harmony in the face of external circumstances. Many stories in *I Remember! I Remember!* (1961) show a concordance between the subject and the temperament of the author. They are the work of a mature, complex, and extraordinarily subtle personality. In manner and development, in delicacy of mood and feeling, in their wise understanding of human nature, they represent further refinement of feeling in O'Faoláin and a more sophisticated control of emotion. To match this subtlety he has worked out

a new technique. Depending on understatement and on meaning achieved through an interrelation of elements within the story, a resonance of moods, images, and incidents, they are the result of an exact and deliberate kind of writing. Every good short story, he has written in his perceptive and germinal commentaries in *Short Stories, A Study in Pleasure* (1961), has some bright destination, and every step into the story must lead towards its point of illumination.

These later stories are linked thematically with **"Lovers of the Lake"** and the preceding satires and comedies. O'Faoláin's growing respect for the deeper psychological experiences of his characters causes him to concentrate now on the universal themes of time and change, the impermanence of youth and age, and the accommodations of middle age. He leads his characters to a realization of the transitory quality of life and measures the value of individual endeavor within the perspective of man's littleness in an immense world. There is a sad awareness of the price paid for growth, for the individual's response to the challenge of life, his submission to the fate within his own character. One of the characters in **"One Night in Turin"** reflects on this complex idea:

> "We make happiness easily when we are young, because we are full of dreams, and ideals, and visions, and courage. We make our own world that pushes away the other world. . . . But you know what happens to us. That little flame in us that could burn up the world when we're young—we sell a bit of it here, and a bit of it there, until, in the end, we haven't as much of it left in us as would light a cigarette." "And yet," she said, frowning through him, "it is there, to the end. You always feel you might blow on it, make it big again, go on to the very end, without giving up, find the thing, discover the thing, invent the thing, call it anything you like, that you'd always been wanting."

The sadness comes from the idea that merely to live is to suffer or to cause suffering in others. All progress is made at the expense of loss either in one's self or in others, and it is the recognition of that truth that is at the heart of these stories.

One of the most valuable achievements of *I Remember! I Remember!* is the creation of a distinctive and perfectly suited voice through which the stories move to their moment of sad truth. It is comfortingly friendly and open, moving along the surface of the story in a deceptively artless and casual manner. Even the style seems uncontrived and flowing; it appeals to the ear. Upon examination, however, it shows deliberate craft in its balance of elements within the sentence and the paragraph. But it suits the narrator in its unhurried pace, its pausing for small and apparently irrelevant ideas and feelings; essentially it is his conversational manner, so that style and character are one.

The new voice makes for flexibility of approach; it brings in the omniscient author under the disguise of the trustworthy voice that deals maturely and tolerantly, in a gentle and wise manner, with its subject. We are made happily aware that it will make no uncomfortable demands upon us. There is no trace of the haunted, compulsive manner, the reforming zeal, or the apocalyptic tone. We feel relaxed, soothed by the voice. It is a fine achievement, because once we have submitted to its grace and friendliness, its exquisite courtesy, we are in its power. The opening paragraph of **"A Touch of Autumn"** illustrates some of these comments on style and manner:

> It was, of all people, Daniel Cashen of Roscommon who first made me realize that the fragments of any experience that remain in a man's memory, like bits and scraps of a ruined temple, are preserved from time not at random but by the inmost desires of his personality.

The relaxation in mood and manner is partly the result of O'Faoláin's detachment, almost an indifference, from the Irish scene. But he is still interested in the subject of frustration. "I am concerned," he has said recently, "about the freedom of the individual in an environment which is very often constricting to him. I'm interested in the growth of the personality within the individual creature" ["On Writing: An Interview," *Mademoiselle* 56, 1963]. Each of the stories in *I Remember! I Remember!* is a reflection of that concern. The approach is different but the subject is essentially the same as in his earlier books. His characters are no longer caught within the web of social, political, or religious conflicts; they are not usually struggling either to overcome the particular deficiencies of a particular society nor revealing in the ambivalent, contradictory manner of their lives the unsettled state of Irish society. The restricting factors now are internal and an inescapable part of every man. Individuals are seen now as the victims of their own nature. The stories gain in universality by being released from the local pressures of an Irish setting. But there is a loss in amplification; the stories no longer express a whole generation and a whole society. They forfeit this distinctive intensity of dilation. The context of human endeavor is defined now in the light of the limitations of opportunity and choice that attend any man's growth. It is the realization of these limitations, as it strikes various characters, that they seek to present.

The basic technique used to bring about this realization is contrast; by reflecting on past events and becoming aware of change, characters gain insight into their own lives and their own natures. The general philosophical truths that emerge come from the exploration of small, seemingly trivial incidents. By analogy and association one is led to consider universal aspects of human existence. Such a result is a tribute to the craft of these stories as well as to the validity of their content. The short story justifies itself as a distinctive genre because of its ability to derive insights of this nature from limited material.

> What usually happens is that the situation explodes or dissolves, as a result of some simple trigger-incident, when out of human tension between those two or three people, the main character breaks through to some sort of truth-to-self, or truth-about-self, which had up to then been hidden from him, or which he had weakly or stupidly dodged. [*Short Stories, A Study in Pleasure*].

"A Touch of Autumn in the Air" is a good example of

O'Faoláin's methods. There is the casual manner and the device of the engaging narrator. There is the surprise in having the basic truth revealed unconsciously by Daniel Cashen. That truth is that the things we remember are indicative of the inmost desires of the personality. In his old age Daniel Cashen finds himself remembering incidents from an autumn vacation spent as a boy on a farm with Kitty Bergin, his sweetheart cousin. The images that have remained are ones that gave him in the past a feeling of human littleness. Now they return to undermine his confidence and cause him to question the value of his life as a businessman. It is the manner in which these effects are created that gives this story its vitality. Little is explicitly stated but much is suggested and implied. Through contrasts in images, incidents, situations, and characters the central effect is achieved. In isolation no single image, or incident, or character would cause the moment of realization.

In the manner of a character in a novel by Conrad and for a similar psychological reason Daniel Cashen does not go directly to the main memory. Nevertheless all relates to the emergent idea that he had as a boy an intuitive recognition of his own smallness. He remembers an afternoon when he watched a river flowing and a time when he saw men standing in a river, ducking a protesting boy and laughing at his screams. In both cases the flow of time is present in the water and the sense of human generations passing while natural objects remain. Attendant images support the general effect: soft, surrounding fields, clouds moving slowly, and the silence of the silence of the countryside. Space and silence, the vastness of the land, the mysterious forces of nature, all speak to the small boy. In his major memory Daniel Cashen describes going with Kitty Bergin from his aunt's warm cottage "one sunny, mistified October morning" to the men in the fields. Again there is the vast, level plain, the flat river basin, and two men shrunken under a vast sky.

As well as being haunted by such sensory impressions of his lost boyhood, Daniel Cashen's memory also contains the idea of growth and separation. This time it is an incident that becomes suggestive. The children bring two letters to the men in the fields. Two sons have left home; one works in the mines at Castlecomer, the other is studying for the priesthood in Dublin. When the father reads their letters it is clear that the sons have gone beyond his experience of life. That estrangement and loss, which affects both the children and the parents, is present also in the account the son in Dublin gives of visiting a convent to see a local girl: "Saint Joachim's has nice grounds, but the trams pass outside the wall and she said that for the first couple of weeks she could hardly sleep at all." Her loneliness in the unfamiliar city is made more sad by the impression that the men never cared much for the girl anyway and so have little sympathy or understanding of her situation now.

Loneliness, separation, growth and change, the drift from the rural background, the individual response to life, all reflect on Daniel Cashen's own life. The feelings and ideas evoked by the account of the men's response to the letters are similar to our understanding of and response to his present state; they express his condition. Now as an old man he remembers the warm, sensory pleasures of that morning, its sense of security and peace, its evidence of a traditional way of life, and at the same time he remembers the feeling of disruption and change that the morning brought. Its moments of joy and its promise of love and happiness are further indications of this complex effect. Kitty Bergin was his girl, they shared the pleasures of that vacation, she wrestled with him in the field, she also pretended to be a nun and he felt the touch of impending loss. But they jogged home together in the cart, and even then the migratory geese and the autumn moon provided an overtone of sadness:

> As they ambled along so, slowly, chatting and chewing, the donkey's hooves whispering through the fallen beech leaves, they heard high above the bare arches of the trees the faint honking of the wild geese called down from the north by the October moon.

It is a beautiful story. Daniel Cashen's discovery of what he has sacrificed comes gradually and tangentially through these lucid and luminous impressions. Self-made, rich, hardheaded, and surrounded by concrete evidence of his success as a businessman, he is perplexed by a few images of a youthful time, a girl he never married, and a peaceful, patriarchal way of life. He is teased into the idea that perhaps he has bartered too much of that warm, simple life for worldly success. His last, revealingly pathetic act is to leave his money to his cousins on that childhood farm. The title story is also concerned with memory and with the concept of loss as inseparable from growth. It announces its theme in the first sentence: "I believe that in every decisive moment of our lives the spur to action comes from that part of the memory where desire lies dozing, awaiting the call to arms." The setting is the little Irish town of Ardagh, where Sarah Cotter lives. She is a plain, kindly, innocent creature who has been confined to an invalid chair since the age of eleven. She is distinguished by a phenomenally retentive memory but has to depend on what others tell her and on what she reads for her information. Twice a year her sister Mary comes, a lively, travelled, and experienced girl who is married to a Continental buyer for a New York store. She and her husband alternate between New York and Switzerland, where they have a small house and where their children go to school. Mary, however, has never told Sarah she passes through Shannon Airport about six times a year. Sarah thinks she goes to Europe twice and visits Ardagh each time. At the end of the story Mary lies even more and tells Sarah her husband is sick, that she will not be travelling back and forth to Europe, but that she will come to visit Sarah "lots of times."

Told in that blunt way it is a cruel story in which Mary's abandonment of Sarah seems selfish and thoughtless. But it is not presented in such a harsh manner. Mary leaves to protect herself from the blinding accuracy of Sarah's memory. What Sarah remembers is the factual record of what Mary or someone else has told her. There is no feeling in it, no life. It is a contradiction and a denial of memory as Mary experiences it. Incidents remembered from the past and told to Sarah by Mary have a warm romantic

glow about them. But when Sarah speaks of the same incidents the glow of feeling is lost. The result is a distortion, as Mary complains:

> "I told her the bones and all she has of anything now is the bones. I can't remember the bones. All I have is the feeling I had at the time. Or else I can't remember at all."

Sarah's indelibly factual recollection is therefore an assault on Mary's own remembrance of things past, and in the conflict between fact and feeling, fact invariably triumphs. It is to escape the defeat of her own memories that Mary is forced to leave Sarah and to discontinue her visits. Sarah's memory is a vault in which the happiness of youth, her girlish escapades, her glorified memory of a man friend are all immured.

Furthermore, after twelve years of marriage Mary needs her memories and cannot afford to have them taken away or exposed as inaccurate. There are many hints of personal troubles: her husband does not love and admire her as he did; she has suffered because of another man; she has had to leave the gentle, unhurried way of life in Ardagh for the elegance, the sophistication, and the acquired pleasures of America and Europe. With the passing of time her sense of estrangement is stronger. All she has are the feelings recaptured from her youth. If she cannot be allowed their consoling warmth she is diminished. Therefore, against her deepest instincts, she decides to leave; it is an inevitable decision to which everything in the story leads. The separation of the sisters has been apparent in many small ways: in the earlier lies about Mary's life in Europe; in the thrust and parry of their conversation in which Mary tries to protect herself from Sarah's sharp memory; and in the simple fact that Mary finds it increasingly difficult to keep up with Sarah's conversation about local people and local issues. But it is a decision made and revealed in the story in the light of many extenuating and explanatory circumstances. Central to it is the fact that to possess herself Mary has to keep her memory intact and that to survive she has to hurt Sarah. That abandonment is saved from cruelty by our awareness of her attachment to the scenes of her childhood, her need for their warm, deceiving comfort. Again it is not a matter of direct statement but of inference:

> The Franciscan belfry was reflected in an islanded pool among the gravel at the bend of the river, and in the pool a sweep of yellow from the far hills that rose to the farthest mountains over whose rounded backs the sailing clouds had long ago seemed so often to call her to come away. Today the clouds were one solid, frozen mass, tomblike, and she could not tell if they moved at all.

Such indirect effects are not dominant in O'Faoláin's recent collection, *The Heat of the Sun, Stories and Tales*. They play a smaller part, because the tale, the main genre in this book, allows more time and space for character development, for a succession and variety of incidents, for descriptive passages, for reflections, for many moods, and even for plot. Since effects are created on a broad scale, there is less reliance on compression and suggestibility.

Fluctuations of emotion and decision form the rhythmic pattern of these stories. And whereas in the previous collection O'Faoláin had been sadly, sometimes subjectively, often tenderly, concerned with man's liability to err, to suffer, and to be self-deceived, he is now mainly amused. Ironic contrasts and reversals reveal complications and lead to insight. But the way is luminous and the tone is dry. (pp. 129-136)

> *Maurice Harmon, in his* Seán O'Faoláin: A Critical Introduction, *University of Notre Dame Press, 1966, 221 p.*

John W. Hughes (essay date 1971)

[*In the following review of* The Talking Trees, and Other Stories, *Hughes discusses O'Faoláin's perceptions of Ireland.*]

Seán O'Faoláin has constructed another Daedalean maze, and we must now decide whether that elusive Minotaur, the chaotic conscience of the Irish race, has been caught within the entanglements of his prose. O'Faoláin describes an Ireland where some of the younger priests read Simone de Beauvoir, where the leap from feudalism into modern industrial society is finally becoming an actuality, and where sex is no longer the unspeakable area of life that it was in the pre-Leopold Bloom days. It's all the more striking, therefore, to find a mood of "spiritual paralysis" hovering over *The Talking Trees*—the same kind of paralysis that James Joyce discerned in the Dublin of seventy years ago.

In each of these stories O'Faoláin probes for the frustrations and conflicts lurking beneath the bland discontents of contemporary Ireland. In **"Of Sanctity and Whiskey"** a painter named Luke Regan returns to his old college, St. Killian's, to paint the portrait of one of his former teachers. Brother Hilary Harty, who has since become head of the college, welcomes Luke with open arms (this is, you must remember, an up-to-date Ireland where artists are supposedly cherished). But the portrait of Brother Hilary that gradually emerges is not what Luke or his ecclesiastical employers expected, for the buried anger and pain in the artist's memory begin to guide the movements of his brush. The face on the canvas starts to resemble that of a beast, and for good reason: Luke suddenly remembers the savage beatings that Brother Hilary would inflict upon students who weren't able to reel off the parts of speech in their proper order. Luke's alcoholic self-destruction, and the burning of his painting by a puritanical Anglo-Irish shrew, give an appropriately apocalyptic conclusion to this parable about the fate of the Irish artist.

"Brainsy" and **"Feed My Lambs"** contain similar treatments of the "priest-ridden" Irish soul, although in each of these stories the victims are themselves members of the clergy. Brainsy is a saintlike genius of a brother who is removed from the classroom by his conformist superiors and given the permanent assignment of plucking weeds in the vegetable garden. Such is the fate of a saint in what used to be called "The Island of Saints and Sages." **"Feed My Lambs"** is a subtle Chekhovian story about a young priest who becomes sexually attracted to a married woman. Spiritual paralysis descends like a wet blanket from heaven, and prevents the priest from getting any further than a kiss.

O'Faoláin's sense of the absurd and the grotesque is almost Beckett-like in these stories, and it keeps him from succumbing to the wispy sentimentality that mars a great deal of his previous fiction. **"Of Sanctity and Whiskey"** is probably the best story in this collection precisely because O'Faoláin projects onto Luke Regan what he fears to be the destiny of any writer who tells the unvarnished truth about the Emerald Isle. O'Faoláin has often criticized the Flaubert-Joyce tradition of "naturalism," but each of the stories I have mentioned succeeds by contrasting the grotesque reality of Irish repressiveness with the humorous Gaelic sentimentality that has so often served to blot it out.

O'Faoláin descends from a long line of Irish satirists, and when things get too sticky for his satire—when passion or death enters the picture—he regresses into the giddy provincialism that can be heard any evening in the pubs of Dublin or in the bars on Third Avenue.

—*John W. Hughes*

"Hymeneal" is an example of O'Faoláin's tendency to wrap a protective layer of sentiment around some of his characters. Phil Doyle, a sterile bureaucrat, retires from his post as Inspector of Schools and decides to withdraw to a cottage in a barren area of County Clare. He hopes to write a book about his career, but the seclusion that Phil finds so attractive has the opposite effect on his vivacious wife, Abby. She is about to go bonkers from all the peace and quiet when they learn that Phil's old friend Failey has been killed in a car crash. They hurry off to Dublin, where Phil discovers that Failey had been Abby's lover before their marriage. As in Joyce's "The Dead," the husband is chastened by the knowledge of his wife's secret love.

But O'Faoláin repeats the mistake of some of his earlier stories: he tries to rewrite Joyce with a happy ending. For as **"Hymeneal"** draws to an overly extended close, a veil of Irish mist begins to surround the stark outlines of Phil's selfish and wasted existence. O'Faoláin, disguised as Phil, enters the story and begins to meditate on St. Martin and the theme of rebirth. The tale ends on a note of dreary optimism that conflicts with the basic thrust of the action. It would almost seem that the author has imposed the Christian rebirth theme upon his character in order to conceal the tragic implications (Luke Regan again) of what he has written.

"The Planets of the Years" is a successful story (up until the turgidly lyrical ending) because the memories of an Irishwoman who has spent her life working in America as a domestic servant are evoked so poignantly:

"Slieve Callan," she murmured, and I saw its whiteness rising like music under the low clouds moving imperceptibly from twenty miles away across the wrinkled Shannon. . . .

The timeless loveliness of Ireland is set off against the woman's slavish existence, and O'Faoláin achieves a perfect fusion of the Chekhovian flashback and the Flaubertian *mot juste*. But O'Faoláin often fails to keep his eye on the object; his mastery of plot is frequently accompanied by a stylistic pseudo-lyricism, a kind of Celtic Mannerism that trivializes the perceptions and fantasies and dialogue of his characters.

" **'Our Fearful Innocence'** " skirts cautiously around the themes of adultery and romanticism, and eventually gets lost amidst the mushy bogs of this Celtic Mannerism:

I loved to visit them on nights when the east wind rattled their windows or blew white spindrift across the water, nights when the three of us would sit before the fire and drink a jorum, and have long wandering arguments about the craziest things. . . .

The narrator, an engineer, is such a mild-mannered fellow that he tends to romanticize his adulterous desire for his friend's wife, who is herself an incurable romantic. Her death from leukemia only serves to compound the mystery of their fearful innocence, and the story concludes on a note of eerie nature-mysticism that reminds one unhappily of the Celtic Twilight. O'Faoláin has been a progressive force in Ireland over the last thirty years, and it's out of character for him to set up such a simplistic dichotomy between progress and tradition. He has long understood, as did Joyce before him, that Yeats's élitist primitivism (which was only a part of the total Yeats) could (and did) lead into a fascist chauvinism, and it's difficult to understand why " **'Our Fearful Innocence'** " is so wrongheaded about the relationship between innocence, romanticism, and evil.

O'Faoláin descends from a long line of Irish satirists, and when things get too sticky for his satire—when passion or death enters the picture—he regresses into the giddy provincialism that can be heard any evening in the pubs of Dublin or in the bars on Third Avenue. O'Faoláin shows the true nature of this provincialism in **"Thieves,"** where a cruel anti-Semitism intrudes upon a quiet Easter Sunday morning in the city of Cork. It is certainly brave of the author to mention this unsavory aspect of a society that is supposed to be founded on the Semitic idea of loving one's neighbor. But the reader may wonder why the glee of the little girls who witness it is allowed to divert our attention from the ugly underside of Irish Catholicism that has just been exposed. Or is this childish glee just another manifestation of those hidden forces?

Seán O'Faoláin has brought courage and skill to the making of these stories, but the resolution of such problems is beyond his imaginative grasp. One is forced to conclude that the Irish Minotaur—the old sow who devours her farrow in more ways than one—has, in this case, escaped from the Daedalean labyrinth. (pp. 30-1)

John W. Hughes, in a review of "The Talking

Trees, and Other Stories," in The Saturday Review, *New York, Vol. LIV, No. 6, February 6, 1971, pp. 30-1.*

Katherine Hanley   (essay date 1971)

[*In the following essay, Hanley traces O'Faoláin's evolution as a short fiction writer through an analysis of "A Meeting," "Passions," and "A Touch of Autumn in the Air."*]

Seán O'Faoláin's fondness for the short story—even were it not evident in his collections—is continually repeated in his autobiographical and critical works. He is candid about its demands, enthusiastic about its possibilities, and always alert for its raw material. One of the best introductions to O'Faoláin's opinions on the short story form is the preface to **The Heat of the Sun,** his 1963 collection, in which he differentiates between story, tale, and novel. A short story, he says:

is like a child's kite, a small wonder, a brief, bright moment. It has its limitations; there are things it can do and cannot do, but, if it is good, it moves in the same elements as the largest work of art—up there, airborne. The main thing a writer of a short story wants to do is to get it off the ground as quickly as possible, hold it there, taut and tense, playing it like a fish. The reader will never know how much time was spent on getting it airborne, how often it flopped, stumbled and dragged along the ground in all those first efforts, those discarded first drafts, those false beginnings, that were cut out once it was up—so much dismissed, forgotten but necessary labour. The limits of the Short Story are apparent. It may not wander far; it has to keep close to its base-point, within the bounds of place, time, and character; it will only carry a few characters, three at least, at best not more than three; there is not time or space, for elaborate characterisation . . . and there is often no plot, nothing more than a situation, and only just enough of that to release a moment or two of drama, enough to let the wilful kite swirl, change colour, catching the winds of mood.

So the short story writer, for O'Faoláin, must have an unusually keen sensitivity to ideas, an ability to snatch the one small thing and make it work. There is no room for loose writing and no quarter for the conventional and the tried; too much is at stake. The writing is hard work; no believer in frenzied inspiration, O'Faoláin remarks that "half the art of writing is rewriting" ["Looking Back at Writing," *Atlantic,* CXCVIII, December 1956]. Neither is the finished story to be regarded as an automatic success: "stories, like whiskey, must be allowed to mature in the cask."

Speaking of his own work, O'Faoláin is equally direct and only occasionally tongue-in-cheek. [In his *The Short Story*] he has said of the genre that it is "an emphatically personal exposition," and his own stories, particularly the early ones, appear to bear this out. Of the works in his first volume, **Midsummer Night's Madness** (1932), O'Faoláin writes [in his **The Stories of Seán O'Faoláin**] "they belong to a period, my twenties. They are very romantic, as their weighted style shows." They are definitely "young" stories; their heavy dependence on romantic words like *dawn, dew, adamant,* and *dusk* and their recurring motifs of the hunted exile, the solitary thinker, the burning but impractical patriot give them an unreal quality as well. Characterized by frequent first person narration, they are involved and often passionate episodes drawn from "an experience which had left me dazed—the revolutionary period in Ireland." They are good stories, these early pieces, and it is certainly significant that O'Faoláin although commenting freely on their shortcomings, has nevertheless left them unrevised.

The short story writer, for O'Faoláin, must have an unusually keen sensitivity to ideas, an ability to snatch the one small thing and make it work.

—*Katherine Hanley*

A Purse of Coppers, the 1937 collection, moves away from the early romanticism and into what O'Faoláin terms "a certain adjustment and detachment." The glamour of the revolution has considerably diminished and there is a greater and deliberate clarity of vision. There is more pessimism in this volume as well; O'Faoláin is not bitter, but into stories like **"A Broken World," "A Meeting,"** and **"Discord"** he injects a darkness which makes this volume one of his most interesting.

The stories tend to be neater, their structure more definite. At times, in **"The Confessional,"** for instance, O'Faoláin experiments well with humor, although in places like **"Mother Matilda's Book,"** it is nearer pathos.

After 1949 O'Faoláin widens his perspective considerably. Instead of disillusioned and groping thinkers, we get a range of human beings, some small, others magnificent, some comic, others near-tragic, who explore their surroundings and themselves and the new Ireland in which they are set. *Teresa,* the 1947 collection, contains beautifully wry satire of a self-deceived novice in religious life; a near-bitter statement of man's power to inject guilt in **"The Man Who Invented Sin"**; an impressionistic tonepoem in **"The Silence of the Valley"**; a small tragedy in **"The End of a Good Man"**; high comedy in **"The Woman who Married Clark Gable"**; and half a dozen other excellent pieces. In *I Remember! I Remember!,* the 1961 volume, O'Faoláin continues moving toward greater detachment and objectivity. That this is so not because the writer ceases to be involved in the stories: he continues to study his own surroundings and takes his art from them, following advice given him by W. B. Yeats: "You must write yourself into yourself. There is no other way." The stories play one against the other, contrasting youth and age, illusion and reality.

In 1963 O'Faoláin described himself as "a romantic with

a hopeless longing for classical order." It is not, I think, forcing things to suggest that early O'Faoláin is predominantly romantic, with form, although always scrupulously discernible, also romantic. The author and/or narrator likes to comment and interpret and the diction is rich with adjectives. Later O'Faoláin moves toward greater subtlety, toward understatement. The stories tend to be more spare (although, interestingly, several are longer as O'Faoláin elaborates on plot and experiments with the more drawn-out tale). So there is, as the author notes, a development away from the romantic, emotional, and verbose and toward realism, detachment, and the compact.

Since generalizations about a writer have validity only if they can be demonstrated, it is of particular value to take three O'Faoláin stories and study them one against the other to illustrate the author's development. **"A Meeting,"** from the 1937 volume, *A Purse of Coppers,* **"Passion,"** from the 1947 *Teresa,* and **"A Touch of Autumn in the Air,"** from the 1959 *I Remember! I Remember!* are three stories, written approximately ten years apart, having as subject matter the past recollected in the present. All are brief, all use the first person, all make use of a "small wonder." They are good stories, although not among those frequently studied; their lack of critical attention makes them more attractive subjects for analysis. In them we may see, I think, a progressive restraint, a movement from the carefully stated to the unsaid, from the simple to the elaborately cryptic.

"A Meeting" is a post-Revolutionary story. In the decaying village of Burnt Hill the narrator meets Sally Dunn, former messenger and intriguer in the movement. He reminisces with her about the earliest days of excitement and glamour, visits her home briefly, walks with her through the bog talking of the past and present, and realizes, as they part, that Sally's memories, however doctored and decorated, can no longer sustain her. It is a simple story, carefully restricted with its two characters; there is no plot, only the "small wonder" of the meeting and the final wonder that the "old tales" have lost their magic. Sally is settled now in apathetic domesticity, with a dentist husband and three children. Her "memories of the old days— pamphlets from Russia, poems by this rebel leader who was shot in action and that one who died on a hunger strike—" are, the narrator discovers, still in her parlor but "down on the lowest shelf behind the armchair." She is caught, unable to people her world with memories but unsuited to the post-war life of the village, rejecting golf and cards as trite and concerned about the factory to be built in the "disused barracks" (the symbolism is poignant here). She frets over modern times:

> I wonder ought we have factories spreading like that all over Ireland? We might end with cities like Manchester or Glasgow? And look at all these people making money out of it all. It's hard to tell. . . .

"A Meeting" illustrates O'Faoláin's statement that the stories in *A Purse of Coppers* shows his own reactions "after I had more or less come out of the daze" of Revolution enthusiasm. The narrator is perfectly juxtaposed to Sally: he sees the end of the dream, although he can remember the magic it used to work on him, and he accepts the necessity of going on (it is significant that he is only visiting the village and leaves on a train at the end of the story); Sally, in contrast, is aware that the dream has ended but has no replacement and so nurses her fragments. In her yearning to prolong the bits of the old dream she begs the narrator to "meet her again, some day in Limerick," to talk again:

> We'll talk like the old days. There's so much I want to talk about! I can't remember it now. We'll talk until the cows come home! And then talk again until the cocks begin to crow! Won't we?

And the narrator, knowing, as Sally knows, that of course they never will, answers, "Of course we will!"

The story is perfectly structured. O'Faoláin opens with two paragraphs on the once-prosperous town and its decay, the "broken line of shops," the barracks "crumbling to pieces." Sally Dunn and her dreams, once prosperous in romance and danger, are decayed as well. O'Faoláin, though, is not content to show this truth; he must also say it. The ending of the story announces "message" with unnecessary clarity:

> We never met again. I doubt if either of us wanted it or expected it. You cannot have your memories and eat them.

The story works too hard, I think, for the reader. Everything is done for him; all the lessons are spelled out. The writing is superb, evocative and gentle, but there is too much of it.

"Passion" is less explicit. Again the theme is the past seen through the perspective of the present, although the form of this story—a sort of letter-soliloquy to an absent love—is unique in the O'Faoláin collections. Here the narrator moves back twenty years to an evening spent with his uncle and aunt in Cork. He is child-observer more than participant, and the incident in which his Uncle Conny refuses his six prized Easter lilies for the child who has died, only to have them beaten down by a raging storm that night, is told with excellent dialogue and a minimum of development. The characters, Conny and the aunt, untold through their comments, the aunt with her truisms about death—"Once we're dead we're soon forgotten"—and Conny with his pathetic possessiveness—"me poor little six Easter lilies that I reared, that I looked after as if they were me own children." And the scene, the "soft, wet night" in the warm kitchen with the fire, the card game, the child-narrator secure but puzzled by his uncle's reactions, contrasts beautifully with the storm which "sailed on the muddy water through the city" and "batters into the mud" Conny's cherished flowers.

As he did in the earlier story, the narrator recalls the incident after it has passed. Again he frames it, not this time by describing the town but by looking at far-off Dublin through the window. As before, there is a conclusion, this time more ambiguous and consequently more effective because the narrator himself experiences a sort of epiphany as he thinks of Conny's possessive love and—with a start—his own:

> Or is it, dearest one, that all passion is an unhappiness? Are we always looking forward to our joy, or thinking back on it, or so drunk with it that we cannot realize it?

The final address to the love, pleading that their meeting be soon, returns us firmly to the present. In this story O'Faoláin offers the reader less and asks more of him. We are not told what to think nor are we expected, necessarily, to agree with the narrator; his questions leave the story open-ended. **"Passion"** is, I think, a better story than **"A Meeting,"** less romantic and more detached.

"A Touch of Autumn in the Air," the most recent story of the three, is the longest and most cryptic. Again O'Faoláin limits himself to two characters, the narrator and Daniel Cashen, owner of a blanket mill. The story is set not in a small village but in the lobby of a modern hotel, moving backward then sixty years to Cashen's childhood in "what was at that time called the Queen's County." Cashen is a successful small businessman, possessed of a considerable fortune and little human warmth, and it is he, "of all people," the story begins, who shows the narrator that "the fragments of any experience that remain in a man's memory, the bits and scraps of his ruined temple, are preserved from time not at random but by the inmost desires of his personality." It is Daniel Cashen who remembers, jogged by the casual remark that "there was a touch of autumn in the air." Cashen's memories are old and idyllic—his uncle's farm on an October morning, his young cousin Kitty Bergin, a letter from another cousin studying to be a priest, the cousin's visit to a neighbor's daughter, now Sister Fidelia. Kitty and Danny, both struck with the apparent meaninglessness of leaving the country, play at making Kitty into Sister Fidelia and finish their cutting of fern by sharing old-fashioned Conversation Lozenges and listening to "the faint honking of the wild geese called down from the North by the October moon." What Daniel Cashen has now, sixty years later, is a large fortune and a fragmented memory of that long-ago autumn, set in motion by an old nun he sees in a book-shop, a sweets-and-toys-shop, and a faint crescent moon. And he is pained without knowing why. The narrator knows, at least in part:

> The pain in his eyes was the pain of a man who has begun to lose one of the great pleasures of life in the discovery that we can never truly remember anything at all, that we are for a great part of our lives at the mercy of uncharted currents of the heart.

He consoles Cashen by pulling him back to the present:

> "I hope the Blankets are doing well?"
>
> "Aha!" he cried triumphantly. "Better than ever."

The story moves into a plot of sorts at the very end as Cashen dies a week after the chance meeting and leaves his hundred and fifty thousand pounds to "his relatives by birth, most of them living in what used to be called, in his boyhood, the Queen's County."

"A Touch of Autumn in the Air" requires—and repays—considerable involvement from the reader. It is, of course, a story about Daniel Cashen but it is, more importantly, a story about the time and memory and the autumn or hint of death that always surrounds memory. O'Faoláin displays magnificent sensitivity by choosing for his central character the relatively unattractive and unsympathetic Cashen. He is not the mellow Irishman nor the dreamy romantic; he is simply a dry industrialist puzzled by scraps of remembrance and unable to throw them into clear focus. Because it leaves much unsaid, the story is pregnant with suggestion. Although the narrator has moralized and interpreted during the tale, he allows the ending to stand simply with Cashen's bequest to his relatives who are also tied to his memories. The story keeps a perfect tension between sadness and bitterness; there is no cynicism here, only a gentleness which would be driven out were O'Faoláin to insert a message. By holding back, he delivers it perfectly. So the three stories have moved from saying everything to suggesting everything, from statement to hint. It is also of interest to compare the function of narrator in each and then to look for a bit at O'Faoláin's style.

The narrator plays an increasingly simple part in the stories. In **"A Meeting"** he figures prominently, has all the answers, and makes all the judgments. In **"Passion"** he is a child, observing without fully comprehending but drawing perceptive conclusions years later when warmed by passion and possession of his own. In **"A Touch of Autumn in the Air"** he is foil to Daniel Cashen, learning from the older man's inability to learn but taught by Cashen's bequest at the end. Instead of judge and interpreter, the narrator is here humbled recipient of an essential truth. He is gentler here, more likeable. In general, O'Faoláin's stories follow this trend, the earlier ones featuring the first person and the later ones putting him in the shadows to observe with the reader. Several of the later stories, **"In the Bosom of the Country," "Lovers of the Lake," "Before the Daystar," "£1000 for Rosebud,"** and **"A Sweet Colleen,"** for instance, use straight third-person narration, thus giving O'Faoláin even greater detachment and objectivity.

The O'Faoláin style, careful and evocative, develops through the three stories. **"A Meeting"** depends heavily on similes, most of them simple ones: "the street becomes gapped like an old man's mouth," "the river was as calm as a dream," "the bog was dry as dust and in the heat it trembled like a marriage," and so throughout the story. The same technique is used in **"Passion"**: "everything was as still as before dawn," "it was about as big as a table," "the lights of Dublin are bright as youth," "it was like hearing an old, old tune on a brass band." Similes, by making comparisons explicit for the reader, do most of the work for him; he need only read them and agree. In **"A Touch of Autumn in the Air"** the reader is given almost no similes (there are three, all of them strikingly original) and is asked instead to work with metaphor: "the bits and scraps of his ruined temple," "a few trivial things stuck up above the tides of forgetfulness," "the jigsaw of his youth"; "Cashen was playing archaeology with his boyhood, trying to deduce a whole self out of a few dusty shards." The writing is tighter now, and the story is the richer for the absence of the many copulative verbs which cluttered the early pieces.

O'Faoláin likes to create tone through his openings. In **"A Meeting"** we get all the early O'Faoláin words in the first few paragraphs: *melancholy, calm, dream, mossy.* **"Passion"** employs similar diction—*melancholy, soft, haze, weeping, dawn,* in the first two paragraphs—although here the words are more functional as the narrator points out that it is precisely these ideas which move him backward in memory. And in the opening of **"A Touch of Autumn in the Air"** we have only stark statement and fact, no romanticism: "It was, of all people, Daniel Cashen of Roscommon who first made me realize that the fragments of any experience that remain in a man's memory, the bits and scraps of his ruined temple, are preserved from time not at random but by the inmost desire of his personality." The tone is realistic here; although not harsh, it is not made poetic.

All of the stories begin at a point in the present, circle backward in time, and return to the present, **"A Meeting"** with regret and pathos, **"Passion"** with wonder and a certain pain, **"A Touch of Autumn in the Air"** with gentle clarity and humility. And perhaps these states of mind might well sum up O'Faoláin's own development. It is not, let it be firmly noted, a development from bad to good or from clumsy apprentice to master craftsman. Early O'Faoláin exhibits artistry just as does later O'Faoláin. But a discernible movement is there and it is exciting to watch the growth of a writer through exploration and discovery and openness to the exacting demands of his craft. (pp. 3-11)

> Katherine Hanley, "The Short Stories of Seán O'Faoláin: Theory and Practice," in Éire-Ireland, Vol. VI, No. 3, Fall, 1971, pp. 3-11.

Julian Moynahan (essay date 1976)

[*Moynahan is an American novelist and critic. In the following essay, he discusses O'Faoláin's depictions of the effects of Ireland's modernization in* Foreign Affairs, and Other Stories.]

From the early masterpiece, **"Midsummer Night Madness,"** set in the era of the Anglo-Irish War of 1919-21, to **"Lovers of the Lake,"** a story about adulterous lovers going on pilgrimage to St. Patrick's Purgatory in Lough Derg, O'Faoláin's fiction has been remarkable, in an Irish context, for the attention it gives to passionate love and sexuality along with the more familiar Irish literary obsessions of religion, politics, family and autobiography. In **"Lovers of the Lake"** the man, an agnostic Dublin surgeon, follows his mistress around the torturous sequence of "stations" on the grim penitential island as a sort of lover's compliment. The woman, on the other hand, is a true believer, although she has scarcely less expectation of giving up her lover than she has of divorcing a husband who has ceased to appeal to her. Add that both these people are affluent, well-educated, urbane and well-traveled, genuinely representative of the Roman Catholic middle-class elite which has been running things in the Republic for the last generation or so, and one will understand why this story has been called by some critics the first modern Irish story.

The eight tales in O'Faoláin's new collection [*Foreign Affairs, and Other Stories*] five of which have appeared in *Playboy,* are very much in the vein of **"Lovers,"** and exploit some of the ironies and tensions that emerge as the Irish, both the people and the institutions, undergo "modernization." Perhaps the strongest tension of all is between this modernizing process and certain elements in the national attitude that conspire to thwart it. Thus, in **"The Faithless Wife,"** a French diplomat stationed in Dublin lays siege to Mrs. O'Sullivan, a Dublin boutique owner with the figure and complexion of Boucher's Mlle. O'Murphy, and is surprised and delighted by the speed and enthusiasm with which she inserts her rosy self between his silken sheets. He learns in the short run that Irish women can be very good in bed, and in the long run that they are deeply evasive in conduct, this evasiveness being the other side of an inalienable fidelity to religious rule and the custom of monogamy.

The Irish male's first line of defense against the Irish woman's devotion to monogamy is of course bachelorhood, with or without the donning of a Roman collar, and O'Faoláin, over the years, has made something of a specialty out of bachelor stories. In the present collection the bachelor theme emerges at numerous points, but with some unlooked-for developments. In **"Falling Rocks, Narrowing Road, Cul-de-sac, Stop"** we are given a country librarian, a doctor and a priest who, as a matter of course, go on picnics together; but almost before we have done exclaiming "Where but in Ireland!" the priest, who has been experimenting with Esalen-type encounter sessions as a substitute for private confession, legs it off to Stockholm with a sexy teenager recruited from his flock, and the doctor, who has been off women since undergoing homosexual rape at age 12 at an English boarding school, gets married to the girl's widowed mother. That the women in the case are German, not Irish, may explain these belated conversions to the cult of Venus. Or maybe not.

With a lifetime of practice behind him, Seán O'Faoláin, who is just as old as the present century, contrives some of these stories with a delightful appearance of casualness, even carelessness. **"How to Write a Short Story"** makes mock of the Maupassant kind of story by introducing a character who wants to write one but finds he can't fit the reminiscences his friend offers him into its tight and crafty formulas. And **"Liberty,"** a quite mysterious tale about a woman psychiatrist who loves and finally marries one of the patients she looks after in a rural asylum, keeps its mystery to the end, tantalizing the reader with suggestions of allegory, appearing as an evocative fragment of some larger fictional structure that the author lost, abandoned, or never got around to spelling out during the course of the stay.

O'Faoláin, a distinguished travel writer, knows Europe in intricate detail and deploys such knowledge effectively in several of these stories. But for me the two best stories in the collection are set practically in their author's backyard, only a few miles down the coast from where he lives in Dun Laoghaire. **"An Inside Outside Complex,"** placed in the rather tacky tourist resort of Bray during the off sea-

son, gives us Bertie Bolger, a spruce young bachelor and antique dealer of 41, who takes to peeking in the few lighted windows he passes on his evening walk and ends up contracting an appallingly bad marriage with one of the ladies he spies upon. After a trial separation he returns to her, drawn by the warm glow of her cottage light, and the story ends, neither happily nor unhappily, yet with the disturbing suggestion that the only difference between marriage and the single state for the Irishman is that the bachelor is out in the cold looking in and the married man is inside the not so tender trap looking out.

The other story, **"Murder at Cobbler's Hulk,"** occurs at a point along the beautiful, vacant beach between Greystones, a town once much frequented during summer by Welsh clergymen and their families, and the town of Wicklow. Here it suffices to say that it is funny, outrageous and wonderful, with as many twists in it as a corkscrew. The short story is not dead while O'Faoláin lives.

> *Julian Moynahan, "Lovers and Other Irishmen," in* The New York Times Book Review, *January 25, 1976, p. 6.*

Joseph Duffy (essay date 1976)

[*In the following favorable review of* The Finest Short Stories of Seán O'Faoláin, *Duffy discusses the defining characteristics of O'Faoláin's short fiction.*]

> And I would have all know that when all falls
> In ruin, poetry calls out in joy,
> Being the scattering hand, the bursting pod,
> The victim's joy among the holy flame,
> God's laughter at the shattering of the world.
>   [W. B. Yeats, *The King's Threshold*]

In "Anonymiad", the final story of John Barth's *Lost in the Funhouse,* a "nameless minstrel" glories in the composition of what he "came to call fiction":

> I found that by pretending that things had happened which in fact had not, and that people existed who didn't, I could achieve a lovely truth which actuality obscures—especially when I learned to abandon myth and pattern my fabrications on actual people and events.

Later he launches his last endeavour—his masterpiece—in a sealed wine jug into unknown seas. The minstrel imagines his work drifting "age after age" and in its voyage passing a "hairsbreadth from the unknown man or woman to whose heart, of all hearts in the world, it could speak fluentist, most balmy . . . until it too must perish, with all things deciphered and undeciphered: men and women, stars and sky."

This fiction about fiction comes from a volume of fiction about fiction. That it, like much of Barth's work, should be concerned with the process of writing is indicative of the self-consciousness about subject-matter, and therefore about reality, felt by the best American writers of this time. But the sentiments of the "nameless minstrel" are poignantly conventional: a confidence in the validity of the production; a pride of craftsmanship; a serenity and detachment from the finished work; and a terror about its extinction before its "lovely" truth had been recognised by a receptive audience. I would not want to be the man "too preoccupied" to be touched by what is "fluentist, most balmy" in Seán O'Faoláin's fiction, especially since his own criticism displays such sensitivity and intelligence about other writers. Nevertheless, my understanding of the work collected in *The Finest Short Stories of Seán O'Faoláin* must inevitably come to grips with the limitations as well as the attainments of the traditional short-story form which he has practiced over so many years.

There are twenty-seven stories in this volume, most of them averaging ten pages. A few are very short; some, including three from the earliest period, are quite long. Their level of competence is consistently high, and there are no failures, unless it is **"A Born Genius"** which seems to be an inchoate novel. Even what for this American may be classified as excessively Irish 'stuff' like **"The Old Master"**, **"Mother Mathilda's Book"**, **"Persecution Mania"**, **"An Enduring Friendship"**, and **"Childy-bawn"** are well-crafted verbal nudges. At least one of the stories, **"The Silence of the Valley"**, is in my judgment a classic piece of short fiction. The imaginative energy of O'Faoláin's fiction is directed mainly towards figures and incidents shaped and coloured by religious, political and sexual contingencies. That set of concerns would alone justify the term 'traditional' because a value or moral quality is evidently assigned to the varieties of conduct generated by one or the other of these forces. Such cultural, social and biological phenomena are assumed to have meaning as well as existence. Although a post-humanist perception might doubt this possibility of meaning and consequently of values or moral order, the raising of such a valid question simply poses the dilemma about all art in our time. Certainly, however, the matter of interest should be confronted, particularly in the religious texture of the fiction—and secondarily in the political. If, for example, the assumption of concern for Catholicism or even Christianity as a familiar aspect of everyday life seems now to be a merely local or topical attitude, can such an assumption be acceptable even vicariously in another time or in another place, or is it at best diminished to the appeal of quaintness? These doubts do not deny the craft of the fiction, but they are seriously directed at the confident presentation of subject-matter in some of the stories here.

The form of these stories is also, appropriately, 'traditional'. For their effect they depend upon the appearance of 'discovery' they impart to the reader. That 'discovery' may be communicated through an unravelling of plot or character complication so that either an anticipated or an unexpected resolution of the fictive problem occurs. The major narrative space of **"Teresa"** encloses the yearning of a young nun for a more austere religious observance than that provided by her order, while the brief concluding space reveals the same figure as a married woman (wife of a Protestant) on an ambiguously motivated visit to the convent she had abandoned. At the conclusion of **"Lovers of the Lake"**, the 'lovers', after what had seemed to be a capricious and sceptical pilgrimage to Lough Derg, renounce their affair as they are on the passionate point of resuming it: "Hand in hand they walked slowly back to the hotel, to their separate rooms."

On the other hand, the 'discovery' may not refer to an overt change in an established character or situation but rather to an understanding a fictive figure comes to about his own condition or to an understanding conveyed to the reader by the fiction itself, an understanding to which the figures and incidents contribute but in which they do not participate. The last sentence of **"Admiring the Scenery"** represents Hanafan, a teacher, unnoticed in his corner of a train compartment, "weeping to himself, the drops creeping through his tightly closed eyes." The occasion for his tears are the unspoken details of a past love affair inferred from an anecdote related to his travelling companions. Earlier Hanafan had said that " 'every man lives out his own imagination of himself' ", and his tears are presumably an acknowledgement of failure to live out the full dimensions of his imagination of self. Both categories of 'discovery'—those of recognition and of understanding—are meant to provoke recognition or understanding in the reader and suggest thereby a relationship of the narrative to reality. A verisimilitude is consequently expected which will support this implied relationship between life outside the fiction and the imagined life within. Moreover, the humanistic assumptions behind the fiction also suggest the susceptibility of life to the ordering capacity of art: concurrence of meaning may be evoked between reality and art.

Because of obvious space limitations, the author of short fiction lacks the novelist's opportunity for developing character and incident, for complicating plot, and for elaborating theme. A dominant impression, which is what the short story aspires to, must be achieved (if it is to be gained at all) through the economic precision with which the specifics of the story—the surface data and techniques—are handled. That tactful and disciplined arrangement accounts for the 'discovery' which is the silent harmony of the fiction: the abstraction which cannot exist without the words of the story and which cannot be put into words, not even into the words of the story. **"The Trout"**, for example, is a very short account of a child who releases a trapped fish from a pool. By her gestures the young girl realises that human effort, not "fairy godmothers", lies behind any form of deliverance. But the story assigns a value larger than the fictive girl's 'discovery' to the generous imagination behind her trivial action; the 'discovery' of the story itself is the perception of miraculous energy flowing through the commonplace.

While **"The Trout"** is slight, it is properly inaccessible to clarifying analysis. **"Teresa"**, however, is carefully developed and yet ends in the mere accessibility of its ironic conclusion. The ambiguity of that brief scene of the returned ex-nun is the occasion for the careful preparation (as non-preparation) of the preceding narrative, as is the renunciation of the couple in **"Lovers of the Lake"** for the long account of the religious routine at Lough Derg. These latter stories are unsatisfactory precisely because their apparently gratuitous conclusions are so accessible to technical analysis. Although **"Teresa"** and **"Lovers of the Lake"** make more overt claims about themselves as fiction than **"The Trout"** does, their fixed, discernible and transparent arrangement earns less respect.

"A Broken World", the title of this essay, is also the title of one of O'Faoláin's stories. And the story title itself may refer, perhaps unconsciously, to the lines from *The King's Threshold*. At any rate, poetry's calling out in joy, which Yeats associates with "God's laughter at the shattering of the world", characterises the finest imaginative wisdom of O'Faoláin's writing. For the most part, the substance of this fiction represents with wit, melancholy and compassion the mystery in the dour cares of ordinary life: the mystery in the common expectations and disappointments experienced in onerous solitude and fragile communion by fictive figures between silence and silence. The joy comes in the distanced imagination of unity present in the best work. That imagination is expressed directly at the conclusion of **"A Broken World"** and is implicit in the arrangement of **"The Silence of the Valley",** the masterpiece of this collection. In both stories a group of strangers come together briefly to form a community which remembers or observes life, and then separate. While the dispersal of figures and incidents occurs within the fictive space, the stories themselves endeavour to uphold a unity above and beyond its represented fragments.

In **"A Broken World,"** a priest, a farmer, and a narrator of unspecified occupation travel for a time in the same compartment of a train heading for Dublin, the destination of the narrator. As he looks from the carriage to the dark snowy countryside, the priest recalls with bitterness his first parish in County Wicklow and the impoverished mountain people, descendants of servants from the now closed and gutted great houses, intermarrying, dwindling in population, and farming patches of land "reclaimed from the furze". That remembered world, which has apparently not changed, was broken between the cabins and bleak land of the parish, the prosperous houses and acreage in the valley below, and the boarded-up homes of the gentry lying empty in enormous wasted parks. When the narrator asks why, with the passing of the large landowners, the mountain people and the prosperous farmers could not make a complete world of their own, the priest shrugs his shoulders in the direction of their companion with the "dull, stupid eyes" and then laughs "an extraordinary inhuman kind of laugh that ended in a noise like a little groan." After the priest's departure, the farmer informs the narrator that the priest has been silenced for " 'politics' "—an attempt to take over a large estate with the aid of " 'ten or twenty foolish young lads.' " Although the farmer is as solid as Wordsworth's leech gatherer, he provides no consolation for his fellow traveller. Solitude and the deprivations of rural life, which gave a remote majesty to the leech gatherer, have simply dehumanised the farmer:

> In his sleep he was as motionless as a rock; but you could not say he was 'like a rock' because he was like nothing on earth but himself, everything about him was so personal to him. Unless, because he was so much a random accumulation of work and season and all that belongs to the first human that was ever made, I chose to say, as I glared at him snoring in his corner, that time and nature had engendered something no more human than a rock.

Alone at last, the narrator tries in his imagination to refute the brutish insensitivity of the farmer and the "self-corrosion" of the priest whose dream of life as "a moral unity" was betrayed by the real world of his first parish. In a passage reminiscent of and counter to the conclusion of "The Dead", the narrator admits the "truth" of "the wintry moment" outside: " . . . that under that white shroud, covering the whole of Ireland, life was lying broken and hardly breathing." And his last thoughts are of the morning to come when "Ireland, under its snow, would be silent as a perpetual dawn." Between the night of the passage of the train around the city to the sea and the approaching morning, the solitary traveller nearing his destination speculates on a romantic version of a world made whole:

> What image of life that would fire and fuse us all, what music bursting like the spring, what triumph, what engendering love, so that those breasting mountains that now looked cold should appear brilliant and gay, the white land that seemed to sleep should appear to smile, and these people who huddled over the embers of their lives should become like peasants who held the hand of Faust with their singing one Easter morning?

Exception may be taken here to the lyric explicitness of the long passage which concludes the story so radiantly, just as criticism might be made of Joyce's conclusion—considerably more purple in its rhetoric—which finishes that story so darkly. Still, the traveller's silent song—for that is what it is—rises out of acknowledgement of the indifferent land which has claimed the spirit of the farmer in an effort to find again the harmony lost to the priest. As the narrator observes from the empty train chugging through a snowy night towards a cold dawn, there are occasions of great hope that imaginative rhythms inspire and of great desolation that the heavy earth provokes so that men "have no other choice but to live splendidly, or gather up at least enough grace for a quick remove." **"The Silence of the Valley"** also begins with a perception of the land, a country place with one or two farm houses and a fishing hotel about a lake, where in winter "great cataracts slide down the mountain face", while in summer only "the tinkle of the ghost of one of these falls" may be heard. Even the winter's "echoes of falling water are fitful" and summer's "tiny muted sounds" "creep" out of "vacancy . . . intermittently." In this quiet valley five visitors gather at the bar of the hotel, an American soldier, "blond, blankly handsome"; a priest, "jovial, fat, ruddy"; an "incorrigible Celt", "a dark young man with pince-nez"; a "red-mopped" Scots girl whose "deep-set eyes ran from gloom to irony, to challenge, to wild humour"; and a school inspector, "a sack of a man".

During the subsequent narrative, from the evening of one May day to the night of the next, the group talks desultorily, a tramp sings sentimental and merry songs in "a fine tenor voice", some eels are caught and roasted, and a local cobbler dies, is waked, and is buried. On the second night, in final fictive assembly, the group move from the bar to the dining room where they sit down to a meal of salmon purchased that morning from "a mountainy lad" for whom the catch had been " 'only a night's sport and a walk over the mountain.' " Through the dining-room window the Scots girl sees "how the moon touched the trees on the island with a ghostly tenderness" and sees as well the gleam of "one clear star above the mountain wall". Breaking off her temporary isolation from the group, she responds "quietly" to the American's observation about the weather: " 'Yes, it will be another fine day tomorrow.' " And her "severe eyebrows", initially described as floating "as gently as a veil in the wind", which at sight of the star "had floated upward softly for sheer joy", now sink "very slowly like a falling curtain".

The contours of the story are smooth and muted so that no incident of life or even of death dominates. When the narrative is compressed and recapitulated, there seems to be a banality of the figures, the situation and the environment. But it is the momentous banality of the earth and common human experience conveyed by the fiction's arrangement of its specifics. A human rhythm of life and death, ritualised in eating, drinking, talking, singing, walking and burying, moves with the natural rhythms of evening, day and night in the lake valley. The closing observations join the inscrutable macrocosmic distance of moon and star from earth to the inscrutable microcosmic distance of one human figure from the others.

The gritty concerns of religion, politics, and sex—those small disturbances of man, which were said to be primary in O'Faoláin's fiction—are not vaporised in the apparent self-effacement of this narrative: the cobbler's widow is alternately ribald and grieving and an erotic pungency rises from the political chaffing between Irishman and Scots. But these details, important in the reading, are abstracted at last into the distanced perception of the whole work, its imaginative position. For what is "fluentist, most balmy" in the "lovely truth" of this fiction which reckons with the remote and the proximate, the mysterious and the familiar, the motley and the singular, is its final silence. There, the imagination flecked with feeling confronts origin and terminus and the movement between—all at once. (pp. 30-6)

David Dempsey on O'Faoláin's characters:

Seán O'Faoláins characters are most attractive when they are being victimized. The agent of their doom may be a personal flaw or a *homme fatal* flaw. It may be too much innocence. It may be money, memory, or merely Irish rectitude. But the doom is not very final, and sympathy for the victim is never far away. It is custom, intolerance, and fanaticism, not people, that O'Faoláin condemns. The people are perplexed and misguided, rather than evil, and most of them survive their situations to try again. "The Irish . . . are really at their best in misfortune," the author reminds us, as in one way or another he has been reminding us for thirty-five years.

David Dempsey, in a review of The Heat of the Sun, and Other Stories, *in* The Saturday Review, *October, 1966.*

Joseph Duffy, "A Broken World: The Finest Short Stories of Seán O'Faoláin," in Irish University Review, *Vol. 6, No. 1, Spring, 1976, pp. 30-6.*

Joseph Storey Rippier   (essay date 1976)

[*In the following excerpt, Rippier asserts that O'Faoláin's later short fiction exhibits a developing maturity, especially in his characterization.*]

In the later work O'Faoláin is clearly on his own. The influence of other writers, in particular of Joyce and Moore, has been shrugged off. There is a definite move away from the intense, occasionally mannered techniques found in some of the first stories.

Altogether an increasing sense of relaxation is conveyed in two main ways: through the method of presentation, and through the words O'Faoláin uses. The rather literary style of many of the early stories gives way to a much more informal manner. Although he often draws on the other arts, O'Faoláin now less frequently brings in allusions to painting or music in the struggle to stress or add depth to what he writes. This does not mean that the reader is being written down to, or that the writer is being any less fastidious in his choice of vocabulary. O'Faoláin merely turns his back on earlier models, to be free to express himself in the superficially simpler language of every day. Through this he breaks one link between himself and what he writes—at least for the reader—because the reader will not be tempted to think that there is one language for literature and another for him, thus automatically, unconsciously accepting that what is written comes directly from the writer, represents the way he sees things. Simple diction clears the mind, while metaphor may dazzle or bemuse.

In his analysis of Hemingway's technique and style, H. E. Bates has something rather similar to say:

> What Hemingway went for was that direct pictorial contact between eye and object, between object and reader. To get it he cut out a whole forest of verbosity. He got back to clean fundamental growth. He trimmed off explanation, discussion, even comment; he hacked off all metaphorical floweriness; he pruned off the dead, sacred clichés; until finally, through the sparse trained words, there was a view. (*The Modern Short Story*, 1968)

The later O'Faoláin stories are seldom directly subjective, even if there is often a first-person narrator. The writer, or the narration, is merely the medium through which events are passed on to the reader. A deliberate attempt appears to have been made to work in mediate, rather than in immediate, terms. Joyce explains this process towards the end of *Portrait*:

> The narrative is no longer personal. The personality of the artist passes into the narrator itself, flowing round and round the persons like a vital sea. This progress you will see easily in that old English ballad "Turpin Hero" which begins in the first person and ends in the third person. . . . The personality of the artist, at first a

cry or a cadence or a mood and then a fluid and lambent narrative, finally refines itself out of existence, impersonalises itself so to speak.

O'Faoláin is never able to "impersonalise" himself totally to reach that final stage demanded of the writer by Joyce. O'Faoláin appears to be convinced that the second stage is as much as can be expected, indeed even desired, so that while the subjective may be diminished, there remains that distilled sense of what he calls "communicated personality".

O'Faoláin continues to tell stories. Much still remains beneath the surface, but Joycean "epiphanies" are rarely found (a striking exception being **"The Silence of the Valley"**).

As in the earlier work, O'Faoláin often writes round a central idea which is sometimes tucked away in the text. In the two stories to be examined in this chapter, these ideas are the relationship of pity to love (**"Up the Bare Stairs"**), and of pride to humility (**"Lady Lucifer"**).

A difference in the handling of the material becomes noticeable. Whereas in such stories as **"Admiring the Scenery"** and **"The Old Master"**, O'Faoláin also works from a central statement (in **"Admiring the Scenery"** it is "Every man lives out his own imagination of himself"; in **"The Old Master"**, "such men have no life but their own drama") the characters representing these statements are never permitted to go beyond living out their own limitations. They are men whose existences remain stunted and blighted. It is the difference between being asked to feel with a Hanafan (**"Admiring the Scenery"**) about whom and about whose previous life one learns little, and with the doctor in **"Lady Lucifer"** who has faced up to the problems of life and mastered them. This is not to suggest that the writer has an obligation to present only characters who have come to terms with themselves and with the world around them, but rather that the method successfully employed in **"Admiring the Scenery"** is not one which is always to be applied. Certainly it imposes limits on what a writer can and cannot do, limits which he may feel to be intolerable. It might possibly be argued that this is one of the distinctions between the short story and the tale, although reference to shorter pieces in the later collections would show that even in these O'Faoláin tends to reveal more, enabling him to go deeper.

In **"Up the Bare Stairs"** for example, a younger O'Faoláin might well have introduced Nugent in quite another way. Instead of permitting Nugent to tell what happened in chronological fashion, leaving out nothing essential, O'Faoláin would probably have had Nugent talk all round this one crucial event in his life. He might have described his professional career, he might have mentioned the parents without discussing what they did to him; he might have referred to the teacher-priest, without so clearly describing the effect Angelo had on him. He does none of these things.

Whereas in **"Admiring the Scenery"** one sees only the marks which unexplained sorrow have burned into Hanafan's features, in **"Up the Bare Stairs"** one is told what lies behind the lines on Nugent's face.

Further ease of manner comes in the person of the narrator; through this, an awareness of the presence, or lack of it, of the writer. No writer, in spite of what Joyce advocates, can absent himself completely. At best a seeming absence will be attained. In a story like **"Dividends"** the narrator is even named. But calling the narrator, Seán, does not necessarily mean that the reader will consider the identity of the narrator to be of great importance, or that what the narrator feels and says, is what the story is about. The Seán of **"Dividends"** is an older, worldly-wise narrator who casts a knowing, mocking eye on what passes before him. He is no longer the passionate, impressionable, named narrator of **"Midsummer Night Madness"** whose changing, changeable viewpoint so powerfully influences the direction in which the reader's thoughts are bent. Generally, the "I" figure of the later stories sees, hears, speaks, without being as directly involved as he is in stories like **"Fugue"** or **"Midsummer Night Madness"**. Even where the narrator is not immediately concerned, as for example in **"A Broken World"**, he is still drawn to take a more active part through some issue which is introduced in the course of the story, or through strong feelings which are aroused at what is said to him. The narrator in **"A Broken World"** cannot just listen passively to the priest and country farmer he meets on the train. He has a point of view of his own which is expressed; he is part of a triangular situation. The narrator in **"Up the Bare Stairs"** remains disinterested. It is possible that he is, or stands for, Seán O'Faoláin. This would not make any difference to an appreciation of the story. The narrator listens while a perfect stranger tells him the story of his life. The two men have certain formative experiences in common—their home town of Cork and the school which both attended. These two facts are coincidental and merely, after the conversation has started, provoke Nugent to tell the story of his life. The very structure of the story tends to support this assertion. The narrator does not speak once while Nugent tells of his early life. He comes in at the beginning to introduce the story, and at the end to round it off. He expresses an opinion, it is true, but it is the response one could expect of a person who is hearing something for the first time. In **"A Broken World"** the narrator constantly argues with the other two men, interrupting and commenting all the way through. He is drawn into a discussion in which he is forced to take sides. The narrator in **"Up the Bare Stairs"** stresses that Nugent's story does not touch his own life:

> Then he leaned forward and let down all his reserves. As he began my heart sank. It was the favourite theme of every successful man. 'How I Began.' But as he went on I felt mean and rebuked. I doubt if he had ever told anyone and before he finished I could only guess why he chose to tell me now.

At the beginning of the other story the narrator first describes the priest as "a bloody bore", but then finds himself ever more deeply embroiled in an altercation over Ireland.

Where an opinion is expressed in the later stories it is often done in such an urbane, self-deprecatory manner as to suggest that the narrator's judgement is as fallible as anybody else's. This may be seen as a natural development from attitudes noticed in the first stories. Even there, even in a story like **"Midsummer Night Madness"**, the impetuous young narrator finds that his harsh, one-sided, rigidly defended attitudes, if not changed, become modified as he looks at the other two men: the youthful, hopelessly irresponsible revolutionary, and the old man, representative of a dying landowner class.

At the same time, comment, criticism, or condemnation may emerge from under the later urbanity. For all the light-heartedness of **"The Man Who Invented Sin"**, the narrator does speak his mind to condemn narrow-mindedness, and to express his sadness at those who refuse or who are unable to be honest with themselves. But even where he censures (for example when he is shocked that Majellan should later in life feel that the innocent fun he and the other monk, Virgilius, had had in the company of two nuns while attending a course on Gaelic, had been wrong) O'Faoláin can still show understanding for the vagaries of human behaviour. The monk admits:

> 'You mightn't understand it, now! But it's not good to take people out of their rut. I didn't enjoy that summer.' I said I understood that. After a few more words, we parted. He smiled, said he was delighted to see I was looking so well, and went off, stooping his way back to his monastery in the slum.

Thus in the later stories a rather different impression is left with the reader, both where there is a narrator and where another narrative method is adopted; the impression of a writer who knows where he stands, who is concerned, but who is no longer acting out his own fate through his writing, no longer identifying personally with the characters he creates. As a mature artist O'Faoláin stands back, permitting his characters to make or unmake mistakes, being aware of man's eternal unpredictability. He would no doubt agree with Somerset Maugham:

> I think what has chiefly struck me in human beings is their lack of consistency. I have never seen people all of a piece. It has amazed me that the most incongruous traits should exist in the same person and for all that yield a plausible harmony. (*The Summing Up*)

In his study on Seán O'Faoláin, Maurice Harmon discusses this realisation of the opposing forces at work within the individual:

> The appearance of **"Lady Lucifer"** shows O'Faoláin working out a rationale. In the course of this story the whole problem raised in *Purse of Coppers* is discussed. The alternative solutions are traditional: exile to a more adventurous and competitive existence where one can realize one's self to the fullest extent, or retirement within the hermitage of an accepted insufficiency. The chief character is a specialist in mental diseases, a rational, scientific Irishman, who has travelled much outside the country. Like many characters in *Purse of Coppers* he is a man of divided loyalties—emotionally and atavistically drawn to the country of his birth, imaginatively and intellectually attracted to the wider world

outside. His defence of that attraction contrasts with his enjoyment of the quiet, rural setting in which the story takes place. Men of ambition, he argues, need a full life; man's pride in himself demands it. The Irish, he says, have too much humility and therein lies the cause of their failure. His argument contains familiar references to loss, damnation, and inner disunity:

> "Pride and humility aren't opposites. They're two sides of the same thing . . . If a man is born proud he must feed his pride. It was something given to him. Once he starts the humility tack he's lost. Lost and damned. Drowned in the opposite of his own pride. Show me your humble man and I'll show you the pride coiled up in his humility devouring it like a worm. Show me your proud man and I'll show you the humility flowering beneath his pride like a crocus under the snow . . ."

> The significant point about the doctor's defence is that it enables him to face up to his divided state successfully. He is the first to move beyond the condition of loss. He does so by an acceptance of human nature as inherently composed of opposing forces. Like the priest in **"A Broken World"** he is concerned with the "compositum" of one's being, the full life. For both, anything that denies the achievement of a full personality is harmful, mentally and spiritually. But whereas the priest was defeated by his knowledge of evil, the doctor was not. His positive stance is based on a sane and healthy point of view. "All our emotions," he says, "are a tension of opposites. It depends from hour to hour which way the balance swings." (*Seán O'Faoláin: A Critical Introduction,* 1966)

Ireland and the Irish remain the subjects of the stories, even where the action is placed abroad. O'Faoláin continues to look for what is universal in the tiny world of Ireland, so that while the men and women who people his work are seen in Irish surroundings, the reader comes to realise how eternally similar are the problems of man even when the outer circumstances are disguised by local customs, local colour.

More or less exclusive recourse to a certain milieu however can bring with it problems of a special kind: for example, that what is generally believed to be "typically Irish" may come to be used in the same way. There is a difference, a very important difference, between the bachelor main character in **"Unholy Living and Half Dying"** who is recognisably, but not exclusively, Irish, and Benjy Spillane (**"Childybawn"**), a man who is so tied to his mother that he can only marry when he is nearly fifty, after his mother has died. Whereas Cardew's problem is one which can be seen within a much larger framework (loneliness, ageing, death), Benjy Spillane, his mother, and the girl he finally marries, are held in the strait-jacket of a situation which is seen as "typical", hopeless, amusing. Little attempt is made to go beyond surface recording, the reader being asked to laugh at a situation whose implications are potentially tragic.

Increasingly O'Faoláin writes about city dwellers whose

contact with nature is minimal. Even in the early work most of the characters were no longer part of a pastoral tradition whose influence was still perceptible, but dying. Nevertheless in **"Midsummer Night Madness"** the presence of nature was not only felt, but became a living, associative entity. The narrator on occasion was one with nature. Later, O'Faoláin cannot just turn his back on what lies beyond the city boundaries. Here too, a change both in attitude towards and description of nature will be found. Sometimes this even takes the form of an expressed indifference. At the beginning of **"Up the Bare Stairs"**, the narrator says of Nugent:

> After a casual interest in the countryside as we left Kingsbridge he had wrapped a rug about his legs, settled into his corner and dozed.

These later stories are fixed firmly in the present. Only occasionally are there references back. Earlier there was often a sense of the past still living on (e.g. **"Fugue"**, **"A Broken World"**). Such links become more and more tenuous, and in a story like **"The Silence of the Valley"**, are seen to have been irrevocably broken.

So far O'Faoláin's work has been examined chronologically. There is no implication in this that maturity is necessarily to be equated with greater excellence. The lasting worth of many of the early stories remains undisputed. As Graham Greene said in his review of *A Purse of Coppers*:

> **"The Old Master"**, **"Sinners"**, **"Admiring the Scenery"**, all have the same superb grasp, the first closed simultaneously on the particular character, his environment and the general moral background of the human mind failing always to live up to its own beliefs . . . One salutes, in these stories, an immense creative humour, as broad in speech as Joyce's gloom. (*The Spectator,* 1937)

Two stories, **"Lady Lucifer"** and **"Up the Bare Stairs"**, have been chosen for particular attention in this [essay]. Both have technical and contentual features which have been met with in earlier stories:

> Third-person narrative.
> Three friends going out into the country.
> One of them telling a story.
> Discussion of nature, revealing attitudes to it.
> Story within a story.
>   **("Lady Lucifer", "Admiring the Scenery")**

> First person narrative.
> Meeting on a train.
> Encounter with a stranger.
> Story of crucial incident in stranger's life.
>   **("A Broken World", "Midsummer Night**
>   **Madness", "Fugue", "Up the Bare Stairs")**
>   (pp. 91-8)

. . . . .

She had me by the two arms now, her full bosom almost touching mine, so close to me that I could see the pouches under her eyes, her mouth dragged down wet and sensual, the little angry furrow between her eyebrows. The wind shook the heavy leaves of the chestnuts and as they scattered benediction on us the light from the lit-

tle Gothic window shone on these wet leaves, and on her bosom and chest and knees. For a second I thought her blue apron drooped over her too rich, too wide hips. Since I did not speak she shook me like a dog and growled at me as fiercely as a dog.

                                    ("Midsummer Night Madness")

There was nothing remarkable about this third man except that he had handlebar moustaches and a long black coat and a black hat that came down low on his forehead and shaded his melancholy face; when he spoke, however, his face was gentle as the fluting of a dove. There was nothing resigned about him; his oblong face was blackberry-colored where he shaved and delicate as a woman's where he did not. His eyes were lined with a myriad of fine wrinkles. They were cranky tormented eyes, and his mouth was thin and cold and hard.

                                    ("Admiring the Scenery")

The doctor was poling. He wore brief cream bathing-trunks: a finely-built, sandy-haired man, serious but not severe. He had studied in Vienna, New York, and London; he was a specialist in mental diseases; he was just back from six years with the British Army in the East; he bore himself with the authority of experience and power.

                                    ("Lady Lucifer")

All the way from Dublin my travelling companion had not spoken a dozen words. After a casual interest in the countryside as we left Kingsbridge he had wrapped a rug about his legs, settled in his corner and dozed.

He was a bull-shouldered man, about sixty, with coarse, sallow skin stippled with pores, furrowed by deep lines on either side of his mouth: I could imagine him dragging these little dykes open when shaving. He was dressed so conventionally that he might be a judge, a diplomat, a shopwalker, a shipowner or an old-time Shakespearian actor: black coat, striped trousers, grey spats, white slip inside his waistcoat, butterfly collar folded deeply and a black cravat held by a gold clasp with a tiny diamond.

The backs of his fingers were hairy: he wore an amethyst ring almost as big as a bishop's. His temples were greying and brushed up in two sweeping wings—wherefore the suggestion of an actor. On the rack over his head was a leather hat-case with the initials 'F.J.N.' in Gothic lettering. He was obviously an Englishman who had crossed the night before.

                                    ("Up the Bare Stairs")

These passages have been taken from stories written over a period of some twenty years. It cannot be asserted that they demonstrate all the ways in which O'Faoláin portrays character. However, careful examination of them can lead to an awareness of differences in descriptive technique, of the writer's consistent, increasing endeavour to let the words he chooses do the work on their own, with less and less reliance on vocabulary which earlier was described as "Romantic allusive", and "Romantic visual".

The stories remain the property of the writer for as long

as he is writing, but there may be a temptation—whether conscious or unconscious—to try to hold on to a story afterwards by wishing to make the reader see what is in the writer's mind by building in persuaders of one kind or another. The reader may therefore come to the story only at third or fourth remove. The writer has it first. He may then pass it on to a narrator who also often expresses an opinion, thereby possibly influencing the reader.

This may be noted in the first passage, where little clear information is given. O'Faoláin is not setting a scene to be appreciated visually; the result is an emotional effect. Most of the descriptive words do not describe: they imply. The narrator sees the gypsy girl in terms of himself, so that while there are adjectives which establish her physical appearance, (e.g. "full"), such words do even more. Taken together with the other adjectives, the general, cumulative effect is not visual. The reader is led—wittingly or unwittingly—not so much to see the girl but to accept what the narrator feels about her. Although the narrator is not to be deliberately affected by or involved with the girl, even the surroundings and language are loaded with emotional association: the season (May), the dark night, the lighting which is provided by beams coming through a window. It is a "Gothic" window. The chestnuts do not scatter raindrops, but "benediction". This could be a scene from a sentimental novel: the fallen, abandoned woman, framed in the light from a window, shut out from society. The Gothic window might even suggest that she is standing outside a church. The associations which radiate from such language are almost unlimited, even if they will tend to go in directions consciously or unconsciously predetermined by the author.

It will be helpful to refer to another passage in which again a powerfully emotional effect is achieved:

> Looking at her soft eyes, and at her soft hair, my eyes wandered down to the first shadows of her breasts: she caught my glance and looked down at her warm bosom and then at me and she smiled. As I moved to her I saw the little broken corner of her tooth: I had no word to say; so I sat beside her before the leaping flames and put my arms around her and felt in the cup of my hollow palm the firm casque of her breast. Smiling at me as a sick woman might smile upon a doctor who brought her ease from pain she slipped my hand beneath her blouse to where I felt her warm protruding nipple, and I leaned to her for a kiss.
>
> ("Fugue")

The narrator (the author's medium) is telling what lies in front of his eyes, so that the reader is able to form his own impression. Of course the writer wishes to make the reader's mind work in a particular way, but in this case the scene has been set long in advance. The boy and girl have met. The reader knows that they are attracted to each other. There is no mystery, the relationship of the two young people has been adequately (though not exhaustively) established. Little is known or revealed about the gypsy girl, except that she is Stevey Long's girl-friend and that she is worried.

There are still vague, suggestive words throughout the

passage from **"Fugue"** ("soft hair", "soft eyes"; in particular, "warm bosom"). The words help to convey not so much the physical attraction, but the need of comfort on the part of the boy. "Bosom" suggests the maternal, especially since a different term is used just before this, "the first shadows of her breasts". There is an effective mixture of the visual with the suggestive, which is not to imply that the visual may not be suggestive too.

A little before this, the setting of the table and the preparations for a simple meal have been mentioned. All of these carry with them to the narrator and to the reader a feeling of being at home, out of the cold, no longer on the run. Factual information is given, including the comment that the girl's teeth are not regular, the implication being that the girl is not just dreamed of, but visualised; she is mortal, not sublime. The writer and reader do not take off for loftier, dizzier heights where the mind no longer functions

It is interesting now to switch to another passage in which the girl makes her first entrance:

> Used to this sort of thing, and pitying us, she came down, barefooted, her black hair around her, a black cloak on her shoulders not altogether drawn over her pale breast, a candle blown madly by the wind slanting in her hand.

This time the light does not come from a source which in itself is suggestive. The girl carries a candle whose weak flame enables the narrator to see the girl in black, and not quite white. Her breast, for example, is described as "pale". This is a very good word here. "White" would have brought in associations (virginity, purity) which could lead to predetermination of the picture the reader creates for himself from the few details he is given. All the words are chosen to enable the reader to use the narrator's eyes without—because this is quite unnecessary—being distracted by what is in the narrator's mind. The only expression which might in the context seem a little intemperate is "madly". A small flame caught by even a breeze flickers wildly, so that "madly" is appropriate, accurate, and as a contrast to what precedes it, very effective. Altogether this paragraph faithfully records what is registered by somebody coming in from the dark. In the case of the gypsy, the approach is not direct. O'Faoláin's use of the adjective "rich", when applied to the girl's hips, retrospectively considered, is ironic. At this point in the story its impact is different.

The extracts so far examined came from stories which have a narrator. Although there is no direct narrator in **"Admiring the Scenery"** the author stands very close behind the reader, never once letting the story get away on its own, constantly, though not always openly, influencing the way it is to be understood. In the passage quoted, for example, there are only three clear statements about Hanafan's appearance. His complexion is dark from shaving, he has wrinkles round his eyes, his lips are thin. All the rest is deduction on the part of the writer from these few facts. After this opening section, any mention of Hanafan or of what he does or says, is accompanied by words like "melancholy" or "gentle". The cumulative effect is for the reader to become more and more aware of a tragic happening in Hanafan's life. The writer is not content to let the facts speak for themselves because he is not prepared to reveal them all (particularly the one piece of information which would explain why Hanafan is a broken man) with the result that the writer has to bend everything in the story to establish a sense of total despair. O'Faoláin sees not the event as such, but the effect on Hanafan, as being important. Hence nature, the weather, the language, the other characters, the literary allusions, the setting, the story within the story, all are mobilised to concentrate the reader's attention to the last on a figure broken by sorrow.

Close examination has shown that **"Admiring the Scenery"** is a very carefully constructed story. It is perhaps an example of that formality which may only be found in art, because art often demands a pattern which is never found in life.

It is almost with a sense of relief that one turns now to the passage from **"Lady Lucifer"** in which the doctor is introduced. This is the man who will later tell the story within the story. Not everything is related, but nowhere in this story can one find the almost subliminal technique noted in **"Admiring the Scenery"**. Nor is the narrator the main character.

There are no words in the passage which carry emotional overtones. All that is said of the doctor is that he has sandy

Seán O'Faoláin, circa 1979.

hair and that he has a good figure. His facial expression is referred to briefly, but not in the same manner as with Hanafan. The description of Hanafan is highly metaphorical, deliberately evasive. One is told that he is a teacher. That is all. In the case of the doctor, just a few details of his professional career are given. Nothing is said about the kind of man he is, except that he "bore himself with the authority of experience and power". This is not suggestion, but direct statement.

The doctor's features are only indirectly mentioned: "serious, but not severe". Description of physical appearance is kept to a minimum. This is very typical of twentieth century short stories, although not always of O'Faoláin (as the passage from **"Up the Bare Stairs"** demonstrates). It is of course O'Faoláin who writes these words, and even bald statements of fact suggest something. Here they do no more than conjure up the appearance and background of a man about whom there are no unanswered questions because none are posed or provoked.

Both in **"Lady Lucifer"** and **"Up the Bare Stairs"** a much more factually descriptive technique is employed, even though there is a narrator in **"Up the Bare Stairs"**. He introduces Nugent ("my travelling companion"), looking at him across a railway compartment, attempting to imagine from what he sees, the kind of man Nugent is. Twice he makes statements in which he says what Nugent's appearance suggests: "He was dressed so conventionally that he might . . ." and "His temples were greying and brushed up in two sweeping wings—wherefore the suggestion of . . ." Neither of his assumptions is correct. There is no reason why they should be. He is only doing what any curious person might do when sharing a carriage with a stranger—he looks at that person, trying to deduce background and character from externalities. How different this is from **"Midsummer Night Madness"** where the narrator on occasion knows more than he should. For example, as has been seen already, the narrator has no reason for referring to the girl's hips as "too rich, too wide", unless—and that is not likely—he is judging the girl's appearance from an aesthetic point of view. The remark could then be interpreted as negative comment on the girl's figure. The narrator, and through him the author, is indulging in language which is initially confusing, only retrospectively to be understood as ironic.

In the description of Nugent, a statement is made—a very unequivocal one—which also turns out to be ironic: "He was obviously an Englishman who had crossed the night before". Nugent is Irish. Here the narrator seems to be basing his assumption on what he has in front of him. It is perfectly reasonable for him to do so. Yet the reader is being misled because the narrator knows that Nugent is not English. In this instance the writer quite obviously wishes the reader to feel his own way into the story. Nevertheless O'Faoláin is playing a kind of trick since he does not have to introduce Nugent in this way. He could just as easily have told the reader who Nugent was right from the start, so that even here, it is only an apparent lack of interference on the part of the writer. Admittedly the mistaken nationality is cleared up very early on in the story. It serves merely to bring the reader to experience with the narrator, not to influence the way the reader's mind will work.

This may be appreciated better if reference is once more made to the technique of evasiveness examined earlier in **"Admiring the Scenery"**. Two examples will suffice. Hanafan is introduced with the words, "There was nothing remarkable about this third man." There most certainly is. Even more striking is a statement which comes later. Hanafan is talking about the station-master:

> . . . "he had no sense and the people used to make a hare of him. He couldn't sing any more than I could. He had a small little voice, a small range too, but it had no strength or sweetness; there was no richness in it."

> The teacher said these words, strength, sweetness, richness, with a luscious curl of his thin lips around the fruit of sound. His eyes widened. Clearly he was seeing nothing but the old station master. Earnestly he went on, a small glow on each cheek.

Perhaps Hanafan was seeing the station-master; the reader is certainly being encouraged to think so. Yet the adverb "clearly" must here be understood as a distractor, particularly as the language used by Hanafan becomes increasingly emotional as he talks about this one night. Since Hanafan was not related to the station-master, there is no reason at all for his excitement. The deliberately distractive intent behind the use of "clearly" is confirmed in the following sentence: "Earnestly he went on, a small glow on each cheek." Why should Hanafan be so roused by the memory of a foolish old man? The explanation must be that he is thinking of something else which he does not mention and which O'Faoláin wishes to be withheld.

To return now to the description of Nugent, elsewhere in the introductory passage, there is—apart from the points already discussed—no evidence of the writer attempting to influence the reader. Physical details are given, also details of dress from which the narrator proceeds to draw conclusions as to the man's profession and background. O'Faoláin stresses the unremarkability—although he does not say Nugent was unremarkable: "He was dressed so conventionally that he might be. . . ." There is a marked lack of metaphorical expression. The adjectives employed are simple, ("bull-shouldered", "coarse", "sallow", "deep", "little", "black", "striped", "grey", "white") they do not have anything more than their usual meaning. In contrast to the doctor (**"Lady Lucifer"**) Nugent's features are dwelt on at some length. In both cases the effect is visual, the reader being offered a greater or lesser amount of information on which to build up his own impression. Here he is neither overtly nor unconsciously being influenced by the writer—except and in so far as everything in the story comes from O'Faoláin.

The doctor's two friends are introduced equally briefly;

> In the stern the priest lay like Velasquez's picture of "Old Silenus lolling in the sunshine", his bare paunch, immensely pink, spilling over his black trousers . . .

> The clerk was only a bank clerk by avocation:

his inward life was in his writing; he wrote novels and stories, over the name of Malachy Lucas.

If one again thinks back to the introduction of the other two men in **"Admiring the Scenery"**, one is immediately struck by the differences. Here all that one learns of the priest is that he is fat, an impression which is emphasized through the comparison with Silenus. O'Faoláin makes a point of explaining that the comparison comes not from him, but from the clerk ("It was he who had said that the priest was like old Silenus") almost suggesting that the writer no longer wishes to use such imagery, or does not intend that the reader shall be unconsciously influenced. Of course there is a further possibility that O'Faoláin's ascribing the remark to the clerk could be interpreted as reflecting more on Malachy than on the priest. Malachy is a dreamy, introspective man to whom such remarks come naturally. Elsewhere, both in the early and later work, O'Faoláin also compares his characters with models chosen from the arts—the Scottish girl (**"The Silence of the Valley"**) with Beethoven, Barbara (**"A Sweet Colleen"**) with Rossetti.

Of the priest in **"Admiring the Scenery"** O'Faoláin says that he was a man who had, "finally solved his problems in a spirit of good-humoured regret." In this story it was noticed that certain adjectives ("sad" and "gentle") accompanied both Hanafan and the priest through the story, so that these attributes came to be associated with the two men. This does not happen in **"Lady Lucifer"**, although it would be untrue to assert that O'Faoláin no longer employs such devices in other stories. In her chapter on **"Unholy Living and Half Dying"**, Suzanne Dockrell-Grünberg has shown how O'Faoláin, while writing in a seemingly light-hearted manner, can all the time keep referring to a central point in the story—death. (pp. 98-105)

In this story it is not so much the repetition of the same adjectives which helps the writer to establish the mood in the mind of the reader, but rather by using words or allusions which have to do with death, or which could be seen as having to do with death, that O'Faoláin successfully builds up a sense of the mortality of all things.

The objects and people around Cardew are mute yet expressive witnesses to the fact that he and they must pass away ("the stamp is on you", "the dying fire", "hollowed cheeks", "slow as a hearse", "faint knocking", "intense vacancy", "low tide"). While making such a statement, one must also realise that there is a difference between constantly referring to a character in a story as "gentle" or "sad", and surrounding him with objects and people, or having things happen to him, which remind him that he too will die. In both cases the reader may come to an awareness of the truth which the writer is offering through his story. Nevertheless, the reader does have a choice in **"Unholy Living and Half Dying"**. Although O'Faoláin is responsible for every word in the story, he still leaves it to the reader to interpret the signs, to take the hints—if he wishes to.

Even the beginning of the story, where Jacky Cardew is introduced, is not as unequivocal as it might at first appear:

Jacky Cardew is one of those club bachelors who are so well-groomed, well-preserved, pomaded, medicated, and self-cosseted that they seem ageless—the sort of fixture about whom his pals will say when he comes unstuck around the age of eighty, "Well, well! didn't poor old Jacky Cardew go off very fast at the end?"

This is a humorous, colloquial description. Physical details are given, but they suggest a type rather than an individual. Again it is up to the reader to imagine for himself. Nugent, although O'Faoláin devotes nearly a page to his description, is not more present than Cardew. Both men are given exteriors which would comfortably fit many of a certain type.

In **"Lady Lucifer"** and **"Up the Bare Stairs"**, the story is taken up by one of the main figures, although not immediately. This is particularly interesting in the case of **"Up the Bare Stairs"**. The narrator ("I") says not a word until Nugent has finished telling the story of his life, another example of the writer permitting the story to take its own course, of not endeavouring to over-ensure that the reader's thoughts will move in the right direction. In **"A Broken World"**, a much earlier story, the narrator constantly interrupts, talks and argues with the other characters, has an opinion which he expresses. He also sums up at the end. Nugent has his say without interruption. Afterwards the two men talk to each other for a few minutes before the train comes into the station. The narrator makes no final comments on what he has heard. The story closes with the narrator looking on as Nugent leaves the train and meets his relations on the platform.

The doctor (**"Lady Lucifer"**) tells the story of the asylum to illustrate a remark which he makes: "Pride and humility aren't opposites. They're two sides of the same thing." There is no reason for supposing that the doctor was personally involved in what happened at the asylum—or only in his professional capacity as a doctor. He obviously finds the woman in the tragedy attractive, but afterwards, in what he says when telling the story, it seems that he stands outside the affair which he uses merely in support of his argument. He tells the whole story, so far as one can judge. Hanafan, for example, left out one essential—what happened on that one night in the past. However there is a rather curious tendency on the part of the doctor and Nugent to describe others in language which is reminiscent of the early stories. For example, the doctor talking of the girl at the asylum:

> She was a beautiful girl. Tall as a spear. Dark as night. Her two eyes were two brown jewels set under her forehead. She was one of the most beautiful girls I have ever seen.

This is imagery which in theory should make the reader's mind work, since it is highly allusive. Expressions such as "Tall as a spear. Dark as night" are suggestive but they do not in fact lead the reader to try to imagine what the girl really looked like. Should he do so, he would become bewildered. "Spears", "night", "jewels", an accumulation of images, all trying very hard to convey beauty, instead, through the quick sequence of different nouns, tending to confuse rather than enlighten or clarify. These words

could suggest all kinds of ideas: the mysterious, the East, almost the supernatural. Indeed when the doctor first refers to the girl he says "She was like a goddess dressed in a wave."

In talking of Davidson, the doctor uses similar, if somewhat modified language: "Davidson, a gentle drooping fellow with a girlish complexion." This inferential description is repeated later: "I remember Davidson asking him about Africa, in his soft, drooly voice."

Additional points emerge from the references to Davidson. He loves the girl but is not loved by her. He cannot break with her, nor, when he is the only one to notice that Motherway (who returns to the asylum after a period of years and is about to marry the girl) is mad, does he say anything. He is "soft" in that he cannot tell the girl the truth. Retrospectively there is even a sinister, tragic, ring to the repetitive description of Davidson in such terms. Here one might see chinks in the hard, or apparently hard, shell of the doctor. He has made his way in life. So has Nugent. But at what cost? They are both capable of deep feeling, have learned to be mistrustful of it. Perhaps that is the reason why both, when describing others in a crisis situation, indulge in language which is emotional. For example, when Nugent mentions Angelo—even the names, Angelo, Motherway, have clear associations—

> There was a time when I thought he was the nicest little man in the whole school. Very handsome. Cheeks as red as a girl, black bristly hair, blue eyes and the most perfect teeth I've ever seen between a man's lips.

The suggestion appears to be that feminine features on a man are dangerous. Davidson is also described as "girlish". Both Davidson and Angelo are innocents who are easily injured. Perhaps theirs is the kind of innocence which Graham Greene so often attacks. For Greene, the fact of not knowing, or of being unaware, is considered inexcusable, punishable. In *The Quiet American,* Pyle's ingenuous attitude to Communism results in the killing of women and children. Neither Davidson nor Angelo is guilty of sins of this magnitude. Both however fail to act at moments of crisis, so that those towards whom they are emotionally attracted are hurt.

Elsewhere too, this negative innocence may be read into physical appearance. In **"The Man Who Invented Sin"**, for example:

> Brother Majellan was very different, a gentle, apple-cheeked man with big glasses, a complexion like a girl, teeth as white as a hound's, and soft, beaming eyes. He was an intelligent, beaming man.

Even Hanafan is briefly referred to in this way: "his oblong face . . . delicate as a woman's." Later in the story Majellan is censured by the narrator for refusing to see that in spite of what the local priest had pretended, there was no guilt attached to the relationship of the two nuns and two monks during those happy weeks spent together many years before.

However there is a difference. **"The Man Who Invented Sin"** is told by a narrator throughout. In **"Up the Bare**

Stairs" and "**Lady Lucifer**", Angelo, Davidson, Motherway and the girl are described by Nugent and the doctor, who enter the story after the beginning. Whereas both men generally speak modestly, eschewing the flamboyant, the moment they start to relate the past, their language changes. There are at least two sides to their personalities. The softer side, the side they do not often show, is still there. In this instance its existence is revealed through the passion expressed in their diction. It may be remembered that Hanafan's appearance and language also change when he talks about the past. The contrast here is between a man who is aware of the emotions, who gives them their due—if limited—place and a Hanafan who is broken by his sensitive nature.

Delineation of character in depth is not attempted in "**Up the Bare Stairs**" and "**Lady Lucifer**". The incidents, other characters, background, conversations, all are so chosen to have a bearing on the central statement. Hence the two other men in "**Lady Lucifer**" are shown in contrast to the doctor. They have not taken up the challenge of life. From what he says, it seems that the priest has taken refuge in the church. If he could, the clerk would act similarly by settling in the country where he feels he would have the right surroundings for inspiration.

The doctor is clearly aware of the state of mind of his two friends. When the three of them discuss where they would ideally like to live and the two others express a desire to retire to the country, the doctor interjects:

> "Lucas, you're not much over thirty. Isn't it a bit early to want to renounce the world?" The priest grinned. "I renounced the world at twenty-four."

The verb "renounce" is repeated twice in this paragraph—a word which implies a deliberate decision to opt out of life. Furthermore the implications of standing still, of not wishing to face reality, go even further. The two men may be considered against the larger background of Ireland and the Irish. O'Faoláin quotes the example of Liam O'Flaherty (through the doctor)—a man who left Ireland—and of the stories he wrote of those who remained behind:

> "The daft ones stayed at home and went into the woods and wrote poetry. Take care, Lucas."

The good physique of the doctor is mentioned several times ("finely-built", "soldierly") whereas the priest is very fat. May there not in this be more than a suggestion that not entering the world, brings with it both mental and physical decay? In this story, the other characters—particularly the two friends—are foils to the doctor. Whereas Hanafan and the priest in "**Admiring the Scenery**" were linked by common adjectives, here it is the differences which the reader is able to appreciate for himself.

It is perhaps even possible to see here that central split in character which Conrad reveals in his major novels; that danger-point which lies between the life of the imagination and the life which is kept firmly under control, where the calls of duty and common sense keep the door bolted and barred on doubts and hesitation. (pp. 105-10)

Joseph Storey Rippier, in his The Short Stories of Seán O'Faoláin: A Study in Descriptive Techniques, *Colin Smythe, 1976, 162 p.*

Guy Le Moigne   (essay date 1979)

[*In the following excerpt, Le Moigne presents an overview of O'Faoláin's short fiction.*]

[O'Faoláin's] lifelong dedication to the writing craft is reflected in what one must describe as a considerable amount of fictional and nonfictional work (a most inadequate distinction, in fact, since in a few instances the boundary-line appears on close scrutiny to be rather elusive). The short stories sometimes, especially in the extremely creative period of the thirties, look like occasional accretions. Some critics have even blamed O'Faoláin for being indiscriminately prolific, wishing that he had devoted more of his precious time to writing short fiction. That kind of statement is obviously based on the assumption that his other works are only derivative. Still, leaving aside the question of evaluating his achievement in those respective fields, the impression that prevails on moving from one work to another is one of unity and continuity. His literary production as a whole proceeds from a persistent quest for style and perception and for a synthesis of both. That basic concern is variously expressed in his versatile, many-faceted writing, whether he gives his main themes discursive treatment or imaginative embodiment. There is a very close interrelationship between his historical biographies, travel books, critical writings, essays, autobiography, his one play, *She Had to Do Something,* and his fiction. The insights which he gained through his relentless curiosity, whether he probed into the past of his own country looking for constructive political thought-patterns that would reconcile the revolutionary spirit with a pragmatic attitude or went exploring foreign cultures in a constant search for wholeness and unity, gradually transformed his vision and consequently his approach to short-story writing. One feels however that the interaction between the various genres is much more intricate. The reconstruction of the historical past of his country, for instance, in such biographies as *King of the Beggars* or *The Great O'Neill,* especially of those periods which he deemed highly significant, setting useful and essential guidelines for the future, gave free play to his fictional gifts and enabled him to develop new skills. The search for perception became inseparable from the search for a style that he could claim his own. All those works therefore played a decisive part in the emergence of that "personal way of seeing and saying" which one recognizes unmistakably as one moves from one story to another. Yet despite this variety of his literary pursuits it is through his stories that O'Faoláin's development as a writer can be most fully traced.

The short narrative under its two species: the "short story" and the "tale", a much-quoted distinction which O'Faoláin established in his preface to **The Heat of the Sun,** is indeed a genre to which he has remained faithful all his life. His exploration of the technical resources of that literary medium enabled him to treat with increasing subtlety and sophistication an ever-widening range of themes and subjects that reflected a persistent quest for a mature, articulate vision capable of holding together the many contradictions of man's nature including his own. Certainly no other tribute would be more appropriate to do justice to his achievement as a short-story writer than the one he himself paid to his forerunner and favourite model, Anton Tchekhov:

> . . . he is one of the most heartening examples of skilful self-management, of the art of keeping the lines clear from beginning to end of the journey.

Seán O'Faoláin's "love-affair" with the short-story has been going on now for over half a century. It began at an early age. He was in his early teens when he saw his first work in print. Other juvenilia, stories and poems, came in its trail and were published in Cork local papers. But it took him another decade before he found his own voice. He made a decisive breakthrough with the publication of **"In Lilliput"**—a story later included in **Midsummer Night Madness** (1932),—in *The Irish Statesman* of February 6th 1926.

> . . . It was my first tiny success, yet showing already how through form or order I was liberated into myself, to good effect,

he commented later in *Vive Moi!*, as he painstakingly pinpointed the various stages in his slow development as a writer.

As his work now stands, his credentials as a professional short story writer are based on the 85 stories and tales collected in the eight volumes which have been published at regular intervals since 1932. Not much would be gained by adding to O'Faoláin's own canon the comparatively few minor pieces that might be gleaned in various papers and magazines, except perhaps the odd satisfaction of bringing the total number close to a hundred. As his later collection, **Foreign Affairs and Other Stories** (1976), shows, he still writes highly entertaining tales in a masculine, youthful prose. But all the same this is a small output compared with the twenty volumes produced by Guy de Maupassant in the space of fifteen years or the dozen stories or so that Anton Tchekhov could write within a year as he went through bursts of creative activity. Seán O'Faoláin was to forestall that kind of objection in his preface to a selection of his stories [**The Stories of Seán O'Faoláin**] which he published in mid-career:

> Story after story by Maupassant is journeyman stuff. I can now reread only the Chekhovs that I have ticked off on the contents page . . . I have learned in my thirty-odd years of serious writing only one sure lesson: that stories, like whiskey, must be allowed to mature in the cask. And that takes so much time! . . .

In an interview given in the same period he added:

> I truly don't believe that anyone can do more than about three of them a year. He can't, that is, if they are good ones . . . [Lewis Nichols, "Talking with Mr. O'Faoláin," *New York Times Book Review* LXII, 1957]

As far as he was concerned, this was a fairly optimistic estimate, for he was well below that target. This pace of pro-

duction remained steady during the following years. The only noticeable change was that he displayed an increased predilection for the longer form of the tale more suitable for the new themes he was handling.

By his constant advance and change in subject-matter and style, by his devotion to his craft, O'Faoláin has lived several lives in one.

—Guy Le Moigne

Seán O'Faoláin could hardly be viewed as a capricious writer who works by fits and starts. By his constant advance and change in subject-matter and style, by his devotion to his craft, he has lived several lives in one. He is undoubtedly something of a bifrontal writer. Behind the artist whose style acquires increasing panache, bringing at times his stories movingly close to the lyric, hides a strong disciplinarian. He has constantly practised the kind of asceticism that enabled him to submit his writing to exacting formal standards. Besides obvious gifts of imagination and feeling he was endowed with a fine intellect which expanded considerably through academic training, something he has always been grateful for. Yet instead of stemming the creative impulse this formidable critical faculty helped him to marshal his sometimes contradictory natural gifts and impulses and thus to achieve progressively that unique balance between feeling and intelligence in a poetic mind. But at the same time it set him apart from those instinctive writers such as Faulkner, Gorki, Seán O'Casey etc. . . , whom he described in *The Vanishing Hero* as having more genius than talent, writing out of the depths of an inexhaustible imagination. In a recent self-portrait [in his "A Portrait of the Artist as an Old Man"], he labelled himself as a "writer of talent", i.e. a writer dogged by that self-consciousness which Henry James saw as one of the distinctive features of modern writers. Concern with the formal requirements of his art played an important part in his development, but remained subordinated to a truthful, scrupulous translation of his groping search for a vision of life that would afford "cohesion plus variety", in other words, "unity of thought". As far as the short narrative is concerned he is no experimental writer, except perhaps in some of his most recent tales where he makes sporadic attempts at updating his fictional idiom under the influence of contemporary American writers. He remains to a large extent a traditionalist.

He has adopted and made his own the modern form of the short story inherited from his Irish predecessors, George Moore and James Joyce, and their French or Russian forerunners.

This self-consciousness far from being detrimental to his artistic development impelled him to work out for himself the critical standards he desperately needed to protect himself from the prevailing complacency engendered by that Celtic foible, the art of indiscriminate praise. They were singularly lacking, as he often complained, in a country which remained "a paradise for the *homme sensuel moyen*, that untranslatable compound of sense, sensibility, and mere sensation, a purgatory for the artist, and a hell for the intellectual" ["On Being an Irish Writer," *The Spectator* CXCI, 1953]. One of his characters, Pat Lenihan, on whom falls the burden of impersonating the fate of the artist in post-revolutionary Ireland, exclaims: "What's the use? Who hears me? . . . Who could tell in this hole of a city whether I was good or bad? . . ." This was O'Faoláin's own dilemma, although he was well on the way of resolving it. Following the early advice of Daniel Corkery and the pattern set by James Joyce, he went looking for models beyond the local sphere not in order to desert his native material but so as to enhance it and impart to it a universal relevance through a wider range of narrative and stylistic means. He went far afield in his exploration of Russian, French, English and American literature without neglecting the Irish tradition, learning from other writers' experience, measuring their achievement and probing into the personal and technical struggle involved in each case.

Of those influences the most decisive is undoubtedly that of Anton Chekhov with whom he is often associated in laudatory articles or reviews that occasionally describe him as "Chekhov in Erin". This is probably stretching the parallel too far. Seán O'Faoláin who made much of the Russian short-story writer in his critical writings is partly to blame for this. But his restatement of the question in a recent interview is useful in reminding critics that they should not follow blindly the leads which they are offered:

> You know, people have talked about Chekhov and Turgenev and so forth, and certainly I learned from them. But the man who's really influenced me and whom I really admired was Shaw, who cut through all the sentimentality. He was able to hold quite tenderly the things that were important to him, and still know that sometimes they had to be looked at objectively. [W. L. Webb, "An Interview" in *The Guardian*, 1976]

Yet one cannot help but notice how strikingly close this evaluation runs to his earlier appraisal of Chekhov's blend of realism and poetic feeling [in his *The Short Story*]:

> What sometimes deludes the sophisticated is the poetry in which he seems to drown this banality, so that they see the beautiful mists and fail to see behind these mists the hard, mocking mind of the doctor, the moralist and the judge.

O'Faoláin obviously praised in Chekhov the selfsame qualities which he had been admiring in a fellow-Irishman but which were this time invested in his own medium.

Such remarks passed on writers that have meant so much to him reveal by implication the main dilemma with which he was confronted in his own creative work. When O'Faoláin's stories strike us as being Chekhovian in manner or mood, he is not merely imitating him but striving in his own idiosyncratic terms after that balance between personal emotion and objective treatment. This kinship

became more conspicuous over the years as O'Faoláin moved towards more intimate, introspective subjects, focusing his stories on increasingly complex shades of feeling, bringing them sometimes close to the mood of a lyric or of an elegy. But the influence of the Russian artist together with that of other story-writers whom he studied appears much earlier through the command which he gradually gained over his medium of expression, as he began hovering around areas of experience attuned to his own inflammable sensibility. In stories of the mid-thirties included in *A Purse of Coppers* (1937) such as **"Sinners"**, **"Admiring the Scenery"**, **"A Meeting"** or **"Discord"**. there is evidence of a subtler approach to short-story writing. Some of them are elegiac in tone, they are all saturated with a sense of dejection, of quiet despair. But at the same time through the varied, imaginative interplay between atmosphere and mood, between the past and the present they acquire a much greater level of suggestiveness that goes along with a tightened, less episodic structure. They stand in sharp contrast to earlier stories in the same volume that suffer either from heavy-handed didacticism in the case of **"A Born Genius"** and, to a lesser extent, **"A Broken World"**, excessive indulgence in slapstick comedy or satirical treatment in **"The Old Master"** and **"Sullivan's Trousers"** or from authorial manipulation of the kind found in **"Egotists"** and **"Kitty the Wren"**.

But despite their flaws and in particular their overexplicitness and occasional discursiveness these stories are not wholly unsuccessful. They indicate that O'Faoláin is gradually mastering the techniques of a form more modern than the one consistently used in the tales of *Midsummer Night Madness*. The prose-line shows signs of greater simplicity, which in itself is no mean achievement when one considers his earlier predilection for lengthy, involved periods running at times one page long on the crest of romantic lyricism. This time scenic presentation, i.e. sequences of scenes linked up by short descriptive segments almost acting as stage-directions, tends to prevail over summary narrative. The long expository sequences of the first tales are likewise superseded by more abrupt openings that take us right into the heart of the action or of the situation or into some odd corner of the narrator's consciousness, thus imparting to the story a greater immediacy and directness. Through those stylistic and narrative innovations brought to the structure of the story as well as the tentative exploration of new modes such as comedy, satire and pathos, O'Faoláin achieved a much greater concentration and compactness in his narratives. But one feels that the pendulum has swung to the other extreme and that the remedies used have been too drastic. A greater objectivity is achieved but at the expense of those emotional, poetic qualities that cause the reader of the first tales to overlook their occasional clumsiness and frequent mannerisms. The stories are much more compact, they show evidence of a more sophisticated craftsmanship, but by and large they rely too much on statement instead of working through suggestion and implication, which would make the experience of reading them much more rewarding. This failure is partly remedied in the following stories which improve considerably on those new skills, blending poetic suggestiveness and realistic treatment. O'Faoláin thus hit upon a basic formula that enabled him to solve his artistic dilemma and which he kept developing and extending towards more refined and varied stylistic and narrative forms.

In view of the turn taken by his evolution over recent years one may wonder whether the more leisurely and traditional form of the "tale" has not been the genre that suited O'Faoláin best. This was how he defined it in contradistinction to the short story proper:

> A tale is quite different. Like a small plane it is much more free, carries a bit more cargo, roves farther, has time and space for more complex characterisation, more changes of mood, more incidents and scenes, even more plot . . . It has its own problems, however, for the writer, whose toughest task is to orchestrate his Tale into a single, satisfying shape of flight. [*The Heat of the Sun*]

There is in O'Faoláin a suppressed novelist who needs a broader canvas than the one currently allotted to the short-story. In that respect he falls short of that complete self-abnegation which he considered as "the absolute essential of the modern short story". He relishes the part of the narrator and carries it with gusto in the manner of the 18th century novelists and those writers who took the tradition into the following century. There is something Dickensian, for instance, in the touch of caricature based on animal imagery that almost invariably emphasizes the physical and moral peculiarities of his characters. He needs some space to give free play to those pictorial gifts which enable him to conjure place, atmosphere and scenery, to describe with artful casualness the dwellings and garb of his people. It is no surprise that in his critical writings he should draw parallels between his craft and the painter's art. His characters are fully realized as physical human beings rooted in their social and geographic environment, shaped by their own choices but also by the force of circumstance. "Reification", one of his favourite critical concepts, in other words, the painter's trick, is the only explanation for this illusion of reality. There is something profoundly healthy about his prose which combines sensuous imagery, romantic feeling and a robust sense of humour. It enhances the mystery and beauty of the gift of life. A most companionable writer, his aim is not only to instruct, but above all to entertain, i.e. share with the reader his own delight in man's physicality, inner resources and oddities.

More than the earlier stories the tales of the second period reveal O'Faoláin's obsession with the classical ideal. There is sufficient evidence of this in the greater degree of contrivance in his plots as well as in the increased refinement of his idiom. The first feature has not escaped critics' notice. As Roger Garfitt pointed out [in his "Constants in Contemporary Irish Fiction," *Two Decades of Irish Writing*, Douglas Dunn, ed.]:

> Perceptive as the stories are, their limitation is that rather than being drawn from the daily process of living they tend to be set at chance crossroads somewhere on the edges of experience.

Likewise the complexity and ambiguity of the themes are gradually matched by a more ornate, florid idiom. This growing aestheticism sometimes goes to the point of affectation as literary and artistic reminiscences keep intruding. The story is viewed at a second remove, as it were, as we follow its reverberations through the narrator's mind, this at the expense of dramatic immediacy. In O'Faoláin's hands the short story has grown into a highly civilized, sophisticated art, not to say aristocratic, meant for those select few who, in Malraux's words, are literature and art addicts. The stories as a result have a haunting quality, a kind of hypnotic effect. In the staccato opening of **"The Inside Outside Complex"**, for instance, O'Faoláin employs a short-hand style laced with slightly archaic, quaint words. This is bravura comic writing, and the element of exaggeration is, of course, part and parcel of the comic mode. For in most cases art, especially the writer's comic gifts and lyricism, disguises artifice. This more rambling form does not necessarily preclude suggestiveness. As one reviewer rightly emphasized:

> He knows exactly how much to explain and when to remain silent. "who was it," one of his characters wonders, "said the last missing bit of every jigsaw is God" . . . [Paul Gray, in his "Celtic Twilight," *Time Magazine*, January 26, 1976]

Few writers have emphasized as much as O'Faoláin did that the business of writing is a slow, arduous process. He may be, as he himself put it, "a besotted romantic" in many respects, but he has all his wits about him when he talks about the creative process, dispelling all the romantic fallacies that are too often associated with that human activity. "Writing is a long, long lifetime study", he reminds us in *Vive Moi!*. Short-story writing is a craft. It cannot do away with time, the necessity of mastering skills, the necessity of growth and change. But what distinguishes it from other crafts is the extent to which it involves the self of the writer. The most difficult obstacles to overcome are not technical but personal, especially in the case of the short story which is essentially, as O'Faoláin kept insisting, "an emphatically personal exposition" [in his *The Short Story*]. W.B. Yeats's advice: "Write yourself into yourself" kept ringing into his ears and urged him to seek out the means of attaining that balance between style and personality.

Quite understandably, when he fails in this, his stories lack the human depth and warmth that irradiate from his best stories and tales. They are not necessarily technical failures. They sound less convincing mainly on account of the choice of subject or even occasionally of setting, and in a few cases on account of the choice of satire, a mode alien to his own genius given to gentle teasing but hardly to derisive harassment of his fictional creations. This paradox will be found again and again. There are situations and themes close to his own personal experience which O'Faoláin handles almost instinctively in a manner that often inclines us to forget the amount of painstaking work that lies behind those achievements. On the other hand, scenes that are, for instance, set in the destitute areas of his hometown, Cork, are not as shrewdly realized as in Frank O'Connor's stories. He is more at home with literate figures—teachers, clerical figures in the first period, and then professionals in his later stories and tales where the settings are nearly always urban and even cosmopolitan—characters belonging to the Irish middle-class. Seldom does his imaginative sympathy enable him to venture outside this narrow social spectrum. But there are a few successful forays, as in **"Midsummer Night Madness"** where the sympathies of the young narrator gradually veer towards that hated symbol of the Ascendancy, the pathetic figure of old Henn. Likewise if his use of demotic idiom may often sound contrived, it can occasionally be quite effective. One notable instance is represented by that fascinating artifact entitled **"The Heat of the Sun"**, where literary reminiscences from *Cymbeline* play upon the beauty and the squalor of a pathetic encounter in the slums of Dublin between a young sailor ashore and a neglected wife whose husband, a mildly eccentric, garrulous barman, is dying in hospital.

But as a rule there are obvious limitations to O'Faoláin's range of inspiration which are predetermined by his life-pattern and the moral, spiritual and religious questions that have kept obsessing him. Whenever he transgresses them, he seems to betray his own gifts. Should he strike out too far from his own home-ground, as it were, his stories are marred by artificiality, implausibility and contrivance. Fortunately failure is averted owing to his zestful sense of comedy. Besides those pitfalls were to be avoided as O'Faoláin having overcome some of the moral and spiritual uncertainties that had bedevilled him began in mid-career drawing more extensively upon personal memories of childhood and youth, reviving some of the material previously used in his three novels, *A Nest of Simple Folk, Bird Alone, Come Back to Erin,* and dealing with themes intimately related to his own development as a human being. Paradoxically enough, he achieved a much greater measure of freedom by surrendering to the passion of memory, which fabled itself into art.

The use of autobiographical material is one of the most persistent features of his stories and tales. Any critic biassed against a biographical approach to literary works would have in O'Faoláin's case to make important concessions just as Paul Valéry who initiated this modern trend had to in his comparative study of Villon and Verlaine:

> But in the present case, he unwillingly admitted, the biographical issue cannot be dismissed. It has to be taken into account, and I must do what I have just condemned.

Confessions made by an artist, he added, are often far from being factually accurate. If he tells the truth, he does not tell the whole truth and he does not only tell the truth:

> An artist selects his material, even when he confesses himself. And all the more so perhaps when he confesses himself. He tones things down or heightens them, here and there . . .

O'Faoláin has written a great deal about himself. Afraid of insincerity, he spent much of his life attempting to understand the deep contradictions within himself. His biographies and travel books were, as is often the case, partly autobiographical. This he readily admits, in *South to Sicily,* for example, when he points out straightaway: "One travels inside oneself. It's all done with mirrors". But it is

mostly his account of the first thirty years of his life, *Vive Moi!,* and a recent self-portrait commissioned by *The Irish University Review* which have established him as a master of that peripheral fictional genre. The comment he appended to an overtly autobiographical story, **"The Kitchen"**, first published in the same review, makes a rather successful attempt at drawing a line between autobiography and this dramatized version of a personal experience.

One of the aspects of the creative process that has engaged his attention most is doubtless the part played by memory. Many of his stories tend to be retrospective in some way or other. And in his characters' lives reminiscences are wedded with aspirations as they move uneasily towards some moment of greater awareness. The workings of memory are continuously scrutinized, most strikingly so in the title-piece of *I Remember! I Remember!* which almost reads like a counterpart to Paul Claudel's dramatization of the opposition between "Animus" and "Anima", setting at variance factual memory and affective memory. This parable makes clear that in life as well as in art memories alone will not suffice. Imagination must reactivate and fecundate remembered images recent or remote and turn them into inspiring thoughts and works of art through an unexpected blend of memory and imagination. If O'Faoláin's stories are so densely permeated by memories of his life including those recalled from books, these are remembered and remoulded into new creations.

Recurrent interferences between biographical facts and fiction reveal an oversubjective preoccupation which is however often transcended through dramatic detachment and humour, his two chief methods of objectivization. One must admit though that stories by O'Faoláin remain above all pieces of writing "wrested from the tensions of his life" and of his personality. As a result his vision of life is essentially agonistic. The various obstacles, either subjective or external, he had to come to terms with either during his formative years or during his career as a man of letters have led him to regard life as a succession of challenges. The theme that increasingly fascinated him was that of the limitations to individual self-fulfillment. Yet what imparts to this central obsession its particular urgency and poignancy is the knowledge of the "potential wholeness and integrity of human nature" that had been forced upon him during those brief phases when he felt at one with himself and the world, for instance, as a youngster overcome by his first vision of love, a youth taking part in the struggle for national independence "privileged to see men at their finest" or as an adult joining the Empire of the Roman Catholic Church. Aching memories of those "few bright hours of grace" reminiscent of the bliss of the paradise of early infancy when one lives "in the waking sleep of childish content, a hibernatory cocoon of total happiness" will persistently haunt his fiction. His stories therefore frequently circle round a sense of loss, the emotional frustration caused either by the social pressures that are brought to bear upon the individual, by one's miscalculations or mismanagement of the business of life, or more fundamentally by man's time-bound condition. Many of his characters are burdened with feelings of nostalgia for blissful moments or missed opportunities at one stage or another in their past lives. The pathos of their lives reminds us very much of Boethius's maxim quoted by old Theo in *A Nest of Simple Folk*:

> *Fuisse felicem et non esse, omnium est infelicissimum genus*; to have been happy at one time and then to be unhappy after, isn't that the greatest unhappiness in the whole world?

But this truth cuts both ways. As we are reminded in such stories as **"Liars", "Feed my Lambs"** or **"Our Fearful Innocence"**, brief moments of fulfillment however ambiguous are treasured ever after and enable one to take an otherwise unpleasant and sterile existence in one's stride without being overpowered by despair.

O'Faoláin's stories frequently circle round a sense of loss, the emotional frustration caused either by the social pressures upon the individual, by one's miscalculations or mismanagement of the business of life, or more fundamentally by man's time-bound condition.

—Guy Le Moigne

What distinguishes O'Faoláin from most of his contemporaries, and this is a constant feature of his work, is the fact that the theme of man's estrangement from his true self, his fellow-being and his environment is not absolutely taken for granted. There is no sense of irretrievability, for man can be redeemed. What perplexes him rather is the uneven course of man's life and the fact that he only seems to achieve "complete integrity . . . in moments as brief, if one compares them with the whole span of a human life, as a lighthouse blink". O'Faoláin's inveterate idealism goes against the grain of the tenets of the age.

The key-image in his work that embodies those ambivalent feelings is undoubtedly that of exile. He progressively extended it into an all-comprehensive metaphor of modern man's predicament. Like all organic images in an artist's work, it is deeply rooted in his own experience. Before actually leaving his country for a few years he had been like every Irishman both frightened and fascinated by that alternative. "Change your place, change your fate" may not always sound as a romantic fallacy especially when the individual finds himself confronted, as O'Faoláin did, with the various strictures laid on him by faith, family and fatherland. This is no better at times than suffering from the pangs of actual exile. It is no surprise that in a story of the thirties, **"The Born Genius"**, he came to describe Cork, his native town, as a "city of exile". He was to make more explicit what he meant by this in *An Irish Journey*:

> Cork is no place for sensitive folk. I have known more men of real talent, who in another atmosphere might have been fruitful, become frustrated and warped in this city than I have ever met in any other of its size. To succeed here you have to have the skin of a rhinoceros, the dissim-

ulation of a crocodile, the agility of a hare, the speed of a hawk. Otherwise for every young Corkonian the word is—"Get out—and get out *quick*".

There is about O'Faoláin a harsh streak. It is part of the survivor kit without which he would not have developed into a complete human being, let alone a full-fledged artist. But such pages largely eclipsed by lyrical celebrations of the hidden beauties of Cork are written obviously out of "that hatred born of jealousy without which there is no true love". The image of exile in whatever guise it recurs through his fiction is always linked up with an ingrown tendency to perceive reality in dualistic terms, to respond to it both intellectually and emotionally.

Exile became an explicit concern of his second and third volumes of short stories, **A Purse of Coppers** and **Teresa.** They dramatize in various forms the condition of individuals whose emotional and spiritual development is almost invariably thwarted in the dispiriting scene of post-revolutionary Ireland. Their state of alienation is ascribed to the disruption of the social fabric and the lack of a workable alternative that would fill the Irish people with a renewed sense of purpose. In **"The Silence of the Valley"** characters belonging to the new generation are brought close to the remnants of an organic social tradition now almost extinct. Still the stories may at times convey the faint hope that the lonely people of Ireland can be reunited:

> What image of life that would fire and fuse us all, what music bursting like the spring, what triumph, what engendering love, so that those breast mountains that now looked cold should appear brilliant and gay, the white land that seemed to sleep should appear to smile, and these people who huddled over the embers of their lives should become like the peasants who held the hand of Faust with their singing one Easter morning? . . .

In **Midsummer Night Madness**, O'Faoláin's first collection of stories, the basic conflicts were already outlined. When one considers it in retrospect, it appears to a large extent as a kind of seminal work. It contains potentialities of development almost left untapped by the stories of the middle period too much concerned with local and historical conditioning. It makes more allowance for "the inevitable desires of the heart" and the inner tensions of emotional growth. These tales of the Irish rebellion in which O'Faoláin transposed the excitement and the nightmare of his involvement in the Civil War as a Republican pinpoint the various stages of growing disillusionment with Irish nationalism and the gradual release through love. They are steeped in luscious romantic imagery of the Irish countryside touched with the pathos of collapsing dreams.

Later stories extended the theme of loneliness and exile considerably as they revealed its psychological, moral and spiritual implications through a greater variety of modes using such ingredients as pathos, comedy and poetry in shifting combinations. Still the part played by external circumstances is not overlooked, but brought in with greater subtlety and complexity. It is seldom given the emphatic treatment it receives in **"Brainsy"**, where the narrator confronted with the unrecognizable, corpse-like appearance of an old friend he had known earlier as a young man and a pal full of zest for life cannot refrain from thinking:

> . . . why must everybody in Ireland live like an express train that starts off for heaven full of beautiful dreams, and marvellous ambitions and, halfway, bejasus, you switch off the bloody track down some sideline that brings you back to exactly where you began . . .

This is all the same quite a successful story through its deft balance between poignancy and poetic symbolism. The concluding images leave a lasting imprint upon the reader's mind.

Stories and tales belonging to that period evince on the whole a much greater serenity and are much more subdued than during the first half of O'Faoláin's artistic career. They reflect a change of outlook that came with the discovery that freedom lies in acquiescence. But this does not lead to smug optimism. There is still a strong undercurrent of nostalgia that seems to contaminate his work. The plaintive note which is often struck culminates in those elegiac moments that recur throughout his later prose.

The greater measure of self-acceptance led to a renewal of inspiration, a quickening of new creative energies, especially a refined sense of humour and comedy. They developed as he went on exploring the ambiguities of man's nature, the intricate workings of memory in *I Remember! I Remember!,* the various shapes of passion in *The Heat of the Sun,* the pains of growth and change in *The Talking Trees,* the trickiness of the course of illicit love in *Foreign Affairs,* concerns which enabled him to achieve a more supple mixture of particulars and universality:

> I would, then, in my late life-acceptance, embracing as much as I had the courage to embrace of all of life's inherent evil and weakness, try to write, however tangentially, about those moments of awareness when we know three truths at one and the same moment: that life requires of each of us that we should grow up and out whole and entire, that human life of its nature intricately foils exactly this, and that the possibility of wholeness is nevertheless as constant and enormous a reality as the manifold actuality of frustration, compromise, getting caught in some labyrinth, getting cut short by death. [*Vive Moi!*]

He found at last that "concordance between temperament and subject" in which the secret of the short story lies. He became increasingly fascinated with those inner obstacles to self-fulfillment which people tend to create through their boundless capacity for self-delusion, conveying the suggestion that a self-imposed moral and spiritual exile is infinitely worse than the one forced upon us by circumstance. Very often man brings the pangs of emotional deprivation upon himself through his own foolishness and folly. Middle-aged, affluent celibates, O'Faoláin's sad-eyed clowns, are often made to carry that burden. Many of his recent stories that are cast in the comic mode display the concerns of a moralist perplexed by his fellow-man's incompetence in existential matters. He has chosen as his province the vagaries of the human heart. His sense of fun always combines psychological insight with an extraordinary mixture of sound humour tinged with gentle scepticism and the sentimentality of an irrepressible romantic. His stories and tales belong to a tradition which beyond Stendhal and Chekhov, two of his favourite models, can be traced back to the sentimental works of the 18th century, Mozart's operas and Sterne's prose-fiction for instance, which Saul Bellow in *To Jerusalem and Back* described as "comedies in which cries are torn from the heart". (pp. 208-24)

> *Guy Le Moigne, "Seán O'Faoláin's Short-Stories and Tales," in* The Irish Short Story, *edited by Patrick Rafroidi and Terence Brown, Humanities Press, Inc., 1979, pp. 205-26.*

Bruce Allen (essay date 1983)

[*In the following mixed review of* The Collected Stories of Seán O'Faoláin, *Allen praises technical aspects of O'Faoláin's short fiction, but criticizes the volume's uneven tone.*]

This enormous volume [*The Collected Stories of Seán O'Faoláin*] includes everything that appeared in the eminent Irish writer's eight previously published collections, plus half a dozen "uncollected stories" dated 1982. Among these 90 "stories and tales" are several undeniable classics, and a few dozen effective entertainments. But, on balance, this is uneven work, unworthy of his publisher's claim that Seán O'Faoláin is "one of the great story-tellers since the death of Chekhov."

What he is is a remarkably skillful and sophisticated technician who can render a small private world in such evocative, echoing detail that its universal relevance is instantly suggested; a chronicler of local conflicts who's adept at presenting two sides of a contretemps. He's one of the masters of realistic dialogue, and he can bring a character to life in a quick, vivid paragraph.

Why, then, do I not feel O'Faoláin qualifies as a great writer? The answer lies partly in his very virtuosity (his ability to create someone or something fascinating, and his habit of shifting impatiently to focus elsewhere), and partly in the distance and distastefulness I infer from his many portrayals of Ireland at war with England and itself. O'Faoláin was a republican fighter during the Civil War, but his subsequent writings are far from a glorification of his country's rebellious history. He seems to connect Ireland's truculent separatist spirit with its people's material poverty and their virtual enslavement to obsolete political and religious ideas. It's as if Ireland is a ghost that haunts its own citizens, and Seán O'Faoláin is so appalled by their superstitiousness and timidity he's unable to take them fully seriously.

This curious coolness is evident even in O'Faoláin's best work, much of which appeared in his first two collections, *Midsummer Night Madness,* (1932) and *A Purse of Coppers* (1937). These stories of revolutionary ardor and social disruption are often conveyed to us by a young (usually idealistic) listener-narrator, who's quick to imply judgments on the characters he thus observes. O'Faoláin has called these early stories "very romantic." They are, and they aren't. **"Fugue"** describes the helplessness of two young Irish rebels pursued by English officers, and **"Lilliput"** celebrates a Mother Courage-like figure, a Cork tinkerwoman undaunted by the violence all around her. Yet **"The Small Lady"** contrasts a pleasure-loving, treacherous Englishwoman against her Irish enemies (and captors), to the credit of neither "side": The revolutionaries' idealism is no less flawed than is her decency.

Several of the stories are still more cynical. **"The Bomb Shop"** dramatically depicts a commitment to violence that draws even unwilling souls into its orbit. **"The Patriot"** ironically contrasts a disillusioned young rebel with a passionately committed republican "orator." The young man turns to the consolations of marital love; the old man continues to fight his never-ending battles.

There are numerous criticisms of the persistence of revolutionary sentiment throughout people's later lives. The two elderly protagonists of **"No Country for Old Men"** react differently to their accidental involvement in latter-day "underground" violence: One embraces the danger eagerly; the other laments that they are only shadows of their former vigorous selves.

But the revolution is scarcely O'Faoláin's only target. We see strong condemnations of Ireland's mindless puritanism in **"The Old Master,"** about a village intellectual's dismay over his neighbors' contempt for a visiting Russian ballet troupe. ("They know nothing. The beauty of the world. The grace of the human body. All lost on them.") The same sentiment is handled far more artfully in the fine story **"A Born Genius,"** which tells of a promising young tenor's failure to put aside his inherited prejudices and adapt to an offered "new life" in America.

Several of O'Faoláin's thinnest, glibbest stories picture ignorant or dishonest priests and nuns; a few are critical of Roman Catholic rigidity. **"Teresa"** is an engrossing story about a young girl's inconsistent wish to become a nun, and eventual rejection of the religious life; it's interesting because its title character is honest and complex, and because her vacillating devotion is attractively and movingly portrayed. **"The Man Who Invented Sin"** describes the experiences of four young novices—two men and two women—on a boating party and then following the accusation that their innocent high spirits have skirted impropriety—a charge that has a lasting, cramping effect on their later lives. This celebrated story (probably its author's best) features one of O'Faoláin's finest strokes—a vision of the elderly priest-accuser (as he walked away, "his elongated shadow waved behind him like a tail") as the devil.

Later works, from the 1950s and after, offer more general laments for the passing of the "old ways" (**"The Silence of the Valley"**) and portrayals of people inhibited by the past; then some find they can't escape its grip (**"The Fur Coat"**), others long for lives different from the ones they've chosen (**"A Touch of Autumn in the Air," "The Sugawn Chair"**).

This autumnal mood is still more dominant in O'Faoláin's very recent work, of which not much need be said. The stories from **The Talking Trees** and **Foreign Affairs** . . . bring their hidebound locals out of Ireland, into other countries, and into erotic involvements, handled with an increasing sexual explicitness that's far from O'Faoláin's best manner. His narrative skills have remained undiminished, and he's never less than entertaining. But of the final two dozen or so stories in this collection, the only one I'd strongly recommend is **"Hymeneal,"** the portrayal of an elderly couple in retirement that builds toward its protagonist's surprised understanding of the kind of person ("an irate man full of cold principle") he has always been.

It will not do, as I've indicated, to compare Seán O'Faoláin with the short-story masters—certainly not with James Joyce (whose Olympian view of Ireland's cultural paralysis he shares and imitates), or Henry James (with whom he seems to beg comparison). Still, his best work will be remembered and should be properly valued. (pp. 21-2)

Bruce Allen, "Seán O'Faoláin Collection: Evocative but Uneven," in The Christian Science Monitor, *October 12, 1983, pp. 21-2.*

John Hildebidle (essay date 1989)

[*In the following excerpt, Hildebidle delineates differences between O'Faoláin's early and late fiction.*]

In the opening pages of **"Midsummer Night Madness,"** at the very beginning of the first of O'Faoláin's collections of stories, a young Corkonian called by the author's own given name, John, experiences a moment of great and continuing significance in O'Faoláin's fiction:

> For a second I looked back into the city, down through the smoke at the clustered chimney-pots and roofs on whose purples and greens and blues the summer night was falling as gently as dust, falling too on the thousand tiny beacons winking and blinking beneath me to their starry counterparts above. It was just the curfew hour and the last few laggard couples went hurrying past me, their love-making ended abruptly for the night, lest the Tans in their roaring Lancia patrol-cars should find them conspicuous on the empty white streets of the city. Then I turned to the open fields and drew in a long draught of their sweetness, their May-month sweetness, as only a man could who had been cooped up for months past under one of those tiny roofs, seeing the life of men and women only through a peep-hole in a window-blind, seeing these green fields only in the far distance from an attic skylight. Mounting my bicycle I left the last gas-lamp behind, and the pavement end, and rode on happily into the open country.

> Yet, though the countryside was very sweet to me after all those months among the backyards, worried and watchful lest I should run into a chance patrol or raiding party, I kept listening, not to the chorus of birds, not to the little wind in the bushes by the way, but nervously to every distant, tiny sound . . .

Although O'Faoláin did in time learn to restrain his tendency to indulge in rather extended and even florid scene-painting, he never lost his taste for vistas—one of the clearest traces of that Romanticism (in this case, rather of the Wordsworthian variety) which he is often willing to acknowledge in himself. But Johnny's Janus-view back and forward is much more than a stylistic tic, or even an obsessively persistent bit of memory. It is in fact a topographical enactment of a conflict of loyalties and intentions which is at the heart of all of O'Faoláin's fiction; and Johnny's position—apparently ready to leave (and with good reason) but in fact still irremediably attached to the place he has left—is a characteristic one for O'Faoláin's protagonists.

In this instance, behind and below (the hint of hellishness is not accidental) lies Cork, for O'Faoláin as for Frank O'Connor the most representative (one might even say symptomatic) place in Ireland. Ahead and above lies the open country (and, if it is west, the truly, unequivocally, never-Anglicized Ireland where O'Faoláin as a young man went to learn Gaelic). That way lies an apparent escape from an attic room, the sort of enclosure abounding in Cork, a "tight little city" full of "lean, long suffocating clausuras of seclusion, smugness, and security . . . [of] mental suffocation and total resistance to all new ideas" [*Vive Moi!*].

Viewed from within the attic the city had shouted an unequivocal message: the necessity of escape, of permanent exile: "Never come back!" But at the precise point where exile begins, the city's iconic message seems to change. The roofs which had "cooped" John and blocked his view out toward the countryside take on a seductive beauty.

The city which had seemed a place of death now appears to achieve some sort of healing union with nature, in which night can fall gently and calmly. Cork for a moment seems full of light and color and even—in the shape of the laggard couples—of human passion. We might easily forget the smoke, the dust, the emptiness. Fortunately perhaps, John knows those things too well; and can see too well the particular historical circumstance which intensifies the city's usual refusal to countenance any liveliness—the curfew, enforced by the mechanical, inhuman Tans.

When only a few pages later he takes a second look, John is struck by "how near and how far I was to the roofs and chimneys I had left." The mix of attachment and distance is a sign of the conflict of emotions O'Faoláin always feels when he looks at the city, "one of those towns you love and hate." What draws him most forcefully perhaps is the power of memory and experience; O'Faoláin, like the young John, *knows* Cork as he does no other place, and as he never will the countryside toward which he turns his hopeful steps. That "free" country will prove to be hardly edenic; or rather, like any true Eden, it contains temptation and entrapments. In **"Midsummer Night Madness,"** as throughout the collection to which that story gives its name, part of the danger is circumstantial: Black-and-Tan patrols or various factions of warring Irishmen. But the central difficulty cannot be assigned wholly to political conflict, as O'Faoláin's characters learn soon enough when they are at large in an Ireland that has, officially at least, ceased to be at war with itself or with England.

The very openness of the country, so seductively appealing from the claustral attic window, threatens to engulf the individual. It can become, as it does in the later story **"Love's Young Dream,"** a place of terrible isolation, a literal and metaphorical waste land:

> I lay down under the shelter of a furze clump . . . Once I thought I heard the coughing of a sheep. Then I realized that I was hearing only the wind rattling through some withered thistles near my feet. The wind, the darkness, the stars, the lights [of distant cottage windows], the size of the plain [of the Curragh] dwindled and isolated me. My isolation turned all those human and sky-borne lights into my guides and companions . . . I remember shouting out in my excitement, without knowing what I meant. "The lights! The lights!"— as if I wanted some pyrotechnic convulsion in nature to occur, some flashing voice to speak. Only the wind whispered. Only the dried thistles coughed.

In the city, the passional human organism must do battle with the suffocating power of moralistic provincialism and political warfare. On the plain, the individual is threatened by utter diminution and the death of all contact, human or divine. Worst of all, the voyage out of the attic may become a voyage into the wilderness of the self. As the young husband in **"Discord"** says of his life, "There's that fear always over me—being isolated—getting away from life—getting wrapped into myself. Everyone living in the country has that feeling sometimes. It's a bit terrifying."

Young John, pausing between memory and new experience, between enclosure and—he hopes—the open field of opportunity which is the future, escaping from a city where love must hide, is a prototype of the young men (and, less often, young women) who are at the center of O'Faoláin's early fiction. Perhaps because the struggle to free Ireland has not yet turned upon itself, John begins his adventure in the countryside with his youthful optimism still intact: "There was enough romance left in the revolution for me to be excited." But romance diminishes sharply as John meets the despotism of reality in a decaying Big House still occupied by its owner, an Anglo-Irish "old devil" named Henn, an aging sensualist with an appropriate fondness for Mozart's *Don Giovanni*.

Henn is both the prisoner and the host of a rebel commandant, Stevey Long, and the master, perhaps the lover, of a pregnant serving-girl, Gypsy Gammle. It immediately becomes difficult for John to keep his bearings, since his revolutionary principles are sound and his appreciation of women predictably combines adolescent longing and respectable Catholic chivalry. Long, who ought to be a hero (although John's mission is to urge him to end an unexplained period of inactivity), proves to be a troubling figure (although not yet quite so coldhearted as he will be a few stories later, in **"The Death of Stevey Long"**); he refuses to acknowledge the unborn child he has fathered and connives, indeed coerces, a marriage between Henn and Gypsy. Henn ought to be easy to despise; indeed, he has been nearly a legendary villain to John: "as children we thought [him] more terrifying than any of the ogres in the fairy-books.'' But Johnny cannot dismiss Henn's claim to have spent a life working to improve the lot of the Irish. "I tried to change them," Henn insists, the first of a long line of characters in O'Faoláin's work to lament or condemn the unwillingness of the Irish to change productively. John learns to examine, even to revise, his idealized sense of how things ought to be; he finds, to his surprise, that "this Hall and estate and countryside had an unpleasant, real life of its own."

The story exemplifies a dynamic of enclosure, escape, and re-enclosure that is fundamental to all of O'Faoláin's early fiction. John flees his Cork attic, confronts the beauty (and the danger) of the "free" country, and then is once again "housed." Old Henn's Red House shares with the attic a sense of constriction and the death of hope, especially for Henn and Gypsy, both of whom are prisoners, the one actual, the other virtual. But the Red House is not only a prison; it is also the scene of intense human passion and sexuality. This might be thought to work against the danger of suffocation and compression, but in the perversely upside-down world of this story it serves too often only to intensify those damning elements. So John flees again, returning to his "back-yard bedroom in Cork."

Each of the individual stories within the collection *Midsummer Night Madness* offers a similarly complex "housing" of the warring principles of constraint and of passion. The collection as a whole begins, as we have seen, with the first moments of Johnny's "escape." It ends, in **"The Patriot,"** when one Bernard, a young Irregular, learns a painful lesson about the death of revolutionary idealism in an isolated hotel which has been commandeered by the indolent, incompetent rebel leadership. He then returns to another hotel, where he can turn away from that bankrupt patriotism and toward his new wife, Norah: "He drew the blind down slowly . . . and slowly he turned to her where she smiled to him in the dark."

Bernard's gesture seems to be a quiet reversal of the defeat that commonly occurs in the previous stories. But the note of promise is at best a faint one amid the disillusionments which the other stories record. Nowhere in *Midsummer Night Madness*—or, for that matter, in *A Purse of Coppers* or *A Nest of Simple Folk* or *Bird Alone* or *Come Back to Erin*—does passion clearly find time or room to breathe. Nor will the exterior world offer relief; it proves, even in contrast to the horrors of enclosure, to be little more than a field of transition. John's earlier sense of opportunity must be set against the hard truth which a dark woman in **"Fugue"** states directly, pointing our attention once again back to Cork:

> You would soon tire of these mountains! The city, though, that's where I'd like to live. There's company there, and sport and educated people, and a chance to live whatever life you choose! . . . This farm is bare and high. The land is poor. And this townland has a Northern aspect. . . . It's a cruel country to have to live in.

If we were inclined to find something a bit hopeful in the closing moments of **"The Patriot,"** we would soon be corrected by *A Purse of Coppers.* That book mimics the topo-

graphic "shape" of O'Faoláin's first collection of stories. It begins, in the story **"A Broken World,"** with yet another protagonist in transit and away from Cork, in this case on a train and, ominously, headed toward Dublin. It ends with enclosure, of a much darker sort than the darkness hiding Bernard and Norah. The final story, **"There's a Birdy in a Cage,"** is a tale in which two lovers are separated; one (who appears in the story only by way of memory) is "free—yet"; the other, Helena Black, within whose consciousness the narrative ultimately settles, is left with a vision of irrevocable isolation:

> Quite clearly, and with absolute honesty and accuracy, she saw her life stretched out before her; and she faced it with courage, for there were many dreams that allured her by the way, and many hopeless possibilities that delayed her. . . . She was caught as, sooner or later, all human beings are caught in that coil of things from which there is no escape.

Like many another enclosed O'Faoláin character—like young John, while he was in his attic—Helena looks out a window; but in what is, in its quiet way, the absolute low point of despair in O'Faoláin's fiction, she does not even achieve a view of the outside, nor of any life beyond the limits of her cage. She can see only the window itself, "the moisture on the window-panes."

And indeed the whole of *A Purse of Coppers* lays out O'Faoláin's most claustral and bleak view of Ireland and of life. Those who can see clearly are left broken and alone, either to be ignored or ridiculed. Those whose ambition has not yet altogether leaked out must flee—to America, of course. But once there, they are likely to find in the brave new world only disappointment and a nostalgic pull back to Ireland. Others, like the ex-rebel Sally Dunn in **"A Meeting,"** can still recall the grand aspirations of the Revolution, its brave, innocent vision of "a rich flowering of the old Ireland, with all its simple ways, pieties, values, traditions"; they endure—in large part as a result of that memory—lives of melancholy and inarticulate confusion:

> I don't know. We are going to have a factory now in the disused barracks. The slum-people have taken over all the living-quarters. And they're turning it into another slum. I don't know. Honest to God, I don't know! I wonder ought we have factories like that spreading all over Ireland? We might end up with cities like Manchester or Glasgow? And look at all these vulgar people making money out of it all. It's hard to tell . . . You know, it's . . .

The land is in the power of provincial moralizers and censorious villagers and embittered clerics. The population at large is given to an absurd pseudo-Gaelicism whose one test for the irrelevance of any bit of modernity is the imagined past: "Our forefathers had no buses, and they were happy. If I were the President I'd pass a law forbidding the use of all motor-vehicles" (**"Sullivan's Trousers"**). The Ireland of *A Purse of Coppers* is, as the first story in the collection argues at great length, **"A Broken World."**

The problem is not contradictions. As O'Faoláin will later formulate it in a story called **"The Human Thing,"** there is something inevitable about them: "The truth about every place is the sum of everybody's contradictions." It is fair to say that O'Faoláin with his "double-sided nature" sees in human character and indeed in the very nature of things an array of opposites—imagination and fact, dream and reality, romanticism and realism, idealism and practicality, faith and skepticism, intelligence and sensibility. But in the Ireland of the 1930s what seems fatally visible is the total absence of any meeting-point, the failure of any element of unification. As the narrator at the end of **"A Broken World"** wonders, looking out over a snowy and shrouded landscape remarkably like the one Gabriel sees in the closing moments of Joyce's "The Dead," "What image of life . . . would fire and fuse us all [?]"

And that is what is most tragic about the defeat of revolutionary idealism. For all its faults, and in spite of its decay into brutal squabbling, the revolutionary idea of Ireland had seemed to O'Faoláin to be just such a fusing image. Remembering, in *Vive Moi!*, "an autumn day of sun and shower" when he took part in a muster of the Irish Volunteers, O'Faoláin speaks of "that moment [when] life became one with the emotion of Ireland":

> In that moment I am sure every one of us ceased to be single or individual and became part of one another, in union, almost like coupling lovers. It was a supreme experience to know that you may not only admire your fellow men, or respect them, or even like them, but that you can love them so much that they have no faults, no weaknesses, so that you will never distrust them even for a second, and will forgive them every slightest minor fault or flaw as they will yours. This extraordinarily heart-lifting revelation, this gaiety, this liberation of the spirit, was to stay with us all through the exciting years to come. If any of the youths and young men of those days should chance to read these lines today I am sure that he will make no wonder of them. He will acknowledge that I am describing something very simple that happened to us all when we were not bald or gray, paunching, tired or skeptical, when in our generous youth we lived and were ready to die for one of the most wild, beautiful and inexhaustible faiths possible to man—faith in one's fellows.

The very passion and ideality of this faith, and the degree to which it is ultimately based on individuals, may help explain the rapidity and inevitability of its decay. It also explains why in the stories of *Midsummer Night Madness* the disillusioning force is the unreliability and complexity of people, not the pressure of events.

However long the "exciting years" lasted, they were long over by 1937. Absent any new faith to take the place of the old, those forces which had once been fused work out their individual courses—which is to say, they each decay into a characteristic extreme. Idealism, for example, turns to a kind of self-absorbed and self-induced madness. In *Vive Moi!* O'Faoláin remembers Eileen Gould saying to him (and for him, an accusation levelled by an attractive woman is always close to the mark): "You are all abstract fanatics. You are suffering, if you are suffering, not out of love for your fellow men but out of love for your own ruth-

less selves," an assessment to which O'Faoláin can only agree: "We were all idealists, self-crazed by abstractions, lost in the labyrinths of the dreams to which we had retreated from this pragmatical pig of a world."

So too passionate emotion becomes sentimentalism. The endurance and stability that remain admirable in the life of the peasantry, and which help explain the sheer survival of anything Irish under years of foreign rule, become mere obstinacy, a reactionary refusal to face the new facts of a post-industrial world. Religion, no longer balancing intelligence and sensibility becomes a rigid and asexual moralism. In *An Irish Journey*, O'Faoláin speaks of "the confused, ambiguous, mingled nature of this modern Ireland"; but it would be more accurate to say that O'Faoláin—at least the O'Faoláin of the 1930s—charges his country with an utter failure to "mingle." Even memory, in his view unquestionably the most powerful and necessary force in the human mind and thus too in human behavior, cannot avoid a decline into the nostalgic despair of Sally Dunn. (pp. 130-38)

. . . . .

By reducing the prominence of a particularly Irish language of politics, O'Faoláin allows the fundamental calculus of selfhood to appear more clearly to a non-Irish reader. He will not abandon an Irish setting, however, nor turn from his effort to understand the peculiarities of that nation, those resistances to individual human aspiration which arise from a recognizably Irish mingling of religion, moralism, and—to use again his favorite concept—provinciality.

For Teresa, the young and troubled novice whose decisive trip to the shrine of St. Therese Martin et Lisieux is told in the story **"Teresa"** (also the title of O'Faoláin's first postwar story collection), the issue is neither political commitment nor geographic exile. The journey, like so many journeys in O'Faoláin's fiction, is at once physical and spiritual, a testing of her vocation. She is another absolutist: "If I can't be a saint, I don't *want* to be a nun!" And the fear that lies beneath that aspiration is that, if her vocation proves false, she will be wholly at a loss: "If I find out there [at the shrine] that I have no vocation, what'll I do?" Like O'Faoláin's revolutionaries, she has defined herself altogether in terms of her intense faith; the death, even the weakening of that ideal feels to her very much like the utter dissolution of her being. Sister Patrick, the good-hearted but worldly older nun who accompanies Teresa, cannot understand the younger woman's intensity; Teresa's announcement that she will join the strictest of orders, the Carmelites, leaves Sister Patrick speechless and "as restless as if she were in bodily agony."

Teresa tells Sister Patrick that she seeks "the death of Love," but it is love, human love, which prevails in the end. She flees the nunnery, and we last see her married, and what is more to a Protestant. Bringing her husband, George, to see the convent, she realizes what she has left and what she has become: "She felt that the woods enclosed a refuge from the world of which she had, irrevocably, become a part." There is no apparent reason for her to regret her decision; no sign whatever that her husband is anything but adoring, if perhaps a bit thick-witted; and yet there is regret: "Ah, George! George! You will never know what I gave up to marry you!" Her renunciation is in its way an exact reversal of her initial "intention"; she has chosen love over its death, human contact over a "saintly" life of withdrawal and devotion. Oddly, her choice seems in part to be based on a distaste for the middle ground, even among the devout; she finds the amiable Sister Patrick, whose vocation demands of her neither anguished thought nor physical pain, to be an unsatisfactory companion and a poor example of the cloistered life.

Teresa will not accept the particular compromise the older woman has made between the human and the divine. Teresa—apparently an idealist to the very end—prefers the abandonment of her ideals to any such compromise, any life of (by her standards) lukewarm and sentimental faith and modest good works. But even having made the choice, she remains marked by the necessity of having to choose. Like so many of the figures we have met in O'Faoláin's fiction, she cannot forego the retrospective view toward a refuge that had never really existed for her; a life of simplicity and order that she had more imagined than lived or seen.

The fundamental terms in O'Faoláin's later fiction are not exile and return but love and memory; the fundamental question is no longer where to live so much as it is with whom to live, and how; the "chance" to be taken, although it still may involve questions of nationality and religion, is at heart the chance inherent in any human relationship.

—*John Hildebidle*

In O'Faoláin's later fiction, those whose dreams are put to the hard test of reality do not come through the conflict unscarred; but neither do they seem as broken and self-exiled as those in his earlier fiction, and especially in his first three novels and *A Purse of Coppers.* The people who suffer the greatest pain are not those who make their renunciations in favor of human love; rather, they are those whose ideal (or vocation) cannot escape the bonds of abstract duty—those who decide, or are forced to decide, to shut out the disorientation, passions, confusions of life as it is customarily lived and, like Brother Majellan in **"The Man Who Invented Sin,"** fall back on the melancholy belief that "it's not good to take people out of their rut."

Against that self-defeated, and self-defeating, resignation, O'Faoláin arrays voices and lives like that of Rose Powis, the "Rosebud" of the much later story **"£1000 for Rosebud,"** who demands of her reluctant Irish lover Milo "Why don't you chance it . . . ? We could be very happy. We could make a go of it. . . . It's not such a big chance to take." Teresa's flight from the convent is one such

chance; and that it is a flight into love and marriage makes her even more representative of the people whom O'Faoláin chooses to observe. Each of his first three novels (although *A Nest of Simple Folk* only minimally) and many of his early stories, especially those in **Midsummer Night Madness,** are concerned with the possibility of human love, and with the particular obstructions which political faith and political conflict present to it. But the failed loves in those stories reach their sad end not so much because of external forces as because of individual hesitancies and obstinacies; the lovers whom John sees scurrying away from the Tans as the curfew comes to Cork are in worse danger from a force within each of them which cuts off love. (pp. 152-54)

That the individual is formed (and indeed often deformed) by outside forces—by parents; by teachers; by political leaders; by Ireland itself, and especially by Cork; even by lovers—had long been a concern of O'Faoláin, not only in his fiction but in his biographies as well. They are all in some way investigations of the degree to which even dominant public figures are shaped by the political and cultural contexts in which they live and act. In his earlier stories, it is a rare individual indeed who can triumph; who can even survive in an approximately whole and contented condition. The moments of escape are few and temporary, as we have seen; the more usual outcome is defeat and betrayal. In his later stories O'Faoláin does not deny the very real possibility of defeat. But defeat is no longer the ground-note in O'Faoláin; it is at least balanced, and often outweighed, by people who endure and even (in a modest way) prosper. At the center, for instance, of one of O'Faoláin's richest stories, **"The Silence of the Valley,"** we encounter an old woman presiding over the funeral of her husband, a cobbler and storyteller:

> The crowd seeped in among the trees. The widow sat in the center of the chapel steps, flanked on each side by three women. She was the only one who spoke and it was plain from the way her attendants covered their faces with their hands that she was being ribald about each new arrival; the men knew it too, for as each one came forward on the sward, to meet the judgment of her dancing, wicked eyes, he skipped hastily into the undergrowth, with a wink or a grin at his neighbors.

That same powerful, clear-eyed figure reappears in many guises, not all of them so unequivocally admirable. If it would not be quite right to call them happy, they are nonetheless content, no matter how unprepossessing their lives may seem viewed from the outside. Many of the characters in O'Faoláin's earlier fiction managed, at moments, to catch sight of such lives, but the glimpse usually served only to prove how impossible the order and satisfaction of those lives were to emulate. In the later stories the view is longer, deeper; and the lesson to be learned therefrom is less despairing.

Take, for example, **"The Planets of the Years."** It is yet another tale of exile, of the peculiar sort to be found in these later stories. The narrator, a young Irishwoman, is married to a dedicated scholar at work on a life of the obscure "Henri Estienne, a character about whom I knew nothing except that he was a sixteenth-century French wit whose most famous *mot* is 'If youth but knew, if age but could.' " That endeavor takes the scholar and his wife to a less-than-gracious corner of Cambridge, Massachusetts; and the scholar's dedication leaves the wife with time on her hands, much of which she spends wishing she were back in Ireland. That wish, which she is forming into a letter to her sister, is interrupted (or perhaps answered) by an unannounced visit from two strangers, the older of whom, an "ancient" woman, stays even now in the narrator's memory, but strangely transformed (as memory almost always is in O'Faoláin) by imagination:

> Whenever I think back to her now I always see an old peasant woman wearing a black coif, bordered inside with a white goffered frill that enclosed a strong, apple-ruddy face netted by the finest wrinkles. I know this is quite irrational. She cannot have been dressed that way at all. I am probably remembering not her but my old grandmother Anna Long from the town of Rathkeale who came to live in our house in Limerick city when I was a child, and who was the first person I ever heard talking in Irish.

The old woman had spent thirty-five years as a maid-of-all-work in the house where the narrator now lives; she came with her middle-aged niece to see the house one more time. To her, the house is full of lively memories against the contrasting reality of the house as it now is—pleasant enough, but no longer her home. To the narrator, the old woman's memories announce, in painful detail, a terrible burden of work: breakfast trays to be carried upstairs, "baskets and baskets of washing" done by hand at a stone trough in the basement. "You must have been happy here," she says to the old woman diplomatically, only to realize how inapplicable the word is. But there is a word that will serve: "I was contented all day and every day as I never was before or since. I found my first and only home in this blessed house."

To the narrator, an exile longing for home, the old woman has one more lesson, derived from her only visit to her native Ireland; and it is a lesson which O'Faoláin has offered before, with particular reference to Cork: "I did not enjoy it. It was not the way I remembered it to be. Whenever you go back to any place . . . across the planets of the years, nothing is the way it was when you were young. Never go back, girl!" Here, "back" is a matter not so much of place as of time. As the protagonist of *And Again?* puts it, in a neatly ambiguous phrase, "No present joy is ever quite the same thing as memory will later make it." To O'Faoláin that is a statement of fundamental fact, not of preference; what the old woman in **"The Planets of the Years"** has managed to retain is the emotional force of memory combined with an awareness that life is lived not in the past but in the present, what O'Faoláin is fond of calling the Now—something even Frankie Hannafey had been able, in his own melodramatic terms, to understand, although not in the end to enact: "life that makes itself out desperately and magnificently of the Now and the Nakedness" (*Come Back to Erin*). That Now is the substance upon which memory will inevitably work; but it must be lived, insofar as possible, outside memory's shadow.

The old woman somehow manages both to be sentimentalist and realist; to hold on to the enlivening, sustaining power of her richly colored memory of the home she once had without sacrificing her ability to compare it accurately with the inevitably changed present condition of things. The encounter with the old woman brings no simple wisdom to the narrator, no sense that this last visit has been the occasion of the old woman's "rejoicing in her last backward look," no diminution of her sense of the sadness of the old woman's life. "Somewhere there had been a lost childhood. Somewhere, at some time, in some house, there had been a vision of home." But neither does the encounter leave her, like Sally Dunn or Frankie Hannafey, embittered even by her own nostalgia. She turns again to her interrupted letter; and to her wish to return to an Ireland which is not a vision of the past but the scene of her future, the vision of home in which her sister and she and her husband and their as-yet-unborn child will live out their lives. The final image is one not of separation and exile but of return; yet another window, yet another snow-scape, but this time with a different import: "How gently the lighted snow kept touching that window-pane, melting and vanishing, and, like love, endlessly returning across the planets of the years."

The fundamental terms in O'Faoláin's later fiction are not exile and return but love and memory; the fundamental question is no longer where to live so much as it is with whom to live, and how; the "chance" to be taken, although it still may involve questions of nationality and religion, is at heart the chance inherent in any human relationship. The point of decision must now be located more in time than in space:

> All that matters is the fear of being on the brink of some essential revelation which we fear as much as we need it. These brinks, these barriers, these *No Road* signs recur and recur. They produce our most exhausting and hateful dreams. They tell us every time that we have to be born all over again, grow, change, free ourselves yet once again. Each teetering moment is as terrible as the imaginary point of time in Eastern philosophy when a dying man, who knows that within a few seconds he will be reincarnated, clings to life in terror of his next shape or dies in the desire to know it.
>
> ("**Love's Young Dream**")

The older language, of enclosure and escape, of entrapment and movement, is still apparent, but now the themes of O'Faoláin's last novel, *And Again?* come up. That novel begins with a moment not unlike that "imaginary point of time in Eastern philosophy" and as its title suggests, it is much concerned with recurrence. But the fundamental terms of the decisions which these "brinks and barriers" mark are now wholly inward; the conflict is between dream and those actions which will put the dream to the test.

We have seen the moment when Teresa's vision of sainthood "fails" this test—although O'Faoláin, who has always rather distrusted abstract standards of purity of action, seems on the whole to call it not a failure but a step into adulthood. The dreams often die hard, and the individual cannot always bear the stress of that inevitable test. But even the most shocking revelations need not be destructive. And in any case, not to undergo the test of experience is an acquiescence to self-entrapment, as the old Cork peasants (in fact, the Whelans) who appear in **"The Sugawn Chair"** and **"The Kitchen"**, prove, but never realize.

Men who twist the real to fit their particular imaginative projections can only be suffered, not admired, whatever their charm and energy. This applies to the Irish Don Juan (and "a natural revolutionary . . . born in the wrong place and time") Charlie Carton (**"Charlie's Greek"**) and to Clarence Michael Dunally, whose aspirations to a place in society Rose Powis must in the end flee (**"£1000 for Rosebud"**). The disillusionment which had, in its earlier, political context, seemed sadly inevitable, now appears necessary and even healthy; but it is not a case of abandoning dreams altogether. Those who find happiness are likely to do so by way of balance, even if it is momentary; a balance which, not surprisingly, is still often acted out spatially, for instance by Bertie Bolger, erstwhile bachelor and "conflator" of antiques in **"An Inside Outside Complex."** The story, as its title may suggest, represents either the logical extreme or a near-parody of O'Faoláin's lifelong interest in the view through windows; Bertie achieves his moment of happiness, both ideal and real, looking both out and in at the same moment, by means of mirrors. Such moments of satisfactorily double vision are hard to come by; neither dream nor reality is usually so obedient to the human will.

Dreams, even though they are rooted in memory and thus (at some remove) in the real past, are to a large degree *constructed;* but they are hard indeed to maintain. Walter Hunter, for example, in **"One Night in Turin,"** imaginatively transforms Molly O'Sullivan into a figure of romantic possibility. This task takes years, both of recalling the night which gives the story its title—a night when he watched her sing the role of Amina in Bellini's *La Sonnambula*—and of keeping just near enough to watch her transform herself into "the Countess Maria Rinaldi." Walter proves to be rather a silly man, and we soon learn how far his image of Molly/Maria is from the reality of her life. But it turns out that the night he so lovingly recalls is a genuine, if complex, moment of happiness, for both of them:

> "I don't know," he gasped. "I was so lonely! And I was so happy!"
>
> She threw up her chin and she laughed the strangest laugh, a laugh like a breaking wave, curling and breaking between pride and regret.
>
> "I was happy too. If you only knew! I often wonder was I ever quite so happy since. . . . "

His disappointment when the dream will not engender a common future for the two of them is thus to some degree healed by his remaining faith in the act of dreaming itself: "A dream? Ah, well! It wasn't such a bad dream. If only I hadn't tried to make it become real. Still, isn't this the way most of us spend our lives, waiting for some island or other to rise out of the mist, become cold and clear,

and . . . so . . . " The story has given us ample time to see Walter clearly and from the outside; but O'Faoláin arranges it so that Walter's hesitant credo is the final word.

To have had the dream at all is of value; another disappointed lover, Mary Anne Gogan, learns this lesson as well, and it can bring her solace even when she returns from a romantic trip to Italy to her usual, rather grey life near Limerick (**"The Time of Their Lives"**). Hearing news of the marriage of the rather comical Italian count whom she had herself nearly married, she judges the affair, and the count, kindly:

> It [that is, to have accepted his proposal] would not have been honest, and it would not have worked. But nothing he had ever done had worked. Nothing ever would work. However! He'd had something. They had both had something. Something precious, brief, and almost true that, she felt proudly certain, neither of them would ever forget.

The motive power behind this machine of dream and realization is memory, from which dreams are made, by which dreams are kept—"precious, brief, and almost true"—long after the despotism of reality has done its work. The nature and operation of memory is perhaps the most predominant theme in O'Faoláin's later fiction, culminating both in his own autobiography—which might more precisely and fairly be called a memoir—and in his last and warmest novel, *And Again?* It may be more accurate to call it a puzzle rather than a theme; for what O'Faoláin asks again and again is: "Why do I remember X when I have forgotten Y?" (*Vive Moi!*). The story **"A Touch of Autumn in the Air"** begins with an answer: "It was, of all people, Daniel Cashen of Roscommon who first made me realize that the fragments of any experience that remain in a man's memory, like bits and scraps of a ruined temple, are preserved from time not at random but by the inmost desires of his personality." That personality, however, may be lost; Cashen, "a caricature of the self-made, self-educated, nineteenth-century businessman," finds himself "playing archaeology with his boyhood, trying to deduce a whole self out of a few dusty shards. It was, of course, far too late." The memories at the core of many another O'Faoláin story prove no less compelling, and no more easily decipherable.

And the effort to encompass, to comprehend (which is to say, to arrange) memory, to find pattern amid randomness has its perilous side. The apparent enthusiasm in the title **"I Remember! I Remember!"** proves to be a sign of something much darker; and the story as a whole is perhaps O'Faoláin's most provocative consideration of the varieties of memory. It begins by proposing a link between memory and action: "I believe that in every decisive moment of our lives the spur to action comes from that part of the memory where desire lies dozing, awaiting the call the arms." The story centers on Sarah Cotter, and especially on "her infallible memory," which at first seems admirable, even if the narrator's appreciation of it is couched in rather peculiar terms: "If she were not so childlike, so modest, so meekly and sweetly resigned, she could be a Great Bore, as oppressively looming as the Great Bear." Her life is, in a sense, all memory; and not even quite *her* memory; crippled since the age of eleven, she "has lived for some twenty-five years in, you might almost say, the same corner of the same room of the same house" in "the little town of Ardagh"—perhaps the most utterly enclosed character in all of O'Faoláin's fiction. She lives for, and by, the chance to talk with others; most especially with her sister Mary, long ago married to an American, living half the year in New York, half the year in Switzerland. Mary visits rarely. The story proves to be an explanation of her ceasing altogether to visit Sarah, and of the sense of threat which, at first, seems almost a trick of the narrator's voice: "I have met nobody who does not admire [Sarah], nobody has the least fault to find with her, apart from her invulnerable memory, which all Ardagh both enjoys and fears, and whose insistence can kill like the sirocco."

That memory is, if you will, the victim of its own accuracy; Sarah can recall every detail that is reported to her. Mary too has a rich memory; but of an altogether different sort, which retains not fact and detail but emotion: "All I have is the feeling I had at the time. Or else I can't remember at all." To Mary, Sarah's memory is a sort of vampirism—and both the persuasiveness of her voice and the narrator's decision to let the story be told not from outside but from within her mind and perceptions make it hard to believe she is not speaking for O'Faoláin. Mary complains to her husband:

> It's not just that it's disconcerting to be reminded about things you've said, or discarded or forgotten years and years ago. Oh, if it was only that! She brings out these bits and scraps of things I've forgotten since I was ten, . . . grubby, pointless, silly, worn, stupid things—and she says, 'That's you.' . . . She knows more about me than I know myself. I keep on wondering what else does she know about me that I don't know. What's she going to produce next? Isn't my life my own, goddammit, to keep or to lose or to throw away if I want to? Am I me? Or am I her? I sometimes think I'm possessed by that old Chucklepuss the way some people are possessed by the devil!

Mary at first tries to defeat Sarah's memory on its own ground, "by catching [Sarah] out in an error of fact"; but that puts at risk what is richest in her own memory, and it is in any case a doomed effort. The only answer is escape; and as she leaves for the last time Sarah's little room, she draws the curtains, as if either to hide her departure or to seal her sister utterly in the little room.

And Again?, as we will see, is much concerned about the accuracy of memory, its tendency to operate not as a precise record or even as the key to character but as a fluid, emotionally charged, reconstructing principle, a force which (as Robert Younger, who has a rather florid style, puts it in that novel) can be "poured over actuality, detaching a mood from its context, so lifting it that it becomes isolated . . . Memory [idealizes] life, shedding it into literature." Sarah Cotter's memory is like the work of naturalist writers whom O'Faoláin so roundly and repeatedly condemns in *The Short Story,* full of a mistaken belief in objectivity and a devotion to a precise—and to O'Faoláin, unselected and thus imaginatively dead—

record of what is, or what has been. Against them O'Faoláin places the work of Stendhal, whom Robert Younger cites as well: "True feeling leaves no memory" (*And Again?*). What may be of equal importance to O'Faoláin is the inverse: how much true feeling resides in, is fed by memory—but only of the properly imaginative sort.

More is at issue in **"I Remember! I Remember!"** than just memory. Mary's husband is, ominously, rather like a more worldly, more mobile Sarah; he too wants to know Mary utterly and in detail; his "memory is just as unerring as Sarah's; and his interest in Mary's past just as avid." The imaginative richness of Mary's recollections he dismisses as a "wonderful Irish gift for fantasy." The misunderstanding is fundamental; the marriage, seemingly happy and healthy, is growing stale; and lost amid the bits and pieces which Sarah can recall so clearly, and can understand so poorly, are the evidences of an old affair of Mary's. Her husband's apparently loving desire to know her, like Sarah's similar desire, is a wish to remake, to possess her in a devilish and corrupting sense.

For O'Faoláin's characters love rather too often involves a kind of imaginative projection of the self on to and into the beloved: a kind of egotism, in other words. Corney Crone, with his usual mixture of self-accusation and pride, of self-analysis and resignation, looks at Elsie Sherlock—they are not yet lovers; hardly more than friends, in fact—and sees a strange transformation:

> Her curls under her father's old hat became the curls of all the women in the world: her waist was the waist of a statue: she was losing her identity for me already, merged into myself. But that is the misfortune of my nature, that all things end by becoming me until, now, nothing exists that is not me.
>
> *(Bird Alone)*

Corney is an extreme case. Besides, he is young, with no real knowledge of women, or even of Elsie for that matter, against which to test and alter his generalized abstraction. This is also the problem of the young narrator, very like O'Faoláin save for being a Dubliner and eventually a medical student, who recalls the events of **"Love's Young Dream."** He too knows too little; like Mary Carton's husband, he wants

> to know what there is to know; to possess life and be its master. The moment I found out nobody knows, I had exposed myself to myself. I would never do it again. The shame of it was too much to bear. Like everybody else I would pretend the rest of my life. I would compound; I would invent—poetry, religion, common sense, kindness, good cheer, the sigh, the laugh, the shrug, everything that saves us from having to admit that beauty and goodness exist here only for as long as we create and nourish them by the force of our dreams, that there is nothing outside ourselves apart from our imaginings.

Perhaps so; Corney (and of course that much earlier Irishman, Bishop Berkeley) could agree; but the flow of the rhetoric, the admirable catalog of products, can hardly defend the desperate solipsism at the heart of this epiphanic moment.

Yet the predominance of imagination in love is argued elsewhere in O'Faoláin; by the cynical T. J. Mooney, for instance, in **"One Man, One Boat, One Girl"**: "Why is it in the name of all that's holy that fellows see things in girls that simply aren't there?" Mooney, who likes to think he has an objective view of human relations (in a life which avoids them altogether), offers several definitions of love:

> I have decided . . . that in what is commonly
> called love man creates woman after his own un-
> likeness. In love woman is man's image of what
> he is not. In love man is his own creator, midwife
> and gravedigger, awake, asleep, dreaming or
> hypnotizing. . . . Love, my dear, poor boy, is a
> sedative disguised as a stimulant. It's a mirror
> where man sees himself as a monster, and
> woman as a thing of untarnished beauty.

But despite Mooney, O'Faoláin's women are not so willing as he assumes to be so "created." The individualistic— and, sadly, doomed—Jill Jennings in **"Our Fearful Inno-cence"** turns away from the amorous Jerry Doyle with the explanation, "You are not in love with me. You are only in love with an imaginary me. Somebody you've made up inside in your head." Her clearheadedness is echoed by Molly/Maria in **"One Night in Turin"** and (eventually) by Rose Powis in **"£1000 for Rosebud."** Indeed, a whole chorus of women's voices is raised against men's idealized abstractions, political and philosophical, optimistic or pessimistic: a line stretching from Bee Hannafey in *Come Back to Erin* down to Eileen Gould O'Faoláin in *Vive Moi!* and Nana in *And Again?*

Imagination, even in a delusive form, can have its place— that seems to be the comic point of **"The Woman Who Married Clark Gable"** and of **"Marmalade."** Both stories are about marriage, which is on the whole a rare and unhappy phenomenon in O'Faoláin's earlier work. In his later fiction marriage becomes the fundamental testing ground of the "chance" which Rose Powis so urgently proposes; of the possibility and contour of human relations generally. Given his belief in the power of dream and memory, and in the self-creating and projective imagination, O'Faoláin sees a common element in relationships which we might, for convenience, call the Pygmalion theme. It is the tendency—not usually ill-intended, but dangerous nonetheless—to want to "improve" or to convert the beloved. The closest O'Faoláin himself comes to giving a mythic label to this behavior occurs in **"Liberty,"** when Doctor Reynolds, thinking of Jack Cornfield, whom she loves and will in due course marry, asks "Am I his female Orpheus?" But as we will see, her "rescue" of Cornfield from the hell of madness and self-isolation is only one particular (albeit particularly rich and important) variant on the theme; and the beloved need not seem damned to attract the lover's transforming impulses.

In one sense, this is a later version of a theme that has been of interest to O'Faoláin since the beginning, a domestic version of the desire to effect change which has long marked his characters (and for that matter himself, in his public role as revolutionary, editor, social critic).

O'Faoláin had observed the efforts of the revolutionaries to build a new, independent, and culturally lively Ireland, only to find they have contributed to the creation of a dreary Eden of suffocating enclosure and complacency in which, among other things, any gesture of intellectual or artistic independence was to be rigorously suppressed. In a parallel vein, ambitions of parents for their children may engender change of a kind that is radically at odds with what the parents had intended. Parental ambitions breed, or at least foster, a spirit of rebellion rather than a taste for bourgeois respectability. Likewise, Corney Crone's attempt to find or construct in Elsie Sherlock an image of his own independence of mind drives her deeper and deeper into moral doubt and dogmatic religious guilt, to the point of despair and self-destruction.

Within the marriages in O'Faoláin's later fiction, the desire to remake the beloved is usually less explicit and not so clearly self-defeating or damnable. As in the case of Corney Crone, the context is often religious, as it is when the widowed Anna insists that her long-time lover Frank Keene, a lukewarm Protestant and ex-soldier, convert to Catholicism and marry her (**"In the Bosom of the Coun-try"**). Frank is reluctant but in the end willing; his conversion to a faith more precise and "complicating" than she can comprehend takes its course with the help of a priest who turns out to have an interest in old war stories that matches Frank's own. Frank has a view of love whose bitter edge is reminiscent of what we heard from T. J. Mooney: "Love is like jungle warfare at night, it keys you up, you feel things you can't see. . . . Love lives in sealed bottles of regret." Frank undertakes the conversion in the familiar hope that he might understand Anna better; what he accomplishes is more or less the reverse. But the outcome is hardly bitter; they do marry, apparently happily; Frank's friendship with the priest is real and important; and the groom even achieves a kind of visionary insight: "Heaven is a gift. The heart is the center."

In that result Anna is perhaps no more than an initiator, in contrast to the redoubtable Moll Wall's more thorough, more controlled, and more self-aware remaking of Georgie Atkinson. Georgie is by birth, name, and manner "an Edwardian hangover," uncomfortable in post-World War II Ireland (**"Foreign Affairs"**). Moll is a realist, even a bit of a skeptic, especially about men. She is an anomaly at her job in the Department of External Affairs in the Dublin government, being solitary, female, and Jewish—and intelligent enough to be fully capable of running the place, albeit from behind the scenes. Having made her Georgie, she is in the end willing to accept him fully—if not quite willing to call it happiness:

> Happy? I remember what happened to poor
> Pygmalion. He worked for years on a statue of
> the perfect woman and found himself left with
> a chatterbox of a wife. I think of all the years I
> have devoted to my chatterbox. . . . Never
> mind. I am really very fond of poor old George.
> I always have been. And he needs me.

Moll, unlike Pygmalion, has never thought of Georgie as perfect; the union of fondness with need is not a grand passion perhaps, but neither is it an impossible basis on which to live.

The statue does not always prove susceptible to the shaper's hand. O'Faoláin seems to think that Henry James understood this too, if we are to judge by O'Faoláin's brief "sequel" to *The Wings of the Dove,* in which an older Morton Densher observes the Kate Croy whom—so he thinks—he played a large part in creating. A more interesting and less derivative case is that of Jack Cornfield and his female Orpheus, Dr. Reynolds (**"Liberty"**). Georgie Atkinson and Frank Keene are amiable and not especially bright; essentially comic characters. Jack Cornfield has at least the dimensions of something more poignant and significant. He is a journalist and was once a novelist who had, like O'Faoláin himself, recomposed his own life into fiction. Something of an exile from birth (born in England but Irish and Catholic by parentage, he flees in young manhood from "insensitive and brutal England" to Dublin, only to flee once more, back to "cruel, cloddish England"); a refugee from a difficult, perhaps even a violent, marriage—he is, as the story makes explicit, a kind of Crusoe, albeit hardly as self-reliant as Defoe's. He acts out, again and again, the old O'Faoláin dynamic of escape and return: England to Dublin to England to an Irish asylum, from which he escapes to London once more and—as the story begins—to which he has just returned.

Dr. Reynolds's desire to help him, indeed to restore him to life and health, is rooted in part in her own sense of need and fondness: she knows her own ugliness but also her own passion. She sees in Cornfield a project (to use an unduly mechanical word for it) that is the distant echo of O'Faoláin's own lifelong hope of changing, enlivening, saving Ireland; to her Cornfield, despite his mixed heritage and unusual life, is an example of a "well-established male Irish type":

> He is simply a sound, healthy, ordinary, bad-tempered man whom we have ruined by domesticating, nationalizing, habituating, acclimatizing or, in the neologistic gobbledygook of our bombastic profession, institutionalizing so thoroughly that he is now afraid to live a normal life. . . . Self-absorbed? Self-pitying? Egocentric? Chip on the shoulder? Truculent? Timid? Incurably self-referential? All that. . . .

Save him she does, by unorthodox means: they run off together, marry, move back to the ground floor of a house near the asylum. As the "cure" proceeds he becomes less and less enclosed, more and more able to wander the streets of the village; and at last he is eager to go off beyond the mountains which encircle them; at last, too, he announces that he needs no help—leaving the doctor to confront directly the distance between intention and effect, between things as they are (and people as they are) and things as she would have them. "This was, no doubt, since it had so happened, and, after all, Saint Augustine once said that whatever is is right, exactly what was to be expected, but it was not at all what she had wanted." This is not resignation, but what O'Faoláin in *Vive Moi!* calls "the frank acceptance of the nature of life"; the difference being that the resignation which O'Faoláin has for so long seen at work in Ireland saps ambition and postpones action of body and mind, whereas this mood allows, indeed in a wry way *encourages* more effort—not any longer to

shape Jack, who is no longer a statue, but to live with him in a mood of something like real contentment. The story does not end with the doctor looking out a window, like so many earlier, defeated O'Faoláin figures, but taking up the small task of setting the table to receive the meal her husband is happily cooking. Imprisonment is on her mind (by way of yet another quotation); but so is hospitality and welcome.

Dr. Reynolds has, in small, lived through the contact between idealistic aspiration and the resistances of the real. Earlier in the story, the still "insane" Jack explains his withdrawal by way of one more of the doctor's favorite epigrams: "It simply happens that I do not like this horrible world. And that is your own word. Or, you said it, quoting Bertrand Russell, 'This world,' you said he said, 'is horrible! Horrible! Horrible! Once we admit that we can enjoy the beauty of it.' "

To which the doctor replies: "His Lordship might just as well have said, 'This world is lovely! Lovely! Lovely! Once we admit that we are ready to suffer the horrors of it.' " The witty parallelism of the two versions of Russell's assertion corresponds to the balance within either version of horror and affectionate joy. In a very rough sense one can plot the course of O'Faoláin's fiction between Jack's and the doctor's citations: the early fiction exists within a world that is, if not always truly horrible, then at least grim and threatening, and yet characters find, or try to find, moments of joy; the world of the later fiction seems considerably less dark, considerably more full of human connection rooted in knowledge *and* emotion, but it is hardly a world without suffering. (pp. 155-68)

> *John Hildebidle, "Seán O'Faoláin: The Cave of Loneliness," in his* Five Irish Writers: The Errand of Keeping Alive, *Cambridge, Mass.: Harvard University Press, 1989, pp. 129-72.*

FURTHER READING

Criticism

Chamberlain, John. "Seán O'Faoláin's Fine Tales of the Irish Rebellion." *The New York Times Book Review* (27 March 1932): 7.

> Places the stories in *Midsummer Night Madness* within the context of Irish history.

Dempsey, David. "Irish Eyes Smile on Fate." *The Saturday Review* 49 (15 October 1966): 40-1.

> Concludes that O'Faoláin's *The Heat of the Sun* is a "mixed bag," with the shorter stories more successful than the more extensive "tales."

Doyle, Paul A. *Seán O'Faoláin.* New York: Twayne Publishers, 1968, 156 p.

> Critical survey of O'Faoláin's career, including a primary and annotated selective secondary bibliography.

Finn, James. "High Standards and High Achievement." *The Commonweal* LXVI, No. 17 (26 July 1957): 428-29.

> Maintains that the short fiction included in *The Finest Stories of Seán O'Faoláin* "will not only resist the harsh passage of time but will gain added luster."

Greene, Graham. "Irish Short Stories." *The Spectator* 159, No. 5710 (3 December 1937): 1014.

> Favorable review of *A Purse of Coppers*.

Harmon, Maurice. *Seán O'Faoláin: A Critical Introduction*. Notre Dame, Ind.: University of Notre Dame Press, 1966, 221 p.

> Important critical study of O'Faoláin's work. The bibliography includes entries on O'Faoláin's major and minor works, and also his editorials in the literary magazine *The Bell*.

Kelleher, John V. "Loneliness Is the Key." *The New York Times Book Review* (12 May 1957): 5, 23.

> Explores the theme of loneliness in *The Finest Stories of Seán O'Faoláin*.

O'Faoláin, Seán. "A Story, and a Comment." *Irish University Review* 1, No. 1 (Autumn 1970): 86-97.

> Presents O'Faoláin's short story "The Kitchen," his comments on the work, and his literary aims and philosophy.

Pryce-Jones, David. Review of *The Talking Trees, and Other Stories*, by Seán O'Faoláin. *The New York Times Book Review* (1 November 1970): 5.

> Asserts that "this collection is vulnerable because of its general mood of regret, of the waste of days, of might-have-beens."

Rippier, Joseph Storey. *The Short Stories of Seán O'Faoláin: A Study in Descriptive Technique*. Gerrards Cross, Buckinghamshire: Colin Smythe, 1976, 162 p.

> Examines O'Faoláin's use of language and characterization in several stories and also discusses his influences. Rippier also includes a primary and secondary bibliography.

Saul, George Brandon. "The Brief Fiction of Seán O'Faoláin." *Colby Library Quarterly* VII, No. 2 (June 1965): 69-74.

> Brief survey of O'Faoláin's short fiction collections.

Tamplin, Ronald. "Seán O'Faoláin's 'Lovers of the Lake.'" *Journal of the Short Story in English: Les Cahiers de la Nouvelle*, No. 8 (Spring 1987): 59-69.

> Analysis of the characters and themes of O'Faoláin's short story "Lovers of the Lake."

Bruno Schulz

1892-1942

Polish short story writer and critic.

INTRODUCTION

Schulz is considered one of twentieth-century Poland's greatest writers. His reputation rests on a small body of extant work: the short story collections *Sklepy cynemonowe* (*The Street of Crocodiles*) and *Sanatorium pod klepsydra* (*Sanatorium under the Sign of the Hourglass*). An amalgam of autobiography, fantasy, and philosophy, Schulz's stories are often compared to the dreamlike works of Surrealism, Symbolism, and Expressionism while at the same time representing a highly individual achievement in world literature.

Schulz was born in Drohobycz, a provincial town that became part of Poland when that country regained independence from the Austro-Hungarian Empire in 1918. The youngest son of a Jewish textiles merchant, Schulz studied architecture for three years at Lvov Polytechnikum. While he did not attain a degree at the Polytechnikum, his proficiency in graphics later earned him a teaching post at a high school in Drohobycz. According to his biographer, Jerzy Ficowski, Schulz loathed his job and devoted his spare time to writing and drawing. Somewhat reclusive, Schulz rarely left his hometown and relied on correspondence for much of his communication with other writers and artists. Among his correspondents was Deborah Vogel, a poet who edited the literary journal *Cuszjtar*. In his letters to Vogel he included strange and fantastic narratives based on his childhood experiences. At Vogel's suggestion, Schulz shaped these stories into his first book, *The Street of Crocodiles*. Published in 1934, this volume impressed the Warsaw literati and won a golden laurel from the Polish Academy of Letters. Schulz published only one more book in his lifetime, *Sanatorium under the Sign of the Hourglass*, although he had been working on a novel entitled *Mesjaz* (which translates as "The Messiah") when he was fatally shot by a soldier in Nazi-occupied Drohobycz in 1942. The manuscript is believed to have been lost or destroyed during World War II.

The Street of Crocodiles and *Sanatorium under the Sign of the Hourglass* have been compared to the fiction of Franz Kafka and Marcel Proust. In their fiction Kafka and Schulz transform banal places, people, and events into highly symbolic and often grotesque narratives. For example, in *The Street of Crocodiles*, the narrator's father's physical and mental deterioration is symbolized by metamorphoses into a bird, cockroach, and crab. Many critics contend that Schulz's writing resembles Proust's in its obsession with childhood and time. In his stories Schulz devotes much attention to the narrator's impressions of his past and to the process of memory itself.

Unlike *The Street of Crocodiles*, which focuses primarily on the narrator's peculiar father, *Sanatorium under the Sign of the Hourglass* deals mostly with the experiences of the narrator himself, who resides in a chimerical world where time and space are mutable. In one episode, for instance, the narrator visits his dead father in a strange sanatorium, where the older man carries on a posthumous existence. In an essay on *Sanatorium under the Sign of the Hourglass*, Emil Breiter observed that "[Schulz] tears the mask off the world by depriving it of the principle of causality, both temporal and spatial. In the apparent chaos that rules in 'supernumerary time' . . . or in illusory space, . . . the writer preserves such discipline in reasoning, shaping, and observation that one would think he existed in the clearest of realms, one perfectly ordered and free from contradictions."

PRINCIPAL WORKS

SHORT FICTION

Sklepy cynamonowe 1934
  [*The Street of Crocodiles*, 1963; published in England as

Cinnamon Shops, and Other Stories, 1963]
Sanatorium pod klepsydra 1937
[Sanatorium under the Sign of the Hourglass, 1978]
The Complete Fiction of Bruno Schulz 1989

OTHER MAJOR WORKS

Letters and Drawings of Bruno Schulz: With Selected Prose
1988

CRITICISM

Colleen M. Taylor   (essay date 1969)

[*In the excerpt below, Taylor explores the theme of the return to childhood in several of Schulz's stories.*]

There are definite psychological similarities between [Marcel Proust and Bruno Schulz]: both were sickly, neurotic, sexually abnormal (Schulz was a self-admitted masochist), introspective, and shared a fear of "le néant" which they sought to eliminate through art, by, as Sartre said, "creating the feeling that (they) are essential in relation to the world, that is, essential to (their) creation." Both sought through art a confirmation of their existence. Proust, according to [Leo Bersani] "had a fearful fantasy of losing the self unless it could be fixed in some external picture," while Schulz, who "leaned toward nothingness" (Gombrowicz) and hated the present, looked back to his childhood as a period of authenticity when he was not yet alienated from himself and the external world. And although Schulz, like Proust, used a narrator, Józef, distinct in name from himself, *Cinnamon Shops* was, he wrote, "an autobiography . . . or rather a genealogy of the soul."

Nevertheless, the works of Schulz and Proust are quite different in form, in style, and in their authors' reactions to the past. In sheer size, the difference is striking: Schulz wrote only one purely autobiographical work, *Cinnamon Shops*, a small (about one hundred pages) collection of fifteen loosely connected stories, while only eight of the thirteen stories of *Sanatorium under the Water Clock* are autobiographical in nature. Proust approaches the past with the powerful, rational intellect of the mature writer; he carefully analyzes his past experiences, reproducing in detail the external world and his past perceptions of it and, on this basis, draws general conclusions about his experience, his personality, and the human condition. Schulz's treatment of the past, on the other hand, is neither analytical, intellectual, nor realistic. Rather, he describes the world as he saw it *during* his childhood in a highly lyrical, emotionally charged prose, without drawing conclusions or offering explanations; he returns in his creative imagination to that time when the dividing line between imagination and external reality has not been drawn and the mind is not yet trapped in what Rimbaud called "the prison of reason." Hence his art is often of a fantastic, surreal-

istic nature: his father is changed into a crab, a cockroach, and a bird, his aunt becomes a pile of ashes, while rooms fill with strange vegetable growths, fiery bars appear in the air, and even time is speeded up and slowed down. These are among the occurrences in the world of "festivals and miracles" which Schulz describes and which in many respects is the diametric opposite of the world in which Schulz, as a child and as an adult, actually lived.

For Schulz's return to childhood in his art represents, on one level, a reaction against the historical and social conditions of his era, especially the physical and moral ugliness of twentieth-century industrial life.

The stores of the Street of Crocodiles were filled with cheap shoddy goods—*tandeta* 'trash,' a word which is frequently met with in interwar Polish literature as a symbol of the ugliness, pretension, and moral decay of the postwar world. Contrasted to it, Schulz presents his ideal—the world of the Cinnamon Shops, so called for their rich mahogany panelling, in which rare, beautiful wares were sold: Bengal lights, parrots, mandrake roots, homunculi in jars, old folio volumes. This world is also identified with his father, a silk merchant of the old school who is eventually ruined by the rise of the unscrupulous merchants of the Street of Crocodiles, becomes physically and mentally ill, and dies. In the story **"Martway sezon" ("The Dead Season")**, he writes:

> Horrified by the spreading dissipation, he shut himself up in the lonely service of a high ideal. His hands never let go of the reins, he never allowed himself to relax the rigor, to lapse into comfortable certainty.
>
> Balanda, Ska, and those other dilettantes of the guild could allow themselves that, for the hunger for perfection, the asceticism of high mastery, was alien to them. My father looked with pain upon the decline of the guild. Who among the present-day generation of silk merchants still knew the fine traditions of the past art . . . who of them could reach the extreme finesse of style in the exchange of notes, memoranda, and letters? Who still knew all the charm of commercial diplomacy, the diplomacy of the good old school?

The rise of a crude but vigorous class of capitalists at the expense of the old, dignified merchantry is a familiar theme in European literature of the early twentieth century: *Buddenbrooks* by Thomas Mann (whose works Schulz knew well and with whom he corresponded) is perhaps the best example. Indeed, much of the literature of the postwar period was a reaction against the ugliness and misery of modern urban life. The French Surrealists were in rebellion against the smug philistinism of the French bourgeoisie, while certain of the German Expressionists attacked the squalor of the city and the cruelty of the ruling industrial class. Some of the latter hoped for a brave new world in the future; Schulz's utopia, however, was in the past, in the world of his childhood. Schulz's paintings especially reveal striking affinities with those of the Expressionists, especially Georg Grosz and Max Beckmann, by their distorted Gothic figures, mask-like faces, and the "demonic" nature of their subject matter (to use St. I. Witkiewicz's word), which reveals the "evil based in the human soul." Expressionism had been introduced into Poland by Przybyszewski and the Zdrój group, and Schulz studied for six months at the Vienna Academy of Fine Arts in 1910. Schulz's prose, too, has certain Expressionist characteristics: the emotional lyricism, which borders on rhetoric, his preoccupation with sex, and its extreme subjectivity.

But Schulz's rejection of the present was also motivated by his own psychological and economic problems. After his father's death in 1905, he was forced to discontinue his art studies and support his family: his mother, his aunt, and, later, his older sister. After some difficulty he found a job teaching at the local gymnasium in Drohobycz, a job for which his natural shyness made him unfit. He hated both his work and the lack of domestic privacy. . . . (pp. 456-58)

Thus, lonely and oppressed by his environment, Schulz sought relief in memories of a happier time. As he said to a student, Andrzej Chciuk: "The most beautiful and most intimate thing in a man are his memories from youth, from childhood. Yes, rather from childhood. People without childhoods to which they can return in memory are color-blind. How wonderful it is that layers of memories can be unfolded before our eyes . . . as when a flower in a movie, growing slowly, is speeded up. Memory is an element: at times we curse it, at times bless it." Schulz sought to recreate these memories in his art. But his childhood was not "realistically" portrayed; rather, Schulz emphasizes its most attractive features, especially in *Cinnamon Shops.* It is as if a spotlight were turned upon certain things while the background remains in darkness. Such an analogy is not out of place here, for one of the distinctive features of Schulz's style in his use of light and color: he literally "paints" with words, which reflects his artistic training.

Colors have strong emotional connotations and perform a symbolic function in Schulz's work. Bright colors are associated with those things that Schulz values and loves: the Cinnamon Shops, his father's aviary, nature, and his hero Maximilian in **"Wiosna"** (**"Spring"**) which begins with a panegyric to the color red. . . . (p. 459)

On the other hand, the most damning epithet in Schulz's lexicon is "grey" or "colorless." He writes of the "grey days of winter, hardened with boredom," the "grey world" of his villain, the Emperor Franz Joseph, who bans the color red from his court (**"Spring"**). In **"The Street of Crocodiles"** he writes: "Only a few people noticed the peculiar characteristic of that district: that fatal lack of color, as if that shoddy, quickly growing area could not afford the luxury of it. Everything was grey there, as in black-and-white photographs or in cheap illustrated catalogues." (p. 459)

Schulz occasionally describes members of his family in his work, as he does in **"August"**; **"Pan Karol"** and **"Dodo"** (his cousin) are the other major examples of this. But his work is dominated by one figure: that of his father, Jakub, the central personage in approximately half of Schulz's

stories. The beginning of his father's physical and mental illness marked the end of Schulz's childhood. . . . (p. 460)

Schulz's attitude toward his father has little in common with that of Kafka, although the importance of the father in their works is often pointed out by critics as proof of the writers' essential kinship. Kafka feared and hated his practical, domineering father, while Schulz felt only love and admiration for his father as an impractical "defender of the lost cause of poetry."

And this admiration took on a special form in his work. In an article entitled "Mityzacja rzeczywistości" ("The Mythologization of Reality") Schulz states: "All poetry is mythologization and aspires to the restoration of myths about the world. The mythologizing of the world is not yet finished."

The figures of Adela, the family maid, the archetype of "woman as destroyer," his aunt, the local half-wit Touya, and other characters in his work can be regarded as attempts to raise the specifics of his private life to the level of the universal.

But the most important example of Schulz's "mythologization of reality" is his elevation of his father to the status of a semi-divine figure: Jakub is compared, among other things, to a Heresiarch, an Old Testament Prophet, Atlas, a magus, and St. George. Many of these comparisons are from the Old Testament, for Schulz, although not a practicing Jew, was fascinated by the ritual and tradition of Judaism. In the story **"Noc wielkiego sezonu"** (**"Night of the Great Season"**) Old Testament imagery is prevalent: his father in his shop is compared to a prophet blowing a shofar against the background of the "folds and valleys of a fantastic Canaan" (the bales of cloth which are "touched with the wand of Moses"), while the "worshippers of Baal"—the greedy customers—stand at the "bottom of that Sinai which rose from my father's anger." . . . And at the end of the story **"Dead Season"** his father is visited by a mysterious black-bearded man who, "like the angel with Jacob," engages in a deadly struggle with him. "Of what?" asks the narrator. "Of the name of God? Of the Covenant?" No one knew, although from that day on began "seven long years of harvest for the store."

But Schulz's father is identified with another world: with those "doubtful, risky, and equivocal regions which we shall call for short the Regions of the Great Heresy." This is manifested in two ways: in his pagan-like closeness to the animal world and in his theories on Demiurgy by which he seeks to emulate the Creator Himself.

Perhaps what Schulz most admired in his father was his unending battle against the boredom and stagnation of the provincial town and his own household. . . .

[In **"Ptaki"** (**"Birds"**)] his father imports exotic birds' eggs from all over the world to construct a brilliant aviary, pulsating with life, color, and motion. His father's passionate interest in animals was that of the huntsman and the artist, notes Schulz, but also the result of a "deeper biological sympathy of one creature for another" which was to have "uncanny, complicated, essentially sinful and unnatural" results. For Schulz's father is, in fact, so near to the world of animals that the narrator cannot distinguish them. His father resembles a certain stuffed condor, which even uses his chamber pot, so that after his father's death, the narrator is convinced he has been reincarnated as the stuffed bird. He also suspects that his father has become a cockroach and, later, a crab in **"Ostatnia ucieczka ojca"** (**"The Last Flight of Father"**).

However, we must point out that these "metamorphoses" are different from those in the work of Kafka. Gregor Samsa's transformation into an insect in "Metamorphosis" is sudden, apparently without cause, and can be interpreted as an externalization of his feelings of guilt and worthlessness. Kafka narrates the story in a simple, matter-of-fact style, without explanation, and almost from Samsa's point of view, so that the reader accepts the basic premise and the subsequent events of the story as real events. The reader of Schulz's work, however, is not sure whether a metamorphosis did occur—that is, whether Schulz expects us to assume the reality of the event, as does Kafka, or whether he is simply re-creating a child's imaginative processes. That is, the narrator in Schulz's work cannot be regarded as a reliable reporter on external, *objective* reality. Moreover, in Schulz's work a metamorphosis is never a sudden change, but rather the end result of a gradual process, the culmination of the "fermentation of material" for which "ordinary objects were only masks." Spiritual forces in Schulz's world can materialize: the father's resemblance to the condor increased with time because of his sympathy for the noble bird and ends in his reincarnation in his form. . . . Schulz again is mythologizing by returning to a pagan view of the world in which the line between animals and men is not yet finely drawn, and, as in the old myths, men and gods change into animals, and vice versa.

Schulz's father enters the "Regions of the Great Heresy" in another way: he is also a creator and, in his theories, is the double of Schulz the writer. In **"Traktat o manekinach"** (**"Treatise on Tailors' Dummies"**), a series of three lectures made by Jakub to Adela and some sewing girls, Schulz expresses his own views on art and creativity. Jakub says: "We have lived for too long under the terror of the matchless perfection of the Demiurge. For too long the perfection of his creation has paralyzed our own creative instinct. We don't wish to compete with him. We have no ambition to emulate. We wish to be creators in our own, lower sphere; we wish to have the privilege of creation, we want creative delights, we want—in one word—Demiurgy." That is, the artist is an independent creator who constructs in his work a reality distinct from external reality, so that art is no longer a reproduction of existence, but rather an addition, a supplement to it. Art was not to be mimetic or "realistic": Jakub proposes the creation of a "generatio aequivoca . . . a species half organic, pseudo-fauna and pseudo-flora, the result of a fantastic fermentation of matter." This concept of art is again close to that of the Expressionists with their slogan "Los von der Natur" and the Surrealists who "saw art as a building process, not an expression or statement of existence as it is" [Anna Balakian]. And Schulz's own art exemplifies his theory, for in it he has created a self-contained, independent universe governed by immanent laws. Metamor-

phoses occur, objects take on lives of their own, while even physical laws are suspended. Schulz's representation of time and space is especially unusual in that time is given physical properties: it can be stretched, expanded, shrunk. . . . (pp. 460-63)

Without lapsing into pseudo-Freudian theorizing, one might submit that Schulz's later devotion to his father in his art stems in part from his feelings of guilt because of his childhood attraction to his mother, his "siding with the enemy." But more important is the love, nostalgia, and gratitude he must have felt toward this strange, ill, lonely man waging his heroic struggle against the boredom and stagnation of life in his family and in Drohobycz. The gratitude may also stem from the writer's belief that his own gifts of imagination and creativity are inherited from the defender of the "lost cause of poetry."

Schulz's return in his art to the period of childhood is motivated not only by nostalgia and a desire to escape present reality: he also sought to regain his childhood consciousness and the freshness of vision which lies at the roots of the creative process. (p. 466)

Childhood is the time of man's most active relationship to reality, which is not systematized by experience or custom, but is seen for the first time in a fresh and individual way. Schulz once wrote to a friend, "My ideal is 'to mature' into childhood. That would be a true maturity." And the child's creative vision of reality is the subject of the first two stories of *Sanatorium under the Water Clock*: **"The Book"** and **"The Genial Epoch."** (p. 467)

The story **"Emeryt"** (**"The Retired Man"**) is one of Schulz's most unusual treatments of the return to childhood. It reveals not so much the influence of Western European literary developments, but the impact of Schulz's friend and colleague, Witold Gombrowicz. The two contemporaries could hardly have been more dissimilar. Gombrowicz, with his customary arrogance, wrote, "Bruno worshipped me. I did not worship him," and admitted that he was never able to finish reading even one of Schulz's stories. But he also admitted that it was Schulz alone who understood his character and his art; he praised Schulz's review of his novel *Ferdydurke*. He and Schulz did share one thing: their concern for experimentation with form, which meant to them more than merely the structure and style of a work of art—it concerned the total relationship of man to himself and to his world. For both writers, the time of childhood offered revelation of the central problem.

Schulz's story **"The Retired Man"** is narrated in the first person by a retired office worker (one of the rare cases when the author is not himself the narrator) who begins by talking about his strange "condition": "a great sobriety . . . a lack of all burdens, a lightness, irresponsibility, levelling of differences. . . . Nothing holds me and nothing ties me down, a lack of support, limitless freedom. . . ." His problem is ontological: deprived of work and society by retirement, he can no longer define himself; his existence, "like that of all retired people," is precarious, and he fears that the fall winds may carry him away. He dreams of becoming a pastry seller, a chimney sweep, even a tree, for these "know the boundaries of their conditions and what is suitable for them." To return to his old office and be knocked about *po koleżeńsku* by the director is pleasant, for it confirms his existence. But the retired man finds a solution to his problem and relief for his existential anguish. While watching children playing in the park, he was "confused and delighted at their fresh, lively behavior . . . their impetuous *savoir vivre.*" Hence he himself goes to the local gymnasium and enrolls in the first class as a student. The director, a pompous pedagogue reminiscent of Gombrowicz's Professor Pimko, tells him: "A very laudatory and worthy decision. I understand you want to rebuild your education from the roots up, from the basics. I always maintain that grammar and the multiplication table are the basis of character building." He asks the retired man a multiplication question, and when he cannot answer, he happily realizes that at last he has returned to the state of total ignorance and innocence. The children accept him, and he becomes their leader, the center of countless intrigues and pranks. The culmination of his delight is his beating by the director, when he can only lisp helplessly. "I was really now a child," he says. But the ending of the story is enigmatic: he is carried away into the air by the winds he had earlier feared. What this probably means is that his existence is still inauthentic, for a mere adoption of the forms of childhood is not a valid means of self-definition; his existence is still precarious. Childhood, Schulz implies, is the happiest, most creative period of life—but its physical reality is lost, and can be recaptured only temporarily in imagination, dreams, and art. Moreover, in this story he reveals the negative side of childhood: the helplessness and passivity of a child before the forces of adult authority (although the retired man-child enjoys his beating by the director).

[Both] Schulz and Gombrowicz recognize the superiority of childhood over maturity in terms of freedom from externally imposed modes of being. But the two writers emphasize different aspects of childhood: Schulz looks with nostalgia on the child's freshness of vision and imaginative power, while Gombrowicz tends to stress the absence of moral and social values and categories. But both regard childhood as a lost Paradise of spontaneity, freedom, and a "sense of the endless possibilities of existence." (p. 470)

Against the world of boredom, conventions, and form— the Austro-Hungarian Empire, the dreary vulgarity of Drohobycz and the Street of Crocodiles, the school where he taught, the lack of privacy and his own psychological fears and weaknesses—Schulz in his work opposes the world of the artist and the child, the world of his father and the Cinnamon Shops, where reality is not restricted but rather freed through the power of man's imagination. Indeed, when reading Schulz one is convinced of the truth of Baudelaire's famous dictum: "Genius is childhood recaptured at will." (p. 471)

> *Colleen M. Taylor, "Childhood Revisited: The Writings of Bruno Schulz," in* Slavic and East-European Journal, *Vol. XIII, No. 4, Winter, 1969, pp. 455-72.*

John Updike   (essay date 1979)

[*Considered a perceptive observer of the human condition and an extraordinary stylist, Updike is one of America's most distinguished men of letters. In the following excerpt from his introduction to the Penguin Edition of* Sanatorium under the Sign of the Hourglass, *he outlines salient stylistic traits and themes in Schulz's short fiction.*]

I. B. Singer, a pleasanter genius from the same between-the-wars Poland, said of Schulz, "He wrote sometimes like Kafka, sometimes like Proust, and at times succeeded in reaching depths that neither of them reached." The striking similarities—Marcel Proust's inflation of the past and ecstatic reaches of simile, Franz Kafka's father-obsession and metamorphic fantasies—point toward an elusive difference: the older men's relative orthodoxy within the Judeo-Christian presumptions of value, and the relative nakedness with which Schulz confronts the mystery of existence. Like Jorge Luis Borges, he is a cosmogonist without a theology. The harrowing effort of his prose (which never, unlike that of Proust or Kafka, propels us onward but instead seems constantly to ask that we stop and re-read) is to construct the world anew, as if from fragments that exist after some unnameable disaster.

> **The harrowing effort of Schulz's prose is to construct the world anew, as if from fragments that exist after some unnameable disaster.**
>
> **—*John Updike***

What might this disaster be? His father's madness, I would guess. "Madness" may be too strong a term— "retreat from reality," certainly. "In reality he was a Drogobych merchant, who had inherited a textile business and ran it until illness forced him to abandon it to the care of his wife. He then retired to ten years of enforced idleness and his own world of dreams": thus Celina Wieniewska, who has so finely translated Schulz's two volumes into English, outlines the facts of the case in her preface to *The Street of Crocodiles.* In that volume the story *"Visitation"* says of the father's retirement: "Knot by knot, he loosened himself from us; point by point, he gave up the ties joining him to the human community. What still remained of him—the small shroud of his body and the handful of nonsensical oddities—would finally disappear one day, as unremarked as the gray heap of rubbish swept into a corner, waiting to be taken by Adela to the rubbish dump." The many metamorphoses of Schulz's fictional father-figure, culminating in the horrifying crab form he assumes in **"Father's Last Escape,"** the sometimes magnificent delusional systems the old man spins, and the terrible war of diminishment versus enlargement in the imagery that surrounds this figure have their basis in an actual metamorphosis that must have been, to the victim's son, more frightening than amusing, more humiliating than poetic.

In Kafka, by contrast, the father threatens by virtue of his potency and emerges as less frail than he at first seems. In both cases the father occupies the warm center of the son's imagination. The mother is felt dimly and coolly and gets small thanks for her efficiency and sanity. At least, however, Schulz's mother is not entirely absent from his re-created world; in the writings of Søren Kierkegaard—yet another bachelor son of a fascinating, if far from reassuring, father—the mother is altogether absent. From the mother, perhaps, men derive their sense of their bodies; from the father, their sense of the world. From his relationship with his father Kafka construed an enigmatic, stern, yet unimpeachable universe; Schulz presents an antic, soluble, picturesque cosmos, lavish in its inventions but feeble in its authority. In **"Tailors' Dummies"** (from **The Street of Crocodiles**) he has his father pronounce: "If, forgetting the respect due to the Creator, I were to attempt a criticism of creation, I would say 'Less matter, more form!' "

Sensitive to formlessness, Schulz gives even more attention than Samuel Beckett to boredom, to life's preponderant limbo, to the shoddy swatches of experience, to dead seasons, to those negative tracts of time in which we sleep or doze. His feeling for idle time is so strong that the adamant temporal medium itself appears limp and fickle to him:

> We all know that time, this undisciplined element, holds itself within bounds but precariously, thanks to unceasing cultivation, meticulous care, and a continuous regulation and correction of its excesses. Free of this vigilance, it immediately begins to do tricks, run wild, play irresponsible practical jokes, and indulge in crazy clowning. The incongruity of our private times becomes evident.

"The incongruity of our private times"—the phrase encapsulates a problematical feature of modern literature, its immurement in the personal. Abandoning kings and heroes and even those sagas of hearsay that inspired Joseph Conrad and Thomas Hardy, the writer seems condemned to live, like the narrator of **"Loneliness"** (in **Sanatorium under the Sign of the Hourglass**), in his old nursery. Limited, by the empirical bias of this scientific age, to incidents he has witnessed, to the existence he has lived minute by drab minute, the writer is driven to magnify, and the texture of magnification is bizarre. More purely than Proust or Kafka Schulz surrendered to the multiple distortions of obsessed reflection, giving us now a father as splendid as the glittering meteor, "sparkling with a thousand lights," and in other places a father reduced to rubbish.

Schulz's last surviving work, the small novella **"The Comet"** (published at the end of **The Street of Crocodiles**), shows Father himself at the microscope, examining a fluorescent homunculus that a wandering star has engendered in the quiet of the stove's pitch-dark chimney shaft, while Uncle Edward, whom Father's sorcery has transformed into an electric bell, sounds the alarm for the end of the world, which does not come. In these vivid, riddling images an ultimate of strangeness is reached, and a degree of religious saturation, entirely heterodox, unknown in literature since William Blake. Indeed, Schulz's blazing

skies, showing "the spirals and whorls of light, the pale-green solids of darkness, the plasma of space, the tissue of dreams," carry us back to the pagan astronomers, their midnight wonder and their desolate inklings of a superhuman order. (pp. 492-95)

Schulz's verbal art strikes us—stuns us, even—with its overload of beauty. But, he declares, his art seeks to serve truth, to fill in the gaps that official history leaves. "Where is truth to shelter, where is it to find asylum if not in a place where nobody is looking for it . . .?" Schulz himself was a hidden man, in an obscure Galician town, born to testify to the paradoxical richness, amid poverty of circumstance, of our inner lives. (p. 497)

> *John Updike, "Eastern Europeans," in his* Hugging the Shore: Essays and Criticism, *Alfred A. Knopf, Inc., 1983, pp. 491-97.*

C. P. Ravichandra   (essay date 1985)

[*In the excerpt below, Ravichandra analyzes the imagery in "August."*]

Bruno Schulz's **"August"** poses a new problem of analysis. The skein of semantics is not easily unravelled in spite of

Dust jacket for the first edition of Cinnamon Shops, *1933.*

the vivid experiential content, a fast moving narrative. The clue lies, perhaps, in the choice of primal images. The difficulty of interpretation could also lie in the alter-identity of the author as the central character of the story.

The story, which hardly runs to eight pages, in English translation, has in it what embodies modernism: the ability to form whorl after whorl a complex system of analogous experience. The power of suggestion is realized through a variety of syntactical experiments to drive home the apposed sensibility of a child in a garish world.

August is an adumbrating presence with its febrile aspect. The world is encysted by the month. The child is seen slowly metastasizing in this atmosphere, from an obfuscated condition to the vitiating adult world. August is the mandrel on which the child is turned, milled.

Placed in the total scheme of Schulz's collection, *The Street of Crocodiles*, the opening lines of **"August"** gain a telescoped nuance: "In July my father went to take the waters and left me, with my mother and elder brother, a prey to the blinding white heat of summer days." The tone and the mood of the story is set by these lines. The child cannot get out of it. The conjunctive "and" succeeded by the objective case "left me" denotes an irreparable situation at once isolating the child in its company. The protective shield is not the mother but the father. Now that he is absent, the child is almost desolate. From then on all events of life start growing strangely meaningful as the child has to, by itself, interpret all encounters. The patriarch will not anymore lead the child through the labyrinth.

Schulz draws from the vast repertory of linguistic skill at his command the necessary tools to oppose the mood created by the earlier sentence. The next lines are of pure joy, of great celebration: "Dizzy with light, we dipped into that enormous book of holidays, its pages blazing with sunshine and scented with the sweet melting pulp of golden pears." It is not always possible to effectively juxtapose the inanimate and the animate. But therein lies Schulz's strength. For him, words are like marbles that come alive in the fingers of a child. Like in a game of marbles, his words strike each the other to explode into a universe of meanings not obscure but opulent. The child is tempted into forgetting the absence. Almost Keatsian in its effusiveness, the images flood the scene and cloy the senses.

The delirious passage quoted above comes with a sudden turn from the sober narrative of the first line. As in all works of any poetic merit, in this too, the associational element provides a richness and helps in adding to the structural evolution of the story. Such effulgence is seen leading Schulz to create the character of Adela. She is the Pomona of this world, returning from the market with a basket full of season's spoils and splendour. Schulz weaves a fascinating web of her description into the design of the story. She at once evokes both wonder and a feeling of revulsion. She is associated simultaneously with plenty and butchery, her basket holding fruits and "the raw material of meals with a yet undefined taste, the vegetative and terrestrial ingredients of dinner, exuding a wild and rustic smell." The adumbrative use of both romantic, surrealistic, and the

harsh, almost horrific descriptions on one hand help to exalt and on the other puncture the exalted in a subtle manner. Another interesting aspect of Adela is the fact that it is through her that the child is exposed to the richness of the month, also it is she who diffuses the harsh glare of the August sun by drawing shades on the window. Perhaps, it is Adela who, after the father, offers in her being, some sort of a shelter to the child who is seen emerging from the cocoon of innocence into the world of sensational experience.

The next stage of significance is the one where the child emerges from within the house out on to the street for a walk with its mother. Schulz's black humour reaches one of its many heights in the following description of the child's observation of the effect of sunlight on the people crowding Stryjska Street:

> The passers-by, bathed in melting gold, had their eyes half closed against the glare, as if they were drenched with honey. Upper lips were drawn back, exposing the teeth. Everyone in this golden day wore that grimace of heat—as if the sun had forced his worshippers to wear identical masks of gold. The old and the young, women and children, greeted each other with these masks, painted on their faces with thick gold paint; they smiled at each other's pagan faces—the barbaric smiles of Bacchus.

The entire universe of Schulz's story now changes into a paganistic celebration with a touch of the phantasmal. The celebration reverberates with silence—a silence that descends on the reader with all its import of the underworld. Such is the metamorphoses which Schulz achieves.

The next paragraph exposits how the eye also observes, paradoxically, that the "Market square was empty and white-hot, swept by hot winds like biblical desert." August, divested of all its enchanting, alluring aspect, now manifests in all its harsh nature. The only objects that appear alive in such a world are the acacias. And rightly so. All else is garbed in emptiness. What relieves this atmosphere is a bunch of indolent youth who play at an inscrutable game.

Thus the contrastive pictures and the evoked stillness commingle to intimate in unmistakable terms the act of growing up in that one predestined act of stepping out of the shaded room.

The first section of the story ends with child passing the urban part of Stryjska Street and entering the suburban section. Here the child faces a very different world. Now, it is the heartland of August in this suburbia. And the description gathers momentum with the striking metaphor of the sunflower. Undoubtedly, it is the patriarch who is the enormous sunflower, towards the end of his days. And the blue bells and dimity flowers are the family which remains insensitive to the tragic import of his life. The sunflower image is the actuated expression of the child's non-verbalized fears. It is only apparent when it is seen in the context of the entire of *The Street of Crocodiles.*

The second section begins in an impressionistic manner. The richly dramatized syntax almost lulls the reader to perceive everything in a benign fashion. But what Schulz attempts, and quite successfully at that, is to show how August has merely produced, with all its potency, a proliferation in weeds. Now, it is Touya, the half-wit girl, who seems to usurp the crown of August from Adela. The half-wit and the season thus grow to be the apotheosis of each other. Curiously, Touya, we see, is the offspring of Maria, the saffron-yellow woman, who scrubs everything with saffron. What we do not forget is the fact that August dusts all under its sky with a golden tint. The ironic reversal effected here through Maria to subvert the aspect of August is but obvious.

Schulz's mockery finds an expression through a new device as he makes Adela the agent who summons the child to the strange world of Maria and Touya—the kingdom of death and the world of anoetic sexuality. If Maria's death implies, for the child, a certain evil presence in the world, Touya's sexual propinquity without any real objective reference is an element which cannot be comprehended for what it is by the child. We see the child's sensibility altering in a determinate manner only when confronted with Maria's death. The syntax picks up pace and flows like an eruption of lava: "And, as if taking advantage of her sleep, the silence talked, the yellow, bright, evil silence delivered its monologue, argued and loudly spoke its vulgar maniacal soliloquy." The reflective sentence that follows the account of Maria's death is in reality a note on the oppressive month that August has grown to be.

In the third section, the child enters the magical world of Aunt Agatha. At the outset the portals of Agatha's house seem to offer a way out from the world of death and of sterile force. The all absorbing mind of the child now attempts to grasp in realistic terms the ethereal world of Agatha. That perhaps signifies an attempt on the part of any growing consciousness to come to terms with whatever is mystical, and/or beyond the physical. The child is susceptible to what at first appears to be a surrealistic idyll of Agatha's world. The "lush green" garden yields to an ephemeral world: "In these pink, green, and violet balls were enclosed bright shining worlds, like the ideally happy pictures contained in the peerless perfection of soap bubbles." The pity is that whatever concrete identity such a world possesses is as that of the soap bubbles.

The doors of Agatha's house exert an influence of their own. They are living presences by crossing which one enters a new sphere of experience. And what cannot be wished away is the knowledge that these doors are always open like those of hell. And Agatha in all her stateliness is the Proserpina of this world. It is only in her stateliness that Agatha is in contrast with the emaciated Maria. For Agatha's fertility is ultimately not much different from that of Touya, "It was an almost self-propagating fertility, a femininity without rein, morbidly expansive." But if Touya's morbid sexual urge which remains unfulfilled is due to her warped nature. Agatha's unrequited sexuality is due to the inadequacy of the male (rather, she renders the male inadequate). She is "the heroism of womanhood triumphing by fertility over the shortcomings of nature, over the insufficiency of the male." Such is her nature. Uncle Mark is the epitome of her contempt for the male.

Schulz's gibe at Agatha is directed through her children. Lucy sees in the most innocent of queries a "secret allusion to her most sensitive maidenhood." Her uncontrolled blushings, an abnormal cephalic condition, and a generally unwholesome appearance are all a logical result of Agatha's own aberrated existence. And Emil at first appears as exotic as the far off places which he has visited. The child craves for his attention and gets it in plenty. For, Emil's globe trotting has resulted in his being a voyeur and a pervert.

Thus Schulz evolves an entire universe of perversity. In such a world the unsuspecting mind for ever grows a victim to the process of unnaturalization. It is a world where the awakening consciousness is forever confined and subjected to a terrible isolation. The "finger-thumb opposition" leads in such a climate not to the logical development of a heightened dexterity but to "a shiver of uneasiness," the result of a comprehension of the febrile nature of the world in which one lives. And that is the theme song of August. (pp. 1-6)

> C. P. Ravichandra, "The Febrile World of Bruno Schulz: An Analysis of 'August'," in The Literary Criterion, *Vol. XX, No. 3, 1985, pp. 1-6.*

Schulz on "reality" in *Cinnamon Shops*:

Cinnamon Shops proposes a certain formula for reality; it posits a special kind of substance. The substance of that reality is in a state of continual fermentation, germination, latency. There are no inanimate, durable, or fixed objects. Everything trespasses beyond its own limits, persists in a given form only long enough to quit it. Life there is conducted by the precept of pan-masquerade. Reality assumes certain forms for show, for sport, for the fun of it. One person may be a human, another a cockroach; but these are forms only, they do not get to the quick of it; they are but skins that in a moment will be shed. Postulated here is a radical monism by which everything is reduced to mask. Life means the conscription of innumerable masks; the migration of forms is its very essence. An aura of pan-irony emanates from that backstage atmosphere where the actors, after quitting their costumes, mock the pathos of their parts. There is an inherent irony, a tease, a clownish ribbing in the very fact of individual existence. . . .

Whether any meaning is left to a reality freed from all illusion is not for me to say. I can only testify that it could not be endured if it did not afford compensation in some other dimension. In a way, we derive a deep satisfaction from this loosening of reality; we have an interest in this bankruptcy of reality.

Bruno Schulz, in "An Interview with Bruno Schulz," Cross Currents 6, 1987.

Russell E. Brown   (essay date 1985)

[*In the following essay, Brown examines the theme of*

metamorphosis in Schulz's short stories, particularly as it applies to the fictional father figure.]

Bruno Schulz (1892-1942) wrote two collections of fiction, *The Street of Crocodiles* (*Sklepy cynamonowe*, 1934) and *Sanatorium under the Sign of the Hourglass,* (*Sanatorium pod klepsydrą* 1937), plus a few separately published short stories. Their central theme is the presentation of his father, a loving, but also ambivalent, description of the last years of the textile merchant of Drohobycz (1846-1915) and especially of his relations with his son, called Joseph in the stories. These are not chronologically arranged, but represent independent efforts to describe and assess the central figure in the author's life. Many of the stories do not even mention his father, but are devoted to other family members and to fringe members of the Galician provincial city. Yet Schulz's main purpose is an elegy to the father, only secondarily a portrayal of family and community. The narrator Joseph himself is strangely passive, content to observe and report the life of his fascinating father, not himself in action, hardly even evaluating or judging him.

Far from creating a realistic and historically exact portrayal of his childhood world, as might be found in Proust or Thomas Mann's *Buddenbrooks* (1901), Schulz transforms the autobiographical base of his work into myths of origins, lifework, illness and death, which are strikingly original and beautiful even in the unchained literature of the twentieth century. For example, his father's physical and mental decline is expressed in a number of magical transformations into lower life forms—like a bird, cockroach, or crab—and thus after his death the son can visit him in a sanatorium where the father reconstructs a feeble image of his former existence.

Schulz's use of the motif of animal transformations recalls to modern readers Franz Kafka's story, *The Metamorphosis* (1912). Indeed the use of this device, along with the preoccupation with his father, has been enough to earn Schulz the dubious title of the Polish Kafka, a title many critics are quick to deny.

The transformation of Gregor Samsa occurs to a son, not to a father as in Schulz, and as a specific punishment for an inadequate and guilty life, corresponding to the death sentence of Kafka's *The Trial* from the same period. The *Ungeziefer* (vermin) which Samsa becomes is the "appropriate punishment" applied in Greek mythology to humans like Narcissus, turned into a flower because of his vanity.

Schulz applies his animal transformations not to himself, but to his beloved father. They are not punishment for a crime or false way of life, or part of a father-son conflict, for Schulz admires and emulates his fictional father, who produces imaginative attempts to create artistic universes, even discourses on the nature of modern art—which the biographical cloth-merchant of Galicia never could have delivered. Rather than punishment or condemnation of his father, the various metamorphoses accompany, exemplify, or demonstrate his illness, insanity, even his bankruptcy in business and in marriage. Since there are a number of transformations, usually ending in death, scattered

throughout the two collections of stories, a certain provisional playful quality obtains. Having expressed a certain aspect of his father's personal and spiritual downfall, each can then be revoked, superseded by the next poetic version of his suffering, alienation and disappearance.

The father's transformation may also arise as a wilful and revolutionary accompaniment to his creative efforts, for example in **"Birds."** There he begins by collecting eggs of exotic birds, then hatches them to create a fantastic aviary in the attic of birds which are at once beautiful and deformed, extravagant products of a fevered, desperate vision. They are justified as part of the war against boredom, a defense of "the lost cause of poetry." Accompanying this artistic project the father himself becomes, or merges with, one of the birds, a condor, which is kept in the attic where it is recognized to "be" the father by both Joseph and his mother, "although we never discussed the subject." In an earlier story, **"Visitation,"** the father had imitated the pose of the large stuffed vulture hanging on the apartment wall. And in a later story, **"Cockroaches,"** the stuffed bird, now again called a condor, survives in deteriorating condition after the father has perished. So, disregarding chronology, Schulz shows first the creation of the birds in the attic area, with the father joining them as a live condor; "later" father and stuffed vulture coexist in the family living quarters, and still later a stuffed condor outlives the father.

Olga Lukashevich interprets the condor choice of birds as an illustration of the father's failure to become a more splendid and beautiful bird—although it may be noted that none of the birds created by the father are healthy specimens. As she points out, "the condor—the largest of the vultures—is a scavenger who does not hunt but feeds on carrion; and he is ordinarily associated with death and decay." ("Bruno Schulz's 'The Street of Crocodiles.' A study in Creativity and Neurosis" in *The Polish Review* 13 (1968), p. 69).

Joseph's father himself "explains" the preservation of the dead or transformed family member within the home by means of the practices of primitive peoples:

> Ancient mythical tribes used to embalm their dead. The walls of their houses were filled with bodies and heads immured in them: a father would stand in a corner of the living room—stuffed, the tanned skin of a deceased wife would serve as a mat under the table. (**"Treatise on Tailors' Dummies: Conclusion"**)

Thus Schulz's use of ancient myth is not naive or unconscious, but a sophisticated system of allusion and modern adaptation. The father predicts his own "future" fate as a stuffed bird or crab tolerated long after his death within the family home. Of course Schulz's transformed fathers have a chameleon aspect not seen in primitive folklore: they can revive, escape to still further metamorphoses.

But to return to the episode of bird creation: driven from the attic by Adela in a fit of spring-cleaning and philistine contempt for the artist or just for men, the birds return to the city in the last story of *The Street of Crocodiles,*

"Night of the Great Season" in nightmare fashion, crippled and blind:

> Nonsensically large, stupidly developed, the birds were empty and lifeless inside. All their vitality went into their plumage, into external adornment. They were like exhibits of extinct species in a museum, the lumber room of a birds' paradise.

These lines contain a manifest level of allusion to works of art, like Schulz's own stories, which he thereby characterizes himself internally in an ironic, self-deprecating mode. The invasion of birds is greeted with stone-throwing by the general populace, by "merry-makers," and soon "the plateau was strewn with strange, fantastic carrion." Just as Adela drove the birds from the attic, the public is hostile to the beautiful flawed products of an admittedly mad creator.

But then, in **"Cockroaches,"** the father who "was then no more with us," survives as the stuffed condor of the aviary; he stands on a shelf in the living room, sadly deteriorated, moth-eaten and without eyes, sawdust emerging from the sockets. Here, the bird-form of the father lacks the parallel reference to artistic creation seen in **"The Birds"**; it refers only to mortality of a family member and to the attitudes of the survivors.

In this story also, the mother is joined with Adela in a conspiracy of women against the helpless, disintegrating father. After she refuses to answer the question of whether the stuffed bird is really the father, Joseph asks her "What is the meaning then of all the stories and the lies which you are spreading about Father?" The embarrassed mother, not above being "coy like a woman with a strange man," weakly changes the subject to cockroaches, another example of transformation the father has undergone which is less incriminating for her and Adela.

This bird example of animal metamorphosis is the most fully developed in Schulz's work, displaying the aspect of artistic creativity and fantasy which is a model for Schulz's own art, along with the aspect of a symbolic treatment of the real father's own real decline and fall. It also shows the usually muted theme of feminine hostility, and the son's feeble attempt to come to his father's rescue.

Other transformations such as that of the cockroaches included in the same story are less complete and rich. The cockroaches have not been created by the father, who initially shares the revulsion of other family members for them, wildly stabbing them with a javelin, until he falls under their spell, hiding as they do, crawling like them, his body stained with black spots "like the scales of a cockroach." In a reductionist "explanation" Schulz writes:

> My father at that time no longer possessed that power of resistance which protects healthy people from the fascination of loathing. Instead of fighting against the terrible attraction of that fascination, my father, a prey to madness, became completely subjected to it.

Although in both cases, the birds and the cockroaches, the father's own change is triggered by the appearance of many of the species he is to become, in the former case the change is benign, beautiful and linked to artistry, while the latter case is pure nightmare without redeeming features or meanings. Therefore the mother interrupts a discussion of the stuffed condor for father's more horrible cockroach metamorphosis which she believes Joseph would be able neither to defend nor to identify with.

In line with the arbitrariness, interchangeability and temporary quality of these transformations—against which a Kafka can appear elementary—she finally denies he has been transformed at all:

> Don't torture me, darling; I have told you already that Father is away, travelling all over the country: he now has a job as a commercial traveler. You know that he sometimes comes home at night and goes away again before dawn.

Thematically related to the cockroach transformation are the father's becoming a fly in **"Dead Season"** (*Sanatorium,* and a gnat in **"Eddie"** (*Sanatorium*), both as a temporary reaction to these insects pestering him. In the former example, the narrator gives another gratuitous explanation of the change:

> Yet, looking at it dispassionately, one had to take my father's transformation *cum grano salis.* It was much more the symbol of an inner protest, a violent and desperate demonstration from which, however, reality was not absolutely absent. One has to keep in mind that most of the events described here suffer from summer aberrations . . .

Thus various "minor" transformations of the father occur to which even the narrator warns us not to attach much significance. Taken as a group they show the vulnerability and dissolution of a formerly integrated bourgeois personality as the father descends through madness and illness into death. Although Joseph may defend the father, as in **"Cockroaches,"** he is just as likely to display the same embarrassment, the averting of eyes which other family members display. At such moments he is far indeed from the solidarity of his pre-mother mythic origins in **"The Book"** or the perception of the father in **"Birds"** as a prototype artist and forerunner to the writer Bruno Schulz himself.

Only one other animal transformation of the father is imbued with mythopoeic significance, that into a crab in **"Father's Last Escape,"** the story which concludes *Sanatorium.*

"Last" is not meant here in a final sense temporally, as there is even a kind of survival from this extreme example of death transformation; for Joseph in another story, **"Sanatorium,"** now again in human form, visits his father after death. In **"Father's Last Escape,"** Joseph's mother brings a crab (or a large scorpion) in from the stairs. He is recognized as the father: surrealistically, "in spite of the metamorphosis, the resemblance was incredible." As in other cases, such as his transformation to a cockroach, the father continues to haunt the family for a long time, even insisting on appearing at dinnertime and narrowly avoiding being stamped on by a visiting uncle.

But now an "unbelievable deed" takes place. Whereas the

other transformations of the father were voluntary, self-generated, and self-terminated, the mother now intervenes to finish off the father. She cooks him and serves him for dinner. When all refuse in horror to eat him, he is put in the sitting room, on a table next to the album of family photographs. He even gradually comes back to life after *this* ordeal.

> One morning, we found the plate empty. One leg lay on the edge of the dish, in some congealed tomato sauce as aspic that bore the traces of his escape. Although boiled and shedding his legs on the way, with his remaining strength he had dragged himself somewhere to begin a homeless wandering and we never saw him again.

Here Schulz, after various evocations of the animal-transformation motif, has achieved a new level of symbolic statement, discovering a new myth that was buried in the metaphors of his father's fall. Father becomes a human sacrifice, which in primitive rituals is to be eaten by the tribe, as echoed in the Christian Eucharist ritual.

Father's death is not a purely personal event, it is a sacrifice for the family, who could now, like Joseph, absorb and incorporate his magical, godlike qualities through eating him. It would also be a way finally to put a halt to the endless series of transformations, to his long drawn-out process of dying, freeing the family and Joseph for other interests and activities. Since they do not actually accept the proposal of the mother, the father is neither released from his torments, nor does the son win the potency and other godlike attributes his father possessed. But, as in the case of the original father-son union which preceded the materialization of the mother, Schulz has here achieved an archetypal recall of primitive ritual which transcends the autobiographical commonplace situation of a father's sickness and death.

The mother's act of cooking the father—or preparing him for sacrificial consumption—is momentarily challenged by the aghast son, who, nevertheless, soon retreats from "she" to the "we" of family unity, implying an acceptance of personal responsibility, as a member of the murderous family, for his father's sacrifice. And yet he, and the others, are too civilized to actually eat him, to carry out to the end the primeval ritual of becoming a father, a leader, a powerful warrior, by consuming his body.

Joseph could thereby again reach the primitive myth level of the story of his origins, **"The Book,"** where a father has a son without a mother: that of the ancient Greek gods who ate one another. He also would have thereby achieved that union he so desired to recapture—"alone in our room" the father in his own body literally, a room which the mother, in spite of her seductive, treacherous ways, could then never enter. Maleness would be linked to maleness; the son would be the father in a way which could never be reversed. Instead Joseph has to make the lonely trip to the sanatorium of his dead father where he will neither be satisfactorily united with his father nor from which he will ever return to the normal world. This is the myth of Orpheus, of the trip to the underworld.

Before leaving the topic of animal transformations, however, it should be noted that these are not employed only for the father. In Schulz's cosmology, where matter and time are both freed of their normal common-sense predictability and regularity, all life and even lifeless matter is always capable of sudden, self-directed spurts of metamorphosis. These casual, cosmic changes generally lack the poignant, tragic quality of the father's changes since the narrator Joseph and the author Schulz have no particular emotional commitment to the subject of their transformations.

Thus Aunt Perasia, otherwise not mentioned in the two books, appears during the **"Gale"** (*The Street of Crocodiles*). Angered at the clumsy preparation of a chicken for cooking, which results in its brief return to life while being scorched, as well as by the general confusion of the terrible storm, Aunt Perasia, like the father with roaches, assumes the role of the creature which has irritated her. First she shrinks to chicken size, then makes stilts out of two splinters to approximate chicken legs, whereupon she scampers about the kitchen like a bird. She then repeats the scorching episode: "became smaller and smaller, black and folded like a wilted, charred sheet of paper, oxidized into a petal of ash, disintegrating into dust and nothingness." This surrealistic end of a relative is noted by the family merely "with regret"; they soon return to their activities "with some relief." The father also had disintegrated, a "gray heap of rubbish," after other transformation, in **"Visitations."**

The father himself describes another transformation, this time from human to inanimate object, in the **"Treatise on Tailors' Dummies."** His brother "as a result of a long and incurable illness" has turned into the "rubber tube of an enema" carried about on a cushion by a cousin who has to sing lullabies to him.

In **"The Comet,"** a story published separately (1938) after the two books of stories, the father becomes a mad scientist, engaging in experiments in chemistry and mesmerism. Out of the ornate carvings on the back of a dining room chair he creates a relative, Aunt Wanda (**"The Comet,"** published together with *The Street of Crocodiles*). He then turns Uncle Edward into a bell or buzzer which his wife often activates, "in order to hear that loud and sonorous sound in which she recognized the former timbre of her husband's voice in moments of irritation."

But these caprices, transformations of human beings to inanimate objects, applied mostly to minor relatives from the endless supply of uncles and aunts, have little to do with Schulz's recreation of archaic myth-materials in the saga of his father. Instead, they are surrealist fantasies of a modern quality, connected with Schulz's and others' speculations about the nature of matter and time.

A last example: the firemen in **"My Father Joins the Fire Brigade"** (*Sanatorium*) spend their winters curled up in chimneys, like cocoons, or hibernating animals: "They sleep upright, drunk with raspberry syrup . . . You must pull them out by their ears and take them back to their barracks . . ." Here the metamorphosis is temporary, seasonal, and reversible. We are far from the sentimental portrayals of the father's dilemma.

Schulz's portrayals of his father's metamorphoses are like fairy tales in that the victim is guiltless, but the transformations are not capricious, being appropriate signs of both the father's mortality and his creativity. Therefore, here more like the classical fables, no rescue is possible: the loving son cannot rescue his father from the nightmare of kaleidoscope transformations, which although sometimes self-healing or self-cancelling, are all steps in an inevitable procession to the land of the dead, the sanatorium where the father lives among the ruins of his former way of life.

Furthermore, the alienation between son and father also precludes any fairy tale type rescue; indifference, boredom, embarrassment, even occasional gestures of hostility prevent Joseph from seriously trying to reestablish the mystical father-son harmony of that so-distant time before the appearance of the mother. Having early abandoned hope of a return to the pre-mother paradise of "our room, which at that time was as large as the world" (**"The Book"**), Joseph seeks the recovery of The Book alone, in the degenerate forms which are the only ones available to him: the mail-order catalogue, Rudolph's stamp collection (**"Spring"**), his drawings (**"The Age of Genius"**). Meanwhile the transformations of his father, which prefigure both the son's mortality and creativity are chronicled in the main with a bemused detachment. The mixture of ambivalence and resignation in face of, on the whole, admirable, heroic efforts of the father, while autobiographically anchored by the death of the father in reality twenty years before, is nevertheless a puzzling feature in the fiction of Bruno Schulz. The ancient father-son materials lead either to duel or to a reunion. (pp. 373-80)

> *Russell E. Brown, "Metamorphosis in Bruno Schulz," in* The Polish Review, *Vol. XXX, No. 4, 1985, pp. 373-80.*

Russell E. Brown   (essay date 1987)

[*In the excerpt below, Brown analyzes Schulz's use of the myth of traveling to an underworld after death in "Sanatorium under the Sign of the Hourglass."*]

One of the archaic myths which Bruno Schulz employs in his poetic reconstruction of the father-son relationship is a visit to the underworld, the land of the dead. Unlike other myths, especially the animal transformations illustrating the father's disintegration which occur throughout Schulz's two books of fiction, [*The Street of Crocodiles* and *Sanatorium under the Sign of the Hourglass*], the myth of a visit to the land beyond death is contained in a single story, '**Sanatorium under the Sign of the Hourglass**', the title story of his second book.

One of the great archetypes of world literature, such visits range from the Greek Orpheus and Odysseus and the Babylonian *Gilgamesh* through Dante's *Divine Comedy* and Goethe's *Faust* (Part Two), to many modern examples. The purpose of the perilous journey may be to visit or rescue a deceased loved one, as in the cases of Orpheus and Gilgamesh, or to get information about how to proceed in some specific earthly project (Odysseus), about man's fate after death in general (Dante), or even about the future of

living men or nations on earth. Schulz's Joseph visits the land beyond death for the first reason.

Whereas the entry to this world in the great models of world literature was either down, beneath the earth's surface (as in Dante, *Gilgamesh* or *Faust* or in Greek-Roman models, across a body of water by boat, Joseph proceeds by railroad to the sanatorium where his father now resides. This substitution of modern technology is familiar from modern versions like Kasack's *Die Stadt hinter dem Strom* (1949) or Thomas Mann's *Der Zauberberg* (1924)—if the latter can be considered in this tradition—where Schulz, who was influenced by Mann, especially in his modern adaptations of myth, may have even found the 'sanatorium' setting since it is not thematically consistent with his hometown, family-based work. But aside from minor features, like the arrival by train, the empty corridors, perhaps the immediate visit to the sanatorium restaurant and the long periods of sleep, Schulz's sanatorium fable bears little resemblance to Thomas Mann's, where a broad panorama of (living) European society is assembled on a Swiss mountain for the treatment of tuberculosis. Joseph's father, on the other hand, seems to be the only patient in his sanatorium. It might be noted that Schulz's father died of tuberculosis, along with cancer.

Hans Castorp unexpectedly remains on the magic mountain for seven years, achieving a kind of *Bildung* in the process; Joseph's planned brief visit is also lengthened indefinitely. In a way he, too, is treated as a patient, or an extension of his father the patient, sharing the same room, even the same bed.

Joseph's journey to the sanatorium, which begins with a train ride, continues with a foot march through a forest (Dante?) where he crosses a foot-bridge into the main entrance of the sanatorium. The foot-bridge, which separates the world of the living from that of the dead, may be a kind of brief homage to Kafka—*Das Schloss* begins in the same way—or it suggests the river borders to the underworld of classical mythology, the Styx, Acheron, Lethe. It is part of the proliferation of entry-motifs to the underworld (train, hill, dark forest, foot-bridge), which Schulz builds between the normal world and the special mythic area, like a summary of the beginnings of related epics.

Jerzy Ficowski in a summary of mythological elements in the Sanatorium story says, 'The Sanatorium is Hades transplanted to this side of the Styx and at the same time a metaphor of art—Schulz's art—as the redeemer of the past' ('The Schulzian Tense, or the Mythic Path to Freedom' in *Polish Perspectives* 10 (1967) No. 11).

The 'classic' matter of a Bruno Schulz story is the recall, reconstruction, or mythopoeic heightening of scenes from the author's childhood, particularly as the childhood scenes commemorate and elegize the central figure of his life: his father Jacob. Bruno, who is named Joseph in the exclusively first-person narratives, experiences the world as a child and it is the child's intensity of perception, as well as the child's freedom from convention and mechanical ways of organizing reality which justify the fantastic metaphors and transformations, the flights of fancy which make Schulz's work unique and memorable. Here Schulz is working in a literary context beyond his own personal formula.

The narrator of **'Sanatorium'** is also not the boy of other stories, recording the fall of his father within the family circle as a child might experience it. Joseph is now a grown man as various erotic incidents reveal: he has ordered a pornographic book by mail, or in discussing the manners of young women he calls himself parenthetically 'a young man who still has a certain amount of interest in such things.' And yet, characteristic of the blurred chronology of Schulz's work, his dead father is wearing a suit 'which he had made only the previous summer.' That is, the father's death occurred less than a year ago, when Joseph's perceptions, as recorded in stories of that period, were still those of a child.

In spite of such temporal inconsistencies, however, the narrator is now clearly an adult; his father even asks him to help out in the family business, a possibility never contemplated in his father's last days. **'Sanatorium'** is written from the perspective of Schulz at the time of composition, rather than the time twenty years earlier (in 1915) when his father died.

The visit to the underworld myth of the story, uprooted from Schulz's 'natural' setting of his own childhood on the market square of Drohobycz with his father's textile business, the servant girl Adela, and an endless series of aunts and uncles, is alien to Schulz's central concern: the return to, and recovery of the, past. Perhaps he chose it as an experiment in an attempt to move beyond the compulsive confines of his initial subject matter. If Schulz's career as a writer had continued normally without the catastrophe of World War Two and the destruction of Poland, Drohobycz, and the extermination of the Jews, he would have had to move into new fictional territory, as Kafka did in the twelve years left to him after his 'breakthrough' of 1912. Schulz in this transitional work has freed the narrator from the child perspective, has changed the setting from the purely autobiographical local home setting to a world-myth underworld, and still is able to write about his father, now receding and diminishing, 'curled up, small as a kitten.'

Schulz has assembled a number of familiar elements from the epic monuments of underworld visits as well as the superstitions connected with death. A good example of the latter occurs when Joseph looks into a mirror in his father's room at the sanatorium and is unable to see his own reflection. In the language of popular Gothic tradition or the ghost story, this means that Joseph himself is already dead. But this suggestion is never followed up; indeed Joseph is able to flee the sanatorium later and return to the railroad-link to the world. Thus he is not dead yet, although he is never able actually to get back home: in an allusion to another topos, conceivably inspired by Kafka's *Ein Landarzt,* Joseph ends as an eternal traveller like the wandering Jew.

Along with the oppressive darkness of the area around the sanatorium, a special kind of sweet air pervades in the adjoining city, causing inebriation, indolence, sleepiness. Suggestive of fleshly decay, it also recalls the special air of

the courts in Kafka's *Der Prozess,* which Schulz and his fiancee translated into Polish. The darkness is also echoed in the 'black vegetation,' including a black fern displayed prominently everywhere where one expects flowers. Schulz has tacked this phenomenon onto a description of the way young women act in the region, to which the black ferns have no connection, as if he suddenly decided to add another Gothic feature to the original myth.

Upon Joseph's arrival at the sanatorium he is told that everybody is asleep. When he points out that it is daytime, not night, the chambermaid says, 'Here everybody is asleep all the time. . . Besides, it is never night here." Later Joseph describes life 'in this town' as full of people sleeping everywhere not only in bed but in restaurants, cabs, even standing up when out for a walk. The motif of the dead as sleepers, of Lethos, the stream of forgetfulness of the Underworld, is here pushed to comic absurdity. We also note in the maid's statement the absence of day and night, the eternal twilight of Hades.

Perhaps the most striking classical motif-borrowing occurs in the appearance of a fierce black dog guarding the sanatorium entrance. This is Cerberus, the (three-headed) guard-dog whom Odysseus and other heroes have to overcome to gain passage into the underworld. In Schulz's story he is treated with unexpected kindness by the frightened Joseph and as a result assumes human form. In classical mythology, Cerberus can be tamed by offering him cake, as do Psyche and Aeneas. Hercules even captures the dog and brings him to the world of the living briefly (12th task), while Joseph brings the dog-man to his father's room. Another interpretation of this creature will be offered below.

Having established the main myth, the visit to the underworld in *Sanatorium* and characteristic motifs associated with this archetypal situation, one may point to a complementary, if not opposed, level of interpretation.

In most mythological versions of the land beyond death, great numbers of souls are assembled, either in sad boredom or suffering the torments of endless punishment. But Joseph's father lives in a sanatorium where he is the only patient Joseph ever sees during his stay. Although there are corridors of numbered rooms, a restaurant with uncleared tables, even tips left behind, Joseph never meets any other occupants of the sanatorium and begins to suspect his father is the only patient. Of the presumably large staff that would be needed for such an institution, only a chambermaid and the chief doctor ever materialize. An elaborate system of deception seems in operation to prevent Joseph from learning the true state of affairs.

Near the Sanatorium, however, there is a well-populated town, where Joseph's father has started a new textile business. Inviting Joseph to visit him there, he assumes Joseph has a prior knowledge of the town. And indeed he finds his way easily: 'What a strange, misleading resemblance it bore to the central square of our native city!' The magical reconstruction of their hometown is immediately rationalized by Joseph: 'How similar, in fact, are all the market squares in the world! Almost identical houses and shops!' But Joseph's father has passed away into a world which is a copy of his own lifetime world, a more rundown or deteriorating version perhaps, but nevertheless an environment where he can for a time continue his former life of selling cloth. His shop is full of customers, his shop assistants hurry about even more than in the "old days" at home. As American Indians imagined a 'happy hunting ground' in the life after death, where some activities of their former life, like hunting and fishing, would continue, so Schulz here shows the dead merchant starting a new business in an almost identical town beyond the grave.

And yet the father's condition is not permanent or stabilized. A further physical deterioration is taking place in him, so that he will soon be too weak to continue the business. He seems to hope Joseph will be willing to take his place:

> You should look into the store more often, Joseph. The shop assistants are robbing us. You can see that I am no longer equal to the task. I have been lying here sick for weeks, and the shop is being neglected, left to ruin itself.

Not only do we have a mirror image of the city and business in the other world, but the father is in the same condition of failing health and sanity as he was at home. He was dying there, and here he is also dying. We may ask where he will be sent after this second death, since he is *already* in the place after death, the underworld. However, classical myths of life after death also include this idea of final disappearance of the soul after a stay in Hades.

The linkage of these two worlds, before and after death, is further demonstrated by the fact that a system of communication apparently functions between them. Not only is there a railroad connection in and out but the father can ask if there was any mail from home. Back in normal life Joseph had ordered a pornographic book from a bookseller who now inexplicably sends him a package direct to this father's new business address.

These facts all suggest that another level of meaning for the sanatorium world is that it is simply the same world the family has always lived in, a new metaphorical arrangement of the familiar materials Schulz has always worked with: life at home in Drohobycz. At least in the business and public aspects of the life of father and son there is only a continuation, thus undermining the 'visit to the underworld' mythic theme.

Joseph, now admittedly older, in his description of life in this 'new' place gives the above-mentioned characterization of the air of superiority which young women display in public, an analysis which has absolutely nothing to do with male-female relations in the afterlife, but corresponding to the author's mistress-slave syndrome of dominant women and servile men, seen in Schulz's art work and also in stories like **'Treatise on Tailors' Dummies.'** Schulz here apparently 'forgets' that he is in the world of the dead, interrupting his ghost story for a normal (for him) evocation of the mysterious power of women, especially the magnetism of feet, 'shapely and graceful in their spotless footwear'. Such attractions can hide blemishes, especially in the face, an observation which one finds also, for example, in the 'home' world of **The Street of Crocodiles**.

Furthermore, the invasion of an enemy army, as well as the appearance of native fascist militia in the town, undermine the level of mythic visit to the underworld. Nothing seems more incompatible with a society of the dead than war or political unrest in such a setting. As in the analysis of young ladies' charms, Schulz is interpolating in a 'naive' way untransformed material from his own (real-life) situations, dropping the mask of allegory or archetype. Rather than an inconsistency or mistake on the author's part, these features may lead us to a different way of reading the story. Schulz is really writing about the real world through a facade of allusion to myth, a fantasy-reorganization of autobiography which can, however, be abandoned at will. The dead father who has left Drohobycz, is found again in the same world, still on the point of final decline to death—after he supposedly has already died. **Sanatorium** belongs to the whole set of stories about father's death, none of which precludes a new later story.

If in the town there is 'business as usual', what of the sanatorium? Surely that is an element irreconcilable with a mere fantasy reconstruction of autobiographical reminiscence. If locale and business are normally 'in place,' the sanatorium, which is where father (and son) sleep in a single bed, must correspond to the home, the living quarters of the diminished family. As in the idyll of **'The Book,'** at the beginning of Joseph's life, female characters while present, are remote, do not penetrate the room itself which father and son share.

The fact that there seem to be no other patients living at the sanatorium thus would no longer be a confusing bit of mystification, as Joseph believes, but would correspond to the real situation which the sanatorium masks. As Joseph's home was the place where the sick and dying father was kept (the sole patient there), so is he kept here in the appropriate substitute building of a hospital.

The flirtatious chambermaid, criticized for neglecting her duties as she hurries about on mysterious errands, corresponds to Adela, the seductive, dominating maid servant of the home-world stories. Adela attracted all the males in her proximity, even the sexually latent Joseph; here the corresponding maid, while acting seductively is not shown actually winning the attention of the few men present in the sanatorium environment. But Joseph who is now interested in pornography interprets her breathless appearance as follows: 'She had run out of a room, as if having torn herself from someone's importuning arms... She was only awaiting an opportunity to leap behind the half-opened door.' The voyeuristic Joseph used to watch Adela at home, speculating about her relations with men. As the chambermaid leads Joseph to the doctor one may be reminded of the promiscuous Leni, the servant of Joseph K.'s lawyer in *Der Prozess*, which Schulz, as noted, transmitted to Polish readers.

Even though the father, perhaps senile, is now indifferent to her charms, the chambermaid provides the same erotic impulse from the socially inferior servant level, so commonly received by bourgeois men before the First World War, reflected in Schulz's work as well as in that of Kafka or of Thomas Mann. In many a tale of middle-class families, sexual initiation is provided by female servants (*Amerika, Felix Krull*).

Another part of the sexual constellation is, of course, the 'proper' woman, both a mother and a wife, from the same social class. She is perceived either as essentially neuter in an erotic sense or as a tyrant who inhibits natural animal expressions of all kinds in the immediate related males, as for example Aunt Agatha with Uncle Mark in **'August'** (*The Street of Crocodiles*).

Without the hypothesis that the sanatorium may be, aside from a place for the dead, a poetically transformed version of home, the appearance of Joseph's mother in the corridors would be totally perplexing, as indeed it is to Joseph:

> "Mother!" I exclaim in a voice trembling with excitement, and my mother turns her face to me and looks at me for a moment with a pleading smile. Where am I? What is happening here? What maze have I become entangled in?

What Joseph does not understand in his conscious purpose of narrating a mythical visit to the underworld, but nevertheless unwittingly reveals to us, is that the sanatorium on another level is really an alternative image of life at home, in Drohobycz, *before* the death of the father. For here in the underworld the father is still dying, still losing his textile business; both the seductive maid and the ineffectual mother are present.

The next problem is the role of Dr. Gotard. In this world he has taken over many of the functions the father used to perform at home, going for long walks with Joseph, holding philosophical discourse similar to the **'Treatise'**, maintaining the primary relation with the female servant (they are the only two staff members visible). His beard, the enema bottle he hurries past with in the night, and his excessive periods of sleep—not necessary for a supernatural 'official' of Hades—relate him to Joseph's father, for example, in **'Visitation'** (*Crocodiles*). The father and Dr. Gotard are both authority figures, the head men of enterprises, the textile shop and the sanatorium respectively. The two are linked in Joseph's chain of thought as well: 'My father was somewhere in the thick of a revolution or in a burning shop' is followed, illogically, by 'Dr. Gotard was unavailable.' The logic for Joseph is that they are in effect the same person: if the father is busy, Dr. Gotard is 'unavailable.' Since Joseph's mother is next mentioned, Dr. Gotard is also placed within a listing of family members.

The father is thus doubled, present in two manifestations, the original familiar one and another incorporating many of his features and habits. So too is the son, who also has a *Doppelgänger* in the sanatorium: the guard dog who becomes, or really always was, a man.

It is interesting to watch Joseph, or Bruno Schulz, shifting gears in the description of the fearful dog. Having introduced him originally as a motif from the Hades myth, he now discovers the potential the tormented creature has as a variation of Joseph himself. When the dog has stretched his chain to the limit and is unable to reach Joseph, the latter is able to identify him for the first time:

> ... only now did I see him clearly. How great is the power of prejudice! How powerful the hold of fear! How blind I had been! It was not a dog, it was a man. A chained man, whom, by a simplifying metaphoric wholesale error, I had taken for a dog. I don't want to be misunderstood. He was a dog, certainly, but a dog in human shape. The quality of a dog is an inner quality and can be manifested as well in human as in animal shape.

Thus Joseph admits to what he wittily calls 'a simplifying metaphoric wholesale error'; the simplification was to view the dog solely as one kind of metaphor, that deriving from the archetype, and not to see until now that he is also a man like Joseph, as we will see, another Joseph.

The dog has been explained above as a mythic component, the classical three-headed dog Cerberus. His other function is to express aspects of the son, to provide a variant son for the father. Just as the son and his lost friend in *Das Urteil* of Kafka can be viewed as aspects of the same person (the businessman Kafka by day, the artist Kafka by night) so the fierce dog whom Joseph initially fears may be reduced to an alternative Joseph.

Firstly, he is chained to the institution of the sanatorium and its chief, as Joseph is dependent on the family business and its fascinating head, even following him beyond his demise on the difficult journey to the underworld. He looks initially like 'an intellectual or a scholar,' 'wearing a black suit,' and the narrator thinks he might be 'Dr. Gotard's unsuccessful elder brother.' This hypothesis is psychologically revealing: a brother of the chief doctor may be equated with the son of a textile business owner; the dog-man is unsuccessful like Joseph, and like Schulz himself (who had a highly successful elder brother, Izydor, in real life). Schulz seems to be inviting us here to consider the possible identification of Joseph and the dog-man with such parallels, but he quickly withdraws the statements made thus far: 'the first impression was false. . . he looked more like a bookbinder, a tubthumper, a vocal party member.' These speculations, along with his description as exceedingly primitive and ugly, produce a new set of new ironic associations with Joseph and especially with the author Bruno Schulz. Schulz is a writer of books, which a bookbinder then binds; he is also part of the literary process, either completing or inhibiting the art of Schulz. The term party-member is also meaningful if we think of the party as a family; in Schulz's family he was indeed the vocal one, writing the chronicle of his family, which would otherwise be forgotten.

The ugliness which is stressed ironically only reflects Schulz's own image of himself physically as shown in the self-caricatures of his art work. The ferocity the dog-man seems to possess may reflect the anger which Schulz felt at losing his father, first from the prefemale paradise of his earliest memories, then to sickness and death, anger at his inability to marry or otherwise lead a sexually fulfilling life, and finally anger at failure in his own adult career, as contrasted to that of his successful older brother.

The bookbinder was wearing a decent black suit, but had bare feet. Like father and doctor he wears the uniform of conventional propriety and authority, but his feet reveal an incomplete socialization. He is still partly a primitive savage, a person too poor to be able to afford shoes, or a child too small to need them. Joseph summarizes: 'I must drop this horrible friendship with a bookbinder who smells of dog and who is watching me all the time.' Friendship, watching, are indicators of the interchangeability and interdependency of the two; the smell of dog is ironically self-depreciating, like the dog's ugliness.

Desperate to escape this creature, which shows more of Joseph to himself than he wishes to see, perhaps providing the self-image he sought in the mirror unsuccessfully ('I must ask for a new looking glass.'), he leads the dog-man to his father's room where, promising to get him some cognac, Joseph rushes away to the railway station. On the way he imagines the father's return to his room and 'his confrontation with the terrible beast.' But these reflections and the act itself are vindictive only if the dog-man and Joseph are two separate characters: Cerberus and the visitor from the living world in the archetype, respectively. For in the second system of interpretation what Joseph has done in taking the dog-man to his father's room is neither illogical nor cruel. It is natural for Joseph, or this part of him, to go back to his father, to whom his anger will be no more a threat than it has ever been; it is also natural that a part of Joseph wants to escape a full confrontation between father and son, the *union mystico* of sleeping together in the same bed, their practice at the sanatorium. His fears for his father's safety, after betraying him, are hypocritical but unnecessary in the parallel-world context: the father's fate may be death and disappearance, even from this second world, but it will not be at the hands of a son.

In addition to the use of a single black guard-dog, which has the double function of being a classical underworld motif, Cerberus, and of being an alter ego, a part of Joseph, a variation of the black dog motif occurs:

> Packs of black dogs are often seen in the vicinity of the sanatorium. Of all shapes and sizes they run at dusk along the roads and paths, engrossed in their own affairs, silent, tense, and alert.

Here the dogs are a political and social phenomenon, an animal parallel to the enemy and the local armed civilians. Again, the initial intention of the author to provide a modern reworking of the archetypal visit to the land of the dead is interrupted for the incompatible purpose of evoking the world of the living. But though they have nothing to do with the Cerberus motif, they do relate to the other use of the black dog-man: as a repressed diabolic component of Joseph himself. Beyond the individual analysis, men in society have both a predatory animal locked within, and a herd instinct, a susceptibility to mass hysteria and insanity. Thus they can be motivated by fascist or militaristic ideologies to threaten civilized society, running through the streets on silent, as yet unrevealed missions of violence. Here the black colour, which relate the packs of dogs to Cerberus-Joseph is probably also a reference to the black shirts of European fascism.

Aside from the guarding-of-Hades aspect then, Schulz uses threatening black dogs, both singly and in groups, to

Stryjska Street, the model for "The Street of Crocodiles," from a 1910 postcard.

refer to evil, sub-human tendencies in modern man, in the narrator and in society in general, which threaten the family and the state. Joseph specifically links the two examples of the beast within man in the text: 'Nothing is to be done about this plague of dogs, but why does the management of the Sanatorium keep an enormous Alsatian on a chain...' Here Joseph, without consciously realizing the symbolism of each example of black dogs which the author intended, implicitly denies the possibility of meaningful action against fascist-military threats to society, but ponders the relevance of the sanatorium dog, which will soon be revealed to be an enraged man, another son to be placed in his father's room.

Thus the sanatorium which Schulz constructed as a modern, mythopoeic reworking of the ancient archetype of a visit to the land of the dead can also be read as a poetic masking of his normal field of interest, with the usual cast of characters, occupations, and relationships, with the father not yet dead but still on the verge of death (as he was in real life for ten years). But in this apparently merely literary setting, this mythopoeic revival of a well-known archetypal situation, Schulz may split himself into two actors, to reveal the angry beast which lurks behind his childish apathy and voyeurism and also to show himself as a coward who flees the spectacle of his father's tragic fate. For while the dog-man is only an imaginary threat (his father, for example, 'walks past the beast with indifference whenever we go out together.'), he does express a secret wish of the son: to attack and destroy his father personally. The father and his business are actually much more in danger from the invading army and the local uprising in the city; but even these, a foreshadowing of the destruction of Poland and the Jews, will not touch him, since they were still twenty-five years away at the time of his death in 1915, when Schulz's real father died at the age of sixty-nine. The invading army was to spell the doom rather of the son, the author who instead of riding endlessly on a train, singing songs to earn a little money, was to lose his poetic voice in the collapse of Poland, and then his life at the hands of the Gestapo in 1942. (pp. 35-46)

> Russell E. Brown, "Bruno Schulz's Sanatorium Story: Myth and Confession," in Polish Perspectives, *Vol. XXX, No. 3, March, 1987, pp. 35-46.*

V. S. Pritchett   (essay date 1990)

[*A contemporary English writer, Pritchett is respected for his mastery of the short story and for what critics describe as his judicious, reliable, and insightful literary criticism. In the following essay, he examines comic aspects in the stories in* The Street of Crocodiles.]

The ridiculous or preposterous father is a subject irresistible to the comic genius. The fellow is an involuntary god, and the variety of the species extends over the knockabout and the merely whimsical to the full wonder of incipient myth. To this last superior class the fantastic father invented by Bruno Schulz in **The Street of Crocodiles** belongs; the richness of the portrait owes everything to its brushwork and to our private knowledge that the deepest roots of the comic are poetic and even metaphysical.

Few English-speaking readers have ever heard of Schulz, and I take from his translator, Celina Wieniewska, and the thorough introduction by Jerzy Ficowski, the following notes on a very peculiar man. Schulz came of a Jewish family of dry goods merchants in the dull little town of Drogobych in Poland—it is now in the USSR—where he became a frustrated art master in the local high school and lived a solitary and hermetic life. The family's trade separated them from the ghetto; his natural language was Polish. The only outlet for his imagination seems to have been in writing letters to one or two friends, and it is out of these letters that his stories in this and other volumes grew. They were a protest against a boredom amounting to melancholia. He became famous, but found he could not live without the Drogobych he hated and he was caught there when the war began and the Nazis put him into the ghetto. It is said that a Gestapo officer who admired his drawings wangled a pass for him to leave the ghetto; one night when he took advantage of his freedom and was wandering among the crowds in the streets he was recognised and shot dead in a random shooting-up of the crowd. He was fifty years old.

It is not surprising to find comic genius of the poetic kind in serious and solitary men, but to emerge it has to feed on anomalies. We might expect—or fear—that Schulz would be a Slavonic droll in the Polish folk tradition, but he is not. Distinctly an intellectual, he translated Kafka's *The Trial* and was deep in *Joseph and His Brothers*—to my mind the most seminal of Thomas Mann's works; hence his sense of life as a collusion or conspiracy of improvised myths. Note the word 'improvised'.

Drogobych had suddenly become an American-type boom town owing to the discovery of oil, and the fantasy of Schulz takes in the shock of technology and the new cult of things and the pain of the metamorphosis. His translator is, rightly I think, less impressed by his literary sources in Kafka or surrealism than by the freedom of the painter's brush—his prose, she says, has the same freedom and originality as the brush of Chagall.

'Our Heresiarch'—as Schulz calls his secretive father, in **The Street of Crocodiles**—blossoms into speeches to his family or the seamstresses and assistants in his dress shop. He rambles into theories about the Demiurge and our enchantment with trash and inferior material. He discourses on the agonies of Matter:

> Who knows . . . how many suffering, crippled, fragmentary forms of life there are, such as the artificially created life of chests and tables quickly nailed together, crucified timbers, silent martyrs to cruel human inventiveness. The terrible transplantation of incompatible and hostile races of wood, their merging into one misbegotten personality.

Misbegetting is one of his obsessions.

> Only now do I understand the lonely hero who alone had waged war against the fathomless, elemental boredom that strangled the city. Without any support, without recognition on our part, that strangest of men was defending the lost cause of poetry.

The awed seamstresses cutting out dresses to fit the draper's model in their room are told the model is alive.

Where is poetry born? In the solitary imagination of the child who instantly sees an image when he sees a thing, where the wallpaper becomes a forest, the bales of cloth turn into lakes and mountains. In this way, the father has the inventive melancholy of Quixote. The delightful thing about him is that he is the embarrassing, scarcely visible nuisance in shop and home. It is hard to know where he is hiding or what he is up to. He is an inquiring poltergeist, coated with human modesty; even his faintly sexual ventures, like studying a seamstress's knee because he is fascinated by the structure of bones, joints, and sinews, are as modest as Uncle Toby's confusion of the fortress of Namur with his own anatomy. A minor character, like Adela the family servant, sets off the old man perfectly. She comes to clean out his room.

> He ascribed to all her functions a deeper, symbolic meaning. When, with young firm gestures, the girl pushed a long-handled broom along the floor, Father could hardly bear it. Tears would stream from his eyes, silent laughter transformed his face, and his body was shaken by spasms of delight. He was ticklish to the point of madness. It was enough for Adela to waggle

her fingers at him to imitate tickling, for him to rush through all the rooms in a wild panic, banging the doors after him, to fall at last flat on the bed in the farthest room and wriggle in convulsions of laughter, imagining the tickling which he found irresistible. Because of this, Adela's power over Father was almost limitless.

This is a small matter compared with his ornithological phase when he imports the eggs of birds from all parts of the world and hatches them in the loft. The birds perched on curtains, wardrobes, lamps. (One—a sad condor—strongly resembles him.) Their plumage carpeted the floor at feeding time. The passion in due course took an 'essentially sinful and unnatural turn'.

> . . . my father arranged the marriages of birds in the attic, he sent out matchmakers, he tied up eager attractive brides in the holes and crannies under the roof, . . .

In the spring, during the migration, the house was besieged by whole flocks of cranes, pelicans, peacocks. And father himself, in an absent-minded way, would rise from the table,

> wave his arms as if they were wings, and emit a long-drawn-out bird's call while his eyes misted over. Then, rather embarrassed, he would join us in laughing it off and try to turn the whole incident into a joke.

It is a sign of Schulz's mastery of the fantastic that, at the end of the book, he has the nerve to describe how after many years the birds returned to the house—a dreadful spectacle of miscegenation, a brood of freaks, degenerate, malformed:

> Nonsensically large, stupidly developed, the birds were empty and lifeless inside. All their vitality went into their plumage, into external adornment. . . . Some of them were flying on their backs, had heavy misshapen beaks like padlocks, were blind, or were covered with curiously coloured lumps.

In a curious passage the father compares them to an expelled tribe, preserving what they could of their soul like a legend, returning to their motherland before extinction—a possible reference to the Diaspora and the return.

Like an enquiring child, the father is wide open to belief in metamorphoses as others are prone to illness: for example he has a horror of cockroaches and, finding black spots on his skin, prepares for a tragic transformation into the creature he dreads by lying naked on the floor. But it is in the father's ornithological phase that we see the complexity of Schulz's imagination. The whole idea—it is hinted—may spring from a child's dream after looking at pictures of birds; it is given power by being planted in the father; then it becomes a grotesque nightmare; and finally we may see it as a parable, illustrating the permutations of myths which become either the inherited wastepaper of the mind or its underground. Incidentally—and how recognisable this is in childish experience—there is an overwhelming picture of the ragged idiot girl of the town sleeping on the rubbish heap, who suddenly rises from the fly-infested dump to rub herself in terrible sexual frenzy against a tree.

Under the modesty of Schulz the senses are itching in disguise. Each episode is extraordinary and carried forward fast by a highly imaged yet rational prose which is especially fine in evoking the forbidden collective wishes of the household or the town: when a comet appears in the sky and a boy comes home from school saying the end of the world is near, the whole town is enthusiastic for the end of the world. When a great gale arrives, the town becomes a saturnalia of things at last set free to live as matter wants to live. There is the admonitory farce when loose-living Uncle Edward agrees to reform and to submit to the father's discovery of mesmerism and the magic of electricity. Uncle Edward is eager to shed all his characteristics and to lay bare his deepest self in the interests of Science, so that he can achieve a 'problem-free immortality'.

> The dichotomy 'happy/unhappy' did not exist for him because he had been completely integrated.

Schulz's book is a masterpiece of comic writing: grave yet demented, domestically plain yet poetic, exultant and forgiving, marvellously inventive, shy and never raw. There is not a touch of whimsy in it. (pp. 128-32)

> *V. S. Pritchett, "Bruno Schulz: Comic Genius," in his* Lasting Impressions: Selected Essays, *Chatto & Windus, 1990, pp. 128-32.*

Susan Miron   (essay date 1992)

[*In the excerpt below, Miron assesses Schulz's short fiction and its influence on contemporary writers on the occasion of the centenary year of his birth.*]

Bruno Schulz, the morbidly shy, reclusive, hypersensitive Polish-Jewish writer, would surely be stunned to find he had, in his centenary, become as mythical a literary presence as the exotic entourage he so ingeniously invented in his own drawings and short stories. This unlikely object of nearly cultish adulation would most likely find this fame as puzzling as his admirers have found him. The recent flurry of books by Schulz that have appeared in the space of two years—the volume of drawings, his letters, and his collected fiction—shock, confound, overwhelm, and astonish with their abundance of sensory data, voluptuous prose, and hallucinatory splendor. Yet, despite this impressive triptych [**The Complete Fiction of Bruno Schulz,** The Drawings of Bruno Schulz, and Letters and Drawings of Bruno Schulz: With Selected Prose], the man behind these images seems as much a mystery as ever, an enigma whose essence is better translated into fiction than biography, as his surfacing in several contemporary novels attests. Cynthia Ozick's bewitching novel, The Messiah of Stockholm, is a deeply felt and brilliantly imagined homage to Schulz and to his lost novel, The Messiah, rescued and reimagined here if only for a moment of fictional time. A. B. Yehoshua uses part of a Schulz story as an epigraph in A Late Divorce, and David Grossman devotes some hundred pages to "Bruno" in See Under: Love. (p. 161)

Singled out for murder by an SS agent on "Black Thursday," November 19, 1942, Schulz was buried by a friend late that evening in the Jewish cemetery in his small town of Drohobycz (then part of Poland, earlier part of the Austro-Hungarian Empire, now part of the Soviet Union). In *See Under: Love,* Grossman imagines the Schulz of **The Street of Crocodiles** eluding his killers by jumping into the sea at Danzig and turning into a salmon. In reality, both his grave and the graveyard, like the manuscript of his lost novel, *The Messiah,* have disappeared, perhaps fittingly for an artist whose life, death, drawings, and stories have themselves become the mythical threads out of which other writers' stories have since been woven. How ironic that the writer who lived all his life in a small provincial town, who kept at a distance even those he loved, allowing them access only through the gateway of letter-writing, has so touched his readers that many cannot bear the thought of his death and, in protest, have rewritten and reimagined his fate, launching what he would have called "a counter-offensive of fantasy" against reality itself.

Schulz owes his posthumous reputation not only to the tireless Jerzy Ficowski, who for forty years has conducted a treasure hunt for Schulz's lost writings and drawings, but also to Philip Roth, who, as general editor of Penguin's *Writers of the Other Europe Series,* introduced Schulz to American readers (In dedicating *The Messiah of Stockholm* to Roth, Cynthia Ozick thanked him for introducing her to Schulz.) Ficowski has claimed that Schulz's work "was so distinctive that it had no precedents in Polish and European literature nor any worthy followers or successors." Yet Schulz certainly knew German literature: he loved Thomas Mann (his letters to Mann are lost), wrote a brilliant afterword to *The Trial,* and adored Rilke. He certainly knew and reviewed with great insight modern Polish literature. Danilo Kis, the recipient just before his death of the Bruno Schulz Prize, given to a writer underrecognized in the United States, does seem a successor of sorts. Kis, whose fiction is as father-fixated as Schulz's, once quipped to John Updike, "Schulz is my god." Even Kis's choice of title for his novel *Hourglass* is reminiscent of Schulz's second novel, **Sanatorium at the Sign of the Hourglass.** (pp. 161-62)

Schulz did not have his first book of stories, **Cinnamon Shops,** published until he was forty. The stories began life as a series of postscripts dropped off into a mailbox, part of a correspondence now lost, with a Polish-Jewish writer, Debora Vogel. Eventually the postscripts broke free of their epistolary moorings and were discovered by another influential Polish woman, Zofia Nalkowska, who became Schulz's patroness and persuaded the publishing house of Rój to publish this unknown writer from the provinces. By contrast, from an early age he impressed teachers, friends, and galleries with his artwork.

Schulz began to illustrate his stories some ten years before his literary debut. He designed the dust jackets for **Cinnamon Shops** (1934) and **Sanatorium under the Sign of the Hourglass** (1937), and he created drawings for each book, although only the thirty-three for **Sanatorium** were used. Jerzy Ficowski believes that Schulz himself wrote the copy on the original dust jacket of **Sanatorium**:

> The author illustrates his work himself. This

very striving to finish the task with his own hands makes us think about the inspiration of priests and craftsmen of the Middle Ages.

During the Nazi occupation of Drohobycz, Schulz was hired as a "house Jew" by the Gestapo officer Felix Landau, to paint signs and family portraits and perform light carpentry. Although Schulz was given false documents to help him escape, he never got the chance to use these "Aryan papers." Walking in the ghetto on the way to buy food, he was shot twice in the head by Landau's rival, Karl Guenther. Schulz was kept alive for a year serving Landau, who boasted he had a Jewish artist-slave that he sustained with a slice of bread and a bowl of soup. One of Schulz's tasks at Landau's was to decorate Landau's son's room with fairy tales, later described by one of Schulz's former students (quoted in the *Drawings*):

> Even then Schulz remained faithful to his artistic method: the figures of kings, knights, and squires painted in a fantastic, legendary scenery in the house of the Gestapo officer displayed distinctively non-Aryan features. Those were the people Schulz were living with at the time. Their emaciated, tormented faces were rendered with unbelievable resemblance. And those miserable people, transferred by Schulz's imagination from the world of tragic reality, reappeared in his paintings with splendor and glory as kings seated in their thrones in sable furs and crowns, as knights on white horses surrounded by their squires, as sovereign rulers riding in their golden carriages. . . .

In much the same way that Schulz's letters expose his fragile emotional make-up and his frequent descents into near-malfunctioning, his drawings, so many of which are self-portraits, reveal even more striking obsessions and neuroses; one feels a discomfort watching this artist go public under the misguided assumption that he is portraying nothing terribly offensive or grotesque. While looking at the volume of his artwork can induce queasiness or even embarrassment, one cannot easily put it down. Utterly spellbinding, it offers a glimpse into a tormented soul fixated on degradation, whose prose only alludes to tendencies which spring into full bloom under the art pen. As a reviewer of his own writing, Schulz's self-perception dazzles us; he sent this description to the Italian publisher of a translation of **Cinnamon Shops**:

> The keynote to **Sanatorium** is the dream of renewal of life through the power of delight, the unleashing of inspiration, the primeval human belief that the dammed-up loveliness of things, hampered and hidden though it is, only awaits an inspired being to break its bonds and release a flood of happiness over all the world. . . . Those reveries about shuffling off the coils of the body, about a revaluation of life through poetry, have found in Schulz a new homeland, a climate of their own, in which, watchful, they burgeon forth in tropical vegetation: a legendary childhood of wonder, elation, and metamorphosis.

Schulz's letters, too, are full of explanations about his mythologizing of reality, the role of art ("to be a probe sunk into the nameless"), and his need for isolation, which so directly conflicted with his need for "a friend, a kindred spirit, a partner for voyages of discovery." Reading these confessions, one often feels the same sense of trespassing that occurs while looking at the drawings; beneath what Adam Zagajewski has called "the captivating sentences of his downy prose," there lurked tremendous anguish, frustration, and sense of failure, "something like the collapse of my whole personality."

It is rare that one finds a critical piece or blurb about Schulz which does not mention Kafka; some have even dubbed him "the Polish Kafka." Like Kafka's, Schulz's letters seem to answer a need to communicate while remaining alone; "isolated from the stuff of daily life," Schulz put it. Each wrote far more letters than fiction. Both were surprisingly candid about their infirmities and neuroses in their letters; both sustained long and involved correspondences with fiancées whom they never married, instead living their adult lives with family members, working at jobs which left them little time for writing. The uncanny likenesses between these two men's lives, letters, and fiction of father-fixations and unforgettable metamorphoses is striking. While Kafka, in his notorious letter to his father, declared, "All my writing is about you," Schulz might have said something similar, having in his fiction created one of literature's most outlandish and fantastic fathers, whose own metamorphosing adventures make Gregor Samsa's seem almost pedestrian.

Schulz is credited as having helped to introduce Kafka's fiction to Poland. He wrote a lengthy and incisive afterword to *The Trial*, which appeared only in the 1936 edition. He lent his name to the translation done by Jozefina Szelínska, to encourage its publication, although he is often mistakenly credited with the translation itself. If Kafka was obsessed by space, Schulz was similarly obsessed by time. In one letter he admits to being dominated by:

> . . the virginity of time. Just as for some rajah of melancholy and insatiable disposition any woman brushed by a male glance is already tainted and thereby unfit for anything but the silken noose, so for me any piece of time someone has laid claim to, has even casually mentioned in passing, is already marred, spoiled, unfit for consumption. I can't stand people laying claim to my time. They make the scrap they touched nauseating to me. I am incapable of sharing time, of feeding on somebody's leftovers.

Time is examined and transmogrified throughout Schulz's fiction, where it occupies a starring role alongside Father, who undergoes as many mutations and transformations (crab, cockroach, horsefly) as Schulzian time. Neither Father nor time can stay put in their original format. They exist in a state of constant flux, mutating and disappearing at will. Time appears in **"The Night of the Great Season"** as "that great eccentric" which "begets sometimes other years, different, prodigal years which—like a sixth, smallest toe—grow a thirteenth month . . . a hunchback month, a half-wilted shoot, more tentative than real." In **"The Age of Genius,"** Schulz explains that while ordinary events are arranged within time, strung along its length as on a thread, other events have occurred too late, that is,

"after the whole of time has been distributed, divided, and allotted." What is to be done with these events:

> . . . hanging in the air, homeless, errant? Could it be that time is too narrow for all events? Could it happen that all seats within time might have been sold? Is there perhaps some kind of bidding for time?

Time, and the "framework of uninterrupted chronology" with our "scrupulous habit of reporting on used-up hours" are all but forsaken in the hilarious story, **"Sanatorium under the Sign of the Hourglass,"** where the "quick decomposition of time" ceases to interest people, who, instead, accept time free of vigilance. "It immediately begins to do tricks, play irresponsible jokes, and indulge in crazy clowning." The staff of the sanatorium have put back the clock, reactivating time past, with all its possibilities, so that which might have happened in "ordinary time" can be undone. Thus, Father, dead in other locales, is offered a possibility of recovery, although the staff admits that his death "throws a certain shadow on his existence here." In a letter to a critic who had written about *Cinnamon Shops*, Schulz claims that the kind of art he cares about is "precisely a regression, childhood revisited. My ideal goal is to 'mature into childhood.' " Schulz's fiction and artwork act as extended elegies to childhood, his family, and Drohobycz, keeping each alive through spectacular acts of metamorphoses. (pp. 163-66)

Susan Miron, "Bruno Schulz Redux," in Partisan Review, *Vol. LIX, No. 1, Winter, 1992, pp. 161-66.*

FURTHER READING

Baranczak, Stanislaw. "His First Short Story Was a Postscript." *Los Angeles Times Book Review* (11 February 1990): 2, 10.

> Positive review of *The Complete Fiction of Bruno Schulz* in which the critic states: "Schulz's work appears the extreme consequence of 20th-Century fiction—its evolution toward the lyrical rather than the epic, the fantastic rather than the realistic, the subjective rather than the objective modes of narration and vision."

Brown, Russell E. "Bruno Schulz and World Literature." *Slavic and East European Journal* 34, No. 2 (1990): 224-46.

> Establishes Schulz's place "in the literary universe *outside* his native Polish language and culture." The critic also discusses major influences on Schulz's writing.

Budurowycz, Bohdan. "Galicia in the Work of Bruno Schulz." *Canadian Slavonic Papers* 28, No. 4 (December 1986): 359-68.

> Explores the significance of Schulz's native Galicia to his fiction.

Iribarne, Louis. "On Bruno Schulz." *Cross Currents: A Yearbook of Central European Culture*, No. 6 (1987): 173-77.

> Introduction to four previously unpublished fictional

writings and one letter, which Iribarne translated. He comments: "[Each] of these pieces can be read as a Schulzian commentary on the art of writing, on a poesy that seeks to reunite the sublime and the base."

Klawans, Stuart. "Metamorphoses: Bruno Schulz's Hothouse Flowers." *VLS*, No. 70 (December 1988): 12-15.
    Appreciative overview of Schulz's literary output and life.

Ozick, Cynthia. "The Phantasmagoria of Bruno Schulz." In her *Art & Ardor*, pp. 224-28. New York: Alfred A. Knopf, 1983.
    Highly praises *The Street of Crocodiles*, comparing Schulz's writing to that of Isaac Babel, I. B. Singer, and Franz Kafka.

Robins, Nicholas. "The Golem." *London Magazine* 32, Nos. 9-10 (December-January 1993): 50-8.
    Detailed view of Schulz's personal life and its relationship to his fiction.

Schulz, Bruno. "An Essay for S. I. Witkiewicz." In *Four Decades of Polish Essays*, edited by Jan Kott, pp. 106-10. Evanston, Ill.: Northwestern University Press, 1990.
    Schulz reveals the imagery, symbolism, and themes of his early drawings and their importance to his fiction.

John Updike

1932-

(Full name John Hoyer Updike) American novelist, short story writer, critic, poet, essayist, playwright, and author of children's books.

INTRODUCTION

A major contemporary American author, Updike is particularly noted for the subtle moral complexity of his writings, which frequently emphasize Christian morality and mythology. Updike's major subject matter in his novels and short stories, particularly since the mid-1960s, has been the domestic life of the American middle class and its attendant rituals: marriage, sex, fidelity, and divorce. Against the mundane settings of American suburbia, Updike presents average people—usually men—searching for aesthetic or religious meaning in the secular awareness of their own mortality. Updike has stated that his books emphasize "insolvable dilemmas," and the dialectical tension in his work is often the result of his characters' struggles to determine what is morally right in a constantly changing world.

Born in Shillington, Pennsylvania, Updike attended Harvard University, where he was editor of the Harvard *Lampoon.* He graduated *summa cum laude* in 1954 and began contributing pieces to the *New Yorker,* a magazine with which he is frequently affiliated. In the early 1950s Updike's first story, "Friends in Philadelphia," was published in the *New Yorker,* and he served as a reporter for the magazine's "Talk of the Town" column from 1955 to 1957. *The Carpentered Hen and Other Tame Creatures,* his first major work and first poetry collection, was published in 1959 as were the short story collection *The Same Door* and the novel *The Poorhouse Fair,* which established him as a major contemporary novelist. Updike has won numerous literary prizes: a National Book Award for *The Centaur* in 1963, an O. Henry Award for "The Bulgarian Poetess" in 1966, a National Book Critics Circle Award in criticism for *Hugging the Shore* in 1983, and a 1991 Pulitzer Prize in fiction for *Rabbit at Rest,* the concluding novel in his *Rabbit* tetralogy.

Updike's earliest short story collections—*The Same Door* and *Pigeon Feathers, and Other Stories*—introduce subjects which occupy much of his later fiction: nostalgia, escapism, the struggle to attain faith, married life, and the search for truth. The themes of religious uncertainty and doubt are also prominently featured, particularly in *Pigeon Feathers,* which includes such critically acclaimed and frequently anthologized stories as "A & P," "Flight," "Lifeguard," and "Pigeon Feathers." In the title work Updike describes an adolescent's attempts to rationalize the existence of a supreme being. After reading what he considers a blasphemous passage in H. G. Wells's *The Outline*

of History portraying Jesus as a political agitator, the protagonist, David, finds his worldview and faith shaken. Noticing the malevolent forces of nature, David becomes resentful and antagonistic, doubting the traditional tenets of his Christian upbringing, which assert the existence of a benevolent deity. Ironically, he finds consolation after killing the pigeons in his parents' barn: David's faith in a supreme being is reaffirmed when he observes the delicate structure and patterns of the birds' feathers. Many of the stories from *The Same Door* and *Pigeon Feathers* are set in Olinger, Pennsylvania, a fictionalized version of Updike's hometown, and were collected in *Olinger Stories: A Selection.* Frequently viewed as memory pieces about Updike's own youth and small-town America, these stories are infused with nostalgia and depict the disillusionment individuals experience when they fail to achieve their expectations.

Incorporating themes of adultery, estrangement, and isolation, *The Music School* emphasizes the primacy of sex, sexuality, and humanity's elusive search for meaning in the modern world. Critic George W. Hunt maintains that *The Music School,* which includes the Bech story "The Bulgarian Poetess," also explores the problems of artistic identity and the creative process. The character Henry Bech, more formally introduced and developed in *Bech: A Book* and *Bech Is Back*, is often considered Updike's literary alter ego and a vehicle through which Updike commented on the American literary scene of the 1950s and 1960s. Unlike Updike, Bech is Jewish, frequently suffers from writer's block, and is willing to commercialize his writing to suit the prurient tastes of contemporary reading audiences.

Museums and Women, and Other Stories, Updike's sixth short fiction collection, delineates the relationship between time, fear, death, faith, and contentment. The story "The Day of the Dying Rabbit," for instance, documents a family's various reactions—hope, despair, disgust, and grief—to a gravely ill animal. In such stories as "Museums and Women," "The Witnesses," and "I Will Not Go, Except Thou Bless Me," Updike similarly traces various individuals' attempts to commemorate brief moments of happiness as recompense for the sadness that their future holds. *Museums and Women* additionally features a section entitled "Other Modes," which departs from Updike's usual setting of middle-class America and includes whimsical stories about amoebae, dinosaurs, and a legend about Jesus, which states that he escaped crucifixion by fleeing to Japan.

Updike's later collections continue to focus on problems of faith, self-awareness, and memory, but critics note a growing preoccupation with family life, aging and deterioration, divorce, death, and the need to accept the past. For example, "The Egg Race" and "Domestic Life in America," both from *Problems, and Other Stories*, feature characters who recognize their failure to live up to the moral standards of loved ones. These concerns are more prominently displayed in *Too Far to Go: The Maple Stories*, which collects tales about characters who first appeared in "Snowing in Greenwich Village" from *The Same Door*. Often considered his most polished collection, *Too Far to Go* traces the decline of the Maples' marriage. Critics observe that the pieces in Updike's most recent volume, *Trust Me*, retain his growing concern with death, sickness, and old age, but, according to Updike, these stories are about "the theme of trust, betrayed or fulfilled." Possibly as a response to charges that his stories frequently feature essentially the same protagonist and are autobiographical in content, Updike has said that *Trust Me* presented him with new stylistic and thematic challenges: "I was determined to try to write short stories about people, who, in no way, could seem to be me, and also, perhaps, to broaden my short stories in both the amount of time they take and the amount of space they take. I have some spacious stories, continent-spanning stories, in this book, and a few stories that take a couple from their 20s to their deaths. So there was some deliberate attempt to broaden my palette."

In assessing Updike's literary status, many commentators perceive a link between his short fiction and his novels—they maintain that the former are a prelude to his longer works—but critics generally agree that Updike excels in the short story genre. With their focus on family life, the past, and moral crises, Updike's stories are often consid-

ered "lyrical meditations" on existential issues and the problems of the American middle class. Jonathan Yardley observed: "[Updike is] a far more accomplished and confident writer of stories than of novels. Perhaps he does not take them so seriously, and thus unwittingly frees himself from the solemnity into which the novels too frequently collapse; perhaps he really is, as was often said of him when he was young, a miniaturist; perhaps the form of the story liberates him from preoccupation with plot, at which he is something less than masterly, and permits him to concentrate upon the loving accumulation of domestic detail, at which he is superb. Whatever the case, it is in his short stories that we find Updike's most assured work, and no doubt it is upon the best of them that his reputation ultimately will rest."

PRINCIPAL WORKS

SHORT FICTION

The Same Door 1959
Pigeon Feathers, and Other Stories   1962
Olinger Stories: A Selection 1964
The Music School 1966
Bech: A Book 1970
Museums and Women, and Other Stories 1972
Problems, and Other Stories 1979
Too Far to Go: The Maple Stories   1979; also published as *Your Lover Just Called: Stories of Joan and Richard Maple*, 1980
Bech Is Back 1982
Trust Me 1987

OTHER MAJOR WORKS

The Carpentered Hen and Other Tame Creatures (poetry) 1958; also published as *Hoping for a Hoopoe*, 1959
The Poorhouse Fair (novel) 1959
Rabbit, Run (novel) 1960
The Magic Flute [with Warren Chappell] (children's book) 1962
The Centaur (novel) 1963
Telephone Poles, and Other Poems (poetry) 1963
The Ring [with Warren Chappell] (children's book) 1964
Assorted Prose (essays) 1965
A Child's Calendar (children's poetry) 1965
Of the Farm (novel) 1965
Verse: The Carpentered Hen and Other Tame Creatures/Telephone Poles, and Other Poems (poetry) 1965
Couples (novel) 1968
Three Texts from Early Ipswich (drama) 1968
Bottom's Dream (children's book) 1969
Midpoint, and Other Poems (poetry) 1969
Rabbit Redux (novel) 1971
Seventy Poems (poetry) 1972
Buchanan Dying (drama) 1974
A Month of Sundays (novel) 1975

CRITICISM

R. B. Larsen (essay date 1972)

[*In the following essay, Larsen argues that many of Updike's best stories are not plot-driven but "lyrical meditations" on the "large, problematic areas of human existence."*]

The often acerbic critical controversy over the stature of John Updike continues, unabated by the publication of *Rabbit Redux*. It is still too early to tell, of course, how durable will be the total work of a writer so surprisingly fertile and inventive. One thing seems indisputable even now, though: his mastery of the short story form. The little that has been said of the stories of Updike is often phrased in superlatives: "Updike's craft sometimes falters," says Charles T. Samuels [in his *John Updike*, 1969], "but it serves him unerringly in . . . that quick glimpse of character or way of life that constitutes a modern story. Of this last form, he is a master." [In her *John Updike: Yea Sayings*, 1971], Rachael Burchard observes that "Updike reaches his highest range of accomplishment in this medium." Guerin LaCourse claims [in "The Innocence of John Updike," *Commonweal* 77 (8 February 1963)] that Updike's "most telling work . . . has been his short stories," while the Hamiltons state categorically [in their *John Updike*, 1967], "What Updike has to say he says first in his short stories. His novels are, in a sense, second tries." Yet an intensive study of the stories *in toto* remains nonexistent. While it is beyond the scope of this article to analyze the tone and tenor of the more than one hundred stories (over a third of them uncollected) Updike has published to date, a brief attempt at propaedeutics can be made in arriving at the particular type of story under consideration, the lyrical meditation.

Even after the strikingly modish *Rabbit Redux*, the short story seems as significant a part of Updike's achievement as it was for Hemingway and Fitzgerald. Many of Updike's efforts bear the hallmarks of good short fiction in American since Poe: discipline, structural soundness, a unity of theme or effect, a sense of wonder at life—all results of the "care and skill" which, Poe said, the form demands. Yet they do not follow the direction taken early by Poe and almost universally since World War II, the depiction of brooding psychomachia that seems in our time to have transfixed the epigoni of Lawrence and Faulkner. Rather they are content to portray, if not (to borrow Howells' phrase) "the more smiling aspects of life," then at least those nonviolent, sublunary events that form the backbone of contemporary American experience. It Updike's characters are not happy, their frustrations drive them neither to madness nor to morbidity. The intelligent, rational, yet sensitive minds of the protagonists preclude psychopathic behavior merely as a function of their (albeit sometimes hypertrophic) observation of life's stable minutiae.

It is in the lyrical meditation that Updike allows precise intelligence and linguistic *delicatesse* their greatest play. The *lyrical* (meaning imaginative and image-filled subjective prose-poetry) *meditation* (meaning contemplation of large, problematic areas of human experience) is not a story in the conventional sense: it bears only vestigial "characterization" and makes no concessions to standard devices of "plot." It is more closely related to Hawthorne's "pure essays" (our guide Poe's term for such pieces as "Snow-Flakes" and "The Sisters Years") or Washington Irving's sketches (both Updike and Irving had intensive art training and hence exhibit the painterly eye) than it is to something out of *Dubliners* or *Go Down, Moses*. Ranging uninhibitedly but always anchored to a central image or concept, it is often incremental in manner: meaning accrete through small revelations as the story works toward making concrete one or more monadic abstractions. In arriving at illumination it employs what Northrop Frye calls [in *Anatomy of Criticism*, 1957] "*dianoia*, the idea or poetic thought (something quite different, of course, from other kinds of thought) that the reader gets from the writer." In arriving there, too, it often requires of the reader a greater mental involvement than he is accustomed to giving the A+B+C plotted story. Yet it is typically neither an exhibition of stylistic dandyism nor the type of solemn lucubration that the word *meditation* sometimes implies: it is, metaphorically, a miniature geography of a region of human experience, elaborated with erudition and wit and a full measure of the author's renowned verbal magic, often partly parodic. Drawing upon story and essay and poem for its form, it succeeds in overcoming the usual limitations of its models: the storyline of the story, the prosaic logic of the essay, the often obscure ellipticality of the poem. It is a sophisticated writer's most sophisticated accomplishment.

Some of the stories categorizable as lyrical meditations are **"Wife-Wooing" "Harv Is Plowing Now," "Lifeguard," "The Dark," "The Indian," "The Music School." "Museums and Women," "Plumbing,"** and **"The Baluchitherium."** It is the first three of these, relatively early and hence prototypical, that will be examined here. The rest are left for the reader's delectation, hopefully with a set of guidelines for orientation to this striking new inflection of the short story form.

The earliest meditation is **"Wife-Wooing,"** one of Updike's many treatments of conjugal love, and surely one of his most soaringly lyrical. In fact, the rollicking language of the story is in part a sort of mock-mock-Joyce, an elaborate caricature of Anglo-Saxon poetry that both tips its hat and winks at the Irish master, even as it explicitly acknowledges its debt. Basically, it is a slight story of a young husband and father who, trying to save his wife from kitchen drudgery so that she will be in the mood (he hopes) for sex later on, brings supper home from a hamburger emporium and proceeds to court her ineffectually. Updike manages to flesh out so apparently feeble a fictional skeleton with reverberations that sound down to our most fundamental patterns of behavior.

For the Anglo-Saxon mode of the story is not mere fancy dressing, however much it adds to the humor. It is used to underscore certain significant parallels between modern man and his primitive ancestors that only recently neo-evolutionists like Desmond Morris (Updike has published an amusing poem called "The Naked Ape") and Robert Ardrey have restored to the popular consciousness. The setting of the story is quite clearly mock-savage, husband and family in their suburban "intimate cave," squatting "before a fire"—in the fireplace, of course. The meal itself was "wrestled warm from the raw hands of the hamburger girl in the diner a mile away, a ferocious place slick with savagery" and "young predators"; Beowulf-like, the narrator "wielded his wallet, and won my way back." As he verbally carries on the wooing, struggling with the indifference of his wife to honeymoon memories and the intrusions of the children as they sloppily eat, he is reminded of the timeless ritual of blood that accompanies successful early courtship: the defloration of the female. Tactfully handled, partially assimilated into the civilized image of a cathedral rosewindow, this remembered act is a key to the point Updike is making about unchanging human situations ("We pay dear in blood for our peaceful homes."), and, indeed, is indispensable to the remarkable way in which the *dianoia* and the story are completed in four telling paragraphs.

His wife has dropped off to sleep, his seductive efforts unsuccessful: it is the next day, a Monday. Our domestic-atavistic hero "arrows off to work," to the "inanimate, adamant joys of job." Returning that evening with his "head enmeshed in a machine," returning, that is, from earning his family's sustenance he assumes the heroic (or, anthropologically, *male-role*) dimension that he lacked on Sunday, his day off. Foundering on a problem he has brought home from work, "churning with cigarettes" as he tries (it is implied) to make more secure his position as a breadwinner, he is "taken by surprise at a turning" when his wife plants a kiss on his lips, a prelude to the lovemaking which he has, along with his salary, truly earned tonight. The "momentous moral" with which the story concludes ("An expected gift is not worth giving.") is playfully deceptive; this wittily imaginative meditation has successfully seduced us to a fresh concept of the "modern" hearth and home, of domesticity itself.

The conflation of ancient past and deceptively deep present that undergirds **"Wife-Wooing"** is much more explicit in **"Harv Is Plowing Now,"** a gemlike story that has gone virtually unnoticed by critics (in their booklength study the Hamiltons do not mention it). More serious than **"Wife-Wooing,"** it is a meditation on the meaning of history, objective and personal, and it manages to crowd into its six pages an almost bewildering richness of thought and image, couched once more in Updike's most lyrical prose style—one gets the feeling that these meditations are the author's truest labors of love. A regularly plotted story could not hope to contain the density of such a piece, simply because it would be largely involved with delineation of event and personality. But we do not feel cheated out of a story, for there is ample compensation—and, indeed, an intriguingly archetypal title-character—in the thought-fruit the story bears on its elegant limbs.

If there is a fault to the piece, it is that there is no trunk, only the three or four convoluted branches that grow, miraculously, off the airy abstraction of history and the author's "strong impulse to mix memory and desire" [Arthur Mizener, *The Sense of Life in the Modern Novel*, 1964]. Memory and desire are precisely the identifiable human elements that invest history—again, objective or personal—with meaning: in this case, the memory of a strange childhood friend (we are back in Olinger, momentarily) and the desire on the part of the narrator to reunite with a lost love. A clue to the analogy that binds the elements of the story together is contained in the odd first line (Poe: "If his very initial sentence tend not to the outbringing of this [single] effect, then he has failed in his first step."): "Our lives submit to archaeology." Before the meaning of this opening conundrum is clear, we are thrust back into the narrator's past to the lyrically evoked image of Harv, a fat, silent farmboy who plowed the neighboring land each spring:

> The linked silhouettes of the man and the mule moved back and forth like a slow brush repainting the parched pallor of the winter-faded land with the wet dark color of loam. It seemed to be happening *in me;* and as I age with this century, I hold within myself this memory, this image unearthed from a pastoral epoch predating my birth, this deposit lower than which there is only the mineral void.

Without pause for reflection, we are then shifted to the story's next limb, a brief recounting of a British archaeological expedition's discovery, beneath eight feet of unmarked clay that was itself buried under sedimental layers of Sumerian ruins, of an antediluvian Ur-city called al'Ubiad. At midpoint in the story a connection is established and the first sentence illuminated: "My existence is similarly stratified." The narrator is impelled to dig back through the shambles a woman has made of his life to the magically prelapsarian place where Harv "eternally plows." A painfully relived process, it demonstrates the general workings of history—a merely apparent randomness in the progression of events—through the particularized events of significance in a man's life. Upon this delicately extended metaphor the tale is poised.

The second half of the story is a compressed retelling of

the long period during which the woman (his wife then) shaped his life, analogized with a remarkably consistent virtuosity—the thing has to be read carefully to be appreciated—to an archaeological exploration. The concluding page or so brings us right up to the present, employing, for effect, curt dialogue (rare in a meditation). The man and his ex-wife meet on a beach, talk desultorily, and, discovering that the fire of love really is extinguished, go their separate ways. At that precise moment, bereft of his woman for good ("I am infinitesimal, lost, invisible, nothing," he is able to reach back ontologically into the past, to delve down to that cathectic deposit for what he must have, to know that his life (and history itself) is more than just a series of ruins piled adventitiously atop one another: "Standing on the slope of sand, I know what is happening across the meadow, on the far side of the line where water and air maintain their elemental truce. Harv is plowing now." At bottom, such concrete events and images are all that can be apprehended of life's great abstractions; it is to such trivial yet wondrously evocative *exempla* that the lyrical meditation is attuned.

"Lifeguard" is among the most widely known of Updike's stories. Yet it has apparently been misread slightly in the two commentaries on it to date. In trying to force Updike into a standard modern-Protestant mold, the Hamiltons cite the story's depiction of a world "wooed away from eternal truth" [in their *The Elements of John Updike*, 1971], while Mizener speaks rather too solemnly of "the real horror of death" in this "humanist parable."

The story is a meditation not only on religion but on a rather extreme religious sensibility, and thus contains a strong flavor of irony that has evidently gone unsavored. The most obvious indication of this irony is, again, the language of the story, a partial parody more subtle than the one in **"Wife-Wooing,"** but equally effective for its purposes. Here the theological Mannerism of the seventeenth century is gently satirized, the Brownean essay which unintentionally camouflages, to modern eyes, the fervor of its religious sentiment behind an ornate rhetoric. It is precisely his antique language that creates a barrier between the lifeguard, narrator and us, and makes hieratical captiousness out of what should be plainest sincerity (the rhetoric, of course, is the persona's, not Updike's). The stilted, alternately self-righteous and self-conscious tone wholly befits the idle lifeguard: a hero-archetype in an unheroic time, an ectomorph in mesomorphy's bronzed skin.

But it is an *attitude* which conducts us to the central irony: the discrepancy between what the lifeguard is and what he imagines himself to be, and the larger implication, not accidental in an author enamored of Karl Barth, of a discrepancy between what religion (or, better, faith) can do and what it cannot do. It cannot, like the lifeguard, who bears unmistakable signs of a Christ complex ("I have given my youth. . . . "), predicate its entire existence upon a need for or an expectation of some ultimate redemption—there is no way to elicit response from the Beyond in the form of an eleventh-hour rescue. Thus it is that the deluded lifeguard waits in vain for "a call." The point of the meditation is neither to prove nor to disprove the reality of benevolent supernatural forces; rather it is simply to show that in an age when "people no longer go to church" and "oblivion is sensible and sanitary" among the multitudes that "blacken the beach," spiritual lifeguards become selfbound, even narcissistic ornaments. Note, again, the all-important first sentence: "Beyond doubt, I am a splendid fellow"—beyond doubt (i.e., in faith) he may be, but there is neither the desire nor the means for anyone to know for certain in an Age of Doubt. The ultimate irony perhaps redounds to the narrator himself, who, in bidding "So: be joyful" is only extending his uselessness by bulwarking the "vast tangle of humanity" against crisis. But this last point, as with so much in matters of religion, is ambiguous—and quite contrivedly so, Updike being fully aware that there are not easy answers, here least of all.

Ambiguity itself is one of the many delights of the lyrical meditation. Subsuming whole worlds of experience under the abstractions it engages, it ensures against facile exhaustion of meaning and thus more greatly rewards the sedulous reader. Ignoring what are often called the "conventions" of the short story, it is an autonomous form that arrogates to itself what it needs of poetry and the essay and offers, where appropriate, universal problems in place of plot and archetypes in place of character. And in celebrating the concrete and minute in experience as a vital aspect of the human condition, it becomes perhaps the most infrangible accomplishment of an author around whom critical whirlpools will, no doubt, continue to swirl. (pp. 33-9)

> *R. B. Larsen, "John Updike: The Story as Lyrical Meditation," in* Thoth, *Vol. 13, No. 1, Winter, 1972-73, pp. 33-9.*

Robert Detweiler   (essay date 1972)

[*Detweiler is an American critic and educator. In the essay below, he offers a thematic analysis of several of the stories collected in* The Same Door.]

The Same Door, published in 1959, is a collection of sixteen short stories written over a period of five years and originally published, some in different form, in *The New Yorker;* and they represent various stages of Updike's maturity. The first story, **"Friends from Philadelphia,"** was also Updike's first commercially published fiction, written in 1954 after his graduation from Harvard. The others were composed during his 1955 scholarship year at Oxford, during his two-year tenure as *New Yorker* staff writer (1955-57), and during his first two years as an independent novelist. Consequently, the stories have little formal unity as a collection, and any attempt to generalize about them is confounded by exceptions.

Certain aspects of casual unity are created by a consistent authorial attitude toward life and by a recurrent structural technique. Updike himself articulates the attitude in the foreword to a later collection called *Olinger Stories.* Answering the complaint that one of those stories seems to have no point, he comments "The point, to me, is plain, and is the point, more or less, of all these Olinger stories. *We are rewarded unexpectedly.* The muddled and inconsequent surface of things now and then parts to yield us a gift." This point is the one made as well, if sometimes negatively so, in ***The Same Door;*** and it expresses a conviction of the author that becomes more determinative as the body of his fiction grows. Updike is a Christian, if not a "religious" writer in the accepted sense, and the centrality of grace in the Protestant experience finds its way into his art through the expression of the gift or the reward.

The particular unifying technique is similar to the construction of the Joycean "epiphany," at least according to the way in which that much-debated term has been generally understood. Somewhat as in Joyce's *Dubliners,* ***The Same Door*** stories, instead of attempting the brutal surprise or the psychological shock, concentrate on producing the gradual revelation—the culminating knowledge-plus-emotion that dawns upon the protagonist following his crucial experiences and upon the reader after he has finished the story. Also, as in Joyce's stories, Updike's epiphanies, while they do not depend upon an overt religious context (except in **"Dentistry and Doubt"**), translate fundamentally religious or at least moral experiences into artistic imagery and action. The revelatory moment does not result from any sensational conflicts or climactic scenes, for these are not stories of deep passion, violence, or death. They occur in the midst of daily life, mixing with the stuff of the mundane; and the insight slowly materializes through a fine fusion of memories, reflexes and some subtle catalyst of the unexpected. Against the wonted beat of familial or vocational being, a counterpoint insinuates itself in these stories that at last upsets the rhythm and forces the characters and reader to pause and then to reconsider the whole composition.

Although the sixteen stories span a period from the very beginning of Updike's career to his establishment as a respected young artist, one finds little difference in the quality of the fiction. **"Friends from Philadelphia,"** the first tale, shows some evidence of a neophyte author in search of a style; but the result is not a weak story by any means: it is, at its worst, a narrative that does not sound like the later, familiar Updike. The sentences are often short and choppy, dialogue predominates, and very little of the metaphoric interplay that marks the later fiction is present. The story succeeds, however, along other lines. Through careful characterization via dialogue, Updike reveals the sensitive uncertainty of late adolescence in contrast to the bluff confidence of adults who have located their secure little niches in society.

The tale is simple enough. Fifteen-year-old John Nordholm, who lives a mile outside Olinger, hikes into town to buy the wine that his parents need to entertain expected guests from Philadelphia. Since he is too young to buy alcohol, he stops by the Lutz home and asks if the father will buy it for him. Mr. Lutz himself arrives home later slightly drunk and agrees to drive John and the teenage Lutz daughter to the liquor store. He allows John (underage) to drive the new family car to the store, takes John's two dollars, and soon reappears with the wine. When they arrive at the Nordholm house, John asks hesitantly for his change and receives it along with the bottle. As Lutz and his daughter drive away, young John Nordholm discovers that the wine is Château Mouton-Rothschild 1937.

The charm of the story, along with the semi-sophisticated banter between the teenagers and the description of the television-addicted Mrs. Lutz in her darkened room, is in the ambivalent kindness of Mr. Lutz. His is an unexpectedly gracious act, for the wine obviously cost much more than the innocent boy anticipated; and the man does not humiliate him in front of the snide daughter by refusing to give change or by divulging the quality and price of the wine. But his gesture is also a patronizing one that increases Mr. Lutz's self-esteem at the expense of the Nordholms. John's schoolteacher-father can't afford good wine or a new car as the uneducated but prosperous Mr. Lutz can, and young John is left with the ironic reward. He is gifted for his family's poverty but suffers condescension for it as well. The revelation of the story, therefore, is that kindness has its price, perhaps, and that receiving grace demands its own kind of maturity.

The second narrative, **"Ace in the Hole,"** could be a preliminary sketch for *Rabbit, Run.* Fred "Ace" Anderson, like Harry Angstrom, is a twenty-six-year-old ex-high school basketball star, married, father of a small child, and the sad product of maternal domination. On the particular day of the story, he has been fired from his job—not for the first time—as a used-car salesman; and he returns home to await the arrival of his working wife and to appease somehow her anticipated anger at his latest failure. The story is packed with the complications and baggage of young American marriage. Evey, the wife, is Roman Catholic; and Ace is Protestant—a sore point between them. Their life is saturated with TV, pop music, beer, and the omnipresent cigarettes. They appear to have married directly out of high school when they were too young and when they had developed no skills; and they survive in a precarious financial state. Evey has matured, but Ace has not. He lives in the illusion of his teenage glory and is a childish egotist. Updike describes in detail how Ace lovingly combs his long, sleek hair in front of the mirror; and he stresses that, while Ace has just lost his job—a reason for actual concern—he is really bothered because a mention of his high-scoring record in the local sports news that day has employed his name of Fred instead of Ace.

That evening Evey takes rather stoically the news of the firing (Ace's mother has already told her), but the irresponsible young husband soon irritates her into bitter recriminations. Then Ace turns on his charm. He distracts her by applauding their baby daughter's antics, then persuades her to dance with him to the sound of dinner music on the radio. The tale ends with the two of them, everything unresolved, dancing a quickening swing step in the isolation of the drab apartment, trying pathetically to relive the popularity of their carefree high school days.

Updike has, amazingly, already found his métier in **"Ace in the Hole."** The story offers less in terms of plot and action than **"Friends from Philadelphia"** but much more in terms of pure mood created out of sheer verbal craftsmanship. It is, much like *Rabbit, Run,* a sustained metaphor of nervous movement and a tension of opposites. Ace is always in motion: driving the car, smoking hastily, tapping a foot in rhythm, running home from his mother's house with the small daughter in his arms—still shifting restlessly on life's basketball court, trying to score and to be the hero again with the effortlessness of the natural. But Ace is not a natural in the workaday world. An indulgent mother and cheap early fame have spoiled him, and he is already a clear-cut failure at the approaching prime of life. The antagonistic characters, his opposites, make his plight the more obvious. The prowling high school youths who insult him at the traffic light only show him (like the boys playing back-alley basketball at the start of *Rabbit, Run*) the reckless innocence that he has lost. His weary and dispirited wife, with her dogged common sense, makes him seem more of a loser.

Apart from a sexual innuendo, the title has a double sense. The protagonist is Ace "in the hole": jobless, unprepared to be a man, and threatened with a spouse nearly ready to leave him. But he also *has* his ace in the hole: his animal charm and his instincts that will help him to survive even if he ruins others in the process. The story is an inversion of the maturation pattern, for the events that should jolt the initiate into growing up at last only cause him to fight reality with a wasteful nervous energy. **"Ace in the Hole"** seems authentic because it fashions a modern American type, the teenage hero seduced by quick success into thinking that the adult world is easy to conquer but who soon suffers disillusion and the gradual degeneration into bumhood. Olinger can be too kind, the family-community can be too generous, when it offers its sons what they should strive a lifetime to deserve—and then permits grace to turn quickly into judgment. Updike has forced more news about one dead end along the American way of life into one brief story than many writers manage to report in a whole novel. It is no wonder that he returned to the theme and the place and expanded the microform into *Rabbit, Run*.

In [**"Tomorrow and Tomorrow and So Forth"**] (the third in the collection), young Mark Prosser is teaching *Macbeth* to a class of restless eleventh-graders; the narration is third-person, from Prosser's point of view. Updike's later familiar blending of the lofty and the trivial (on which *The Centaur* is based) appears here for the first time with clarity. It is carried in the title: **"Tomorrow and Tomorrow and So Forth"** joins the beginning of the famous Shakespearean soliloquy with the callous teenage disregard for highflown language, just as the inane teenage paraphrases of the speech clash with the quite incisive analysis that Prosser gives the bored students—and that is lost, of course, on them. That incongruity, introduced by the pupils' barbarizing of a classic, is deepened and then justified and resolved in the central action of the story.

Just before the period is over, Prosser intercepts a note passed from the provocative Gloria Angstrom to a boyfriend in which she confesses that "He's heavenly with poetry. I think I love him. I really do *love* him." Prosser detains the girl after class and lectures to her firmly but kindly about the dangers of using love's vocabulary too lightly; she leaves on the verge of tears. Immediately after, while Prosser is enjoying this surprising evidence of his professional-masculine charm, another teacher enters to tell him the gossip of the day: Gloria has written the same sort of note about two other faculty members and had them pur-

posely discovered. Prosser has obviously been duped, and he is angered by the girl's duplicity; but he also comprehends that the trick has backfired on her: "The girl had been almost crying; he was sure of that."

Updike manages to project, in the unpredictable extremes of a youthful mind, a pettiness and a potential nobility that contribute together to the imaged truths of the story. As Prosser discovers, "a terrible tenderness" marks adolescents; and that oxymoron contains the power of the narrative. A young girl can use her budding sexuality to play an irritating trick on her instructors, but she will also respond to an honest encounter. The experience holds a gift for pupil and teacher. He takes her seriously, in their private discussion after class, in spite of her immaturity; and she answers with an acknowledgment of respect for him that was hidden hitherto behind the façade of mischief. "This petty pace from day to day" is quickened and made worthwhile by the occasional spontaneous meeting of two momentarily unmasked selves.

"Snowing in Greenwich Village," the seventh of *The Same Door* series, is one of the most impressive performances in the collection. It shifts from the Olinger setting to Manhattan and introduces Richard and Joan Maple, a young married couple who appear again, older and unhappier, in *The Music School* and in four uncollected short stories. Very little actually happens in the narration; instead, it shows the author absorbed in his persistent but delicate probing of interacting personalities. Richard (in the advertising trade) and Joan have just moved to West Thirteenth Street in the Village and have invited an old acquaintance over for the evening, Rebecca Cune, a girl with "a gift for odd things."

The three drink sherry and converse, but the talk is dominated by Rebecca's wry recollections of the strange people she has known. Joan, who has a cold and has not been at all witty in the conversation, is roused by the clatter of horses of mounted policemen. She rushes to the window, sees snow falling outside, and hugs her husband in a moment of unguarded intimacy while their guest watches blandly. When Rebecca leaves, Richard walks her home and follows her upstairs, aroused, to see her apartment. At her door as he prepares to leave, they are poised to embrace; but Richard destroys the critical moment with a joke that misfires, and departs.

The undertone of sexual competition pervades the tale. Joan and Rebecca are at cautious odds from the start, and Updike contrasts them graphically: Joan's angular "Modiglianiesque" features give her an air of simplicity, but Rebecca is a da Vinci type whose constant enigmatic smile reminds one of the mystery of the tantalizing Mona Lisa portrait. Beneath the purposefully casual conversation, one is made to feel the unnamed struggle. Richard is the prize, Joan the defender of her property, and Rebecca the predator. Joan's weapon is her defenselessness; Rebecca's, her cool and cryptic reserve that promises a hidden excitement. Richard is caught between loyalty toward his wife, who is put at a disadvantage by the off-beat discussion, and Rebecca's novel attractiveness. The chatting remains discreet, but the adultery motif accompanies it through the repeated references to beds: in the first paragraph, Richard lays Rebecca's coat and scarf on their marriage bed; Rebecca relaxes on the floor in the living room with her arm on the Hide-a-Bed (while Joan sits straightbacked on a chair); Rebecca tells about the bedroom troubles she had in sharing her apartment with a pair of lovers; and, when Richard at the end visits her apartment, he is surprised to see the double bed that dominates the room. The subtlety of the imagery matches the subtlety of the invitation to extra-marital adventure.

Updike is a Christian, if not a "religious" writer in the accepted sense, and the centrality of grace in the Protestant experience finds its way into his art through the expression of the gift or the reward.

—Robert Detweiler

But Rebecca's strength is also her weakness. Her knack for comic recitation gradually emerges as the extent of her substance. She achieves her unique personality at the expense of others, exaggerating their foibles to fit the style of her performance. That Rebecca is a predator in every way Richard suddenly grasps after his wife's impulsive embrace, as he sees Joan and himself from Rebecca's viewpoint. She will twist the moment of tenderness into a joke when she narrates the scene to other friends: the simple wife with the sniffles who hugs her husband in ludicrous joy because it happens to be snowing. But Richard's discovery does not make her less desirable; for when Richard escorts her home (at Joan's insistence—a smart if risky strategy, since it forces her opponent's move), they hold an embarrassed dialogue that masks the tension of presexual encounter and that continues inside her apartment.

Updike produces the tension by allowing the inane comments to fill the void of anticipation. The crucial moment, exquisitely described, occurs at the door when Richard acts to leave; and the result could go either way. Rebecca, very close to him in the shadows, is waiting for him to make the move. If he does, he betrays his wife; if he doesn't, he becomes the ridiculous male. He tries a joke and stutters; the timing and the situation are ruined. He is free but at the expense of his pride.

Since this is Richard Maple's story, one must inquire what unexpected gift he receives. It may be, in part, the thrill of the just-missed extra-marital adventure; but, more likely, it is that he does *not* become intimately involved. He has had the quick glance into the tantalizing maze of illicit romance but also the luck, or the grace, to avoid its penalties—emotional, social, and moral. The revelation of mutual attraction between a man and a woman is a joy not only because it reassures one of his desirability but also because it indicates an elementary kind of human communication. A fine line may exist between lust and love, but the libido need not always incite to sexual consummation; it

can produce other kinds of knowledge as well. Lust can teach.

The thirteenth story, **"A Gift from the City,"** employs the technique of inversion. James and Liz are a well-to-do young couple with a baby daughter who live on Tenth Street in Greenwich Village. Liz telephones her husband at work on a Friday afternoon to tell him that a poor Negro from North Carolina has been at her door asking for work and that she has given him ten dollars and sent him away. But the man wants to come back on Saturday evening to thank the husband as well for their generosity. That prospect upsets James; and, when the Negro actually does appear the next evening, James in his embarrassment gives him twenty dollars more. James and Liz are afraid now that they have a permanent dole on their hands and are not sure if they should believe his story: that he has just arrived from the South with wife and family and has a construction job promised him for the following week. Friends of the couple argue that the man is a fraud. When James returns home from work on Monday evening, Liz informs him that the Negro has been there once more, and that she sent him away without any money. He does not appear again, and the equilibrium of their life is restored.

The title is double-edged and signifies the inversion that gives the story its rationale. James tells the Negro to accept the thirty dollars from them "as a gift from the city." What he and his wife do not see, in their genteel materialist pride, is that the Negro himself is the real gift from the city to them. Whether he is a small-time swindler or someone in genuine need, he is involved in a struggle for survival; and he is offered to them as a unique introduction to the destitution that characterizes the other side of metropolitan living. But James and Liz, for all their humanitarian impulses and notions of decency, do not really want to *know* the Negro. James is insulted when the black man refers to them as his only friends in New York. The scene in which James sees a similarity between the Negro's head and a new shaver he has designed is revealing. James is immersed in a world of things, and philanthropy must remain nicely objective and distant in that schema. He is easy prey for panhandlers on the street because he is so acutely fearful of a personal involvement that will unbalance his neatly arranged way of life.

James thinks twice of magic circles around his wife and child that would protect them from the hundred daily dangers of Manhattan living. In the first reference, he is sorry that love is too immaterial to protect his dearest ones; but, by the end of the story, in his frustration over the resilient Negro, he believes that he has "sold his life, his chances" for his wife's sake and that she should make her own enchanted circles. But love in this story is too dependent on the modern symbols of affluence for its effectiveness and is perhaps more a matter of egotistic possession than of shared affection. In any case, James and Liz are in a charmed circle that they have unwittingly drawn around themselves and from which they cannot escape. Because of their economic and social success, they are separated from much of the real humanity of the city. In spite of their broadmindedness, they are morally narrow; they have chosen not to help; and, through their wealth, they are made spiritually poor. To be able to give graciously is also a gift; and the couple, by refusing to meet the Negro in all his potential, are denying themselves the gift they most need.

If "A Gift from the City" concludes with an ironic word about peace of mind and moral compromise, "The Happiest I've Been," the final story of the collection, returns with considerable nostalgia to the context of a fading moral innocence. John Nordholm (as Updike states it in the Foreword to *Olinger Stories*), having taken his turn as protagonist in "Friends from Philadelphia," narrates the story in the first person as a nineteen-year-old college student who is home in Olinger for the Christmas vacation. The tale is stylistically different from the others in *The Same Door.* It is essentially plotless and has the form of a reminiscence, a series of smoothly connected vignettes that one would guess to be transposed autobiography— Updike's personally experienced Shillington into the fictive Olinger of 1951. Yet the story evokes a mood that marks a transitional stage in one's maturing rather than a specific history and geography. It is the period of the end of youthful innocence, when one practices the rites of adulthood half-willingly to demonstrate sophistication, yet lingers with the more familiar and less complicated habits of late adolescence.

John is picked up in the evening by Neil, a friend of his, to drive to a girlfriend's New Year's party in Chicago, seventeen hours distant; but, once beyond parental ken, they decide to attend first in Olinger a party given by former high school classmates. They stay at the party until three in the morning and then take two girls home to nearby Riverside. Margaret, one of the girls, invites the others into her parent's home for early coffee; while Neil and the other girl pet in the darkened house, John and Margaret sit and talk until she falls asleep in his arm. As dawn breaks, the two boys finally leave for Chicago. Neil has John drive the car and sleeps beside him as the trip begins.

Except for "A Gift from the City," this is the longest story of the collection and one of Updike's favorites—a fact that in itself does not necessarily insure its quality; but the author does achieve his artistic ends through control of narrative idiom, perspective, and manipulation of an efficient metaphoric pattern. John tells the story in a retrospective late-teenager style—one relatively free of Updike's now ripened elaborate diction—that infuses his experience with a simple, forthright authenticity. But the angle of vision is not therefore wholly a teenager's; it is a double view that tempers the precious hours of the youthful past with the increased wisdom of the present.

The result is a certain discrepancy of moods and tones that creates the sense of loss now beginning to invade Updike's fiction and appearing strongest in *The Centaur* and *The Music School.* This mood is indicated in the adverbial superlative of the title ("The *Happiest* I've Been") and in the shadow of sadness that lingers over the careful description. Updike quotes Henri Bergson in the preface to *The Same Door:* "How many of our present pleasures, were we to examine them closely, would shrink into nothing more than memories of past ones!" That realization, which ap-

plies exactly to this story, is also Wordsworthian: with increasing self-consciousness comes the loss of natural, spontaneous joy, so that the stylizing mind must reconstruct its pleasures artificially out of the past.

But even if that much of the romantic survives in Updike, he possesses the discipline to fashion a universally meaningful event out of a private memory and to create thereby sentiment instead of sentimentality. "The Happiest I've Been" broadens into a modern maturation ritual, replete with the archetypal accoutrements, that does not simply dress up the old forms of twentieth-century art but also adds a new interpretive dimension. The season, the party, and the trip embody and symbolize the transitional nature of the experience that introduces a new stage of maturity. It is nearly New Year (the classmates pretend that it *is* New Year's Eve), the time to begin formally a fresh kind of existence; and the trip has echoes of the *rite de passage.* John leaves the old farm and his gnarled grandmother and aging parents for young, robust Chicago and the girlfriend awaiting him there; and, of course, the actual journey begins at the pristine moment of dawn. It is an emphatic moment of separation from family and home and the start of the independent journey through adult life.

The party particularly has ritual elements. It is a last meeting in youthful irresponsibility; less a reunion than a final celebration of oneness; still held in a parental home, but in one from which the parents are absent. The games, the alcoholic drinks, the dancing, all combined with a constant awareness of *the time,* blend the playfulness of adolescence with the growing sophistication of impending adulthood. When at midnight "everyone" tries to kiss the only married girl of the group, the concentrated ritual duality becomes most apparent; it is an embracing of the new state of being attempted through a playful gesture.

The new relevance of the maturation pattern appears after the party among the privacy of the two couples. The movement is from the group to individuals, from the tribe to self-conscious formal structures. For John Nordholm, the revelation of beginning maturity that promises goodness for the future and that makes him the happiest he's been comes through the double incident of demonstrated faith that others have in him: "There was knowing that twice since midnight a person had trusted me enough to fall asleep beside me." The nostalgia for an irretrievable carefree past is balanced by a pride in the assumed responsibility of adult relationships. One trusts one's sexual being, one's safety, with the other person; and there is joy in accepting the burden of that faith.

Here once more, finally, is the theme of the unexpected gift that runs through all the stories. To be treated as an adult, and the ability to respond as one, are two of life's subtle presents; to be introduced to the challenges of manhood through the expressed new trust of old friends is a surprising graciousness of nature, or of fate. Indeed, Updike might interpret it as an extension of God's blessing into one's deepening self-conscious existence.

The other stories in the collection present variations on the themes and motifs already described. "Dentistry and Doubt" concerns an American divinity student at Oxford who, plagued by Luther-like struggles with the devil, finds solace in a visit to an English dentist when the man working on his teeth prompts him into recalling a faith-restoring quotation. The story ends with an apt natural metaphor: as the student watches birds through the window, he sees two wrens snatch a crumb from a blackbird—like a pair of weak humans outsmarting Satan.

In **"The Kid's Whistling,"** a young commercial artist who is working overtime during the Christmas season and who is annoyed by the incessant piping of a stockboy is paid a touchy visit in his department-store office by his impatient wife. She leaves, he ruins the TOYLAND sign he was lettering, and discovers it was because "the kid had stopped whistling." The irritations of life, whether they are the minor bothers caused by fellow workers or the more constant frictions of marriage, become as familiar and as much second nature as the established comforts. They are also a kind of communication, and one learns to depend upon them to maintain the rhythms of human endeavor.

"Toward Evening," which is more of a sketch than a short story, is the only one of its kind in the book. Rafe, a young New Yorker, takes a bus home from work to his wife and baby daughter on the Upper West Side. Some undefined rift separates him and his wife that evening, and he retreats into whimsical, cynical conjecture about the pointless construction of the huge Spry sign that shines across from the New Jersey side of the Hudson River. When the gift of human response is not forthcoming, it seems, one feels himself abandoned in the mechanized and vulgar meaninglessness of the age.

"Who Made Yellow Roses Yellow?" contrasts the suave Manhattan playboy Fred Platt with his old Ivy League classmate Clayton Clayton, the middle-class plodder who has made good as a big business executive. Just returned from France, Platt wants a job with Clayton's firm but is too proud to ask directly. When they meet for lunch, Fred offers hints that Clayton, still dazzled by his friend's worldly-wise front, doesn't take seriously. Frustrated by his failure, Fred insults the bewildered Clayton with school-primer French as they separate. Fred Platt is one of Updike's few thoroughly unpleasant character creations (Freddy Thorne in *Couples* is a more recent one), but he is also pathetic. Caught in the web of his own perverse personality, he cannot really meet anyone else on honest terms; and he seems doomed to isolation in his shallow social superiority. Even the last name (Platt is German for "flat" or "low") reinforces the sense of underlying failure.

"Sunday Teasing," in turn, is a subtly cruel story of a marriage relationship; and Updike uses in it the trick of fiction within fiction to impose the effect. The young couple Arthur and Macy, after a discussion about family affection with their Sunday dinner guest, retire for the evening; and Macy reads a depressing French short story that she passes on to her husband. He explains its essence to her—it concerns a "perceptive man caged in his own weak character"—and he then defends the hero's apparently harsh treatment of the heroine. When Macy begins to cry in confusion, Arthur humors her and puts her to bed. One real-

izes gradually that Arthur is also very aware but very weak, and the skillfully placed aspects of the story fall into line. Unamuno's *The Tragic Sense of Life* (which Arthur is reading), Arthur's distorted understanding of Protestant individuality, his playful demand that Macy mimic the Garbo line, "You're fooling me."—all these assume a terrible irony. Arthur does not, perhaps cannot, love his wife; but he doesn't have the courage to tell her. Instead, he keeps them both suspended in a painful illusion of communion. Behind his self-righteous Christian pose, he is sinning against her and himself.

In **"His Finest Hour,"** George and Rosalind Chandler intervene in a bloody marital quarrel in a neighboring Manhattan apartment. A month later, they receive an extravagant gift of flowers from the neighbors "to show that everything was right between our families." The Chandlers move to Arabia; homesick for America, George's first vision is always of a profusion of flowers in the shabby West Side rooms. This is a story of the unexpected and unrecognized reward, but George Chandler's "finest hour" is not when he ends the quarrel but when he and his wife are the surprised recipients of the flowers from the people they had thought to despise.

In **"A Trillion Feet of Gas,"** a young New York couple are enduring the lengthy visit of a mildly obnoxious British houseguest. At a party, the three meet a windy Texas businessman, "a States' Righter, a purchaser of Congressmen, a pillar of reaction," who entrances them all with his blunt, crude power. His vulgarity finally puts the carping Englishman on the defensive; and in his quasi-capitulation, before so much "gas," to America's "hideous vigor," he enters into a kind of comradeship at last with his hosts.

"Incest" begins with the description of a titillating dream that Lee, a young husband, relates to his wife at supper; and it ends with him asleep and dreaming again. In between, he plays with his spoiled baby daughter while his exhausted wife rests; and he manages to lull the child to sleep with a bedtime story. As the title suggests, the story probes the complexity of a marriage involvement from the male perspective. In a sense, Lee is married not just to his wife but to her aggressive mother, whom she resembles, and also to his demanding child. The dream of the other woman, then, illustrates the familiar wish-fulfillment of basic Freudianism; but it also shows the husband's acceptance of his actual situation. In the end of the dream, he finds himself washing the mysterious blonde girl with a garden hose. She could be his daughter grown up, his secret ideal woman, his mother-in-law, or all three merged. In any case, "the task, like rinsing an automobile, was more absorbing than pleasant or unpleasant"; and such a reaction, Updike would say, is the reality of most of our experiences.

In **"Intercession,"** Paul, the golf duffer, meets a lonely and insulting teenage boy on a Connecticut green. Exasperated by the boy's behavior, Paul does not see that it is a clumsy way of begging for companionship; and, instead of giving him the aid he needs, Paul challenges him to a round of golf for money. The boy refuses and goes away; Paul quits his playing and heads for his car, vaguely aware of failure but not of his central role in it.

In **"The Alligators,"** which returns to the Olinger setting, Joan Edison is the new girl from Baltimore who enters the Olinger fifth grade in mid-semester. The class taunts her about her city ways; but Charlie (the protagonist), although he takes part in the persecution, secretly loves her and determines to confess it to her and become her champion against his classmates' torment. But, by the time he is ready to make his move, Joan has become "queen of the class." Charlie, an only child, has misinterpreted the strange manifestations of adolescent affection; he understands too late that the others all along teased her to make her one of them. As the eternal outsider, Charlie does not comprehend the rites of initiation; and, because he is so young, his alienation is all the more pitiful.

"The same door" as a metaphor of communication is physically or figuratively present in all of the stories of the collection. It can function literally, as with Richard and Rebecca frozen in the tension of sexual attraction at the door of her darkened walk-up, or the poor Negro waiting outside the Village apartment for help from strangers, or George Chandler entering timidly to intervene in the neighbors' marital battle. Or it can be the symbolic door between husband and wife, between old friends, or between chance acquaintances. Some doors are opened quickly and gladly, others are opened only to be slammed shut, some are quietly closed, and some are never opened at all. The image of the door, a familiar object of ordinary life, is fitting and effective for Updike's purpose: to show that the formative events of one's being occur within the framework of the common, and that the common moments can be redeemed or lost through the quality of one's response to others. (pp. 15-30)

Robert Detweiler, in his John Updike, *Twayne Publishers, Inc., 1972, 183 p.*

Alice Hamilton and Kenneth Hamilton (essay date 1974)

[*The Hamiltons are the authors of* John Updike: A Critical Essay *(1967) and* The Elements of John Updike *(1970). In the essay below, they discuss Updike's treatment of time and radiance in* Museums and Women.]

In his autobiographical sketch, "The Dogwood Tree: A Boyhood" John Updike writes:

> Is the true marvel of Sunday skaters the pattern of their pirouettes or the fact that they are silently upheld? Blankness is not emptiness; we may skate upon an intense radiance we do not see because we see nothing else. And in fact there is a color, a quiet but tireless goodness that things at rest, like a brick wall or a small stone, seem to affirm.

Updike's successive collections of short stories show that the theme of a silent, upholding radiance has never been far from his mind. From **The Same Door** (1959) to **Museums and Women and Other Stories** (1972), his latest collection, this theme is constantly present.

In **The Same Door** and the collection following, **Pigeon Feathers and Other Stories,** Updike returns very frequently to memories of childhood and adolescence in order to recapture moments of radiance. The center for his stories of childhood is the fictional town of Olinger—corresponding to Shillington, Pennsylvania, the actual town where he grew up. Updike explains that in pronouncing Olinger we are to make the "O" long and the "g" hard and to accent the first syllable. So he is saying to the time of his early experiences of radiance, "Oh! linger." For, as Wordsworth also knew when he wrote his *Immortality* Ode, the radiance found in childhood seems to fade with the passing of time. Updike's third collection of short stories **The Music School** (1966) contains only one Olinger story; and the narrator of the title story says in the opening sentence, "I exist in time." How time carries away the capacity for vision is illustrated in the next collection, **Bech: A Book.** This volume contains seven stories about a novelist who, having written one masterpiece at the beginning of his career, feels himself grow old as he broods over the loss of his inspiration. Now, in **Museums and Women and Other Stories,** Updike's theme of lost radiance appears again and again. The narrator of the title story ends his narrative by speaking about the failure of "my search for the radiance that had faded behind me."

The destructive power of time is a perennial *motif* in world literature, so it is not surprising to find Updike concerning himself with it. Nevertheless, there is more to Updike's handling of this subject than a lament over departed glory or an attempt to relive, in backward glances, what once was and now is no more. He seems to believe in the upholding power of radiance that continues even when we have ceased to see it; and he reassures us that time is not an invincible enemy.

This aspect of Updike's treatment of the theme of radiance in **Museums and Women** is the subject of this essay.

Museums and Women is divided into three sections. The first section opens with the title story, narrated by a young man called William Young. William begins by describing the first museum he visited and how he began to make a connection between museums and women. When William was a boy his mother had taken him often to the local museum. He had felt then "that she was pointing me through these corridors toward a radiant place she had despaired of reaching."

In this same museum William met the first girl he loved. More accurately, he thought he loved her as a result of his mother's promptings. Yet, even then in his schooldays, he displayed a "timid rapacity" in attempting to grasp the radiance to be found in both museums and women, and the radiance eluded him. His mother remained a mystery to him, and he never declared his love for the freckled girl whom he worshipped from a distance. While Old Father William (as described by Robert Southey and by Lewis Carroll) was young in spirit, Updike's William Young seems to have been born old. At least, he was old in his inability to respond spontaneously to the experience of radiance.

The museum of William's childhood housed a collection

of bronze statuettes which affected him "in their smallness like secret thoughts of mine projected into dimension and permanence." Of these his mother said, "Billy, they seem such unhappy little people." William could not doubt the truth of her observation. The statuettes looked as though "caught in a tarnished fate," and he yearned to rescue them, to touch and comfort them. Yet he held back, "afraid of breaking the seal of their sullen, furious underworld."

William was convinced that the dread he felt when he looked at the statuettes did not emanate from them. It came "as if from another living person in the room." The only other living person actually around was his mother. Yet William says, "as if." So his secret thoughts must have been about growing up. To grow into the adult world is to despair (as his mother did) of ever reaching radiance. That other living person in the room was William's adult self. And the child did not dare to reach out to comfort the unhappy little people for fear that by so doing he would break the seal of their underworld and find himself sharing, prematurely, their tarnished fate.

William, though early old in intuition, was to remain immature when he reached adulthood. His "timid rapacity" was to keep him permanently "Young." Thus he stayed the Billy whom his mother had introduced to museums and to women. He went on seeking the radiant place to which his mother had pointed him, even when he knew that radiance had faded behind him. The story goes on to tell how, many times during his adult life, women and museums were connected in his experience; and how he came to realize that each fresh experience would result merely in increasing disenchantment.

Unlike William Young, Updike himself considers it very needful to know, and to act, one's age. In all his short-story collections the principal characters tend to be portrayed at the same age as his own and to be preoccupied with the problems attendant upon this particular stage of life. Updike is now forty. When, at the end of his thirty-fifth year, he wrote the long autobiographical poem "Midpoint" he pictured himself as having come to the top of the Hill of Life and about to descend its farther side. *Museums and Women* presents characters most of whom are similarly past the top of the hill and now, fearfully or curiously, taking a look at that downward slope which is henceforth the only view available to them.

Already, in his opening story, Updike introduces *motifs* which reoccur through the rest of the book. The mood of dread felt by William Young in the presence of the bronze statuettes is a present reality for most of the characters of the other stories. That other living person whom the boy senses is now a present reality— the aging adult who has seen the seal come off the "sullen, furious underworld" so that dread has become the prevailing spiritual climate. Most of the characters whom Updike describes could be called unhappy little people. Their lives are neither striking nor glorious; and, like the bronze statuettes, they bear the marks of tarnish that come with the passing of the years. The little figures were all nudes. Updike's characters, too, are naked. They are exposed to the elements without any protective covering of cultural tradition or re-

ligious faith to temper the winds of ill-fortune. Like William Young, they are conscious of radiance having faded behind them. As he does, they look back nostalgically to scattered moments of happiness—or almost-happiness—in the past. And they view with apprehension a future offering only diminishing returns, if indeed it has not already closed against all promise. Those who are bolder or more realistic than William, to be sure, occupy themselves with plans and stratagems and hopes of a kind. Yet all know that the past which is beyond recall has narrowed their options for the future. They know that repeated experiences of failure make the prospect of the days to come empty of any really new beginnings. To salvage a little from the wreck of time has become an increasingly urgent task—even when all that is salvageable is a small stock of memories.

Just as Updike is unlike William Young in facing the process of aging, so he may well be unlike him also in not being afraid to offer comfort to the unhappy little people who are his contemporaries and whose tarnished fate he shares. Supposing that his earlier intuition expressed in "The Dogwood Tree" still holds good, the blankness experienced by those descending the Hill of Life need not be emptiness. Perhaps at forty, when his characters do not see radiance, they are too ready to affirm that it is not there; too anxious to affirm that it has vanished beyond recall with the passing of their youth. Perhaps, Updike suggests, though the immediate, joyful experience of radiance is an experience peculiar to childhood and adolescence, maturity may have its own vision also, a vision affirming in less ecstatic fashion the permanent goodness at the heart of things.

Comfort, in its basic sense of strengthening (*confortare*), can come only through an enlarged vision. Men in a condition of grief have to be led to see that their situation is less desperate than they had imagined. If hopes were dupes, fears may be liars. Genuine comfort, then, must be a summons to realism. Such realism in the context of fading radiance is commended by Wordsworth in his *Immortality* Ode:

> What though the radiance which was once so
>   bright
> Be now forever taken from my sight,
> Though nothing can bring back the hour
> Of splendor in the grass, of glory in the flower,
> We will grieve not, rather find
> Strength in what remains behind;
> In the primal sympathy
> Which having been must ever be;
> In the soothing thoughts that spring
> Out of human suffering;
> In the faith that looks through death,
> In years that bring the philosophic mind.

The stories in *Museums and Women* have a great deal to say about what remains behind after youthful radiance has faded. The question that Updike raises is whether his generation has eyes to see these things and minds to estimate them rightly—whether indeed years have brought the philosophic mind. And he seems to suggest that lack of spiritual maturity to match biological maturity is the chief reason why so many people today remain unhappy little people. One story, entitled **"I Will Not Let Thee Go, Except Thou Bless Me,"** tells how Tom Brideson looks back upon his years in Connecticut before moving to a new home in Texas. He thinks of how he has seen his friends and their wives aging. He has witnessed the many-faceted events of their lives, "—a heap of organic incident that in a village of old would have moldered into wisdom. But he was not wise, merely older."

Wordsworth says that the philosophic mind finds strength from three constants: primal sympathy, consolation arising out of suffering, and the faith looking through death. Death is certainly very much present to Tom Brideson, but not the faith to look through it. About to depart from his home, he thinks, "Departure rehearses death." He realizes that his friends have already dismissed him as one who no longer belongs to their world, and thus is not real. His one-time mistress Maggie tells him that, while five years ago he was life and death to her, now he is nothing. Out of suffering—and Maggie is suffering from a feverish chill—nothing that is soothing comes to him. Yet, unexpectedly, Tom learns the truth about "primal sympathy/Which having been must ever be." His wife Lou describes how Maggie kissed her warmly on the mouth when saying goodbye. By means of this act Maggie has assured Tom that he will carry something through the death known as departure. The mistress, whom he leaves behind in every sense, has imprinted her living affection for him upon the wife who goes with him into the unknown future.

Tom Brideson is, perhaps, luckier than most in being given clear (if belated) evidence of human sympathy. His situation is not desperate since he faced merely a rehearsal for death, not death itself. **"The Witnesses,"** in contrast, shows that many today experience little except the most vestigial remnants of strength to offset grief.

In **"The Witnesses"** death enters directly and in its most widely feared from. The narrator, Herbie, begins by explaining how only yesterday he was told that Fred Prouty had died of cancer. Fred, the husband of two ex-wives, had been at school and college with him but was no close friend. Herbie recalls the last occasion when Fred had been in his home. At that time Fred was still married to his first wife, Marjorie. He had phoned and invited himself and "a friend" over for drinks. The friend turned out to be Priscilla, his new love. Herbie and his wife Jeanne found the visit embarrassing, and Jeanne pronounced it "extremely dreary." Later, meeting Fred casually, Herbie learned from him that his sole purpose had been to let his moment of happiness with Priscilla be witnessed so it would not be totally lost. Fred, who was then divorced from Priscilla and fast going to pieces, confessed, "I had never known I could be so happy. God. I wanted you and Jeanne to see us together before it went bad."

"The Witnesses" raises the question as to whether anything at all can be salvaged from the wreck of time. Fred Prouty wished his fleeting moment of happiness to be seen, so as to rescue it from oblivion. The witnesses whom he had chosen, however, saw merely something extremely dreary. Human sight is partial, and primal sympathy may be sought and seemingly be sought in vain. Things that were briefly good go bad, and death gathers good and bad

together and writes *finis*. Yet even in the situation of near despair the human spirit grasps at a straw of comfort, refusing to believe that the victory of time over radiance can be total.

"The Witnesses" portrays a low point in human comfort. **"When Everyone Was Pregnant"** portrays a high point, one in which the philosophic mind gropes its way towards a faith that looks through death. The unnamed narrator of this story—we know only that he is "in securities"—writes while sitting on a moving train. He sees the train as an image of time. He has been reading about the revival of the fashions of the Fifties, and he notes, "But *my* Fifties won't come back." The Fifties represent to him the era of creativity for his life, the days when his wife Nancy and all her friends seemed to be perpetually pregnant. Those days are over. He writes:

> Notes not come to anything. Lives not come to anything. Life a common stock that fluctuates in value. But you cannot sell, you must hold, hold till it dips to nothing. The big boys sell you out.

> Edgar to blinded Gloucester: Ripeness is all. Have never exactly understood. Ripeness is all that is left? Or, deeper and more hopeful, ripeness is all that matters? Encloses all, answers all, justifies all. Ripeness is God.

The man on the moving train knows that all the investments of life come to nothing. The radiant era when everyone was pregnant with new life cannot be brought back. Nevertheless, he is "in securities" and will not grieve. The blind Gloucesters of our age need to be reminded that the destructiveness of time does not in validate the creativity that time makes possible.

In **Museums and Women** images of vision are omnipresent, and frequently these images are taken from photography. If you are to capture radiance in an enduring photographic record, what lens will you use on your camera? The narrator of **"When Everyone Was Pregnant"** speaks in this way. Recalling the years of the Cold War and the easing of tensions with Eisenhower's "precarious peace" in Korea, he writes, "Viewed the world through two lenses since discarded: fear and gratitude. Young people now are many things but they aren't afraid, and aren't grateful." At the end of the story he says, "The decades slide seaward, taking us along. I am still afraid. Still grateful."

Updike is a self-confessed religious writer. Fear and gratitude are the two responses that a religious person believes to be owing, most of all, to God. But in an age that has largely lost its vision of God the direct response of faith is seldom found. The man of the train comes very near to this response when he says, "Ripeness is God," and affirms that fear and gratitude must be permanent features of our attitude toward our existence. Only when the truths belonging to faith are known are we "in securities." Updike also suggests, however, that every movement of the human spirit seeking comfort reaches out unconsciously for the strength that God alone can give. Thus even Fred Prouty exclaims, "God. I wanted you and Jeanne to see us. . . ." Unconsciously, Fred is asking for more than a human witness to preserve his moment of radiance. Similarly, **"I Will Not Let Thee Go, Except Thou Bless Me"** connects the human wish for comfort in a parting message from a former mistress with Jacob's wrestling with God.

The religious believer affirms that, if men are to have a secure vision of life's radiance, they must acknowledge the source of all radiance in God Himself. Updike makes such an acknowledgment in the epigraph he has chosen for *Museums and Women.* On the dedication page of the book there stands the following scriptural passage:

> He has made everything beautiful in its time; also he has put eternity into man's mind, yet so that he cannot find out what God has done from the beginning to the end.
>
> I know that there is nothing better for them than to be happy and enjoy themselves as long as they live;
>
> also that it is God's gift to man that every one should eat and drink and take pleasure in all his toil. (Ecclesiastes 3: 11-13 Revised Standard Version)

The reason for Updike's going to Ecclesiastes for his affirmation of faith is not hard to discover. His concern is with the wisdom that should come with maturity. Ecclesiastes belongs to that part of the Bible known as Wisdom Literature. The Book records the words of Koheleth, the Preacher or Professor who represents the biblical version of "the philosophic mind." Already in *Rabbit Redux* (1971) Updike had declared indirectly that the teaching of Ecclesiastes was peculiarly adapted to the needs of our current society. Now he makes explicit the topicality of Koheleth's words.

In our day there is no general recognition concerning the universe that "God has made it so, in order that men should fear before him" (Eccles. 3:14). In the consciousness of most Americans the fear of God is not taken for granted. If God is recognized at all it is unconsciously. This point is illustrated in **"The Day of the Dying Rabbit."** The narrator of the story is a professional photographer with six children. His youngest child Godfrey is a four-year-old boy who was born with club feet. In the family Godfrey is affectionately called "God."

A photographer, of course, is an expert in seeing. Updike's photographer refers several times to the different vision achieved through the human eye and through the camera lens. He says that he is anxious to make a record of one August day that became set apart from other days because a dying rabbit had been brought into the family holiday cottage. He does not know exactly how the rabbit's coming affected them so greatly; thus he simply writes down what happened during the time that it was with them.

The dying rabbit is left by a stray cat that has caught and mauled it. Its back being broken, it is doomed from the start; yet the children try to nurse it back to life. Its right eye, which the cat has clawed, is white and cloudy "like isinglass." It lies until death with this damaged eye uppermost. The events of the next twenty-four hours, therefore, are seen as it were through a "cloudy glass." These are ordinary enough events, common to any family on holiday: visits from neighbors; the children boating and swimming; a tennis game; and a beach picnic to end the day. The rab-

bit dies in the afternoon. The photographer speaks of the picnic party, sitting around a fire while the darkness gathers, as "survivors." Yet he had felt himself excitedly happy in his efforts to capture on film "the dying light."

The different members of the family are variously affected by the dying animal. Looking back, the photographer records how he and his wife were stirred to make love on the first evening of the rabbit's arrival. (Its continued breathing had filled them with hope.) His daughters, at first solicitous over nursing the helpless creature, were later indifferent to or disgusted by the event of its death. They refused to look at the body. Jimmy, the older boy, alone was grief-stricken. He had recently been made aware of death as a real part of human existence, and he tried to hide his tears "by thumping God." Godfrey, in fact, had picked the rabbit up and then dropped it. So Jimmy had an excuse, though he was more likely following the universal human reaction and blaming God for the presence of evil in the world.

Jimmy and his father, nevertheless, discovered that there is always radiance, even in mankind's dark night of the spirit. As they paddled their kayak home after the picnic, all was blackness around them. Then the photographer saw "in the hazed sky overhead, a single unsteady star." Suddenly, they were surrounded by a phosphorescent radiance. Their paddle strokes "called into visibility a rich arc of sparks, animalcula hailing our passage with bright shouts." Then Jimmy calmly announced that they were about to hit something. They had reached land and bumped into the bank. "With this bump, and my awakening laugh, the day of the rabbit ended."

The photographer describes the day of the rabbit as being "singular in its, let's say, *gallantry,*" while other days had been "merely happy days." Gallantry is associated with nobility and courage—the virtues of chivalry. Elsewhere Updike has evidenced through his fiction his sense of the serious lack of these particular virtues in modern America. The vision of radiance given to the photographer and his elder son comes because, instead of being content with "merely happy days," they have had the courage to face the facts of death and of the dark night of human loneliness. Through the "glass" of the rabbit's eye they have seen that the same universe containing grief and loss contains radiance too.

When Jimmy and his father run their kayak into the bank they are reminded that, in spite of moments of radiance, the material world is a brute fact preventing men from continuing to sail forever in the joy which radiance brings. The bank is described as "a mass, gray etched on gray, higher than a man." No man, then, can simply jump over this featureless obstacle.

The second part of *Museums and Women* is headed "Other Modes." It begins with a story examining the brute face of matter. **"The Sea's Green Sameness,"** which first appeared in 1960, is the only story in the collection written prior to 1965. We can be reasonably sure that it stands where it does for a good reason, and that it is integral to the theme of *Museums and Women.*

The narrator of **"The Sea's Green Sameness"** is an unnamed writer on a beach. He notices the likeness and difference between the sea and a printed page. Both are surfaces covered with marks. "But this page yields a meaning, however slowly, whereas the marks on the sea are everywhere the same. That is the difference between Art and Nature." The writer—after saying many pertinent things about the craft of writing—goes on to say that he has something new to contribute to human knowledge concerning the sea. The sea can be viewed as a vertical wall, impenetrable yet ever inviting us to break through it. The invitation seems to come from "the outside" of the wall, and from "another heart beating" as though in answer to the writer's own heart. The writer connects this unknown reality with "the thing itself"—that is, with the meaning he tries to express through his art. He ends by asking, "What is it? Its breadth, its glitter, its greenness and sameness balk me. *What is it? If I knew, I could say.*"

Gray land (**"The Day of the Dying Rabbit"**) and green sea (**"The Sea's Green Sameness"**) both symbolize Nature, that solidity against which we "bump" and the meaning of which eludes all our efforts. What is it? Updike asked that question, so intensely, twelve years ago. He now seems to believe that he has found, if not an answer, at least a clue to why no answer is forthcoming. Koheleth preaches that God "has put eternity into man's mind, yet so that he cannot find out what God has done from the beginning to the end." Koheleth also affirms that "there is nothing new under the sun" (Eccles. 1:9). That "something new" which Updike wished to contribute to human knowledge concerning the sea, may turn out not to be so new after all. The other heart beating on the outside of the wall which is the physical world may be the heart of the Living God. If so, then "the thing itself" is the eternity of God that is always in man's heart. Yet the wall of Nature remains just as impenetrable as ever. There is no answer, from this side, to the question of what Nature is. Man cannot find out what God has done from the beginning to the end. This answer concerning the hiddenness of God in nature is the answer of true wisdom. In the Book of Job (a Wisdom Book also) the limits of human knowledge are made clear:

> Can you find out the deep things of God?
> Can you find out the limit of the Almighty?
> It is higher than heaven—what can you do?
> It is deeper than Sheol—what can you know?

We can never stop putting the question concerning Nature, "What is it?" Out of Nature herself no answer to our question can ever come. For Nature is infinitely various—yet eternally the same.

In the section "Other Modes" Updike has several stories that at first sight seem merely whimsical. These are stories illustrated by "stolen" manuscript drawings and engravings from books of natural history. **"Under the Microscope"** describes a modern cocktail party, the hosts and guests being minute pond creatures. **"During the Jurassic"** is another cocktail party. This time the characters are brontosauri. **"The Baluchitherium"** is a tape-recorded interview with the largest mammal of all time, an animal known only by the survival of a few bone fragments. The interview, however, proves the Baluchitherium to be, as

befits a species with a much larger brain cavity than man's, the possessor of the most advanced culture the world has ever seen. Even the Baluchitherium, though, believes in his species' destiny to inherit the future. He cannot imagine the day in which he and his civilization will be forgotten. **"The Invention of the Horse Collar"** is a fantasy set in the Dark Ages. The invention of the horse collar—and thus of horse power—prefigures the end of the Age of Ignorance and the coming of technology and our own Age of Knowledge. Yet the New Age is inaugurated by a fratricide in which two villeins, Canus and Ablatus, act out the story of Cain and Abel.

"There is nothing new under the sun." This seems to be the burden of these tales that span the extremes of the natural world and of human civilization, "from the beginning to the end." Wherever man looks around God's creation he cannot find out any definite evidence of meaning and purpose. A similar conclusion underlies the final story in this section. **"Jesus Upon Honshu"** is based on a news item in the *Times* telling of a Japanese legend that Jesus did not die on the Cross, but fled to the island of Honshu. Updike reconstructs a possible biography of the founder of Christianity on this basis. Instructed in His youth by Japanese sages, Jesus was enabled to initiate in Palestine the religious movement named after Him. Then He returned to Japan, married, and died at the great age of 106. Seeing that His grandson so much resembled His own father Joseph, Jesus was at last persuaded of the truth of the cyclical view of history held in Japan, although He had earlier argued "that there was also a vertical principle in the world, something thrusting, which did not repeat." That He was some kind of god was assumed by His neighbors in Honshu. He had extraordinary powers, extending to the raising of the dead. Yet, in the end, He could not alter the natural processes of aging, or the natural fact that each generation must give place to the next. He too had to die in the end. And, if He thought of Himself always as the unique Son of God, "in this, at least, He resembled all men."

"Jesus on Honshu" ends the second section of *Museums and Women.* It takes to its final conclusion the attempt to find the meaning of man's existence on this side of the wall. If we read the face of Nature to draw our wisdom from what we see there, we must be left believing that all religions—like everything else in this world—are eternally the same. Man would like to imagine himself a divine creature. Yet he is really no more than an animal, and he can be surpassed by any animal to whom Nature may choose to give a larger brain. All his knowledge can bring him but one certainty: he must die, so that Nature can go on repeating herself.

Seen from our side of the wall, then, the universe seems to have no meaning and to carry no comfort. Nevertheless, this is only to be expected if we inhabit a world where the Creator has so ordered His creation that man "cannot find out what God has done from the beginning to the end."

Karl Barth has always been one of Updike's guides in matters of faith. In *The Epistle to the Romans* Barth addresses himself to the problem of Nature's seeming opaqueness. Noting that both Ecclesiastes and Job emphasize "the archetypal, unobservable, undiscoverable majesty of God," Barth goes on to say,

> The insecurity of our whole existence, the vanity and utter questionableness of all that is and what we are, lie as in a text-book open before us. What are all those enigmatic creatures of God—a zoological garden, for example,—but so many problems to which we have no answer. But God only, God Himself, is the Answer. And so the boundary which bars us in and which, nevertheless, points beyond itself, can *since the creation of the world* be clearly seen *through the things that are made* by God.

It is hard to avoid the conjecture that this particular passage of Barth's *Romans* must have been in Updike's mind when he was writing **Museums and Women.** In "Other Modes" Updike has taken the subject-matter of his stories from that "boundary which bars us in and which, nevertheless, points beyond itself." That such is his theme, he was indicated by beginning the section with **"The Sea's Green Sameness."** Then he has written about "all those enigmatic creatures of God," describing the extremes to be found in the zoological garden of evolution. He has even "stolen" the illustrations for the zoological stories from text-books. Together, his stories present "the vanity and utter questionableness of all that is and of what we are"—set under the quotation from Ecclesiastes.

What is more important than these details is the context of Barth's remarks in the passage quoted. Barth is discussing Romans 1:19-21, where the central argument of St. Paul is that "the invisible things" of God are "clearly seen" in the creation. He not only calls upon the Wisdom Literature of the Old Testament to explain why the things of God are invisible to men. He also emphasizes that, if men fail to see God in His creation this is because they are reluctant to see clearly how God is both "the hidden abyss" and "the hidden home at the beginning and end of all our journeyings." For Updike, the question of seeing clearly is raised again and again in **Museums and Women.** Where are men to find the right lens through which to capture that which lies on the other side of the boundary which bars us in? And, again, in other stories, Updike picks up Barth's other metaphor and describes the journeyings we make, reluctant to leave the home that we know because unaware of the God who is our hidden home in both our departures and our arrivals.

Yet, if Barth has provided Updike with an approach to the wisdom of Ecclesiastes and has linked the opaqueness of Nature with Paul's understanding of what it means to see clearly, Updike has developed these themes in his own way. He has related them to his *motif* of radiance. In a world where the things of God are invisible to men, the invisible God gives us glimpses of the radiance of "His everlasting power and divinity" (Rom. 1:20). It is the characteristic of radiance, after all, to allow us to see light in all its glorious power without revealing the Source from which the light radiates. We see the effect, but the Cause of the effect remains invisible.

Updike first spoke of radiance in connection with Sunday skaters. In the story **"Man and Daughter in the Cold"** he

explains why it is that radiance fades from our consciousness with the passing of childhood. He makes the point that the radiance coming from eternity is too rarified—too ice-cold—for flesh and blood creatures such as we are to endure except in the innocence and toughness of youth.

The father in **"Man and Daughter in the Cold"** is a college professor suffering from emphysema and conscious that he is already journeying toward death. Skiing in New Hampshire, he sees his daughter radiant and skillful in the biting cold of the mountain-top. (". . . the cold her element. Her womanhood soon enough to be smothered in warmth.") He flounders after her, and finds that his face is like a spectre's. So the teacher learns his lesson. "Space seemed love, bestowed to be free in, and coldness the price. He felt joined to the great dead whose words it was his duty to teach." As Koheleth—one of the great dead—insists, there is a season for everything under heaven (Eccles. 3:1). Even his daughter's face is touched by frost-bite, showing that she is leaving her childhood behind her. He in his advancing ill-health has resented his students' youth and careless energy. Now he is conscious of happiness that is selfless as he sees life in the youthful steps of his daughter. He has no jealousy as he sees this life to be "a pageant that would leave him behind."

The radiance of eternity is traditionally imaged as a perfect circle. Updike suggests that we can no more see that circle than we can see the invisible God. Yet we are given moments when arcs of the circle are revealed to us. Seeking radiance in women and museums, William Young sees the body of a sphinx in a Boston museum and afterwards finds its head in the Louvre. Each portion carries the same S-curve. William, thinking of the women he has known, muses, "So, too, the women were broken arcs of one curve." William's grief is that he cannot have all the arcs together; and thus he concludes that radiance has faded behind him. The wisdom of Koheleth teaches that men should enjoy themselves as long as they live, not jealously desiring a wholeness impossible in space and time. Each arc of radiance justifies itself, for each is an intimation of the goodness at the heart of things.

At the beginning of **"The Day of the Dying Rabbit,"** the rabbit is brought into the holiday cottage through the "arc" of a screen door swinging. At the end of the story, the photographer and his son find how their paddles "called into visibility a rich arc of sparks." The day of the rabbit, making them more than merely happy, begins and ends with an arc.

The arc of radiance appears in another context in the story called **"The Deacon."** The deacon is an electrician, over fifty, whose name is Miles. Every seven years or so he moves to another part of the country. Though he has been a deacon in several different denominations, he is not a religious man. His trade has given him a materialistic view of things and he has no place for the supernatural. "God, concretely considered, had a way of merging with that corner of the church ceiling that showed signs of water leakage." Moving to New England, Miles gives up church-going. Then he lets his wife persuade him to try the local Congregational church. One night he goes to attend a meeting in the white wooden building and finds that he is the only one there.

Miles looks around the shabby sanctuary with distaste. "Waste. Nothing but waste, salvage and waste. And weariness." Outside there is a high wind and cold rain is falling. He "feels the timbers of this ark" are holding, and he realizes why he has come. It is "to share the pride of this ancient thing that will not quite die, to have it all to himself." He sees it as a preparation for death. While "the rain rattles like a robber to get in," he knows that it is good to be at home.

Inside the shabby Congregational church Miles learns what the man of wisdom ought to know, namely, the truth proclaimed in God's words to Job:

> Or who shut in the sea with doors,
> when it burst forth from the womb;
> When I made the clouds its garment,
> and thick darkness its swaddling band,
> and prescribed bounds for it, and set bars and
>   doors,
> and said, 'Thus far shall you come, and no far-
>   ther,
> and here shall your proud waves be stayed'?

The breaking-forth of the primeval waters is one of the oldest images of chaos and death. All that Miles has known of God by looking at the signs of water-leakage on church ceilings, is that He is the One who keeps the waters in their place. Now he knows more. The white wooden "ark" of the old church in New England has become for him an arc of the radiant white circle of eternity. That radiance is always there, although men may have to travel "miles" before they become aware of it. Miles, a man of no continuing city, is seeking one to come (Heb. 13:14)—asking for a preparation for death—and now he knows that he is at home. As Karl Barth reminds us, God is the hidden home at the beginning and the end of all our journeyings.

The deacon has been given the keys of the church by its minister. He is surprised to find that the front door key "seems magically small." The God who has bolts and bars to restrain the bounds of the waters has also given the keys of the Kingdom of Heaven to the keepers of the Church against which the powers of death shall never prevail (Matt. 16:19-9). In spite of all appearances, "this ancient thing" will not quite die, and the magically small key that places an individual inside the ark (arc) is faith.

All of Updike's writing is directed to the finding of the key that will open "the same door" through which we came into the world and through which we must pass out. Abyss, funnel, hole; these are the words that he has associated with death, when death is seen by the defective eyes of men without faith. The problem is how defective eyesight can be helped, so that the "hidden abyss" can be seen as the "hidden home" from which we came and to which we return.

Faith, joy, and happiness come from the trust that knows both fear and gratitude. This fear and this gratitude are the "selfless" lenses through which we can see clearly that God is the hidden abyss, the hidden home. In this wisdom

of maturity, in this "quiet but tireless goodness" we shall find our rest and our security. (pp. 56-71)

Alice Hamilton and Kenneth Hamilton, "John Updike's 'Museums and Women and Other Stories'," in Thought, *Vol. XLIX, No. 192, March, 1974, pp. 56-71.*

Updike on the Short Story:

What you need in a novel is for several ideas to come somehow together in an interesting way. But with a short story you need only one spark to begin writing. So it is fairly spontaneous, and I think the better ones I've written have resulted from a fairly direct "delivery" from inspiration to production. Otherwise, you tend to cool on the idea and forget what excited you.

John Updike, in an interview with Charlie Reilly, in Canto, *1980.*

John Updike (essay date 1974)

[*In the following essay, first delivered as a speech at the March 1974 Festival of Arts in Adelaide, South Australia, Updike discusses his literary motivations, ambitions, and aims.*]

My Title ["Why Write?"] offers me an opportunity to set a record of brevity at this Festival of Arts; for an adequate treatment would be made were I to ask, in turn, "Why not?" and sit down.

But instead I hope to explore, for not too many minutes, the question from the inside of a man who, rather mysteriously to himself, has earned a livelihood for close to twenty years by engaging in the rather selfish and gratuitous activity called "writing." I do *not* propose to examine the rather different question of what use is writing to the society that surrounds and, if he is fortunate, supports the writer. The ancients said the purpose of poetry, of writing, was to entertain and to instruct; Aristotle put forward the still fascinating notion that a dramatic action, however terrible and piteous, carries off at the end, in catharsis, the morbid, personal, subjective impurities of our emotions. The enlargement of sympathy, through identification with the lives of fictional others, is frequently presented as an aim of narrative; D. H. Lawrence, with characteristic fervor, wrote, "And here lies the vast importance of the novel, properly handled. It can inform and lead into new places the flow of our sympathetic consciousness, and can lead our sympathy away in recoil from things that are dead." Kafka wrote that a book is an ax to break the frozen sea within us. The frozen sea within himself, he must have meant; though the ax of Kafka's own art (which, but for Max Brod's posthumous disobedience, Kafka would have taken with him into the grave), has served an analogous purpose for others. This note of pain, of saintly suffering, is a modern one, far removed from the serene and harmonious bards and poets of the courts of olden time. Listen to Flaubert, in one of his letters to Louise Colet:

I love my work with a love that is frenzied and perverted, as an ascetic loves the hair shirt that scratches his belly. Sometimes, when I am empty, when words don't come, when I find I haven't written a single sentence after scribbling whole pages, I collapse on my couch and lie there dazed, bogged in a swamp of despair, hating myself and blaming myself for this demented pride which makes me pant after a chimera. A quarter of an hour later everything changes; my heart is pounding with joy. Last Wednesday I had to get up and fetch my handkerchief; tears were streaming down my face. I had been moved by my own writing; the emotion I had conceived, the phrase that rendered it, and satisfaction of having found the phrase—all were causing me to experience the most exquisite pleasure.

Well, if such is the writer at work, one wonders why he doesn't find a pleasanter job; and one also wonders why he appears himself to be the chief market for his own product.

Most people sensibly assume that writing is propaganda. Of course, they admit, there is bad propaganda, like the boy-meets-tractor novels of socialist realism, and old-fashioned propaganda, like Christian melodrama and the capitalist success stories of Horatio Alger or Samuel Smiles. But that some message is intended, wrapped in the story like a piece of crystal carefully mailed in cardboard and excelsior, is not doubted. Scarcely a day passes in my native land that I don't receive some letter from a student or teacher asking me *what I meant to say* in such a book, asking me to elaborate more fully on some sentence I deliberately whittled into minimal shape, or inviting me to speak on some topic, usually theological or sexual, on which it is pleasantly assumed I am an expert. The writer as hero, as Hemingway or Saint-Exupéry or D'Annunzio, a tradition of which Camus was perhaps the last example, has been replaced in America by the writer as educationist. Most writers teach, a great many teach writing; writing is furiously taught in the colleges even as the death knell of the book and the written word is monotonously tolled; any writer, it is assumed, can give a lecture, and the purer products of his academic mind, the "writings" themselves, are sifted and, if found of sufficient quality, installed in their places on the assembly belt of study, as objects of educational contemplation.

How dare one confess, to the politely but firmly inquiring letter-writer who takes for granted that as a remote but functioning element of his education you are duty-bound to provide the information and elucidating essay that will enable him to complete his term paper, or his Ph.D. thesis, or his critical *opus*—how dare one confess that the absence of a swiftly expressible message is, often, *the* message; that reticence is as important a tool to the writer as expression; that the hasty filling out of a questionnaire is not merely irrelevant but *inimical* to the writer's proper activity; that this activity is rather curiously private and finicking, a matter of exorcism and manufacture rather than of top-lofty proclamation; that what he makes is ideally as ambiguous and opaque as life itself; that, to be blunt, the social usefulness of writing matters to him primarily in that it somehow creates a few job opportunities—in Australia, a few government grants—a few opportunities to live as a writer.

Not counting journalists and suppliers of scripts to the media, hardly a hundred American men and women earn their living by writing, in a wealthy nation of two hundred million. Does not then, you ask, such a tiny band of privileged spokesmen owe its country, if not the trophy of a Nobel Prize, at least the benign services of a spiritual aristocracy? Is not the writer's role, indeed, to speak for humanity, as conscience and prophet and servant of the billions not able to speak for themselves? The conception is attractive, and there are some authors, mostly Russian, who have aspired to such grandeur without entirely compromising their gifts. But in general, when a writer such as Sartre or Faulkner becomes a great man, a well-intentioned garrulity replaces the specific witness that has been theirs to give.

The last time I dared appear on a platform in a foreign land, it was in Kenya, where I had to confess, under some vigorous questioning from a large white man in the audience, that the general betterment of mankind, and even the improvement of social conditions within my own violently imperfect nation, were *not* my basic motivation as a writer. To be sure, *as a citizen* one votes, attends meetings, subscribes to liberal pieties, pays or withholds taxes, and contributes to charities even more generously than—it turns out—one's own President. But as a writer, for me to attempt to extend my artistic scope into all the areas of my human concern, to substitute nobility of purpose for accuracy of execution, would certainly be to forfeit whatever social usefulness I *do* have. It has befallen a Solzhenitsyn to have experienced the Soviet labor camps; it has befallen Miss Gordimer and Mr. Mtshali to suffer the tensions and paradoxes and outrages of a racist police state; social protest, and a hope of reform, is in the very fiber of their witness. But a writer's witness, surely, is of value in its circumstantiality. Solzhenitsyn's visible and brave defiance of the Soviet state is magnificent; but a novel like *The First Circle* affords us more than a blind flash of conditioned and—let's face it—chauvinistic indignation; it affords us entry into an unknown world, it offers a complex and only implicitly indignant portrait of how human beings live under a certain sort of political system. When I think of the claustrophobic and seething gray world of *The First Circle,* I am reminded in texture of Henry Miller's infamous Paris novels. Here, too, we have truth, and an undeniable passion to proclaim the truth—a seedy and repellent yet vital truth—though the human conditions Miller describes are far removed from any hope of political cure. And Miller, in his way, was also a martyr: as with Solzhenitsyn, his works could not be published in his native land.

We must write where we stand; wherever we do stand, there is life; and an imitation of the life we know, however narrow, is our only ground. As I sat on that stage in Kenya, a symbolic American in a corner of that immense range of peoples symbolically called The Third World, I felt guilty and bewildered that I could not hear in my formidable accuser's orotund phrases anything that had to do with my practice of the writer's profession; I was discomfited that my concerns—to survive, to improve, to make my microcosms amusing to me and then to others, to fail, if fail I must, through neither artistic cowardice nor laziness, to catch all the typographical errors in my proofs, to see that my books appear in jackets both striking and fairly representative of the contents, to arrange words and spaces and imagined realities in patterns never exactly achieved before, to be able to defend any sentence I publish—I was embarrassed that my concerns were so ignoble, compared to his. But, once off the stage (where a writer should rarely be), I tend to be less apologetic, and even to believe that my well-intentioned questioner, and the silent faces in the same audience looking to me to atone for America's sins real and supposed, and the touching schoolchildren begging me by letter to get them through the seventh grade—that none of these people have any felt comprehension of my vocation.

Why write? As soon ask, why rivet? Because a number of personal accidents drift us toward the occupation of riveter, which pre-exists, and, most importantly, the riveting-gun exists, and we love it.

Think of a pencil. What a quiet, nimble, slender and then stubby wonder-worker he is! At his touch, worlds leap into being; a tiger with no danger, a steam-roller with no weight, a palace at no cost. All children are alive to the spell of pencil and crayons, of making something, as it were, from nothing; a few children never move out from under this spell, and try to become artists. I was once a rapturous child drawing at the dining-room table, under a stained-glass chandelier that sat like a hat on the swollen orb of my excitement. What is exciting that child, so distant from us in time and space? He appears, from the vantage of this lectern unimaginable to him, to be in the grip of two philosophical perceptions.

One, mimesis demands no displacement; the cat I drew did not have to fight for food or love with the real cat that came to the back porch. I was in drawing *adding* to the world rather than rearranging the finite amount of goods within it. We were a family struggling on the poverty edge of the middle class during the Depression; I was keen to avoid my father's noisy plight within the plague of competition; pencil and paper were cheap, unlike most other toys.

And, Two, the world called into being on the pencilled paper admitted of connections. An early exercise, whose pleasure returns to me whenever I assemble a collection of prose or poetry or whenever, indeed, I work several disparate incidents or impressions into the shape of a single story, was this: I would draw on one sheet of paper an assortment of objects—flowers, animals, stars, toaster, chairs, comic-strip creatures, ghosts, noses—and connect them with lines, a path of two lines, so that they all became the fruit of a single impossible tree. The exact age when this creative act so powerfully pleased me I cannot recall; the wish to make collections, to assemble sets, is surely a deep urge of the human mind in its playful, artistic aspect. As deep, it may be, as the urge to hear a story from beginning to end, or the little ecstacy of extracting resemblances from different things. Proust, of course, made simile the cornerstone of his theory of aesthetic bliss, and Plato, if

I understand him right, felt that that which a set of like objects have in common *must* have a separate existence in itself, as the *idea* which delivers us, in our perception of the world, from the nightmare of nominalism. At any rate, to make a man of pencil and paper is as much a magical act as painting a bison with blood on the wall of a cave; a child, frail and overshadowed, and groping for his fate, herein *captures* something and, further, brings down praise from on high.

I have described the artistic transaction as being between the awakening ego and the world of matter to which it awakes; but no doubt the wish to please one's parents enters early, and remains with the artist all his life, as a desire to please the world, however displeasing his behavior may seem, and however self-satisfying the work pretends to be. We are surprised to discover, for instance, that Henry James hoped to make lots of money, and that James Joyce read all of his reviews. The artist's personality has an awkward ambivalence: he is a cave dweller who yet hopes to be pursued into his cave. The need for privacy, the need for recognition: a child's vulnerability speaks in both needs, and in my own reaction to, say, the beseeching mail just described, I detect the live ambiguity—one is avid to receive the letters, and loath to answer them. Or (to make some reference to the literary scene I know best) consider the striking contrast between the eager, even breathless warmth of Saul Bellow's fiction, inviting our love and closeness with every phrase, and Bellow's own faintly haughty, distinctly edgy personal surface. Again, J. D. Salinger wrote a masterpiece, *The Catcher in the Rye,* recommending that readers who enjoy a book call up the author; then he spent his next twenty years avoiding the telephone. A writer, I would say, out of no doubt deficiencies of character, has constructed a cave-shaped organ, hollow more like a mouth than like an ear, through which he communicates with the world at one remove. Somewhat, perhaps, as his own subconscious communicates with him through dreams. Because the opportunities for feedback have been reduced to letters that need not be answered and telephones that can be unlisted, to an annual gauntlet of reviews and non-bestowal of prizes, the communication can be more honest than is any but the most trusting personal exchange; yet also great opportunities for distortion exist unchecked. For one more of these rather subterranean and reprehensible satisfactions of writing that I am here confessing is that the world, so balky and resistant and humiliating, can in the act of mimesis be rectified, adjusted, chastened, purified. Fantasies defeated in reality can be fully indulged; tendencies deflected by the cramp of circumstances can be followed to an end. In my own case I have noticed, so often it has ceased to surprise me, a prophetic quality of my fictions, even to the subsequent appearance in my life of originally fictional characters. We write, that is, out of latency as much as memory; and years later our laggard lives in reality act out, often with eerie fidelity, the patterns projected in our imaginings.

But we have come too far, too fast, from that ambitious child making his pencil move beneath the stained-glass chandelier. In my adolescence I discovered one could write with a pencil as well as draw, without the annoying need to consult reality so frequently. Also, the cave beneath the written page holds many more kinds of space than the one beneath the drawing pad. My writing tends, I think, to be pictorial, not only in its groping for visual precision but in the way the books are conceived, as objects in space, with events and persons composed within them like shapes on a canvas. I do not recommend this approach; it is perhaps a perversion of the primal narrative urge. Storytelling, for all its powers of depiction, shares with music the medium of time, and perhaps its genius, its most central transformation, has to do with time, with rhythm and echo and the sense of time not frozen as in a painting but channelled and harnessed as in a symphony.

But one can give no more than what one has received, and we try to create for others, in our writings, aesthetic sensations we have experienced. In my case, some of these would be: the graphic precision of a Dürer or a Vermeer, the offhand-and-backwards-feeling verbal and psychological accuracy of a Henry Green, the wonderful embowering metaphors of Proust, the enigmatic concreteness of Kafka and Joyce, the collapse into components of a solved mathematical problem, the unriddling of a scrupulous mystery story, the earth-scorning scope of science fiction, the tear-producing results of a truly humorous piece of writing. Writing, really, can make us do rather few substantial things: it can make us laugh, it can make us weep, and if it is pornography and we are rather young, it can make us come. It can also, of course, make us sleep; and though in the frequent discussion of the writer's social purpose this soporific effect is unfailingly ignored, I suspect it is the most widespread practical effect of writing—a book is less often a flaming sword or a beam of light than a bedtime toddy. Whatever the use, we hope that some members of society will find our product useful enough to purchase; but I think it would be a hypocrisy to pretend that these other people's welfare, or communication with them, or desire to ennoble or radicalize or terrify or lull them, is the primary reason why one writes.

No, what a writer wants, as every aspiring writer can tell you, is to *get into print.* To transform the changing shadows of one's dimly and fitfully lived life into print—into metal or, with the advent of offset printing, into rather mysteriously electrified rubber—to lift through the doubled magic of language and mechanical reproduction our own impressions and dreams and playful constructions into another realm of existence, a multiplied and far-flung existence, into a space far wider than that which we occupy, into a time theoretically eternal: *that* is the siren song that holds us to our desks, our dismal revisions, our insomnia panics, our dictionaries and encyclopedias, our lonely and, the odds long are, superfluous labor. "Of making many books there is no end; and much study is a weariness of the flesh." A weariness one can certainly feel entering even a modestly well-stocked bookstore. Yet it is just this involvement in the world of commerce and industry, this imposition of one's otherwise evanescent fancies upon the machinery of manufacture and distribution, that excites the writer's ego, and gives an illusion of triumph over his finitude.

Although, as a child, I lived what was to become my material and message, my wish to write did not begin with that material and message; rather, it was a wish to escape from it, into an altogether better world. When I was thirteen, a magazine came into the house, *The New Yorker* by name, and I loved that magazine so much I concentrated all my wishing into an effort to make myself small and inky and intense enough to be received into its pages. Once there, I imagined, some transfigured mode of being, called a "writer's life," would begin for me. My fantasy was not entirely fantastic, as my domineering position on this platform and the first-class airplane tickets that brought me halfway around the world testify. But what I would not altogether insincerely ask you to accept is something shabby, precarious, and even craven about a writer's life.

Among artists, a writer's equipment is least out-of-reach—the language we all more or less use, a little patience at grammar and spelling, the common adventures of blundering mortals. A painter must learn to paint; his studio is redolent of alchemic substances and physical force. The musician's arcanum of specialized knowledge and personal dexterity is even more intimidating, less accessible to the untrained, and therefore somehow less corruptible than the writer's craft. Though some painters and musicians go bad in the prime of their lives, far fewer do, and few so drastically, as writers. Our trick is treacherously thin; our art is so incorrigibly amateur that novices constantly set the world of letters on its ear, and the very phrase "professional writer" has a grimy sound. Hilaire Belloc said that the trouble with writing was that it was never meant to be a profession, it was meant to be a hobby. An act of willful play, as I have described it.

So I have not spoken up to now of language, of the joys of using it well, of the role of the writer as a keeper of the keys of language, a guardian of usage and enforcer of precision. This does not seem to me a very real notion, however often it is put forward. Language goes on evolving in the street and in the spoken media, and well-written books are the last places it looks for direction. The writer follows after the spoken language, usually timidly. I see myself described in reviews as a doter upon words. It is true, I am grateful to have been born into English, with its polyglot flexibility and the happy accident, in the wake of two empires, of its worldwide currency. But what I am conscious of doting on is not English *per se,* its pliable grammar and abundant synonyms, but its potential, for the space of some phrases or paragraphs, of becoming reality, of engendering out of imitation another reality, infinitely lesser but thoroughly possessed, thoroughly human.

Pascal says, "When a natural discourse paints a passion or an effect, one feels within oneself the truth of what one reads, which was there before, although one did not know it. Hence one is inclined to love him who makes us feel it, for he has not shown us his own riches, but ours." The writer's strength is not his own; he is a conduit who so positions himself that the world at his back flows through to the readers on the other side of the page. To keep this conduit scoured is his laborious task; to be, in the act of writing, anonymous, the end of his quest for fame.

Beginning, then, with cunning private ambitions and a childish fascination with the implements of graphic representation, I find myself arrived, in this audible search for self-justification, at an embarrassed altruism. Beginning with the wish to make an impression, one ends wishing to erase the impression, to make of it a perfect transparency, to make of oneself a point of focus purely, as selfless as a lens. One begins by seeking celebrity and ends by feeling a terrible impatience with everything—every flattering attention, every invitation to speak and to impersonate a wise man, every hunger of the ego and of the body—an impatience with everything that clouds and clots our rapt witness to the world that surrounds and transcends us. A writer begins with his personal truth, with that obscure but vulnerable and, once lost, precious life that he lived before becoming a writer; but, those first impressions discharged—a process of years—he finds himself, though empty, still posed in the role of a writer, with it may be an expectant audience of sorts and certainly a habit of communion. It is then that he dies as a writer, and becomes an inert cultural object merely, or is born again, by re-submitting his ego, as it were, to fresh drafts of experience and refined operations of his mind. *To remain interested*—of American novelists, only Henry James continued in old age to advance his art; most, indeed, wrote their best novels first, or virtually first. Energy ebbs as we live; success breeds disillusion as surely as failure; the power of hope to generate action and vision lessens. Almost alone the writer can reap profit from this loss. An opportunity to sing louder from within the slackening ego is his. For his song has never been all his own: he has been its excuse as much as its source. The little tyrant's delight in wielding a pencil always carried with it an empathy into the condition of *being* a pencil; more and more the writer thinks of himself as an instrument, a means whereby a time and a place make their mark. To become less and transmit more, to replenish energy with wisdom—some such hope, at this more than mid-point of my life, is the reason why I write. (pp. 29-39)

> *John Updike, "Four Speeches," in his* Picked-Up Pieces, *Alfred A. Knopf, 1975, pp. 16-39.*

William Peden   (essay date 1975)

[*An American critic and educator, Peden has written extensively on Thomas Jefferson and American history. In the following excerpt, in which he surveys Updike's short fiction, Peden argues that Updike's best work in the genre—"a triumph of the art of the usual"—emphasizes the ordinary and the unexceptional.*]

John Updike (1932-) is so talented as to be alarming, so versatile and prolific as to evoke amazement. Still in his early forties, he is the author of six novels, including the National Book Award-winning *The Centaur;* three volumes of verse; four juveniles; a closet drama; a collection of miscellaneous prose pieces; and five collections of short stories: *The Same Door* (1959), *Pigeon Feathers* (1962), *The Music School* (1966), *Bech: A Book* (1970), and *Museums and Women* (1972), along with *Olinger Stories* (1964), a selection from his first two collections.

Many of Updike's earliest stories are set in the small town of Olinger, Pennsylvania, the fictional name for Shillington, where he was born and raised; in or around New York

City, where he began his professional career with the *New Yorker;* and in New England, where he has lived for years. The settings of the short fiction of his three later collections range from these locales to England to Russia to Charlotte Amalie as he became a peripatetic State Department-sponsored citizen of the universe. From the beginning he has had a marvelous eye and ear, an unquenchable desire to explore what is new, sensitivity, a retentive memory, a hungry concern for the drama beneath the surface of ordinary incidents and characters. Even his least consequential stories exhibit enormous technical skill and artistry: the "perfect marriage," as has frequently been observed, of "ambition to performance."

Very smooth, very relaxed, most of these early fictions are concerned with problems, reflections, and minor revelations in the lives of sensitive and/or egotistical adolescents and young people—intellectuals, pseudointellectuals, married couples, youthful parents—and center on such unexceptional situations as two former classmates having lunch together, a young schoolteacher's difficulty with his Shakespeare class, a young married couple's return from Boston to New York with their two infant children, a quiet evening visit of an émigré professor with two of his former students.

The larger sorrows or tragedies of life are quite naturally absent from such stories. Updike's characters live moderately comfortable lives. Depression and war exist for them, if at all, only as vague memories, as remote from their actual experience as the Black Plague or the Napoleonic conquests. They live in reasonably well-furnished apartments with reasonably well-stocked bookshelves, record cabinets, and pantries. They seem to know a good sherry from a poor one, and are as likely as not to read Proust or Gide before retiring.

Despite the absence of any larger catastrophes, however, most of Updike's characters are far from happy. They are introspective and easily disturbed, by matters extending from the inconsequential to the significant. They love each other and are good parents, but the early morning yammering of their children or the sticking of the electric toaster will sometimes set their teeth fearfully on edge. They are susceptible to insomnia; they have hard-to-shake-off colds; because of their allergies they must watch their diets; they suffer from fears of inadequacy, of being conspicuous, of being outmanned or threatened in one way or another. Doing anything in public for the first time, "carving a roast, taking communion, buying a tuxedo," makes one young man's chest "feel fragile and thin"; a young wife sees "homosexuals everywhere"; one young husband and father wishes "there were such a thing as enchantment, and he could draw, with a stick, a circle of safety" around his wife and child; another, told by a doctor that he has fungus of the eyelids, immediately thinks of how beautiful his eyelashes were in his adolescence and visualizes "his face with the lids bald and the lashes lying scattered on his cheeks like insect legs"; still another, denied his marital pleasures, is pleased the following morning to see that his wife looks "ugly . . . Wan breakfast light bleaches you blotchily, drains the goodness from your thickness, makes the bathrobe a limp stained tube flapping disconsolately, exposing sallow décolletage. The skin between your breasts a sad yellow. I feast with the coffee on your drabness."

At their best, and taken singly, these stories are a triumph of the art of the usual; Updike possesses a genius for recording, as it were, the flicker of the eyelid that becomes an epiphany, and his small apartments, automobiles stuck in the snow, and mildly frustrating Sunday afternoons, which make his characters reflect that "this was the sort of day when you sow and not reap," are sharply observed and brilliantly recorded. At their least successful, or taken in large, sustained doses, however, they seem trivial rather than significant: characteristic is **"Flight,"** in which a young married writer, Allen Dow, returns to his home in Pennsylvania. "At the age of seventeen," Allen tells us, "I was poorly dressed and funny-looking, and went around thinking about myself in the third person." Here begins a seemingly interminable series of reminiscences, about his mother, about *her* mother and his father and *her* father and her grandfather, and how and where his mother was educated and how she had to go to work in a department store selling cheap fabrics at $14.00 a week, and how he, Allen Dow, made out with the girls when he was in high school, particularly when at the age of seventeen he was chosen, along with three girls, to represent his high school in a debate at another high school a hundred miles away from Olinger, and how he and Molly Bingaman, one of the girl debaters, made it ("her lipstick smeared in little unflattering flecks into the skin around her mouth; it was as if I had been given a face to eat"), and how he finally breaks from his mother by having a series of almost consummated sexual encounters with Molly, after the last of which he "went to the all-night diner just beyond the Olinger town line and ate three hamburgers, ordering them one at a time, and drank two glasses of milk."

All I can say is that by this time it is of little concern to me whether Allen Dow ate three hamburgers that night, ordering them one at a time, and drank two glasses of milk, or ate two hamburgers and drank three glasses of milk, ordering *them* one at a time.

A similar preoccupation with the unexceptional characterizes most of the stories in *The Music School* and *Museums and Women.* As his young married couples approach maturity or middle age, their youthful petulance and irritability deepen into despair or disenchantment, or manifest themselves in hostility or paranoia. They are lonely, dissatisfied with their wives or mistresses, at odds with their children, their jobs, their society. The opening line of **"In Football Season,"** the first story of *The Music School*—"Do you remember a fragrance girls acquire in autumn? . . . so faint and flirtatious on those afternoon walks through the dry leaves . . . banked a thousandfold and . . . heavy as the perfume of a flower shop on the dark slope of the stadium . . ."—is almost like the prelude to an elegy, an elegy with infinite variations upon the same themes, repeated in story after story. "Now I peek into windows and open doors and do not find that air of permission. It has fled the world. Girls walk by me carrying their invisible bouquets from fields still steeped in grace,

and I look up in the manner of one who follows with his eyes the passage of a hearse . . ."

There is a similar tone in the title story of *Museums and Women:* the protagonist, reflecting upon some of the women in life—mother, wife, discarded love object—concludes "it appeared to me that now I was condemned, in my search for the radiance that had faded behind me, to enter more and more museums, and to be a little less exalted by each new entrance, and a little more quickly disenchanted by the familiar contents beyond."

All of Updike's unhappy people do not, like the voice in Dylan Thomas' poem, sing in their chains in such tempered tones. The natural course of love, one character comments, is "passion, consummation, contentment, boredom, betrayal." "We are all pilgrims, faltering toward divorce," echoes another; still another, after recovering from a broken affair, "discovered himself so healed that his wound ached to be reopened." Like Richard Maples, the most unpleasant of all Updike's antiheroes, who appears and reappears with his wife and four children in several of *The Music School* and *Museums and Women* pieces, Updike's characters have "been married too long." They approach middle age ungracefully, angrily, or pitifully. They suffer from maladies real or imagined: about to donate blood for the first time, Richard almost funks out; in Rome, his feet ache hideously and he has unbearable stomach pains while visiting the Forum; on the day he is to accompany his wife on a Boston protest march, he has a terrible cold; having had his aching teeth capped, he gets drunk and smashes up a new car; eventually, persevering in his hideous marriage and wallowing like a medieval madman in his own excrement, he revels in his cuckoldry: you "whore," my "virgin bride," he cries to his wife. "Tell me everybody!" ("You honestly *are* hateful," Joan tells him in the first of the Maples stories. "It's not just a pose.")

At their best, stories like these are a devastating commentary on various aspects of contemporary manners; at their least successful, as they are in what seem to me more than a few trivial pieces like **"The Orphaned Swimming Pool,"** the less said the better.

But then there is Henry Bech, author of "one good book and three others, the good one having come first," whom we first meet in **"The Bulgarian Poetess"** in *The Music School,* and subsequently in *Bech: A Book,* which seems to me Updike's major collection of short fiction and perhaps his best book to date.

For Bech—Prurient, perceptive, pursued, paranoid, passionate, and I might add permanent Henry Bech—is a comic masterpiece (and if there is any other factor that weakens so many of Updike's flawlessly put together stories it is the lack of a saving sense of humor). Bech is a compound, as he comments in his foreword to **"Dear John,"** of "some gentlemanly Norman Mailer" and of "gallant, glamorous Bellow, the King of the Leprechauns," with a "childhood . . . out of Alex Portnoy and . . . [an] ancestral past out of I. B. Singer," together with a "whiff of Malamud" and "something Waspish, theological, scared, and insulatingly ironical that derives . . . from you."

Whatever his ancestry, literary or otherwise, Bech *towers.* Bech in Russia for a month of cultural exchange at the expense of the State Department; Bech in Rumania sporting an astrakhan hat he has purchased in Moscow; Bech in Bulgaria, falling in undeclared love with the Bulgarian poetess; Bech smoking pot for the first time and switching mistresses; Bech overwhelmed by *angst* at a girls' college in Virginia; Bech swinging and having a hasty love affair and being undone by a double-talking journalist in London; Bech entering the heaven of literary lions—these are superb stories. This horny, hairy, middle-aged, likable, outrageous, unforgivable, self-searching, ponderous, light-footed spin-off from the suffering, self-contemplative Bellow-Malamud-Roth-et al.-Jewish-intellectual protagonist soars far beyond the level of caricature; with Bech, Updike has created a character so real that it is difficult to believe he did not always exist . . . and, in effect, he always has, at least in American life and literature.

John Updike has had his ups and downs, from the almost hysterical acclaim that greeted his earliest books, the subsequent fall from grace with *The Centaur* and *Couples,* and the rather dismal failure of *Buchanan Dying,* along with the unsought and sometimes dubious distinction of having become a favorite subject for term papers and doctoral dissertations. As with [John] O'Hara, there is a temptation—one that must stubbornly be resisted until it is demonstrably valid—to think that anyone as prolific as Updike cannot really be too good. Despite the occasional shallowness, the rhetorical flourishes, the repetitiveness and what to me seems the imitativeness of the "Other Modes" sequence of *Museum and Women,* he is still the most talented and exciting short story writer under fifty in America today. His many good-to-excellent stories plus *Bech* in toto are a notable achievement. (pp. 47-53)

> William Peden, "Metropolis, Village, and Suburbia: The Short Fiction of Manners," in his *The American Short Story: Continuity and Change, 1940-1975,* revised edition, Houghton Mifflin Company, 1975, pp. 30-68.

When I was younger I thought of myself as a short-story writer. . . . They were what I expected to make my living by. Now that the novels are the breadwinners, I still feel grateful to the short-story form.

—John Updike, in Edwin McDowell's "Fine-Tuning a Collection," in The New York Times Book Review, *26 April 1987.*

Robert J. Nadon   (essay date 1979)

[*In the essay below, Nadon examines Updike's perspective on farm and small-town life as represented by the*

"middle landscape" in The Olinger Stories, *viewing the volume as an extension of Updike's own experiences and upbringing in Shillington, Pennsylvania.*]

I believe John Updike's literary path leads to the fictional town of Olinger, "a shadow of 'Shillington,' " his real home town. In Updike's moral geography, Olinger is an embodiment of the middle landscape tradition that Leo Marx tells us in *The Machine in the Garden* is a persistent force in the American imagination. The concept of the middle landscape as an American ideal is best formulated by Crèvecoeur in his famous *Letters:* " . . . it is natural to conceive that those who live near the sea, must be very different from those who live near the woods; the intermediate space will afford a separate and distinct class." Crèvecoeur's geographical determinism ("Men are like plants; the goodness and flavor of the fruit proceeds from the peculiar soil and exposition in which they grow") is very much alive in the *Olinger Stories.* Indeed, Updike acknowledges that the sensibility which was formed by Shillington has produced a "state of mind . . . that in my subjective geography is still the center of the world." It is also a literal and figurative middle ground between the territory *Of the Farm* and the urban milieu which is always a presence in his fiction. In fact, the middleness of Olinger becomes itself the challenge of his literary endeavor: "To transcribe middleness with all its grits, bumps, and anonymities, its fullness of satisfaction and mystery: is it possible . . . or worth doing?"

In Crèvecoeur's triptych, the middle landscape is a modified nature that lies between city and woods. Updike echoes this division of place and then transports it:

> For the city and the woods and the ominous places were peripheral; their glamour and menace did not intrude into the sunny area where I lived. . . . My geography went like this: in the center of the world lay our neighborhood of Shillington [Olinger]. Around it there was greater Shillington, and around that, Berks County. Around Berks County there was the State of Pennsylvania, the best, the least eccentric, state in the Union. Around Pennsylvania, there was the United States, with a greater weight of people on the right and a greater weight of land on the left. For clear geometrical reasons, not all children could be born, like me, at the center of the nation.

The weight of the land counterposed with the weight of the people, with Updike's small town of Shillington standing immobile as the fulcrum, is an appropriate image with which to crystalize Updike's rural-urban balance and his own use of his small-town past as the very center of his literary being.

In Updike's non-fictional prose, he returns again and again to his boyhood and the town of Shillington. In "The Dogwood Tree: a Boyhood" he comments on the "exceptional effect" which the "site" of his boyhood had upon him. In a world in which "change is the order of things," Shillington was the embodiment of immutability, steadfastness. Like Olinger, it somehow managed to exist outside of time and place, not subject to the forces that worked upon the rest of the world. Shillington, in spite of its nearness to Reading, "retained a rural flavor." Most of the people were "not long off the farm." Corn grew between the school and the alley and one old lady still wore a bonnet. "When I walked down the street to school, the houses called, 'Chonny.' I had a place to be." Updike, with perhaps feigned modesty, writes that the places of his childhood are "impossible" to describe because they were so fundamental to him. "They have the neutral color of my own soul." The dogwood tree referred to in the title of the essay is a reference to a tree that Updike's parents planted at his birth. At age thirteen, Updike revisited Shillington, and noted the shadow of the dogwood tree against the formerly blank brick wall of his house as he drove away. He writes: "I turned away before it would have disappeared from sight, and so it is that my shadow has always remained in one place."

The shadow of Shillington and all that it has come to symbolize falls on all of Updike's work. Like Bellow's association of "reality" with St. Dominique street, to the young author "everything outside Olinger . . . seemed relatively unreal." This small-town sensibility is carried to New York and becomes the editorial "we" of the pieces that Updike did for the "Talk of the Town" series. "Who, after all, could that indefatigably fascinated, perpetually peripatetic 'we' be but a collection of dazzled farm boys?"

Updike not only uses the *persona* of the farm boy to capture "the lyric glimpses of the city," but he transplants the pastoral world to the heart of the city and makes it, again in a familiar device, the center of the world. In his piece, "Bryant Park," Updike contrasts the quiet interior atmosphere of the park with the noisy bustle of the urban surroundings. Even the people of the park are different from the others; they "are the quiet people," unlike the secretary and "her counterpart the businessman" who are "on their way to somewhere else. It abruptly occurred to us that we were near the center of the world." "Where but here, in Bryant Park, was the bull's eye of our city? As surely as if we were in the Forum of 160, on the Ile de la Cité in 1260, or in Piccadilly Circus in 1860, we sat, now, in 1960, in the center of Western Civilization." Ironically, what makes New York the center of Western civilization is not the skyscraper, the businessman, "the antique jumble of high architecture," or the maze of advertising signs, but rather its hint of a nostalgic past and of the residents of the park who are not, like the businessman "children of the morning," but rather a "quiet, uneasy, twilight lot."

Updike has commented on cities in his non-fiction prose, and although they exist outside the charmed world of Olinger they hold a particular meaning and promise. In Updike's subjective geography, Reading (Alton), Pennsylvania, holds a special place. It is "a very powerful and fragrant and obscure city." After a half-page catalog of olfactory images, he concludes: "Reading's smells were most of what my boyhood knew of the Great World that was suspended, at a small but sufficient distance, beyond my world." Reading and all other cities, in contrast to the "reality" of Shillington, become for the young Updike a dream of the future, a place of promise and fulfillment. If Olinger is boyhood and the past, the city is manhood and the future. But what the city is in the imagination of the

young boy and what it will become in reality to the young man are the subject matter of much of Updike's later fiction and not the concern of this [essay].

Updike draws heavily on his own and his family's past in the eleven short stories collected under the title, *Olinger Stories,* and in three of his five novels: *Rabbit, Run, The Centaur* and *Of the Farm.* His other two novels, *The Poorhouse Fair* and *Couples,* reflect the Olinger sensibility, but to a much lesser degree. The former works, which I will call the Olinger materials, are an extended treatment of the city-country dialogue. Updike acknowledges that the hero in each of the Olinger stories "wears different names . . . but he is at bottom the same boy, a local boy—This selection could be called *A Local Boy.*" Updike's local boy resembles in many ways the stereotyped small-town boy of nineteenth-century fiction which Page Smith reconstructs in his book *As a City Upon a Hill.* Like Smith's ideal type, Updike's boy heroes have a sense of belonging to the whole community; they are unaware of the limitations of their environment and instead feel that the environment is rich in mystery and complexity; they succumb to the small town "world of intimacy, warmth, acceptance, and security." The child embraces the town as his symbolic home; it becomes the object of his later search in the complexities of the urban world to which he graduates. The twentieth century embodiment of this mythic quest for the home town is, of course, Thomas Wolfe's work with its "you-can't-go-home-again" refrain.

The central force which operates in the Olinger material is the small town versus the farm, with a variant minor theme of the lure of the city. Most often the protagonists in the central conflict are the young boy and all he represents—boyhood, the present, the small-town—and his mother, who represents the farm, the past, his heritage. Related to this central cluster of conflicts is the pull of the city, represented by the boy's father and oftentimes the boy himself when he envisions his future in the city. Overly simplified, the conflict between farm and city is the parental conflict of father and mother over the boy's destiny. Updike focuses the battle on the literal neutral ground of the small town, an amalgam of both worlds, where the boy is spiritually at home. The forces that surround him, including his grandparents as well as his parents, conspire to root him out of his spiritual home and transplant him elsewhere. Updike writes in the straight autobiographical piece, "Dogwood Tree": "For all of them—for all four of my adult guardians—Shillington was a snag, a halt in a journey that had begun elsewhere. *Only I belonged to the town.* The accidents that had planted me here made uneasy echoes in the house . . . but their source was beyond my vision."

In **"Flight,"** the hero's mother asserts her desire to have her son escape the snag of Olinger. Having climbed to the top of Shade Hill overlooking Olinger, the mother, digging her fingers into the boy's hair, announces, "There we all are, and there we'll all be forever. . . . Except you, Allen. You're going to fly." The mother's greatest fear is that Allen will not take flight and escape Olinger, but that he will "stick and die in the dirt." All of the forces and characters of this early fiction are lined up to move the boy-heroes out of the dead center of the small town toward either the land or the people, the farm or the city.

At age thirteen Updike was moved to the land. In **"Pigeon Feathers"** the narrator tells us of the effect of the move on the family: the father rushes off to Olinger every chance he gets, performing "needless errands. A city boy by birth, he was frightened of the farm and seized any excuse to get away." Grandmother dabbles around the kitchen, always getting in the way. "Strange, out in the country, amid eighty acres, they were crowded together." The parents carry on an endless argument about organic farming, the father insisting that "the earth is nothing but chemicals." " 'George, if you'd just walk out on the farm you'd know it's not true. The land has a soul.' 'Soil, has, no, soul,' he said, enunciating stiffly, as if to a very stupid class." The mother continues the agrarian rhetoric with the argument that this "country was made by farmers. George Washington was a farmer." The father replies: "George Washington's dead. In this day and age only the misfits stay on the farm. The lame, the halt, the blind. The morons with one arm. Human garbage. They remind me of death, sitting their with their mouths open." This debate continues through most of the short stories and reaches its climax in the novel, *The Centaur*. The argument is reborn in *Of the Farm* when the boy, now an adult, replaces the voice of father, who dies at the end of *The Centaur*.

In **"Flight"** it is the grandfather who is revealed to be anti-farm. Early in life he had exchanged the "indignity of farming" for the "dignity of finance." He was driven to the town because of a rebuff by his father. ". . . it is not love of land but its absence that needs explaining." Just the reverse appears to be the case for the mother. She, too, is rebuffed by her father in her desire to go to New York. Out of pique, she marries the boy's father who takes her to Wilmington, only to have the Depression force them back to the white house in Olinger. The narrator sums up these generational conflicts "As if each generation of parents commits atrocities against their children which by God's decree remain invisible to the rest of the world." What Updike seems to be suggesting is that it is not the farm nor small town *per se* that engenders either love or hate, but rather the human personalities that come to be associated with place that motivates one either to accept or reject certain geographic settings. In any case, it is the women in Updike's early fiction who come to be associated with the farm and the men who identify with the city.

The young heroes in the Olinger stories do not share a love for the farm or even for the "land" as we normally use the term. Instead, they are especially attached to the earth, or dirt, of the small town. This attachment is spoken of in one of the last of the Olinger stories by the young hero now become adult, married, and with children of his own. The title, **"Packed Dirt, Churchgoing, A Dying Cat, A Traded Car,"** singles out the "different things that move us," and it is the "sight of bare earth that has been smoothed and packed by the passage of human feet" that is reassuring and pleasurable to the adult narrator.

> Such spots abound in small towns: the furtive break in the playground fence dignified into a thoroughfare, the trough of dust underneath each swing, the blurred path worn across a wedge of grass, the anonymous little mound or embankment polished by pay and strewn with pebbles like the confetti aftermath of a wedding. Such unconsciously *humanized intervals of clay*, to humble and common even to have a name, remind me of my childhood, when one communes with dirt down among the legs, as it were, of presiding fatherly presences. The earth is our playmate then, and the call to supper has a piercingly sweet eschatological ring. (critic's emphasis)

The religious diction of this passage indicates Updike's attempt to make a little epiphany of this common experience. The narrator goes on to describe his child's fear of the bulldozing machine tearing up the neighboring lot, leaving it raw and gouged. However, it was not long before the play of children's feet had "worn the sharpness away." This "small modification," "this small work of human erosion, seemed precious to me . . . it had been achieved accidentally, and had about it that repose of grace that is beyond willing." He then raises this action to a symbolic level: "We in America have from the beginning been cleaving and baring the earth, attacking, reforming the enormity of nature we were given, which we took to be hostile. We have explored, on behalf of all mankind, this paradox: the more matter is outwardly mastered, the more it overwhelms us in our hearts." This reshaping of the *earth* is not the traditional cultivation of the *land* which we associate with the agrarian ideal. It is a much more "urbanized" coming to terms with the American landscape. He goes on: "Evidence—gaping right-of-ways, acres mercilessly scraped, bleeding mountains of muddy fill—surrounds us of a war that is incapable of ceasing, and it is good to know that there are enough of us to exert a counter-force. If craters were to appear in our landscape tomorrow, the next day there would be usable paths threading down the blasted sides." The alteration of the landscape is not denounced out of hand as a ravishment of God's countryside, but instead is interpreted as a mingling of the human, establishing a "human legacy." He concludes: "As our sense of God's forested legacy to us dwindles, there grows, in these worn, rubbed, and patted patches, a sense of human legacy—like those feet of statues of saints which have lost their toes to centuries of kisses. One thinks of John Dewey's definition of God as the union of the actual and the ideal." Updike, in this passage, has shifted the emphasis from the traditional religious value associated with "land" to a more secularized, humanized landscape based upon "dirt."

In the following section of the story, on churchgoing, Updike reverses his strategy and makes the church in the city function like the worn path in the raw countryside. "In Manhattan, Christianity is so feeble its future seems before it. One walks to church past clattering cafeterias and ravaged newsies in winter weather that is always a shade of Lent, on pavements spangled with last night's vomit. The expectantly hushed shelter of the church is like one of those spots worn bare by a softball game in a weed-filled vacant lot. The presence of the city beats like wind at the glowing windows." The presence of the church in the city works to "humanize" the city, just as the worn paths work to humanize the weed-filled vacant lot. The city in this passage is certainly viewed negatively, but the city with its multiplicity of churches allows the narrator to visit a different church each Sunday, retaining his anonymity and permitting him freedom from the coercive commitments one might find in a small town. "To be known by face and name and financial weight robs us of our unitary soul, enrolls us against those Others. We are the others. It is of the essence to be a stranger in church." Paradoxically, anonymity, a city value, has been converted into a means of establishing a sense of community, of eliminating the I-Other relationship traditionally associated with city living.

In summary, the Olinger materials are invaluable in defining Updike's esthetic of middleness and his early small-town sensibility. In the cultural shift of life styles and values that America has made from rural to small town, from small town to city, Updike locates himself as a child literally and figuratively "at home" in the small town. Like America itself, however, he envisions his future as destined for the city. The city is for him full of promise and excitement. In the Olinger stories the rural life is totally rejected and apparently has no hold over his early imagination. Updike's subsequent fiction, however, reveals that the promise of the city has so far gone unfulfilled and that the lure of the farm (as we see in his novel *Of the Farm*) cannot be rejected as easily as he thinks.

If Updike continues to be a major writer, what his early fiction tells us is still important. The middle landscape of small town and humanized dirt still play a role in his imagination and, perhaps, ours. The urbanized landscape in which most Americans live has not replaced the inner landscape of the imagination that was shaped by small town influences. The town of Olinger is still a hometown for Updike and he is, at least fictionally, "always coming back," as he tells us in one of the concluding stories: "He became a child again in this town, where life was a distant adventure, a rumor, an always imminent joy." (pp. 62-8)

> *Robert J. Nadon, "Updike's 'Olinger Stories':*
> *In the Middle Landscape Tradition," in* Per-
> *spectives on Contemporary Literature, Vol. 5,*
> *1979, pp. 62-8.*

Suzanne Henning Uphaus   (essay date 1980)

[*In the following excerpt, Uphaus provides a thematic and stylistic analysis of "Pigeon Feathers," "A & P,"* and Too Far to Go.]

Updike received recognition first as a writer of short stories, and he has published almost as many collections of short stories as novels. Most of these stories were previously published in *The New Yorker* or some other magazine. Because of limitations of space, and because of the overwhelming number of Updike's short stories, I will be able only to generalize about them. I will then concentrate briefly on two of the most frequently anthologized short stories and one collection.

There are many similarities between Updike's short stories and his novels, and many of the observations . . . made about the novels hold true for the stories as well. As in the

novels, the short stories are often concerned with how the natural world (whether evidenced by pigeons or sexual encounters) relates to the supernatural. A frequent theme in both genres is the consideration of social and familial obligations as sacrifice, resulting in a diminishing of the protagonist's artistic or religious or sexual freedom. The nostalgia for the past, the tenuousness of middle-class institutions, particularly marriage and the family, the suspicion that Updike has always had for what seems, on the surface, to be heroic and unselfish action, all these are frequent themes in the short stories.

In the short stories Updike concentrates not as much on the event as upon the effect of outward events upon the protagonist. While the same may be said of the novels, Updike realizes that as a genre, novels demand more action simply to sustain their length. Because of their brevity, the short stories can sustain uninterrupted introspection, a spareness of overt action, in a way that novels cannot. Thus the genre of the short story allows Updike to present selected and detailed vignettes focused on the nuances of the protagonist's reaction to events.

For those readers used to dime-store thrillers, the plots in the short stories may seem bare: in one a man takes his daughter to a music lesson, in another a father tells his child a bedtime story, in many the temptations toward or suspicions of adultery are suffered but seldom confirmed. Moreover, within the brevity of the short story, Updike's remarkable style, unfailingly precise, often lyrical, occasionally ironic, becomes even more noticeable than in the novels.

Perhaps the most sustained stylistic achievement in any of the short stories comes in the frequently anthologized story **"Pigeon Feathers."** David is the young protagonist, an adolescent who has been plunged into religious doubt by his almost accidental reading of H. G. Wells's account of Jesus. Wells describes Jesus as "an obscure political agitator, a kind of hobo, in a minor colony of the Roman Empire," who "by an accident impossible to reconstruct . . . survived his own crucifixion and presumably died a few weeks later." Outraged by the sacrilege of this account, David's first reaction is astonishment that the man who had written such "blasphemy" had not been struck by lightning but had been allowed to continue writing, "to grow old, win honors, wear a hat, write books that, if true, collapsed everything into a jumble of horror."

In the weeks following, David's doubt and depression grow, as does his sense of alienation from his family and acquaintances. This sense of alienation is reinforced by the fact that David is an only child who has just moved, with his family, from town to farm. (These details correspond to events in Updike's own adolescence). The nature he contemplates in the loneliness of the farm reminds him of the persistence of death and decay in the natural cycle. In the darkness of the outhouse one night, David experiences a moment of consummate horror as he contemplates the possibility of his own death, without resurrection. He questions the minister during a church confirmation class but the other children laugh at his impertinence, and the clergyman, answering, reveals his own disbelief in the resurrection of each individual.

Weeks later, when David is asked by his mother to shoot the pigeons who are fouling furniture stored in the barn, he accepts the task with increasing eagerness. Since the universe has been revealed to him as possibly uncaring, there has developed a streak of meanness within David, a reflexive lack of caring. Into the darkness of the barn comes the destroyer, with his new gun, a fifteenth birthday present. The pigeons are his helpless victims.

In describing the pigeons, Updike's style becomes lyrical and precise. The sound of their cooing "flooded the vast interior with its throaty, bubbling outpour." David aims at a pigeon that is "preening and cooing in a throbbing, thrilled, tentative way" and shoots at its "tiny, jauntily cocked head." The bird, "pirouetting rapidly and nodding its head as if in frantic agreement," finally falls. As the cooing of the remaining pigeons becomes shriller, their "apprehensive tremolo made the whole volume of air seem liquid."

When David buries his victims, he notices, for the first time, the intricate individual design of each bird. The pattern of each feather is carefully and precisely colored. Each feather is trimmed to fulfill its purpose. One pigeon has plumage "slate shades of blue," another is "mottled all over in rhythms of lilac and gray." David becomes convinced that "the God who had lavished such craft upon these worthless birds would not destroy His whole Creation by refusing to let David live forever."

There is irony, of course, in this final statement of the story. David thinks that the birds are worthless, although they have shown so much to him. Moreover, in the self-centered manner of adolescents, he believes the universe has been created for his own pleasure, and that his death would imply its destruction; thus, David concludes he will "live forever."

In the lyrical description of the birds, Updike frequently uses words associated with the arts, with music, with dancing, and in the burial scene, with painting. Words like "tremolo" and "pirouetting" and the detailed description of the color and pattern of the feathers reinforce Updike's ultimate purpose, to suggest the existence of a design, and thus a Designer, in the natural world. While philosophical objections could be (and have been) made to the argument of design as proof of God's existence, the tone of gentle irony in the final paragraph assures us of Updike's control of his theme. As Robert Detweiler writes [in his *John Updike*]:

> The point is that Updike, through symbolic action and analogy, has written a moving religious narrative that does not presume to convince one of the objective truth of Christian faith, but that does testify to an individual's achievement of it.

Updike's story **"A & P"** is perhaps his most popular; it has been anthologized in many college texts. **"A & P"** derives its impact from the narrative voice, comic contrast, and the ironic distance between the intentions of the protagonist and what he actually accomplishes.

Sammy, the narrator, is a nineteen-year-old checkout clerk at an A & P market in a New England town that is close to a wealthy beach colony. The narrative voice is established immediately as familiar and colloquial, using the present tense for dramatic impact; it is as if the young narrator is recounting the incident to a friend. "In walks these three girls in nothing but bathing suits," he begins. "I'm in the third checkout slot, with my back to the door, so I don't see them until they're over by the bread."

Much of the humor in the story comes from Sammy's response to the girls. Mesmerized by his initial sight of them, he rings up "a box of HiHo crackers" twice, enraging his customer. When the girls come into view again, Sammy's attention becomes fixed on the "queen" of the three. She walks with poised nonchalance, barefoot, with the straps of her bathing suit off her shoulders; "as a result the suit had slipped a little on her," Sammy tells us, to reveal where her tan ends. She leads the other girls down one aisle, to the meat counter, and up another aisle, appearing by the checkout lanes with a jar of "Fancy Herring Snacks in Pure Sour Cream." They come to Sammy's lane, and from the "hollow at the center of her nubbled pink" bathing suit top, the queen lifts a folded dollar. As Sammy watches this maneuver he tells us, "The jar went heavy in my hand."

At this point the manager of the store appears. Lengel, a Sunday school teacher, is affronted by the indignity of the girls shopping in his store in such attire. "We want you decently dressed when you come in here," he tells the girls, who blush, suddenly embarrassed. Enraged that Lengel has humiliated the girls, Sammy says, " 'I quit' . . . quick enough for them to hear, hoping they'll stop and watch me, their unsuspected hero." But the girls "keep right on going," and Sammy is left to carry out his heroic gesture, remove his apron and his bow tie, ring up No Sale on the register, and leave, jobless and alone. The final sentence registers Sammy's awareness of "how hard the world was going to be for me hereafter."

The irony of Sammy's heroism reflects Updike's conviction, obvious in many of his works, that the heroic gesture is often meaningless and usually arises from selfish rather than unselfish impulses. Sammy wants to be noticed by the girls, but he isn't. They are of a social class beyond his, for he is a town boy, they are summer vacationers, from families who snack on herring in sour cream as they sip their cocktails. Sammy is aware of the gulf between them; the only way he can get them to notice him is to differentiate himself from what he sees, through their eyes, as the hopeless provincialism of the small town that insists on "decent dress" in its supermarkets. When the manager rebukes the girls, "Queenie" (as Sammy calls the leader), begins to get "sore now that she remembers her place, a place from which the crowd that runs the A & P must look pretty crummy. Fancy Herring Snacks flashed in her very blue eyes."

But the comic tone of the story is also created by the contrast between the usual customers at the A & P and these girls. Sammy is painfully aware of female appearances, and he describes the matrons he sees daily on his job in terms that are representative of his age group. There is a "witch about fifty with rouge on her cheekbones and no eyebrows" who screeches when he rings up her purchase twice. There are "a few house-slaves in pin curlers." There is "an old party in baggy gray pants" buying four giant cans of pineapple juice, and there are "women with six children and varicose veins mapping their legs." They are described repeatedly as "sheep" who are "pushing their carts down the aisle." When Sammy closes down his register and quits, he tells us the middle-aged matrons knock against each other to get to another checkout counter "like scared pigs in a chute."

On the other hand, the three girls, and especially the queen, are described in intimate and pleasurable detail. The queen has "long white prima-donna legs," and "oaky hair that the sun and salt had bleached." But to prevent the story from becoming maudlin, Updike often uses Sammy's youthful and unromantic descriptive powers. The dollar bill that the girl lifts from her cleavage is uncreased by Sammy "tenderly as you may imagine, it just having come from between the two smoothest scoops of vanilla I had ever known. . . . " As he waits breathlessly at the checkout for the girls to appear from one of the aisles, Sammy describes "the whole store" as being "like a pinball machine and I didn't know which tunnel they'd come out of." The maudlin is also prevented by Updike's precise eye for detail; there is no soft-focused romanticism here. The girls appear against a background of "Diet Delight peaches," stacked dog food, packaged spaghetti, and cheap plastic toys.

Sammy's quitting has been described, by [Detweiler] as "the reflex of the still uncorrupted, of the youth still capable of the grand gesture because he has not learned the sad wisdom of compromise." Sammy's loneliness at the end of the story is the result of this gesture: the girls have taken no notice of him, but he has alienated himself from the town by presuming to judge its standards.

The short stories by Updike that are most familiar to readers of *The New Yorker* are the seventeen that trace the history and eventual dissolution of the marriage of Joan and Dick Maple. In 1979 these were collected into a volume entitled *Too Far To Go* and made into a television movie of the same name. The stories, written over a span of twenty-three years, follow the outward events of Updike's own first marriage: Dick Maple, like Updike, married in the early fifties when he was twenty-one; both couples had four children, separated after twenty-one years, and finally received one of the first no-fault divorces granted in the state of Massachusetts.

Most of the Maple stories are told from the point of view of Dick Maple who, like many of Updike's protagonists, suffers insomnia and frequent minor illnesses (a nervous stomach in Rome, a mysterious fever the day of a civil rights demonstration, innumerable colds). He recognizes that these are possibly psychosomatic, as his doctor suggests in the final story. These illnesses reflect Dick Maple's uneasy relationship with his own body; when it is not irritating him with illness, it plagues him with sexual hungers. His character reveals an uncomfortable conjunction of independence and insecurity, both aggravated not so much by his wife as by his married state.

In contrast, Joan Maple is revealed in these stories as being, for the most part, competent and conscientious.

Caricature of John Updike by David Levine.

Dick finds her mysterious and distant, describing her as "solid but hidden," and finally, as "a secret woman he could never reach and had at last wearied of trying to reach." In the early stories she is clearly in control. In **"Wife-Wooing"** she refuses her husband's advances only to initiate sex with him the next night, when he is not expecting it. In the next story, **"Giving Blood,"** several years and one child later, she has convinced Richard, over his squeamish objections, to go to Boston with her to give blood for her cousin who is ill.

But in this story there is a new note of friction in the marriage. During the drive to Boston each accuses the other of flirting at a party the night before. Dick coolly accuses Joan of smugness and sexlessness. But joined by the strange sacrificial ceremony of giving blood, they make peace over the late breakfast in a restaurant, with Dick pretending that he is Joan's romantic suitor on a date until he finds his wallet empty and must take money from his wife.

Subsequent stories show them drawing further apart. They "had talked and thought about separation," but their "conversations, increasingly ambivalent and ruthless as accusation, retraction, blow and caress alternated and canceled, had the final effect of knitting them ever tighter together in a painful, helpless, degrading intimacy." One story centers on a mysterious telephone caller; each accuses the other that it must be his or her lover. In another, Dick warmly embraces a divorced woman whom he and

Joan have been driving home from a party, and in another, he comes upon his wife and a mutual friend embracing in the kitchen of his house.

The accusations and suppositions, Dick's occasional attraction to his wife, and his frequent rejection of her continue through the stories. It is like an elaborate dance in which, pledged to keep each other as partners, the couple, perhaps because of this enforced commitment, draws farther and farther apart. The concentration in these stories is always on the couple; lovers remain shadowy background figures whose implied presence is incidental and not the cause of the distance between the couple.

It is ironic that this distance, rather than closeness, is the end result of so many, ultimately futile, conversations. The Maples talk endlessly over the years, but all these words fail to draw them closer. Thus, one of the effects of these stories is to demonstrate the limitations of words as a means of communication, as the writer depends on them to convey this message to the reader.

After twenty-one years of marriage, the Maples do decide to separate, and the story **"Separating"** records their painful breaking of the news to their children, now young adults and adolescents. Dick and Joan, concerned about the effect of the news they feel they must inflict upon the children, have waited months for the right moment. But, as [Erica Jong wrote in a review of *Too Far To Go* appearing in *New Republic* (September 1979)], "there turns out to be no proper moment for such a revelation." While the girls respond with a quiet stoicism, the younger son at first shouts at his parents accusingly, then jokes, and then dissolves in tears in a scene that rings painfully true. The older son seems to accept the separation with calm, yet as he kisses his father good night he moans in his ear the unanswerable question, "Why?"

Perhaps the Maples' closest moment is, ironically, in the courthouse right after their divorce is legalized. The final story of the volume, **"Here Come the Maples,"** links Richard's memories of his wedding with the formalities and red tape of getting a divorce. He must get a copy of their marriage license, and in doing so, Dick finds himself remembering, with increasing detail, his wedding day, the day they began what they are now about to end. When the Maples arrive in court they are as nervous as any young bride and groom, although their marriage is about to be dissolved, not solemnized. To the judge's questions Dick and Joan answer, "I do," echoing the marriage ceremony. As the ceremony ends, Dick turns to his former wife and kisses her, remembering to do what, twenty-two years before at their wedding ceremony, he had forgotten.

In her review of the Maple stories Erica Jong has written, "Their separation and divorce are the more poignant for their not hating each other. The title of this collection might well be 'No Fault.' " In the Maple stories Updike has succeeded in being impartial and unblaming. It is always much easier to blame than to understand, and yet Updike has avoided this temptation. Out of his impartiality he has created a series of stories both poignant and sensitive. (pp. 121-30)

Suzanne Henning Uphaus, in her John Up-

dike, *Frederick Ungar Publishing Co., 1980, 149 p.*

Updike on the pleasures of writing and the creative process:

Writers tend to complain and say what agony it is, and there are days when you wonder why you're doing it, but, by and large, I am immensely pleased to have been able to make a living at it. To do something creative had been my ambition from when I was small. There are satisfactions at almost every point of the writing process. To begin at the end, it's certainly pleasing to get the finished book. If the book is well received, it's pleasant to enjoy the reception and to spend the checks when they arrive, and all that. I suppose the chief happiness is actually the finished book, holding it in your hand, something you've made and something that's pretty much yours—yours and the printer's.

At the other end, of course, the moment of inspiration can be exciting, when you have a sudden idea that feels like a real idea. In between, there's a certain amount of drudgery; but each morning's work—I tend to work in the morning—there has to be some inspiration, some sense of having caught a little bit of life and put it down in words or having improved on a previously written sentence. For the fiction writer, there's some pleasure in being able to take the confusion of a lived life and turn it into patterns to, in a way, relive your life via these fictional characters, in a productive way, to save something of the flux, and put it down in permanent form. So, yes, I do enjoy almost every aspect of the writing profession.

John Updike, in an interview with Rebekah Presson, in New Letters, *1992.*

George W. Hunt (essay date 1980)

[*An American educator, critic, and clergyman, Hunt won a Book of the Year award from the Modern Language Association for his* John Updike and the Three Great Secret Things: Sex, Religion, and Art, *from which this excerpt is taken. In the first part of the excerpt, portions of which appeared in slightly different form in the journal* Short Story Fiction, *he argues that the pieces in* The Music Room—*best represented by the story* "Leaves"—*concern the problems of creativity, artistic identity and self-awareness, and the relationship between nature and reality. In the second part of the excerpt, Hunt asserts that* Bech: A Book *provides discourse on the problems faced by the American writer in the 1960s.*]

The Music School collection holds a distinctive place in the Updike corpus because it contains several stories that, in addition to more familiar Updike themes, specifically engage the issues of artistic self-consciousness and the act of composition itself. In the story **"The Bulgarian Poetess,"** published in March 1965, Updike created a spokesman who would explicitly engage these issues, Henry Bech. In 1970 he told an audience why he felt compelled to invent Henry Bech:

Now, as for the Bech stories. . . . For a writer, life becomes overmuch a writer's life. Things happen to you that wouldn't happen to anybody else, and a way of using this to good advantage, of course, is to invent another writer. At first, he is very much an alter ego, but then, in the end, not so. At any rate I have used the writer in *Bech* as a subject in order to confess sterility in a truthful way. . . . In my book, I tried to—and I believe I did—package and dispose of a certain set of tensions and anxieties which I have as a practicing writer.

But Bech's character is only the most obvious alter ego in *The Music School* collection. Most of the remaining stories reveal a narrator or character wrestling with similar "writerly" problems of sterility and creativity and the tensions that result. A cursory reading, though, might miss this artistic aspect. The primary and ostensible theme of almost every story is that of the mystery of sexuality and sexual relationships examined in the light of their sterility or vitality. Subordinate, but concomitant with it, is the secondary theme of the mysterious relationship between the imagined and the real, between artistic re-creation and Creation, between the sterile and vitalizing processes of the mind. Updike's later story **"Museums and Women,"** published in 1967, will explicitly conjoin these two "mysteries," but several stories in this collection do so with greater subtlety. The most obvious clue, however, that Updike is addressing these twin themes is found in the epigraph chosen for *The Music School,* a quotation from Wallace Stevens' poem, "To the One of Fictive Music":

> Now, of the music summoned by the birth
> That separates us from the wind and the sea,
> Yet leaves us in them, until earth becomes,
> By being so much of the things we are,
> Gross effigy and simulacrum, none
> Gives motion to perfection more serene
> Than yours, out of our imperfections wrought,
> Most rare or ever of more kindred air
> In the laborious weaving that you wear.

These lines represent well Stevens' continuing poetic theme: that the apparent dichotomy which exists between the realm of reality, disorder, and the actual (earth) and the realm of the imagination, order, and the ideal (music) is bridged only through Art. The "One" addressed in the poem is the Muse of poetry who personifies man's power of imagination and memory. The "birth" referred to in the first line is that of human consciousness which separates us from nature (wind and sea) "yet so leaves us" in it that we see in nature a "gross effigy" of ourselves. But "the music summoned by the birth" of consciousness is Art which tries to unite man and nature, and none is more perfect and "rare" than poetry. Yet poetry is of a "kindred air" since as the bridge between, the more the poem retains of ourselves, the closer it brings us to nature.

Updike's choice of this epigraph is most apt since most of the stories deal with the "Stevensian" theme of re-creating reality and the past via imagination and memory. The intractable "natural" reality that challenges this re-creative effort is that of Woman in the mystery of her sexuality. This is most apparent in **"The Stare," "In Football Season," "The Morning," "Leaves," "Harv is Plowing Now,"**

and **"The Bulgarian Poetess."** In each of these stories the sexual challenge is associated with the artistic challenge to *imagine* and so re-create the object of pursuit; implied in this effort, furthermore, is the narrator's desire for a new form of union, so that, in a Stevens-like way, the story not only recounts that effort but *becomes* the new form of union as well.

At first the brilliantly designed story **"The Music School"** seems excepted—until we note that the adulterous narrator, now "unfaithful" to his wife and "faltering toward divorce," had been "unfaithful" to the novel he once planned to write and so now, "though unmusical," he waits in a music school attempting to sort out answers to both infidelities. In this and the other stories, composition and theme, frame and form are one in that each story's inner dynamic is heuristic in a composite way. We find the narrator, explicitly or not, seeking "connections" amid remembered or imagined events so that the resultant structure (i.e. where these connections intersect) both shapes and is shaped by this heuristic movement. Throughout, there is threefold pursuit, as there is continually in the poetry of Wallace Stevens: 1) pursuit of the elusive, disordered reality (Nature and Woman); 2) the conscious effort to draw upon the resources of the imagination through the medium of metaphor; and finally, 3) the heuristic movement outward which becomes simultaneously a search for the self, the symbolic center of the pursuit. But the goal and instrument of these three quests are the same: recovery and re-creation.

The dense and difficult story **"Harv is Plowing Now"** illustrates well this triple-layered attempt at recovery. In it the controlling metaphor is that of an archeological excavation. Just as the archeologist "unearths" both the precious and the dross, and a farmer like Harv plows the dead earth in order to revitalize it, so too the narrator-artist must mine his memory (memory of a Woman) in order to effect a re-creation by reimagining, thus issuing in a "resurrection" of his very self at the story's end.

Like Updike's technique of dialectical movement, Stevens' poetry always proceeds in a series of antithetical terms, such as chaos and order, imagination and reality, stasis and change; these antitheses are rarely resolved in his poetry, and, if so, then briefly, only to return again. Like Updike, Stevens gropes for a final formulation about art and reality, but, also like him, he knows that it cannot be stated, for man is a temporal being and reality is in flux.

But, in addition to this dialectical procedure, there is perhaps an even more significant "technical" affinity. For Wallace Stevens, poetry was "an act of the mind," and so art was itself the process whereby "the mind turns to its own creations and examines them." By "creations" here he meant primarily *metaphor,* for he admitted in *The Necessary Angel* that

> Poetry is almost incredibly one of the effects of analogy . . . almost incredibly the outcome of figures of speech or, what is the same thing, the outcome of the operation of one imagination on another through the instrumentality of the figures. To identify poetry and metaphor or metamorphosis is merely to abbreviate the last re-

mark. There is always an analogy between nature and the imagination, and possibly poetry is merely the strange rhetoric of that parallel. . . .

For Stevens, the artist's imaginative alertness regarding the manifold potential of the metaphor allows him to shape reality in new ways since the metaphor is his instrument for exploring unsuspected resemblances between things, thereby bringing reality's hidden secrets to the surface. It is *through* the metaphor that reality and imagination meet. The metaphor itself, then, becomes for Stevens a vehicle of discovery, a method of movement, and, finally, an instrument for the integration of experience.

The narrator of Updike's story **"The Sea's Green Sameness"** wrestles with the problematic relationship between Art and Nature; years later, Updike commented on this story by saying:

> I believe that narratives should not be *primarily* packages for psychological insight, though they can contain them, like raisins in buns. But the substance is the dough, which feeds the story-telling appetite, the appetite for motion, for suspense, for resolution. The author's deepest pride, as I have experienced it, is not in his incidental wisdom but in his ability to keep an organized mass of images moving forward, to feel life engendering itself under his hands. . . .

When we reflect on these comments in the light of Stevens, we realize that in Updike too the "dough" that feeds the "story-telling appetite" and "keeps a mass of images moving" throughout his fiction is mainly metaphor. Plot is generally of secondary interest in his fiction; a plot outline of any of his novels always sounds shapeless and random. So too, seldom are his characters dramatic in themselves; rather, it is their recorded perceptions, rather than their human idiosyncrasies, that engage our attention. "Life is engendered" in his fiction most successfully *through* metaphor. For example, a characteristic hitherto overlooked is that *each* of Updike's novels is metaphor-centered (of course, usually in multiple fashion), and the title itself often signals the controlling metaphor. This is more obvious in *Rabbit, Run* where the metaphor of movement is ironically aimless, or in *Rabbit Redux* where "returns" are explored in manifold modes, or in *Of the Farm* where each of the characters "becomes" the farm-metaphor from various perspectives, or in *Couples* where "coupling" is not only the recurrent activity but where so many events are seen in double-focus and so many characters seem duplicates of each other, or in *The Centaur* where, by drawing upon the Chiron myth (a universalized metaphor), he broadens, deepens, and twists the divine/human analogies throughout. (pp. 104-08)

Updike is sometimes castigated for over-writing, for "forever moving from event to embroidery, from drama to coy detail," in Richard Gilman's phrase [in his *The Confusion of Realms*, 1969], but it is this Stevens-like probing of the manifold potential of metaphor that provides a likely explanation for this characteristic and not perverse artiness. J. Hillis Miller reminds us [in *Poets of Reality*, 1965] that this was an intentional strategy for Stevens, that the "Most salient quality of *Harmonium* is the elegance, the finicky fastidiousness, even sometimes the ornate foppish-

ness, of the language. . . . These words cooperate with the words around them to create an atmosphere as rich and strange as that of a painting by Matisse or Dufy, and as much a new revelation of reality."

One might object at this point that such an Updike-Stevens "connection" seems tenuous since many artists besides Stevens have used metaphor as an instrument for discovering and shaping their view of reality. What makes Stevens' aesthetic somewhat distinctive, of course, is his additional conviction that metaphor is a vehicle for *self*-discovery, the means whereby the self, estranged from a world external to it, is capable of bridging this divide and achieving, however briefly, an integration.

It is precisely this conviction that many stories in Updike's *The Music School* address; or, more accurately, it is *in and through* the fiction that we find Updike the artist consciously wrestling with the reality/imagination dichotomy and its relation to the self. *The Music School* stories are not only special in Updike's *corpus* but create, in a sense, a new genre in the American short story tradition. For a good many of these stories are not narratives at all, but are *lyric meditations* in prose, more closely akin to the poetry of Stevens than our more usual categories. As in Stevens' poetry, many of these stories are structured as inquiries wherein the central character, often a first-person narrator, is being compelled to pursue the implications of real or imagined events from the past in an attempt to find some "connective" resolution. Updike himself has characterized "this mode of mine" as the "abstract-personal"— which has a Stevensian ring—and is well aware that some critics have "expressed impatience with my lace-making, so called." But, as with Stevens, here such "lace-making" is all.

A more detailed investigation of these parallel heuristic movements in all the major stories found in *The Music School* would demand a book-length study itself. For our purposes it is sufficient to concentrate on one dense and difficult story entitled **"Leaves,"** which critics have overlooked, and offer it as a paradigm for such an investigation. Coincidentally, Updike selected **"Leaves"** as his *best* story upon being asked to contribute to Rust Hills' anthology called *Writer's Choice*. His comments about it are worth noting and enlighten our argument thus far.

> [**"Leaves"**] is in a mode of mine, the abstract-personal, not a favorite with my critics. One of them, reviewing *The Music School,* expressed impatience with my lace-making, so-called. Well, if **"Leaves"** is lace, it is taut and symmetrical lace, with scarce a loose thread. It was written after long silence, swiftly, unerringly as a sleepwalker walks. No memory of any revision mars my backwards impression of it. The way the leaves become the pages, the way the bird becomes his description, the way the bright and multiform world of nature is felt rubbing against the dark world of the trapped ego—all strike me as beautiful, and of the order of artistic "happiness" that is given rather than attained. The last image, the final knot of lace, is an assertion of transcendental faith scaled, it seems to me, nicely to the mundane.

"Leaves" is a very brief story, only nine paragraphs long, but in its integration of imagery and subtlety of structure it represents well Updike's successful effort to engage the Reality-Art-Imagination relationships, and as a prose-poem it exemplifies the Stevens epigraph.

The title **"Leaves"** itself suggests multiple meanings, each warranted in the story, for the word "leaves" can connote the product of Nature (as in grape leaves), and, as a verb, can indicate departure, loss, and time. Significantly, it can also suggest a book's "leaves," its pages, which are the outcome of art. The story is ostensibly a confession-meditation in that the narrator, now isolated in a forest retreat, is essaying to recover from the emotional disaster of imminent divorce by "sorting out the events" of his predicament. The story's framework is both heuristic and cruciform. The crux or X pattern is manifest in the sequence of reflections as the narrator pursues the "connections" among them.

The opening paragraph is reminiscent of the Stevens epigraph, for in it the narrator realizes that his previous self-absorption has blinded him to the paradoxical discovery that, on the one hand, although he and Nature are independent, his "curiosity" or attention now unites them and, on the other hand, although physically part of Nature, his spiritual consciousness—now ironically the source of his guilt—also separates him from it.

> The grape leaves outside my window are curiously beautiful. "Curiously" because it comes upon me as strange, after the long darkness of self-absorption and fear and shame in which I have been living, that things are beautiful, that independent of our catastrophes they continue to maintain the "effect," which is the hallmark and specialty of Nature. Nature: this morning it seems to me very clear that Nature may be defined as that which exists without guilt. Our bodies are in Nature; our shoes, their laces, the little plastic tips of the laces—everything around us and about us is in Nature, and yet something holds us away from it, like the upward push of water which keeps us from touching the sandy bottom. . . .

This discernment about Nature and yet "that something that holds us back" from it, in turn, issues in another realization: man's limited power to make contact with and arrest Nature through language. Here the elusive natural object is a blue jay. The bird itself might "leave," but a book's "leaves" might capture it—another "curious" relationship for reflection.

> A blue jay lights on a twig outside my window. Momentarily sturdy, he stands astraddle, his dingy rump toward me, his head alertly frozen in silhouette. . . . See him? I do, and, snapping the chain of my thought, I have reached through glass and seized him and stamped him on this page. Now he is gone. And yet, there, a few lines above, he still is, "astraddle," rump "dingy," his head "alertly frozen." A curious trick, possibly useless, but mine.

The third paragraph then merges these self-nature, art-nature contrasts and congruities and develops them by introducing the story's controlling images. These images will be re-"connected" and transformed in the story's final paragraph.

> The grape leaves where they are not in each other's shadow are golden. Flat leaves, they take the sun flatly, and turn the absolute light, sum of the spectrum and source of all life, into the crayon yellow with which children render it. Here and there, wilt transmutes this lent radiance into a glowing orange, and the green of the still tender leaves—for green persists long into autumn, if we look—strains from the sunlight a fine-veined chartreuse. The shadows these leaves cast upon each other, though vagrant and nervous in the wind that sends friendly scavenging rattles scurrying across the roof, are yet quite various and definite, containing innumerable barbaric suggestions of scimitars, flanged spears, prongs, and menacing helmets. The net effect, however, is innocent of menace. On the contrary, its intricate simultaneous suggestion of shelter and openness, warmth and breeze, invites me outward; my eyes venture into the leaves beyond. I am surrounded by leaves. The oak's are tenacious claws of purplish rust; the elm's, scant feathers of a feminine yellow; the sumac's, a savage, toothed blush. I am upheld in a serene and burning universe of leaves. Yet something plucks me back, returns me to that inner darkness where guilt is the sun.

Reality and imagination conjoin by contrast. The shadowless "flat leaves" of Nature, by taking the sunlight "flatly," spontaneously transmute the sun's real shape and color the way a child's crayon would. A parallel transmutation takes place as well. The "shadows these leaves cast" take on a human coloration and suggest to the narrator's imagination a simultaneity of opposites, for they are at once barbaric and menacing, yet open and inviting. Invited outward, only his eyes can venture *into* the leaves; once there, he perceives, amid other ferocious shapes, that the elm leaves are "feminine yellow." Yet "something plucks him back," his realization of his ironic contrast with Nature. Whereas Nature's leaves, in receiving the sun flatly, had transmuted it, his guilt-consciousness which is *his* sun finally transmutes the "serene and burning universe of leaves" and returns him to the darkness of self-isolation.

The apprehension of his private predicament leads him to reflect upon its "connective" implications. Leaf-related imagery is introduced once more, but here its use dramatizes the ironic contrast between Nature and the human spirit. The implication is clear: despite the union of descriptive "images," *actual* union between spirit and Nature *seems* impossible; only a sharpening of one's awareness of our dialectical predicament seems possible.

> . . . And once the events are sorted out—the actions given motivations, the actors assigned psychologies, the miscalculations tabulated, the abnormalities named, the whole furious and careless growth pruned by explanation and rooted in history and returned, as it were, to Nature—what then? Is such a return serious? Can our spirits really enter Time's haven of mortality and sink composedly among the mulching

leaves? No: we stand at the intersection of two kingdoms, and there is no advance and no retreat, only a sharpening of the edge where we stand.

The fifth paragraph, and hence "middle" section of this nine-paragraph story, concerns the "sharpening edge" of memory, for the narrator remembers "most sharply" the black of his wife's V-shaped dress as she "leaves" to get her divorce.

> I remember most sharply the black of my wife's dress as she left our house to get her divorce. The dress was a soft black sheath, with a V neckline, and Helen always looked handsome in it; it flattered her pallor. This morning she looked especially handsome, her face utterly white with fatigue. Yet her body, that natural thing, ignored our catastrophe, and her shape and gestures were incongruously usual. She kissed me lightly in leaving. . . . And I, satisfied at last, divorced, studied my children with the eyes of one who had left them, examined my house as one does a set of snapshots from an irrevocable time, drove through the turning landscape as a man in asbestos cuts through a fire, met my wife-to-be—weeping yet smiling, stunned yet brave—and felt, unstoppably, to my horror, the inner darkness burst my skin and engulf us both and drown our love. The natural world, where our love had existed, ceased to exist. My heart shied back; it shies back still. I retreated. As I drove back, the leaves of the trees along the road stated their shapes to me. There is no more story to tell. By telephone I plucked my wife back; I clasped the black of her dress to me, and braced for the pain.

This paragraph recapitulates and broadens the color and fire imagery noted above, and the remembered "leaving" introduces a new "natural" association, for as his wife "leaves," her body, "that natural thing," appears unconscious of the catastrophe of their divorce. Here Updike returns to a frequent association in his fiction—that between women and Nature. This association provides the central symbolic thread uniting the novel *Of the Farm,* where the wife, Peggy, is allied throughout with "stupid Nature." In *Rabbit Redux* Rabbit, not unlike the narrator here, reflects that he alone experiences guilt because "women and nature forget." A rather subtle explanation for this association is offered in the story **"The Bulgarian Poetess"** from *The Music School* collection. There the novelist, Henry Bech, observes that sexual love is "a form of nostalgia. We fall in love . . . with women who remind us of our first landscapes." Bech is, of course, a fictional creation; however, two years before, in a review of De Rougemont's *Love Declared* Updike expressed remarkably similar sentiments by observing that a "woman loved, momentarily eases the pain of time by localizing nostalgia, the vague and irrecoverable objects of nostalgic longing are assimilated . . . the images we hoard in wait for the woman who will seem to body them forth include the inhuman—a certain slant of sunshine, a delicate flavor of dust. . . ." In short, contemplation of the beloved Woman simultaneously returns the lover to remembered natural landscapes, "images" he hoards, and to his very

self. This paragraph recounts this process artfully, for the narrator gradually realizes that his imminent divorce from "that natural thing" (his wife) has thus divorced him from "the natural world" (the leaves) and from his very self; only upon returning to his wife do the leaves again state "their shapes" to him.

This "middle" memory-interlude is brief, and the next paragraph returns us to the present time and his painful dread of what the future might bring. He fears his wife's rejection, for, with that rejection, "the curious beauty of the leaves will be eclipsed again." Earlier, the blue jay had spurred on his imagination; his writing about him "had seized and stamped him on the page" and made him "mine." Now, however, a spider is sighted, hanging "like a white asterisk," and, unlike the earlier blue jay, it "feels a huge alien presence."

> I catch myself in the quaint and antique pose of the fabulist seeking to draw a lesson from a spider, and become self-conscious. I dismiss self-consciousness and do earnestly attend to this minute articulated star hung so pointedly before my face; and am unable to read the lesson. The spider and I inhabit contiguous but incompatible cosmoses. Across the gulf we feel only fear. The telephone remains silent. The spider reconsiders its spinning. The wind continues to stir the sunlight.

Their "natural" alienation is his major realization: man's "self-consciousness" inevitably places him in tension with Nature, and yet he continually seeks "fables" there. The depiction of the spider, seen as an "articulated star," seems a deliberate pun to imply this "fabulist" power in man, a power both re-active and creative. What, then, of art, of man's endeavor to bridge this gulf through language? This key question returns us to the story's central image of "leaves."

> In walking in and out of this cottage, I have tracked the floor with a few dead leaves, pressed flat like scraps of dark paper. And what are these pages but leaves? Why do I produce them but to thrust, by some subjective photosynthesis, my guilt into Nature, where there is no guilt?

At this point of apparent impasse, suddenly the narrator notices the vital green amid the shades of brown and that beyond the evergreens "there is a low, blue hill. . . . *I see* it, for the first time in months I see it. I see it as a child, fingers gripping and neck straining, glimpses the roof of a house over a cruelly high wall." Just as in the third paragraph where a child's vision transmuted sunlight, here his child-like vision alters everything. This experience triggers a recent memory.

> Under my window, the lawn is lank and green and mixed with leaves shed from a small elm, and I remember how, the first night I came to this cottage, thinking I was leaving my wife behind me, I went to bed alone and read, in the way one reads stray books in a borrowed house, a few pages of an old edition of *Leaves of Grass.* And my sleep was a loop, so that in awaking I seemed still in the book, and the light-struck sky quivering through the stripped branches of the

young elm seemed another page of Whitman, and I was entirely open, and lost, like a woman in passion, and free, and in love, without a shadow in any corner of by being. It was a beautiful awakening, but by the next night I had returned to my house.

The memory of this all-too-brief but "beautiful awakening"—its significant associations, the unexpected short-lived union of both Nature and Art in his imagination wherein the branches of the elm and the page-leaves of Whitman unite to make him feel "like a woman in passion"—all these not only once brought him awake but do so again in recollection. The story ends with appropriate images of illumination, for no longer is Nature wholly "barbaric" and alien; the remembered union of Art and Nature alters everything, and, just as the "flat leaves" transmuted the sunlight, imagination can so transmute guiltless Nature that "sunlight falls flat at my feet like a penitent."

> The precise barbaric shadows on the grape leaves have shifted. The angle of illumination has altered. I imagine warmth leaning against the door, and open the door to let it in; sunlight falls flat at my feet like a penitent.

In both technique and theme we recognize similarities here between Updike and Wallace Stevens. Like so many of Stevens' poems, this story develops *through* an imaginative exploration of the potential implications of the central *metaphor*. The plurisignificant metaphor becomes an instrument for discovery, therefore, the vehicle for grappling with the mysterious relationship between natural reality and man's imaginative consciousness. The poem, or the story here, not only records this process of discovery and the problems engaged, but is the process.

Furthermore, not only does this story proceed like a Stevens "meditation," but it deals specifically with the Stevens problematic and, in a sense, reads like a commentary on the Stevens epigraph. In **"Leaves,"** the "real" autumn leaves at the story's start are both inviting and repulsive, and make the narrator aware that he is "at the intersection of two kingdoms"; these real leaves then merge with a memory of his wife's "leaving" so that once again "real nature" (symbolized by the spider) seems alien, for they "inhabit . . . incompatible cosmoses." These memories and thoughts then conjoin with his recollection of the imaginative *Leaves of Grass* which, in its turn, once had united with the elm tree "leaves" in his own imaginative "awakening," so that, finally, memory of this previous union of "leaves" brings a "new angle of illumination" to the real autumn leaves which he now imagines falling "flat at my feet like a penitent." The story's structure, then, records the central theme in Stevens: that, despite the apparent dichotomy between the realms of imagination and reality, a reciprocal interpenetration is possible, and the "leaves" of an artist's book can capture it briefly—"it" being a merger of reality, memory, and imagination. Nature informs the artistic imagination, and, in turn or reciprocally, his imagination *trans*forms Nature and the artwork is born.

In closing we should observe further, however, that the story's last lines ("The angle of illumination has altered. I imagine warmth leaning against the door, and open the door to let it in; the sunlight falls flat at my feet like a penitent.") also introduce a religious perspective to the scene that is non-Stevensian. As we heard Updike himself express it, these lines betray the further recognition "of the order of artistic 'happiness' that is given rather than attained. The last image, the final knot of lace, is an assertion of transcendental faith scaled, it seems to me, nicely to the mundane."

We have noted at length . . . that Updike's perception of the opposition between Creation and Nothingness induces moral as well as ontological questions. Man's self-consciousness, his sense of ontological alienation from Nature and Creation that **"Leaves"** explores, can inspire the Stevensian impulse to bridge the conflict via the imagination. Their brief union is achieved through metaphor, as this story demonstrates.

However, this dialectical opposition prompts other questions as well and addresses other chambers deeper than the imagination. For, as Auden emphasized in *The Dyer's Hand,* the imagination of the artist is itself "a natural human faculty and therefore retains the same character whatever a man believes. The only difference can be in the way he interprets the data." Unlike the imagination, then, that other aspect of consciousness we call conscience is rooted in specifically moral, not aesthetic, instincts and its promptings issue from a wholly different wellspring of beliefs about one's alienation from Creation.

Auden's "data" are common; interpretation is all. **"Leaves"** records *both* the transcendental movement outward of the trapped ego understood in aesthetic terms, and the equally transcendental movement in faith of the morally trapped ego as it seeks a different kind of "reconciliation," i.e. forgiveness, a realization that can only be "given rather than attained"—in short, a grace. (pp. 108-16)

. . . .

[*Bech: A Book*] addresses the more specialized problems an artist faces, as well as those more generally shared anxieties experienced on the American scene. The ever-shifting point of view, the multi-leveled irony, the varying psychic stimuli the different settings evoke, the doubling back in time-focus, the inclusion of comments on "classical" American authors, the scheme of question and answer interviews that subtly both unite and disrupt the ongoing "story," all of these devices contribute to the realization that Bech is definitely Bech, a writer by instinct and profession, and yet Bech is us as well, an American us in the post-Kennedy 1960's. To consign *Bech: A Book* to the category "comic satire" about writer's block is to misread its other, more universal intent.

Bech is called *A Book* rather than a novel, not because it lacks imaginative unity, but, no doubt, because it was conceived and architected in piecemeal fashion. Updike has admitted that when he returned in 1964 from Russia and Eastern Europe as a representative in a writers' exchange, he had collected some impressions peculiar to a writer. To convey these he invented the Jewish writer Henry Bech as a vehicle for those impressions and wrote **"The Bulgarian Poetess."** That story, which also appears in *The Music School* collection, went on to win the O. Henry award for the finest short story that year. Spurred on by this success, he then wrote **"Bech in Rumania"** and **"Rich in Russia,"** after an abortive try at a long Russian Journal, the remains of which are now included as an appendix to *Bech: A Book.* Domestic inspirations from America's changing scene in the 1960's led him to compose **"Bech Takes Pot Luck"** in an American setting; then a London story **"Bech Swings?"** made a Bech collection feasible. To complete it and unify loose strands, Updike wrote **"Bech Panics"** as a bridge chapter and **"Bech Enters Heaven"** to give it a final shape. Since the publication of this collection Updike has written three more Bech stories, and so a sequel can be expected. Like Rabbit, Bech lives on, ever ready to return.

In an interview in 1970, the year *Bech* was published, Updike, in a quote worth repeating, addressed the more specialized aspects of the collection.

> Now as for the *Bech* stories. . . . For a writer, life becomes overmuch a writer's life. Things happen to you that wouldn't happen to anybody else, and the way of using this to good advantage, of course, is to invent another writer. At first, he is very much an alter ego, but then, in the end, not so. At any rate, I have used the writer in *Bech* as a subject to confess sterility in a truthful way. . . . In my book I tried to— and I believe I did—package and dispose of a certain set of tensions which I have as a practicing writer. . . . Mine is merely a kind of complaint about the curious position the American writer now finds himself in; he is semi-obsolete, a curious fellow without any distinct sense of himself as a sensible professional.
> (pp. 154-55)

Bech in many ways is everything that Updike is not: he is a blocked writer, a bachelor, a Jewish celebrity whose emotional and imaginative roots are urban, a World War II veteran whose initial successes were published in the now defunct *Liberty* and *Collier's* magazines. To further that distance, Updike provides Bech with an extensive bibliography of primary and secondary sources, itself an hilarious gem, wherein we find a list of popular and scholarly dissections of Bech's work, the titles of which betray the scholars' mounting frustration with Bech's *oeuvre*. Updike apparently experienced as much delight in composing this bibliography as the reader receives. But, besides the artistic reasons, Updike admitted that the "bibliography was also a matter of working off various grudges, a way of purging my spleen. I've never been warmly treated by the *Commentary* crowd—insofar as it is a crowd—and so I made Bech its darling."

To compound the fun Updike has Bech write the foreword to the collection (an enterprise that takes him eight days), and Bech gives a rather restrained and quizzical blessing to its contents. The foreword is addressed to the author John and, should we mistake who that John might be, Bech subtly informs us that the "Bech" one discovers

within these pages is not necessarily all Henry but a literary gumbo concocted and flavored by "John."

> . . . in Bulgaria (eclectic sexuality, bravura narcissism, thinning curly hair), I sound like a gentlemanly Norman Mailer; then that London glimpse of *silver* hair glints more of the gallant, glamorous Bellow. . . . I got a whiff of Malamud in your city breezes, and I am paranoid to feel my "block" an ignoble version of the more or less noble renunciations of H. Roth, D. Fuchs, and J. Salinger? Withal, something Waspish, theological, scared, and insulatingly ironical that derives, my wild surmise is, from you.

That last sentence alerts us to the fact that, when we discover satiric nudges in *Bech: A Book,* the object of the jab is more often Updike himself, his own prose style, and familiar fictive angsts than Henry Bech. In fact, Updike considers *Bech* not "satirical, really; it was never really a concern of mine to poke fun at the Jewish writer, or the New York-Jewish literary establishment in this country. I hope I always gave Bech my full sympathy, my full empathy."

At the risk of dampening the rich fun in the book, it is important to emphasize that the figure of Bech himself and his Jewish background are introduced not in order to exploit ethnic particularities but to provide Updike with a symbolic figure whose problems and fears are able to represent both the literary situation and the ambivalent moral and cultural status of contemporary America in the 1960's. Here Bech's Jewishness is emblematic in multiple ways. First of all, when one thinks of a literary establishment since World War II, i.e. those writers who have repeatedly met with artistic success and have eloquently given a distinctive pattern of insight to American literature, it is quite evident that a sizeable number come from Jewish backgrounds. To be an important writer in the 1960's and to be Jewish were hardly synonymous, of course, but the expectation was keen enough not to seem far-fetched, although likely. Who, then, better than a Bech could embody those strains and anxieties proper to an American writer? Furthermore, once Bech was chosen, who better could exemplify the gradual and yet seemingly abrupt transition that had taken place within the American conscience and consciousness since World War II? In that 1970 interview Updike offered a telling observation on this very point by saying:

> All the graces we think of as Jewish reflect a totality of embrace of the world. It's something you feel in the Jewish sensibility that isn't elsewhere— although you do find something like it in Southern writing. Conceivably, the war ruined our sense of the world being divided and charged in every particle, a sense of the world that I think various Protestant writers have tended to view as part demonic. But it seems to me that the Jewish Americans kept up the belief a little longer—it is implied, at least, in their mental activities of all sorts. They arrived at the written page equipped with the belief in the instinctual importance of human events. . . .

However, I'm not sure there are going to be increasing waves of such writing from those with a Jewish background.

Bech's sterility and dread, therefore, are not restricted to a professional writer's "block" alone but are symptomatic of the immobility, futility, and desperation perceived by sensitive souls throughout American culture. That sanguine resourcefulness, once so characteristic of the American temperament and personified in its image of itself as the American Adam, was renewed for a time, in transformed fashion, by the energy and distinctive optimism of Jewish writers after World War II. As Updike himself observed, even the familiar Jewish "victim" figure was of a special sort in that "along with this sense of being a victim is an underlying tone that the world is somehow getting better under these awful conditions . . . there's always available some other kind of triumph, or the thought that what happens is in some way good for them, or, at least, the balm that is inevitable." One might add, then, that the post-War Jewish victim was not so unlike Billy Budd or Hester Prynne after all, and that the Jewish writer sincerely expected his own "barbaric yawp" to be heard, for he presumed the ears to hear were out there, anxious to hear his "song" and travel the open road with him as guide.

But by the mid-60's with his Whitmanesque *Travel Light* behind him, Bech finds himself at an impasse; both the old frontier and the New Frontier are gone, and he dwells in an America that is emotionally unrecognizable. Perhaps the finest parallel text to use in appreciating **Bech** and its themes is to be found in a speech Updike gave at the American Enterprise Institute in 1976 entitled "The Plight of the American Writer." In this address Updike relates the financial, political, and linguistic advantages American writers enjoy vis-à-vis their foreign confreres, but then adds that, despite these assets, "the profession of the writer in the United States has been sharply devalued in the last thirty years and has suffered loss both in the dignity assigned to it and the sense of purpose that shapes a profession from within." Unlike his foreign counterparts, the American writer lacks a "cohesive and tangible audience." Ironically, the very absence of artistic restrictions—not only political but also sexual—inhibits the writer in a sense, cutting him off from "the vocabulary of gesture and innuendo that society invents to circumvent its taboos [which] are so precious to art; one thinks of the moment when Hester Prynne in *The Scarlet Letter* takes off her cap and lets her hair fall down in the forest. . . ." Those very restrictions under which pre-1955 writers labored were challenges to their imaginations and elicited from them the "ingenuities of correlative symbolism, euphemism, and telling omission."

However, in an era where everything is permitted, explicitness is all and yet, imaginatively, not enough; when everything can be said, one wonders whether anything in particular is worth saying or saying in a special way. Bech's writing block is thus not a private affair, for Bech is the quintessential post-War adult: granted unlimited freedom of speech but without anything to say. Like his country, his own past success has inhibited him and, seemingly, rendered him speechless. Unsurprisingly, Bech will find imaginative refreshment only during the travel chapters; at least abroad he will be inspired to think big (and

that only) about his next novel *Think Big*. By contrast, on the home front he will be continually terrified by visions of decay and death and impotence. Impotence is a key metaphor here. In that Washington address Updike observed:

> If any law at all can be proposed, it is that art flourishes *before* a national potency has been fulfilled; Elizabethan poetry has more patriotic energy than Victorian; the Americans of the 1850's wrote with a confidence impossible to those of the 1950's. Not now could Melville write, "The world is as young today as when it was created; and this Vermont morning dew is as wet to my feet, as Eden's dew to Adam's."

This image of the American Adam amid freshness flourished in an era of pre-potency. Yet, we ought not forget that Nature herself continually presented a Janus-face even in this idyllic Eden. For those members of the party of Hope, the American wilderness was seen as wild but wonderful, meant to be tamped by Adam's feet and floriate through his sweat: Nature was his given, the New World was his oyster. On the other hand, as Hawthorne's ambiguous use of forest imagery and Melville's of the sea suggest, thoughts of an intractable Nature generated terrors as well, evoking sensations of hostility, brutality, and loneliness. Indeed, Nature and the land were part of the American promise; but that promise, reflecting the Old Testament covenant, guaranteed both life and death, vitality and decay.

The excellent [story] **"Bech Panics"** reenacts this primordial American ambivalence and updates it. Earlier in **"The Bulgarian Poetess"** [story], we had been told that, upon arriving in Sofia, Bech stayed in his hotel room all night, behind a locked door, reading Hawthorne (namely, "Roger Malvin's Burial"). "The image of Roger Malvin lying alone, dying, in the forest—'Death would come like the slow approach of a corpse, stealing gradually towards him through the forest, and showing its ghostly and motionless features from behind a nearer and yet a nearer tree'—frightened him. Bech fell asleep early and suffered from swollen, homesick dreams." For Bech, a man professionally prone toward creating images, this image of Roger Malvin will be re-created within him, just as Hawthorne the artist's personal dilemma is his.

In **"Bech Panics"** Bech is invited to give a series of lectures at a girl's school in Virginia at the beginning of Spring. The earth-smells of the countryside coming to life oddly fill him with dread and a fear of dying. His anguish is compounded by his contact with the virginal vitality and sexual innocence of these girls whose "limbs [were] still ripening toward the wicked seductiveness Nature intended."

> Their massed fertility was overwhelming; their bodies were being broadened and readied to generate from their own cells a new body to be pushed from the old, and in time to push bodies from itself, and so on into eternity, an ocean of doubling and redoubling cells within which his own conscious moment was soon to wink out.

Confronted by Nature's twin powers of creative newness

and foreseeable decay, Bech enters upon an existential crisis in these Edenesque surroundings, a crisis that reads like a parallel text to Kierkegaard's description of it in *The Concept of Dread*. He begins to wonder: "Who was he? A Jew, a modern man, a writer, a bachelor, a lover, a loss. . . . A fleck of dust condemned to know it is a fleck of dust." This identity crisis reaches its climax (as does the recurring imagery) while Bech walks alone in a wooded area on the outskirts of the campus.

> . . . the grandeur of the theatre in which Nature stages its imbecile cycle struck him afresh and enlarged the sore accretion of fear he carried inside him as unlodgeable as an elastic young wife carries within her womb her first fruit. . . . He felt increasingly hopeless; he could never be delivered of this. In a secluded, sloping patch of oaks, he threw himself down with a grunt of decision onto the damp earth, and begged Someone, Something, for mercy. He had created God. And now the silence of the created universe acquired for Bech a miraculous quality of willed reserve, of divine tact that would let him abjectly pray on a patch of mud and make no answer. . . .

Bech thus becomes a new species of the American Adam, one unforeseen by the optimists of a century ago. In his essay "The Plight of the American Writer," Updike outlines the unique development in American history that culminates in Bech's peculiar crisis. He argues that the very abundance of riches available in our virgin wilderness, combined with our rapid success in taming and exploiting it, made a new sort of individualism possible. Updike states that this individualism was further abetted by the ethos of Protestantism, an ethos that still characterized America right up to its expansionism via the moon-shots.

> The communal theocracy of the Puritan settlements, and the solidarity of the pioneers in the face of danger, are makeshift fabrics compared to the ecclesiastical and feudal interdependence of the Old World; by rejecting the mediating institutions of Catholicism, Luther and Calvin freed men to be independent, competitive, and lonely; and so Americans are. Also, by giving to the individual conscience full responsibility for relations with God, Protestantism, with its Puritan shading, conjured up a new virtue: *sincerity*. . . .
>
> The same passion for sincerity, however, tends to bind the writer to confessional honesty and to an intensity which cannot be consistently willed.

This paragraph reads like a profile of Henry Bech, for Bech is no longer, strictly speaking, a Jew except racially; the American ethos has done its work too well for that. Bech, instead, is now Everyamerican and those visions of abundance and vitality, which a century ago sparked exhilaration, now generate nightmares. Furthermore, to be both an individual and sincere—those virtues demanded especially of the American writer—inevitably issues in loneliness and the dread of the self–lie. The fears of Hawthorne and others have come true, for America and Bech embody them. After he recovers from this incident in the woods, Bech becomes embarrassed and angry that he cried to Someone, Something for mercy; as we learn in the comic final chapter, Bech's idea of "Heaven" and the "God he created" have been elsewhere for too long. His Heaven is the image of success, of making it, a distinctively American view of Heaven. Unfortunately, such a Heaven, being self-created and empty of mediation, inevitably is divorced from real Earth and its teeming vitality. Words like "immortality" and "eternity" have lost their spiritual connotation of permanence; now these words enjoy only an earthly meaning, that of endless multiplication, of a "massed fertility that is overwhelming," of teeming propagation without end or purpose.

Bech is childless, artistically sterile, and frightened at Nature's manic potency; nonetheless, he, like so many other Updike heroes, instinctively and yet almost by default (i.e. *faute de mieux*), adopts the contemporary identification of genital success with other more truly generative achievements. The post-pill paradise, rather than any other image of Eden, captivates the mind, and sex seems the only viable entry into recovering the deeper yearnings of the race and of the self. Sex is the emergent religion and the emergent Aesthetic as well, for the former Religious Quest for a Heavenly Paradise now is transposed into a Sexual and Artistic Quest. As a result, "Immortality" is no longer to be sought in union with God but is sought in a woman's arms or in the Nobel Prize.

Bech's writing block thus becomes symbolic of more than a literary crisis, for he unites these two emerging views of Heaven, identifying the sexual with the aesthetic. Unfortunately, as usual though, man must always die in order to get to Heaven. Throughout [*Bech: A Book*], Bech is ever in quest for an Eve-like figure; for him women are "supernatural creatures," vessels of special powers, alien forms as elusive as fictional inspirations have been for him. We are told that his "transactions with these supernatural creatures imbued him, more keenly each time, with his own mortality. His life seemed increasingly like that sinister fairy story in which each granted wish diminishes a magic pelt that is in fact the wisher's life. But perhaps, Bech thought, one more woman, one more leap would bring him safe into that high calm pool of immortality where Proust and Hawthorne and Catullus float, glassy-eyed and belly up."

When he meets the Bulgarian poetess, Bech feels that he might have finally discovered that prototype of Woman he had been seeking, that ideal to which De Rougemont refers. He and the poetess engage in a conversation about the Art of Fiction; but inevitably in Updike, this one Great Secret is allied with the other two [sex and religion]. Here the religious referent is not explicit, but the conversation implicitly touches upon those postlapsarian Adam and Eve realizations that each person reenacts in solitude.

> Vera calmly intruded. "Your personae are not moved by love?" "Yes, very much. But as a form of nostalgia. We fall in love, I tried to say in the book, with women who remind us of our first landscape. A silly idea. I used to be interested in love. I once wrote an essay on the orgasm—you know the word?—"

She shook her head. He remembered that it meant Yes. "—on the orgasm as perfect memory. The one mystery is, what are we remembering?"

But Bech and the poetess must part. His nostalgia, his quest for immortality, his efforts at retrieving memory and mystery will be directed elsewhere. This is what makes the book's final chapter, **"Bech Enters Heaven,"** at once so poignant and comic. Bech's memory and nostalgia, frustrated in the areas of Sex and Religion, have too long concentrated on their possible redemption through Art. His Eden has become a reminiscence of that grey building in northwest Manhattan to which his mother dragged him as a boy. Now no longer a boy and so with Eden behind him, he must face forward: what was Paradise past, an Eden, has become Paradise future, a Heaven.

However, Memory and Hope must always meet in Irony, and in irony the book ends with Bech being inducted into this literary Olympus of his and his mother's dreams; at last he has won immortality amid the mummies of the literary establishment.

> The light in his eyes turned to warm water. His applause ebbed away. He sat down. Mildred nudged him. Josh Glazer shook his hand, too violently. Bech tried to clear his vision by contemplating the backs of the heads. They were blank: blank shabby backs of a cardboard tableau lent substance only by the credulous, by old women and children. His knees trembled, as if after an arduous climb. He had made it, he was here, in Heaven. Now what?

(pp. 155-63)

Joyce Carol Oates on Updike's oeuvre:

Out of contradictory forces that, taken very seriously, have annihilated other writers or reduced them to fruitless angry quarrels in the guise of literary works, Updike has fashioned a body of writing that is as rich, mysterious, and infinitely rewarding as life itself—which, in fact, it *is,* finally claiming no intellectual or moral excuse for its own being. It is uniquely Updike's, and uniquely American. Updike exiled from America is unthinkable, and America without Updike to record it—unthinkable as well. His special value for us is his willingness to be disarmed of perspective, to allow his intensely-realized worlds to flower with something of the mysterious effortlessness of nature itself, and to attempt to spiritualize the flesh since, for many in our time, the "flesh" may be all that remains of religious experience. The charge that Updike is too fascinated with the near-infinitesimal at the cost of having failed to create massive, angry works of art that more accurately record a violent time is unfair, because it is far more difficult to do what Updike does. Like [his protagonists] he accepts the comic ironies and inadequacies of ordinary life.

Joyce Carol Oates, in her "Updike's American Comedies,"
in Modern Fiction Studies, *Autumn 1975.*

George W. Hunt, S. J., in his John Updike and the Three Great Secret Things: Sex, Religion, and Art, *William B. Eerdmans Publishing Company, 1980, 232 p.*

Jane Barnes   (essay date 1981)

[*Barnes is an American educator, critic, and novelist. In the following essay, in which she examines* Too Far to Go, Problems, *and several of Updike's earlier stories, Barnes argues that many of Updike's works feature essentially the same protagonist and emphasize themes of family life.*]

In 1979, two collections of John Updike's stories appeared, [**Too Far To Go** and **Problems**]. Rather than review these books by themselves, I want to discuss the stories in the new collections that round out one distinct phase of Updike's involvement with themes of family life. It is a phase which began with the Olinger stories and which follows a single narrator through his adolescence, marriage, and divorce. From story to story, this narrator appears in slightly different guises—his name changes, he lives in different towns or cities. Of course, not all the narrators of all the stories are this narrator; but from the Olinger fictions to the most recent ones, certain traits of character and key repetitions from a particular life story identify several heroes as one man.

To a great extent, the tension in these stories derives from the conflict between the illusions fueling the adult from the past and the demands made on him as a parent and husband in the present. His childhood hopes, desires, dreams are frustrated by family life, and Updike's narrator is constantly turning back—less and less, however, to rediscover his childhood's glory. As he passes through his cycles of hope, discouragement, and liberation, his childhood becomes the text which he earnestly studies for clues to who he is and what he should do and how he got into his situation in the first place. Over the 20 or so years during which Updike has published stories, much of the drama has been generated by the narrator's changing view of his relation to his mother and father, as well as the changing way he regards their marriage. In fact, his first marriage seems largely undertaken in imitation of his parents'. The narrator's slow coming to terms with his unhappiness in the marriage, his falling in love, and gradual accumulation of the nerve to act (to divorce and remarry)— all these occur because of revisions in his understanding of the past.

In the early Olinger stories, during the narrator's boyhood, he is subject to the willful, frustrated, hard-working adults who roam the house like lions pacing the narrow dimensions of their cage. The narrator is a gifted only child who is both admired and excluded by his contemporaries. Within his family, a once prosperous group who've fallen on hard times, his talents give him a special role. His mother's parents and his parents share a large house; suppressed furies make it feel small, and the boy's sensitivities pick up every last feathery vibration of the conflicts binding the adults. From the start, he is also conscious of his mother's urging him to take advantage of his gifts, to fly, to escape the fate she has suffered.

In **"Flight,"** the narrator looks up from the newspaper while he is reading to his grandfather.

> It would dawn on me then that his sins were likely no worse than any father's. But my mother's genius was to give the people closest to her mythic intensity. I was the phoenix. My father and grandmother were legendary invader-saints, she springing out of some narrow vein of Arab blood in the German race and he coming over from the Protestant wastes of New Jersey, both of them serving and enslaving their mates with their prodigious powers of endurance and labor. For my mother felt that she and her father alike had been destroyed by marriage, made captive by people better yet less than they. It was true my father loved Mom Baer, and her death made him seem more of an alien than ever. He, and her ghost, stood to one side, in the shadows but separate from the house's dark core, the inheritance of frustration and folly that had descended from my grandfather to my mother and me, and that I, with a few beats of my grown wings, was destined to reverse and redeem.

It is worth quoting this passage at length because so much that unravels in the later stories is tied here in intricate knots. Updike's narrator returns repeatedly to these key elements: his understanding that his mother and father are unhappily married, that his mother is the larger spirit of his two parents, that his father represents virtue, and that he, the boy, is divided between them. As a boy, while he is still his mother's son, his sense of division is not as intense as it becomes in later years, after the narrator has married and is himself a father.

But during his own boyhood, he tailors himself to her unconscious demands. Several stories contain variations on the boy's sense that his mother is not happy, "that the motion that brought us again and again to the museum was an agitated one, that she was pointing me through these corridors toward a radiant place she had despaired of reaching." Repeatedly, the mother in these stories thirsts for culture for her son. Sometimes this drive is recollected ironically, so that she appears as a kind of no-nonsense improver—a sort of Carrie Nation of the mind; but, more frequently, the mother is the muse of transcendence, a destination which she believes, however vaguely, however wrong-headedly, can be reached through art. For her son, she is the first woman to be associated with art, but afterwards, women and art will represent the mysteries he wants most to understand.

In fact, Updike did grow up to be an artist, and though there is probably an autobiographical connection between the author and his central narrator, the important thing here is to settle what is set forth in the fiction. In terms of the narrator's profession, things are rather shadowy, as if his job were of third or fourth importance in his life. In one story, the narrator has "a job teaching mathematics to ex-debutantes at a genteel college on the Hudson." In another, he is an "assistant professor at a New Hampshire college." In **"Wife-Wooing,"** the narrator's job is a poetic composite of all men's work. "Stone is his province, the winning of coin. The maneuvering of abstractions. Making heartless things run. Oh the inanimate adamant joy of

jobs!" Richard Maple, the narrator of the central series of stories about a marriage that fails, commutes to an unnamed occupation. Like all the other narrators, Richard Maple's primary task is not business, but self-awareness. More than that, his first responsibility is to know the *meaning* of life; what he should do, how he should live.

For this man, women are the carriers of the mystery within which meaning may lie. His various, not to say conflicting, desires for them create the moral problem he struggles to solve. Yet when he marries, he marries young (long before he has had any real experience with women), and he chooses someone who is both "better and less" than he. "She was a fine-arts major, and there was a sense in which she contained the museum, had mastered all the priceless and timeless things that would become through her, mine as well. She had first appeared to me as someone guarding the gates." With one difference, the wife's limiting or critical relation to the narrator is almost exactly what he perceived his father's was to his mother. The difference is that his wife's superiority is one of class, as if he'd understood all his mother's urgings as a simple plea to climb the social ladder. Still, the effect of his wife's upper class is like that of his father's virtue, and in one of its manifestations (civic duty), is exactly the same, It is impossible not to feel that the narrator is repeating the pattern of his parents' unhappy marriage. He seems to be taking on his mother's suffering, in part because he identifies with her and does not want some pleasure she will never have herself. He assumes her suffering out of a desire to solve it, so that he might find an answer both of them can use.

However, once the narrator becomes a father his interest in his own father begins to increase, if not actually to shift away from his mother. The boy in the Olinger stories saw his father as a "ditherer." The young father regards the same man as a "potential revelation" and competes with his wife "partly in the vain hope of the glory his father now and then won in the course of his baffled quest." But this rising identification also complicates the narrator's sense of his role in his marriage. The closer he comes to his father—the more, in other words, that he is conscious of his responsibility—the more trapped he feels. As his sense of being forced to match his wife's virtue increases, his sense of diminishment waxes proportionately. He has not solved the suffering in his parents' marriage; he has repeated it.

The level of domestic irritation begins to rise. "He felt caught in an ugly middle position, and though he as well felt his wife's presence in the cage with him, he did not want to speak with her, work with her, touch her, anything." He begins to be unfaithful, though, at first, this does not involve him in any real conflict. Having lapsed into the familiar unhappy pattern of his parents' marriage, he takes the unhappiness in marriage as an eternal truth. There is nothing to do but pursue what little pleasure one can find (this pleasure, however, brings no real joy because nothing ever really changes) and wait for death. Then everything is suddenly, unexpectedly, and completely altered. He falls in love.

Though his ostensible problem is being torn between his wife and his mistress, this division is the twin of loyalties that were originally torn between his mother and father. On the one hand, romantic love satisfies the raised expectations he received from his mother; on the other, his wife and children have the claim of duty, a claim raised in the narrator's estimation by his adult appreciation of his father's strengths. Yet even while love forces the narrator to face his divisions clearly, love also seems to offer a whole new resolution to his conflict. "Seeing her across a room standing swathed in the beauty he had given her, he felt a creator's, a father's pride."

His mistress and the love they share offer him the chance to become the author of his own happiness. Their love is not just a chance to be free, but also to be his own father, his own man. At the same time, the narrator in love identifies himself with "the creator," the artist, and says that "in this museum I was more the guide; it was I who could name the modes and deliver the appreciations . . . I had come to the limit of unsearchability. From this beautiful boundary I could imagine no retreat."

He may not retreat, but for a long time he is unable to move forward. A series of stories reveal the narrator as lacking either the nerve, the passion, or perhaps the cruelty necessary to leave his wife. The love, which at first offered a clear alternative to his unhappiness, begins to subside, some of it actually seems to slosh back into the marriage—as if his emotions were like the water on the floor of a rocking boat. Though he does not act, he does seem changed, lovingly released in a new way. Nonetheless, while his love spreads out to the world in general—to his wife, his mistresses (he seems to start to have many again), his children, his dog—he still has not satisfied his specific yearning. He is much happier, but his life again becomes static. Once more, his conflicts are so well-balanced that he is paralyzed.

During this period, which stretches through several years, his memories of his childhood begin to serve a new purpose. In the Olinger stories, the narrator's childhood seems to be recollected out of a nostalgia for the past, and in the interest of drawing the original battle lines that marked the little boy's character. In the later stories, once the central crisis of the narrator's marriage has occurred, the stories about childhood seem to go in search of some liberating insight. And in **"Solitaire,"** the narrator finds what he is looking for. He has always regarded his parents' marriage as a difficult one, but he had never doubted its solidity. Having seen their perseverance as a support to himself, as a standard to meet and an example to follow, he comes to see how he kept them together, not they him. In **"Solitaire,"** the narrator plays cards and remembers his mother playing the same game years before.

> He knew now that her mind had been burdened in that period. Everything was being weighed in it. He remembered very faintly—for he had tried to erase it immediately—her asking him if he would like to go alone with her far away, and live a new life. *No,* must have been his answer, *Mother don't* . . . And she, too, must have felt a lack of ripeness, for in the end she merely moved them all a little distance, to a farm where he grew up in solitude and which at first opportunity he left, a farm where now his father and

mother still performed, with an intimate expertness that almost justified them, the half-comic routines of their incompatibility. In the shrill strength of his childish fear he had forced this on them; he was, in this sense, their creator, their father.

The narrator is forced to recognize how he literally kept his parents married, requiring them to stay together on his account. (The echo of this is heard in **"Avec La Bebe-sitter,"** after the narrator has fallen in love with another woman; he and his wife agree to stay together "for the children's sake.") But the more important understanding which comes out of this reexamination of the past is that he sees himself as his parents' "creator, their father." The Freudian logic or compulsion, tactful and twice-removed as it is in these stories, collapses as the narrator assumes the imaginative responsibility for his parents. All along, they have been *his* fictions, and insofar as he has imitated or denied them, he has relinquished crucial authority. But that is just the point: in seeing how the knot is of his own intellectual making (and not a hard, universal law), the narrator frees himself from the binding psychoanalytic tie. **"Solitaire"** ends: "He was a modern man, not superstitious even alone with himself; his life must flow from within. He had made his decision, and sat inert, waiting for grief to be laid upon him."

After this, the narrator slowly pulls away from his marriage, though as he arrives at his decision to divorce, he once more sees less and less difference between his wife and mistress. In **"Domestic Life in America,"** a story from *Problems,* coming home after a visit first to his wife and then to his mistress, the narrator is struck by the time 10:01 (and temperature 10°: things are the same and their sameness is repeated infinitely). Like his women, the hours and minutes are perfect mirror opposites. But the tone of the story is different from the defeated tone of earlier stories when the narrator saw unhappy marriage as the unchangeable human condition. Though the narrator now sees himself as driven back and forth between two sets of equally draining demands, one of the women (his mistress) gives him something he wants. She offers him sexual happiness, and, finally, he has reached a point where he regards himself as free to choose on the basis of his desires, whatever they are.

In the end, the influence his mother has on his life has declined to the extent that the once overpowering, magical fulfillment she urged him toward has become sexual contentment. At various times, Updike has represented sex as glorious or lost or the only alternative to the death of religion. In **"Domestic Life in America,"** sex is a simple human connection which makes him feel more at home on earth. He has come to choose this because he has given up on the morality that belongs to his wife and father. Yet he does not escape judgment. The virtue which he has found so frustrating in his wife, that very quality which made his father both "better and less" than his mother, that same virtue has the last word. His wife and father have been good, but diminishing, reducing life so it will be small enough for virtue to cover neatly its complexity. But what this means is that, by the narrator's own definition, embracing the complexity is both vital and immoral.

In **"The Egg Race,"** another story from *Problems,* the narrator goes back to a high school reunion where a classmate says, "You aren't half the man your father was." The narrator agrees. His father has emerged from the past as the real hero by whose standards Updike's narrator feels he has failed. In **"The Egg Race,"** the narrator speaks of having left his wife for another woman: "He had long contemplated this last, but would never have done it had his father been alive." Though he's made his way out of the charmed circle of the childhood world he shared with his parents, they have clearly left their mark on the shape he finally assumes. The individual he becomes actually unites his parents again, but in a form that declares his separation, his distinctness. He chooses the path his mother wanted for him, the road to a happier life, but by doing so, he leaves her behind. At the same time, he goes against the example set for him by his father (who, after all, stayed with his wife), and so always knows how he is fallen. I recently read in an essay by Freud that a very long labor will cause the imprint of the mother's pelvic bone to be impressed on the baby's skull; I can't think of a better analogy to describe the influence of his parents and their marriage on the final form of the narrator's character.

As the narrator comes to view himself as the author of his parents' marriage, so the author of the narrator seems increasingly to write out of a simple, coherent core. Both books of short stories published in 1979, *Too Far To Go* and *Problems,* demonstrate how fully fledged the author's understanding is of his narrator's place in his domestic world. *Too Far To Go* collects all the Maple stories, the first of which was written in 1956. None of them suffers from the stylistic excesses that mark other stories—as if the Maple series were the best stories from any given stage of Updike's developing perception. At each stage, Updike has written many stories about the insight of that stage, but the Maple stories represent his most polished statement. An exception to this is **"Domestic Life in America"** in which the narrator is named Fraser, though everything else about his life—his divorce, his wife, children, mistress—are straight out of Richard Maple's résumé, including the clarity of the story's style.

Because of the purity and sureness of the writing, the Maple stories are a clear medium for the narrator's moral dilemmas. The medium is rendered clearer still by the fact that the Maples' experience is considered all by itself, in terms of Richard and Joan and their children. The stories about the narrator's most romantic passion are not written through or for Richard Maple; yet it is known throughout the series that he has had love affairs, and he ultimately leaves Joan for another woman. Tonally, the stories are dominated by the itchy, loving irritation of Mr. and Mrs. which can't include the wilder reaches of emotion. That life swells in secret, and I make the assumption that the unhappily married narrator in the stories about a raging love affair is actually Richard Maple stepping outside his marriage. This is an assumption based on the differences and limitations of tone. The tone of the Maples' domestic affection outlaws lyricism in a literary as well as an emotional sense. Yet Richard seems to benefit from the experience of other narrators, which is why I imagine they are all one man.

But there are other links between the Maple series and the wider exploration of all of Updike's stories about marriage, family, and adulterous love. In *Too Far To Go,* the central problem between man and wife is sex. He wants it more than she does (sometimes it seems she doesn't want any). His sexual frustration, in its most profound implications as "unlived life" (Lawrence's phrase), reminds us of the unhappiness which allied the younger narrator with his mother. In *Too Far To Go,* Richard Maple's frustrated longing meets Joan Maple's cool reserve much as in the Olinger stories the mother's restlessness collided with the father's more temperate nature. Like that father, Joan is both "better and less" than Richard; his slow advances toward freedom and love identify his journey with the narrator, who realizes his mother's dream against his father's restrictions.

In the first story in *Too Far To Go,* **"Snowing in Greenwich Village,"** that dream exists as the young husband's niggling lust for a woman dinner guest. In **"Here Come the Maples,"** the last story in the collection, the couple gets divorced. Richard has fought for his desires and won, though it means failing his father even as he sheds him. Richard says to his eldest son, after he has told the boy about the separation, "I hate this. *Hate* this. My father would have died before doing it to me." In the course of the collection, what starts as weakness, slyly acknowledged, becomes a transforming force. The Maple's disagreement about sex is, in the end, a debate between the claims of society and the claims of the self. For a long time, Joan's side—the former—has more power in the marriage because she has rules to go by and Richard has not.

There are times when this makes her less appealing than her husband. In *Too Far To Go,* two stories specifically contrast her virtue with his irresponsibility— **"Giving Blood"** and **"Marching Through Boston."** Both are about her insistence on doing something for people they have no real personal connection with and his sense of being deprived of her most important affections. **"Marching Through Boston"** is a comic masterpiece about Joan's involvement with the 1960's Civil Rights Movement. Despite a bad cold, Richard goes with her to a march in Boston, gets a worse cold, and comes home wildly raving, "Ah kin heeah de singin' an' de banjos an' de cotton balls a burstin' . . . an' mebbe even de what folks up in de Big House kin shed a homely tear or two. . . . ' He was almost crying; a weird tenderness had crept over him in bed, as if indeed he had given birth, birth to his voice, a voice crying for attention from the depths of oppression." His charm carries the day; he wins the story hands down. Joan gets no points in the reader's heart, despite the fact that she is out saving the world.

In other stories, Richard's attunement to the "life that flows within" makes him quite awful. For one thing, in the earlier stories, he is hopelessly ambivalent. This compares badly with Joan's prim, but unswerving commitment to duty. In **"Twin Beds in Rome,"** Richard's move toward and retreat from divorce are emotionally exhausting to no avail. The lust which troubled him at the start of the marriage has graduated to love, but the fact that he addresses it to his mistress *as well* as his wife seems self-indulgent. Joan's dutifulness is clear, constructive, restful. In **"Waiting Up,"** Richard's dependence on his wife's virtue is actually disgusting. The story describes him waiting for Joan's return from an encounter with Richard's mistress and *her* husband. It's not exactly clear what the encounter was supposed to accomplish, but it was deliberately planned and executed in a thoroughly grown-up way. Possibly its purpose is for Joan to smooth over the social awkwardness of the affair having been discovered. In any case, the meeting doesn't change the situation. At the end, Richard persists in wanting both women, and the fact that he does makes us prefer the claims of society in the form of Joan over the claims of the self in the form of this selfish vacillator.

About halfway through *Too Far To Go,* it has become obvious that both of them have lovers. We have to assume that Joan's adultery is at least partially retaliatory, but regardless of what drives her to it, the fact that they are both having affairs and both know it brings them equally low. At first, in **"Your Lover Just Called,"** there is a little spurt of intimacy and rediscovery which comes with Richard's first realizing that Joan is attractive to other men. This accelerates in **"Eros Rampant"** when he learns that she has also been involved in complete love affairs. Finally, however, in **"Red-Herring Theory,"** they seem more petty than racy. They bicker about whom the other is really sleeping with. Joan's red-herring theory is that he pretends to be interested in one woman as a way of drawing attention from his real mistress of the moment. Set after a party, the story is as gritty as the overflowing ashtrays the Maples are cleaning up. The reader longs for one of these characters to make some sweeping, noble gesture, to renounce something, anything—even if it's just to give up smoking. In this story, they seem to have been endlessly treading the same dirty water, both of them, getting nowhere, stirring the same pain round and round and round.

Just as we lose patience with their problems, a new spiritual strength appears in their relationship. They pass beyond sexual discontent and competition. In **"Sublimating,"** they actually decide to give sex up between themselves (and thus to stop arguing about it). Other lovers are still in the background, but there is new clarity to Richard and Joan's characters—like windows which have just been washed. This sharpness does not bring them closer together. In fact, in **"Nakedness,"** the last story before the Maples tell their children they are separating, various bodies are stripped, but all that's exposed is Richard and Joan's individual loneliness within the marriage. We don't know about Joan, but Richard's thoughts about his mistress have a loving, solid—one might say husbandly—ring. His encounters with his wife are hollow. He nurses his insults about her in the privacy of his thoughts. " 'My God,' Joan said, 'It's like Masaccio's *Expulsion from the Garden.'* And Richard felt her heart in the fatty casing of her body plump up, pleased with this link, satisfied to have demonstrated once again to herself the relevance of a humanistic education to modern experience." If he once loved her for her erudition, he now no longer does.

"Separating," another excellent story, does not surprise us

with its news about the end of the Maple's marriage. It is remarkable as a revelation of Richard's changed character. He has altered slowly through the stories, but here he emerges, speaking with real authority. He has mixed feelings of love and guilt, hope and regret, but he no longer slides back and forth between the two poles of his ambivalence. He has made a decision in favor of the woman he really wants. As cruel irony would have it, his self-assertion robs his wife of the support of everything she's stood for. When he leaves her, Joan's virtue does not keep her warm. In **"Divorcing: A Fragment,"** she has lost her control; she is miserable; she begs him to come back after a year and a half of separation. There is the horrible suggestion that without a self to suppress, duty hasn't got a leg to stand on. It turns out that her virtue was just her form of selfishness, her method of keeping her husband. It was also her way of denying him, as his self-assertion is his way of denying her.

At the end of the collection, their roles are reversed. **"Here Come the Maples"** is the story of the couple's moment before the judge. Richard's values are triumphant. He knows what he wants and insists that his wife play by his rules. Joan is as fragile and accommodating as her young husband had once been when she was the keeper of the social order. If only because the author takes sides, lavishing his gifts on Richard's subtleties, we do, too. In the course of time, Joan will probably make a comeback as the world's most wonderful person, but at the end of *Too Far To Go,* we feel that Richard's upper hand is more than just a win. It seems like a step in the right direction of freedom, truth, and love.

Updike seems to write the way spiders spin: weaving his webs to catch life as it passes, spinning, spinning as much to survive as to astonish. He is probably the most prolific gifted writer of his generation, though the quality of his outpouring is uneven. The problem of picking and choosing between what is good and what is less good is related, I think, to his subject. As a rule, the stories about the particular narrator I have described seem to be better than Updike's other stories. These others fall into several categories: experimental (**"Under the Microscope," "During the Jurassic"**), descriptive (**"The Indian," "Son"**), and— for lack of a better word—journalistic (**"When Everyone Was Pregnant," "One of My Generation," "How to Love America"**). All of these stories have in common the absence of such literary conventions as character, plot, or dialogue. They seem to serve the purpose of unburdening the author's receptive mind of all the different kinds of information that he breathes in from his environment.

What distinguishes the stories about the narrator is the emotion irradiating the finely spun structures. They are more truly felt than the experimental or journalistic stories which seem too much like demonstrations of the author's facility with language and data. At the same time, the stories about the narrator also vary; between the earliest stories and the most recent ones, while the narrator is struggling to come to terms with sex and love, the style is often puffy, sometimes it seems downright anxious—as though the author were really not sure of the material. In the course of Updike's development, the problem of meaning has been complicated by and interlocked with the problem of handling his talent. At moments, he seems to have been swept away by sheer youthful delight, as though his gift were a marvelous toy; other times, a terrible piety seems to have possessed him, as though he could only live up to his promise by taking his Style seriously. And then his intelligence, along with his remarkable observing powers, presented real problems by crowding his attention with an embarrassment of impressions, details, facts.

These distractions get the upper hand when the author's moral grasp of his material is weakest. In **"Packed Dirt, Churchgoing, A Dying Cat, A Traded Car,"** for instance, the overwriting goes hand in hand with the falsely ancient tone of the young man. He comes home to see his sick father in the hospital, his thoughts coated by a world weariness worthy of a very old person who'd seen nothing but war, torture, and death. In fact, the narrator is a young, suburban husband who's seen nothing but peace and domesticity, whose real problem (as he confesses to a hitchhiker) is that he doesn't see the point of his virtuous life. This is not quite the same thing as confronting the void, though there is a tendency in Updike's stories to inflate American boredom into French existentialist despair. At his worst, there is more sneakiness than evil in Updike, more opportunism than moral questing in his restless, curious narrator.

Then, too, though the narrator is clearly a self-centered person, it is not clear that his suffering is more than the pinch we all feel trying to live decently with others. His suffering sometimes seems like pure whining—his philosophizing nothing more than a complaint that spouses can cramp a person's sexual style. It is generally assumed that Updike's stories about domestic life are autobiographical. This assumption seems to be made out of a worldly wisdom which allows all sophisticated people to connect what is known about the author through articles *i.e.*, that Updike has been married, divorced, and recently remarried) and what happens in the fictional life of his central hero (who has been married, divorced, and recently remarried). It *is* hard not to wonder if the narrator hasn't benefited from Updike's possible experience. At the start, the narrator is a timid, even a cowardly man. That he slowly, but surely has his way with women probably has less to do with a change in his personal charm and more with the unadmitted fact that the author's fame made him desirable and gave him unexpected opportunities, ones which Updike passed on to his narrator. There are times when the narrator's cheerlessness about his adulteries seems just insupportable, only explicable by something having been left out—such as the fact that this is not the typical experience of a lusty suburban male, but rather the typical experience of a celebrity who suddenly finds himself in sexual demand. The narrator's depression would be more believable if it *were* openly identified as the cynicism a famous author might feel towards a rise in his desirability that had nothing to do with his true human self.

Yet having made these criticisms, I want to disassociate myself from the knowing, worldly assumption that Updike's work must be autobiographical. I want to consider the role of autobiography in these stories, but I want to do it from the inside out. Instead of talking about them as reflections of the author's life, I want to discuss their importance in his development as a writer.

Updike himself makes the connection between the human content and the author's art. he speaks of his hero's sense of being the "creator" of both his parents and his mistress. From the start, we know the narrator regards women and art as equally mysterious, if not equivalents. We know that women have dominated his experience, that they are the media through which he comes to terms with the past, learns to love and begins to act for himself. When the author refers to the narrator's sense of himself as the artist of his private life, the association of women with art naturally teams up with Updike's identification with his hero. We can take this as the primary, the *essential* starting point of any discussion of the role of autobiography.

Having begun, there are several paths open to us, all leading to **"Domestic Life in America"** as a culmination of the art the author has evolved through his hero's quest. Through time, the resonance in these stories has deepened, the authorial voice has become true, simpler, wiser. As a collection, ***Problems*** is marked by the author's growth as a writer, but the best stories in the book are best because they are about the subject which is most crucial to Updike. In those, form and feeling are one; the problem raised and the problem solved matter because the human heart is at stake; the drama is literally tied to it like a creature punished in the flames.

The narrator is not that complicated a character, but he seeks complexity out. As he has explored the varieties of erotic experience and conflict, Updike's style has reflected the alteration in values and depths and types of feeling. The best Olinger stories provide us with a model of what Updike's recent stories have returned to. In **"Flight," "Pigeon Feathers," "A Sense of Shelter,"** there is more fancy writing than there is in ***Too Far to Go*** or ***Problems,*** but in both groups of stories the writing all serves a purpose. In the long run, the unruly impulses in his style seem to have been brought under control by the same principle that liberates the narrator from the past.

"His life must flow from within." As the narrator clarifies his values, as he becomes his own man, free of his ties to the past, Updike's style becomes simpler again. In **"Domestic Life in America,"** there are few unnecessary words, almost no irrelevant descriptions. There is a very clean-cut relationship between content and art, between the narrator's inner state and the story's language and design. In fact, it is a photograph of the narrator's feelings at this moment in his life, yet the story has more power than this description of stasis might imply. It has the power of Updike's best writing—his quick insight, wit, and catlike tread. I associate this purity of style with another source of power in the story: it reveals a new resolution of conflicts which the narrator has been wrestling with from the start.

"Domestic Life in America" describes Fraser's visit to his estranged wife and two of their children, followed by a trip to his mistress's household. The parts mirror each other like two halves of an inkblot. Though there are different people in each place, they present the same degree of difficulty. Fraser's guilty relationship to his own children is no better than his problematic relationship to his mistress's offspring. The reminders of death he finds at his first wife's do not go away when he goes to his next wife's. At the first, he is involved in the burial and emotion attending the death of their dog, a yellow Labrador. As he arrives at his mistress's house, he sees her pinching mealybugs off her plants and killing them. It is almost a tie between the trade-offs each woman involves. The wife, of course, has claim to his guilt; but in her intelligence, her nonchalance under pressure, her decisiveness, Jean also seems personally more attractive than Fraser's mistress. Gerta is rather vulgar, though humorous, and much more selfish than the woman he has left for her.

The sexual pleasure Fraser finds with his mistress is compared to the pleasure he always got coming home from work and diving into the channel beside his land. "It was as when, tired and dirty from work, Fraser had stripped and given himself to that sustaining element, the water in the center of the channel, which answered every movement of his with a silken resistance and buoyed him above its own black depth." While this comparison shows yet another similarity between the two households, it also contains the essence of their difference. There is pleasure for him in both places; and that pleasure has something to do with the unconscious (underwater) life of the senses. But his first wife contributes to this satisfaction only insofar as she is an aspect of his property. If she were all he had, he would have lost what made him happy as her husband. Though he owns nothing with his mistress, though he is actually a trespasser on her property (the gift of her husband), still Fraser is happy with her.

The equations between one household and the other mount as the story progresses, culminating in Fraser's glimpse of the time and temperature as he returns to Boston: 10:01 and 10°. The perfection of this image sets the drama in final clarity before us, recalling the whole history of the narrator's problem even while it casts this dilemma in a new form. The series of numbers demonstrate the similarity between the narrator's choices, but as the witness he is also another actor—one who can and does tip the balance.

Originally, the narrator was paralyzed because every action involved a life-and-death struggle. He could not move without moving against someone else. For the young narrator, identification with one parent meant attacking the other. For Richard Maple, giving his wife her way meant giving up his own. Finally, however, the narrator is compelled to act because not acting hurts himself. No one else is going to act on his behalf; he has to. But for him to reach this point the problem has had to change. The extreme either/or that characterized the important people in his life has subsided. The narrator slowly but surely has incorporated into himself the parts of his parents which, at first, he served alternately as absolutes. He takes his own shape, and as he does, the opposing principles in the universe around him cease to clash so violently. The sense of futility so often present in the early stories is transformed, not because the problem goes away, but because the narrator has

become engaged in it. **"Domestic Life in America"** is there as proof. The narrator is alive and well by virtue of his willingness to pursue what he wants. He has accepted the fact that this will hurt others, and does what he can to take responsibility for his part in the dog-eat-dog reality. He cannot change his feelings, but he does not hide or suppress them. While he also fulfills his obligations at the level of finances and work, the most important form his responsibility takes is acting on what he perceives to be "the real relation between things."

This last is from Marx, who also said that people would only know what these real relations were once they had rid themselves of their illusion. Through time, the narrator's illusions have worn away, allowing the difficult, tiring, moving human truth to emerge. The relationships which have had various kinds of power over the narrator turn out to be commanding for the simplest reason. These people, after all, are not the symbols he once envisioned. They are just the people he happened to know in life. He probably would have known them anyway, even if they had not fit into his sense of how the world was divided.

Division has haunted the narrator and informed the writer's art. It grew out of the boy's understanding of the differences between his parents and grew into his conflict between marriage and wife, on the one hand, and love and mistress, on the other. For some time, the division between parents and women was also between duty and self, morality and pleasure. In **"Domestic Life in America,"** the element of compulsion, of one thing versus another, has fallen away. There is still strife and conflict, but it is between characters who are both good and bad, who are as mixed as the blessings they enjoy and the penalties they pay. The arguments which the narrator worked out through them were always only partially true about the human beings. And the real debate was always one the narrator was having with them about his own nature. (pp. 79-98)

> *Jane Barnes, "John Updike: A Literary Spider," in* The Virginia Quarterly Review, *Vol. 57, No. 1, Winter, 1981, pp. 79-98.*

Donald J. Greiner   (essay date 1981)

[An American educator and critic, Greiner has written extensively about Updike, Robert Frost, and John Hawkes. In the following excerpt, which offers a thematic analysis of Pigeon Feathers, *Greiner emphasizes Updike's use of detail, memory, and time in the collection.]*

In many cases, a reviewer's praise of or reservation about **Pigeon Feathers** depends upon his attitude toward Updike's talent for locating a moment in time and then describing the details which make it special. . . . [Some] readers believe that his lingering over the details of life, the ambiguities of the daily routine, and the nuances of the smallest gesture indicates a narrow vision which brands him as unworthy of the designation "major author." I disagree. As the [line "What is the past, after all, but a vast sheet of darkness in which a few moments, pricked apparently at random, shine" from **"The Astronomer"**] suggests, Updike knows that we understand the past only as we seize upon the few shining moments of memory in the vast blankness of forgetfulness. We may misunderstand the "pricked" moment, or we may misinterpret its affinity with the present, but the effort to see it must be made. So many of the stories in the first two collections detail the threats to the security one gains in a precise evaluation of the moment that Updike will probably always have to endure the criticism that he is a minor author because he writes about little things. To insist upon this argument is, however, to suggest that loss of family stability, the insecurity of maturity and age, the conflict between marriage and imagination, and the pressures of memory are not dilemmas of immense proportions. Updike may praise in **"Archangel"** "Certain moments, remembered or imagined, of childhood," but he is concerned with more than that.

The epigraph to **Pigeon Feathers** from Kafka's "A Report to An Academy" sets the tone:

> In revenge, however, my memory of the past has closed the door against me more and more. I could have returned at first, had human beings allowed it, through an archway as wide as the span of heaven over the earth, but as I spurred myself on in my forced career, the opening narrowed and shrank behind me; I felt more comfortable in the world of men and fitted it better; the strong wind that blew after me out of my past began to slacken; today it is only a gentle puff of air that plays around my heels; and the opening in the distance, through which it comes and through which I once came myself, has grown so small that, even if my strength and my will power sufficed to get me back to it, I should have to scrape the very skin from my body to crawl through.

Updike scrapes the skin—willingly. As if hurrying backward, stretching toward moments already experienced but not yet obliterated, he protests against the slamming of the door. Like Kafka's narrator, he finds that his archway is no longer as wide as the span of heaven.

He cannot, for example, tell the complete story of his Grandmother's thimble or of Fanning Island: "For I thought that this story, fully told, would become without my willing it a happy story, a story full of joy; had my powers been greater, we would know. As it is, you, like me, must take it on faith." He has pursued his career, so the opening to the past has narrowed and shrunk. But it has not closed. **Pigeon Feathers** is Updike's race with time, his homage to the ghosts of the past. He *will* remember and create. yet the collection also looks forward, for it is his offering to the gods of immortality, part of an achievement on which he will stake his future. This tension informs many of the stories in **Pigeon Feathers.** Yearning toward the future necessitates grappling with the past.

Jack and Clare face this challenge in the first story, **"Walter Briggs."** Generally ignored except to be dismissed as a piece of fluff, **"Walter Briggs"** is an excellent beginning to a collection largely concerned with the nagging demands of memory. Updike carefully sets the time with references to Archbishop Cushing, Khrushchev, and Nas-

ser—this is a tale of the 1950s. Yet the specific decade is not as important to the story as the difficulty involved in remembering the past. Updike structures the story along the lines of a rough parallel: The two-year old daughter fantasizes a make-believe "Miss Duni" just as Jack and Clare probe their memories in an effort to recall a name from a past that might as well be fantasy.

Neither the child Jo nor the mother Clare cares about identifying Miss Duni. They merely enjoy the memory game. But Jack needs a "minimal element of competition" to excite him. To declare, as Robert Detweiler does, that Jack's ability finally to say "Walter Briggs" affirms his "joy about and satisfaction from their mutual past" is to overlook the sense of competition he feels with Clare. His determination to remember Walter Briggs contrasts with the easy tone of playfulness expressed by his wife and daughter. Usually their name game is fun, a bit of nonsense he and Clare play when "whiling away enforced time together." But this time the game breaks down because while they can describe guests at a party they are apparently returning from, they cannot call names. When they stumble while trying to name adults at the camp where they spend their honeymoon, we know that the highlights of their past together are beginning to shade away into that gray area no longer significant to the valuable persistence of memory: "Walter Buh, buh—isn't that maddening?"

They remember everything else about the man. He was fat, played bridge every night, was good at shuffleboard, fished near the men's tents, stayed behind after the closing of camp to help dismantle the metal pier, spent winters in Florida, and wore droopy hats. But they cannot recall his last name just as Jo cannot identify Miss Duni.

The point of the story is not the recovery of a name but Jack's compulsion to defeat Clare: " 'I can remember their professions but not their names,' he said, anxious to put in something for himself, for he felt his wife was getting ahead of him at this game." Frustrated nearly to the point of childishness, Jack gets hung up on this trifling blockage in the narrow passageway to his past. Inability to call the name from his memory affects his mood and attitude toward the present. But Clare keeps the game in perspective, side-stepping the stumbling block called "Briggs" to dance ahead: "It made him jealous, her store of explicit memories. . . but she moved among her treasures so quickly and gave them so generously he had to laugh at each new face and scene offered him, because these were memories they had collected together."

Although he is jealous, he tries to enjoy her easy access to their happy past. But his unfortunate sense of competition with Clare will not let him laugh as freely as he might. Upset not only at his "unsatisfactory showing" in the game but also at his realization that "their past was so much more vivid to her presumably because it was more precious," he enters his reluctant memory after Clare falls asleep:

> All around the cabin had stood white pines stretched to a cruel height by long competition, and the cabin itself had no windows, but broken screens. Pausing before the threshold, on earth

littered with needles and twigs, he unexpectedly found what he wanted; he lifted himself on his elbow and called "Clare" softly, knowing he wouldn't wake her, and said, "Briggs. Walter Briggs."

Shared experiences turn commonplace moments into the kind of private highlights a couple may build a lifetime upon, and thus scraping the skin on the door of memory may be a blessed act. But the ending of this story is ambiguous. Is Jack's quiet comment a triumph for them, an affirmation of his past with Clare, or is it a way for him to assert himself against her? Because of the description of the pines around their honeymoon cabin "stretched to a cruel height by long competition," the latter interpretation seems more likely. Jack's victory is ironic because Clare is innocently unaware of the intensity of his competition with her. The future of their marriage is as fragile as his memory of their past.

The transition from Jack's story to Clyde Behn's in **"The Persistence of Desire"** is smooth, for Clyde goes beyond Jack to plunge into his past. As he tells Janet, he is "always coming back." The marvelous first sentence, stressing the linoleum checkerboard pattern, pinpoints Clyde's sense of living in areas of intensity alternating between his present identity in Massachusetts and his "disconsolate youth" in Pennsylvania. Clyde, unfortunately, has faulty eyes, so he returns to his hometown to visit his childhood ophthalmologist and to stand once again between the "two infinities of past and future." The metaphor of eyes in need of corrective lenses exposes his distorted view of the past and thus his uneasiness in the present.

Updike's gift for the minute detail which contributes to the sense of reality allows him to describe Dr. Pennypacker's waiting room and simultaneously to point to Clyde's dilemma. The checkerboard floor suggests Behn's sense of intersection. The new clock on the table shows the time in Arabic numbers and thus with each digit change drops another moment of the present into "the brimming void." Upset by this stark revelation of lost time, Clyde looks to the familiar grandfather clock for comfort. Its hands are stopped. Unfortunately, his life has not. His comfort in this suggestion of frozen time where the past is only a checkerboard away is reflected in the accidental meeting with his old flame Janet. Hoping to recapture a sense of past love, he tries to ignore the flow of each moment to the void. He fails to understand, for example, when he reads that the human body replaces its cells *in toto* every seven years. Clyde prefers the old cells, the old self. Memory, he hopes, stops time. Updike's allusion in the title to the limp timepieces in Salvador Dali's 1931 surrealistic painting *The Persistence of Memory* is unobtrusive and effective. Understating both the allusions and Clyde's urge to validate his past, Updike suggests the distorted nature of Clyde's desire and yet the poignancy of his need.

Both are contrasting colors on the checkerboard. Clyde is lonely in the waiting room and thus is grateful when the door opens to reveal his boyhood love. He is like a child again trying to hold on to some moment of pleasure long since terminated in the flow that turns experience to memory. His persistence of desire is misguided because it fails

to help him validate his past in order to reaffirm his present. He prefers, instead, to neutralize the present in order to relive the past. Unhappily, he is unaware of his dilemma: "Poor Janet, Clyde felt; except for the interval of himself—his splendid, perishable self—she would never see the light." But Clyde needs corrective lenses, too. Faulty eyesight affects his ability to cope. He tells Dr. Pennypacker that his twitching eyelid makes it difficult for him to think. For example, he admits to Janet that he is "incredibly happy" with his wife, yet he acts as if he still has an adolescent crush on her: "Happiness," he says, "isn't everything."

The description of Pennypacker's examination goes to the heart of the matter: "Clyde, blind in a world of light, feared that Pennypacker was inspecting the floor of his soul." Clyde's soul may be stale. Told that he may lose his eyelashes due to a fungus, he worries more about vanity than disease. Similarly, he is upset that Janet has forgotten what he remembers as an intense teen-age romance. In his conceit, he imagines that by marrying another woman he has deprived her of something special which is, of course, himself. Thus he glories in the guilt that he may have mistreated her. His vanity requires confirmation by his memory that he has made Janet unhappy by breaking off the affair. When she responds that she does not hate him, he is angry because her reply does not corroborate his view of the past: "Son of a bitch, so I'm a bother. I knew it. You've just forgotten, all the time I've been remembering; you're so *damn* dense. I come in here a bundle of pain to tell you I'm sorry and I want you to be happy, and all I get is the back of your neck." The narrator's suggestion that Clyde resembles a thirsty blind man begging for sustenance makes the point. His nostalgia is too close to sentimentality.

Pennypacker, however, is a no-nonsense man dealing with the present. His job is to supply corrective lenses which, he cannot realize, Clyde needs in more ways than one. His prescription punctures at least some of Clyde's illusions: Drops for the fungus, adjustable nose pads for the strain despite Clyde's vain but expected protest that they leave ugly dents, and instructions to wear glasses all the time because he is no longer in the third grade. "Thus Clyde was dismissed into a tainted world where things evaded his focus."

But not quite yet—Janet is still in the waiting room. Placing a note into his pocket, she slips out the door. Clyde, of course, thrills to this touch of conspiracy, to what he imagines is a promise of things to come which ironically will be a return to what he remembers of things long ago. But Updike knows better. Describing Clyde as an "actor snug behind the blinding protection of the footlights," and as a man who can no longer see the face of the new clock, he stresses the childlike blindness of Clyde's faith in the memory of desire. Eyes blurred by Pennypacker's drops, Clyde cannot read Janet's note: He wiggles it. He holds it at arm's length. He moves it toward his defective eyes. The note will not yield a single word. Nothing. Unwilling to give up and unaware of his problem, he decides that he can nevertheless detect Janet's identity in the shape of the handwriting. Desire quickens. He returns the note to his shirt pocket as if it were the armor needed to shield his wounded heart. The point is that he wants not Janet but the boy who once loved her. The note means more to him than her body because remembered happiness is more sustaining than current pleasure. In Updike's fiction, love may make either a museum piece out of the vanished past or an improbable goal for the unrealized future, but in the present it loses its magic. Clyde cherishes the note as a passageway to the past. Eyes still distorted, he steps into the streets of his boyhood: "The maples, macadam, shadows, houses, cement, were to his violated eyes as brilliant as a scene remembered; he became a child again in this town, where life was a distant adventure, a rumor, an always imminent joy." Nostalgia and the possibility of defeat go together. Unless he can use the note to purge his past and to face his present, the persistence of memory and the romance of desire will reduce him to a child.

Unlike many of Updike's stories about the allure of the past, **"The Persistence of Desire"** shows the main character confronting the object of his memory. The question left purposely unanswered at the end is whether memory will give way to reality. With the unreadable note in his pocket, a symbol of the unobtainable past of his life, Clyde will have to accept the distinction between the demands of the present and the lure of memory or else stop living, like the grandfather clock. Although these stories are not specifically about Updike, he has his own adolescence in mind when he writes the Olinger tales. Those years, he explains, provide a sense of unity to his canon:

> In a sense my mother and father, considerable actors both, were dramatizing my youth as I was having it, so that I arrived as an adult with some burden of material already half-formed. There is, true, a submerged thread connecting certain of the fictions, and I guess the submerged thread is the autobiography. . . . My own sense of childhood doesn't come from being a father, it comes from having been a child. We're all so curiously alone. But it's important to keep making signals through the glass.

The signals are not clear when Updike steps away from Olinger in *Pigeon Feathers.* Although the stories set in England draw upon his experience as an art student at Oxford, he is not as committed to that part of his past and thus he does not bring to these tales the complexities of emotion and perspective which make the Olinger fictions so effective. In **"Still Life,"** for example, his sensitive young man is in London, but Leonard Hartz is out of place. A slender, earnest American with "an unromantically round head" studying in the British Constable School of Art, he is alone in a strange city where chemists' shops are not drugstores and where tea parlors are not luncheonettes: "The American movies so readily available reaffirmed rather than relieved his fear that he was out of contact with anything that might give him strength." Leonard is the kind of unconfident art student who, when he attempts to draw copies of cast classical statuary, neglects his own idealism to sketch in even the casting seams.

His lack of confidence unfortunately extends to his relationship with the female students. Updike's quiet comic touch shapes the description in which Leonard sizes up Robin not as a potential lover but as an artist checking over a model: "like a piece of fine pink ceramic her ankle kept taking, in Seabright's phrase, his eye." **"Still Life"** stresses their differences and, by extension, the culture gap between the two countries. He is calm, patient, quiet; she is bouncy, breathless, blithe. Yet when Leonard is about to be embarrassed by an American acquaintance from his hometown, Robin rescues him with a "preposterous" lie. Unfortunately for Leonard, his lack of confidence with Robin is so pronounced that he inadvertently begins to assume a fatherly role with her. When she asks his advice about painting technique and then about modeling in the nude for the American friend Jack Fredericks, he fears that he is being "neutralized." His still life with Robin decays as quickly as the cabbage and onions they have arranged together. Reassigned to the classical statuary, she tells him that she never posed for Fredericks because he is a "dreadful bore." But her dismissal of Fredericks does not leave the way open for Leonard. The culture gap is too great. All he can do is agree that "All Americans are bores." Their tentative romance never gets beyond the state of still-life objects: Shy American boy, confident British girl. Arrange, focus, and paint. **"Still Life"** is competent but not distinguished, perhaps because the tone of wistful loss and the theme of the always receding past are absent. One suspects that Updike is too far removed from the story to care with more than his skill. Such is not the case with **"Flight."**

[In *American Writers: A Collection of Literary Biographies*, edited by Leonard Ungar], Charles Thomas Samuels calls **"Flight"** perhaps the "most brilliantly written of the autobiographical tales," and I certainly agree. Although it is the first story in the collection told in the first person, **"Flight"** is a companion piece with **"The Persistence of Desire"** and **"A Sense of Shelter."** Updike is especially good in suggesting the dual perspective of the boy going through the unsettling competition with his mother and of the mature man looking back on the experience. Not only does Allen Dow recall the time when he speaks of himself in the third person; he also remembers that the struggle with Mother has been going on for years. "Years before, when I was eleven or twelve, just on the brink of ceasing to be a little boy, my mother and I. . . ." From the vantage point of maturity, he now realizes that at age seventeen he was poorly dressed, funny-looking, and conscious that "a special destiny made me both arrogant and shy."

His sense of being special is ambiguous. Partly the result of Mrs. Dow's own frustration with her drab life, Allen's supposed specialness is also her most important dream for herself and her son. If we accuse her of trying to live through Allen, we must also recognize that her aspirations for his escape from the small town of Olinger save him from a similar frustration. **"Flight"** is the story of a mother-son relationship at a time in the boy's life when the father seems busy or asleep. Mrs. Dow prefigures the complex Mrs. Robinson in *Of the Farm* just as Mr. Dow becomes the Centaur. "Impulsive and romantic and inconsistent," the mother grudgingly accepts her static life in Olinger only because she is convinced that her son is going to "fly." But getting him into flight is her problem and his despair. She tells him at age twelve that he is special, and he thus becomes "captive to a hope she had tossed off and forgotten." Since she fears his "wish to be ordinary," she protests when he tries to fly the nest with Molly Bingaman without abandoning the limits of Olinger. This point is crucial to the story. Mrs. Dow is not so much against Molly as she is fearful that Molly will tie Allen to his hometown.

Updike is especially perceptive in capturing the uneasy ambivalence of Allen's predicament. He sketches in the sense of generations by describing in a few paragraphs the tensions that identify Allen's ancestors as far back as his great-grandfather. "Perhaps," says the mature Allen, "prolonged fear is a ground of love." Wondering if "each generation of parents commits atrocities against their children," he uses the memory of his adolescent love of Molly to ponder his relationship with his mother. The genius of **"Flight"** is that Allen's recollection of Mrs. Dow is as inconsistent as he claims she is. His descriptions hit the mark: She is precocious yet believes in ghosts; handsome, she has a deprecating smile; a fabric snob with a generous clothes allowance, she marries the penniless son of a minister; and though she obeys her own father, she, like Allen, tries to escape Olinger. The key to the relationship between Allen and his mother may be found in the mature Allen's realization that he has misunderstood her attitude toward her own father all along, that she fights with him not because of desperation or anger but because she cannot leave him alone. The same is true in the mutual relationship between mother and son. Allen needs to tell this story in order to understand a past which continues to puzzle him. Without the past, of course, there is no meaningful present and thus no basis for growth and knowledge. Allen's story is paradoxically both his most strenuous flight from and his most determined effort to know his roots. Plunging into the past in order to tell his tale, he hopes to soar from memory toward the future. He realizes now that he has successfully found his role in his mother's dreams for him, for Mrs. Dow is above all a mythmaker, a frustrated woman who gives those closest to her "mythic immensity." Allen is her phoenix. Believing that she and her father have been destroyed by marriage, she raises her son as a hero who will fly from the desolation of her domestic life and thereby redeem her.

No wonder she discourages his attraction to teen-aged girl friends. The second half of **"Flight"** details Allen's journey with three girls during his senior year in high school to debate at another school over one hundred miles from Olinger. There, away from mother and the inhibiting routine of home, Allen discovers the "beautiful skin, heartbreaking skin" of Molly to whom he has before not paid the slightest attention. He mistakenly thinks she frees him. He jokes with Molly, dances with Molly, and for the first time in his life stays up past midnight talking with Molly. From today's perspective, he has forgotten the details of what must have been a pivotal night in his adolescence: "What did we say? I talked about myself." Yet the experience lodges in his memory, and we suspect that his attraction to Molly has itself become mythologized in his mind as the first serious step away from mother.

How wrong he is at the time. Mrs. Dow sees the ostensible outward-bound footprint for what it is, a step toward married life in Olinger. Still clinging to the dream that her son will somehow soar from the small town and thereby atone for her own disappointing life, she counterattacks as soon as Allen returns from the trip: "Don't go with little women, Allen. It puts you too close to the ground." Unfortunately for the teen-ager, but luckily for the man, friends, teachers, and both sets of parents conspire to separate him from Molly: "The entire town seemed ensnarled in my mother's myth, that escape was my proper fate. It was as if I were a sport that the ghostly elders of Olinger had segregated from the rest of the livestock and agreed to donate in time to the air." His youthful vanity, as he now remembers, is so great that he believes all of Olinger focuses upon his plight. In his bewilderment, Allen criticizes Molly because the affair makes him see an "ignoble, hysterical, brutal aspect" of his mother. But things are not that simple. He recognizes now, although he fails to do so as a teen-ager, that Mrs. Dow's apparent pettiness results as much from the daily presence of her dying father as from her desire for Allen's flight. The competing tensions from two generations of men nearly exhaust her.

Like Clyde Behn, Allen Dow returns to memory to discover who he was all those years ago, but unlike Clyde, he does not like all that he finds.

> [Molly] gave herself to me anyway, and I had her anyway, and have her still, for the longer I travel in a direction I could not have taken with her, the more clearly she seems the one person who loved me without advantage. I was a homely, comically ambitious hillbilly, and I even refused to tell her I loved her, to pronounce the word "love"—an icy piece of pedantry that shocks me now that I have almost forgotten the context of confusion in which it seemed wise.

Allen inadvertently conspires with his mother to hurt Molly, and he realizes now that his attraction to her was not only desire but also rebellion. Innocent Molly is the injured loser. His angry retort to Mrs. Dow that he will reject a girl she disapproves of only this one time prompts her reply, "Goodbye, Allen." She launches him into flight.

But this dismissal to the world is partly ironic, for, as we know from the story, Allen's flight takes him both forward into adulthood and back into memory where the tensions remain and the wounds do not heal. The key phrase in the above quotation is his realization that he has traveled a direction in which he "could not have taken" Molly. We may not like Mrs. Dow, but her vision for Allen, no matter how selfish, is correct. Molly would have tied him down. Only Mrs. Dow knows that potential artists have to soar.

The genius of stories like **"Flight"** is that Updike fashions ambiguity about time and memory out of sketches of unextraordinary domestic life. Recognizable people do ordinary things. He shows the unresolvable complications that often rest at the center of mundane relationships. Nothing much happens in **"Flight,"** but the story reveals a lifetime. So does **"A Sense of Shelter."** A companion piece to **"Flight,"** this story has attracted many critics who continue to disagree about the ending: What is William Young's future as he leaves Mary Landis at the end of the story? Surely Arthur Mizener's reading [in his *Modern Short Stories: The Uses of Imagination,* 1967] is questionable: "He succeeds, and escapes back into the warm, stuffy world of the high school." R.W. Reising disagrees, [in "Updike's 'A Sense of Shelter'," *Studies in Short Fiction* 7 (Fall 1970)], suggesting that William escapes from the high school toward his happy future. [Other critics] seem more correct when they note the irony of the ending. William's "humiliated, ugly, educable self" may feel "clean and free" as he thinks about the days ahead, but the details of the story undercut his sense of a carefree tomorrow.

As in **"Flight,"** Updike mentions the mother (who this time likes the girl), the confused high-school boy trying to come of age, and the sweetheart who represents a first step away from home. There are differences, however, which make **"A Sense of Shelter"** not a retelling of **"Flight"** but its own tale. The primary distinction is point of view. Told in the third person as William lives the experience, **"A Sense of Shelter"** does not touch as much on the processes of memory which frame many of the stories in *Pigeon Feathers.* We see William's high-school world as he does, but the point of view is omniscient enough to encourage irony created by narrative distance. In addition, **"A Sense of Shelter"** focuses not on a boy and his mother but on a boy and his girl. Finally, William Young and Allen Dow have different attitudes toward school, home, and the demands of small-town life. While Allen hopes to take flight toward his future, William struggles into his present. He loves the protection of familiarity too much. Note his reaction to the gloomy schoolroom on a dreary day: "The feeling the gloom gave him was not gloomy but joyous: he felt they were all sealed in, safe. . . the smells of tablet paper and wet shoes and varnish and face powder pierced him with a vivid sense of possession."

Yet no matter how snug and secure he feels behind the protective walls of the school, the outside beyond the window must eventually beckon. William resists the invitation. Not only does he see the parking lot as a blackboard in reverse; he also rejects the fresh air coming in from the barely opened window. William has the kind of mind which deals in precise observations. He knows, for example, that the temperature is "exactly" thirty-two degrees, but we notice that the snow fails to cover the tire tracks which William sees as scars on the possibility of perfection. He is poised, in effect, between thawing and freezing.

It is not as if William is exceptionally popular or admired and is thus reluctant to abandon the domain of acknowledged successes. He is a senior, a teacher's pet, and an occasional winner of a school election, but according to the student's definition of success, he does not fit in: No girl friend, no gang of buddies, no seat on the bus. Within his self-defined world, he is king, a benevolent master to unappreciative but respectful subjects. Yet his definition of life is so insular that his notion of kingship is ironic. **"A Sense of Shelter"** tells of William Young's effort to invite someone else into his world:

> So, his long legs blocking two aisles, he felt regal even in size and, almost trembling with happiness under the high globes of light beyond whose

lunar glow invisible snowflakes were drowning on the gravel roof of his castle, believed that the long delay of unpopularity had been merely a consolidation, that he was at last strong enough to make his move. Today he would tell Mary Landis he loved her.

From the initial description of Mary, we know what William will have to learn: She has grown beyond him. She approaches adulthood with her full breasts and poise while he looks at her from an angle of vision shaped by a second-grade memory when she grabbed his schoolbag and outran him. William has loved her, so he thinks, ever since, but she is still way out in front. Closer now to flawed maturity than to childhood perfection, Mary is the reality on the other side of the classroom window. Her hardness is suggested by her reputation as being sexually initiated, but she is also sympathetic, patient, and kind. She is the heroine who has stepped outside of the shelter, a character we may not wish to emulate but one we should respect. William, however, wants to make her the queen of his sheltered world. Updike needs only one sentence to show how far apart they are. When Mary enters a teen-age hangout, buys cigarettes, and steps back outside, William "yearned to reach out, to comfort her, but he was wedged deep in the shrill booths, between the jingling guts of the pinball machine and the hillbilly joy of the jukebox." He has yet to give up childish things, whereas she has left shelter to enter the world of snow. William prepares thirty lines of Vergil and answers all of the questions in Social Science, but Mary dates a man she meets while working as a waitress in a nearby town.

One suspects that William has never been there. A womb-like retreat, the school is coziest to him when the halls are nearly empty after hours, leaving him free to wander without the crowds of unappreciative "casual residents." His plans for the future depend upon school, for he romanticizes earning a Ph.D. and teaching at college, "section man, assistant, associate, *full* professor, possessor of a dozen languages and a thousand books, a man brilliant in his forties, wise in his fifties, renowned in his sixties, revered in his seventies, and then retired, sitting in the study lined with acoustical books until the time came for the last transition from silence to silence, and he would die, like Tennyson, with a copy of *Cymbeline* beside him on the moon-drenched bed." Mary is not of this world, and she knows it.

Holding on to the past and his crush on Mary, William fails to see that life is passing him by. He is alienated from girls, peers, parents, and self. The deflation of dreams begins when she calls the school an idiotic building which she longs to leave. Thus it is significant that when he bungles his declaration of love, he senses a panel pushed open in his world of closed surfaces. We suspect that he will never walk through it, but Mary wears a scarf, likened to a halo, and is ready to step through the door. As his myth of king and queen together dissolves following Mary's gentle refusal of his love, he takes the opposite direction toward the school basement: "Between now and the happy future predicted for him he had nothing, almost literally nothing, to do." Updike's juxtaposition of "happy" and "nothing" suggests a clue to the unanswered question about William's future: Will he ever walk outside to live, or will he graduate from nothing to nothing, a copy of *Cymbeline* beside his bed instead of an experienced woman in it? Nothingness seems to be in store for him, for *Cymbeline* supports his tendency to idealize his lover. A king within his imaginary world, William loses his queen when he refuses to acknowledge the door opening from shelter to snow. He exchanges an illusion of his past for an illusion of his future.

The prospects for maturity and love are far more promising in **"Wife-wooing."** A widely anthologized, justly praised piece, **"Wife-wooing"** is more a lyrical meditation than a conventional short story. Like the traditional tale, it has character, movement, and resolution, but it is much more concerned with patterns of language and nuances of tone than dramatic action. In one sense, the play on words is the plot of **"Wife-wooing."**

Young adults often admit that they are stunned by this story, that they reread it aloud to savor the pleasures of Updike's rhythmical prose and the luxuriance of sustained love. Not everyone agrees. [In his "John Updike: Style in Search of a Center," *Sewanee Review* 75 (October-December 1967)] Richard H. Rupp calls **"Wife-wooing"** "Browning gone wild," a "silly" description of an experience in which Updike "resorts instead to self parody." These comments miss the mark. What attracts readers to this poetic account of adult love is that the principals are a married couple with children. Many young adults are on the threshold of their own marriages when they read this meditation, and they find in it the promise of domestic difficulties overcome, of romance alive beyond the first years together. How seriously they take the line, "courting a wife takes tenfold the strength of winning an ignorant girl." Even at an age when most are still exchanging fraternity pins and engagement rings, they know the truth of that comment and hope that the word "wife" does "not end the wooing."

"Wife-wooing" appeals, however, to all kinds of readers. The meditation is as much about art as about sex, and in an indirect way, it is Updike's homage to James Joyce, an author who could express the eroticism of "smackwarm woman's thigh" as well as "feel the curious and potent, inexplicable and irrefutably magical life language leads within itself." In this sense, women resemble language. Both are mysterious, powerful, and above all creative. Yet the husband's language is also partly a parody of Joyce. The soaring prose, full of alliteration and caesura, adds to the humor as the husband suggests an affinity between modern lover and Anglo-Saxon poet. Gently mocking himself while seriously declaring his love for the bare-thighed woman beside him, he likens his family eating hamburgers in front of the fireplace to primitive lovers before the fire.

The narrator senses the creative unity of language and woman, but he feels let down watching his family eat the fast-food dinner. One reason is that he lacks Joyce's power. Like an Anglo-Saxon poet, he sings of his exploits: "I wielded my wallet, and won my way back." But Joyce's "smackwarm" is better. Another reason is that he is not a hero, no Leopold Bloom enshrined in fiction, much less

Ulysses enshrined in myth. Rather than wrestle meat from the forest and then circle back to his cave, he drives to the nearest hamburger joint. Although he is serious about his declaration of love, he can view himself with irony. Note the self-mockery in his mock-heroic description of the diner: "a ferocious place, slick with savagery, wild with chrome; young predators snarling dirty jokes menaced me, old men reached for me with coffee-warmed paws." One cannot help but like such a narrator.

Most of all he worries that erotic love no longer binds man and wife after seven years of marriage and three children. Looking at his wife's exposed thighs as she sits with knees drawn up in front of the fireplace, he is aware of the demands which the children beside her make. The little girl asks questions, "enunciating angrily, determined not to let language slip on her tongue." The two-year-old boy cannot quite grab language which the husband describes as "thick vague handles swirling by." He has a similar problem: How does he communicate the mystery of love and sexual desire to a "cunning" woman he has known for so long? Where is the pleasure of surprise when "we sense everything between us, every ripple, existent and non-existent; it is tiring"? The point is that all of these expressions are in his mind. Unlike Joyce, he has not yet found a way to translate his emotion into language equally fervent: "Once my ornate words wooed you." When the wife ignores his unspoken invitation to sexual love in order to read a book about Richard Nixon, he is angry and then glad when, the next morning, he notices that, not yet dressed, she is drab.

One can only marvel at the end of **"Wife-wooing."** Returning home from a day's run with the rat race in the city, so preoccupied with a business problem that his wife serves his supper as "less than a waitress," he hardly notices when once more she goes upstairs with the book about Nixon:

> So I am taken by surprise at a turning when at
> the meaningful hour of ten you come with a kiss
> of toothpaste to me moist and girlish and quick;
> the momentous moral of this story being, An ex-
> pected gift is not worth giving.

The quiet irony is that she woos him. Surprises are still possible, even after seven years of marriage. She acts with her body and creates a love scene for him; he reacts with words and creates a love story for us.

The religious implications which inform much of Updike's nonfiction prose and which direct the thematic content of many of his short stories as early as **"Dentistry and Doubt"** in *The Same Door* are especially important in **"Pigeon Feathers."** The most ambitious story in the collection, **"Pigeon Feathers"** explores an identity crisis as adolescent David Kern faces the idea of his mortality for the first time. The theological implications are impressively worked out, but the story does not seem to me as memorable as **"Wife-wooing," "Flight,"** or **"The Persistence of Desire."**

Mundane events produce crises of the soul: David and his family have moved away from the relative security of the past. The move from town to country farm, recalling Updike's own childhood move from Shillington to Plowville, becomes a metaphor for David's suffering as a spiritual refugee and, in turn, for the alienation of all men who bother to think about their condition. The story suggests that formal religion is little more than a refuge against the shock of recognition but that personal faith may sustain the soul. As David realizes immediately, things are "upset, displaced, rearranged." Disorientation in the world of the quotidian thus becomes a metaphor for questions in the world of metaphysics. What better way to regain order than by arranging the books that have been hastily switched from moving crates to library shelves? But as David handles the books, most of which date back to his mother's college days, he senses the "ominous gap between himself and his parents, the insulting gulf of time that existed before he was born." Dipping into volume two of H.G. Wells's *The Outline of History,* he stares into "unreal and irrelevant worlds." His displacement gains momentum when he reads Wells's account of Jesus' death which denies Christ's divinity and which accounts for the genesis of a new religion called Christianity by discussing the "credulous imagination of the times." Jesus, says Wells, was just another political rebel. Convinced that this account of history is false, David is initially more outraged than frightened: "This was the initial impact—that at a definite spot in time and space a brain black with the denial of Christ's divinity had been suffered to exist." The problem is that David cannot supply rational objections to Wells's story of Christianity. It is not so much that he worries about the challenge to Christ's divinity but that his faith in God's ability and willingness to touch his life has been shaken. David finds the steps too easy from questions about Jesus to hints of his own oblivion to, worst of all, doubts about the existence of God. His "enemy's" point seems impregnable: "Hope bases vast premises on foolish accidents, and reads a word where in fact only a scribble exists."

His parents cannot help. They seem to have more troubles than he does. Preoccupied with their own domestic squabbles because Mr. Kern does not want to live on a farm, they argue whether the land has a soul. Mr. Kern's insistence that the soil is nothing but chemicals seems to ally him with H.G. Wells, while Mrs. Kern seems to echo David's faith by attributing mysterious essence to the farmland. Yet she unwittingly increases his fear by advising him about the present when he needs assurance about eternity. She fails to understand his belief that God has to be different from His creation and thus is not just *in* the land.

David needs proof. Triggered by the move to the farm, his disorientation so affects him that he begins to have visions not only of his own death but also of final extinction. He seems surrounded by possibilities of annihilation: His father's condemnation of alcohol and cholesterol, his mother's comments on heart attacks and dead earthworms, his grandmother's Parkinson's disease, the pigeons he is later asked to slaughter. The point is that he unwittingly illustrates Wells's argument that men read a word where only a scribble exists except that in his confusion he interprets everything negatively. Even his science fiction novels seem

to confirm "his impending oblivion." Worst of all is his horrifying revelation while sitting in the outhouse:

> Without warning, David was visited by an exact vision of death: a long hole in the ground, no wider than your body, down which you are drawn while the white faces above recede. You try to reach them but your arms are pinned. Shovels pour dirt into your face. There you will be forever, in an upright position, blind and silent, and in time no one will remember you, and you will never be called.

Surely Updike has in mind here the famous story about Martin Luther who is reported to have had his epiphany about matters of doctrine while seated in the privy. David consults, after all, a Lutheran minister about his despair. His problem is that his thoughts in the outhouse lead him to fears of personal annihilation. Questions of Christ's divinity suddenly seem secondary. He needs to learn Luther's message that not reason but faith leads to salvation. His mother's explanation about the soul's presence in the land is ridiculous to a boy who now associates the land with privy holes, graves, and the tunnel to final death.

At first his defenses hold. An unabridged dictionary, for example, defines "soul" in a way to confirm its separate existence. His prayer suggests at least the possibility of reassurance: "All he needed was a little help; a word, a gesture, a nod of certainty, and he would be sealed in, safe." He hopes that Reverend Dobson, whom Mr. Kern has described as too intelligent for a bunch of farmers, will be his major defense, but David is too smart for Dobson. One need only read the exchange between the Lutheran minister and the searching boy in catechetical class to note Dobson's inability to discuss the resurrection of the body or to sense David's despair. In David's eyes, the minister's obtuseness betrays Christianity. Defining heaven as like Abraham Lincoln's goodness living on does not settle crises of metaphysical disorientation. David cannot explain what he wants heaven to be, but he hopes that it is something. As he says in response to his mother's comment that Dobson may have made a mistake: "It's not a *question* of his making a mistake! It's a question of dying and never moving or seeing or hearing anything ever again." Mrs. Kern's offer of the farm's beauty as proof of God's existence is not enough. Neither is Plato's Parable of the Cave. David is alone.

Ironically, he has his religious experience when he is asked to kill. Pigeons foul the furniture in the barn, says Grandmother. She wants them shot. Note Updike's description of the barn as if it were a rustic church: "A barn, in day, is a small night. The splinters of light between the dry shingles pierce the high roof like stars, and the rafters and crossbeams and built-in ladders seem, until your eyes adjust, as mysterious as the branches of a haunted forest." The irony is that as he begins to shoot the pigeons in the mysterious old building, he finds that he enjoys the slaughter. From despair to delight, he is suddenly a master, a "beautiful avenger," God-like in his ability to sweep away creatures that dirty the beauty of creation. While he is shooting, he may not realize the allusion to dying humans, but we do: "Out of the shadowy ragged infinity of the vast barn roof these impudent things dared to thrust their heads, presumed to dirty its starred silence with their filthy timorous life, and he cut them off, tucked them back neatly into the silence." Examining the dead bodies before burying them, David sees for the first time the gorgeous designs of color and feathers, the intricate unity of pattern and flesh, the proof of care on the part of the creator. This experience means much more to him than his earlier investigation of his dog's ears, for he associates the animal's odor with holes in the ground and thus death: "And in the smell of the dog's hair David seemed to descend through many finely differentiated layers of earth: mulch, soil, sand, clay, and the glittering mineral base." Beautiful designs on creatures of the air are different.

Still, the ending is ambiguous. David's faith is restored because he is now convinced that the God who "had lavished such craft upon these worthless birds would not destroy His whole Creation by refusing to let David live forever." One may indeed accept his revelation of eternal life. In **"Archangel"** the angel offers gifts which are "as specific as they are everlasting." The message of the angel is the promise of God's love. Offering no proof of his truth, the angel only urges man to accept. For those who read **"Pigeon Feathers"** in this light, David is fortunate to take the message in the feathers on faith. How much better a dead pigeon is than Lincoln's goodness when it comes to looking for proof of God's love. At least he may touch the feathers as perhaps God touched the bird. H.G. Wells may not care about Christ, but God cares about David. Additional support for an affirmative reading of the story may be found in Updike's superb essay on Karl Barth, entitled "Faith in Search of Understanding," in which Updike shows his knowledge of theological arguments which explain the non-rational basis of faith. But in spite of this evidence, one should not dismiss the possibility for irony. David makes a leap of faith from pattern in the feathers to design in the universe, but the fact remains that he does not gain his insight until he kills. His act is not a matter of losing one's life to save it but of slaughtering defenseless birds. If David is supposed to learn the lesson that faith thrives on acceptance instead of reason, he may fail when he interprets the pigeon feathers as if they were rational proof. Perhaps his violent road to faith is as absurd as Wells's determined attempt to nullify it. In either case, the paradox of slaughter and salvation lifts this story beyond the simplicity of religious formula.

Later in the collection, in **"Packed Dirt, Churchgoing, A Dying Cat, A Traded Car,"** we learn that David Kern survives the adolescent religious crisis to become the regular adult churchgoer. But in the last section of this four-part story, he confronts another religious dilemma: Are men judged by the soul's convictions or the body's deeds? Is the sensation of lust the same as the sin of adultery? David now suspects that a universe which would permit adultery would also sanction death—his death. Updike shows that contemplation of annihilation is not limited to the naive questioning of adolescents. David Kern has grown up, but he is still afraid: "I seemed already eternally forgotten. The dark vibrating air of my bedroom seemed the dust of my grave; the dust went up and up and I prayed upward into it, prayed, prayed for a sign, any glimmer at all, any microscopic loophole or chink in the chain of evidence,

and saw none." The minute intricacies of pigeon feathers will not help him this time. Reasoning that the God who permits his fear is unworthy of existence, he totters on the brink of despair. David has lost touch with the packed-dirt paths made by children and suggestive of grace.

Thus he has little to answer his mother with when, visiting her and his hospitalized father, she tells him that Mr. Kern no longer believes. Her telephone call on his birthday turns out to be a summons to death. Unexpectedly, he feels relief at the message, for he still has a childlike confidence in his father as a man who can defeat all adversaries. How, then, can he accept his dad's loss of faith? He learns that the beauty of his father's life is that he gives others faith, not so much in the specifics of religious mystery but in the grace of a job well done. David hurries to help his sick father but leaves buoyed by the old man's humor. His journey back home in an old car about to be traded is a renewal of the soul's voyage. Death and life are one, a truth he learns in England when he helps a dying cat on the night of his child's birth and which is reinforced here when the father falls ill on David's birthday. Mr. Kern may have lost religious faith, but as the doctor points out, the old man's heart is not yet blocked. Thus the strong gain from the weak: "I felt I would ascend straight north from his touch."

More important, he learns a lesson which sustains him as a writer and which in turn supports us. Earlier, he is asked by a hitchhiking sailor to explain the reason for writing. He cannot answer then, but now, following the visit to the ailing father, he can: "We in America need ceremonies, is I suppose, sailor, the point of what I have written." His first crucial ceremony takes place when, as a boy, he handles the dead pigeons. But as an adult, he needs more than one revelation. Grown now from adolescent to author, he uses his art to keep us in touch with our rituals, our memories, ourselves. Writers preserve the ceremonies which sustain humanity. They show how things which have served well in the past are not to be sloughed off in the present as easily as a traded car, "dismissed without a blessing, a kiss, a testament, or any ceremony of farewell." Driving back through the dark, he is consoled as his old car brings him safely home to a vision of permanent stars in the black night of the soul.

The metaphysical considerations of **"Pigeon Feathers"** give way to the deceptive simplicity of **"Home,"** an exquisite sketch not to be interpreted as much as admired for its mastery of the small detail. Returning home from England with his wife and newly born child, Robert notices that his mother has "the face of a woman whose country has never quite settled what to do with its women." His father, who has lost his teeth to age, stands "perfectly erect, like a child that has just learned to stand." Updike *knows* how mothers kiss returning sons on the cheek while father and son shake hands with averted eyes. He may be our master of the fiction of domestic crisis because he knows the way the kitchen looks and what the family says.

Robert's problem resembles that of most of the young men in this collection: What to make of memory and the persistence of the past. It is as though Updike writes these stories in order to answer the problem that Robert poses to himself when he reveals that they will spend a month with his parents in Pennsylvania before he begins teaching college girls in New York: "He had looked forward to this month; it would be the longest he would have been in Pennsylvania with his wife, and he had a memory of something he had wanted to describe, to explain, to her about his home. But exactly what that was, he had forgotten." Robert is David Kern grown up, returning to the same farm where epiphanies are found in dead pigeons and where parents always squabble. Although he has escaped the small town and the outhouse through education, marriage, and travel, the landmarks of the past are still home to him. Flight may have been necessary, but it leaves him "feeling hollow, fragile, transparent." He needs to return to touch base with his heritage much the same way Updike needs to write to prop open the door to memory. Updike knows that the trip home is always engaged with a sense of "guilty urgency" which quietly but painfully exacerbates the prodigal with "disappointment, apology, and lost time." When we learn that Robert, as if still a child, is upset because his aging parents cannot solve the many mysteries of life, we know that his flight from home has not been dramatic or final.

But **"Home"** is not all nostalgia and loss. Renewal is as important to the process as guilt. The confrontation between the furious, vulgar, squat Pennsylvania Dutchman in the florid Hawaiian shirt and Robert's calm father, standing as tall as Uncle Sam while trying patiently to understand the source of the fury beneath the obscenities, is a master stroke of comedy. The father wins the battle of cross-purposes but only because each misunderstands the other. Laughter is directed not so much at the angry driver as with Robert's bewildered father. **"Home"** is his story after all. Criticism is mixed with admiration, similar to our feelings about George Caldwell in *The Centaur,* and we sense that Updike sees the father as a kind of flawed saint muddling through one more catastrophe. The father's awkward innocence, so earnest in its expression, refreshes the tired son and reacquaints him with the security of continuity which has been threatened by a foreign country and a new child. As if he were a boy again, looking up to his dad, Robert is excited as the car approaches the familiar folds of land. He is almost home.

Variations on the validity of a sense of shelter and its contrasts with the more impersonal outside world are also important to **"A & P"** and **"Lifeguard."** Very little happens in either, but both are about the demands of heroism. William Young refuses to leave the warm shelter of the school, Robert crosses an ocean with a wife and baby before returning home, and Sammy, the hero of **"A & P,"** finally steps outside to the parking lot.

"A & P" is one of Updike's most popular and anthologized tales. Told in the first person from Sammy's point of view, the story calls attention not to the tone of nostalgia but the brashness of his colloquialism. The first sentences suggest his confidence: "In walks these three girls in nothing but bathing suits. I'm in the third check-out slot, with my back to the door, so I don't see them until they're over by the bread. The one that caught my eye first was the one in the plaid green two-piece." Sammy's sym-

pathy with the teeny boppers is established immediately by the contrast between the girls and the typical cash-register watcher, "a witch about fifty with rouge on her cheekbones and no eyebrows" who gives him a hard time for ringing up a box of HiHo crackers twice. Admiring the three girls for daring to enter the grocery store dressed in bathing suits, he especially likes the one who wears her straps down and her head high. He also enjoys the shock on the faces of the housewives in pin curlers who do a double take to corroborate this breach in decorum: "these are usually women with six children and varicose veins mapping their legs... there's people in this town haven't seen the ocean for twenty years."

The sketch turns on the offhand comment that his parents think the outcome sad. We know then that despite the colloquial immediacy of the tale, **"A & P"** is the record of an incident which Sammy has already lived through but not forgotten. His response to the situation has made an impact upon him which he continues to ponder. When Lengel, the store manager who teaches Sunday school, criticizes the three girls with the comment, "this isn't the beach," Sammy's sense of heroism is aroused. Lengel utters his sarcasm as if the A & P were a great sand dune and he the head lifeguard, but no one is saved. Like a hero in a story by J.D. Salinger performing a quixotic gesture, Sammy accepts the role of the girls' unsuspected hero and announces to Lengel that he quits.

He does not agree with his parents that the outcome is sad. Someone must stand up for embarrassed teen-agers in bathing suits with straps down. But this quixotic gesture does him no good. The girls never hear him declare himself their protector, and they do not wait for him in the parking lot with favors and thanks. Indeed, when he steps outside, he is in the ugly world of harried housewives with varicose veins: "There wasn't anybody but some young married screaming with her children about some candy they didn't get by the door of a powder-blue Falcon station wagon." Sammy does not want to quit his job, but he believes that he must go through with the gesture. His protest throws him out of the artificially ordered world of the A & P, where the third checkout slot looks directly up the row to the meat counter, and into the parking lot where mothers yell at children while pretty girls in bathing suits do not notice small acts of heroism. Worse, they do not care.

Sammy's brash slang covers his sentimental act which neither the teen-agers nor the world accepts. His sacrificial action is incongruous but nevertheless mildly moving. The irony is that the girls never need his help. They stand up well under the Victorianism of Lengel and the stares of the other shoppers. As one of the girls retorts, "We *are* decent." Sammy learns that no one welcomes or even tolerates idle idealism. Rather than insist on a principle, he has merely shown off: "My stomach kind of fell as I felt how hard the world was going to be to me hereafter."

The world is just as hard on the unnamed narrator of **"Lifeguard,"** but he misses both the point and the irony of his position. Once again Updike explores the complexities of mundane heroism in a sketch based on an elaborate analogy between a lifeguard and God. The first-person narrator is a divinity student nine months of the year, but although his occupation is more intellectual than Sammy's job in the A & P, he also finds himself surrounded by teen-aged girls in bathing suits when he assumes his lifeguard duties in the summer. Yet this lifeguard is no Sammy. His tone is different. Confident, haughty, and conscious of the image he projects, he ponders problems while Sammy acts hastily. His first statement throws the reader: "Beyond doubt, I am a splendid fellow." Is he egotistical? Pedantic? Childish? One suspects Updike's irony in the opening sentence, for it the lifeguard is beyond doubt, he has no need of faith. He seems too smug. Perhaps he unwittingly loves himself more than the sunbathing masses he would comfort. If they do not need him he will praise himself.

The lifeguard's language is a parody of the religious sermon, and his stilted rhetoric stands between himself and those he hopes to convert, including the reader. Calling his elevated guard's station a throne, he explains that he is disguised by the sun in the summer so that he no longer resembles the pale student of divinity who spends most of the year in seminary libraries wrestling with the complexities of Paul Tillich, Karl Barth, and Kierkegaard. Is he God disguised as Christ when he ascends to his summer throne to cast a watchful eye over those who may one day be in danger? He at least thinks so. The teeny boppers say that his tan contrasting with the white pith helmet gives him a "delightfully edible appearance." One hears echoes of "this is my body." His lifeguard's chair is decorated with a red cross, and his daily ascent to the throne reminds him of climbing "into an immense, rigid, loosely fitting vestment." As if anticipating protests against his analogies, he hastens to define the point of his monologue which he calls a sermon: "I rest my eyes on a sheet of brilliant sand printed with the runes of naked human bodies. That there is no discrepancy between my studies, that the texts of the flesh complement those of the mind, is the easy burden of my sermon."

He is indeed hard-pressed to justify his sexual desire, so he cloaks lust in rhetoric. Arguing that discrepancies exist between the ways ancient theologians and modern thinkers discuss God's relationship to the world, he suggests that humanism erodes the demands of divinity. Just as the sea is no longer a metaphor of divine mystery but only a place to play, so God is no longer an awe-inspiring idea but a lifeguard watching, as opposed to watching over, bathing suits and bodies. Humanity parades before his throne. The old, the matronly, the young with toddlers—they all come. But most of all the young women in skimpy bathing suits catch the eye, especially the lifeguard's. Who can miss the irony of a would-be God ogling "the dimpled blonde in the bib and diapers of her Bikini, the lambent fuzz of her midriff shimmering like a cat's belly. Lust stuns me like the sun." Lest any reader accuse him of emulating Elmer Gantry, of confusing godliness and the desires of the flesh, he hastens to explain that lust is related to love and that love is the sister of salvation: "To desire a woman is to desire to save her. . . . Every seduction is a conversion." He would like to convince us that sexual intercourse which is neither predatory nor hurried unlocks the shadows of the soul, that in sex all lovers approach the immen-

sity of immortality, but we are not so sure. For immediately following his effort to link sex and salvation, he defines his calling to lift the masses into eternal life: "It is not a light task; the throng is so huge, and its members so individually unworthy." One hears again his opening statement with the echo that only he is worthy.

Yet one of the delights of **"Lifeguard"** is the ambiguity. If the story is not ironic, the shepherd correctly seeks his flock at the beach where they congregate instead of in church. They take his presence for granted, yet he is always there. Bidding them to be joyful, he awaits their call for help, "a call, it saddens me to confess, that I have yet to hear." But irony seems to apply. He has not heard their call because they cannot understand his rhetoric. Perhaps it is ironic that he is not in church either, but surely his contorted effort to justify lust in terms of salvation smacks of sophistry. The answer to the question of irony depends upon how the reader reacts to the opening sentence. If the lifeguard is a pompous ass, boasting about his greatness and deluded about his worthiness, then his monologue is suspect, an elaborate analogy by a puffed-up would-be hero. God is absent. But if he utters a truth in the first statement, a truth he must speak himself since no one hurrying to the beach will acknowledge him, then his meditation is a sermon from a mount marked with a red cross and well stocked with suntan lotion. God loves. The former reading seems more acceptable. This divinity student fails to see that intellect and reason, which he has in abundance, do not replace love and faith.

In both **"A & P"** and **"Lifeguard,"** the first-person narrators are defined largely by their tones and vocabularies. No one else supplies background information or details to round out character. Updike experiments with opposite extremes of voice, for Sammy is casual and colloquial while the lifeguard is pompous and pedantic. Sammy initially seems so confident that he may irritate some readers. Surveying the three girls as they wander the aisles, he assumes that his perspective and judgment are naturally correct. When he describes the girls, we wonder if his lyrical flights of language expose the inadequacy of his slang as he stretches to show why these teen-agers deserve his sacrifice: Breasts, for example, become two smooth scoops of vanilla. We can see him longing to ring up the purchase of *that* ice cream. Yet the end of the story suggests that all is not self-righteousness and slang. Sammy has sympathy and a sense of outrage. However ironic, his sacrificial gesture is as refreshing as his colloquial candor. We finish the story sensing that he is more than just another A & P employee with an eye for cute behinds. An observer of his social world, he resolves not just to record but also to act upon his impressions.

The lifeguard's language is just the opposite. A student of theology and thus a reader of abstract ideas expressed in abstruse prose, his tone is stilted and his vocabulary formal. Many readers are so taken aback by the opening sentence that they can only assume the lifeguard's monologue echoes the academic jargon he has heard in the classroom and read in the library. At least Sammy's two scoops of vanilla are real. Perhaps the lifeguard's words parody the theologians' by showing how meaningless intellectualisms can be disguised in important sounding language. Reading on, however, we suspect a contrast developing between the erosion of theological speculations once designed to define the relationship of God and man, and the lifeguard's need to reconcile religious convictions and the demands of the flesh. He speaks largely in abstractions, the way he has been trained to think, but he hopes that his concern for religious speculations will not nullify the goal for which they are conceived in the first place. Language may belie his conviction, but it also unfortunately hampers his communication.

Jack faces a similar problem in the exquisite five-page sketch **"The Crow in the Woods."** One of the most moving pieces in *Pigeon Feathers,* this story joins **"Walter Briggs"** and **"Should Wizard Hit Mommy?"** as the three Jack and Clare tales. The domestic tension forecast for this marriage in **"Walter Briggs"** is not yet an open sore, but Jack's sense of intimacy with his family and nature at the end of **"The Crow in the Woods"** does not ward off the possibility of alienation. We linger in Updike's luxurious gift for natural description and domestic detail when we follow Jack through the early dawn with a slight hangover and a child who needs attention. Note the sense of security and magic as Jack awakens to a world suddenly white:

> All the warm night the secret snow fell so adhesively that every twig in the woods about their little rented house supported a tall slice of white, an upward projection which in the shadowless glow of early morning lifted depth from the scene, made it seem Chinese, calligraphic, a stiff tapestry hung from the gray sky, a shield of lace interwoven with black thread.

Nearly stunned by the beauty, Jack is ready for a vision despite the demands of his child and the desire for sleep.

Against the wondrous backdrop of nature's surprise, Jack tries to do a favor for Clare. She may sleep while he cares for the baby. There is no crisis in this sketch, only gently comic snapshots of Jack's domestic inadequacy and the poignancy of resolution when his vision of universal love finds a mundane balance in Clare's declaration of pragmatic routine. Leaving her in bed, he manages to change the baby's diaper. But he cannot find the cereal. He cannot fit the tray to the high chair. He cannot place the little girl's legs in the chair. Inadequate to the tasks but proud that he has tried, and relieved when Clare, unable to sleep and thus unable to accept his gesture, appears in the kitchen, he watches her deliver without effort warm baby cereal and orange juice. To his eyes already full with the beautiful snow, Clare is magical like the earth which has blessed them with last night's unexpected gift. It is as if heaven has visited them with grace in the guise of snow: "Like her sister the earth, the woman puts forth easy flowers of abundance." Surrounded by a white world, they seem insulated in a world of love.

No longer in charge of necessary domestic duties which he is unequipped to perform, Jack turns to the window and looks at the snow-covered earth. For him the hour, the morning, the world are magic. Yet the apparently inviolable surface of whiteness is shattered when a huge crow dives to land on a high branch, its black bulk destroying

the lacy patterns like flak. To Jack's surprise, the crow settles down as if uniting with the white world. Harmony is inexplicably restored in the mystical balance of extremes suggested by white and black, ephemeral vision and domestic routine. Stunned again, Jack calls to Clare to look: "The woman's pragmatic blue eyes flicked from his face to the window where she saw only snow and rested on the forgotten food steaming between his hands. Her lips moved: 'Eat your egg.' " Thus are we called back to the things of this world.

Meditations like **"The Crow in the Woods"** illustrate the advance that Updike has made in *Pigeon Feathers* over *The Same Door.* The tone is surer, the pursuit of the past more fervent, and the prose more lyrical, all signs of Updike at his best. Richard H. Rupp, no fan of Updike's work, says that in *Pigeon Feathers* Updike cannot "close the gap between style and emotion, between the outside and the inside." But it seems to me that Updike is a master at revealing the possibilities for ever-expanding mystery in the homeliness of the ordinary detail. **"The Crow in the Woods"** does indeed illustrate the unity of the "outside and inside," literally in terms of outdoors and indoors, artistically in terms of style and emotion, and thematically in terms of reality and vision. Those who believe otherwise might read **"The Blessed Man of Boston, My Grandmother's Thimble, and Fanning Island"** in which Updike mentions the importance of details to the author who hopes to celebrate the mystery in the mundane: "But we would-be novelists have a reach as shallow as our skins. We walk through volumes of the unexpressed and like snails leave behind a faint thread excreted out of ourselves. From the dew of the few flakes that melt on our faces we cannot reconstruct the snowstorm."

The narrator decides that he will never write a novel about the blessed man of Boston because while he can fix the exact detail, he cannot fathom the man's life. Yet Updike does admirably well turning out dozens of short stories, many of which pivot on his genius for catching precisely the minute detail which mirrors a snowstorm or a lifetime: "Details are the giant's fingers." Much of the business of *Pigeon Feathers* is with memory and the necessity of scraping the skin to crawl through the always narrowing door of time. The little moments of the past matter. Often no larger than a grandmother's thimble, the apparently insignificant details of the past loom large in the present when they fill in a bit of the mystery about where we have been and who we are. The writer's duty— and privilege— is to honor the delicate task of transporting these details and moments to the page for all who will accept the gift. Art redeems. Thus the writer's request: "O Lord, bless these poor paragraphs, that would do in their vile ignorance Your work of resurrection." Updike knows what Jack learns in **"The Crow in the Woods"**: "that we have no gestures adequate to answer the imperious gestures of nature." But the man of imagination tries. *Pigeon Feathers* is Updike's homage to the relentlessly closing door of memory and the mysterious detail of now. Then other memories come, tap his elbow, and lead him away. (pp. 96-124)

Donald J. Greiner, in his The Other John Updike: Poems, Short Stories, Prose, Play, *Ohio University Press, 1981, 297 p.*

Updike on *Trust Me*:

[*Trust Me* is], I think, the longest of my collections, and it's a book I'm pleased with. For a number of years now I've been more a novelist than a short-story writer, but I do, occasionally, write the odd short story and have been trying, deliberately, to get out of the autobiographical mode, which was a vein I worked and worked again.

I was determined to try to write short stories about people who, in no way, could seem to be me, and also, perhaps, to broaden my short stories in both the amount of time they take and the amount of space they take. I have some spacious stories, continent-spanning stories, in this book, and a few stories that take a couple from their 20s to their deaths. So there was some deliberate attempt to broaden my palette.

John Updike, in an interview with Rebekah Presson, in
New Letters, *1992.*

Jonathan Yardley   (essay date 1987)

[*Yardley is an American journalist, educator, and biographer. In the following review, he offers a mixed assessment of* Trust Me *but enthusiastically praises Updike's abilities as a short story writer.*]

John Updike's ninth collection of short stories finds him once again in "the suburban cat's-cradle" territory upon which he has exercised rights of ownership for more than three decades. The scene is at once wholly familiar and slightly different: familiar because the territory itself is virtually unchanged, different because its occupants, like their creator, have grown older. Where in the past Updike wrote about the lives of the relatively youthful, in *Trust Me* he is more concerned with "middle-aged restlessness"—with the dislocations, both actual and psychological, that take place as the flesh grows weaker and the end becomes more visible.

These 22 stories are united, we are advised, by "the theme of trust, betrayed or fulfilled," and certainly that is so. But too much should not be made of this for, as one who writes chiefly about domestic matters, Updike has always, inescapably, dealt with trust; it is, after all, the rock upon which domestic life rests or founders. Rather, what most strongly unites these stories is Updike himself, with all his considerable strengths and his no less considerable weaknesses; for better and for worse one is constantly aware in these stories that Updike is at the controls, creating the world in his own terms.

He is, we are reminded once again, a far more accomplished and confident writer of stories than of novels. Perhaps he does not take them so seriously, and thus unwittingly frees himself from the solemnity into which the novels too frequently collapse; perhaps he really is, as was often said of him when he was young, a miniaturist; per-haps the form of the story liberates him from preoccupation with plot, at which he is something less than masterly, and permits him to concentrate upon the loving accumulation of domestic detail, at which he is superb. Whatever the case, it is in his short stories that we find Updike's most assured work, and no doubt it is upon the best of them that his reputation ultimately will rest.

That having been said, it must be added that with a few happy exceptions the stories in *Trust Me* are not among Updike's most successful. They are uniformly facile and knowing, and almost without fail they give pleasure, a quality not to be taken lightly. But only intermittently do they seem to have engaged their author's full attention; more often he seems to have put his word processor on automatic pilot and to have let it steer him through all the old familiar places. The cocktail parties, the affairs, the country weekends, the divorces, the cookouts, the hasty assignations, the commuter trains, the station wagons, the city apartments, the gin and tonics—Updike has been there for so long that he can summon it all up with scarcely a shrug, and too often a shrug is all he seems able to muster.

In one of these stories Updike writes: "In the pattern of his generation he had married young, had four children, and eventually got a divorce." That is the pattern of these stories as well: marriage, parenthood and divorce, with middle- aged dread thrown in for good measure. The men and women are now in their 40s, some even in their 50s, but they still are preoccupied with sex, still pair off in random and illicit couplings, still remain essentially isolated from each other in "our essential solitude." They talk the usual talk of the suburbs, which over the years has not become notably more interesting, and they still somehow manage to find room in their self-preoccupied lives for their children, about whom Updike writes with genuine tenderness.

It is in his short stories that we find Updike's most assured work, and no doubt it is upon the best of them that his reputation ultimately will rest.

—*Jonathan Yardley*

Yet the ardor of youth is gone, for Updike as for his characters. He clearly yearns to summon up the old energy and passion, but they have faded. In **"Leaf Season,"** a long and quite pointless story about a gaggle of adults and children on an annual excursion to Vermont, Updike strains so hard to be jolly and affectionate and avuncular that the story quickly degenerates under the weight of all this manufactured merriment. Three decades ago, when Updike first began writing stories about the Maples and then about the many families of *Couples,* these scenes were fresh and, to the reader encountering them for the first time, illuminating; by now they have been played too often, though, and it is time to move on to others.

Indeed it is when Updike does move along that the stories in *Trust Me* improve markedly. When he explores new territory, or old territory with a new twist, his interest brightens and his perceptions become markedly more acute. **"Getting into the Set,"** for example, is a wickedly funny depiction of the high costs and small rewards of social climbing, one that exposes the essential emptiness and complacency of what passes for an American aristocracy. In **"The Wallet"** an old man is reduced to near-panic when the order to which he is accustomed dissolves about him, and then is restored to equanimity—and given a new acceptance of his mortality—when that order is itself restored. In **"Killing"** a divorced woman makes the decision to allow her father to die peacefully, without benefit of life-support technology, then must come to terms with the guilt and confusion this decision understandably provokes.

In each of these stories Updike attempts what is for him something relatively new, and in each he succeeds admirably. In none of them does his prose take on that lush, preening, self-conscious air to which he is from time to time susceptible, and in all of them he gives the impression of being quite happy to look at new scenes and to look at life from new angles. He is sharper in these than in any of the others—writing in **"Killing,"** for example, about a nursing home with "its cloaked odors, its incessant television, its expensive false order and hypocrisy of false cheer, its stifling vulgarity." There's nothing artificial about the feeling—the anger—in those words; Updike is engaged, and it shows in what he writes.

Interestingly, none of these three stories was originally published in *The New Yorker,* the magazine with which Updike has been intimately connected since 1955. Like most of his readers I have long assumed that his best fiction is published there; yet **"Getting into the Set"** appeared in *Vanity Fair,* **"The Wallet"** in *Yankee,* and **"Killing"** in *Playboy.* On the evidence of the 13 stories in *Trust Me* that first came out in *The New Yorker,* that magazine—at least under its previous editorship—seems hospitable only to stories by Updike that retrace familiar ground. But at this stage in his career familiar ground is no longer especially rewarding, for his readers or, apparently, for him; it's when he finds something new that he springs to life, so it is to be hoped that he feels emboldened to do so more often.

Jonathan Yardley, "John Updike: For Better, for Worse," in Book World, *May 10, 1987, p. 3.*

Marilynne Robinson (essay date 1987)

[*In the review below, Robinson, an American novelist, offers a favorable assessment of* Trust Me.]

I once read that if the universe, having come to the end of its explosion, collapses on itself, time will run backward. On no good grounds I imagine this as meaning that suburbs will grow new, then raw, and will then recede,

that surgeons and scientists will daily master the use of cruder instruments; that every life will be shadowed by the inevitable onset of callowness, childhood, and dreaded infancy. In such a world retrospection would be visionary, and events would be rescued from seeming entropy, from mere accident and mere loss. So it is in [the 22 stories in John Updike's *Trust Me*], which assume for their characters a past of such density that it stands on the temporal landscape as stolidly as an empty house—promising comfort, needing care, full of habit and purpose somehow interrupted and abandoned.

For most of these characters it is a past not remote, yet thrown into deep perspective by estrangement, whether a divorce or an intimation of mortality or a realization that has altered the aspect of memory. It is as if the terrible fragility of families were being compensated for, redeemed by the emergence of an afterlife in this life, a stoic Elysium of adult children and second marriages from which old error and disruption can be viewed with tenderness and calm.

The collection's title, *Trust Me,* is a brave, sad, insinuating phrase if ever there was one. It is trust that knits up the world in these stories, a stuff peculiarly liable to fraying and raveling. When the promises implicit in words like father, daughter, wife or friend have proved somehow impossible to keep, only then does it become clear what had been promised, and attempted, and what courage and folly and hope there was in the attempt.

The best of these stories are luminous with compassion, and full of the deep humor very sad tales have when their burden is that we are all frail creatures in a mysterious and perilous world. The plainest objects and events bloom in these stories as if they had at last found their proper climate. In the conclusion to **"Deaths of Distant Friends"** there is a description of a dead dog which is splendid:

> The thunderbolt had hit my former pet by moonlight, his heart full of marshy joy and his stomach fat with garbage, and he had lain for days with ruffling fur while the tides went in and out. The image makes me happy, like the sight of a sail popping full of wind and tugging its boat swiftly out from shore.

The passage is, altogether, a virtuoso's laughing demonstration that gorgeousness inheres in anything.

Some of these stories seem to me less than wonderful. They involve New England social-climbing, and the affairs of edgy, and unrealized women. Mr. Updike's interest in the former is Godlike—not, in this context, a synonym for creditable. In terms of divine attention, surely any sparrow fighting a down draft enjoys priority over the dance of social spheres in the elderly towns of Massachusetts. If these spheres must be tended to it can only be on the grounds that everything must finally be tended to, not because, in themselves, they compel attention. The conflict in **"More Stately Mansions"** between a Yankee descended from mill owners and an Italian descended from mill workers is a patient recounting of two minor strains of bad behavior. In this story and in **"A Constellation of Events"** and **"The Other,"** intimate relations are entered into with or by women who are characterized by nothing so much as the perplexed and fascinated distance from which the author views them. These women have an aunt-ish tendency to deflect the imagination from any thought that passion could actually touch them.

Having said this, I may now praise with added emphasis the stories that are wonderful, indeed, beginning with **"The City,"** a sort of inversion of Tolstoy's *Death of Ivan Ilych*. In Tolstoy's work, the protagonist dies in the bosom of his family, which is irked and indifferent and refuses to attach importance to the seriousness of his illness, and to the ultimate seriousness of death itself. In **"The City,"** a traveling computer salesman learns from a novel discomfort in his bowels the lonely fact that things are not as they should be. He grows worse in a hotel room, and entrusts himself finally to the care of a municipal hospital.

The city of the title, which remains nameless, could be any one of scores of cities in the American interior. It has a calm, distinctive, rural accent, an unselfconscious diversity of population, a renewed center, a few skyscrapers, an art museum containing one or two indubitable treasures. Here Carson, the main character, falls into the net of generalized, grand-scale solicitude. He is rescued and healed by strangers, among strangers. Convention would have this a cold and anomic experience, but in this story it is beautiful.

All we know about Carson is that for a long time his family has been divorced, scattered and estranged. As a commercial traveler he has become a connoisseur of minor cities. Felled by his illness in a hotel bathroom, he notes the shapes of porcelain fixtures viewed from the underside, and the delicate evening light rimming the surfaces of the rented furniture. His vision is the kind one sees in Edward Hopper paintings. For him, and for the story, the intimate and the impersonal are not exclusive categories.

The hospital is itself romanticized by a sick man's wistful eagerness to see competence in those on whom he must depend, and by his sensitivity to the vigor of those who are young and well, and by his quiet pleasures in convalescence. But his perceptions, if heightened, still persuade. He notes the sporting interest of one doctor in doing surgery on him, the strained courtesy that makes another allow him 20 minutes of his time, the youthful and festive atmosphere in the operating room. He regards all this sheer life with an admiring compassion, which is otherworldly and esthetic, too, as if those on the fraying edge of life are, like esthetes, excused from making the more finicky moral judgments.

In a lovely passage a young black nurse appears in the middle of the night to take Carson's blood pressure. After this wordless visitation the hospital begins to seem a cache of the humanly beautiful. The art treasure in this city happens to be "a priceless Hieronymus Bosch," and the beauty is of an unsentimental kind that embraces obesity and bandages and "old ladies shrivelling to nothing in a forest of flowers."

It is the callous habit of piety to subsume all births under Birth and all deaths under Death and to deal with them impersonally, ritualistically. So cathedrals manage their

stony joy. Something of the kind happens here. The plain sprawl of urban life is made potent in this equivocal monument. So far does this quiet story transform its materials that when at the end the nameless city is compared to an anonymous prostitute one feels a delicate compliment is paid to them both.

In **"Still of Some Use"** a man helps his former wife empty their former house with the help of his two sons who had lived there as children. They have parked a pickup below the attic window and they fling things to be discarded into it, including any number of board games, which, lacking a piece or two, still "presented a forceful semblance of value: the springs of their miniature launchers still reacted, the logic of their instructions would still generate suspense, given a chance." There seems a lurking potential for a return to a time when "excitement had flowed along the paths of these stylized landscapes" —of household, marriage, childhood, fatherhood—whose pieces are scattered and whose rules are misplaced. The metaphor may sound overbearing, but in context the games evoke the possibilities that seem to lurk in families for moments of peaceable communion, the hope and obligation of parents especially, always dashed or slighted in some degree at least, the intention set aside too often and then remembered again too late.

Often in these stories Mr. Updike achieves a sense of the mind in its mysterious landscape. It is not an eccentric mind but one called up through confident allusion to common experience. It occupies landscape not of dream and the subconscious nor of social realism, but of the worn paths and familiar places of vernacular experience, come directly out of childhood. When he describes "a sound of tidy retching, like that of a cat who has eaten a bird bones and all," or a furnace "whirring and softly stinking to itself," he is exploiting this most intimate and universal stratum where cultures spawn and jokes hatch, the untranslatable world of fetish and amulet, of synesthesia, memory and suggestion, the backyard, the old neighborhood of the human psyche.

In **"Killing"** a woman decides to forgo the medical intervention that would prolong the life of her old father, and then suffers out his protracted death. She sits by his bedside re-enacting a time in her childhood when, somehow briefly released from the strictures of male reticence, he sat beside her bed and talked to her, to help her sleep. She endures the fluent sympathy of her former husband, made possible by his newly complete detachment from her. The totemic potency of the silent old man, and the powerful memory of his brief, uncharacteristic attentiveness— "perhaps her recollection had expanded a few incidents into a lengthy episode"—evoke the power of memory to conjure with the causal and linear, and of the mind to find or invest value where it will, even in the evasive dignity and baffled emotion of old-fashioned men.

"The Lovely Troubled Daughters of Our Old Crowd" describes the grown children who once played together at the peripheries of the buoyant social lives of their young parents. What the girls glimpsed of infidelity was enough to have kept them from entrusting themselves to adult life when the time came. They still haunt their hometown "as if searching for something they missed." The transgressions the narrator remembers rather nostalgically, seeking to account for the fear he sees in these young women, are not remarkable—suburban cordiality overstepping its limits. He sees their importance for the first time in these inhibited lives. The disproportion between cause and effect, the manners of one generation sealing the fate of the next, set the conventional in a sharp, transforming light.

"Unstuck" is a good-humored story about a newly married couple not yet at ease with one another and still alarmed by unmastered appliances and the mass of expectations implied in ordinary householding, the competences it is embarrassing to lack and to acquire under the eyes of neighbors, and especially under the eyes of one's wife.

"Deaths of Distant Friends" is a sort of reverie, concluding in a comic and charitable view of death itself:

> In truth—how terrible to acknowledge—all three of these deaths make me happy, in a way. Witnesses to my disgrace are being removed. The world is growing lighter. Eventually there will be none to remember me as I was in those embarrassing, disarrayed years when I scuttled without a shell, between houses and wives, a snake between skins, a monster of selfishness, my grotesque needs naked and pink, my social presence beggarly and vulnerable. The deaths of others carry us off bit by bit, until there will be nothing left; and this, too, will be, in a way, a mercy.

That great Death should be enlisted to expunge our little disgraces seems disproportionate only if one discounts that teeming republic of private experience, to which Mr. Updike appeals here again.

"Made In Heaven" is a story of notable sensitivity from a writer whose intuitions about women I would never call unerring. A man is attracted to a woman by her religiousness. He marries her, and falls in beside her, or so he believes, taking pleasure in her piety. Finally he learns he has displaced her, dispossessed her of her peace. The piety of women is a rock on which every church is built, and this story seems to me to say something just and true about women, which is that they cherish religion as a form of solitude.

There are other stories in this collection I find estimable, and others still whose virtues it is not in my gift to discover. At the end I find myself searching for language to describe the very palpable pleasure that comes with experiencing in a writer authority and also humor and elegance and honesty and generosity of spirit.

The distancing that works so powerfully in this book is the farthest thing in the world from alienation. Mr. Updike has claimed a wide terrain for his own by writing about our world as if it were home to him. (pp. 1, 44-5)

> Marilynne Robinson, "At Play in the Backyard of the Psyche," in The New York Times Book Review, *April 26, 1987, pp. 1, 44.*

Stephen M. Chanley (essay date 1987)

[*In the essay below, Chanley analyzes Updike's use of Christian mythology in the critically acclaimed short story "Pigeon Feathers."*]

O Linger, Pennsylvania—"a square mile of middle-class homes" whose "population numbers less than 5,000, predominantly Protestant and of German descent," and where "the Lord's Prayer is daily recited in the schools"—is the setting for all of the short stories of Updike's 1964 collection **Olinger Stories.** Excepting **"In Football Season,"** each of the eleven stories first appeared in *The New Yorker,* then in the collections **The Same Door** and **Pigeon Feathers and Other Stories,** prior to their assembly by Updike . . . under the **Olinger Stories** title. They represent what might be considered the thematic hallmark of his early career.

Aside from their setting, the stories are unified by similar characters, moods, and themes that unquestionably arose from Updike's childhood and adolescent experiences in Shillington, Pennsylvania. The synthesis of those characters, moods, and themes was born of a process of catharsis to express certain unspoken abstractions and revelations toward which Updike was impelled at the early part of his literary career. The family in each is in essence the same, though their names change; the boy, whose age and circumstances vary, "is at bottom the same boy." In **"Pigeon Feathers,"** for example, the longest of the Olinger-set short stories, Updike's protean family assumes the identity of the Kerns: the father, George; the mother, Elsie; and the son, David. With respect to the Olinger-set novels, it is more similar to *The Centaur,* with its adolescent protagonist and his concerns, than to *Of the Farm,* with its fully adult hero and his.

As with all the Olinger Stories, **"Pigeon Feathers"** shares the theme that, in the words of Updike, "We are rewarded unexpectedly. . . . The muddled and inconsequent surface of things now and then parts to yield us a gift." The unexpected reward in this case belongs to David Kerns, for **"Pigeon Feathers"** is a rite-of-passage story where the adolescent learns to accept death as part of the natural order after his unquestioning childhood faith in Christianity is shaken for the first time. Updike uses Christianity or "Christian mythology" while tracing David's spiritual maturation to illustrate that Christianity, or any mythology that helps man to better conceptualize the universal order and his station therein, is relative in its application in that the most appropriate test of its "truth" lies in its effectiveness for the individual.

The mood and circumstance of the story become manifest in the first sentence: "When they moved to Firetown, things were upset, displaced, rearranged." The Kerns, in moving from the secure familiarity of their Olinger home to the uncertain novelty of their Firetown farm, cast their son David in a setting where he must struggle to fit in: "like the furniture, he had to find a new place." His "new place," as we shall see, isn't merely a place in his new rural setting, but also his place in the universal order, his place in the realms of life and death. Amid the shuffled red caneback sofa and blue wing chair, disconcerting in their new stations, David tries to "work off his disorientation" by organizing a jumble of books, which in itself indicates his striving toward order. While leafing through one of the books, H.G. Wells's *The Outline of History,* he is struck by a previously unfathomable idea, one which ultimately proves central to the conflict in the story: Jesus Christ was merely a man who, by fluke of circumstance, was mythicized and mistakenly characterized as something preternatural.

> He had been an obscure political agitator, a kind of hobo, in a minor colony of the Roman Empire. By an accident impossible to reconstruct, he (the small *h* horrified David) survived his own crucifixion and presumably died a few weeks later. A religion was founded on the freakish accident. The credulous imagination of the times retrospectively assigned miracles and supernatural pretensions to Jesus; a myth grew, and then a church, whose theology at most points was in direct contradiction of the simple, rather communistic teachings of the Galilean.

Although shocked by the passage, David's first response is not one of fright, but rather one of surprise that such thoughts—"that, if true, collapsed everything into a jumble of horror"—had been "permitted to exist in an actual human brain." Such threats to the universal order, in other words, thinks David, ought not to be tolerated.

After trying for a time, in vain, to refute Wells's claim, scrambling for "objections that would defeat the complacent march of these black words," David acquiesces to the truth of "the enemy's point: Hope bases vast premises on foolish accidents and reads a word where in fact only a scribble exists." Thus is the quandary posed: that which is devoid of empirically demonstrable facts affords no certainty; faith in God proves only justified or bankrupt when it is too late to choose to embrace or reject Christian dogma. Confronted with such a profound dilemma, the fourteen year old is forced, for the first time, to critically evaluate what had till now been a certainty, forced to reassess and puzzle out his spiritual beliefs. Confronted with Wells's discounting of the mythification of Jesus as "the ornamental and unwise additions of the unintelligently devout" and its consequential threat to the boy's sense of order, David is cast in a perplexity he must resolve so as to pass into maturity.

Although not in apparent conformity with the monomythic pattern, whereby a hero's quest or life cycle follows that of the seasons, David's initiation does seem to nonetheless conform with the archetypal test-motif, whereby a hero undergoes successfully a series of trials, which are linear in their progression, before arriving at his destination or achieving his goal. For instance, he does not, like Jesus and Lazarus, complete a cycle by rising after a real or symbolic death; rather, his quest, and its subsequent fulfillment with his maturation, concludes with his passage into a different state than that from whence he began. Each of his trials, it should be mentioned, differs from the traditional sense in that they are more akin to being steps in an intellectual investigation than to actual trials, where various heroic qualities (courage, strength, cunning, etc.) are tested and proven.

Prior to the beginning of his trials, or steps along the path between innocence and experience, though, David is further called to action by visions of death and universal chaos following his reading of Wells. While in the outhouse, he has an "exact vision of death," a vision of burial as the final resting place of the body *and* soul, where, "blind and silent, . . . no one will remember you, and you will never be called." The vision is significant because, for the first time in his life, he conceives of death *sans* Heaven, death *sans* the consciousness of an immortal soul, death *sans* the orderliness suggested in Christian doctrine. Following the shock of that revelation, and stripped of his former certitude in Christian mythology, his mind is seized by images of an imminent collapse of universal order: "the dilation of the sun, the triumph of the insects, the crabs on the shore in *The Time Machine.*" And until he adopts a mythology, either Christian or some other, which serves as a system of ordering the universe, he will be vexed by the concept of death and afterlife.

The desire to quell that vexation induces the first step toward his spiritual maturity: consulting the Webster's dictionary about the meaning of *soul.* Met with a definition that specifies the soul's separate existence from that of the body, David is comforted, though for but a short time. He is moved, shortly thereafter in the next task, to ask Christ for a sign of proof, in the form of touching David's upheld hands. That, too, yields minimal comfort. Sometime between these first tasks, though, the adolescent again ponders death: this time in the form of an image that, as we shall see, is not only a recurrent one in the story, but also one of considerable metaphorical import.

Lying in bed, David sees a crack of light coming from the jarred door of his parents' room, which triggers a thought concerning the last moments of consciousness before death: "Surely there would be, in the last five minutes, in the last second, a crack of light, showing a door from the dark room to another, full of light." The metaphor here might be taken in several senses: most immediately, the darkness of David's room symbolizes his ignorance and inability to grapple with his mortality, while the light of his parents' room symbolizes their wisdom and ability to deal with death; in another sense, it suggests that life is a "dark room," where the ignorance and malevolence that darkness symbolizes reigns, while the afterlife is one "full of light," full of the wisdom and benevolence symbolized by light; in yet another sense, the crack of light symbolizes a glimmer of hope for David, that for at least the final five minutes or last second of this life, where he is figuratively kept in the dark, he will know for certain whether or not faith in God is warranted.

The third step in David's initiation is to consult the Reverend Mr. Dobson, his catechism instructor, in hopes of finding an answer to his spiritual uncertainty: "About the Resurrection of the Body—are we conscious between the time when we die and the Day of Judgment?" Dobson, however, is unable to provide any adequate answers. His responses, instead, confuse David further with their indistinction, such as in his description of Heaven as "the way the goodness Abraham Lincoln did lives on after him." Such a description of Heaven, as a sort of residual benevolence that continues on in this life, "amounts to saying," according to David, "there isn't any Heaven at all," at least in the sense of being something separate and distinct from this life. The other children in the class, it is important to note, are surprised by David's indiscretion in asking such questions. They are presumably in the stage that David was in prior to reading Wells, the stage where Christian mythology is accepted without question, the stage of immaturity bereft of independent theological/mythological inquiry. They are characterized by the narrator as dumb animals, the girls being "dull white cows," the boys "narrow-faced brown goats," who are "herded on Sunday afternoons" into catechism classes they can never hope to understand. In that light, then, perhaps Dobson's answers are adequate for the majority of students, whose queries are shallow and easily satisfied, if not adequate for David.

Flustered by that inadequacy, David leaves the class bearing, vicariously, Dobson's "burden and fever of being a fraud," and is moved, in his fourth step, to find the answer for himself in the Bible, which he had "never tried reading. . . for himself before." He searches for a passage that specifically reveals Jesus' power to grant admission into another, more ideal life: "where Jesus says to the one thief on the cross, 'Today shalt thou be with me in paradise.' " David's search, however, is abandoned when he is embarrassed at being found reading "the apparatus of piety" by his mother. Following his experience with Dobson, he hates everything associated with organized Christianity, its "fusty churches, creaking hymns, ugly Sunday-school teachers and their stupid leaflets," except the "promise they [hold] out, . . . that in the most perverse way. . . [makes] every good and real thing. . . possible." David seems to resent the fact that by virtue of being a social institution, having to be applicable to a great many people, organized Christianity perforce must not cater to the needs of the individual but rather to the needs of the whole. Organized Christianity, in other words, functions as one body, composed of all its parishioners, who lost their individuality in exchange for identifying with a greater unit, which is united by its worship of Christ. David, it seems, realizes the benefit of Christianity, though he cannot affect the selflessness of its organized manifestation, since he somehow believes that, as an exceptional individual, he merits exemption from death. The casting off of that belief, that he mustn't die, is imperative to David's attainment of maturity.

David's mother attempts, before his next task, to help resolve his dilemma, after he explains his reason for consulting the Bible, by revealing to him her system of making sense of the universe, her adopted mythology. Simply put, she draws spiritual sustenance from nature, the pure state of our physical surroundings, in a sort of Wordsworthian rapture. The harmonious relationship of man and nature, including both its physical and metaphysical aspects, is central to her conception of the universal order. When David asks her, for instance, who made God, "Why, Man," she beams. By that, she means that God, as the personified entity revered in so many religions, is a product of human mythmaking. God and his work, she tells David, are embodied in nature: ". . . you have the *evidence.*

Look out the window at the sun; at the fields." David, however, cannot adopt her mythology, which, as she also suggests, dictates that there is only the decay and subsequent physical assimilation into nature after this life. Her mythology, according to David, therefore means that everything is "just an ocean of horror," and is rejected by the youth forthwith.

David's fifth step toward maturity is his reading of Plato's parable of the cave, which also marks the reappearance of the dark-room/beam-of-light metaphor. This step is significant because it is the first one in which his action comes after the suggestion or action of another, which indicates his gradual loss of individuality. In this case, he acts after his mother's suggestion. The parable, which illustrates that what man sees and believes to be real is merely an illusion comparable to shadows on the back of a cave, fits into the story's scheme because it suggests that pure truth, represented by blinding sunlight, is incomprehensible to man. What is comprehensible to man, though, is the shadows or myths that he creates, which serve to buffer or mediate between himself and pure truth. David, however, finds no solace or relevance to himself in the philosophical doctrine, but is instead "puzzled. . . [by] its queer softness and tangled purity."

After exhausting all the apparent and immediate steps to finding answers— consulting the dictionary, praying for a sign, asking a clergyman, looking in the Bible, reading the work of a great philosopher—David's next step is to attempt to escape his vexation by neglecting to address it. This sixth step follows a period of his feeling comforted in crowds, not only because the surrounding people shared with him a human mortality and seem not to notice, but also because he imagined that perhaps one of them might be close at hand who, like him, "recognized that we cannot, *cannot,* submit to death." Until that person emerges, however, David is determined to escape his plight by "drown[ing] his hopelessness in the clatter and jostle" of a pinball machine and other such "merciful distraction." "All quiet hours [seem]," to David, "invitations to dread"; thus, together with his father, he contrives reasons to linger in Olinger to "escape the farm," which, to David, particularly harkens memories of the mortality that plagues him, with its own dark-room/beam-of-light symbol.

> Every delay postponed the moment when they must ride together down the dirt road into the heart of the dark farmland, where the only light was the kerosene lamp waiting on the dining-room table, a light that drowned their food in shadow and made it sinister.

David, however, is no longer able to find sanctuary in Olinger after school ends there, and his father, an Olinger school teacher, finds summer work in a place that affords David no such reprieve from his thoughts.

A significant development in David's maturation process then follows when, for his fifteenth birthday, his parents give him a Remington .22 rifle. On the surface level, there's something inherently ironic about commemorating a birth with the awarding of a tool whose primary purpose is to kill. However, perhaps it isn't as incongruous as it first seems, when birth and death are properly considered to be both related and part of the natural order. The rifle symbolizes a physical maturation, if not a spiritual one, since, in Freudian symbolism, it is a phallic object. Immediately upon receiving the rifle, David improves his marksmanship through target practice, which signifies, then, his attempt to adapt to his new status. This attempted adaptation to his physical maturation also diverts, "somewhat like a pinball machine," his woes regarding his spiritual maturation.

Another symbol, not incidentally, comes to light at this juncture when the Kernses' new puppy, Copper, emerges as a symbol of innocence. The puppy, who David takes with him during target practice, "hate[s] the gun but love[s] the boy." When the puppy is frightened by the gunshots, David feels alternately willing, then not willing, to comfort Copper, which suggests that he is still on the threshold between man and boy. Giving this comfort soothes his own remaining innocence, since, "to a degree, [it] return[s] comfort to [David]." Comforting the dog is also significant, because in doing so David marvels at the "finely differentiated layers of earth" in the animal's coat, which signifies his coming to realize the intricate beauty of nature as well as the relationship of all living creatures to it. This is an important development because it illustrates his further loss of the individuality that in part troubles him with his mortality. He is now able to incorporate his mother's mythology, her feelings of sanctity in nature, whereas before, "he wondered what joy she found in such [nature] walks; to him the brown stretches of slowly rising and falling land expressed only a huge exhaustion."

David's seventh and last step is perhaps the only one which is truly a task; it is akin, for example, to Arthur's pulling a sword from a stone, because it is here that David successfully completes a task that ultimately proves his worth and is consequently rewarded with his complete passage into physical and spiritual maturity. His final step comes, again, after the suggestion of another person: yet another indication of his hastening loss of individuality. He is asked by his mother, who, out of discomfort, seemingly tries to ascribe the idea to kill a flock of pigeons in the barn to the grandmother. Such a suggestion on the part of the mother is heroic: earlier in the story she is distraught over the killing of earthworms, yet, apparently realizing that it will ultimately aid her son, she sacrifices her own values in asking David to kill the pigeons. Updike himself, interestingly, has revealed his sentiments on the matter by referring to David as "the boy who wrestles with H.G. Wells and murders pigeons."

After initially declining to perform the task, David agrees. With his rifle in hand, he silently enters the barn. Before proceeding to his task, however, David shouts at Copper to go away, and closes the door on the puppy, which symbolizes the casting off of his innocence prior to actually undergoing his rite of passage in a way that is similar to Goodman Brown's symbolic casting off of his faith prior to his rite of passage, when he leaves his wife behind.

Free of his innocence, therefore, but armed with his new physical prowess, David ventures forth into the darkness of the barn, which is yet another dark-room/beam-of-light metaphor: "A barn, in day, is a small night." The image is made explicit when the barn is said to be almost completely dark, save for the light coming through some holes "about as big as basketballs, . . . under the ridge of the roof." David begins by shooting the birds as they near these holes of light, but soon becomes skilled at killing them in the dark, after his eyes are "at home in the dusty gloom," which, perhaps, suggests his gradual adaptation to the shadows, or illusory truths of this life, after concentrating on the pure but incomprehensible truth of an afterlife.

Of all the pigeons that he kills, both in the light and in the dark, however, the second one proves to be the most significant to his experience. Instead of falling to the barn floor after it is shot, such as the others, it lies dead in the hole of light. The "imperfection" of its death bothers David, who shoots its carcass numerous times in an effort to knock it to the ground. Frustrated in his attempt after shooting an entire clip, David accepts it as being something beyond his power to change and desists in his attempt to dislodge it from the middle state between light and dark. It is perhaps here that he realizes his limitations or the futility of influencing the nature of death; although he can impose death on the pigeon, he cannot affect the course that death will take. Such, he realizes, is the case with his own death. With that in mind, and with his task successfully completed, David emerges from the barn into a state of physical maturity and spiritual wisdom: "He stepped with his rifle into the light."

There is some obvious validity, it behooves us to discuss, to the contention that David's final task is archetypal, in that his entering the dark barn, conquering the fear of death, and emerging into the sunlight represents the archetypal hero's requisite journey to the underworld (death) and subsequent return (rebirth). However, such a treatment of his task fails to acknowledge the precedent set by the other dark-room/beam-of-light metaphors in the story, in which the darkness doesn't represent death, in the traditional literary sense, but rather earthly life, which is shrouded in the shadows of nontruth. Furthermore, the cyclical progression of the monomythic hero's journey, of which the death/rebirth phase is a part, is not apparent in **"Pigeon Feathers."**

In any event, although his final step toward maturation is successfully completed by killing the pigeons in the barn, David has yet to completely synthesize his revelations into a mythology that helps him to conceptualize the universal order and "build his fortress against death" until he buries the pigeons. He begins that synthesis, however, immediately upon emerging from the barn, when he incorporates some of his father's stoical acceptance of death into his own beliefs. That is suggested not only by the facts that David uses the term "poor devils" and carries his gun in a careless manner, which are made explicit characteristics of his father in the story, but also by his mother's comment when he emerges from the barn: "Don't smirk. You look like your father." (His father, incidentally, is so thoroughly comfortable with the idea of death, that his favorite expression is "That reminds me of death.") Nonetheless, it is the burial of the pigeons that marks the epiphany in

David, which results in his adoption of a mythology or system for ordering the universe.

While preparing to lay the birds in a freshly dug hole, David marvels at the infinite detail, iridescent luster, and exquisite beauty inherent to the pigeons' lifeless bodies.

> . . . across the surface of the infinitely adjusted yet somehow effortless mechanics of the feathers played idle designs of color, no two alike, designs executed, it seemed, in a controlled rapture, with a joy that hung level in the air above and behind him.

"Yet," David realizes, despite the sublime intricacy with which these pigeons are wrought, "these birds [breed] in the millions and [are] exterminated as pests." This revelation, above everything else, causes him to realize that no matter how special he had previously assumed himself to be, he must, like even the most beautiful creatures, of which there are many, succumb to death, which is as much a part of nature as life. With this epiphany, "crusty coverings" are lifted from David, and a passage follows that is perhaps the key to the story, insofar as understanding the mythology that David adopts following his revelation.

> . . . he was robed in this certainty: that the God who had lavished such craft upon these worthless birds would not destroy His whole Creation by refusing to let David live forever.

His "crusty coverings," in other words, give way to a robe of certainty, which represents his personal mythology. The passage is purposely ambiguous to lend itself to two related interpretations, both of which apparently illustrate David's conception of the universal order: one interpretation is that God will refuse to let David live forever, because not refusing to do so would destroy His whole creation, of which death is an integral part; the other interpretation is that the refusal to let David live forever is of no consequence—it will not destroy the works of a God whose creation is so glorious that even its worthless creatures are beautiful. The importance of David's loss of individuality, which gradually came about along his various steps, is apparent in this universal scheme, which is something of a conglomerate of his mother's reverence of nature and his father's wholehearted acceptance of death.

With the formulation of that mythology, which David embraces as the one most relevant to himself, he successfully completes the spiritual quest that began after his lifelong belief in Christian mythology was shaken by reading H.G. Wells. Through the progression of steps that he undertakes in the story, starting with looking in the most obvious places for his answer, David gradually loses his individuality and comes to accept death as a part of nature. By losing his individuality and adopting a mythology, which serves as a mediator between himself and an incomprehensible universe, David is able to find his place in the cosmic order. In a sense, what he accomplishes on a macrocosmic level parallels what people who join a church do on a microcosmic level: by forfeiting their individual concerns, they become part of something larger and greater than themselves. And in both cases, to be sure, much is facilitated by a mythology. (pp. 251-63)

Steven M. Chanley, "Quest for Order in 'Pigeon Feathers': Updike's Use of Christian Mythology," in Arizona Quarterly, *Vol. 43, No. 3, Autumn, 1987, pp. 251-63.*

Alison Lurie   (essay date 1988)

[*An American novelist, nonfiction writer, and critic, Lurie won a 1985 Pulitzer Prize in fiction for her novel* Foreign Affairs (1984). *In the following laudatory review of* Trust Me, *in which she faults critics who belittle Updike's literary stature, Lurie praises his use of detail and ability to evoke the past, concluding that the stories in* Trust Me *reflect a growing concern with death, aging, and sickness.*]

The American reading public prefers famous writers to suffer. The approved pattern is a meteoric rise like that of a Roman candle, exploding into brilliance at its apogee and then descending and becoming extinguished in the glare of newer fountains of colored fire. The descent ideally will be haunted by demons of a particularly nasty sort and end in a classical purgation of terror and fear, with biographers and critics scrambling round to pick up the holy cinders.

A writer who achieves the initial detonation yet does not fall apart—who remains high in the empyrean, producing another and yet another burst of red and green stars, risks provoking first discomfort and then a lethal mixture of boredom and spite. Over the years something of the sort has begun to happen to John Updike. Critics are irritated to realize that after over three decades of success he has not become an alcoholic or a drug addict, suffered a debilitating illness or a serious bout of writer's block; nor has he lost his gift for social observation, his intellectual acuity and erudition, his love of the sensual world, or his remarkable, poetic talent for description. Voices have begun to be raised suggesting that Updike does what he does too easily for it to be really good (as if sweat were a kind of golden glaze). It has been said that his work is "all surface" and fails to show the marks of a painful struggle with words and ideas.

Years ago I had a summer volunteer job on a highbrow magazine in New York. There, when someone complained that an article was too closely argued or too novel intellectually, the editor I most admired would remark sardonically: "The fish swims too well." Updike, like these imaginary fish, began to be criticized because he swam too well. He was blamed for doing exactly what he had been praised for earlier, even though it was admitted, sometimes grudgingly, that nobody did it half so skillfully.

Rationally speaking, such criticism seems perverse and ungrateful. Updike's stories about middle- and upper-middle-class people in the northeastern United States were and are marvelously subtle, sociologically accurate, beautifully observed and yet more beautifully written, opening out at unexpected moments into both comedy and tragedy. At his best he is, more truly than John Cheever, the Chekhov of American suburbia. In such tales his tone, even at the start, was elegiac; perhaps it is significant that his first novel dealt with the lives of the elderly inhabitants of a poorhouse.

No matter what the subject of Updike's stories, underlying even the most lighthearted was a sense of the inevitable ravages of time. The memory of some moment of past happiness or unhappiness—usually linked to physical details of weather and scenery—often in the end weighed heavier than the original event. Over and over again that kind of "spot of time" (in the Wordsworthian sense) was re-created for the reader in words just as it had been re-created for the narrator or central character in memory, accumulating a still greater freight of nostalgia and distance.

Updike's latest volume of stories, *Trust Me,* displays his many talents wonderfully. Here again is his unerring instinct for the language, the clothes, the cuisine, the characteristic chatter of a particular place and time. In **"More Stately Mansions,"** for instance, he is spot-on about the tastes and attitudes and speech patterns of two erotically involved couples in a declining mill town: one rising working-class Italian, one declining WASP. In **"The City"** he portrays with great clarity the almost supernatural experience of a traveling sales representative who finds himself in a strange midwestern hospital with acute appendicitis.

Unlike many contemporary observers of middle-class mores and possessions, Updike doesn't employ his acute sense of detail just to provide atmosphere. **"Still of Some Use,"** for instance, describes how a man helps his ex-wife clean out the attic of their former home. They find "dozens of forgotten, broken games": Monopoly, Comic-Strip Lotto, Drag Race, Mousetrap. Not only are the games exactly the right ones for the people and the period; they all slowly and silently become metaphors of the family life of which they were once a part.

One of Updike's most attractive qualities is his ability to make much of little— to open out the simplest encounter or incident into significance. In **"Unstuck,"** a new but erotically failing marriage gets another chance when the husband and wife work successfully together to get their car out of a snowbank. The sexual overtones in their efforts are so delicately sketched that the joke remains latent until the last few lines:

> He walked to his car and opened the door and got in beside his wife. The heater had come on; the interior was warm. He repeated, "You were great." He was still panting.
>
> She smiled and said, "So were you."

Though Updike is best known for his tales of middle-class life, he can and does move successfully beyond these limits. **"Poker Night,"** for instance, is the first-person narrative of a factory worker and long-time poker buff who has just discovered he has cancer and gone home to tell his wife.

> Alma did and said all the right things, of course. She cried but not so much I'd panic and came up with a lot of sensible talk about second opinions and mysterious remissions and modern medicine and how we'd take it a day at a time and had to have faith.

But she wasn't me. I was me.

> While we were talking across the kitchen table there was a barrier suddenly that I was on one side of and she was on the other, overweight and over fifty as she was. . . . I had handed her this terrible edge.

> You could see it in her face, her mind working. She was considering what she had been dealt; she was thinking how to play her cards.

Over the years, Updike has been deservedly praised for his detached sympathy for his characters, including those that other writers might implicitly or explicitly condemn. In **"Killing,"** for example, an estranged husband pretends to try to comfort his wife, whose father has just died. It is clear that Martin, the husband, is or has become a rather dreadful person:

> Martin was lethal in his new manner, all efficient vitality, hugging the children ardently, talking to each with a self-conscious and compressed attentiveness unknown in the years when he had absent-mindedly shared their home. He even presumed to tap Anne on the bottom as she stood at the stove. . . .

> "Anne, dear," [he remarked] "tell us all why you can't seem to replace the burned-out light bulbs. Is it the unscrewing or the screwing in that frightens you?"

And yet in the end Updike allows Anne to recognize her part in the breakup of the marriage and in what Martin has become, and to forgive him; as Updike implicitly does.

The title of the book, and its jacket copy, suggest that "the theme of trust. . . runs through" this collection. Trust and mistrust, however, have always been part of Updike's world. What is new here is a growing consciousness of illness, aging, and death, which have begun to threaten not only parents and children and friends, but the central characters in these tales. (p. 3)

Alison Lurie, "The Woman Who Rode Away," in The New York Review of Books, *Vol. XXXV, No. 8, May 12, 1988, pp. 3-4.*

FURTHER READING

Bibliography

Olivas, Michael A. *An Annotated Bibliography of John Updike Criticism 1967-1973, and A Checklist of His Works.* New York: Garland Publishing, Inc.: 1975, 91 p.
    Provides annotated references to recent criticism on Updike.

Taylor, C. Clarke. *John Updike: A Bibliography.* Kent, Ohio: Kent State University Press, 1968, 82 p.
    Lists works by and about Updike through the 1960s.

Criticism

Bayley, John. "Falling in Love with the Traffic Warden." *London Review of Books* 9, No. 17 (1 October 1987): 6-8.
    Favorable assessment of *Trust Me*. Bayley observes: "No writer today is less abstract and cagey in the modern manner, than John Updike. He boldly identifies the quality of his art, and the entertainment and comfort it gives, with the discards of existence, artefacts and trivialities of being, and the way consciousness clings to them."

Bloom, Harold, ed. *John Updike*. New York: Chelsea House Publishers, 1987, 172 p.
    Reprints essays on Updike's work in various genres by such noted critics as Joyce Carol Oates, Cynthia Ozick, and Donald J. Greiner.

Brookner, Anita. "The Pleasures of the Suburbs." *The Spectator* 259, No. 8305 (19 September 1987): 44-5.
    Praises Updike's attention to detail and focus on the ordinary in *Trust Me*.

Burchard, Rachael C. "The Short Stories." In her *John Updike: Yea Sayings*, pp. 133-59. Carbondale and Edwardsville: Southern Illinois University Press, 1971.
    Surveys Updike's earliest short story collections.

Hamilton, Alice, and Hamilton, Kenneth. "Long Thoughts in Short Stories" and "Harmony and Discord." In their *John Updike: A Critical Essay*, pp. 22-30, pp. 40-6. Grand Rapids, Mich.: William B. Eerdmans, 1967.
    Offers a brief thematic assessment of *The Same Door, Pigeon Feathers,* and *The Music School*, noting: "What Updike has to say, he says first in his short stories. His novels are, in a sense, second tries."

———. *The Elements of John Updike*. Grand Rapids, Mich.: William B. Eerdmans, 1970, 267 p.
    Thematic and stylistic critique of Updike's writings. Several chapters include discussion of his short fiction, particularly the Maple stories.

Kleiman, Ed. "John Updike's 'Giving Blood': An Experiment in Genre." *Studies in Short Fiction* 29, No. 2 (Spring 1992): 153-60.
    Argues that in "Giving Blood" Updike emphasizes the themes of rebirth, innocence, and hope, and thus departs from the theme of marital discord that links the other stories in *Too Far to Go*.

Luscher, Robert M. "John Updike's *Olinger Stories*: New Light among the Shadows." *Journal of the Short Story in English* 11 (Autumn 1988): 99-117.
    Discusses the order in which the pieces in *Olinger Stories* appear and how the collection functions as a memorial to Updike's past, his desire to return to the small town of his youth, and a "ceremony of farewell."

———. *John Updike: A Study of the Short Fiction*. New York: Twayne, 1993, 242 p.
    Critical overview and analysis of Updike's work in the short story genre.

McNaughton, William R., ed. *Critical Essays on John Updike*. Boston: G. K. Hall and Co., 1982, 308 p.
    Reprints reviews and critical studies of Updike's works. Includes essays by Anthony Burgess, Granville Hicks, and Alfred Kazin.

Pinsker, Sanford. "John Updike and the Distractions of Henry Bech, Professional Writer and Amateur American Jew." *Modern Fiction Studies* 37, No. 1 (Spring 1991): 97-111.
    Argues that the protagonist of *Bech: A Book* and *Bech Is Back* afforded Updike the opportunity to comment on the American literary scene of the 1950s and 1960s.

Shurr, William H. "The Lutheran Experience in John Updike's 'Pigeon Feathers'." *Studies in Short Fiction* 14, No. 4 (Fall 1977): 329-35.
    Asserts that although "Pigeon Feathers" incorporates elements from the narrative Romance and the theme of the American naif, the story's focus is on theological issues.

Tanner, Tony. Review of *Museums and Women, and Other Stories*, by John Updike. *The New York Times Book Review* (22 October 1972): 5, 24.
    Favorable assessment of *Museums and Women* which, Tanner assets, describes "Updike's vision of American life."

Thorburn, David, and Eiland, Howard, eds. *John Updike: A Collection of Critical Essays*. Englewood Cliffs, N.J.: Prentice-Hall, 1979, 222 p.
    Includes essays on several of Updike's novels and short story collections. Five chapters are devoted to *The Same Door, Pigeon Feathers, The Music School, Bech: A Book,* and *Museums and Women*.

Tracy, Bruce H. "The Habit of Confession: Recovery of the Self in Updike's 'The Music School'." *Studies in Short Fiction* 21, No. 4 (Fall 1984): 339-55.
    Analyzes the relationship between plot, voice, self-identity, and narrative structure in "The Music School." Tracy concludes that this work "succeeds on two levels: it is a satire of the dehumanizing impulse native to our major cultural artifacts–science and religion; and it is, in addition, an affirmation of humanistic value present in an aesthetic stance both in life and in art where creative action appears to be the predictable result of claiming personal responsibility for one's baffling circumstances in life."

Waxman, Robert E. "Invitations to Dread: John Updike's Metaphysical Quest." *Renascence* XXIX, No. 4 (Summer 1977): 201-10.
    Examines the influence of Karl Barth's and Blaise Pascal's philosophical and theological writings on Updike's work through an analysis of the short stories "The Blessed Man of Boston, My Grandmother's Thimble, and Fanning Island" and "Packed Dirt, Churchgoing, A Dying Cat, A Traded Car."

Wells, Walter. "John Updike's 'A & P': A Return Visit to Araby." *Studies in Short Fiction* 30, No. 2 (Spring 1993): 127-33.

Views "A & P" as a retelling of James Joyce's short story "Araby."

Additional coverage of Updike's life and career is contained in the following sources published by Gale Research: *Contemporary Authors*, Vols. 1-4, rev. ed.; *Contemporary Authors Bibliographical Series*, Vol. 1; *Contemporary Authors New Revision Series*, Vols. 4, 33; *Contemporary Literary Criticism*, Vols. 1, 2, 3, 5, 7, 9, 13, 15, 23, 34, 43, 70; *Dictionary of Literary Biography*, Vols. 2, 5; *Dictionary of Literary Biography Documentary Series*, Vol. 3; *Dictionary of Literary Biography Yearbook: 1980* and *1982*; *Major 20th-Century Writers*; and *World Literature Criticism*.

Appendix:

Select Bibliography of General Sources on Short Fiction

BOOKS OF CRITICISM

Allen, Walter. *The Short Story in English.* New York: Oxford University Press, 1981, 413 p.

Aycock, Wendell M., ed. *The Teller and the Tale: Aspects of the Short Story* (Proceedings of the Comparative Literature Symposium, Texas Tech University, Volume XIII). Lubbock: Texas Tech Press, 1982, 156 p.

Averill, Deborah. *The Irish Short Story from George Moore to Frank O'Connor.* Washington, D.C.: University Press of America, 1982, 329 p.

Bates, H. E. *The Modern Short Story: A Critical Survey.* Boston: Writer, 1941, 231 p.

Bayley, John. *The Short Story: Henry James to Elizabeth Bowen.* Great Britain: The Harvester Press Limited, 1988, 197 p.

Bennett, E. K. *A History of the German Novelle: From Goethe to Thomas Mann.* Cambridge: At the University Press, 1934, 296 p.

Bone, Robert. *Down Home: A History of Afro-American Short Fiction from Its Beginning to the End of the Harlem Renaissance.* Rev. ed. New York: Columbia University Press, 1988, 350 p.

Bruck, Peter. *The Black American Short Story in the Twentieth Century: A Collection of Critical Essays.* Amsterdam: B. R. Grüner Publishing Co., 1977, 209 p.

Burnett, Whit, and Burnett, Hallie. *The Modern Short Story in the Making.* New York: Hawthorn Books, 1964, 405 p.

Canby, Henry Seidel. *The Short Story in English.* New York: Henry Holt and Co., 1909, 386 p.

Current-García, Eugene. *The American Short Story before 1850: A Critical History.* Twayne's Critical History of the Short Story, edited by William Peden. Boston: Twayne Publishers, 1985, 168 p.

Flora, Joseph M., ed. *The English Short Story, 1880-1945: A Critical History.* Twayne's Critical History of the Short Story, edited by William Peden. Boston: Twayne Publishers, 1985, 215 p.

Foster, David William. *Studies in the Contemporary Spanish-American Short Story.* Columbia, Mo.: University of Missouri Press, 1979, 126 p.

George, Albert J. *Short Fiction in France, 1800-1850.* Syracuse, N.Y.: Syracuse University Press, 1964, 245 p.

Gerlach, John. *Toward an End: Closure and Structure in the American Short Story.* University, Ala.: The University of Alabama Press, 1985, 193 p.

Hankin, Cherry, ed. *Critical Essays on the New Zealand Short Story.* Auckland: Heinemann Publishers, 1982, 186 p.

Hanson, Clare, ed. *Re-Reading the Short Story.* London: MacMillan Press, 1989, 137 p.

Harris, Wendell V. *British Short Fiction in the Nineteenth Century.* Detroit: Wayne State University Press, 1979, 209 p.

Huntington, John. *Rationalizing Genius: Ideological Strategies in the Classic American Science Fiction Short Story.* New Brunswick: Rutgers University Press, 1989, 216 p.

Kilroy, James F., ed. *The Irish Short Story: A Critical History.* Twayne's Critical History of the Short Story, edited by William Peden. Boston: Twayne Publishers, 1984, 251 p.

Lee, A. Robert. *The Nineteenth-Century American Short Story.* Totowa, N. J.: Vision / Barnes & Noble, 1986, 196 p.

Leibowitz, Judith. *Narrative Purpose in the Novella.* The Hague: Mouton, 1974, 137 p.

Lohafer, Susan. *Coming to Terms with the Short Story.* Baton Rouge: Louisiana State University Press, 1983, 171 p.

Lohafer, Susan, and Clarey, Jo Ellyn. *Short Story Theory at a Crossroads.* Baton Rouge: Louisiana State University Press, 1989, 352 p.

Mann, Susan Garland. *The Short Story Cycle: A Genre Companion and Reference Guide.* New York: Greenwood Press, 1989, 228 p.

Matthews, Brander. *The Philosophy of the Short Story.* New York: Longmans, Green and Co., 1901, 83 p.

May, Charles E., ed. *Short Story Theories.* Athens, Oh.: Ohio University Press, 1976, 251 p.

McClave, Heather, ed. *Women Writers of the Short Story: A Collection of Critical Essays.* Englewood Cliffs, N. J.: Prentice-Hall, 1980, 171 p.

Moser, Charles, ed. *The Russian Short Story: A Critical History.* Twayne's Critical History of the Short Story, edited by William Peden. Boston: Twayne Publishers, 1986, 232 p.

New, W. H. *Dreams of Speech and Violence: The Art of the Short Story in Canada and New Zealand.* Toronto: The University of Toronto Press, 1987, 302 p.

Newman, Frances. *The Short Story's Mutations: From Petronius to Paul Morand.* New York: B. W. Huebsch, 1925, 332 p.

O'Connor, Frank. *The Lonely Voice: A Study of the Short Story.* Cleveland: World Publishing Co., 1963, 220 p.

O'Faolain, Sean. *The Short Story.* New York: Devin-Adair Co., 1951, 370 p.

Orel, Harold. *The Victorian Short Story: Development and Triumph of a Literary Genre.* Cambridge: Cambridge University Press, 1986, 213 p.

O'Toole, L. Michael. *Structure, Style and Interpretation in the Russian Short Story.* New Haven: Yale University Press, 1982, 272 p.

Pattee, Fred Lewis. *The Development of the American Short Story: An Historical Survey.* New York: Harper and Brothers Publishers, 1923, 388 p.

Peden, Margaret Sayers, ed. *The Latin American Short Story: A Critical History.* Twayne's Critical History of the Short Story, edited by William Peden. Boston: Twayne Publishers, 1983, 160 p.

Peden, William. *The American Short Story: Continuity and Change, 1940-1975.* Rev. ed. Boston: Houghton Mifflin Co., 1975, 215 p.

Reid, Ian. *The Short Story.* The Critical Idiom, edited by John D. Jump. London: Methuen and Co., 1977, 76 p.

Rhode, Robert D. *Setting in the American Short Story of Local Color, 1865-1900.* The Hague: Mouton, 1975, 189 p.

Rohrberger, Mary. *Hawthorne and the Modern Short Story: A Study in Genre.* The Hague: Mouton and Co., 1966, 148 p.

Shaw, Valerie, *The Short Story: A Critical Introduction.* London: Longman, 1983, 294 p.

Stephens, Michael. *The Dramaturgy of Style: Voice in Short Fiction.* Carbondale, Ill.: Southern Illinois University Press, 1986, 281 p.

Stevick, Philip, ed. *The American Short Story, 1900-1945: A Critical History.* Twayne's Critical History of the Short Story, edited by William Peden, Boston: Twayne Publishers, 1984, 209 p.

Summers, Hollis, ed. *Discussion of the Short Story.* Boston: D. C. Heath and Co., 1963, 118 p.

Vannatta, Dennis, ed. *The English Short Story, 1945-1980: A Critical History.* Twayne's Critical History of the Short Story, edited by William Peden. Boston: Twayne Publishers, 1985, 206 p.

Voss, Arthur. *The American Short Story: A Critical Survey.* Norman, Okla.: University of Oklahoma Press, 1973, 399 p.

Walker, Warren S. *Twentieth-Century Short Story Explication: New Series, Vol. 1: 1989-1990.* Hamden, Conn.: Shoe String, 1993, 366 p.

Ward, Alfred C. *Aspects of the Modern Short Story: English and American.* London: University of London Press, 1924, 307 p.

Weaver, Gordon, ed. *The American Short Story, 1945-1980: A Critical History.* Twayne's Critical History of the Short Story, edited by William Peden. Boston: Twayne Publishers, 1983, 150 p.

West, Ray B., Jr. *The Short Story in America, 1900-1950.* Chicago: Henry Regnery Co., 1952, 147 p.

Williams, Blanche Colton. *Our Short Story Writers.* New York: Moffat, Yard and Co., 1920, 357 p.

Wright, Austin McGiffert. *The American Short Story in the Twenties.* Chicago: University of Chicago Press, 1961, 425 p.

CRITICAL ANTHOLOGIES

Atkinson, W. Patterson, ed. *The Short-Story.* Boston: Allyn and Bacon, 1923, 317 p.

Baldwin, Charles Sears, ed. *American Short Stories.* New York: Longmans, Green and Co., 1904, 333 p.

Charters, Ann, ed. *The Story and Its Writer: An Introduction to Short Fiction.* New York: St. Martin's Press, 1983, 1239 p.

Current-García, Eugene, and Patrick, Walton R., eds. *American Short Stories: 1820 to the Present.* Key Editions, edited by John C. Gerber. Chicago: Scott, Foresman and Co., 1952, 633 p.

Fagin, N. Bryllion, ed. *America through the Short Story.* Boston: Little, Brown, and Co., 1936, 508 p.

Frakes, James R., and Traschen, Isadore, eds. *Short Fiction: A Critical Collection.* Prentice-Hall English Literature Series, edited by Maynard Mack. Englewood Cliffs, N.J.: Prentice-Hall, 1959, 459 p.

Gifford, Douglas, ed. *Scottish Short Stories, 1800-1900.* The Scottish Library, edited by Alexander Scott. London: Calder and Boyars, 1971, 350 p.

Gordon, Caroline, and Tate, Allen, eds. *The House of Fiction: An Anthology of the Short Story with Commentary.* Rev. ed. New York: Charles Scribner's Sons, 1960, 469 p.

Greet, T. Y., et. al. *The Worlds of Fiction: Stories in Context.* Boston: Houghton Mifflin Co., 1964, 429 p.

Gullason, Thomas A., and Caspar, Leonard, eds. *The World of Short Fiction: An International Collection.* New York: Harper and Row, 1962, 548 p.

Havighurst, Walter, ed. *Masters of the Modern Short Story.* New York: Harcourt, Brace and Co., 1945, 538 p.

Litz, A. Walton, ed. *Major American Short Stories.* New York: Oxford University Press, 1975, 823 p.

Matthews, Brander, ed. *The Short-Story: Specimens Illustrating Its Development.* New York: American Book Co., 1907, 399 p.

Menton, Seymour, ed. *The Spanish American Short Story: A Critical Anthology.* Berkeley and Los Angeles: University of California Press, 1980, 496 p.

Mzamane, Mbulelo Vizikhungo, ed. *Hungry Flames, and Other Black South African Short Stories.* Longman African Classics. Essex: Longman, 1986, 162 p.

Schorer, Mark, ed. *The Short Story: A Critical Anthology.* Rev. ed. Prentice-Hall English Literature Series, edited by Maynard Mack. Englewood Cliffs, N. J.: Prentice-Hall, 1967, 459 p.

Simpson, Claude M., ed. *The Local Colorists: American Short Stories, 1857-1900.* New York: Harper and Brothers Publishers, 1960, 340 p.

Stanton, Robert, ed. *The Short Story and the Reader.* New York: Henry Holt and Co., 1960, 557 p.

West, Ray B., Jr., ed. *American Short Stories.* New York: Thomas Y. Crowell Co., 1959, 267 p.

Short Story
Criticism
Indexes

Literary Criticism Series
Cumulative Author Index

SSC Cumulative Nationality Index
SSC Cumulative Title Index

How to Use This Index

The main references

Calvino, Italo
1923-1985.....CLC 5, 8, 11, 22, 33, 39,
73; SSC 3

list all author entries in the following Gale Literary Criticism series:

CLC = Contemporary Literary Criticism
CLR = Children's Literature Review
CMLC = Classical and Medieval Literature Criticism
DC = Drama Criticism
LC = Literature Criticism from 1400 to 1800
NCLC = Nineteenth-Century Literature Criticism
PC = Poetry Criticism
SSC = Short Story Criticism
TCLC = Twentieth-Century Literary Criticism

The cross-references

See also CANR 23; CA 85-88;
obituary CA 116

list all author entries in the following Gale biographical and literary sources:

AAYA = Authors & Artists for Young Adults
AITN = Authors in the News
BLC = Black Literature Criticism
BW = Black Writers
CA = Contemporary Authors
CAAS = Contemporary Authors Autobiography Series
CABS = Contemporary Authors Bibliographical Series
CANR = Contemporary Authors New Revision Series
CAP = Contemporary Authors Permanent Series
CDALB = Concise Dictionary of American Literary Biography
CDBLB = Concise Dictionary of British Literary Biography
DLB = Dictionary of Literary Biography
DLBD = Dictionary of Literary Biography Documentary Series
DLBY = Dictionary of Literary Biography Yearbook
HW = Hispanic Writers
MAICYA = Major Authors and Illustrators for Children and Young Adults
MTCW = Major 20th-Century Writers
SAAS = Something about the Author Autobiography Series
SATA = Something about the Author
WLC = World Literature Criticism, 1500 to the Present
YABC = Yesterday's Authors of Books for Children

Literary Criticism Series
Cumulative Author Index

Aldanov, Mark (Alexandrovich)
    1886(?)-1957 .... **TCLC 23**
    See also CA 118

Aldington, Richard 1892-1962 ...... **CLC 49**
    See also CA 85-88; DLB 20, 36, 100

Aldiss, Brian W(ilson)
    1925- .... **CLC 5, 14, 40**
    See also CA 5-8R; CAAS 2; CANR 5, 28;
    DLB 14; MTCW; SATA 34

Alegria, Claribel 1924- .... **CLC 75**
    See also CA 131; CAAS 15; HW

Alegria, Fernando 1918- .... **CLC 57**
    See also CA 9-12R; CANR 5, 32; HW

Aleichem, Sholom .... **TCLC 1, 35**
    See also Rabinovitch, Sholem

Aleixandre, Vicente 1898-1984 ... **CLC 9, 36**
    See also CA 85-88; 114; CANR 26;
    DLB 108; HW; MTCW

Alepoudelis, Odysseus
    See Elytis, Odysseus

Aleshkovsky, Joseph 1929-
    See Aleshkovsky, Yuz
    See also CA 121; 128

Aleshkovsky, Yuz .... **CLC 44**
    See also Aleshkovsky, Joseph

Alexander, Lloyd (Chudley) 1924- .. **CLC 35**
    See also AAYA 1; CA 1-4R; CANR 1, 24,
    38; CLR 1, 5; DLB 52; MAICYA;
    MTCW; SATA 3, 49

Alfau, Felipe 1902- .... **CLC 66**
    See also CA 137

Alger, Horatio, Jr. 1832-1899 ..... **NCLC 8**
    See also DLB 42; SATA 16

Algren, Nelson 1909-1981 .... **CLC 4, 10, 33**
    See also CA 13-16R; 103; CANR 20;
    CDALB 1941-1968; DLB 9; DLBY 81,
    82; MTCW

Ali, Ahmed 1910- .... **CLC 69**
    See also CA 25-28R; CANR 15, 34

Alighieri, Dante 1265-1321 .... **CMLC 3**

Allan, John B.
    See Westlake, Donald E(dwin)

Allen, Edward 1948- .... **CLC 59**

Allen, Roland
    See Ayckbourn, Alan

Allen, Woody 1935- .... **CLC 16, 52**
    See also AAYA 10; CA 33-36R; CANR 27,
    38; DLB 44; MTCW

Allende, Isabel 1942- .... **CLC 39, 57**
    See also CA 125; 130; HW; MTCW

Alleyn, Ellen
    See Rossetti, Christina (Georgina)

Allingham, Margery (Louise)
    1904-1966 .... **CLC 19**
    See also CA 5-8R; 25-28R; CANR 4;
    DLB 77; MTCW

Allingham, William 1824-1889 ... **NCLC 25**
    See also DLB 35

Allison, Dorothy 1948- .... **CLC 78**

Allston, Washington 1779-1843 .... **NCLC 2**
    See also DLB 1

Almedingen, E. M. .... **CLC 12**
    See also Almedingen, Martha Edith von
    See also SATA 3

Almedingen, Martha Edith von 1898-1971
    See Almedingen, E. M.
    See also CA 1-4R; CANR 1

Alonso, Damaso 1898-1990 .... **CLC 14**
    See also CA 110; 131; 130; DLB 108; HW

Alov
    See Gogol, Nikolai (Vasilyevich)

Alta 1942- .... **CLC 19**
    See also CA 57-60

Alter, Robert B(ernard) 1935- ..... **CLC 34**
    See also CA 49-52; CANR 1

Alther, Lisa 1944- .... **CLC 7, 41**
    See also CA 65-68; CANR 12, 30; MTCW

Altman, Robert 1925- .... **CLC 16**
    See also CA 73-76

Alvarez, A(lfred) 1929- .... **CLC 5, 13**
    See also CA 1-4R; CANR 3, 33; DLB 14,
    40

Alvarez, Alejandro Rodriguez 1903-1965
    See Casona, Alejandro
    See also CA 131; 93-96; HW

Amado, Jorge 1912- .... **CLC 13, 40**
    See also CA 77-80; CANR 35; DLB 113;
    MTCW

Ambler, Eric 1909- .... **CLC 4, 6, 9**
    See also CA 9-12R; CANR 7, 38; DLB 77;
    MTCW

Amichai, Yehuda 1924- ...... **CLC 9, 22, 57**
    See also CA 85-88; MTCW

Amiel, Henri Frederic 1821-1881 .. **NCLC 4**

Amis, Kingsley (William)
    1922- ...... **CLC 1, 2, 3, 5, 8, 13, 40, 44**
    See also AITN 2; CA 9-12R; CANR 8, 28;
    CDBLB 1945-1960; DA; DLB 15, 27,
    100; MTCW

Amis, Martin (Louis)
    1949- .... **CLC 4, 9, 38, 62**
    See also BEST 90:3; CA 65-68; CANR 8,
    27; DLB 14

Ammons, A(rchie) R(andolph)
    1926- .... **CLC 2, 3, 5, 8, 9, 25, 57**
    See also AITN 1; CA 9-12R; CANR 6, 36;
    DLB 5; MTCW

Amo, Tauraatua i
    See Adams, Henry (Brooks)

Anand, Mulk Raj 1905- .... **CLC 23**
    See also CA 65-68; CANR 32; MTCW

Anatol
    See Schnitzler, Arthur

Anaya, Rudolfo A(lfonso) 1937- .... **CLC 23**
    See also CA 45-48; CAAS 4; CANR 1, 32;
    DLB 82; HW; MTCW

Andersen, Hans Christian
    1805-1875 .... **NCLC 7; SSC 6**
    See also CLR 6; DA; MAICYA; WLC;
    YABC 1

Anderson, C. Farley
    See Mencken, H(enry) L(ouis); Nathan,
    George Jean

Anderson, Jessica (Margaret) Queale
    .... **CLC 37**
    See also CA 9-12R; CANR 4

Anderson, Jon (Victor) 1940- .... **CLC 9**
    See also CA 25-28R; CANR 20

Anderson, Lindsay (Gordon)
    1923- .... **CLC 20**
    See also CA 125; 128

Anderson, Maxwell 1888-1959 ..... **TCLC 2**
    See also CA 105; DLB 7

Anderson, Poul (William) 1926- .... **CLC 15**
    See also AAYA 5; CA 1-4R; CAAS 2;
    CANR 2, 15, 34; DLB 8; MTCW;
    SATA 39

Anderson, Robert (Woodruff)
    1917- .... **CLC 23**
    See also AITN 1; CA 21-24R; CANR 32;
    DLB 7

Anderson, Sherwood
    1876-1941 ...... **TCLC 1, 10, 24; SSC 1**
    See also CA 104; 121; CDALB 1917-1929;
    DA; DLB 4, 9, 86; DLBD 1; MTCW;
    WLC

Andouard
    See Giraudoux, (Hippolyte) Jean

Andrade, Carlos Drummond de ...... **CLC 18**
    See also Drummond de Andrade, Carlos

Andrade, Mario de 1893-1945 ..... **TCLC 43**

Andrewes, Lancelot 1555-1626 .... **LC 5**

Andrews, Cicily Fairfield
    See West, Rebecca

Andrews, Elton V.
    See Pohl, Frederik

Andreyev, Leonid (Nikolaevich)
    1871-1919 .... **TCLC 3**
    See also CA 104

Andric, Ivo 1892-1975 .... **CLC 8**
    See also CA 81-84; 57-60; MTCW

Angelique, Pierre
    See Bataille, Georges

Angell, Roger 1920- .... **CLC 26**
    See also CA 57-60; CANR 13

Angelou, Maya 1928- .... **CLC 12, 35, 64, 77**
    See also AAYA 7; BLC 1; BW; CA 65-68;
    CANR 19; DA; DLB 38; MTCW;
    SATA 49

Annensky, Innokenty Fyodorovich
    1856-1909 .... **TCLC 14**
    See also CA 110

Anon, Charles Robert
    See Pessoa, Fernando (Antonio Nogueira)

Anouilh, Jean (Marie Lucien Pierre)
    1910-1987 ...... **CLC 1, 3, 8, 13, 40, 50**
    See also CA 17-20R; 123; CANR 32;
    MTCW

Anthony, Florence
    See Ai

Anthony, John
    See Ciardi, John (Anthony)

Anthony, Peter
    See Shaffer, Anthony (Joshua); Shaffer,
    Peter (Levin)

Anthony, Piers 1934- .... **CLC 35**
    See also CA 21-24R; CANR 28; DLB 8;
    MTCW

Antoine, Marc
    See Proust, (Valentin-Louis-George-Eugene-)
    Marcel

Antoninus, Brother
See Everson, William (Oliver)

Antonioni, Michelangelo 1912- ..... **CLC 20**
See also CA 73-76

Antschel, Paul 1920-1970...... **CLC 10, 19**
See also Celan, Paul
See also CA 85-88; CANR 33; MTCW

Anwar, Chairil 1922-1949 .... **TCLC 22**
See also CA 121

Apollinaire, Guillaume .. **TCLC 3, 8, 51; PC 7**
See also Kostrowitzki, Wilhelm Apollinaris
de

Appelfeld, Aharon 1932- ...... **CLC 23, 47**
See also CA 112; 133

Apple, Max (Isaac) 1941-........ **CLC 9, 33**
See also CA 81-84; CANR 19; DLB 130

Appleman, Philip (Dean) 1926- ..... **CLC 51**
See also CA 13-16R; CANR 6, 29

Appleton, Lawrence
See Lovecraft, H(oward) P(hillips)

Apteryx
See Eliot, T(homas) S(tearns)

Apuleius, (Lucius Madaurensis)
125(?)-175(?) .... **CMLC 1**

Aquin, Hubert 1929-1977......... **CLC 15**
See also CA 105; DLB 53

Aragon, Louis 1897-1982....... **CLC 3, 22**
See also CA 69-72; 108; CANR 28;
DLB 72; MTCW

Arany, Janos 1817-1882........ **NCLC 34**

Arbuthnot, John 1667-1735......... **LC 1**
See also DLB 101

Archer, Herbert Winslow
See Mencken, H(enry) L(ouis)

Archer, Jeffrey (Howard) 1940- .... **CLC 28**
See also BEST 89:3; CA 77-80; CANR 22

Archer, Jules 1915- .... **CLC 12**
See also CA 9-12R; CANR 6; SAAS 5;
SATA 4

Archer, Lee
See Ellison, Harlan

Arden, John 1930- .... **CLC 6, 13, 15**
See also CA 13-16R; CAAS 4; CANR 31;
DLB 13; MTCW

Arenas, Reinaldo 1943-1990 .... **CLC 41**
See also CA 124; 128; 133; HW

Arendt, Hannah 1906-1975 .... **CLC 66**
See also CA 17-20R; 61-64; CANR 26;
MTCW

Aretino, Pietro 1492-1556 .... **LC 12**

Arguedas, Jose Maria
1911-1969 .... **CLC 10, 18**
See also CA 89-92; DLB 113; HW

Argueta, Manlio 1936-........... **CLC 31**
See also CA 131; HW

Ariosto, Ludovico 1474-1533........ **LC 6**

Aristides
See Epstein, Joseph

Aristophanes
450B.C.-385B.C....... **CMLC 4; DC 2**
See also DA

Arlt, Roberto (Godofredo Christophersen)
1900-1942 .... **TCLC 29**
See also CA 123; 131; HW

Armah, Ayi Kwei 1939-........ **CLC 5, 33**
See also BLC 1; BW; CA 61-64; CANR 21;
DLB 117; MTCW

Armatrading, Joan 1950-......... **CLC 17**
See also CA 114

Arnette, Robert
See Silverberg, Robert

Arnim, Achim von (Ludwig Joachim von
Arnim) 1781-1831 .... **NCLC 5**
See also DLB 90

Arnim, Bettina von 1785-1859.... **NCLC 38**
See also DLB 90

Arnold, Matthew
1822-1888 .... **NCLC 6, 29; PC 5**
See also CDBLB 1832-1890; DA; DLB 32,
57; WLC

Arnold, Thomas 1795-1842 ...... **NCLC 18**
See also DLB 55

Arnow, Harriette (Louisa) Simpson
1908-1986 .... **CLC 2, 7, 18**
See also CA 9-12R; 118; CANR 14; DLB 6;
MTCW; SATA 42, 47

Arp, Hans
See Arp, Jean

Arp, Jean 1887-1966............... **CLC 5**
See also CA 81-84; 25-28R

Arrabal
See Arrabal, Fernando

Arrabal, Fernando 1932- ... **CLC 2, 9, 18, 58**
See also CA 9-12R; CANR 15

Arrick, Fran..................... **CLC 30**

Artaud, Antonin 1896-1948 ..... **TCLC 3, 36**
See also CA 104

Arthur, Ruth M(abel) 1905-1979.... **CLC 12**
See also CA 9-12R; 85-88; CANR 4;
SATA 7, 26

Artsybashev, Mikhail (Petrovich)
1878-1927 .... **TCLC 31**

Arundel, Honor (Morfydd)
1919-1973 .... **CLC 17**
See also CA 21-22; 41-44R; CAP 2;
SATA 4, 24

Asch, Sholem 1880-1957 .... **TCLC 3**
See also CA 105

Ash, Shalom
See Asch, Sholem

Ashbery, John (Lawrence)
1927- ...... **CLC 2, 3, 4, 6, 9, 13, 15, 25,**
41, 77
See also CA 5-8R; CANR 9, 37; DLB 5;
DLBY 81; MTCW

Ashdown, Clifford
See Freeman, R(ichard) Austin

Ashe, Gordon
See Creasey, John

Ashton-Warner, Sylvia (Constance)
1908-1984 .... **CLC 19**
See also CA 69-72; 112; CANR 29; MTCW

Asimov, Isaac
1920-1992 ...... **CLC 1, 3, 9, 19, 26, 76**
See also BEST 90:2; CA 1-4R; 137;
CANR 2, 19, 36; CLR 12; DLB 8;
DLBY 92; MAICYA; MTCW; SATA 1,
26, 74

Astley, Thea (Beatrice May)
1925- .... **CLC 41**
See also CA 65-68; CANR 11

Aston, James
See White, T(erence) H(anbury)

Asturias, Miguel Angel
1899-1974 .... **CLC 3, 8, 13**
See also CA 25-28; 49-52; CANR 32;
CAP 2; DLB 113; HW; MTCW

Atares, Carlos Saura
See Saura (Atares), Carlos

Atheling, William
See Pound, Ezra (Weston Loomis)

Atheling, William, Jr.
See Blish, James (Benjamin)

Atherton, Gertrude (Franklin Horn)
1857-1948 .... **TCLC 2**
See also CA 104; DLB 9, 78

Atherton, Lucius
See Masters, Edgar Lee

Atkins, Jack
See Harris, Mark

Atticus
See Fleming, Ian (Lancaster)

Atwood, Margaret (Eleanor)
1939- ..... **CLC 2, 3, 4, 8, 13, 15, 25, 44;**
SSC 2
See also BEST 89:2; CA 49-52; CANR 3,
24, 33; DA; DLB 53; MTCW; SATA 50;
WLC

Aubigny, Pierre d'
See Mencken, H(enry) L(ouis)

Aubin, Penelope 1685-1731(?)........ **LC 9**
See also DLB 39

Auchincloss, Louis (Stanton)
1917- .... **CLC 4, 6, 9, 18, 45**
See also CA 1-4R; CANR 6, 29; DLB 2;
DLBY 80; MTCW

Auden, W(ystan) H(ugh)
1907-1973 ...... **CLC 1, 2, 3, 4, 6, 9, 11,**
14, 43; PC 1
See also CA 9-12R; 45-48; CANR 5;
CDBLB 1914-1945; DA; DLB 10, 20;
MTCW; WLC

Audiberti, Jacques 1900-1965 ...... **CLC 38**
See also CA 25-28R

Auel, Jean M(arie) 1936-.......... **CLC 31**
See also AAYA 7; BEST 90:4; CA 103;
CANR 21

Auerbach, Erich 1892-1957 .... **TCLC 43**
See also CA 118

Augier, Emile 1820-1889 .... **NCLC 31**

August, John
See De Voto, Bernard (Augustine)

Augustine, St. 354-430 .... **CMLC 6**

Aurelius
See Bourne, Randolph S(illiman)

Austen, Jane
      1775-1817 .... **NCLC 1, 13, 19, 33**
      See also CDBLB 1789-1832; DA; DLB 116;
      WLC

Auster, Paul 1947- .... **CLC 47**
      See also CA 69-72; CANR 23

Austin, Frank
      See Faust, Frederick (Schiller)

Austin, Mary (Hunter)
      1868-1934 .... **TCLC 25**
      See also CA 109; DLB 9, 78

Autran Dourado, Waldomiro
      See Dourado, (Waldomiro Freitas) Autran

Averroes 1126-1198 .... **CMLC 7**
      See also DLB 115

Avison, Margaret 1918- .... **CLC 2, 4**
      See also CA 17-20R; DLB 53; MTCW

Axton, David
      See Koontz, Dean R(ay)

Ayckbourn, Alan
      1939- .... **CLC 5, 8, 18, 33, 74**
      See also CA 21-24R; CANR 31; DLB 13;
      MTCW

Aydy, Catherine
      See Tennant, Emma (Christina)

Ayme, Marcel (Andre) 1902-1967... **CLC 11**
      See also CA 89-92; CLR 25; DLB 72

Ayrton, Michael 1921-1975 .... **CLC 7**
      See also CA 5-8R; 61-64; CANR 9, 21

Azorin .... **CLC 11**
      See also Martinez Ruiz, Jose

Azuela, Mariano 1873-1952 .... **TCLC 3**
      See also CA 104; 131; HW; MTCW

Baastad, Babbis Friis
      See Friis-Baastad, Babbis Ellinor

Bab
      See Gilbert, W(illiam) S(chwenck)

Babbis, Eleanor
      See Friis-Baastad, Babbis Ellinor

Babel, Isaak (Emmanuilovich)
      1894-1941(?) .... **CLC 73**
      See also CA 104; TCLC 2, 13

Babits, Mihaly 1883-1941 .... **TCLC 14**
      See also CA 114

Babur 1483-1530................. **LC 18**

Bacchelli, Riccardo 1891-1985 ..... **CLC 19**
      See also CA 29-32R; 117

Bach, Richard (David) 1936- .... **CLC 14**
      See also AITN 1; BEST 89:2; CA 9-12R;
      CANR 18; MTCW; SATA 13

Bachman, Richard
      See King, Stephen (Edwin)

Bachmann, Ingeborg 1926-1973..... **CLC 69**
      See also CA 93-96; 45-48; DLB 85

Bacon, Francis 1561-1626 .... **LC 18**
      See also CDBLB Before 1660

Bacovia, George................. **TCLC 24**
      See also Vasiliu, Gheorghe

Badanes, Jerome 1937- .... **CLC 59**

Bagehot, Walter 1826-1877 ...... **NCLC 10**
      See also DLB 55

Bagnold, Enid 1889-1981 .... **CLC 25**
      See also CA 5-8R; 103; CANR 5, 40;
      DLB 13; MAICYA; SATA 1, 25

Bagrjana, Elisaveta
      See Belcheva, Elisaveta

Bagryana, Elisaveta
      See Belcheva, Elisaveta

Bailey, Paul 1937- .... **CLC 45**
      See also CA 21-24R; CANR 16; DLB 14

Baillie, Joanna 1762-1851 .... **NCLC 2**
      See also DLB 93

Bainbridge, Beryl (Margaret)
      1933- .... **CLC 4, 5, 8, 10, 14, 18, 22, 62**
      See also CA 21-24R; CANR 24; DLB 14;
      MTCW

Baker, Elliott 1922- .... **CLC 8**
      See also CA 45-48; CANR 2

Baker, Nicholson 1957- .... **CLC 61**
      See also CA 135

Baker, Ray Stannard 1870-1946... **TCLC 47**
      See also CA 118

Baker, Russell (Wayne) 1925- ...... **CLC 31**
      See also BEST 89:4; CA 57-60; CANR 11,
      41; MTCW

Bakshi, Ralph 1938(?)- .... **CLC 26**
      See also CA 112; 138

Bakunin, Mikhail (Alexandrovich)
      1814-1876 .... **NCLC 25**

Baldwin, James (Arthur)
      1924-1987 ...... **CLC 1, 2, 3, 4, 5, 8, 13,
            15, 17, 42, 50, 67; DC 1; SSC 10**
      See also AAYA 4; BLC 1; BW; CA 1-4R;
      124; CABS 1; CANR 3, 24;
      CDALB 1941-1968; DA; DLB 2, 7, 33;
      DLBY 87; MTCW; SATA 9, 54; WLC

Ballard, J(ames) G(raham)
      1930- .... **CLC 3, 6, 14, 36; SSC 1**
      See also AAYA 3; CA 5-8R; CANR 15, 39;
      DLB 14; MTCW

Balmont, Konstantin (Dmitriyevich)
      1867-1943 .... **TCLC 11**
      See also CA 109

Balzac, Honore de
      1799-1850 ....'.. **NCLC 5, 35; SSC 5**
      See also DA; DLB 119; WLC

Bambara, Toni Cade 1939- .... **CLC 19**
      See also AAYA 5; BLC 1; BW; CA 29-32R;
      CANR 24; DA; DLB 38; MTCW

Bamdad, A.
      See Shamlu, Ahmad

Banat, D. R.
      See Bradbury, Ray (Douglas)

Bancroft, Laura
      See Baum, L(yman) Frank

Banim, John 1798-1842 .... **NCLC 13**
      See also DLB 116

Banim, Michael 1796-1874 ...... **NCLC 13**

Banks, Iain
      See Banks, Iain M(enzies)

Banks, Iain M(enzies) 1954- .... **CLC 34**
      See also CA 123; 128

Banks, Lynne Reid .... **CLC 23**
      See also Reid Banks, Lynne
      See also AAYA 6

Banks, Russell 1940- .... **CLC 37, 72**
      See also CA 65-68; CAAS 15; CANR 19;
      DLB 130

Banville, John 1945- .... **CLC 46**
      See also CA 117; 128; DLB 14

Banville, Theodore (Faullain) de
      1832-1891 .... **NCLC 9**

Baraka, Amiri
      1934- ... **CLC 1, 2, 3, 5, 10, 14, 33; PC 4**
      See also Jones, LeRoi
      See also BLC 1; BW; CA 21-24R; CABS 3;
      CANR 27, 38; CDALB 1941-1968; DA;
      DLB 5, 7, 16, 38; DLBD 8; MTCW

Barbellion, W. N. P.............. **TCLC 24**
      See also Cummings, Bruce F(rederick)

Barbera, Jack 1945- .... **CLC 44**
      See also CA 110

Barbey d'Aurevilly, Jules Amedee
      1808-1889 .... **NCLC 1**
      See also DLB 119

Barbusse, Henri 1873-1935 .... **TCLC 5**
      See also CA 105; DLB 65

Barclay, Bill
      See Moorcock, Michael (John)

Barclay, William Ewert
      See Moorcock, Michael (John)

Barea, Arturo 1897-1957 .... **TCLC 14**
      See also CA 111

Barfoot, Joan 1946- .... **CLC 18**
      See also CA 105

Baring, Maurice 1874-1945 .... **TCLC 8**
      See also CA 105; DLB 34

Barker, Clive 1952- .... **CLC 52**
      See also AAYA 10; BEST 90:3; CA 121;
      129; MTCW

Barker, George Granville
      1913-1991 .... **CLC 8, 48**
      See also CA 9-12R; 135; CANR 7, 38;
      DLB 20; MTCW

Barker, Harley Granville
      See Granville-Barker, Harley
      See also DLB 10

Barker, Howard 1946- .... **CLC 37**
      See also CA 102; DLB 13

Barker, Pat 1943- .... **CLC 32**
      See also CA 117; 122

Barlow, Joel 1754-1812 .... **NCLC 23**
      See also DLB 37

Barnard, Mary (Ethel) 1909- .... **CLC 48**
      See also CA 21-22; CAP 2

Barnes, Djuna
      1892-1982 ... **CLC 3, 4, 8, 11, 29; SSC 3**
      See also CA 9-12R; 107; CANR 16; DLB 4,
      9, 45; MTCW

Barnes, Julian 1946- .... **CLC 42**
      See also CA 102; CANR 19

Barnes, Peter 1931- .... **CLC 5, 56**
      See also CA 65-68; CAAS 12; CANR 33,
      34; DLB 13; MTCW

Baroja (y Nessi), Pio 1872-1956 .... **TCLC 8**
      See also CA 104

Baron, David
      See Pinter, Harold

Baron Corvo
See Rolfe, Frederick (William Serafino Austin Lewis Mary)

Barondess, Sue K(aufman)
1926-1977 . . . . **CLC 8**
See also Kaufman, Sue
See also CA 1-4R; 69-72; CANR 1

Baron de Teive
See Pessoa, Fernando (Antonio Nogueira)

Barres, Maurice 1862-1923 . . . . . . **TCLC 47**
See also DLB 123

Barreto, Afonso Henrique de Lima
See Lima Barreto, Afonso Henrique de

Barrett, (Roger) Syd 1946- . . . . **CLC 35**
See also Pink Floyd

Barrett, William (Christopher)
1913-1992 . . . . **CLC 27**
See also CA 13-16R; 139; CANR 11

Barrie, J(ames) M(atthew)
1860-1937 . . . . **TCLC 2**
See also CA 104; 136; CDBLB 1890-1914;
CLR 16; DLB 10; MAICYA; YABC 1

Barrington, Michael
See Moorcock, Michael (John)

Barrol, Grady
See Bograd, Larry

Barry, Mike
See Malzberg, Barry N(athaniel)

Barry, Philip 1896-1949 . . . . **TCLC 11**
See also CA 109; DLB 7

Bart, Andre Schwarz
See Schwarz-Bart, Andre

Barth, John (Simmons)
1930- . . . . . . **CLC 1, 2, 3, 5, 7, 9, 10, 14,
27, 51; SSC 10**
See also AITN 1, 2; CA 1-4R; CABS 1;
CANR 5, 23; DLB 2; MTCW

Barthelme, Donald
1931-1989 . . . . . . **CLC 1, 2, 3, 5, 6, 8, 13,
23, 46, 59; SSC 2**
See also CA 21-24R; 129; CANR 20;
DLB 2; DLBY 80, 89; MTCW; SATA 7,
62

Barthelme, Frederick 1943- . . . . **CLC 36**
See also CA 114; 122; DLBY 85

Barthes, Roland (Gerard)
1915-1980 . . . . **CLC 24**
See also CA 130; 97-100; MTCW

Barzun, Jacques (Martin) 1907- . . . . **CLC 51**
See also CA 61-64; CANR 22

Bashevis, Isaac
See Singer, Isaac Bashevis

Bashkirtseff, Marie 1859-1884 . . . **NCLC 27**

Basho
See Matsuo Basho

Bass, Kingsley B., Jr.
See Bullins, Ed

Bass, Rick 1958- . . . . **CLC 79**
See also CA 126

Bassani, Giorgio 1916- . . . . **CLC 9**
See also CA 65-68; CANR 33; DLB 128;
MTCW

Bastos, Augusto (Antonio) Roa
See Roa Bastos, Augusto (Antonio)

Bataille, Georges 1897-1962 . . . . **CLC 29**
See also CA 101; 89-92

Bates, H(erbert) E(rnest)
1905-1974 . . . . **CLC 46; SSC 10**
See also CA 93-96; 45-48; CANR 34;
MTCW

Bauchart
See Camus, Albert

Baudelaire, Charles
1821-1867 . . . . **NCLC 6, 29; PC 1**
See also DA; WLC

Baudrillard, Jean 1929- . . . . **CLC 60**

Baum, L(yman) Frank 1856-1919 . . . **TCLC 7**
See also CA 108; 133; CLR 15; DLB 22;
MAICYA; MTCW; SATA 18

Baum, Louis F.
See Baum, L(yman) Frank

Baumbach, Jonathan 1933- . . . . . . **CLC 6, 23**
See also CA 13-16R; CAAS 5; CANR 12;
DLBY 80; MTCW

Bausch, Richard (Carl) 1945- . . . . . . **CLC 51**
See also CA 101; CAAS 14; DLB 130

Baxter, Charles 1947- . . . . **CLC 45, 78**
See also CA 57-60; CANR 40; DLB 130

Baxter, George Owen
See Faust, Frederick (Schiller)

Baxter, James K(eir) 1926-1972 . . . . **CLC 14**
See also CA 77-80

Baxter, John
See Hunt, E(verette) Howard, Jr.

Bayer, Sylvia
See Glassco, John

Beagle, Peter S(oyer) 1939- . . . . **CLC 7**
See also CA 9-12R; CANR 4; DLBY 80;
SATA 60

Bean, Normal
See Burroughs, Edgar Rice

Beard, Charles A(ustin)
1874-1948 . . . . **TCLC 15**
See also CA 115; DLB 17; SATA 18

Beardsley, Aubrey 1872-1898 . . . . . **NCLC 6**

Beattie, Ann
1947- . . . . **CLC 8, 13, 18, 40, 63; SSC 11**
See also BEST 90:2; CA 81-84; DLBY 82;
MTCW

Beattie, James 1735-1803 . . . . **NCLC 25**
See also DLB 109

Beauchamp, Kathleen Mansfield 1888-1923
See Mansfield, Katherine
See also CA 104; 134; DA

**Beauvoir, Simone (Lucie Ernestine Marie
Bertrand) de**
1908-1986 . . . . **CLC 1, 2, 4, 8, 14, 31, 44,
50, 71**
See also CA 9-12R; 118; CANR 28; DA;
DLB 72; DLBY 86; MTCW; WLC

Becker, Jurek 1937- . . . . **CLC 7, 19**
See also CA 85-88; DLB 75

Becker, Walter 1950- . . . . **CLC 26**

Beckett, Samuel (Barclay)
1906-1989 . . . . . . **CLC 1, 2, 3, 4, 6, 9, 10,
11, 14, 18, 29, 57, 59**
See also CA 5-8R; 130; CANR 33;
CDBLB 1945-1960; DA; DLB 13, 15;
DLBY 90; MTCW; WLC

Beckford, William 1760-1844 . . . . **NCLC 16**
See also DLB 39

Beckman, Gunnel 1910- . . . . **CLC 26**
See also CA 33-36R; CANR 15; CLR 25;
MAICYA; SAAS 9; SATA 6

Becque, Henri 1837-1899 . . . . **NCLC 3**

Beddoes, Thomas Lovell
1803-1849 . . . . **NCLC 3**
See also DLB 96

Bedford, Donald F.
See Fearing, Kenneth (Flexner)

Beecher, Catharine Esther
1800-1878 . . . . **NCLC 30**
See also DLB 1

Beecher, John 1904-1980 . . . . **CLC 6**
See also AITN 1; CA 5-8R; 105; CANR 8

Beer, Johann 1655-1700 . . . . **LC 5**

Beer, Patricia 1924- . . . . **CLC 58**
See also CA 61-64; CANR 13; DLB 40

Beerbohm, Henry Maximilian
1872-1956 . . . . **TCLC 1, 24**
See also CA 104; DLB 34, 100

Begiebing, Robert J(ohn) 1946- . . . . . **CLC 70**
See also CA 122; CANR 40

Behan, Brendan
1923-1964 . . . . **CLC 1, 8, 11, 15, 79**
See also CA 73-76; CANR 33;
CDBLB 1945-1960; DLB 13; MTCW

Behn, Aphra 1640(?)-1689 . . . . **LC 1**
See also DA; DLB 39, 80, 131; WLC

Behrman, S(amuel) N(athaniel)
1893-1973 . . . . **CLC 40**
See also CA 13-16; 45-48; CAP 1; DLB 7,
44

Belasco, David 1853-1931 . . . . **TCLC 3**
See also CA 104; DLB 7

Belcheva, Elisaveta 1893- . . . . **CLC 10**

Beldone, Phil "Cheech"
See Ellison, Harlan

Beleno
See Azuela, Mariano

Belinski, Vissarion Grigoryevich
1811-1848 . . . . **NCLC 5**

Belitt, Ben 1911- . . . . **CLC 22**
See also CA 13-16R; CAAS 4; CANR 7;
DLB 5

Bell, James Madison 1826-1902 . . . **TCLC 43**
See also BLC 1; BW; CA 122; 124; DLB 50

Bell, Madison (Smartt) 1957- . . . . . . **CLC 41**
See also CA 111; CANR 28

Bell, Marvin (Hartley) 1937- . . . . . **CLC 8, 31**
See also CA 21-24R; CAAS 14; DLB 5;
MTCW

Bell, W. L. D.
See Mencken, H(enry) L(ouis)

Bellamy, Atwood C.
See Mencken, H(enry) L(ouis)

Bonnefoy, Yves 1923-........ **CLC 9, 15, 58**
See also CA 85-88; CANR 33; MTCW

Bontemps, Arna(ud Wendell)
1902-1973 .... **CLC 1, 18**
See also BLC 1; BW; CA 1-4R; 41-44R;
CANR 4, 35; CLR 6; DLB 48, 51;
MAICYA; MTCW; SATA 2, 24, 44

Booth, Martin 1944-............. **CLC 13**
See also CA 93-96; CAAS 2

Booth, Philip 1925-.............. **CLC 23**
See also CA 5-8R; CANR 5; DLBY 82

Booth, Wayne C(layson) 1921- ..... **CLC 24**
See also CA 1-4R; CAAS 5; CANR 3;
DLB 67

Borchert, Wolfgang 1921-1947 ..... **TCLC 5**
See also CA 104; DLB 69, 124

Borel, Petrus 1809-1859........ **NCLC 41**

Borges, Jorge Luis
1899-1986 ... **CLC 1, 2, 3, 4, 6, 8, 9, 10,
13, 19, 44, 48; SSC 4**
See also CA 21-24R; CANR 19, 33; DA;
DLB 113; DLBY 86; HW; MTCW; WLC

Borowski, Tadeusz 1922-1951 ...... **TCLC 9**
See also CA 106

Borrow, George (Henry)
1803-1881 .... **NCLC 9**
See also DLB 21, 55

Bosman, Herman Charles
1905-1951 .... **TCLC 49**

Bosschere, Jean de 1878(?)-1953... **TCLC 19**
See also CA 115

Boswell, James 1740-1795.......... **LC 4**
See also CDBLB 1660-1789; DA; DLB 104;
WLC

Bottoms, David 1949-............. **CLC 53**
See also CA 105; CANR 22; DLB 120;
DLBY 83

Boucicault, Dion 1820-1890...... **NCLC 41**

Boucolon, Maryse 1937-
See Conde, Maryse
See also CA 110; CANR 30

Bourget, Paul (Charles Joseph)
1852-1935 .... **TCLC 12**
See also CA 107; DLB 123

Bourjaily, Vance (Nye) 1922- .... **CLC 8, 62**
See also CA 1-4R; CAAS 1; CANR 2;
DLB 2

Bourne, Randolph S(illiman)
1886-1918 .... **TCLC 16**
See also CA 117; DLB 63

Bova, Ben(jamin William) 1932-.... **CLC 45**
See also CA 5-8R; CANR 11; CLR 3;
DLBY 81; MAICYA; MTCW; SATA 6,
68

Bowen, Elizabeth (Dorothea Cole)
1899-1973 ...... **CLC 1, 3, 6, 11, 15, 22;
SSC 3**
See also CA 17-18; 41-44R; CANR 35;
CAP 2; CDBLB 1945-1960; DLB 15;
MTCW

Bowering, George 1935-........ **CLC 15, 47**
See also CA 21-24R; CAAS 16; CANR 10;
DLB 53

Bowering, Marilyn R(uthe) 1949-... **CLC 32**
See also CA 101

Bowers, Edgar 1924- .... **CLC 9**
See also CA 5-8R; CANR 24; DLB 5

Bowie, David .... **CLC 17**
See also Jones, David Robert

Bowles, Jane (Sydney)
1917-1973 .... **CLC 3, 68**
See also CA 19-20; 41-44R; CAP 2

Bowles, Paul (Frederick)
1910- .... **CLC 1, 2, 19, 53; SSC 3**
See also CA 1-4R; CAAS 1; CANR 1, 19;
DLB 5, 6; MTCW

Box, Edgar
See Vidal, Gore

Boyd, Nancy
See Millay, Edna St. Vincent

Boyd, William 1952-........ **CLC 28, 53, 70**
See also CA 114; 120

Boyle, Kay
1902-1992 ..... **CLC 1, 5, 19, 58; SSC 5**
See also CA 13-16R; 140; CAAS 1;
CANR 29; DLB 4, 9, 48, 86; MTCW

Boyle, Mark
See Kienzle, William X(avier)

Boyle, Patrick 1905-1982.......... **CLC 19**
See also CA 127

Boyle, T. Coraghessan 1948-.... **CLC 36, 55**
See also BEST 90:4; CA 120; DLBY 86

Boz
See Dickens, Charles (John Huffam)

Brackenridge, Hugh Henry
1748-1816 .... **NCLC 7**
See also DLB 11, 37

Bradbury, Edward P.
See Moorcock, Michael (John)

Bradbury, Malcolm (Stanley)
1932- .... **CLC 32, 61**
See also CA 1-4R; CANR 1, 33; DLB 14;
MTCW

Bradbury, Ray (Douglas)
1920- .... **CLC 1, 3, 10, 15, 42**
See also AITN 1, 2; CA 1-4R; CANR 2, 30;
CDALB 1968-1988; DA; DLB 2, 8;
MTCW; SATA 11, 64; WLC

Bradford, Gamaliel 1863-1932..... **TCLC 36**
See also DLB 17

Bradley, David (Henry, Jr.) 1950- .. **CLC 23**
See also BLC 1; BW; CA 104; CANR 26;
DLB 33

Bradley, John Ed 1959-.......... **CLC 55**

Bradley, Marion Zimmer 1930-..... **CLC 30**
See also AAYA 9; CA 57-60; CAAS 10;
CANR 7, 31; DLB 8; MTCW

Bradstreet, Anne 1612(?)-1672 .... **LC 4**
See also CDALB 1640-1865; DA; DLB 24

Bragg, Melvyn 1939-............. **CLC 10**
See also BEST 89:3; CA 57-60; CANR 10;
DLB 14

Braine, John (Gerard)
1922-1986 .... **CLC 1, 3, 41**
See also CA 1-4R; 120; CANR 1, 33;
CDBLB 1945-1960; DLB 15; DLBY 86;
MTCW

Brammer, William 1930(?)-1978 .... **CLC 31**
See also CA 77-80

Brancati, Vitaliano 1907-1954..... **TCLC 12**
See also CA 109

Brancato, Robin F(idler) 1936- ..... **CLC 35**
See also AAYA 9; CA 69-72; CANR 11;
SAAS 9; SATA 23

Brand, Max
See Faust, Frederick (Schiller)

Brand, Millen 1906-1980 .... **CLC 7**
See also CA 21-24R; 97-100

Branden, Barbara .... **CLC 44**

Brandes, Georg (Morris Cohen)
1842-1927 .... **TCLC 10**
See also CA 105

Brandys, Kazimierz 1916-......... **CLC 62**

Branley, Franklyn M(ansfield)
1915- .... **CLC 21**
See also CA 33-36R; CANR 14, 39;
CLR 13; MAICYA; SAAS 16; SATA 4,
68

Brathwaite, Edward (Kamau)
1930- .... **CLC 11**
See also BW; CA 25-28R; CANR 11, 26;
DLB 125

Brautigan, Richard (Gary)
1935-1984 .... **CLC 1, 3, 5, 9, 12, 34, 42**
See also CA 53-56; 113; CANR 34; DLB 2,
5; DLBY 80, 84; MTCW; SATA 56

Braverman, Kate 1950- .... **CLC 67**
See also CA 89-92

Brecht, Bertolt
1898-1956 ..... **TCLC 1, 6, 13, 35; DC 3**
See also CA 104; 133; DA; DLB 56, 124;
MTCW; WLC

Brecht, Eugen Berthold Friedrich
See Brecht, Bertolt

Bremer, Fredrika 1801-1865 ..... **NCLC 11**

Brennan, Christopher John
1870-1932 .... **TCLC 17**
See also CA 117

Brennan, Maeve 1917-............. **CLC 5**
See also CA 81-84

Brentano, Clemens (Maria)
1778-1842 .... **NCLC 1**

Brent of Bin Bin
See Franklin, (Stella Maraia Sarah) Miles

Brenton, Howard 1942-........... **CLC 31**
See also CA 69-72; CANR 33; DLB 13;
MTCW

Breslin, James 1930-
See Breslin, Jimmy
See also CA 73-76; CANR 31; MTCW

Breslin, Jimmy .... **CLC 4, 43**
See also Breslin, James
See also AITN 1

Bresson, Robert 1907- .... **CLC 16**
See also CA 110

Breton, Andre 1896-1966... **CLC 2, 9, 15, 54**
See also CA 19-20; 25-28R; CANR 40;
CAP 2; DLB 65; MTCW

Breytenbach, Breyten 1939(?)- .. **CLC 23, 37**
See also CA 113; 129

Campana, Dino 1885-1932 . . . . **TCLC 20**
See also CA 117; DLB 114

Campbell, John W(ood, Jr.)
1910-1971 . . . . **CLC 32**
See also CA 21-22; 29-32R; CANR 34;
CAP 2; DLB 8; MTCW

Campbell, Joseph 1904-1987 . . . . **CLC 69**
See also AAYA 3; BEST 89:2; CA 1-4R;
124; CANR 3, 28; MTCW

Campbell, (John) Ramsey 1946- . . . . **CLC 42**
See also CA 57-60; CANR 7

Campbell, (Ignatius) Roy (Dunnachie)
1901-1957 . . . . **TCLC 5**
See also CA 104; DLB 20

Campbell, Thomas 1777-1844 . . . . **NCLC 19**
See also DLB 93

Campbell, Wilfred . . . . **TCLC 9**
See also Campbell, William

Campbell, William 1858(?)-1918
See Campbell, Wilfred
See also CA 106; DLB 92

Campos, Alvaro de
See Pessoa, Fernando (Antonio Nogueira)

Camus, Albert
1913-1960 . . . . **CLC 1, 2, 4, 9, 11, 14, 32,**
63, 69; DC 2; SSC 9
See also CA 89-92; DA; DLB 72; MTCW;
WLC

Canby, Vincent 1924- . . . . **CLC 13**
See also CA 81-84

Cancale
See Desnos, Robert

Canetti, Elias 1905- . . . . . . **CLC 3, 14, 25, 75**
See also CA 21-24R; CANR 23; DLB 85,
124; MTCW

Canin, Ethan 1960- . . . . **CLC 55**
See also CA 131; 135

Cannon, Curt
See Hunter, Evan

Cape, Judith
See Page, P(atricia) K(athleen)

Capek, Karel
1890-1938 . . . . **TCLC 6, 37; DC 1**
See also CA 104; 140; DA; WLC

Capote, Truman
1924-1984 . . . . . . **CLC 1, 3, 8, 13, 19, 34,**
38, 58; SSC 2
See also CA 5-8R; 113; CANR 18;
CDALB 1941-1968; DA; DLB 2;
DLBY 80, 84; MTCW; WLC

Capra, Frank 1897-1991 . . . . **CLC 16**
See also CA 61-64; 135

Caputo, Philip 1941- . . . . **CLC 32**
See also CA 73-76; CANR 40

Card, Orson Scott 1951- . . . . **CLC 44, 47, 50**
See also CA 102; CANR 27; MTCW

Cardenal (Martinez), Ernesto
1925- . . . . **CLC 31**
See also CA 49-52; CANR 2, 32; HW;
MTCW

Carducci, Giosue 1835-1907 . . . . . . **TCLC 32**

Carew, Thomas 1595(?)-1640 . . . . **LC 13**
See also DLB 126

Carey, Ernestine Gilbreth 1908- . . . . **CLC 17**
See also CA 5-8R; SATA 2

Carey, Peter 1943- . . . . **CLC 40, 55**
See also CA 123; 127; MTCW

Carleton, William 1794-1869 . . . . . **NCLC 3**

Carlisle, Henry (Coffin) 1926- . . . . . . **CLC 33**
See also CA 13-16R; CANR 15

Carlsen, Chris
See Holdstock, Robert P.

Carlson, Ron(ald F.) 1947- . . . . **CLC 54**
See also CA 105; CANR 27

Carlyle, Thomas 1795-1881 . . . . . . **NCLC 22**
See also CDBLB 1789-1832; DA; DLB 55

Carman, (William) Bliss
1861-1929 . . . . **TCLC 7**
See also CA 104; DLB 92

Carossa, Hans 1878-1956 . . . . **TCLC 48**
See also DLB 66

Carpenter, Don(ald Richard)
1931- . . . . **CLC 41**
See also CA 45-48; CANR 1

Carpentier (y Valmont), Alejo
1904-1980 . . . . **CLC 8, 11, 38**
See also CA 65-68; 97-100; CANR 11;
DLB 113; HW

Carr, Emily 1871-1945 . . . . **TCLC 32**
See also DLB 68

Carr, John Dickson 1906-1977 . . . . . . **CLC 3**
See also CA 49-52; 69-72; CANR 3, 33;
MTCW

Carr, Philippa
See Hibbert, Eleanor Alice Burford

Carr, Virginia Spencer 1929- . . . . **CLC 34**
See also CA 61-64; DLB 111

Carrier, Roch 1937- . . . . **CLC 13, 78**
See also CA 130; DLB 53

Carroll, James P. 1943(?)- . . . . **CLC 38**
See also CA 81-84

Carroll, Jim 1951- . . . . **CLC 35**
See also CA 45-48

Carroll, Lewis . . . . **NCLC 2**
See also Dodgson, Charles Lutwidge
See also CDBLB 1832-1890; CLR 2, 18;
DLB 18; WLC

Carroll, Paul Vincent 1900-1968 . . . . **CLC 10**
See also CA 9-12R; 25-28R; DLB 10

Carruth, Hayden 1921- . . . . **CLC 4, 7, 10, 18**
See also CA 9-12R; CANR 4, 38; DLB 5;
MTCW; SATA 47

Carson, Rachel Louise 1907-1964 . . . **CLC 71**
See also CA 77-80; CANR 35; MTCW;
SATA 23

Carter, Angela (Olive)
1940-1992 . . . . . . **CLC 5, 41, 76; SSC 13**
See also CA 53-56; 136; CANR 12, 36;
DLB 14; MTCW; SATA 66;
SATA-Obit 70

Carter, Nick
See Smith, Martin Cruz

Carver, Raymond
1938-1988 . . . **CLC 22, 36, 53, 55; SSC 8**
See also CA 33-36R; 126; CANR 17, 34;
DLB 130; DLBY 84, 88; MTCW

Cary, (Arthur) Joyce (Lunel)
1888-1957 . . . . **TCLC 1, 29**
See also CA 104; CDBLB 1914-1945;
DLB 15, 100

Casanova de Seingalt, Giovanni Jacopo
1725-1798 . . . . **LC 13**

Casares, Adolfo Bioy
See Bioy Casares, Adolfo

Casely-Hayford, J(oseph) E(phraim)
1866-1930 . . . . **TCLC 24**
See also BLC 1; CA 123

Casey, John (Dudley) 1939- . . . . **CLC 59**
See also BEST 90:2; CA 69-72; CANR 23

Casey, Michael 1947- . . . . **CLC 2**
See also CA 65-68; DLB 5

Casey, Patrick
See Thurman, Wallace (Henry)

Casey, Warren (Peter) 1935-1988 . . . **CLC 12**
See also CA 101; 127

Casona, Alejandro . . . . **CLC 49**
See also Alvarez, Alejandro Rodriguez

Cassavetes, John 1929-1989 . . . . **CLC 20**
See also CA 85-88; 127

Cassill, R(onald) V(erlin) 1919- . . . **CLC 4, 23**
See also CA 9-12R; CAAS 1; CANR 7;
DLB 6

Cassity, (Allen) Turner 1929- . . . . **CLC 6, 42**
See also CA 17-20R; CAAS 8; CANR 11;
DLB 105

Castaneda, Carlos 1931(?)- . . . . **CLC 12**
See also CA 25-28R; CANR 32; HW;
MTCW

Castedo, Elena 1937- . . . . **CLC 65**
See also CA 132

Castedo-Ellerman, Elena
See Castedo, Elena

Castellanos, Rosario 1925-1974 . . . . . **CLC 66**
See also CA 131; 53-56; DLB 113; HW

Castelvetro, Lodovico 1505-1571 . . . . . **LC 12**

Castiglione, Baldassare 1478-1529 . . . **LC 12**

Castle, Robert
See Hamilton, Edmond

Castro, Guillen de 1569-1631 . . . . **LC 19**

Castro, Rosalia de 1837-1885 . . . . . **NCLC 3**

Cather, Willa
See Cather, Willa Sibert

Cather, Willa Sibert
1873-1947 . . . . . . **TCLC 1, 11, 31; SSC 2**
See also CA 104; 128; CDALB 1865-1917;
DA; DLB 9, 54, 78; DLBD 1; MTCW;
SATA 30; WLC

Catton, (Charles) Bruce
1899-1978 . . . . **CLC 35**
See also AITN 1; CA 5-8R; 81-84;
CANR 7; DLB 17; SATA 2, 24

Cauldwell, Frank
See King, Francis (Henry)

Caunitz, William J. 1933- . . . . **CLC 34**
See also BEST 89:3; CA 125; 130

Causley, Charles (Stanley) 1917- . . . . . **CLC 7**
See also CA 9-12R; CANR 5, 35; CLR 30;
DLB 27; MTCW; SATA 3, 66

Caute, David 1936-.............. **CLC 29**
See also CA 1-4R; CAAS 4; CANR 1, 33;
DLB 14

Cavafy, C(onstantine) P(eter)...... **TCLC 2, 7**
See also Kavafis, Konstantinos Petrou

Cavallo, Evelyn
See Spark, Muriel (Sarah)

Cavanna, Betty .... **CLC 12**
See also Harrison, Elizabeth Cavanna
See also MAICYA; SAAS 4; SATA 1, 30

Caxton, William 1421(?)-1491(?)..... **LC 17**

Cayrol, Jean 1911-.............. **CLC 11**
See also CA 89-92; DLB 83

Cela, Camilo Jose 1916-...... **CLC 4, 13, 59**
See also BEST 90:2; CA 21-24R; CAAS 10;
CANR 21, 32; DLBY 89; HW; MTCW

Celan, Paul .... **CLC 53**
See also Antschel, Paul
See also DLB 69

Celine, Louis-Ferdinand
.... **CLC 1, 3, 4, 7, 9, 15, 47**
See also Destouches, Louis-Ferdinand
See also DLB 72

Cellini, Benvenuto 1500-1571 .... **LC 7**

Cendrars, Blaise
See Sauser-Hall, Frederic

Cernuda (y Bidon), Luis
1902-1963 .... **CLC 54**
See also CA 131; 89-92; HW

Cervantes (Saavedra), Miguel de
1547-1616 .... **LC 6, 23; SSC 12**
See also DA; WLC

Cesaire, Aime (Fernand) 1913-.. **CLC 19, 32**
See also BLC 1; BW; CA 65-68; CANR 24;
MTCW

Chabon, Michael 1965(?)- .... **CLC 55**
See also CA 139

Chabrol, Claude 1930-............ **CLC 16**
See also CA 110

Challans, Mary 1905-1983
See Renault, Mary
See also CA 81-84; 111; SATA 23, 36

Challis, George
See Faust, Frederick (Schiller)

Chambers, Aidan 1934-........... **CLC 35**
See also CA 25-28R; CANR 12, 31;
MAICYA; SAAS 12; SATA 1, 69

Chambers, James 1948-
See Cliff, Jimmy
See also CA 124

Chambers, Jessie
See Lawrence, D(avid) H(erbert Richards)

Chambers, Robert W. 1865-1933... **TCLC 41**

Chandler, Raymond (Thornton)
1888-1959 .... **TCLC 1, 7**
See also CA 104; 129; CDALB 1929-1941;
DLBD 6; MTCW

Chang, Jung 1952-.............. **CLC 71**

Channing, William Ellery
1780-1842 .... **NCLC 17**
See also DLB 1, 59

Chaplin, Charles Spencer
1889-1977 .... **CLC 16**
See also Chaplin, Charlie
See also CA 81-84; 73-76

Chaplin, Charlie
See Chaplin, Charles Spencer
See also DLB 44

Chapman, George 1559(?)-1634...... **LC 22**
See also DLB 62, 121

Chapman, Graham 1941-1989 ..... **CLC 21**
See also Monty Python
See also CA 116; 129; CANR 35

Chapman, John Jay 1862-1933 ..... **TCLC 7**
See also CA 104

Chapman, Walker
See Silverberg, Robert

Chappell, Fred (Davis) 1936-.... **CLC 40, 78**
See also CA 5-8R; CAAS 4; CANR 8, 33;
DLB 6, 105

Char, Rene(-Emile)
1907-1988 .... **CLC 9, 11, 14, 55**
See also CA 13-16R; 124; CANR 32;
MTCW

Charby, Jay
See Ellison, Harlan

Chardin, Pierre Teilhard de
See Teilhard de Chardin, (Marie Joseph)
Pierre

Charles I 1600-1649.............. **LC 13**

Charyn, Jerome 1937- .... **CLC 5, 8, 18**
See also CA 5-8R; CAAS 1; CANR 7;
DLBY 83; MTCW

Chase, Mary (Coyle) 1907-1981 ...... **DC 1**
See also CA 77-80; 105; SATA 17, 29

Chase, Mary Ellen 1887-1973....... **CLC 2**
See also CA 13-16; 41-44R; CAP 1;
SATA 10

Chase, Nicholas
See Hyde, Anthony

Chateaubriand, Francois Rene de
1768-1848 .... **NCLC 3**
See also DLB 119

Chatterje, Sarat Chandra 1876-1936(?)
See Chatterji, Saratchandra
See also CA 109

Chatterji, Bankim Chandra
1838-1894 .... **NCLC 19**

Chatterji, Saratchandra .... **TCLC 13**
See also Chatterje, Sarat Chandra

Chatterton, Thomas 1752-1770 .... **LC 3**
See also DLB 109

Chatwin, (Charles) Bruce
1940-1989 .... **CLC 28, 57, 59**
See also AAYA 4; BEST 90:1; CA 85-88;
127

Chaucer, Daniel
See Ford, Ford Madox

Chaucer, Geoffrey 1340(?)-1400 ..... **LC 17**
See also CDBLB Before 1660; DA

Chaviaras, Strates 1935-
See Haviaras, Stratis
See also CA 105

Chayefsky, Paddy .... **CLC 23**
See also Chayefsky, Sidney
See also DLB 7, 44; DLBY 81

Chayefsky, Sidney 1923-1981
See Chayefsky, Paddy
See also CA 9-12R; 104; CANR 18

Chedid, Andree 1920-............ **CLC 47**

Cheever, John
1912-1982 ...... **CLC 3, 7, 8, 11, 15, 25,
64; SSC 1**
See also CA 5-8R; 106; CABS 1; CANR 5,
27; CDALB 1941-1968; DA; DLB 2, 102;
DLBY 80, 82; MTCW; WLC

Cheever, Susan 1943-.......... **CLC 18, 48**
See also CA 103; CANR 27; DLBY 82

Chekhonte, Antosha
See Chekhov, Anton (Pavlovich)

Chekhov, Anton (Pavlovich)
1860-1904 ...... **TCLC 3, 10, 31; SSC 2**
See also CA 104; 124; DA; WLC

Chernyshevsky, Nikolay Gavrilovich
1828-1889 .... **NCLC 1**

Cherry, Carolyn Janice 1942-
See Cherryh, C. J.
See also CA 65-68; CANR 10

Cherryh, C. J. .... **CLC 35**
See also Cherry, Carolyn Janice
See also DLBY 80

Chesnutt, Charles W(addell)
1858-1932 .... **TCLC 5, 39; SSC 7**
See also BLC 1; BW; CA 106; 125; DLB 12,
50, 78; MTCW

Chester, Alfred 1929(?)-1971....... **CLC 49**
See also CA 33-36R; DLB 130

Chesterton, G(ilbert) K(eith)
1874-1936 .... **TCLC 1, 6; SSC 1**
See also CA 104; 132; CDBLB 1914-1945;
DLB 10, 19, 34, 70, 98; MTCW;
SATA 27

Chiang Pin-chin 1904-1986
See Ding Ling
See also CA 118

Ch'ien Chung-shu 1910-.......... **CLC 22**
See also CA 130; MTCW

Child, L. Maria
See Child, Lydia Maria

Child, Lydia Maria 1802-1880 .... **NCLC 6**
See also DLB 1, 74; SATA 67

Child, Mrs.
See Child, Lydia Maria

Child, Philip 1898-1978 .... **CLC 19, 68**
See also CA 13-14; CAP 1; SATA 47

Childress, Alice 1920-.......... **CLC 12, 15**
See also AAYA 8; BLC 1; BW; CA 45-48;
CANR 3, 27; CLR 14; DLB 7, 38;
MAICYA; MTCW; SATA 7, 48

Chislett, (Margaret) Anne 1943-.... **CLC 34**

Chitty, Thomas Willes 1926-....... **CLC 11**
See also Hinde, Thomas
See also CA 5-8R

Chomette, Rene Lucien 1898-1981 .. **CLC 20**
See also Clair, Rene
See also CA 103

Chopin, Kate .... **TCLC 5, 14; SSC 8**
See also Chopin, Katherine
See also CDALB 1865-1917; DA; DLB 12, 78

Chopin, Katherine 1851-1904
See Chopin, Kate
See also CA 104; 122

Chretien de Troyes
c. 12th cent. - .... **CMLC 10**

Christie
See Ichikawa, Kon

Christie, Agatha (Mary Clarissa)
1890-1976 ...... **CLC 1, 6, 8, 12, 39, 48**
See also AAYA 9; AITN 1, 2; CA 17-20R; 61-64; CANR 10, 37; CDBLB 1914-1945; DLB 13, 77; MTCW; SATA 36

Christie, (Ann) Philippa
See Pearce, Philippa
See also CA 5-8R; CANR 4

Christine de Pizan 1365(?)-1431(?) .... **LC 9**

Chubb, Elmer
See Masters, Edgar Lee

Chulkov, Mikhail Dmitrievich
1743-1792 .... **LC 2**

Churchill, Caryl 1938- .... **CLC 31, 55**
See also CA 102; CANR 22; DLB 13; MTCW

Churchill, Charles 1731-1764........ **LC 3**
See also DLB 109

Chute, Carolyn 1947-............. **CLC 39**
See also CA 123

Ciardi, John (Anthony)
1916-1986 .... **CLC 10, 40, 44**
See also CA 5-8R; 118; CAAS 2; CANR 5, 33; CLR 19; DLB 5; DLBY 86; MAICYA; MTCW; SATA 1, 46, 65

Cicero, Marcus Tullius
106B.C.-43B.C............... **CMLC 3**

Cimino, Michael 1943-............ **CLC 16**
See also CA 105

Cioran, E(mil) M. 1911-........... **CLC 64**
See also CA 25-28R

Cisneros, Sandra 1954-............ **CLC 69**
See also AAYA 9; CA 131; DLB 122; HW

Clair, Rene....................... **CLC 20**
See also Chomette, Rene Lucien

Clampitt, Amy 1920- .... **CLC 32**
See also CA 110; CANR 29; DLB 105

Clancy, Thomas L., Jr. 1947-
See Clancy, Tom
See also CA 125; 131; MTCW

Clancy, Tom.................... **CLC 45**
See also Clancy, Thomas L., Jr.
See also AAYA 9; BEST 89:1, 90:1

Clare, John 1793-1864........... **NCLC 9**
See also DLB 55, 96

Clarin
See Alas (y Urena), Leopoldo (Enrique Garcia)

Clark, (Robert) Brian 1932-........ **CLC 29**
See also CA 41-44R

Clark, Eleanor 1913-............ **CLC 5, 19**
See also CA 9-12R; CANR 41; DLB 6

Clark, J. P.
See Clark, John Pepper
See also DLB 117

Clark, John Pepper 1935- .... **CLC 38**
See also Clark, J. P.
See also BLC 1; BW; CA 65-68; CANR 16

Clark, M. R.
See Clark, Mavis Thorpe

Clark, Mavis Thorpe 1909- ...... **CLC 12**
See also CA 57-60; CANR 8, 37; CLR 30; MAICYA; SAAS 5; SATA 8, 74

Clark, Walter Van Tilburg
1909-1971 .... **CLC 28**
See also CA 9-12R; 33-36R; DLB 9; SATA 8

Clarke, Arthur C(harles)
1917- ...... **CLC 1, 4, 13, 18, 35; SSC 3**
See also AAYA 4; CA 1-4R; CANR 2, 28; MAICYA; MTCW; SATA 13, 70

Clarke, Austin 1896-1974........ **CLC 6, 9**
See also CA 29-32; 49-52; CAP 2; DLB 10, 20

Clarke, Austin C(hesterfield)
1934- .... **CLC 8, 53**
See also BLC 1; BW; CA 25-28R; CAAS 16; CANR 14, 32; DLB 53, 125

Clarke, Gillian 1937- .... **CLC 61**
See also CA 106; DLB 40

Clarke, Marcus (Andrew Hislop)
1846-1881 .... **NCLC 19**

Clarke, Shirley 1925-............. **CLC 16**

Clash, The .... **CLC 30**
See also Headon, (Nicky) Topper; Jones, Mick; Simonon, Paul; Strummer, Joe

Claudel, Paul (Louis Charles Marie)
1868-1955 .... **TCLC 2, 10**
See also CA 104

Clavell, James (duMaresq)
1925- .... **CLC 6, 25**
See also CA 25-28R; CANR 26; MTCW

Cleaver, (Leroy) Eldridge 1935- .... **CLC 30**
See also BLC 1; BW; CA 21-24R; CANR 16

Cleese, John (Marwood) 1939- ..... **CLC 21**
See also Monty Python
See also CA 112; 116; CANR 35; MTCW

Cleishbotham, Jebediah
See Scott, Walter

Cleland, John 1710-1789 .... **LC 2**
See also DLB 39

Clemens, Samuel Langhorne 1835-1910
See Twain, Mark
See also CA 104; 135; CDALB 1865-1917; DA; DLB 11, 12, 23, 64, 74; MAICYA; YABC 2

Cleophil
See Congreve, William

Clerihew, E.
See Bentley, E(dmund) C(lerihew)

Clerk, N. W.
See Lewis, C(live) S(taples)

Cliff, Jimmy.................... **CLC 21**
See also Chambers, James

Clifton, (Thelma) Lucille
1936- .... **CLC 19, 66**
See also BLC 1; BW; CA 49-52; CANR 2, 24; CLR 5; DLB 5, 41; MAICYA; MTCW; SATA 20, 69

Clinton, Dirk
See Silverberg, Robert

Clough, Arthur Hugh 1819-1861.. **NCLC 27**
See also DLB 32

Clutha, Janet Paterson Frame 1924-
See Frame, Janet
See also CA 1-4R; CANR 2, 36; MTCW

Clyne, Terence
See Blatty, William Peter

Cobalt, Martin
See Mayne, William (James Carter)

Coburn, D(onald) L(ee) 1938- ...... **CLC 10**
See also CA 89-92

Cocteau, Jean (Maurice Eugene Clement)
1889-1963 .... **CLC 1, 8, 15, 16, 43**
See also CA 25-28; CANR 40; CAP 2; DA; DLB 65; MTCW; WLC

Codrescu, Andrei 1946- .... **CLC 46**
See also CA 33-36R; CANR 13, 34

Coe, Max
See Bourne, Randolph S(illiman)

Coe, Tucker
See Westlake, Donald E(dwin)

Coetzee, J(ohn) M(ichael)
1940- .... **CLC 23, 33, 66**
See also CA 77-80; CANR 41; MTCW

Coffey, Brian
See Koontz, Dean R(ay)

Cohen, Arthur A(llen)
1928-1986 .... **CLC 7, 31**
See also CA 1-4R; 120; CANR 1, 17; DLB 28

Cohen, Leonard (Norman)
1934- .... **CLC 3, 38**
See also CA 21-24R; CANR 14; DLB 53; MTCW

Cohen, Matt 1942-................ **CLC 19**
See also CA 61-64; CANR 40; DLB 53

Cohen-Solal, Annie 19(?)- .... **CLC 50**

Colegate, Isabel 1931- .... **CLC 36**
See also CA 17-20R; CANR 8, 22; DLB 14; MTCW

Coleman, Emmett
See Reed, Ishmael

Coleridge, Samuel Taylor
1772-1834 .... **NCLC 9**
See also CDBLB 1789-1832; DA; DLB 93, 107; WLC

Coleridge, Sara 1802-1852....... **NCLC 31**

Coles, Don 1928- .... **CLC 46**
See also CA 115; CANR 38

Colette, (Sidonie-Gabrielle)
1873-1954 ...... **TCLC 1, 5, 16; SSC 10**
See also CA 104; 131; DLB 65; MTCW

Collett, (Jacobine) Camilla (Wergeland)
1813-1895 .... **NCLC 22**

Collier, Christopher 1930-......... **CLC 30**
See also CA 33-36R; CANR 13, 33; MAICYA; SATA 16, 70

Dannay, Frederic 1905-1982 ...... **CLC 11**
See also Queen, Ellery
See also CA 1-4R; 107; CANR 1, 39;
MTCW

D'Annunzio, Gabriele
1863-1938 .... **TCLC 6, 40**
See also CA 104

d'Antibes, Germain
See Simenon, Georges (Jacques Christian)

Danvers, Dennis 1947- .... **CLC 70**

Danziger, Paula 1944- .... **CLC 21**
See also AAYA 4; CA 112; 115; CANR 37;
CLR 20; MAICYA; SATA 30, 36, 63

Dario, Ruben .... **TCLC 4**
See also Sarmiento, Felix Ruben Garcia

Darley, George 1795-1846 .... **NCLC 2**
See also DLB 96

Daryush, Elizabeth 1887-1977 .... **CLC 6, 19**
See also CA 49-52; CANR 3; DLB 20

Daudet, (Louis Marie) Alphonse
1840-1897 .... **NCLC 1**
See also DLB 123

Daumal, Rene 1908-1944 .... **TCLC 14**
See also CA 114

Davenport, Guy (Mattison, Jr.)
1927- .... **CLC 6, 14, 38**
See also CA 33-36R; CANR 23; DLB 130

Davidson, Avram 1923-
See Queen, Ellery
See also CA 101; CANR 26; DLB 8

Davidson, Donald (Grady)
1893-1968 .... **CLC 2, 13, 19**
See also CA 5-8R; 25-28R; CANR 4;
DLB 45

Davidson, Hugh
See Hamilton, Edmond

Davidson, John 1857-1909 .... **TCLC 24**
See also CA 118; DLB 19

Davidson, Sara 1943- .... **CLC 9**
See also CA 81-84

Davie, Donald (Alfred)
1922- .... **CLC 5, 8, 10, 31**
See also CA 1-4R; CAAS 3; CANR 1;
DLB 27; MTCW

Davies, Ray(mond Douglas) 1944- .. **CLC 21**
See also CA 116

Davies, Rhys 1903-1978 .... **CLC 23**
See also CA 9-12R; 81-84; CANR 4

Davies, (William) Robertson
1913- .... **CLC 2, 7, 13, 25, 42, 75**
See also BEST 89:2; CA 33-36R; CANR 17;
DA; DLB 68; MTCW; WLC

Davies, W(illiam) H(enry)
1871-1940 .... **TCLC 5**
See also CA 104; DLB 19

Davies, Walter C.
See Kornbluth, C(yril) M.

Davis, Angela (Yvonne) 1944- ...... **CLC 77**
See also BW; CA 57-60; CANR 10

Davis, B. Lynch
See Bioy Casares, Adolfo; Borges, Jorge
Luis

Davis, Gordon
See Hunt, E(verette) Howard, Jr.

Davis, Harold Lenoir 1896-1960 .... **CLC 49**
See also CA 89-92; DLB 9

Davis, Rebecca (Blaine) Harding
1831-1910 .... **TCLC 6**
See also CA 104; DLB 74

Davis, Richard Harding
1864-1916 .... **TCLC 24**
See also CA 114; DLB 12, 23, 78, 79

Davison, Frank Dalby 1893-1970 ... **CLC 15**
See also CA 116

Davison, Lawrence H.
See Lawrence, D(avid) H(erbert Richards)

Davison, Peter 1928- .... **CLC 28**
See also CA 9-12R; CAAS 4; CANR 3;
DLB 5

Davys, Mary 1674-1732 .... **LC 1**
See also DLB 39

Dawson, Fielding 1930- .... **CLC 6**
See also CA 85-88; DLB 130

Dawson, Peter
See Faust, Frederick (Schiller)

Day, Clarence (Shepard, Jr.)
1874-1935 .... **TCLC 25**
See also CA 108; DLB 11

Day, Thomas 1748-1789 .... **LC 1**
See also DLB 39; YABC 1

Day Lewis, C(ecil)
1904-1972 .... **CLC 1, 6, 10**
See also Blake, Nicholas
See also CA 13-16; 33-36R; CANR 34;
CAP 1; DLB 15, 20; MTCW

Dazai, Osamu .... **TCLC 11**
See also Tsushima, Shuji

de Andrade, Carlos Drummond
See Drummond de Andrade, Carlos

Deane, Norman
See Creasey, John

**de Beauvoir, Simone (Lucie Ernestine Marie
Bertrand)**
See Beauvoir, Simone (Lucie Ernestine
Marie Bertrand) de

de Brissac, Malcolm
See Dickinson, Peter (Malcolm)

de Chardin, Pierre Teilhard
See Teilhard de Chardin, (Marie Joseph)
Pierre

Dee, John 1527-1608 .... **LC 20**

Deer, Sandra 1940- .... **CLC 45**

De Ferrari, Gabriella .... **CLC 65**

Defoe, Daniel 1660(?)-1731 .... **LC 1**
See also CDBLB 1660-1789; DA; DLB 39,
95, 101; MAICYA; SATA 22; WLC

de Gourmont, Remy
See Gourmont, Remy de

de Hartog, Jan 1914- .... **CLC 19**
See also CA 1-4R; CANR 1

de Hostos, E. M.
See Hostos (y Bonilla), Eugenio Maria de

de Hostos, Eugenio M.
See Hostos (y Bonilla), Eugenio Maria de

Deighton, Len .... **CLC 4, 7, 22, 46**
See also Deighton, Leonard Cyril
See also AAYA 6; BEST 89:2;
CDBLB 1960 to Present; DLB 87

Deighton, Leonard Cyril 1929-
See Deighton, Len
See also CA 9-12R; CANR 19, 33; MTCW

Dekker, Thomas 1572(?)-1632 ...... **LC 22**
See also CDBLB Before 1660; DLB 62

de la Mare, Walter (John)
1873-1956 .... **TCLC 4**
See also CA 110; 137; CDBLB 1914-1945;
CLR 23; DA; DLB 19; MAICYA;
SATA 16; WLC

Delaney, Franey
See O'Hara, John (Henry)

Delaney, Shelagh 1939- .... **CLC 29**
See also CA 17-20R; CANR 30;
CDBLB 1960 to Present; DLB 13;
MTCW

Delany, Mary (Granville Pendarves)
1700-1788 .... **LC 12**

Delany, Samuel R(ay, Jr.)
1942- .... **CLC 8, 14, 38**
See also BLC 1; BW; CA 81-84; CANR 27;
DLB 8, 33; MTCW

Delaporte, Theophile
See Green, Julian (Hartridge)

De La Ramee, (Marie) Louise 1839-1908
See Ouida
See also SATA 20

de la Roche, Mazo 1879-1961 ...... **CLC 14**
See also CA 85-88; CANR 30; DLB 68;
SATA 64

Delbanco, Nicholas (Franklin)
1942- .... **CLC 6, 13**
See also CA 17-20R; CAAS 2; CANR 29;
DLB 6

del Castillo, Michel 1933- .... **CLC 38**
See also CA 109

Deledda, Grazia (Cosima)
1875(?)-1936 .... **TCLC 23**
See also CA 123

Delibes, Miguel .... **CLC 8, 18**
See also Delibes Setien, Miguel

Delibes Setien, Miguel 1920-
See Delibes, Miguel
See also CA 45-48; CANR 1, 32; HW;
MTCW

DeLillo, Don
1936- ..... **CLC 8, 10, 13, 27, 39, 54, 76**
See also BEST 89:1; CA 81-84; CANR 21;
DLB 6; MTCW

de Lisser, H. G.
See De Lisser, Herbert George
See also DLB 117

De Lisser, Herbert George
1878-1944 .... **TCLC 12**
See also de Lisser, H. G.
See also CA 109

Deloria, Vine (Victor), Jr. 1933- .... **CLC 21**
See also CA 53-56; CANR 5, 20; MTCW;
SATA 21

Del Vecchio, John M(ichael)
1947- .... **CLC 29**
See also CA 110; DLBD 9

de Man, Paul (Adolph Michel)
1919-1983 .... **CLC 55**
See also CA 128; 111; DLB 67; MTCW

Author Index

Dunlap, William 1766-1839 . . . . . . **NCLC 2**
See also DLB 30, 37, 59

Dunn, Douglas (Eaglesham)
1942- . . . . **CLC 6, 40**
See also CA 45-48; CANR 2, 33; DLB 40;
MTCW

Dunn, Katherine (Karen) 1945- . . . . . **CLC 71**
See also CA 33-36R

Dunn, Stephen 1939- . . . . **CLC 36**
See also CA 33-36R; CANR 12; DLB 105

Dunne, Finley Peter 1867-1936 . . . . **TCLC 28**
See also CA 108; DLB 11, 23

Dunne, John Gregory 1932- . . . . **CLC 28**
See also CA 25-28R; CANR 14; DLBY 80

**Dunsany, Edward John Moreton Drax
Plunkett** 1878-1957
See Dunsany, Lord; Lord Dunsany
See also CA 104; DLB 10

Dunsany, Lord . . . . **TCLC 2**
See also Dunsany, Edward John Moreton
Drax Plunkett
See also DLB 77

du Perry, Jean
See Simenon, Georges (Jacques Christian)

Durang, Christopher (Ferdinand)
1949- . . . . **CLC 27, 38**
See also CA 105

Duras, Marguerite
1914- . . . . . . **CLC 3, 6, 11, 20, 34, 40, 68**
See also CA 25-28R; DLB 83; MTCW

Durban, (Rosa) Pam 1947- . . . . **CLC 39**
See also CA 123

Durcan, Paul 1944- . . . . **CLC 43, 70**
See also CA 134

Durrell, Lawrence (George)
1912-1990 . . . . **CLC 1, 4, 6, 8, 13, 27, 41**
See also CA 9-12R; 132;
CDBLB 1945-1960; DLB 15, 27;
DLBY 90; MTCW

Durrenmatt, Friedrich
. . . . **CLC 1, 4, 8, 11, 15, 43**
See also Duerrenmatt, Friedrich
See also DLB 69, 124

Dutt, Toru 1856-1877 . . . . **NCLC 29**

Dwight, Timothy 1752-1817 . . . . . . **NCLC 13**
See also DLB 37

Dworkin, Andrea 1946- . . . . **CLC 43**
See also CA 77-80; CANR 16, 39; MTCW

Dwyer, Deanna
See Koontz, Dean R(ay)

Dwyer, K. R.
See Koontz, Dean R(ay)

Dylan, Bob 1941- . . . . . . **CLC 3, 4, 6, 12, 77**
See also CA 41-44R; DLB 16

Eagleton, Terence (Francis) 1943-
See Eagleton, Terry
See also CA 57-60; CANR 7, 23; MTCW

Eagleton, Terry . . . . **CLC 63**
See also Eagleton, Terence (Francis)

Early, Jack
See Scoppettone, Sandra

East, Michael
See West, Morris L(anglo)

Eastaway, Edward
See Thomas, (Philip) Edward

Eastlake, William (Derry) 1917- . . . . . **CLC 8**
See also CA 5-8R; CAAS 1; CANR 5;
DLB 6

Eberhart, Richard (Ghormley)
1904- . . . . **CLC 3, 11, 19, 56**
See also CA 1-4R; CANR 2;
CDALB 1941-1968; DLB 48; MTCW

Eberstadt, Fernanda 1960- . . . . **CLC 39**
See also CA 136

Echegaray (y Eizaguirre), Jose (Maria Waldo)
1832-1916 . . . . **TCLC 4**
See also CA 104; CANR 32; HW; MTCW

Echeverria, (Jose) Esteban (Antonino)
1805-1851 . . . . **NCLC 18**

Echo
See Proust, (Valentin-Louis-George-Eugene-)
Marcel

Eckert, Allan W. 1931- . . . . **CLC 17**
See also CA 13-16R; CANR 14; SATA 27,
29

Eckhart, Meister 1260(?)-1328(?) . . **CMLC 9**
See also DLB 115

Eckmar, F. R.
See de Hartog, Jan

Eco, Umberto 1932- . . . . **CLC 28, 60**
See also BEST 90:1; CA 77-80; CANR 12,
33; MTCW

Eddison, E(ric) R(ucker)
1882-1945 . . . . **TCLC 15**
See also CA 109

Edel, (Joseph) Leon 1907- . . . . . . **CLC 29, 34**
See also CA 1-4R; CANR 1, 22; DLB 103

Eden, Emily 1797-1869 . . . . **NCLC 10**

Edgar, David 1948- . . . . **CLC 42**
See also CA 57-60; CANR 12; DLB 13;
MTCW

Edgerton, Clyde (Carlyle) 1944- . . . . **CLC 39**
See also CA 118; 134

Edgeworth, Maria 1767-1849 . . . . . . **NCLC 1**
See also DLB 116; SATA 21

Edmonds, Paul
See Kuttner, Henry

Edmonds, Walter D(umaux) 1903- . . **CLC 35**
See also CA 5-8R; CANR 2; DLB 9;
MAICYA; SAAS 4; SATA 1, 27

Edmondson, Wallace
See Ellison, Harlan

Edson, Russell . . . . **CLC 13**
See also CA 33-36R

Edwards, G(erald) B(asil)
1899-1976 . . . . **CLC 25**
See also CA 110

Edwards, Gus 1939- . . . . **CLC 43**
See also CA 108

Edwards, Jonathan 1703-1758 . . . . **LC 7**
See also DA; DLB 24

Efron, Marina Ivanovna Tsvetaeva
See Tsvetaeva (Efron), Marina (Ivanovna)

Ehle, John (Marsden, Jr.) 1925- . . . . **CLC 27**
See also CA 9-12R

Ehrenbourg, Ilya (Grigoryevich)
See Ehrenburg, Ilya (Grigoryevich)

Ehrenburg, Ilya (Grigoryevich)
1891-1967 . . . . **CLC 18, 34, 62**
See also CA 102; 25-28R

Ehrenburg, Ilyo (Grigoryevich)
See Ehrenburg, Ilya (Grigoryevich)

Eich, Guenter 1907-1972 . . . . **CLC 15**
See also CA 111; 93-96; DLB 69, 124

Eichendorff, Joseph Freiherr von
1788-1857 . . . . **NCLC 8**
See also DLB 90

Eigner, Larry . . . . **CLC 9**
See also Eigner, Laurence (Joel)
See also DLB 5

Eigner, Laurence (Joel) 1927-
See Eigner, Larry
See also CA 9-12R; CANR 6

Eiseley, Loren Corey 1907-1977 . . . . . **CLC 7**
See also AAYA 5; CA 1-4R; 73-76;
CANR 6

Eisenstadt, Jill 1963- . . . . **CLC 50**
See also CA 140

Eisner, Simon
See Kornbluth, C(yril) M.

Ekeloef, (Bengt) Gunnar
1907-1968 . . . . **CLC 27**
See also Ekelof, (Bengt) Gunnar
See also CA 123; 25-28R

Ekelof, (Bengt) Gunnar . . . . **CLC 27**
See also Ekeloef, (Bengt) Gunnar

Ekwensi, C. O. D.
See Ekwensi, Cyprian (Odiatu Duaka)

Ekwensi, Cyprian (Odiatu Duaka)
1921- . . . . **CLC 4**
See also BLC 1; BW; CA 29-32R;
CANR 18; DLB 117; MTCW; SATA 66

Elaine . . . . **TCLC 18**
See also Leverson, Ada

El Crummo
See Crumb, R(obert)

Elia
See Lamb, Charles

Eliade, Mircea 1907-1986 . . . . **CLC 19**
See also CA 65-68; 119; CANR 30; MTCW

Eliot, A. D.
See Jewett, (Theodora) Sarah Orne

Eliot, Alice
See Jewett, (Theodora) Sarah Orne

Eliot, Dan
See Silverberg, Robert

Eliot, George
1819-1880 . . . . **NCLC 4, 13, 23, 41**
See also CDBLB 1832-1890; DA; DLB 21,
35, 55; WLC

Eliot, John 1604-1690 . . . . **LC 5**
See also DLB 24

Eliot, T(homas) S(tearns)
1888-1965 . . . . . **CLC 1, 2, 3, 6, 9, 10, 13,
15, 24, 34, 41, 55, 57; PC 5**
See also CA 5-8R; 25-28R; CANR 41;
CDALB 1929-1941; DA; DLB 7, 10, 45,
63; DLBY 88; MTCW; WLC 2

Elizabeth 1866-1941 . . . . **TCLC 41**

Elkin, Stanley L(awrence)
1930- ... CLC 4, 6, 9, 14, 27, 51; SSC 12
See also CA 9-12R; CANR 8; DLB 2, 28;
DLBY 80; MTCW

Elledge, Scott .... CLC 34

Elliott, Don
See Silverberg, Robert

Elliott, George P(aul) 1918-1980 ..... CLC 2
See also CA 1-4R; 97-100; CANR 2

Elliott, Janice 1931- .... CLC 47
See also CA 13-16R; CANR 8, 29; DLB 14

Elliott, Sumner Locke 1917-1991 ... CLC 38
See also CA 5-8R; 134; CANR 2, 21

Elliott, William
See Bradbury, Ray (Douglas)

Ellis, A. E. .... CLC 7

Ellis, Alice Thomas .... CLC 40
See also Haycraft, Anna

Ellis, Bret Easton 1964- .... CLC 39, 71
See also AAYA 2; CA 118; 123

Ellis, (Henry) Havelock
1859-1939 .... TCLC 14
See also CA 109

Ellis, Landon
See Ellison, Harlan

Ellis, Trey 1962- .... CLC 55

Ellison, Harlan 1934- .... CLC 1, 13, 42
See also CA 5-8R; CANR 5; DLB 8;
MTCW

Ellison, Ralph (Waldo)
1914- .... CLC 1, 3, 11, 54
See also BLC 1; BW; CA 9-12R; CANR 24;
CDALB 1941-1968; DA; DLB 2, 76;
MTCW; WLC

Ellmann, Lucy (Elizabeth) 1956- .... CLC 61
See also CA 128

Ellmann, Richard (David)
1918-1987 .... CLC 50
See also BEST 89:2; CA 1-4R; 122;
CANR 2, 28; DLB 103; DLBY 87;
MTCW

Elman, Richard 1934- .... CLC 19
See also CA 17-20R; CAAS 3

Elron
See Hubbard, L(afayette) Ron(ald)

Eluard, Paul .... TCLC 7, 41
See also Grindel, Eugene

Elyot, Sir Thomas 1490(?)-1546 ..... LC 11

Elytis, Odysseus 1911- .... CLC 15, 49
See also CA 102; MTCW

Emecheta, (Florence Onye) Buchi
1944- .... CLC 14, 48
See also BLC 2; BW; CA 81-84; CANR 27;
DLB 117; MTCW; SATA 66

Emerson, Ralph Waldo
1803-1882 .... NCLC 1, 38
See also CDALB 1640-1865; DA; DLB 1,
59, 73; WLC

Eminescu, Mihail 1850-1889 ..... NCLC 33

Empson, William
1906-1984 .... CLC 3, 8, 19, 33, 34
See also CA 17-20R; 112; CANR 31;
DLB 20; MTCW

Enchi Fumiko (Ueda) 1905-1986.... CLC 31
See also CA 129; 121

Ende, Michael (Andreas Helmuth)
1929- .... CLC 31
See also CA 118; 124; CANR 36; CLR 14;
DLB 75; MAICYA; SATA 42, 61

Endo, Shusaku 1923- ..... CLC 7, 14, 19, 54
See also CA 29-32R; CANR 21; MTCW

Engel, Marian 1933-1985 .... CLC 36
See also CA 25-28R; CANR 12; DLB 53

Engelhardt, Frederick
See Hubbard, L(afayette) Ron(ald)

Enright, D(ennis) J(oseph)
1920- .... CLC 4, 8, 31
See also CA 1-4R; CANR 1; DLB 27;
SATA 25

Enzensberger, Hans Magnus
1929- .... CLC 43
See also CA 116; 119

Ephron, Nora 1941- .... CLC 17, 31
See also AITN 2; CA 65-68; CANR 12, 39

Epsilon
See Betjeman, John

Epstein, Daniel Mark 1948- .... CLC 7
See also CA 49-52; CANR 2

Epstein, Jacob 1956- .... CLC 19
See also CA 114

Epstein, Joseph 1937- .... CLC 39
See also CA 112; 119

Epstein, Leslie 1938- .... CLC 27
See also CA 73-76; CAAS 12; CANR 23

Equiano, Olaudah 1745(?)-1797 ...... LC 16
See also BLC 2; DLB 37, 50

Erasmus, Desiderius 1469(?)-1536.... LC 16

Erdman, Paul E(mil) 1932- .... CLC 25
See also AITN 1; CA 61-64; CANR 13

Erdrich, Louise 1954- .... CLC 39, 54
See also AAYA 10; BEST 89:1; CA 114;
CANR 41; MTCW

Erenburg, Ilya (Grigoryevich)
See Ehrenburg, Ilya (Grigoryevich)

Erickson, Stephen Michael 1950-
See Erickson, Steve
See also CA 129

Erickson, Steve .... CLC 64
See also Erickson, Stephen Michael

Ericson, Walter
See Fast, Howard (Melvin)

Eriksson, Buntel
See Bergman, (Ernst) Ingmar

Eschenbach, Wolfram von
See Wolfram von Eschenbach

Eseki, Bruno
See Mphahlele, Ezekiel

Esenin, Sergei (Alexandrovich)
1895-1925 .... TCLC 4
See also CA 104

Eshleman, Clayton 1935- .... CLC 7
See also CA 33-36R; CAAS 6; DLB 5

Espriella, Don Manuel Alvarez
See Southey, Robert

Espriu, Salvador 1913-1985 .... CLC 9
See also CA 115

Espronceda, Jose de 1808-1842... NCLC 39

Esse, James
See Stephens, James

Esterbrook, Tom
See Hubbard, L(afayette) Ron(ald)

Estleman, Loren D. 1952- .... CLC 48
See also CA 85-88; CANR 27; MTCW

Evan, Evin
See Faust, Frederick (Schiller)

Evans, Evan
See Faust, Frederick (Schiller)

Evans, Marian
See Eliot, George

Evans, Mary Ann
See Eliot, George

Evarts, Esther
See Benson, Sally

Everett, Percival
See Everett, Percival L.

Everett, Percival L. 1956- .... CLC 57
See also CA 129

Everson, R(onald) G(ilmour)
1903- .... CLC 27
See also CA 17-20R; DLB 88

Everson, William (Oliver)
1912- .... CLC 1, 5, 14
See also CA 9-12R; CANR 20; DLB 5, 16;
MTCW

Evtushenko, Evgenii Aleksandrovich
See Yevtushenko, Yevgeny (Alexandrovich)

Ewart, Gavin (Buchanan)
1916- .... CLC 13, 46
See also CA 89-92; CANR 17; DLB 40;
MTCW

Ewers, Hanns Heinz 1871-1943 ... TCLC 12
See also CA 109

Ewing, Frederick R.
See Sturgeon, Theodore (Hamilton)

Exley, Frederick (Earl)
1929-1992 .... CLC 6, 11
See also AITN 2; CA 81-84; 138; DLBY 81

Eynhardt, Guillermo
See Quiroga, Horacio (Sylvestre)

Ezekiel, Nissim 1924- .... CLC 61
See also CA 61-64

Ezekiel, Tish O'Dowd 1943- .... CLC 34
See also CA 129

Fagen, Donald 1948- .... CLC 26

Fainzilberg, Ilya Arnoldovich 1897-1937
See Ilf, Ilya
See also CA 120

Fair, Ronald L. 1932- .... CLC 18
See also BW; CA 69-72; CANR 25; DLB 33

Fairbairns, Zoe (Ann) 1948- .... CLC 32
See also CA 103; CANR 21

Falco, Gian
See Papini, Giovanni

Falconer, James
See Kirkup, James

Falconer, Kenneth
See Kornbluth, C(yril) M.

Falkland, Samuel
See Heijermans, Herman

Fallaci, Oriana 1930- . . . . **CLC 11**
  See also CA 77-80; CANR 15; MTCW

Faludy, George 1913- . . . . **CLC 42**
  See also CA 21-24R

Faludy, Gyoergy
  See Faludy, George

Fanon, Frantz 1925-1961 . . . . **CLC 74**
  See also BLC 2; BW; CA 116; 89-92

Fanshawe, Ann . . . . **LC 11**

Fante, John (Thomas) 1911-1983 . . . **CLC 60**
  See also CA 69-72; 109; CANR 23;
   DLB 130; DLBY 83

Farah, Nuruddin 1945- . . . . **CLC 53**
  See also BLC 2; CA 106; DLB 125

Fargue, Leon-Paul 1876(?)-1947 . . . **TCLC 11**
  See also CA 109

Farigoule, Louis
  See Romains, Jules

Farina, Richard 1936(?)-1966 . . . . **CLC 9**
  See also CA 81-84; 25-28R

Farley, Walter (Lorimer)
  1915-1989 . . . . **CLC 17**
  See also CA 17-20R; CANR 8, 29; DLB 22;
   MAICYA; SATA 2, 43

Farmer, Philip Jose 1918- . . . . **CLC 1, 19**
  See also CA 1-4R; CANR 4, 35; DLB 8;
   MTCW

Farquhar, George 1677-1707 . . . . **LC 21**
  See also DLB 84

Farrell, J(ames) G(ordon)
  1935-1979 . . . . **CLC 6**
  See also CA 73-76; 89-92; CANR 36;
   DLB 14; MTCW

Farrell, James T(homas)
  1904-1979 . . . . **CLC 1, 4, 8, 11, 66**
  See also CA 5-8R; 89-92; CANR 9; DLB 4,
   9, 86; DLBD 2; MTCW

Farren, Richard J.
  See Betjeman, John

Farren, Richard M.
  See Betjeman, John

Fassbinder, Rainer Werner
  1946-1982 . . . . **CLC 20**
  See also CA 93-96; 106; CANR 31

Fast, Howard (Melvin) 1914- . . . . . . **CLC 23**
  See also CA 1-4R; CANR 1, 33; DLB 9;
   SATA 7

Faulcon, Robert
  See Holdstock, Robert P.

Faulkner, William (Cuthbert)
  1897-1962 . . . . . **CLC 1, 3, 6, 8, 9, 11, 14,
               18, 28, 52, 68; SSC 1**
  See also AAYA 7; CA 81-84; CANR 33;
   CDALB 1929-1941; DA; DLB 9, 11, 44,
   102; DLBD 2; DLBY 86; MTCW; WLC

Fauset, Jessie Redmon
  1884(?)-1961 . . . . **CLC 19, 54**
  See also BLC 2; BW; CA 109; DLB 51

Faust, Frederick (Schiller)
  1892-1944(?) . . . . **TCLC 49**
  See also CA 108

Faust, Irvin 1924- . . . . **CLC 8**
  See also CA 33-36R; CANR 28; DLB 2, 28;
   DLBY 80

Fawkes, Guy
  See Benchley, Robert (Charles)

Fearing, Kenneth (Flexner)
  1902-1961 . . . . **CLC 51**
  See also CA 93-96; DLB 9

Fecamps, Elise
  See Creasey, John

Federman, Raymond 1928- . . . . . . **CLC 6, 47**
  See also CA 17-20R; CAAS 8; CANR 10;
   DLBY 80

Federspiel, J(uerg) F. 1931- . . . . **CLC 42**

Feiffer, Jules (Ralph) 1929- . . . . **CLC 2, 8, 64**
  See also AAYA 3; CA 17-20R; CANR 30;
   DLB 7, 44; MTCW; SATA 8, 61

Feige, Hermann Albert Otto Maximilian
  See Traven, B.

Fei-Kan, Li
  See Li Fei-kan

Feinberg, David B. 1956- . . . . **CLC 59**
  See also CA 135

Feinstein, Elaine 1930- . . . . **CLC 36**
  See also CA 69-72; CAAS 1; CANR 31;
   DLB 14, 40; MTCW

Feldman, Irving (Mordecai) 1928- . . . . **CLC 7**
  See also CA 1-4R; CANR 1

Fellini, Federico 1920- . . . . **CLC 16**
  See also CA 65-68; CANR 33

Felsen, Henry Gregor 1916- . . . . **CLC 17**
  See also CA 1-4R; CANR 1; SAAS 2;
   SATA 1

Fenton, James Martin 1949- . . . . **CLC 32**
  See also CA 102; DLB 40

Ferber, Edna 1887-1968 . . . . **CLC 18**
  See also AITN 1; CA 5-8R; 25-28R; DLB 9,
   28, 86; MTCW; SATA 7

Ferguson, Helen
  See Kavan, Anna

Ferguson, Samuel 1810-1886 . . . . . **NCLC 33**
  See also DLB 32

Ferling, Lawrence
  See Ferlinghetti, Lawrence (Monsanto)

Ferlinghetti, Lawrence (Monsanto)
  1919(?)- . . . . **CLC 2, 6, 10, 27; PC 1**
  See also CA 5-8R; CANR 3, 41;
   CDALB 1941-1968; DLB 5, 16; MTCW

Fernandez, Vicente Garcia Huidobro
  See Huidobro Fernandez, Vicente Garcia

Ferrer, Gabriel (Francisco Victor) Miro
  See Miro (Ferrer), Gabriel (Francisco
   Victor)

Ferrier, Susan (Edmonstone)
  1782-1854 . . . . **NCLC 8**
  See also DLB 116

Ferrigno, Robert 1948(?)- . . . . **CLC 65**
  See also CA 140

Feuchtwanger, Lion 1884-1958 . . . . . **TCLC 3**
  See also CA 104; DLB 66

Feydeau, Georges (Leon Jules Marie)
  1862-1921 . . . . **TCLC 22**
  See also CA 113

Ficino, Marsilio 1433-1499 . . . . **LC 12**

Fiedler, Leslie A(aron)
  1917- . . . . **CLC 4, 13, 24**
  See also CA 9-12R; CANR 7; DLB 28, 67;
   MTCW

Field, Andrew 1938- . . . . **CLC 44**
  See also CA 97-100; CANR 25

Field, Eugene 1850-1895 . . . . **NCLC 3**
  See also DLB 23, 42; MAICYA; SATA 16

Field, Gans T.
  See Wellman, Manly Wade

Field, Michael . . . . **TCLC 43**

Field, Peter
  See Hobson, Laura Z(ametkin)

Fielding, Henry 1707-1754 . . . . **LC 1**
  See also CDBLB 1660-1789; DA; DLB 39,
   84, 101; WLC

Fielding, Sarah 1710-1768 . . . . **LC 1**
  See also DLB 39

Fierstein, Harvey (Forbes) 1954- . . . **CLC 33**
  See also CA 123; 129

Figes, Eva 1932- . . . . **CLC 31**
  See also CA 53-56; CANR 4; DLB 14

Finch, Robert (Duer Claydon)
  1900- . . . . **CLC 18**
  See also CA 57-60; CANR 9, 24; DLB 88

Findley, Timothy 1930- . . . . **CLC 27**
  See also CA 25-28R; CANR 12; DLB 53

Fink, William
  See Mencken, H(enry) L(ouis)

Firbank, Louis 1942-
  See Reed, Lou
  See also CA 117

Firbank, (Arthur Annesley) Ronald
  1886-1926 . . . . **TCLC 1**
  See also CA 104; DLB 36

Fisher, M(ary) F(rances) K(ennedy)
  1908-1992 . . . . **CLC 76**
  See also CA 77-80; 138

Fisher, Roy 1930- . . . . **CLC 25**
  See also CA 81-84; CAAS 10; CANR 16;
   DLB 40

Fisher, Rudolph 1897-1934 . . . . **TCLC 11**
  See also BLC 2; BW; CA 107; 124; DLB 51,
   102

Fisher, Vardis (Alvero) 1895-1968 . . . . **CLC 7**
  See also CA 5-8R; 25-28R; DLB 9

Fiske, Tarleton
  See Bloch, Robert (Albert)

Fitch, Clarke
  See Sinclair, Upton (Beall)

Fitch, John IV
  See Cormier, Robert (Edmund)

Fitgerald, Penelope 1916- . . . . **CLC 61**

Fitzgerald, Captain Hugh
  See Baum, L(yman) Frank

FitzGerald, Edward 1809-1883 . . . . **NCLC 9**
  See also DLB 32

Fitzgerald, F(rancis) Scott (Key)
  1896-1940 . . . . **TCLC 1, 6, 14, 28; SSC 6**
  See also AITN 1; CA 110; 123;
   CDALB 1917-1929; DA; DLB 4, 9, 86;
   DLBD 1; DLBY 81; MTCW; WLC

Fitzgerald, Penelope 1916- . . . . . . **CLC 19, 51**
  See also CA 85-88; CAAS 10; DLB 14

Friedan, Betty (Naomi) 1921- ...... **CLC 74**
See also CA 65-68; CANR 18; MTCW

Friedman, B(ernard) H(arper)
1926- .... **CLC 7**
See also CA 1-4R; CANR 3

Friedman, Bruce Jay 1930- .... **CLC 3, 5, 56**
See also CA 9-12R; CANR 25; DLB 2, 28

Friel, Brian 1929- .... **CLC 5, 42, 59**
See also CA 21-24R; CANR 33; DLB 13;
MTCW

Friis-Baastad, Babbis Ellinor
1921-1970 .... **CLC 12**
See also CA 17-20R; 134; SATA 7

Frisch, Max (Rudolf)
1911-1991 ..... **CLC 3, 9, 14, 18, 32, 44**
See also CA 85-88; 134; CANR 32;
DLB 69, 124; MTCW

Fromentin, Eugene (Samuel Auguste)
1820-1876 .... **NCLC 10**
See also DLB 123

Frost, Frederick
See Faust, Frederick (Schiller)

Frost, Robert (Lee)
1874-1963 .... **CLC 1, 3, 4, 9, 10, 13, 15,
26, 34, 44; PC 1**
See also CA 89-92; CANR 33;
CDALB 1917-1929; DA; DLB 54;
DLBD 7; MTCW; SATA 14; WLC

Froy, Herald
See Waterhouse, Keith (Spencer)

Fry, Christopher 1907- .... **CLC 2, 10, 14**
See also CA 17-20R; CANR 9, 30; DLB 13;
MTCW; SATA 66

Frye, (Herman) Northrop
1912-1991 .... **CLC 24, 70**
See also CA 5-8R; 133; CANR 8, 37;
DLB 67, 68; MTCW

Fuchs, Daniel 1909- .... **CLC 8, 22**
See also CA 81-84; CAAS 5; CANR 40;
DLB 9, 26, 28

Fuchs, Daniel 1934- .... **CLC 34**
See also CA 37-40R; CANR 14

Fuentes, Carlos
1928- ...... **CLC 3, 8, 10, 13, 22, 41, 60**
See also AAYA 4; AITN 2; CA 69-72;
CANR 10, 32; DA; DLB 113; HW;
MTCW; WLC

Fuentes, Gregorio Lopez y
See Lopez y Fuentes, Gregorio

Fugard, (Harold) Athol
1932- .... **CLC 5, 9, 14, 25, 40; DC 3**
See also CA 85-88; CANR 32; MTCW

Fugard, Sheila 1932- .... **CLC 48**
See also CA 125

Fuller, Charles (H., Jr.)
1939- .... **CLC 25; DC 1**
See also BLC 2; BW; CA 108; 112; DLB 38;
MTCW

Fuller, John (Leopold) 1937- .... **CLC 62**
See also CA 21-24R; CANR 9; DLB 40

Fuller, Margaret .... **NCLC 5**
See also Ossoli, Sarah Margaret (Fuller
marchesa d')

Fuller, Roy (Broadbent)
1912-1991 .... **CLC 4, 28**
See also CA 5-8R; 135; CAAS 10; DLB 15,
20

Fulton, Alice 1952- .... **CLC 52**
See also CA 116

Furphy, Joseph 1843-1912 .... **TCLC 25**

Fussell, Paul 1924- .... **CLC 74**
See also BEST 90:1; CA 17-20R; CANR 8,
21, 35; MTCW

Futabatei, Shimei 1864-1909 ..... **TCLC 44**

Futrelle, Jacques 1875-1912 ..... **TCLC 19**
See also CA 113

G. B. S.
See Shaw, George Bernard

Gaboriau, Emile 1835-1873 ...... **NCLC 14**

Gadda, Carlo Emilio 1893-1973 .... **CLC 11**
See also CA 89-92

Gaddis, William
1922- .... **CLC 1, 3, 6, 8, 10, 19, 43**
See also CA 17-20R; CANR 21; DLB 2;
MTCW

Gaines, Ernest J(ames)
1933- .... **CLC 3, 11, 18**
See also AITN 1; BLC 2; BW; CA 9-12R;
CANR 6, 24; CDALB 1968-1988; DLB 2,
33; DLBY 80; MTCW

Gaitskill, Mary 1954- .... **CLC 69**
See also CA 128

Galdos, Benito Perez
See Perez Galdos, Benito

Gale, Zona 1874-1938 .... **TCLC 7**
See also CA 105; DLB 9, 78

Galeano, Eduardo (Hughes) 1940-... **CLC 72**
See also CA 29-32R; CANR 13, 32; HW

Galiano, Juan Valera y Alcala
See Valera y Alcala-Galiano, Juan

Gallagher, Tess 1943- .... **CLC 18, 63**
See also CA 106; DLB 120

Gallant, Mavis
1922- .... **CLC 7, 18, 38; SSC 5**
See also CA 69-72; CANR 29; DLB 53;
MTCW

Gallant, Roy A(rthur) 1924- .... **CLC 17**
See also CA 5-8R; CANR 4, 29; CLR 30;
MAICYA; SATA 4, 68

Gallico, Paul (William) 1897-1976 ... **CLC 2**
See also AITN 1; CA 5-8R; 69-72;
CANR 23; DLB 9; MAICYA; SATA 13

Gallup, Ralph
See Whitemore, Hugh (John)

Galsworthy, John 1867-1933 .... **TCLC 1, 45**
See also CA 104; CDBLB 1890-1914; DA;
DLB 10, 34, 98; WLC 2

Galt, John 1779-1839 .... **NCLC 1**
See also DLB 99, 116

Galvin, James 1951- .... **CLC 38**
See also CA 108; CANR 26

Gamboa, Federico 1864-1939 ..... **TCLC 36**

Gann, Ernest Kellogg 1910-1991 .... **CLC 23**
See also AITN 1; CA 1-4R; 136; CANR 1

Garcia, Christina 1959- .... **CLC 76**

Garcia Lorca, Federico
1898-1936 .. **TCLC 1, 7, 49; DC 2; PC 3**
See also CA 104; 131; DA; DLB 108; HW;
MTCW; WLC

Garcia Marquez, Gabriel (Jose)
1928- .... **CLC 2, 3, 8, 10, 15, 27, 47, 55;
SSC 8**
See also Marquez, Gabriel (Jose) Garcia
See also AAYA 3; BEST 89:1, 90:4;
CA 33-36R; CANR 10, 28; DA;
DLB 113; HW; MTCW; WLC

Gard, Janice
See Latham, Jean Lee

Gard, Roger Martin du
See Martin du Gard, Roger

Gardam, Jane 1928- .... **CLC 43**
See also CA 49-52; CANR 2, 18, 33;
CLR 12; DLB 14; MAICYA; MTCW;
SAAS 9; SATA 28, 39

Gardner, Herb .... **CLC 44**

Gardner, John (Champlin), Jr.
1933-1982 ..... **CLC 2, 3, 5, 7, 8, 10, 18,
28, 34; SSC 7**
See also AITN 1; CA 65-68; 107;
CANR 33; DLB 2; DLBY 82; MTCW;
SATA 31, 40

Gardner, John (Edmund) 1926- ..... **CLC 30**
See also CA 103; CANR 15; MTCW

Gardner, Noel
See Kuttner, Henry

Gardons, S. S.
See Snodgrass, W(illiam) D(e Witt)

Garfield, Leon 1921- .... **CLC 12**
See also AAYA 8; CA 17-20R; CANR 38,
41; CLR 21; MAICYA; SATA 1, 32

Garland, (Hannibal) Hamlin
1860-1940 .... **TCLC 3**
See also CA 104; DLB 12, 71, 78

Garneau, (Hector de) Saint-Denys
1912-1943 .... **TCLC 13**
See also CA 111; DLB 88

Garner, Alan 1934- .... **CLC 17**
See also CA 73-76; CANR 15; CLR 20;
MAICYA; MTCW; SATA 18, 69

Garner, Hugh 1913-1979 .... **CLC 13**
See also CA 69-72; CANR 31; DLB 68

Garnett, David 1892-1981 .... **CLC 3**
See also CA 5-8R; 103; CANR 17; DLB 34

Garos, Stephanie
See Katz, Steve

Garrett, George (Palmer)
1929- .... **CLC 3, 11, 51**
See also CA 1-4R; CAAS 5; CANR 1;
DLB 2, 5, 130; DLBY 83

Garrick, David 1717-1779 .... **LC 15**
See also DLB 84

Garrigue, Jean 1914-1972 .... **CLC 2, 8**
See also CA 5-8R; 37-40R; CANR 20

Garrison, Frederick
See Sinclair, Upton (Beall)

Garth, Will
See Hamilton, Edmond; Kuttner, Henry

Garvey, Marcus (Moziah, Jr.)
1887-1940 .... **TCLC 41**
See also BLC 2; BW; CA 120; 124

Gary, Romain . . . . **CLC 25**
See also Kacew, Romain
See also DLB 83

Gascar, Pierre . . . . **CLC 11**
See also Fournier, Pierre

Gascoyne, David (Emery) 1916- . . . . **CLC 45**
See also CA 65-68; CANR 10, 28; DLB 20;
MTCW

Gaskell, Elizabeth Cleghorn
1810-1865 . . . . **NCLC 5**
See also CDBLB 1832-1890; DLB 21

Gass, William H(oward)
1924- . . . **CLC 1, 2, 8, 11, 15, 39; SSC 12**
See also CA 17-20R; CANR 30; DLB 2;
MTCW

Gasset, Jose Ortega y
See Ortega y Gasset, Jose

Gautier, Theophile 1811-1872 . . . . . **NCLC 1**
See also DLB 119

Gawsworth, John
See Bates, H(erbert) E(rnest)

Gaye, Marvin (Penze) 1939-1984 . . . **CLC 26**
See also CA 112

Gebler, Carlo (Ernest) 1954- . . . . **CLC 39**
See also CA 119; 133

Gee, Maggie (Mary) 1948- . . . . **CLC 57**
See also CA 130

Gee, Maurice (Gough) 1931- . . . . **CLC 29**
See also CA 97-100; SATA 46

Gelbart, Larry (Simon) 1923- . . . **CLC 21, 61**
See also CA 73-76

Gelber, Jack 1932- . . . . **CLC 1, 6, 14, 79**
See also CA 1-4R; CANR 2; DLB 7

Gellhorn, Martha Ellis 1908- . . . **CLC 14, 60**
See also CA 77-80; DLBY 82

Genet, Jean
1910-1986 . . . **CLC 1, 2, 5, 10, 14, 44, 46**
See also CA 13-16R; CANR 18; DLB 72;
DLBY 86; MTCW

Gent, Peter 1942- . . . . **CLC 29**
See also AITN 1; CA 89-92; DLBY 82

George, Jean Craighead 1919- . . . . . . **CLC 35**
See also AAYA 8; CA 5-8R; CANR 25;
CLR 1; DLB 52; MAICYA; SATA 2, 68

George, Stefan (Anton)
1868-1933 . . . . **TCLC 2, 14**
See also CA 104

Georges, Georges Martin
See Simenon, Georges (Jacques Christian)

Gerhardi, William Alexander
See Gerhardie, William Alexander

Gerhardie, William Alexander
1895-1977 . . . . **CLC 5**
See also CA 25-28R; 73-76; CANR 18;
DLB 36

Gerstler, Amy 1956- . . . . **CLC 70**

Gertler, T. . . . . **CLC 34**
See also CA 116; 121

Ghalib 1797-1869 . . . . **NCLC 39**

Ghelderode, Michel de
1898-1962 . . . . **CLC 6, 11**
See also CA 85-88; CANR 40

Ghiselin, Brewster 1903- . . . . **CLC 23**
See also CA 13-16R; CAAS 10; CANR 13

Ghose, Zulfikar 1935- . . . . **CLC 42**
See also CA 65-68

Ghosh, Amitav 1956- . . . . **CLC 44**

Giacosa, Giuseppe 1847-1906 . . . . . **TCLC 7**
See also CA 104

Gibb, Lee
See Waterhouse, Keith (Spencer)

Gibbon, Lewis Grassic . . . . **TCLC 4**
See also Mitchell, James Leslie

Gibbons, Kaye 1960- . . . . **CLC 50**

Gibran, Kahlil 1883-1931 . . . . **TCLC 1, 9**
See also CA 104

Gibson, William 1914- . . . . **CLC 23**
See also CA 9-12R; CANR 9; DA; DLB 7;
SATA 66

Gibson, William (Ford) 1948- . . . **CLC 39, 63**
See also CA 126; 133

Gide, Andre (Paul Guillaume)
1869-1951 . . . . . **TCLC 5, 12, 36; SSC 13**
See also CA 104; 124; DA; DLB 65;
MTCW; WLC

Gifford, Barry (Colby) 1946- . . . . **CLC 34**
See also CA 65-68; CANR 9, 30, 40

Gilbert, W(illiam) S(chwenck)
1836-1911 . . . . **TCLC 3**
See also CA 104; SATA 36

Gilbreth, Frank B., Jr. 1911- . . . . **CLC 17**
See also CA 9-12R; SATA 2

Gilchrist, Ellen 1935- . . . . **CLC 34, 48**
See also CA 113; 116; CANR 41; DLB 130;
MTCW

Giles, Molly 1942- . . . . **CLC 39**
See also CA 126

Gill, Patrick
See Creasey, John

Gilliam, Terry (Vance) 1940- . . . . **CLC 21**
See also Monty Python
See also CA 108; 113; CANR 35

Gillian, Jerry
See Gilliam, Terry (Vance)

Gilliatt, Penelope (Ann Douglass)
1932- . . . . **CLC 2, 10, 13, 53**
See also AITN 2; CA 13-16R; DLB 14

Gilman, Charlotte (Anna) Perkins (Stetson)
1860-1935 . . . . **TCLC 9, 37; SSC 13**
See also CA 106

Gilmour, David 1949- . . . . **CLC 35**
See also Pink Floyd
See also CA 138

Gilpin, William 1724-1804 . . . . **NCLC 30**

Gilray, J. D.
See Mencken, H(enry) L(ouis)

Gilroy, Frank D(aniel) 1925- . . . . **CLC 2**
See also CA 81-84; CANR 32; DLB 7

Ginsberg, Allen
1926- . . . . . . **CLC 1, 2, 3, 4, 6, 13, 36, 69;**
PC 4
See also AITN 1; CA 1-4R; CANR 2, 41;
CDALB 1941-1968; DA; DLB 5, 16;
MTCW; WLC 3

Ginzburg, Natalia
1916-1991 . . . . **CLC 5, 11, 54, 70**
See also CA 85-88; 135; CANR 33; MTCW

Giono, Jean 1895-1970 . . . . **CLC 4, 11**
See also CA 45-48; 29-32R; CANR 2, 35;
DLB 72; MTCW

Giovanni, Nikki 1943- . . . . **CLC 2, 4, 19, 64**
See also AITN 1; BLC 2; BW; CA 29-32R;
CAAS 6; CANR 18, 41; CLR 6; DA;
DLB 5, 41; MAICYA; MTCW; SATA 24

Giovene, Andrea 1904- . . . . **CLC 7**
See also CA 85-88

Gippius, Zinaida (Nikolayevna) 1869-1945
See Hippius, Zinaida
See also CA 106

Giraudoux, (Hippolyte) Jean
1882-1944 . . . . **TCLC 2, 7**
See also CA 104; DLB 65

Gironella, Jose Maria 1917- . . . . **CLC 11**
See also CA 101

Gissing, George (Robert)
1857-1903 . . . . **TCLC 3, 24, 47**
See also CA 105; DLB 18

Giurlani, Aldo
See Palazzeschi, Aldo

Gladkov, Fyodor (Vasilyevich)
1883-1958 . . . . **TCLC 27**

Glanville, Brian (Lester) 1931- . . . . . . **CLC 6**
See also CA 5-8R; CAAS 9; CANR 3;
DLB 15; SATA 42

Glasgow, Ellen (Anderson Gholson)
1873(?)-1945 . . . . **TCLC 2, 7**
See also CA 104; DLB 9, 12

Glassco, John 1909-1981 . . . . **CLC 9**
See also CA 13-16R; 102; CANR 15;
DLB 68

Glasscock, Amnesia
See Steinbeck, John (Ernst)

Glasser, Ronald J. 1940(?)- . . . . **CLC 37**

Glassman, Joyce
See Johnson, Joyce

Glendinning, Victoria 1937- . . . . **CLC 50**
See also CA 120; 127

Glissant, Edouard 1928- . . . . **CLC 10, 68**

Gloag, Julian 1930- . . . . **CLC 40**
See also AITN 1; CA 65-68; CANR 10

Gluck, Louise (Elisabeth)
1943- . . . . **CLC 7, 22, 44**
See also Glueck, Louise
See also CA 33-36R; CANR 40; DLB 5

Glueck, Louise . . . . **CLC 7, 22**
See also Gluck, Louise (Elisabeth)
See also DLB 5

Gobineau, Joseph Arthur (Comte) de
1816-1882 . . . . **NCLC 17**
See also DLB 123

Godard, Jean-Luc 1930- . . . . **CLC 20**
See also CA 93-96

Godden, (Margaret) Rumer 1907- . . . **CLC 53**
See also AAYA 6; CA 5-8R; CANR 4, 27,
36; CLR 20; MAICYA; SAAS 12;
SATA 3, 36

Godoy Alcayaga, Lucila 1889-1957
See Mistral, Gabriela
See also CA 104; 131; HW; MTCW

Gray, Thomas 1716-1771 . . . . **LC 4; PC 2**
See also CDBLB 1660-1789; DA; DLB 109;
WLC

Grayson, David
See Baker, Ray Stannard

Grayson, Richard (A.) 1951- . . . . **CLC 38**
See also CA 85-88; CANR 14, 31

Greeley, Andrew M(oran) 1928- . . . . **CLC 28**
See also CA 5-8R; CAAS 7; CANR 7;
MTCW

Green, Brian
See Card, Orson Scott

Green, Hannah . . . . **CLC 3**
See also CA 73-76

Green, Hannah
See Greenberg, Joanne (Goldenberg)

Green, Henry . . . . **CLC 2, 13**
See also Yorke, Henry Vincent
See also DLB 15

Green, Julian (Hartridge)
1900- . . . . **CLC 3, 11, 77**
See also CA 21-24R; CANR 33; DLB 4, 72;
MTCW

Green, Julien 1900-
See Green, Julian (Hartridge)

Green, Paul (Eliot) 1894-1981 . . . . . . **CLC 25**
See also AITN 1; CA 5-8R; 103; CANR 3;
DLB 7, 9; DLBY 81

Greenberg, Ivan 1908-1973
See Rahv, Philip
See also CA 85-88

Greenberg, Joanne (Goldenberg)
1932- . . . . **CLC 7, 30**
See also CA 5-8R; CANR 14, 32; SATA 25

Greenberg, Richard 1959(?)- . . . . **CLC 57**
See also CA 138

Greene, Bette 1934- . . . . **CLC 30**
See also AAYA 7; CA 53-56; CANR 4;
CLR 2; MAICYA; SAAS 16; SATA 8

Greene, Gael . . . . **CLC 8**
See also CA 13-16R; CANR 10

Greene, Graham
1904-1991 . . . . **CLC 1, 3, 6, 9, 14, 18, 27,
37, 70, 72**
See also AITN 2; CA 13-16R; 133;
CANR 35; CDBLB 1945-1960; DA;
DLB 13, 15, 77, 100; DLBY 91; MTCW;
SATA 20; WLC

Greer, Richard
See Silverberg, Robert

Greer, Richard
See Silverberg, Robert

Gregor, Arthur 1923- . . . . **CLC 9**
See also CA 25-28R; CAAS 10; CANR 11;
SATA 36

Gregor, Lee
See Pohl, Frederik

Gregory, Isabella Augusta (Persse)
1852-1932 . . . . **TCLC 1**
See also CA 104; DLB 10

Gregory, J. Dennis
See Williams, John A(lfred)

Grendon, Stephen
See Derleth, August (William)

Grenville, Kate 1950- . . . . **CLC 61**
See also CA 118

Grenville, Pelham
See Wodehouse, P(elham) G(renville)

Greve, Felix Paul (Berthold Friedrich)
1879-1948
See Grove, Frederick Philip
See also CA 104

Grey, Zane 1872-1939 . . . . **TCLC 6**
See also CA 104; 132; DLB 9; MTCW

Grieg, (Johan) Nordahl (Brun)
1902-1943 . . . . **TCLC 10**
See also CA 107

Grieve, C(hristopher) M(urray)
1892-1978 . . . . **CLC 11, 19**
See also MacDiarmid, Hugh
See also CA 5-8R; 85-88; CANR 33;
MTCW

Griffin, Gerald 1803-1840 . . . . **NCLC 7**

Griffin, John Howard 1920-1980 . . . . **CLC 68**
See also AITN 1; CA 1-4R; 101; CANR 2

Griffin, Peter . . . . **CLC 39**

Griffiths, Trevor 1935- . . . . **CLC 13, 52**
See also CA 97-100; DLB 13

Grigson, Geoffrey (Edward Harvey)
1905-1985 . . . . **CLC 7, 39**
See also CA 25-28R; 118; CANR 20, 33;
DLB 27; MTCW

Grillparzer, Franz 1791-1872 . . . . . . **NCLC 1**

Grimble, Reverend Charles James
See Eliot, T(homas) S(tearns)

Grimke, Charlotte L(ottie) Forten
1837(?)-1914
See Forten, Charlotte L.
See also BW; CA 117; 124

Grimm, Jacob Ludwig Karl
1785-1863 . . . . **NCLC 3**
See also DLB 90; MAICYA; SATA 22

Grimm, Wilhelm Karl 1786-1859 . . **NCLC 3**
See also DLB 90; MAICYA; SATA 22

**Grimmelshausen, Johann Jakob Christoffel
von** 1621-1676 . . . . **LC 6**

Grindel, Eugene 1895-1952
See Eluard, Paul
See also CA 104

Grossman, David 1954- . . . . **CLC 67**
See also CA 138

Grossman, Vasily (Semenovich)
1905-1964 . . . . **CLC 41**
See also CA 124; 130; MTCW

Grove, Frederick Philip . . . . **TCLC 4**
See also Greve, Felix Paul (Berthold
Friedrich)
See also DLB 92

Grubb
See Crumb, R(obert)

Grumbach, Doris (Isaac)
1918- . . . . **CLC 13, 22, 64**
See also CA 5-8R; CAAS 2; CANR 9

Grundtvig, Nicolai Frederik Severin
1783-1872 . . . . **NCLC 1**

Grunge
See Crumb, R(obert)

Grunwald, Lisa 1959- . . . . **CLC 44**
See also CA 120

Guare, John 1938- . . . . **CLC 8, 14, 29, 67**
See also CA 73-76; CANR 21; DLB 7;
MTCW

Gudjonsson, Halldor Kiljan 1902-
See Laxness, Halldor
See also CA 103

Guenter, Erich
See Eich, Guenter

Guest, Barbara 1920- . . . . **CLC 34**
See also CA 25-28R; CANR 11; DLB 5

Guest, Judith (Ann) 1936- . . . . **CLC 8, 30**
See also AAYA 7; CA 77-80; CANR 15;
MTCW

Guild, Nicholas M. 1944- . . . . **CLC 33**
See also CA 93-96

Guillemin, Jacques
See Sartre, Jean-Paul

Guillen, Jorge 1893-1984 . . . . **CLC 11**
See also CA 89-92; 112; DLB 108; HW

Guillen (y Batista), Nicolas (Cristobal)
1902-1989 . . . . **CLC 48, 79**
See also BLC 2; BW; CA 116; 125; 129;
HW

Guillevic, (Eugene) 1907- . . . . **CLC 33**
See also CA 93-96

Guillois
See Desnos, Robert

Guiney, Louise Imogen
1861-1920 . . . . **TCLC 41**
See also DLB 54

Guiraldes, Ricardo (Guillermo)
1886-1927 . . . . **TCLC 39**
See also CA 131; HW; MTCW

Gunn, Bill . . . . **CLC 5**
See also Gunn, William Harrison
See also DLB 38

Gunn, Thom(son William)
1929- . . . . **CLC 3, 6, 18, 32**
See also CA 17-20R; CANR 9, 33;
CDBLB 1960 to Present; DLB 27;
MTCW

Gunn, William Harrison 1934(?)-1989
See Gunn, Bill
See also AITN 1; BW; CA 13-16R; 128;
CANR 12, 25

Gunnars, Kristjana 1948- . . . . **CLC 69**
See also CA 113; DLB 60

Gurganus, Allan 1947- . . . . **CLC 70**
See also BEST 90:1; CA 135

Gurney, A(lbert) R(amsdell), Jr.
1930- . . . . **CLC 32, 50, 54**
See also CA 77-80; CANR 32

Gurney, Ivor (Bertie) 1890-1937 . . . **TCLC 33**

Gurney, Peter
See Gurney, A(lbert) R(amsdell), Jr.

Gustafson, Ralph (Barker) 1909- . . . . **CLC 36**
See also CA 21-24R; CANR 8; DLB 88

Gut, Gom
See Simenon, Georges (Jacques Christian)

Guthrie, A(lfred) B(ertram), Jr.
1901-1991 . . . . CLC 23
See also CA 57-60; 134; CANR 24; DLB 6;
SATA 62; SATA-Obit 67

Guthrie, Isobel
See Grieve, C(hristopher) M(urray)

Guthrie, Woodrow Wilson 1912-1967
See Guthrie, Woody
See also CA 113; 93-96

Guthrie, Woody . . . . CLC 35
See also Guthrie, Woodrow Wilson

Guy, Rosa (Cuthbert) 1928- . . . . CLC 26
See also AAYA 4; BW; CA 17-20R;
CANR 14, 34; CLR 13; DLB 33;
MAICYA; SATA 14, 62

Gwendolyn
See Bennett, (Enoch) Arnold

H. D. . . . . CLC 3, 8, 14, 31, 34, 73; PC 5
See also Doolittle, Hilda

Haavikko, Paavo Juhani
1931- . . . . CLC 18, 34
See also CA 106

Habbema, Koos
See Heijermans, Herman

Hacker, Marilyn 1942- . . . . CLC 5, 9, 23, 72
See also CA 77-80; DLB 120

Haggard, H(enry) Rider
1856-1925 . . . . TCLC 11
See also CA 108; DLB 70; SATA 16

Haig, Fenil
See Ford, Ford Madox

Haig-Brown, Roderick (Langmere)
1908-1976 . . . . CLC 21
See also CA 5-8R; 69-72; CANR 4, 38;
CLR 31; DLB 88; MAICYA; SATA 12

Hailey, Arthur 1920- . . . . CLC 5
See also AITN 2; BEST 90:3; CA 1-4R;
CANR 2, 36; DLB 88; DLBY 82; MTCW

Hailey, Elizabeth Forsythe 1938- . . . CLC 40
See also CA 93-96; CAAS 1; CANR 15

Haines, John (Meade) 1924- . . . . CLC 58
See also CA 17-20R; CANR 13, 34; DLB 5

Haldeman, Joe (William) 1943- . . . . . CLC 61
See also CA 53-56; CANR 6; DLB 8

Haley, Alex(ander Murray Palmer)
1921-1992 . . . . CLC 8, 12, 76
See also BLC 2; BW; CA 77-80; 136; DA;
DLB 38; MTCW

Haliburton, Thomas Chandler
1796-1865 . . . . NCLC 15
See also DLB 11, 99

Hall, Donald (Andrew, Jr.)
1928- . . . . CLC 1, 13, 37, 59
See also CA 5-8R; CAAS 7; CANR 2;
DLB 5; SATA 23

Hall, Frederic Sauser
See Sauser-Hall, Frederic

Hall, James
See Kuttner, Henry

Hall, James Norman 1887-1951 . . . TCLC 23
See also CA 123; SATA 21

Hall, (Marguerite) Radclyffe
1886(?)-1943 . . . . TCLC 12
See also CA 110

Hall, Rodney 1935- . . . . CLC 51
See also CA 109

Halliday, Michael
See Creasey, John

Halpern, Daniel 1945- . . . . CLC 14
See also CA 33-36R

Hamburger, Michael (Peter Leopold)
1924- . . . . CLC 5, 14
See also CA 5-8R; CAAS 4; CANR 2;
DLB 27

Hamill, Pete 1935- . . . . CLC 10
See also CA 25-28R; CANR 18

Hamilton, Clive
See Lewis, C(live) S(taples)

Hamilton, Edmond 1904-1977 . . . . CLC 1
See also CA 1-4R; CANR 3; DLB 8

Hamilton, Eugene (Jacob) Lee
See Lee-Hamilton, Eugene (Jacob)

Hamilton, Franklin
See Silverberg, Robert

Hamilton, Gail
See Corcoran, Barbara

Hamilton, Mollie
See Kaye, M(ary) M(argaret)

Hamilton, (Anthony Walter) Patrick
1904-1962 . . . . CLC 51
See also CA 113; DLB 10

Hamilton, Virginia 1936- . . . . CLC 26
See also AAYA 2; BW; CA 25-28R;
CANR 20, 37; CLR 1, 11; DLB 33, 52;
MAICYA; MTCW; SATA 4, 56

Hammett, (Samuel) Dashiell
1894-1961 . . . . CLC 3, 5, 10, 19, 47
See also AITN 1; CA 81-84;
CDALB 1929-1941; DLBD 6; MTCW

Hammon, Jupiter 1711(?)-1800(?) . . NCLC 5
See also BLC 2; DLB 31, 50

Hammond, Keith
See Kuttner, Henry

Hamner, Earl (Henry), Jr. 1923- . . . CLC 12
See also AITN 2; CA 73-76; DLB 6

Hampton, Christopher (James)
1946- . . . . CLC 4
See also CA 25-28R; DLB 13; MTCW

Hamsun, Knut . . . . TCLC 2, 14, 49
See also Pedersen, Knut

Handke, Peter 1942- . . CLC 5, 8, 10, 15, 38
See also CA 77-80; CANR 33; DLB 85,
124; MTCW

Hanley, James 1901-1985 . . . CLC 3, 5, 8, 13
See also CA 73-76; 117; CANR 36; MTCW

Hannah, Barry 1942- . . . . CLC 23, 38
See also CA 108; 110; DLB 6; MTCW

Hannon, Ezra
See Hunter, Evan

Hansberry, Lorraine (Vivian)
1930-1965 . . . . CLC 17, 62; DC 2
See also BLC 2; BW; CA 109; 25-28R;
CABS 3; CDALB 1941-1968; DA;
DLB 7, 38; MTCW

Hansen, Joseph 1923- . . . . CLC 38
See also CA 29-32R; CAAS 17; CANR 16

Hansen, Martin A. 1909-1955 . . . . . TCLC 32

Hanson, Kenneth O(stlin) 1922- . . . . CLC 13
See also CA 53-56; CANR 7

Hardwick, Elizabeth 1916- . . . . CLC 13
See also CA 5-8R; CANR 3, 32; DLB 6;
MTCW

Hardy, Thomas
1840-1928 . . . . . . TCLC 4, 10, 18, 32, 48;
SSC 2
See also CA 104; 123; CDBLB 1890-1914;
DA; DLB 18, 19; MTCW; WLC

Hare, David 1947- . . . . CLC 29, 58
See also CA 97-100; CANR 39; DLB 13;
MTCW

Harford, Henry
See Hudson, W(illiam) H(enry)

Hargrave, Leonie
See Disch, Thomas M(ichael)

Harlan, Louis R(udolph) 1922- . . . . . CLC 34
See also CA 21-24R; CANR 25

Harling, Robert 1951(?)- . . . . CLC 53

Harmon, William (Ruth) 1938- . . . . . CLC 38
See also CA 33-36R; CANR 14, 32, 35;
SATA 65

Harper, F. E. W.
See Harper, Frances Ellen Watkins

Harper, Frances E. W.
See Harper, Frances Ellen Watkins

Harper, Frances E. Watkins
See Harper, Frances Ellen Watkins

Harper, Frances Ellen
See Harper, Frances Ellen Watkins

Harper, Frances Ellen Watkins
1825-1911 . . . . TCLC 14
See also BLC 2; BW; CA 111; 125; DLB 50

Harper, Michael S(teven) 1938- . . CLC 7, 22
See also BW; CA 33-36R; CANR 24;
DLB 41

Harper, Mrs. F. E. W.
See Harper, Frances Ellen Watkins

Harris, Christie (Lucy) Irwin
1907- . . . . CLC 12
See also CA 5-8R; CANR 6; DLB 88;
MAICYA; SAAS 10; SATA 6, 74

Harris, Frank 1856(?)-1931 . . . . TCLC 24
See also CA 109

Harris, George Washington
1814-1869 . . . . NCLC 23
See also DLB 3, 11

Harris, Joel Chandler 1848-1908 . . . TCLC 2
See also CA 104; 137; DLB 11, 23, 42, 78,
91; MAICYA; YABC 1

Harris, John (Wyndham Parkes Lucas)
Beynon 1903-1969 . . . . CLC 19
See also CA 102; 89-92

Harris, MacDonald
See Heiney, Donald (William)

Harris, Mark 1922- . . . . CLC 19
See also CA 5-8R; CAAS 3; CANR 2;
DLB 2; DLBY 80

Harris, (Theodore) Wilson 1921- . . . . CLC 25
See also BW; CA 65-68; CAAS 16;
CANR 11, 27; DLB 117; MTCW

Harrison, Elizabeth Cavanna 1909-
See Cavanna, Betty
See also CA 9-12R; CANR 6, 27

Harrison, Harry (Max) 1925- ...... **CLC 42**
See also CA 1-4R; CANR 5, 21; DLB 8;
SATA 4

Harrison, James (Thomas) 1937-
See Harrison, Jim
See also CA 13-16R; CANR 8

Harrison, Jim .... **CLC 6, 14, 33, 66**
See also Harrison, James (Thomas)
See also DLBY 82

Harrison, Kathryn 1961- .... **CLC 70**

Harrison, Tony 1937- .... **CLC 43**
See also CA 65-68; DLB 40; MTCW

Harriss, Will(ard Irvin) 1922- ...... **CLC 34**
See also CA 111

Harson, Sley
See Ellison, Harlan

Hart, Ellis
See Ellison, Harlan

Hart, Josephine 1942(?)- .... **CLC 70**
See also CA 138

Hart, Moss 1904-1961 .... **CLC 66**
See also CA 109; 89-92; DLB 7

Harte, (Francis) Bret(t)
1836(?)-1902 .... **TCLC 1, 25; SSC 8**
See also CA 104; 140; CDALB 1865-1917;
DA; DLB 12, 64, 74, 79; SATA 26; WLC

Hartley, L(eslie) P(oles)
1895-1972 .... **CLC 2, 22**
See also CA 45-48; 37-40R; CANR 33;
DLB 15; MTCW

Hartman, Geoffrey H. 1929- .... **CLC 27**
See also CA 117; 125; DLB 67

Haruf, Kent 19(?)- .... **CLC 34**

Harwood, Ronald 1934- .... **CLC 32**
See also CA 1-4R; CANR 4; DLB 13

Hasek, Jaroslav (Matej Frantisek)
1883-1923 .... **TCLC 4**
See also CA 104; 129; MTCW

Hass, Robert 1941- .... **CLC 18, 39**
See also CA 111; CANR 30; DLB 105

Hastings, Hudson
See Kuttner, Henry

Hastings, Selina.................... **CLC 44**

Hatteras, Amelia
See Mencken, H(enry) L(ouis)

Hatteras, Owen .... **TCLC 18**
See also Mencken, H(enry) L(ouis); Nathan,
George Jean

Hauptmann, Gerhart (Johann Robert)
1862-1946 .... **TCLC 4**
See also CA 104; DLB 66, 118

Havel, Vaclav 1936- .... **CLC 25, 58, 65**
See also CA 104; CANR 36; MTCW

Haviaras, Stratis .... **CLC 33**
See also Chaviaras, Strates

Hawes, Stephen 1475(?)-1523(?) ..... **LC 17**

Hawkes, John (Clendennin Burne, Jr.)
1925- ...... **CLC 1, 2, 3, 4, 7, 9, 14, 15,
27, 49**
See also CA 1-4R; CANR 2; DLB 2, 7;
DLBY 80; MTCW

Hawking, S. W.
See Hawking, Stephen W(illiam)

Hawking, Stephen W(illiam)
1942- .... **CLC 63**
See also BEST 89:1; CA 126; 129

Hawthorne, Julian 1846-1934 ..... **TCLC 25**

Hawthorne, Nathaniel
1804-1864 .... **NCLC 39; SSC 3**
See also CDALB 1640-1865; DA; DLB 1,
74; WLC; YABC 2

Haxton, Josephine Ayres 1921- .... **CLC 73**
See also CA 115; CANR 41

Hayaseca y Eizaguirre, Jorge
See Echegaray (y Eizaguirre), Jose (Maria
Waldo)

Hayashi Fumiko 1904-1951 ...... **TCLC 27**

Haycraft, Anna
See Ellis, Alice Thomas
See also CA 122

Hayden, Robert E(arl)
1913-1980 ...... **CLC 5, 9, 14, 37; PC 6**
See also BLC 2; BW; CA 69-72; 97-100;
CABS 2; CANR 24; CDALB 1941-1968;
DA; DLB 5, 76; MTCW; SATA 19, 26

Hayford, J(oseph) E(phraim) Casely
See Casely-Hayford, J(oseph) E(phraim)

Hayman, Ronald 1932-............ **CLC 44**
See also CA 25-28R; CANR 18

Haywood, Eliza (Fowler)
1693(?)-1756 .... **LC 1**

Hazlitt, William 1778-1830 ...... **NCLC 29**
See also DLB 110

Hazzard, Shirley 1931- .... **CLC 18**
See also CA 9-12R; CANR 4; DLBY 82;
MTCW

Head, Bessie 1937-1986........ **CLC 25, 67**
See also BLC 2; BW; CA 29-32R; 119;
CANR 25; DLB 117; MTCW

Headon, (Nicky) Topper 1956(?)- ... **CLC 30**
See also Clash, The

Heaney, Seamus (Justin)
1939- ...... **CLC 5, 7, 14, 25, 37, 74**
See also CA 85-88; CANR 25;
CDBLB 1960 to Present; DLB 40;
MTCW

Hearn, (Patricio) Lafcadio (Tessima Carlos)
1850-1904 .... **TCLC 9**
See also CA 105; DLB 12, 78

Hearne, Vicki 1946- .... **CLC 56**
See also CA 139

Hearon, Shelby 1931-............. **CLC 63**
See also AITN 2; CA 25-28R; CANR 18

Heat-Moon, William Least......... **CLC 29**
See also Trogdon, William (Lewis)
See also AAYA 9

Hebert, Anne 1916- .... **CLC 4, 13, 29**
See also CA 85-88; DLB 68; MTCW

Hecht, Anthony (Evan)
1923- .... **CLC 8, 13, 19**
See also CA 9-12R; CANR 6; DLB 5

Hecht, Ben 1894-1964 .... **CLC 8**
See also CA 85-88; DLB 7, 9, 25, 26, 28, 86

Hedayat, Sadeq 1903-1951....... **TCLC 21**
See also CA 120

Heidegger, Martin 1889-1976 ...... **CLC 24**
See also CA 81-84; 65-68; CANR 34;
MTCW

Heidenstam, (Carl Gustaf) Verner von
1859-1940 .... **TCLC 5**
See also CA 104

Heifner, Jack 1946- .... **CLC 11**
See also CA 105

Heijermans, Herman 1864-1924 ... **TCLC 24**
See also CA 123

Heilbrun, Carolyn G(old) 1926-..... **CLC 25**
See also CA 45-48; CANR 1, 28

Heine, Heinrich 1797-1856 .... **NCLC 4**
See also DLB 90

Heinemann, Larry (Curtiss) 1944- .. **CLC 50**
See also CA 110; CANR 31; DLBD 9

Heiney, Donald (William) 1921- ..... **CLC 9**
See also CA 1-4R; CANR 3

Heinlein, Robert A(nson)
1907-1988 ...... **CLC 1, 3, 8, 14, 26, 55**
See also CA 1-4R; 125; CANR 1, 20;
DLB 8; MAICYA; MTCW; SATA 9, 56,
69

Helforth, John
See Doolittle, Hilda

Hellenhofferu, Vojtech Kapristian z
See Hasek, Jaroslav (Matej Frantisek)

Heller, Joseph
1923- .... **CLC 1, 3, 5, 8, 11, 36, 63**
See also AITN 1; CA 5-8R; CABS 1;
CANR 8; DA; DLB 2, 28; DLBY 80;
MTCW; WLC

Hellman, Lillian (Florence)
1906-1984 ...... **CLC 2, 4, 8, 14, 18, 34,
44, 52; DC 1**
See also AITN 1, 2; CA 13-16R; 112;
CANR 33; DLB 7; DLBY 84; MTCW

Helprin, Mark 1947- ..... **CLC 7, 10, 22, 32**
See also CA 81-84; DLBY 85; MTCW

Helyar, Jane Penelope Josephine 1933-
See Poole, Josephine
See also CA 21-24R; CANR 10, 26

Hemans, Felicia 1793-1835 ...... **NCLC 29**
See also DLB 96

Hemingway, Ernest (Miller)
1899-1961 .... **CLC 1, 3, 6, 8, 10, 13, 19,
30, 34, 39, 41, 44, 50, 61; SSC 1**
See also CA 77-80; CANR 34;
CDALB 1917-1929; DA; DLB 4, 9, 102;
DLBD 1; DLBY 81, 87; MTCW; WLC

Hempel, Amy 1951- .... **CLC 39**
See also CA 118; 137

Henderson, F. C.
See Mencken, H(enry) L(ouis)

Henderson, Sylvia
See Ashton-Warner, Sylvia (Constance)

Henley, Beth .... **CLC 23**
See also Henley, Elizabeth Becker
See also CABS 3; DLBY 86

Henley, Elizabeth Becker 1952-
See Henley, Beth
See also CA 107; CANR 32; MTCW

Henley, William Ernest
1849-1903 .... **TCLC 8**
See also CA 105; DLB 19

Hennissart, Martha
See Lathen, Emma
See also CA 85-88

Henry, O. . . . . **TCLC 1, 19; SSC 5**
See also Porter, William Sydney
See also WLC

Henryson, Robert 1430(?)-1506(?). . . . **LC 20**

Henry VIII 1491-1547. . . . . **LC 10**

Henschke, Alfred
See Klabund

Hentoff, Nat(han Irving) 1925- . . . . . **CLC 26**
See also AAYA 4; CA 1-4R; CAAS 6;
CANR 5, 25; CLR 1; MAICYA;
SATA 27, 42, 69

Heppenstall, (John) Rayner
1911-1981 . . . . **CLC 10**
See also CA 1-4R; 103; CANR 29

Herbert, Frank (Patrick)
1920-1986 . . . . **CLC 12, 23, 35, 44**
See also CA 53-56; 118; CANR 5; DLB 8;
MTCW; SATA 9, 37, 47

Herbert, George 1593-1633 . . . . **PC 4**
See also CDBLB Before 1660; DLB 126

Herbert, Zbigniew 1924- . . . . **CLC 9, 43**
See also CA 89-92; CANR 36; MTCW

Herbst, Josephine (Frey)
1897-1969 . . . . **CLC 34**
See also CA 5-8R; 25-28R; DLB 9

Hergesheimer, Joseph
1880-1954 . . . . **TCLC 11**
See also CA 109; DLB 102, 9

Herlihy, James Leo 1927- . . . . **CLC 6**
See also CA 1-4R; CANR 2

Hermogenes fl. c. 175- . . . . **CMLC 6**

Hernandez, Jose 1834-1886. . . . . . **NCLC 17**

Herrick, Robert 1591-1674 . . . . **LC 13**
See also DA; DLB 126

Herring, Guilles
See Somerville, Edith

Herriot, James 1916- . . . . **CLC 12**
See also Wight, James Alfred
See also AAYA 1; CANR 40

Herrmann, Dorothy 1941- . . . . **CLC 44**
See also CA 107

Herrmann, Taffy
See Herrmann, Dorothy

Hersey, John (Richard)
1914-1993 . . . . **CLC 1, 2, 7, 9, 40**
See also CA 17-20R; 140; CANR 33;
DLB 6; MTCW; SATA 25

Herzen, Aleksandr Ivanovich
1812-1870 . . . . **NCLC 10**

Herzl, Theodor 1860-1904 . . . . **TCLC 36**

Herzog, Werner 1942- . . . . **CLC 16**
See also CA 89-92

Hesiod c. 8th cent. B.C.- . . . . **CMLC 5**

Hesse, Hermann
1877-1962 . . . . **CLC 1, 2, 3, 6, 11, 17, 25,
69; SSC 9**
See also CA 17-18; CAP 2; DA; DLB 66;
MTCW; SATA 50; WLC

Hewes, Cady
See De Voto, Bernard (Augustine)

Heyen, William 1940- . . . . **CLC 13, 18**
See also CA 33-36R; CAAS 9; DLB 5

Heyerdahl, Thor 1914- . . . . **CLC 26**
See also CA 5-8R; CANR 5, 22; MTCW;
SATA 2, 52

Heym, Georg (Theodor Franz Arthur)
1887-1912 . . . . **TCLC 9**
See also CA 106

Heym, Stefan 1913- . . . . **CLC 41**
See also CA 9-12R; CANR 4; DLB 69

Heyse, Paul (Johann Ludwig von)
1830-1914 . . . . **TCLC 8**
See also CA 104; DLB 129

Hibbert, Eleanor Alice Burford
1906-1993 . . . . **CLC 7**
See also BEST 90:4; CA 17-20R; CANR 9,
28; SATA 2; SATA-Obit 74

Higgins, George V(incent)
1939- . . . . **CLC 4, 7, 10, 18**
See also CA 77-80; CAAS 5; CANR 17;
DLB 2; DLBY 81; MTCW

Higginson, Thomas Wentworth
1823-1911 . . . . **TCLC 36**
See also DLB 1, 64

Highet, Helen
See MacInnes, Helen (Clark)

Highsmith, (Mary) Patricia
1921- . . . . **CLC 2, 4, 14, 42**
See also CA 1-4R; CANR 1, 20; MTCW

Highwater, Jamake (Mamake)
1942(?)- . . . . **CLC 12**
See also AAYA 7; CA 65-68; CAAS 7;
CANR 10, 34; CLR 17; DLB 52;
DLBY 85; MAICYA; SATA 30, 32, 69

Hijuelos, Oscar 1951- . . . . **CLC 65**
See also BEST 90:1; CA 123; HW

Hikmet, Nazim 1902-1963 . . . . **CLC 40**
See also CA 93-96

Hildesheimer, Wolfgang
1916-1991 . . . . **CLC 49**
See also CA 101; 135; DLB 69, 124

Hill, Geoffrey (William)
1932- . . . . **CLC 5, 8, 18, 45**
See also CA 81-84; CANR 21;
CDBLB 1960 to Present; DLB 40;
MTCW

Hill, George Roy 1921- . . . . **CLC 26**
See also CA 110; 122

Hill, John
See Koontz, Dean R(ay)

Hill, Susan (Elizabeth) 1942- . . . . **CLC 4**
See also CA 33-36R; CANR 29; DLB 14;
MTCW

Hillerman, Tony 1925- . . . . **CLC 62**
See also AAYA 6; BEST 89:1; CA 29-32R;
CANR 21; SATA 6

Hillesum, Etty 1914-1943 . . . . **TCLC 49**
See also CA 137

Hilliard, Noel (Harvey) 1929- . . . . . . **CLC 15**
See also CA 9-12R; CANR 7

Hillis, Rick 1956- . . . . **CLC 66**
See also CA 134

Hilton, James 1900-1954 . . . . **TCLC 21**
See also CA 108; DLB 34, 77; SATA 34

Himes, Chester (Bomar)
1909-1984 . . . . **CLC 2, 4, 7, 18, 58**
See also BLC 2; BW; CA 25-28R; 114;
CANR 22; DLB 2, 76; MTCW

Hinde, Thomas . . . . **CLC 6, 11**
See also Chitty, Thomas Willes

Hindin, Nathan
See Bloch, Robert (Albert)

Hine, (William) Daryl 1936- . . . . **CLC 15**
See also CA 1-4R; CAAS 15; CANR 1, 20;
DLB 60

Hinkson, Katharine Tynan
See Tynan, Katharine

Hinton, S(usan) E(loise) 1950- . . . . . **CLC 30**
See also AAYA 2; CA 81-84; CANR 32;
CLR 3, 23; DA; MAICYA; MTCW;
SATA 19, 58

Hippius, Zinaida . . . . **TCLC 9**
See also Gippius, Zinaida (Nikolayevna)

Hiraoka, Kimitake 1925-1970
See Mishima, Yukio
See also CA 97-100; 29-32R; MTCW

Hirsch, E(ric) D(onald), Jr. 1928- . . . **CLC 79**
See also CA 25-28R; CANR 27; DLB 67;
MTCW

Hirsch, Edward 1950- . . . . **CLC 31, 50**
See also CA 104; CANR 20; DLB 120

Hitchcock, Alfred (Joseph)
1899-1980 . . . . **CLC 16**
See also CA 97-100; SATA 24, 27

Hoagland, Edward 1932- . . . . **CLC 28**
See also CA 1-4R; CANR 2, 31; DLB 6;
SATA 51

Hoban, Russell (Conwell) 1925- . . **CLC 7, 25**
See also CA 5-8R; CANR 23, 37; CLR 3;
DLB 52; MAICYA; MTCW; SATA 1, 40

Hobbs, Perry
See Blackmur, R(ichard) P(almer)

Hobson, Laura Z(ametkin)
1900-1986 . . . . **CLC 7, 25**
See also CA 17-20R; 118; DLB 28;
SATA 52

Hochhuth, Rolf 1931- . . . . **CLC 4, 11, 18**
See also CA 5-8R; CANR 33; DLB 124;
MTCW

Hochman, Sandra 1936- . . . . **CLC 3, 8**
See also CA 5-8R; DLB 5

Hochwaelder, Fritz 1911-1986 . . . . . . **CLC 36**
See also Hochwalder, Fritz
See also CA 29-32R; 120; MTCW

Hochwalder, Fritz . . . . **CLC 36**
See also Hochwaelder, Fritz

Hocking, Mary (Eunice) 1921- . . . . . **CLC 13**
See also CA 101; CANR 18, 40

Hodgins, Jack 1938- . . . . **CLC 23**
See also CA 93-96; DLB 60

Hodgson, William Hope
1877(?)-1918 . . . . **TCLC 13**
See also CA 111; DLB 70

Hoffman, Alice 1952- . . . . **CLC 51**
See also CA 77-80; CANR 34; MTCW

Hoffman, Daniel (Gerard)
1923- . . . . **CLC 6, 13, 23**
See also CA 1-4R; CANR 4; DLB 5

Hughes, Colin
See Creasey, John

Hughes, David (John) 1930- .... **CLC 48**
See also CA 116; 129; DLB 14

Hughes, (James) Langston
1902-1967 ..... **CLC 1, 5, 10, 15, 35, 44;
DC 3; PC 1; SSC 6**
See also BLC 2; BW; CA 1-4R; 25-28R;
CANR 1, 34; CDALB 1929-1941;
CLR 17; DA; DLB 4, 7, 48, 51, 86;
MAICYA; MTCW; SATA 4, 33; WLC

Hughes, Richard (Arthur Warren)
1900-1976 .... **CLC 1, 11**
See also CA 5-8R; 65-68; CANR 4;
DLB 15; MTCW; SATA 8, 25

Hughes, Ted
1930- .... **CLC 2, 4, 9, 14, 37; PC 7**
See also CA 1-4R; CANR 1, 33; CLR 3;
DLB 40; MAICYA; MTCW; SATA 27,
49

Hugo, Richard F(ranklin)
1923-1982 .... **CLC 6, 18, 32**
See also CA 49-52; 108; CANR 3; DLB 5

Hugo, Victor (Marie)
1802-1885 .... **NCLC 3, 10, 21**
See also DA; DLB 119; SATA 47; WLC

Huidobro, Vicente
See Huidobro Fernandez, Vicente Garcia

Huidobro Fernandez, Vicente Garcia
1893-1948 .... **TCLC 31**
See also CA 131; HW

Hulme, Keri 1947- .... **CLC 39**
See also CA 125

Hulme, T(homas) E(rnest)
1883-1917 .... **TCLC 21**
See also CA 117; DLB 19

Hume, David 1711-1776............ **LC 7**
See also DLB 104

Humphrey, William 1924- .... **CLC 45**
See also CA 77-80; DLB 6

Humphreys, Emyr Owen 1919-..... **CLC 47**
See also CA 5-8R; CANR 3, 24; DLB 15

Humphreys, Josephine 1945-.... **CLC 34, 57**
See also CA 121; 127

Hungerford, Pixie
See Brinsmead, H(esba) F(ay)

Hunt, E(verette) Howard, Jr.
1918- .... **CLC 3**
See also AITN 1; CA 45-48; CANR 2

Hunt, Kyle
See Creasey, John

Hunt, (James Henry) Leigh
1784-1859 .... **NCLC 1**

Hunt, Marsha 1946-............. **CLC 70**

Hunter, E. Waldo
See Sturgeon, Theodore (Hamilton)

Hunter, Evan 1926- .... **CLC 11, 31**
See also CA 5-8R; CANR 5, 38; DLBY 82;
MTCW; SATA 25

Hunter, Kristin (Eggleston) 1931-... **CLC 35**
See also AITN 1; BW; CA 13-16R;
CANR 13; CLR 3; DLB 33; MAICYA;
SAAS 10; SATA 12

Hunter, Mollie 1922-............. **CLC 21**
See also McIlwraith, Maureen Mollie
Hunter
See also CANR 37; CLR 25; MAICYA;
SAAS 7; SATA 54

Hunter, Robert (?)-1734............ **LC 7**

Hurston, Zora Neale
1903-1960 .... **CLC 7, 30, 61; SSC 4**
See also BLC 2; BW; CA 85-88; DA;
DLB 51, 86; MTCW

Huston, John (Marcellus)
1906-1987 .... **CLC 20**
See also CA 73-76; 123; CANR 34; DLB 26

Hustvedt, Siri 1955-............. **CLC 76**
See also CA 137

Hutten, Ulrich von 1488-1523....... **LC 16**

Huxley, Aldous (Leonard)
1894-1963 ..... **CLC 1, 3, 4, 5, 8, 11, 18,
35, 79**
See also CA 85-88; CDBLB 1914-1945; DA;
DLB 36, 100; MTCW; SATA 63; WLC

Huysmans, Charles Marie Georges
1848-1907
See Huysmans, Joris-Karl
See also CA 104

Huysmans, Joris-Karl............. **TCLC 7**
See also Huysmans, Charles Marie Georges
See also DLB 123

Hwang, David Henry 1957-........ **CLC 55**
See also CA 127; 132

Hyde, Anthony 1946-............. **CLC 42**
See also CA 136

Hyde, Margaret O(ldroyd) 1917- ... **CLC 21**
See also CA 1-4R; CANR 1, 36; CLR 23;
MAICYA; SAAS 8; SATA 1, 42

Hynes, James 1956(?)-............ **CLC 65**

Ian, Janis 1951- .... **CLC 21**
See also CA 105

Ibanez, Vicente Blasco
See Blasco Ibanez, Vicente

Ibarguengoitia, Jorge 1928-1983 .... **CLC 37**
See also CA 124; 113; HW

Ibsen, Henrik (Johan)
1828-1906 .... **TCLC 2, 8, 16, 37; DC 2**
See also CA 104; DA; WLC

Ibuse Masuji 1898-............... **CLC 22**
See also CA 127

Ichikawa, Kon 1915-............. **CLC 20**
See also CA 121

Idle, Eric 1943-.................. **CLC 21**
See also Monty Python
See also CA 116; CANR 35

Ignatow, David 1914-...... **CLC 4, 7, 14, 40**
See also CA 9-12R; CAAS 3; CANR 31;
DLB 5

Ihimaera, Witi 1944- .... **CLC 46**
See also CA 77-80

Ilf, Ilya........................ **TCLC 21**
See also Fainzilberg, Ilya Arnoldovich

Immermann, Karl (Lebrecht)
1796-1840 .... **NCLC 4**

Inclan, Ramon (Maria) del Valle
See Valle-Inclan, Ramon (Maria) del

Infante, G(uillermo) Cabrera
See Cabrera Infante, G(uillermo)

Ingalls, Rachel (Holmes) 1940-..... **CLC 42**
See also CA 123; 127

Ingamells, Rex 1913-1955 .... **TCLC 35**

Inge, William Motter
1913-1973 .... **CLC 1, 8, 19**
See also CA 9-12R; CDALB 1941-1968;
DLB 7; MTCW

Ingelow, Jean 1820-1897 .... **NCLC 39**
See also DLB 35; SATA 33

Ingram, Willis J.
See Harris, Mark

Innaurato, Albert (F.) 1948(?)- .. **CLC 21, 60**
See also CA 115; 122

Innes, Michael
See Stewart, J(ohn) I(nnes) M(ackintosh)

Ionesco, Eugene
1912- .... **CLC 1, 4, 6, 9, 11, 15, 41**
See also CA 9-12R; DA; MTCW; SATA 7;
WLC

Iqbal, Muhammad 1873-1938 ..... **TCLC 28**

Ireland, Patrick
See O'Doherty, Brian

Irland, David
See Green, Julian (Hartridge)

Iron, Ralph
See Schreiner, Olive (Emilie Albertina)

Irving, John (Winslow)
1942- .... **CLC 13, 23, 38**
See also AAYA 8; BEST 89:3; CA 25-28R;
CANR 28; DLB 6; DLBY 82; MTCW

Irving, Washington
1783-1859 .... **NCLC 2, 19; SSC 2**
See also CDALB 1640-1865; DA; DLB 3,
11, 30, 59, 73, 74; WLC; YABC 2

Irwin, P. K.
See Page, P(atricia) K(athleen)

Isaacs, Susan 1943- .... **CLC 32**
See also BEST 89:1; CA 89-92; CANR 20,
41; MTCW

Isherwood, Christopher (William Bradshaw)
1904-1986 .... **CLC 1, 9, 11, 14, 44**
See also CA 13-16R; 117; CANR 35;
DLB 15; DLBY 86; MTCW

Ishiguro, Kazuo 1954- ..... **CLC 27, 56, 59**
See also BEST 90:2; CA 120; MTCW

Ishikawa Takuboku
1886(?)-1912 .... **TCLC 15**
See also CA 113

Iskander, Fazil 1929-............. **CLC 47**
See also CA 102

Ivan IV 1530-1584 .... **LC 17**

Ivanov, Vyacheslav Ivanovich
1866-1949 .... **TCLC 33**
See also CA 122

Ivask, Ivar Vidrik 1927-1992...... **CLC 14**
See also CA 37-40R; 139; CANR 24

Jackson, Daniel
See Wingrove, David (John)

Jackson, Jesse 1908-1983 .... **CLC 12**
See also BW; CA 25-28R; 109; CANR 27;
CLR 28; MAICYA; SATA 2, 29, 48

Jones, D(ouglas) G(ordon) 1929-.... **CLC 10**
See also CA 29-32R; CANR 13; DLB 53

Jones, David (Michael)
1895-1974 .... **CLC 2, 4, 7, 13, 42**
See also CA 9-12R; 53-56; CANR 28;
CDBLB 1945-1960; DLB 20, 100; MTCW

Jones, David Robert 1947-
See Bowie, David
See also CA 103

Jones, Diana Wynne 1934- .... **CLC 26**
See also CA 49-52; CANR 4, 26; CLR 23;
MAICYA; SAAS 7; SATA 9, 70

Jones, Edward P. 1951-........... **CLC 76**

Jones, Gayl 1949-.............. **CLC 6, 9**
See also BLC 2; BW; CA 77-80; CANR 27;
DLB 33; MTCW

Jones, James 1921-1977.... **CLC 1, 3, 10, 39**
See also AITN 1, 2; CA 1-4R; 69-72;
CANR 6; DLB 2; MTCW

Jones, John J.
See Lovecraft, H(oward) P(hillips)

Jones, LeRoi .... **CLC 1, 2, 3, 5, 10, 14**
See also Baraka, Amiri

Jones, Louis B. .... **CLC 65**

Jones, Madison (Percy, Jr.) 1925-... **CLC 4**
See also CA 13-16R; CAAS 11; CANR 7

Jones, Mervyn 1922-......... **CLC 10, 52**
See also CA 45-48; CAAS 5; CANR 1;
MTCW

Jones, Mick 1956(?)-............. **CLC 30**
See also Clash, The

Jones, Nettie (Pearl) 1941- .... **CLC 34**
See also CA 137

Jones, Preston 1936-1979 .... **CLC 10**
See also CA 73-76; 89-92; DLB 7

Jones, Robert F(rancis) 1934-...... **CLC 7**
See also CA 49-52; CANR 2

Jones, Rod 1953- .... **CLC 50**
See also CA 128

Jones, Terence Graham Parry
1942-..................... **CLC 21**
See also Jones, Terry; Monty Python
See also CA 112; 116; CANR 35; SATA 51

Jones, Terry
See Jones, Terence Graham Parry
See also SATA 67

Jong, Erica 1942-......... **CLC 4, 6, 8, 18**
See also AITN 1; BEST 90:2; CA 73-76;
CANR 26; DLB 2, 5, 28; MTCW

Jonson, Ben(jamin) 1572(?)-1637...... **LC 6**
See also CDBLB Before 1660; DA; DLB 62,
121; WLC

Jordan, June 1936-......... **CLC 5, 11, 23**
See also AAYA 2; BW; CA 33-36R;
CANR 25; CLR 10; DLB 38; MAICYA;
MTCW; SATA 4

Jordan, Pat(rick M.) 1941- .... **CLC 37**
See also CA 33-36R

Jorgensen, Ivar
See Ellison, Harlan

Jorgenson, Ivar
See Silverberg, Robert

Josipovici, Gabriel 1940-........ **CLC 6, 43**
See also CA 37-40R; CAAS 8; DLB 14

Joubert, Joseph 1754-1824 .... **NCLC 9**

Jouve, Pierre Jean 1887-1976...... **CLC 47**
See also CA 65-68

Joyce, James (Augustine Aloysius)
1882-1941 .... **TCLC 3, 8, 16, 35; SSC 3**
See also CA 104; 126; CDBLB 1914-1945;
DA; DLB 10, 19, 36; MTCW; WLC

Jozsef, Attila 1905-1937......... **TCLC 22**
See also CA 116

Juana Ines de la Cruz 1651(?)-1695 ... **LC 5**

Judd, Cyril
See Kornbluth, C(yril) M.; Pohl, Frederik

Julian of Norwich 1342(?)-1416(?) .... **LC 6**

Just, Ward (Swift) 1935-........ **CLC 4, 27**
See also CA 25-28R; CANR 32

Justice, Donald (Rodney) 1925- .. **CLC 6, 19**
See also CA 5-8R; CANR 26; DLBY 83

Juvenal c. 55-c. 127 .... **CMLC 8**

Juvenis
See Bourne, Randolph S(illiman)

Kacew, Romain 1914-1980
See Gary, Romain
See also CA 108; 102

Kadare, Ismail 1936- .... **CLC 52**

Kadohata, Cynthia................. **CLC 59**
See also CA 140

Kafka, Franz
1883-1924 ...... **TCLC 2, 6, 13, 29, 47;
SSC 5**
See also CA 105; 126; DA; DLB 81;
MTCW; WLC

Kahn, Roger 1927-............... **CLC 30**
See also CA 25-28R; SATA 37

Kain, Saul
See Sassoon, Siegfried (Lorraine)

Kaiser, Georg 1878-1945 .... **TCLC 9**
See also CA 106; DLB 124

Kaletski, Alexander 1946-......... **CLC 39**
See also CA 118

Kalidasa fl. c. 400- .... **CMLC 9**

Kallman, Chester (Simon)
1921-1975 .... **CLC 2**
See also CA 45-48; 53-56; CANR 3

Kaminsky, Melvin 1926-
See Brooks, Mel
See also CA 65-68; CANR 16

Kaminsky, Stuart M(elvin) 1934-... **CLC 59**
See also CA 73-76; CANR 29

Kane, Paul
See Simon, Paul

Kane, Wilson
See Bloch, Robert (Albert)

Kanin, Garson 1912-.............. **CLC 22**
See also AITN 1; CA 5-8R; CANR 7;
DLB 7

Kaniuk, Yoram 1930-............. **CLC 19**
See also CA 134

Kant, Immanuel 1724-1804 ...... **NCLC 27**
See also DLB 94

Kantor, MacKinlay 1904-1977 ...... **CLC 7**
See also CA 61-64; 73-76; DLB 9, 102

Kaplan, David Michael 1946- ...... **CLC 50**

Kaplan, James 1951-............. **CLC 59**
See also CA 135

Karageorge, Michael
See Anderson, Poul (William)

Karamzin, Nikolai Mikhailovich
1766-1826 .... **NCLC 3**

Karapanou, Margarita 1946-....... **CLC 13**
See also CA 101

Karinthy, Frigyes 1887-1938...... **TCLC 47**

Karl, Frederick R(obert) 1927-..... **CLC 34**
See also CA 5-8R; CANR 3

Kastel, Warren
See Silverberg, Robert

Kataev, Evgeny Petrovich 1903-1942
See Petrov, Evgeny
See also CA 120

Kataphusin
See Ruskin, John

Katz, Steve 1935-................ **CLC 47**
See also CA 25-28R; CAAS 14; CANR 12;
DLBY 83

Kauffman, Janet 1945-............ **CLC 42**
See also CA 117; DLBY 86

Kaufman, Bob (Garnell)
1925-1986 .... **CLC 49**
See also BW; CA 41-44R; 118; CANR 22;
DLB 16, 41

Kaufman, George S. 1889-1961..... **CLC 38**
See also CA 108; 93-96; DLB 7

Kaufman, Sue .... **CLC 3, 8**
See also Barondess, Sue K(aufman)

Kavafis, Konstantinos Petrou 1863-1933
See Cavafy, C(onstantine) P(eter)
See also CA 104

Kavan, Anna 1901-1968......... **CLC 5, 13**
See also CA 5-8R; CANR 6; MTCW

Kavanagh, Dan
See Barnes, Julian

Kavanagh, Patrick (Joseph)
1904-1967 .... **CLC 22**
See also CA 123; 25-28R; DLB 15, 20;
MTCW

Kawabata, Yasunari
1899-1972 .... **CLC 2, 5, 9, 18**
See also CA 93-96; 33-36R

Kaye, M(ary) M(argaret) 1909-..... **CLC 28**
See also CA 89-92; CANR 24; MTCW;
SATA 62

Kaye, Mollie
See Kaye, M(ary) M(argaret)

Kaye-Smith, Sheila 1887-1956..... **TCLC 20**
See also CA 118; DLB 36

Kaymor, Patrice Maguilene
See Senghor, Leopold Sedar

Kazan, Elia 1909-........... **CLC 6, 16, 63**
See also CA 21-24R; CANR 32

Kazantzakis, Nikos
1883(?)-1957 .... **TCLC 2, 5, 33**
See also CA 105; 132; MTCW

Kazin, Alfred 1915- .... **CLC 34, 38**
See also CA 1-4R; CAAS 7; CANR 1;
DLB 67

Klein, A(braham) M(oses)
  1909-1972 .... **CLC 19**
  See also CA 101; 37-40R; DLB 68

Klein, Norma 1938-1989 .... **CLC 30**
  See also AAYA 2; CA 41-44R; 128;
  CANR 15, 37; CLR 2, 19; MAICYA;
  SAAS 1; SATA 7, 57

Klein, T(heodore) E(ibon) D(onald)
  1947- .... **CLC 34**
  See also CA 119

Kleist, Heinrich von 1777-1811.... **NCLC 2**
  See also DLB 90

Klima, Ivan 1931-................ **CLC 56**
  See also CA 25-28R; CANR 17

Klimentov, Andrei Platonovich 1899-1951
  See Platonov, Andrei
  See also CA 108

Klinger, Friedrich Maximilian von
  1752-1831 .... **NCLC 1**
  See also DLB 94

Klopstock, Friedrich Gottlieb
  1724-1803 .... **NCLC 11**
  See also DLB 97

Knebel, Fletcher 1911-1993 .... **CLC 14**
  See also AITN 1; CA 1-4R; 140; CAAS 3;
  CANR 1, 36; SATA 36

Knickerbocker, Diedrich
  See Irving, Washington

Knight, Etheridge 1931-1991 ...... **CLC 40**
  See also BLC 2; BW; CA 21-24R; 133;
  CANR 23; DLB 41

Knight, Sarah Kemble 1666-1727 ..... **LC 7**
  See also DLB 24

Knowles, John 1926- ...... **CLC 1, 4, 10, 26**
  See also AAYA 10; CA 17-20R; CANR 40;
  CDALB 1968-1988; DA; DLB 6; MTCW;
  SATA 8

Knox, Calvin M.
  See Silverberg, Robert

Knye, Cassandra
  See Disch, Thomas M(ichael)

Koch, C(hristopher) J(ohn) 1932- ... **CLC 42**
  See also CA 127

Koch, Christopher
  See Koch, C(hristopher) J(ohn)

Koch, Kenneth 1925- .... **CLC 5, 8, 44**
  See also CA 1-4R; CANR 6, 36; DLB 5;
  SATA 65

Kochanowski, Jan 1530-1584....... **LC 10**

Kock, Charles Paul de
  1794-1871 .... **NCLC 16**

Koda Shigeyuki 1867-1947
  See Rohan, Koda
  See also CA 121

Koestler, Arthur
  1905-1983 .... **CLC 1, 3, 6, 8, 15, 33**
  See also CA 1-4R; 109; CANR 1, 33;
  CDBLB 1945-1960; DLBY 83; MTCW

Kogawa, Joy Nozomi 1935-....... **CLC 78**
  See also CA 101; CANR 19

Kohout, Pavel 1928-............. **CLC 13**
  See also CA 45-48; CANR 3

Koizumi, Yakumo
  See Hearn, (Patricio) Lafcadio (Tessima
  Carlos)

Kolmar, Gertrud 1894-1943 ...... **TCLC 40**

Konrad, George
  See Konrad, Gyoergy

Konrad, Gyoergy 1933- ...... **CLC 4, 10, 73**
  See also CA 85-88

Konwicki, Tadeusz 1926-..... **CLC 8, 28, 54**
  See also CA 101; CAAS 9; CANR 39;
  MTCW

Koontz, Dean R(ay) 1945-....... **CLC 78**
  See also AAYA 9; BEST 89:3, 90:2;
  CA 108; CANR 19, 36; MTCW

Kopit, Arthur (Lee) 1937- .... **CLC 1, 18, 33**
  See also AITN 1; CA 81-84; CABS 3;
  DLB 7; MTCW

Kops, Bernard 1926-.............. **CLC 4**
  See also CA 5-8R; DLB 13

Kornbluth, C(yril) M. 1923-1958.... **TCLC 8**
  See also CA 105; DLB 8

Korolenko, V. G.
  See Korolenko, Vladimir Galaktionovich

Korolenko, Vladimir
  See Korolenko, Vladimir Galaktionovich

Korolenko, Vladimir G.
  See Korolenko, Vladimir Galaktionovich

Korolenko, Vladimir Galaktionovich
  1853-1921 .... **TCLC 22**
  See also CA 121

Kosinski, Jerzy (Nikodem)
  1933-1991 .... **CLC 1, 2, 3, 6, 10, 15, 53, 70**
  See also CA 17-20R; 134; CANR 9; DLB 2;
  DLBY 82; MTCW

Kostelanetz, Richard (Cory) 1940-.. **CLC 28**
  See also CA 13-16R; CAAS 8; CANR 38

Kostrowitzki, Wilhelm Apollinaris de
  1880-1918
  See Apollinaire, Guillaume
  See also CA 104

Kotlowitz, Robert 1924-............ **CLC 4**
  See also CA 33-36R; CANR 36

Kotzebue, August (Friedrich Ferdinand) von
  1761-1819 .... **NCLC 25**
  See also DLB 94

Kotzwinkle, William 1938- ... **CLC 5, 14, 35**
  See also CA 45-48; CANR 3; CLR 6;
  MAICYA; SATA 24, 70

Kozol, Jonathan 1936-........... **CLC 17**
  See also CA 61-64; CANR 16

Kozoll, Michael 1940(?)-.......... **CLC 35**

Kramer, Kathryn 19(?)-........... **CLC 34**

Kramer, Larry 1935- .... **CLC 42**
  See also CA 124; 126

Krasicki, Ignacy 1735-1801 .... **NCLC 8**

Krasinski, Zygmunt 1812-1859 .... **NCLC 4**

Kraus, Karl 1874-1936 .... **TCLC 5**
  See also CA 104; DLB 118

Kreve (Mickevicius), Vincas
  1882-1954 .... **TCLC 27**

Kristeva, Julia 1941- .... **CLC 77**

Kristofferson, Kris 1936-.......... **CLC 26**
  See also CA 104

Krizanc, John 1956-,............. **CLC 57**

Krleza, Miroslav 1893-1981........ **CLC 8**
  See also CA 97-100; 105

Kroetsch, Robert 1927- ...... **CLC 5, 23, 57**
  See also CA 17-20R; CANR 8, 38; DLB 53;
  MTCW

Kroetz, Franz
  See Kroetz, Franz Xaver

Kroetz, Franz Xaver 1946- .... **CLC 41**
  See also CA 130

Kroker, Arthur 1945-............. **CLC 77**

Kropotkin, Peter (Aleksieevich)
  1842-1921 .... **TCLC 36**
  See also CA 119

Krotkov, Yuri 1917-.............. **CLC 19**
  See also CA 102

Krumb
  See Crumb, R(obert)

Krumgold, Joseph (Quincy)
  1908-1980 .... **CLC 12**
  See also CA 9-12R; 101; CANR 7;
  MAICYA; SATA 1, 23, 48

Krumwitz
  See Crumb, R(obert)

Krutch, Joseph Wood 1893-1970.... **CLC 24**
  See also CA 1-4R; 25-28R; CANR 4;
  DLB 63

Krutzch, Gus
  See Eliot, T(homas) S(tearns)

Krylov, Ivan Andreevich
  1768(?)-1844 .... **NCLC 1**

Kubin, Alfred 1877-1959 .... **TCLC 23**
  See also CA 112; DLB 81

Kubrick, Stanley 1928-............ **CLC 16**
  See also CA 81-84; CANR 33; DLB 26

Kumin, Maxine (Winokur)
  1925- .... **CLC 5, 13, 28**
  See also AITN 2; CA 1-4R; CAAS 8;
  CANR 1, 21; DLB 5; MTCW; SATA 12

Kundera, Milan
  1929-............ **CLC 4, 9, 19, 32, 68**
  See also AAYA 2; CA 85-88; CANR 19;
  MTCW

Kunitz, Stanley (Jasspon)
  1905- .... **CLC 6, 11, 14**
  See also CA 41-44R; CANR 26; DLB 48;
  MTCW

Kunze, Reiner 1933-............. **CLC 10**
  See also CA 93-96; DLB 75

Kuprin, Aleksandr Ivanovich
  1870-1938 .... **TCLC 5**
  See also CA 104

Kureishi, Hanif 1954(?)-.......... **CLC 64**
  See also CA 139

Kurosawa, Akira 1910-............ **CLC 16**
  See also CA 101

Kuttner, Henry 1915-1958........ **TCLC 10**
  See also CA 107; DLB 8

Kuzma, Greg 1944-............... **CLC 7**
  See also CA 33-36R

Kuzmin, Mikhail 1872(?)-1936 .... **TCLC 40**

Kyd, Thomas 1558-1594 . . . . . . **LC 22; DC 3**
See also DLB 62

Kyprianos, Iossif
See Samarakis, Antonis

La Bruyere, Jean de 1645-1696 . . . . . . **LC 17**

Lacan, Jacques (Marie Emile)
1901-1981 . . . . **CLC 75**
See also CA 121; 104

Laclos, Pierre Ambroise Francois Choderlos
de 1741-1803 . . . . **NCLC 4**

La Colere, Francois
See Aragon, Louis

Lacolere, Francois
See Aragon, Louis

La Deshabilleuse
See Simenon, Georges (Jacques Christian)

Lady Gregory
See Gregory, Isabella Augusta (Persse)

Lady of Quality, A
See Bagnold, Enid

La Fayette, Marie (Madelaine Pioche de la
Vergne Comtes 1634-1693 . . . . . . **LC 2**

Lafayette, Rene
See Hubbard, L(afayette) Ron(ald)

Laforgue, Jules 1860-1887 . . . . **NCLC 5**

Lagerkvist, Paer (Fabian)
1891-1974 . . . . **CLC 7, 10, 13, 54**
See also Lagerkvist, Par
See also CA 85-88; 49-52; MTCW

Lagerkvist, Par
See Lagerkvist, Paer (Fabian)
See also SSC 12

Lagerloef, Selma (Ottiliana Lovisa)
1858-1940 . . . . **TCLC 4, 36**
See also Lagerlof, Selma (Ottiliana Lovisa)
See also CA 108; CLR 7; SATA 15

Lagerlof, Selma (Ottiliana Lovisa)
See Lagerloef, Selma (Ottiliana Lovisa)
See also CLR 7; SATA 15

La Guma, (Justin) Alex(ander)
1925-1985 . . . . **CLC 19**
See also BW; CA 49-52; 118; CANR 25;
DLB 117; MTCW

Laidlaw, A. K.
See Grieve, C(hristopher) M(urray)

Lainez, Manuel Mujica
See Mujica Lainez, Manuel
See also HW

Lamartine, Alphonse (Marie Louis Prat) de
1790-1869 . . . . **NCLC 11**

Lamb, Charles 1775-1834 . . . . **NCLC 10**
See also CDBLB 1789-1832; DA; DLB 93,
107; SATA 17; WLC

Lamb, Lady Caroline 1785-1828 . . **NCLC 38**
See also DLB 116

Lamming, George (William)
1927- . . . . **CLC 2, 4, 66**
See also BLC 2; BW; CA 85-88; CANR 26;
DLB 125; MTCW

L'Amour, Louis (Dearborn)
1908-1988 . . . . **CLC 25, 55**
See also AITN 2; BEST 89:2; CA 1-4R;
125; CANR 3, 25, 40; DLBY 80; MTCW

Lampedusa, Giuseppe (Tomasi) di . . . **TCLC 13**
See also Tomasi di Lampedusa, Giuseppe

Lampman, Archibald 1861-1899 . . **NCLC 25**
See also DLB 92

Lancaster, Bruce 1896-1963 . . . . **CLC 36**
See also CA 9-10; CAP 1; SATA 9

Landau, Mark Alexandrovich
See Aldanov, Mark (Alexandrovich)

Landau-Aldanov, Mark Alexandrovich
See Aldanov, Mark (Alexandrovich)

Landis, John 1950- . . . . **CLC 26**
See also CA 112; 122

Landolfi, Tommaso 1908-1979 . . . **CLC 11, 49**
See also CA 127; 117

Landon, Letitia Elizabeth
1802-1838 . . . . **NCLC 15**
See also DLB 96

Landor, Walter Savage
1775-1864 . . . . **NCLC 14**
See also DLB 93, 107

Landwirth, Heinz 1927-
See Lind, Jakov
See also CA 9-12R; CANR 7

Lane, Patrick 1939- . . . . **CLC 25**
See also CA 97-100; DLB 53

Lang, Andrew 1844-1912 . . . . **TCLC 16**
See also CA 114; 137; DLB 98; MAICYA;
SATA 16

Lang, Fritz 1890-1976 . . . . **CLC 20**
See also CA 77-80; 69-72; CANR 30

Lange, John
See Crichton, (John) Michael

Langer, Elinor 1939- . . . . **CLC 34**
See also CA 121

Langland, William 1330(?)-1400(?) . . . **LC 19**
See also DA

Langstaff, Launcelot
See Irving, Washington

Lanier, Sidney 1842-1881 . . . . **NCLC 6**
See also DLB 64; MAICYA; SATA 18

Lanyer, Aemilia 1569-1645 . . . . **LC 10**

Lao Tzu . . . . **CMLC 7**

Lapine, James (Elliot) 1949- . . . . . . **CLC 39**
See also CA 123; 130

Larbaud, Valery (Nicolas)
1881-1957 . . . . **TCLC 9**
See also CA 106

Lardner, Ring
See Lardner, Ring(gold) W(ilmer)

Lardner, Ring W., Jr.
See Lardner, Ring(gold) W(ilmer)

Lardner, Ring(gold) W(ilmer)
1885-1933 . . . . **TCLC 2, 14**
See also CA 104; 131; CDALB 1917-1929;
DLB 11, 25, 86; MTCW

Laredo, Betty
See Codrescu, Andrei

Larkin, Maia
See Wojciechowska, Maia (Teresa)

Larkin, Philip (Arthur)
1922-1985 . . . . **CLC 3, 5, 8, 9, 13, 18, 33,**
39, 64
See also CA 5-8R; 117; CANR 24;
CDBLB 1960 to Present; DLB 27;
MTCW

Larra (y Sanchez de Castro), Mariano Jose de
1809-1837 . . . . **NCLC 17**

Larsen, Eric 1941- . . . . **CLC 55**
See also CA 132

Larsen, Nella 1891-1964 . . . . **CLC 37**
See also BLC 2; BW; CA 125; DLB 51

Larson, Charles R(aymond) 1938- . . . **CLC 31**
See also CA 53-56; CANR 4

Latham, Jean Lee 1902- . . . . **CLC 12**
See also AITN 1; CA 5-8R; CANR 7;
MAICYA; SATA 2, 68

Latham, Mavis
See Clark, Mavis Thorpe

Lathen, Emma . . . . **CLC 2**
See also Hennissart, Martha; Latsis, Mary
J(ane)

Lathrop, Francis
See Leiber, Fritz (Reuter, Jr.)

Latsis, Mary J(ane)
See Lathen, Emma
See also CA 85-88

Lattimore, Richmond (Alexander)
1906-1984 . . . . **CLC 3**
See also CA 1-4R; 112; CANR 1

Laughlin, James 1914- . . . . **CLC 49**
See also CA 21-24R; CANR 9; DLB 48

Laurence, (Jean) Margaret (Wemyss)
1926-1987 . . **CLC 3, 6, 13, 50, 62; SSC 7**
See also CA 5-8R; 121; CANR 33; DLB 53;
MTCW; SATA 50

Laurent, Antoine 1952- . . . . **CLC 50**

Lauscher, Hermann
See Hesse, Hermann

Lautreamont, Comte de
1846-1870 . . . . **NCLC 12**

Laverty, Donald
See Blish, James (Benjamin)

Lavin, Mary 1912- . . . . . . **CLC 4, 18; SSC 4**
See also CA 9-12R; CANR 33; DLB 15;
MTCW

Lavond, Paul Dennis
See Kornbluth, C(yril) M.; Pohl, Frederik

Lawler, Raymond Evenor 1922- . . . . **CLC 58**
See also CA 103

Lawrence, D(avid) H(erbert Richards)
1885-1930 . . . . **TCLC 2, 9, 16, 33, 48;**
SSC 4
See also CA 104; 121; CDBLB 1914-1945;
DA; DLB 10, 19, 36, 98; MTCW; WLC

Lawrence, T(homas) E(dward)
1888-1935 . . . . **TCLC 18**
See also Dale, Colin
See also CA 115

Lawrence Of Arabia
See Lawrence, T(homas) E(dward)

Lawson, Henry (Archibald Hertzberg)
1867-1922 . . . . **TCLC 27**
See also CA 120

Lawton, Dennis
See Faust, Frederick (Schiller)

Laxness, Halldor . . . . **CLC 25**
See also Gudjonsson, Halldor Kiljan

Layamon fl. c. 1200- . . . . **CMLC 10**

Laye, Camara 1928-1980 . . . . **CLC 4, 38**
See also BLC 2; BW; CA 85-88; 97-100;
CANR 25; MTCW

Layton, Irving (Peter) 1912- . . . . **CLC 2, 15**
See also CA 1-4R; CANR 2, 33; DLB 88;
MTCW

Lazarus, Emma 1849-1887 . . . . **NCLC 8**

Lazarus, Felix
See Cable, George Washington

Lazarus, Henry
See Slavitt, David R(ytman)

Lea, Joan
See Neufeld, John (Arthur)

Leacock, Stephen (Butler)
1869-1944 . . . . **TCLC 2**
See also CA 104; DLB 92

Lear, Edward 1812-1888 . . . . **NCLC 3**
See also CLR 1; DLB 32; MAICYA;
SATA 18

Lear, Norman (Milton) 1922- . . . . . . **CLC 12**
See also CA 73-76

Leavis, F(rank) R(aymond)
1895-1978 . . . . **CLC 24**
See also CA 21-24R; 77-80; MTCW

Leavitt, David 1961- . . . . **CLC 34**
See also CA 116; 122; DLB 130

Leblanc, Maurice (Marie Emile)
1864-1941 . . . . **TCLC 49**
See also CA 110

Lebowitz, Fran(ces Ann)
1951(?)- . . . . **CLC 11, 36**
See also CA 81-84; CANR 14; MTCW

le Carre, John . . . . **CLC 3, 5, 9, 15, 28**
See also Cornwell, David (John Moore)
See also BEST 89:4; CDBLB 1960 to
Present; DLB 87

Le Clezio, J(ean) M(arie) G(ustave)
1940- . . . . **CLC 31**
See also CA 116; 128; DLB 83

Leconte de Lisle, Charles-Marie-Rene
1818-1894 . . . . **NCLC 29**

Le Coq, Monsieur
See Simenon, Georges (Jacques Christian)

Leduc, Violette 1907-1972 . . . . **CLC 22**
See also CA 13-14; 33-36R; CAP 1

Ledwidge, Francis 1887(?)-1917 . . . **TCLC 23**
See also CA 123; DLB 20

Lee, Andrea 1953- . . . . **CLC 36**
See also BLC 2; BW; CA 125

Lee, Andrew
See Auchincloss, Louis (Stanton)

Lee, Don L. . . . . **CLC 2**
See also Madhubuti, Haki R.

Lee, George W(ashington)
1894-1976 . . . . **CLC 52**
See also BLC 2; BW; CA 125; DLB 51

Lee, (Nelle) Harper 1926- . . . . . . **CLC 12, 60**
See also CA 13-16R; CDALB 1941-1968;
DA; DLB 6; MTCW; SATA 11; WLC

Lee, Julian
See Latham, Jean Lee

Lee, Lawrence 1903- . . . . **CLC 34**
See also CA 25-28R

Lee, Manfred B(ennington)
1905-1971 . . . . **CLC 11**
See also Queen, Ellery
See also CA 1-4R; 29-32R; CANR 2

Lee, Stan 1922- . . . . **CLC 17**
See also AAYA 5; CA 108; 111

Lee, Tanith 1947- . . . . **CLC 46**
See also CA 37-40R; SATA 8

Lee, Vernon . . . . **TCLC 5**
See also Paget, Violet
See also DLB 57

Lee, William
See Burroughs, William S(eward)

Lee, Willy
See Burroughs, William S(eward)

Lee-Hamilton, Eugene (Jacob)
1845-1907 . . . . **TCLC 22**
See also CA 117

Leet, Judith 1935- . . . . **CLC 11**

Le Fanu, Joseph Sheridan
1814-1873 . . . . **NCLC 9**
See also DLB 21, 70

Leffland, Ella 1931- . . . . **CLC 19**
See also CA 29-32R; CANR 35; DLBY 84;
SATA 65

Leger, (Marie-Rene) Alexis Saint-Leger
1887-1975 . . . . **CLC 11**
See also Perse, St.-John
See also CA 13-16R; 61-64; MTCW

Leger, Saintleger
See Leger, (Marie-Rene) Alexis Saint-Leger

Le Guin, Ursula K(roeber)
1929- . . . . . . **CLC 8, 13, 22, 45, 71; SSC 12**
See also AAYA 9; AITN 1; CA 21-24R;
CANR 9, 32; CDALB 1968-1988; CLR 3,
28; DLB 8, 52; MAICYA; MTCW;
SATA 4, 52

Lehmann, Rosamond (Nina)
1901-1990 . . . . **CLC 5**
See also CA 77-80; 131; CANR 8; DLB 15

Leiber, Fritz (Reuter, Jr.)
1910-1992 . . . . **CLC 25**
See also CA 45-48; 139; CANR 2, 40;
DLB 8; MTCW; SATA 45;
SATA-Obit 73

Leimbach, Martha 1963-
See Leimbach, Marti
See also CA 130

Leimbach, Marti . . . . **CLC 65**
See also Leimbach, Martha

Leino, Eino . . . . **TCLC 24**
See also Loennbohm, Armas Eino Leopold

Leiris, Michel (Julien) 1901-1990 . . . **CLC 61**
See also CA 119; 128; 132

Leithauser, Brad 1953- . . . . **CLC 27**
See also CA 107; CANR 27; DLB 120

Lelchuk, Alan 1938- . . . . **CLC 5**
See also CA 45-48; CANR 1

Lem, Stanislaw 1921- . . . . **CLC 8, 15, 40**
See also CA 105; CAAS 1; CANR 32;
MTCW

Lemann, Nancy 1956- . . . . **CLC 39**
See also CA 118; 136

Lemonnier, (Antoine Louis) Camille
1844-1913 . . . . **TCLC 22**
See also CA 121

Lenau, Nikolaus 1802-1850 . . . . . . **NCLC 16**

L'Engle, Madeleine (Camp Franklin)
1918- . . . . **CLC 12**
See also AAYA 1; AITN 2; CA 1-4R;
CANR 3, 21, 39; CLR 1, 14; DLB 52;
MAICYA; MTCW; SAAS 15; SATA 1,
27

Lengyel, Jozsef 1896-1975 . . . . **CLC 7**
See also CA 85-88; 57-60

Lennon, John (Ono)
1940-1980 . . . . **CLC 12, 35**
See also CA 102

Lennox, Charlotte Ramsay
1729(?)-1804 . . . . **NCLC 23**
See also DLB 39

Lentricchia, Frank (Jr.) 1940- . . . . . . **CLC 34**
See also CA 25-28R; CANR 19

Lenz, Siegfried 1926- . . . . **CLC 27**
See also CA 89-92; DLB 75

Leonard, Elmore (John, Jr.)
1925- . . . . **CLC 28, 34, 71**
See also AITN 1; BEST 89:1, 90:4;
CA 81-84; CANR 12, 28; MTCW

Leonard, Hugh
See Byrne, John Keyes
See also DLB 13

**Leopardi, (Conte) Giacomo (Talegardo
Francesco di Sales Save**
1798-1837 . . . . **NCLC 22**

Le Reveler
See Artaud, Antonin

Lerman, Eleanor 1952- . . . . **CLC 9**
See also CA 85-88

Lerman, Rhoda 1936- . . . . **CLC 56**
See also CA 49-52

Lermontov, Mikhail Yuryevich
1814-1841 . . . . **NCLC 5**

Leroux, Gaston 1868-1927 . . . . **TCLC 25**
See also CA 108; 136; SATA 65

Lesage, Alain-Rene 1668-1747 . . . . **LC 2**

Leskov, Nikolai (Semyonovich)
1831-1895 . . . . **NCLC 25**

Lessing, Doris (May)
1919- . . . . . **CLC 1, 2, 3, 6, 10, 15, 22, 40;
SSC 6**
See also CA 9-12R; CAAS 14; CANR 33;
CDBLB 1960 to Present; DA; DLB 15;
DLBY 85; MTCW

Lessing, Gotthold Ephraim
1729-1781 . . . . **LC 8**
See also DLB 97

Lester, Richard 1932- . . . . **CLC 20**

Lever, Charles (James)
1806-1872 . . . . **NCLC 23**
See also DLB 21

Leverson, Ada 1865(?)-1936(?) . . . . **TCLC 18**
See also Elaine
See also CA 117

Longfellow, Henry Wadsworth
1807-1882 .... NCLC 2
See also CDALB 1640-1865; DA; DLB 1,
59; SATA 19

Longley, Michael 1939- .... CLC 29
See also CA 102; DLB 40

Longus fl. c. 2nd cent. - .... CMLC 7

Longway, A. Hugh
See Lang, Andrew

Lopate, Phillip 1943- .... CLC 29
See also CA 97-100; DLBY 80

Lopez Portillo (y Pacheco), Jose
1920- .... CLC 46
See also CA 129; HW

Lopez y Fuentes, Gregorio
1897(?)-1966 .... CLC 32
See also CA 131; HW

Lorca, Federico Garcia
See Garcia Lorca, Federico

Lord, Bette Bao 1938- .... CLC 23
See also BEST 90:3; CA 107; CANR 41;
SATA 58

Lord Auch
See Bataille, Georges

Lord Byron
See Byron, George Gordon (Noel)

Lord Dunsany .... TCLC 2
See also Dunsany, Edward John Moreton
Drax Plunkett

Lorde, Audre (Geraldine)
1934- .... CLC 18, 71
See also BLC 2; BW; CA 25-28R;
CANR 16, 26; DLB 41; MTCW

Lord Jeffrey
See Jeffrey, Francis

Lorenzo, Heberto Padilla
See Padilla (Lorenzo), Heberto

Loris
See Hofmannsthal, Hugo von

Loti, Pierre .... TCLC 11
See also Viaud, (Louis Marie) Julien
See also DLB 123

Louie, David Wong 1954- .... CLC 70
See also CA 139

Louis, Father M.
See Merton, Thomas

Lovecraft, H(oward) P(hillips)
1890-1937 .... TCLC 4, 22; SSC 3
See also CA 104; 133; MTCW

Lovelace, Earl 1935- .... CLC 51
See also CA 77-80; CANR 41; DLB 125;
MTCW

Lowell, Amy 1874-1925 .... TCLC 1, 8
See also CA 104; DLB 54

Lowell, James Russell 1819-1891 .. NCLC 2
See also CDALB 1640-1865; DLB 1, 11, 64,
79

Lowell, Robert (Traill Spence, Jr.)
1917-1977 ... CLC 1, 2, 3, 4, 5, 8, 9, 11,
15, 37; PC 3
See also CA 9-12R; 73-76; CABS 2;
CANR 26; DA; DLB 5; MTCW; WLC

Lowndes, Marie Adelaide (Belloc)
1868-1947 .... TCLC 12
See also CA 107; DLB 70

Lowry, (Clarence) Malcolm
1909-1957 .... TCLC 6, 40
See also CA 105; 131; CDBLB 1945-1960;
DLB 15; MTCW

Lowry, Mina Gertrude 1882-1966
See Loy, Mina
See also CA 113

Loxsmith, John
See Brunner, John (Kilian Houston)

Loy, Mina .... CLC 28
See also Lowry, Mina Gertrude
See also DLB 4, 54

Loyson-Bridet
See Schwob, (Mayer Andre) Marcel

Lucas, Craig 1951- .... CLC 64
See also CA 137

Lucas, George 1944- .... CLC 16
See also AAYA 1; CA 77-80; CANR 30;
SATA 56

Lucas, Hans
See Godard, Jean-Luc

Lucas, Victoria
See Plath, Sylvia

Ludlam, Charles 1943-1987 ..... CLC 46, 50
See also CA 85-88; 122

Ludlum, Robert 1927- .... CLC 22, 43
See also AAYA 10; BEST 89:1, 90:3;
CA 33-36R; CANR 25, 41; DLBY 82;
MTCW

Ludwig, Ken .... CLC 60

Ludwig, Otto 1813-1865 .... NCLC 4
See also DLB 129

Lugones, Leopoldo 1874-1938 ..... TCLC 15
See also CA 116; 131; HW

Lu Hsun 1881-1936 .... TCLC 3

Lukacs, George .... CLC 24
See also Lukacs, Gyorgy (Szegeny von)

Lukacs, Gyorgy (Szegeny von) 1885-1971
See Lukacs, George
See also CA 101; 29-32R

Luke, Peter (Ambrose Cyprian)
1919- .... CLC 38
See also CA 81-84; DLB 13

Lunar, Dennis
See Mungo, Raymond

Lurie, Alison 1926- ...... CLC 4, 5, 18, 39
See also CA 1-4R; CANR 2, 17; DLB 2;
MTCW; SATA 46

Lustig, Arnost 1926- .... CLC 56
See also AAYA 3; CA 69-72; SATA 56

Luther, Martin 1483-1546 .... LC 9

Luzi, Mario 1914- .... CLC 13
See also CA 61-64; CANR 9; DLB 128

Lynch, B. Suarez
See Bioy Casares, Adolfo; Borges, Jorge
Luis

Lynch, David (K.) 1946- .... CLC 66
See also CA 124; 129

Lynch, James
See Andreyev, Leonid (Nikolaevich)

Lynch Davis, B.
See Bioy Casares, Adolfo; Borges, Jorge
Luis

Lyndsay, SirDavid 1490-1555 .... LC 20

Lynn, Kenneth S(chuyler) 1923- .... CLC 50
See also CA 1-4R; CANR 3, 27

Lynx
See West, Rebecca

Lyons, Marcus
See Blish, James (Benjamin)

Lyre, Pinchbeck
See Sassoon, Siegfried (Lorraine)

Lytle, Andrew (Nelson) 1902- ...... CLC 22
See also CA 9-12R; DLB 6

Lyttelton, George 1709-1773 .... LC 10

Maas, Peter 1929- .... CLC 29
See also CA 93-96

Macaulay, Rose 1881-1958 ..... TCLC 7, 44
See also CA 104; DLB 36

MacBeth, George (Mann)
1932-1992 .... CLC 2, 5, 9
See also CA 25-28R; 136; DLB 40; MTCW;
SATA 4; SATA-Obit 70

MacCaig, Norman (Alexander)
1910- .... CLC 36
See also CA 9-12R; CANR 3, 34; DLB 27

MacCarthy, (Sir Charles Otto) Desmond
1877-1952 .... TCLC 36

MacDiarmid, Hugh ..... CLC 2, 4, 11, 19, 63
See also Grieve, C(hristopher) M(urray)
See also CDBLB 1945-1960; DLB 20

MacDonald, Anson
See Heinlein, Robert A(nson)

Macdonald, Cynthia 1928- ...... CLC 13, 19
See also CA 49-52; CANR 4; DLB 105

MacDonald, George 1824-1905 ..... TCLC 9
See also CA 106; 137; DLB 18; MAICYA;
SATA 33

Macdonald, John
See Millar, Kenneth

MacDonald, John D(ann)
1916-1986 .... CLC 3, 27, 44
See also CA 1-4R; 121; CANR 1, 19;
DLB 8; DLBY 86; MTCW

Macdonald, John Ross
See Millar, Kenneth

Macdonald, Ross ..... CLC 1, 2, 3, 14, 34, 41
See also Millar, Kenneth
See also DLBD 6

MacDougal, John
See Blish, James (Benjamin)

MacEwen, Gwendolyn (Margaret)
1941-1987 .... CLC 13, 55
See also CA 9-12R; 124; CANR 7, 22;
DLB 53; SATA 50, 55

Machado (y Ruiz), Antonio
1875-1939 .... TCLC 3
See also CA 104; DLB 108

Machado de Assis, Joaquim Maria
1839-1908 .... TCLC 10
See also BLC 2; CA 107

Machen, Arthur .... TCLC 4
See also Jones, Arthur Llewellyn
See also DLB 36

Machiavelli, Niccolo 1469-1527 ...... **LC 8**
See also DA

MacInnes, Colin 1914-1976...... **CLC 4, 23**
See also CA 69-72; 65-68; CANR 21;
DLB 14; MTCW

MacInnes, Helen (Clark)
1907-1985 .... **CLC 27, 39**
See also CA 1-4R; 117; CANR 1, 28;
DLB 87; MTCW; SATA 22, 44

Mackay, Mary 1855-1924
See Corelli, Marie
See also CA 118

Mackenzie, Compton (Edward Montague)
1883-1972 .... **CLC 18**
See also CA 21-22; 37-40R; CAP 2;
DLB 34, 100

Mackenzie, Henry 1745-1831 .... **NCLC 41**
See also DLB 39

Mackintosh, Elizabeth 1896(?)-1952
See Tey, Josephine
See also CA 110

MacLaren, James
See Grieve, C(hristopher) M(urray)

Mac Laverty, Bernard 1942-....... **CLC 31**
See also CA 116; 118

MacLean, Alistair (Stuart)
1922-1987 ....**CLC 3, 13, 50, 63**
See also CA 57-60; 121; CANR 28; MTCW;
SATA 23, 50

Maclean, Norman (Fitzroy) 1902-1990
See also CA 102; 132; SSC 13

MacLeish, Archibald
1892-1982 ....**CLC 3, 8, 14, 68**
See also CA 9-12R; 106; CANR 33; DLB 4,
7, 45; DLBY 82; MTCW

MacLennan, (John) Hugh
1907- .... **CLC 2, 14**
See also CA 5-8R; CANR 33; DLB 68;
MTCW

MacLeod, Alistair 1936- .... **CLC 56**
See also CA 123; DLB 60

MacNeice, (Frederick) Louis
1907-1963 .... **CLC 1, 4, 10, 53**
See also CA 85-88; DLB 10, 20; MTCW

MacNeill, Dand
See Fraser, George MacDonald

Macpherson, (Jean) Jay 1931-...... **CLC 14**
See also CA 5-8R; DLB 53

MacShane, Frank 1927-.......... **CLC 39**
See also CA 9-12R; CANR 3, 33; DLB 111

Macumber, Mari
See Sandoz, Mari(e Susette)

Madach, Imre 1823-1864........ **NCLC 19**

Madden, (Jerry) David 1933- .... **CLC 5, 15**
See also CA 1-4R; CAAS 3; CANR 4;
DLB 6; MTCW

Maddern, Al(an)
See Ellison, Harlan

Madhubuti, Haki R.
1942- .... **CLC 6, 73; PC 5**
See also Lee, Don L.
See also BLC 2; BW; CA 73-76; CANR 24;
DLB 5, 41; DLBD 8

Madow, Pauline (Reichberg) .... **CLC 1**
See also CA 9-12R

Maepenn, Hugh
See Kuttner, Henry

Maepenn, K. H.
See Kuttner, Henry

Maeterlinck, Maurice 1862-1949 ... **TCLC 3**
See also CA 104; 136; SATA 66

Maginn, William 1794-1842...... **NCLC 8**
See also DLB 110

Mahapatra, Jayanta 1928-........ **CLC 33**
See also CA 73-76; CAAS 9; CANR 15, 33

Mahfouz, Naguib (Abdel Aziz Al-Sabilgi)
1911(?)-
See Mahfuz, Najib
See also BEST 89:2; CA 128; MTCW

Mahfuz, Najib .... **CLC 52, 55**
See also Mahfouz, Naguib (Abdel Aziz
Al-Sabilgi)
See also DLBY 88

Mahon, Derek 1941-............. **CLC 27**
See also CA 113; 128; DLB 40

Mailer, Norman
1923- ...... **CLC 1, 2, 3, 4, 5, 8, 11, 14,
28, 39, 74**
See also AITN 2; CA 9-12R; CABS 1;
CANR 28; CDALB 1968-1988; DA;
DLB 2, 16, 28; DLBD 3; DLBY 80, 83;
MTCW

Maillet, Antonine 1929-.......... **CLC 54**
See also CA 115; 120; DLB 60

Mais, Roger 1905-1955 .... **TCLC 8**
See also BW; CA 105; 124; DLB 125;
MTCW

Maitland, Sara (Louise) 1950-...... **CLC 49**
See also CA 69-72; CANR 13

Major, Clarence 1936-....... **CLC 3, 19, 48**
See also BLC 2; BW; CA 21-24R; CAAS 6;
CANR 13, 25; DLB 33

Major, Kevin (Gerald) 1949-....... **CLC 26**
See also CA 97-100; CANR 21, 38;
CLR 11; DLB 60; MAICYA; SATA 32

Maki, James
See Ozu, Yasujiro

Malabaila, Damiano
See Levi, Primo

Malamud, Bernard
1914-1986 ...... **CLC 1, 2, 3, 5, 8, 9, 11,
18, 27, 44, 78**
See also CA 5-8R; 118; CABS 1; CANR 28;
CDALB 1941-1968; DA; DLB 2, 28;
DLBY 80, 86; MTCW; WLC

Malcolm, Dan
See Silverberg, Robert

Malherbe, Francois de 1555-1628..... **LC 5**

Mallarme, Stephane
1842-1898 .... **NCLC 4, 41; PC 4**

Mallet-Joris, Francoise 1930-...... **CLC 11**
See also CA 65-68; CANR 17; DLB 83

Malley, Ern
See McAuley, James Phillip

Mallowan, Agatha Christie
See Christie, Agatha (Mary Clarissa)

Maloff, Saul 1922-............... **CLC 5**
See also CA 33-36R

Malone, Louis
See MacNeice, (Frederick) Louis

Malone, Michael (Christopher)
1942- .... **CLC 43**
See also CA 77-80; CANR 14, 32

Malory, (Sir) Thomas
1410(?)-1471(?) .... **LC 11**
See also CDBLB Before 1660; DA;
SATA 33, 59

Malouf, (George Joseph) David
1934- .... **CLC 28**
See also CA 124

Malraux, (Georges-)Andre
1901-1976 ...... **CLC 1, 4, 9, 13, 15, 57**
See also CA 21-22; 69-72; CANR 34;
CAP 2; DLB 72; MTCW

Malzberg, Barry N(athaniel) 1939-... **CLC 7**
See also CA 61-64; CAAS 4; CANR 16;
DLB 8

Mamet, David (Alan)
1947- .... **CLC 9, 15, 34, 46**
See also AAYA 3; CA 81-84; CABS 3;
CANR 15, 41; DLB 7; MTCW

Mamoulian, Rouben (Zachary)
1897-1987 .... **CLC 16**
See also CA 25-28R; 124

Mandelstam, Osip (Emilievich)
1891(?)-1938(?) .... **TCLC 2, 6**
See also CA 104

Mander, (Mary) Jane 1877-1949... **TCLC 31**

Mandiargues, Andre Pieyre de....... **CLC 41**
See also Pieyre de Mandiargues, Andre
See also DLB 83

Mandrake, Ethel Belle
See Thurman, Wallace (Henry)

Mangan, James Clarence
1803-1849 .... **NCLC 27**

Maniere, J.-E.
See Giraudoux, (Hippolyte) Jean

Manley, (Mary) Delariviere
1672(?)-1724 .... **LC 1**
See also DLB 39, 80

Mann, Abel
See Creasey, John

Mann, (Luiz) Heinrich 1871-1950... **TCLC 9**
See also CA 106; DLB 66

Mann, (Paul) Thomas
1875-1955 .... **TCLC 2, 8, 14, 21, 35, 44;
SSC 5**
See also CA 104; 128; DA; DLB 66;
MTCW; WLC

Manning, David
See Faust, Frederick (Schiller)

Manning, Frederic 1887(?)-1935 ... **TCLC 25**
See also CA 124

Manning, Olivia 1915-1980 ...... **CLC 5, 19**
See also CA 5-8R; 101; CANR 29; MTCW

Mano, D. Keith 1942- .... **CLC 2, 10**
See also CA 25-28R; CAAS 6; CANR 26;
DLB 6

Mansfield, Katherine... **TCLC 2, 8, 39; SSC 9**
See also Beauchamp, Kathleen Mansfield
See also WLC

Manso, Peter 1940- .... **CLC 39**
See also CA 29-32R

Mantecon, Juan Jimenez
See Jimenez (Mantecon), Juan Ramon

Manton, Peter
See Creasey, John

Man Without a Spleen, A
See Chekhov, Anton (Pavlovich)

Manzoni, Alessandro 1785-1873 . . **NCLC 29**

Mapu, Abraham (ben Jekutiel)
1808-1867 . . . . **NCLC 18**

Mara, Sally
See Queneau, Raymond

Marat, Jean Paul 1743-1793 . . . . **LC 10**

Marcel, Gabriel Honore
1889-1973 . . . . **CLC 15**
See also CA 102; 45-48; MTCW

Marchbanks, Samuel
See Davies, (William) Robertson

Marchi, Giacomo
See Bassani, Giorgio

Margulies, Donald . . . . **CLC 76**

Marie de France c. 12th cent. -. . . . **CMLC 8**

Marie de l'Incarnation 1599-1672. . . . **LC 10**

Mariner, Scott
See Pohl, Frederik

Marinetti, Filippo Tommaso
1876-1944 . . . . **TCLC 10**
See also CA 107; DLB 114

Marivaux, Pierre Carlet de Chamblain de
1688-1763 . . . . **LC 4**

Markandaya, Kamala . . . . **CLC 8, 38**
See also Taylor, Kamala (Purnaiya)

Markfield, Wallace 1926- . . . . **CLC 8**
See also CA 69-72; CAAS 3; DLB 2, 28

Markham, Edwin 1852-1940 . . . . . **TCLC 47**
See also DLB 54

Markham, Robert
See Amis, Kingsley (William)

Marks, J
See Highwater, Jamake (Mamake)

Marks-Highwater, J
See Highwater, Jamake (Mamake)

Markson, David M(errill) 1927- . . . . **CLC 67**
See also CA 49-52; CANR 1

Marley, Bob . . . . **CLC 17**
See also Marley, Robert Nesta

Marley, Robert Nesta 1945-1981
See Marley, Bob
See also CA 107; 103

Marlowe, Christopher
1564-1593 . . . . **LC 22; DC 1**
See also CDBLB Before 1660; DA; DLB 62;
WLC

Marmontel, Jean-Francois
1723-1799 . . . . **LC 2**

Marquand, John P(hillips)
1893-1960 . . . . **CLC 2, 10**
See also CA 85-88; DLB 9, 102

Marquez, Gabriel (Jose) Garcia . . . . . . **CLC 68**
See also Garcia Marquez, Gabriel (Jose)

Marquis, Don(ald Robert Perry)
1878-1937 . . . . **TCLC 7**
See also CA 104; DLB 11, 25

Marric, J. J.
See Creasey, John

Marrow, Bernard
See Moore, Brian

Marryat, Frederick 1792-1848 . . . . **NCLC 3**
See also DLB 21

Marsden, James
See Creasey, John

Marsh, (Edith) Ngaio
1899-1982 . . . . **CLC 7, 53**
See also CA 9-12R; CANR 6; DLB 77;
MTCW

Marshall, Garry 1934- . . . . **CLC 17**
See also AAYA 3; CA 111; SATA 60

Marshall, Paule 1929- . . **CLC 27, 72; SSC 3**
See also BLC 3; BW; CA 77-80; CANR 25;
DLB 33; MTCW

Marsten, Richard
See Hunter, Evan

Martha, Henry
See Harris, Mark

Martin, Ken
See Hubbard, L(afayette) Ron(ald)

Martin, Richard
See Creasey, John

Martin, Steve 1945- . . . . **CLC 30**
See also CA 97-100; CANR 30; MTCW

Martin, Violet Florence
1862-1915 . . . . **TCLC 51**

Martin, Webber
See Silverberg, Robert

Martin du Gard, Roger
1881-1958 . . . . **TCLC 24**
See also CA 118; DLB 65

Martineau, Harriet 1802-1876. . . . **NCLC 26**
See also DLB 21, 55; YABC 2

Martines, Julia
See O'Faolain, Julia

Martinez, Jacinto Benavente y
See Benavente (y Martinez), Jacinto

Martinez Ruiz, Jose 1873-1967
See Azorin; Ruiz, Jose Martinez
See also CA 93-96; HW

Martinez Sierra, Gregorio
1881-1947 . . . . **TCLC 6**
See also CA 115

Martinez Sierra, Maria (de la O'LeJarraga)
1874-1974 . . . . **TCLC 6**
See also CA 115

Martinsen, Martin
See Follett, Ken(neth Martin)

Martinson, Harry (Edmund)
1904-1978 . . . . **CLC 14**
See also CA 77-80; CANR 34

Marut, Ret
See Traven, B.

Marut, Robert
See Traven, B.

Marvell, Andrew 1621-1678. . . . . **LC 4**
See also CDBLB 1660-1789; DA; DLB 131;
WLC

Marx, Karl (Heinrich)
1818-1883 . . . . **NCLC 17**
See also DLB 129

Masaoka Shiki. . . . . **TCLC 18**
See also Masaoka Tsunenori

Masaoka Tsunenori 1867-1902
See Masaoka Shiki
See also CA 117

Masefield, John (Edward)
1878-1967 . . . . **CLC 11, 47**
See also CA 19-20; 25-28R; CANR 33;
CAP 2; CDBLB 1890-1914; DLB 10;
MTCW; SATA 19

Maso, Carole 19(?)- . . . . **CLC 44**

Mason, Bobbie Ann
1940- . . . . **CLC 28, 43; SSC 4**
See also AAYA 5; CA 53-56; CANR 11,
31; DLBY 87; MTCW

Mason, Ernst
See Pohl, Frederik

Mason, Lee W.
See Malzberg, Barry N(athaniel)

Mason, Nick 1945- . . . . **CLC 35**
See also Pink Floyd

Mason, Tally
See Derleth, August (William)

Mass, William
See Gibson, William

Masters, Edgar Lee
1868-1950 . . . . **TCLC 2, 25; PC 1**
See also CA 104; 133; CDALB 1865-1917;
DA; DLB 54; MTCW

Masters, Hilary 1928- . . . . **CLC 48**
See also CA 25-28R; CANR 13

Mastrosimone, William 19(?)- . . . . . . **CLC 36**

Mathe, Albert
See Camus, Albert

Matheson, Richard Burton 1926- . . . **CLC 37**
See also CA 97-100; DLB 8, 44

Mathews, Harry 1930- . . . . **CLC 6, 52**
See also CA 21-24R; CAAS 6; CANR 18,
40

Mathias, Roland (Glyn) 1915- . . . . . . **CLC 45**
See also CA 97-100; CANR 19, 41; DLB 27

Matsuo Basho 1644-1694. . . . . **PC 3**

Mattheson, Rodney
See Creasey, John

Matthews, Greg 1949- . . . . **CLC 45**
See also CA 135

Matthews, William 1942- . . . . **CLC 40**
See also CA 29-32R; CANR 12; DLB 5

Matthias, John (Edward) 1941- . . . . . . **CLC 9**
See also CA 33-36R

Matthiessen, Peter
1927- . . . . **CLC 5, 7, 11, 32, 64**
See also AAYA 6; BEST 90:4; CA 9-12R;
CANR 21; DLB 6; MTCW; SATA 27

Maturin, Charles Robert
1780(?)-1824 . . . . **NCLC 6**

Matute (Ausejo), Ana Maria
1925- . . . . **CLC 11**
See also CA 89-92; MTCW

Maugham, W. S.
See Maugham, W(illiam) Somerset

Maugham, W(illiam) Somerset
    1874-1965 .... **CLC 1, 11, 15, 67; SSC 8**
    See also CA 5-8R; 25-28R; CANR 40;
    CDBLB 1914-1945; DA; DLB 10, 36, 77,
    100; MTCW; SATA 54; WLC

Maugham, William Somerset
    See Maugham, W(illiam) Somerset

Maupassant, (Henri Rene Albert) Guy de
    1850-1893 .... **NCLC 1; SSC 1**
    See also DA; DLB 123; WLC

Maurhut, Richard
    See Traven, B.

Mauriac, Claude 1914- .... **CLC 9**
    See also CA 89-92; DLB 83

Mauriac, Francois (Charles)
    1885-1970 .... **CLC 4, 9, 56**
    See also CA 25-28; CAP 2; DLB 65;
    MTCW

Mavor, Osborne Henry 1888-1951
    See Bridie, James
    See also CA 104

Maxwell, William (Keepers, Jr.)
    1908- .... **CLC 19**
    See also CA 93-96; DLBY 80

May, Elaine 1932- .... **CLC 16**
    See also CA 124; DLB 44

Mayakovski, Vladimir (Vladimirovich)
    1893-1930 .... **TCLC 4, 18**
    See also CA 104

Mayhew, Henry 1812-1887 ...... **NCLC 31**
    See also DLB 18, 55

Maynard, Joyce 1953- .... **CLC 23**
    See also CA 111; 129

Mayne, William (James Carter)
    1928- .... **CLC 12**
    See also CA 9-12R; CANR 37; CLR 25;
    MAICYA; SAAS 11; SATA 6, 68

Mayo, Jim
    See L'Amour, Louis (Dearborn)

Maysles, Albert 1926- .... **CLC 16**
    See also CA 29-32R

Maysles, David 1932- .... **CLC 16**

Mazer, Norma Fox 1931- .... **CLC 26**
    See also AAYA 5; CA 69-72; CANR 12,
    32; CLR 23; MAICYA; SAAS 1;
    SATA 24, 67

Mazzini, Guiseppe 1805-1872 .... **NCLC 34**

McAuley, James Phillip
    1917-1976 .... **CLC 45**
    See also CA 97-100

McBain, Ed
    See Hunter, Evan

McBrien, William Augustine
    1930- .... **CLC 44**
    See also CA 107

McCaffrey, Anne (Inez) 1926- ...... **CLC 17**
    See also AAYA 6; AITN 2; BEST 89:2;
    CA 25-28R; CANR 15, 35; DLB 8;
    MAICYA; MTCW; SAAS 11; SATA 8,
    70

McCann, Arthur
    See Campbell, John W(ood, Jr.)

McCann, Edson
    See Pohl, Frederik

McCarthy, Cormac, Jr. .... **CLC 4, 57**
    See also McCarthy, Charles, Jr.
    See also DLB 6

McCarthy, Mary (Therese)
    1912-1989 ... **CLC 1, 3, 5, 14, 24, 39, 59**
    See also CA 5-8R; 129; CANR 16; DLB 2;
    DLBY 81; MTCW

McCartney, (James) Paul
    1942- .... **CLC 12, 35**

McCauley, Stephen (D.) 1955- ..... **CLC 50**

McClure, Michael (Thomas)
    1932- .... **CLC 6, 10**
    See also CA 21-24R; CANR 17; DLB 16

McCorkle, Jill (Collins) 1958- ..... **CLC 51**
    See also CA 121; DLBY 87

McCourt, James 1941- .... **CLC 5**
    See also CA 57-60

McCoy, Horace (Stanley)
    1897-1955 .... **TCLC 28**
    See also CA 108; DLB 9

McCrae, John 1872-1918 .... **TCLC 12**
    See also CA 109; DLB 92

McCreigh, James
    See Pohl, Frederik

McCullers, (Lula) Carson (Smith)
    1917-1967 .. **CLC 1, 4, 10, 12, 48; SSC 9**
    See also CA 5-8R; 25-28R; CABS 1, 3;
    CANR 18; CDALB 1941-1968; DA;
    DLB 2, 7; MTCW; SATA 27; WLC

McCulloch, John Tyler
    See Burroughs, Edgar Rice

McCullough, Colleen 1938(?)- ...... **CLC 27**
    See also CA 81-84; CANR 17; MTCW

McElroy, Joseph 1930- .... **CLC 5, 47**
    See also CA 17-20R

McEwan, Ian (Russell) 1948- ... **CLC 13, 66**
    See also BEST 90:4; CA 61-64; CANR 14,
    41; DLB 14; MTCW

McFadden, David 1940- .... **CLC 48**
    See also CA 104; DLB 60

McFarland, Dennis 1950- .... **CLC 65**

McGahern, John 1934- .... **CLC 5, 9, 48**
    See also CA 17-20R; CANR 29; DLB 14;
    MTCW

McGinley, Patrick (Anthony)
    1937- .... **CLC 41**
    See also CA 120; 127

McGinley, Phyllis 1905-1978 ...... **CLC 14**
    See also CA 9-12R; 77-80; CANR 19;
    DLB 11, 48; SATA 2, 24, 44

McGinniss, Joe 1942- .... **CLC 32**
    See also AITN 2; BEST 89:2; CA 25-28R;
    CANR 26

McGivern, Maureen Daly
    See Daly, Maureen

McGrath, Patrick 1950- .... **CLC 55**
    See also CA 136

McGrath, Thomas (Matthew)
    1916-1990 .... **CLC 28, 59**
    See also CA 9-12R; 132; CANR 6, 33;
    MTCW; SATA 41; SATA-Obit 66

McGuane, Thomas (Francis III)
    1939- .... **CLC 3, 7, 18, 45**
    See also AITN 2; CA 49-52; CANR 5, 24;
    DLB 2; DLBY 80; MTCW

McGuckian, Medbh 1950- .... **CLC 48**
    See also DLB 40

McHale, Tom 1942(?)-1982 .... **CLC 3, 5**
    See also AITN 1; CA 77-80; 106

McIlvanney, William 1936- .... **CLC 42**
    See also CA 25-28R; DLB 14

McIlwraith, Maureen Mollie Hunter
    See Hunter, Mollie
    See also SATA 2

McInerney, Jay 1955- .... **CLC 34**
    See also CA 116; 123

McIntyre, Vonda N(eel) 1948- ..... **CLC 18**
    See also CA 81-84; CANR 17, 34; MTCW

McKay, Claude .... **TCLC 7, 41; PC 2**
    See also McKay, Festus Claudius
    See also BLC 3; DLB 4, 45, 51, 117

McKay, Festus Claudius 1889-1948
    See McKay, Claude
    See also BW; CA 104; 124; DA; MTCW;
    WLC

McKuen, Rod 1933- .... **CLC 1, 3**
    See also AITN 1; CA 41-44R; CANR 40

McLoughlin, R. B.
    See Mencken, H(enry) L(ouis)

McLuhan, (Herbert) Marshall
    1911-1980 .... **CLC 37**
    See also CA 9-12R; 102; CANR 12, 34;
    DLB 88; MTCW

McMillan, Terry (L.) 1951- ..... **CLC 50, 61**
    See also CA 140

McMurtry, Larry (Jeff)
    1936- .... **CLC 2, 3, 7, 11, 27, 44**
    See also AITN 2; BEST 89:2; CA 5-8R;
    CANR 19; CDALB 1968-1988; DLB 2;
    DLBY 80, 87; MTCW

McNally, Terrence 1939- ...... **CLC 4, 7, 41**
    See also CA 45-48; CANR 2; DLB 7

McNamer, Deirdre 1950- .... **CLC 70**

McNeile, Herman Cyril 1888-1937
    See Sapper
    See also DLB 77

McPhee, John (Angus) 1931- ...... **CLC 36**
    See also BEST 90:1; CA 65-68; CANR 20;
    MTCW

McPherson, James Alan
    1943- .... **CLC 19, 77**
    See also BW; CA 25-28R; CAAS 17;
    CANR 24; DLB 38; MTCW

McPherson, William (Alexander)
    1933- .... **CLC 34**
    See also CA 69-72; CANR 28

McSweeney, Kerry .... **CLC 34**

Mead, Margaret 1901-1978 .... **CLC 37**
    See also AITN 1; CA 1-4R; 81-84;
    CANR 4; MTCW; SATA 20

Meaker, Marijane (Agnes) 1927-
    See Kerr, M. E.
    See also CA 107; CANR 37; MAICYA;
    MTCW; SATA 20, 61

Medoff, Mark (Howard) 1940- . . . **CLC 6, 23**
See also AITN 1; CA 53-56; CANR 5;
DLB 7

Meged, Aharon
See Megged, Aharon

Meged, Aron
See Megged, Aharon

Megged, Aharon 1920- . . . . **CLC 9**
See also CA 49-52; CAAS 13; CANR 1

Mehta, Ved (Parkash) 1934- . . . . **CLC 37**
See also CA 1-4R; CANR 2, 23; MTCW

Melanter
See Blackmore, R(ichard) D(oddridge)

Melikow, Loris
See Hofmannsthal, Hugo von

Melmoth, Sebastian
See Wilde, Oscar (Fingal O'Flahertie Wills)

Meltzer, Milton 1915- . . . . **CLC 26**
See also AAYA 8; CA 13-16R; CANR 38;
CLR 13; DLB 61; MAICYA; SAAS 1;
SATA 1, 50

Melville, Herman
1819-1891 . . . . . . **NCLC 3, 12, 29; SSC 1**
See also CDALB 1640-1865; DA; DLB 3,
74; SATA 59; WLC

Menander
c. 342B.C.-c. 292B.C. . . . . **CMLC 9; DC 3**

Mencken, H(enry) L(ouis)
1880-1956 . . . . **TCLC 13**
See also CA 105; 125; CDALB 1917-1929;
DLB 11, 29, 63; MTCW

Mercer, David 1928-1980. . . . . **CLC 5**
See also CA 9-12R; 102; CANR 23;
DLB 13; MTCW

Merchant, Paul
See Ellison, Harlan

Meredith, George 1828-1909 . . . **TCLC 17, 43**
See also CA 117; CDBLB 1832-1890;
DLB 18, 35, 57

Meredith, William (Morris)
1919- . . . . **CLC 4, 13, 22, 55**
See also CA 9-12R; CAAS 14; CANR 6, 40;
DLB 5

Merezhkovsky, Dmitry Sergeyevich
1865-1941 . . . . **TCLC 29**

Merimee, Prosper
1803-1870 . . . . **NCLC 6; SSC 7**
See also DLB 119

Merkin, Daphne 1954- . . . . **CLC 44**
See also CA 123

Merlin, Arthur
See Blish, James (Benjamin)

Merrill, James (Ingram)
1926- . . . . **CLC 2, 3, 6, 8, 13, 18, 34**
See also CA 13-16R; CANR 10; DLB 5;
DLBY 85; MTCW

Merriman, Alex
See Silverberg, Robert

Merritt, E. B.
See Waddington, Miriam

Merton, Thomas
1915-1968 . . . . **CLC 1, 3, 11, 34**
See also CA 5-8R; 25-28R; CANR 22;
DLB 48; DLBY 81; MTCW

Merwin, W(illiam) S(tanley)
1927- . . . . . . **CLC 1, 2, 3, 5, 8, 13, 18, 45**
See also CA 13-16R; CANR 15; DLB 5;
MTCW

Metcalf, John 1938- . . . . **CLC 37**
See also CA 113; DLB 60

Metcalf, Suzanne
See Baum, L(yman) Frank

Mew, Charlotte (Mary)
1870-1928 . . . . **TCLC 8**
See also CA 105; DLB 19

Mewshaw, Michael 1943- . . . . **CLC 9**
See also CA 53-56; CANR 7; DLBY 80

Meyer, June
See Jordan, June

Meyer, Lynn
See Slavitt, David R(ytman)

Meyer-Meyrink, Gustav 1868-1932
See Meyrink, Gustav
See also CA 117

Meyers, Jeffrey 1939- . . . . **CLC 39**
See also CA 73-76; DLB 111

Meynell, Alice (Christina Gertrude Thompson)
1847-1922 . . . . **TCLC 6**
See also CA 104; DLB 19, 98

Meyrink, Gustav . . . . **TCLC 21**
See also Meyer-Meyrink, Gustav
See also DLB 81

Michaels, Leonard 1933- . . . . **CLC 6, 25**
See also CA 61-64; CANR 21; DLB 130;
MTCW

Michaux, Henri 1899-1984 . . . . . . **CLC 8, 19**
See also CA 85-88; 114

Michelangelo 1475-1564. . . . . **LC 12**

Michelet, Jules 1798-1874 . . . . **NCLC 31**

Michener, James A(lbert)
1907(?)- . . . . **CLC 1, 5, 11, 29, 60**
See also AITN 1; BEST 90:1; CA 5-8R;
CANR 21; DLB 6; MTCW

Mickiewicz, Adam 1798-1855 . . . . . **NCLC 3**

Middleton, Christopher 1926- . . . . . . **CLC 13**
See also CA 13-16R; CANR 29; DLB 40

Middleton, Stanley 1919- . . . . **CLC 7, 38**
See also CA 25-28R; CANR 21; DLB 14

Migueis, Jose Rodrigues 1901- . . . . . **CLC 10**

Mikszath, Kalman 1847-1910 . . . . . **TCLC 31**

Miles, Josephine
1911-1985 . . . . **CLC 1, 2, 14, 34, 39**
See also CA 1-4R; 116; CANR 2; DLB 48

Militant
See Sandburg, Carl (August)

Mill, John Stuart 1806-1873 . . . . . **NCLC 11**
See also CDBLB 1832-1890; DLB 55

Millar, Kenneth 1915-1983 . . . . **CLC 14**
See also Macdonald, Ross
See also CA 9-12R; 110; CANR 16; DLB 2;
DLBD 6; DLBY 83; MTCW

Millay, E. Vincent
See Millay, Edna St. Vincent

Millay, Edna St. Vincent
1892-1950 . . . . **TCLC 4, 49; PC 6**
See also CA 104; 130; CDALB 1917-1929;
DA; DLB 45; MTCW

Miller, Arthur
1915- . . . . **CLC 1, 2, 6, 10, 15, 26, 47, 78;**
DC 1
See also AITN 1; CA 1-4R; CABS 3;
CANR 2, 30; CDALB 1941-1968; DA;
DLB 7; MTCW; WLC

Miller, Henry (Valentine)
1891-1980 . . . . **CLC 1, 2, 4, 9, 14, 43**
See also CA 9-12R; 97-100; CANR 33;
CDALB 1929-1941; DA; DLB 4, 9;
DLBY 80; MTCW; WLC

Miller, Jason 1939(?)- . . . . **CLC 2**
See also AITN 1; CA 73-76; DLB 7

Miller, Sue 1943- . . . . **CLC 44**
See also BEST 90:3; CA 139

Miller, Walter M(ichael, Jr.)
1923- . . . . **CLC 4, 30**
See also CA 85-88; DLB 8

Millett, Kate 1934- . . . . **CLC 67**
See also AITN 1; CA 73-76; CANR 32;
MTCW

Millhauser, Steven 1943- . . . . **CLC 21, 54**
See also CA 110; 111; DLB 2

Millin, Sarah Gertrude 1889-1968 . . **CLC 49**
See also CA 102; 93-96

Milne, A(lan) A(lexander)
1882-1956 . . . . **TCLC 6**
See also CA 104; 133; CLR 1, 26; DLB 10,
77, 100; MAICYA; MTCW; YABC 1

Milner, Ron(ald) 1938- . . . . **CLC 56**
See also AITN 1; BLC 3; BW; CA 73-76;
CANR 24; DLB 38; MTCW

Milosz, Czeslaw
1911- . . . . **CLC 5, 11, 22, 31, 56**
See also CA 81-84; CANR 23; MTCW

Milton, John 1608-1674. . . . . **LC 9**
See also CDBLB 1660-1789; DA; DLB 131;
WLC

Minehaha, Cornelius
See Wedekind, (Benjamin) Frank(lin)

Miner, Valerie 1947- . . . . **CLC 40**
See also CA 97-100

Minimo, Duca
See D'Annunzio, Gabriele

Minot, Susan 1956- . . . . **CLC 44**
See also CA 134

Minus, Ed 1938- . . . . **CLC 39**

Miranda, Javier
See Bioy Casares, Adolfo

Miro (Ferrer), Gabriel (Francisco Victor)
1879-1930 . . . . **TCLC 5**
See also CA 104

Mishima, Yukio
. . . . **CLC 2, 4, 6, 9, 27; DC 1; SSC 4**
See also Hiraoka, Kimitake

Mistral, Frederic 1830-1914 . . . . . . **TCLC 51**
See also CA 122

Mistral, Gabriela. . . . . **TCLC 2**
See also Godoy Alcayaga, Lucila

Mistry, Rohinton 1952- . . . . **CLC 71**

Mitchell, Clyde
See Ellison, Harlan; Silverberg, Robert

Author Index

Morrison, James Douglas 1943-1971
  See Morrison, Jim
  See also CA 73-76; CANR 40

Morrison, Jim . . . . **CLC 17**
  See also Morrison, James Douglas

Morrison, Toni 1931- . . . . **CLC 4, 10, 22, 55**
  See also AAYA 1; BLC 3; BW; CA 29-32R;
    CANR 27; CDALB 1968-1988; DA;
    DLB 6, 33; DLBY 81; MTCW; SATA 57

Morrison, Van 1945- . . . . **CLC 21**
  See also CA 116

Mortimer, John (Clifford)
  1923- . . . . **CLC 28, 43**
  See also CA 13-16R; CANR 21;
    CDBLB 1960 to Present; DLB 13;
    MTCW

Mortimer, Penelope (Ruth) 1918- . . . . **CLC 5**
  See also CA 57-60

Morton, Anthony
  See Creasey, John

Mosher, Howard Frank 1943- . . . . . . **CLC 62**
  See also CA 139

Mosley, Nicholas 1923- . . . . **CLC 43, 70**
  See also CA 69-72; CANR 41; DLB 14

Moss, Howard
  1922-1987 . . . . **CLC 7, 14, 45, 50**
  See also CA 1-4R; 123; CANR 1; DLB 5

Mossgiel, Rab
  See Burns, Robert

Motion, Andrew 1952- . . . . **CLC 47**
  See also DLB 40

Motley, Willard (Francis)
  1912-1965 . . . . **CLC 18**
  See also BW; CA 117; 106; DLB 76

Mott, Michael (Charles Alston)
  1930- . . . . **CLC 15, 34**
  See also CA 5-8R; CAAS 7; CANR 7, 29

Mowat, Farley (McGill) 1921- . . . . . **CLC 26**
  See also AAYA 1; CA 1-4R; CANR 4, 24;
    CLR 20; DLB 68; MAICYA; MTCW;
    SATA 3, 55

Moyers, Bill 1934- . . . . **CLC 74**
  See also AITN 2; CA 61-64; CANR 31

Mphahlele, Es'kia
  See Mphahlele, Ezekiel
  See also DLB 125

Mphahlele, Ezekiel 1919- . . . . **CLC 25**
  See also Mphahlele, Es'kia
  See also BLC 3; BW; CA 81-84; CANR 26

Mqhayi, S(amuel) E(dward) K(rune Loliwe)
  1875-1945 . . . . **TCLC 25**
  See also BLC 3

Mr. Martin
  See Burroughs, William S(eward)

Mrozek, Slawomir 1930- . . . . **CLC 3, 13**
  See also CA 13-16R; CAAS 10; CANR 29;
    MTCW

Mrs. Belloc-Lowndes
  See Lowndes, Marie Adelaide (Belloc)

Mtwa, Percy (?)- . . . . **CLC 47**

Mueller, Lisel 1924- . . . . **CLC 13, 51**
  See also CA 93-96; DLB 105

Muir, Edwin 1887-1959 . . . . **TCLC 2**
  See also CA 104; DLB 20, 100

Muir, John 1838-1914 . . . . **TCLC 28**

Mujica Lainez, Manuel
  1910-1984 . . . . **CLC 31**
  See also Lainez, Manuel Mujica
  See also CA 81-84; 112; CANR 32; HW

Mukherjee, Bharati 1940- . . . . **CLC 53**
  See also BEST 89:2; CA 107; DLB 60;
    MTCW

Muldoon, Paul 1951- . . . . **CLC 32, 72**
  See also CA 113; 129; DLB 40

Mulisch, Harry 1927- . . . . **CLC 42**
  See also CA 9-12R; CANR 6, 26

Mull, Martin 1943- . . . . **CLC 17**
  See also CA 105

Mulock, Dinah Maria
  See Craik, Dinah Maria (Mulock)

Munford, Robert 1737(?)-1783 . . . . . . **LC 5**
  See also DLB 31

Mungo, Raymond 1946- . . . . **CLC 72**
  See also CA 49-52; CANR 2

Munro, Alice
  1931- . . . . **CLC 6, 10, 19, 50; SSC 3**
  See also AITN 2; CA 33-36R; CANR 33;
    DLB 53; MTCW; SATA 29

Munro, H(ector) H(ugh) 1870-1916
  See Saki
  See also CA 104; 130; CDBLB 1890-1914;
    DA; DLB 34; MTCW; WLC

Murasaki, Lady . . . . **CMLC 1**

Murdoch, (Jean) Iris
  1919- . . . . . . **CLC 1, 2, 3, 4, 6, 8, 11, 15,
                        22, 31, 51**
  See also CA 13-16R; CANR 8;
    CDBLB 1960 to Present; DLB 14;
    MTCW

Murphy, Richard 1927- . . . . **CLC 41**
  See also CA 29-32R; DLB 40

Murphy, Sylvia 1937- . . . . **CLC 34**
  See also CA 121

Murphy, Thomas (Bernard) 1935- . . . **CLC 51**
  See also CA 101

Murray, Albert L. 1916- . . . . **CLC 73**
  See also BW; CA 49-52; CANR 26; DLB 38

Murray, Les(lie) A(llan) 1938- . . . . . **CLC 40**
  See also CA 21-24R; CANR 11, 27

Murry, J. Middleton
  See Murry, John Middleton

Murry, John Middleton
  1889-1957 . . . . **TCLC 16**
  See also CA 118

Musgrave, Susan 1951- . . . . **CLC 13, 54**
  See also CA 69-72

Musil, Robert (Edler von)
  1880-1942 . . . . **TCLC 12**
  See also CA 109; DLB 81, 124

Musset, (Louis Charles) Alfred de
  1810-1857 . . . . **NCLC 7**

My Brother's Brother
  See Chekhov, Anton (Pavlovich)

Myers, Walter Dean 1937- . . . . **CLC 35**
  See also AAYA 4; BLC 3; BW; CA 33-36R;
    CANR 20; CLR 4, 16; DLB 33;
    MAICYA; SAAS 2; SATA 27, 41, 70, 71

Myers, Walter M.
  See Myers, Walter Dean

Myles, Symon
  See Follett, Ken(neth Martin)

Nabokov, Vladimir (Vladimirovich)
  1899-1977 . . . . . **CLC 1, 2, 3, 6, 8, 11, 15,
                        23, 44, 46, 64; SSC 11**
  See also CA 5-8R; 69-72; CANR 20;
    CDALB 1941-1968; DA; DLB 2;
    DLBD 3; DLBY 80, 91; MTCW; WLC

Nagai Kafu . . . . **TCLC 51**
  See also Nagai Sokichi

Nagai Sokichi 1879-1959
  See Nagai Kafu
  See also CA 117

Nagy, Laszlo 1925-1978 . . . . **CLC 7**
  See also CA 129; 112

Naipaul, Shiva(dhar Srinivasa)
  1945-1985 . . . . **CLC 32, 39**
  See also CA 110; 112; 116; CANR 33;
    DLBY 85; MTCW

Naipaul, V(idiadhar) S(urajprasad)
  1932- . . . . **CLC 4, 7, 9, 13, 18, 37**
  See also CA 1-4R; CANR 1, 33;
    CDBLB 1960 to Present; DLB 125;
    DLBY 85; MTCW

Nakos, Lilika 1899(?)- . . . . **CLC 29**

Narayan, R(asipuram) K(rishnaswami)
  1906- . . . . **CLC 7, 28, 47**
  See also CA 81-84; CANR 33; MTCW;
    SATA 62

Nash, (Frediric) Ogden 1902-1971 . . **CLC 23**
  See also CA 13-14; 29-32R; CANR 34;
    CAP 1; DLB 11; MAICYA; MTCW;
    SATA 2, 46

Nathan, Daniel
  See Dannay, Frederic

Nathan, George Jean 1882-1958 . . . **TCLC 18**
  See also Hatteras, Owen
  See also CA 114

Natsume, Kinnosuke 1867-1916
  See Natsume, Soseki
  See also CA 104

Natsume, Soseki . . . . **TCLC 2, 10**
  See also Natsume, Kinnosuke

Natti, (Mary) Lee 1919-
  See Kingman, Lee
  See also CA 5-8R; CANR 2

Naylor, Gloria 1950- . . . . **CLC 28, 52**
  See also AAYA 6; BLC 3; BW; CA 107;
    CANR 27; DA; MTCW

Neihardt, John Gneisenau
  1881-1973 . . . . **CLC 32**
  See also CA 13-14; CAP 1; DLB 9, 54

Nekrasov, Nikolai Alekseevich
  1821-1878 . . . . **NCLC 11**

Nelligan, Emile 1879-1941 . . . . **TCLC 14**
  See also CA 114; DLB 92

Nelson, Willie 1933- . . . . **CLC 17**
  See also CA 107

Nemerov, Howard (Stanley)
  1920-1991 . . . . **CLC 2, 6, 9, 36**
  See also CA 1-4R; 134; CABS 2; CANR 1,
    27; DLB 6; DLBY 83; MTCW

Neruda, Pablo
1904-1973 ..... **CLC 1, 2, 5, 7, 9, 28, 62;**
PC 4
See also CA 19-20; 45-48; CAP 2; DA; HW;
MTCW; WLC

Nerval, Gerard de 1808-1855...... **NCLC 1**

Nervo, (Jose) Amado (Ruiz de)
1870-1919 .... **TCLC 11**
See also CA 109; 131; HW

Nessi, Pio Baroja y
See Baroja (y Nessi), Pio

Neufeld, John (Arthur) 1938- ...... **CLC 17**
See also CA 25-28R; CANR 11, 37;
MAICYA; SAAS 3; SATA 6

Neville, Emily Cheney 1919-....... **CLC 12**
See also CA 5-8R; CANR 3, 37; MAICYA;
SAAS 2; SATA 1

Newbound, Bernard Slade 1930-
See Slade, Bernard
See also CA 81-84

Newby, P(ercy) H(oward)
1918- .... **CLC 2, 13**
See also CA 5-8R; CANR 32; DLB 15;
MTCW

Newlove, Donald 1928- .... **CLC 6**
See also CA 29-32R; CANR 25

Newlove, John (Herbert) 1938-..... **CLC 14**
See also CA 21-24R; CANR 9, 25

Newman, Charles 1938-......... **CLC 2, 8**
See also CA 21-24R

Newman, Edwin (Harold) 1919- .... **CLC 14**
See also AITN 1; CA 69-72; CANR 5

Newman, John Henry
1801-1890 .... **NCLC 38**
See also DLB 18, 32, 55

Newton, Suzanne 1936- .... **CLC 35**
See also CA 41-44R; CANR 14; SATA 5

Nexo, Martin Andersen
1869-1954 .... **TCLC 43**

Nezval, Vitezslav 1900-1958 ...... **TCLC 44**
See also CA 123

Ngema, Mbongeni 1955- .... **CLC 57**

Ngugi, James T(hiong'o)........ **CLC 3, 7, 13**
See also Ngugi wa Thiong'o

Ngugi wa Thiong'o 1938-.......... **CLC 36**
See also Ngugi, James T(hiong'o)
See also BLC 3; BW; CA 81-84; CANR 27;
DLB 125; MTCW

Nichol, B(arrie) P(hillip)
1944-1988 .... **CLC 18**
See also CA 53-56; DLB 53; SATA 66

Nichols, John (Treadwell) 1940-.... **CLC 38**
See also CA 9-12R; CAAS 2; CANR 6;
DLBY 82

Nichols, Leigh
See Koontz, Dean R(ay)

Nichols, Peter (Richard)
1927- .... **CLC 5, 36, 65**
See also CA 104; CANR 33; DLB 13;
MTCW

Nicolas, F. R. E.
See Freeling, Nicolas

Niedecker, Lorine 1903-1970.... **CLC 10, 42**
See also CA 25-28; CAP 2; DLB 48

Nietzsche, Friedrich (Wilhelm)
1844-1900 .... **TCLC 10, 18**
See also CA 107; 121; DLB 129

Nievo, Ippolito 1831-1861 .... **NCLC 22**

Nightingale, Anne Redmon 1943-
See Redmon, Anne
See also CA 103

Nik.T.O.
See Annensky, Innokenty Fyodorovich

Nin, Anais
1903-1977 ..... **CLC 1, 4, 8, 11, 14, 60;**
SSC 10
See also AITN 2; CA 13-16R; 69-72;
CANR 22; DLB 2, 4; MTCW

Nissenson, Hugh 1933-.......... **CLC 4, 9**
See also CA 17-20R; CANR 27; DLB 28

Niven, Larry .... **CLC 8**
See also Niven, Laurence Van Cott
See also DLB 8

Niven, Laurence Van Cott 1938-
See Niven, Larry
See also CA 21-24R; CAAS 12; CANR 14;
MTCW

Nixon, Agnes Eckhardt 1927-...... **CLC 21**
See also CA 110

Nizan, Paul 1905-1940........... **TCLC 40**
See also DLB 72

Nkosi, Lewis 1936-................ **CLC 45**
See also BLC 3; BW; CA 65-68; CANR 27

Nodier, (Jean) Charles (Emmanuel)
1780-1844 .... **NCLC 19**
See also DLB 119

Nolan, Christopher 1965-......... **CLC 58**
See also CA 111

Norden, Charles
See Durrell, Lawrence (George)

Nordhoff, Charles (Bernard)
1887-1947 .... **TCLC 23**
See also CA 108; DLB 9; SATA 23

Norfolk, Lawrence 1963-.......... **CLC 76**

Norman, Marsha 1947- .... **CLC 28**
See also CA 105; CABS 3; CANR 41;
DLBY 84

Norris, Benjamin Franklin, Jr.
1870-1902 .... **TCLC 24**
See also Norris, Frank
See also CA 110

Norris, Frank
See Norris, Benjamin Franklin, Jr.
See also CDALB 1865-1917; DLB 12, 71

Norris, Leslie 1921-.............. **CLC 14**
See also CA 11-12; CANR 14; CAP 1;
DLB 27

North, Andrew
See Norton, Andre

North, Anthony
See Koontz, Dean R(ay)

North, Captain George
See Stevenson, Robert Louis (Balfour)

North, Milou
See Erdrich, Louise

Northrup, B. A.
See Hubbard, L(afayette) Ron(ald)

North Staffs
See Hulme, T(homas) E(rnest)

Norton, Alice Mary
See Norton, Andre
See also MAICYA; SATA 1, 43

Norton, Andre 1912- .... **CLC 12**
See also Norton, Alice Mary
See also CA 1-4R; CANR 2, 31; DLB 8, 52;
MTCW

Norway, Nevil Shute 1899-1960
See Shute, Nevil
See also CA 102; 93-96

Norwid, Cyprian Kamil
1821-1883 .... **NCLC 17**

Nosille, Nabrah
See Ellison, Harlan

Nossack, Hans Erich 1901-1978..... **CLC 6**
See also CA 93-96; 85-88; DLB 69

Nosu, Chuji
See Ozu, Yasujiro

Nova, Craig 1945-.............. **CLC 7, 31**
See also CA 45-48; CANR 2

Novak, Joseph
See Kosinski, Jerzy (Nikodem)

Novalis 1772-1801 .... **NCLC 13**
See also DLB 90

Nowlan, Alden (Albert) 1933-1983 .. **CLC 15**
See also CA 9-12R; CANR 5; DLB 53

Noyes, Alfred 1880-1958 .... **TCLC 7**
See also CA 104; DLB 20

Nunn, Kem 19(?)-............... **CLC 34**

Nye, Robert 1939- .... **CLC 13, 42**
See also CA 33-36R; CANR 29; DLB 14;
MTCW; SATA 6

Nyro, Laura 1947-............... **CLC 17**

Oates, Joyce Carol
1938-...... **CLC 1, 2, 3, 6, 9, 11, 15, 19,**
33, 52; SSC 6
See also AITN 1; BEST 89:2; CA 5-8R;
CANR 25; CDALB 1968-1988; DA;
DLB 2, 5, 130; DLBY 81; MTCW; WLC

O'Brien, E. G.
See Clarke, Arthur C(harles)

O'Brien, Edna
1936- ... **CLC 3, 5, 8, 13, 36, 65; SSC 10**
See also CA 1-4R; CANR 6, 41;
CDBLB 1960 to Present; DLB 14;
MTCW

O'Brien, Fitz-James 1828-1862... **NCLC 21**
See also DLB 74

O'Brien, Flann........ **CLC 1, 4, 5, 7, 10, 47**
See also O Nuallain, Brian

O'Brien, Richard 1942-........... **CLC 17**
See also CA 124

O'Brien, Tim 1946-........ **CLC 7, 19, 40**
See also CA 85-88; CANR 40; DLBD 9;
DLBY 80

Obstfelder, Sigbjoern 1866-1900... **TCLC 23**
See also CA 123

O'Casey, Sean
1880-1964 .... **CLC 1, 5, 9, 11, 15**
See also CA 89-92; CDBLB 1914-1945;
DLB 10; MTCW

O'Cathasaigh, Sean
  See O'Casey, Sean

Ochs, Phil 1940-1976............ **CLC 17**
  See also CA 65-68

O'Connor, Edwin (Greene)
  1918-1968 .... **CLC 14**
  See also CA 93-96; 25-28R

O'Connor, (Mary) Flannery
  1925-1964 .... **CLC 1, 2, 3, 6, 10, 13, 15,
                  21, 66; SSC 1**
  See also AAYA 7; CA 1-4R; CANR 3, 41;
    CDALB 1941-1968; DA; DLB 2;
    DLBY 80; MTCW; WLC

O'Connor, Frank.......... **CLC 23; SSC 5**
  See also O'Donovan, Michael John

O'Dell, Scott 1898-1989.......... **CLC 30**
  See also AAYA 3; CA 61-64; 129;
    CANR 12, 30; CLR 1, 16; DLB 52;
    MAICYA; SATA 12, 60

Odets, Clifford 1906-1963 .... **CLC 2, 28**
  See also CA 85-88; DLB 7, 26; MTCW

O'Doherty, Brian 1934-........... **CLC 76**
  See also CA 105

O'Donnell, K. M.
  See Malzberg, Barry N(athaniel)

O'Donnell, Lawrence
  See Kuttner, Henry

O'Donovan, Michael John
  1903-1966 .... **CLC 14**
  See also O'Connor, Frank
  See also CA 93-96

Oe, Kenzaburo 1935-.......... **CLC 10, 36**
  See also CA 97-100; CANR 36; MTCW

O'Faolain, Julia 1932-....... **CLC 6, 19, 47**
  See also CA 81-84; CAAS 2; CANR 12;
    DLB 14; MTCW

O'Faolain, Sean
  1900-1991 .... **CLC 1, 7, 14, 32, 70;
                SSC 13**
  See also CA 61-64; 134; CANR 12;
    DLB 15; MTCW

O'Flaherty, Liam
  1896-1984 .... **CLC 5, 34; SSC 6**
  See also CA 101; 113; CANR 35; DLB 36;
    DLBY 84; MTCW

Ogilvy, Gavin
  See Barrie, J(ames) M(atthew)

O'Grady, Standish James
  1846-1928 .... **TCLC 5**
  See also CA 104

O'Grady, Timothy 1951- .... **CLC 59**
  See also CA 138

O'Hara, Frank
  1926-1966 .... **CLC 2, 5, 13, 78**
  See also CA 9-12R; 25-28R; CANR 33;
    DLB 5, 16; MTCW

O'Hara, John (Henry)
  1905-1970 .... **CLC 1, 2, 3, 6, 11, 42**
  See also CA 5-8R; 25-28R; CANR 31;
    CDALB 1929-1941; DLB 9, 86; DLBD 2;
    MTCW

O Hehir, Diana 1922- .... **CLC 41**
  See also CA 93-96

Okigbo, Christopher (Ifenayichukwu)
  1932-1967 .... **CLC 25; PC 7**
  See also BLC 3; BW; CA 77-80; DLB 125;
    MTCW

Olds, Sharon 1942-............ **CLC 32, 39**
  See also CA 101; CANR 18, 41; DLB 120

Oldstyle, Jonathan
  See Irving, Washington

Olesha, Yuri (Karlovich)
  1899-1960 .... **CLC 8**
  See also CA 85-88

Oliphant, Margaret (Oliphant Wilson)
  1828-1897 .... **NCLC 11**
  See also DLB 18

Oliver, Mary 1935-........... **CLC 19, 34**
  See also CA 21-24R; CANR 9; DLB 5

Olivier, Laurence (Kerr)
  1907-1989 .... **CLC 20**
  See also CA 111; 129

Olsen, Tillie 1913- ..... **CLC 4, 13; SSC 11**
  See also CA 1-4R; CANR 1; DA; DLB 28;
    DLBY 80; MTCW

Olson, Charles (John)
  1910-1970 ..... **CLC 1, 2, 5, 6, 9, 11, 29**
  See also CA 13-16; 25-28R; CABS 2;
    CANR 35; CAP 1; DLB 5, 16; MTCW

Olson, Toby 1937- .... **CLC 28**
  See also CA 65-68; CANR 9, 31

Olyesha, Yuri
  See Olesha, Yuri (Karlovich)

Ondaatje, (Philip) Michael
  1943- .... **CLC 14, 29, 51, 76**
  See also CA 77-80; DLB 60

Oneal, Elizabeth 1934-
  See Oneal, Zibby
  See also CA 106; CANR 28; MAICYA;
    SATA 30

Oneal, Zibby .... **CLC 30**
  See also Oneal, Elizabeth
  See also AAYA 5; CLR 13

O'Neill, Eugene (Gladstone)
  1888-1953 .... **TCLC 1, 6, 27, 49**
  See also AITN 1; CA 110; 132;
    CDALB 1929-1941; DA; DLB 7; MTCW;
    WLC

Onetti, Juan Carlos 1909-....... **CLC 7, 10**
  See also CA 85-88; CANR 32; DLB 113;
    HW; MTCW

O Nuallain, Brian 1911-1966
  See O'Brien, Flann
  See also CA 21-22; 25-28R; CAP 2

Oppen, George 1908-1984 .... **CLC 7, 13, 34**
  See also CA 13-16R; 113; CANR 8; DLB 5

Oppenheim, E(dward) Phillips
  1866-1946 .... **TCLC 45**
  See also CA 111; DLB 70

Orlovitz, Gil 1918-1973 .... **CLC 22**
  See also CA 77-80; 45-48; DLB 2, 5

Orris
  See Ingelow, Jean

Ortega y Gasset, Jose 1883-1955 ... **TCLC 9**
  See also CA 106; 130; HW; MTCW

Ortiz, Simon J(oseph) 1941- .... **CLC 45**
  See also CA 134; DLB 120

Orton, Joe .... **CLC 4, 13, 43; DC 3**
  See also Orton, John Kingsley
  See also CDBLB 1960 to Present; DLB 13

Orton, John Kingsley 1933-1967
  See Orton, Joe
  See also CA 85-88; CANR 35; MTCW

Orwell, George .... **TCLC 2, 6, 15, 31, 51**
  See also Blair, Eric (Arthur)
  See also CDBLB 1945-1960; DLB 15, 98;
    WLC

Osborne, David
  See Silverberg, Robert

Osborne, George
  See Silverberg, Robert

Osborne, John (James)
  1929- .... **CLC 1, 2, 5, 11, 45**
  See also CA 13-16R; CANR 21;
    CDBLB 1945-1960; DA; DLB 13;
    MTCW; WLC

Osborne, Lawrence 1958- .... **CLC 50**

Oshima, Nagisa 1932- .... **CLC 20**
  See also CA 116; 121

Oskison, John M(ilton)
  1874-1947 .... **TCLC 35**

Ossoli, Sarah Margaret (Fuller marchesa d')
  1810-1850
  See Fuller, Margaret
  See also SATA 25

Ostrovsky, Alexander
  1823-1886 .... **NCLC 30**

Otero, Blas de 1916- .... **CLC 11**
  See also CA 89-92

Otto, Whitney 1955-.............. **CLC 70**
  See also CA 140

Ouida .... **TCLC 43**
  See also De La Ramee, (Marie) Louise
  See also DLB 18

Ousmane, Sembene 1923- .... **CLC 66**
  See also BLC 3; BW; CA 117; 125; MTCW

Ovid 43B.C.-18th cent. (?)... **CMLC 7; PC 2**

Owen, Hugh
  See Faust, Frederick (Schiller)

Owen, Wilfred (Edward Salter)
  1893-1918 .... **TCLC 5, 27**
  See also CA 104; CDBLB 1914-1945; DA;
    DLB 20; WLC

Owens, Rochelle 1936-............. **CLC 8**
  See also CA 17-20R; CAAS 2; CANR 39

Oz, Amos 1939- ... **CLC 5, 8, 11, 27, 33, 54**
  See also CA 53-56; CANR 27; MTCW

Ozick, Cynthia 1928-...... **CLC 3, 7, 28, 62**
  See also BEST 90:1; CA 17-20R; CANR 23;
    DLB 28; DLBY 82; MTCW

Ozu, Yasujiro 1903-1963 .... **CLC 16**
  See also CA 112

Pacheco, C.
  See Pessoa, Fernando (Antonio Nogueira)

Pa Chin
  See Li Fei-kan

Pack, Robert 1929-.............. **CLC 13**
  See also CA 1-4R; CANR 3; DLB 5

Padgett, Lewis
  See Kuttner, Henry

Padilla (Lorenzo), Heberto 1932- . . . . **CLC 38**
See also AITN 1; CA 123; 131; HW

Page, Jimmy 1944- . . . . **CLC 12**

Page, Louise 1955- . . . . **CLC 40**
See also CA 140

Page, P(atricia) K(athleen)
1916- . . . . **CLC 7, 18**
See also CA 53-56; CANR 4, 22; DLB 68;
MTCW

Paget, Violet 1856-1935
See Lee, Vernon
See also CA 104

Paget-Lowe, Henry
See Lovecraft, H(oward) P(hillips)

Paglia, Camille (Anna) 1947- . . . . **CLC 68**
See also CA 140

Paige, Richard
See Koontz, Dean R(ay)

Pakenham, Antonia
See Fraser, Antonia (Pakenham)

Palamas, Kostes 1859-1943 . . . . **TCLC 5**
See also CA 105

Palazzeschi, Aldo 1885-1974 . . . . . . **CLC 11**
See also CA 89-92; 53-56; DLB 114

Paley, Grace 1922- . . . . **CLC 4, 6, 37; SSC 8**
See also CA 25-28R; CANR 13; DLB 28;
MTCW

Palin, Michael (Edward) 1943- . . . . . **CLC 21**
See also Monty Python
See also CA 107; CANR 35; SATA 67

Palliser, Charles 1947- . . . . **CLC 65**
See also CA 136

Palma, Ricardo 1833-1919 . . . . **TCLC 29**

Pancake, Breece Dexter 1952-1979
See Pancake, Breece D'J
See also CA 123; 109

Pancake, Breece D'J . . . . **CLC 29**
See also Pancake, Breece Dexter
See also DLB 130

Panko, Rudy
See Gogol, Nikolai (Vasilyevich)

Papadiamantis, Alexandros
1851-1911 . . . . **TCLC 29**

Papadiamantopoulos, Johannes 1856-1910
See Moreas, Jean
See also CA 117

Papini, Giovanni 1881-1956 . . . . . . **TCLC 22**
See also CA 121

Paracelsus 1493-1541 . . . . **LC 14**

Parasol, Peter
See Stevens, Wallace

Parfenie, Maria
See Codrescu, Andrei

Parini, Jay (Lee) 1948- . . . . **CLC 54**
See also CA 97-100; CAAS 16; CANR 32

Park, Jordan
See Kornbluth, C(yril) M.; Pohl, Frederik

Parker, Bert
See Ellison, Harlan

Parker, Dorothy (Rothschild)
1893-1967 . . . . **CLC 15, 68; SSC 2**
See also CA 19-20; 25-28R; CAP 2;
DLB 11, 45, 86; MTCW

Parker, Robert B(rown) 1932- . . . . . . **CLC 27**
See also BEST 89:4; CA 49-52; CANR 1,
26; MTCW

Parkes, Lucas
See Harris, John (Wyndham Parkes Lucas)
Beynon

Parkin, Frank 1940- . . . . **CLC 43**

Parkman, Francis, Jr.
1823-1893 . . . . **NCLC 12**
See also DLB 1, 30

Parks, Gordon (Alexander Buchanan)
1912- . . . . **CLC 1, 16**
See also AITN 2; BLC 3; BW; CA 41-44R;
CANR 26; DLB 33; SATA 8

Parnell, Thomas 1679-1718 . . . . **LC 3**
See also DLB 94

Parra, Nicanor 1914- . . . . **CLC 2**
See also CA 85-88; CANR 32; HW; MTCW

Parrish, Mary Frances
See Fisher, M(ary) F(rances) K(ennedy)

Parson
See Coleridge, Samuel Taylor

Parson Lot
See Kingsley, Charles

Partridge, Anthony
See Oppenheim, E(dward) Phillips

Pascoli, Giovanni 1855-1912 . . . . . . **TCLC 45**

Pasolini, Pier Paolo
1922-1975 . . . . **CLC 20, 37**
See also CA 93-96; 61-64; DLB 128;
MTCW

Pasquini
See Silone, Ignazio

Pastan, Linda (Olenik) 1932- . . . . . . **CLC 27**
See also CA 61-64; CANR 18, 40; DLB 5

Pasternak, Boris (Leonidovich)
1890-1960 . . . . . **CLC 7, 10, 18, 63; PC 6**
See also CA 127; 116; DA; MTCW; WLC

Patchen, Kenneth 1911-1972 . . . **CLC 1, 2, 18**
See also CA 1-4R; 33-36R; CANR 3, 35;
DLB 16, 48; MTCW

Pater, Walter (Horatio)
1839-1894 . . . . **NCLC 7**
See also CDBLB 1832-1890; DLB 57

Paterson, A(ndrew) B(arton)
1864-1941 . . . . **TCLC 32**

Paterson, Katherine (Womeldorf)
1932- . . . . **CLC 12, 30**
See also AAYA 1; CA 21-24R; CANR 28;
CLR 7; DLB 52; MAICYA; MTCW;
SATA 13, 53

Patmore, Coventry Kersey Dighton
1823-1896 . . . . **NCLC 9**
See also DLB 35, 98

Paton, Alan (Stewart)
1903-1988 . . . . **CLC 4, 10, 25, 55**
See also CA 13-16; 125; CANR 22; CAP 1;
DA; MTCW; SATA 11, 56; WLC

Paton Walsh, Gillian 1937-
See Walsh, Jill Paton
See also CANR 38; MAICYA; SAAS 3;
SATA 4, 72

Paulding, James Kirke 1778-1860 . . **NCLC 2**
See also DLB 3, 59, 74

Paulin, Thomas Neilson 1949-
See Paulin, Tom
See also CA 123; 128

Paulin, Tom . . . . **CLC 37**
See also Paulin, Thomas Neilson
See also DLB 40

Paustovsky, Konstantin (Georgievich)
1892-1968 . . . . **CLC 40**
See also CA 93-96; 25-28R

Pavese, Cesare 1908-1950 . . . . **TCLC 3**
See also CA 104; DLB 128

Pavic, Milorad 1929- . . . . **CLC 60**
See also CA 136

Payne, Alan
See Jakes, John (William)

Paz, Gil
See Lugones, Leopoldo

Paz, Octavio
1914- . . . . **CLC 3, 4, 6, 10, 19, 51, 65;**
PC 1
See also CA 73-76; CANR 32; DA;
DLBY 90; HW; MTCW; WLC

Peacock, Molly 1947- . . . . **CLC 60**
See also CA 103; DLB 120

Peacock, Thomas Love
1785-1866 . . . . **NCLC 22**
See also DLB 96, 116

Peake, Mervyn 1911-1968 . . . . **CLC 7, 54**
See also CA 5-8R; 25-28R; CANR 3;
DLB 15; MTCW; SATA 23

Pearce, Philippa . . . . **CLC 21**
See also Christie, (Ann) Philippa
See also CLR 9; MAICYA; SATA 1, 67

Pearl, Eric
See Elman, Richard

Pearson, T(homas) R(eid) 1956- . . . . **CLC 39**
See also CA 120; 130

Peck, John 1941- . . . . **CLC 3**
See also CA 49-52; CANR 3

Peck, Richard (Wayne) 1934- . . . . . . **CLC 21**
See also AAYA 1; CA 85-88; CANR 19,
38; MAICYA; SAAS 2; SATA 18, 55

Peck, Robert Newton 1928- . . . . **CLC 17**
See also AAYA 3; CA 81-84; CANR 31;
DA; MAICYA; SAAS 1; SATA 21, 62

Peckinpah, (David) Sam(uel)
1925-1984 . . . . **CLC 20**
See also CA 109; 114

Pedersen, Knut 1859-1952
See Hamsun, Knut
See also CA 104; 119; MTCW

Peeslake, Gaffer
See Durrell, Lawrence (George)

Peguy, Charles Pierre
1873-1914 . . . . **TCLC 10**
See also CA 107

Pena, Ramon del Valle y
See Valle-Inclan, Ramon (Maria) del

Pendennis, Arthur Esquir
See Thackeray, William Makepeace

Pepys, Samuel 1633-1703 . . . . **LC 11**
See also CDBLB 1660-1789; DA; DLB 101;
WLC

Percy, Walker
1916-1990 . . . . **CLC 2, 3, 6, 8, 14, 18, 47,
65**
See also CA 1-4R; 131; CANR 1, 23;
DLB 2; DLBY 80, 90; MTCW

Perec, Georges 1936-1982 . . . . **CLC 56**
See also DLB 83

Pereda (y Sanchez de Porrua), Jose Maria de
1833-1906 . . . . **TCLC 16**
See also CA 117

Pereda y Porrua, Jose Maria de
See Pereda (y Sanchez de Porrua), Jose
Maria de

Peregoy, George Weems
See Mencken, H(enry) L(ouis)

Perelman, S(idney) J(oseph)
1904-1979 . . . **CLC 3, 5, 9, 15, 23, 44, 49**
See also AITN 1, 2; CA 73-76; 89-92;
CANR 18; DLB 11, 44; MTCW

Peret, Benjamin 1899-1959 . . . . **TCLC 20**
See also CA 117

Peretz, Isaac Loeb 1851(?)-1915 . . . **TCLC 16**
See also CA 109

Peretz, Yitzkhok Leibush
See Peretz, Isaac Loeb

Perez Galdos, Benito 1843-1920 . . . **TCLC 27**
See also CA 125; HW

Perrault, Charles 1628-1703 . . . . **LC 2**
See also MAICYA; SATA 25

Perry, Brighton
See Sherwood, Robert E(mmet)

Perse, St.-John . . . . **CLC 4, 11, 46**
See also Leger, (Marie-Rene) Alexis
Saint-Leger

Perse, Saint-John
See Leger, (Marie-Rene) Alexis Saint-Leger

Peseenz, Tulio F.
See Lopez y Fuentes, Gregorio

Pesetsky, Bette 1932- . . . . **CLC 28**
See also CA 133; DLB 130

Peshkov, Alexei Maximovich 1868-1936
See Gorky, Maxim
See also CA 105; DA

Pessoa, Fernando (Antonio Nogueira)
1888-1935 . . . . **TCLC 27**
See also CA 125

Peterkin, Julia Mood 1880-1961 . . . . **CLC 31**
See also CA 102; DLB 9

Peters, Joan K. 1945- . . . . **CLC 39**

Peters, Robert L(ouis) 1924- . . . . **CLC 7**
See also CA 13-16R; CAAS 8; DLB 105

Petofi, Sandor 1823-1849 . . . . **NCLC 21**

Petrakis, Harry Mark 1923- . . . . **CLC 3**
See also CA 9-12R; CANR 4, 30

Petrov, Evgeny . . . . **TCLC 21**
See also Kataev, Evgeny Petrovich

Petry, Ann (Lane) 1908- . . . . . . **CLC 1, 7, 18**
See also BW; CA 5-8R; CAAS 6; CANR 4;
CLR 12; DLB 76; MAICYA; MTCW;
SATA 5

Petursson, Halligrimur 1614-1674 . . . . **LC 8**

Philipson, Morris H. 1926- . . . . **CLC 53**
See also CA 1-4R; CANR 4

Phillips, David Graham
1867-1911 . . . . **TCLC 44**
See also CA 108; DLB 9, 12

Phillips, Jack
See Sandburg, Carl (August)

Phillips, Jayne Anne 1952- . . . . . **CLC 15, 33**
See also CA 101; CANR 24; DLBY 80;
MTCW

Phillips, Richard
See Dick, Philip K(indred)

Phillips, Robert (Schaeffer) 1938- . . . **CLC 28**
See also CA 17-20R; CAAS 13; CANR 8;
DLB 105

Phillips, Ward
See Lovecraft, H(oward) P(hillips)

Piccolo, Lucio 1901-1969 . . . . **CLC 13**
See also CA 97-100; DLB 114

Pickthall, Marjorie L(owry) C(hristie)
1883-1922 . . . . **TCLC 21**
See also CA 107; DLB 92

Pico della Mirandola, Giovanni
1463-1494 . . . . **LC 15**

Piercy, Marge
1936- . . . . **CLC 3, 6, 14, 18, 27, 62**
See also CA 21-24R; CAAS 1; CANR 13;
DLB 120; MTCW

Piers, Robert
See Anthony, Piers

Pieyre de Mandiargues, Andre 1909-1991
See Mandiargues, Andre Pieyre de
See also CA 103; 136; CANR 22

Pilnyak, Boris . . . . **TCLC 23**
See also Vogau, Boris Andreyevich

Pincherle, Alberto 1907-1990 . . . **CLC 11, 18**
See also Moravia, Alberto
See also CA 25-28R; 132; CANR 33;
MTCW

Pinckney, Darryl 1953- . . . . **CLC 76**

Pineda, Cecile 1942- . . . . **CLC 39**
See also CA 118

Pinero, Arthur Wing 1855-1934 . . . **TCLC 32**
See also CA 110; DLB 10

Pinero, Miguel (Antonio Gomez)
1946-1988 . . . . **CLC 4, 55**
See also CA 61-64; 125; CANR 29; HW

Pinget, Robert 1919- . . . . **CLC 7, 13, 37**
See also CA 85-88; DLB 83

Pink Floyd . . . . **CLC 35**
See also Barrett, (Roger) Syd; Gilmour,
David; Mason, Nick; Waters, Roger;
Wright, Rick

Pinkney, Edward 1802-1828 . . . . . **NCLC 31**

Pinkwater, Daniel Manus 1941- . . . . **CLC 35**
See also Pinkwater, Manus
See also AAYA 1; CA 29-32R; CANR 12,
38; CLR 4; MAICYA; SAAS 3; SATA 46

Pinkwater, Manus
See Pinkwater, Daniel Manus
See also SATA 8

Pinsky, Robert 1940- . . . . **CLC 9, 19, 38**
See also CA 29-32R; CAAS 4; DLBY 82

Pinta, Harold
See Pinter, Harold

Pinter, Harold
1930- . . **CLC 1, 3, 6, 9, 11, 15, 27, 58, 73**
See also CA 5-8R; CANR 33; CDBLB 1960
to Present; DA; DLB 13; MTCW; WLC

Pirandello, Luigi 1867-1936 . . . . . **TCLC 4, 29**
See also CA 104; DA; WLC

Pirsig, Robert M(aynard)
1928- . . . . **CLC 4, 6, 73**
See also CA 53-56; MTCW; SATA 39

Pisarev, Dmitry Ivanovich
1840-1868 . . . . **NCLC 25**

Pix, Mary (Griffith) 1666-1709 . . . . **LC 8**
See also DLB 80

Pixerecourt, Guilbert de
1773-1844 . . . . **NCLC 39**

Plaidy, Jean
See Hibbert, Eleanor Alice Burford

Plant, Robert 1948- . . . . **CLC 12**

Plante, David (Robert)
1940- . . . . **CLC 7, 23, 38**
See also CA 37-40R; CANR 12, 36;
DLBY 83; MTCW

Plath, Sylvia
1932-1963 . . . . . **CLC 1, 2, 3, 5, 9, 11, 14,
17, 50, 51, 62; PC 1**
See also CA 19-20; CANR 34; CAP 2;
CDALB 1941-1968; DA; DLB 5, 6;
MTCW; WLC

Plato 428(?)B.C.-348(?)B.C. . . . . **CMLC 8**
See also DA

Platonov, Andrei . . . . **TCLC 14**
See also Klimentov, Andrei Platonovich

Platt, Kin 1911- . . . . **CLC 26**
See also CA 17-20R; CANR 11; SATA 21

Plick et Plock
See Simenon, Georges (Jacques Christian)

Plimpton, George (Ames) 1927- . . . . . **CLC 36**
See also AITN 1; CA 21-24R; CANR 32;
MTCW; SATA 10

Plomer, William Charles Franklin
1903-1973 . . . . **CLC 4, 8**
See also CA 21-22; CANR 34; CAP 2;
DLB 20; MTCW; SATA 24

Plowman, Piers
See Kavanagh, Patrick (Joseph)

Plum, J.
See Wodehouse, P(elham) G(renville)

Plumly, Stanley (Ross) 1939- . . . . . . **CLC 33**
See also CA 108; 110; DLB 5

Poe, Edgar Allan
1809-1849 . . . **NCLC 1, 16; PC 1; SSC 1**
See also CDALB 1640-1865; DA; DLB 3,
59, 73, 74; SATA 23; WLC

Poet of Titchfield Street, The
See Pound, Ezra (Weston Loomis)

Pohl, Frederik 1919- . . . . **CLC 18**
See also CA 61-64; CAAS 1; CANR 11, 37;
DLB 8; MTCW; SATA 24

Poirier, Louis 1910-
See Gracq, Julien
See also CA 122; 126

Poitier, Sidney 1927- . . . . **CLC 26**
See also BW; CA 117

Polanski, Roman 1933- .... **CLC 16**
See also CA 77-80

Poliakoff, Stephen 1952- .... **CLC 38**
See also CA 106; DLB 13

Police, The .... **CLC 26**
See also Copeland, Stewart (Armstrong);
Summers, Andrew James; Sumner,
Gordon Matthew

Pollitt, Katha 1949- .... **CLC 28**
See also CA 120; 122; MTCW

Pollock, (Mary) Sharon 1936- ...... **CLC 50**
See also DLB 60

Pomerance, Bernard 1940- .... **CLC 13**
See also CA 101

Ponge, Francis (Jean Gaston Alfred)
1899-1988 .... **CLC 6, 18**
See also CA 85-88; 126; CANR 40

Pontoppidan, Henrik 1857-1943 ... **TCLC 29**

Poole, Josephine .... **CLC 17**
See also Helyar, Jane Penelope Josephine
See also SAAS 2; SATA 5

Popa, Vasko 1922- .... **CLC 19**
See also CA 112

Pope, Alexander 1688-1744 .... **LC 3**
See also CDBLB 1660-1789; DA; DLB 95,
101; WLC

Porter, Connie 1960- .... **CLC 70**

Porter, Gene(va Grace) Stratton
1863(?)-1924 .... **TCLC 21**
See also CA 112

Porter, Katherine Anne
1890-1980 ...... **CLC 1, 3, 7, 10, 13, 15,
27; SSC 4**
See also AITN 2; CA 1-4R; 101; CANR 1;
DA; DLB 4, 9, 102; DLBY 80; MTCW;
SATA 23, 39

Porter, Peter (Neville Frederick)
1929- .... **CLC 5, 13, 33**
See also CA 85-88; DLB 40

Porter, William Sydney 1862-1910
See Henry, O.
See also CA 104; 131; CDALB 1865-1917;
DA; DLB 12, 78, 79; MTCW; YABC 2

Portillo (y Pacheco), Jose Lopez
See Lopez Portillo (y Pacheco), Jose

Post, Melville Davisson
1869-1930 .... **TCLC 39**
See also CA 110

Potok, Chaim 1929- .... **CLC 2, 7, 14, 26**
See also AITN 1, 2; CA 17-20R; CANR 19,
35; DLB 28; MTCW; SATA 33

Potter, Beatrice
See Webb, (Martha) Beatrice (Potter)
See also MAICYA

Potter, Dennis (Christopher George)
1935- .... **CLC 58**
See also CA 107; CANR 33; MTCW

Pound, Ezra (Weston Loomis)
1885-1972 ...... **CLC 1, 2, 3, 4, 5, 7, 10,
13, 18, 34, 48, 50; PC 4**
See also CA 5-8R; 37-40R; CANR 40;
CDALB 1917-1929; DA; DLB 4, 45, 63;
MTCW; WLC

Povod, Reinaldo 1959- .... **CLC 44**
See also CA 136

Powell, Anthony (Dymoke)
1905- .... **CLC 1, 3, 7, 9, 10, 31**
See also CA 1-4R; CANR 1, 32;
CDBLB 1945-1960; DLB 15; MTCW

Powell, Dawn 1897-1965 .... **CLC 66**
See also CA 5-8R

Powell, Padgett 1952- .... **CLC 34**
See also CA 126

Powers, J(ames) F(arl)
1917- .... **CLC 1, 4, 8, 57; SSC 4**
See also CA 1-4R; CANR 2; DLB 130;
MTCW

Powers, John J(ames) 1945-
See Powers, John R.
See also CA 69-72

Powers, John R. .... **CLC 66**
See also Powers, John J(ames)

Pownall, David 1938- .... **CLC 10**
See also CA 89-92; DLB 14

Powys, John Cowper
1872-1963 .... **CLC 7, 9, 15, 46**
See also CA 85-88; DLB 15; MTCW

Powys, T(heodore) F(rancis)
1875-1953 .... **TCLC 9**
See also CA 106; DLB 36

Prager, Emily 1952- .... **CLC 56**

Pratt, E(dwin) J(ohn)
1883(?)-1964 .... **CLC 19**
See also CA 93-96; DLB 92

Premchand .... **TCLC 21**
See also Srivastava, Dhanpat Rai

Preussler, Otfried 1923- .... **CLC 17**
See also CA 77-80; SATA 24

Prevert, Jacques (Henri Marie)
1900-1977 .... **CLC 15**
See also CA 77-80; 69-72; CANR 29;
MTCW; SATA 30

Prevost, Abbe (Antoine Francois)
1697-1763 .... **LC 1**

Price, (Edward) Reynolds
1933- .... **CLC 3, 6, 13, 43, 50, 63**
See also CA 1-4R; CANR 1, 37; DLB 2

Price, Richard 1949- .... **CLC 6, 12**
See also CA 49-52; CANR 3; DLBY 81

Prichard, Katharine Susannah
1883-1969 .... **CLC 46**
See also CA 11-12; CANR 33; CAP 1;
MTCW; SATA 66

Priestley, J(ohn) B(oynton)
1894-1984 .... **CLC 2, 5, 9, 34**
See also CA 9-12R; 113; CANR 33;
CDBLB 1914-1945; DLB 10, 34, 77, 100;
DLBY 84; MTCW

Prince 1958(?)- .... **CLC 35**

Prince, F(rank) T(empleton) 1912- .. **CLC 22**
See also CA 101; DLB 20

Prince Kropotkin
See Kropotkin, Peter (Aleksieevich)

Prior, Matthew 1664-1721.......... **LC 4**
See also DLB 95

Pritchard, William H(arrison)
1932- .... **CLC 34**
See also CA 65-68; CANR 23; DLB 111

Pritchett, V(ictor) S(awdon)
1900- .... **CLC 5, 13, 15, 41**
See also CA 61-64; CANR 31; DLB 15;
MTCW

Private 19022
See Manning, Frederic

Probst, Mark 1925- .... **CLC 59**
See also CA 130

Prokosch, Frederic 1908-1989 .... **CLC 4, 48**
See also CA 73-76; 128; DLB 48

Prophet, The
See Dreiser, Theodore (Herman Albert)

Prose, Francine 1947- .... **CLC 45**
See also CA 109; 112

Proudhon
See Cunha, Euclides (Rodrigues Pimenta) da

Proust, (Valentin-Louis-George-Eugene-)
Marcel 1871-1922 .... **TCLC 7, 13, 33**
See also CA 104; 120; DA; DLB 65;
MTCW; WLC

Prowler, Harley
See Masters, Edgar Lee

Prus, Boleslaw .... **TCLC 48**
See also Glowacki, Aleksander

Pryor, Richard (Franklin Lenox Thomas)
1940- .... **CLC 26**
See also CA 122

Przybyszewski, Stanislaw
1868-1927 .... **TCLC 36**
See also DLB 66

Pteleon
See Grieve, C(hristopher) M(urray)

Puckett, Lute
See Masters, Edgar Lee

Puig, Manuel
1932-1990 .... **CLC 3, 5, 10, 28, 65**
See also CA 45-48; CANR 2, 32; DLB 113;
HW; MTCW

Purdy, A(lfred) W(ellington)
1918- .... **CLC 3, 6, 14, 50**
See also Purdy, Al
See also CA 81-84

Purdy, Al
See Purdy, A(lfred) W(ellington)
See also CAAS 17; DLB 88

Purdy, James (Amos)
1923- .... **CLC 2, 4, 10, 28, 52**
See also CA 33-36R; CAAS 1; CANR 19;
DLB 2; MTCW

Pure, Simon
See Swinnerton, Frank Arthur

Pushkin, Alexander (Sergeyevich)
1799-1837 .... **NCLC 3, 27**
See also DA; SATA 61; WLC

P'u Sung-ling 1640-1715 .... **LC 3**

Putnam, Arthur Lee
See Alger, Horatio, Jr.

Puzo, Mario 1920- .... **CLC 1, 2, 6, 36**
See also CA 65-68; CANR 4; DLB 6;
MTCW

Pym, Barbara (Mary Crampton)
1913-1980 .... **CLC 13, 19, 37**
See also CA 13-14; 97-100; CANR 13, 34;
CAP 1; DLB 14; DLBY 87; MTCW

Remizov, Aleksei (Mikhailovich)
  1877-1957 . . . . **TCLC 27**
  See also CA 125; 133

Renan, Joseph Ernest
  1823-1892 . . . . **NCLC 26**

Renard, Jules 1864-1910 . . . . **TCLC 17**
  See also CA 117

Renault, Mary . . . . **CLC 3, 11, 17**
  See also Challans, Mary
  See also DLBY 83

Rendell, Ruth (Barbara) 1930- . . **CLC 28, 48**
  See also Vine, Barbara
  See also CA 109; CANR 32; DLB 87;
    MTCW

Renoir, Jean 1894-1979 . . . . **CLC 20**
  See also CA 129; 85-88

Resnais, Alain 1922- . . . . **CLC 16**

Reverdy, Pierre 1889-1960 . . . . **CLC 53**
  See also CA 97-100; 89-92

Rexroth, Kenneth
  1905-1982 . . . . . . **CLC 1, 2, 6, 11, 22, 49**
  See also CA 5-8R; 107; CANR 14, 34;
    CDALB 1941-1968; DLB 16, 48;
    DLBY 82; MTCW

Reyes, Alfonso 1889-1959 . . . . **TCLC 33**
  See also CA 131; HW

Reyes y Basoalto, Ricardo Eliecer Neftali
  See Neruda, Pablo

Reymont, Wladyslaw (Stanislaw)
  1868(?)-1925 . . . . **TCLC 5**
  See also CA 104

Reynolds, Jonathan 1942- . . . . **CLC 6, 38**
  See also CA 65-68; CANR 28

Reynolds, Joshua 1723-1792 . . . . **LC 15**
  See also DLB 104

Reynolds, Michael Shane 1937- . . . . **CLC 44**
  See also CA 65-68; CANR 9

Reznikoff, Charles 1894-1976 . . . . **CLC 9**
  See also CA 33-36; 61-64; CAP 2; DLB 28,
    45

Rezzori (d'Arezzo), Gregor von
  1914- . . . . **CLC 25**
  See also CA 122; 136

Rhine, Richard
  See Silverstein, Alvin

R'hoone
  See Balzac, Honore de

Rhys, Jean
  1890(?)-1979 . . . . **CLC 2, 4, 6, 14, 19, 51**
  See also CA 25-28R; 85-88; CANR 35;
    CDBLB 1945-1960; DLB 36, 117; MTCW

Ribeiro, Darcy 1922- . . . . **CLC 34**
  See also CA 33-36R

Ribeiro, Joao Ubaldo (Osorio Pimentel)
  1941- . . . . **CLC 10, 67**
  See also CA 81-84

Ribman, Ronald (Burt) 1932- . . . . **CLC 7**
  See also CA 21-24R

Ricci, Nino 1959- . . . . **CLC 70**
  See also CA 137

Rice, Anne 1941- . . . . **CLC 41**
  See also AAYA 9; BEST 89:2; CA 65-68;
    CANR 12, 36

Rice, Elmer (Leopold)
  1892-1967 . . . . **CLC 7, 49**
  See also CA 21-22; 25-28R; CAP 2; DLB 4,
    7; MTCW

Rice, Tim 1944- . . . . **CLC 21**
  See also CA 103

Rich, Adrienne (Cecile)
  1929- . . . . **CLC 3, 6, 7, 11, 18, 36, 73, 76;
                                                    PC 5**
  See also CA 9-12R; CANR 20; DLB 5, 67;
    MTCW

Rich, Barbara
  See Graves, Robert (von Ranke)

Rich, Robert
  See Trumbo, Dalton

Richards, David Adams 1950- . . . . . . **CLC 59**
  See also CA 93-96; DLB 53

Richards, I(vor) A(rmstrong)
  1893-1979 . . . . **CLC 14, 24**
  See also CA 41-44R; 89-92; CANR 34;
    DLB 27

Richardson, Anne
  See Roiphe, Anne Richardson

Richardson, Dorothy Miller
  1873-1957 . . . . **TCLC 3**
  See also CA 104; DLB 36

Richardson, Ethel Florence (Lindesay)
  1870-1946
  See Richardson, Henry Handel
  See also CA 105

Richardson, Henry Handel . . . . **TCLC 4**
  See also Richardson, Ethel Florence
    (Lindesay)

Richardson, Samuel 1689-1761 . . . . **LC 1**
  See also CDBLB 1660-1789; DA; DLB 39;
    WLC

Richler, Mordecai
  1931- . . . . **CLC 3, 5, 9, 13, 18, 46, 70**
  See also AITN 1; CA 65-68; CANR 31;
    CLR 17; DLB 53; MAICYA; MTCW;
    SATA 27, 44

Richter, Conrad (Michael)
  1890-1968 . . . . **CLC 30**
  See also CA 5-8R; 25-28R; CANR 23;
    DLB 9; MTCW; SATA 3

Riddell, J. H. 1832-1906 . . . . **TCLC 40**

Riding, Laura . . . . **CLC 3, 7**
  See also Jackson, Laura (Riding)

Riefenstahl, Berta Helene Amalia 1902-
  See Riefenstahl, Leni
  See also CA 108

Riefenstahl, Leni . . . . **CLC 16**
  See also Riefenstahl, Berta Helene Amalia

Riffe, Ernest
  See Bergman, (Ernst) Ingmar

Riley, James Whitcomb
  1849-1916 . . . . **TCLC 51**
  See also CA 118; 137; MAICYA; SATA 17

Riley, Tex
  See Creasey, John

Rilke, Rainer Maria
  1875-1926 . . . . **TCLC 1, 6, 19; PC 2**
  See also CA 104; 132; DLB 81; MTCW

Rimbaud, (Jean Nicolas) Arthur
  1854-1891 . . . . **NCLC 4, 35; PC 3**
  See also DA; WLC

Ringmaster, The
  See Mencken, H(enry) L(ouis)

Ringwood, Gwen(dolyn Margaret) Pharis
  1910-1984 . . . . **CLC 48**
  See also CA 112; DLB 88

Rio, Michel 19(?)- . . . . **CLC 43**

Ritsos, Giannes
  See Ritsos, Yannis

Ritsos, Yannis 1909-1990 . . . . . **CLC 6, 13, 31**
  See also CA 77-80; 133; CANR 39; MTCW

Ritter, Erika 1948(?)- . . . . **CLC 52**

Rivera, Jose Eustasio 1889-1928 . . . **TCLC 35**
  See also HW

Rivers, Conrad Kent 1933-1968 . . . . . . **CLC 1**
  See also BW; CA 85-88; DLB 41

Rivers, Elfrida
  See Bradley, Marion Zimmer

Riverside, John
  See Heinlein, Robert A(nson)

Rizal, Jose 1861-1896 . . . . **NCLC 27**

Roa Bastos, Augusto (Antonio)
  1917- . . . . **CLC 45**
  See also CA 131; DLB 113; HW

Robbe-Grillet, Alain
  1922- . . . . . . **CLC 1, 2, 4, 6, 8, 10, 14, 43**
  See also CA 9-12R; CANR 33; DLB 83;
    MTCW

Robbins, Harold 1916- . . . . **CLC 5**
  See also CA 73-76; CANR 26; MTCW

Robbins, Thomas Eugene 1936-
  See Robbins, Tom
  See also CA 81-84; CANR 29; MTCW

Robbins, Tom . . . . **CLC 9, 32, 64**
  See also Robbins, Thomas Eugene
  See also BEST 90:3; DLBY 80

Robbins, Trina 1938- . . . . **CLC 21**
  See also CA 128

Roberts, Charles G(eorge) D(ouglas)
  1860-1943 . . . . **TCLC 8**
  See also CA 105; DLB 92; SATA 29

Roberts, Kate 1891-1985 . . . . **CLC 15**
  See also CA 107; 116

Roberts, Keith (John Kingston)
  1935- . . . . **CLC 14**
  See also CA 25-28R

Roberts, Kenneth (Lewis)
  1885-1957 . . . . **TCLC 23**
  See also CA 109; DLB 9

Roberts, Michele (B.) 1949- . . . . **CLC 48**
  See also CA 115

Robertson, Ellis
  See Ellison, Harlan; Silverberg, Robert

Robertson, Thomas William
  1829-1871 . . . . **NCLC 35**

Robinson, Edwin Arlington
  1869-1935 . . . . **TCLC 5; PC 1**
  See also CA 104; 133; CDALB 1865-1917;
    DA; DLB 54; MTCW

Robinson, Henry Crabb
  1775-1867 . . . . **NCLC 15**
  See also DLB 107

Robinson, Jill 1936-............. **CLC 10**
See also CA 102

Robinson, Kim Stanley 1952-...... **CLC 34**
See also CA 126

Robinson, Lloyd
See Silverberg, Robert

Robinson, Marilynne 1944-........ **CLC 25**
See also CA 116

Robinson, Smokey................. **CLC 21**
See also Robinson, William, Jr.

Robinson, William, Jr. 1940-
See Robinson, Smokey
See also CA 116

Robison, Mary 1949-............. **CLC 42**
See also CA 113; 116; DLB 130

Roddenberry, Eugene Wesley 1921-1991
See Roddenberry, Gene
See also CA 110; 135; CANR 37; SATA 45

Roddenberry, Gene................ **CLC 17**
See also Roddenberry, Eugene Wesley
See also AAYA 5; SATA-Obit 69

Rodgers, Mary 1931-............. **CLC 12**
See also CA 49-52; CANR 8; CLR 20;
MAICYA; SATA 8

Rodgers, W(illiam) R(obert)
1909-1969 .... **CLC 7**
See also CA 85-88; DLB 20

Rodman, Eric
See Silverberg, Robert

Rodman, Howard 1920(?)-1985..... **CLC 65**
See also CA 118

Rodman, Maia
See Wojciechowska, Maia (Teresa)

Rodriguez, Claudio 1934-......... **CLC 10**

Roelvaag, O(le) E(dvart)
1876-1931 .... **TCLC 17**
See also CA 117; DLB 9

Roethke, Theodore (Huebner)
1908-1963 ...... **CLC 1, 3, 8, 11, 19, 46**
See also CA 81-84; CABS 2;
CDALB 1941-1968; DLB 5; MTCW

Rogers, Thomas Hunton 1927-.... **CLC 57**
See also CA 89-92

Rogers, Will(iam Penn Adair)
1879-1935 .... **TCLC 8**
See also CA 105; DLB 11

Rogin, Gilbert 1929-............. **CLC 18**
See also CA 65-68; CANR 15

Rohan, Koda .... **TCLC 22**
See also Koda Shigeyuki

Rohmer, Eric................... **CLC 16**
See also Scherer, Jean-Marie Maurice

Rohmer, Sax .... **TCLC 28**
See also Ward, Arthur Henry Sarsfield
See also DLB 70

Roiphe, Anne Richardson 1935-... **CLC 3, 9**
See also CA 89-92; DLBY 80

Rojas, Fernando de 1465-1541 ..... **LC 23**

**Rolfe, Frederick (William Serafino Austin
Lewis Mary)** 1860-1913..... **TCLC 12**
See also CA 107; DLB 34

Rolland, Romain 1866-1944....... **TCLC 23**
See also CA 118; DLB 65

Rolvaag, O(le) E(dvart)
See Roelvaag, O(le) E(dvart)

Romain Arnaud, Saint
See Aragon, Louis

Romains, Jules 1885-1972 .... **CLC 7**
See also CA 85-88; CANR 34; DLB 65;
MTCW

Romero, Jose Ruben 1890-1952 ... **TCLC 14**
See also CA 114; 131; HW

Ronsard, Pierre de 1524-1585....... **LC 6**

Rooke, Leon 1934-............ **CLC 25, 34**
See also CA 25-28R; CANR 23

Roper, William 1498-1578.......... **LC 10**

Roquelaure, A. N.
See Rice, Anne

Rosa, Joao Guimaraes 1908-1967... **CLC 23**
See also CA 89-92; DLB 113

Rosen, Richard (Dean) 1949-...... **CLC 39**
See also CA 77-80

Rosenberg, Isaac 1890-1918....... **TCLC 12**
See also CA 107; DLB 20

Rosenblatt, Joe .... **CLC 15**
See also Rosenblatt, Joseph

Rosenblatt, Joseph 1933-
See Rosenblatt, Joe
See also CA 89-92

Rosenfeld, Samuel 1896-1963
See Tzara, Tristan
See also CA 89-92

Rosenthal, M(acha) L(ouis) 1917-... **CLC 28**
See also CA 1-4R; CAAS 6; CANR 4;
DLB 5; SATA 59

Ross, Barnaby
See Dannay, Frederic

Ross, Bernard L.
See Follett, Ken(neth Martin)

Ross, J. H.
See Lawrence, T(homas) E(dward)

Ross, Martin
See Martin, Violet Florence

Ross, (James) Sinclair 1908-....... **CLC 13**
See also CA 73-76; DLB 88

Rossetti, Christina (Georgina)
1830-1894 .... **NCLC 2; PC 7**
See also DA; DLB 35; MAICYA;
SATA 20; WLC

Rossetti, Dante Gabriel
1828-1882 .... **NCLC 4**
See also CDBLB 1832-1890; DA; DLB 35;
WLC

Rossner, Judith (Perelman)
1935-................... **CLC 6, 9, 29**
See also AITN 2; BEST 90:3; CA 17-20R;
CANR 18; DLB 6; MTCW

Rostand, Edmond (Eugene Alexis)
1868-1918 .... **TCLC 6, 37**
See also CA 104; 126; DA; MTCW

Roth, Henry 1906-........... **CLC 2, 6, 11**
See also CA 11-12; CANR 38; CAP 1;
DLB 28; MTCW

Roth, Joseph 1894-1939......... **TCLC 33**
See also DLB 85

Roth, Philip (Milton)
1933-...... **CLC 1, 2, 3, 4, 6, 9, 15, 22,
31, 47, 66**
See also BEST 90:3; CA 1-4R; CANR 1, 22,
36; CDALB 1968-1988; DA; DLB 2, 28;
DLBY 82; MTCW; WLC

Rothenberg, Jerome 1931-....... **CLC 6, 57**
See also CA 45-48; CANR 1; DLB 5

Roumain, Jacques (Jean Baptiste)
1907-1944 .... **TCLC 19**
See also BLC 3; BW; CA 117; 125

Rourke, Constance (Mayfield)
1885-1941 .... **TCLC 12**
See also CA 107; YABC 1

Rousseau, Jean-Baptiste 1671-1741 ... **LC 9**

Rousseau, Jean-Jacques 1712-1778... **LC 14**
See also DA; WLC

Roussel, Raymond 1877-1933 ..... **TCLC 20**
See also CA 117

Rovit, Earl (Herbert) 1927-........ **CLC 7**
See also CA 5-8R; CANR 12

Rowe, Nicholas 1674-1718.......... **LC 8**
See also DLB 84

Rowley, Ames Dorrance
See Lovecraft, H(oward) P(hillips)

Rowson, Susanna Haswell
1762(?)-1824 .... **NCLC 5**
See also DLB 37

Roy, Gabrielle 1909-1983...... **CLC 10, 14**
See also CA 53-56; 110; CANR 5; DLB 68;
MTCW

Rozewicz, Tadeusz 1921-........ **CLC 9, 23**
See also CA 108; CANR 36; MTCW

Ruark, Gibbons 1941-............. **CLC 3**
See also CA 33-36R; CANR 14, 31;
DLB 120

Rubens, Bernice (Ruth) 1923-... **CLC 19, 31**
See also CA 25-28R; CANR 33; DLB 14;
MTCW

Rudkin, (James) David 1936- ...... **CLC 14**
See also CA 89-92; DLB 13

Rudnik, Raphael 1933-............. **CLC 7**
See also CA 29-32R

Ruffian, M.
See Hasek, Jaroslav (Matej Frantisek)

Ruiz, Jose Martinez.............. **CLC 11**
See also Martinez Ruiz, Jose

Rukeyser, Muriel
1913-1980 ....**CLC 6, 10, 15, 27**
See also CA 5-8R; 93-96; CANR 26;
DLB 48; MTCW; SATA 22

Rule, Jane (Vance) 1931-......... **CLC 27**
See also CA 25-28R; CANR 12; DLB 60

Rulfo, Juan 1918-1986............ **CLC 8**
See also CA 85-88; 118; CANR 26;
DLB 113; HW; MTCW

Runeberg, Johan 1804-1877...... **NCLC 41**

Runyon, (Alfred) Damon
1884(?)-1946 .... **TCLC 10**
See also CA 107; DLB 11, 86

Rush, Norman 1933-............. **CLC 44**
See also CA 121; 126

Shue, Larry 1946-1985 . . . . **CLC 52**
See also CA 117

Shu-Jen, Chou 1881-1936
See Hsun, Lu
See also CA 104

Shulman, Alix Kates 1932- . . . . . . **CLC 2, 10**
See also CA 29-32R; SATA 7

Shuster, Joe 1914- . . . . **CLC 21**

Shute, Nevil . . . . **CLC 30**
See also Norway, Nevil Shute

Shuttle, Penelope (Diane) 1947- . . . . . **CLC 7**
See also CA 93-96; CANR 39; DLB 14, 40

Sidney, Mary 1561-1621 . . . . **LC 19**

Sidney, Sir Philip 1554-1586 . . . . **LC 19**
See also CDBLB Before 1660; DA

Siegel, Jerome 1914- . . . . **CLC 21**
See also CA 116

Siegel, Jerry
See Siegel, Jerome

Sienkiewicz, Henryk (Adam Alexander Pius)
1846-1916 . . . . **TCLC 3**
See also CA 104; 134

Sierra, Gregorio Martinez
See Martinez Sierra, Gregorio

Sierra, Maria (de la O'LeJarraga) Martinez
See Martinez Sierra, Maria (de la
O'LeJarraga)

Sigal, Clancy 1926- . . . . **CLC 7**
See also CA 1-4R

Sigourney, Lydia Howard (Huntley)
1791-1865 . . . . **NCLC 21**
See also DLB 1, 42, 73

Siguenza y Gongora, Carlos de
1645-1700 . . . . **LC 8**

Sigurjonsson, Johann 1880-1919 . . . **TCLC 27**

Sikelianos, Angelos 1884-1951 . . . . **TCLC 39**

Silkin, Jon 1930- . . . . **CLC 2, 6, 43**
See also CA 5-8R; CAAS 5; DLB 27

Silko, Leslie Marmon 1948- . . . . **CLC 23, 74**
See also CA 115; 122; DA

Sillanpaa, Frans Eemil 1888-1964 . . . **CLC 19**
See also CA 129; 93-96; MTCW

Sillitoe, Alan
1928- . . . . **CLC 1, 3, 6, 10, 19, 57**
See also AITN 1; CA 9-12R; CAAS 2;
CANR 8, 26; CDBLB 1960 to Present;
DLB 14; MTCW; SATA 61

Silone, Ignazio 1900-1978 . . . . **CLC 4**
See also CA 25-28; 81-84; CANR 34;
CAP 2; MTCW

Silver, Joan Micklin 1935- . . . . **CLC 20**
See also CA 114; 121

Silver, Nicholas
See Faust, Frederick (Schiller)

Silverberg, Robert 1935- . . . . **CLC 7**
See also CA 1-4R; CAAS 3; CANR 1, 20,
36; DLB 8; MAICYA; MTCW; SATA 13

Silverstein, Alvin 1933- . . . . **CLC 17**
See also CA 49-52; CANR 2; CLR 25;
MAICYA; SATA 8, 69

Silverstein, Virginia B(arbara Opshelor)
1937- . . . . **CLC 17**
See also CA 49-52; CANR 2; CLR 25;
MAICYA; SATA 8, 69

Sim, Georges
See Simenon, Georges (Jacques Christian)

Simak, Clifford D(onald)
1904-1988 . . . . **CLC 1, 55**
See also CA 1-4R; 125; CANR 1, 35;
DLB 8; MTCW; SATA 56

Simenon, Georges (Jacques Christian)
1903-1989 . . . . **CLC 1, 2, 3, 8, 18, 47**
See also CA 85-88; 129; CANR 35;
DLB 72; DLBY 89; MTCW

Simic, Charles 1938- . . . **CLC 6, 9, 22, 49, 68**
See also CA 29-32R; CAAS 4; CANR 12,
33; DLB 105

Simmons, Charles (Paul) 1924- . . . . . **CLC 57**
See also CA 89-92

Simmons, Dan 1948- . . . . **CLC 44**
See also CA 138

Simmons, James (Stewart Alexander)
1933- . . . . **CLC 43**
See also CA 105; DLB 40

Simms, William Gilmore
1806-1870 . . . . **NCLC 3**
See also DLB 3, 30, 59, 73

Simon, Carly 1945- . . . . **CLC 26**
See also CA 105

Simon, Claude 1913- . . . . . . **CLC 4, 9, 15, 39**
See also CA 89-92; CANR 33; DLB 83;
MTCW

Simon, (Marvin) Neil
1927- . . . . **CLC 6, 11, 31, 39, 70**
See also AITN 1; CA 21-24R; CANR 26;
DLB 7; MTCW

Simon, Paul 1942(?)- . . . . **CLC 17**
See also CA 116

Simonon, Paul 1956(?)- . . . . **CLC 30**
See also Clash, The

Simpson, Harriette
See Arnow, Harriette (Louisa) Simpson

Simpson, Louis (Aston Marantz)
1923- . . . . **CLC 4, 7, 9, 32**
See also CA 1-4R; CAAS 4; CANR 1;
DLB 5; MTCW

Simpson, Mona (Elizabeth) 1957- . . . **CLC 44**
See also CA 122; 135

Simpson, N(orman) F(rederick)
1919- . . . . **CLC 29**
See also CA 13-16R; DLB 13

Sinclair, Andrew (Annandale)
1935- . . . . **CLC 2, 14**
See also CA 9-12R; CAAS 5; CANR 14, 38;
DLB 14; MTCW

Sinclair, Emil
See Hesse, Hermann

Sinclair, Iain 1943- . . . . **CLC 76**
See also CA 132

Sinclair, Iain MacGregor
See Sinclair, Iain

Sinclair, Mary Amelia St. Clair 1865(?)-1946
See Sinclair, May
See also CA 104

Sinclair, May . . . . **TCLC 3, 11**
See also Sinclair, Mary Amelia St. Clair
See also DLB 36

Sinclair, Upton (Beall)
1878-1968 . . . . **CLC 1, 11, 15, 63**
See also CA 5-8R; 25-28R; CANR 7;
CDALB 1929-1941; DA; DLB 9; MTCW;
SATA 9; WLC

Singer, Isaac
See Singer, Isaac Bashevis

Singer, Isaac Bashevis
1904-1991 . . . . **CLC 1, 3, 6, 9, 11, 15, 23,
38, 69; SSC 3**
See also AITN 1, 2; CA 1-4R; 134;
CANR 1, 39; CDALB 1941-1968; CLR 1;
DA; DLB 6, 28, 52; DLBY 91;
MAICYA; MTCW; SATA 3, 27;
SATA-Obit 68; WLC

Singer, Israel Joshua 1893-1944 . . . **TCLC 33**

Singh, Khushwant 1915- . . . . **CLC 11**
See also CA 9-12R; CAAS 9; CANR 6

Sinjohn, John
See Galsworthy, John

Sinyavsky, Andrei (Donatevich)
1925- . . . . **CLC 8**
See also CA 85-88

Sirin, V.
See Nabokov, Vladimir (Vladimirovich)

Sissman, L(ouis) E(dward)
1928-1976 . . . . **CLC 9, 18**
See also CA 21-24R; 65-68; CANR 13;
DLB 5

Sisson, C(harles) H(ubert) 1914- . . . . . **CLC 8**
See also CA 1-4R; CAAS 3; CANR 3;
DLB 27

Sitwell, Dame Edith
1887-1964 . . . . **CLC 2, 9, 67; PC 3**
See also CA 9-12R; CANR 35;
CDBLB 1945-1960; DLB 20; MTCW

Sjoewall, Maj 1935- . . . . **CLC 7**
See also CA 65-68

Sjowall, Maj
See Sjoewall, Maj

Skelton, Robin 1925- . . . . **CLC 13**
See also AITN 2; CA 5-8R; CAAS 5;
CANR 28; DLB 27, 53

Skolimowski, Jerzy 1938- . . . . **CLC 20**
See also CA 128

Skram, Amalie (Bertha)
1847-1905 . . . . **TCLC 25**

Skvorecky, Josef (Vaclav)
1924- . . . . **CLC 15, 39, 69**
See also CA 61-64; CAAS 1; CANR 10, 34;
MTCW

Slade, Bernard . . . . **CLC 11, 46**
See also Newbound, Bernard Slade
See also CAAS 9; DLB 53

Slaughter, Carolyn 1946- . . . . **CLC 56**
See also CA 85-88

Slaughter, Frank G(ill) 1908- . . . . . . **CLC 29**
See also AITN 2; CA 5-8R; CANR 5

Slavitt, David R(ytman) 1935- . . . . **CLC 5, 14**
See also CA 21-24R; CAAS 3; CANR 41;
DLB 5, 6

Tabori, George 1914- . . . . CLC 19
See also CA 49-52; CANR 4

Tagore, Rabindranath 1861-1941. . . . TCLC 3
See also CA 104; 120; MTCW

Taine, Hippolyte Adolphe
1828-1893 . . . . NCLC 15

Talese, Gay 1932- . . . . CLC 37
See also AITN 1; CA 1-4R; CANR 9;
MTCW

Tallent, Elizabeth (Ann) 1954- . . . . . CLC 45
See also CA 117; DLB 130

Tally, Ted 1952- . . . . CLC 42
See also CA 120; 124

Tamayo y Baus, Manuel
1829-1898 . . . . NCLC 1

Tammsaare, A(nton) H(ansen)
1878-1940 . . . . TCLC 27

Tan, Amy 1952- . . . . CLC 59
See also AAYA 9; BEST 89:3; CA 136

Tandem, Felix
See Spitteler, Carl (Friedrich Georg)

Tanizaki, Jun'ichiro
1886-1965 . . . . CLC 8, 14, 28
See also CA 93-96; 25-28R

Tanner, William
See Amis, Kingsley (William)

Tao Lao
See Storni, Alfonsina

Tarassoff, Lev
See Troyat, Henri

Tarbell, Ida M(inerva)
1857-1944 . . . . TCLC 40
See also CA 122; DLB 47

Tarkington, (Newton) Booth
1869-1946 . . . . TCLC 9
See also CA 110; DLB 9, 102; SATA 17

Tarkovsky, Andrei (Arsenyevich)
1932-1986 . . . . CLC 75
See also CA 127

Tartt, Donna 1964(?)- . . . . CLC 76

Tasso, Torquato 1544-1595 . . . . LC 5

Tate, (John Orley) Allen
1899-1979 . . . . CLC 2, 4, 6, 9, 11, 14, 24
See also CA 5-8R; 85-88; CANR 32;
DLB 4, 45, 63; MTCW

Tate, Ellalice
See Hibbert, Eleanor Alice Burford

Tate, James (Vincent) 1943- . . . CLC 2, 6, 25
See also CA 21-24R; CANR 29; DLB 5

Tavel, Ronald 1940- . . . . CLC 6
See also CA 21-24R; CANR 33

Taylor, Cecil Philip 1929-1981 . . . . . CLC 27
See also CA 25-28R; 105

Taylor, Edward 1642(?)-1729 . . . . LC 11
See also DA; DLB 24

Taylor, Eleanor Ross 1920- . . . . CLC 5
See also CA 81-84

Taylor, Elizabeth 1912-1975 . . . CLC 2, 4, 29
See also CA 13-16R; CANR 9; MTCW;
SATA 13

Taylor, Henry (Splawn) 1942- . . . . . CLC 44
See also CA 33-36R; CAAS 7; CANR 31;
DLB 5

Taylor, Kamala (Purnaiya) 1924-
See Markandaya, Kamala
See also CA 77-80

Taylor, Mildred D. . . . . CLC 21
See also AAYA 10; BW; CA 85-88;
CANR 25; CLR 9; DLB 52; MAICYA;
SAAS 5; SATA 15, 70

Taylor, Peter (Hillsman)
1917- . . . . . . CLC 1, 4, 18, 37, 44, 50, 71;
SSC 10
See also CA 13-16R; CANR 9; DLBY 81;
MTCW

Taylor, Robert Lewis 1912- . . . . CLC 14
See also CA 1-4R; CANR 3; SATA 10

Tchekhov, Anton
See Chekhov, Anton (Pavlovich)

Teasdale, Sara 1884-1933 . . . . TCLC 4
See also CA 104; DLB 45; SATA 32

Tegner, Esaias 1782-1846 . . . . NCLC 2

Teilhard de Chardin, (Marie Joseph) Pierre
1881-1955 . . . . TCLC 9
See also CA 105

Temple, Ann
See Mortimer, Penelope (Ruth)

Tennant, Emma (Christina)
1937- . . . . CLC 13, 52
See also CA 65-68; CAAS 9; CANR 10, 38;
DLB 14

Tenneshaw, S. M.
See Silverberg, Robert

Tennyson, Alfred
1809-1892 . . . . NCLC 30; PC 6
See also CDBLB 1832-1890; DA; DLB 32;
WLC

Teran, Lisa St. Aubin de . . . . CLC 36
See also St. Aubin de Teran, Lisa

Teresa de Jesus, St. 1515-1582 . . . . . . LC 18

Terkel, Louis 1912-
See Terkel, Studs
See also CA 57-60; CANR 18; MTCW

Terkel, Studs . . . . CLC 38
See also Terkel, Louis
See also AITN 1

Terry, C. V.
See Slaughter, Frank G(ill)

Terry, Megan 1932- . . . . CLC 19
See also CA 77-80; CABS 3; DLB 7

Tertz, Abram
See Sinyavsky, Andrei (Donatevich)

Tesich, Steve 1943(?)- . . . . CLC 40, 69
See also CA 105; DLBY 83

Teternikov, Fyodor Kuzmich 1863-1927
See Sologub, Fyodor
See also CA 104

Tevis, Walter 1928-1984 . . . . CLC 42
See also CA 113

Tey, Josephine . . . . TCLC 14
See also Mackintosh, Elizabeth
See also DLB 77

Thackeray, William Makepeace
1811-1863 . . . . NCLC 5, 14, 22
See also CDBLB 1832-1890; DA; DLB 21,
55; SATA 23; WLC

Thakura, Ravindranatha
See Tagore, Rabindranath

Tharoor, Shashi 1956- . . . . CLC 70

Thelwell, Michael Miles 1939- . . . . . CLC 22
See also CA 101

Theobald, Lewis, Jr.
See Lovecraft, H(oward) P(hillips)

The Prophet
See Dreiser, Theodore (Herman Albert)

Theriault, Yves 1915-1983 . . . . CLC 79
See also CA 102; DLB 88

Theroux, Alexander (Louis)
1939- . . . . CLC 2, 25
See also CA 85-88; CANR 20

Theroux, Paul (Edward)
1941- . . . . CLC 5, 8, 11, 15, 28, 46
See also BEST 89:4; CA 33-36R; CANR 20;
DLB 2; MTCW; SATA 44

Thesen, Sharon 1946- . . . . CLC 56

Thevenin, Denis
See Duhamel, Georges

Thibault, Jacques Anatole Francois
1844-1924
See France, Anatole
See also CA 106; 127; MTCW

Thiele, Colin (Milton) 1920- . . . . CLC 17
See also CA 29-32R; CANR 12, 28;
CLR 27; MAICYA; SAAS 2; SATA 14,
72

Thomas, Audrey (Callahan)
1935- . . . . CLC 7, 13, 37
See also AITN 2; CA 21-24R; CANR 36;
DLB 60; MTCW

Thomas, D(onald) M(ichael)
1935- . . . . CLC 13, 22, 31
See also CA 61-64; CAAS 11; CANR 17;
CDBLB 1960 to Present; DLB 40;
MTCW

Thomas, Dylan (Marlais)
1914-1953 . . . . TCLC 1, 8, 45; PC 2;
SSC 3
See also CA 104; 120; CDBLB 1945-1960;
DA; DLB 13, 20; MTCW; SATA 60;
WLC

Thomas, (Philip) Edward
1878-1917 . . . . TCLC 10
See also CA 106; DLB 19

Thomas, Joyce Carol 1938- . . . . CLC 35
See also BW; CA 113; 116; CLR 19;
DLB 33; MAICYA; MTCW; SAAS 7;
SATA 40

Thomas, Lewis 1913- . . . . CLC 35
See also CA 85-88; CANR 38; MTCW

Thomas, Paul
See Mann, (Paul) Thomas

Thomas, Piri 1928- . . . . CLC 17
See also CA 73-76; HW

Thomas, R(onald) S(tuart)
1913- . . . . CLC 6, 13, 48
See also CA 89-92; CAAS 4; CANR 30;
CDBLB 1960 to Present; DLB 27;
MTCW

Thomas, Ross (Elmore) 1926- . . . . . . CLC 39
See also CA 33-36R; CANR 22

Thompson, Francis Clegg
See Mencken, H(enry) L(ouis)

Thompson, Francis Joseph
1859-1907 . . . . TCLC 4
See also CA 104; CDBLB 1890-1914;
DLB 19

Thompson, Hunter S(tockton)
1939- . . . . CLC 9, 17, 40
See also BEST 89:1; CA 17-20R; CANR 23;
MTCW

Thompson, Jim 1906-1977(?) . . . . . . CLC 69

Thompson, Judith . . . . CLC 39

Thomson, James 1700-1748 . . . . LC 16

Thomson, James 1834-1882 . . . . . . NCLC 18

Thoreau, Henry David
1817-1862 . . . . NCLC 7, 21
See also CDALB 1640-1865; DA; DLB 1;
WLC

Thornton, Hall
See Silverberg, Robert

Thurber, James (Grover)
1894-1961 . . . . . . CLC 5, 11, 25; SSC 1
See also CA 73-76; CANR 17, 39;
CDALB 1929-1941; DA; DLB 4, 11, 22,
102; MAICYA; MTCW; SATA 13

Thurman, Wallace (Henry)
1902-1934 . . . . TCLC 6
See also BLC 3; BW; CA 104; 124; DLB 51

Ticheburn, Cheviot
See Ainsworth, William Harrison

Tieck, (Johann) Ludwig
1773-1853 . . . . NCLC 5
See also DLB 90

Tiger, Derry
See Ellison, Harlan

Tilghman, Christopher 1948(?)- . . . . . CLC 65

Tillinghast, Richard (Williford)
1940- . . . . CLC 29
See also CA 29-32R; CANR 26

Timrod, Henry 1828-1867 . . . . NCLC 25
See also DLB 3

Tindall, Gillian 1938- . . . . CLC 7
See also CA 21-24R; CANR 11

Tiptree, James, Jr. . . . . CLC 48, 50
See also Sheldon, Alice Hastings Bradley
See also DLB 8

Titmarsh, Michael Angelo
See Thackeray, William Makepeace

**Tocqueville, Alexis (Charles Henri Maurice
Clerel Comte)** 1805-1859 . . . . . NCLC 7

Tolkien, J(ohn) R(onald) R(euel)
1892-1973 . . . . CLC 1, 2, 3, 8, 12, 38
See also AAYA 10; AITN 1; CA 17-18;
45-48; CANR 36; CAP 2;
CDBLB 1914-1945; DA; DLB 15;
MAICYA; MTCW; SATA 2, 24, 32;
WLC

Toller, Ernst 1893-1939 . . . . TCLC 10
See also CA 107; DLB 124

Tolson, M. B.
See Tolson, Melvin B(eaunorus)

Tolson, Melvin B(eaunorus)
1898(?)-1966 . . . . CLC 36
See also BLC 3; BW; CA 124; 89-92;
DLB 48, 76

Tolstoi, Aleksei Nikolaevich
See Tolstoy, Alexey Nikolaevich

Tolstoy, Alexey Nikolaevich
1882-1945 . . . . TCLC 18
See also CA 107

Tolstoy, Count Leo
See Tolstoy, Leo (Nikolaevich)

Tolstoy, Leo (Nikolaevich)
1828-1910 . . . . . . TCLC 4, 11, 17, 28, 44;
SSC 9
See also CA 104; 123; DA; SATA 26; WLC

Tomasi di Lampedusa, Giuseppe 1896-1957
See Lampedusa, Giuseppe (Tomasi) di
See also CA 111

Tomlin, Lily . . . . CLC 17
See also Tomlin, Mary Jean

Tomlin, Mary Jean 1939(?)-
See Tomlin, Lily
See also CA 117

Tomlinson, (Alfred) Charles
1927- . . . . CLC 2, 4, 6, 13, 45
See also CA 5-8R; CANR 33; DLB 40

Tonson, Jacob
See Bennett, (Enoch) Arnold

Toole, John Kennedy
1937-1969 . . . . CLC 19, 64
See also CA 104; DLBY 81

Toomer, Jean
1894-1967 . . . . . . CLC 1, 4, 13, 22; PC 7;
SSC 1
See also BLC 3; BW; CA 85-88;
CDALB 1917-1929; DLB 45, 51; MTCW

Torley, Luke
See Blish, James (Benjamin)

Tornimparte, Alessandra
See Ginzburg, Natalia

Torre, Raoul della
See Mencken, H(enry) L(ouis)

Torrey, E(dwin) Fuller 1937- . . . . . . CLC 34
See also CA 119

Torsvan, Ben Traven
See Traven, B.

Torsvan, Benno Traven
See Traven, B.

Torsvan, Berick Traven
See Traven, B.

Torsvan, Berwick Traven
See Traven, B.

Torsvan, Bruno Traven
See Traven, B.

Torsvan, Traven
See Traven, B.

Tournier, Michel (Edouard)
1924- . . . . CLC 6, 23, 36
See also CA 49-52; CANR 3, 36; DLB 83;
MTCW; SATA 23

Tournimparte, Alessandra
See Ginzburg, Natalia

Towers, Ivar
See Kornbluth, C(yril) M.

Townsend, Sue 1946- . . . . CLC 61
See also CA 119; 127; MTCW; SATA 48,
55

Townshend, Peter (Dennis Blandford)
1945- . . . . CLC 17, 42
See also CA 107

Tozzi, Federigo 1883-1920 . . . . TCLC 31

Traill, Catharine Parr
1802-1899 . . . . NCLC 31
See also DLB 99

Trakl, Georg 1887-1914 . . . . TCLC 5
See also CA 104

Transtroemer, Tomas (Goesta)
1931- . . . . CLC 52, 65
See also CA 117; 129; CAAS 17

Transtromer, Tomas Gosta
See Transtroemer, Tomas (Goesta)

Traven, B. (?)-1969 . . . . CLC 8, 11
See also CA 19-20; 25-28R; CAP 2; DLB 9,
56; MTCW

Treitel, Jonathan 1959- . . . . CLC 70

Tremain, Rose 1943-. . . . . CLC 42
See also CA 97-100; DLB 14

Tremblay, Michel 1942-. . . . . CLC 29
See also CA 116; 128; DLB 60; MTCW

Trevanian (a pseudonym) 1930(?)-. . . CLC 29
See also CA 108

Trevor, Glen
See Hilton, James

Trevor, William
1928- . . . . CLC 7, 9, 14, 25, 71
See also Cox, William Trevor
See also DLB 14

Trifonov, Yuri (Valentinovich)
1925-1981 . . . . CLC 45
See also CA 126; 103; MTCW

Trilling, Lionel 1905-1975 . . . . CLC 9, 11, 24
See also CA 9-12R; 61-64; CANR 10;
DLB 28, 63; MTCW

Trimball, W. H.
See Mencken, H(enry) L(ouis)

Tristan
See Gomez de la Serna, Ramon

Tristram
See Housman, A(lfred) E(dward)

Trogdon, William (Lewis) 1939-
See Heat-Moon, William Least
See also CA 115; 119

Trollope, Anthony 1815-1882 . . NCLC 6, 33
See also CDBLB 1832-1890; DA; DLB 21,
57; SATA 22; WLC

Trollope, Frances 1779-1863 . . . . . NCLC 30
See also DLB 21

Trotsky, Leon 1879-1940 . . . . TCLC 22
See also CA 118

Trotter (Cockburn), Catharine
1679-1749 . . . . LC 8
See also DLB 84

Trout, Kilgore
See Farmer, Philip Jose

Trow, George W. S. 1943-. . . . . CLC 52
See also CA 126

Troyat, Henri 1911- . . . . CLC 23
See also CA 45-48; CANR 2, 33; MTCW

Trudeau, G(arretson) B(eekman) 1948-
See Trudeau, Garry B.
See also CA 81-84; CANR 31; SATA 35

Trudeau, Garry B. . . . . **CLC 12**
See also Trudeau, G(arretson) B(eekman)
See also AAYA 10; AITN 2

Truffaut, Francois 1932-1984 . . . . . . **CLC 20**
See also CA 81-84; 113; CANR 34

Trumbo, Dalton 1905-1976 . . . . **CLC 19**
See also CA 21-24R; 69-72; CANR 10;
DLB 26

Trumbull, John 1750-1831 . . . . **NCLC 30**
See also DLB 31

Trundlett, Helen B.
See Eliot, T(homas) S(tearns)

Tryon, Thomas 1926-1991 . . . . **CLC 3, 11**
See also AITN 1; CA 29-32R; 135;
CANR 32; MTCW

Tryon, Tom
See Tryon, Thomas

Ts'ao Hsueh-ch'in 1715(?)-1763 . . . . . . **LC 1**

Tsushima, Shuji 1909-1948
See Dazai, Osamu
See also CA 107

Tsvetaeva (Efron), Marina (Ivanovna)
1892-1941 . . . . **TCLC 7, 35**
See also CA 104; 128; MTCW

Tuck, Lily 1938- . . . . **CLC 70**
See also CA 139

Tunis, John R(oberts) 1889-1975 . . . **CLC 12**
See also CA 61-64; DLB 22; MAICYA;
SATA 30, 37

Tuohy, Frank . . . . **CLC 37**
See also Tuohy, John Francis
See also DLB 14

Tuohy, John Francis 1925-
See Tuohy, Frank
See also CA 5-8R; CANR 3

Turco, Lewis (Putnam) 1934- . . . **CLC 11, 63**
See also CA 13-16R; CANR 24; DLBY 84

Turgenev, Ivan
1818-1883 . . . . **NCLC 21; SSC 7**
See also DA; WLC

Turner, Frederick 1943- . . . . **CLC 48**
See also CA 73-76; CAAS 10; CANR 12,
30; DLB 40

Tusan, Stan 1936- . . . . **CLC 22**
See also CA 105

Tutuola, Amos 1920- . . . . **CLC 5, 14, 29**
See also BLC 3; BW; CA 9-12R; CANR 27;
DLB 125; MTCW

Twain, Mark
. . . . **TCLC 6, 12, 19, 36, 48; SSC 6**
See also Clemens, Samuel Langhorne
See also DLB 11, 12, 23, 64, 74; WLC

Tyler, Anne
1941- . . . . **CLC 7, 11, 18, 28, 44, 59**
See also BEST 89:1; CA 9-12R; CANR 11,
33; DLB 6; DLBY 82; MTCW; SATA 7

Tyler, Royall 1757-1826 . . . . **NCLC 3**
See also DLB 37

Tynan, Katharine 1861-1931 . . . . . . **TCLC 3**
See also CA 104

Tytell, John 1939- . . . . **CLC 50**
See also CA 29-32R

Tyutchev, Fyodor 1803-1873 . . . . . **NCLC 34**

Tzara, Tristan . . . . **CLC 47**
See also Rosenfeld, Samuel

Uhry, Alfred 1936- . . . . **CLC 55**
See also CA 127; 133

Ulf, Haerved
See Strindberg, (Johan) August

Ulf, Harved
See Strindberg, (Johan) August

Unamuno (y Jugo), Miguel de
1864-1936 . . . . **TCLC 2, 9; SSC 11**
See also CA 104; 131; DLB 108; HW;
MTCW

Undercliffe, Errol
See Campbell, (John) Ramsey

Underwood, Miles
See Glassco, John

Undset, Sigrid 1882-1949 . . . . **TCLC 3**
See also CA 104; 129; DA; MTCW; WLC

Ungaretti, Giuseppe
1888-1970 . . . . **CLC 7, 11, 15**
See also CA 19-20; 25-28R; CAP 2;
DLB 114

Unger, Douglas 1952- . . . . **CLC 34**
See also CA 130

Unsworth, Barry (Forster) 1930- . . . . **CLC 76**
See also CA 25-28R; CANR 30

Updike, John (Hoyer)
1932- . . . . . . **CLC 1, 2, 3, 5, 7, 9, 13, 15,
23, 34, 43, 70; SSC 13**
See also CA 1-4R; CABS 1; CANR 4, 33;
CDALB 1968-1988; DA; DLB 2, 5;
DLBD 3; DLBY 80, 82; MTCW; WLC

Upshaw, Margaret Mitchell
See Mitchell, Margaret (Munnerlyn)

Upton, Mark
See Sanders, Lawrence

Urdang, Constance (Henriette)
1922- . . . . **CLC 47**
See also CA 21-24R; CANR 9, 24

Uriel, Henry
See Faust, Frederick (Schiller)

Uris, Leon (Marcus) 1924- . . . . **CLC 7, 32**
See also AITN 1, 2; BEST 89:2; CA 1-4R;
CANR 1, 40; MTCW; SATA 49

Urmuz
See Codrescu, Andrei

Ustinov, Peter (Alexander) 1921- . . . . **CLC 1**
See also AITN 1; CA 13-16R; CANR 25;
DLB 13

V
See Chekhov, Anton (Pavlovich)

Vaculik, Ludvik 1926- . . . . **CLC 7**
See also CA 53-56

Valenzuela, Luisa 1938- . . . . **CLC 31**
See also CA 101; CANR 32; DLB 113; HW

Valera y Alcala-Galiano, Juan
1824-1905 . . . . **TCLC 10**
See also CA 106

Valery, (Ambroise) Paul (Toussaint Jules)
1871-1945 . . . . **TCLC 4, 15**
See also CA 104; 122; MTCW

Valle-Inclan, Ramon (Maria) del
1866-1936 . . . . **TCLC 5**
See also CA 106

Vallejo, Antonio Buero
See Buero Vallejo, Antonio

Vallejo, Cesar (Abraham)
1892-1938 . . . . **TCLC 3**
See also CA 105; HW

Valle Y Pena, Ramon del
See Valle-Inclan, Ramon (Maria) del

Van Ash, Cay 1918- . . . . **CLC 34**

Vanbrugh, Sir John 1664-1726 . . . . . . **LC 21**
See also DLB 80

Van Campen, Karl
See Campbell, John W(ood, Jr.)

Vance, Gerald
See Silverberg, Robert

Vance, Jack . . . . **CLC 35**
See also Vance, John Holbrook
See also DLB 8

Vance, John Holbrook 1916-
See Queen, Ellery; Vance, Jack
See also CA 29-32R; CANR 17; MTCW

**Van Den Bogarde, Derek Jules Gaspard Ulric
Niven** 1921-
See Bogarde, Dirk
See also CA 77-80

Vandenburgh, Jane . . . . **CLC 59**

Vanderhaeghe, Guy 1951- . . . . **CLC 41**
See also CA 113

van der Post, Laurens (Jan) 1906- . . . **CLC 5**
See also CA 5-8R; CANR 35

van de Wetering, Janwillem 1931- . . **CLC 47**
See also CA 49-52; CANR 4

Van Dine, S. S. . . . . **TCLC 23**
See also Wright, Willard Huntington

Van Doren, Carl (Clinton)
1885-1950 . . . . **TCLC 18**
See also CA 111

Van Doren, Mark 1894-1972 . . . . . **CLC 6, 10**
See also CA 1-4R; 37-40R; CANR 3;
DLB 45; MTCW

Van Druten, John (William)
1901-1957 . . . . **TCLC 2**
See also CA 104; DLB 10

Van Duyn, Mona (Jane)
1921- . . . . **CLC 3, 7, 63**
See also CA 9-12R; CANR 7, 38; DLB 5

Van Dyne, Edith
See Baum, L(yman) Frank

van Itallie, Jean-Claude 1936- . . . . **CLC 3**
See also CA 45-48; CAAS 2; CANR 1;
DLB 7

van Ostaijen, Paul 1896-1928 . . . . . **TCLC 33**

Van Peebles, Melvin 1932- . . . . . . **CLC 2, 20**
See also BW; CA 85-88; CANR 27

Vansittart, Peter 1920- . . . . **CLC 42**
See also CA 1-4R; CANR 3

Van Vechten, Carl 1880-1964 . . . . . . **CLC 33**
See also CA 89-92; DLB 4, 9, 51

Van Vogt, A(lfred) E(lton) 1912- . . . . . **CLC 1**
See also CA 21-24R; CANR 28; DLB 8;
SATA 14

Wiesel, Elie(zer)   1928- . . . . . **CLC 3, 5, 11, 37**
See also AAYA 7; AITN 1; CA 5-8R;
CAAS 4; CANR 8, 40; DA; DLB 83;
DLBY 87; MTCW; SATA 56

Wiggins, Marianne   1947- . . . . **CLC 57**
See also BEST 89:3; CA 130

Wight, James Alfred   1916-
See Herriot, James
See also CA 77-80; SATA 44, 55

Wilbur, Richard (Purdy)
1921- . . . . **CLC 3, 6, 9, 14, 53**
See also CA 1-4R; CABS 2; CANR 2, 29;
DA; DLB 5; MTCW; SATA 9

Wild, Peter   1940- . . . . **CLC 14**
See also CA 37-40R; DLB 5

Wilde, Oscar (Fingal O'Flahertie Wills)
1854(?)-1900 . . . . **TCLC 1, 8, 23, 41;**
SSC 11
See also CA 104; 119; CDBLB 1890-1914;
DA; DLB 10, 19, 34, 57; SATA 24; WLC

Wilder, Billy . . . . **CLC 20**
See also Wilder, Samuel
See also DLB 26

Wilder, Samuel   1906-
See Wilder, Billy
See also CA 89-92

Wilder, Thornton (Niven)
1897-1975 . . . . . . **CLC 1, 5, 6, 10, 15, 35;**
DC 1
See also AITN 2; CA 13-16R; 61-64;
CANR 40; DA; DLB 4, 7, 9; MTCW;
WLC

Wilding, Michael   1942- . . . . **CLC 73**
See also CA 104; CANR 24

Wiley, Richard   1944- . . . . **CLC 44**
See also CA 121; 129

Wilhelm, Kate . . . . **CLC 7**
See also Wilhelm, Katie Gertrude
See also CAAS 5; DLB 8

Wilhelm, Katie Gertrude   1928-
See Wilhelm, Kate
See also CA 37-40R; CANR 17, 36; MTCW

Wilkins, Mary
See Freeman, Mary Eleanor Wilkins

Willard, Nancy   1936- . . . . **CLC 7, 37**
See also CA 89-92; CANR 10, 39; CLR 5;
DLB 5, 52; MAICYA; MTCW;
SATA 30, 37, 71

Williams, C(harles) K(enneth)
1936- . . . . **CLC 33, 56**
See also CA 37-40R; DLB 5

Williams, Charles
See Collier, James L(incoln)

Williams, Charles (Walter Stansby)
1886-1945 . . . . **TCLC 1, 11**
See also CA 104; DLB 100

Williams, (George) Emlyn
1905-1987 . . . . **CLC 15**
See also CA 104; 123; CANR 36; DLB 10,
77; MTCW

Williams, Hugo   1942- . . . . **CLC 42**
See also CA 17-20R; DLB 40

Williams, J. Walker
See Wodehouse, P(elham) G(renville)

Williams, John A(lfred)   1925- . . . . **CLC 5, 13**
See also BLC 3; BW; CA 53-56; CAAS 3;
CANR 6, 26; DLB 2, 33

Williams, Jonathan (Chamberlain)
1929- . . . . **CLC 13**
See also CA 9-12R; CAAS 12; CANR 8;
DLB 5

Williams, Joy   1944- . . . . **CLC 31**
See also CA 41-44R; CANR 22

Williams, Norman   1952- . . . . **CLC 39**
See also CA 118

Williams, Tennessee
1911-1983 . . . . . **CLC 1, 2, 5, 7, 8, 11, 15,**
19, 30, 39, 45, 71
See also AITN 1, 2; CA 5-8R; 108;
CABS 3; CANR 31; CDALB 1941-1968;
DA; DLB 7; DLBD 4; DLBY 83;
MTCW; WLC

Williams, Thomas (Alonzo)
1926-1990 . . . . **CLC 14**
See also CA 1-4R; 132; CANR 2

Williams, William C.
See Williams, William Carlos

Williams, William Carlos
1883-1963 . . . . **CLC 1, 2, 5, 9, 13, 22, 42,**
67; PC 7
See also CA 89-92; CANR 34;
CDALB 1917-1929; DA; DLB 4, 16, 54,
86; MTCW

Williamson, David (Keith)   1942- . . . . **CLC 56**
See also CA 103; CANR 41

Williamson, Jack . . . . **CLC 29**
See also Williamson, John Stewart
See also CAAS 8; DLB 8

Williamson, John Stewart   1908-
See Williamson, Jack
See also CA 17-20R; CANR 23

Willie, Frederick
See Lovecraft, H(oward) P(hillips)

Willingham, Calder (Baynard, Jr.)
1922- . . . . **CLC 5, 51**
See also CA 5-8R; CANR 3; DLB 2, 44;
MTCW

Willis, Charles
See Clarke, Arthur C(harles)

Willy
See Colette, (Sidonie-Gabrielle)

Willy, Colette
See Colette, (Sidonie-Gabrielle)

Wilson, A(ndrew) N(orman)   1950- . . **CLC 33**
See also CA 112; 122; DLB 14

Wilson, Angus (Frank Johnstone)
1913-1991 . . . . **CLC 2, 3, 5, 25, 34**
See also CA 5-8R; 134; CANR 21; DLB 15;
MTCW

Wilson, August
1945- . . . . **CLC 39, 50, 63; DC 2**
See also BLC 3; BW; CA 115; 122; DA;
MTCW

Wilson, Brian   1942- . . . . **CLC 12**

Wilson, Colin   1931- . . . . **CLC 3, 14**
See also CA 1-4R; CAAS 5; CANR 1, 22,
33; DLB 14; MTCW

Wilson, Dirk
See Pohl, Frederik

Wilson, Edmund
1895-1972 . . . . **CLC 1, 2, 3, 8, 24**
See also CA 1-4R; 37-40R; CANR 1;
DLB 63; MTCW

Wilson, Ethel Davis (Bryant)
1888(?)-1980 . . . . **CLC 13**
See also CA 102; DLB 68; MTCW

Wilson, John   1785-1854 . . . . **NCLC 5**

Wilson, John (Anthony) Burgess
1917- . . . . **CLC 8, 10, 13**
See also Burgess, Anthony
See also CA 1-4R; CANR 2; MTCW

Wilson, Lanford   1937- . . . . **CLC 7, 14, 36**
See also CA 17-20R; CABS 3; DLB 7

Wilson, Robert M.   1944- . . . . **CLC 7, 9**
See also CA 49-52; CANR 2, 41; MTCW

Wilson, Robert McLiam   1964- . . . . . **CLC 59**
See also CA 132

Wilson, Sloan   1920- . . . . **CLC 32**
See also CA 1-4R; CANR 1

Wilson, Snoo   1948- . . . . **CLC 33**
See also CA 69-72

Wilson, William S(mith)   1932- . . . . . **CLC 49**
See also CA 81-84

Winchilsea, Anne (Kingsmill) Finch Counte
1661-1720 . . . . **LC 3**

Windham, Basil
See Wodehouse, P(elham) G(renville)

Wingrove, David (John)   1954- . . . . . . **CLC 68**
See also CA 133

Winters, Janet Lewis . . . . **CLC 41**
See also Lewis, Janet
See also DLBY 87

Winters, (Arthur) Yvor
1900-1968 . . . . **CLC 4, 8, 32**
See also CA 11-12; 25-28R; CAP 1;
DLB 48; MTCW

Winterson, Jeanette   1959- . . . . **CLC 64**
See also CA 136

Wiseman, Frederick   1930- . . . . **CLC 20**

Wister, Owen   1860-1938 . . . . **TCLC 21**
See also CA 108; DLB 9, 78; SATA 62

Witkacy
See Witkiewicz, Stanisław Ignacy

Witkiewicz, Stanisław Ignacy
1885-1939 . . . . **TCLC 8**
See also CA 105

Wittig, Monique   1935(?)- . . . . **CLC 22**
See also CA 116; 135; DLB 83

Wittlin, Jozef   1896-1976 . . . . **CLC 25**
See also CA 49-52; 65-68; CANR 3

Wodehouse, P(elham) G(renville)
1881-1975 . . . **CLC 1, 2, 5, 10, 22; SSC 2**
See also AITN 2; CA 45-48; 57-60;
CANR 3, 33; CDBLB 1914-1945;
DLB 34; MTCW; SATA 22

Woiwode, L.
See Woiwode, Larry (Alfred)

Woiwode, Larry (Alfred)   1941- . . . **CLC 6, 10**
See also CA 73-76; CANR 16; DLB 6

Wojciechowska, Maia (Teresa)
1927- . . . . **CLC 26**
See also AAYA 8; CA 9-12R; CANR 4, 41;
CLR 1; MAICYA; SAAS 1; SATA 1, 28

Wolf, Christa 1929- .... **CLC 14, 29, 58**
See also CA 85-88; DLB 75; MTCW

Wolfe, Gene (Rodman) 1931-....... **CLC 25**
See also CA 57-60; CAAS 9; CANR 6, 32;
DLB 8

Wolfe, George C. 1954- .... **CLC 49**

Wolfe, Thomas (Clayton)
1900-1938 .... **TCLC 4, 13, 29**
See also CA 104; 132; CDALB 1929-1941;
DA; DLB 9, 102; DLBD 2; DLBY 85;
MTCW; WLC

Wolfe, Thomas Kennerly, Jr. 1930-
See Wolfe, Tom
See also CA 13-16R; CANR 9, 33; MTCW

Wolfe, Tom .... **CLC 1, 2, 9, 15, 35, 51**
See also Wolfe, Thomas Kennerly, Jr.
See also AAYA 8; AITN 2; BEST 89:1

Wolff, Geoffrey (Ansell) 1937- ..... **CLC 41**
See also CA 29-32R; CANR 29

Wolff, Sonia
See Levitin, Sonia (Wolff)

Wolff, Tobias (Jonathan Ansell)
1945- .... **CLC 39, 64**
See also BEST 90:2; CA 114; 117; DLB 130

Wolfram von Eschenbach
c. 1170-c. 1220 .... **CMLC 5**

Wolitzer, Hilma 1930-........... **CLC 17**
See also CA 65-68; CANR 18, 40; SATA 31

Wollstonecraft, Mary 1759-1797..... **LC 5**
See also CDBLB 1789-1832; DLB 39, 104

Wonder, Stevie .... **CLC 12**
See also Morris, Steveland Judkins

Wong, Jade Snow 1922-........... **CLC 17**
See also CA 109

Woodcott, Keith
See Brunner, John (Kilian Houston)

Woodruff, Robert W.
See Mencken, H(enry) L(ouis)

Woolf, (Adeline) Virginia
1882-1941 .... **TCLC 1, 5, 20, 43; SSC 7**
See also CA 104; 130; CDBLB 1914-1945;
DA; DLB 36, 100; DLBD 10; MTCW;
WLC

Woollcott, Alexander (Humphreys)
1887-1943 .... **TCLC 5**
See also CA 105; DLB 29

Woolrich, Cornell 1903-1968....... **CLC 77**
See also Hopley-Woolrich, Cornell George

Wordsworth, Dorothy
1771-1855 .... **NCLC 25**
See also DLB 107

Wordsworth, William
1770-1850 ...... **NCLC 12, 38; PC 4**
See also CDBLB 1789-1832; DA; DLB 93,
107; WLC

Wouk, Herman 1915-........ **CLC 1, 9, 38**
See also CA 5-8R; CANR 6, 33; DLBY 82;
MTCW

Wright, Charles (Penzel, Jr.)
1935-.................. **CLC 6, 13, 28**
See also CA 29-32R; CAAS 7; CANR 23,
36; DLBY 82; MTCW

Wright, Charles Stevenson 1932- ... **CLC 49**
See also BLC 3; BW; CA 9-12R; CANR 26;
DLB 33

Wright, Jack R.
See Harris, Mark

Wright, James (Arlington)
1927-1980 .... **CLC 3, 5, 10, 28**
See also AITN 2; CA 49-52; 97-100;
CANR 4, 34; DLB 5; MTCW

Wright, Judith (Arandell)
1915- .... **CLC 11, 53**
See also CA 13-16R; CANR 31; MTCW;
SATA 14

Wright, L(aurali) R. 1939-........ **CLC 44**
See also CA 138

Wright, Richard (Nathaniel)
1908-1960 .... **CLC 1, 3, 4, 9, 14, 21, 48,
74; SSC 2**
See also AAYA 5; BLC 3; BW; CA 108;
CDALB 1929-1941; DA; DLB 76, 102;
DLBD 2; MTCW; WLC

Wright, Richard B(ruce) 1937- ...... **CLC 6**
See also CA 85-88; DLB 53

Wright, Rick 1945-............... **CLC 35**
See also Pink Floyd

Wright, Rowland
See Wells, Carolyn

Wright, Stephen 1946-............ **CLC 33**

Wright, Willard Huntington 1888-1939
See Van Dine, S. S.
See also CA 115

Wright, William 1930-............ **CLC 44**
See also CA 53-56; CANR 7, 23

Wu Ch'eng-en 1500(?)-1582(?)........ **LC 7**

Wu Ching-tzu 1701-1754 .... **LC 2**

Wurlitzer, Rudolph 1938(?)- ... **CLC 2, 4, 15**
See also CA 85-88

Wycherley, William 1641-1715 .... **LC 8, 21**
See also CDBLB 1660-1789; DLB 80

Wylie, Elinor (Morton Hoyt)
1885-1928 .... **TCLC 8**
See also CA 105; DLB 9, 45

Wylie, Philip (Gordon) 1902-1971... **CLC 43**
See also CA 21-22; 33-36R; CAP 2; DLB 9

Wyndham, John
See Harris, John (Wyndham Parkes Lucas)
Beynon

Wyss, Johann David Von
1743-1818 .... **NCLC 10**
See also MAICYA; SATA 27, 29

Yakumo Koizumi
See Hearn, (Patricio) Lafcadio (Tessima
Carlos)

Yanez, Jose Donoso
See Donoso (Yanez), Jose

Yanovsky, Basile S.
See Yanovsky, V(assily) S(emenovich)

Yanovsky, V(assily) S(emenovich)
1906-1989 .... **CLC 2, 18**
See also CA 97-100; 129

Yates, Richard 1926-1992 ..... **CLC 7, 8, 23**
See also CA 5-8R; 139; CANR 10; DLB 2;
DLBY 81, 92

Yeats, W. B.
See Yeats, William Butler

Yeats, William Butler
1865-1939 .... **TCLC 1, 11, 18, 31**
See also CA 104; 127; CDBLB 1890-1914;
DA; DLB 10, 19, 98; MTCW; WLC

Yehoshua, Abraham B. 1936- ... **CLC 13, 31**
See also CA 33-36R

Yep, Laurence Michael 1948-...... **CLC 35**
See also AAYA 5; CA 49-52; CANR 1;
CLR 3, 17; DLB 52; MAICYA; SATA 7,
69

Yerby, Frank G(arvin)
1916-1991 .... **CLC 1, 7, 22**
See also BLC 3; BW; CA 9-12R; 136;
CANR 16; DLB 76; MTCW

Yesenin, Sergei Alexandrovich
See Esenin, Sergei (Alexandrovich)

Yevtushenko, Yevgeny (Alexandrovich)
1933- .... **CLC 1, 3, 13, 26, 51**
See also CA 81-84; CANR 33; MTCW

Yezierska, Anzia 1885(?)-1970 ..... **CLC 46**
See also CA 126; 89-92; DLB 28; MTCW

Yglesias, Helen 1915-........... **CLC 7, 22**
See also CA 37-40R; CANR 15; MTCW

Yokomitsu Riichi 1898-1947 ...... **TCLC 47**

Yonge, Charlotte (Mary)
1823-1901 .... **TCLC 48**
See also CA 109; DLB 18; SATA 17

York, Jeremy
See Creasey, John

York, Simon
See Heinlein, Robert A(nson)

Yorke, Henry Vincent 1905-1974 ... **CLC 13**
See also Green, Henry
See also CA 85-88; 49-52

Young, Al(bert James) 1939-....... **CLC 19**
See also BLC 3; BW; CA 29-32R;
CANR 26; DLB 33

Young, Andrew (John) 1885-1971.... **CLC 5**
See also CA 5-8R; CANR 7, 29

Young, Collier
See Bloch, Robert (Albert)

Young, Edward 1683-1765........... **LC 3**
See also DLB 95

Young, Neil 1945-................ **CLC 17**
See also CA 110

Yourcenar, Marguerite
1903-1987 .... **CLC 19, 38, 50**
See also CA 69-72; CANR 23; DLB 72;
DLBY 88; MTCW

Yurick, Sol 1925-................ **CLC 6**
See also CA 13-16R; CANR 25

Zamiatin, Yevgenii
See Zamyatin, Evgeny Ivanovich

Zamyatin, Evgeny Ivanovich
1884-1937 .... **TCLC 8, 37**
See also CA 105

Zangwill, Israel 1864-1926........ **TCLC 16**
See also CA 109; DLB 10

Zappa, Francis Vincent, Jr. 1940-
See Zappa, Frank
See also CA 108

Zappa, Frank.................... **CLC 17**
See also Zappa, Francis Vincent, Jr.

Zaturenska, Marya   1902-1982. . . . **CLC 6, 11**
  See also CA 13-16R; 105; CANR 22

Zelazny, Roger (Joseph)   1937- . . . . . **CLC 21**
  See also AAYA 7; CA 21-24R; CANR 26;
    DLB 8; MTCW; SATA 39, 57

Zhdanov, Andrei A(lexandrovich)
    1896-1948 . . . . **TCLC 18**
  See also CA 117

Zhukovsky, Vasily   1783-1852 . . . . **NCLC 35**

Ziegenhagen, Eric . . . . **CLC 55**

Zimmer, Jill Schary
  See Robinson, Jill

Zimmerman, Robert
  See Dylan, Bob

Zindel, Paul   1936- . . . . **CLC 6, 26**
  See also AAYA 2; CA 73-76; CANR 31;
    CLR 3; DA; DLB 7, 52; MAICYA;
    MTCW; SATA 16, 58

Zinov'Ev, A. A.
  See Zinoviev, Alexander (Aleksandrovich)

Zinoviev, Alexander (Aleksandrovich)
    1922- . . . . **CLC 19**
  See also CA 116; 133; CAAS 10

Zoilus
  See Lovecraft, H(oward) P(hillips)

Zola, Emile (Edouard Charles Antoine)
    1840-1902 . . . . **TCLC 1, 6, 21, 41**
  See also CA 104; 138; DA; DLB 123; WLC

Zoline, Pamela   1941- . . . . **CLC 62**

Zorrilla y Moral, Jose   1817-1893 . . **NCLC 6**

Zoshchenko, Mikhail (Mikhailovich)
    1895-1958 . . . . **TCLC 15**
  See also CA 115

Zuckmayer, Carl   1896-1977. . . . . . . **CLC 18**
  See also CA 69-72; DLB 56, 124

Zuk, Georges
  See Skelton, Robin

Zukofsky, Louis
    1904-1978 . . . . **CLC 1, 2, 4, 7, 11, 18**
  See also CA 9-12R; 77-80; CANR 39;
    DLB 5; MTCW

Zweig, Paul   1935-1984. . . . . **CLC 34, 42**
  See also CA 85-88; 113

Zweig, Stefan   1881-1942 . . . . **TCLC 17**
  See also CA 112; DLB 81, 118

SSC Cumulative Nationality Index

ALGERIAN
Camus, Albert **9**

AMERICAN
Aiken, Conrad **9**
Anderson, Sherwood **1**
Baldwin, James **10**
Barnes, Djuna **3**
Barth, John **10**
Barthelme, Donald **2**
Beattie, Ann **11**
Benét, Stephen Vincent **10**
Bierce, Ambrose **9**
Bowles, Paul **3**
Boyle, Kay **5**
Cable, George Washington **4**
Capote, Truman **2**
Carver, Raymond **8**
Cather, Willa **2**
Cheever, John **1**
Chesnutt, Charles Wadell **7**
Chopin, Kate **8**
Crane, Stephen **7**
Dunbar, Paul Laurence **8**
Elkin, Stanley **12**
Faulkner, William **1**
Fitzgerald, F. Scott **6**
Freeman, Mary Wilkins **1**
Gardner, John **7**
Gass, William H. **12**
Gilman, Charlotte Perkins **13**
Harte, Bret **8**
Hawthorne, Nathaniel **3**
Hemingway, Ernest **1**
Henry, O. **5**
Hughes, Langston **6**
Hurston, Zora Neale **4**
Irving, Washington **2**
Jackson, Shirley **9**

James, Henry **8**
Jewett, Sarah Orne **6**
Le Guin, Ursula K. **12**
London, Jack **4**
MacLean, Norman **13**
Marshall, Paule **3**
Mason, Bobbie Ann **4**
McCullers, Carson **9**
Melville, Herman **1**
Nabokov, Vladimir **11**
Oates, Joyce Carol **6**
O'Connor, Flannery **1**
Olsen, Tillie **11**
Paley, Grace **8**
Parker, Dorothy **2**
Poe, Edgar Allan **1**
Porter, Katherine Anne **4**
Powers, J. F. **4**
Salinger, J. D. **2**
Singer, Isaac Bashevis **3**
Steinbeck, John **11**
Taylor, Peter **10**
Thurber, James **1**
Toomer, Jean **1**
Twain, Mark **6**
Updike, John **13**
Vonnegut, Kurt, Jr. **8**
Walker, Alice **5**
Warren, Robert Penn **4**
Welty, Eudora **1**
Wharton, Edith **6**
Wright, Richard **2**

ARGENTINIAN
Borges, Jorge Luis **4**
Cortazar, Julio **7**

AUSTRIAN
Kafka, Franz **5**

CANADIAN
Atwood, Margaret **2**
Gallant, Mavis **5**
Laurence, Margaret **7**
Munro, Alice **3**

COLUMBIAN
García Márquez, Gabriel **8**

CUBAN
Calvino, Italo **3**

CZECHOSLOVAKIAN
Kafka, Franz **5**

DANISH
Andersen, Hans Christian **6**
Dinesen, Isak **7**

ENGLISH
Ballard, J. G. **1**
Bates, H. E. **10**
Bowen, Elizabeth **3**
Carter, Angela **13**
Chesterton, G. K. **1**
Clarke, Arthur C. **3**
Conrad, Joseph **9**
Doyle, Arthur Conan **12**
Hardy, Thomas **2**
Kipling, Rudyard **5**
Lawrence, D. H. **4**
Lessing, Doris (Newbold Jones) **6**
Lovecraft, H. P. **3**
Maugham, W. Somerset **8**
Saki **12**
Wells, H. G. **6**
Wodehouse, P. G. **2**
Woolf, Virginia **7**

SSC Cumulative Title Index

Title Index

Title Index

Title Index

Title Index

Title Index

Title Index